KT-439-112

207 857

LAROUSSE
ENCYCLOPEDIA OF
WINE

hamlyn

LAROUSSE
ENCYCLOPEDIA OF
WINE

GENERAL EDITOR : CHRISTOPHER FOULKES

NORWICH CITY COLLEGE LIBRARY

207857

641.2203

LAROUSSE ENCYCLOPEDIA OF WINE
Published in Great Britain by Hamlyn in 2001
First published in 1994 by Larousse

———

Managing editors: Claude Naudin, Laure Flavigny
Art director: Frédérique Longuépée

Edited and designed by Segrave Foulkes
8 King's Road, Kingston upon Thames KT2 5HR (United Kingdom)
Introductory essay: Michael Broadbent
Managing editor: Carrie Segrave
Designers: Nigel O'Gorman, Roger Walton
Maps: European Map Graphics
Picture researchers: Samantha Lawrence, Liz Eddison
Illustration: Trevor Lawrence, Clare Roberts
Other contributors: see page 624

———

Edition fully updated in 2001 by Larousse

Managing editor: Colette Hanicotte
Editor: Rupert Hasterok
Art director: Emmanuel Chaspoul assisted by Sophie Compagne,
Jacqueline Bloch and Olivier Caldéron
Proof reading: Annick Valade assisted by Sophie de Kayser
Production: Annie Botrel
Cover design: Véronique Laporte
Translation from French: Alison Hughes in association
with First Edition Translations Ltd, Cambridge

Contributors to the updated edition: Michel Dovaz, Oscar Caballero, Claude Dovaz,
Mathilde Hulot, René Lambert, Valérie de Lescure, Toshio Matsuura, Ingrid Nakajo,
José de Païva, Constantin Stergides, Tamara Thorgevsky.

Edition partially updated in 2004 by Larousse
Contributors: Paul Strang (Midi and South-West of France), Michel Dovaz (other French wine regions),
Georges Lepré (vintage charts)
Translation and proof reading: Regan Kramer

Copyright © Larousse 1994 for the first edition
Copyright © Larousse 2004 for this new edition

All rights reserved under International and Pan-American Copyright convention.
No part of this publication may be reproduced, stored in retrieval system or transmitted in any form or by any means,
electronic, mechanical, photocopying, recording or otherwise, without the prior permission of the copyright owners.

ISBN 0 600 60475 6
Hamlyn, a division of Octopus Publishing Group Limited
2-4 Heron Quays
London
E14 4JP

Printed in Italy

FOREWORD

Today's wine lover has the vineyards of the world to command. In a short generation, a cluster of wine lands have emerged from deserved obscurity to range alongside Europe's classics. The world's list of fine wine zones, once restricted to a few regions of France, a river valley in Germany and two corners of Iberia, has expanded twenty-fold. The roll-call of good, reliable everyday wines has grown longer still. More people have easy access to more good wine than ever before.

This cornucopia has inspired not excess but enthusiasm. Wine has become the enjoyable study of millions, who delight to compare and contrast, to match food and wine, vintages and occasions. Even more are happily bringing wine into their everyday life, discovering value and quality, exploring nuances of flavour and finding out why some bottles are sublime, others mundane.

Guidelines, not laws

A sense of worry often accompanies wine: is this the right bottle? Is it too cool, too warm, too young or too old? Will it match the food, or clash with it? Nearly always the wisdom of yesterday is confirmed, not overturned, by the science of today. There is however one area in which science has made a real difference to the ways we think about wine. It is winemaking. The whole process of making wine, from vineyard to cellar, has been turned upside down by technical advances and the growth in scientific understanding. Classically excellent wines are, most tasters agree, even better, while new centres of excellence are emerging constantly. There is no longer only one "correct" way to make wine. The growth in choice throws the spotlight on the winemaker, and makes the customer's rôle more challenging, and rewarding, as the range of wine expands.

Building the memory-bank

No written word, or picture, can substitute for actually tasting wine. It is the only way to build real knowledge of wine. Some wine lovers — mostly, it must be said, professionals in wine — make notes about every bottle they taste. For most of us, the substitute for this enviable efficiency is the mental note. It is made in those few seconds of concentration when we let the wine have our whole attention, expressing itself through our senses. With a very little practice, the brain becomes a memory-bank of tastes. One wine excites memories of another: the special flavours of a certain region's wines, of those made from a particular grape, even of a particular vintage are stored away and triggered by trying a new wine.

How this Encyclopedia was compiled

This Encyclopedia is the work of a collective of well-informed writers and experts from around the world, who have contributed their special knowledge to the whole. As conductor of this orchestra I have the luck to be able to thank them for their skill and work; as any honest conductor should, I can say that their efforts needed only guidance, not direction.

The Larousse Encyclopedia of Wine is a reference to what wines are made where, what they taste like and which examples are the best. It cannot be comprehensive: millions of named wines are made. It can and does profile every wine zone whose produce will be found in commerce, describe the characteristics of the wines and suggest good examples. Armed with this outline knowledge, the reader can feel confident exploring the rich, charming and ever-changing variety that is the world of wine.

CHRISTOPHER FOULKES

Contents

WINE: THE TASTE, THE ENJOYMENT

WINE LANDS OF THE WORLD

USING THE ENCYCLOPEDIA

The *Larousse Encyclopedia of Wine* is a reference guide to the world's vineyards and an aid to enjoying their fruits. It is arranged in two main sections.

The first section is called *Wine: the Taste, the Enjoyment.* Starting on page 19, it offers a guide to the world of wine from its history, through choosing wine, wine laws, the keeping and serving of wine, and on to tasting and to wine and food partnerships. The section concludes with how wine is made, exploring why radical changes in tecchnology and approach are improving the wines we drink.

The second section, starting on page 125, profiles the Wine Lands of the World: France, then the other European countries, then on to the New World of wine. Within each national chapter are sections on the wine regions. For all major areas, the level of detail grows to encompass specific châteaux, estates and producers. Thirty-eight new maps, created especially for this Encyclopedia, and hundreds of photographs illuminate the wine zones.

A third, reference, section gathers facts and statistics, a glossary of wine terms and a set of vintage charts. A comprehensive index offers a route to information: names of wines, vineyards, producers and properties.

To find out about a particular region or district, consult the Contents. For most countries and regions, an overall introduction sets the scene, explains about local wine laws, grape varieties and wine styles, and discusses the detailed local divisions. These areas are then profiled in greater or lesser depth depending upon their importance.

To find out about a specific named wine, refer to the Contents if its location is known, or consult the Index. For example, if a wine label is clear that the wine is from the Napa region of California, or the Mâcon region of Burgundy, the Contents will lead to the California Chapter, and the Napa section. Equally, the Burgundy chapter has a section on the Mâconnais.

Why regional chapters differ

The way each district is organized differs. In some places, the "unit" — the name seen on the label — is the estate. Call it a château, an estate, a quinta or a winery, it is the way wine there works and is sold. In other places, the geographical names are uppermost. Here, wine is sold according to its vineyard or area of origin. Many people may own land and make wine from the same named vineyard — and, indeed, a single producer may own plots in several villages in the region. The wine lover relies for wine identification upon official rules which stipulate how vineyard and locality names can be used.

QUICK REFERENCE

For advice and information on the following turn to these pages:

A wine Index
An area Contents list or index
A producer Index
Choosing wine By sweetness/dryness, pages 28-33; by style, pages 28-33; by grape variety, pages 34-42
Serving wine Pages 59-74
Buying wine Pages 47-49
Which vintage to choose Page 581
Food and wine Pages 81-90; specific foods and suggested partnerships, pages 91-98
Tasting wine Pages 75-80
How wine is made Pages 99-124.
What wine terms mean Glossary, *see* page 594
Reading a winc labcl Pages 44-46; reference section pages 576-580
Statistics and wine regions Reference section, *see* page 586

It follows that in regions where estate names are paramount, it is these that are listed in the Encyclopedia's Producers pages. Where vineyards and districts dominate, there are pages which profile these, with producers listed by name only.

Wine estates and producers

No wine reference book can list all wine producers, châteaux, estates or vineyards. For instance, California and Australie each have more than 700 wine producers, Bordeaux has more than 4,000 named châteaux, Burgundy has 10,000 growers.

The selection process is agonizing, and it works, however imperfectly, according to three criteria. First, is the wine good? Second, is it made and sold in such a quantity that the wine lover may expect to find it? Third, is there a track-record of consistent quality? Even with these "filters" many good wine producers will not be listed. Some make very litte; others sell it all to one customer. Exclusion is not condemnation. Wherever possible, the Encyclopedia provides the detail needed to make an informed judgement about wines, even if the individual estate or producer, vineyard or village is not listed. This may be in the form of overall appraisals of the style of wine made in a district, or from a given grape variety.

Units and conversions

Metric and imperial units are used, with the latter in brackets. Yield is in hectolitres of wine per hectare of land, or hl/ha. A hectolitre is 100 litres. Wine production is in cases. A case of wine is defined as 12 bottles of 75cl each, one case therefore holding 9 litres of wine; there are approximately 11 cases to the hectolitre. Temperature is expressed in centigrade/Celsius, with Fahrenheit in brackets. ❑

TYPES OF PAGES

The Encyclopedia is built up using various types of pages. This allows speedy identification of the start of a chapter, or a particular kind of text. Some of the most important page styles are illustrated here.

On the right is a page opening a chapter. Pages in this style begin important subject areas in Section I, and major regions such as Bordeaux and Burgundy and major wine countries such as Germany, Italy and Spain. Facing this is a map page. There are 38 maps in the Encyclopedia, each placed close to the start of the relevant chapter.

Step-by-step pages provide a sequence of photographs to guide the reader through practical tasks, such as opening sparkling wine and decanting. This style of page is also used to illustrate wine-making techniques.

Boxed text punctuates chapter pages, providing greater detail on subjects such as reading a label, wine laws or local grape varieties and (in minor regions) wine zones and producers.

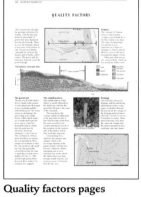

Quality factors pages explore the environmental conditions underlying the character of wines from specific places. They supply geological cross-sections and other data, plus notes on key influences, be they climatic, topographical or human.

Pages with four columns profile a region's wines and producers. These are organized by areas and/or château, estate or winery, as appropriate. Profiles of significant producers are displayed on panels.

THE ENJOYMENT OF WINE

by
MICHAEL BROADBENT

The very word "wine" conjures up a pleasurable image. Not, for each of us, the very same image. It might range from the biblical to the distinctly profane, encompassing everyday use as a simple beverage to something approaching an art form — something to quaff, something to discuss. It is easy to forget that wine begins life as an agricultural product, converted skilfully by nature from the grape with the aid of man into a potable liquid of immense variety that can be bottled, transported and consumed outside its area of origin and, at its best, left to mature in bottle. Wine is a commodity. From the earliest civilizations known it has been traded. Grower, winemaker, wine merchant: all are ancient and honourable callings.

Above all, wine is made to be enjoyed. Bottles, adorned by an infinite variety of labels, can be gazed at, stored, collected like stamps, traded for profit — but, sooner or later, the contents must be consumed. This requires neither skill nor knowledge; yet to venture further, to know, to understand, adds immeasurably to one's appreciation. The aim of this Encyclopedia is to provide information, to answer questions, to clear away the mist from the mystique. My first mentor in the business of wine happened also to be a wine writer; a well-read gentleman with the — to me at the time — irritating habit of quoting from ancient classics, notably *The Deipnosophists of Athenaeus*. Quite recently I purchased a reprint from a specialist wine bookseller in America, and solemnly ploughed through the eight volumes: Greek text on the left, translation on the right. What struck me was that in ancient Greece and Rome the variety of wine and its uses were surprisingly wide. The references to wine, the appreciation of its manifold facets and effects, were of a high order without being pretentious — indeed, some were distinctly down to earth, even bawdy.

This was some 2,000 years or more ago. Yet we think that there is something relatively new about "winespeak", or about widespread consumption of wine; that the only habitual consumers were to be found in wine-producing countries — dotted first around the shores of the Aegean, then Italy, followed in due course by France and Spain. But by the time of Edward III, wine was as common a tipple as ale in London, and both were a great deal safer to drink than water. The commerce in wool and wine dominated the English economy. Wine merchants were as rich as Croesus, even lending money to the king. Those were the days! Now, the only money we "lend" is in the form of duties and taxes.

Wine and the senses

On to basics. What is the attraction of wine? First and foremost it appeals to the senses: of sight, of smell and of taste. To a lesser extent, of touch: its sensuous, silky, tactile feel. And to a rather frivolous extent to the sense of hearing: the explosion of a champagne cork, the more discreet but equally anticipatory pop of a drawn cork, and the tantalizing swirl as the wine is poured into the glass. The colour. A so-called "white" wine that ranges from almost colourless through pale green tinges to yellow gold; the even more varied and subtle reds, vivid purple through cherry to soft red brown; tawny, ruby, sparkling, viscous.

Smell. The most evocative of all our senses, working on several planes, to make the mouth water, to set the gastric juices in motion; to detect the "varietal" characteristics, revealing the grape from which the wine has been made. Note the hidden depths and subtle enchantment of a superb wine, fully mature, as its bouquet blossoms in the glass.

Finally, its taste: the first sip, the touch on the tongue and the various impressions as the wine crosses the palate. Some wines, like great burgundy, expand in the mouth; some have persistent flavour and ethereal aftertaste. At the same time, unconsciously, the wine is doing a job. Sparkling wine refreshes, teases, adds gaiety to life. Dry sherry — an unfairly neglected wine — is surely the perfect apéritif, the salty tang of a fino anticipating the meal, setting the gastric juices in motion. There is a white wine for every occasion, a fruity Riesling to sip and chat over, Chardonnay with fish, with chicken. With the main course, the meat course, a multitude of reds from which to choose. But what with the pudding? Not, I beg of you, a fine Sauternes, even less an *Auslese* from the Rheingau. These sweet wines are killed stone dead by most sweet dishes. Sauternes with cheese, please — or, if you are rich, with pâté de foie gras at the beginning of a sumptuous dinner. The most suitable pudding wines are, happily, among the least expensive. My personal recommendations are either Muscat de Beaumes-de-Venise or a well-chilled Moscato d'Asti. After dinner, a 10- or 20-year-old tawny or vintage port. Alternatively, Malmsey, the sweetest of that most versatile of wines, Madeira. Verdelho mid-morning, Sercial before a meal, Bual mid-afternoon — much more satisfying than tea!

Learning about wine

So much to choose from, so much to learn. How best to start? Shop around. Find a good retailer. If he is the sort who prints a list, study it, buy a mixed case or two. Open a bottle and, before a meal, give the wine a preview taste, looking up the wine in

this Encyclopedia. Read about where it comes from, perhaps how it is made, about its characteristics and style should be. Then gaze at its colour, bring the glass to the nose, sip and make a brief note. Try to describe it in your own words. At least write down its name and whether or not you like it.

As a rather old-fashioned sort of person, trained in the wine trade when merchants handled mainly the "classics" (by which I mean bordeaux, burgundy, the wines of Germany, Loire, Rhône, sherry, port and champagne), these tend to be my touchstones. Though the latter half of my career at Christie's has been mainly concerned with mature and rare wines, as a writer and consumer I have always taken an active interest in more recent vintages and wines of other regions. The reader might have noted that the wines of Italy did not appear in my list of "classics". This is quite simply because in the mid-1950s to mid-1960s, when I did my stint as a wine merchant, Italian wines were generally considered unreliable and in England, at any rate, they were associated with cheap and cheerful Italian restaurants. Even today one sees quite good Italian wines standing upright on shelves in steamy, unairconditioned restaurants. With the exception of one or two major, long-established family wineries, Italian wines did not come into their own until the mid-1980s.

Let me demonstrate how I learned more about them. I did precisely what I advise any beginner. I read the list of a specialist Italian wine importer and retailer, ordered mixed cases, usually just two bottles each of a couple of dozen different wines, and sat down to taste them with a wine map and book at hand.

Where does one begin? It is simply not possible to taste, to drink — let alone to know about — all the wines of the world. In many ways we are living in a consumer paradise: all the world seems to be deep in the throes of making wine, and the combination of modern winemaking and intense competition should — in theory at least — result in better quality at lower prices. What in practice is happening is that there is a surfeit of choice, added to which the great barrage of wine-writing can simply add to the confusion. In England and America, at any rate, it would seem that newspaper editors and wine journalists conspire to discover obscure wines, preferably at giveaway prices.

To be fair, they do give an airing to new and perhaps struggling wine areas and, of course, they provide the adventurous drinker with a challenge, the occasional disappointment making up for the equally occasional delight. The plain fact of the matter is that, particularly in the "New World", farmers know how to grow good grapes, and winemakers now know perfectly well what to do with them. To the newcomer this might seem obvious. Yet only a generation ago viticulture and viniculture were relatively hit and miss. In some parts of the world viticulture did not exist. Take New Zealand. To our forefathers a country once uniquely devoted to the production and export of butter and lamb, it now makes and markets a host of attractive and reasonably-priced wines.

Winemaking goes international

In the more traditional European wine districts the transition has also been noticeable, if not as spectacular. Vine tending and winemaking had been very much a father-to-son tradition. The owner of a small vineyard might make only twenty-five wines in his working life. Almost literally, a new breed has arisen. In Burgundy, sons in their 20s and early 30s will now be trained in oenology, and members of this new generation form tasting groups to exchange ideas and assess the relative merits of their neighbours' wines. They also travel. For example, in Alsace, Johnny Hugel's two nephews spent time in California and Australia, working in vineyards and wineries, studying new techniques, before coming back to the family business in Riquewihr.

I cannot emphasize strongly enough how much attitudes have changed. As recently as the mid-1970s the French were rather smugly self-confident.

Then, in Paris in 1976, a California Chardonnay and Cabernet Sauvignon came out top in a blind tasting against white burgundy and red bordeaux. French pride was dented, but at this stage they did not fully grasp the significance; fortress France would repel American boarders! What eventually dawned was the realization that French exports of wine could be affected. I personally noticed this first-hand, as a regular visitor to the United States. In the early 1970s hardly any serious wine drinkers along the eastern seaboard, from Florida up to New York State, had California wine in their cellars. A decade later this changed, and nowadays "domestic" wines line the shelves of retailers, dominate restaurant lists and occupy serious space in commodious and air-conditioned private cellars.

The spread of wine culture is so important that it is worth mentioning how this happened. The pioneers, notably in California, had the climate and the determination. What they first concentrated on was the vine stock. Enthusiastic and skilled winemakers like Robert Mondavi came to Europe in the mid-1960s to discover what was responsible for the flavour and character of red bordeaux, of red and white burgundy, of fine German wines. They deduced that it was the grape variety: respectively Cabernet Sauvignon, Pinot Noir, Chardonnay and Riesling. Importing these vinestocks, they created what are now universally known as "varietal" wines. Given amenable climate and soil conditions, clever winemakers first made bordeaux and burgundy look-alikes, then wines of their own distinctive style — usually fuller and more fruity than the original.

The growth of the international Cabernet Sauvignon and Chardonnay market has been phenomenal. It has spread back into Europe, to the east — Bulgaria, for example — and even to Italy, where classic native grape varieties such as Sangiovese had been sacrosanct. Pinot Noir, hitherto considered a difficult grape variety to handle, is now making great strides. Among the dry whites, Sauvignon Blanc is tremendously fashionable; Riesling somewhat less so.

Vive la différence

But, one might ask, is this altogether a good thing? On the one hand there is comfort in a familiar name, suggesting a certain recognizable style, be it red or white. On the other hand it is not only relegating to the sidelines other traditional grape varieties, of which there are a surprising number in the older European wine areas, but (equally important) is inducing winemakers to change the style of their wines so that it is more in accord with an internationally-accepted style.

Of course, not only wine is affected by the global market patterns. It is not the only product with a local market, custom-worn taste and standards, that has failed to meet a more sophisticated international clientèle. Drab, oily, oxidized, sloppily-made wines were produced not only in remote Italian villages and on the flatter plains of Spain but also, even in my lifetime, in the Graves district of Bordeaux. I am all in favour of healthy grapes and competent winemaking, but I am saddened by inexorably creeping uniformity in wine. Rather like the international news on television — fleeting, trivialized, repetitive — our taste parameters are fast being reduced, neutralized. Watch out!

How will modern wines age?

It is generally agreed that the overall quality of winemaking has improved, which is all to the good; though there is, alas, still far too much poor wine. But what about quality wine? Are the great growths of Bordeaux as good as they used to be? Will they keep as long, develop as well? This question is sometimes asked with (though few have tasted it) pre-phylloxera claret in mind: the formidable and fabled 1865s and 1870s.

Lafite, for example, of the latter vintage was still superb — indeed faultless — in magnums a century later. Will there be another 1945 and 1961? In both these years nature did the pruning: severe frosts reduced the crop and concentrated the remaining grapes which ripened fully during the ensuing summer and harvest time. So freak weather conditions are part of the answer. Quality is directly the result not only of ideal conditions during the growing season but of prudent husbandry, pruning, grape selection; of careful winemaking and final selection of the very best vats.

Undoubtedly, thanks to sophisticated pesticides and rot control, it is possible to make palatable wine in conditions that formerly would have been considered near disastrous. But for fine wine there is no substitute for healthy grapes.

It is said that there has been a deliberate tendency to make easy-to-drink, fruity wine, even on classic estates. To a certain extent this is true, but it is my firm opinion that in order to survive long term, the great domaines of Burgundy, the major châteaux of Bordeaux, must take an uncompromising stand. In a world of harsh competition only quality will survive. Weather and economic conditions are cyclical. Happily, there were an exceptional number of extremely good vintages in the ten years from 1981 to 1990. Enjoy the splendid results while the going is good.

I shall end with my "credo": I believe in wine. I believe in its health-giving qualities. It is the most supreme of all beverages. It appeals to the senses: its colour thrills and fills one with eager anticipation; its fragrance is evocative and pleasing and whets the appetite; it tastes good. Not only does its flavour intrigue and delight, but the natural acidity refreshes and the tannin of a red wine cleans the mouth, preparing it for the next mouthful of food. It completes these unofficial duties by aiding the digestion, relaxing the appreciative imbiber and stimulating pleasant thoughts and civilized conversation.

Explore the world of wine and *enjoy* its many riches.

Michael Broadbent

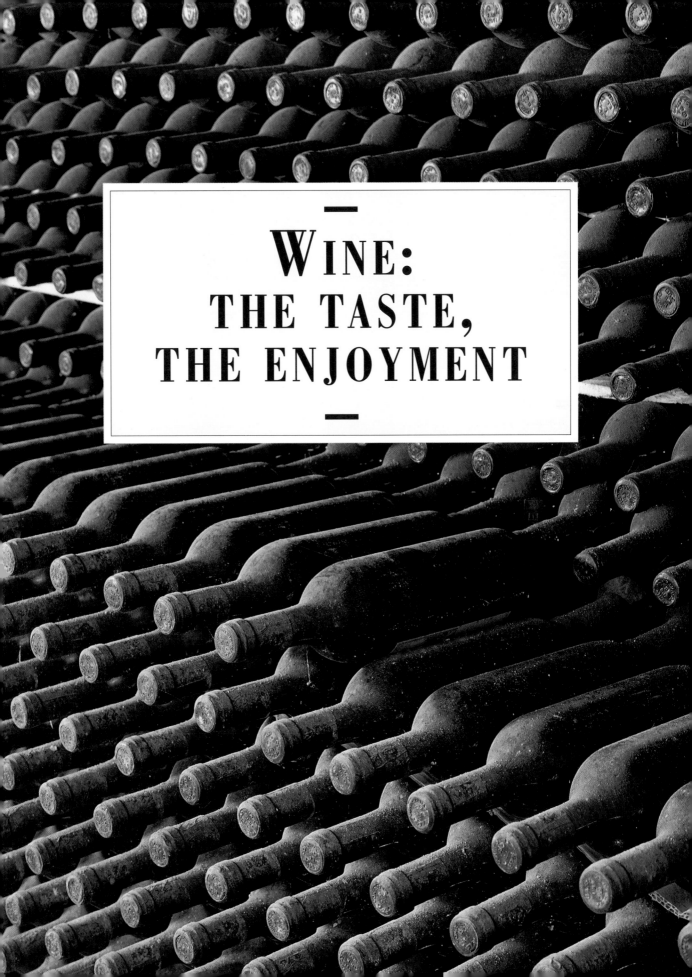

WINE:
THE TASTE,
THE ENJOYMENT

The next hundred pages take wine from its misty origins to the latest frontiers of wine-making technology. On the way there is advice on, and discussion of, the techniques and knowledge that can make wine more enjoyable.

This section covers practical matters to do with enjoying wine. The second, longer, section of the book covers the world's wine lands, exploring the great variety of wines made today. Use the first section to understand and enjoy wine at its best; the second to discover which wines to enjoy.

A programme for enjoyment

A corkscrew, a mug and a sunny spot for a picnic are all you need to gain enormous pleasure from a bottle of wine. Yet how much is lost if the wine is warm, not chilled; if the corkscrew breaks the cork; if the wine itself clashes with the food in the picnic basket. This section aims to enhance the pleasure.

The section begins with the History of Wine, then comes a chapter on Choosing Wine. This includes profiles of the main grape varieties used across the world and an outline of the different style groups — from dry white to fortified — that wines fall into. Lists of wines make it clear which is light, which is heavy, which is dry, which is sweet. If there is a particular style of wine that you like, or you find that your favourite red wines all come from the Cabernet Sauvignon grape, this chapter will help you find more examples to try. The chapter concludes with background information on wine laws and labels, and some advice on buying wine.

The chapter on Keeping Wine explains why wine — almost uniquely among foods and drinks — can change and improve with age, and sets out the guidelines for successful wine storage.

The important practicalities of Serving Wine, from temperature to care of glasses, come next. This chapter includes step-by-step descriptions of decanting and other processes. Then a chapter covers the art and science of Tasting Wine. This skill can be used to judge and appraise wine for value and quality, and can be developed into an absorbing pursuit in its own right. A chapter on Wine and Food partnerships, including an extensive list of suggestions for wines to match different dishes, conclude the "guidelines" chapters.

The modern way of making wine, which is at once the heir to millenia of tradition and the focus of exciting change, is covered in detail in Wine-making Today, followed by a chapter on what happens next: the maturing of wine and its onward progress to our tables. This discusses oak-ageing and other cellar techniques which can make such an enormous difference to the character of a wine.

The realm of the senses

Wine enjoyment is magnified if the knowledge gained goes beyond the technical and the mundane, and enters the realm of the senses. Winetasting and appreciation is not an arcane or even complicated art, and it has moved from a technique of the trade to a hobby for the *amateur* because it uniquely links the aesthetic, the technical and the sensuous.

It is when wine demands a second thought, at a set-piece dinner for family or friends, or at a large party, that knowledge and skill pay real dividends in enjoyment. While every wine gains from thoughtful choice and serving, not all wines have a lot to say. Ordinary wines stay ordinary, however heavy the glassware and seductive the candlelight. This is not to say that only expensive wine is enjoyable: there are many more minor wines worth a second taste today than there were even just a few years ago. The advice and information set out here will help you avoid the traps and enhance the pleasures of wine, both on an everyday basis and on those occasions when wine matters more.

However, the many rules and standards, classifications and rankings, set out by the wine world cannot guarantee excellence and character. There is no substitute for the practical; it is up to the wine lover to seek out and enjoy the good and avoid the merely correct. Equipped with that corkscrew and a well-chosen bottle, you are ready to start the search.

THE HISTORY OF WINE

WHO MADE THE FIRST WINE AND WHERE WAS THE FIRST VINEYARD
ARE TANTALIZING QUESTIONS. WINE HAS BEEN LINKED WITH OUR
CULTURE FOR SEVEN MILLENNIA, AND INSPIRES IT STILL.

In many cultures, wine has been considered a necessary accompaniment to a banquet. At the time this mosaic was created, the 1st or 2nd century AD, the Romans had already defined which of their vineyards made the best wines.

Wine has a long history, and individual bottles of wine can have their story too. These two aspects add greatly to wine's fascination, but wine's place in our cultural history is the larger and grander theme. Wine was one of the first things that Man created, and it has held a special place in many cultures. The history of wine is also an intriguing story of technical innovation, as Man applied his intelligence to the problems posed by the first chemical reactions that he encountered: fermentation and oxidation. No-one can know who made the first wine. The great classical civilizations of Greece and Rome traced it back into their prehistory, and built legends around its discovery. Ancient Egypt has left us wine lists and wall paintings. Indeed, the Egyptians recorded the vintage, vineyard and winemaker on individual jars of wine: the first wine labels. The Babylonians laid down laws to regulate the running of a wine-shop, and wrote vivid descriptions of a magical, jewel-bearing vineyard in the *Epic of Gilgamesh*, the earliest imaginative writing there is: it appears to have been written in the 18th century BC. Wine can be, and is, made from wild grapes. The grape is the one fruit that, with its concentrated sugars and ample juice, has an inherent tendency to ferment. Fermentation makes alcohol, and this will take place when the grapes are ripe and the juice released comes into contact with yeast — there in plenty, in wild form, on the skins of the grapes. So if the grape juice is held in a container, wine will make itself. Pure conjecture leads us to a Stone Age man who placed ripe grapes in a vessel — clay pot, wooden bowl or skin bag — and, perhaps forgetting them, left them to ferment. In warm conditions this will happen in hours rather than days, and in days there will be wine of a sort. Who was the first to drink this intoxicating and delightful juice? We can never know, but perhaps he or she also had the first wine-induced headache. At feasts, in religious ceremonies, as antiseptic, as medicine: wine has played many rôles. But only comparatively recently in its history came the biggest breakthrough: when the ability to age wine was mastered, allowing us to keep it perhaps for years, improving in cask or bottle, fine wine was born.

The first vineyard

The accidental making of wine probably happened wherever wild grapes grew and people lived. A much greater step was the cultivation of the vine. Archaeologists can tell from grape pips found in ancient settlements whether the grapes were wild or cultivated. Cultivated pips have been unearthed in the Caucasus, the region at the eastern end of the Black Sea. They date from 7,000 years ago. Somewhere in this region — in what is now Turkey, or Georgia, or Armenia — which is well suited by climate and relief to the growing of the vine, and where the vine indeed once grew wild, the first vineyard was planted.

Wine's link with religion

The most significant thing that happened in the early history of wine was that the classical Greeks, and later the Romans, made it an important part of their lives. Because of this, and especially because of the part it played in religions and rituals, wine became a major theme in Western culture, rather than a minor detail. China had wine at the same time as ancient Greece, but made little fuss about it. The cultivated grapevine came and went in the cities of Persia and India without leaving much trace. America never discovered it at all, despite the wild vines that flourish there and the sophisticated cultures that existed before Columbus.

From Greek and Roman ritual one can trace a direct line to Christian practice and belief. The use of wine in the Sacrament has direct links with Jewish ritual, but the strongest similarities are with the Greek worship of Dionysus, god of wine, and his Roman equivalent, Bacchus. It was Dionysus who, in legend, brought the vine to Greece — from Asia Minor, today's Turkey. Dionysus, the son of Zeus, was born twice (the myth is confused, to our ears at least), the second time in a virgin birth to a mortal woman. He was the vine; his blood was wine.

Even the horse is drunk in this Bacchic orgy from ancient Rome.

WINE GODS

Dionysus was only one wine god among many, and similar legends appear in other cultures with remarkable consistency.

An inscription from 2,700 BC names the Sumerian deity Gestin, which means "mother vine-stock". Another Sumerian god was Pa-gestin-dug or "good vine-stock". His wife Nin-kasi was "the lady of the inebriating fruit".

In Egypt, Osiris was the god of wine, though wine itself was sometimes called "the tears of [the god] Horus" or "the sweat of Ra" (the sun god).

Christ said: "I am the true vine". But the Jewish religion made no links between God and wine, nor did it allow libations — the offering of wine to the gods so common in Babylonian, Greek and other religions. Wine is important to Jewish ritual, but its abuse is frowned upon. Christians suppressed Dionysus, or Bacchus, once theirs had become the dominant religion. The abandoned behaviour at Bacchic revels was anathema to the early bishops — especially as it involved women.

Rome, growing in power as Greece declined, took over Greek gods along with much else. Dionysus was identical to Bacchus — the latter name was used in the Greek cities of Lydia, in Asia Minor. Bacchus evolved from wine god into saviour. His cult became popular among women, slaves and the urban poor — and emperors tried to ban it without much success. Christianity, the growth of which became inextricably linked with the expansion of the Roman Empire, took over many Bacchic symbols and rites, and at first attracted the same groups of people. The meaning of the Eucharist is a more complex subject than can be dealt with here; it is sufficient to note that wine became vital, in a real sense, to Christian observance. A source of wine for the Sacrament was as necessary to a Christian church as a priest, perhaps more so. It was this fact that was to carry wine through the Dark Ages that followed the decline of Rome, when Europe was engulfed in barbarism.

WINE REGIONS OF THE ANCIENT MEDITERRANEAN

The Egyptians, the Sumerians and the Romans named their vineyards and debated about which were the best. The land that the Bible calls Canaan — Phoenicia, or Syria — was famous for its wine. "The wine in the presses of Daha is as copious as running water," wrote an Egyptian chronicler. Daha was somewhere in the Canaan region, where Egypt traded for timber — and wine. And according to the Bible, it was from Canaan that the Israelites brought back a bunch of grapes so large that it needed two strong men to carry it. The Old Testament is full of references to vineyards.

The Romans were careful to define the best Italian vineyards. Falernum, south of Rome, was the greatest, with the estate of Faustus accounted the best "château". The wines of Alba — today's Colli Albani — were rated almost as good. The great wine port of Roman Italy was Pompeii, where one wine merchant was rich enough to build both the theatre and the amphitheatre. The Romans also esteemed the wines of Spain and Greece, and, in Imperial times, those of Gaul (France), the Rhineland, the Danube and even Britain. Many wine regions of today trace their origins to Roman vineyards.

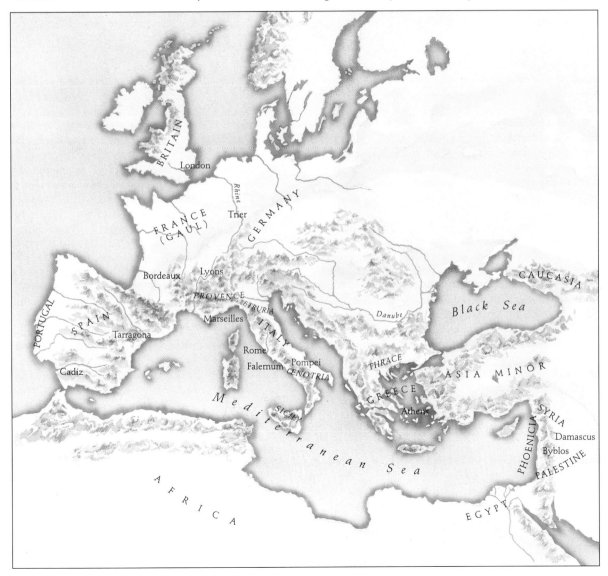

Monks and merchants

Wine had become indelibly written on the Mediterranean way of life. But there was no stability north of the Alps. In the face of waves of cruel invaders, the settled arts — vineyards among them — were in deep peril. Only the Church, with its need for wine and its power to organize and confer continuity, kept the vines growing. As Europe emerged into recorded history again, it was around the monasteries and cathedrals that vines were to be found.

The monks did more than make wine: they improved it. The medieval Cistercians of Burgundy were the first to study the soil of the Côte d'Or, and to transform vineyards by selecting the best vines, experimenting with pruning, and choosing plots without frost and in which grapes ripened best. They built walls around the best vineyards: the *clos* which still survive, if in name only, are testimony to the keen-eyed monks of centuries ago. An outpost of Cistercians at Kloster Eberbach did the same thing in the Rheingau. All this effort was to make wine not just for the Mass, but for the market: the monks were a central part of the medieval wine trade.

Medieval life gradually became more settled, allowing the expansion of vineyards and the revival of trade in wine. Wine had never entirely died out as a trading commodity: the pirate-filled western seas of the Dark Ages had seen merchant ships creeping from Bordeaux or the Rhine's mouth to Britain, Ireland and further north. The meanest barbarian chief felt that his station called for wine at feast-times, the remotest hermit needed wine for the Sacrament.

With restored trade came the great wine-fleets: hundreds of ships at a time plying to London or the north German ports. Rivers became important trade routes: wine casks are heavy and cumbersome, and water-borne transport suits them best.

For medieval man, wine or beer was not a luxury but a necessity.

Cities had impure — often dangerous — water supplies. Wine was an antiseptic, a component of the primitive medicine of the time. It was added to water to alleviate its endemic pollution. Water was rarely drunk by itself, in cities at least. "Water is not wholesome sole by itself, for an Englishman," wrote Andrew Boorde, an English scholar, in 1542.

Large quantities of wine were traded. Bordeaux's exports to England in the 14th century were so great that the average annual total was not exceeded until 1979. Edward II of England ordered the equivalent of over a million bottles to celebrate his wedding to Isabella of France in 1308. Under Elizabeth I almost three centuries later the English were drinking over 40 million bottles of wine a year. The population at the time was 6.1 million.

The rise of the connoisseur

The demand for wine as an everyday beverage kept winegrowers and merchants busy for many centuries. Around the end of the 17th century came a new demand: for wine that was an aesthetic experience. Of course the Romans searched their Empire for the finest vintages, and kings and abbots of the medieval era expected the best. What was new in France, and especially in England, was the rise of a social group with money and taste, who would pay a premium for fine wine. In France the courtiers of the Regency period (1715–1723) demanded — and got — a copious flow of better, and more sparkling, champagne. In England in the same period the grandees of the government, headed by Prime Minister Robert Walpole, sought out the finest red wines from Bordeaux.

It is to this generation that we can trace fine wine as we know it today. Up to this point, wine was drunk within a year of its making; as the new vintage approached, the price of the "old" wine fell. But by 1714 a Paris merchant was writing to his Bordeaux agent asking specifically for

"good, fine wine, old, black and velvety". The secrets of maturing and improving wines had been mastered, and the age of fine wines had begun.

Arnaud de Pontac, *président* of the *parlement* of Bordeaux around 1660, and owner of Château Haut-Brion, is generally credited with pioneering this new approach. He set out to make a new kind of wine, applying the techniques that were later to become routine: small crops, careful selection, and rigorous winemaking and cellar practice. The aim was, of course, to gain a reputation and command a high price. In London, Haut-Brion sold for more than three times the price of other good wine.

Within a generation other Bordeaux estates — led by Latour, Lafite and Margaux — had followed suit. Refinement followed refinement: the best vine varieties were selected, vineyards were drained, ageing and cellar care became a precise art. Fine wine was being made on a large scale.

For ordinary wine to be made on a similar scale France had to wait for the Industrial Revolution. The growth of towns, filled with thirsty workers, redoubled the demand for cheap wine. The railways allowed it to be met — from the wide, hot lands of the Midi.

The vine plagues

It was in the Midi in the 1860s that the most devastating of vine plagues first appeared. Phylloxera is a tiny insect, a pin-prick in size, which can kill vines by feeding on their roots. It was introduced, by accident, from North America when steamers began to make ocean voyages so swift that the pest could survive the crossing on imported plants. It spread across Europe: hardly a vine was spared. After four decades of destruction, the solution was found: vines grafted onto rootstocks of American vines are immune. Phylloxera was not the only problem: two diseases, oïdium or powdery mildew, and downy mildew, affected Europe's vines in the same period.

In France, many phylloxera-affected vineyards were never replanted. Few vineyards other than the most prestigious could by then compete with the mass-production of southern France and Italy.

The 20th century

In many respects it took much of the 20th century for the wine world to recover from the crisis of the late 19th. After World War I, wine consumption in Europe rose to new heights, but the wine itself, drawn from the southern vineyards and from North Africa, was very poor. Even great wines — from Bordeaux, Burgundy, the Rhein and Mosel — sold for low prices: their once-prosperous drinkers had been hit by wars and slumps. The brightest spots were the New World vineyards of western USA, Australia, South Africa and New Zealand, where immigrants from Europe's wine lands developed virgin soil in benign climates.

The quest for authenticity

The struggle to recover from phylloxera and economic crises led to the growth of regulation over wine and vineyards. The French system of appellations of origin (AOC), and the others around the world that have been based (in part at least) upon it, stemmed from a desire to combat fraud. This took the form of passing off ordinary wine under great names, and in adulterating wine. Riots in Champagne in 1911, against wine from outside the region being sold as champagne, were but the most dramatic in a series of protests. After World War I the French government put the AOC system in place. This guarantees authenticity and controls quality. Grape varieties, vineyard boundaries, pruning methods — everything is subject to regulation.

The discovery of control

Science began to influence wine, with research programmes into vine breeding, fermentation and cellar care proliferating. With knowledge came control, and yields became more predictable, and larger. At the same time the worldwide fashion for wine-drinking took off. Countries which had not drunk wine on a large scale for centuries — England, the USA, Canada, the Scandinavian nations — gained the wine habit. The classic vineyards were able to respond with copious, and excellent, vintages — the 1980s and 1990s were decades of superlatives. And the top wines from the New World began to match the European classics' quality, and to enlarge the frontiers of taste. For winemakers, the late 20th century has been a time of prosperity. For wine drinkers, it has been a golden age, with more good wine, at relatively cheaper prices, than ever before. The sufferers have been the mass-market producers, hit by the rapid decline in the quantity — but not the quality — of wine drunk in Italy, Portugal, Spain and France.

The future promises to bring yet more wine-producing countries into already crowded markets. Modern techniques can rapidly improve the wines of backward areas: witness the results of Australian and American investment in the Midi, Hungary and Italy. For the wine drinker, more and better wine at lower prices is the prospect. For the winemaker, the demands will be great.   □

Vineyard workers rioted in 1911 over the import of wine from outside Champagne.

HISTORICAL WINE PRICES

The production of wine, and its price, have fluctuated widely over the centuries as climate changes and the vagaries of trade have constrained both the possible yield and the potential market. The price of wine is also linked to supply and demand: competition from other wines — even other drinks — has depressed prices of some famous wines. Conversely, shortages have forced prices up.

Wine's keeping qualities insulate it from the dramatic rises and falls of more ephemeral crops, but there have been lengthy periods when winemaking has not been a paying proposition, while the occasional boom period has brought wealth to the vineyard areas.

The great wines of Bordeaux have been recognized as superior since the early 18th century, and this makes the rise and fall of their prices of particular interest. There have been only limited swings in the fashion for these wines, and not many true competitors.

The rise of premium wines

From the Bordeaux archives it is possible to trace the rise of the quality wines, designed for keeping and from specific, named, estates. In 1647 we find that the price of the soft, early-drinking *palus* wines, made on the rich riverside land, were higher than those of the Graves and Médoc. Two generations later, in 1714, fine wines from named châteaux — Pontac (now Haut-Brion), Latour, Lafite, Margaux — cost five times as much as the *vin courant* — the basic red bordeaux made for early drinking. The First Growths had emerged, and established their premium prices — a situation that endures to this day.

The archives of Château Latour, a First Growth by reputation for three centuries and in law since 1855, provide a particularly full set of figures for wine production and prices: *see* graph below.

Prices fluctuated, from a low of 250 francs a *tonneau* (a cask of 900 litres) in 1809 to a maximum of 6,000 francs in 1867. The owners of Latour sold their wine to the Bordeaux *négocians*, the price being fixed each year. In some periods the proprietors arranged fixed-price contracts: the graph shows this in the 1840s, 1880s and 1900s.

Golden age and slump

Some periods of high prices were due to reduced production and thus scarcity, a pattern constantly repeated. The oïdium disease in 1853–4 reduced the crop, and prices shot up to the highest levels known for a century. A 30-year "golden age" followed — but then came the mildew and phylloxera diseases, which hit confidence in wine as a beverage as well as in its supply. It took a generation for claret to recover its image, and in the important British market champagne and whisky became fashionable, to the detriment of red wine. This crisis was followed by a series of wars and slumps which kept the price low until the 1960s. Many Bordeaux vineyards were abandoned as they were unprofitable.

Price and rank

Prices in Bordeaux were used as the basis for the 1855 Classification, a ranking of châteaux which is still in use. The study of prices and the ranking of châteaux into tiers of *crus* ("growths") dates from the early 18th century. The first half of the 19th century saw several lists, more and less official, culminating in the formal hierarchy of the Médoc and Sauternes estates of 1855 (*see* pp146 and 164). The brokers who drew up the list used as their data the prices the various wines had obtained over the previous generation. The marketplace was the true measure of wine quality, price set the rank of each wine.

Fluctuations in the price of wine

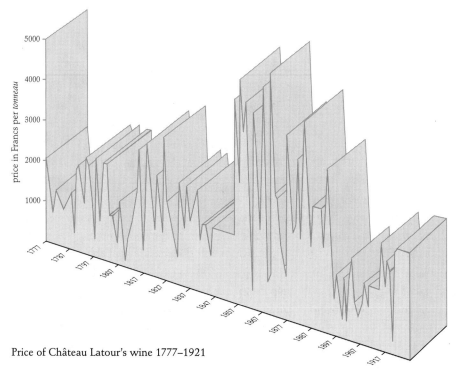

Price of Château Latour's wine 1777–1921

CHOOSING WINE

A SHOP MAY DISPLAY HUNDREDS OF WINES FROM AROUND THE
WORLD. CHOOSING A BOTTLE IS EASIER IF YOU REMEMBER THAT
MOST WINES FALL INTO ONE OF SEVERAL MAIN STYLE GROUPS.

Looking at the label will tell you where a wine comes from,
and can give many clues as to how it will taste. The price
may determine whether it is a wine for a special occasion
or one for everyday drinking.

The wine lover today has an enormous range of wines from which to choose. A wine store in a big cosmopolitan city may sell the produce of 20 or even 40 countries. Even in winemaking countries, which traditionally have drunk local wine, the mass-market stores increasingly scour the world for the novel, the good-value, the excellent. With this plethora of choice come new and often unfamiliar ways of labelling wine, even of describing wine, to confront the consumer.

Wines differ according to origin, grape variety, technique of manufacture and age. Origin is the most important clue to a wine's character, and the biggest section of this book, Wine Lands of the World, describes winemaking countries and regions, the wine styles made, and what they taste like. The grape variety used in a wine has assumed major importance since New World wine lands such as California and Australia burst upon the scene. These lands generally label and name their wine according to the name of the grape, a trend that has spread back to Europe, where it was previously rarely seen apart from in Italy, Germany and Alsace. Winemaking techniques have changed dramatically since 1960, and have a chapter to themselves. Finally, the age of a bottle of wine has an important bearing on its character. The chapter on wine and time explains why age matters, and the charts in the reference section of this book offer a guide to the recent vintages. When choosing a bottle of wine that you intend to drink in the near future — rather than keeping it to improve in the bottle — your first consideration should be the occasion on which you intend to open it. Do you want a cool thirst-quencher or a wine to sip and savour? Do you want an everyday wine for an informal occasion, or a serious bottle for an important dinner? Choosing wine to match food is discussed in a separate chapter; the greatest food and wine partnerships are those where the flavours of the dish match the character of the wine.

So much choice can be daunting, but with a little help a structure falls into place, and the world's wines become both accessible and enjoyable. In the next few pages we offer a resumé of wine styles, grouped by colour and character.

CHOOSING WHITE WINES

Are you looking for a white wine to serve as a long refreshing drink, or as a special treat — a glass full of intense flavours? Price may be a rough guide, but the cost — and availability — of any wine will depend on where you are in the world: what may be a treat in New York may be almost everyday in Italy.

White wine may be bone dry, lusciously sweet, or anywhere in between — individual wines are discussed in the main section of the encyclopedia — but can be divided into six main styles.

Light, dry wines are intended for drinking young, are not aged in oak, are bottled with no residual sugar and are low in extract (the components that give a wine substance, or body). These may be served well chilled, and are delightful for everyday drinking, with or without food.

Medium-bodied and full, dry white wines have increasingly more extract, and although technically dry they have the almost sweet richness of ripe fruit. Either may have been matured in oak vats and/or bottles, and the fullest style may be capable of further ageing in bottle.

Certain grape varieties make particularly aromatic wines; these may be dry or medium-dry.

Medium-sweet wines are usually bottled before all the grape sugar has been converted into alcohol (*see* Winemaking, p110). Light and low in alcohol, their soft sweetness makes them less suitable with food. Sweetest of all are the powerfully flavoured wines, usually served in small glasses.

Some wines are made in more than one style: Orvieto, for example, may be dry (*secco*) or medium-sweet (*abboccato*).

A wine may also vary according to the way it is made. Such differences are most apparent when comparing wines that have been

Whites from around the world: Burgundy, Germany, California and Australia.

fermented or matured in wood with those that have not. Traditionally Rioja, both white and red, is aged in oak barrels, leading to a full wine with a vanilla aroma. Modern Rioja winemakers allow minimum contact with the wood, giving wine that is lighter and fresher-tasting.

When winemakers choose to name their wines by grape variety, much depends on the climate of the producing region. A Chardonnay from the Alto Adige in northern Italy will taste crisp and fresh, with the acidity of grapes ripened in a cool region, while an Australian Chardonnay will display the tropical fruit character of fully ripe grapes.

Much also depends on the intention of the winemaker. Thus a Riesling from Alsace will always be made dry, while German Rieslings (unless marked *trocken*/dry) tend to have more than a hint of sweetness. □

USING THE CHARTS

The charts list some of the most frequently encountered wine names from around the world, grouping wines that are similar in style. They begin with the lightest styles and go on to more characterful, or sweeter, wines.

The name given in the chart is usually what you will see on the label: as explained elsewhere in the Encyclopedia, in some countries the name of the region is the key to the style, while others place more emphasis on grape variety.

The numbers down the left-hand side of each chart indicate the approximate degree of alcohol — although alcohol content may vary slightly from producer to producer, and from vintage to vintage.

Look for the name of a wine that you know you like: the names nearest to it may be very different in flavour, but will be similar in style. You will then be able to try a wine from an unfamiliar region, or from a higher or lower price bracket.

WHITE WINE STYLES

These charts give as broad a range as possible (*see* box opposite). Names given are those usually found on the label: the area name (eg Bergerac), classification (eg Kabinett Trocken) or the grape variety (eg Pinot Blanc).

1. LIGHT, DRY

9%Vol	Gros Plant (France)
	Kabinett Trocken (Germany, Austria)
	Vinho Verde (Portugal)
10%Vol	English wines
11%Vol	Bergerac Sec (France)
	Kabinett Halbtrocken (Germany, Austria)
	Navarra (Spain)
	Pinot Blanc (from anywhere)
	Pouilly sur Loire (France)
	Soave (Italy)
12%Vol	Anjou (France)
	Bianco di Custoza (Italy)
	Chasselas, Fendant (Switzerland)
	Chenin Blanc, Steen (South Africa)
	Entre-deux-Mers (France)
	Gaillac (France)
	Frascati Secco (Italy)
	Muscadet (France)
	Nuragus di Cagliari (Italy)
	Saumur (France)
	Trebbiano & Verdicchio (Italy)

2. MEDIUM-BODIED, DRY

10%Vol	Spätlese Trocken (Germany)
11%Vol	Colombard (South Africa)
	Penedès (Spain)
	Rioja — new-style unoaked (Spain)
	Sémillon/Chardonnay (Australia)
	Vernaccia di San Gimignano (Italy)
12%Vol	Chablis (France)
	Chardonnay (from virtually anywhere)
	Côtes du Rhône (France)
	Graves (France)
	Lugana (Italy)
	Mâcon-Villages (France)
	Orvieto Secco (Italy)
	Pouilly Fumé (France)
	Alsace Riesling (France)
	Rueda (Spain)
	Sancerre (France)
	Silvaner, Sylvaner (from anywhere)
13%Vol	Coteaux du Languedoc, Picpoul de Pinet (France)
	Jurançon Sec, Vin Jaune (France)

3. FULL, DRY

11%Vol	Pomino (Italy)
	Torgiano (Italy)
12%Vol	Burgundy Premier and Grand Cru (France)
	Chablis Premier and Grand Cru (France)
	Gavi (Italy)
	Graves Cru Classé (France)
	Grechetto (Italy)
	Rías Baixas (Spain)
	Riesling, Johannisberg Riesling (Australia, New Zealand, California, South Africa)
	Rioja — traditional oak-aged (Spain)
	Sémillon (Australia)
	Vermentino di Gallura (Italy)
	Vouvray (France)
13%Vol	Châteauneuf-du-Pape (France)
	Pouilly-Fuissé (France)
	St-Véran (France)
	Savennières (France)
	Vendange Tardive (France)
14%Vol	Hermitage Blanc (France)

4. AROMATIC

11%Vol	Müller-Thurgau, Riesling-Sylvaner (Germany, Switzerland, Danube lands)
	Optima (Germany)
	Pinot Grigio (Italy)
	Seyval Blanc (from anywhere)
	Scheurebe (Germany)
12%Vol	Fumé Blanc (California)
	Grüner Veltliner (Austria)
	Muscat (from anywhere)
	Muscat-Ottonel (Austria, Danube lands)
	Pinot Gris, Ruländer, Tokay (Alsace, France)
	Retsina (Greece)
	Sauvignon Blanc (USA, Australia, New Zealand, South Africa, Brazil)
	Tocai Friulano (Italy)
	Viognier (from anywhere)
13%Vol	Condrieu (France)
	Gewürztraminer (from anywhere)

5. MEDIUM-SWEET

6%Vol	Moscato d'Asti (Italy)
7%Vol	
8%Vol	Lambrusco (Italy)
	Mosel QbA (Germany)
9%Vol	Liebfraumilch (Germany)
	Rhein QbA (Germany)
10%Vol	Riesling Kabinett, Riesling Spätlese (Germany, Austria)
11%Vol	Frascati Amabile (Italy)
	Laski Rizling, Olaszrizling, Welschriesling (Danube lands)
12%Vol	Chenin Blanc (California, South Africa)
	Côtes de Bergerac (France)
	Gaillac Moelleux (France)
	Orvieto Abboccato (Italy)
	Malvoisie (Switzerland)
13%Vol	Jurançon (France)
	Late-harvest Riesling (California, Australia)
	Vouvray Moelleux (France)
14%Vol	Recioto di Soave (Italy)

6. SWEET

9%Vol	Botrytized wines (from anywhere)
10%Vol	Riesling Auslese (Germany)
	Trockenbeerenauslese (Germany, Austria)
11%Vol	Eiswein (Germany, Austria, Canada)
	Moscatel de Valencia (Spain)
12%Vol	Beerenauslese (Germany, Austria)
13%Vol	Bonnezeaux, Coteaux du Layon (France)
	Premières Côtes de Bordeaux (France)
	Quarts-de-Chaume (France)
	Sélection de Grains Nobles (France)
	Vin Jaune (France)
14%Vol	Monbazillac (France)
	Moscato di Pantelleria (Italy)
	Sauternes, Barsac, Cérons, Loupiac, Ste-Croix-du-Mont (France)
	Tokaji Aszú (Hungary)
15%Vol	Orange Muscat (California, Australia)
	Vin Santo (Italy)
16%Vol	
17%Vol	
18%Vol	Malvasia delle Lipari (Italy)

CHOOSING RED WINES

Most red wines are made to taste dry, thus removing one of the major style variants. Red wines vary according to weight and astringency. They also differ more than white wines in their longevity: some are made to be drunk young — like most white wines — others can improve with age for decades. A long-lived red wine will give little pleasure in its youth: *see* Wine and Time, pp50–54 for guidelines on when to drink which wines.

Rosé wines vary relatively little: few are made to age, and they differ mostly in sweetness. Some, such as Rosé d'Anjou and California "blush" wines, are fairly sweet, others, including most Spanish and Provence rosés, are dry.

Red wines in the "light, fresh, unaged" category are intended to be drunk young. They are made from grapes such as Gamay, Cabernet Franc and other varieties which produce un-tannic wines (broadly speaking, it is the tannin that allows red wine to age).

Medium-bodied red wines form the largest single class. It includes many wines of high quality and even more of medium status. Some of these can go on to age into the "mature quality" class.

The "assertive, powerful" class includes wines made to display strong flavours and tannins, usually (especially from the New World) with plenty of fruit flavours. Most of these wines have the structure to age.

Mature quality wines are those from classic areas, and great vintages in lesser areas, which have undergone bottle-ageing. These wines deserve a special category because the taste of maturity is a distinct one.

The "specialities" listed here include the exceptions to the rule that most red wine is dry. In ancient Mediterranean tradition, wines made

The classic reds of France, burgundy and bordeaux, flanked by Italy and Spain.

from semi-dried grapes — with a high level of sugar to be converted into alcohol — are strong and sometimes sweet. In Italy this style of winemaking is known as *passito* or *recioto*. Italian wines labelled *liquoroso* are fortified (*see* p33).

Some wines are hard to place: are they in this "specialities" group or are they fortified? The answer is in the winemaking technique, but in taste terms there can be little to choose between a wine made from sun-dried grapes, but not fortified, and one which is made from freshly-picked grapes and then stiffened with brandy.

Red wines may move from group to group according to vintage: a good vintage in a classic area such as Bordeaux or Burgundy will move many wines up into the assertive and powerful class from their normal status as medium-bodied.

The prestigious grape varieties which form the basis of Bordeaux's and Burgundy's red wines, Cabernet Sauvignon and Pinot Noir, have been planted enthusiastically in the New World wine lands of California, Washington, Oregon, South America, Australia and New Zealand, as well as in many eastern European countries along the Danube and around the Black Sea. The wines may be of an everyday, medium-bodied style, or may rival the French originals — particularly those from top producers and good vintages in California, Oregon, Australia, Chile and South Africa.

In these areas, where there is no accepted, traditional wine style, the choice of wines can be complicated. Style is up to the winemaker, who may change his or her mind from one vintage to the next. Careful study of a bottle's back label can provide clues. □

ROSÉ AND RED WINE STYLES

These charts give as broad a range as possible (*see* box, p28). Names given are those usually found on the label: the area name (eg Buzet), classification (eg Bordeaux Cru Classé) or the grape variety (eg Barbera).

1. ROSÉ

10%Vol	Blush wines, White Zinfandel, White Grenache (California)
	Weissherbst (Germany)
11%Vol	Œil de Perdrix (Switzerland)
	Portuguese wines
12%Vol	Anjou (France)
	Bardolino Chiaretto (Italy)
	Bergerac (France)
	Bordeaux Clairet (France)
	Cabernet d'Anjou (France)
	Cabernet de Saumur (France)
	Provence rosé wines (France)
	Navarra (Spain)
	Rioja (Spain)
	Vin Gris (from anywhere)
13%Vol	Cirò (Italy)
	Lirac (France)
	Marsannay (France)
	Salice Salentino (Italy)
	Tavel (France)
14%Vol	California wines (not blush)

2. LIGHT, FRESH, UNAGED

10%Vol	Spätburgunder (Germany, Austria)
11%Vol	Blauer Zweigelt (Austria)
	Bardolino (Italy)
	Vin de Savoie (France)
12%Vol	Anjou (France)
	Barbera (from virtually anywhere)
	Beaujolais, including Nouveau (France)
	Bergerac (France)
	Bourgueil (France)
	Buzet (France)
	Cannonau di Sardegna (Italy)
	Chinon (France)
	Dolcetto (Italy)
	Dôle (Switzerland)
	Dornfelder (Germany)
	Gaillac (France)
	Grignolino (Italy)
	Monica di Sardegna (Italy)
	Alsace Pinot Noir (France)
	Saumur (France)
	Valpolicella (Italy)

3. MEDIUM-BODIED

12%Vol	Bairrada (Portugal)
	Beaujolais-Villages and Cru (France)
	Bordeaux — except Cru Classé
	Bourgogne AOC, Passetoutgrain (France)
	Cabernet Sauvignon (Europe, New Zealand)
	Cabernet Sauvignon/Shiraz (Australia)
	Chianti (Italy)
	Corbières, Côtes du Roussillon, Fitou (France)
	Merlot (from virtually anywhere)
	Minervois (France)
	Montepulciano d'Abruzzo (Italy)
	Navarra (Spain)
	Pinot Noir (New World)
	Ribera del Duero, Rioja (Spain)
	Rosso Conero, Rosso Piceno (Italy)
	Valdepeñas (Spain)
	Valtellina (Italy)
	Vino da tavola (Italy)
13%Vol	Barbera d'Alba (Italy)
	Coteaux du Languedoc (France)
	Côtes du Rhône (France)

4. ASSERTIVE, POWERFUL

12%Vol	Burgundy Premier and Grand Cru (France)
	Cabernet Sauvignon (New World)
	Cahors (France)
	Cornas, Côte Rôtie, Crozes-Hermitage (France)
	Dão, Douro (Portugal)
	Madiran (France)
	Montefalco (Italy)
	Nebbiolo (from virtually anywhere)
	Penedès (Spain)
	Pinotage (South Africa)
	Pomino (Italy)
	St-Joseph (France)
	Torgiano (Italy)
13%Vol	Barbaresco, Barolo (Italy)
	Brunello di Montalcino (Italy)
	Châteauneuf-du-Pape (France)
	Cirò (Italy)
	Collioure (France)
	Shiraz (Australia, South Africa)
	Zinfandel (California)
14%Vol	Château Musar (Lebanon)

5. MATURE QUALITY

12%Vol	Bordeaux Cru Classé (France)
	Burgundy Premier and Grand Cru — from top vintages (France)
	Cabernet Sauvignon (New World, top vintages)
	Chianti Classico Riserva (Italy)
	Graves (France)
	Pessac-Léognan (France)
	Pinot Noir (New World, top vintages)
	Rioja Reserva, Gran Reserva (Spain)
	Vino da tavola (Italy's best)
13%Vol	Hermitage (Rhône)
	Vino Nobile di Montepulciano (Tuscany)

6. SPECIALITIES

14%Vol	Sagrantino di Montefalco (Italy)
	Valpolicella Amarone (Italy)
15%Vol	Black Muscat (California, Australia)
	Commandaria (Cyprus)
	Mavrodaphne (Greece)
	Vin Santo (Italy)
16%Vol	Recioto della Valpolicella (Italy)
17%Vol	Priorato (Spain)

CHOOSING SPARKLING WINES

Sparkling wines vary greatly in quality, character and style. The French prototype, champagne, is imitated around the world. At its best champagne is dry but not austere, with a full but fine flavour coming from the use of classic grape varieties and from bottle-ageing.

Other sparkling wines vary from close competitors to champagne, made from the same grapes and in the same way, to wines which are closer to fizzy drinks: full of froth, sometimes with fresh fruit flavours, sometimes with little taste at all. The winemakers of Champagne are fiercely protective of their name; wines from anywhere else in the world made by the method traditionally used in Champagne (*see* p114 and pp214–216) are no longer allowed to use the term *méthode champenoise* on their labels; look for the words *méthode classique* (classic method), *méthode traditionnelle* (traditional method), or "fermented in bottle". All should denote quality wines made by the second-fermentation method.

Champagne may be the first choice for a celebration, but its price may render it prohibitive. All the sparkling wines listed here are above the basic, industrially-produced level and should not disappoint.

The first group — light, dry sparkling wines — all show regional identity and individuality. Most of the French and Spanish sparklers are made from more neutral-tasting grapes than is champagne and in consequence have less weight and perhaps more acidity.

Sparkling wines from Germany and Italy use more highly-flavoured grapes and tend to be medium, rather than dry, in taste. These wines are for drinking young and ice-cold, and are usually cheap enough to serve in quantity — the ultimate refreshers.

Italian Chardonnay; champagne.

In the second group, the long-lasting taste, fineness of aroma, cleanness of style and length of finish of good champagne sets it above most of its competitors.

Other fine, dry sparkling wines are conscious imitators of champagne, although the New World is developing its own styles of sparkling wine as vineyards mature. New World wines tend to be fuller and softer than champagne, though with enough bottle-age they can show the same complex flavours of maturity.

Sweet sparkling wines range from the very light, Muscat-based wines of Italy to champagnes that have been made with additional *dosage* to taste sweet. These are often intended to accompany desserts, but beware: too sweet a pudding will overwhelm most wines: a dessert wine should always be a little sweeter than the dessert. □

1. LIGHT, DRY

11%Vol	Brut sparkling wine (from anywhere except Champagne)
	Cava (Spain)
	Prosecco (Italy)
	Sekt (Germany)
	Sparkling Saumur (France)
	Asti Spumante (Italy)
12%Vol	Blanquette de Limoux (France)
	Clairette de Die (France)
	Crémant d'Alsace (France)
	Crémant de Bourgogne (France)
	Crémant de Loire (France)
	St-Péray (France)
	Seyssel (France)
	Vouvray (France)
13%Vol	Sparkling Shiraz (Australia)

2. FINE, DRY

12%Vol Champagne — brut, brut nature (France)

Chardonnay/Blanc de Blancs sparkling wine (from virtually anywhere)

Classic-method sparkling wine (the best from the New World, especially California, Australia, New Zealand)

Pinot Noir/Blanc de Noirs sparkling wine (from virtually anywhere)

3. SWEET

6%Vol	Moscato d'Asti (Italy)
7%Vol	Asti Spumante (Italy)
8%Vol	
9%Vol	
10%Vol	Lambrusco (Italy)
	Sweet Sekt (Germany)
	Sweet sparkling wine (from virtually anywhere)
11%Vol	Sweet Prosecco (Italy)
12%Vol	Champagne — demi-sec, doux (France)
	Clairette de Die Tradition (France)

CHOOSING FORTIFIED WINES

The classic Iberian fortified wines — sherry, port, málaga and madeira — and Italy's marsala, have a wide spectrum of tastes, from austerely dry to positively sweet. Wines may be sweet when young, but can mature into relative dryness, as with vintage port. This maturing is done by the winemaker in virtually all cases, vintage port being the exception. Most fortified wines are very much controlled by their makers, who decide on the style and blend accordingly (*see* Sherry and Málaga, pp424–430, Port and Madeira, pp440-447, Marsala, p391).

All sherries start off dry, and gain their sweetness from the blending in of sweeter wine. Manzanilla and fino sherries are never sweetened, but amontillado and oloroso, although classically dry, are often made as a medium or sweet wine.

Montilla wines are not necessarily fortified, but they are made in much the same way as sherry and come in a similar range of styles.

Port gains its sweetness from naturally sweet grapes. Because the fermentation is stopped before the sugar is all converted to alcohol, the port tastes sweet. Age lends dryness: old tawnies, and especially old (bottle-aged) vintage port, become drier.

Countries such as Australia and South Africa, that have imitated the classic Iberian styles, sherry and port, make wines ranging from dry to very sweet; the style will be indicated on the label.

France's *vins doux naturels* (*see* p283) fall into two types: the red wines of Banyuls, Maury and Rivesaltes are aged — sometimes for several years — in order to achieve their complex nutty tastes; the white wines made from Muscat grapes are best drunk fresh and young.

The French products known as *vins de liqueur*, such as pineau des

Vintage port and sherry.

Charentes, floc de Gascogne and macvin du Jura, although they are fortified to have an alcohol content of between 16 and 22%Vol, are not true wines (the grape juice is not fermented before fortification) and are not included in these charts

Italian wines that use the word *liquoroso* on the label are always fortified, and usually sweet.

Fortified wines cover quite a wide range of strengths. Some are lightly fortified, with 14–15%Vol of alcohol, while most ports and some sherries weigh in at 20%Vol, which is twice as strong as many table wines.

Some fortified wines are shipped from their region of production at a higher strength than the wine sold locally. This is especially true of fino sherry, which can have quite a distinctly different character in Jerez from, say, London. This is a relic of the old purpose of fortification. □

1. DRY	
14%Vol	Dry/fino Montilla (Spain)
15%Vol	Manzanilla sherry (Spain)
16%Vol	Fino sherry (Spain)
	Málaga Seco (Spain)
17%Vol	Dry Amontillado sherry (Spain)
	Oloroso sherry (Spain)
	Sercial madeira (Portugal)
18%Vol	Marsala Secco (Italy)
19%Vol	Dry white port (Portugal)
20%Vol	Oloroso Viejo sherry (Spain)

2. MEDIUM	
16%Vol	Málaga Pajarete (Spain)
17%Vol	
18%Vol	Medium Amontillado sherry (Spain)
19%Vol	Palo Cortado sherry (Spain)
	Verdelho madeira (Portugal)
20%Vol	Aged tawny port (Portugal)
	Vintage port (Portugal)

3. SWEET	
15%Vol	Cream/dulce Montilla (Spain)
	Muscat de Beaumes-de-Venise, Muscat de Frontignan,
	Muscat de Rivesaltes (France)
	Samos Muscat (Greece)
16%Vol	Málaga Dulce (Spain)
	Banyuls, Maury, Rivesaltes (France)
17%Vol	Aleatico di Gradoli liquoroso (Italy)
	Marsala Dolce (Italy)
	Bual madeira (Portugal)
	Cream sherry (Spain)
18%Vol	Liqueur Muscat (Australia)
	Muscat de Setúbal (Portugal)
19%Vol	Malmsey madeira (Portugal)
	Port-style wine (USA, Australia, South Africa)
20%Vol	Ruby port, LBV port (Portugal)
	Young tawny port (Portugal)
21%Vol	Moscato Passito di Pantelleria liquoroso (Italy)

GRAPE VARIETIES

Grape varieties are landmarks on the map of wine. The wine drinker finds it useful to know the variety used because this is a major clue to the taste and character of the wine in the bottle. A wine made from Chardonnay, for example, will have certain taste characteristics, wherever in the world it is made. The grape variety is only one ingredient in the taste — winemaking technique and the land it grows on can be much stronger influences — but a knowledge of the main grape varieties is a most useful tool in wine choice.

The cultivated grape vine is the distant descendant of a wild forest plant whose habit is to climb up and trail through trees. This can still be seen in the Caucasus, and vines are still trained up trees and arbors in Italy, northern Spain and Portugal. The severely pruned bush that is the modern vine bears little resemblance to this wild plant, but the genetic inheritance can be traced even though *vitis vinifera* has since evolved into several thousand varieties. Specific varieties are chosen by winemakers for their various attributes, both in ease of cultivation and the quality they confer on the wine they produce.

The behaviour of varieties in the vineyard is discussed in the chapter on Winemaking (*see* p99). Here, we consider the wine drinker and the character that the classic varieties give to the wine in the glass.

Despite the very large number of vine varieties, a few have been selected by winemakers as having special characteristics, and these have become increasingly international. These varieties all originate in classic European vineyards, and they are linked in the minds of wine lovers and winemakers across the world

Cabernet Sauvignon

Cabernet Franc

with classic French and other wines. European wine legislation, especially that of France, dictates the variety to be grown: all red burgundy from the Côte d'Or, the heart of the region, is made from Pinot Noir, nearly all white burgundy from Chardonnay. In other areas a mix of varieties is permitted: red bordeaux is made from a varying proportion of Cabernet Sauvignon, Cabernet Franc, Merlot and a few minor grapes.

In some European countries, such as Italy and Spain, French varieties are being introduced to complement the local, traditional, vines. Thus Cabernet Sauvignon is grown in Tuscany, and Chardonnay in Catalonia, to make new styles of wine.

Winemakers in the New World have taken these and other classic varieties and planted them widely. A debate continues as to whether a classic variety can allow winemakers to reproduce the taste of the European

original in other vineyards. The emerging consensus is that varietal character, while a strong influence on eventual wine taste, is only one factor among many. The very location of the vineyard, the climate, soil and other factors unique to that vineyard, will affect the way the vine grows and the flavour of the grapes it bears. And then the whole process of winemaking comes into play.

Most of the world's wine is made from non-classic varieties. These may be grown for traditional reasons, or because they are prolific and easy to cultivate, or because a variety is particularly suited to the local conditions. It is a mistake to think that only classic varieties can make good wine. The worldwide move to the dozen or so classics endangers local vines, which have their own special characteristics and which preserve valuable genetic material.

Throughout the encyclopedia, local varieties are discussed where appropriate.

Identifying the grape

Labels of European *appellation* wines rarely show which grape is used in a wine: until quite recently it was very much the exception. The New World vineyards of California led the way in widespread use of variety names, making American consumers familiar with Chardonnay as the name of a wine as well as of a vine variety. A drinker of red burgundy cannot tell from the label that the wine is made from Pinot Noir: it is assumed that a wine conforming to the appropriate *appellation contrôlée* will be Pinot Noir. Among the classic French wine areas, only in Alsace is varietal labelling the norm for *appellation contrôlée* wine. In other areas it is actually illegal.

The development of *vins de pays* has brought varietal labelling to France. Growers use variety names to signal that their wine uses an internationally known grape rather than the indigenous ones which the rules may also permit.

CABERNET SAUVIGNON

Cabernet Sauvignon and its cousin Cabernet Franc (*see* below) are the foundation of red bordeaux. The Cabernet Sauvignon has been the most successful of the classic varieties in travelling the world: it is planted wherever wine is made, and its character is strong enough to present a recognizable basic taste whatever the context.

The variety developed in Bordeaux, and began to be noted by name in the late 18th and early 19th centuries. The Château Latour archives hold a letter from the *régisseur*, Lamothe, recording his plan in 1808 to plant "8,000 cuttings of the best variety, the Cabernet; they will be planted with care".

Cabernet Sauvignon gives low yields, and is thus only grown where quality wine is the aim. It produces small berries, with thick and very dark skins, which means that there is a low ratio of pulp to skin. This gives a wine that is tannic and very dark in colour. Consequently it is often blended with other varieties, such as Cabernet Franc and Merlot. This is the recipe for the "Bordeaux blend" which has become popular in many New World vineyards as 100% Cabernet Sauvignon has proved too austere. The variety is a late ripener, which restricts its use in the cooler vineyards of France, such as the Loire: Cabernet Franc ripens earlier. It requires moderate temperatures: in over-warm conditions, and with rich soil, the wine can be "jammy", lacking in acidity and with dominant vegetal, "grassy" flavours. Despite this, and while the meagre Médoc gravel seems to provide the ideal soil for Cabernet Sauvignon, it will flourish under most conditions.

Tasters identify Cabernet Sauvignon through its colour: dark red with a little purple in it when very young. The colour fades towards brick red with age. The aroma prompts mentions of blackcurrants in young wines, cedar-wood on more mature ones. The taste of young Cabernet Sauvignon is often harsh because of the abundant tannins. It reacts well to oak-ageing, so tasters look for oak notes, and appreciate the harmony between the variety's fruit, tannins and the contribution of new oak when the wine is aged in new casks. Un-oaked Cabernet Sauvignon will be softer, more direct in taste. Cabernet Sauvignon has a good capacity to mature: great red bordeaux from a good vintage will improve for decades.

Apart from Bordeaux (where it is blended with Merlot, Cabernet Franc and other more minor varieties), Cabernet Sauvignon is found elsewhere in south-west France in wines such as Bergerac; in the Midi and elsewhere in *vins de pays*; in the central Loire where it is blended with Cabernet Franc; in the rest of Europe as a modern introduction into Spain and north and central Italy (though isolated plantations date back a century in Rioja, the Duero and Chianti).

In eastern Europe, Bulgaria has 35,000ha (85,000 acres) of Cabernet Sauvignon — as much as Bordeaux — and has established a thriving export market to the UK and Scandinavia for its wares. It is also grown in Romania, Moldova, Russia, Georgia, Greece, Turkey and the Lebanon.

In the USA, California produces serious, quality wines from its 15,000ha (37,000 acres) of Cabernet Sauvignon (1995), mostly in the North Coast counties. It is used as a single variety and, increasingly, blended with other varieties. Chile has had Cabernet Sauvignon vineyards for a century, with very good results.

Australia has had success with the variety in Coonawarra in South Australia, in the Hunter Valley of New South Wales, and in isolated cool vineyards in other areas. New Zealand has had less success, but Cabernet Sauvignon vines need a long time to become truly mature (12–15 years) and many of New Zealand's vines are still young. South Africa grows the variety with some success: it is at its best blended with Merlot and Cabernet Franc.

CABERNET FRANC

While this red variety is grown in Bordeaux, it is nearly always in a minority in blends with Cabernet Sauvignon and Merlot. The exception is St-Emilion, where the Premier Grand Cru Château Cheval Blanc is made from 60% or more Cabernet Franc. A typical Médoc or Graves classed-growth will have 12–15% Cabernet Franc, though *petits châteaux* are likely to have more. It is dominant in the central Loire vineyards of Touraine, where wines such as Saumur, Bourgueil and Chinon are essentially Cabernet Franc. Unlike its cousin, it has been little exported, and its status rests with its contribution to the classic Bordeaux blend. Some Cabernet Franc is grown in California, but outside France the grape is most popular in north-east Italy, in the Veneto and Friuli-Venezia Giulia.

In the Loire, where it can be tasted unblended, Cabernet Franc produces a relatively light red wine which only rarely has the capacity to age. Occasional hot years produce Loire reds which improve with bottle-age, but most are drunk young. The Cabernet Franc lacks the tannin, acidity and structure of Cabernet Sauvignon, offering in their place fresh fruit aromas, a characteristic taste of soft fruits, and an earthy taste.

CHARDONNAY

The most successful white grape in the international spread of classic varieties, Chardonnay became established as the name of a style in California in the wine boom of the 1970s and 1980s. Winemakers around the world have attempted to replicate some of the success of Chardonnay in its home vineyards of Burgundy and Champagne. This process has demonstrated that Chardonnay is a profoundly adaptable variety, capable of making a wide range of wine styles in a wide range of locations.

The vine is easy to grow, and it tolerates a wide range of climates, from the cold of Champagne to the warmth of Australia.

The classic, benchmark Chardonnays are the white wines of the Côte d'Or, Chablis and Mâcon, and the sparkling wine of Champagne. In burgundy, Chardonnay is used alone; in champagne it is normally blended with the black grapes Pinot Noir and Pinot Meunier. Champagne made from pure Chardonnay is called, and is labelled, *blanc de blancs*.

White burgundy marries the tastes of Chardonnay and oak, a pairing that has been tried everywhere Chardonnay is grown. Oak casks are used to ferment the wine in Burgundy, as well as to age it. This treatment is restricted by its cost to the very best wines: most Chardonnay is simpler, made with normal methods.

Tasters find strong fruit flavours in Chardonnay: in hotter climates, the fruits move away from the citrus of burgundy towards the banana/pineapple end of the spectrum. The best Chardonnays, such as white burgundies, age well: others, especially those with no oak-ageing, are made for early drinking. With Chardonnay, much depends upon the intentions of the winemaker.

CHENIN BLANC

Chenin Blanc is a variety of usually unexciting if predictable quality. In one area — the Loire — it can make long-lived white wines which emerge from an acidic youth to a maturity of complex, luscious sweetness. In South Africa, California and other areas it is used to make medium-dry wines of inoffensive and commercial character. It is an adaptable variety.

The great Chenin-based Loires are Vouvray, Bonnezeaux, and other Anjou *appellations* (*see* pp238–241). The winetaster finds these wines a challenge, for without intimate knowledge of Loire vintages it is hard to tell if they will be sweet, moderately sweet or almost dry. Age plays its part too: few white wines live as long as sweet Chenin Blanc-based wines in a great vintage.

The variety is suited to late-harvest wines from grapes affected by noble rot (*botrytis cinerea*). The Layon Valley of Anjou, and Vouvray, are the prime areas for this. Chenin Blanc ripens late, and picking can take place as late as November. The resulting wines are sweet, with the noble rot accentuating the sweetness.

GAMAY

Gamay's oft-quoted denunciation by the Burgundian Duke Phillip the Bold, who in the year 1395 ordered it banned from the vineyards of the Côte d'Or, has stained its character in the eyes of subsequent generations of wine lovers. Yet even the most fair-minded admit that Gamay is hardly a classic. It owes its place in this survey to the fact that it makes Beaujolais, one of the most widely known (if not always widely drunk) light red wines in the world.

Gamay is rich in ripe fruit aromas and flavours. If the winemaking method traditional (and still current) in Beaujolais, *macération carbonique*, (*see* p112) is used, Gamay wine keeps this simple, direct, fruity character. In wine made from Gamay, it is the grape which is dominant in the mix of factors. True, there are carefully defined *crus* in Beaujolais, each with its *terroir*, and they can be distinguished, but their use of Gamay gives them more in common than their subtleties differentiate them.

Gamay is also grown in the Loire Valley, and in a few vineyards in central France, and outside France is found on any scale only in California. Here, confusion over names (there is a "Gamay Beaujolais" which is no such thing) makes it difficult to discover whether actual Gamay is being grown.

Gamay wine is not long-lived, the exception being *cru* Beaujolais in outstanding vintages.

GEWÜRZTRAMINER

In German "Gewürz" means spicy, a clue to the character of this white-wine grape, which is at home in the vineyards on both sides of the Rhine in Alsace and south Germany, and in northern Italy and Austria. Traminer is considered by some to be the same vine, though in parts of Germany a distinction is made.

Wine made from Gewürztraminer is one of the most recognizable of all. It has a pronounced fruitiness overlaid by aromatic, spicy notes. If made badly, it can be coarse; if the fruit is underripe it can be under-flavoured, but good Alsace and Baden examples have a mouth-filling intensity, though acidity is nearly always low. Gewürztraminer's taste has been likened to ripe grapefruit, lychees, or mangoes. It is often more recognizable by its aroma: hard to describe, easy to recognize and remember.

Gewürztraminer has had limited success outside its central European home, partly due to its intolerance of warm conditions, when its wine can turn out too flabby and blowzy. Some Gewürztraminer is grown in California and in New Zealand.

MERLOT

Merlot is to the right-bank vineyards of Bordeaux what Cabernet Sauvignon is to the left-bank, Médoc, districts. It is the key to the great red wines of St-Emilion and Pomerol, though not always dominant in percentage terms in the blend. The important rôle it plays in some great names (Ch Petrus, particularly) has led California winemakers to experiment with the variety.

On a less exalted level, Merlot is widely grown in southern France, where it increasingly figures on *vins de pays* labels, and in northern Italy. Many of the minor Bordeaux regions grow more Merlot than Cabernets. Merlot is used even in the Médoc because it ripens earlier than Cabernet Sauvignon. However, this makes it vulnerable to spring frosts and it is also susceptible to *coulure* and other damage, and in some vintages Merlot vines yield hardly any grapes: 1984 is remembered in Bordeaux as a vintage made almost entirely from Cabernet.

Merlot made unblended offers a soft, earthy, fruity taste, a dark, rich colour, and a simple and direct aroma. Most Merlot wine is made to be drunk young; the exceptions, such as the great Pomerols, age into a wine of superb complexity. It is not yet clear whether New World Merlots will match this longevity, but much money and effort is being put behind it.

Merlot

Chardonnay

Gewürztraminer

Chenin Blanc

Gamay

Riesling

Pinot Noir

Nebbiolo

Sauvignon Blanc

Muscat

MUSCAT

More a family of grapes than a single variety, Muscat wines are instantly recognizable to anyone who has tasted a Muscat table grape. The taste is about the only common factor in this vast family. Some are black, some reddish, some white in colour. The wines made from Muscat grapes vary just as widely: from sparkling white to the rich, dark, fortified wines of Australia.

It is thought possible that the Muscat vine is the oldest variety there is, and even that other *vitis vinifera* vines are descended from it. Such theories are unprovable, but it is a fact that classical Greece grew Muscat or something similar, and that a vine that the Roman author Pliny described was Muscat. Greece still has Muscat vines, and the places where Greek colonists settled, from the Crimea to Marseilles, still grow it.

There are at least 200 members within the Muscat family. Some are better than others: Muscat Blanc à Petits Grains is generally considered the best. It thrives in relatively hot conditions, such as are found in the southern French vineyards of Frontignan, where it is used in *vins doux naturels*. The same vine occurs in the Rhône Valley at Beaumes-de-Venise, and also nearby at Die, where the wine is sparkling. In Italy and Spain, the vine is important and known as Moscato and Moscatel respectively.

Australia has taken Muscat Blanc à Petits Grains and produced a remarkable and unique style of wine: liqueur Muscat. Until detailed studies were done, it was thought that the Australian vineyards contained several varieties of Muscat. However, Muscat Blanc à Petits Grains mutates readily, changing in grape colour from white to red-brown. This has led to confusion, with the various colours being given names such as White, or Brown, Muscat. Truly, they are all Muscat Blanc à Petits Grains.

Other Muscat varieties, such as Muscat of Alexandria, produce

CHOOSING WINE/GRAPE VARIETIES 39

higher yields but the wine is of lesser quality. It is, however, widely grown in countries as various as Greece, Australia and South Africa. Muscat Ottonel, a 19th-century crossing, is widespread in central Europe, from Alsace eastwards via Austria and Hungary to Romania.

Muscat vines vary in the style of wine produced according to the degree of concentration and of Muscat flavour. Muscat Blanc à Petits Grains produces the grapiest, most intense wine. It is rare, however, for labels to indicate which type of Muscat is used in a wine.

NEBBIOLO

Italy's main contribution to the ranks of classic vine varieties, Nebbiolo, is at home in the valleys of Piedmont, where it makes Barolo and Barbaresco. However, the vine is hardly grown outside Italy, with only a few vines in North and South America. Nebbiolo's Piedmont home vineyards are hilly, and misty in autumn and cold in winter. The grapes ripen late in the season, sometimes as late as November, and need the warmth that south-facing slopes can offer. They are dark, tough-skinned and high in acidity, meaning that wood-ageing is almost essential to tame the resulting wine.

Nebbiolo wines are famously long-lived, and need time in bottle, and in the decanter, to soften their tannins and bring out their bouquets. The inherent bitterness in the Nebbiolo grape can become astringent if the wine is not well made.

PINOT NOIR

Infuriating to grow, fascinating to taste, Pinot Noir is the grape of great red burgundy. Unlike its white counterpart Chardonnay, Pinot Noir has resisted attempts to duplicate the Côte d'Or taste elsewhere. That does not stop winemakers trying, such is the allure of classic burgundy.

Pinot Noir has an ancient history, with documents tracing it back to 14th-century Burgundy, and folklore

taking it beyond to Roman Gaul. With age goes an unstable genetic character, leading to many mutations, and a great susceptibility to disease. Recent genetic work has multiplied the number of clones of the vine available. Some of these clones increase disease-resistance, but produce inferior wine.

It is possible that some of the problems faced by Pinot Noir growers around the world stem from the use of inferior clones. Clonal variation is also shown by the wide range of wine styles made in the Côte d'Or, which is a Pinot Noir monoculture. Whatever the clone, Pinot Noir poses problems for growers. It is in danger from spring frosts, from summer rain (which leads to rot) or excess summer heat and from cool autumns which inhibit ripeness. It never makes much wine: yields must be kept low if quality wine is the aim.

Outside Burgundy, Pinot Noir makes great wine in Champagne, where it is almost always blended with (red) Pinot Meunier and (white) Chardonnay in that most famous of sparkling wines. Pinot Noir is widely grown elsewhere in the world, but its claims to greatness are contested. Spätburgunder (the German name for Pinot Noir) is growing deeper in colour and drier in style since lower yields and *barrique*-ageing took over from the sweet versions. Pinot Noirs made in Italy and eastern Europe often disappoint with their lack of character and intensity of flavour. In California, and even more in the Pacific Northwest of the USA, avid experimentation has produced a wide range of Pinot Noir wines, both in style and quality. Perhaps Oregon has the best track record so far, but unaccountable disappointments mar the progress being made. Australia has only recently begun to discover, or rediscover, the cool vineyard sites needed by this variety.

The taste of Pinot Noir is hard to define: much depends upon *terroir* and winemaking, more so than with other red varieties. Light versions

hint at soft fruits; more solid wines, with oak in their ageing, develop complexity and density, while still retaining a relatively pale colour and a hint of ripe fruits (cherry, Morello cherry).

RIESLING

Germany has produced one true classic vine, the white-wine grape Riesling. The variety is perfectly adapted to the cool, steep, river-slope vineyards of Germany, so much so that the classic German vineyards, as opposed to the everyday ones, are almost wholly given over to this aristocratic vine.

The virtues of Riesling are that it makes a wine that balances acidity and sweetness. It ripens late in the year, but this can mean superb sweet wines if the autumn is warm. Riesling also resists winter cold, surviving frosts that kill other vines. Against it is its relatively low yield — by German standards.

Riesling can make dry or sweet wines, wines for early drinking and wines that can age for decades. The best take advantage of the variety's acidity, which adds interest to even the sweetest wines.

The variety is grown in the best vineyards of Germany's Mosel and Rhine Valleys, in Austria and southeast down the Danube, and in northern Italy. In France it is restricted to Alsace, where its wine is typically stronger in alcohol, and drier, than the German versions. In the New World Riesling does well in California, New Zealand and Australia. In such warmer climates the balanced acidity of the German prototype wines can be lacking. Late-harvest Rieslings can be successful, but are usually "fatter" in style than German wines. Riesling should not be confused with the Welsch or Laski Riesling, which is inferior.

SAUVIGNON BLANC

This variety was not regarded as a classic until the discovery, by fashionable Paris followed by the rest of the world, of the wines of Sancerre and Pouilly Fumé in the 1960s. Sauvignon Blanc had been used to make these two Upper Loire white wines for generations, but it was the vine's place in Bordeaux that attracted what little attention it got. For, with Sémillon, it is a component of white Graves and Sauternes. These wines were on the world's fine wine lists when Sancerre and Pouilly were forgotten villages in central France.

Today, the Sauvignon Blanc style — fresh, acidic and assertive yet with enough fruit to be enjoyable — is known worldwide. Winemakers in New Zealand and California have taken the variety and produced wines which have undercut the Loire prototypes in price on the export market, and sometimes overtaken them in quality. Yet it is still to Bordeaux that the wine lover turns for Sauvignon Blanc wines which have the capacity to age, to gain complexity and to be truly fine wines.

Sauvignon Blanc is acquiring a new role in Bordeaux, that of rejuvenator of tired wine styles. When producers of Entre-deux-Mers, Graves and basic AOC Bordeaux wish to add some zest to their wine, they increase the Sauvignon component at the expense of Sémillon. It is not that simple, of course: Sauvignon's rise is in part to do with its affinity with modern winemaking. Cool fermentation, skin contact, maturation in tank rather than cask, all suit Sauvignon Blanc. So many of the Sauvignon Blanc wines trumpeted as the "new" wines of old *appellations* are as much due to improved techniques as to the extra Sauvignon. In many ways these wines are France's answer to the New World: New Zealand, especially, has caused a stir with a flood of often excellent, and usually inexpensive, Sauvignon Blanc wines.

The traditional style of Sauvignon Blanc wines, in Sancerre and Pouilly, may have been better than legend would tell. So much poor wine was made, often by large firms remote from the vineyards, that there is a danger of losing contact with the traditional style. This tradition involved low yields, fermentation in oak (sometimes new oak): a generally Burgundian approach. A few growers, such as Didier Dagueneau (*see* p246) of Pouilly, are reviving this approach, with impressive results. They may be able to prove that Sauvignon Blanc can make wine capable of ageing, and that it deserves more respect as a variety. But the vast majority of Sauvignon Blanc wines are, and will be, simple in taste and structure, and designed to be drunk young.

Sauvignon Blanc's international spread is now wide, following the boom in fashion. Australia is mostly too warm for the variety — New Zealand supplies the wine. Chile has yet to match New Zealand for clean, fruity Sauvignon Blanc wines — but the signs are that it will.

In California Sauvignon Blanc has been designed by Robert Mondavi into a new kind of wine: Fumé Blanc. This clever adaptation uses a short period of oak-ageing to transform California Sauvignon Blanc from a flat, rather grassy-tasting wine to something akin to Pouilly Fumé. Italy, Slovenia, Austria and Bulgaria have varying amounts of Sauvignon Blanc; it is perhaps in Austria that it does best.

Sauvignon Blanc requires cool conditions and a poor soil if it is to emulate the Upper Loire. In warmer regions — even Bordeaux — it can take on a rather vegetal style, lacking the acidity and crisp fruit of the Loire prototype. The warmer the region, the more influence careful winemaking can have on the style.

Sauvignon Blanc is a junior partner in white Graves and Sauternes, at least in quality terms. The balance of varieties varies from château to château, with Sémillon usually in the majority in Sauternes, though both varieties are subject to noble rot if conditions are right. Sauvignon Blanc takes over as the majority component of Graves, with some properties growing 100% Sauvignon Blanc. The Pessac-Léognan *appellation* insists on at least 25% Sauvignon Blanc.

SEMILLON

Sémillon is highly unfashionable among both winemakers and wine drinkers, and is rarely thought of as a single-variety grape. The name Sémillon on the label does not encourage sales in the way that Chardonnay or Sauvignon Blanc does. Indeed its main role is to be blended with Sauvignon Blanc in sweet wines such as Sauternes, but this obscures the variety's usefulness in dry ones. It partners Sauvignon Blanc in great white Graves, and alone it has made some superb, long-maturing dry wines in Australia's Hunter Valley. These wines are not widely known, and their need for long ageing works against them.

Sémillon's virtues include reliable cropping, a good yield and resistance to vineyard diseases. In all these respects it is the superior of Sauvignon Blanc. It also responds well to oak-ageing, something which the superior white Graves wines have been demonstrating for generations. But, unlike Chardonnay, Sémillon has not caught the imagination of New World winemakers eager to emulate the classic French wine styles. This is due partly to the grape's vices, which include a tendency for its juice to oxidize easily during the winemaking process. Another problem — and opportunity — with Sémillon is that their thin skin makes the grapes liable to rot. This is good news if the rot is "noble" *botrytis cinerea*, but bad if the rot is the dreaded grey variety which can ruin a crop while the grapes are on the vine.

In France, Sémillon is concentrated in the Gironde, around Bordeaux, and in nearby areas like Monbazillac. There are fair-sized Sémillon vineyards in Chile, the Argentine, South Africa and Australia. Outside France it is only in Australia, and in particular in the Hunter Valley of New South Wales, that Sémillon has made its mark. Elsewhere in New South Wales it is grown in the Murrumbidgee zone and blended with other grapes to produce good everyday wines.

SYRAH

Syrah is yet another classic French variety which has been exported, and its benchmark wine style emulated, around the world. Syrah is the grape of the great Rhône wines, including Hermitage and Côte Rôtie, and it is a component of Châteauneuf-du-Pape and others. Australia has taken to Syrah with enthusiasm, partly because it was one of the first grapes planted there. California is less enamoured, but a group of winemakers is working vigorously to promote the variety and its Rhône cousins. Indeed, the homeland of Syrah, the Rhône, has much in common climatically with many New World vineyards.

Historians suggest that Syrah originated in what is now Iran, at the town of Shiraz. Ancient Greek, or even earlier, seafarers brought the vine westward, and it was being grown in southern France before the Romans arrived. Australians today call the vine Shiraz.

Syrah is relatively easy to grow as long as the climate is warm, and the crop is reliable and relatively large. It poses challenges to the winemaker, especially if it is used unblended. In everyday wines, the best use for Syrah is as a *cépage améliorateur* — a vine that can add spice and interest to a blend of undistinguished grapes. Subsidies have encouraged its planting in southern France, and the distinctive smoky, rich notes of Syrah can be tasted in many a *vin de pays* from Provence round to the Aude.

If used unblended — as it is in the northern Rhône wines — Syrah needs careful winemaking and also, ideally, ageing in oak. The expense of this can be justified only in *appellations* such as Hermitage which command a premium price. A great Syrah wine can be as long-lived, complex and expensive as a first-growth claret. The connection with Bordeaux is an old one: until a century ago, Hermitage was regularly added to red bordeaux to add colour and flavour and to make the wine suitable for the important English market. Claret that had undergone this enhancement (which today would be illegal adulteration) was said to be *hermitagé*. In a sense, the practice of using Syrah to add flavour to *vins de pays* is a revival of this practice.

Australia continues the tradition, by blending Syrah with Cabernet Sauvignon. This makes a relatively soft, accessible wine. Unblended Australian Syrah (or Shiraz) is potentially a better wine; but here, as in California, growers find it vital to choose warm, well-drained hillsides for the vine. Which is exactly the description of the hill of Hermitage, the vine's archetypical home.

TEMPRANILLO

Tempranillo is the key grape of most serious Spanish red wines, including Rioja, Ribera del Duero and the fine reds of Catalonia. To the wine drinker Tempranillo carries hints of the Burgundy grape, Pinot Noir, in its aroma and taste. Science does not support theories, which doubtless

Tempranillo

Syrah

Zinfandel

Sémillon

stem from the taste, that the vine was carried into northern Spain from France by pilgrims. Whatever its origins, Tempranillo has established itself as Spain's senior red variety. It goes under a range of names across the peninsula, and is known in Portugal as Tinta Roriz. It is grown under this name in the Douro for port and table wines.

Rioja is the most widely-known Tempranillo-based wine. The grape is not the only one used, but the better the Rioja, the more likely it is to have a majority of Tempranillo in the blend. The variety grows best in the Rioja Alta and Rioja Alavesa subzones, where it receives the moderate rainfall it needs. Tempranillo ripens early, making it suitable for the high, cool areas, such as Rioja and Ribera del Duero. It also suits the limestone soils of these regions.

Tempranillo produces wine of good colour, relatively low acidity and with an affinity for oak-ageing. The Tempranillo is low in tannin, so other grapes, such as Mazuelo and Cabernet Sauvignon, are sometimes added to the blend to compensate.

Spain has kept Tempranillo to itself. Portugal apart, the only other large plantings are in the Argentine.

ZINFANDEL

All American wines are made from grape varieties of European origin, French in particular, but also Italian, Spanish, German, Hungarian, and so on. The only wine which may be considered typically American is made from the Zinfandel grape, known colloquially as *Zin*. The grape was probably imported to the USA around 1850. Its origin is thought to be the Primitivo of southern Italy, itself a descendant of the Klavac Mali, a little-known vine of Dalmatia. Zinfandel is transformed into every colour of wine that exists, and even into a sort of port wine. The very pale rosé is called *blush*. The best Zinfandels are deep red, fruity wines with markedly spicy flavours appearing towards the fourth year. □

OTHER MAJOR VARIETIES

These are some of the most widespread major varieties; other, more local varieties are discussed in their relevant chapters. *See also* p107.

Aleatico Red grape with an intense perfume, making deep-coloured, often sweet and strong wine. Grown in several regions of Italy, and now in Chile (small plantings in Australia and California).

Aligoté White grape from Burgundy; makes dry, fairly acidic white wine of varying quality, Bourgogne Aligoté. Also grown in Bulgaria, Romania, California.

Barbera Versatile red, good acidity; widespread in Italy and California.

Carignan/Cariñena France's most widely planted red grape, yielding high quantities of deep-coloured, alcoholic, tannic wine.

Chasselas White grape grown mainly in Switzerland, for a soft, dry white wine. Also in the upper Loire, Alsace, Savoie and Germany (as Gutedel).

Cinsaut Medium-quality, low-tannin red. Likes heat; used for blending in Midi, Lebanon, North and South Africa.

Colombard West France white; very successful in California, South Africa. Flowery young wines with crisp acidity.

Cot *See* Malbec, p107.

Folle Blanche High-yielding, highly acidic white variety used for Gros Plant in Muscadet, and in blends in California.

Fumé Blanc Synonym for Sauvignon Blanc in California, New Zealand, Australia, South Africa.

Garnacha/Grenache Spain's (and the world's) most widely-planted red-wine grape, Garnacha Tinta/Grenache Noir grows well in hot, dry climates; used for blending and for good, fruity rosé. Found in the Rhône, Provence, Corsica, Midi, California, Australia, and South Africa.

Malvasia/Malvoisie Good-quality aromatic white grape, producing deep-coloured, full wines, and adding its character to blends. The variety gave its name to the sweetest style of madeira. The "Malvoisie" of Switzerland and parts of France is actually Pinot Gris.

Marsanne Used for dry white wines in the northern Rhône; also grown in Switzerland and Australia.

Mazuelo Spanish name for Carignan.

Melon de Bourgogne White grape used to make dry white Muscadet wine.

Sometimes called Pinot Blanc in California.

Mourvèdre Sturdy red grape, usually blended with Syrah, Grenache and Cinsaut in the Rhône, Provence and Midi (AOC Bandol).

Müller-Thurgau Germany's most-planted grape, producing fairly neutral white wine. Also used in Hungary. Better, floral-scented Müller-Thurgau is made in New Zealand, N Italy, Austria, England and Luxembourg.

Muscadelle Aromatic white grape used in white bordeaux blends, and for rich dessert liqueur Tokays in Australia.

Muskat-Silvaner German/Austrian synonym for Sauvignon Blanc.

Palomino White grape low in acidity and sugar, used in sherry (also planted in California, Australia and South Africa).

Pedro Ximénez Very sweet white grape used for sherry and Montilla Moriles. Outside Spain, it can be found in Australia, California and South Africa.

Pinot Blanc White that can make delicate, appley-aroma wines, particularly in Alsace. Known as Weissburgunder in Germany and Austria, Pinot Bianco in Italy; is increasingly popular in California. A good base for sparkling wines.

Pinot Gris May be red or white; its wine is usually a deep-coloured, full-bodied dry white. Known as Tokay d'Alsace in France, Ruländer in Germany, Pinot Grigio in Italy, Szürkebarát in Hungary; also found in Romania.

Ruländer *See* Pinot Gris.

Seyval Blanc Hybrid grape with high acidity, making dry white wine with neutral or grapefruity character in England, New York State and Canada.

Shiraz Synonym for Syrah, grown in Australia and South Africa.

Silvaner/Sylvaner White, making wine high in acidity, low in aroma, except from good producers in Alsace and Franken (Germany). Useful in blends.

Steen Chenin Blanc in South Africa.

Tokay d'Alsace *See* Pinot Gris.

Trebbiano/Ugni Blanc Very prolific, highly acidic, often characterless white grape, widely planted throughout world.

Weissburgunder *See* Pinot Blanc.

Welschriesling White; unrelated to Riesling, but makes light, aromatic wines of very variable quality in Austria, N Italy (Riesling Italico), and throughout S-E Europe (Laski Rizling, Olaszriesling).

BOTTLE SIZES AND SHAPES

When choosing wine, the shape and size of the bottle offers some useful clues. Some regions have traditional bottle shapes and sizes.

The world standard size for a wine bottle has emerged as 75cl — three-quarters of a litre. Nearly all fine and internationally-traded wine is bottled in this size or its multiples. The litre size is widely used, mostly for everyday wines; the half-bottle, holding 37.5cl, is also found. Until the early 1980s, there were quite wide variations from the 75cl norm. Older wines will still be found in bottles holding between 70 and 80cl.

The evolution of the bottle

The bottle is central to the improvement of wine through ageing (*see* pp50–51). The first bottles were merely serving vessels, used as a decorative, though costly and fragile, way of bringing wine to table. It took a 17th-century breakthrough in glass-making, first made in England and soon taken up in Holland and France, to provide a supply of strong bottles. The key was a coal-burning furnace — charcoal had been banned by King James I because it consumed vital ship-building timber — made extra-hot by the use of a wind-tunnel. These bottles were strong, dark in colour (and thus opaque to light), regular in shape and above all cheap: the ideal containers for maturing wine.

By the mid-18th century the original globe shape had evolved into the tall cylinder we know today, suitable for "binning" — storing on its side with the cork moist, the necessary posture for bottle-ageing of the wine.

The effect of bottle size

Varying bottle sizes provide more than a convenient amount of wine: size also affects the way wine ages. Wine matures faster in a smaller bottle and slower in a larger one —

a point well worth remembering when buying wine. This is due to the amount of oxygen available to fuel the reductive processes (*see* p51). Many wine lovers find that a magnum (1.5 litres, or two normal bottles) provides optimum ageing conditions.

Traditional shapes and colours

Most wines are bottled in three basic shapes, illustrated on pp28 and 30. For reds, there are the bottles with a sloping shoulder used in Burgundy and the Rhône, and the straighter-sided, high-shouldered sort used in Bordeaux. Both are green; white wines from the same regions adopt identical shapes to the local reds, with burgundies in green and bordeaux in clear glass. The third main shape is the tall "flute" of the Rhine and Mosel. Rhine

BOTTLE SIZES

Fine-wine regions have many traditional sizes in addition to the standard 75cl:

Champagne

The champagne pint is virtually extinct.

Pint	40cl	
Magnum	1.5 litres	2 bottles
Jeroboam	3 litres	4 bottles
Rehoboam	4.5 litres	6 bottles
Methuselah	6 litres	8 bottles
Salmanazar	9 litres	12 bottles
Balthazar	12 litres	16 bottles
Nebuchadnezzar	15 litres	20 bottles

Bordeaux

Note that a Bordeaux Jeroboam differs from that of Champagne.

Magnum	1.5 litres	2 bottles
Marie-Jeanne	2.5 litres	3 bottles
Double-magnum	3 litres	4 bottles
Jeroboam	4.5 litres	6 bottles
Imperial	6 litres	8 bottles

Port

Here, a Jeroboam is the Champagne size.

Magnum	1.5 litres	2 bottles
Tappit Hen	2.25 litres	3 bottles
Jeroboam	3 litres	4 bottles

wines use brown glass, Mosels and Alsace wines, green.

Other wine regions use all of these. Italy and Spain offer all variations of shape and colour, with few consistent themes; though brown glass is normal for Italian reds.

Some regions preserve traditional shapes: Germany's Franken region and nearby districts have the *bocksbeutel* — a squat, bulbous flat-sided bottle. The Jura has its own shape and size for Château-Chalon: the short *clavelin* of 62cl reflects the amount left from a litre after the evaporation of six years in cask. Other, less venerable, shapes include the Provence "skittle" and the similar bottle used for Italy's Verdicchio. Vintage port uses a variant on the high-shouldered, straight-sided bottle, with a slight bulge in the neck. The straw wrapping on Chianti's flask or *fiasco*, little used today, is a relic of the protective sheafs necessary when glass was very fragile.

Champagne and other sparkling wines use a sloping-shouldered bottle made of thick glass to with stand the pressure of the gases inside.

Modern wine bottles

Some New World wine producers adopt bordeaux-shape bottles for Cabernet Sauvignon wines, burgundy-style ones for Chardonnay and Pinot Noir. However, bottle size and shape is increasingly a marketing tool: new wines in Italy announce themselves with expensive, heavy glass and unusual colours (a very dark green is fashionable) and shapes. Some German producers use burgundy-shaped bottles for Pinot Blanc (Weissburgunder) and other wines. Half-bottles are increasingly used for sweet wines and other specialities, and the 50cl size is being used in Italy for wines such as Recioto de Soave which are sipped rather than gulped. □

WINE LAWS AND LABELS

Wine labels are among the most informative on any product. Labels need to be detailed because the buyer needs to know quite a lot about a wine — where it comes from, who made it, and preferably from which grapes and in which year — before he or she can judge its quality and value. Labels are also the interface between the complex laws and regulations which govern the wine world and the consumer. These laws cover quality control, health standards and authenticity. The last is most useful: vital information about where the wine comes from.

Decoding a label

The seemingly complex collection of details on a wine label can be swiftly decoded. Nearly every winemaking country sets out what must (and must not) be printed on labels. International treaties have harmonized these laws so that wine can be traded across the world bearing labels which will be legal in importing countries. Thus, for example, the New World habit of calling a wine, say, "claret" or "burgundy" — an attempt, of greater or lesser accuracy, to describe the style intended — is fast being discontinued. The current state of these regulations is set out, country by country, in a series of charts on pp576–580.

What might be called the non-specific, or legal, information is listed below. Other details, such as place of origin and/or producer, often also appear: they are discussed below under The Importance of Place.

Origin In broad terms, the first thing to look for on a label is the country of origin. This is compulsory and is expressed as, for example, "produce of France".

Quality level Then comes the quality level. Not all countries have an official hierarchy, but the European countries of the EC do. The EC divides wine into table wine — the most basic sort — and quality wine. Quality wine is in the majority in France, Germany and other countries. Within this band are specific national quality categories such as *Appellation d'origine contrôlée* (France) and *Qualitätswein* (Germany). If the wine in the bottle is entitled to one of these, the label will say so. It must further tell you which region the wine comes from. This book concentrates on quality wine, which usually gives a clue to its taste on its label. Table wine, by contrast, can make only very general claims to a region — and at its most basic level may even blend grapes from several different countries.

Capacity This is the amount in the bottle, which in Europe may be expressed as 75cl or 750ml or 0.75litres: *see* p43.

Alcohol content Shown as a percentage or degree (*see* box p46).

Vintage The vintage is not compulsory information: some wines, such as most champagne and virtually all sherry, are blended from different vintages. If a date is given,

WORLD WINE LABELS

The information found in wine labels around the world is discussed in more detail throughout the Encyclopedia in the individual country chapters: see below. There is also a comparative chart, What the Quality Wine Label Shows, in the Reference Section, p576.

France General p140, Bordeaux p142, Burgundy p185, Champagne p216, Rhône p250.
Germany p314, **Switzerland** p353, **Austria** p 357.
Italy p363, **Spain** p403, **Portugal** p433
USA pp476 and 480
Australia pp533 and 536
New Zealand p559.

national laws will stipulate how much of the wine must be from that vintage: it is not always 100%.

The importance of place

It matters where wine comes from. It matters so much that in Burgundy, for example, the names of specific fields are legally protected. Put that way, wine's unique status is thrown into relief. Other agricultural products do not enjoy such subtlety. Cheese is perhaps the closest to wine, and indeed the French authorities lay down *appellation contrôlée* zones and rules for cheeses too. With wine, the source of the grapes and the place where the wine was made are essential knowledge.

The whole question of why this is so is explored in the introduction to the Wine Lands of the World section of this Encyclopedia (*see* pp125-132). Here it is worth noting that most — certainly all European — labelling systems stress location above other factors.

From region to vineyard

Labels get complicated when they attempt to pin down the source of the wine. This is because most wine laws recognize several layers of detail. A wine may be from a broad region, from a village or district within the region, from a closely defined quality zone — the best hillside in a village — or from a specific vineyard or farm.

Each country, and each region, has a slightly different approach. The French system puts the most stress on the location of the producing vineyard, but even so the French regions vary widely in the level of detail they provide. In Champagne, for instance, it is quite rare for the label to describe the source of the grapes within the broad 32,000ha (79,000 acres) of vineyards which are entitled to use

LABEL INFORMATION

Burgundy

The appellation name — *Gevrey-Chambertin Premier Cru* — is in large print, the name of the vineyard — *Petite Chapelle* — legally must be in smaller type.

The actual title of the AOC — *Appellation Gevrey-Chambertin 1er Cru Contrôlée* — appears above the vintage date, *1990*.

"*Mis en bouteille au domaine*": the wine is bottled at source.

The name of the producer — *Domaine Rossignol-Trapet* — is accompanied by a signature. The word "*propriétaire*" and the address identify the domaine.

The alcohol level (*13%*) and the amount in the bottle (*75 cl*) must be stated.

Produce of France, printed at the top of the label, is obligatory in wine destined for export.

Bordeaux

The name *Château Latour* takes prominence: the appellation — *Pauillac* — and even the vintage being relegated to the small print.

Grand Vin means the main wine of the château; many Bordeaux châteaux also make a second wine (*see* p149).

Premier Grand Cru Classé is the status of the wine. It refers to the 1855 classification of the Médoc (*see* p146).

"*Mise en bouteille au château*" shows that it is bottled at source.

"*Produce of France*" and the capacity are legal requirements: see Burgundy above.

The name and address of the bottler (and producer), here a *Société Civile*, must be given.

Germany

Lingenfelder, the name of the estate, takes prominence. The vintage, and the grape variety — *Riesling* — come next.

Halbtrocken indicates that the wine is medium-dry. *Spätlese* is the quality category, *Freinsheimer Goldberg* the vineyard name. The suffix "*er*" means of the village of Freinsheim. *Rheinpfalz* is the region.

The information "*Erzeugerabfüllung*" or "*Estate Bottled*" is given in German and English.

The alcohol level and capacity are obligatory, following EC practice.

The bottom line contains the estate address, the quality category (*Qualitätswein mit Prädikat*, or *QmP*) and the official testing number (*Amtliche Prüfungsnummer*, or *APNr*).

the Champagne Appellation d'Origine Contrôlée (AOC). In nearby Burgundy, AOCs apply to the broad region, to communes within it and so on, in a sort of Russian doll system, down to individual vineyards which may be as small as less than a hectare (two acres).

It would be helpful if every wine showed the region it comes from, with the more detailed location added if appropriate. This is not the practice, however, in many places. The consumer is expected to know, for instance, that the Barolo zone is in the Piedmont region of northern Italy, and that Echezeaux is a small but grand vineyard in a particular corner of Burgundy.

Germany offers more clues, insisting that the region be named; but the length of German names, combined sometimes with the difficulties of black-letter script, make the information hard to disentangle. Again, the burden placed on the consumer is an unreasonable one: to remember the names and qualities of Germany's 2,000 or so named vineyards.

Spain and Portugal nearly always mention the region, in addition to the name of the producer and/or estate.

Producers
Producers may be identified on the label, or the wine may carry only the name of the region or district. Most legal systems insist that the bottler be named: this allows faulty or fraudulent wine to be traced. The bottler may not be the maker: the concern bottling the wine may be a merchant firm which buys wine from many sources: *see* p123.

If the wine is bottled by its maker, the label usually says so. The term "château" implies producer-bottling, and French law is being tightened to insist on this. Producer-bottling is not the only way to find a wine from a single producer, though: some merchants handle the bottling for winemakers. More often, however, a merchant will blend wines from several sources.

Place names and New World wine
New World wine lands are only just getting round to systematizing the use of place names. Until the 1980s, more stress was put on the name of the producer and the grape variety. The need to harmonize laws to aid exports, along with an increasing consumer awareness of the nuances of location, have combined to bring in location labelling laws in all wine countries.

The United States uses a Viticultural Area system which is described in detail on p476. Wines can, if they meet the rules, be labelled as coming from a state, a county, or a specially defined area which can be as large as half a state (such as California's North Coast VA) or as small as one vineyard (such as Napa Valley Atlas Peak VA in California).

Australia introduced a similar system in 1994, based on zones and regions. New Zealand's appellation system is due for implementation in 1995, while South Africa has had a system of Wine of Origin regions, with a narrower category of districts, since the 1970s.

Why appellations are controversial
The officials who draw up maps of wine zones bear a heavy burden. If land is placed within a prestige zone, it may increase in value by an enormous extent. In Europe, the

ALCOHOL CONTENT
In most countries of the world it is compulsory to state on the label the alcoholic strength of a wine. This may be expressed as a percentage of the total volume of liquid — say, 12% alcohol by volume (abv) —, as used in this Encyclopedia, or as degrees of alcohol (12°).

Under EC law, wine is defined as being between 8.5 and 15% alcohol by volume. Certain quality wines (as distinct from table wines) may fall outside this range; Italy's Moscato d'Asti, for example, has around 6% alcohol by volume, while fortified wines such as sherry and port may contain up to 21%.

boundaries are often hallowed by tradition, but even in Champagne the limits of the AOC have been controversial. In Italy, the boundaries of some wine zones (DOCs) owed more to politics than viticulture; zones were too large, or in a few cases had no real right to exist. A massive tidying-up operation is underway to eliminate doubtful DOCs (*see* p360).

New World countries that move to establish wine zones on a legal basis face problems. First, setting the boundaries raises the vexed question of whose land is in and whose out. Second, once a zone is established it can be impossible for new land to be planted outside the zone. If a vineyard area is new — and all the ones outside Europe are — then no-one can be sure that the best land has yet been discovered and planted. To set a wine zone's boundaries is to inhibit experiment.

Other label information
Wine laws in some countries insist on further detail. Most places demand that the name of the bottler be printed; this can be illuminating if the wine is not bottled in the region it comes from, showing that the wine was bottled not by a local estate but by a *négociant*. In Germany, each quality wine label carries a number which shows when and where the batch of wine was officially tested.

As well as the legal information, many wines carry further details and advice. This is often in the form of a back label. The text may tell how the wine was made, with useful detail such as whether the wine was oakaged, which will influence taste and longevity. There may be hints on serving the wine, how long it can be kept, and whether it is dry or sweet.

Sometimes, too, there is a more personal note from the producer, This can be pure hype, but occasionally provides fascinating insights into what goes into the making of a wine. These back labels are most common in New World countries, and in Europe on supermarket wines. □

BUYING WINE

Because there are so many wines in the world, and of such widely varying quality, buying decisions can become complex. Price may limit your choice, but today's range of wines is wide at every price level. It is helpful to narrow down the range by using the style categories in the Choosing Wine chapter (pp27–33). After that, keep an open mind: today there are many more wines, from many more places, than even the most expert taster has tried. With new vintages arriving and old ones developing and changing in bottle, even well-informed wine merchants cannot hope to know more than a fraction of the available wines.

The many ways to buy
There are many ways to buy wine, from dealing direct with the producer to visiting a famous city-centre store. In between come wine clubs, direct mail merchants, and stores of all sizes, from specialist wine merchants to edge-of-town supermarkets. You can even buy wine "pre-owned": the major auction houses have thriving wine departments. Each outlet will be trying to suit different customers. Some aim to sell large amounts of very cheap wine; others concentrate on a certain part of the world or a type of wine, or offer a high level of service (which will be reflected in the prices). Many wine lovers use several sources of supply: they visit a wine warehouse in search of bargains and bin-ends, they buy from a wine merchant or a mail-order company which has expertise in one region, and they pick up everyday wine from the supermarket with the family groceries.

Consult the experts
It is worthwhile using expert advice when buying wine. In the past this meant going to a wine merchant and accepting what they had to sell.

A chance to taste — and buy direct.

Today there is plenty of informed comment in the press on which wines are worth trying. Journalists may recommend wines which promptly sell out as readers try to buy them — which points up how limited the supply of many good wines can be. Books, especially annual ones, will update you on the condition of vintages and will pick out rising stars and up-and-coming regions. Be aware, though, that even specialist writers can taste only a small percentage of the wines available. They also have their personal likes and dislikes. To tie yourself to the recommendations of just one expert is to restrict your choice, increase your bills (star wines always rise in price) and miss half the fun of wine, which is discovering for yourself which wines you like best.

Cultivate wine merchants, from the august traditionalists to the bright young staff at well-run chain stores. Many of them have wide experience, and today many are trained by wine education authorities. In a good store the staff will have tasted the wines and can advise on their maturity, fitness for various food combinations and general character.

Bin-ends and discount stock
The bargain-lover will find plenty of wine at attractive prices in what the wine trade calls "bin-ends". These are small amounts of wine which the merchant wishes to sell fast. The normal reason is to clear the way for a new vintage, or to reduce over-stocks of wines which have proved unpopular. Many merchants hold bin-end sales once or twice a year, and the good ones will describe the wines, saying which are in need of drinking soon, which have a minor flaw, and which are merely from unfashionable places. Careful scouring through such offers can yield bargains. Some stores specialize in such bin-ends, and in bankrupt stock from the wine trade. These can be the source of bargains, but beware tired and poor vintages.

Watch out too for the transatlantic trap: see Auctions, p49. The careful consumer can, however, profit from merchants' mistakes. Sometimes, too, bottles will appear with damaged labels. Try a bottle: if the wine is good buy more; you can always decant it. Other bargains can be found in second- and even third-label wines (see Bordeaux), which, especially in prolific vintages or times of economic recession, can find their way onto the market at good prices. Occasionally you will find wines labelled "from vines at..." a well-known property. These are from young vines not entitled to the appellation, or surplus production. They are worth trying.

Wine lists
Wine merchants may issue lists, even catalogues, of their wines. Lists vary from the bald to the loquacious, and good ones from merchants you grow

to trust become invaluable. They will have details of vintages: how individual wines are maturing. New wines will be featured; if your favourite merchant lists them, they will be worth a try. And they will offer accounts of visits to producers, which make the wines much more real.

Buying direct

Buying wine direct from the maker is both romantic and practical, and it can save money. Most wine areas have plenty of producers willing to sell at the winery gate. Some places make a holiday out of buying, with guided tours, shops, picnic areas and even restaurants. In other places, especially in Europe, it is more a matter of picking up a few bottles at the cellar door.

Most direct sellers provide tastings. The proprietor hopes you will buy after tasting, and it is normal to buy a couple of bottles — unless the wine is bad. It is hard to make an instant judgement about a wine, and if you are keen to find a good source of supply in a locality it pays to buy samples from several places and taste them at your leisure.

New World wineries often have a wide range of wine styles on offer. In Europe most makers will be specialists, though in many regions both red and white wines will be found. Buying direct thus limits your choice. Many wine lovers buy from three or four producers in different regions. It is pleasant to build up a relationship with them, and to observe the way their vintages differ and develop.

There is a small amount of essential paperwork in buying direct. Be sure to get a receipt, and keep it, especially if you are buying in a country not your own and taking the wine home. Find out the regulations about taxes and other possible restrictions before you buy, particularly in large quantities.

Transporting the wine must be considered. A few bottles in the back of the car will be no problem, but remember that a car in summer is a bad environment for wine: it can be ruined by high temperatures. Wine is heavy: a case of 12 standard-sized bottles weighs about 18kg (41lbs); more if the cases are wooden ones or if the estate uses expensive, heavy bottles. Adding a few cases to a heavily laden holiday car may overload the suspension. For large amounts, consider a special buying trip in spring or autumn. This avoids warm weather and crowded roads, and the wine producers will have more time to talk. No-one, however, will be very pleased to see you at harvest time.

Choosing a supplier   When buying direct, choose your supplier with care. Some of the signs offering wine for sale will be more genuine than others. Buy from someone who makes and bottles the wine at the property. In some areas, vineyard owners take their grapes to a wine-making cooperative and get back a share of the co-op's production as bottled wine. The wine may be adequate, but it will have little to do with the place you buy from: it is cheaper to go direct to the co-op.

Not every estate will sell wine direct — or, if it does, it may be at quite high prices. In many areas direct sales conflict with the custom of dealing with *négociants*. Properties may hesitate to sell to cellar-door customers for fear of upsetting their relationships with the wine trade. In some cases, estates cannot sell direct for tax or legal reasons. While this may stop you buying First Growths or *Grands Crus* direct, there will be plenty of less prestigious wines on offer nearby.

Where the wine properties are small, direct purchase is the only way to be sure of a supply of the wine. This is true of "boutique" wineries in the USA and Australia, of small growers in Burgundy, in the Loire and in other parts of France, and in Germany. Ask to be put on the mailing list of properties you like: these mailings will tell you when new wines are to be released, and it is often possible to buy direct from the property by mail.

Bulk or bottle?   Many cooperatives and other producers of everyday wine sell both bottled and bulk wine. Large plastic containers make wine cheaper, but the wine in them will not keep for long. Buy them for a holiday home, or to take back for immediate drinking, but for wine to be kept stick to bottles. A few people buy wine in casks or other large quantities to bottle at home: this is perfectly possible, the equipment needed being a hand-corking machine, plenty of clean bottles and several assistants. There is rarely any problem finding the assistants.

Door-to-door sales

Some producers use agents who visit consumers and sell their wines, which are then despatched by mail or carrier. This was and is traditional in parts of Bordeaux, especially the Libournais. Buying from these agents can be a good way of obtaining otherwise unknown wines from obscure châteaux. Be wary of dealers who offer to set up wine tastings in your home or workplace. Their margins will be high, the quality often dubious, and it is hard to resist buying.

Buying en primeur

Some wines are offered for sale before being bottled. The consumer is asked to reserve a quantity of wine for later delivery. This is done for two reasons: to secure stock of a rare wine, and to buy at a low price in times of inflation. A third reason is speculation (*see* Auctions, below). The buyer who parts with money for wine that is still in the vat is placing a great deal of trust in the supplier. The merchant, in turn, is relying on a *négociant* or a producer to honour a contract two years hence. There have been several occasions when companies have defaulted on these contracts, or simply gone broke, and the legal position of the consumer is often unclear. If buying wine *en primeur* (also called buying futures), deal only with the most reliable merchants, and keep all paperwork.

The only real reason for buying *en primeur* is to safeguard supplies. The wine trade finds it costly to hold stocks of wine until they are mature: modern accountants look askance at the old practice of cellaring wine for a decade or so. In addition some wines are made in small amounts and may not be obtainable via the stores. The consumer may feel the sacrifice of tying up cash in wine is worthwhile to be sure of having mature stocks of favourite wines. This also allows control of storage conditions: you can cellar it yourself, or pay your (trusted) supplier to keep it for you.

The question of saving money depends upon too many variables for prediction. If the wine is scarce to start with, and will grow scarcer, it may rise in price and it may be possible to sell part or all of the stock bought *en primeur* at a profit. This can misfire: wine prices fall as well as rise; vintages and châteaux may not fulfil their early promise.

Auctions

The wine trade uses auctions to move surplus stock, and a small but influential group of wine lovers buys and sells fine and old wines — "collectables". Occasionally these auctions hit the headlines when century-old bottles sell for very high prices. Most fine wine bought and sold at auction is from the last three decades: vintages that are ready to drink or will soon become so.

Fine-wine auctions are held in London, Geneva, Amsterdam and some American cities. The most widely traded wine is red bordeaux, with vintage port, white bordeaux and burgundy also represented at most sales. Buyers should obtain a catalogue and check the terms of business carefully: a buyer's premium, and in some cases value added tax and duty, will need to be added to the price. Check also the sizes of the lots, usually (but not always) multiples of a dozen bottles. The source of the wine is important: the catalogue will give details.

In addition to fine-wine sales, some auction houses hold sales of cheaper, everyday wines. These can include wines from bin-ends and bankrupt stocks.

E-commerce

A large number of web sites now offer wine on-line, including stock *en primeur*. Some of them are run by châteaux or producers, others by specialized merchants.

Wine in restaurants

In a restaurant, your choice is in large measure made for you by whoever draws up the wine list. A good list will offer wines which complement the food, and at a range of prices. If the list reveals care and thought, the house wine should be as reliable as the more expensive bottles.

Wine lists Many restaurants do not draw up their own lists but rely on a wholesaler who supplies both wine and printed list. Experienced diners will spot these by the narrow range of wine. A regular clue is the inclusion of "generic" wines rather than those of individual properties or growers: Médoc or St-Emilion instead of a named *petit château*. In restaurants with these lists, do not hesitate to ask to see the unopened bottle before making a choice. The label may offer clues to quality in the form of a property or *négociant's* name.

As general quality improves, truly bad wine in restaurants is becoming rarer. Lessen your chances of disappointment by sticking to areas with a reasonable reputation. Remember that little bad, or even boring, wine is exported to Europe from the "New World" wine lands: it is not worth the shipping costs to import really ordinary wine. Also these countries are trying to gain a reputation. Sadly, the converse is not true: Europe exports some poor wines as well as very fine wines, and the term "produce of Italy, France or Germany" on a label is no guarantee.

Some wine lovers avoid ordering fine or rare wines in a restaurant, reasoning that they have no way of knowing whether the wine has been well stored or if it will be properly handled. Vintage port is hard to get in restaurants not because it is expensive but because no-one can be trusted to decant it.

Restaurant tactics Having made your choice, be sure to look at the label before the bottle is opened: it should be shown to you. Watch as the waiter removes the capsule and cork. This reassures you that the wine is what you have chosen — the right year, if one was stated, and wine. It also gives a good clue to the competence of the *sommelier*.

Tasting the wine is more than a ritual: few bottles are bad, but when they are they should be rejected. When tasting a rare and expensive wine, check the glasses before the wine is poured. Sniff quickly at the inside of the glass (it may have picked up off odours in storage or washing), and pour a little water into the glass and swill it around. This will sometimes release the smell of dishwasher chemicals. If a glass is dirty or tainted, ask for a fresh one and sniff again.

When offered a sample of wine, look at it quickly: is the colour clear and bright? Then sniff: a corked bottle (*see* Wine faults, p79) will be obvious. Taste to see if the wine is fresh and clear-cut in taste, and to assess its temperature. Reasons for rejecting a wine are if it is corked, if it is the obvious victim of poor storage and is tired and old, or if it has a fault such as excess sulphur.

White wines should be served, and kept, cold. Many restaurants serve red wines too warm: they can be improved by gentle chilling. Ask for an ice bucket. If a second bottle is ordered, taste it, too — preferably in a fresh glass. There is no reason to suppose it will not be faulty just because the first bottle was good.

Ignore all this advice when drinking ordinary, everyday wine in a casual way — except the rule about rejecting bad wine, just as you would bad food.   □

KEEPING WINE

WINE HAS A RARE QUALITY AMONG ALL OUR FOODS AND DRINKS:
IT CAN IMPROVE FOR YEARS. GOOD WINE CAN GET BETTER, BUT NOT ALL
WINE IMPROVES WITH AGE, AND WINES AGE AT DIFFERENT RATES.

The heart of many a traditional wine estate is the bottle cellar, where old vintages rest in cobwebbed peace. This is the private cellar of the Rioja *bodega* Viña Tondonia in Haro, northern Spain.

When it was found that a good vintage could get better if kept, wine made the leap from an ephemeral beverage to something close to the sublime. For most of the time that wine has been made, the newest wine has been considered the best. This meant that medieval wine merchants would hasten to sell the "old" stock when a vintage was approaching, for they knew that customers would prefer the fresh new wine. The customers also took it for granted that wine would get worse if kept. Merchants had no idea why wine became vinegar, and did not suspect that poor winemaking, dirty storage casks and exposure of wine to the air would hasten its decline. The Romans, and many cultures since, have found that good wine tightly stoppered — be it in a pottery amphora, a well-made cask or a glass bottle — can get better, not worse, with age. Roman vintages were prized at a century old. But it was not until the 18th century that wine began to be made deliberately, on a large scale, to be aged. Winemakers, in Bordeaux and elsewhere, began to exploit the quality of wine that allows it to gain in taste and subtlety if it is aged. There are two kinds of ageing: in a wooden cask or other container, and in the bottle. The first is entirely the job of the winemaker, and the second may also be partly under the winemaker's control. But bottle-ageing is more the job of the merchant or, increasingly, the final purchaser of the wine. Some wines need no ageing, and are ready to drink when sold. Others gain from a few months in bottle; but they, and the first group, rapidly lose freshness if kept in bottle too long. It is just as important to know which wines to drink soon as it is to know which need to be kept. It is useful to know how a given wine has been matured if you want to establish the optimum time to drink it. For instance, some Spanish and Italian wines are matured for long periods in cask and bottled when virtually ready to drink. Bottle-age adds little if anything to these wines, for they are already mature when bottled. Wines such as vintage port are bottled after little cask-ageing and need long years in bottle to mature. Others, such as red bordeaux, spend up to two years in new oak casks, then must spend more years in bottle.

WINE AND TIME

Why does wine change over time? Even the most brilliant research chemist cannot give a full answer to this question. Pasteur's work in the 19th century showed that oxidation affects wine exposed to air. Oxidation slowly (sometimes quickly) destroys the colour in a wine, turning both red and white wines brown. A cut banana, or apple, suffers the same fate. But Pasteur's hypothesis that this process takes place in a corked bottle seems incorrect. Not enough air passes through the cork to allow oxidation. What is going on is a process of reduction: the small amount of oxygen present in the wine is fuelling various chemical reactions, which themselves involve bacteria, enzymes and other components of the wine. Wine is a complex chemical: over 800 individual components have been identified in it.

Tannins and acids

The main reactions that the oxygen is fuelling involve the colouring matter the wine gets from the grapes, the tannin it gains from stalks and skins (and sometimes the casks), plus the acids that are present in grapes. These processes gently and slowly strip the wine of its hard edges, in every sense: in a red wine colour changes from deep purple to red, then to a faded brick or mahogany. Tannin is softened, as is acidity.

What is happening in the bottle is not just the removal of negative, harsh flavours and powerful, brash colours. The wine is gaining more and more complex scents — the experts say "aromas" — and more interesting and subtle tastes as it ages.

Every wine goes through these changes — except for very simple ones which are fiercely filtered, or pasteurized, during the process of making or bottling.

How long is long enough?

Great red wines, fortified wines and sweet white wines can age and gain in character for decades. This is because — in very simple terms — they have plenty of fat to live on. For a wine to age for a long time, and become complex and interesting in the process, it must have very great qualities at the beginning. Rare is the wine that starts simple and ages to complexity, though some great wines can taste simple in youth

YOUTH, MATURITY AND AGE

The life cycle of a wine can be shown on a simple graph. There are two variables, shown by the two axes on the chart. One is time: shown along the bottom. The other is quality: shown along the side. A wine rises to a peak, over a greater or lesser period, and then falls. The height of the peak of quality depends on the intrinsic quality of the wine and the characteristics of the vintage it comes from. Thus a poor year will never make a wine that scales the ultimate quality heights, and a mediocre wine district or château will not either, however good the vintage.

Different wines develop at different rates. Some are precocious: they rise fast to their peak, and fall fast from it. Beaujolais among reds, and many white wines, fit this profile. Other wines — such as red bordeaux — take longer to rise to their peak, stay at it longer, and decline more slowly.

The graph only shows examples, and each wine is different. However the profile concept is useful when thinking about the maturity of a wine.

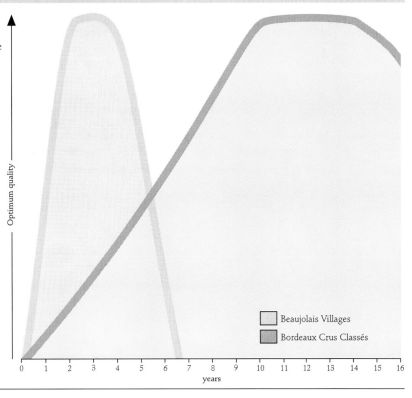

Beaujolais Villages

Bordeaux Crus Classés

owing to tannin or acidity masking their underlying flavours.

Some wines are made to age, some to drink while young. This is partly a decision of the winemaker, partly a matter of *terroir*, grape variety and weather. Each of these factors bears upon an individual wine.

To explore one example: the 1980 red bordeaux could never last as long as the 1982s because 1980 was a cool, damp year, while 1982 was a warm, dry one. In particular, the weather was good at the right times in 1982, and poor at the wrong times in 1980; the overall weather statistics for the two years, in terms of rainfall, were (on paper) very similar. The 1982 grapes were very ripe, the skins were well coloured, the rain in October was late and did not dilute the juice. With super-ripe grapes, winemakers felt able to expose the wine to plenty of new oak in its initial cask-ageing. This adds tannins and other complexity-inducing components to the young wine. All in all, the 1982 wines are predicted to have a life of decades, while the 1980s were mostly past their best by 1990.

Wines made under the same climatic conditions may differ in their ability to age owing to underlying *terroir*, linked to the mixture of grape varieties used. Different grape varieties grown in adjacent vineyards will make wines with very different ageing potential: Gamay and Pinot Noir grown in Beaujolais and Burgundy are examples. Gamay wine is low in acidity and tannin, high in fruit. It develops fast, but has a short potential life span (*see* graph, p51). Pinot Noir has more tannin and complexity, and thus has the ability to age for far longer.

A winemaker may decide to make two wines from the same estate: one which is destined to age, the other for early drinking. His decisions as to the length of time the new wine spends in the fermentation vat, how the wine is aged, and when it is bottled, will contribute to the varying characters of the two wines.

All these factors are explored in more detail in the chapter on Winemaking, starting on p99.

The process of decline
Eventually, the reductive processes inside the bottle will contribute to its decline. The fruit flavours will begin to fade; the acidity (always present, sometimes masked) will start to dominate; the aromas will lose their freshness. The wine is now past its best and in time it will decay and die.

Keeping conditions
A wine will age differently in different conditions. Temperature plays the biggest part in altering the rate of change. These factors are to a large extent under the control of the wine merchant and the final purchaser, and are discussed on the next six pages.

Choosing wines to age
There are two main reasons to buy young wine to age: to ensure you have the wines you want, which may be unavailable in shops when they reach maturity; and to control the cellaring conditions. Of lesser importance is the possible financial saving and/or profit, which is discussed on p48.

Beyond these reasons is the basic question: will the wine age well? The list on p54 groups wines according to their likely keeping time. It should be remembered that vintages play a big part in the ability of wines to age.

Most wines in an ageing cellar will be red. Fewer white wines need time to mature. Most wine buyers fall into a pattern of buying white wines as they need them, and using storage space (and money) on red and fortified wines. Remember the rule about buying young what cannot be bought old. Each region has some wines that are made in small amounts, and are in great demand. Buy these young, or not at all — unless you can pay a premium price. Examples are clarets such as Château Petrus, California's currently fashionable Cabernets, the best domaine-

bottled burgundies. There are only 7,000 bottles of Romanée-Conti a year, and the whole world wants them. Most classed-growth clarets are made on a much larger scale and can be bought through the wine trade later in their lives. At the other end of the spectrum, minor wines from obscure districts can be worth cellaring and they should be bought when found, for they rarely appear on merchants' lists.

How much wine to buy?
How much can you afford? There is rarely too much wine in a cellar, and if there is, there will always be someone to buy it. The great auction houses regularly sell off the surplus contents of cellars large and small.

Wines that last longest need most space: a serious red bordeaux, for example, may not reach its peak for eight or ten years, but may stay at or near its best for a decade after that. If you expect to drink three bottles a year of such wine, you need three dozen. If a wine — a red burgundy, say, of moderate quality — is expected to improve for four years and then stay at its best for another four, then a dozen will do.

For most wine lovers, space and money will impose constraints. Think of your wine collection, or cellar, as having three parts: day-to-day wines; the "working" fine wine selection; and maturing wines. The aim should be to have a "working" cellar holding enough mature wine to cover your foreseeable needs — dinner parties, family occasions — and a surplus for impromptu pleasure. Thirdly there are the long-term wines: those which you are nursing towards maturity. Eventually, it is to be hoped, these wines will start to flow into the "working" cellar, avoiding the need for outside purchases — except for more young wine to provide continuity.

A number of software programs are now on offer, which help the wine lover to manage stocks in his wine cellar.   □

WINE COLOUR AND AGE

As wines age and mature in bottle, they change colour. Red wines grow steadily lighter, white wines grow darker. Reds vary, according to type of wine and age, from deep plummy purple through various shades of red to tawny-orange and mahogany. Whites range from virtually colourless when young through gold to deep ochre. Sweet white wines are usually darker when young, and can age to a yellow-brown hue.

Red burgundy   On the left a four-year-old wine, showing the characteristic mid-red, with slight brick-red notes, of wine made from Pinot Noir. On the right a 12-year-old wine, still with some depth of red but distinct signs of age in the mahogany-orange at the rim.

Red bordeaux   On the left, a three-year-old wine shows its relative youth in the bright red colour fading to white, rather than brown, at the rim. On the right is a mature wine: a *cru bourgeois* at 11 years old. The deep red has faded, and a distinct orange note shows at the edge.

Port   The sample on the left is a ruby port: young, perhaps three years old, and that on the right is a ten-year-old tawny. Both have aged in large vats. The tawny has lost much of its deep purple colour and gained an attractive brick-red hue.

German wine   The left-hand glass contains a young Mosel Riesling Kabinett, the right-hand one a similar wine at 20 years old. The young wine is virtually colourless, having a slight green-gold tinge. The older wine has darkened to mid-gold.

WINES TO KEEP

The following list gives broad guidelines on how long to keep wines. Wines are divided into five groups:

Y Wines that must be drunk young. Their best quality is freshness; bottle-age does nothing to improve them. Drink within a year of the vintage, or within 2–3 months of purchase. Many such wines have no vintage date on the label. Wine stores with a fast turnover will sell Group Y wines that are fresh and at their best: beware stores — and restaurants — with a slower turnover of stock.

I Drink at 1–3 years old. These wines need a brief period in bottle to settle, blend their flavours, soften acidity or tannin, and allow flavours to emerge.

II Drink at 3–5 years old. These wines gain more subtlety from bottle maturation.

III Drink at 5–8 years old. Classic wines which demand bottle-age to show their true quality.

IV Wines that reach their best at 8+ years: refer to vintage charts. These are the great wines from the best vintages.

Within categories there will be big variations: the best wines from an area, and the best vintages, mean longer-lasting wine. Refer to the vintage charts in the Reference Section for guidance. In poor vintages, treat all Group II–IV wines as Group II.

GROUP Y

France All *vins de table*; white *vins de pays*; most red *vins de pays* except those from classic grape varieties or named estates; Muscadet except from named estates; *nouveau* wines; Côtes du Rhône; whites from the South-West such as Gaillac and Bergerac; Provence white and rosé wines.

Germany *Tafelwein* and *Landwein*; branded (non-vineyard-specific) QbA wines and wines such as Liebfraumilch.

Italy Most whites except noble grape varieties.

New World Blended or "jug" wines, white and red.

Other South-east European whites; Vinho Verde; most Spanish whites; most rosé wines; most sparkling wines, except champagne (*see* Group I); fino and manzanilla sherry.

GROUP I

France White wines: good-quality Muscadet; other Loire whites including Sancerre and Pouilly; Chablis; regional AOC white burgundies; most Alsace; most white bordeaux (including Graves) from non-classed growths. Non-vintage champagne gains from an extra year in bottle.
Red wines: Provence; Midi wines such as Hérault and Corbières; South-West reds such as Cahors; bordeaux from minor appellations and *petits châteaux*; red burgundy from normal to light vintages, and generic appellations; Beaujolais *crus*; Loire reds.

Germany Most QbA wines, except very good vintages and top vineyards and/or producers.

Italy and Spain Most reds except *riservas/reservas*; all whites; all sherry except those in Group Y.

New World Chardonnays and Sauvignon Blancs; most red wines except those from quality areas and producers.

GROUP II

France White wines: the best Alsace; most good dry white Loires that are not in Group I, but not sweet Vouvrays and other Chenin Blanc wines, which need longer; good white burgundy; Graves and Sauternes from good but not top châteaux; Jurançon; vintage champagne.
Red wines: all those from Midi, Provence, South-West and Rhône wines not in lower groups; bordeaux such as Médoc, St-Emilion, Fronsac, Pomerol from all except classed growths in good vintages; burgundy below *Premier Cru* level, and at it in all but the best vintages.

Germany QmP wines up to and including *Auslese*, though not from the best vintages.

Italy and Spain Most *riserva/reserva* and *gran reserva* reds; Cabernet Sauvignons.

New World Top-quality Chardonnays; all but the best reds from Cabernet Sauvignon, Syrah and other grapes from quality areas.

GROUP III

France White wines: the best Graves and Sauternes — only the greatest wines (Château d'Yquem etc) need longer; Vouvray and other Chenin Blanc wines from hot vintages; *sélection de grains nobles* Alsace; top white burgundy; the best vintages of champagne.
Red wines: good, but not the greatest, red burgundy; great burgundies from average years; good northern Rhône wines and Châteauneuf; most bordeaux classed growths, except from the best years and top châteaux.

Germany The best *Auslesen* and above; *Eiswein*. These can improve — sometimes for decades — but most can be drunk within their first decade.

Italy and Spain Top Barolos from good vintages; the best Rioja *reservas* and *gran reservas*; the best "super" *vini di tavola*.

New World Top Cabernet Sauvignons; best Australian Shiraz and Sémillon.

GROUP IV

France White wines: the very best Sauternes and sweet Loire wines; *Grand Cru* burgundy.
Red wines: top (*Grand Cru*) burgundy from fine vintages; bordeaux classed growths from fine vintages; Rhônes from the best properties in fine vintages.

Others The richest QmPs from the top vintages in Germany; vintage port.

Very much a Group IV wine.

STORING WINE

Wine kept for more than a few weeks needs proper storage conditions. It can be hard to achieve these in many homes, and some wine lovers use commercial cellars or storage facilities for their fine wines and long-term storage. However, much can be done to make even the most unpromising apartment wine-friendly. The main needs for wine storage are listed in the box on p58.

Basic storage conditions

Wine needs to be kept still, dark and at a constant temperature. Humidity should be on the high side, ventilation should be good, and there should be no intrusive smells. Temperature is the hardest factor to regulate, which sometimes means that the others are neglected. Vibration and movement will harm wine, especially old wines with a deposit. Avoid storing wine where it may have to be moved; do not put it near domestic machines. Strong light, too, can harm wine, especially white wines. However tempting it is to display bottles in dining room or kitchen, keep them in the dark and they will be better for it. Avoid spaces where other items, such as fuel oil, paint or vegetables, are stored. Fumes can taint the wine, even through the cork, and vegetable matter and foodstuffs can introduce fungal and other pests. The high humidity is to stop corks drying out — also the reason why bottles must be stored on their sides. (If the cellar is very damp, elastic bands help keep the labels on.) Free circulation of air avoids musty smells and rot.

Temperature

The ideal is a constant, low temperature. The range can be 5–18°C (41–64°F), but somewhere in the middle of this range, around 10–12°C (50–55°F) is the optimum. More important than the actual temperature is the range through which it fluctuates, and more important still is the short-term fluctuation. If the cellar slowly moves from 12°C (55°F) in winter to 20°C (68°F) in summer, no great harm will be done. But if it fluctuates by this amount every day, or week, then there will be problems. The wine in the bottles will expand and contract, the cork will suffer, and eventually the wine will begin to "weep" around the cork, leaving a sticky deposit around the capsule.

Achieving cellar conditions

Best of all is a rock-dug cellar or cave. Almost as good are the stone or brick-built cellars beneath old houses. Check these for hot-water pipes, which can raise the temperature: lag pipes if necessary. Make sure that cellars are well ventilated, but be prepared to inhibit ventilation in any extremes of weather — hot or cold.

A large quantity of the same wine can be kept in a "bin".

Ensure cleanliness, but be careful if fungicides are used to treat or clean brickwork or wood: these can leave a taint. The floor should ideally be porous to allow the humidity to be kept high. A layer of gravel on part or all of the floor can be watered to raise humidity.

If there is no cellar, and it is not possible to create one (*see* right), there are two choices: to insulate a cupboard or part of a room, or to invest in purpose-built, temperature-controlled cabinets. Cooling units can be bought which will allow a large cupboard or small room, or an inadequate cellar, to be kept at the correct temperature. Some cabinets are effectively refrigerators with accurate temperature control, adjustable between 6°C and 15°C (42–59°F). Others have both warming and cooling circuits, allowing them to cope with a wide range of ambient temperatures. Such cabinets can be used in places such as outbuildings or garages which are prone to wide temperature fluctuations. Purpose-built wine cabinets have air filters to avoid mould growth. Do not use a cabinet with a lamp, like a refrigerator: these may jam on, producing harmful light and heat. The most sophisticated cabinets, designed for restaurant use, have compartments at various temperatures to hold white and red wines at the right level for serving.

Racks and shelves

The next requirement is orderly, safe storage. Shelves and racks need to be secure and easy to reach, and there must be a simple way to discover which wine is where. The traditional cellar had "bins" or large compartments in which wines were stacked. This assumes large amounts of the same wine. Today racks holding a dozen bottles, and individual bottles, are more use. The best racks are metal, which cannot rot, though wood and metal ones are much used and will last for many years. All-metal racks can tear labels if you are not careful.

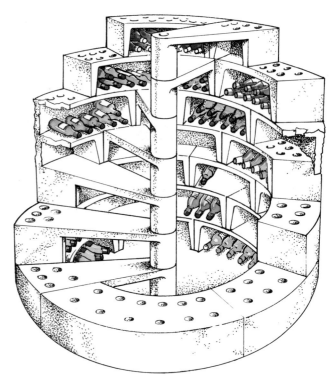

The **spiral cellar** (above) is a modular concrete construction: it is buried in a pit, lined with a waterproof membrane, which is dug beneath a house or outbuilding and accessed via a trap-door. It provides the benefits of a cellar for those homes without one. These cellars can be obtained in several sizes.

Wine which is packed in wooden cases can be kept in them, but there is a small risk of dry rot. Cases should not be placed directly on the floor: place battens beneath them. Cardboard cases should be viewed as temporary storage only, as they will rot in damp conditions, and possibly introduce smells and mould. Wooden cases should be kept if there is a chance that the wine will be sold. Original cases reassure the buyer at auction and can enhance the value of the wine. This is particularly true of magnums and larger sizes.

The cellar book

A cellar book — a ledger with columns for wine bought and consumed — helps keep track of the constant flow of wine. In practice, with many single bottles or small lots of wine, it is hard to keep a cellar book up to date. Use one for logging wine bought by the case, and/or for

The **temperature-controlled cabinet** (above) is useful in apartments, where cellars are not available. It has heating and cooling elements and can be set to maintain a constant internal temperature.

IN THE CELLAR

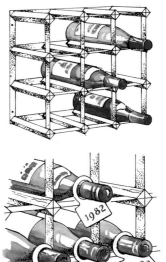

The ideal wine cellar (above) has plenty of racks and bins of various sizes, a table for decanting and note-keeping, and of course the right conditions of temperature, humidity and ventilation. The racks shown here, set in a diamond pattern, provide space for a dozen, or fewer, bottles of the same wine. Most cellars also include racks for single bottles (*see* below). The floor can be covered with gravel, which can be watered to raise humidity.

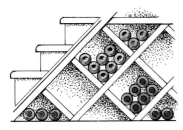

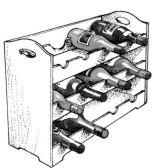

Wine can be stored virtually anywhere — see above — if basic conditions can be ensured. Keep bottles in the dark, and insulate racks beneath stairs from vibration.

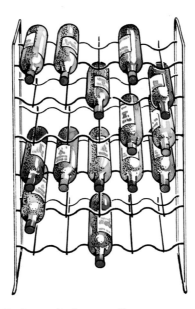

Racks can be free-standing.
These are made of wire-covered plastic and hold the bottles at a slight slope.

Racks can be fixed to a wall, when they will need stout screws or bolts to handle the weight.
Use tags or labels (above) to mark individual bottles.

long-term storage. A system for labelling racks and bins is even more useful. Individual labels or wipe-clean tags can identify bottles, or racks can be labelled with a grid system so that bottles can be pinpointed in a ledger. If wine is kept in wooden cases, ensure that the case end, with the wine name and vintage, is visible.

Wine collecting

Some wine lovers consider the contents of their cellar as a collection, rather like a library of rare books or an album of postage stamps. Any collection should have a theme, and wine collectors have amassed some remarkable hoards of wines from certain châteaux or districts, and even of large-format bottles from particular properties. These collec-

tions provide the raw material for very special tastings, at which fellow wine lovers can compare the qualities of the various vintages of a given wine, or can contrast the wines of different estates in the same vintages.

A collector will take enormous care over the storage conditions of the cellar, as some or all of the wines will be very old and thus fragile. Labels and cases will also require more care, for the bottle itself is part of the "collectable" and, indeed, will be the only souvenir when the wine has been drunk.

A wine collection, as opposed to a domestic cellar, may well have more large-sized bottles, from magnums upwards. These will not fit into most normal racks, and storage space will have to be especially designed and

built for them. Large-format bottles often have their own wooden cases.

Collecting strategies

The wine collector, unlike the investor, will not restrict the cellar to the "blue chip" wines which are certain to command an easy auction sale. As noted above, many strategies can be adopted, the common feature of all being some kind of logic. The collector will seek out faultless examples, and when wines cannot be bought *en primeur* they will be sourced from impeccable cellars where storage conditions are known. In turn, the collector hopes that when the time comes to drink, or perhaps to sell, the wine, its provenance — the collector's cellar — will add lustre to its reputation.   □

STORAGE CONDITIONS

The main needs for successful wine storage can be summed up as follows:

Temperature. *See p55.* When establishing a cellar, use a maximum–minimum thermometer to take readings at different points, and keep notes. It will become clear that some corners are warmer or cooler than others. If possible, isolate the source of temperature change and neutralize it. For example, lag hot pipes and block off very cold draughts. Insulate doors leading to heated parts of the house with polystyrene or glass fibre. The aim is a balanced temperature that does not rise or fall too rapidly. Continue to use the maximum–minimum thermometer until you have a picture of the annual temperature fluctuation.

Darkness   Light harms wine; especially white and sparkling wines. Ensure the cellar is dark, blocking off any light from outside, even from a ventilator on a sunny wall.

Artificial light is necessary for access and use of the cellar, but do not make it too bright, and be careful never to leave the lights on.

Cleanliness   If possible, clean the cellar thoroughly before storing any wine in it. Use a disinfectant, preferably without a scent, to kill mould, insects and other organic life. Then paint the walls with a porous paint such as whitewash: it is not a good idea to seal brick or stone walls as this inhibits natural ventilation and humidity control, and can cause condensation.

Humidity   Ideally, relative humidity should be 75–80%. Excess humidity rots labels, cardboard boxes and (eventually) corks; but if humidity is too low, corks may dry out.

You can raise humidity by covering the floor with a layer of gravel and watering it.

Dehumidifiers can be used to extract excess moisture from the air, but these are expensive and only worth

considering in large cellars. Deal with excess humidity in small cellars through drainage and improved ventilation, and by sealing off moisture sources such as very damp walls. Labels can come unstuck in a damp cellar: an elastic band will stop a special bottle from becoming anonymous.

Ventilation   Air circulation is essential, though this may clash with the need to keep temperature low. A true cellar should have air bricks or ventilators allowing air from the outside to enter and circulate. These can be blocked in very cold or very warm weather. If the cellar has north- and south-facing walls, place ventilators as low as possible on the north side, and high up on the south side. This utilizes the natural flow of air, with warm air being extracted from the upper ventilator by the convection effect of the warm south-facing wall, and cool air from the north side flowing in to replace it.

Freedom from vibration
The kind of harsh vibration caused by domestic machinery, or a nearby road, can harm wine. Racks will insulate the bottles to some extent.

Orderliness   It should be easy to find any wine, and to discover wines of the same sort in adjacent racks. Use labels or a logging system (*see* p56).

Accessibility   Wine once stored should be left alone. Therefore it should not be necessary to move one bottle or case to get at another. Avoid rigid racking systems that cannot be altered to cope with changes.

Angle of storage   Wine must be stored horizontally, to keep the cork moist. Some collectors fit racks and bins with a very gentle backwards slope to encourage deposits to form near the base of the bottle, while the cork stays moist. Place labels uppermost, so that the deposit will then form on the opposite side of the bottle.

SERVING WINE

CARE IN SERVING, THE RIGHT TEMPERATURE, THE CHOICE OF THE CORRECT
GLASS, CAN HELP GET THE BEST FROM EVERY BOTTLE,
BE IT AN EVERYDAY WINE OR A PRECIOUS OLD VINTAGE.

The severe simplicity of plain white table linen, white and gold china and classically-shaped crystal glasses allow wine and food to give of their best. Glasses with tulip-shaped bowl and tall, thin stem are ideal for white wine.

Serving wine covers what to do between choosing which bottles of wine to open and enjoying them in the glass. One can — indeed should — be very relaxed about this on most occasions. A corkscrew and a glass are all you need when the wine is simple, the occasion informal, the decision to open a bottle perhaps spontaneous. But even a simple bottle tastes better at the right temperature. Even a minor wine is best appreciated in the right glass. And if the wine is a little more serious, the occasion more formal, so much pleasure can be gained from following the right procedures when serving wine.

The techniques of serving follow on from those of storing wine (see pp55–58). Allow wine time: a bottle that is rushed to table, straight from a shopping bag, can never be at its best. This matters little with everyday wines, but finer, older ones do suffer from being moved, and regain their balance and character only after a period of rest, preferably in a cool, dark place. With some fine wines — those prone to develop a deposit in bottle — stability is vital. It is best to plan ahead and stand such wines up two days before drinking to allow the deposit to settle on the bottom, rather than the side, of the bottle. Temperature is the next thing to consider when serving wine, as it takes a while to alter. Allow time for bottles to chill — or warm up — before a meal. Then, check on the quantity, type and — most neglected, but most important — the cleanliness of the glasses you will require (see pp71–72). And always include water glasses, and jugs or bottles of chilled water, on the table. Assemble decanters as necessary, checking that they too are clean and free of trapped, stale air and lingering odours (see pp68–70).

Finally, consider the order of service: which wine comes first? Will there be two wines on the table at once, so guests can compare them? This is normal for groups of wine lovers, but can be an eye-opener for other guests too. If two wines are to be served, mark the glasses so that everyone knows which wine is which. Small elastic bands around the stem, or a dab of washable white paint on the glass foot, are two ways to distinguish between identical glasses. Or use glasses of distinctly different styles.

TEMPERATURE

More wine is ruined by being too warm than too cold. A wine that is served cool can be warmed: the atmosphere of the room, and even the drinker's hands cupped round the glass, will rapidly heat it. A wine which is warm when poured is hard to chill, and it may well have passed the point of pleasure.

In general, white wines should be served cooler than reds. But there is a sliding scale between the two, not a step. The rubric "white wines at refrigerator temperature, red wines at room temperature" is only partly true. Different styles of white wine demand different serving temperatures, and many, if not most, reds are best served cooler than the dining room's ambient temperature.

The idea of "room temperature" dates from when our ancestors dined in what to us would be cold rooms. Wine would be stored in a cellar (which was colder still), so it made sense to bring it into the dining room in advance to let it emerge from its deep cellar chill. Today our wine storage may be at the right temperature to serve red wines, and allowing them to warm up to the centrally-heated pitch of the dining room or kitchen does them harm, not good.

It is possible, even amusing, to use a thermometer to tell exactly when a wine has reached the recommended level. On the other hand, a degree or two either way will not ruin the pleasure of the wine, while the fuss with the thermometer may well spoil your evening. Use a thermometer a few times to get used to how a bottle at, say, 10°C (50°F) feels to the touch. Then put the thermometer away and rely on your own senses.

Why do wines taste better at different temperatures? Warmth allows aroma compounds to volatilize, which is a complex way of saying that the wine's pleasant bouquet is

Insulated container and ice bucket.

given a chance to emerge. Different wines have different mixtures of compounds, and so give of their best at varying temperatures. This is most applicable to red wines, but complex white wines should not be served too cold because what makes them interesting — the tastes and aromas of quality and maturity — will be more apparent when they are warmer.

The reason white wines should be cold is to do with acidity. Warmth accentuates acidity, making some white wines taste harsh. When cool, this acidity allies with the fruity freshness of the wine to become appetizing and refreshing. Expectations have their influence, too: whites are expected to taste refreshingly chilly, so they should be.

Reaching the right temperature

How wine is stored is a big contributor to easy temperature control: those with a cool cellar, or a cooled cabinet, will have white wines nearly cold enough at any time. Note that purpose-made wine storage cabinets are not as cold as domestic

refrigerators. Do not keep wines, especially good wine, in an ordinary refrigerator for any period longer than a day or two, as they grow tired and flat and can even pick up taints from other foods stored nearby.

An ice bucket is the quickest way to cool wine. Water as well as ice is essential: cubes of ice surrounded by air are useless as air is a poor conductor of heat, and cannot extract the warmth from the bottle. Add water, which does conduct heat, and the bottle will rapidly chill, taking 10–15 minutes to cool from 20°C to 8°C (68 to 46°F). A refrigerator takes 1.5–2 hours to do the job — longer in hot weather. Once a wine is cool, an ice bucket with less ice and more water will keep it so, but beware of over-chilling. An insulated container keeps a cool bottle cool for some hours. A wrapping of wet newspaper has the same effect on a picnic.

To warm a wine, bring it into a gently warm room and let it stand quietly for two to three hours. (If the dining room is hot, the hall may be cooler.) Do not place the wine near sources of heat such as stoves or radiators: the heat will set up currents in the wine, making it cloudy if there is a deposit, and in extreme cases affecting the taste. A very cold bottle of red wine can be gently warmed in a bucket of warm water.

Temperature and occasions

If the weather is hot, wine will rapidly reach the ambient temperature, no matter what temperature the wine was to start with. The same is true of wine placed in severely air-conditioned rooms. In a hot climate, serve wines cooler than normal. In cold weather (even if the room is warm), young red wine should not be served too chilled.

Old, precious wines need careful treatment as they may be damaged by extremes of temperature, and by temperature change. Ideally, drink whites at cellar temperature (meaning the temperature they are stored at). Let old reds warm up gently from cellar temperature.

Wines served outdoors will need extra care. Whites can be kept cool in insulated bags and boxes, or even buried in the earth. The ideal picnic spot will have a stream or pool to hand: remember to tie string round the bottle necks and tie the other end to something solid.

In boats, the coolest place will be under the floorboards, where the proximity of the sea will cool the wine. Do not neglect red wines, which can easily become far too warm if stood in the sun. Offer them, and your guests, some shade.   □

For perfectionists: wine thermometer and pipette for measuring alcoholic degree.

TEMPERATURE CHART

WINE STYLE	EXAMPLES	
Sparkling wines		
Simple sparkling wines	Cava, Crémants, Saumur, Sekt, non-vintage champagne	6–8°C (43–46°F)
Sweet sparkling wines	Sweet champagne, Moscato d'Asti	6–8°C (43–46°F)
Finest sparkling wines	Vintage champagne, luxury *cuvées*	8–10°C (46–50°F)
White wines		
Simpler sweet white wines	Anjou blanc, German QbAs, Loupiac, Muscats	6–8°C (43–46°F)
Simpler crisp, dry whites	Muscadet, Sancerre, Sauvignon Blancs, Alsace	6–8°C (43–46°F)
More complex dry white wines	Burgundy, Graves, Chardonnays, Rioja	9–11°C (48–52°F)
Medium-sweet wines	German *Spätlese*, Auslese, Rieslings	10–12°C (50–54°F)
The finest sweet wines	Sauternes, *Ausbruch*, late-harvest wines	11–13°C (52–55°F)
The finest dry white wines	Mature white burgundies, Graves, the best New World Chardonnays	10–12°C (50–54°F)
Rosé wines	Simpler rosés should be coldest	6–8°C (43–46°F)
Red wines		
Young, fresh red wines	Loire reds, simple Beaujolais, Côtes du Rhône	10–12°C (50–54°F)
Straightforward red wines	Simple young bordeaux and burgundies	14–15°C (57–59°F)
Serious mature red wines especially Pinot Noir wines	Burgundies	16–17°C (61–63°F)
Fully mature fine red wines, especially Cabernet wines	Classed-growth bordeaux, Côte-Rôtie, Cabernet Sauvignon	17–18°C (63–64°F)
Fortified wine		
Dry	Fino sherry and New World equivalents	9–11°C (48–52°F)
Medium	Amontillado sherry, sercial madeira, white port	10–12°C (50–54°F)
Sweet	Oloroso and cream sherries, bual and malmsey madeiras	15–16°C (59–61°F)
	Tawny and ruby port and New World equivalents. Tawny can be chilled in summer to, say, 8–10°C (46–50°F)	15–16°C (59–61°F)
	Vintage port	16–18°C (61–64°F)
	Vins doux naturels	8–10°C (46–50°F)

OPENING WINE

The first corkscrew, it is believed, was adapted from a worm-like steel device made to extract bullets from guns. The corkscrew (or bottle screw) became necessary when the habit of corking bottles became widespread in the 18th century.

Cork is used to seal nearly every bottle of wine, apart from those holding simple wines, which are sold with screw caps. It has been found to be the best form of closure, despite the difficulties and costs inherent in dealing with a natural rather than synthetic material. Cork is cut from the bark of a particular kind of oak tree, an evergreen found in the western Mediterranean lands and Portugal.

The virtues of cork are that it is impermeable and elastic, and takes on the shape of the neck of the bottle, thus forming an excellent seal. It will last a very long time, and it is unaffected by changes in temperature. The only things that affect corks are dryness — if a bottle is stood upright, rather than horizontally, the cork will dry out — and various bacteriological and insect pests. Corks are sterilized before use to combat these, but a tiny proportion of corks will develop mould, which can penetrate the cork and taint the wine. This is the origin of the term "corked" or "corky". Wine from such a bottle will smell unmistakably flat, musty and unpleasant. A few fragments of cork floating in a wine do not mean it is "corked".

Opening the bottle

The wine should be at the right temperature before opening the bottle, which should not be shaken unduly. An old wine, which may have a deposit, should be handled especially carefully (see p68).

The first step is to remove the capsule (see opposite). This may be of lead on fine wines, of tinfoil, or of

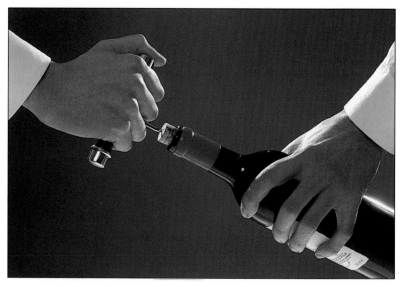

Hold the bottle securely and pull the corkscrew slowly and firmly.

various kinds of plastic. Very old bottles may have wax capsules: they must be chipped off. Old corkscrews had a hammer to do this, and a brush to remove the dust. Many capsules will tear off, some may need a knife, or the tip of the corkscrew. Some capsules are usually left on as they form part of the identity of a wine: traditional German estates use colour-coded capsules to identify the various grades of wine.

Once the capsule is off, clean the neck and rim with a cloth or tissue. □

TYPES OF CORKS

Corks come in various grades suited to different wines. The standard width is 24mm (1in), which is compressed by a corking machine into a standard bottle neck width of 18.5mm (0.75in). Champagne corks are wider — about 31mm (1.25in): they undergo greater compression in order to withstand the pressure of a sparkling wine.

Fine wine — long corks The great châteaux use long corks of the highest quality to protect wines that are expected to last decades. Wines in the private reserve cellars of the great châteaux are re-corked every 25 years.

Shorter corks are used for faster-maturing wines.

Composite corks are formed from fragments of cork glued together. They are used for everyday wines and in part of the champagne cork (see below).

Plastic 'corks', coloured or imitating the cork pattern, are a reliable seal for the medium-range wines for which they are mostly used.

Champagne corks are formed from several layers of cork: two discs of natural cork at the bottom, in contact with the wine, composite cork at the top. The "mushroom" shape comes because the cork is inserted only halfway in, so only the lower half is compressed. The mushroom top is held in place by a cage of wire and a metal disc.

Branded corks By law, all champagne corks must carry the word "champagne" and, if relevant, the vintage. Many other winemakers also print the origin and vintage of the wine, as well as the maker's name on the cork.

USING A CORKSCREW

The technique depends upon the type of corkscrew used, but the preparatory stages (*see* steps 1–3) are just as important. Some sommeliers cut off part of the capsule, as shown; amateurs may prefer to remove it all.

Once the cork is out, examine it. Check the printed brand on the side is correct. Squeeze the cork to check if it is elastic, therefore young; or hard, which indicates age. Finally sniff the cork: it should smell gently of wine, not mouldy cellars.

1 Carefully cut the capsule right round the neck of the bottle with a sharp knife. The corkscrew known as the "waiter's friend" has a knife in the handle for cutting foil.

2 Use the knife to ease off the top of the capsule. With lead capsules, remove entirely or trim to well below the rim so that the wine does not touch the lead.

3 Wipe the rim of the bottle and the top of the cork with a clean cloth. Do not worry if there is mould on the cork: it is normally just a sign that the cellar where the bottle was stored was damp.

4 Insert the corkscrew thread, taking care to hit the centre of the cork. (Check the screw: some have off-centre tips. Aim to centre the screw, not the tip.) Turn steadily until the screw is almost, but not quite, through the cork. This can be hard to judge as cork lengths vary.

5 Slowly remove the cork from the bottle. The continuous-thread type of corkscrew, pictured here, extracts the cork in a continuous turning movement; with other types, gently pull the cork out. (If it breaks, try re-inserting the screw at an angle.)

CHOOSING A CORKSCREW

Considering that the device has been around for three centuries, and has excited so much ingenuity and artistry that there are thousands of designs, there are a lot of bad corkscrews. Anyone who opens more than one or two bottles a year should invest in a proper one. There are two main aspects to the design.

First, the screw, the part that actually penetrates the cork, must be the right shape. Avoid those that look more like a gimlet or drill than a spiral. These will tend to drill a hole in the cork, and will not grip it. The result, on pulling, is a shower of cork dust with the cork still in the bottle, or broken in half. Look for a screw formed in a spiral, with an open centre (*see* opposite). This will grip the cork properly. The tip should be sharp.

Second, consider the design of the pulling mechanism. The simplest sort, with a handle set T-shaped to the screw, leaves your arm and shoulder muscles to provide the pulling power, which is acceptable for the fit and strong — though even they will be defeated by very tight corks. Look for a corkscrew with a leverage action that braces the corkscrew against the neck of the bottle. The simplest sort is the "waiter's friend", which has a claw-shaped arm attached to one end of the handle. This is lodged against the bottle neck. This corkscrew is effective with practice, but be sure to buy one with a long enough, properly formed screw.

Another design of corkscrew is the butterfly, which has twin handles operating through a ratchet mechanism onto the screw shank to lever the cork out once the screw is inserted. The principle of these is excellent, but many unfortunately have the wrong sort of screw.

Counter-screw or double-action mechanism corkscrews are the easiest to use. A common design is the

The waiter's friend in action.

boxwood double-action, which has two handles, one of which drives the corkscrew, while the other rotates the wooden screw set around it to extract the cork. The outer body provides the locator for the wooden screw, and the handle for the user.

PROBLEM CORKS

Some corks refuse to come out of the bottle: if this is the case, try the following remedies.

Sticking corks Warm the bottle neck under a warm tap to wet and expand the glass, not the cork. Or apply a corkscrew at an angle.

Broken corks Use a corkscrew with care at an angle in the part of the cork still in the bottle. If this fails, push the cork into the wine. When pouring the first glass, use the corkscrew to hold the cork away from the neck, after which it will float on the surface of the wine.

Cork fragments in the wine These can be ignored or, if intrusive, the wine can be poured through a filter (*see* p69) into a clean bottle, decanter or carafe.

An advantage of this sort is that it is easy to position the screw over the centre of the cork. Metal variations of this basic design were common in the 19th century, and reproductions can be bought today. Some used a handle working through a bevelled gear onto the shaft.

The Screwpull® is a modern design that is extremely easy and effective to use. It has a plastic body which rests on the neck of the bottle. The very long screw is wound down into the cork, and continued winding draws the cork out of the bottle almost effortlessly. The Screwpull® has the added advantage of ensuring that the screw hits the centre of the cork. This device was designed by an American oil engineer, Herbert Allen, using the principles of oil drills. A luxury version has a handle to provide the leverage, bringing the cork out with one easy movement.

Avoid devices that pump air or gas into the bottle. Faulty bottles have been known to crack or explode under such treatment. □

CORKSCREWS

Corkscrew designs range from the early 19th-century engineered elegance of the metal-bevelled twin screw (centre left) to the very latest in corkscrew technology: the Screwpull Professional (bottom left). Simple T-shaped corkscrews demand some strength.

Waiter's friend

Butterfly pattern

Classic simple corkscrew

19th-century twin screw

Modern reproduction

Screwpull®

Screwpull® Professional

Modern spring-aided

Boxwood double-action

OPENING SPARKLING WINES

Sparkling wines have no need of a corkscrew, but they need care. The wine in the bottle is under pressure, and clumsy opening can send the cork shooting out with alarming force. The froth that accompanies this is a great waste of wine — even in the most ostentatious of celebrations — but the wayward cork can be a real danger.

Safety measures

The first rule about opening sparkling wine is never to point the bottle at anyone — or at a window or mirror. The second rule is to keep a hand over the cork. This can be hard, with the wire cage to fiddle with, but the right technique ensures that the cork is under control at all times.

Warm sparkling wine is not only unappetizing, it is dangerous. Warm wine and gas have a greater volume and will explode with greater ferocity. The cork from a chilled bottle is far less likely to get out of control. So chill the bottle well first. And keep the bottle still: shaking stirs up the gas.

Use a clean cloth to lift the bottle from the ice bucket, if one is being used. Dry the bottle and tear off the foil capsule so that the wire cage is visible. You will note that the wire is twisted at the ends. Gently untwist this loop. The wire should still be round the flange at the neck of the bottle and thus holding the cork down, but from now on keep a thumb over the cap.

Once the wire is untwisted, hold tightly onto the cork with one hand and remove the wire with the other. Take the wire, and the metal cap, right off the cork. Keep a thumb over the cork.

Releasing the cork

The secret of opening is to hold the cork tightly, and twist the bottle gently with the other hand. This

Perfectly controlled removal of the cork.

applies leverage to the cork, and makes it easier to remove than when twisting the cork and holding the bottle still. It also lessens the risk of the cork breaking in half, leaving the lower half still in the bottle. If this

OPENING VINTAGE PORT

Because port ages for a long time in bottle, the corks of vintage port bottles are often old, crumbly and hard to remove. Vintage port has to be decanted (*see* pp68–69), and so the cork must be removed when the bottle is horizontal. Alternatively, stand the bottle upright for 48 hours before decanting to allow the crust, or deposit, to fall to the bottom. Sometimes getting the cork out can require unusual measures. Port tongs are the traditional solution. These long-handled metal tongs fit neatly around the bottle neck. The ends are heated in a fire until red-hot, then clamped around the bottle neck. After a minute, moisture is applied with a wet rag. The neck should crack cleanly below the cork. This is not a method for the novice.

happens, pierce the cork with a needle or sharp tool to release the pressure, then use a corkscrew — but carefully. The wine will be less sparkling, but the bottle will have been opened much more safely.

As you turn the bottle, you will feel the cork begin to move as the pressure of the gas in the wine pushes it up. When you detect this, gently ease the cork out with fingers and thumb.

Have a glass ready, and pour a little wine straight into it before there is a chance of any escaping. Hold it slanted: the wine will froth less if it slides rather than falls to the bottom. If you first chill the glasses, the bubbles (known as *mousse*) will last longer and the wine will stay cooler longer.

Pliers and stars

A pair of champagne pliers, or a champagne "star", are useful if you plan to open several bottles of sparkling wine for a party. The pliers are designed to grip the mushroom top of the cork and add leverage. The star fits into the four grooves on the top and sides of the cork left by the wire cage. With both devices, take care to hold the top of the cork with the palm of your hand or fingers to avoid sudden eruptions.

Closers

Stoppers or closers can be bought which grip around the bottle neck and keep most of the sparkle in a half-empty bottle of wine. The best sorts are effective for several days. Stoppers or closers can also be used when you need to open several bottles of sparkling wine at a time. Open the bottles in advance, replacing the corks with stoppers. The wine will be perfect for several hours — if it is chilled — and this routine will ensure that serving sparkling wine is made much easier. □

OPENING SPARKLING WINES

Sparkling wine should always be served chilled. A cold bottle is not only more pleasant, but it is safer: the eruption of gas is less forceful. Avoid shaking or other undue movement of the bottle as this too excites the gas. When opening, ensure that the bottle is pointed away from anyone, or anything fragile.

1 Tear the foil off, exposing the wire cage and the metal cap that cover the cork.

3 Remove wire and cap. Remember to keep holding the cork with your other hand.

4 Grasp the cork with one hand, the bottle with the other, and then twist the bottle — rather than the cork — gently.

5 When the cork begins to move out, ease it further with fingers and thumb. Have a glass at the ready to catch the first "rush", if necessary.

2 Gently untwist the loop of wire that is part of the cage, holding a thumb over the cork as you do so.

DECANTING

Most wine is at its best served straight from the bottle, without further fuss. Some wines, however, gain by being moved from their bottle into a decanter, a carafe — or even a jug. Decanting helps wine in two ways: it frees a wine from any solid matter, or sediment, that may have gathered in the bottle, and it allows contact with air, which may speed up the wine's maturation. The first is a practical necessity if the wine has a deposit. Each type of decanting demands a different technique (*see* opposite).

Decanting used to be essential for most red wines, as deposits of solid matter accumulated in the bottle as the wines aged. In order to enjoy a clear, bright glass of wine, free from unsightly sludge, wine was carefully poured from its bottle into a clean container. Today, wine-making techniques are different, and only a few red wines develop such a deposit.

Decanting: for and against

Wines that have thrown a deposit must be decanted, and the only questions are about practicalities. The debate over whether or not to decant other wines centres on the age of the wine and the time it is allowed to spend in the decanter. Enthusiasts for decanting say that young wines can be softened, rounded and have their taste generally improved by decanting an hour, even several hours, before they are drunk.

The counter-argument is that a lengthy period can allow the wine to lose crispness and vitality. Older wines may be freshened by decanting — but they may lose some of their precious aromas in the process.

Few doubt that the aeration caused as one pours the wine into a decanter is beneficial. Even white wines, especially mature ones, gain from this. The air releases aromas and tastes which are dormant in the wine. The question is when to do this: just before serving, or earlier.

Another argument for decanting is that it allows young wines to "age" quickly; to mimic the effect of bottle-ageing. This is more controversial: no-one is quite sure how and why wines age in bottle; the chemical reaction involved is complex and not fully understood.

Beware of decanting too soon: wines that are mature, or even past their peak, will fade quickly in the decanter. It is always best to allow too little rather than too much time. The beneficial effects of aeration will continue when the wine is poured from decanter to glass, and wines can be aerated by gentle swirling in the glass to speed up the "decanter effect".

How to decant

Decanting is an easy operation, but the weight of tradition it carries has sometimes obscured this. All that is needed is a steady hand and a good light. Work on a white surface out of choice: it makes it easier to see the wine through the neck of the bottle. An essential precaution is cleanliness. Too often decanters are not entirely clean, or are full of musty smells from being stored in a closed cupboard. The counsel of perfection is to rinse both decanter and glasses with mineral or well water before use. This is to dispel taints from chemically treated mains water, and any odours from storage. Funnels and filter cloths should be equally clean.

The vessel used can be either a purpose-made decanter, or a simple jug or carafe. ◻

WHICH WINES TO DECANT?

■ These red wines are likely to have a deposit and should be decanted:
Bordeaux *Cru Classé* and top *cru bourgeois* wines more than five years old.
Burgundy *Premier Cru* and *Grand Cru* wines more than ten years old.
Rhône Hermitage and other Northern Rhône reds and Châteauneuf-du-Pape more than five years old.
Other French Top Provence, Madiran, selected *vins de pays*.
Italy Barolo, top *vini da tavola* such as Sassicaia. Chianti seldom has a deposit.
Spain Vega Sicilia, top Penedès wines over seven years old. Few Riojas will have a deposit.
Portugal Vintage port, crusted port. Late-bottled vintage and tawny need not be decanted.
New World wines Cabernet Sauvignon and Shiraz wines over five years old from California, Australia and Chile.

■ These younger red wines will usually benefit from the aeration of decanting:
Bordeaux *Crus Classés* under five years old, *crus bourgeois* and *petits châteaux* under three years old.
Burgundy All Beaujolais, Côte d'Or village wines and *Premiers Crus* drunk under three years old.
Rhône Red wines under four years old.
Other French Most *vins de pays*, Provence and Midi wines, Loire reds.
Rest of the world All quality red wines drunk at under three years old, everyday red wines even when young.

■ Some white wines can benefit from decanting just before serving:
Germany Fine Rhein and Mosel wines more than ten years old.
Spain Good oak-aged white Riojas.
France Old white Loire wines, mature white Graves, *vendange tardive* wines from Alsace.

■ Some wines should not be decanted: Very old red bordeaux and burgundy (stand bottles up for 24–48 hours prior to serving to let deposit settle), mature white wines except those listed above, young white wines, sparkling wines.

THE TECHNIQUES OF DECANTING

Decanting young wines is straightforward. The purpose is to expose them to air, to let them soften and to let flavour emerge. Older wines need more care; they are decanted to separate them from their deposit. With young wine, simply open the bottle and pour the wine into a clean container (right), using a funnel if you like to help avoid spillage. If the young wine splashes against the sides of the carafe, so much the better; it aids aeration. Let the wine stand, uncovered, for at least one hour before drinking, in the room in which the meal is to be served. This allows the wine's temperature to rise gently from cellar level. Decant a very old wine just before serving and then put the stopper in the decanter. This stops the wine fading due to too much contact with the air. Take care not to disturb older wines before decanting. If possible, stand the bottle up gently the day before so the deposit sinks to the bottom. If the bottle is still lying down, the deposit will be along its lower side: use a basket or cradle to carry it to the decanter.

1 Remove the capsule which covers the cork. Gently withdraw the cork while the bottle is still lying in the basket. Wipe the bottle mouth with a clean cloth.

2 Light the candle or torch and place behind the bottle. Lift the bottle very carefully to keep the deposit where it has settled. Pour the wine slowly and steadily through the funnel.

3 Keep pouring in a steady stream. Do not allow the wine to "glug" in the bottle neck and swill around: that will disturb the sediment. The candle or torch illuminates the neck of the bottle: when the bottle is nearly empty, watch carefully for the first signs of the deposit. If you look through the neck at the light behind it, you will see when the black, cloudy sediment begins to enter the neck.

4 Stop pouring as the deposit appears in the neck. The wine in the decanter will be clear and bright: the deposit stays in the bottle. The filter in this silver decanting funnel is to catch the heavier, flaky deposit of vintage port. Most wines have a finer, powdery deposit.

CHOOSING A DECANTER

G reat and innocent pleasure can
be derived from the choosing
and using of wine artefacts such as
corkscrews and decanters. These
days many handsome modern and
reproduction decanters are made,
some of which are illustrated right.

History of decanters
Carafes or flasks came before
decanters. There was little distinction, in fact, between a bottle and a
flask until corks became common-
place in the 18th century. Both did
the same job: to bring wine from the
cask in the cellar to the table.

The earliest decanters, dating from
around 1730, had features of contemporary bottles, including a ridged
neck to allow the stopper to be fixed
on with string. Most early decanters
were mallet-shaped — with a squat
body and a tall neck. One oddity of
the early 18th century was the cruci-
form decanter, where the body was
divided into four sections to allow
rapid cooling of the wine when the
decanter was immersed in ice.

Later in the 18th century globe
and shaft shapes evolved, followed
by elegant tapering shapes. Neck
rings, common on late 18th-century
decanters, evolved to make tapering
decanters easier to hold. All these
basic shapes are reproduced today.
Modern decanters have reverted to
the plain glass of early 18th-century
designs after a period in the 19th century when decoration and especially
heavily cut glass were in vogue.

The ideal decanter
Connoisseurs seek out the classic
decanters of the late 18th century,
and modern reproductions, because
they offer near-perfect conditions for
fine wine. A decanter should be of
good, clear glass; it should be big
enough (there is nothing worse than
having a 650ml decanter and a 750ml

A reproduction 18th-century decanter (left), a magnum and a modern decanter.

bottle of wine) and it should not be
difficult to keep clean.

Most wine lovers look for clear
glass decanters, leaving the cut-glass
and decorated ones for spirits such as
whisky or brandy. Clear glass shows
off the colour of the wine. The neck of
the decanter should be broad enough
to allow easy decanting, and there
should be a stopper that fits.

Decanters come in bottle and
magnum sizes. The latter are most
useful: a magnum of wine may be an
occasional treat, but it is usually fine
wine and therefore deserves decanting. Do not pour two bottles of the
same wine into a magnum unless you
have tasted a little from each first.
There may well be variation between
two bottles of the same wine (it is
a traditional Bordeaux adage that
"there are no great old wines, only
great old bottles of wine"), and one
may even be corked, or otherwise

out of condition. Pour that into a
decanter containing sound wine and
you have lost two bottles. Of course,
a magnum can be split between two
bottle-sized decanters. Even larger
bottles (*see* p43) demand a fleet of
decanters — or well-washed bottles.

Carafes
Young wines sometimes gain from
decanting, too, and for them a jug
or stopperless carafe is the best vessel. A more rustic appearance can
work well, too; perhaps even using
glass with a slight texture or colour,
which would be inappropriate for
fine wine. Use a litre carafe or jug for
a standard bottle of wine, to allow
the wine to be poured in vigorously.

Carafes or jugs can also be used
when drinking wine from a large
container, such as a "wine cask" or
"bag-in-box", to keep a check on how
much is being drunk.   □

CARING FOR GLASS

Many an important winetasting has been marred by dirty glasses. They need not be visibly dirty: the film left by detergents can be undetectable by eye or nose when the glass is empty, but it can react with wine (or water) to produce a bad taste. This is a common problem in hotels and restaurants which use dishwashers, and it has happened (to the immense embarrassment of host and butler) more than once even at dinners at important wine châteaux.

Washing glasses

Glasses look impervious to taint, but they can pick up and hold smells: these can come from washing or drying or storing, and all can be easily avoided with proper care.

It is best to avoid washing wine glasses in dishwashers. An exception can be made for everyday glasses, but it is best for all wine glasses to be washed by hand, using plenty of hot water. Small amounts of mild washing-up liquid can be used if necessary, but plain hot water is best. If the glasses are washed soon after use, no detergent will be necessary.

The glasses should be rinsed straight away in plenty more clean hot water, regularly changed, and then dried while still warm and damp. Dry and polish the glasses using a clean linen or cotton cloth which itself has been well rinsed after washing. A cloth is capable of adding a detergent smell to glasses. Avoid new cloths which will leave dust and threads on the glass.

Storing glass

Storage can add taints to glasses. New glasses packed in cardboard will smell and taste of cardboard until very thoroughly washed, and the habit of storing glasses in their boxes should be discouraged for the same reason. If you hire or borrow glasses,

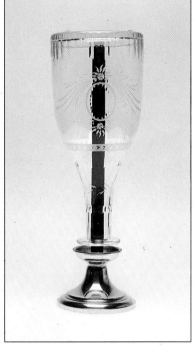

Decanter drier in action.

perhaps when having a large party, check them before use for detergent and storage smells.

The best place to store glasses is a closed cupboard outside the kitchen, which will inevitably have a steamy atmosphere. Stand the glasses the right way up, or hang them from racks. If stood upside-down on their bowls they will pick up taints from the shelf. Take them out well before the meal so that they lose any "cupboard" smells.

Decanters and carafes

Decanters must be clean. They should be cleaned in the same way as glasses — with plenty of hot water and plenty of rinsing. Getting them dry is harder. Polish the outside with a cloth as you would with glasses, and drain moisture from the inside by inverting the decanter. If very hot water is used, more moisture will

evaporate from the decanter. To drain the decanter, use a stand (*see* picture) or wedge it upside down in a warm cupboard. The stand has a smooth wooden rod over which the decanter is placed, and a heavily weighted base for stability. Most households have a warm airing cupboard into which a decanter can be wedged to allow draining of excess moisture.

Extra care is necessary when storing decanters as they can trap stale air which will taint the wine when the decanter is next used. After the decanter has been cleaned and is completely dry, store it unstoppered: if the stopper is in place it will trap air in the decanter and lead to staleness. Before using a decanter which has been stored for some time, rinse well with clean, untainted water.

With time, all decanters seem to become stained and discoloured. Sometimes stains can be carefully removed with a flexible bottle brush. Another remedy is the soluble powder sold for cleaning false teeth: a solution made from this product removes stains from decanters if they are left full overnight.

Decanter stoppers frequently get lost, especially with antique decanters. A stopper is not strictly necessary, certainly if the wine is to be consumed at one sitting, but wines like vintage port, which will survive in a decanter for some days, demand a stopper. It is also prudent to stopper red wines that have been decanted before a meal, unless you want to accelerate the softening process by encouraging further contact with air. It is sometimes possible to find replacement stoppers, but beware of those that are not quite a perfect fit: they can subsequently damage the neck of the decanter. A used champagne cork makes a utilitarian-looking stopper for many decanters, but does the job effectively.   □

CHOOSING GLASSES

Wine tastes different, and better, when drunk from the right sort of glass. This observation, seemingly esoteric and perhaps even precious, has been proved in carefully-conducted comparative tastings.

The important factors in choosing a glass are shape, size and material, in that order. Then comes tradition: most wine regions have their own well-loved shapes and even colours for glasses to suit their local wine.

But overwhelming all other considerations is cleanliness (*see* p71). A dirty glass — which need not look dirty but which carries a taint — will ruin any wine.

Glass shape

A wine glass must, first of all, have an in-turned top. The bowl must narrow towards the top to allow the aromas of the wine to be trapped and funnelled up towards you. A shallow bowl will present a large surface area of wine to the air, and there will be nothing to trap the aromas. Half the pleasure of the wine will be wasted.

The next essential is a long enough stem to allow the glass to be held without the hand coming into contact with the bowl. A glass of chilled white wine will be warmed rapidly by the hand.

Glass size

A glass should be large enough to accommodate a measure of wine, leaving the glass no more than a quarter or a third full. If the glass is too small or too full, the wine cannot be swirled around to release its aromas; and the glass cannot be tilted to view it (*see* Tasting, p77).

A normal serving of wine would be around 90ml/3fl oz (one-eighth of a bottle). So a glass should hold at least 270ml/9fl oz. Many glasses designed for red wines hold more. Avoid exaggerated glasses of the sort

The Vinum and Sommelier ranges of glasses made by Riedel were designed after much research to suit specific types of wine. From left to right, Vinum red bordeaux, red burgundy, white wine, champagne and Rhein wine glasses.

used in some restaurants where the normal measure of red wine forms a mere puddle in the bottom. These have a specialist use: they promote volatilizing of the aromas in a young wine on the large surface area — but they should not be used with old, delicate wines. A large glass, but not too large, is the ideal for fine red wines. Aim for one with a capacity of 350–400ml/12–14fl oz.

The exception to the size rule is the champagne flute — a tall, slender glass designed to show off the colour and bubbles of sparkling wine. It is filled three-quarters full, presenting a column of wine to be appreciated.

Glass material

Wine glasses at their best should be clear, and made from unadorned, uncut glass. Heavily cut crystal glasses, and glasses decorated with gold leaf, may be attractive in themselves, but they get in the way of the enjoyment and appreciation of wine. Coloured glass makes it impossible to judge colour. The best material for a wine glass is the finest crystal that cost and practicality allows. Crystal glass gives optimum clarity: its thinness means that your view of the wine is unimpaired.

This much is straightforward: what is harder to pin down scientifically is the enhanced tasting pleasure that a fine, thin glass gives compared to a thick-edged machine-made glass. Comparative tastings have left experts in little doubt that the fineness of the glass does contribute to our tactile and tasting enjoyment. But material is a lesser concern than shape or size, and many wine lovers avoid the inevitably costly fine crystal glasses because the worry of an expensive breakage impinges on the pleasure of the occasion. □

An all-purpose white-wine glass with tall, thin stem and tulip-shaped bowl.

Red bordeaux and similar wines show at their best in this larger, well-shaped glass.

Designed for mature red burgundy, this glass is large enough to "swirl" the wine, releasing the aromas.

The ISO standard tasting glass is the international norm for professional tastings.

Glass for port and sherry, based on the Jerez *copita*.

Flute for champagne and other sparkling wines.

WINE AT TABLE

In civilizations from ancient Greece onwards, wine-drinking has traditionally been highly formalized. Toasts, speeches, an elaborate order of service — all conspire to lengthen the evening and to limit the amount of wine consumed. Wine-drinking to ancient Greeks and Egyptians, and to the peoples of the Caucasus to this day, was a recreation, a social occasion, as well as a meal-time necessity. From these traditions we get toasts, and although these are now drunk regularly only in a ceremonial way on formal occasions, nearly every language has its terms for saluting your friends with a raised glass: Salut! Cheers! Prost! Slainte! Good health!

The duty of the host

If the formality has lessened, surviving customs such as this are all, once examined, reflections of the oldest tradition of them all: that of the host's sacred duty to the guests.

This is even true of that seemingly most arcane of customs, "passing the port". Happily the delights of a fine vintage port to crown the meal are no longer reserved for the men (women were once expected to retire to tea and gossip in the "withdrawing room"). But port, traditionally (and practically) served in a decanter, is still passed around a table clockwise. The host is expected to fill the glasses of the guests sitting to his right and left, pour a little wine into his own glass and then to pass the port to his left. Each diner fills his or her glass and passes the port decanter onwards, always to the left.

Why to the left? There are many concocted explanations, but there is no mystique: it is easier to take the weight of the decanter with your right hand, from the person on your right. But the central point of the custom of "passing the port" is merely the host's concern that no-one should monopolize what was often the most costly wine. It is interesting to reflect that this ritual passage of the decanter, often derided as old-fashioned, is the last survival of a pattern of hospitality going back to pre-Classical times.

Food, wine and fashion

Custom, too, dictates the order of service of wines, and their place on the menu. This is explored in the Wine and Food chapter (*see especially* p82). The conventions are: white wine before red, young before old, light before heavy, dry before sweet, minor before fine or rare. White wines accompany the first courses in a meal, red ones the main or later courses.

Do not serve assertive, aromatic wines such as Gewürztraminer and expect a delicate burgundy to show at its best just afterwards. Powerful young wines can overwhelm fading old ones.

Wines from very different wine-making traditions can clash, even if the conventions of order are followed. Think of the weight and character of the wine, and reflect that neighbours make good partners: a Sancerre followed by a Chinon; a white Graves, then a Médoc. Grape variety pairings often work well, contrasting wines from the same grape but from different regions, even different continents.

All these "principles" seem no more than practical common sense — and so they are. However, what is rarely appreciated is how ephemeral they are. They change over time, and from country to country.

Only 60 years ago, a revolutionary change came over the menus of the Oxford and Cambridge colleges: red wines began to be served with food. Until the 1930s, dinner for the Fellows at Christ's College, Cambridge, involved no fewer than nine courses — all washed down with white wine. After dinner the dons settled down with the vintage port, and with a classed-growth claret.

The pattern was an international one: André Simon, the French-born writer and gastronome and founder of the International Wine and Food Society, gave a dinner in 1907, the 14 courses of which included lamb and pheasant. The wines were sherry, Mosel and — with the game — champagne. Then port to finish.

This tradition went back a century, in England at least, with hock and champagne the wines to go with food, and not a red to be seen until the cheese course at earliest, with port and claret to follow. How will the next century regard our food and wine conventions?

Customs of service

Restaurants preserve an etiquette of service which is rarely practised today at private dinners. The host is given the wine to taste (in case of a faulty bottle — not to decide whether he or she likes it); then it is served to the women at table, starting on the host's right and working clockwise. Next it is the turn of the men, and finally the host. At a private meal, the host, who is usually the wine waiter as well, should discreetly taste a little of the wine before serving it to the guests. Wines at home can be corked or tainted, just as in restaurants.

When a wine is chosen to match a dish, be sure to serve it at the same time. It is a common problem in restaurants that the wine can arrive too late. If two wines are served together for guests to compare, leave a short interval between them to ensure everyone has some of the first wine (in the right glass — *see* p72) before pouring the second. Always supply plenty of water at table.   □

HOW TO TASTE WINE

TASTING WINE MEANS TAKING CARE TO STUDY THE QUALITIES A
WINE HAS TO OFFER, AS DISTINCT FROM MERELY DRINKING AND
ENJOYING IT. THE TECHNIQUES AND LANGUAGE ARE OUTLINED HERE.

The way a wine looks and smells are important clues to its quality and potential. Studying appearance and aroma are the first steps in the tasting process, which leads to a better appreciation and enjoyment of wine.

All day long we see, hear, feel, smell and taste. Most of the time we do so automatically: our senses react to stimuli in our surroundings, our minds barely aware of that reaction. When we taste wine we attempt to register consciously as many as possible of the sensations it has to offer, in order to increase our enjoyment and knowledge of it. Surprisingly, perhaps, this is not that complicated or difficult an art. It is simply a matter of building up a good memory-bank of wine tastes. You may not be able immediately to emulate those fictional connoisseurs who would say "Ah! Corton-Charlemagne — the '89 vintage," and add, crushingly, "the south side of the vineyard" (this was easier in days past when all fine wine was French, apart from a little German hock). But you will soon learn to recognize the particular taste and smell of the Cabernet Sauvignon grape, whether it comes from Bordeaux or Bulgaria; the taste of a wine made in a hot country rather than a cooler one; and tell new wine from older. After that, apparently dizzying feats of memory become largely a matter of elimination. Learning how to taste enhances the pleasure we get from wine, and makes it possible to choose wine with care. An experienced taster can judge when a wine will be ready to drink, enabling the selection of immature wines for cellaring. Careful tasting also allows the recognition of the rare faults in wine. For tasting, you need three things: first, the skills to allow the efficient use of your senses, so that you can interpret the sensations of sight, smell, taste and touch that you experience as you taste. Second, a vocabulary with which you can describe your reactions. Third, a set of criteria by which you can judge what you have tasted. The skills are easy to learn, and the vocabulary, like any language, simply needs working at. You need time to develop standards so that you can make judgements that are more than purely subjective. This is because you need to taste a range of wines to acquire the necessary perspective. Anybody can become a good taster if they want to. Most of us are born with more or less the same capacity to taste, and although individual sensitivities may vary widely, winetasting depends much more on practice than on any natural gift.

HOW TO START

To become a proficient winetaster you need to be able to make the most of your abilities. There are some things you can do to enhance your tasting skill:

■ **Taste as widely** as you can, in terms of both styles and quality.

■ **Always compare** wines with a common theme, which could be a region, a grape variety or a style such as sparkling wine. This makes recognition, description and discrimination easier.

■ **Establish** a regular procedure when sampling wines, and stick to it.

■ **Develop** your vocabulary, taking time to search for the right words.

■ **Begin** by tasting with an experienced taster who can guide you.

■ **Taste "blind"** so you are forced to rely on your senses alone and can judge without preconception.

The technique of tasting

Watch an experienced winetaster at work, and the process seems simple: a glance, a sniff, a sip and a spit. Then a note is made, and on to the next wine. This expertise can be acquired, as can the few "tools" needed. The photographs opposite show the process step by step.

The first stage in tasting a wine is to examine colour, then smell and finally taste. In a tasting note these would usually be described under the headings of appearance, nose and palate, followed by a conclusion.

Glasses

A tasting glass needs to be clear, plain, quite roomy (a capacity of 200–230ml is ideal) and inward-curving at the top. This "tulip" shape, widely available, holds and concentrates the aromas rising from the wine, and also helps prevent spillage when the wine is swirled around or when the glass is tilted to examine its colour. There is an ISO (International Standards Organisation) glass, which the professionals use, which is both an excellent tasting tool and a good all-purpose glass for the table.

THE LOOK OF THE WINE

Although less important than tasting and smelling, looking can tell you quite a lot about a wine.

Appearance

Look at the wine against a plain white background: *see* opposite.

■ **Clarity** Check that the wine is clear (no haze or murkiness) and bright. (If it looks dull it may well taste dull, too.) The finest wines often have a noticeable brilliance and lustre to them.

■ **Depth of colour** Look at the degree of colour — is it pale or dark gold? Ruby red, light pink, or brown? A deeply coloured, almost opaque red wine indicates high quality.

■ **Carbon-dioxide bubbles** CO_2 is naturally present in all wines as a by-product of fermentation, but in most non-sparkling wines it is at a level which can be neither seen nor tasted. However, a few bubbles are sometimes visible at the edge of young white wines. In this case the winemaker has deliberately retained a little more of the wine's natural CO_2 in order to enhance its freshness.

Now pick up your glass. The next stage is to examine the colour of the wine in detail.

■ **The colour rim** This gives some idea of the wine's maturity: the more brown or brick-hued it is at its rim, the older and/or readier it is to drink.

■ **White wines** gain colour as they age, moving from the pale yellow of youth, through straw, dark yellow, various shades of gold and finally deepening to amber.

■ **Red wines** lose "redness" as they age, and the rim becomes almost clear. When young they are often bright purple; as time goes by they progress through red, ruby and browny-red hues to the almost mahogany tints of old age.

Viscosity

Swirl the wine in the glass, then hold it up to the light.

Some of it will cling to the sides before forming transparent "tears" or "legs". The richer and more alcoholic the wine the more evident these will be. They can hint at a wine's weight and richness, but they are a crude indicator and no substitute for what your palate tells you. At first you may spill the wine, but the knack is soon acquired.

THE SMELL OF THE WINE

The sense of smell is the most important of our senses for appreciating and enjoying wine, for a very high proportion of what we "taste" is in fact smelled. Just recall how little you can taste food or drink when you have a cold or a blocked nose.

The centre of the sense of smell, the olfactory bulb, is at the top of the nose. Molecules of smell (in vaporized form) find their way to the olfactory bulb via two routes: up the nostrils when we breathe in, and along the passage from throat to nose when we breathe out.

Don't smell too insistently for too long when trying to describe or identify odours in a wine glass. Instead, rest for a few moments and then sniff again. The olfactory bulb is rapidly tired; that is, it adapts quickly to what it senses so that the impact of a given smell soon diminishes. Equally, when away from the smell to which it has "adapted", it recovers rapidly.

Nose

The smell of a wine is described in a general sense as its nose. "Aroma" and "bouquet" are also used, and though technically they refer to different characteristics they are often used interchangeably.

■ **Aroma** refers specifically to smells that come from the grape — fresh, fruity smells that you will experience principally in young wines.

■ **Bouquet** refers to the smells that develop as a result of wine being matured in oak casks, and from its subsequent ageing in bottle. These are generally softer, sweeter and more subtle scents.

The nose of a wine will vary in intensity and distinction according to

THE TECHNIQUES OF TASTING

Appearance can tell you a lot about wine. Tilting the glass away from you until it is almost horizontal will reveal the width and hue of the "rim". The wine's clarity, brightness, depth of colour and carbon-dioxide bubbles are best seen by looking at it from above, with the glass standing on a table.

1 Hold the glass against the light or against a blank background to give a general impression of the colour. Then take your first sniff — before you swirl the wine.

2 Hold your glass by the stem or by the foot so that you can see the wine clearly. To get the wine moving most right-handed people move the glass gently anticlockwise; left-handers find it easier clockwise. In either case very little movement is required.

3 Swirl the wine in the glass, and hold it up to the light. Examine the "legs" or "tears": are they large or small; slow or fast-moving?

4 Sniff the wine before swirling (*see* Step 1), using short sniffs and deeper ones, very gentle sniffs and much sharper ones. Concentrate on the smell, and what it reminds you of. Repeat the process immediately after you have swirled the wine in the glass. Note your thoughts.

5 Taste the wine by taking a reasonably generous mouthful; "chew" it around your mouth for a few seconds, then purse your lips and suck some air into your mouth to "aerate" the wine. Note your conclusions, returning for a repeat sniff if desired.

its age, grape variety (*see* pp34–42), origin and quality, but it should always be clean — that is, free of unpleasant odours. "Closed" and "dumb" are used to describe a wine that does not yet smell of much, but which intuition or experience leads you to expect will become more expressive as it matures.

How to smell

First smell the wine when it is still — before you swirl it in the glass — then swirl it around and smell it again immediately after swirling, as the wine settles: *see* Step 4. There is usually a difference between these two states, especially with finer, more mature wines.

Wines made from noble grape varieties have particularly distinct smells: Cabernet Sauvignon, for example, reminds most people of blackcurrants, Gewürztraminer of lychees and Turkish delight. Grape variety is the first thing to try to identify when "nosing" a wine.

The most frequently found non-grape smells are those of the wood in which the wine has been aged — particularly those associated with new oak: cedar, vanilla and caramel for example.

Winetasters, when smelling, use a combination of short and deeper sniffs, very gentle and also much sharper sniffs. Think about what the smells remind you of.

Vocabulary

There are many words to describe smells, but most of us have no training, or little practice, in using them, so we have to relate a wine's smells to something similar. You will hear wines described as "floral", or "fruity" — or even "vegetal".

- **Floral**: rose, violet, acacia, jasmine, orange blossom.
- **Spicy**: pepper, clove, licorice, aniseed, cinnamon.
- **Fruity**: lemon, grapefruit, blackcurrant, cherry, plum, peach, apricot, apple, melon, gooseberry, pineapple, lychee, raspberry.

- **Vegetal**: straw, undergrowth, greenery, grass, sweet pepper, mint, asparagus, olive, mushrooms.
- **Animal**: gamey, musky, wet wool/fur, leathery.
- **Woody**: resin, pine, oak, cedar, vanilla.
- **Burnt**: singed or roasted notes; tar, toast, coffee, caramel, smoke.
- **Chemical**: yeast, sulphur, nail varnish, vinegar, plastic.
- **Mineral**: chalky, volcanic, earthy, oily, petrolly.
- **Others**: nutty, honeyed, buttery, smoky.

THE TASTE AND TOUCH OF THE WINE

Before actually tasting the wine, it is useful to think about the ways in which we perceive tastes.

ORGANIZING A TASTING

Basic requirements are the same for informal, social occasions and more formal professional tastings.

Time Ideally before a meal; say 11am or 6pm.

Location Should be free of intrusive smells (cooking, tobacco smoke, perfumes; tell any helpers/servers) and have a plain white background against which to examine colour. Daylight is ideal; standard bulbs are better than fluorescent tubes if lighting is artificial.

Decanting Reds with a deposit should be decanted (*see* pp68–69) so that all the wine sampled is clear.

Presentation Serve wines at appropriate temperatures. To taste "blind", cover bottles and number them.

Order There is no perfect order, but in principle: white before red; dry before sweet; light before heavy; and lesser before greater.

Glasses ISO type are best (*see* p76); or at least tulip-shaped. One per person for a stand-up tasting, as many as practical for sit-down tastings.

Spittoons Individual beakers for sit-down tastings, otherwise large shared receptacles: bins or wine-boxes lined with plastic and half-filled with sawdust.

Dry biscuits; water; tasting sheets with room for notes; full details of each wine.

Palate

The tongue distinguishes just four so-called primary tastes: sweet, sour (acid), bitter and salty.

In addition to the four primary tastes, there is an infinite variety of subtle flavours in wine. Generally, the greater variety there is the better.

- **White wines** tend towards the citrus and other tree-fruit flavours: lemon, orange, grapefruit; peach, pear, apricot, apple; also melon, gooseberry, lychee.
- **Red wines** tend to be more reminiscent of red soft fruits: black and red cherry, plum, damson; blackcurrant, redcurrant, blackberry, raspberry, strawberry.
- **Red and white** can both have all sorts of mineral, spice, herb and other common flavours such as bread, yeast, honey, caramel, various nuts.

Touch

Other sensations perceived on the palate (winespeak for "in the mouth") are tactile: body, astringency, temperature and carbon-dioxide bubbles.

- **Body** describes the feel of a wine in the mouth, due principally to alcoholic weight, but also to depth of flavour and the consistency of the liquid. Low alcohol and limited flavour make for watery wines.
- **Astringency** is the dry, gripping sensation on the gums, tongue and palate, due to the effect of tannin.
- **Temperature** The right temperature can enhance a wine's performance, whereas being much too cold or too warm can easily mar its bouquet and flavour. It is important to be aware of the general guidelines for different types of wine (*see* pp60–61).
- **Carbon-dioxide spritz** is an important consideration in the texture of sparkling wines, but is sometimes perceptible as a prickle on the tip of the tongue in still wines.
- **Texture** The general tactile impression of a wine is a significant quality factor. Useful comparisons are often made with the feel of fabrics or other grainy materials: silky, satiny, velvety, for example.

THE ACT OF TASTING

See Step 5. Take the equivalent of a large teaspoonful, about 5–6ml. Try two simple comparative exercises with a good-quality wine such as a Gewürztraminer or Sauvignon Blanc.

Take a sip and swallow it straight down. Take another sip, but this time work the wine well round your mouth for a few seconds (this is called "chewing") before swallowing. Notice how much more of its flavour you can taste.

Take a further sip and "chew" the wine well before swallowing a little and spitting out the rest. With the next sip of wine, in addition to chewing it, purse your lips and suck (not breathe) a little air through the wine two or three times before swallowing a little. Notice how you can taste/smell even more of the wine this way because you have deliberately "volatized" (released) its aromas. Always "chew" and "aerate" for several seconds to get the most out of any wine you are tasting.

Spitting

Winetasters spit simply in order to stay sober when assessing large numbers of wines at one tasting.

MAKING NOTES, JUDGING QUALITY

Notes help you to concentrate, and the very process of searching for words to describe a wine means you taste it attentively. Notes then become a useful record of the development of your own palate at the same time as charting the progress of your wines; both crucial to an understanding of how fine wines age and when you like to drink them.

What to note

In addition to describing colour and bouquet, a good tasting note should combine a relatively objective description of the wine's general style (full-bodied or light, soft or sharp in acidity, modestly or deeply flavoured, etc), along with a description of its flavours and quality as

A professional winetasting.

PRINCIPAL WINE FAULTS

Thanks to modern technology, faults are becoming increasingly rare. Most are easy to detect by sight or smell.

■ **Oxidized wines**
So-called because excess contact with oxygen has spoiled their taste.
White wines have a dull appearance, with a darker colour than normal for age/type: lacklustre straw to brown. Flat, stale smell; dull, sharp taste. Also called maderized.
Red wines too have a dull appearance, browner than normal for age/type. Flat, stale nose with a "sweet and sour" or caramelly smell and taste.
■ **Volatile wines**
Have a noticeable sour vinegar smell from the "volatile" acid: acetic acid, ie vinegar. Thin, sharp, sour taste.
■ **Sulphur-related faults**
Sulphur dioxide: pungent, acrid, suffocating smell, like a safety match on being lit; sharp, dry prickling sensation in throat on tasting.
Hydrogen sulphide: smell of bad eggs, rubber, garlic, rotting vegetation, with tastes to match. Also called reduced.
■ **Corked wine**
Smell of damp and mould completely dominates the bouquet and flavour of the wine. Nothing to do with fragments of cork in the glass, which are harmless.

distinct from its constituent parts. Think of this like describing an individual's height, build and colour first, and then their personality.

How good is the wine?

We have learnt how to perceive and describe the bare bones of a wine — colour, nose, body, tannin, acidity, flavour — but not yet how to judge its quality.

Good wines are well balanced: there is no part that appears deficient or excessive. But remember the proportions of that balance will vary according to origin and grape variety; there is no one "ideal" style.

In general, concentration and depth of flavour are positive features, but these do not alone make for quality. Fine wines will have within that concentration a large variety of complex flavours that will make you want to keep them in your mouth. This quality is called long middle palate, especially in Australia.

Finally, one of the clearest indicators of quality is a long finish, where the wonderful tastes and aromas linger for several seconds or more after swallowing. The longer the finish the better; lesser wines have a short finish.

Conclusion and assessment

This should combine a subjective opinion — whether you like the wine or not — with a more objective assessment of how good it is of its type. The second part will become easier the more widely you taste. You can also note here whether the wine is value for money, whether it is ready to drink, needs keeping, or is well past its best.

Honesty

Be honest with yourself about your impressions, and be definite in your conclusions. If you cannot rely on your notes you will not be able to learn from them. Trust what your palate tells you, at any stage of your tasting career, but equally be prepared to reassess or reinterpret. □

GLOSSARY OF TASTING TERMS

This is a basic list of words for describing wine. The starred words are faults, which are discussed on the previous page. Words that describe the principal components of wine — acid, alcohol and tannin (in CAPITALS) — are grouped under their respective entries.

Acetic *
ACID/ACIDITY Gives life and freshness. Also helps define and prolong wine flavours. Words to describe acidity (from too little to too much) include: *flat, flabby, soft, supple, fresh, lively, crisp, firm, hard, sharp, green, tart, acid*.
ALCOHOL Gives wine its characteristic "weight". Described as (from inadequate to excess): *watery, thin, light, medium-bodied, full-bodied, ample, generous, heady, heavy, alcoholic, hot*.
Aroma Smells that come from the grape rather than from ageing in barrel or bottle, or from vinification. *See also* bouquet.
Aromatic Wines from grapes with a particularly pronounced aroma (eg Gewürztraminer, Muscat, Sauvignon Blanc, Cabernet Sauvignon).
Astringent The drying, gripping sensation on the gums produced by tannin (*qv*).
Austere The hard, unyielding impression given by wine with high tannin or acid, which needs time to soften.
Backward Not ready to drink; needs more bottle-age to mellow.
Balanced Wine whose component parts "balance" each other so that no element appears lacking or obtrusive for its type.
Blackcurrant The smell and taste usually associated

with wines made from Cabernet Sauvignon.
Body The combined impression of weight and consistency on the palate, due mainly, but not solely, to the level of alcohol.
Botrytis *See* noble rot.
Bouquet General term to describe the smell of wine, but particularly used for smells deriving from vinification and barrel- or bottle-age. *See also* aroma.
Buttery A smell and taste often associated with rich, oaked Chardonnay.
Cedary Cedar-wood smell found in wines aged in new French oak.
Closed Referring to the bouquet, it means muted but promising. Can also be used of flavour.
Cloying Sweetness that is "sticky" because it is not balanced by enough acidity.
Coarse Used to describe texture, tannin in particular. Also describes a harsh mousse in sparkling wines.
Complex Indicates quality, describing variety and subtlety in both flavour and bouquet.
Corked *
Drying out Mature wines that are losing their flavour, so allowing their acid, alcohol or tannin to appear obtrusive.
Dumb *See* closed.
Earthy Usually a positive term; recalling damp earth on nose and palate.
Elegant Finesse, harmony and the absence of harsh impressions.
Fierce Harshness from high levels of alcohol and acidity.
Fine High-quality wine.
Finish Tastes and aromas that linger after the wine has been swallowed. *See also* length, short.
Fleshy Rich in flavour, supple in texture. Refers

mainly to reds.
Flinty Mineral taste in crisp dry white wines, such as Chablis and Sancerre.
Fruity Many wines smell or taste of a specific fruit (eg peach, apple, blackcurrant, cherry); others have a pleasant, general "juiciness" of aroma and flavour. A term difficult to avoid, easy to over-use.
Gooseberry A taste and smell mostly associated with Sauvignon Blanc.
Grapey Used to suggest a taste of fresh grape juice. Muscats are almost the only wines to smell and taste just like the fresh grape.
Green Unripe, young. Also refers to acidity (*qv*).
Grip A firm, dry feel on the gums; produced by tannin in red wine.
Harsh Refers to texture.
Herbaceous A smell reminiscent of green plants, or freshly cut grass.
Hollow Empty of flavour and noticeably short (*qv*).
Lean Used critically, means a lack of ripe fruit.
Length/Long The hallmark of a high-quality wine. *See also* finish.
Maderized *
Mature Ready to drink.
Mellow With a soft, agreeable texture.
Noble rot *Botrytis cinerea*, the rot on ripe grapes (Sémillon, Riesling and Chenin Blanc) that can, under the right conditions, considerably enhance the flavour of wines. *See also* p159.
Nutty A smell and taste often found in mature white burgundy, good-quality dry marsala and amontillado sherry.
Oaky Smells (vanilla, cedar wood, caramel, toast) and sometimes slight dryness of

texture that derive from ageing in new oak barrels.
Oxidized *
Peppery Smell of ground black pepper, in port and Rhône wines especially.
Pétillant Lightly sparkling.
Petrolly Agreeable petroleum smell in mature Riesling-based wines.
Raw Harsh impressions from alcohol, acid and tannin in immature wine.
Reduced *
Rich Describes flavour and texture.
Ripe A sweetness of flavour in wines made from very ripe grapes.
Rustic Coarse; a result of primitive or careless winemaking techniques.
Short Lacking in persistence of flavour on the finish (*qv*). *See also* length.
Smoky Smell and/or taste; eg in white Sancerre and northern Rhône reds.
Stewed Like tea brewed too long: dull, vegetal smell; coarse, astringent.
Sulphury *
Supple Soft and gentle, without being flabby.
TANNIN Substance from grape skins that gives red wine its dry, mouth-puckering feel. Described as (from a little to a lot): *fine-grained, soft, matt, dry, rich, firm, tough, coarse, vegetal, stemmy, astringent*.
Thin Dilute and meagre in flavour.
Tired Lacking freshness and zest.
Vanilla The smell and taste most often associated with wines that have been aged in new oak barrels.
Volatile *
Wet wool Smell in unoaked Chardonnay (Chablis) and Sémillon (Sauternes). Also found in wines with too much sulphur.

WINE AND FOOD

CHOOSING WINES TO MATCH A MENU — OR A DISH
TO COMPLEMENT A SPECIAL WINE — OFFERS
SCOPE FOR SOME EXCITING DISCOVERIES.

The joyous marriage of food and wine is evocatively captured
here in Peter Severin Kroyer's painting entitled
Artists' Party, Skagen. Champagne — a dessert, as well as a
special-occasion, wine — is raised in celebration.

When a particular glass of wine meets a certain dish in perfect harmony, a magic spell is woven — both food and wine are improved by the partnership, each revealing new and sometimes unexpected levels of flavour in the other. Such felicitous food and wine marriages are not confined to the highest of *haute cuisine* and the grandest of *crus*. A rich dish of slightly sweet lobster in butter sauce merits its match with an intense, rare, ten-year-old dry white burgundy such as Bâtard-Montrachet, while simply-cooked prawns are equally happy with a wide range of dry white wines, from tangy fino sherry to bone-dry Loire whites such as Muscadet and Pouilly-Fumé or a fresh New Zealand Sauvignon Blanc. Many classic combinations were "discovered" in the early 19th century, when French chefs were in great demand throughout Europe: caviar with champagne, sole with white burgundy, game with red burgundy. Certain "rules" became established: white wine goes with fish, red wine with meat. However, these rules have always been challenged — by meats such as chicken or pork, by different sauces and by the

place of meat in the menu. Wine cannot be matched to food by colour alone; many other factors — the wine's weight and acidity, the grapes' flavours — also come into play. There is also its importance: a great wine, worth serious attention, demands a simple dish. While the upper classes of the 19th century had access to a wide range of food and wine, the less well-off drank whatever was available locally. This brings another guideline: regional specialities are often best accompanied by the wine of that region; after all, they evolved together. There are few better partners to the salted cabbage, or *choucroute*, of north-eastern France than an aromatic dry white Alsace Riesling or Pinot Gris. The almost "meaty" character of Loire salmon is highlighted by the lively local red wines of Chinon and Bourgueil (red wines that certainly go with fish). Italy's array of red wines, from austere Barolo to the lightest Bardolino, partner an equally varied repertoire of dishes. Tastes change with every generation; today people travel far, experiencing new foods, new wines. Our idea of what makes a classic combination may alter; it will certainly expand.

WINE ON THE MENU

Since ancient times, an alcoholic drink such as wine or beer has been a desirable adjunct to food. It stimulates the appetite and relaxes the mind, contributing to the general enjoyment of the meal; its own agreeable taste may open up an additional spectrum of flavours in combination with the food eaten.

Menus through the ages

The medieval banquet would have been impossible to match with wine in today's terms: not only were many of the dishes well spiced (with cinnamon, cloves, ginger and saffron), they were also presented in what appears a very haphazard way, with many dishes placed on the table at each course for diners to help themselves. Wine, perhaps watered, was a beverage, not an object of interest. Spiced wines were served after the meal.

The chefs of the Italian Renaissance were the first to tone down their use of spices and bring a sense of order to the menu. Although menus tended to be arranged more carefully (first cold foods, then roasts, then stews, then desserts), there was still a vast choice of different dishes on the table at each course — and we have little record of the wines that were served. We can only imagine that the wines, like the foods, were chosen for social prestige at great feasts.

Similar menus, with ornately decorated dishes arranged together on the table, held sway for another 200 years, a style of dining known as *service à la française*. During the 19th century this gave way to the more familiar *service à la russe*.

Wines fit for kings

The famous French gourmet Baron Brisse (1813-1876) gave a clear picture of the wines available to rich diners of his day when he set out the following rules. "During the whole of dinner,

well-iced dry and sweet champagne must be served. After the soup: madeira and vermouth. With the fish: burgundies, either Beaune, Volnay or Pommard; clarets, either Mouton, Rausan-Ségla, Léoville, Gruaud-Larose, Lascombes, Pichon-Longueville, Cosd'Estournel or Monrose. Between the cold entrées and the game, offer either Château Yquem or Rhine wine... slightly iced, in green glasses. With the roasts and dressed vegetables: burgundies, La Romanée Conti, Clos Vougeot or Chambertin; clarets, Château Lafite, Margaux, Latour or Haut Brion. With the sweets: sherry. During dessert: sweet wines, such as malmsey, muscatel or tokay."

While the upper classes were displaying their wealth in ostentatious banquets, the newly wealthy middle classes enjoyed the simpler pleasures of good home cooking. The French in the early 19th century were hugely interested in food, as was demonstrated by the instant success of *La Physiologie du Goût*, a study of taste by the judge and gourmet Brillat-Savarin (1755–1826), which offers many fascinating insights into the eating and drinking habits of the time.

Sequence of serving

Few people today would disagree with Brillat-Savarin, who pointed out that "the right order of drinking is from the mildest wines to the headiest and most perfumed". As a general rule, we still serve wines in a certain order throughout a meal: young wines are followed by older vintages, light wines by fuller-bodied or more alcoholic ones, chilled wines by those that have become *chambré* (room temperature), dry wines by sweet.

The rule can be broken judiciously, particularly at the beginning and end of a meal; even Brillat-Savarin began with madeira (hardly a "mild" wine), with "French wines to accompany the

main courses, and African and Spanish wines to crown the meal". Tastes in apéritifs, drunk before the food arrives to stimulate the appetite, vary widely. Only the fact that they are drinks of pronounced character, usually served well chilled, link the vermouths of France and Italy, America's cocktail or gin and tonic, Greece's ouzo and northern Europe's schnapps.

If wine is an important part of a meal, it is often frowned upon to dull the palate with spirits first, but any number of characterful wines (usually white) make admirable apéritifs. Champagne is excellent anywhere in the world; fino or manzanilla sherry is now as popular in Britain as it is in Spain; chilled ruby or tawny port is seen in France as often as sweet white wines (Sauternes, the South-West's Jurançon, Muscat de Beaumes-de-Venise) and aromatic dry Alsace Muscats and Rieslings.

The question of whether to serve cheese followed by pudding, or vice versa, is not so much one of French versus British practice, as one of personal taste. If cheese follows the main course, the red wine served with the meat — or a similar but superior wine — also accompanies the cheese. A sweet dish is then last on the menu, accompanied by a glass of champagne. British households tended to follow meats with sweet dishes, which were served with sweet wines from Sauternes, Barsac or Tokaji. The final course was cheese and dessert, which meant fresh and dried fruit and nuts, with port, oloroso sherry, or Bual or Malmsey madeira.

The regional connection

Many of Europe's traditional dishes have a natural affinity with the wine produced in their region. Cahors and Madiran go with the bean, duck and sausage cassoulets of South-West France; and Switzerland's crisp dry white wines accompany cheese fondue. In Spain, the dry white wines of Rías Baixas, from the local Albariño grape, are drunk with Galicia's famous shellfish; while inland, classic oaky red Riojas are usually served with plainly roast or grilled meat — lamb, pork or kid. The odd, resinated taste of retsina is perfectly at home in a Greek taverna, where the food has strong flavours of herbs, lemons and olive oil, and is often cooked over charcoal.

There are also countless examples of regional cuisine that use local wine in their preparation. France's chicken casseroles range from the best-known coq au vin, made with red burgundy, to coq au vin jaune from the Jura and coq au Riesling from Alsace. Throughout Europe, meat is stewed in wine, be it a French daube, Greek stifado, Italian stufatino or the more specific brasato al Barolo; all such dishes should be eaten with the wine used in the preparation of the dish.

Food first or wine foremost?

In most western countries, where a wide range of wine is readily available, food is usually chosen first, and two or more wines will then be selected to accompany different stages of the menu. When the emphasis is very much on the food — for example with a chef's special tasting menu — the best choice will be a well-structured red wine whose fruity and polished taste will flatter the palate as well as the food: St-Emilion (but not a classed *grand cru*), a 2- to 5- year-old Bergerac or a Beaujolais *cru* with sufficient character (St-Amour, Morgon...) of the same age. If the food requires a white wine, a smooth and fresh Côte de Beaune Chardonnay from one of the smaller *appellations* will be a safe bet.

For an unpretentious cuisine, go for a fruity and refreshing red wine, which should be served lightly chilled: Bourgueil, St-Nicolas-de-Bourgueil, Beaujolais *cru* — Fleurie or Brouilly — or Côte de Provence. To accompany sea food or fish, choose a classic white wine such as Sancerre,

Muscadet or Entre-deux-Mers.

On other occasions, if you have a bottle of fine wine such as a prestigious Bordeaux cru, don't forget that it will show off at its best when accompanied by the tender meat of a roast lamb prepared with some herbs and a little garlic or by more savoury meat such as beef or duck cutlet.

Red burgundy is often thought of as a good match for game, but only Premiers and Grands Crus bottle-aged for some years — for instance, Gevrey-Chambertin, Pommard or even La Romanée or La Tâche — can carry off a gamey dish such as woodcock, pheasant or hare, but also truffles. The same applies to the superb *crus* of the Northern Rhône valley, such as Côte-Rôtie, Hermitage or Cornas. White burgundies, such as a

white Hermitage, should be confined to the highest of *haute cuisine* and need turbot, lobster and langoustines to show them at their best. But don't forget that an Alsace Riesling Grand Cru will also make a perfect marriage with a sophisticated *cuisine* of fish or seafood, or even with the rare caviar.

Vintage port is sometimes considered wasted with cheese — in fact, it goes well with certain kinds of cheese (*see* p96). The same can be said of a mature Maury or Banyuls, fine old oloroso sherry or a good madeira. A special rich sweet white wine (Sauternes, Barsac, mature sweet Vouvray or Quarts-de-Chaume) needs no other accompaniment than buttery biscuits, although such wines make excellent partners for many fruity puddings and some cheeses.

A FRENCH MENU FOR EACH SEASON

Philippe Bourguignon, wine waiter at the Laurent restaurant in Paris, has put together these four menus, one for each season. In keeping with his idea that good eating and drinking does not rule out simplicity, he was keen to select some easy-to-prepare dishes and has limited his wine selection to three bottles.

Spring

Asparagus with an olive oil vinaigrette
Wine: *Condrieu*

Oven-roasted sucking lamb with peas and broad beans
Wine: *a 5-6 year old Médoc*

Saint-nectaire or mature gouda
Wine: *a 5-6 year old Médoc*

Tarte aux fraises
Wine: *medium dry Champagne*

Summer

Terrine of vegetables in aspic jelly
Wine: *Sancerre or Pouilly Fumé*

Grilled rib of beef with summer chanterelles or tomatoes à la provençale
Wine: *a lightly-chilled (12-14°C) Loire red made from Cabernet grapes*
Chinon, Bourgueil or St-Nicolas-de Bourgueil

Mature goats cheeses
Wine: *Sancerre or Pouilly Fumé*

Peach and apricot soup
Wine: *Sauternes or Sainte-Croix-du-Mont*

Autumn

Oysters
Wine: *a 2-5 year-old Chablis 1er cru*

Roasted wild duck
Wine: *a 5-7 year-old red Burgundy such as Gevrey-Chambertin, Pommard, Mercurey*

Roquefort
Wine: *a rancio-style Vieux Banyuls*

Roasted figs
Wine: *a rancio-style Vieux Banyuls*

Winter

Scallops with a truffle butter or a cream sauce
Wine: *a 5-7 year old white Hermitage*

Venison stew
Wine: *5-10 year old Châteauneuf-du-Pape or St-Emilion*

Vacherin and mature Comté
Wine: *a 5-7 year old white Hermitage*

Chocolate cake
Wine: *Rasteau or Maury*

Flavours and textures

The famous Bordeaux winemaker, Emile Peynaud, in his book *Le Goût du vin* explains that, when matching food with wine, "the type and quality of flavours and their intensity" should be taken into account. Alain Senderens, Lucas Carton's famous chef, for his part insists that textures play an important part. He maintains that, to obtain the perfect food and wine match, the tactile qualities of each, both volume and density of texture, must be in harmony. Before making a match, one must therefore understand the character of the dish and the wine and analyse their respective qualities and also any shortcomings.

Although when tasting a wine we use our senses of sight, smell and taste, the latter is most useful when it comes to defining its personality. We use our tongue and taste buds not only to detect the four (unique) taste sensations — sweet, salt, bitter and acid (sour) — but also to ascertain the weight and texture of the wine. Depending on the components of the wine (alcohol, residual sugars, acidity and tannins), it emits a whole array of tactile sensations — from lean to fatty, thin to rich, dry to cloying, silky smooth to rough... —, and thus different flavours. Alcohol gives the wine its fatty element. Sugars mixed with the alcohol amplify its richness. On the other hand, acidity lessens the impression of volume in the mouth and the astringent, sometimes bitter, nature of the tannins tightens up the structure of the wine. The combination of these four components, each time in varying proportions, is what gives a wine its personality. In general, each *appellation* can be categorised in accordance with the style of wines it produces. Thus, a Beaujolais, which is higher in acidity than tannins, has a light, fluid texture which makes it a refreshing wine. In a Pomerol, the alcohol coats the very upfront tannins, giving it a fleshy, velvety texture and thus a strong personality. White wines can be categorised similarly, even though their tannin content is low. The rich, fatty texture of a Meursault, where alcohol prevails over acidity, is entirely different from the fine, firm body of a Riesling, where acidity is more prominent than alcohol.

The same criteria used to analyse the flavours and textures of a wine can also be applied to those of a dish. The consistency of a dish will vary according to its moisture content and textures can range from mushy to dry, tender to crispy, smooth to firm. Rillettes have a different texture from chicken in a cream sauce, a grilled beefsteak or poached salmon. Salt and sweet are the main flavours in cooking, but acid and bitter tastes are also present to a lesser extent, although one is more likely to try to disguise them than emphasise them. In actual fact, saltiness reinforces bitterness, acidity temporarily disguises bitterness and acidity increases the perception of sweetness. All this can in practice be translated into the following recommendations: avoid tannic red wines with salty food as the salt hardens the tannins in the wine — this

AN ITALIAN MENU

Italy has one of the oldest winemaking cultures in Europe with a large range of native grape varieties. Italian cooking is equally as rich and original. Claudio Puglia, chef at La Romantica, a high class Italian restaurant in Paris, offers modern cuisine based on traditional products.

Sardine fillet marinated in balsamic vinegar with a fennel salad
Wine: *Prosecco de Valdobbiadene DOC, Nino Franco Estate*
(a sparkling white from Venetia)

Pasta stuffed with bass in a langoustine jus
Wine: *Fiano di Avellino DOC, Mastroberardino Estate*
(a white wine from Campania)

Fillet of bass with lemon liqueur and leeks
Wine: *Alteni di Brassica Sauvignon IGT, Angelo Gaya*
(a white wine from Campania)

Green risotto with a selection of garden vegetables
Wine: *Dolcetto d'Alba Rossana DOC, Ceretto Estate*
(Piedmont red)

Cushion of veal stuffed with smoked buffalo cheese served with polenta
Wine: *Casale dei Biscari IGT, Torre Vecchia*
(Sicilian red)

Panna cotta in a fresh grenadine syrup
Wine *Brachetto d'Acqui DOC, Castello Banfi*
(sweet sparkling red from Piedmont)

A SPANISH MENU

Spain, with its long agricultural tradition, is the second largest wine producing country in Europe. Despite this fact, with the exception of Sherry and the classic Rioja, its wines are still relatively unknown. Alberto Herraíz, chef at the Fogón Saint-Julien, a Spanish restaurant in Paris, imports his wines direct from all his country's wine growing regions and these are a perfect match for his cuisine based on typical regional products.

Iberian Ham
Wine: *Fino Jerez DO, Fino Quinta or Manzanilla DO, Bodega La Gitana*
(Fortified white wines from the Palomino grape)

Assortment of tapas
Wine: *Penedes DO, Viña del Sol*
(White wine from Parellada grapes)
or Rías Baixas DO, Lagar Cervera
(white wine from Albariño grapes)

Black paella
Wine: *Mancha, Bennangueli*
(red wine from the Cencibel grape)
or Mancha DO, Calzadilla
(red wine from the Tempranillo grape)

Leg of lamb cooked in honey
Wine: *Penedes DO, Gran Sangre de Toro*
(red wine from Carignan and Grenache grapes)
or Rioja DO, Marqués de Riscal
(red wine from Tempranillo and Mazuelo grapes)

Assortment of sweet tapas
Vin : *Montilla Moriles DO, Gran Barquero*
(a sweet white wine from the Pedro Ximénez grape)

is why cheeses rarely go well with red wines — and opt for white wines as the freshness they derive from their acidity will compensate for the salt; serving a sweet wine with a salty dish will make the former taste even sweeter and, if not compensated for by the fatty element, may create a distortion of flavours in the mouth; a dessert with a predominant sweet flavour needs to be partnered with a very sweet wine, otherwise the wine will taste more acidic.

Flavours and strengths

Wine covers a whole spectrum of aromas — from small fresh red berries to cooked black fruits, citrus fruit zest to orange marmalade, green apples to yellow peaches, truffles to undergrowth, fur to cigars — depending on the grape varieties, *terroir* and age. Of differing strengths, these aromas may offer a great gastronomical experience which can be enhanced by a dish. Logically, therefore, the aroma of the wine should be one of the parameters used to select a dish to accompany it. It has however been shown that, in practice, similarity of aromas between a wine and dish is not easy to identify. How do you enhance the green-apple flavour of Muscadet? Certainly not with its classic partner, a seafood platter! Not to mention the hints of petroleum in a Riesling of a certain age. There are however a few examples of this harmony of aromas. Duck cooked with cherries or figs enhances the red and black fruit aromas of a Vintage Banyuls; a dish containing truffles glorifies a mature Hermitage or a truffle-scented Pomerol; an orange or lemon tart brings out the bitter orange taste of a mature Sauternes.

As a general rule, when matching food and wine, it is more important to ensure the aromas in one do not overpower those of the other, and vice versa, than to try to find their equivalent. A wine with a powerful nose served with a fairly flavourless dish will crush the latter, and vice versa. Although oysters go extremely well with Muscadet, the rose and lychee bouquet of a Gewürztraminer would not make for a happy match and yet, the latter parades in front of a spicy dish while a Muscadet would beat a retreat!

The rules of compatibility

These are based on the similarities — be it in texture, flavour, aroma or strength — between the dish and the wine but as explained, the texture and strength of a dish or a wine are generally much more important than similarities of aroma.

AN AMERICAN MENU

Floyd Cardoz, chef at the Tabla restaurant in New York, was born in Bombay and was trained in both India and France. His menu is an example of the new trend in American cooking towards 'fusion cooking', inspired here by Indian cooking. The wines all come from California.

Chilled sweetcorn soup with star anis, cloves, ginger and herbs
Wine: *a dry Gewürztraminer from the Navarro Estate (Anderson Valley, California)*

Prawn, crayfish and squid in a saffron and fennel flavoured bouillon with peas
Wine: *Eleven Oaks Sauvignon Blanc from the Bacok Estate (Santa Barbara, California)*

Steak with a spicy crust served with baby Chinese cabbage, mini taro and horseradish and ginger raita
Wine: *Madrona Ranch Cabernet Sauvignon from the Abreu Estate (Napa Valley, California)*

Vanilla yoghurt sorbet served with a Bing cherry iced soup
Wine: *Muscat Eiswein from the Bonny Doon Estate (Santa Cruz, California)*

Chocolate and almond cake served warm with ginger ice cream and wild blackberry syrup
Wine: *Vintage port from the Saint Amand Estate (California)*

The rules are simple. The textures and strengths must be on an equal footing: serve a dish with a soft consistency with a light wine which is low in tannins and a supple-textured fatty dish with a rich, well-rounded wine. The wine has to have the right amount of strength and character to match the strength of flavour in a dish. If you serve too powerful a wine with a delicate dish, the wine is likely to kill the flavours in the dish and vice versa. For example, a light, dry white wine with good acid content, such as Muscadet or Sancerre, goes well with fish *mousseline*. Fish in a sauce needs a supple white wine with subtle aromas, such as Savennières or Pessac-Léognan. With a cassoulet or a stew, opt for a heady wine such as Madiran, Côtes du Rhône-Villages or Cahors (the fat content in the dishes will mellow the often slightly rustic, tannins in these wines). For a white meat in a cream sauce, stake your bets on the richness and opulence of the white burgundies from Côte de Beaune, such as Mersault. Grilled red meat goes well with an austere, firm-structured red wine such as a Médoc or Libourne claret or a red Côte des Nuits. With subtle-flavoured small game, choose mature red wines whose soft texture and tertiary aromas will marry well with those of the dish. It is important to remember, however, that wine is first and foremost a drink. If eating very salty food, such as charcuterie, salt meats or fish or cheeses, the freshness of a wine with a good acidity will quench the thirst more efficiently than a heady, tannic red. Rillettes are better matched with a pleasant Beaujolais or a Sauvignon Blanc than a Médoc or white Hermitage. On the other hand, a heady, tannic white calls out for a rich dish, the fat content of which will soften the tannins and the alcohol content of the wine will aid digestion. So far as desserts are concerned, the rules of compatibility are based essentially on sweetness. Dishes with a high sugar content, whether tarts, sweets or chocolate cake, can only take a sweet wine as dry whites become terribly acidic and dry reds, bitter and tannic. The custom of serving champagne with desserts at celebrations is an absolute sacrilege unless it is medium-dry or medium sweet. Rosé and dry champagne can, at a pinch, be served with a red fruit dessert which is not too sweet. Chocolate needs to be partnered with natural sweet wines such as Banyuls, Rivesaltes, Maury and port.

Another basic common sense recommendation: match wines and dishes in a similar price range! Drinking Pétrus with sausages may be an interesting taste experience but will do nothing to enhance the qualities of the wine; if you serve calf sweetbreads in a cream sauce with an inexpensive wine you might be missing what could have been a great gastronomic experience.

The rules of contrast

Another way to tackle the matter is to select opposing flavours and textures. A fatty lobster goes better with an acidic white wine such as Muscadet or Gros-Plant than a white Hermitage or a Corton-Charlemagne. This is an excellent example of opposing textures whereby the subtle, salty flavour of the shellfish is enhanced by a wine with more muted aromas. Sweet and sour is another combination of contrasts. The partnership of a wine which is high in residual sugars, such as port, Banyuls or even a Sauternes, with a Roquefort-type blue veined cheese has become a classic. The flavours explode in the mouth yet neither taste is overpowering as they come together in perfect harmony. Both do however share a richness—one has a high fat content, the other is high in sugars and alcohol. The same principle applies to the combination of foie gras terrine and Sauternes or Alsace Sélection de Grains Nobles, duck breast with figs and Banyuls, etc.

The Age of Wine

Since the 1980s winemaking techniques have laid great emphasis on the quality of the raw material, that is the grape itself. Nowadays, many winemakers are looking into the optimum ripeness for harvesting, the stage where the grapes have a high concentration of sugars, a level of acidity referred to as weak 'green' and, for red grapes, ripe tannins. As a result, wines are being consumed much earlier than before thanks to the richness of their fruits. It is no longer necessary to wait three, five, even ten years to enjoy them although it may take a few years before they reach their peak.

A young wine is more concentrated. Its aromas, called primary aromas, are intensely fruity or floral. The

A VIETNAMESE MENU

For several years now our Western palates have been enjoying the discovery of Asian cooking. Often, however, it does seem difficult to find a wine to match these exotic flavours which can be anything from spicy to sweet, including sweet and sour. Robert Vifian, the Vietnamese chef at the famous Tan Dinh restaurant in Paris, and above all a highly skilled wine waiter — over 600 wines on his wine list — has suggested some food and wine matches which should convince us otherwise.

Asam prawn rolls
Wine: *a rich, yet dry Riesling, 3 to 4 years old*

Golden crayfish triangles
with ginko nuts
Wine: *5-6 year old Meursault 1er cru*
or 5-6 year old Puligny-Montrachet 1er cru

Cardamon Veal
Wine: *5-7 year old Volnay*
or 5-6 year old Chambolle-Musigny

Thin slices of beef filet Tan Dinh
(black pepper, star anis, cloves, cinnamon)
Wine: *Pomerol from a good year such as*
85, 89, 90 or St Emilion from a good year
such as 85, 89 or 90

Pineapple Hoanh Thanh
(Wheat pastry parcel with chopped pineapple,
honey, lemon, pepper)
Wine: *a rich, very mature Sauternes 83 or 86*
or a smooth, rich, mature Vouvray 89 or 90

body of the wine is dense and a little harsh as, in the case of red wines, the tannins have not completely softened, and in whites the balance between alcohol and acidity is not yet stable. In wines which have been vinified or aged in new oak barrels, the woody aromas (vanilla, spice, toast) are predominant while the tannins are often more astringent.

An old wine is characterised by the complexity and finesse of its tertiary aromas, referred to as its bouquet, while the texture of the wine is considerably more subtle and refined or, in the worst scenario, leaner. It has to be said however that the elegance the wine has achieved through time does have a certain fragility.

It goes without saying therefore that the age of a wine is an important parameter which must be taken into account when considering wine and food matches. The rule is fairly simple: the younger the wine, the simpler, less sophisticated the dish, to bring out the fruity aromas of the wine. A young wine also requires a dish with a fairly dense texture to compliment its still firm structure. On the other hand, the more a wine ages, the more it demands intricate dishes with complex flavours in keeping with its own and with a supple texture to compensate for its lack of fattiness.

Alain Senderens, in his book *Le Vin à Table,* suggests two possible partnerships for a Châteauneuf-du-Pape, depending on the age of the wine. For a young wine with dominant tannins he suggests a firm-textured casserole of veal heart. To compliment the powerful bouquet and smooth texture of a mature wine, he recommends jugged hare.

Philippe Bourguignon works along the same principles. His book, *L'Accord parfait,* recommends oysters or a terrine with gherkins as the perfect match for the good acidity of a young Chablis, whereas, with an older wine, he prefers fish in butter or a cream sauce, which will enhance the smooth contours of the wine. □

THE 14 MAIN WINE FAMILIES

Wines can be divided into 14 main categories according to their colour and personality.
For each category, the main grape varieties and the most common appellations are listed, together with
advice on food matches. A grape variety may appear in several families as it will be given different
expression in different wines, depending on the terroir in which it was grown.

1 - LIGHT, TAUT, DRY WHITE WINE

Characteristics	easy to drink, light, refreshing palate thanks to a good acidic structure; simple, fairly uncomplex aromas; a fresh finish.
Grape varieties	Aligoté, Chasselas, Chardonnay, Gros-Plant, Jacquère, Melon de Bourgogne, Pinot Blanc, Romorantin, Sauvignon, Sylvaner, Tressallier.
Appellations	Bergerac, Bourgogne Aligoté, Cheverny, Cour-Cheverny, Crépy, Entre-deux-Mers, Mâcon-Villages, Muscadet, Petit Chablis, Pinot Blanc d'Alsace, Pouilly-sur-Loire, St-Pourçain, Sylvaner d'Alsace, Vin de Savoie.
Food matches	simple, straightforward food without too many complex flavours, seafood including oysters, raw or cooked vegetables, snails, frogs legs, grilled fish, fish terrine, fried fish, charcuterie, goat's cheeses.
How to serve?	drink very young, serve very chilled, around 8°C (46°F).

2 - SUPPLE, FRUITY DRY WHITE WINE

Characteristics	full, fresh, fruity palate; expressive fruit and/or floral aromas; a fragrant, thirst-quenching finish.
Grape varieties	Altesse, Chardonnay, Chenin, Clairette, Gros-Manseng, Mauzac, Rolle, Sauvignon, Sémillon, Ugni Blanc, Vermentino.
Appellations	Bandol, Bellet, Cassis, Chablis, Côtes de Blaye, Coteaux d'Aix, Côtes de Provence, Gaillac, Graves, dry Jurançon, Picpoul-de-Pinet, Pouilly Fumé, Pouilly-Fuissé, Montlouis, Roussette de Savoie, Roussette du Bugey, Saint-Véran, Sancerre, Saumur, Vin de Corse.
Food matches	food of varying styles, from the most simple to the most elaborate, but without too many complex aromas; raw or cooked shellfish, seafood pasta, simply cooked or grilled fish, fish mousseline, charcuterie, medium-textured and hard goat's cheeses.
How to serve?	drink within 3 years of bottling, serve chilled, between 8° and 10°C (46-50°F).

3 - FULL-BODIED, DISTINCTIVE DRY WHITE WINE

Characteristics	a meaty white with a rich, distinctive, perfectly balanced palate; complex, elegant aromas; long, persistent finish.
Grape varieties	Chardonnay, Chenin, Marsanne, Riesling, Roussanne, Sauvignon, Sémillon.
Appellations	Châteauneuf-du-Pape, Chablis *premier* and *grand cru*, Chassagne-Montrachet, Corton-Charlemagne, Hermitage, Meursault, Montrachet, Puligny-Montrachet, Pessac-Léognan, Savennières, Vouvray.
Food matches	fairly sophisticated, flavoursome food; mushrooms, scallops, fried fois gras, cooked lobster, fish in a cream sauce, white meat in a cream sauce, creamy cheeses such as Saint-Félicien, Saint-Marcellin, mature goat's cheeses such as Picodon.
How to serve?	should be aged for 3 to 5 years in the bottle before drinking, serve not too chilled, between 10° and 12°C (50-54°F).

Brûlefer

Gewürztraminer

4 - VERY AROMATIC, DRY WHITE WINE

Characteristics	rich, lively palate with distinctive flavours; exuberant fruity aromas, often spicy, sometimes fresh nut or wheat aromas; persistent finish with plenty of character.
Grape varieties	Gewürztraminer, Muscat, Palomino, Riesling, Savagnin, Tokay-Pinot Gris, Viognier.
Appellations	Château-Chalon, Condrieu, Alsace Gewürztraminer, Manzanilla, Alsace Muscat, Alsace Riesling, Alsace Tokay-Pinot Gris, Jura Vin Jaune, sherry.
Food matches	very aromatic food cooked with spices and herbs; meat curry, chicken with a cream and mushroom sauce, lobster *à l'américaine*, salmon with fennel, cooked pressed cheeses (Beaufort, Comté, etc) or strong-flavoured cheeses (Munster, etc).
How to serve?	Muscat and Viognier are to be drunk young and served chilled, between 8° and 10°C (46-50°F); the others should be drunk after 3 to 5 years in the bottle and served not too chilled, between 10° and 12°C (50-54°F).

5 - MEDIUM SWEET AND SWEET WHINE WINES

Characteristics	rich texture from the varying amounts of residual sugars present with a sweet, fatty body balanced by good levels of acidity; significant fruity, honeyed aromas; persistent, aromatic finish.
Grape varieties	Chenin, Gros- and Petit-Manseng, Muscadelle, Riesling, Sauvignon, Sémillon, Tokay-Pinot Gris.
Appellations	Bonnezeaux, Cérons, Coteaux de l'Aubance, Coteaux du Layon, Gewürztraminer Vendanges Tardives or Sélection de Grains Nobles, Monbazillac, Montlouis, Quarts-de-Chaume, Riesling Vendanges Tardives or Sélection de Grains Nobles, Ste-Croix-du-Mont, Tokay-Pinot Gris Vendanges Tardives or Sélection de Grains Nobles, Vouvray.
Food matches	rich, fatty food, either classic or more exotic with spicy or sweet and sour flavours; foie gras, chicken in a spicy cream sauce, duck *à l'orange*, blue-veined cheese such as Roquefort, fruit tart, cream-based desserts such as zabaglione and *crème brûlée*.
How to serve?	drink after a minimum of 3 to 5 years in the bottle, serve chilled, between 8° and 10°C (46-50°F).

6 - LIVELY, FRUITY ROSÉ WINE

Characteristics	crisp, fresh, slightly acidic palate with very fruity aromas, thirst-quenching finish.
Grape varieties	Cabernet Franc, Carignan, Cinsault, Gamay, Grenache, Poulsard, Tibouren.
Appellations	Bellet, Baux de Provence, Coteaux d'Aix, Coteaux varois, Côtes du Luberon, Côtes de Provence, Côtes du Jura, Irouléguy, Palette, Rosé de Loire.
Food matches	light food based on raw or cooked vegetables; mixed salads, vegetable pasta dishes, savoury vegetable tarts, *tapenade, anchoïade*, pizzas, soft or slightly firm goat's cheeses.
How to serve?	drink within one year of bottling, while still very fruity, serve chilled, between 8° and 10°C (46-50°F).

7 - FULL-BODIED, VINOUS ROSÉ WINES

Characteristics	full, versatile palate with good vinosity; fruity aromas, good balance between the acidity and a light tannic structure; refreshing finish.
Grape varieties	Carignan, Grenache, Merlot, Mourvèdre, Négrette, Pinot Noir, Syrah.
Appellations	Bandol, Bordeaux clairet, Coteaux du Languedoc, Côtes du Rhône, Corbières, Lirac, Marsannay, Rosé des Riceys, Tavel.

Sauternes

Food matches	sunshine food based on olive oil, vegetables and fish; aïoli, *bouillabaisse*, aubergine *tian*, ratatouille, mullet, grilled meats, mature goat's cheeses.
How to serve?	drink young, within 2 years of bottling, serve chilled, between 8° and 10°C (46-50°F).

8 - LIGHT, FRUITY RED WINE

Characteristics	quaffable wine full of fruit and freshness; light tannins compensated for by a pleasant acidity; expressive aromas of red fruits and/or flowers; simple, thirst-quenching finish.
Grape varieties	Cabernet Franc, Gamay, Pinot Noir, Poulsard, Trousseau.
Appellations	Anjou, Arbois, Beaujolais, Bourgogne, Bourgueil, Côtes du Forez, Côtes du Jura, Coteaux du Lyonnais, Hautes Côtes de Beaune, Hautes Côtes de Nuits, Alsace Pinot Noir, St-Nicolas de Bourgueil, Sancerre, Saumur-Champigny, Vin de Savoie.
Food matches	simple, fairly uncomplicated food; pork, quiches, meat pâté, chicken liver pâté, rabbit *terrine*, fairly creamy goat's or cow's milk cheeses such as Saint-Marcellin.
How to serve?	drink young, within two years of bottling, serve between 12° and 14°C (54-57°F).

Sangre de Toro

9 - FULL-BODIED, FRUITY RED WINE

Characteristics	a fleshy palate derived from the abundance of fruits, the fullness of the alcohol and the presence of tannins, albeit fairly uncomplicated; red fruit, and often spicy, aromas; fairly persistent finish.
Grape varieties	Cabernet Franc, Cabernet Sauvignon, Carignan, Grenache, Merlot, Mondeuse, Pinot Noir, Syrah.
Appellations	Bergerac, Bordeaux, Bordeaux Supérieur, Buzet, Chinon, Côte de Blaye, Côte de Bourg, Côte de Castillon, Côte chalonnaise, Côtes de Provence, Côtes du Rhône-Villages, Coteaux d'Aix, Coteaux champenois, Crozes-Hermitage, Fronton, St-Joseph.
Food matches	full-flavoured regional fare; small game birds or animals, pâté de campagne, meats in sauces, roasted red meat, grilled meats, uncooked pressed cheeses such as Tomme, Saint-Nectaire.
How to serve?	needs to mature in the bottle for 2 to 3 years before drinking; serve between 15° and 17°C (59-63°F).

10 - COMPLEX, POWERFUL RED WINE WITH A FINE BOUQUET

Characteristics	smooth, fleshy palate derived from a high alcohol content and tannins which require a few years to soften; rich, complex bouquet of fruits, spices and often oaky nuances; persistent, complex finish.
Grape varieties	Auxerrois, Cabernet Franc, Carignan, Grenache, Malbec, Merlot, Mourvèdre, Syrah, Tannat.
Appellations	Cahors, Châteauneuf-du-Pape, Corbières, Côtes du Roussillon-Villages, Coteaux du Languedoc, Gigondas, Madiran, Minervois, Pécharmant, Pomerol, St-Emilion, St-Chinian, Vacqueyras.
Food matches	full-flavoured food with a high fat content; cassoulet, conserve of duck, mushrooms including truffles, escalope of foie gras, dishes in sauces, grilled or roasted red meat, game birds or animals, uncooked pressed cheeses such as Tomme, Cantal.
How to serve?	drink after a minimum of 3 years in the bottle, serve between 15° and 17°C (59-63°F).

Pauillac

11 - COMPLEX, TANNIC, DISTINCTIVE RED WINE

Characteristics	distinctive palate with a taut, dense texture supported by a significant, yet elegant, tannin structure which will only soften after a few years ageing; complex fruity, spicy and often oaky aromas; long distinctive finish.
Grape varieties	Cabernet Sauvignon, Mourvèdre, Syrah.
Appellations	Bandol, Cornas, Côte Rôtie, Graves, Haut-Médoc, Hermitage, Margaux, Médoc, Pauillac, Pessac-Léognan, St-Estèphe, St-Julien.
Food matches	food which is full of flavour and not too fatty; mushrooms including truffles, game birds or animals, grilled or roasted red meat, uncooked pressed cheeses such as Cantal, Saint-Nectaire.
How to serve?	drink after a minimum of 3 years in the bottle, serve between 16° and 17°C (61-63°F).

12 - COMPLEX, ELEGANT, DISTINCTIVE RED WINE

Characteristics	silky, elegant palate supported by fine, still firm young tannins; expressive red fruit aromas with notes of undergrowth; persistent, distinctive finish.
Grape varieties	Pinot Noir
Appellations	good burgundies, Côte de Nuits such as Chambolle-Musigny, Gevrey-Chambertin, Vosne-Romanée, Côte de Beaunes such as Corton, Pommard, Volnay and Côte Chalonnaise such as Mercurey.
Food matches	flavoursome dishes simmered in a wine sauce: coq au vin, eggs *en meurette*, roasted white or red meat, small game birds or animals, fairly mild soft cheeses with a surface mould (Brie, Coulommiers...).
How to serve?	drink after a minimum of 3 years in the bottle, serve between 16° and 17°C (61-63°F).

13 - SPARKLING WINE

Characteristics	fresh, lively, light palate thanks to the bubbles (CO_2); delicate fruit or floral aromas; thirst-quenching finish, more persistent in some cases than others.
Grape varieties	Auxerrois, Cabernet Franc, Chardonnay, Chenin, Clairette, Mauzac, Merlot, Pinot Blanc, Pinot Noir, Pinot Meunier, Sauvignon, Savagnin, Sémillon.
Appellations	Blanquette de Limoux, Champagne, Clairette de Die, Crémant d'Alsace, Crémant de Bordeaux, Crémant de Bourgogne, Crémant du Jura, Gaillac, Montlouis, Saumur, Vouvray.
Food matches	dry: seafood, fish *terrine*, grilled or smoked fish or fish served with a light cream sauce, soft cheeses with a surface mould; sweeter varieties: soft cheeses with a surface mould, fruit desserts, meringue, *crème anglaise*.
How to serve?	while young, serve chilled, between 8° and 10°C (46-50°F).

14 - VINS DOUX NATURELS AND FORTIFIED WINES

Characteristics	sweet, alcoholic palate giving a fatty texture, full or fruit flavours; exuberant fruity aromas, flavoursome finish.
Grape varieties	Cabernet Franc, Cabernet Sauvignon, Folle-Blanche, Colombard, Grenache, Maccabeu, Malvoisie, Merlot, Muscat, Ugni Blanc.
Appellations	Banyuls, Macvin du Jura, Muscat de Beaumes-de-Venise, Muscat de Mireval, Muscat de Rivesaltes, Pineau des Charentes, Porto, Rasteau, Rivesaltes.
Food matches	rich, flavoursome dishes combining sweet and sour, in particular desserts, cooked fresh foie gras, duck with figs, blue-veined cheese such as Roquefort, fruity desserts, chocolate or coffee desserts.
How to serve?	whites: drink very young, serve chilled between 8°C (46°F) and 12°C (R4°F); reds: drink after 3 to 5 years ageing, serve between 12° and 15°C (54-59°F).

Mercurey

MATCHING WINE AND FOOD

The following suggestions include both classic and regional wine partnerships, as well as pairings discovered at professional tastings. However, there are no hard and fast rules. Individuals' taste and culture will have a strong influence on their perception of particular flavours.

COLD STARTERS

Fresh anchovies	white Banyuls, white Châteauneuf-du-Pape, Collioure rosé, Coteaux d'Aix rosé, sherry.
Artichokes in *vinaigrette*	Chinon rosé, white Côtes de Provence, Sancerre.
Artichaut *Barigoule*	Coteaux d'Aix rosé, Côtes de Provence rosé, Lirac rosé, Tavel rosé.
White asparagus	an Alsace Pinot Blanc or Muscat, sherry fino.
Green asparagus	Château-Grillet, Condrieu, Viognier Vin de Pays, dry Muscat, Vin de Pays du Roussillon.
Avocado	Côtes-de-Provence rosé, Mâcon-Villages, Sancerre.
Caviar	*Blanc de Blancs* Champagne, dry Riesling from Alsace or Germany (or chilled vodka).
Foie gras *terrine*	sweet wines such as Sauternes, Coteaux du Layon, Jurançon, Monbazillac, Tokay-Pinot Gris Sélection de Grains Nobles (S.G.N.), Gewürztraminer S.G.N. or a fortified wine such as Vintage Banyuls, port.
Gazpacho	Collioure rosé, Côtes du Rhône-Villages rosé, Tavel, Penedès rosé.
Guacamole	Mexican Cabernet Sauvignon or Californian Chardonnay.
Melon	*vins doux naturels*, Muscat de Beaumes-de-Venise, Muscat de Rivesaltes, Banyuls, Rivesaltes, Ruby port, Sercial or Bual madeira.
Auvergne salad	Beaujolais-Villages, Côtes d'Auvergne, Côtes du Forez.
Walnut and chicory salad	Savagnin-based Jura wine, Arbois, Côtes du Jura, L'Étoile.
Salade niçoise	Bandol rosé, white Bellet, white Cassis, Coteaux d'Aix rosé.
Taramasalata	Pouilly Fumé, Alsace Riesling, Aleppo rosé.

Salade niçoise

HOT STARTERS

Frogs legs	Aligoté de Bourgogne, Petit Chablis, Mâcon-Villages.
Snails *à la bourguignonne*	Aligoté de Bourgogne, white Beaujolais, Chablis, Mâcon-Villages.
Warm fresh foie gras	sweet wines such as Vintage Banyuls and Sauternes, but also full-bodied reds such as Madiran and Cahors.
Garbure	Cahors, Irouléguy, Madiran.
Small provençal pastries	Bandol rosé, white or rosé Bellet, red Côtes du Rhône-Villages, Tavel.
Pizza	Coteaux-d'Aix red or rosé, Coteaux du Luberon red or rosé, Chianti, Valpolicella.
Quenelle of pike	Chablis, Pouilly-Fuissé, St-Véran, Roussette de Savoie.
Quiche Lorraine	Alsace Pinot Blanc or Tokay-Pinot Gris, white wines from Savoie or light red wines such as Beaujolais, Bourgueil or Alsace Pinot Noir.
Onion tart	Alsace Pinot Blanc or Sylvaner.
Fish soufflé	Chablis, white Graves or Pessac-Léognan, Pouilly Fumé, a Napa Valley Fumé Blanc.
Cheese soufflé	Savagnin-based Jura wine, Arbois, Côtes du Jura, Château-Chalon.
Onion soup	Beaujolais-Villages, Entre-deux-Mers, Mâcon-Villages red or white.
Vol au vent	Jura *Vin Jaune*, good Chardonnay such as Corton-Charlemagne, Meursault, Montrachet or Californian Chardonnay.

CHARCUTERIE (SMOKED AND CURED MEATS)

Andouille	Sancerre, Savennières.
Boudin noir	Chinon, Crozes-Hermitage, St-Joseph, Saumur-Champigny.
Spicy chorizo	Cahors, Irouléguy, Rioja.
Cured ham	Collioure, Irouléguy, Pinot Grigio dell'Alto Adige, Soave Classico, a dry Rheingau Riesling, sherry or manzanilla, young Spanish red.
Cooked ham	Beaujolais-Villages or *cru*, Mercurey, Mâcon-Villages red or white.
Smoked ham	Riesling Vendanges Tardives, German Spätlese.
Ham and parsley in aspic jelly	white or red Beaujolais, Chablis, white Mercurey, Pouilly-Fuissé, white St-Romain.
Smooth chicken liver pâté	Beaujolais *cru*, white Beaune, white Ladoix, Meursault.

Grilled lobster

Pâté de campagne	Beaujolais, Chinon, Coteaux du Lyonnais, Côtes du Rhône-Villages, Crozes-Hermitage, Saint-Joseph, Saumur-Champigny.
Game *terrine*	Bergerac, Châteauneuf-du-Pape, Mercurey, Gevrey-Chambertin, Pomerol, St-Emilion, Vacqueyras, Garrafeira from central Portugal.
Rabbit *terrine*	Bourgueil, Cheverny, Cour-Cheverny, St-Nicolas de Bourgueil, Morgon, Moulin-à-Vent.
Rillettes	Montlouis, Sancerre, Vouvray.
Salami	Irouléguy, Tavel, Corsican rosé, Navarran red or rosé, Barbera, Chianti, Montepulciano d'Abruzzo, Rosso Conero, sherry.
Pork sausage	Buzet, Côtes du Rhône, Gigondas, Dolcetto d'Alba, Merlot, Rioja.
Saucisson sec	Crozes-Hermitage, Côtes du Rhône-Villages, Hautes Côtes de Beaune, Hautes Côtes de Nuits, St-Joseph, red Sancerre .
Warm *saucisson* in *brioche*	Morgon, Moulin-à-Vent, St-Joseph.

EGGS

Scrambled eggs with truffles	white Hermitage, Montrachet.
Scrambled eggs	light, fruity reds such as Beaujolais, Gamay de Touraine.
Eggs in aspic jelly	young, fruity wines from the Côte de Beaune, such as Santenay, Maranges.
Eggs *en meurette*	Beaujolais *crus*, red Mâcon, Pinot Noir from the Côte de Beaune or the Côte Chalonnaise.
Salmon eggs	Chablis, Alsace Riesling, Vouvray.
Plain omelette	Beaujolais-Villages, Coteaux du Lyonnais, Côtes du Forez.
Cheese omelette	a Chardonnay and Savagnin-based Jura white.

SEAFOOD AND SHELLFISH

Scallops	*Blanc de Blancs* Champagne, white Châteauneuf-du-Pape, white Hermitage, Pessac-Léognan, a dry Alsace or German Riesling.
Crab	White Cassis, Chablis, Entre-deux-Mers, Gros Plant, Muscadet.

Prawns	white Bergerac, white Cassis, Petit Chablis, Entre-deux-Mers, Gros-Plant, Muscadet, Picpoul-de-Pinet, Friuli Riesling.
Crayfish in *court-bouillon*	Condrieu, white Châteauneuf-du-Pape, dry Alsace Riesling.
Grilled lobster	Corton-Charlemagne, white Hermitage, Pessac-Léognan, Meursault, Alsace Riesling, Savennières, Verdicchio del Castelli di Jesi.
Lobster *à l'américaine*	Alsace Tokay-Pinot Gris, Jura *Vin Jaune*, medium-dry Vouvray.
Oysters	Chablis, Entre-deux-Mers, Gros-Plant, Muscadet, Picpoul-de-Pinet, Alsace Riesling.
Warm oysters	*Blanc de Blancs* Champagne, white Graves, Alsace Riesling, Savennières, Vouvray, Oregon Chardonnay.
Grilled crayfish	Chablis *Premier Cru* or *Grand Cru*, white Hermitage, Pessac-Léognan, Alsace Riesling.
***Langoustine* mayonnaise**	Pouilly Fumé, Sancerre, Chablis.
Mussels in cream sauce	white Bergerac, white Côte de Blaye, Pouilly-Fuissé, white Rully.
Mussels *marinière*	Entre-deux-Mers, Muscadet, Sauvignon de Touraine, Vinho Verde.

FISH

Eel *à la bordelaise*	red Bergerac, red Bordeaux Supérieur, Graves. St-Emilion satellites.
Grilled bass (or sea perch)	white Bellet, white Châteauneuf-du-Pape, white Côtes-de-Provence, Chablis *Premier Cru* or *Grand Cru*.
Bouillabaisse	rosé Bandol, Cassis, rosé Côteaux d'Aix, Tavel.
Salt cod *brandade*	Cassis, white Hermitage, white Saint-Joseph.
Cold hake with mayonnaise	Mâcon-Villages, Alsace Pinot Blanc, white Savoie wine, Alsace Sylvaner.
Fried fish selection	Aligoté de Bourgogne, Gros Plant, Mâcon, Muscadet, Vinho Verde.
Cod with aïoli	white or rosé Bandol, Cassis, white or rosé Côtes-de-Provence, Collioure rosé, Irouléguy rosé, Vinho verde.
Oily fish (herring, mackerel, sardines, swordfish, tuna)	Aligoté de Bourgogne, Gros-Plant, Muscadet, Sancerre, Sauvignon de Touraine, Sylvaner, white Dão, Vinho Verde.
Grilled white fish	dry Chenin Blanc, white Coteaux d'Aix, white Côtes de Provence, Soave, Verdicchio, white Corsican wine, Vaud Chasselas.
White fish in a *beurre blanc*	*Blanc de Blancs* Champagne, dry or medium-dry Vouvray, Meursault, Pessac-Léognan, Puligny-Montrachet, Savennières, Moselle wines.
Raw fish	Chablis *Premier Cru*, white Graves, Meursault, New Zealand Chardonnay.
Fresh-water fish	Chablis, Swiss Chasselas, white Graves, white Mercurey, Montlouis, white Rully, Sancerre, Vouvray, Neuchâtel Chasselas.

Fried fish	Beaujolais, Entre-deux-Mers, Gamay de Touraine, Gros-Plant, Muscadet, Roussette de Savoie, Chardonnay and Savagnin-based Jura white, Friuli Pinot Grigio, Frascati Superiore.
Smoked fish	Chablis *1er cru*, *Blanc de Blancs* Champagne, Poulliy Fumé, Sancerre, Alsace Riesling or Tokay-Pinot Gris, German Spätlese.
Plain fish	white wines of varying intensity depending on whether the fish and its garnish are fatty or not, from the lesser *vins de pays* to the *grands crus* from Burgundy, Bordeaux or Alsace. Some red wines, especially Cabernet Francs from the Loire Valley or Beaujolais Gamays, which are not too tannic, also go perfectly well with fish.
Red Mullet	rosé or red Bandol, Collioure, Côtes de Provence red or white, Soave.
Smoked salmon	*Blanc de Blancs* Champagne, Alsace Riesling, Sancerre (or vodka or a peaty single malt whisky).
Salmon with sorrel	Condrieu, Châteauneuf-du Pape blanc.
Poached salmon	white: white Burgundy, Sancerre, Savennières, dry Vouvray, Sicilian white wine; red: Beaujolais-Villages, Bourgueil, Alsace Pinot Noir.
Grilled sardines	Côtes-de-Provence, white Côtes-du-Rhône-Villages, white Coteaux du Languedoc, white Coteaux d'Aix.
Sole *meunière*	white Bellet, Chablis *Premier Cru* or *Grand Cru*, Sancerre, Alsace Riesling.
Fish terrine	Aligoté de Bouzeron, Chablis, white Graves, Mâcon-Villages, Muscadet, Sancerre, Alsace Sylvaner.
Basque-style tuna	red or rosé Collioure, red or rosé Coteaux du Languedoc, red Côtes du Rhône-Villages, Irouléguy rosé, Tavel.
Fish pie (with cream sauce)	Mâcon-Villages, Pouilly-Fuissé, Alsace Pinot Gris, Bianco di Custoza, Pfälzer Sylvaner, Nahe Müller-Thurgau, Napa Valley Chardonnay.
Turbot with *sauce hollandaise*	Corton-Charlemagne, white Hermitage, Meursault, Pessac-Léognan, Chili Chardonay.

LAMB

Roast lamb	complex, distinctive red wines such as the Bordeaux *crus*, i.e. Graves, Margaux, Pauillac, Pomerol, Saint-Emilion, but also a Bandol from a good year; Rioja Reserva, Ribera del Duero, American, Australian, Chilean and Italian Cabernet Sauvignons.
Lamb couscous	Cahors, Côtes du Rhône-Villages, Madiran, Gigondas, a red from Médéa (Algeria).
Lamb curry	Bergerac, Côtes de Castillon, Côtes de Franc, Côtes du Rhône-Villages, Lalande-de-Pomerol.
Roast shoulder of lamb	Haut-Médoc, Médoc, American, Australian, Chilean and Italian Cabernet Sauvignons, a red from Boulaouane (Morocco).

Leg of lamb with herbs and/or garlic	powerful reds with fine bouquet such as Bandol, Châteauneuf-du-Pape, Côtes du Roussillon-Villages, Coteaux du Languedoc, St-Chinian, Vacqueyras, red Retsina.
Rolled leg of lamb	Côte de Beaune Pinot Noir, Bourgueil, Chinon, Vino Nobile di Montepulciano.
Lamb casserole	Côte de Beaune or Côte Chalonnaise Pinot Noir, Beaujolais *crus*, Navarra (Spain).
Lamb *à la provencale*	red Coteaux d'Aix, red Côtes de Provence, Côtes du Rhône-Villages, Zinfandel.
Saddle of lamb	Côte Rôtie, Hermitage, Médoc, Pomerol, St-Emilion, Vega Sicilia (Douro Valley).

BEEF

Bœuf bourguignon	Chinon, Corbières, Côtes du Rhône-Villages, Mercurey, Minervois, Rully, St-Amour, red Saumur.
Beef *en croûte* **(Beef Wellington)**	Bordeaux, Médoc or Libournais wines, Burgundy Pinot Noir.
Roast beef	well-structured, powerful reds with a fine bouquet such as the wines from the Côte de Nuits, Margaux, Pauillac, Pomerol, St-Emilion, American, Australian and Chilean Merlots.
Carpaccio	Côte Chalonnaise wines, Chianti Classico or Rufina.
Chateaubriand	Gevrey-Chambertin, Graves, Pomerol, Pommard, Saint-Emilion.
Braised Beef	Cahors, Corbières, Côtes du Rhône-Villages, Côtes du Roussillon-Villages, Madiran.
Entrecôte *à la bordelaise*	Bergerac, Bordeaux Supérieur, Côtes de Blaye, Côtes de Castillon, Fronsac, Graves, Aragon (Spain).
Grilled entrecôte	Cabernet Sauvignon wines, Médoc from recent vintages, Vin de Pays d'Oc or a generous young wine such as Châteauneuf-du-Pape, Cornas, Gigondas, Vacqueyras.
Boiled beef with vegetables	Red Anjou, Beaujolais *cru*, Bourgueil, Côtes de Bordeaux, Saumur-Champigny, Pinot d'Alsace, red Sancerre.
Grilled Steak	Chénas, Côtes du Frontonnais, Cornas, Moulin-à-Vent, Chianti Riserva.
Steak *au poivre*	red Côtes du Rhône, Fronton, Californian Zinfandel, Australian Shiraz.
Steak *tartare*	Buzet, Cahors, Crozes-Hermitage, Chilean Merlot, Australian Shiraz.

Roasted loin of lamb

PORK

Andouillette à la crème	white Beaujolais, Chablis, Pouilly-Fuissé, white Rully, St-Véran.
Grilled andouillette	light red wines such as red Anjou, Beaujolais-Villages, Gamay de Touraine, Alsace Pinot Noir, red Sancerre and also dry, fruity whites such as Chablis, Gaillac, white Saumur.
Choucroute	Alsace Tokay-Pinot Gris, Riesling or Sylvaner.
Grilled pork	full, fruity wines such as Bergerac, Crozes-Hermitage, St-Joseph, Saumur-Champigny.
Pork shoulder	light white wines: white Anjou, Mâcon-Villages, Alsace Pinot Blanc or Sylvaner; but also light, fruity reds: Beaujolais, Mâcon-Villages, Alsace Pinot Noir.
Pork and cabbage stew	Brouilly, Mâcon-Villages, red Sancerre.
Roast pork	Crozes-Hermitage, Côte de Beaune, Côtes du Rhône-Villages, St-Joseph, red Bairrada.

VEAL

***Blanquette* of veau**	Beaujolais-Villages, Mâcon-Villages, white Mercurey, white Givry, red Sancerre.
Veal chop	finest Médoc wines such as Pauillac or Saint-Estèphe, Côte de Nuits *crus* such as Gevrey-Chambertin, Chambolle-Musigny.
Veal chop with cream and cider	white Burgundy, Chardonnay and Savagnin-based Jura wines, Californian Chardonnay.
Veal scalloppini	Beaujolais *crus*, Côte de Beaune red wines, red Graves.
Veal liver	Chinon, Pomerol, St-Emilion, red Sancerre.
Osso-bucco	Barbera, Barbaresco, Chianti Classico, Valpolicella.
Veal olives	Beaujolais *crus*, Bourgueil, Burgundy Pinot Noir, S t-Nicolas de Bourgueil.
Sweetbreads in a cream sauce	a good white Burgundy such as Corton-Charlemagne, Meursault, Montrachet, Château-Chalon or Jura *Vin Jaune*, Alsace Tokay-Pinot Gris, medium-dry Vouvray.
Veal kidneys in mustard sauce	fairly young, meaty red such as Chinon, Pomerol, St-Emilion ; Chinon, Morgon, St-Amour, Côte Chalonnaise Pinot Noir.
Roast veal	Beaujolais *crus*, Côte de Beaune Pinot Noir, Valpolicella (Italy).
Calf's head	Beaujolais *crus*, Pouilly-Fuissé, Sancerre rosé, Tavel.
Veal Marengo	Côtes du Rhône-Villages, Costières de Nîmes, Côtes du Ventoux, Dão red, Sangiovese di Romagna (Italy).
Veal Orloff	a white Grand Bourgogne such as Chassagne-Montrachet, Corton Charlemagne, Meursault; also fruity, but full-bodied red wines such as a red burgundy from the Côte de Beaune.

DUCK, GOOSE, PIGEON

Duck *à l'orange*	fairly young sweet wines, Cérons, Loupiac, Monbazillac, Ste-Croix-du-Mont, Sauternes.
Duck with figs or cherries	rich, powerful wines such as Bandol, Châteauneuf-du-Pape but also young fortified wines such as Banyuls, Maury, Rivesaltes.
Glazed duck	Alsace Gewürztraminer or Tokay-Pinot Gris, Arbois, Château-Chalon, Jura *Vin Jaune*.
Duck with olives	Côtes du Rhône-Villages, Gigondas, Vacqueyras, a red from Carthage (Tunisia).
Roast duck	Merlot-based wines, Lalande-de-Pomerol, Pomerol, St-Emilion and also the Côte de Nuits *crus*.
Conserve	Bergerac, Buzet, Cahors, Châteauneuf-du-Pape, Madiran, Pécharmant.
Duck fillet	Bordeaux wines from good vintages, Médoc or Libournais.
Cassoulet	Cahors, Côtes du Frontonnais, Madiran.
Roast goose	mellow reds from Côte Rôtie, Côtes de Nuits, Madiran, Margaux, St-Emilion, but also fine late vintage Tokay-Pinot Gris from Alsace.
Roast pigeon	red Burgundy from a good vintage, a Médoc or Libournais, Bandol, Châteauneuf-du-Pape, Hermitage, Merlot from north-east Italy.
Pigeon *Pastilla*	a fortified wine such as Banyuls, Muscat de Beaumes-de-Venise, Muscat de Rivesaltes, Cap Corse Muscat, Mascara (Algeria).
Wood pigeon *salmi*	Pomerol, St-Emilion, Chilean or Italian Merlots.

POULTRY

Coq au vin	Burgundy Pinot Noir, Moulin-à-Vent.
Stuffed turkey	wines with a fine bouquet: Châteauneuf-du-Pape, Hermitage, Pomerol, Madiran, St-Emilion, American or Chilean Merlots, etc
Turkey with chesnut stuffing	Pinot Noir from the Côte Chalonnaise, such as Mercurey or Givry, or from the Côte de Beaune such as Savigny-les-Beaune, Volnay.
Fatted chicken with truffles	fine Côte de Beaune Chardonnays such as Corton-Charlemagne, Meursault, Montrachet but also white Hermitage, Arbois, Château-Chalon, Jura *Vin Jaune*.
Boiled chicken	Beaujolais, Mâcon blanc, Pouilly-Fuissé, white Rully.
Basque-style chicken	Bordeaux Supérieur, Corbières, Coteaux du Languedoc, Fronton.
Chicken with a creamy morel mushroom sauce	Arbois, Château-Chalon, Jura *Vin Jaune*, a Côte de Beaune Pinot Noir or good Chardonnay.
Roast chicken	Pinot Noir from the Côte de Beaune or the Côte Chalonnaise, Moulin-à-Vent, Zinfandel.
Chicken in a red wine vinegar sauce	Anjou-Villages, Bourgueil, Chinon, St-Nicolas de Bourgueil, Saumur-Champigny.

Blueberry tart

RABBIT

Rabbit *chasseur*	Beaujolais-Villages, Bourgueil, Côte-Chalonnaise, Saumur-Champigny.
Rabbit with mustard sauce	Chénas, Chinon, Mercurey, red Sancerre, St-Joseph.
Roasted rabbit with thyme	Coteaux des Baux, Coteaux d'Aix, Palette, a red Corsican wine.
Rabbit with prunes	Bergerac, Buzet, Côtes de St-Mont, red Gaillac, Pécharmant, Dão red.

GAME

Game	as a general rule, the finest Burgundies, Bordeaux or Vallée du Rhône wines, Valpolicella Amarone (Italy).
Jugged hare	Bandol from a good vintage, Côte Rôtie, *Grand Cru* Côte de Nuits, Châteauneuf-du-Pape, Hermitage, Pomerol, Oregon Pinot Noir.
Roasted haunch of wild boar	Châteauneuf-du-Pape, Côtes du Roussillon-Villages, Corbières, Ch Musar (Lebanon).
Small game birds (young partridge, pheasant, woodcock)	Côte de Beaune or Côte de Nuits Pinot Noir, Rioja.
Small game animals (wild rabbit, hare)	Côte Chalonnaise Pinot Noir, Médoc, St-Emilion, Chilean Merlot.
Marinated game	Cahors, Châteauneuf-du-Pape, Madiran, Gigondas, Vacqueyras, Shiraz.
Haunch of venison *grand veneur*	Côte Rôtie, Hermitage, Corton, Châteauneuf-du-Pape, Barbaresco (Italy).

VEGETABLES *see also starters*

Aubergines	red Coteaux d'Aix, Coteaux du Languedoc, red Côtes de Provence; Greek reds such as Naoussa Xinomavro or Retsina.
Mushrooms	the finest Merlots or Pinot Noirs such as Burgundy or Libournais reds.
Stuffed cabbage	Beaujolais-Villages, Gamay de Touraine, South African Pinotage.
Cauliflower	Côtes-du-Luberon, Dolcetto, Sauvignon de Touraine.
Green beans	white or rosé Sancerre, rosé Coteaux d'Aix, white Côtes de Provence.
Gratin dauphinois	Chardonnay and Savagnin-based Jura wines such as white Arbois but also Savoie white wines from the Roussette grape.
Pasta	light whites, reds or rosés depending on the ingredients of the sauce, Valpolicella or Friuli Merlot.
Pasta with tomato and basil	Côtes du Rhône-Villages rosé, Lirac rosé, Coteaux d'Aix rosé, Dolcetta Alba (Italy).
Seafood pasta	Chablis, Mâcon-Villages, Sancerre, Sauvignon de Touraine, dry Italian whites (Orvieto white).

Pasta with meat sauce	Beaujolais-Villages, Bourgueil, Coteaux du Tricastin, Mâcon-Villages, Alsace Pinot Noir, Chianti, Valpolicella.
Raw vegetables	dry white wines, Aligoté de Bourgogne, Petit Chablis, Sauvignon de Touraine or light red wines made from the Gamay grape, sherry.
Risotto	dry, fruity Italian whites such as Bianco di Custoza, Trebbiano d'Abruzzo, Pinot Grigio; red Italian wines such as Chianti or Spanish reds such as Rioja and La Mancha wines.
Truffles	Pomerol and St-Emilion *grands crus*, also those from the Vallée du Rhône nord Côte Rotie and Hermitage, Barolo (Italy).

DESSERTS

Brioche	Clairette de Die, Alsace Vendange Tardive and Sélection de Grains Nobles, Jura *vin de paille*.
Fruit charlotte	medium-dry Champagne, Muscat-based *vins doux naturels* such as Muscat de Beaumes-de-Venise, Muscat de Rivesaltes, Moscatel de Valence.
Crème brûlée	Muscat-based *vins doux naturels* such as Muscat de Rivesaltes, Muscat de St-Jean-de-Minervois; Jurançon, Pacherenc de Vic-Bilh.
Entremets	dry or medium-dry Champagne, Clairette de Die and also Muscat-based *vins doux naturels*.
Chocolate desserts	red fortified wines such as Banyuls, Maury, Malaga, Port, Rivesaltes.
Spicy desserts	aromatic, sweet wines such as Tokay-Pinot Gris Vendanges Tardives or Sélection de Grains Nobles, Jurançon, Riesling Auslese.
Floating islands	medium-dry rosé Champagne, Muscat-based *vins doux naturels*.
Fruit Zabaglione	sweet wine from the Sauternais, Tokay-Pinot Gris or Gewürztraminer Vendanges Tardives and Sélection de Grains Nobles.
Lemon tart	dessert wines such as Cérons, Jurançon, Sainte-Croix-du-Mont, Sauternes.
Red fruit tart	dry or medium-dry rosé Champagne. Clairette de Die, sparkling Gaillac, Muscat-based *vins doux naturels*.
Tarte Tatin	Sweet white wines from the Loire such as Bonnezeaux, Coteaux du Layon, Coteaux de l'Aubance, sweet Montlouis, Quarts-de-Chaume, sweet Vouvray.

Y Y Y

MATCHING CHEESE AND WINE

It can be fairly tricky to match cheese with wine. Cheese is salty, often very strong-flavoured and some cheeses are more dense than others. These factors must all be taken into account. Accepted practice of serving red wine, often mature, with the cheese course is often incorrect as the subtle taste of the wine is overpowered by the stronger flavour of the cheese. Dry, or sweeter, white wines on the other hand are good partners for cheese, especially if they are young. The fresh acidity of these wines counterbalances the saltiness of the cheese and their fruitiness stands up to the strong flavours. The lack of tannins in white wine also explains why they go so well with cheese as harsh tannins, especially in young red wines, are accentuated by the saltiness of the cheese. When matching wine with cheese, the maturity of the cheese is equally important as the age of the wine. Regional matches, such as Crottin de Chavignol with Sancerre and Munster with Gewürztraminer, are generally a safe bet.

We have listed below the seven main cheese families, giving their main characteristics, the most well known cheeses falling into each category and their classic wine matches. This is followed by an alphabetical list of cheeses with their preferred wines.

FRESH CHEESES

Names	all soft white cow's or goat's cheeses such as Fontainebleau, Petit-Suisse, mozzarella, ricotta, feta, cream cheese.
Characteristics	a soft consistency with a prominent milky taste. Fairly acidic with varying degrees of saltiness.
Matches	when served with sugar or, even better, honey: sweet wines such as muscat-based *vins doux naturels*, Muscat de Rivesaltes, Muscat de Mireval or sweet aromatic wines, Gewürztraminer Vendange Tardive (V.T.), Tokay-Pinot Gris V.T., Jurançon; when seasoned with herbs, salt and pepper: an aromatic dry white such as Condrieu, Alsace Tokay-Pinot Gris, Viognier Vin de Pays.

GOAT'S CHEESES AND SHEEP'S CHEESES *(perhaps containing a little cow's milk)*

Names	Brocciu, Chabichou, Charlolais, Crottin de Chavignol, Pélardon, Pouligny-Saint-Pierre, Saint-Félicien, Saint-Marcellin, Selles-sur-Cher, Valencay.
Characteristics	the cheese can be soft, medium-textured or hard depending on its age. The harder the cheese, the saltier and stronger the taste.
Matches	versatile, fruity dry whites: Chablis, dry Jurançon, Pouilly-Fuissé, dry Vouvray and especially Sauvignon wines such as Sancerre and Pouilly Fumé; also medium-dry Vouvray or Montlouis wines and light reds with very little tannin such as Gamay-based Beaujolais and Gamay de Touraine, Cabernet Francs such as Bourgueil and St-Nicolas de Bourgueil or even a Pinot Noir such as Hautes Côtes de Beaune, Hautes Côtes de Nuits and Alsace Pinot Noirs.

Goat's cheeses

Pélardons

Chabichou

Cabécous

Boutons de culotte

SOFT CHEESES WITH A SURFACE MOULD

Names	Brie, Brillat-Savarin, Camembert, Chaource, Coulommiers.
Characteristics	smooth texture, ranging from mild and creamy to strong and pungent.
Matches	avoid young, tannic red wines. Aim for unoaked fruity reds with few tannins such as Côte Chalonnaise and Côte de Beaune Burgundies, Coteaux Champenois, Côtes du Rhône, Pomerol, St Emilion, red Sancerre; also young *blanc de blancs* Champagnes (as recommended by the wine waiter Philippe Bourguignon).

Soft cheeses with a surface mould

Coulommiers

Camembert A.O.C.

Pithiviers au foin

Boursault

SOFT CHEESES WITH A WASHED RIND

Names	Epoisses, Livarot, Pont-l'Evêque, Langres, Maroilles, Mont d'Or, Munster, Reblochon, Vacherin.
Characteristics	smooth texture with a definite, or even powerful, taste.
Matches	avoid strong, full-bodied reds and go for very aromatic white wines such as dry or Vendange Tardive Alsace Gewürztraminer, finest Meursault, mature Alsace Riesling, Jura *Vin Jaune* and mature champagnes.

BLUE-VEINED CHEESES

Names	Bleu d'Auvergne, Bleu de Bresse, Fourme d'Ambert, Roquefort.
Characteristics	a smooth, often fatty, texture with a strong, salty flavour.
Matches	red or white *vins doux naturels* such as Muscat de Beaume-de-Venise, Banyuls, Rivesaltes and sweet wines such as Coteaux du Layon, Quarts-de-Chaumes, Cérons and Sauternes.

Cooked pressed cheeses

Bel paese

Gaperon

Gouda

Morbier

Saint-Nectaire A.O.C.

Murol and Murolait

UNCOOKED PRESSED CHEESES

Names	Cantal, Edam, Gouda, Mimolette, Morbier, Saint-Nectaire, Tomme de Savoie.
Characteristics	often take the form of a *tomme* cheese, some have a creamy texture and others a fairly dense texture, with a relatively mild flavour.
Matches	mature Bordeaux reds such as Medoc, Pauillac, Pomerol, St-Emilion but the *tomme* cheeses also go well with Jura and Savoie white wines.

COOKED PRESSED CHEESES

Names	Appenzell, Comté, Emmenthal, Fribourg, Gruyère.
Characteristics	a hard texture with a relatively salty taste and often pronounced flavour.
Matches	fairly aromatic dry white wines, preferably made from Savagnin, such as Jura *Vins Jaunes* but also rich, mature whites such as Meursault.

Blue-veined cheeses

Bleu de Gex A.O.C.

Gorgonzola

Fourme d'Ambert A.O.C.

Bleu des Causses A.O.C.

Bleu d'Auvergne A.O.C.

Pont-l'Evêque A.O.C.

Maroilles A.O.C.

Soumaintrain

Vacherin A.O.C.

Bleu de Bresse

Roquefort A.O.C.

Munster A.O.C.

Rigotte

Boulette d'Avesnes

Livarot A.O.C.

Soft cheeses with a washed rind

CHEESES FROM A TO Z
AND THEIR MATCHES

Appenzell	Château-Chalon, Jura *Vin Jaune*.
Banon	red Côtes du Rhône-Villages, white Côtes de Provence, white Coteaux d'Aix.
Beaufort	Château-Chalon, Jura Vin Jaune.
Bleu d'Auvergne	Loupiac, Maury, Ste-Croix-du-Mont, young Sauternes.
Bleu de Bresse	Monbazillac, white Rivesaltes.
Bleu des Causses	Banyuls Vintage, Barsac.
Bleu de Gex	Cérons, Maury, Loupiac.
Brebis basque et corse	dry Jurançon, Muscat de Corse.
Brillat-Savarin	*blanc de blancs* Champagne .
Brie de Meaux et de Melun	Champagne, Pomerol, St-Emilion, red Sancerre.
Brocciu	dry white Corsican wines or Muscat de Corse.
Camembert	sweet cider, Champagne, Coteaux Champenois.
Cantal	red Côtes d'Auvergne, Mercurey, Pomerol, St-Emilion.
Chabichou	white Menetor-Salon, white Sancerre.
Chaource	rosé Champagne, Coteaux Champenois.
Charolais	Chablis, Mâcon-Villages, Saint-Véran.
Chèvre sec	Beaujolais, Mâcon-Villages, Pouilly-Fuissé.
Comté	Château-Chalon, Jura Vin Jaune, mature Meursault.
Coulommiers	young *blanc de blancs* Champagne , Coteaux Champenois.
Crottin de Chavignol	Pouilly Fumé, white Sancerre.
Edam	Chinon, Médoc, Pauillac.
Emmenthal	Roussette de Savoie, white wine from Savoy.
Epoisses	red Bandol, very aromatic Gewürztraminer.
Fontainebleau	Muscat de Beaumes-de-Venise, Muscat de Mireval.
Fourme d'Ambert	Banyuls, Rivesaltes, port.
Fribourg	Château-Chalon, mature Meursault, Jura *Vin Jaune*.
Gouda	Médoc, Madiran, St-Estèphe.
Gruyère	mature Swiss Chasselas, Roussette de Savoie, Roussette du Bugey.

Laguiole	red Bergerac, Côtes du Frontonnais.
Langres	a slightly older Champagne, Marc de Champagne.
Livarot	Gewürztraminer V.T., Tokay-Pinot Gris V.T.
Maroilles	very aromatic Gewürztraminer, Tokay-Pinot Gris V.T.
Mimolette	Pomerol, St-Emilion.
Morbier	white wine from Savoy.
Mont d'Or	mature Swiss Chasselas (Dézaley), Mâcon-Villages, Roussette de Savoie.
Munster	Alsace Gewürztraminer, dry or V.T.
Ossau-Iraty	Jurançon, white Irouléguy.
Pélardon	white or red Châteauneuf-du-Pape, Condrieu, Viognier *Vin de Pays*.
Picodon	red Côtes du Rhône-Villages, white or red St-Joseph.
Pont-l'Evêque	Chassagne-Montrachet, Meursault, mature Alsace Riesling.
Pouligny-Saint-Pierre	Cheverny, white Reuilly, white Sancerre, Sauvignon de Touraine.
Reblochon	Pouilly-Fuissé, Crépy, Roussette de Savoie.
Rocamadour	dry Jurançon, sherry.
Roquefort	Banyuls Vintage, Rivesaltes Rancio, port.
Saint-Félicien	white or red Beaujolais, white St-Joseph.
Saint-Marcellin	red Beaujolais, white Châteauneuf-du-Pape, white St-Joseph.
Saint-Nectaire	Chinon, Médoc, Pauillac.
Sainte-Maure	Bourgueil, dry or medium-dry.
Salers	red Côtes du Rhône-Villages, Mercurey, Pomerol, St-Emilion.
Selles-sur-Cher	Pouilly Fumé, white Sancerre.
Tomme d'Auvergne	Côte d'Auvergne, red Côtes du Rhône-Villages, Mâcon-Villages.
Tomme des Pyrénées	mature Madiran.
Tomme de Savoie	Bourgueil, Chinon, red and white wine from Savoy, such as Roussette de Savoie.
Vacherin	mature Swiss Chasselas (Dézaley), mature Meursault, Roussette de Savoie.
Valencay	Quincy, white or rosé Reuilly, white Sancerre.

WINEMAKING TODAY

WINE IS NOT DIFFICULT TO MAKE, BUT TO MAKE GOOD WINE, CONSISTENTLY, IS VERY CHALLENGING. THE BASIC TECHNIQUES, AND THE DEBATE ABOUT ADVANCED METHODS, ARE EXPLORED HERE.

Selective harvesting is the key to one of the world's finest sweet white wines: the best Sauternes is made only from grapes that have been attacked by the fungal infection known as "noble rot" (*botrytis cinerea*).

The craft of winemaking was one of the first skills mastered by mankind. Over millennia, it developed into an art, with individual secrets and subtleties handed on from one generation to the next. But it was only in the second half of the 20th century that winemaking became a science. Now it is a sometimes uneasy amalgam of all three: craft skills coexist with creative decisions, all underpinned by scientific understanding. Previous generations had few choices to make: local conditions, such as climate, soil and the proximity of a market, shaped the kind of wine that could be made; custom and tradition reinforced these rules and made them all but unbreakable. Today the mysterious process of fermentation, so strange that our ancestors invoked gods to explain it, can be controlled from a computer console. New varieties of vine can be planted: ones more disease-resistant, or perhaps French classics instead of humbler local grapes. Yet the winemaker is uneasily aware that traditional techniques embody priceless wisdom. All over the world of wine, in vineyard and cellar, the same drama is played out: the college-trained, scientific winemaker meets the traditionalist. The wise winemaker acknowledges that all three approaches — traditional local craft, creative insight and scientific analysis — have their part to play if the wines are not to be bland and shorn of identity even though technically perfect. There are many steps between vineyard and glass, and each plays some part in shaping, or spoiling, the wine. Different parts of the process can have conflicting aims. The grower would like top prices for a large crop. The winemaker may feel happier with fruit grown at a lower yield per vine, and per hectare or acre, for such grapes will have more flavour. In turn, the winemaker's desire to make wine that will age well may not be shared by the company accountant, who wants a quick sale, not a cellar-full of unsold wine in expensive barrels.

A paradox is emerging: the winemaker has gained a battery of controls and skills. But the best wines, in old world and new, are often made by leaving things alone; by letting the wine make itself, watched by someone who knows why it is happening and how to put things right if they go wrong.

TRADITIONAL TECHNIQUES

All that is needed to make wine is ripe grapes. Getting them ripe, and healthy, and full of flavour, and harvested at the right moment, is the job of the vineyard worker. The winemaker (who may be the same person) receives the grapes, then creates the conditions for fermentation to take place. It is this biochemical process that is at the heart of all winemaking. The sugar in the ripe grapes is converted, by fermentation, into alcohol.

Modern winemakers attempt, and succeed in, a great degree of control: the traditional attitude was (and is) that nature, dictated by the local environment, should take its course with the minimum of guidance. The local hillside may yield ripe red grapes or tart white ones, depending on climate and soil. Cellars in autumn may be very cool, with consequent slow fermentation and gentle maturation, or lingeringly warm, when the ferment would be fast and hot.

Working with nature may sound relaxed and laudable, but it became the norm only because yesterday's winemakers lacked the techniques to do anything else. Today this simple way is an alternative to more sophisticated ones. It is also the basis of the wine law in countries such as Italy and France, where rules such as *appellations contrôlées* (see pp136–138) dictate which grapes can be grown, where and how.

Wherever wine is made, the same basic skills evolved. Then the basics were adapted to suit local conditions, and these variations in turn evolved into some of the classic wines. Red bordeaux, for instance, is a response to the cool, variable climate, and to the foreign buyers who flocked to the port of Bordeaux, eager for wine. Champagne's quality and style depend as much as anything on the chilly, early autumns and frosty

The age-old method of immersing the grape skins
in the fermenting red wine.

winters of this northern, windswept corner of France, which halted the fermentation while still leaving traces of natural sugar and of yeast, which began to ferment again in the spring. The harnessing of the accidental, natural process led to sparkling wine. And again, in Champagne and in Burgundy, the incentive of a luxury-level market was there to spur on the progression from good to great: Paris, and the royal court.

The environment

Local wine styles are the product of the kinds of grapes, and their degree of ripeness, that a district can grow. The ambient temperature in autumn has a major influence on the progress of fermentation, and many of Europe's quality wines come from the northern edge of the grape-growing zone. Here, the quality of fruit is best, but also the autumns are cool. No mechanical help is needed to

keep the temperature down, and the cool cellars promise long, slow maturation of the finished wine.

The invention of the vineyard

Initially, man did more to modify the vine than to perfect winemaking. Pruning a vine, so it grows as a low bush rather than a rampant climber, was the critical advance, and it was made in ancient Greece. Legend gives credit to a donkey, which ate the shoots of a vine — that then yielded more and better fruit. Pruning and training, grafting and ploughing, became normal in medieval Europe, and techniques have only really changed in the past three decades.

The concept of the specialized, monoculture vineyard goes back to classical times and was adopted by the medieval monks. But many vineyards were scattered strips amid other crops until well into this century. In Italy, mixed crops were the norm until the 1950s, even in exalted areas such as Barolo. Such vineyards provide security to peasant farmers.

Yield

Yesterday's methods were laborious and often failed partially or completely: rot, mildew and insects; rain, wind and frost, had their way and there was little that man could do. Rich growers sent their workers to pick the insects off the vines by hand; poor ones harvested no grapes. Wet summers meant rotten grapes for rich and poor alike, for there were no anti-rot sprays. But traditional vineyard practice, with its hard pruning, did produce low yields per vine and per hectare, and thus grapes in which the flavours were concentrated. Modern techniques (see pp104–105) offer the chance to grow twice or three times as many bunches of grapes — but are they going to make great, long-lived wine?

From grapes to wine

Grapes contain lots of natural sugar, and their skins harbour wild yeasts. Let the yeasts get at the juice, and fermentation will start. The winemaker helps this to happen by gently crushing the grapes to release their juice. Traditionally, this was done by foot. Grapes are still trodden in the port country of northern Portugal, the Greek islands and a few other out-of-the-way places. Port makers reckon it is the gentlest way to crush (though economics mean it is no longer universal).

Red-wine makers put the crushed grapes and juice into a vat and wait for fermentation to start. The process takes as long as it takes, then the wine is run off into another tank, and the residue is finally pressed to extract more juice. Today a press is used; until recently in remote properties the technique was to shovel the grape pulp (marc) into sacks and pile stones on top.

White wine involves the press first rather than last: the grapes are pressed, and the juice alone ferments in a vat or cask. This immediately begins to explain the broad difference in taste and structure between red and white wines. It is not just colour that is picked up from the skins (white wine can be made from red grapes if they are pressed first — champagne, for instance). Tannins and subtle flavouring compounds are infused from the skins and pips during the fermentation of red wine.

The temperature must be just right for fermentation. Old-fashioned

CLASSIC WINE STYLES

The local styles of some European regions have become classics, emulated in other continents.

Red bordeaux   A temperate climate, just warm enough to ripen red grapes, and varieties such as the Cabernets and Merlot, combine with maturation in small oak casks (often new) to make long-lived and complex wines.

Sweet white bordeaux   The microclimate of Sauternes allows the growth of noble rot (see p163); stringent selection of grapes and careful, even fanatical, winemaking converts the affected fruit into the world's best sweet white wines. The key is selection, with new oak sometimes used for ageing.

Red burgundy   Careful choice of terroir, low yields of the right clones of Pinot Noir grapes, pre-fermentation maceration, warm, fairly fast fermentation, then cask-ageing (often in new oak) are the recipe, but vintage variation due to weather is considerable.

White burgundy   Terroir, climate, intensely flavoured Chardonnay fruit and oak for fermentation all play their part in this style, which gains further complexity from ageing in oak casks (often new) and in bottle.

German Riesling   Long ripening into a warm autumn, careful grape selection, slow fermentation in large vats in a cool cellar, and natural clarification as the wine "falls bright" in the vat lead to wines in an intense, long-lived, beautifully balanced style — but the yields must be kept low.

For fortified wine styles — port, sherry, madeira — see pp424–430 and 440–447.

wineries still open doors and windows to cool the vat-house, or light fires to warm it up.

Once the fermentation is under way, nature takes its course. It may be so warm that the new wine becomes too hot and the yeasts are stunned into inactivity. A "stuck" fermentation results. It may start again as things cool down, or it may not. The wine may survive, or it may be totally spoiled.

The fermentation over, the young wine — red or white — will be cloudy: it needs to settle, and then to be gently poured (racked) off its lees (the sediment of spent yeast cells). Then comes a period in cask or tank, which serves to soften and further clarify the wine (see the chapter starting on p117).

The traditional approach

The simple process outlined above is still used in many parts of the world. Treading has been replaced by mechanical crusher-destemmers, but little else has changed. Some of the greatest wines of France, Germany and elsewhere are made according to this philosophy. The attitude extends to using the yeasts naturally present on the grape skins and in the vathouse, rather than adding cultured yeasts. Winemakers consider that the yeasts form part of the environment that shapes the wine.

Until this century no-one scientifically understood the malolactic or second fermentation, which "wakes" the wine in its first spring, seemingly in tune with the budding of the vines (see p109). Long periods in cask had their dangers: evaporation reduced quantity and constant topping up was needed. Dirty casks could lead to oxidation. The wine would sooner or later be sold, in cask, to a merchant. Bottling at the château, with its added authenticity, is a 20th-century practice.

The traditional approach was (and is) one of minimal intervention, but with plenty of chance for things to go badly wrong.   □

THE WINE YEAR

The tasks of the grape farmer have not changed since winemaking began: to regulate growth, fend off weeds, pests and diseases, and harvest the crop at the right time.

The life of a vine
The vine is a perennial plant, like a fruit tree, and it undergoes not only an annual cycle of fruit production, but a life-cycle of its own, moving from birth as a cutting through immaturity to full production, tailing off into old age. A vine can live for a century, but most vineyards replace their vines after they are 40 or so years old. Older vines produce fewer grapes, but the juice from them is usually superior in concentration and flavour; old vines have had time to send their roots deep into the subsoil and establish a true harmony with the *terroir*.

The end product: ripe grapes.

The vine's annual cycle
Vines cannot thrive unless they undergo a dormant winter period.

This dictates where in the world they can be grown, as the dormancy is triggered by cold. The timings that follow relate to vineyards in a temperate climate, in France. In warmer or cooler climates timings will be earlier or later; in the Southern Hemisphere the seasons are reversed.

In early spring, the sap rises in the plant. The swelling of buds on the bare stems comes in March or April. Bud-break — when the buds emerge — is expected in April. The leaves open, followed in late May or early June by embryo bunches of flowers.

Flowering takes place in June: weather is critical now, with rain greatly feared and warm, sunny conditions preferred. The flowers are white and tiny. They set into tiny fruits late in June or July. Through the summer the grapes develop, red-wine grapes changing from green to black, white grapes taking on gold tints.

The end product is a crop of fully ripe grapes, but there is more to be desired than mere sugar. As sugar levels increase, acidity declines. The point at which the grapes are picked depends on the winemaker's analysis of the best balance between sugar and acidity: a maker of sparkling wine will seek more acidity than a red-wine producer. Different grape varieties ripen at different times, but the same vines in different parts of a vineyard may also vary.

A new vineyard
Starting a new vineyard involves a major programme of levelling, sometimes terracing, the land. Easy access for machines is a priority as running costs drop sharply with mechanization. Drainage may have to be improved. Then the land is ploughed, fertilized and disinfected to kill pests.

Training and staking systems must be installed before vines are planted. The pattern of these

THE VINEYARD MONTH-BY-MONTH

The classic calendar of vineyard work remains unchanged in essence since Roman times, but the new approach to vine management described in the following pages has changed the conventional wisdom on many jobs including pruning, training and fertilizing. This calendar recounts the classic method, as practised in France.

January   Pruning. This delicate work is normally done by hand, but machines are becoming common in the New World. "Minimal pruning" technique is used in parts of the New World.
February   Finish pruning.
March   The vine emerges from dormancy. Start ploughing. Vineyards in Champagne and many New World regions are never ploughed: herbicides combat weeds, the ground is left flat.
April   Bud-break. Plant young vines, check and replace stakes and wires.
May   Guard against frost, start spraying. Repeat ploughing to combat weed growth. Organic growers do not

spray, and encourage plant growth between rows to preserve ecological balance.
June   Flowering. Tie in new shoots by hand or machine. Continue spraying.
July   Plough again to keep down weeds, spray as necessary, trim off long vine shoots — by machine in some vineyards. In some years thin out green grapes to reduce crop size. California growers may start to irrigate.
August   Continue to weed and spray, trim excess growth.
September   Begin the harvest. Machines are increasingly common, except in *Grands Crus*. In hot areas, they work at night to keep the grapes cool.
October   Finish the harvest. Spread manure or fertilizer. Organic growers will avoid chemical fertilizer.
November   Trim long shoots, spray against mildew. Plough to bank soil against vine stems as frost protection.
December   Start pruning. Check and maintain drains, culverts, roads and fences. Begin pruning.

depends upon the kind of vine training and pruning system to be adopted. High-trained systems, as used in many modern vineyards (*see* p105) demand elaborate, permanent and expensive structures. Lower training systems need fairly simple posts and wires. Mechanization may dictate wide gaps between rows — and thus fewer vines per hectare — which in turn affects yield (*see* p105).

New vines are planted in spring, either as cuttings grafted onto their rootstocks, or by planting rootstocks one year and "field-grafting" the vine onto the rootstock the next year.

Key vineyard tasks

The yearly cycle, as described in the box left, starts with winter pruning. This is the most skilled job, and there are many pruning systems, each resulting in a different pattern of fruiting canes and buds. The amount, and quality, of grapes from each vine is set by pruning. Another key process, still mostly manual, is summer trimming and tying in of stray shoots.

The practice of thinning bunches in the summer, the *vendange vert* or "green harvest", has become part of the armoury of skills as yields have risen. If a harvest looks like being large, immature bunches are removed from the vines in July to cut the potential crop. This increases the quality of the grapes by concentrating their flavour: makers of quality wine prefer a moderate crop of well-flavoured grapes to a large crop of watery ones.

Every vineyard is threatened by pests and diseases, ranging from cryptogamic or fungal diseases to flocks of birds. The responses range from spraying with increasingly sophisticated chemicals to fencing the vineyards against deer and wild boar. Grey rot, or *botrytis*, the malign form of the famed "noble rot" (*see* p110) is the worst problem in many vineyards. It thrives in warm, damp weather and can ruin an entire crop with speed. There are chemical sprays, but no complete remedy.

How vintages vary

Several periods of the growing season are critical. The first is spring, when frosts can damage the tender young vine growth as late as May. Flowering, in June, establishes the size of the harvest, and its date: late flowering normally means a late vintage. July and August can be dangerous if the weather is damp: mould and rot can strike at the grapes if spraying is not carried out. Sunshine in September is vital to fully ripen the grapes, and a dry harvest period in September/October allows the fruit to be brought in free from swelling due to excess moisture.   □

Harvest in the Médoc: grapes are collected in small baskets to prevent bruising.

REVOLUTION IN THE VINEYARD

Grape farmers are enthusiastic participants in the "green revolution", the application of science to crop-growing. This has boosted yields of wheat and rice, coffee and cotton. Its instigators are an alliance of soil scientists, geneticists, climatologists — representatives of just about every "-ology" between pure physics and water-supply management.

A wheat or rice crop is planted each year and experiments can take place annually. To build up experience in a vineyard takes a generation, with vines taking four years to fruit and then a decade more to reach maturity. So the revolution in the vineyard is at an earlier stage than that in the wheat field, but revolution it is. It has helped to produce dramatic results in the quantity, predictability and quality of wine.

It is a mixed blessing: Europe's "wine lake" crisis was a by-product of this increase in yields; and — as with other crops — taste and flavour sometimes get sacrificed to quantity and predictability.

The seeds of the great changes in the vineyard were sown a century ago, when science was called in to fight a series of vineyard plagues.

The years of troubles
The late 19th century saw grape farmers, especially in Europe, in constant battle against new and virulent pests and diseases. Vines had always been attacked by insects, snails and rot, but the 1860s and 1870s saw the arrival from North America of both the insidious phylloxera louse and cryptogamic (fungal) diseases such as downy mildew and oïdium, also known as powdery mildew.

Phylloxera has a reputation as the destroyer of Europe's vineyards, but oïdium proved harder to control. Phylloxera, an insect with a complex life-cycle, destroys vines by eating

Young vines in New Zealand being sprayed to prevent mildew.

the roots. Luckily, American rootstocks are immune, and Europe's vines were saved by grafting them onto American rootstocks.

Oïdium succumbed to "Bordeaux mixture" — copper sulphate and lime — which when sprayed gives vine leaves a blue tinge. Downy mildew cannot be cured by one process: it requires constant spraying with more and more sophisticated chemicals. Grey rot, or *botrytis* (not the "noble" variety), is similarly devastating and can be treated only by spraying, as are pests such as red spider.

Phase one of the vineyard revolution was the conquering by chemicals of many diseases and pests.

Scientists then turned to improving the quantity and quality of the crop. Traditional vineyards were low-yielding by modern standards. Some, such as those of Spain, still are. The yield per vine and per hectare can be boosted by eliminating rot and pests.

Rootstocks and clones
It took a long time for today's classic grape varieties to settle down as non-mutating strains. Some varieties, such as Pinot Noir, still mutate readily. Vineyard managers learnt by experience to select the best strains, and to propagate from the best plants. The new science of plant genetics has built upon the empirical skills of nurserymen and growers.

When planting vines, a grape-grower has two choices: rootstock and clone. The development of a range of rootstocks has been one of the 20th century's biggest advances. The first concern is resistance to pests, but the grower can also choose rootstocks with greater or less vigour, which are better or worse at extracting minerals from the soil, which prompt the vine to ripen early or late, which can cope with humidity or drought, or which suit certain soils. And clones offer even more choice:

modern vines are propagated by taking tissue from a particular vine and growing innumerable vines from it. The scientists can choose vines which are resistant to disease, which yield large crops and which ripen early. So a vineyard can be planted with thousands of identical vines, which will all crop at once. But high yields usually mean poor flavour. Burgundy, California and Australia have all suffered quality loss from the use of inappropriate clones.

Canopy management

The European *vigneron* prunes his vines hard in winter to encourage vigorous but controlled new growth and reduce yield: the harder the vine is pruned, the fewer the grapes. In summer, leaf growth is at the expense of the fruit: excess foliage is trimmed to encourage the development of the bunches of grapes. Traditional pruning and training establish a balance between leaf growth and fruit and ensure that the grapes mature in optimum conditions. The leaves act as the vine's "lung" in the process of photosynthesis and the grapes ripen due to the effect of sun on the leaves.

The New World grower has had to abandon much of the thinking behind vine control, for New World soils are typically richer than those of the old and the climate is warmer. Used in a warm, fertile area, European techniques promote abundant but poorly-flavoured fruit. The Australian or Californian vineyard technician today manages the "canopy". Canopy management encourages leaf growth in order to reduce yields and achieve greater concentration of flavours in the grapes.

The canopy debate is moving fast into the realms of advanced science. By manipulating all the variables, from vine density through pruning, trellising, irrigation and fertilizing, the sophisticated grower can alter the micro-climate around the vines and to a large extent decide the quality and quantity of the fruit.

A more radical answer is to move the vines to a poorer soil and a cooler climate — which explains the search for hillside sites in California and Australia since the late 1980s.

The yield debate

A hectare of vineyard can hold 1,000 vines — or 10,000. Each vine may yield a basketful of grapes, or a single bunch. These options are open to the wine farmer, though in many cases his choices are constrained by law. French and Italian regulations stipulate the maximum amount of wine

WHAT THE VINE NEEDS

The grape vine needs specific conditions to grow and fruit, and quite restrictive ones to thrive. Much of the science of canopy management (*see* above) is concerned with manipulating these conditions.

Light   The vine is the child of a family of climbing forest plants, adapted to seek daylight by climbing through trees. Like all plants, it needs light to promote photosynthesis, the process of converting sunlight to carbohydrates that is central to plant growth. Sun is not vital: cloudy daylight will do. In high latitudes, longer summer days balance lower sun angles.

Warmth   Like any other plant, the vine only grows within a narrow temperature band. Vines start to grow at 10°C (50°F), do best between 15 and 25°C (59–77°F) and slow down above 25°C. At around 28°C (82°F) moisture will evaporate from the plant's leaves faster than it can be drawn from the ground. Growth and photosynthesis will stop.

Water   The vine in its natural state thrives best in wet, humid conditions. This does not suit the grape-grower as the fruit is easily spoilt by rot or splitting, and yields become too large. Vines will seek moisture by sending down roots, so a vineyard with ground water deep below the surface is ideal. Deep roots ensure against drought and also tap mineral sources. Because large yields are undesirable for quality wine, irrigation is banned in most European vineyards. However, artificial water supply is central to the economics of vineyards in Australia, the USA and South Africa.

that can be made per hectare. German law sets no upper limit, but defines quality levels based upon the sugar level in the grape juice (or "must"); in the New World there are no laws relating to yield.

There are, however, natural constraints on yield. Climate and soil will set limits, as will variety, rootstock and clone. The grower can choose to fertilize his land, or not.

European consensus is that low yields are good, and that a vine growing under stress will produce better wine than one growing rampantly. Stress comes from poor soil, high planting density, hard pruning and minimal fertilization. This view is challenged by experiments (mostly in the New World) that show passable wine being made at what (to Europe) are astonishing yields from lush, fruit-laden vines.

Many experts around the world remain convinced that quality wines are synonymous with relatively low yields. There is a level at 50hl/ha (the standard measure of yield: about 550 cases of wine per hectare, or 225 cases per acre) above which it seems risky to go.

The organic movement

Concern for the environment has led an ever-increasing band of grape-growers — in the New World, France and Germany — to turn away from chemicals; but successful organic viticulture means more than the mere avoidance of synthetic fertilizers, herbicides and pesticides. Plant or animal fertilizers may be chosen, and ecologically benign sprays based on plants or minerals can protect against pests. Certain insect predators are encouraged; unwelcome weeds are removed mechanically. The organic path is not easy — it takes some years before the soil is clear of chemicals, and it can be hard to avoid spray drift from neighbouring vineyards.

Organic philosophy extends to the winemaking process, but good winemakers — organic or not — keep additives to a minimum.   □

VINE AND WINE TRENDS

Cooking styles, vines and wines evolve at the same rate. Traditions, progress and globalisation, concepts which can conflict and which can work together, shape consumer tastes. The latter have changed greatly over the last 500 years, as can be seen from the table below. New cultural and winemaking techniques lie behind the wine evolution.

In the vineyards

Selection by mass and clonal selection tend to produce healthy grapes which achieve perfect ripeness. This is helped by the search for root stocks which speed up the vegetative process; the introduction of new pruning techniques opens up the canopy; vineyards pruned by the lyre method (Bordeaux right bank, United States) are proving interesting, the increased use of *taille en vert* or green pruning reduces the yield and concentrates the flavour of the must;

the use of sorting tables, now common practice, improves the quality of the harvest.

In the vat-house

Nowadays the grapes arriving at wineries are healthier, riper and sweeter. In the 19th and 20th centuries the ripeness of the grape was assessed by measuring the increase in its sugar level and the decrease in its acidity. When both rates stabilised, the grape was said to be ripe. In the latter part of the 20th century, the phenolic maturity was the measure used as it was discovered that alcoholic ripeness and phenolic ripeness were not always the same.

Winemaking can often be a vague, tortuous process. From the end of the second world war, stainless steel vats became de rigueur. In the last decade of the 20th century the wooden cask made a comeback! It is said that wine feels more at home in wooden casks and

remains at a constant temperature, which cannot be said for wine in stainless steel vats. Cask shape has changed over the years and it is unanimously agreed that they should be equally as tall as they are wide or possibly slightly wider (increasing the surface area of the "cap").

Selected yeasts

It has to be said that there is much dispute about the addition of yeasts. The yeast is what starts fermentation. There are "natural" yeasts present on the grape skins and, if necessary, the winemaker can multiply them by the addition of fermenting yeasts. It is becoming increasingly common practice to remove the natural yeasts and replace them by "selected yeasts". These fungi (yeast is a fungus) do not remain neutral, they act as aroma selectors or creators. These practices, although authorised, are not in keeping with the spirit of the terroir. On the other hand, the addition of bacteria to prompt the malolactic fermentation is one of the better practices of modern winemaking.

Ripeness of the grapes

The grapes received by the winemaker are sweet but sometimes the climatic conditions can have disastrous consequences. Chaptalisation, the procedure whereby sugar is added to the must, can make up for a lack of ripeness. Over the last few years substractive or self-enriching methods have been developed, whereby part of the water content is eliminated, thus increasing the concentration of the must. Several procedures can be used:
– the grapes can be removed from the vines and partly dried in a heated tunnel;
– cold pressing which involves freezing, or almost freezing, the grapes so that only the sweetest juice is collected (mainly used for sweet white wines);
– vacuum evaporation carried out in a forced vacuum at room temperature;

HOW CONSUMER TASTES HAVE EVOLVED

	In the past	Today
White	yellow colour	pale gold colour
	well-developed nose and palate	aromas opening up (nose and palate)
	heavy	fresh, pure
	oxidation	oxidation prohibited
	absence of oak	oaky
Rosé	salmon pink/orange colour	purplish/pink colour
	lack of freshness	fresh floral and fruity qualities, no tannins
Red	medium-coloured	highly-coloured
	average extracts	high extracts
	inconsistent ripeness of tannins	ripe tannins
	sometimes light	full-bodied
	un-aged or aged for very short periods	lengthy ageing, new wood

Blanc de Blancs Champagnes and sparkling wines are increasing in popularity. Nouveau wines are becoming very popular. Markets are opening up and new regions, new countries and différent grape varieties are appearing on the scene.

– evaporation under atmospheric pressure, prompted by circulating hot air through the must (Burgundy); and finally

– reverse osmosis which is similar to passing the must through a semi-permeable membrane (Bordeaux).

Whatever the process used, experience has shown that self-enriching should not be used excessively and that 5% evaporation improves the sensory qualities of the wine.

Of course the authorities have shown some concern about these new techniques, whether they apply to the must or the wine, and regulations have been introduced. Thus, in France, any winemaker using them must declare which procedure he has used and also detail the type of products used.

The ageing process

There has also been much research carried out on the ageing process, the purpose of which is to slowly oxygenate the wine and introduce the tannins. These processes can be carried out artificially, either by micro-bullage (oxygenation of the lees) or by adding wood shavings to wine which is stored in neutral casks. Currently wood shavings cannot be used for AOC wines in France but their use is permitted in many countries. Blind tastings have failed to prove the superiority of *barrique*-aged wines.

Fashionable grape varieties

The big international varieties are currently fashionable (*see* p34) but other varieties are increasingly being planted in different regions of various countries and others again are seeing their reputation grow.

The increase in the fortunes of Viognier, a white variety, has been astounding. This grape, which grows very well on decomposed granite, is full of peach, apricot, pear and exotic fruit aromas, but its versatility can often result in flabby wines. Originally, there were only a few hectares of Viognier at Château Grillet (AOC) and Condrieu (AOC) but nowadays there has been somewhat of an invasion and it is

Lyre training allows for a better maturing of the grapes.

planted throughout the Rhône Valley, in Languedoc and as far as Roussillon.

Roussanne is another white variety from the Rhône valley (white Hermitage AOC). It is a high quality, elegant grape with good ageing potential which is being planted increasingly in Languedoc, Savoie, Italy and Australia).

Furmint is a white grape variety from Hungary and Eastern Europe, famously the grape from which Tokay wine is made. Its thick skin is an excellent medium for noble rot.

The red Tuscan grape, Sangiovese, is used to make Chianti but its *pièce de résistance* is the DOCG Brunello de Montalcino, a very expensive wine with good ageing potential (Sangiovese Grosso).

The red Malbec (or Cot) grape was very popular in Bordeaux in the 18th century. It is the main grape in the Cahors appellation, where it is called Auxerrois. It produces excellent wines in Argentina.

Pinotage, a red variety created in South Africa in 1925 by crossing Pinot Noir and Cinsaut, produces elegant, light bodied wines.

Other fashionable varieties include Petit Verdot, Carmenère, Tannat, Mondeuse and Blaufränkisch (reds) and

Mauzac, Clairette and Savagnin (whites).

Crossbred grape varieties

Research centres throughout the world are crossing *Vitis vinifera* varieties to produce crossbreeds, new varieties which undergo trials for several years before being approved. In France, these new varieties are not used in the composition of AOC wines.

The most active research centre is the Hessen Research Institute for Wine, Fruit Growing and Horticulture in Geisenhein in Germany's Rhineland, whose activity goes back very many years. It was here in 1883 that Professor Müller created Germany's most planted grape, Müller-Thurgau, from a sexed crossing of the Riesling and Sylvaner varieties. Other highly aromatic white varieties have been very successful since the war, although they were "invented" in the first half of the 20th century: Scheurebe, another Riesling and Sylvaner crossbreed, was created in 1916 by Professor Scheu, who was also behind the Huxelrebe (Chasselat and Muscat, 1929) and the rich and nervy Faber (Pinot and Müller-Thurgau). Others include the exuberant Morio-Muskat (Sylvaner and Pinot Blanc, invented by Peter Morio), Dr Husfeld's very classic Bacchus (Sylvaner and Riesling/Müller-Thurgau), the rich but sometimes flabby Ortega (Müller-Thurgau and Siegerrebe) and finally the very interesting Kerner (Trollinger (red) and Riesling) which has crossed German frontiers.

All these new varieties were obtained by simple crossing, the only human invention which boils down to the choice of parents. We can therefore cross the Riesling and Traminer ten times and obtain ten different halfbreeds in the same way as a man and woman will produce different children. In the 21st century, once the genotype has been read, things will no longer be left to chance — the genes for the halfbreed will be selected. During the second stage, control of genetically-modified organisms should lead towards *Vitis vinifera* which are resistant to phylloxera.   □

FERMENTATION

The vat-house or *cuvier* of a winery is a magical place at fermentation time. The first thing the visitor notices is a powerful, attractive smell, somewhat akin to baking bread. A gentle warmth emanates from the giant vats of wood, concrete or steel that line the high-ceilinged room. Go close to the vat and you will hear the bubbling, living process at work in the grape juice (or "must"). Decline the workers' invitations to stick your head over the vat: there is no air to breathe, just carbon dioxide rising from the turbulent mass.

This is fermentation, a process that science has only recently fully unravelled, the seemingly magic way in which grape juice becomes wine.

It is both a complex biochemical reaction and a totally natural process. Grapes will ferment if their skin is broken. The sugars inside the ripe, juicy fruit meet the tiny yeast spores or microbes which live providentially on the grape skin and in the cellar — and fermentation begins. The winemaker merely provides the container, or vat, to hold the juice, and helpfully crushes the grapes to allow it to escape. He has recently gained more control over the process, with growing understanding of the microbiology of fermentation. But a better term is guidance: fermentation will inevitably happen; the winemaker can steer it on its path towards wine.

The process of fermentation
The skin of a ripe grape harbours several types of yeast. Only one sort does the vital job of reacting with the glucose and fructose sugars inside to produce alcohol. These yeasts, members of the genus *Saccharomyces cerevisiae,* multiply quickly in the fermenting juice.

This reaction produces heat — which is why cooling fermentation vats is so important — and carbon

Testing the fermenting grape juice.

dioxide gas and ethanol (alcohol). Further by-products include glycerol, esters or flavouring compounds, and various higher alcohols, aldehydes and acids. The yeast also turns some of the malic acid naturally present in the fruit into alcohol, thus lowering the wine's acidity. Some yeasts consume all the malic acid: they are added if the winemaker desires this.

Still more reactions take place in the fermenting must, or in the resulting wine. Some by-products can be useful, such as sulphur dioxide, which acts as a preservative. Others, like the "bad-egg gas" hydrogen sulphide, are less desirable. Yeasts also break down compounds in the grape pulp to produce aromatic substances called phenols, which can add to the aroma and complexity of the wine.

The reaction demands a supply of both sugars and yeast. If the yeast uses up all the sugar, converting it to alcohol, the reaction stops. This is the norm; sometimes there is so much sugar present that the alcohol level rises to the point where it stops

the yeasts working, leaving a strong, but still sweet, wine. If the ambient temperature is low, the yeast may stop work before all the sugar has been used up, leaving a wine with some sugar, and less alcohol than the grapes' ripeness would allow.

The winemaker's rôle
The main steering mechanism at the winemaker's command is temperature. Yeasts work in a fairly narrow band of temperature, between 12°C and 37°C (54–98°F). Traditional winemakers relied upon the autumn weather to provide these temperatures. If it was too cold for the fermentation to start, fires would be lit in the *cuvier* or, *in extremis*, workers would plunge into the vat to add their body heat to the mass of grapes to attempt to start the fermentation.

Once the process is under way, it will generate heat and become self-perpetuating. Often the problem is too much heat. In a warm year, the grapes will arrive warm, the *cuvier* will not be cool enough to lower their temperature, and the vats will be dangerously warm as soon as fermentation starts. The old way to alleviate this was to ventilate the *cuvier*, opening all the windows and doors. Hoses might be brought in to spray water on the outside of the vats — if there was a source of cold water and a pump. In very hot years blocks of ice would be tipped into the vats.

Temperature control first began when pumps allowed the fermenting must to be taken from the vat and passed through a heat exchanger. The stainless steel vat is now almost universal in modern wineries. Steel is a very good conductor of heat, while wood is not. Steel vats can be cooled by pouring cold water over them, allowing it to run down the sides into collecting gutters. Other types have a "jacket" of pipes of cooling fluid.

Yeasts

Natural yeasts, present on the grape skins and in the wider environment, are used in most European areas, though with white wines yeasts are frequently added. The New World prefers to use cultured strains of yeast, bred from samples taken in European vineyards, since different yeasts work best at different temperatures: the winemaker who wishes to control fermentation temperature finds it easier to work with a yeast that suits that level. However, some believe in the virtues of the wild (or "native") yeasts which are part of the *terroir*.

Adding sugar for strength

The amount of alcohol produced, and thus the strength of the final wine, depends upon how ripe the grapes are. In many places grapes are more likely to be overripe, with consequent loss of taste and quality, but in Europe many of the quality wine-producing areas are cool, and thus prone to underripe vintages.

The wine world long ago discovered a way round this: add extra sweetness. This can be done in two ways: adding sugar to the vat, or blending in sweet unfermented grape juice. Adding sugar is considered a little embarrassing in an age when artificial additives are frowned upon, but it is widespread. In France it is called chaptalization after Napoleon I's minister of agriculture, Chaptal. He hoped to promote the use of beet sugar, of which there was a glut.

All the added sugar converts into alcohol, so chaptalization does not sweeten the wine. But sugar made from beet or cane is not grape sugar, and does not have the same natural flavour. Chaptalization was intended to be a rescue operation for poor vintages, but it is now common practice, even in vintages when the grapes have plenty of natural sugar. Chaptalized wine tastes smoother, richer and more appealing earlier on in its maturation. The corollary of this practice is the temptation to increase yields, since low alcohol levels can always be boosted by sugar. (It also opens the door to the illegal practice of diluting wine.)

Chaptalization is permitted in cooler parts of France — including Bordeaux, Burgundy and the Loire — and in some states of the USA, including New York and Oregon. It is forbidden in southern France, Italy, California and in Germany for QmP wines. German QbA wines — the vast majority — can be boosted with concentrated grape juice or saccharose before fermentation (this only sweetens if fermentation is stopped). The addition of actual sugar is illegal.

All countries have regulations to control the use of sugar; in Burgundy, for instance, levels of permitted sugar are set vintage by vintage for each *appellation*. However, these rules are not always observed.

WOOD OR STEEL?

Wooden vats can be cooled, and research at Château Margaux in the Médoc has led the winemaker there, Paul Pontallier, to conclude that wood is preferable to steel. Heat exchangers can be used in conjunction with the regular pumping over of the must (*see* p113) to regulate the fermentation temperature. Steel is, of course, easier to keep clean, but this is a matter of time and money and therefore not a problem at Margaux.

Pontallier feels that the wooden vats have distinct advantages. During the period of maceration, when the new wine stays on its lees to gain colour and tannins from the *marc*, wine in wood stays warmer, because the wood holds the heat. The wooden vats have a different shape from the steel ones, being wider and not so tall. This, Pontallier finds, means more even temperatures in the vat, and a greater area of solid matter (pulp, skin and pips) exposed to the liquid must, which helps the extraction of colour and flavour.

This research, allied with the decisions of other top châteaux to go on using wood rather than introducing steel, has reopened the debate, but stainless steel's advantages at every level of winemaking except the very top seem conclusively established.

Most red burgundy, and much red bordeaux, is routinely chaptalized. Some winemakers stand out against this, saying that it is an unnecessary and detrimental interference with the wine. Until the 1960s, chaptalization was virtually unknown in Bordeaux and many great clarets had quite low alcohol levels, which seemed to have no effect on their longevity. Latour's great steward, Lamothe, tried chaptalization for the first time in 1816. The results were poor, "which made me believe", he wrote, "that when nature withholds the essential ingredients that make up the wine's fine quality, art cannot supply them; only a mediocre result will ever be obtained."

Adding sugar for sweetness

In Germany for QmP wines, and in Italy, unfermented grape juice is used to add sweetness. The German term is *Süssreserve*. The juice must be from the same area, and of the same quality, as the wine. It is added after fermentation and before bottling, to produce a sweeter wine.

The malolactic fermentation

In the spring, as the vine buds begin to break, the wine in the casks in an old-fashioned cellar will begin to "work". It will bubble and murmur, as if in sympathy with the awakening vine. This romantic explanation was accepted for millennia until the malolactic, or secondary, fermentation process was explained. This is carried out by bacteria, not yeasts, which work on the malic acid in the wine and convert it to lactic acid. It is an optional stage: desirable in red wines (and used in nearly all), but not always in whites.

It helps soften acidic whites, and adds a buttery flavour, but can strip flavour and character from warm-climate, fruitier ones. To avoid the malolactic, the wine is filtered or centrifuged to remove the bacteria which cause it. Conversely, it can be triggered by the addition of bacteria, or left to happen naturally in the vat. □

MAKING WHITE WINE

The paramount concern of the maker of white wine is to ensure fruit quality. Even healthy grapes spoil rapidly once off the vine, so speed and cleanliness are important. White grapes must be kept whole to avoid maceration — the juice picking up colour and flavour from the grape skins — and oxidation. Grapes should be moved in small boxes, not large containers, to avoid premature crushing. At a château or other estate winery, overseers will check in the vineyard that the pickers are bringing in ripe, healthy fruit, free of leaves and insects. At a cooperative or commercial winery buying in grapes, rigorous checks on quality and ripeness are made: sugar and acidity levels are measured, and managers are on the alert to reject sub-standard fruit.

The grapes are sometimes pressed in whole bunches, but more often a crusher-destemmer is used to strip the grapes from their stalks and break the skins. The resulting mass of pulp is pumped or tipped straight into a press to extract the juice. The pulp must be kept cool to avoid premature fermentation: modern wineries use chillers.

Some winemakers use a short period of "skin contact", leaving the juice and crushed grapes in a tank to allow flavour pick-up from the skins.

The press
There are several types of white-wine press. All aim to extract maximum juice without crushing the bitter pips, to crush quickly to avoid oxidation, and to provide clear juice with minimum solids. Continuous horizontal presses like giant screws are used in large-scale wineries.

Handling the juice
White grape juice is as delicate and prone to spoiling as white grapes. It emerges from the press cloudy with solid matter in suspension, and must be clarified. Traditionally this is done by allowing the juice to settle in a tank. Today chilling to 0°C (32°F) is often used: this "cold-stabilization" technique cleans the juice by precipitating solids. Bentonite — a kind of clay powder — also aids clarification. Another modern method uses a centrifuge, but this strips out desirable ingredients such as yeast cells and detracts from the taste and complexity of the wine. It is used in large-scale wineries making everyday wine. Sulphur dioxide — a disinfectant — is added to prevent oxidation and to kill micro-organisms which could spoil the must (juice). It can mask all flavour too: modern winemakers use as little as possible.

Fermentation
Most white wines are fermented in stainless steel vats with temperature-control equipment. The modern aim, to ensure maximum fruit and aroma, demands a long, cool fermentation. Temperatures as low as 10°C (50°F) — but more normally 12–15°C (54–59°F) — can be maintained by cooling (or naturally cool cellars). Other wines, such as traditionally-made white burgundies and other Chardonnays, are fermented in 225-litre oak casks. These have been found to be the right size and shape to control the temperature naturally at around 25°C (77°F): any larger, and the wine grows too warm.

High-quality wines, made from naturally concentrated, complex grape juice, can gain longevity and flavour from a warm fermentation; simpler wines will be deadened. Cool fermentation leads to fresher, faster-maturing wine. In cool regions such as Germany, the fermentation may stop as temperatures fall before all the grape sugar is converted into alcohol. This leaves a wine naturally and gently sweet, but prone to renewed fermentation in spring as the weather warms up. This is avoided by filtration, racking and sulphuring.

A secondary, malolactic, fermentation is sometimes used: see p109.

Sweet wines
The best are made from grapes so sweet that fermentation cannot convert all the sugar into alcohol. In favoured areas, growers leave their grapes on the vines until they over-ripen, hoping for *botrytis cinerea* ("noble rot") to develop. This causes the grapes to shrivel, concentrating down the already sweet juice to rich drops. This makes the finest of all; wines like the treasured Sauternes (*qv*), *Trockenbeerenauslese*, Tokaji Aszú and several New World wines.

Dried grapes can also be used, as in France's *vin de paille*, Italy's Vin Santo and other *passito* wines.

Others are made by stopping fermentation artificially — with sulphur dioxide, by filtering or racking the wine, or by fortification (*see* p116) — or simply by adding sugar (*see* p109).

Racking and lees contact
The fermentation over, the wine is normally removed from the vat and the lees (the solids, mostly dead yeast cells) left behind at the bottom of the tank or cask. This process is called "racking". In some regions, such as Muscadet, it is traditional to leave the wine *sur lie* — on its lees, in the same container — until bottling. In Burgundy, white wines, especially good ones, rest on their lees in the casks in which they ferment, and winemakers stir the lees to mix them into the wine. This technique has been taken up by white-wine makers elsewhere to make use of the natural disinfectant qualities of the lees, to add a creamy taste to the wine, and to prompt the malolactic fermentation. □

THE WHITE WINE PROCESS

Fermentation in oak casks (right), especially new oak, is fundamental to making fine white burgundy. The fermenting wine reacts with tannins and other ingredients in the oak, adding flavour and complexity to the wine. New World winemakers are experimenting with this technique.

1 Quality control
Grapes arrive at the winery and are checked for quality before being channelled into a hopper.

2 Pressing: the basket, or vertical, press
Grapes may be de-stalked or pressed in whole bunches. Gentle pressure and a large surface area ensure the cleanest juice.

3 Pressing: the horizontal press
The gentlest modern press is the pneumatic version: the rubber bag inside inflates, pressing the grapes against the slatted sides of the drum.

4 Fermenting in stainless steel
Steel vats can be cooled to control temperature by pouring cold water over them, by passing refrigeration fluid through pipes around the walls, or by putting heat exchangers into the vat.

5 Filtering
Most modern wineries use a filter or centrifuge to clarify wine after it has finished fermenting. Here, filtered wine is checked for clarity.

MAKING RED WINE

It is easier to make red wine than white: the winemaker does more guiding and less shaping. But good, or great, red wine requires infinite pains and great skill. The process described and shown here is that used in Bordeaux, and is the model for hundreds of wineries in other parts of the world. Important variations in other wine areas are noted below.

Red grapes are not pressed, as are white grapes; they are stripped from their stems and crushed to release the juice. The difference is that the red-wine maker wants the skins to stay with the juice during fermentation. The next step is to put the juicy, semi-liquid mass of crushed grapes into a container to let it start to ferment. Some modern wineries have equipment that allows the juice to be kept below fermentation point for a day or two to allow maceration. This boosts the extraction of colour and flavour from the skins. When the temperature is increased, fermentation begins.

The wine ferments in a container called a vat (*cuve*), which traditionally is made of wood, and today could equally be wood, concrete, plastic or stainless steel. Wood has its advocates (*see* p109); the new materials are more hygienic and easier to clean.

Temperature control

Nature will allow the fermentation temperature to rise up to 29–30°C (84–86°F) in the conditions of a temperate autumn climate — such as Bordeaux's. A warm autumn, or an early harvest, may see higher ambient temperatures, and a fast and furious fermentation may take place. This will harm the wine's fruit and delicacy, and if the temperature rises too high (above say 34°C/93°F) the ferment may stop dead.

So in warm weather the winemaker keeps constant watch on the thermometer (in a hyper-modern winery a computer will do this for him) and switches on the cooling system to keep the fermentation at the chosen level. The key is choice. Some winemakers stress cool fermentation: just as with white wines, they are aiming to extract fruit and finesse. Others go for warmer temperatures, perhaps for just a brief period, to get the maximum colour and intensity of flavour. Control allows decisions about the length of the fermentation as well. This option is more the tool of the white-wine maker: red wines have their natural fermentation time, which in Bordeaux can be one week or three, depending on the vintage.

Concentration

The winemaker aims for a concentrated expression of the grapes' flavours and aromas in the finished wine. It is common practice for some juice to be "run off", or *saignée*, very early in the fermentation process. This concentrates the juice remaining in the vat, and can also allow a pale red or rosé wine to be made with the juice that has been run off (in the Bordeaux region this is called *clairet*).

Modern techniques include filtering the juice (tangential filtration or inverse osmosis) in order to remove some of the undesirable elements (including water) and concentrate the must before fermentation. The policy of concentrating the juice as much as possible was fashionable in Bordeaux during the 1980s, when there were some very ripe vintages, but was less popular in the 1990s, when vintages were unreliable and excessive extraction led to vegetal aromas in the wine.

Selection

Once fermentation is over, the Bordeaux technique is to let the new wine remain on its lees — that is, in the vat with the residue of skins, pips and other solids. During this period the malolactic fermentation (*see* p109) normally takes place.

Many serious Bordeaux châteaux will keep different grape varieties, and grapes from different parts of the vineyard, separate. This aids the vital *assemblage*, the process of blending and selecting. The different vats provide a palette of styles and qualities for the winemaker to choose from. Vats of wine from young vines, or outlying patches of land, will be routinely excluded from the *grand vin*. Any vats that are below the required standard will also be excluded. Up to half the wine may be rejected in large or difficult years. It may be blended separately and labelled as a "second wine" (*see* p149) or sold in bulk.

Finally the wine is moved into cask to begin the process of maturing, described on pp117–124.

Variations

Different grape varieties and environments prompt various decisions on the temperature and length of fermentation and the ageing method. Burgundy has its own traditions (*see* pp184–185), and Beaujolais has developed the technique of *macération carbonique* (*see* pp209–210), also used in the Midi and elsewhere. Italy's Barolo (*see* p365) and Chianti (*see* p382), and Spain's Rioja (*see* pp405–406) are made according to local custom, subject to variation by the new generation of winemakers.

Rosé wine

There are two main ways of making rosé wine. In the *saignée* method the wine is made from juice run off in the early stages of red-wine making, described above under Concentration. In the white-wine method, red grapes are pressed just enough to colour the must, then vinification continues as for white wine.   □

THE RED WINE PROCESS

Oak vats (right) are the traditional — and still common — alternative to stainless steel for fermenting red wine. The vats are also used to store the wine once fermentation is over.

1 The crusher-destemmer
This machine strips the grapes from their stems, and lightly crushes them, breaking the skin to release the juice.

2 The fermentation vat
The juice and the crushed mass of grapes and skins are pumped or tipped into a tall vat. Modern stainless steel vats can be cooled more easily than wooden ones.

3 Fermentation
Yeasts — either those naturally present on the grape skins, or cultured yeasts introduced into the vat — start to react with the grape juice (*see* p108).

4 Pumping over
During fermentation a "cap" of skins and pips forms. This must be immersed, to extract colour. Winemakers may use pumps to spray the juice over the cap; a plunger to force the cap down; or a grille which keeps the cap submerged.

5 Ageing
The fermentation complete, the new wine is pumped into tanks or vats, or into small oak barrels for further ageing.

MAKING SPARKLING WINE

Sparkling wine is the most "industrial" of wines. In some cases it is totally mechanical: these wines are made by the various tank methods described below. Others are basically still wines bottled with a little residual sugar; fermentation will continue, giving the wine a slight sparkle, or *pétillance*.

The classic sparkling wine is that made by the method pioneered in Champagne. This requires a second fermentation: still white wine will begin to ferment again if more sugar (and sometimes more yeast) is added. The second fermentation, which takes place in the bottle, produces carbon dioxide gas; the gas is trapped in the bottle, and the result is an effervescent wine.

The basic steps in the elaborate process of champagne are shown opposite. The first important point is the selection of fruit. Harvesting, grape selection and pressing are carried out with enormous care: the aim is very clean juice, low in tannin and without colour from skin contact. Only the juice of the first pressing, called *vin de cuvée*, is used in the best champagne. A second pressing, or *première taille*, will increase the amount of juice available. Once the first fermentation is over the wine is clarified by cold stabilization, fining and/or filtering.

The next critical stage is blending, or *assemblage*. The directors of the company will taste wine from every vat — one from the Côte des Blancs, another from Ay, a third from the Montagne de Reims and so on. There will be samples of Pinot Noir, of Chardonnay, of Pinot Meunier. The aim: to blend a wine that is consistent to the house style, creating a non-vintage champagne that reaches the same high standard year after year. To this end, wine from older years may be added to the blend.

A blend of wine, sugar and yeast, known as *liqueur de tirage*, is added before bottling, in order to stimulate the second fermentation, which takes place inside tightly sealed thick glass bottles, stored horizontally.

Time is the ingredient that makes the best champagne so expensive. While the second fermentation takes only around three months, quality champagne houses leave the wine to rest and mature for at least two years (sometimes 20 or longer).

Removing the sediment is an equally laborious process, traditionally done by skilled *remueurs*. The bottles are transferred to special racks (*pupitres*) which are gradually (over a period of months) tilted until the sediment falls down to the neck. The bottles may then be stored vertically for further maturation.

Disgorging, or removing the sedi-

OTHER BOTTLE-FERMENTED

The term *méthode champenoise* has been banned from use on labels of wines other than champagne, but the process is used in the following regions and wine styles:

France: Loire: Anjou, Saumur, Touraine, Vouvray, Crémant de Loire
Burgundy: Crémant de Bourgogne
Alsace: Crémant d'Alsace
Rhône: Clairette de Die, St-Péray
Midi: Blanquette de Limoux.
Italy: Lombardy, Trentino and elsewhere: labelled *metodo classico* or *metodo tradizionale*.
Spain: wines labelled *cava* from Catalonia and elsewhere.
Germany: some *Sekt* — see p348 — but most is not bottle-fermented.
USA: California, New York State and other regions: labelled "classic method" or "fermented in the bottle".
Australia and New Zealand: the word "Champagne" is now illegal on labels: look for the term bottle-fermented.

ment, is another skilled task. The neck of the bottles is passed through a solution which freezes the sediment into a solid plug. As the cap is removed the plug is forced out by the pressure of gas from the champagne.

Each bottle must now be topped up with *liqueur d'expédition*, a blend of wine and sugar in varying proportions. This process, known as dosage, determines whether the champagne will be completely dry (*brut*) or sweeter in style. After dosage the bottles are immediately corked and labelled. The champagne is now ready for sale.

The technique of the champagne method can be exported, as can the grape varieties, or be applied to other grape varieties, but nowhere has emulated the region's *terroir* — yet. Comforting as this is to the champagne industry, the New World's sparkling-wine makers are catching up fast. Careful site selection, and more mature vineyards, are narrowing the gap.

Other sparkling methods

Other sorts of sparkling wine acquire their fizz outside the bottle, usually by one of the following methods:
Charmat process A tank-based system: wine, sugar and yeast are placed in a large vat for secondary fermentation to take place. The wine is chilled, filtered, transferred under pressure to a second tank, sweetened with *liqueur d'expédition* and bottled.
Transfer method Follows the champagne method until disgorging, when the wine is transferred into pressurized tanks, filtered to remove sediment and rebottled.
Cuve close Synonym for Charmat.
Carbonated The most basic method (forbidden for AOC wines). Carbon dioxide is pumped into the wine, which is then bottled under pressure. □

THE CHAMPAGNE PROCESS

Champagne's second fermentation in bottle (*see* Step 4) results in a residue of dead yeast cells. To remove this, bottles are placed in racks (*pupitres*), and gradually rotated and tilted towards the vertical (right). This work (*remuage*) is increasingly done by machines (*gyropalettes*).

1 Pressing
The champagne basket press is massive, slow and gentle, but many large firms now use pneumatic presses (*see* p111).

2 Fermentation
The oak casks shown here are traditional, but today are only used by two champagne firms. Most use stainless steel vats for the initial fermentation.

3 Blending
Dark suits and white rooms, endless flasks of pale champagne: the aim is a consistent blend, the recipe for which will be used on an enormous scale to mingle the various vats of wine.

The wine is enriched with the *liqueur de tirage*, a blend of sugar, champagne and yeast, and is then bottled.

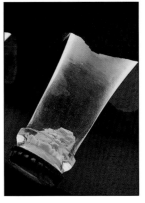

4 Second fermentation
The wine is sealed with a "crown cork". Fermentation takes place inside the bottle, producing carbon dioxide gas and a residue of dead yeast. The bottles are gradually tilted until the residue falls to the neck.

5 Disgorging
After further maturation, the bottles are transferred, still upside down, to a conveyor belt which passes them through a solution that freezes the plug of yeast deposit in the neck. The bottle is opened, the plug shoots out, a dose of sugar is added and the bottle is swiftly closed.

MAKING FORTIFIED WINE

Fortified wines are initially made in the same way as any other: the change comes with the addition of alcohol, in the form of brandy or other spirit. Sherry, port, madeira, the *vins doux naturels* of France, Sicily's marsala: all are fortified. The chief differences are when and how much. There are two main ways to fortify: during fermentation, or after.

The purpose of fortifying was to make wine from hot regions fit to travel, by subduing the ill-understood process of fermentation that often re-started in cask and ruined wines in transit. It is now an intrinsic part of the wine style.

All fortified wines gain a great deal of their character from the maturation process; *see* p117.

Making port
Port is fortified during the fermentation, or more truly the ferment is stopped by adding spirit. The grapes, first crushed and de-stemmed, are tipped into great open stone tanks, called *lagars*. Treading the grapes is traditional, and still current for the finest port. It is laborious (though leavened by music), but considered the best way to extract colour from the tough-skinned port grapes without the risk of over-pressing the pips. Labour costs mean, however, that treading is increasingly only used at a minority of port estates, and then only for the best wine.

The crushed juice then ferments for a matter of hours — perhaps 24 to 36 — not the weeks of the normal red-wine process. The winemaker constantly checks the alcohol level and the degree of sweetness in the fermenting wine. When it has reached the desired level — strong enough, with about 9% of alcohol, but still sweet — the new wine is run off into barrels or tanks, and the *aguardente* or grape spirit added. The

Mature amontillado sherry.

amount of alcohol added is around 25% of the volume of wine. This raises the alcohol level to about 18%, which is higher than the yeasts can stand. The yeasts stop dead, leaving the remaining unfermented grape sugar in the wine, which is now port.

At this early stage the port is a dark red, sweet wine, with a harsh taste of spirit. Port needs time for the spirit to blend with the wine. In its first spring, it is tasted by the winemaker and its destiny — as one of the various styles (*see* p441) — is decided.

Most port is now made in vats following crushing/de-stemming. Various methods are used to mix the must and the cap of skins to extract maximum colour at maximum speed, including pumping over (*see* p113); autovinifiers (vats that utilize carbon dioxide from fermentation to pump the wine over); and giant drums which rotate to mix the fermenting

contents. The addition of alcohol takes place in exactly the same way as with foot-trodden port.

Making sherry
Sherry is a simpler wine to make than port: the complexity comes with ageing and blending. It is initially made like any other white wine, with extra care to prevent oxidation of the low-acid Palomino grapes. At the end of fermentation, the new wine is placed in wooden casks, known as butts, with a little air space above the wine. After a few months, some of the butts develop a thick layer of a special yeast, called *flor*. The sherry is then divided into two categories (*see* p427), and fortified accordingly: lightly (up to about 15.5%) for fino, which is affected by *flor*; more (to about 18%) for oloroso. A further classification about six months later determines the precise style of the sherry.

All sherry is matured in a *solera* (*see* box, p424), a complex system of blending younger wines with older ones over a period of years. During its maturation, fino sherry slowly loses strength. It is fortified again when shipped, to around 15.5–17%. Connoisseurs seek out finos which have not been fortified, or fortified more lightly, for shipping. Oloroso sherries gain extra strength during maturation and are not fortified further.

Other fortified wines
The fortified wines marsala (*see* p397), málaga (*see* p430) and madeira (*see* p446) are all made in a range of styles from dry to sweet. In France's *vins doux naturels* (naturally sweet wines), fermentation is stopped before all the sugar has been converted to alcohol.

Many other countries make wines in port and sherry styles; some grow Portuguese or Spanish grape varieties to achieve a more authentic style.   □

MATURING WINE

THE NEW WINE IS IN THE VAT: ASSERTIVE, AROMATIC AND ROUGH-EDGED.
NOW COMES THE PROCESS THE FRENCH CALL ELEVAGE,
OR THE UPBRINGING OF THE WINE.

Topping up casks to replace wine lost by evaporation is a weekly task in the first year of a red bordeaux's maturing. The loose-fitting glass bungs allow the wine to "work": the gas produced by the malolactic fermentation can escape.

As the last chapter has outlined, winemaking has seen enormous strides in the last three decades, with the process and chemistry becoming well understood. The vineyard too has been the scene of great advances. But the cellar — the whole span from vat to bottle to glass — is still an area of some mystery. Scientists are only now really coming to grips with the ageing, or maturing, process. That oak casks affect the taste of wine matured in them, and that some oak casks are better than others, has been known for centuries — but we are only beginning to discover just why. We are starting to understand how different wines react in varying ways to greater or lesser degrees of ageing. Even the process of bottle-ageing, perhaps the final mystery, is giving up some of its secrets.

The *élevage* — the "bringing up", or maturing — of a wine can make as much difference to its final quality as any other stage in its making. Much can go wrong: many of the poor wines of previous generations were ruined by dirty casks and inadequate cellar care. Now that the biochemistry of wine is better understood, there is no longer any need for this spoilage to occur — except through bad management. Maturing involves intervention: some perfectly natural products of winemaking, inevitably derived from chemical and microbiological reactions, must be removed or inhibited if the wine is to survive in bottle. The château or winery, or the merchant who "brings up" the young wine, puts it through a series of processes to clarify and stabilize the wine, to soften its rough edges and to allow it to improve. This is a gentle metamorphosis: time acting on wine. The container the wine ages in can add to the process, as with new oak casks; or be neutral, if of steel, glass or old wood.

The maturing process takes in the stages whereby the wine trade handles the wine on its way to our tables. The complex and changing world of wine offers opportunities to buy wine direct from the producer. When buying from further down the chain, there are factors that can badly harm wine and which buyers should guard against. Wine in bottle is a fragile thing. The investment of time and trouble that a bottle of fine wine represents must be respected.

THE ART OF ELEVAGE

Elevage, or in English the art of maturing wine, is correctly translated as the educating or upbringing of wine. The French term clearly tells that wine needs care and work to bring out its quality and make it ready to drink. The various processes are described in detail under Work in the Cellar on p120.

How wine is stored during ageing is of significance for the wine drinker, because the storage medium can affect taste and character. One of the first questions to consider about an unfamiliar wine is the way it is aged, or matured, and for how long.

Some wines undergo little or no ageing, though nearly all wines go through certain processes to stabilize them and ready them for bottling. Many white wines are bottled soon after they are made, and drunk not long after that. Other wines, both red and white, spend a greater or lesser time in some form of tank, vat or cask, and then may age further in bottle before being ready to drink. Red wines designed for long ageing, such as bordeaux and Rhônes, can spend more than two years in the cellar before bottling. Bottle-ageing often takes place in the final consumer's cellar: it is discussed under Wine and Time on pp 51–54.

The use of barrels was vital in developing the art of ageing. Later came the bottle — used not just as a serving, but as a storage, vessel: a technique that profoundly altered the way wine aged.

The two forms of ageing — vat or cask, and bottle — may be either complementary or alternatives. Some wines are kept in cask until they are ready to drink, and then bottled. They then require no further bottle-ageing. Others are bottled when still in need of time to soften their tannins and acidity. Examples of the former are tawny port, sherry, *vins doux*

Six egg-whites per *barrique* is the recipe for fining at Château Léoville-Barton.

naturels, many Italian red wines and (traditionally) red and white Rioja. Examples of the latter are vintage port and fine red and white bordeaux and burgundy.

From goatskin to plastic

The first wine container was probably a skin bag. Until well into this century, cheap Spanish wine often gained an added hint of goat through being kept in *borrachas*. These were the skins of goats, or pigs, hair and all — with the hair on the inside — which were lined with pitch to keep them wineproof. The leather *bota*, or bottle, of Spain, which was smaller and less aromatic, was a more civilized container.

The ancient world developed pottery jars, often of enormous size, for storing and transporting wine. The sea-bed of the Mediterranean regularly gives up cargoes of *amphorae* — standard-sized stone jars in which the Greeks, and later the Romans,

traded wine, and other commodities such as oil, across the then known world. The Romans began to make casks from wood once they moved north of the Alps — though it is possible the Celts or Gauls had found the skill before them. The cask or barrel became the main vessel for moving wine around, as can be seen in surviving reliefs, inscriptions and archaeological survivals from the Roman era in France, Britain and Germany.

The cask is a lighter vessel than a stone jar, is more durable, easier to transport and easier to repair. These virtues made it essential to any trade in wine a long time before it was found that casks helped wine mature.

Wood was the dominant material in cellars for both fermentation vats and storage casks until the late 19th century, when concrete and then glass-lined vats began to be used. Today stainless steel and plastic are alternatives (*see* p109). Glass bottles have taken over as the medium of distribution, as well as bottle-ageing, though some wine is sold in plastic containers and in metallic-plastic "bladders" inside cardboard "casks".

Maturation: the pragmatic art

The raising, or bringing up, of wine is a relatively modern part of the wine-making process. The Romans knew that a well-stoppered *amphora* could allow wine to age, but this knowledge was lost with the Dark Ages. The medieval wine merchant, however, viewed youth in wine as a virtue. So did his customers, who found that old wine, kept in half-empty casks, turned inexorably to vinegar. The only skill in evidence was cask-making, which needed a degree of sophistication: casks had to be strong enough to survive the rough and tumble of transport. Wine often went out of condition — turned to vinegar, or started to re-ferment — and no-one knew the cause. The phases of the moon were invoked — a belief more logical than the medieval merchants knew (see below).

The 17th century saw the start of change. The basic processes now in use date from the 17th and 18th centuries. Remarkably, these techniques were discovered by pragmatic cellar masters and merchants, not by scientists. Professor Pascal Ribéreau-Gayon, himself one of the leaders of modern oenology, credits these pre-scientific pragmatists with inventing selection, cask-ageing and the control of bacteria. Sulphur dioxide (*see* below) was used to kill bacteria long before anyone knew bacteria existed.

Sulphur dioxide

Wine contains bacteria that will convert it to vinegar if they have the oxygen they need to begin the reaction. A well-made and full cask contains no oxygen, or only a very little. Then, too, a cold cellar slows the reaction, which is why the German and northern French vineyards were the first places to age wines in cask. A high

Stirring the lees — *bâtonnage* — adds complexity to white wines.

degree of alcohol, found in the sweet wines of the Mediterranean, also inhibits the vinegar bacteria.

But it was the rediscovery (the Romans used it) of sulphur dioxide, in medieval Germany, that allowed wine to be properly stabilized. Sulphur, when burned in a cask prior to filling with wine, kills bacteria and prevents oxidation of the wine. By the early 18th century this was common practice in Bordeaux. This century has seen its use worldwide. It is sometimes over-used: many white wines, from Spain and France especially, gained a name some decades ago for heavy sulphur tastes.

Sulphur dioxide is used in solid, liquid or gas form at several stages. If a white wine is not to undergo malolactic fermentation, sulphur protects it and preserves the malic acid which contributes freshness. In red wine-making, sulphur is a general disinfectant for casks, grapes and wine.

Modern practice is to lessen and sometimes avoid the use of sulphur. Healthy grapes, and scrupulously clean winemaking equipment and premises, make it less necessary. Sulphur's use is also discouraged by mandatory labelling ("contains sulfites") in the USA and Australia. A small fraction of the population is allergic to sulphur, but the labelling law alarms far more. There is at present no EC directive on such labelling.

The purpose of élevage

Elevage is first of all a preventative process. The new wine will have solid matter in suspension which must be removed if these substances are not to cause trouble later. These solids include yeast cells, bacteria, and tiny particles of grape skin and flesh. Removing, wholly or partially, these substances aims to avoid two main problems to which wine is subject. These are re-fermentation, caused by the presence of unfermented sugar and triggered by yeasts remaining in the wine or wild yeasts from the environment, and souring or turning to vinegar. Souring is caused by micro-organisms which need oxygen to act. Additional worries are excess deposit in the wine, which can trigger re-fermentation in bottle or (less serious, but often considered undesirable) a heavy deposit. Young wine also contains dissolved carbon dioxide, a product of fermentation. If this is not removed it can lead to a second fermentation in bottle. Some carbon dioxide adds a refreshing "prickle" or very gentle sparkle in young wines, especially whites. It is sought after in Muscadet bottled *sur lie* — off the lees, without fining.

Minimal intervention
Under various names, including organic winemaking, a doctrine of élevage by minimal intervention has grown up. This posits that as little should be done to wine as possible. It is considered a luxury by many winemakers, especially those making relatively inexpensive wines on a large scale. They cherish the control that modern techniques gives them and rely for survival upon their ability to make decent wine year in, year out.

Reduced intervention can go as far as eschewing pumps, which (believers allege) can "bruise" the wine. The vertical winery, where grapes arrive at the top and work down from crusherdestemmer to vat to cask by gravity, is the dream. This was common in the 19th century, before electricity- and petrol-driven pumps. Some wineries are now run on this principle. There is at present no hard evidence in favour of the no-pumping school, which bases its beliefs more on minimalist philosophy than on science.

Modern winemaking aims at minimum use of any chemical, including sulphur dioxide. Experts point out that, compared with many other foodstuffs, wine undergoes few treatments, and all chemicals used have well-known properties and effects.

It is possible to avoid the use of chemicals entirely, and indeed to restrict the handling of wine to bottling. This requires scrupulous care and cleanliness, with casks topped up frequently to expel air. Tradition calls for racking when the weather is clear, and the moon waning. These conditions often coincide with high atmospheric pressure, which inhibits to a small but useful extent the action of bacteria or yeasts in the wine. The result: more clarity, less sediment from stirred-up lees.   □

WORK IN THE CELLAR

The processes carried out in the cellar aim to stabilize and clarify the new wine. All affect wine character and some, if over-used, can strip a wine of flavour and character. They are all optional — except perhaps topping up and racking — and are avoided by traditionalist winemakers, who also eschew pumping (*see* left).

Unfiltered wines can lead to unease among buyers who are used to bright, clear bottles. With careful handling and storage, and decanting if required, such wines can be perfect; but they are at greater risk from spoilage than manipulated wines.

Fining   The new wine will contain solid matter, such as yeast cells, tiny particles of grape skin and proteins, in suspension. If not removed, this will make the wine cloudy and may cause spoiling. A certain amount stays in quality red wines, leading to the deposit in the bottle. The solids will slowly sink to the bottom of the container if the wine is allowed time. Most wines are further clarified by fining. This involves adding a protein substance to the wine which attracts and precipitates solid matter: both then sink to the bottom of the cask or vat, and the clear wine is racked.

Substances used in fining include whipped egg white, bentonite clay, isinglass and blood.

Fining can, however, remove tannin and other desirable ingredients from a wine, and over-fined wine can be deficient in flavour.

Racking   The moving (by pump or gravity) of the wine from one cask or vat to another. This is done after fining, to separate the clarified wine from the deposit or lees, which stays at the bottom of the old cask. Racking is also done to aerate the wine, especially if an open container is used between the vats and barrels. The classic Bordeaux routine is to rack red wines four times in the first year in cask, and two or three times in the second year.

Filtering   Modern filters can be set to remove specific-sized particles from the wine. This allows yeast cells to be filtered out, as well as other solid matter, preventing secondary fermentation. Filtering is thus an alternative, in whole or part, to the use of sulphur dioxide and other chemical disinfectants.

Centrifuging   The centrifuge spins wine around in a drum, pushing solid matter outwards and extracting it from the wine. Over-use can lead to bland wine, but again it is an alternative to chemicals and filtering.

Pasteurization   A further method of taking bacteria and yeast out of the wine and preventing re-fermentation. The wine is heated to 85°C (185°F) for a short time (there is also a slower, cooler technique). Opponents say this strips the wine of ability to improve in bottle.

Adjusting acidity   Many wines are naturally low in acidity, making them at risk of spoiling. Many New World winemakers add ascorbic acid (or vitamin C) as an anti-oxidant and to adjust taste. In Europe this is permitted in some regions — but not if the wine has been chaptalized (*see* p109).

Topping up   Wine in cask or vat evaporates at a greater or lesser rate depending upon the temperature and humidity of the *chai*. To avoid oxidation, the lost wine is replaced weekly by topping up with the same wine from another cask.

In traditional cellars the casks are first sealed with glass bungs. These fit loosely to allow overflow as the wine "works". Later, wooden bungs are tightly fitted and the casks are turned through 30° to submerge the bung.

White wine techniques   Many white wines undergo no maturation apart from storage in inert steel or glass-lined tanks. A period of very cool storage allows tartrates to precipitate out as crystals.

CASKS AND THE TASTE OF WINE

Wooden casks, when new, confer a definite, vanilla taste on the wine they contain. This is desirable in some but not all cases. In Bordeaux and Burgundy, the properties of new oak casks are exploited, for both red and (to a lesser extent) white wines. But in other equally classic wine regions — the port country, Jerez, Champagne — new wood is avoided. Wood also "breathes", allowing a little air in, and can augment the wine's own tannins, helping its ageing ability.

What does wood do to wine? There are three aspects to consider: the size and shape of the cask, its age, and the wood it is made from. The wood first: oak is the preferred timber because of its strength and relative lightness, its cellular structure and its taste components. The structure of oak wood varies according to its source: winemakers identify close- (or tight) and coarse- (or loose)

Fire makes the cask malleable.

grained sorts. This in turn depends upon the forest from which the tree comes, both its environment and the way it is managed. Slow-growing forests produce the tightest-grained

wood. This affects not only its air intake: such oak also has more aromatic phenol compounds (caused by the trees growing more in spring than summer).

Phenols are among the many substances found in oak which can affect wine: so far, more than 60 have been identified, including 18 different phenols of which vanillin is the most important. The tannins in oak, ellagic tannins, are not the same as those that wine gains from grape skins and stalks. They add astringency, and reinforce the wine's structure.

Even more complex than, but related to, wood structure is the varying pattern of substances in oaks from different forests. Limousin oak, from west-central France, is fast-growing, has an open structure and more tannin (but fewer phenols) than Allier oak from further east, which has less tannin but more aromatics such as eugenol and lactone.

WINES AGED IN OAK

Now alternatives are available, the use of oak casks is a conscious choice. The winemaker or cellar master must make several decisions. The variables are the percentage of new oak, the length of time the wine spends in oak, and the type of oak.

Some wines, and some vintages, will not stand 100% new oak. The winemaker may use a percentage of new casks each year, or may age part of the crop in stainless steel or another inert material.

The time spent in oak will vary, again with wine and vintage. In a light year, the wine will spend less time in cask.

Winemakers, especially in the New World, will select casks from particular kinds of oak, even particular makers, believing that these variables can effect subtle changes to the wine.

The following wines are aged in oak as a deliberate part of the taste-shaping

process, not just because large and inert casks are the local tradition. The list cannot be exhaustive, for oak-ageing is part of the armoury of techniques drawn upon by winemakers the world over, and the decision may change from vintage to vintage. It would be hard to find a wine region where someone is not oak-ageing their wine, for good or ill effect.

WHITE WINES
Australia and New Zealand
Chardonnay, Sémillon
Bordeaux   Graves, Sauternes
Burgundy   Chablis, Côte d'Or, Chalonnais
California   Chardonnay, some Sauvignon Blanc, other whites on an experimental basis
Champagne   A few traditional makers use oak casks for fermentation and initial ageing
Germany   Pinot Blanc and Pinot Gris

Italy   Chardonnay, Vin Santo
Rhône   Some white Hermitage
Spain   Traditional-style white Rioja spends several years in oak

RED WINES
Australia   Cabernet Sauvignon, Pinot Noir, Shiraz
Bordeaux   Classed growths, many *crus bourgeois*; increasingly, lesser wines
Burgundy   Côte d'Or, Chalonnais
California   Cabernet Sauvignon, Pinot Noir, Syrah, some Zinfandel
Italy   Piedmont's Barolo and Barbaresco, "super" *vini da tavola* in Tuscany and elsewhere
Loire   Some traditionally-made Chinon and other reds
Rhône   Syrah and Syrah-based wines such as Hermitage and Côte Rôtie
Spain   Red Rioja, Ribera del Duero and other Tempranillo-based wines, Cabernet Sauvignon

Oak from the Baltic lands, from Slovenia, Croatia, North America — all are used, and each has its qualities. Baltic oak was the staple in Bordeaux for many years, despite the proximity of the French forests, because it was easy to transport the wood in the returning wine-ships. It is also relatively neutral: a quality prized, even in Bordeaux, until this century (*see* below).

How the wood is treated is equally important in determining the character of the finished cask. It must be seasoned by leaving the whole trunk to dry naturally: kiln-drying is less good. The wood should be split, not sawn, into staves. Only the best wood from each trunk should be chosen. The staves in turn need to be matured. Only then does the barrel-maker's art — *see* below— come into play.

The shape and size of the cask
The wine world has standardized the ageing barrel as the "small oak" cask of around 225 litres capacity. This is the size of the traditional Bordeaux *barrique*. The Burgundy

pièce is 228 litres, that of Champagne 220. The size became the norm because two men can easily handle such a cask. But it also provides the optimum surface area of oak to wine. Smaller casks provide more oak-contact, but are uneconomic; bigger ones lessen the interchange between wood and wine.

Now that casks are no longer used to transport the wine, thinner wood can be used. The thickness of the staves matters: a Bordeaux *barrique* is made from fairly thin wood, which allows transpiration of a small amount of oxygen. Thicker wood lowers the oxygen intake.

The age of the cask
New oak is of course most heavily impregnated with flavouring compounds. As the cask is used, tannins and other substances are leached out by the wine, and tartrate crystals from the wine build up on the inside. Eventually the cask becomes inert: it is so coated with tartrate that it gives nothing to the wine. This is fine if you require a container, less of

a help if you want the cask to contribute to the taste of the wine.

New wood breathes more than old: its pores are not clogged with solids from the wine, and thus the oxygen trickle through the wood is at its greatest. New oak contributes more tannin, but also more "softening" substances from the cellulose of the oak, and more of the characteristic vanilla flavour. Once used for a year, the oak contributes less tannin, but also allows less oxidation.

How casks are made
The cooper's ancient art is a fascinating one, but only some of its skills are relevant here. In order to achieve the correct shape, the oak staves are secured at one end by a hoop and bent into place. Heat allows the staves to be bent. Some coopers use steam, others fire, from burning wood or a gas burner. This "toasts" the inside of the cask.

A greater or lesser degree of "toast" affects the character of the wine made in the cask. High toast adds smoky notes and a toasted cask contributes more, and different, phenols. Steam-heated casks lack this dimension — which is why some wineries prefer them.

Caring for casks
A cask should, ideally, never be left empty: when full of wine the wood expands and leaks are cured. Empty casks must be scoured out with water before use, and disinfected with sulphur dioxide.

Old casks and vats can be "refreshed" by chipping the tartrate crystals from the inside. Sometimes casks are taken apart, the oak staves shaved, and re-built. This provides a new oak surface that mimics to some extent the properties of a new cask.

Adding oak flavour
Casks are not vital for oak flavour, oak is. New World wineries sometimes use oak chips suspended in the vat to add oak flavours to wines — a practice frowned upon in Europe. □

Fitting staves to an oak *barrique*.

FROM CHÂTEAU TO TABLE

Once the maturation process is complete, the wine is bottled and leaves the château or *négociant* on its way to the consumer. The task of bottling, the most mundane and technical of the winery processes, conceals an important stage in the life of the wine: the use of the cork.

The perfect stopper

The chapter on serving wine (pp 59–73) describes how corks vary, and how to deal with problem corks at the point of serving. But what is cork? It is an organic anachronism in an age of technical solutions, a survival from Roman times, via the 18th century, that is still used despite attempts to develop a better stopper for wine bottles. Alternatives do exist: plastic and metal closures abound, yet none has displaced cork as the seal not just for fine wine, but for most everyday wine too.

Cork forms a perfect seal because its microscopic cells form "suckers" which cling to the glass of the bottle neck. A cork is impervious to liquid, but allows very small amounts of gas — air — to pass through. It is inert, cannot react with the wine, and cannot be corrupted by it. Only insect pests — weevils — and some moulds can affect it, and these can be avoided by proper cellar conditions. No manufactured material offers the same set of qualities, which is why cork remains paramount.

Cork is taken from the bark of a species of oak tree, *Quercus suber*. The harvesting cycle is a long one, from 9–15 years depending upon the country of origin, and the oaks do not begin to produce bark for usable corks until they are 50–75 years old. Portugal produces the largest amount of cork — about 50% of the world crop — followed by Spain, Algeria and Morocco, France and Italy. Cork oaks thrive only in this

Bottling is the most automated process in wine. Absolute cleanliness is vital.

limited western Mediterranean area.

Wine producers choose corks according to the expected ageing period of their wine. Shortlived white wines have short, low-quality corks; wines such as classed-growth red bordeaux and vintage port demand the best: long corks of the highest quality. Well cellared, a good cork can protect wine for a century, though the great French châteaux re-cork bottles in their own cellars every 20 or 30 years.

Bottles

The glass bottle is almost as important to wine as the cork. Glass is inert, durable and attractive: a combination of virtues as rare as those of the cork. The invention of the strong, mass-produced wine bottle is described elsewhere (*see* p43) but perhaps as important as strength was shape. Until the late 18th century, most bottles were globe- or club-

shaped, and thus hard to store on their sides. The slow evolution of the tall, parallel-sided bottle, which can be "binned" or stored with ease on its side with the cork moist, was most important for fine wine as it allowed long ageing.

Who does what in wine

Many modern wine lovers try to buy direct from the producer. This is possible in wine countries, and as an occasional treat for holidaying Scandinavians, British and other non-winemaking peoples. But even those who live next door to a vineyard have access to only one kind of wine, and the search for variety sends them to a merchant of some kind.

The wine trade has evolved some complex relationships, and these survive to a large extent in European countries: practice buttressed by law. In the USA, Australia and other New World wine lands, the patterns are less rigid. Even so, many states in the USA prohibit direct buying of wine by consumers.

The négociants

The *négociants* of Bordeaux are the best-known among the various sub-species of wine merchant. Their rôle in history was to buy wine from the various châteaux, and to sell it on to (mostly foreign) merchants. Their cellars along the Quai des Chartrons in Bordeaux became legendary, not least for what went on inside. The *négociants* were unblushing about the blending of Rhône and even Spanish wine into the greatest of clarets. The "English" *négociants*, descendants of British and Irish merchants, were most adept at the *"travail de l'Anglais"*. Unlike other adulterators of wine, the Chartronnais were concerned to improve the bordeaux reds, not stretch them. They knew that their northern European clientele wanted claret to be strong, dark and heady — and after a good dash of Hermitage and perhaps even a second fermentation prompted by the use of unfermented must, so it was. Port underwent a similar transformation, more extreme and more permanent.

This to our minds dubious process was but one of the jobs of the traditional *négociant*. He was a *"négociant-éleveur"*, with the rôle not just of trader but of shaper, bringer-up, of the young wine. The wines may have remained in his cellars for several years, and during this time the casks were topped up, racked if necessary and allowed to age gently in the proper environment. It was recognized in Bordeaux that the *négociants'* cellars provided superior ageing conditions. Unlike the over-ground *chais* of the châteaux, the deep, dark cellars behind the Chartronnais's elegant 18th-century premises were ideal for ageing wine.

Château-bottling

It is becoming rare to find a fine wine bottled other than at the estate which grew it. In Bordeaux today, every "château" wine is bottled by the property, at the property. It was not always so: it was only in 1924 that Baron Philippe de Rothschild of Mouton persuaded his fellow propri-etors of the leading châteaux to make it compulsory. Even after that several top châteaux slipped back into selling in bulk until the 1950s. The reasons for château-bottling are authenticity and quality. The drawbacks are expense: cellar space is needed to age the wines for two years; and capital is required to finance them. A wine bottled by the estate which made it is (unless there is a grand fraud under way) what the label says it is. The *négociants* had no such scruples.

The château goes international

The château (and estate) as a brand name is not usual in France, except in Bordeaux, other areas depending tra-ditionally on the vineyard or district name to give the wine its identity. The château was taken up by New World producers who realized the value of the concept. They frequently use the French word "château" to give dignity to their claim to be a wine estate in the classic tradition, though few of the buildings would look at home in the Médoc.

The use of an estate name does not tie production to a given area: a château, and an estate, can expand, as long as it stays within the often wide limits of the AOC. Outside France, the concept can become more elastic still, with some of the grapes being bought from land outside the estate. What, then, is a château-bot-tled wine? The classic definition is that it is a wine made from grapes grown on the estate, and matured and bottled there. The distinction between château-bottled wine and wine sold in bulk is, to the proprietor, crucial: the latter is raw material, the former a finished product.

The modern négoce

Today's *négociants* adopt a different profile. They no longer age and bottle the fine wines: château-bottling has seen to that. They have three main rôles: to acquire château- or domaine-bottled wine and sell it on to wholesalers and export markets; to identify and sell *petits châteaux* and other minor wines; and to blend and market wines of generic appellations and table wines. In many ways the *négociant* is now a broker, introducing two sides, supplier and customer, and taking a percentage. In many areas, especially in Europe where many thousand small producers exist, the *négociant* or broker plays a key role. He or she can track down wines of quality and interest amid the mass of small châteaux and offer them to cus-tomers. Brokers have played a part in bringing domaine-bottled bur-gundies, individual vineyard Pied-mont wines, and the produce of good small German estates to buyers' attention. They are also important in northern Italy and in the world of cooperative cellars in the Midi.

The big buyers

Every wine region sees regular visits from major buyers working for retail concerns. They can influence wine-making considerably. Bringing to the wine world the approach of the food industry — tight quality and price control and a need for consistency — they have shaken up sleepy wine dis-tricts. They call for large amounts of wine, in a regular flow, and without variation. This can be good for areas which need advice on and investment in winemaking and maturation tech-niques. Such buyers sometimes send their own winemakers to shape and control the wine: the "flying wine-maker" phenomenon which has affected the Danube countries, parts of southern France, Spain and Italy. But the demands of the big buyers can suppress individuality by insisting on certain grape varieties or wine styles and above all by demanding large amounts of wine, which means blending. They can also be unsym-pathetic about vintage variations, and can abandon a supplier if a better price is offered. □

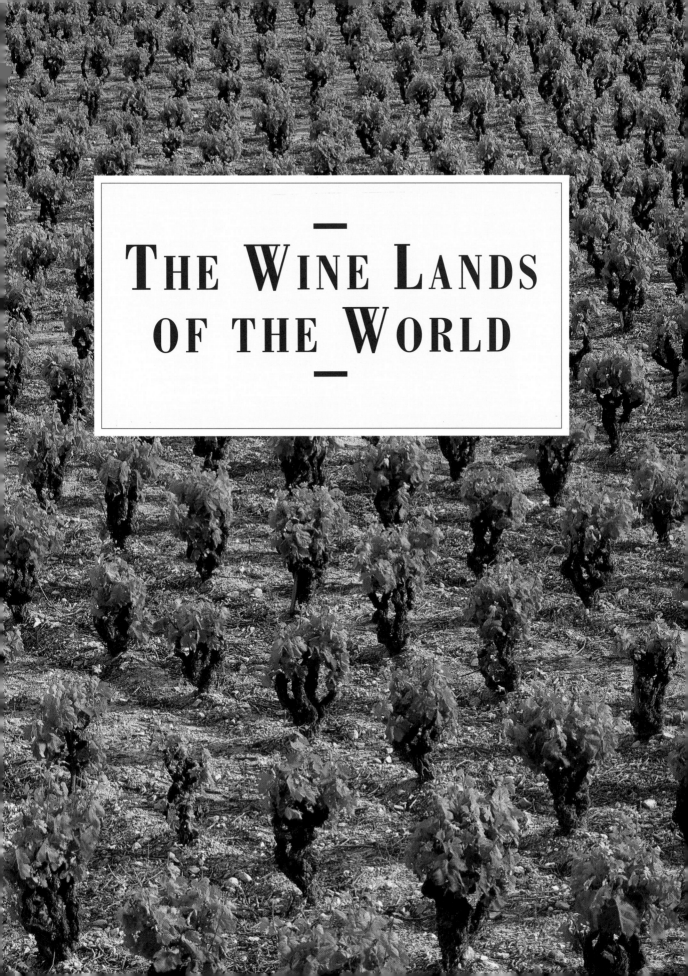

THE WINE LANDS
OF THE WORLD

Wine is made in at least 50 countries, and nearly all of them now export some of their production: wine is the most widely traded and available of drinks. Indeed, no other food product reaches so many places in an identifiable form, for wine is not anonymous. Alone among agricultural products, only wine is labelled according not just to the country or region, but frequently the field, from which it comes.

Once, that field would have been in France. Or perhaps the Mosel Valley in Germany, or Chianti territory in Italy. If you were drinking the fruits of a Californian vineyard, or an Australian one, then you were in America or Australia. In the last two decades we have witnessed an explosion in the choice of wines available — matched only by a revolutionary increase in their general quality.

The wild vine is a native plant of the world's temperate zones, and the cultivated grapevine bred from it is an established crop in regions such as Europe and the eastern Mediterranean, wide parts of the Americas, North and South, and in Australasia. It is less common — for cultural, not climatic reasons — in Asia east of the Mediterranean littoral.

Wine's heartland is the Mediterranean, and it is due to the worldwide dominance of Western culture, which stemmed from the Classical world, that wine is today so ubiquitous. The vast and flourishing vineyards of the New World — in wine terms, the Americas, South Africa, Australia, New Zealand — were founded by Europeans. Today wines from these countries and more join those of Europe's ancient vineyards on the tables of wine lovers the world over.

A technical revolution in winemaking has dramatically raised the quality of wine. Compared to even 20 years ago, there is far less bad wine made. The amount of truly good wine is increasing as the New World's restless innovators challenge the quality dominance of Europe's vineyards. In between, the calibre of ordinary, everyday wine is far higher, thanks to a succession of advances in quality control.

At the same time the quantity of wine made and drunk is in steady decline. This is not surprising: wine is not only a delightful, sometimes luxurious pleasure. For centuries it did duty as medicine, anaesthetic and antiseptic as well as a drink that was usually a lot safer than the local water supply. With better water, and less thirst-inducing manual labour, the world now wants — and is getting — quality rather than quantity. The amount of wine drunk in France halved from 1961 to 1991, though France remains the country where most wine is drunk per head. Italy, Portugal and Spain had similar falls.

Other countries, such as Australia, the USA, Germany and the UK, are drinking more wine. It is here that the interest in wine as a subject of connoisseurship first became widespread. Perhaps because wine is less ubiquitous, it is more closely studied.

Old World, New World
If the trade in wine is worldwide, so too is the traffic in wine ideas, and increasingly in people. The New World countries have been eager observers of European practice for at least a century. The new wine industries continually looked over their shoulders at Europe, profiting from wine-wise immigrants and from a flow of technical information and prototype bottles to emulate. As travel grew easier and cheaper, it became virtually the norm for young Australian and American wine students to spend a few months in Europe. Later, as practitioners, they would be back to scour Bordeaux and Burgundy for vine cuttings, new oak casks — and ideas.

By the 1980s this trade had become two-way. French winemakers, amazed at the boom in sales of New World wines in countries where France had dominated, started to send their sons and daughters to California and Australia. The large champagne companies began to buy land and set up wineries there. Bordeaux's élite followed: Baron Philippe de Rothschild formed a partnership with Bob Mondavi to make Opus One, a wine in the Bordeaux mould and at a First Growth price — but from the Napa Valley. Moueix of Pomerol, Roederer, Mumm, Deutz of Champagne have all followed them to California — and in some cases to Australia and New Zealand too.

Old World, New World fusion: the Opus One winery in California's Napa Valley.

French expertise is also helping to open up new territories. Will China's millions become wine lovers *en masse*? The process has certainly started. And in Japan, and India. The world wine map is not yet complete.

Understanding the world of wine

This marvellous diversity does, however, pose difficulties for consumers. There is too much to choose from: it is hard to work out which wines are best.

The main focus for understanding wine is geographical, which is why the next 400 pages of this Encyclopedia profile the world's wine lands, dividing them into regions and smaller districts as appropriate. At the most local level, there are descriptions of wine villages, wine-producing estates, and individual producers. The focus seems clear: countries have wine zones and smaller districts, producers own vines and make wine. This comforting pattern exists in some places, but not all — and it is changing.

Many New World countries stress other factors above the locality. A glance at the labels of wines in these countries will show many European names: they are those of grapes, the far-travelled varieties that have been planted in virtually every wine country. Consumers in the new wine countries have become familiar with the use of grape variety names as the names of a wine. Chardonnay, or Cabernet Sauvignon, indicates a certain style of wine. European consumers, and legislators, are less happy with this approach. When judging a wine's status and quality, they put the geographical source of the grapes ahead of the variety.

An approach common to all wine lands is the stress on the importance of the winemaker. In the classic regions this is expressed through the property name: a château, or an estate, is a brand name. New World vineyards have their named estates, and also their wine companies: some large; some run by, and named after, individuals. These names come to be shorthand for wine style and quality.

Thus in Australia a consumer may become used to buying wine from a given maker, trusting the company to deliver quality, and knowing the style of wine which that company prefers. The names of grape and maker on the label are the guarantees, not the exact site of the winery. Europe's stress on location is an extra, not an alternative, clue to quality. Wine lovers everywhere are getting used to using all three: location, maker and grape.

WORLD WINE ZONES

The grape vine tolerates a fairly narrow climatic range. It needs a growing season long enough to complete the fruiting cycle, and a period of winter cold to force the vine into dormancy. It needs certain amounts of warmth, water and daylight: *see* p105. It gets these where conditions are not extreme: it is a plant of the temperate zones. The conditions needed are found in two bands between latitudes 30° and 50° north and south.

The temperate bands

These bands run across Europe, Asia and North America; and in the southern hemisphere, South America, South Africa, Australia and New Zealand. Within them, sites which can offer the correct balance of rainfall, temperature and exposure are chosen to grow vines.

Choosing the site

In the northern hemisphere's classic winelands, upland areas are ruled out owing to the effect of altitude, which modifies the effect of latitude and makes the areas too cold, or too windblown, for viticulture. Higher areas are however sought after in Australia, southern Italy and other places where latitude means that summers can be hot. Here, high vineyards will enjoy cooler, and thus more balanced, conditions.

The world's vineyard sites are also increased by areas, otherwise too arid, where irrigation is allowed: common in the southern hemisphere and some parts of the USA. The best vineyard sites are found on slopes: this not only aids drainage (vines hate wet feet), but can also maximize the exposure to the grape-ripening sun.

Areas of flat land are usually avoided, partly because they will grow other crops to greater profit, and partly because their drainage can be poor. The ideal is a gentle slope.

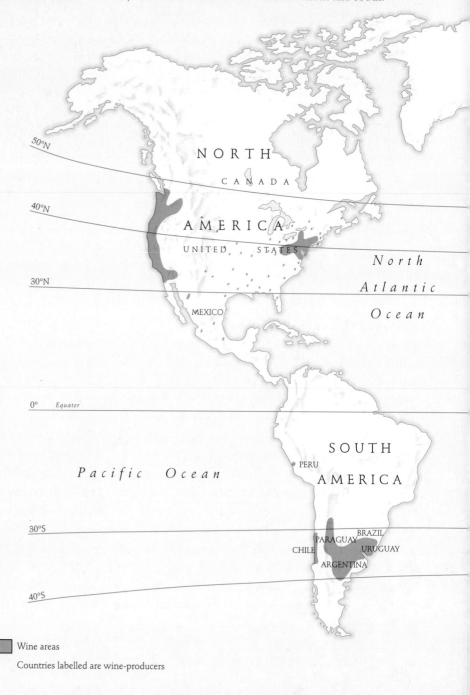

Wine areas

Countries labelled are wine-producers

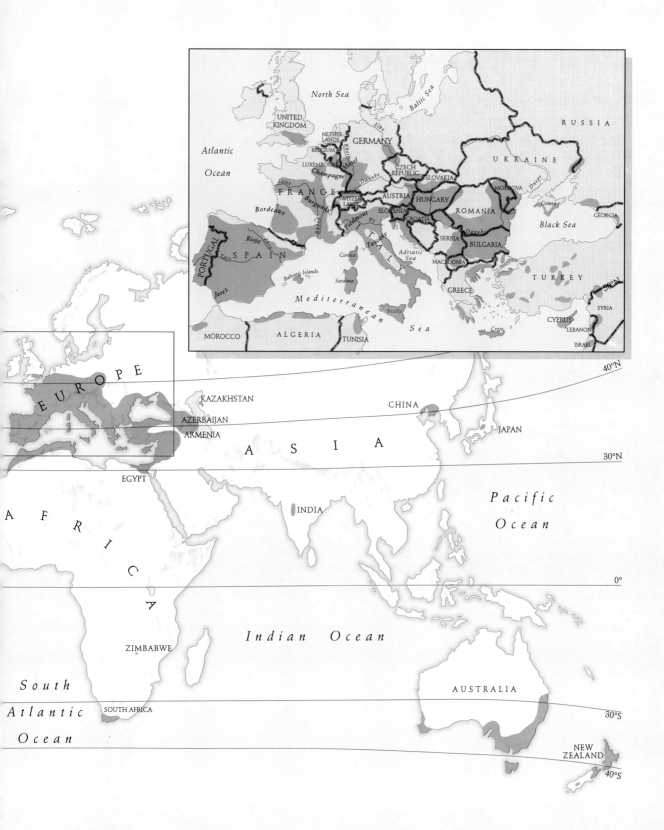

QUALITY WINE ZONES

Within the broad bands of latitude that provide the underlying conditions, why do grapes thrive in some places and not others? And how do wine countries define these zones and regulate them?

CHOOSING THE SITE
Man can manipulate the basic growing conditions — by irrigating in dry areas, for instance — but his biggest contribution to wine quality is to choose the actual vineyard site. Ancient Rome's farmers knew that vines loved a sunny slope, a nearby river. Aspect to the sun, altitude, soil and underlying rock, taken together with climate both general and local, determine why wine from some vineyards is consistently better than that from others. France has developed the concept of *terroir* — the sum of all the factors pertaining to a particular plot of land.

The *terroir* approach is a traditional one and is challenged to some extent by modernists, who say that science can master nature's foibles. Few experienced vinegrowers, however, dispute that site does matter. It is how much it matters that is under discussion.

What the vine needs
Vines need shelter from cold winds, which can desiccate them and damage tender foliage and fruit. They must have adequate warmth to promote growth, and sun to ripen grapes.

More subtle choices concern the type of soil. Soil has four attributes: it supports the vine, supplies moisture, it warms up and cools down at a greater or lesser rate, and it supplies nutrients. Of course, any plant needs nutrients to grow — but nearly all of them can be found as traces in rainwater.

Do the particular nutrients in a vineyard's soils make a difference?

Here we are on holy ground. Château Petrus tastes rich and concentrated because of the iron in the subsoil. Chevalier-Montrachet wine is lighter than its neighbour Montrachet's because the soil is stonier. So says the orthodoxy. Iconoclastic Australians challenge this, averring that there is no scientific proof that the subtly classified soils of (say) Burgundy make the wines different.

Soil and the concept of terroir
Does soil do anything more than hold the vine up? Even to ask such a question in France is to utter sacrilege: the whole edifice of the *appellation d'origine contrôlée* system is founded on delineating the best soils. A Burgundy *Grand Cru* is better than a Burgundy *Premier Cru* because its soil is superior.

This view went unchallenged until California and Australia began to produce seriously good wines — from every kind of soil imaginable. French experts visited the "New World" and found that soil was not at the top of a winemaker's priority list. And there were no lines on maps to say that a certain kind of vine could be grown on this hillside, but not on the next.

New World winemakers look at a vineyard's water supply and temperature. If there is not enough water from rainfall or the water table, they irrigate. If there is not enough warmth, or too much, they plant a vineyard somewhere else. Many New World vineyards were recently sheep pasture or cornfields, and many will be again. It is hard to imagine the hill of Corton, or the gravel of the Médoc, growing anything other than grapes, but in the New World there are no certainties.

Soil is thought to confer special flavours: every French or Italian textbook describes the way in which the

various minerals, clays or limestones in a given soil affect the taste of the wine. This theory has yet to be proved by analysis. Tasters can distinguish between wines from different vineyards. But is it soil they are tasting, or the myriad other factors that influence the grapes and the wine?

There is more to soil than fertility and minerals. Soils differ in their structure: some are open and free-draining and quick to warm up, others (clay) are dense, damp and cool. Vines prefer an open soil, such as gravel, limestone-based soils or even fissured and fragmented rock. In many vineyards there is very little actual soil in the sense that a gardener would know it. Dense, damp soils promote rot and the soil will be slow to warm up. Rich, fertile soil is generally held to be a bad thing when quality, not ordinary, wine is the aim. ("The vine must suffer to produce", as the French saying has it.)

ENSURING THE QUALITY
All quality wines carry a label saying where they come from. The French quality control system is described below at length because it formed the prototype for other European laws, from Italy to Bulgaria, and because its philosophy impregnates the European Community (EC) wine régime including its attitude to non-EC wines.The power of the EC as an enormous importer is clearly shown in the 1990s' flurry of reframing of New World countries' wine laws. Central and eastern Europe, New Zealand and Australia have had to bring their laws in line with EC rules.

How wine laws began
The spur to the development of laws about wine labelling — which is what an appellation system is — was fraud. As commerce in wine grew, and noted wines achieved higher

Proclaiming one's status with pride in St-Emilion.

prices, it became tempting for those selling the wine to lie about its origins. No doubt the Romans had to contend with fake Falernian, and the provenance of a cask of medieval claret must have been hard to establish, but the real problem grew in the late 19th century.

It was then that railways, mass marketing and the growth in consumer demand encouraged a spate of outright fraud. The proprietors of the great Bordeaux châteaux were horrified to find fake Margaux and Latour on the market in Belgium, Germany and England. There was little they could do as the law then stood. In truth, the Bordeaux merchants (and those of elsewhere) had long been cavalier about what was sold under these famous names. The wine was anyway "adjusted" to *le goût anglais*; and a shortage of Médoc wine was easily remedied, thought the 18th-century *négociants*: send for a shipment from the Languedoc.

Water into wine

A writer in the 1860s rounded on the merchants of Burgundy: "When it wishes to be, the wine trade is God, and part of its equipment is the miracle at Cana."

Turning water into wine was perhaps an exaggeration, but turning Algerian red into burgundy was not. Honest growers and merchants needed protection against the fraudsters, and found it in the steady growth of *appellation d'origine* legislation in France. The process started in 1919, but had its origins much earlier. Bordeaux in medieval times had laws which banned wine from inland regions from being sold as bordeaux — but this was more trade rivalry than quality control. The league of winemakers of Rioja in Spain set their own rules in 1560. Chianti became one of the first controlled wine zones when the grand duke of Florence drew the boundaries in 1716. An international convention in

1883 banned the use of false or fictitious denominations of origin.

In France, a law of 1905 was the first step against fraudulent wine labelling, introducing declarations by growers to allow monitoring of how much wine was made and where. The law also said that names of origin must only be used on labels if true. Boundaries of wine zones had therefore to be drawn. But origin was contentious: just how large an area was Champagne, or Bordeaux? Riots in Epernay in 1911 were sparked by the delineation of the Champagne district in a way that many growers resented. The government rapidly devolved the job of drawing up boundaries to local bodies. The 1919 law gave them a framework: wines of *appellation d'origine* status must be made in stated places and by methods in line with local custom ("*les usages locaux, loyaux et constants*").

More was needed than just accurate descriptions of origin; the law must control quality and quantity too. A further law in 1927 meant that appellation authorities could ban grape varieties not thought locally suitable. Yield, and alcoholic degree, were slowly brought into the regulations. However, the law was subject to local implementation and it took many years for even the finest French vineyards to be defined, delineated and controlled. A further step came in 1935, when the all-important word "*contrôlée*" was added. The INAO (*Institut National des Appellations d'Origine Contrôlée*) was founded and to this day it polices the system. AOCs are extended and modified, and wines are promoted to AOC, under the eye of the INAO.

The European wine laws

The European Community (EC) built on the AOC structure and set up a concept of quality wine produced in a delimited region (VQPRD, which initials stand for *vin de qualité produit dans une région determinée*). The Community's rules lay down that only wines made in a named zone can be so labelled, and oblige member countries to control yield, grape varieties and the precise area within each denomination.

Prototypes and facsimiles

The travelling French wine lover of a decade or two ago would fume as wine lists in the USA and elsewhere offered California "Chablis", "Burgundy" or other famous names. This practice was common in Spain up to 1973, when the main market for Spanish "Sauternes" and the others, namely the United Kingdom, agreed to adhere to French labelling laws.

The wines may or may not have had any connection — in style, grape variety or quality — with the prototype, though the colour was usually the same. But the makers undoubtedly felt that a French name would help sell their bottles.

Slowly, the practice of using generic names, as these are called, has been banned. At first the EC wine régime made it impossible for such wines to be imported into Europe. Then treaties between the EC and other countries extended the ban into domestic markets in return for concessions about sales in the EC. Thus the famous Australian "White Burgundy" label is today banished from Sydney and Perth as well as Paris and London.

Champagne has proved a more troublesome case. Though truly a geographical appellation, the word "champagne" has come to refer to the area's method of making wine, using a second fermentation in the bottle. This technique is widely used all around the world. A judgement of the EC that the term *"méthode champenoise"* could not be used on non-champagne wines has left a gap in the terminology. How should such wines be described? And how can they be differentiated from sparkling wines made by other, usually lesser, methods? There is no clear answer. The use of terms such as "traditional method" lacks the clarity that using *"méthode champenoise"* confers.

Laws can enshrine bad practice

Wine laws began, as the French example shows, in an attempt to regulate the making of and trading in wine, guaranteeing minimum standards and authenticity. But in some cases the standards set have turned out to be the wrong ones.

The Italian legislation, for example, sometimes fossilized bad practice rather than preserving fine traditions. Local politics ensured that many zones that achieved the DOC (*denominazione di origine controllata*: the equivalent of the French AOC) had little more than habit to recommend them. Just because a wine has been made in a certain way in a certain valley for generations, that does not make it a good wine. It may become far better if techniques and grapes are reconsidered — but one effect of DOC (and indeed AOC) is to preserve the status quo.

The Italian law has been replaced by a more practical, pragmatic and open-minded one and change should be swift, with fewer and more closely defined DOC wines.

Do laws control the right things?

France posits that the better vineyards must always make better wine, so the quality system classifies land. In Germany, all vineyards are equal: wines from each one have a chance to be rated at the highest quality level. The only variable the law recognizes is grape sugar level. This is analysable, and non-controversial. But it tells the consumer little about wine quality, especially in the lower grades, and it ignores differences between vineyards. In Germany, the myriad vineyard site names were seen as a barrier to understanding wine. Therefore the 1971 wine law grouped many small vineyards under blanket names. These camouflage the origin of the wine, allowing the misunderstanding to arise that wine with a famous name on the label is from that particular village or vineyard, when this is not the case. Many producers, and most wine drinkers,

feel the German law is unhelpful, and it is clearly working to a different philosophy from other wine laws.

Conscientious German growers often limit yields, though the law makes no such demand, and they use vineyard names only when they are justified. The law is struggling to catch up with the best growers.

New World laws

Until recently, New World countries did not regulate the naming of wines. Up to 1994, Australians could apply whatever geographical name they liked. Certain areas became known for quality wines, but unlike those in Europe they had no formal borders. This was potentially misleading to the consumer, but potentially liberating for the winemaker, and in the end the consumer too. For vineyards could be extended, grape varieties tried out, entire new wine regions discovered, all without fear of infringing appellation laws.

Since 1994 in Australia, and from 1995 in New Zealand, a system of appellations is in force and it is illegal to label a wine with a false or misleading geographical origin. Australia calls the defined regions "geographical indications"; New Zealand refers to "certified origin". In the USA state and county names are used, as are Viticultural Areas, which are more closely defined zones that apply viticultural, rather than political, considerations to boundary-setting.

The effect of appellation laws

As soon as a boundary is drawn, land inside it becomes more valuable, and that outside it less. This works with property zoning regulations; it happens with wine laws. Growers in Australia have been split over the rules which define exactly where the Coonawarra and Clare districts begin and end. Champagne endures constant sniping between landowners, who would restrict the AOC areas, and the large producing firms, which would welcome the lower prices that expansion would bring. □

FRANCE

—

FRANCE'S ASTONISHING ARRAY OF QUALITY WINES IS A NATURAL
CONSEQUENCE OF ITS VARIED CLIMATES AND SOILS, FROM THE COOL
CHALKY VINEYARDS OF CHAMPAGNE TO THE SUN-WARMED STONES
OF CHATEAUNEUF-DU-PAPE IN THE SOUTHERN RHONE.

—

Everywhere in the world that wine is made, France is the standard of comparison. Wherever a wine list is drawn up, France seems to belong naturally at the beginning. A generation ago, it could be confidently asserted that France made all the best wines of the world, with the traditional exceptions of the white wines of Germany and the fortified ones of Iberia. Now, France has competitors as well as imitators, even at the very top level of quality. But all would-be makers of great wines aim to match and surpass those of France, and this dominance, a more subtle form of influence than sheer quality leadership, seems unshakeable.

In Cape Town and San Francisco, Sydney and Auckland, winetasters assemble classic French bottles to put their local wines in perspective. In the same places and thousands more, wine merchants will stock French wines, both great and small, to meet the demand both from wine lovers seeking quality and from the wider public whose knowledge of wine may be limited, but who know that France and wine are synonymous.

The range of French wine

One of the reasons for the dominance of French wines is the extraordinary range the country makes. This is thanks to its wide span of climates, which allows light white wines to be made in the Loire, and powerful red ones in the Midi. France has exploited this to assemble a list of wines, or wine regions, which dominate the world. Bordeaux, Burgundy and Champagne each make styles of wine which are unsurpassed, though widely imitated. The great names ring around the world: Mouton-Rothschild, Chambertin, Krug. The second rank — the Loire, Rhône, Alsace — makes wines if anything more inimitable. Then there is the broad spread of appellations and districts making their own wines according to deep-rooted traditions: Cahors and Madiran, Provence, the Jura. All these districts and more make at least some wines of serious quality in world terms. Beyond this again is the whole range of French wines which may be almost unknown outside their home country, or even province, but which offer fascinating and individual flavours. Think of Limoux, with its sparking wines; of the Aveyron hills with their unique Marcillac red; of Bellet near Nice with its unexpectedly good white wines. Then there are the mass-production wine areas where islands of real quality can be found amid the cheap blending wines: the *crus* of Languedoc, the Minervois and Corbières hills.

This list of French wines could have been written at any time in the last two centuries. Indeed, it would have been longer: the phylloxera plague and changing patterns of commerce drove many a *vigneron* from the land, and left many a terraced hillside deserted. But in the 1980s a new wave of innovation swept the French wine regions, especially those of the south — the Midi — and this is prompting the growth of new wines. To the list of French classics, great and minor, can be added classics in the making. In the hills of the Midi a return to old vineyards and vines, allied to the latest in techniques, is yielding wines which stun tasters in New York, Paris and London with their quality. The same is true in Provence, in the wide lands of the southern Rhône, and in the vineyards of the south-west.

Added to this revitalization has been the updating of the more recent, mass-producing, vineyards of the plains. Australian and American techniques and attitudes are shaking up the sad, featureless wine lands here, with open-minded experts finding that the conditions are suitable for good wine from classic grapes. France is now making wines labelled "Chardonnay" and "Cabernet Sauvignon" (in the New World fashion of wines named simply from the *cépage*), from grapes grown in the Midi, processed according to the latest New World thinking and marketed in an outgoing, designer-bottle New World way — with no concessions to classic French wine notions about *terroir* and tradition. This has had more success in export markets than at home, as the French public is taking time to adapt to the idea that the Midi can make interesting wines, but the heartening news for French wine is that these

WINE REGIONS OF FRANCE

Few *départements* south of Paris are wholly without vines, but the main wine regions are those mapped here. Each (with the exception of the small regions of Jura and Savoie) has its own map at the start of its chapter.

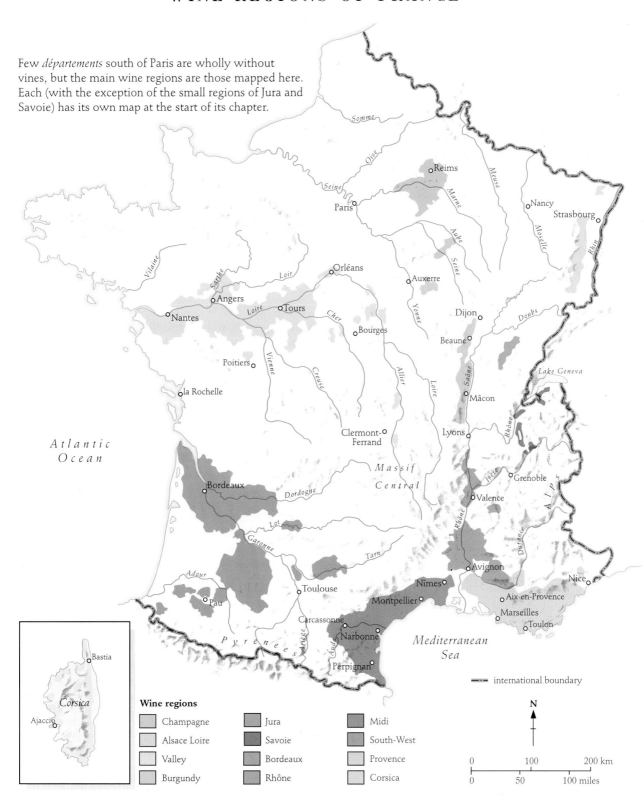

Wine regions

- Champagne
- Alsace Loire
- Valley
- Burgundy
- Jura
- Savoie
- Bordeaux
- Rhône
- Midi
- South-West
- Provence
- Corsica

— ·· — international boundary

0   100   200 km
0   50   100 miles

N

bottles meet and beat New World "varietals" on their own terms in price, presentation and above all flavour.

France is gaining a new wine dimension to add to its classics. And it is important to note that the classic regions, too, have seen what is happening in the wider world and reacted to it. New generations of educated, outward-looking winemakers and proprietors have taken over in Burgundy, the Rhône and Alsace. In Bordeaux, with its tradition of wider horizons, there was less of a revolution, but its homegrown expertise has been spurred on by competition to raise the overall standard of its wine by a discernible step. Even Champagne, which according to its own messengers had achieved perfection a century or so back, has seen changes in viticulture and maturation which have enhanced the quality of the wine.

The scale of French wine

France shares with Italy and Spain the character of a complete wine country. Grapes are grown in more than half the *départements*, or counties, of metropolitan France.

Some 914,000 hectares of vineyard — or 2,260,000 acres — contribute their grapes to the French harvest. This area is smaller than it used to be, but the average annual production of more than 53 million hl, or 583 million cases puts France into second — and sometimes first — place among the wine lands of the world (*see* p588 onwards for detailed figures). Only Italy makes more wine.

More than 30% of French wine is entitled to an *appellation d'origine contrôlée* (AOC). The structure of French wine law is described below, but the dominance of AOC wine is relatively new, and points out an interesting trend in French wine. Much less wine is drunk today than it was even 30 years ago. France's average consumption per head is now around 60 litres a year, down from 140 litres in 1954. However, much more of what is drunk today is now quality wine.

Regulating French wine

The French wine industry is one of the most closely monitored in any agricultural sector anywhere. Each bottle is labelled according to law, and each fits into a quality category. These are, in descending importance, *appellation d'origine contrôlée* (AOC), *vins délimités de qualité supérieure* (VDQS), *vins de pays* and *vins de table*.

Appellation d'Origine Contrôlée (AOC)

The process by which the AOC laws developed has an importance beyond France, and their history is thus outlined in the chapter on the world's quality wine zones (*see* p130).

The AOCs are areas making wine according to local criteria. There are around 450 AOCs in existence. Two aspects are important: one, that the rules are local ones; second, that AOCs exist in tiers or levels. The local nature of the rules is a deliberate attempt to preserve wine traditions and qualities, and to emphasize the uniqueness of each region or locality.

The rules, governed since 1935 by the INAO — the Institut National des Appellations d'Origine (*see* opposite), were drawn up by, and amended in cooperation with, each region's wine producers and merchants. They thus reflect local usage. In Bordeaux the unit of wine is a château. This somewhat mystical and elastic concept is discussed on p142, but it is by no means a fixed patch of land. In Burgundy and elsewhere, by contrast, the specific vineyard takes priority over the person, or persons, who own it.

The AOC rules in the two regions differ accordingly. In Bordeaux there are fairly wide AOCs covering whole communes or even, as in the case of AOC Margaux, five communes. Specific vineyards are not graded, though everyone knows that some land is better than others. Apart from excluding patently unsuitable land — low-lying meadows — the AOC contents itself with establishing AOC Margaux or St-Julien. Within these districts the

châteaux have a pecking order, expressed in the 1855 Classification, the other, later, classifications, and the list of *Crus Bourgeois*. None of these is the concern of the AOC. The labels on bottles of Château Margaux, and on the obscurest backwoods wine, each bear the words "Appellation Margaux Contrôlée".

In Burgundy, a commune the size of Gevrey-Chambertin, comparable in scale with one of the Médoc villages, will have its own AOC but will be further divided into dozens of named vineyards. Some of these will be AOC Gevrey-Chambertin, others will be entitled to the AOC Gevrey-Chambertin *Premier Cru*, and a select few will possess their own AOCs and the status of *Grand Cru*. A small amount of outlying land will, by contrast, be thought unfit to be Gevrey at all and be demoted to mere AOC Bourgogne.

A more manageable example of the same tier approach can be found in many other regions. In the Rhône, the large Côtes du Rhône AOC is dotted with districts entitled to use the Côtes du Rhône-Villages AOC. These are communes deemed to make better wine. A selected few have been further promoted and allowed to use their own name — added on to Côtes du Rhône-Villages. The top tier has escaped from the Côtes du Rhône AOC completely and go under their name alone, such as AOC Gigondas.

■ **AOC regulations** Once an AOC has been defined — the boundaries drawn, and unsuitable land excluded — further rules are set. These specify which grapes can be grown, how much wine can be made, what strength it must reach and (sometimes) not exceed. The permitted grape varieties are those in use in the area when the AOC was drawn up: some are varietal monocultures, others allow a broad choice. Rhône reds from Cornas must be 100% Syrah, whereas at Châteauneuf, down the valley, no fewer than 13 different grapes can be used.

Restrictions on yield are the most debated of the AOC rules. Each AOC has its maximum, expressed as hectolitres of wine per hectare of vineyard (abbreviated normally to hl/ha). A small, prestige AOC will have a lower yield than a more widespread one. This basic yield can be exceeded if the AOC authorities permit it, taking into account the conditions of the vintage. This gives the annual yield or *rendement annuel*. In rare cases this can be below the basic yield.

In addition, a producer can apply for a permit to make more wine: perhaps 20% more. To get this permit he must submit his wine for tasting, and he cannot (as in the past) declare surplus wine as *vin de table* — it must be sent for distillation. It can be seen that the base yield — that is, the figure normally quoted as the maximum for a given AOC — may be exceeded by a large proportion if the officials of the INAO concur.

In some areas production techniques form part of the AOC. Champagne is an example, with detailed regulations about pressing the grapes and maturing the wine.

The AOC rules also regulate details such as density of vines planted per hectare, chaptalization, the use of fertilizers, pruning techniques and the paperwork necessary to monitor the movement of wine.

It is this last aspect that the authorities find hardest to control. Each batch of wine is recorded, and checks are made to correlate vineyard size with the amount of wine produced from it. But once the wine leaves the producer, it is very hard to keep track of every batch.

■ **Protecting the appellations** The AOC system is controlled and nurtured by the INAO, which rightly takes a serious view of its task. It speaks of the "worldwide struggle to protect the *appellations d'origine* from

every possible external threat". These threats include misuse of wine names on other wines — such as sparkling wine labelled as champagne — and on products as various as mustard and perfume.

EC law is in line with the INAO on protection of names, and the European Community has negotiated with other countries, such as Australia, to establish mutual recognition of appellation names.

The INAO concludes its justification of the appellation philosophy like this: "Unlike a brand name, which belongs to a single person or company... the appellation is the joint, inalienable property of the whole community of people working the land to which it applies."

Specific appellations work to protect their own name. The champagne industry is particularly active through the Comité Interprofessionel du Vin de Champagne (CIVC), which has

Right side of the tracks: across the wall these Gevrey-Chambertin vines are rated *Premier Cru*.

fought legal actions in several countries to protect the name "champagne", whether it appears on a wine label or on any other product. Other wine regions have similar bodies.

Vins Délimités de Qualité Supérieure (VDQS)

These are wine areas judged to be less prestigious than *appellations d'origine contrôlées*. They are regulated in the same way, but the zones are drawn along commune boundaries, and thus not as precisely as AOCs.

This category, also under INAO control, is gradually being phased out, with wines promoted to AOC status. At present the VDQS (the full, formal title is *appellation d'origine vins délimités de qualité supérieure*) make up around 1% of the French total.

Vins de Pays

These wines represent some 15% of French production and form a separate group within the larger category of *vins de table* (*see* below), but they have more in common with AOC wines. They come from specific places, and are made according to quite strict rules.

Their growth has been rapid, and accords with the philosophy of diversity which underlies French wine officialdom: there is no absolute pyramid of quality; rather there are separate and parallel ways to regulate wine, of which *vins de pays* is one.

The AOC is the senior system, but that does not place the newest, *vins de pays*, automatically at the bottom of the pile. One of the virtues of the *vin de pays* system is that it allows growers to use grape varieties that AOCs forbid because they are not locally traditional. In many parts of the country the AOCs and *vin de pays* zones overlap, and the latter allow experiments.

Chardonnay vines are, for example, not listed in the Muscadet AOC rules and are therefore forbidden. But the *vin de pays* zone of the Loire Valley (Jardin de la France) allows several grapes not traditional to the region. Thus a Muscadet grower can use some land to experiment with Chardonnay and sell the wine under the *vin de pays* label.

Similar experiments have brought Cabernet Sauvignon and Merlot to the Midi; Viognier, the cherished northern Rhône white grape, to vineyards farther south; and the ubiquitous Chardonnay has spread from its Burgundy heartland to more or less everywhere. On the other hand, *vins de pays* can permit the use of varieties which the *appellation d'origine contrôlée* rejects on quality grounds.

■ **Vins de pays zones** *Vins de pays* come in three categories: regional, departmental and zonal.

Regional *vins de pays* come from the broadest areas. There are four such denominations: Vins de Pays d'Oc (from the Midi, the lower Rhône and Provence); Vins de Pays du Jardin de la France (from the Loire Valley); Vins de Pays du Comté Tolosan (from South-west France); and Vins de Pays des Comtés Rhodaniens (from the northern Rhône and Savoie).

Departmental *vins de pays* apply to each of virtually all the wine-producing *départements* in France, from Meuse in the north-east to Pyrénées-Atlantiques in the south-west.

Zonal *vins de pays* are more restricted in area. They vary in size, taking in sometimes a few communes, sometimes most of a *département*. They are often named after physical features: valleys, perhaps, or ranges of hills.

These zonal wines are concentrated in the Midi, where in many cases they serve to revive vineyards

The famous roof of the Hôtel Dieu, Hospices de Beaune.

left moribund by the growth of the mass-market areas on the coastal plains. Others recognize tiny vineyards buried in the heart of France, or give alternatives to growers in existing AOC areas.

The usefulness of *vins de pays* to growers is that they provide a choice. There is always the fallback of selling the wine as *vin de table*. Some wine can be declared as *vin de pays*, but not all. In most districts, the producer has two or three names to choose from: he may be within a zonal *vin de pays*, but if that name does not suit — it may have restrictive rules, or simply be unknown — the departmental name is available, and in many cases also the regional one.

A Vin de Pays d'Oc, for example, may come from the Aude, and could be labelled as such, or from a specific Aude zone — Coteaux de Narbonne, Val de Dagne and so on.

In addition, the wider departmental and regional *vins de pays* allow blending. A merchant can buy in batches of grapes or wine from across the Midi and still use the name Vin de Pays d'Oc — much in the way that an Australian firm can name a wine "produce of South-East Australia".

■ **Vin de pays regulations** Each area has its list of permitted grape varieties, selected in the case of zonal *vins de pays* from a departmental list. In some cases maxima and minima of certain varieties are laid down: a minimum of 10 or 20% of "classic" grapes is sometimes stipulated to add flavour and distinction to other, less characterful, varieties.

Yields are controlled, though at quite high levels: 80hl/ha is normal for zonal *vins de pays*, though some set limits of 70hl/ha. Departmental *vins de pays* allow 90hl/ha — twice the yield of a top AOC.

Quite strict analytical standards are applied: these measure the minimum natural alcohol, the volatile acidity and the sulphur dioxide levels. A sample of wine from each vat is tested. A panel then tastes each batch before registering the wine as

Carved barrel-end at Louis Roederer Champagne.

being up to *vin de pays* standard. Labelling regulations forbid the use of the words "Château" or "Clos" — these are thought to belong to AOC wines — but "Domaine" is allowed. Unlike most AOCs, *vins de pays* can be labelled with their grape variety, and this is sometimes the main name used on labels.

■ **The future of vins de pays** Some areas have already proved themselves to the point that they have been promoted, or moved sideways, to the lists of VDQS and AOC wines. This implies that a certain style has been established, and that the wine is suitable for the more rigid rules of the senior grades. Other *vins de pays* may well fade away as no-one finds it sensible to use them. The amount of wine which could be *vin de pays* but is labelled *vin de table* — about half the total — shows that not all growers feel that the current system suits their needs.

Vins de tables
Fifty-five per cent of the French vineyard area produces *vin de table*, or simple table wine. This figure

includes the *vins de pays*. Most *vin de table* is red; most comes from the Midi, Provence and Corsica. Labels do not show region of origin, only the country: France. Vintage dates may not be used. Most are blended and sold under brand names.

Special wines
France abounds with specialities. Many AOCs produce sparkling as well as still wine; other zones concentrate on sweet wines.

■ **Sparkling wines** Many sparkling wines are made according to an *appellation contrôlée* — for example champagne and the various *crémants* of Bourgogne, Alsace and the Loire.

Other sparkling wines are made outside the AOC regulations. These employ one of the "industrial" techniques described on pp114–115. The grapes used may come from anywhere in France, or even from elsewhere in the EC. Such wines are labelled with a brand name and the words "Vin Mousseux".

■ **Vins doux naturels (VDNs)** The "natural sweetness" indicated by the name is brought about by fortification, which halts the fermentation and thus leaves grape sugars unfermented in the finished wines. Made according to traditional methods in the Languedoc and Roussillon regions, these wines, of which the best-known is Muscat de Beaumes-de-Venise (*see* p258), are mainly drunk in France, where they are prized as apéritifs. There are several types, and a range of appellations, mostly strung along the Mediterranean coast, which are described in further detail on p283.

■ **Vins de liqueur** Several parts of France have a tradition of adding unfermented grape juice to the local spirit to make a *vin de liqueur,* or *mistelle.* Despite the name, these are not wines. The Pineau des Charentes recipe, for instance, is one part cognac to three parts grape juice. Both ingredients should come from the same estate. The result is a sweet drink, usually white or amber in colour, but occasionally rosé. Production is regulated by an AOC. This is not the case for other *mistelles,* such as the Floc de Gascogne, the Macvin du Jura or the Ratafia from the Champagne region, which belong to the fiscal category of *vins de liqueur,* just as port, sherry and all kinds of imported fortified wines.

Reading a French wine label

Most French labels are models of clarity. The status of the wine will be obvious: look for the words "Appellation Contrôlée", "Vin Délimité de Qualité Supérieure", or "Vin de Pays", to establish region of origin and status. Table wines carry none of these terms, but must use the words "Vin de Table".

Each label includes the address of the person or firm bottling the wine. In the case of *vins de table*, this is sometimes a post code to avoid confusing the consumer by stating a name which is the same as that of an AOC. The first two digits of a French post code give the *département* in which the wine was bottled — not made, note, but bottled. This can

give a clue to the style of a table wine. Many *négociants* are based in Bordeaux (33 is Gironde), or the Loire (44 for the Pays Nantais, 49 for Angers and Saumur). A 21 code indicates the Côte-d'Or *département*, with 71 for the Mâcon and Chalon districts and 69 for Beaujolais. Merchants in Chablis use the code 89.

It is risky to deduce too much from the code, but wines do appear that are made from young vines in AOC vineyards. These can only be called "Vin de Table", and if this is suspected (or heavily hinted by words like "Jeunes Vignes" on the label) a glance at the code will give a

FRENCH WINE TERMS

Terms concerned with winemaking and description are defined in the glossary. Some words specific to France and likely to be found on labels or in wine lists include:

Millésime Vintage; year of production.
Mise en bouteilles au château/domaine Bottled at the estate where the wine is made.
Mise en bouteilles dans nos caves Bottled "in our cellars" — usually a *négociant.*
Négociant Merchant — shorthand term for a buyer of wine who then sells it to wholesalers and exporters. Many sorts and sizes of *négociants* exist:
Négociant-éleveur Buys, nurtures and sells wine. Often responsible for its selection, cellar care and maturation, bottling and then sales. Much concerned with exports.
Négociant-embouteilleur Engaged in bottling and stock-holding wine.
Négociant-expéditeur A shipper or transporter of wine from producing to consuming areas.
Vignoble A vineyard, and in France this can be just one plot, or an entire region: "the Bordeaux *vignoble*". There is no exact translation for the French usage: "winefield" has been tried, but has not caught on. "Wine region", "zone" or "district" are used in this book.
Propriétaire-récoltant Vineyard owner who also makes wines.
Vigneron A wine grower, sometimes a worker in a vineyard.

clue to where the wine comes from. It could, of course, have been trucked across France and merely bottled there. The risk is the buyers'.

The wine trade in France

More than half a million people grow grapes for wine in France, and around 100,000 of them grow grapes for AOC wines. Not all of these growers actually make wine: some sell their grapes to larger concerns, others take their grapes to a wine-producing cooperative. Those who make wine may not sell it under their own name; they may prefer to pass on their wine in bulk to a *négociant*, who blends it with wine from other sources and bottles it under his own label.

Different parts of France offer wines to the consumer in varying ways.

■ **The cooperatives** Winemaking cooperatives, owned by the growers, provide small growers with winemaking and marketing facilities. They date from the first decades of this century, when low prices were forcing *vignerons* from the land. Some co-ops have retained the basic winemaking standards of a generation ago; others have invested in modern equipment and even in oak barrels for ageing.

The best co-ops make it worth growers' while to produce good-quality grapes of classic varieties by paying a premium. Some co-ops even fly in Australian winemakers to advise on the vintage: Australia picks its grapes in February and March, so they are free to work in France in September and October. Those co-ops with a modern approach to winemaking and marketing are an excellent source of good-value wine.

■ **The négociants** Some *négociants* offer wines from individual properties, others blend wine from a range of suppliers and label it with their own name. Many firms do both. Most French wine finds its way into the hands of a *négociant* at some stage, the exceptions being cooperative wines and that sold direct by the grower. □

BORDEAUX

THE VINEYARDS AROUND BORDEAUX ARE THE GREATEST SOURCE
OF FINE WINE IN THE WORLD, AND ALSO OFFER
MANY GOOD, IF LESSER, WINES.

The grandeur of Château Pichon-Longueville Baron
demonstrates the prosperity and confidence of 19th-century
Bordeaux — and of its owners in the 1980s, who lavishly
restored the Pauillac Second-Growth's château.

Leave the great city of Bordeaux in any direction and you will pass through vineyards. The city is the capital of a wine region that can be fairly described as the most important on Earth. It is not the biggest, but it has arguably the finest red wines, and the finest sweet white ones. Then there is the sheer depth of quality: Bordeaux's vineyards supply copious amounts of good wine, and it is wine with individuality. A wine lover can spend a lifetime exploring the many châteaux of Bordeaux and the *appellations* into which they fall.

Bordeaux's wines are predominantly red. The white wines fall into two groups: dry from the Graves and other areas, and sweet ones headed by those from Sauternes. The red wines have a distinct flavour: there is more acidity, more liveliness, than in, say, the weightier wines of the Rhône. The personalities of the dominant Cabernet Sauvignon and Merlot grapes show through. While most red bordeaux show these traits, the best add more: ageing in oak produces an important set of nuances; the finest wines have more concentration, live longer in bottle and evolve in a more complex and a more interesting way. Bordeaux has centuries of experience in making fine wine: the Roman poet Ausonius praised it. The great estates, set on their privileged, gravelly *croupes*, were established early on (Pape-Clément in 1331). Haut-Brion was the first wine estate to sell its wine under its own name, as a branded product, when its owner had it shipped to London in 1660. The diarist Samuel Pepys, writing just three years later, left us a tasting note for "Ho Bryan", describing it as having "a good and most particular taste that I have never met with", and by the start of the 18th century fine wine, capable of improving as it aged, was born.

For centuries before this, England and other northern countries had been buying wine from Bordeaux. When Eleanor of Aquitaine, heiress to the entire western half of France, married Henry Plantagenet in 1152, England and Bordeaux became married too: an alliance that was to last for three centuries. The medieval English called Bordeaux red wine "claret" (from *clairet*) and drank an average of six bottles a head a year. The name claret — and the habit of drinking it — has lasted in England to this day.

Areas and wine styles

The map opposite shows how Bordeaux's vineyards are divided by the Gironde and Garonne into two zones: Left Bank, with its capital the city of Bordeaux, and Right Bank, centred on the smaller port of Libourne. These two have experienced differing histories and have distinct geographic conditions. They show different facets of the overall Bordeaux style of red wine. The Left Bank vineyards, the large Médoc and Graves districts, have always looked to Bordeaux and beyond, to export markets. There are many large estates and well-known châteaux here. Cabernet Sauvignon is the dominant red wine grape. The Right Bank wines — primarily St-Emilion and Pomerol, with a clutch of lesser ones — were shipped through the port of Libourne, or overland, and historically have been less involved with overseas trade. Estates here are typically smaller, and fewer châteaux are household names overseas. Merlot is the main grape variety.

Dry white wine is made in the large area of the Entre-deux-Mers, between the Graves and Libourne, and in Graves itself. Of these, only white Graves aspire to fine wine status. Sweet whites are also made, with the quality area famously concentrated on the left bank of the Garonne in Sauternes and Barsac and some less known appellations, such as Ste-Croix-du-Mont and Loupiac, on the right bank of the Garonne.

Wine on a grand scale

Bordeaux is important to the world's winelovers not just because it makes great wine but because it makes a lot of wine. The vineyards total around 115,000ha (284,000 acres) — bigger than the whole of Germany and four times bigger than California's Napa Valley, which can be considered the American equivalent of the Bordeaux region. The 1980s saw a big increase in the yield per hectare, and thus the amount of wine made from these vineyards: the figure of 5,500,000hl

— 60,000,000 cases of wine — was regularly exceeded. The first time 4,000,000hl was made was in 1979. This is all *appellation contrôlée* wine — only a small amount of non-AOC wine is made within the Gironde area.

Four bottles of bordeaux wine in five are red: this ratio has altered markedly since 1970, before which date there was regularly more white wine made than red.

The idea of the wine château

It was Bordeaux that invented the concept of the wine château. The word may conjure up images of a castle, with turrets and moats: some are like that, but only a few. No-one

APPELLATIONS AND LABELS

The Bordeaux vineyards are divided among 57 *appellations contrôlées* in several tiers. All vineyards of the Gironde *département* are entitled to grow AOC Bordeaux. Bordeaux Supérieur is the same but stricter rules apply for its production.

Within this area are three main groups of *appellations*. On the west, or Left Bank of the Gironde and Garonne rivers are, from south to north, the AOC Sauternes, Barsac, Graves, Pessac-Léognan and Médoc. To the east, on the Right Bank of the Gironde and Dordogne rivers are the Libournais AOC (St-Emilion, Pomerol, Fronsac), the Bourgeais and the Blayais. Between the two rivers is the fourth group: Entre-deux-Mers.

The main groups, such as Médoc, have inner *appellations*: examples are Margaux and St-Julien. These are communes, or parts of communes, and have higher standards than ordinary Médoc. Haut-Médoc is the southern and better half of the Médoc.

Most Bordeaux wine is sold under a château label. Its legal status is the AOC of the commune, but its brand-name, or identity, is the name of the château. Thus Château Lafite is AOC Pauillac, Château Pavie is AOC St-Emilion.

For Bordeaux's classifications *see* Médoc p146 and p149, Pessac-Léognan p159, Sauternes p164, St-Emilion p172.

knows exactly how many "châteaux" there are in Bordeaux — perhaps as many as 7,000, although perhaps only 1,000 actually deserve the term. Most of them are specialized farms of greater or lesser size or grandeur. Few aspire to the status of "château" as understood elsewhere in France.

The wine château in Bordeaux is a unit of land, often owned and farmed by one proprietor, where grapes are grown and wine is made. At the major châteaux, every process up to and including bottling is carried out at the château; very minor properties, on the other hand, will send their grapes or wine to the local cooperative to be turned into finished, bottled wine. Châteaux have vineyards varying in size from a few hectares to 150ha (370 acres) or more. Properties selling wine under their own names range from 20ha (50 acres) upwards — less in Pomerol and St-Emilion. The land may be in one block or in scattered parcels across a commune. Underlying the château concept is the idea of *terroir* (*see* p130) — the individuality of a particular patch of land. From the Bordeaux example has stemmed a worldwide movement towards "estate" wines.

Winemaking

Bordeaux is responsible for setting the styles for several of the world's favourite kinds of wine.

The making of red bordeaux is not complex. It differs little from the straightforward process described on pp112–113. What the Bordeaux winemakers and merchants evolved were two key processes: the *assemblage* and cask maturation. *Assemblage* is the blending of the wines from different grape varieties, and different parcels in the vineyard, to achieve a harmonious whole. This has been refined since the 1970s to involve tasting and selection vat by vat, with those below standard demoted to the château's "second wine" (*see* p149) or even to the commune *appellation*. Wine from young vines, or those in outlying parcels,

WINE REGIONS OF BORDEAUX

On the Left Bank of the Gironde and Garonne rivers are the Médoc, Pessac-Léognan, Graves and Sauternes *appellations*. On the Right Bank are the Libournais (St-Emilion, Pomerol and their "satellites") and the Entre-deux-Mers *appellations*.

Wine regions

- Médoc
- Pessac-Léognan
- Graves
- Sauternes, Barsac, Cérons, Loupiac, Ste-Croix-du-Mont
- Entre-deux-Mers
- Ste-Foy-Bordeaux
- Premières Côtes de Bordeaux
- Côtes de Bordeaux St-Macaire
- St-Emilion and satellites
- Pomerol, Lalande-de-Pomerol
- Côtes de Blaye
- Côtes de Bourg
- Bordeaux-Côtes de Francs
- Fronsac, Canon-Fronsac
- Côtes de Castillon
- Graves de Vayres
- Bordeaux

— Bordeaux appellation boundary
--- *département* boundary
— motorway
— major road
— other road

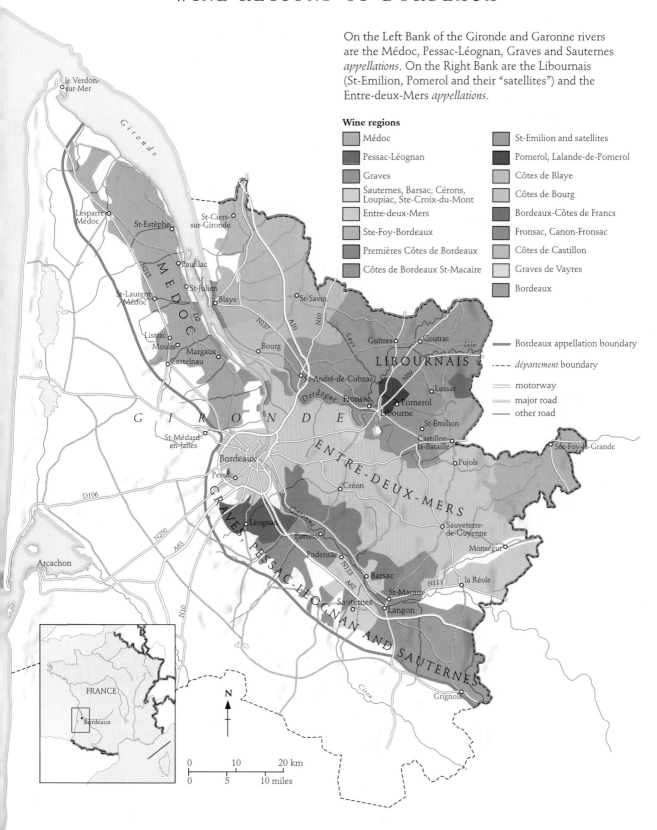

may be routinely removed from the blend. This selection process allows the château to maintain a consistent standard vintage after vintage. In the top properties, a poor vintage may result in more than half of the wine produced being excluded from the main château wine, the *Grand Vin*. Even a large but good vintage may see anything up to half the wine de-selected to maintain the concentration and quality of the *Grand Vin*.

Ageing in oak casks developed in Bordeaux from being a utilitarian way of storing and transporting, to being a vital part of the recipe for the finished wine. Each château makes its own decisions about whether to use new oak *barriques* and, if so, in what proportion; what kind of oak to use; and for how long. New oak adds character and taste to the wine (*see* p121) but not every wine can stand it: *petits châteaux* that use too much new oak can end up with claret that tastes of oak rather than grapes. A top château will use 100% new oak casks each year.

While all red bordeaux is made according to the same methods and from the same grape varieties, and most examples will show a common character, the variations in style can be considerable. The balance of the grape varieties grown makes a big difference: Merlot-dominated wines taste fuller, fatter and softer, and mature earlier, than those based upon Cabernet Sauvignon. The yield of the vineyard will have its effect on the concentration and character of the wine. The location of the vineyard will show in the final taste, with the various areas having their own styles, which are described in the chapters that follow. Once the grapes are picked, the various steps in the wine-making process, especially *assemblage* and ageing, will affect the taste. Rigour in selection and care in wine-making do make a difference, as châteaux show when they outper-form their neighbours — and the expectations set by their *terroir* — when in talented hands. The reverse is also true: a badly run estate can make wine well below the standard that its classification, position and status would suggest.

Over the centuries, the best land in Bordeaux has been planted with grapes, the varieties that perform best have been selected, and invest-ment in the vineyard maintained. So the top estates on the price (and clas-sification) lists are at the top for good reasons. They make a distinct style of red bordeaux: more concentrated, longer-lived, more complex than their *petits châteaux* cousins. Occa-sionally, a small estate rises above its classification, and there are whole areas (like Pomerol until the 1960s) that have been unjustly neglected. But the chance of a new star emerg-ing is far less than in, say, California, where all the options of site, variety and technique are still wide open.

The making of white wine has altered more than red, in Bordeaux and elsewhere, as new methods have

GRAPE VARIETIES

The classic grapes used in the Bordeaux region are described on pp34–41. Below are details of the effect these and other grapes used have on Bordeaux wines.

RED WINES

Bordeaux has established a "recipe" for claret that involves mixing three main and several lesser varieties. The proportions of the mixture are the decision of the winemaker; there is no insistence on one variety, as in Burgundy.

Cabernet Sauvignon   Dominant in the Médoc, especially in the classed growths, where it can be up to 80% of the blend. In the top AOCs (Pauillac, St-Julien, Margaux) the variety finds the well-drained gravel soils it thrives best on. Also important in red Graves. Less dominant in St-Emilion, where it appears in small proportions, or not at all, as the heavier limestone-based soils do not suit it (*see* St-Emilion quality factors, p173). Cabernet Sauvignon-based wines are long-lived, tannic when young, and capable of developing great finesse. Carmenère, a variety listed in the regulations, is another name for Cabernet Sauvignon.

Cabernet Franc   Plays the dominant role in St-Emilion, where it partners Merlot in most wines, but is a minority grape in the Médoc, Graves and most other red-wine districts. It gives less "structure" than Cabernet Sauvignon, but adds fruit and fine aromas.

Merlot   The key to Pomerol; the most important grape in much St-Emilion, and a part of the blend of most Médoc and Graves wines. Merlot brings colour, fruit and suppleness to the blend. It thrives on heavier (and thus colder) soils, where the Cabernets are unhappy.

Malbec   Once quite widely grown in the Médoc, where its early ripening and fruity, deep-coloured wine made it a useful wine to blend with the Cabernets. It has declined due to disease problems, and is now a minority variety.

Petit Verdot   Commonly grown in the Médoc, this variety ripens even later than Cabernet Sauvignon and appreciates warm years. Making up between 5 and 10% of the blends, it yields tannic, age-worthy, aromatic dark wines.

WHITE WINES

The balance between Sauvignon Blanc and Sémillon, the two main quality white wine grapes, alters according to the fashion of the decade and the style of wine required. Sauvignon, with lots of fresh, grassy aromas and a dry finish, became popular in the 1980s. Most white Graves and Sauternes use both, in varying proportions.

Sémillon   The most widely planted white variety, which is responsible for much ordinary white bordeaux and a small, but important, amount of great sweet wine. It can gain from the otherwise dreaded *botrytis* rot which concentrates its sweetness: *see* p163. For dry wines, and some sweet ones, it is blended with Sauvignon Blanc.

Sauvignon Blanc   Important in white Graves, in Sauternes as a minor partner with Sémillon, and in recent years planted widely for dry wines in the Entre-deux-Mers and outlying districts.

Muscadelle   A minor component of dry and sweet white wines, adding perfume and a pungent flavour.

Château Cheval-Blanc is one of the top estates in St-Emilion.

been developed since around 1970. The advent of stainless steel vats, modern presses and temperature control has made it possible for Bordeaux winemakers to make better use of their Sauvignon Blanc and Sémillon grapes, which now reveal pleasant fruity flavours, and to produce well-balanced wines that are enjoyable to drink. In recent years, the best Pessac-Léognan wines have thus reached the level of top quality whites and the vineyards of the Entre-deux-Mers now offer very good whites, which are excellent value for money.

The debate about which direction techniques should take is discussed on p158, and Sauternes' approach to sweet winemaking on p163.

Vintages and ageing

Bordeaux is the one wine region in the world (apart from Champagne) where the weather can make newspaper headlines. The Bordeaux wine trade has become adept, after centuries of practice, at proclaiming "vintages of the century" at least twice in each decade. It has an audience for its claims, and for its laments about poor weather, because Bordeaux is such a dominant name on the fine wine scene.

The location of the region, bordered by the Atlantic, gives it a maritime climate: *see* Quality Factors pages 150 and 173 for details. There is the constant danger of late winter frosts, a cool, wet spring, a damp summer, rain at harvest-time, hail at any time, all of which can affect the size and quality of the grape crop.

Vintages can thus differ markedly. The run of good years in the 1980s raised hopes that new techniques in vineyard and *chai* might have combated the effects of the weather and evened out the annual variations, and that the climate might have altered for the better. But, although the following decade started well with an excellent year, 1991, with a damaging April frost and then September rains, quieted the optimists. The next year was mediocre, while 1993 and 1994 would have been exceptional years but for the September rains. 1995 and 1996, above average, raised expectations which turned out to be too optimistic for the weak 1997. In 1998, wines from the Merlot grape proved much better than those from the Cabernet grape, while 1999 shows uneven results. Modern techniques, plus rigorous selection, have raised the quality of the wines of poor vintages from downright undrinkable to moderate, but nature alone can create the conditions needed for a great vintage.

Bordeaux's top red wines can age for 20 to 30 years and even longer. Great bottles from the 19th century are occcasionally opened with reverence and sampled in silence: the wine can be miraculously good. However, not every red bordeaux is designed to be aged, and it is unclear whether even the top wines as made today will age for as long as their predecessors. Wine merchants will point out exceptions, and some properties in lesser regions make wine to higher standards, but these wines normally get no oak ageing and are designed for drinking while young and fresh. Wines from *petits châteaux* from more noted regions, such as St-Emilion and Médoc, may gain in character and complexity for three to five years in bottle. Classed growths from the Graves, the Médoc and St-Emilion may improve for longer, depending on the vintage. Only the classed growths of the top *appellations*, such as Margaux, Pauillac and St-Julien, will stand decades of ageing.

In general, and it is a generalization set about with exceptions, red wines from the Left Bank (Médoc and Graves) age for longer than those from the Right Bank (St-Emilion and Pomerol). Of course, vintage variation matters too: the 1975 and 1976 wines, both hailed as successes at the time of their birth, have evolved very differently, with the '76s mostly well past their best within 15 years and the '75s taking a long time to emerge from their tannic, heavy shells.

Classifications

Bordeaux in general, and the Médoc in particular, is the land of hierarchies. These widely-traded wines have depended on giving customers clear signals of quality and price, and the 1855 Classification (*see* right) was one of several 19th-century lists drawn up by the wine trade. All the classed growths, as the 1855 châteaux are called, are profiled on the pages that follow.

Classifications existed before 1855: the surviving correspondence of the brokers, merchants and estate stewards of the 18th century is full of mentions of first, second and even third growths. The "Firsts" have remained constant since 1700: Margaux, Haut-Brion, Lafite and Latour, with Mouton coming into the list in the 19th century and officially promoted in 1973. Elsewhere in the

Gironde, the classifications have been, and are, less elaborate. Sauternes was classified at the same time as the Médoc, but Graves had to wait until 1953, and St-Emilion until 1956 (*see* following chapters). Classification implies that the château so honoured is a fixed unit of land. This is not so: a proprietor can buy additional vineyards within the AOC and, even if the land was not part of a classed growth, it becomes so the moment it moves into classed-growth ownership. However, this was challenged by the authorities in 1986 when the St-Emilion classification was revised, and a *Premier Grand Cru* château was demoted for doubling its size. □

THE 1855 CLASSIFICATION

The 1855 Classification (as amended by the 1973 promotion of Ch Mouton Rothschild to Premier Cru status) is still in force. It covers the red-wine châteaux of the Médoc, with one Pessac-Léognan property, Haut-Brion. Châteaux are placed in five classes, from one (the highest) to five. The commission that compiled the list used as a benchmark the prices of each château's wines over the previous century. Some wines have risen in status since 1855, some have fallen, but the classification is still in use today. It shows that by the mid-19th century the landowners of the Médoc had singled out and planted the best land.

Premiers Crus

Ch Lafite-Rothschild, Pauillac
Ch Latour, Pauillac
Ch Margaux, Margaux
Ch Haut-Brion, Pessac-Léognan
Ch Mouton Rothschild, Pauillac

Deuxièmes Crus

Ch Rausan-Ségla, Margaux
Ch Rauzan-Gassies, Margaux
Ch Léoville Las-Cases, St-Julien
Ch Léoville Poyferré, St-Julien
Ch Léoville Barton, St-Julien
Ch Durfort-Vivens, Margaux
Ch Lascombes, Margaux
Ch Gruaud-Larose, St-Julien
Ch Brane-Cantenac, Cantenac-Margaux
Ch Pichon-Longueville Baron, Pauillac
Ch Pichon-Longueville Comtesse de Lalande, Pauillac
Ch Ducru-Beaucaillou, St-Julien
Ch Cos d'Estournel, St-Estèphe
Ch Montrose, St-Estèphe

Troisièmes Crus

Ch Giscours, Labarde-Margaux
Ch Kirwan, Cantenac-Margaux
Ch d'Issan, Cantenac-Margaux

Ch Lagrange, St-Julien
Ch Langoa Barton, St-Julien
Ch Malescot-St-Exupéry, Margaux
Ch Cantenac-Brown, Cantenac-Margaux
Ch Palmer, Cantenac-Margaux
Ch La Lagune, Ludon
Ch Desmirail, Margaux
Ch Calon-Ségur, St-Estèphe
Ch Ferrière, Margaux
Ch Marquis d'Alesme Becker, Margaux
Ch Boyd-Cantenac, Cantenac-Margaux

Quatrièmes Crus

Ch St-Pierre, St-Julien
Ch Branaire-Ducru, St-Julien
Ch Talbot, St-Julien
Ch Duhart-Milon-Rothschild, Pauillac
Ch Pouget, Cantenac-Margaux
Ch La Tour Carnet, St-Laurent
Ch Lafon-Rochet, St-Estèphe
Ch Beychevelle, St-Julien
Ch Prieuré-Lichine, Cantenac-Margaux
Ch Marquis de Terme, Margaux

Cinquièmes Crus

Ch Pontet-Canet, Pauillac
Ch Batailley, Pauillac
Ch Grand-Puy-Lacoste, Pauillac
Ch Grand-Puy-Ducasse, Pauillac
Ch Haut-Batailley, Pauillac
Ch Lynch-Bages, Pauillac
Ch Lynch-Moussas, Pauillac
Ch Dauzac, Labarde-Margaux
Ch d'Armailhac (formerly Mouton Baron Philippe), Pauillac
Ch du Tertre, Arsac-Margaux
Ch Haut-Bages Libéral, Pauillac
Ch Pédesclaux, Pauillac
Ch Belgrave, St-Laurent
Ch de Camensac, St-Laurent
Ch Cos Labory, St-Estèphe
Ch Clerc-Milon, Pauillac
Ch Croizet-Bages, Pauillac
Ch Cantemerle, Macau

WINE DISTRICTS OF THE MEDOC, GRAVES, SAUTERNES

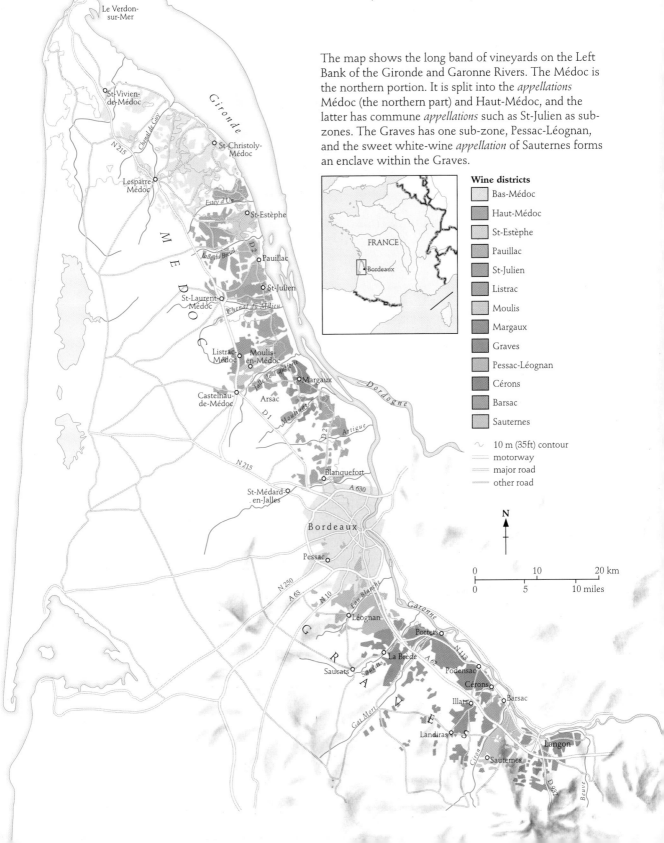

The map shows the long band of vineyards on the Left Bank of the Gironde and Garonne Rivers. The Médoc is the northern portion. It is split into the *appellations* Médoc (the northern part) and Haut-Médoc, and the latter has commune *appellations* such as St-Julien as sub-zones. The Graves has one sub-zone, Pessac-Léognan, and the sweet white-wine *appellation* of Sauternes forms an enclave within the Graves.

Wine districts

Bas-Médoc
Haut-Médoc
St-Estèphe
Pauillac
St-Julien
Listrac
Moulis
Margaux
Graves
Pessac-Léognan
Cérons
Barsac
Sauternes

10 m (35ft) contour
motorway
major road
other road

MÉDOC

The Médoc is an isolated, almost withdrawn place. It is cut off from most of France by the wide brown waters of the Gironde, and from the rest of the world by the Atlantic Ocean. The wine country is a thin band stretching down the eastern side of the Médoc peninsula, between the estuary and the great forest of the Landes, which filters the Atlantic's cooling breezes. This position, allied to some unique subsoil, makes its unremarkable, gentle, gravelly slopes produce great wine.

The key quality factors in the Médoc's environment are analysed on p150. The other ingredients in greatness are the grape varieties which have evolved as the local choice, and Bordeaux's heritage as an international port. Médoc wine, along with that of Graves, was discovered long ago by the northern Europeans, who have bought wine from Bordeaux since Roman times. The great châteaux of the Médoc — Margaux, Latour and Lafite — were known as suppliers of top-class wine three centuries ago. A steady demand from an international clientele enabled the owners of the châteaux to invest in the vineyards, plant the best Cabernet Sauvignon and other vines, drain the subsoil, and construct the best *chais* and *cuviers*.

The châteaux

Prosperity gave the Médoc another legacy: the châteaux. There are more great wine estates here than in any other area in the world, and many of them have symbols of their greatness in their buildings. Proprietors have celebrated their ownership and wealth by building in a variety of styles. There are a few medieval survivors and some later gems· medieval Château Lamarque and 17th-century Château d'Issan are both very fine. Most, though, date from the late 18th

One of St-Estèphe's leading châteaux.

and 19th centuries. The grand turrets and façades of these mansions add a note of distinction to an otherwise

monotonous landscape. The mansions are only one facet of the châteaux: more vital to the wine are the *chais*, the great, grey buildings that house the wine. These overground cellars are unique to the region.

Grape varieties and wine styles

The predominant grape of the Médoc *appellations* is Cabernet Sauvignon, which is blended in varying proportions with Merlot, Cabernet Franc, Malbec and Petit Verdot. The exact proportion of Cabernet Sauvignon in a châteaux's wine is a useful signpost to the style: more Cabernet spells a longer-lived, more austere wine.

A greater contributor to style is the position and status of the vineyard. The top châteaux — mostly those classified in 1855 (*see* p146) — adopt the selection and ageing techniques described on p142. They grow more Cabernet, less Merlot. They

THE MEDOC APPELLATIONS

There is a clear hierarchy of *appellations* in the Médoc:

AOC Médoc   Once this was called Bas-Médoc, the area being lower down the Gironde, but the growers objected and the "Bas" was removed from the AOC. Here, in a big sweep of land north and north-west of St-Seurin, are many small châteaux and some sizeable estates. Much of the wine is made by cooperatives and bought by the merchants who sell blended Médocs.

The land is mostly woods, pasture and marsh, with the vines clustered on gravel mounds. *See* p157 for châteaux.

AOC Haut-Médoc   This *appellation* is a catch-all for every patch of vineyard in the southern half of the region not in either the four prestige riverside *appellations*, or Moulis or Listrac. It extends from the suburbs of Bordeaux in the south up to St-Seurin de Cardonne, north of St-Estèphe.

Most of the land is away from the Gironde, divided from it by Margaux, St-Julien, Pauillac and St-Estèphe. The exceptions are in the south, around Ludon-Médoc and Macau; in a central gap between Margaux and St-Julien, where the communes of Lamarque and Cussac have some good sites; and in the north at St-Seurin.

Five of the *Crus Classés* of the 1855 list (*see* p146) are in Haut-Médoc. There are many more *Crus Bourgeois* and a host of minor growers, many of whom sell their wine through cooperatives, while others search for a market under their own name as *petits châteaux*, capitalizing on the magic name Haut-Médoc on their labels. *See* p157 for châteaux.

Commune AOCs   These, described in detail in the following pages, are the top level of the Médoc hierarchy, covering the good vineyard land in five single communes or (in the case of AOC Margaux) several communes.

occupy the best-drained, gravel-soil land. Away from the favoured *terroirs,* châteaux adapt to heavier soils by planting more Merlot. They use less new oak for ageing. The resulting wines are softer; more agreeable in youth but with less ageing potential. The best estates tend to have old vines. A property which is replanted, perhaps following a period of neglect, will need a decade or more to return to its full potential.

Médoc red wines are distinguishable from St-Emilions and other Right Bank wines by their more austere, refined style and the characteristic aromas and flavours of Cabernet Sauvignon.

The Crus Bourgeois

The 1855 classification of the Médoc classed-growth châteaux is listed on p146. Below the classed growths in prestige (and usually price) are the *Crus Bourgeois.* The term and idea were in use as early as the Middle Ages, and not only with regard to wines of the Médoc. The first formal listings date from a 1932 committee of wine brokers and counted 444 *Crus Bourgeois,* of which 99 were classified as *Supérieurs* and 6 as *Supérieurs Exceptionnels.* However, this classification failed to establish itself in the way that the 1855 classed-growth list had done.

In 1962, a Syndicate of Crus Bourgeois started to draw up a new classification, followed by others, but none received official recognition. The EU authorities tolerate the term on labels, but have refused to include it in the official hierarchy.

Finally, in 2001, a decree issued by the French Ministry of Agriculture laid down conditions for a true classification made up of three categories. The official classification was published in June 2003, listing 247 *Crus Bourgeois,* 8 *Crus Bourgeois Supérieurs,* and 9 *Crus Bourgeois Exceptionnels.* As of the 2003 vintage, these are the only wines allowed to bear the term *Cru Bourgeois* on their label. ☐

The classed growths of the Médoc are large enough, and well-enough known, to select only the best vats for the *grand vin,* the wine sold under the château's main label. What is left after this selection goes into a "second wine" sold under another label. There are no regulations other than those of the *appellation*: what is in the wine is up to the château. But, even though these wines are made from vines that are classed growths or *Crus Bourgeois,* their producers lose, of course, the right to refer to these distinctions on the label. The wine may come from outlying vineyards, from young vines, from vats of wine considered below standard, or from any combination of the above. The selection will vary with the vintage: a good vintage will make a good second wine. A ripe year, such as 1982 or 1986, may have produced an abundant Merlot crop. In order to keep the balance of the *grand vin* as they want it, proprietors will downgrade Merlot vats to the second wine, which will then taste more like a Pomerol than a Médoc.

Latour's archives show that it made a second wine over 200 years ago, and others began early in the 20th century. Château-bottling in the post-World War II era, and the consequent control acquired by the châteaux over their wines, has led to more second wines.

The harvests of the 1980s made selection more vital and provided more wine for second labels. The second wines, from being a speciality known only to the wine trade, came to the notice of consumers.

Second wines are less concentrated and should therefore be drunk sooner. They vary considerably, depending on the status of the parent wine and the selection policy.

Some château proprietors use the name of another château they own as the second-wine label. The buyer is left to wonder if any of the wine comes from the named estate, or if it is just de-selected wine from the great estate.

Occasionally, a "third wine" is produced. A few top estates sell some wine from young vines as straightforward commune AOC wine, entitled to be called just Pauillac, St-Julien, etc. Much of this wine vanishes into *négociants'* blends.

SOME SECOND WINES

First Growths
Lafite-Rothschild: Les Carruades
Latour: Les Forts de Latour
Margaux: Pavillon Rouge du Château Margaux

Second Growths
Brane-Cantenac: Notton
Cos d'Estournel: Pagodes de Cos
Ducru-Beaucaillou: La Croix
Dufort-Vivens: Domaine de Cure-Bourse
Gruaud-Larose: Sarget de Gruaud-Larose
Lascombes: Ségonnes
Léoville Las-Cases: Clos du Marquis
Léoville Poyferré: Moulin-Riche
Montrose: La Dame de Montrose
Pichon-Baron: Les Tourelles de Longueville
Pichon-Lalande: Réserve de la Comtesse
Rauzan-Ségla: Segla

Third Growths
Calon-Ségur: Marquis de Ségur
Cantenac-Brown: Canuet
Lagrange: Fiefs de Lagrange
La Lagune: Le Moulin de Ludon
Malescot-Saint-Exupéry: La Dame de Malescot
Palmer: Alter Ego

Fourth Growths
Beychevelle: Amiral de Beychevelle
Duhart-Milon-Rothschild: Moulin de Duhart
Marquis de Terme: des Gondats
Prieuré-Lichine: de Clairefont
Talbot: Connétable de Talbot

Fifth Growths
Grand-Puy-Ducasse: Artigues-Arnaud
Grand-Puy-Lacoste: Lacoste-Borie
Lynch-Bages: Haut-Bages-Avérous
Pontet-Canet: Les-Hauts-de-Pontet

Crus Bourgeois
Caronne-Ste-Gemme: Parc Rouge de Caronne
Castéra : Bourbon la Chapelle
Chasse-Spleen: L'Oratoire de Chasse-Spleen
Citran: Moulin-de-Citran
Gloria: Peymartin
Labegorce-Zédé: Admiral
Meyney: Prieuré-de-Meyney
Ormes-Sorbet: Conques
Phélan Ségur: Frank Phélan
Siran: S de Siran
Sociando-Mallet: La Demoiselle
Tour-de-By: Roque de By

QUALITY FACTORS

This cross-section through the geology and subsoil of Pauillac, and the key map, show the great beds of gravel that were deposited here by the Gironde. These lie over the bedrock, which is limestone with pockets of clay. The greatest Médoc vineyards are sited on the deepest gravel banks, called *croupes*. The gravel and the limestone beneath it provide good drainage.

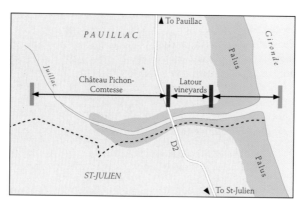

THE MEDOC: SITE AND SOIL

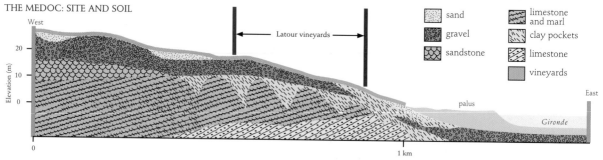

sand

gravel

sandstone

limestone and marl

clay pockets

limestone

vineyards

Position

The vineyard of Château Latour, a First Growth, occupies a gravel bank above the flat riverside *palus* land. The relatively steep slope towards the river is important, as it improves drainage (*see below*) and also allows cool air to ebb away, lessening the danger of frost.

Other great châteaux are also on gravel beds, which are less dominant, further west.

The gravel soil

The gravel soil of the Médoc shows clearly in the picture. A misleading term: the largest stones are plainly pebbles rather than gravel. The stones ensure good drainage; the intervening soil is sandy. Below, a thin topsoil, made up of sandy-clayey gravels, gives way to a firm but penetrable subsoil, which may be sandy gravels (Mouton), limestone (Margaux) or clay (Latour). The combination of these layers has three advantages: the soil and subsoil offer a meagre environment so that the vine produces only small harvests; the penetrable subsoil allows the old vines to push their roots down to depths of 4–5m (13–16ft); and the high permeability does not allow water to be retained or to stagnate.

The rainfall pattern

The rainfall pattern of the Médoc is greatly affected by the shelter provided by the great belt of forest to the west of the vineyards.

The map shows the average rainfall in millimetres in the important month of July. Rain-bearing winds from the west cross the forest country and deposit much of the moisture on the western side of the Médoc, before they reach the vineyards.

Growers hope for a relatively dry summer and autumn, which will encourage ripening of the grapes and provide the best harvest conditions. Winter and spring rain is more welcome, but on the whole the Médoc has more than enough rainfall, and the wet years are more to be feared than the dry ones.

Gravel soil in Pauillac.

Drainage

Gravel soil provides good drainage, and the underlying subterranean water-courses improve it further. Beneath the top soil are the vestiges of the drainage pattern formed when the Gironde's level was lower than it is today. These speed rainwater away from the vineyards. Despite this, the château proprietors have sunk large sums into drains.

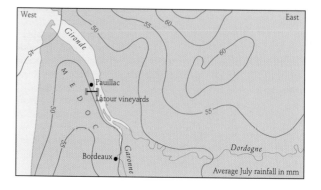

Average July rainfall in mm

ST-ESTEPHE

Here, in the far north of the Haut-Médoc, the land is open, with fewer trees; the vineyards lie on heavier, clay-based soils compared to those further south, and the wines are generally less prestigious. Formerly, they were also considered slow to mature. This is still true of some top châteaux, but much St-Estèphe is now made in a faster-maturing style, with more Merlot in the blend. The St-Estèphe style of wine is still, however, more acidic than that found in Pauillac or St-Julien. This is strict red-wine country.

THE APPELLATION

The commune borders Pauillac, and the southernmost St-Estèphe châteaux, such as Cos d'Estournel, look south across a wide marshy valley to Lafite and Mouton. Indeed, Lafite has a small patch of land across the border in St-Estèphe. To the north is the Médoc *appellation* area, with fewer gravel banks and wilder, marshier land. St-Estèphe has only five classed growths among its châteaux. Here, though, the wine lover will find a good range of affordable clarets, including some famous *Crus Bourgeois*.

Ch Andron-Blanquet

Cru Bourgeois A well-sited 16-ha (40-acre) vineyard on the southern edge of the area, close to Cos d'Estournel, making strong, rich wines which need time to age in the bottle.

Ch Beau-Site

Cru Bourgeois Supérieur A finely-sited vineyard indeed, with the view of the river that locals say good wine demands. The wines are well-made, fleshy and long-lived.

Ch Le Boscq

Cru Bourgeois Supérieur This 16-ha (40-acre) vineyard has been rented out to the *négociant* Dourthe since 1995. The estate has since made regular progress with wine made from equal parts Merlot and Cabernet Sauvignon, to which is added some Petit Verdot. The successful, deep-coloured and very ripe 2000 vintage gives a good idea of the estate's potential.

Ch Calon-Ségur

3ème Cru Classé The most northerly of the Médoc classed growths, sited just outside St-Estèphe village. Long-lasting, solid wines, particularly from the 1995 vintage onwards.

Ch Chambert-Marbuzet

Cru Bourgeois Supérieur Same owners as Haut-Marbuzet (*qv*); makes enjoyable, approachable wine which is ready quite quickly.

Ch Cos d'Estournel

2ème Cru Classé Well-known both for its odd, orientally styled château, whose façade hides the *chais,* and for the consistent excellence of its wine. There is 40% Merlot, and winemaking resorts to the latest technology; but the wines have remained classic in style. Jean-Guillaume Prats, son of Bruno, the former owner, is a brilliant winemaker, who now works for SA Domaine Reybier, the new owner of this 65-ha (161-acre) vineyard.

Ch Cos Labory

5ème Cru Classé Next door to Cos d'Estournel, but different in style: straightforward and early-maturing. Recent vintages have improved.

Ch Le Crock

Cru Bourgeois Supérieur A handsome château whose vineyard borders those of Montrose and Cos d'Estournel. Its impressive wines have remained classic in style. Under the aegis of the Cuvelier family, the château has been renovated and the wineries have been entirely redone.

Ch Haut-Beauséjour

Cru Bourgeois Taken over by Champagne Roederer in 1992, this 20-ha (49-acre) vineyard is planted mainly with Merlot — and 40% Cabernet-Sauvignon — producing characteristic, firm and well-balanced wines.

Ch Haut-Marbuzet

Cru Bourgeois Exceptionnel The vines overlook the river in the south-east corner of the AOC. New oak and competent winemaking produce well-regarded, deep-coloured and high-flavoured wines.

Ch Lafon-Rochet

4ème Cru Classé A fine vineyard facing south towards Lafite, with old vines. There is 55% Cabernet Sauvignon. The best vintages produce a good long-keeping wine.

Ch Lilian Ladouys

Cru Bourgeois Supérieur Another revived château, well-placed on the southern rim of the plateau, and with 48ha (119 acres) of mostly old vines in scattered parcels.

Ch Meyney

Cru Bourgeois Supérieur The Cordier firm of *négociants* own Meyney and ensure its high standards and wide distribution. One of the best *Crus Bourgeois*, and one of the classic St-Estèphes, it is high-flavoured and easy to enjoy.

Ch Montrose

2ème Cru Classé A riverside vineyard, perfectly placed on a slope above the Gironde. The solid, fleshy, long-lasting wines suggest a St-Estèphe version of Latour — as does the site — though the style has softened since the 1989 vintage, after a change in winemaking techniques. In good vintages — such as 1990 and 1996 — among the Médoc's best wines.

Ch les Ormes de Pez

Cru Bourgeois Exceptionnel Owned by the Cazes family of Lynch-Bages (*see* Pauillac), les Ormes de Pez makes easy to enjoy, modern-style wines.

Ch de Pez

Cru Bourgeois Exceptionnel Since the estate has been taken over by Jean-Claude Rouzand of Champagne Roederer, in 1995, the 26-ha (64-acre) vineyard, the winery and the château have all been entirely renovated. These efforts were rewarded by excellent vintages in 1998 and 1999.

Ch Phélan-Ségur

Cru Bourgeois Exceptionnel This property was hit by consistency problems in the early 1980s, but much progress has been made recently, since this 26-ha (64-acre) vineyard was bought up by the Gardinier family. The revival of Phélan-Ségur goes back to 1986 and has been confirmed by the excellent vintages of 1996 and 1998.

Ch Tronquoy-Lalande

Cru Bourgeois Supérieur A familiar wine in export markets, made in the solid St-Estèphe style. The estate's long-keeping wines have firm tannins and always need patience.

PAUILLAC

With three out of the Médoc's four First Growths, and a galaxy of other star châteaux, Pauillac is perhaps the most familiar Médoc commune name. Its wines show a constant style: the Cabernet Sauvignon grape dominates, giving a powerful, long-lived wine that smells and tastes of blackcurrants, cedar-wood and a certain dusty spiciness that immediately suggests Pauillac. Tasters stress the elegance of Pauillac, allied to a structure that allows the best wines to rise to their full stature over perhaps three decades.

THE APPELLATION

There are 18 classed growths, which between them own much of the land, so this is not an AOC for bargain-hunters. Value is to be found in the second (even third) wines of the great châteaux (*see* p149), and the great wines themselves should be appreciated occasionally, for they set standards for the world.

This is red-wine country, with a tiny proportion of white: Mouton-Rothschild makes a white wine, but they are alone among the Pauillac châteaux.

Ch d'Armailhac

5ème Cru Classé Owned by the Rothschilds of Mouton, and called Mouton-Baron-Philippe until 1989, d'Armailhac once formed part of the Mouton estate. The vineyards are adjacent but separate. The wine is classic Pauillac, with less potential to age than its First-Growth neighbour.

Ch Batailley

5ème Cru Classé Long-lived wine is made in an old-fashioned style at a 55-ha (136-acre) estate in the south-west of the commune.

Ch Clerc-Milon

5ème Cru Classé The land is to the east of the great pair of Rothschild First Growths in the north of the commune, with the château itself in the hamlet of Mousset. Clerc-Milon has belonged to the Rothschilds of Mouton since 1970, and a long programme of replanting and modernization is slowly producing results, with the duo of 1985 and 1986 attracting praise.

Ch Croizet-Bages

5ème Cru Classé Unusually for Pauillac, Cabernet Sauvignon is not the main variety here: it is outnumbered by the Merlot and Cabernet Franc vines. The style is thus softer and more open, and the wines mature quite quickly.

Ch Duhart-Milon

4ème Cru Classé Part of the Rothschild jigsaw puzzle on the northern plateau of le Pouyalet, this 63-ha (156-acre) vineyard (which has no actual château) is owned by the Lafite Rothschilds. The land is to the west of Lafite and Mouton, and is bounded to the north by the little Jalle de Breuil stream. The vintages since 1983 have begun to fulfil the potential of the site.

Ch Grand-Puy-Ducasse

5ème Cru Classé New owners have bought more land to bring the vineyard to 40ha (99 acres) and have renovated the château, which is in the centre of Pauillac, away from the vineyard. A wine of consistent standard and classic Pauillac taste, which often represents good value.

Ch Grand-Puy-Lacoste

5ème Cru Classé The Borie family, the owners of Ducru-Beaucaillou (St-Julien), bought this old estate in 1980 and have modernized and improved it, conjuring still better wine from an excellent vineyard of 50ha (124 acres) on the Bages plateau. The style is fruity yet well-structured.

Ch Haut-Bages Libéral

5ème Cru Classé This vineyard, owned by the Merlaut family, is well-placed, with a parcel next to Latour. As with so many Pauillac properties, modernization and replanting have been producing results, with wines that do better justice to the quality of the site and of the grape varieties. Good vintages (such as 1985, 1986 and 1990) are long keepers.

Ch Haut-Batailley

5ème Cru Classé Run by the Borie family (*see* Ducru-Beaucaillou, St-Julien), a 22-ha (54-acre) property without a château but with a name for good wine that matures relatively fast.

Ch Lafite-Rothschild

1er Cru Classé Travellers entering Pauillac from the north glimpse Lafite's modest château, almost hidden behind garden walls and the sizeable *chais*. The 94-ha (232-acre) vineyard is superbly placed on the rim of the northern Pauil-lac plateau, facing across the Jalle de Breuil to St-Estèphe. The soil is gravel (finer here than at Latour in the south), the drainage good. Situation has made Lafite a First Growth since the term was first coined in the early 18th century. It was at this time that Lafite belonged to the great Marquis de Ségur, who also owned both neighbouring Mouton and Latour. It was de Ségur who fixed the boundary between the vineyards of Mouton and Lafite, which in his day were one. Lafite was bought by the Paris bankers the Rothschilds in 1868, and is still owned by them. For many years the estate fell below the heights reached in the 18th and 19th centuries, but since Baron Eric de Rothschild took over as director in 1974 there has been steady improvement. Lafite was the wine to match in the great vintages of the 1980s. Today its wines make a fascinating comparison with neighbouring Mouton, and with Latour at the other end of the commune.

Lafite has 70% Cabernet Sauvignon, compared to Mouton's 85%; and Lafite's 15% Merlot (Mouton: 8%) shows in its lighter style. Lafite is generally held to be the most graceful, refined, even delicate of the First Growths. This quality is balanced by concentration and structure. The result can be almost indestructible: critics predict the 1982 to have a life of 40 years. Only millionaires will be able to watch it mature.

Ch Latour

1er Cru Classé The wines of Latour have been sought after since the Middle Ages. The boundaries of the four-square central block of vineyard have remained unchanged ever since: it is on two gentle riverside mounds of deep gravel which offer perfect drainage, good protection from severe weather and easy access to the Gironde. The whole vineyard is only 60ha (148 acres) — just two-thirds the size of Lafite — and this includes the perimeter plots not used in the *Grand Vin*.

Latour's old-fashioned Cabernet Sauvignon-based style made it a legend for longevity. Modernization — it was the first Médoc estate to install stainless steel vats — has tamed the wine a little, but hardly changed its deep, dark, sturdy character. The excellence of the *terroir* allows Latour to make good wines in poor years. In good years it offers up a dark, chewy monster of a wine that demands patience measured in decades. The impatient turn to its second wine, Les Forts de Latour, and to the occasional bottlings of AOC Pauillac, whose label is graced with Latour's trademark tower.

After 30 years of British ownership, Latour returned to a French owner, businessman François Pinault, in 1993.

Ch Lynch-Bages

5ème Cru Classé Traditional wine from modern equipment is the Cazes family's philosophy here, an approach that bred some of the best wines of the Médoc in the decade 1981–1991. The style is supple and accessible, yet with the concentration and depth of flavour of a truly good Pauillac. A large and superbly sited vineyard of 90ha (222 acres) on fine gravel *croupes* means it is in ample supply. Château Haut-Bages-Avérous is the second wine.

Ch Lynch-Moussas

5ème Cru Classé Yet another château that has shown form after a major renewal programme. The vineyard has 30% Merlot, producing wines in the lighter style which are good value.

Ch Mouton Rothschild

1er Cru Classé. See profile.

Ch Pédesclaux

5ème Cru Classé Small, little-known, but reliable in recent vintages, this estate has only 25ha (62 acres).

Ch Pibran

Cru Bourgeois Supérieur A small estate under the same ownership as Pichon-Baron (*qv*), i.e. the French insurance concern AXA. The château produces deep-coloured wine in a fruity yet muscular style.

Ch Pichon-Longueville Baron

2ème Cru Classé The two Pichons glare at each other across the D2 road just south of the hamlet of St-Lambert. Latour stands back, its entrance beside the contrasting pair of Pichon châteaux, which both date from the Médoc's "golden age" in the mid-19th century. Pichon-Baron — as it is often abbreviated — is west of the road, its turreted château now restored, flanked by an architecturally controversial new *chai* and mirrored in a giant pool. The money for this comes from insurance giant AXA, which owns this and several other châteaux. AXA brought in Jean-Michel Cazes (owner of Ch Lynch-Bages) to run Ch Pichon-Baron.

The vineyard is to the south of the château, facing Latour across the road. With several plots of land added recently, it now covers more than 68ha (168 acres) of vines.

Ch Pichon-Longueville Comtesse de Lalande

2ème Cru Classé Madame May-Eliane de Lencquesaing has stamped her demanding personality on the wines, and the image, of her estate. The results have been spectacular, with Pichon-Comtesse sometimes outpointing the First Growths in competitive tastings. The style is influenced by the *encépagement*: only 45% Cabernet Sauvignon and a high 35% Merlot, making the wine softer and more opulent than most Pauillacs. The château is on the east side of the D2, in an enclave of Latour land. The vineyard is partly in Pauillac and partly (a third) across the Juillac stream in St-Julien.

The second wine is called Réserve de la Comtesse. Because of the rigorous selection policy here, the second wine contains excellent material and is well-regarded in its own right.

Ch Pontet-Canet

5ème Cru Classé A large (78ha/193 acres) and well-placed vineyard, just south of Mouton's. In the mid-1970s, the château, which was very famous during the early 20th century, was bought up by Guy Tesseron, who has produced excellent wines, the best vintages being those of the late 1980s.

CHATEAU MOUTON-ROTHSCHILD

The domaine was a Second Growth until 1973, but due to the brilliant persistence of the late Baron Philippe de Rothschild it was promoted: the only change ever made in the 1855 Classification.

The 75ha (185 acres) of vines lie next to Lafite. There is more Cabernet Sauvignon than at Lafite: 85%, even more than at Latour. Great vintages are incredibly long-lived: opulent, dense and complex. Almost two decades of superb wines (1982, 1985, 1986, 1988, 1989, 1990 and 1998) have only heightened the property's fame.

The château is not impressive, but visitors flock to the superb museum of wine-inspired works of art. Each Mouton vintage is being assigned a work of art reproduced on the label.

ST-JULIEN

Compact and distinctive, St-Julien is the smallest Médoc *appellation* (896ha/2,214 acres), but has a great name, with 11 *Crus Classés* out of a total of some 40 wine producers. The style of wine varies with the château, but when generalizing about St-Julien, tasters tend to use words like quality, consistency and concentration. A typical St-Julien has more finesse than a Pauillac and more structure than a Margaux. Most of the wine is red but, as elsewhere in Médoc, there are also some AOC Bordeaux white wines.

THE APPELLATION
St-Julien takes up a slice of the vinegrowing Médoc between Pauillac, to the north, and the Cussac and de Lamarque AOC Haut-Médoc vineyards to the south. Two east-flowing streams, or *jalles*, form the northern and southern boundaries. The land comprises a series of bold gravel banks, well-drained by the *jalles* and the Gironde.

Ch Beychevelle
4ème Cru Classé A grand 18th-century château, offering distant views across meadows on the banks of the Gironde, with 85ha (210 acres) of vines along the edge of the plateau. The wine is lush and delicious, and in good vintages it ages well. The second wine here is Amiral de Beychevelle.

Ch Branaire-Ducru
4ème Cru Classé The château is close to Beychevelle, but the vineyard consists of plots scattered around the commune. The wine therefore does not show the refined "riverside" elegance of its neighbours, though it does have body and perfume.

Ch Ducru-Beaucaillou
2ème Cru Classé The Borie family owns, and lives at, the château, whose vines stand along the riverside rim of the gravel banks. A consistent quality (especially since 1993) is the hallmark of the wine, which is made in the old-fashioned way. A large proportion of the estate's wine is demoted to the second label, La Croix, thus ensuring the quality of the *Grand Vin*.

Ch Gloria
One of the success stories of the Médoc, this 48-ha (119-acre) vineyard did not exist until the 1940s. The late Henri Martin, who was Mayor of St-Julien, assembled the land from small plots bought all around the commune. Despite this, the wine gained — and has kept — a fine reputation. Gloria is not made for long keeping, but for early enjoyment of its hedonistic character.

Ch Gruaud-Larose
4ème Cru Classé This vineyard of 84ha (207 acres) has made fashionable and consistent wine for 250 years. In 1815 the private notebook of the Bordeaux merchant Lawton described Larose as "substantial, yet fragrant and mellow" — a description that could be used now, with the addendum that the wine needs time to mature. The second wine here is Sarget de Gruaud-Larose.

Once part of Domaines Cordier, the château was bought by the Taillan group (Merlaut) in 1997.

Ch Lagrange
3ème Cru Classé This large — 108-ha (267-acre) — property was bought by the Japanese group Suntory in 1983. Lagrange had millions of yen spent on it in the succeeding decade, with vineyards replanted and expanded, brand-new equipment and air-conditioned *chais* installed. The results have been impressive ever since the 1985 vintage.

The highly regarded second wine here is called Fiefs de Lagrange.

Ch Langoa Barton
3ème Cru Classé The Bartons arrived in Bordeaux from Ireland in 1715, became leading merchants, and then in 1821 bought Ch Langoa. Later in the decade they bought a portion of the Léoville estate (*qv*). The family owns and runs both estates to this day. The winemaking is traditional, as are the prices, making Langoa and Léoville Barton bywords for value. The vineyards cover 16ha (40 acres).

Ch Léoville Barton
2ème Cru Classé See above and below. Léoville was a large estate in the northern corner of St-Julien, facing Latour to the north. Barton's 47-ha (116-acre) portion is reckoned to make slightly better, more concentrated wine than Langoa.

Ch Léoville Las-Cases
2ème Cru Classé This large estate is but half of the old Las-Cases family property, a remarkable spread of fine vineyard that ran from the southern edge of Latour down to Beychevelle, taking up all the good riverside gravel-soil land. The 97ha (240 acres) under this label include the original walled *clos* beside the D2 road.

Powerful, concentrated, long in taste and long-lived in bottle, this is one of the great red wines. Comparisons are often made with its neighbour Latour across the Pauillac border. Clos du Marquis is the second wine.

Ch Léoville Poyferré
2ème Cru Classé The third, 80-ha (198-acre), portion of the great Léoville property was reckoned in the last century to make the best wines of the three Léovilles, but was eclipsed by the others for most of this one. Things began to change with the 1980s' vintages, when Didier Cuvelier took charge and introduced a more rigorous selection. The Poyferré second wine is called Moulin-Riche.

Ch St-Pierre
4ème Cru Classé In the same ownership as Ch Gloria (*qv*), with 17ha (42 acres) of old vines. The wine is solid, dark and flavoursome, and can take a long time to mature. The 1996 is superb.

Ch Talbot
4ème Cru Classé This large (102-ha/252-acre) estate belongs to the Cordier family, who run it with great attention to detail. The wine has many qualities: it is soft, full and rich. In great vintages it can age well; in minor ones it is reliable. The second wine is Connétable de Talbot. There is also a white wine, Caillou Blanc, made from Sauvignon Blanc grapes and aged in new oak.

MARGAUX

The village of Margaux is known worldwide thanks to the fame of its leading château, the First Growth of the same name. The *appellation* has the Médoc's largest list of classed growths — 22 out of the 70 châteaux. The wines of the AOC exhibit a clear style: softer and more opulent and perfumed than the Pauillac wines; yet equally long-lived. With the exception of Ch Margaux's Pavillon Blanc, all the wine is red.

THE APPELLATION

These are the southernmost vineyards of the Médoc, set at first amid trees and meadows, and then dominating the landscape as the gravel banks appear. The gravel is made up of larger stones than further north, and the shingly banks are split by tongues of low-lying, marshy land.

Unlike other Médoc *appellations communales*, the AOC Margaux covers more than just the village of its name: from north to south, it takes in 1,100ha (2,718 acres) in parts of the communes of Soussans, Margaux, Arsac, Cantenac and Labarde.

Beware confusion when looking at labels: the name Margaux can legitimately be used in postal addresses in nine communes, five of them outside the *appellation*. Look for "Margaux" in the AOC name. And Château Margaux is quite a different wine to just "Margaux"...

A central block of vineyards sits on a plateau that runs from Cantenac in the south-east up to Marsac in the Soussans commune; to the south, south-east and west are seven other patches of higher ground with vines. The major growths are sited along the edges of the central plateau: Ch Margaux, Palmer and d'Issan face east, towards the river; Pouget, the Cantenacs and Kirwan face south, across

the marshes, from the southern edge of the gravel.

Atypically, many château buildings are grouped in the village of Margaux, with their land scattered in parcels around the *appellation*.

Ch d'Angludet

Cru Bourgeois Supérieur A 32-ha (79-acre) vineyard in Arsac and Cantenac, to the south of the *appellation*, making tannic and austere wines that keep just as well as classed-growth-quality wine.

Ch Boyd-Cantenac

3ème Cru Classé A small (18-ha/44-acre) estate with powerful, long-lasting wine made from old vines.

Ch Brane-Cantenac

2ème Cru Classé A large well-sited vineyard on the south tip of the main gravel plateau with 85ha (210 acres) of vines. The estate is owned by the Lurton family. Vintages of the 1970s were disappointing, but Henri Lurton has been making superb wines, especially since 1996.

Ch Cantenac-Brown

3ème Cru Classé One of several Médoc estates owned by AXA, a big insurance company. During the 1970s and early 1980s, the wine had a reputation for being hard and charmless. Vintages since 1988 have seen much improve-

ment, as modernization and new management take effect.

Ch Dauzac

5ème Cru Classé Estate of 45ha (111 acres) in Labarde, close to the Gironde. Owned since 1988 by MAIF, a big insurance company, whose investments have improved the quality of recent vintages.

Since the 1993 vintage the property has been managed by André Lurton.

Ch Desmirail

3ème Cru Classé This 30-ha (74-acre) property was recently taken over by Denis Lurton, who has considerably improved the quality.

Ch Deyrem Valentin

Cru Bourgeois Cabernet Sauvignon slightly dominates Merlot in this 13-ha (32-acre) vineyard. A solid Margaux to be kept for 5 or 6 years.

Ch Durfort-Vivens

2ème Cru Classé Yet another Lurton property, with a very high proportion of Cabernet Sauvignon on its 30ha (74 acres). Now run by Gonzague Lurton, its future looks very promising.

Ch Ferrière

3ème Cru Classé Bought up in 1992 by the Taillan-Merlaut group, it produces high-quality wines. The second wine is Les Remparts de Ferrière.

Ch Giscours

3ème Cru Classé One of the success stories of Margaux, a big (75-ha/185-acre) estate at Labarde which has been rescued from dereliction and wholly modernized, extended and replanted over the last 20 years. The wines were excellent in the 1970s, but showed less consistency in the early 1980s. Happily, some vintages, such as 1986, 1988 and 1989, are elegant and attractive wines.

Ch La Gurgue

Cru Bourgeois Supérieur The house is in the centre of Margaux village, the 12.5ha (31 acres) of vineyards situated just west of Ch Margaux. In the same ownership as Ch Chasse-Spleen (*see* Moulis).

Ch Haut Breton Larigaudière

Cru Bourgeois A small estate of just over 12ha (29 acres) in Soussans, also housing a good restaurant specializing in local dishes. The château produces a supple and fruity Margaux.

Ch d'Issan

3ème Cru Classé A romantic, moated château, with vines on 30ha (74 acres) of the best east-facing slopes of the plateau. The wine is approachable quite young but is still long-lived; smooth, with Margaux sweetness; one of the best of the commune and the Médoc. The estate is owned by the Cruse family.

Ch Kirwan

3ème Cru Classé Well placed on the gravel plateau east of Brane-Cantenac, with 35ha (86 acres) of vines, a high proportion being Merlot and Cabernet Franc. Margaux in the softer style, gaining finesse with age. Advice from oenologist Michel Rolland since 1993 has brought out the full potential of this property.

Ch Labégorce

Cru Bourgeois Supérieur This 36-ha (89-acre) estate lies on the Margaux-Soussans border. It changed owners in 1989, and since then big investments have been made, resulting in a solid, long-lived Margaux.

Ch Labégorce-Zédé
Cru Bourgeois Exceptionnel Reliable, good-quality, traditionally made wine from this 35-ha (86-acre) estate in Soussans. The owner, Luc Thienpont, also owns the Pomerol property of Vieux Château-Certan.

Ch Lascombes
2ème Cru Classé A big vineyard on a grand estate restored by Franco-American wine merchant and writer, the late Alexis Lichine, and sold by him to an English brewer. Some years of steady, unexciting wine were followed by encouraging progress in the late 1980s. A new winery was built in 1986, and facilities for visitors are excellent.

Ch Malescot-Saint-Exupéry
3ème Cru Classé Known for its tannic, graceless youth, this wine blossoms with maturity. The house is in the middle of Margaux, the vineyards (24ha/59 acres) to the north of the commune.

Ch Margaux
1er Cru Classé See profile.

Ch Marquis d'Alesme Becker
3ème Cru Classé A small estate, typical of Soussans in size (13ha/32 acres) and in the solid, earthy quality of its wine.

Ch Marquis de Terme
4ème Cru Classé This estate has been owned by the Sénéclause family since 1935. The 40-ha (99-acre) vineyard with a high proportion of Cabernet Sauvignon (55%) and Merlot

(35%) produces a straightforward Margaux.

Ch Marsac-Séguineau
Cru Bourgeois A modest (10-ha/25-acre) vineyard in two parts near Marsac, north of Margaux, producing solid, typical wine.

Ch Martinens
Cru Bourgeois An 18th-century château with 25ha (62 acres) of Merlot-dominated vineyards on the western edge of the Cantenac plateau. Recent investment has improved an already good, consistent Margaux.

Ch Monbrison
Cru Bourgeois Supérieur A little 21-ha (52-acre) vineyard in Arsac, just across the valley from du Tertre, with a good name for solid, elegant wines which repay ageing.

Ch Palmer
3ème Cru Classé Neighbour to Ch Margaux, Palmer made better wine than the First Growth for several vintages in the 1960s and 1970s.

Today Margaux has reasserted its pre-eminence, but Palmer still makes superb wine, the fruit of a fine site on the same gravel bank as Margaux, plus long fermentation and careful selection. There is 40% Merlot, which shows in the wine's style. Long fermentation and rigorous selection explain why Palmer plays in the major leagues.

Ch Pouget
4ème Cru Classé Little-known 10ha (25-acre) classed growth making good wine.

Ch Prieuré-Lichine
4ème Cru Classé Once a priory, the house is next to the Cantenac church. Alexis Lichine (*see* Lascombes) built up this estate, which consists of 68ha (168 acres) in widely scattered plots in the five com-

munes of the Margaux *appellation* zone. His son Sacha sold it to the Ballande group in 1999. The wines are elegant and richer than in the past. The estate also productes a small amount of white wine.

Ch Rausan-Ségla
2ème Cru Classé An example of the dramatic improvements in the Médoc in the 1980s: new stainless steel vats, better vines, a new team — and the estate is back where it was last century, a true Second Growth. Impressive wines from 1988 onwards.

Ch Rauzan-Gassies
2ème Cru Classé Less in the limelight than the other half of the old Rausan estate (*see* above), and less consistent.

Ch Siran
Cru Bourgeois Exceptionnel A showplace château with 24ha (59 acres) at Labarde, producing smooth, silky wines that can age well.

Ch du Tertre
5ème Cru Classé Well hidden in the woods at Arsac, this estate has a large amount of Cabernet Sauvignon on its 50ha (124 acres), planted on an inland outcrop of gravel. Since 1997, Albada Jelgersma, the new owner (and *fermier* of Giscours), has brought about the brillant revival of this property which he has renovated entirely.

Ch La Tour-de-Mons
Cru Bourgeois Supérieur A well-known property in Soussans making reliable, smooth, enjoyable wine from 35ha (74 acres) of predominantly clay-soil vineyard, planted almost equally with Merlot and Cabernet Sauvignon.

——— CHATEAU MARGAUX ———

The *appellation*'s single *Premier Cru* is a superb, even lordly, country estate, its grand 1820 mansion standing within boundaries intact since the 17th century. It has made great wine in every century since, but its revival since 1978, after a period of decline, is as spectacular as anything in Margaux's history. A superbly-sited 78-ha (193-acre) vineyard, 75% Cabernet Sauvignon, on the east slope of the Margaux plateau, is the starting point for the pursuit of excellence in vineyard and *chais*. Great rigour in selection for the *Grand Vin*, with as much as half the crop relegated to the second wine, Pavillon Rouge, has had its effect. Margaux has gained a name for solidity, structure and longevity to match its charm, perfume and personality. A white wine, Pavillon Blanc, is made using 100% Sauvignon Blanc.

OTHER MEDOC APPELLATIONS

Not all Médoc estates are starry classed growths in famous communes: the back country, and the gaps between some of the great communes, hide some good châteaux in the AOC Haut-Médoc. The wide area of the northern AOC Médoc offers another hunting-ground for value. In every case the vines occupy the higher, better-drained land amid the marshes and woods.

AOC MOULIS
The little commune of Moulis, with its hamlet of Grand-Poujeaux, is the smallest Médoc AOC. It lies west of Margaux, and away from the Gironde. The vineyards are on a plateau with gravel sub-soils. The red wines from here are solid, dark and long-lived.

Ch Chasse-Spleen
Cru Bourgeois Exceptionnel One of the best, and best-known, Chasse-Spleen makes wine to classed-growth standard, supple and enjoyable when young, but which can age for ten years.

Ch Dutruch-Grand-Poujeaux
Cru Bourgeois Supérieur One of a series of châteaux with "Poujeaux" in their name, this well-structured wine ages well.

Ch Maucaillou
Cru Bourgeois Supérieur Philippe Dourthe makes well-structured wine with an oaky taste from 69ha (170 acres) of vines, a modern *chai* and lots of new oak.

Ch Poujeaux
Cru Bourgeois Exceptionnel The other estate (with Maucaillou) to contend with Chasse-Spleen as the best in the commune. Good traditional claret: dark, flavoursome and long-lived.

AOC LISTRAC
To the north of Moulis lies Listrac, with several well-known châteaux, making wines in a rather robust, austere style that nonetheless repay keeping. Friendlier and with more fruit in lesser vintages.

Ch Clarke
Cru Bourgeois Supérieur Edmond de Rothschild's will (and money) has conjured a virtually new vineyard out of a neglected corner by planting 53ha (141 acres) of vines on artificially drained stubborn soil. His efforts are showing increasingly good results. In the mid-1980s, the wine had a pleasant fruity flavour; recent vintages are well-structured and have more depth.

Ch Fourcas-Dupré
Cru Bourgeois Supérieur This estate produces a rich and well-balanced claret from 44ha (109 acres).

Ch Fourcas-Hosten
Cru Bourgeois Supérieur This estate produces serious wine from 45% Merlot. Deserves ageing to bring out the richness.

Other Moulis and Listrac châteaux
La Becade, Bel-Air-Lagrave, Biston-Brillette, Brillette, Duplessis-Fabre, Lestage, Mayne-Lalande.

AOC HAUT-MEDOC
Ch Belgrave
5ème Cru Classé Deservedly obscure until recently, this estate has 54ha (133 acres) of well-placed land close to St-Julien. Neglect for decades ended in the late 1980s with new owners, advice and investment. Results now show.

Ch de Camensac
5ème Cru Classé In St-Laurent, the commune inland from St-Julien, and with 65ha (160 acres) of vines owned by the Forner family.

Ch Cantemerle
5ème Cru Classé This very traditional property in the southernmost part of Médoc has been revived by the Domaines Cordier team, headed by Georges Pauli. The high proportion of Merlot in its 67-ha (166-acre) vineyard gives a velvety character and fruity flavours to the wine. Recent vintages (such as 1997 and 1998) have gained high praise.

Ch Citran
Cru Bourgeois Supérieur Sold to the Taillan (Merlaut) group in 1996, this large (97ha (240 acres) estate has been given a new life through major investments. Today, the powerful, harmonious wines are among the best of the *appellation*.

Ch La Lagune
3ème Cru Classé Being outside the famous communes — Lagune is south of Margaux, close to Bordeaux — has deprived the wine from this 65-ha (166-acre) estate of its true standing. The wine is supple and attractive in the scented, silky style typical of Margaux. A new winery being built in 2004 bodes well for even better wine in future.

Ch La Tour-Carnet
4ème Cru Classé Sited in St-Laurent, this *cru* owned by Bernard Magrez has been entirely renovated. The still reliable wine shows a lot more elegance.

Ch Sociando-Mallet
This 65-ha (161-acre) vineyard with a high proportion of Cabernet Sauvignon must be considered a top *Cru Bourgeois*. Great long-lived wines of classed-growth quality.

Other châteaux
D'Agassac, d'Arcins, d'Arsac, Beaumont, Bel-Air, Bel-Orme-Tronquoy-de-Lalande, le Bourdieu, Caronne-Ste-Gemme, Coufran, Dillon, Fonréaud, Hanteillan, de Lamarque, Lanessan, Larose-Trintaudon, Lestage, Liversan, Malescasse, de Malleret, Peyrabon, Puy-Castéra, Ramage-la-Bâtisse, Reysson, Sénéjac, Tour-du-Haut-Moulin.

AOC MEDOC
Ch la Cardonne
Cru Bourgeois Supérieur Now owned by Guy Charloux, this large (87-ha/215-acre) estate is producing well-structured wines with an oaky taste.

Ch Loudenne
Cru Bourgeois Supérieur This beautifully placed property by the Gironde was sold to the Lafragette family in June 2000. Its red wine is light and easy to drink, and its white wine dry and precise.

Ch Rollan-de-By
Cru Bourgeois Supérieur A highly successful well-structured and complex, "silky and delicate" wine from a 40-ha (99-acre) vineyard and brand new equipment. Rollan-de-By's rare "super wine" is called Haut-Condissas and is up to the best classed-growth wine.

Other châteaux
De By, Les Ormes-Sorbet, Patache d'Aux, Potensac, St-Bonnet, La Tour-de-By, Tour Haut Courson, La Tour-St-Bonnet.

PESSAC-LÉOGNAN AND GRAVES

The Graves is a huge region on the west bank of the Garonne River. This region produced the original bordeaux wine long before the Médoc was planted. Estates such as Château Pape-Clément can trace their history back 700 years.

The Pessac-Léognan appellation

The *appellation* of Pessac-Léognan, near the city of Bordeaux, prides itself on its classed-growth estates. It has long been the view of proprietors in the northern part of the region, south of Bordeaux, that their vineyards are superior, because of the *terroir*, to those in the southern Graves. Ten communes in the northern Graves won the right to label their wines with a new *appellation*, Pessac-Léognan, beginning with the 1986 vintage. The new *appellation* covers 55 estates, including all those listed as classed growths in the Graves classification of 1959 (*see* box).

The red Pessac-Léognan style

Such is the soil diversity of the *appellation* that it offers an extremely large range of wines; this becomes immediately evident as soon as one compares two of its red wines — such as Haut-Brion and Domaine de Chevalier — over several decades. These wines may lack the aristocratic power and elegance of the finest Médoc and the lush fruitiness of good St-Emilion or Pomerol, but they are supple and well-balanced with suggestions of black cherries, tobacco and chocolate. The renewal of winemaking techniques has meant a better expression of the various *terroirs* but also, and even more so, of grape varieties. Cabernet Sauvignon is the dominant red grape variety, as in Médoc. Other permitted red grapes are Cabernet Franc, Petit Verdot and Cot (Malbec), but the latter two only account for a very low portion.

Trimming summer growth at Château La Mission-Haut-Brion.

The white Pessac-Léognan style

White wines from the Pessac-Léognan region have become increasingly famous and production of very fine white wines is no longer confined to the reputed Domaine de Chevalier. The blending of the two white grape varieties — Sémillon and Sauvignon Blanc — is no longer the rule as some estates, such as Smith Haut-Lafitte, Malartic-Lagravière and Couhins-Lurton, are now making white wines from pure Sauvignon. During the 1990s, several estates have produced whites that are equal, or superior to those of the Chevalier, Fieuzal and Laville-Haut-Brion estates. While the Sémillon grape adds body to the wine, Sauvignon provides for fruity flavour, and this has made it difficult to predict the quality of wine only from the vintage.

In addition to temperature-controlled fermentation, other techniques are used for improving aromatic qualities, such as *macération pelliculaire* (leaving the must in contact with the skins for a certain period). Another option is the use of new *barriques*, which gives certain white wines an additional oaky taste. Finally, several estates have adopted lees-stirring, which fattens the wine. All these efforts — pioneered by reputed oenologists, such as Denis Dubourdieu and Christophe Ollivier — have been used to achieve a marked improvement in the wines and have been rewarded by the increasing enthusiasm of wine amateurs and, of course, by a certain rise in prices.

Grape varieties for white Pessac-Léognan

There is also much discussion among the region's winemakers as to the respective merits of Sauvignon Blanc and Sémillon. Partisans of the former, such as André Lurton, who owns many estates in Pessac-Léognan, point to the aromatic qualities of the Sauvignon Blanc grape. Indeed, the Pessac-Léognan AOC regulations require at least 25% Sauvignon Blanc. Partisans of the more neutral Sémillon say that its breadth of flavour is better adapted to *barrique*-ageing. In practice almost every estate (except for Châteaux Couhins-Lurton, Smith-Haut-Lafitte, La Garde and Malartic-Lagravière, where Sauvignon Blanc dominates) blends the two.

A third permitted grape variety is the highly aromatic Muscadelle, but it rarely achieves full maturity because of failure and the ease with which it succumbs to disease.

Estates with a strong reputation for white wines — Carbonnieux, Fieuzal, La Louvière, Malartic-Lagravière and Smith-Haut-Lafitte, among others — charge considerably more for their whites than their reds. Some of these white wines demand several years of bottle-age to show at their best, if they are made mainly from the Sémillon grape, while those made from Sauvignon Blanc should be consumed during the first five years for their fruity flavour, especially in lesser vintages.

The Graves appellation

The delimited area of the Graves *appellation* spreads south for about 55km (35 miles) to just beyond the small town of Langon. At its widest the Graves is 20km (12 miles) from east to west. Its large size makes the region hard to characterize, especially since its production is so much more diverse than the other principal regions of Bordeaux, the Médoc and St-Emilion. The Graves produces not only fine red wine, but a considerable amount of white, both dry and sweet. Indeed, the most celebrated sweet white wine in the world, Sauternes (*see* p163), as well as Barsac, are produced in an enclave within the Graves, but there is, inevitably, some overlap between the two areas. For instance, some Sauternes châteaux make dry white wines, which they are not allowed to label AOC Graves, but only AOC Bordeaux.

Despite its size, the Graves is a patchwork of vineyards, producing only half as much as the Haut-Médoc or St-Emilion.

As the name might suggest, the Graves is a region of shallow but well-drained gravel ridges — the "graves" — mingled with sand, sand-stone and some clay. Slopes are very gentle and often sheltered by woods. These well-drained ridges provide the best vineyard sites, and variations between wines are to a large extent due to differing soils. Nonetheless, generalizations are risky, since even within single vineyards there are considerable variations in soil and subsoil. Although the quality of white Graves has increased greatly since the mid-1980s, there has been an expansion in red vineyards compared with white, with red grape varieties accounting for 68% in the region, including Pessac-Léognan, and even for 75% in the Pessac-Léognan area.

A bright future

The Graves is very much a region in transition. The concentration of classified growths in the north has prompted a healthy competition among estates in these districts, which has improved overall quality. The glorious 1980s have allowed for the necessary investments in a region which had been less favoured by Bordeaux wine merchants than, for instance, the Médoc. Today, a number of estates offer excellent wines which are up to classed-growth standard in Pessac-Léognan, and the future of both white and red wines looks bright. Recent investment in new wineries and improved care of vineyards should do better justice to the splendid soils with which the Graves is blessed. The best fine wines of the Graves *appellation*, which have long been eclipsed by those of the Médoc, should thus be able to achieve the success they are deserving. □

THE CLASSIFICATION OF THE PESSAC-LEOGNAN

Estates in the Graves region were classified in 1959 and the following châteaux were designated classed growths. They are all in the northern part of the Graves. All these classed growths, and some 40 others, are entitled to the Pessac-Léognan AOC.

RED WINES
Premier Grand Cru
Ch Haut-Brion

Crus Classés
Ch Bouscaut
Ch Carbonnieux
Dom de Chevalier
Ch de Fieuzal
Ch Haut-Bailly
Ch La Mission-Haut-Brion
Ch Latour-Haut-Brion
Ch La Tour-Martillac
Ch Malartic-Lagravière
Ch Olivier
Ch Pape-Clément
Ch Smith-Haut-Lafitte

WHITE WINES
Crus Classés
Ch Bouscaut
Ch Carbonnieux
Dom de Chevalier
Ch Couhins
Ch Couhins-Lurton
Ch Haut-Brion
Ch La Tour-Martillac
Ch Laville-Haut-Brion
Ch Malartic-Lagravière
Ch Olivier

PESSAC-LEOGNAN PRODUCERS

The *appellation*'s 1,150ha (2,840 acres) of vineyards lie in the communes immediately south and west of Bordeaux. Since the *appellation* came into effect in September 1987 (for the 1986 vintage), the region has produced some fine wines, both white and red. Today, Pessac-Léognan wines are as expensive as a good Médoc or St-Emilion. Their quality is similar, but they differ in the aromatic substances they contain. The communes entitled to the *appellation* are Cadaujac, Canéjan, Gradignan, Léognan, Martillac, Mérignac, Pessac, St-Médard-d'Eyrans, Talence and Villenave-d'Ornon.

Ch Bouscaut
Cru Classé The most beautiful estate of Cadaujac is owned by the family of winemaker Lucien Lurton, who has never been keen on flamboyant wines, preferring subtlety. The white has been barrel-fermented since 1988. The 1999 and 2000 vintages in particular have been a great success.

Ch Carbonnieux
Cru Classé An old and beautiful turreted château, in Benedictine hands in the 18th century, where white Graves was pioneered. This 90-ha (220-acre) Léognan estate is now owned by the Perrin family. Since 1990 the château has been making its red and white wines in a winery with splendidly up-to-date equipment. The white wine is rich and toasty, while the red wine is oaky with supple tannins.

Ch Les Carmes-Haut-Brion
Entirely surrounded by the Bordeaux suburbs, this tiny 4,5-ha (11-acre) Pessac property, blessed with a particularly mild micro-climate and parcels of old vines, should be a jewel. Yet the wines, all red, are medium-bodied with an easy charm and no great staying power.

Domaine de Chevalier
See profile.

Ch Couhins-Lurton
Cru Classé Formerly part of Ch Couhins (now a research station), this 5,5-ha (14-acre) property in Villenave-d'Ornon is owned by André Lurton and planted solely with Sauvignon Blanc. The wines are fermented and aged in new oak.

Ch de Cruzeau
Having been replanted in 1974, this St-Medard-d'Eyrans estate — yet another property owned by Lucien Lurton — produces a straightforward unoaked white, mostly from Sauvignon Blanc, and an austere but stylish oak-aged red.

Ch de Fieuzal
Cru Classé A star estate in Léognan, even more celebrated for its sensational white than for its robust red. The white is fermented and aged in new oak for 16 months, and needs a few years to unfurl its rich flavours. The burly red, with its black-cherry flavours and dense structure, can be superb.

Ch de France
A large (32ha/79 acres) Léognan estate, producing a velvety and charming red wine

and a fully-flavoured well-balanced white aged in new oak, made from 80% Sauvignon Blanc, 10% Sémillon and 10% Muscadelle.

Ch La Garde
This ancient estate in Martillac has been renovated. Its best red wines are vinified in new oak and labelled Réserve. They are rich and silky and intended to be accessible young but capable of ageing in bottle. Quality is impressive and prices sensible. A small amount of elegant white wine is produced from pure Sauvignon Blanc.

Ch Haut-Bailly
Cru Classé Many wine lovers would name Ch Haut-Bailly, in the commune of Léognan, as their favourite red Pessac-Léognan. Made with great skill, it is less powerful and less dense than many other wines but always elegant. Its discreet oaky structure means that it matures reasonably quickly but can age well. Haut-Bailly is often successful in lesser vintages too.

Ch Haut-Brion
1er Grand Cru Classé (1855) In the commune of Pessac, this is the sole red *Premier Grand Cru* of the Graves, and thoroughly deserving of its status; it is a red wine of consummate breed and great consistency. Even in modest vintages such as 1987 and 1991 it produced perfumed and elegant wines. The wine became more for-

ward and voluptuous by the mid-1980s, but still needs several years to show at its best.

The estate is owned and directed by the Duc and Duchesse de Mouchy, the Duchesse being a daughter of the Dillon family which bought the estate in 1935.

Haut-Brion has never rested on its laurels, and its team, under winemaker and manager J B Delmas, is constantly searching to improve the quality of the grapes. A small quantity of highly prized white wine is produced, and in recent years it has been fermented in a considerable percentage of new oak. In unsatisfactory years, such as 1986, no white was released. The second label for red wine, Bahans-Haut-Brion, is one of the best second wines in Bordeaux. La Mission-Haut-Brion (*qv*) has the same owners.

Ch Larrivet-Haut-Brion
This Léognan estate of 45ha (110 acres) has benefited from considerable investment in new cellars. Since 1988 its wines have been very impressive, both the rich spicy white and the firm oaky red. Yields are being kept low, and these efforts should result in increasingly high quality.

Ch Laville-Haut-Brion
Cru Classé This Pessac estate is, in effect, the white wine of Ch La Mission-Haut-Brion (*qv*). Laville is a legendary white wine, and 50-year-old bottles have been much enjoyed. After a rough patch in the 1970s, Laville is back on form. It is perhaps a little less sumptuous than Ch Haut-Brion, which is produced by the same team, but it is an opulent wine by any standards. It is marked in youth by its upbringing in new oak, and needs a decade in bottle to show its best. The price is high, but in great vintages this is a sensational wine.

Ch La Louvière
This handsome château, in the commune of Léognan, is the flagship estate of the ubiquitous André Lurton (he also owns Ch Couhins-Lurton, Ch de Cruzeau and Ch Rochemorin). The white wine is dominated by Sauvignon Blanc, and is a sound oaky wine of some distinction. The red is well structured and ages well.

La Louvière also vinifies Ch Coucheroy, simple but well-made red and white Graves that are very good value.

Ch Malartic-Lagravière
Cru Classé Bought in 1998 by Alfred-Alexandre Bonnie, this 54-ha (133-acre) Léognan estate is probably best known for its all-Sauvignon Blanc white, but recent vintages have been made with 20% Sémillon. The reds have a reputation for severity, but in fact they are supple with ripe tannins. Like the whites, they benefit from a few years in bottle.

Ch La Mission-Haut-Brion
Cru Classé This 22-ha (55-acre) red-wine estate in Pessac lies across the road from Ch Haut-Brion, which acquired the property in 1983, yet the two wines are very different. If Haut-Brion exhibits harmony and finesse above all else, Ch La Mission stresses power and depth of flavour. It has always been an expensive wine, reflecting its owners' conviction that La Mission is close to *Premier Grand Cru* in

quality, and in many vintages it is hard to disagree.

Ch Olivier
Cru Classé At the heart of this Léognan estate stands a splendid medieval moated castle, but until recently the wines have not been as sensational as the architecture. Now that the Bethmann family has bought the property, the wines are improving.

Ch Pape-Clément
Cru Classé What is probably the most ancient surviving vineyard in Bordeaux — it was created in 1300 by Bertrand de Cot, archbishop of Bordeaux, who later became pope Clement V — is now encircled by urban development in the commune of Pessac. For many years the red wine was lacklustre, but with the 1985 vintage there was a dramatic improvement that has continued with every succeeding year. Pape-Clément is a rich, lush wine, full-flavoured and with impressive length in the mouth.

The estate has developed a small vineyard planted with white grape varieties — 2,5ha (6 acres) of Sémillon, Sauvignon Blanc and Muscadelle —, which produces a (not-classified) rare white wine of top quality.

Ch Pique-Caillou
In the commune of Mérignac, this 14-ha (35-acre) estate produces only red wine. This is a supple, soundly made wine that is relatively quick to evolve.

Ch de Rochemorin
Another of André Lurton's properties, this large Martillac estate makes fine fleshy reds and sound whites that are approachable young. Rochemorin is rarely among the top wines in the Lurton portfolio, but it is medium-priced and offers very good value.

Ch Le Sartre
Gradually being renovated by the Perrins of Ch Carbonnieux, this small Léognan estate offers the Carbonnieux style at half the price. The red is better than the white.

Ch Smith-Haut-Lafitte
Cru Classé This large Martillac estate was sold in 1990 for a colossal sum to Daniel and Florence Cathiard, who immediately instigated the necessary improvements in vineyard and cellar, receiving advice from the region's best "flying winemakers". Under its former owners, the *négociant* firm of Eschenauer, this was a dependable source of sound red and white Graves. The first vintages under Cathiard's regime show that their expenditure was worthwhile. The white in particular, an all-Sauvignon Blanc, turns

out to be marvellously balanced, with pleasant fruity flavours. With rigorous selection the second wine, called Les-Hauts-de-Smith, is a highly prized red wine.

Ch La Tour Haut-Brion
Cru Classé Of the same family as Château Haut-Brion, bordering Laville Haut-Brion, this estate produces a red wine with a strong Cabernet Sauvignon flavour from its 4,9-ha (12-acre) vineyard.

Ch La Tour Martillac
Cru Classé Run for over a century by the Kressmann family, this Martillac estate offers reds that are plump and fleshy yet elegant, and impeccably balanced whites that are oaky but retain their youthful fruitiness for many years. The consistency of quality is admirable.

DOMAINE DE CHEVALIER

Cru Classé First planted in 1770, this vineyard in the commune of Léognan makes two of the great wines of Bordeaux. The red is classically elegant, rarely a blockbuster but impeccably made, with a core of fruit wrapped subtly in oak. The white is of equal stature, rare, and very expensive. The secret of Chevalier's greatness lies in the care with which the grapes are grown and harvested. Long before the practice had become established in the Graves, *triage* was routine at Chevalier. The white is barrel-fermented in one-third new oak, spends 18 months in barrels, and is carefully selected. Both red and white wines are sufficiently concentrated to enable them to age for two or three decades. Indeed, the white wine should really not be broached until it is at least eight years old.

GRAVES PRODUCERS

Until the 1970s, many Graves estates, especially in the southern part of the region, sold their wines to *négociants*. Estate-bottling is a relatively recent phenomenon. Now the practice is growing and so is the sophistication of the winemaking, as communes and estates vie with each other to produce more appealing red and white wines. Some concentrate on quality at all costs, producing richly flavoured tannic red wines intended for long ageing; others opt for reds that are easier to drink young. So there remain inconsistencies in style as well as quality.

Estates tend to be clustered in certain communes such as Portets and Langon, where the gravel comes to the surface. Only vines grown on this soil are entitled to the *appellation*; other vineyards, such as those close to the Garonne, are labelled AOC Bordeaux.

Ch d'Archambeau
In the commune of Illats, a source of impeccably made, fresh white wines, and soft delicate reds.

Ch Le Bonnat
This estate in Labrède is owned by Gérard Gribelin of Ch de Fieuzal in Pessac-Léognan (*qv*). The red wines are aged in 40% new oak, and the whites are barrel-fermented and aged in all new oak.

Clos Bourgelat
In the commune of Cérons, a reliable source of soft, fruity reds and crisp whites.

Ch Brondelle
This 62-ha (153-acre) vineyard is sited on a magnificent gravelled hilltop. The red wine gives a prominent part to Cabernet Sauvignon and new oak. The white, made from Sauvignon Blanc and Sémillon, is a wine of pure, modern style, born of steel vats and *macération pelliculaire*.

Ch Cabannieux
This estate of almost 20ha (49 acres) in the northern part of the *appellation* produces a Merlot-dominated red and a fine and distinguished Sémillon-based white.

Ch de Chantegrive
In 25 years the Lévêque family have created from scratch an estate of 92ha (227 acres) in Podensac. *Barrique*-aged wines were introduced only in 1988, but results have been impressive. New oak is used for the white Cuvée Caroline and the red Cuvée Edouard. The estate includes other properties, such as Ch Bon Dieu des Vignes, which are bottled separately.

Clos Floridène
Denis Dubourdieu, who has had an enormous influence on improving white wine vinification in the Graves, owns this small estate in Pujols. He was a pioneer of skin contact and stirring the wine while it rests on its lees, and is a consultant at many Graves estates. The results at Floridène are delicious. At present the whites, aged in new oak, are better than the reds.

Ch du Grand Bos
A vineyard of some 10ha (25 acres) planted with equal portions of Cabernet Sauvignon and Merlot, the first providing structure, the second a supple fruity flavour.

Domaine de Hauret-Lalande
Flowery, perfumed whites from an estate in Cérons owned by the Lalande family of Ch Piada in Barsac.

Ch Haut-Selve
This 24-ha (59-acre) estate is the brainchild of Jean-Jacques Lesgourges. His first red Graves, one of the best, was released in 1996.

Ch Lehoul
This vineyard of some 10ha (25 acres) of wines near Langon, in the southern part of the *appellation*, produces red as well as dry and sweet white wines, all aged in oak. The red wine shows an outstandingly strong fruity flavour (Cabernet and Merlot), the dry white is dominated by the fruity aroma of the Sauvignon grape, and the Sémillon-based sweet wine tends to present a balance between the two.

Ch Magence
Well-known estate in St-Pierre-de-Mons in the southern Graves, producing appealing red and sound white wines.

Ch de Portets
This imposing château overlooking the Garonne is surrounded by 30ha (75 acres) of vineyards in the commune of Portets. The white wine is aged in new oak, and the red spends 18 months in *barriques*. The wines are supple and soundly made.

Ch Rahoul
Famous in the early 1980s for its oaky whites made entirely from Sémillon, this estate is now owned by Alain Thiénot.

Ch Respide-Médeville
Vines at this Toulenne estate are young, but already the rich, tannic reds and barrel-fermented whites are improving.

Ch de Roquetaillade-La-Grange
This large Mazères estate produces Sémillon-dominated white wines and beautifully structured reds which repay keeping.

Ch St-Robert
The Crédit Foncier, a bank, owns this vineyard of over 30ha (74 acres), planted with almost equal portions of Merlot and Cabernet, while Sauvignon is the dominant white grape variety.

Ch Toumilon
This vineyard in the southern part of the *appellation* produces sound red and white wines of consistent quality.

Ch Le Tuquet
This large (35-ha/86-acre) property near Beautiran, bordering the Bordeaux-Langon road, produces a light fruity red and a pleasant, crisp white.

Vieux Ch Gaubert
Dominique Haverlan has built up a small estate in Portets, but has no winery of his own. From leased cellars he makes fine oak-aged wines.

Villa Bel Air
From this large (45-ha/111-acre) vineyard, J M Cazes (Lynch-Bages and AXA) produces Cabernet Sauvignon-based red wines and whites from Sauvignon Blanc and Sémillon, all very elegant and lively, with an oaky flavour.

Other producers
Graves white wines from Sauternes châteaux are a quirk of the AOC laws. Noteworthy wines are Y d'Yquem, R de Rieussec, Château Doisy-Daëne and M de Malle.

SAUTERNES

Sauternes, one of the world's great sweet white wines, comes from the southern Graves region. These luscious, golden wines, which develop deep notes of honey, hazelnuts and oranges, are classic dessert wines, to be enjoyed with puddings or on their own at the end of a meal. In France they are often served chilled as an apéritif, or with foie gras. The *appellation* includes five communes — Sauternes, Fargues, Bommes, Preignac and Barsac. One of these, Barsac, has its own *appellation*, which may be used on the label, although some Barsac producers use the better-known AOC Sauternes.

The grape varieties used are the same as for white Graves: Sauvignon Blanc, Sémillon and Muscadelle. Sémillon is more prone to *botrytis* (*see* below) than Sauvignon, and the most common blend is 80% Sémillon, 20% Sauvignon Blanc, and sometimes a dash of Muscadelle.

The importance of noble rot

Natural conditions tend to produce sweet wines in Sauternes. There is some debate, however, about when the deliberate making of sweet wine started. Credit is given to a local proprietor for introducing the technique from Germany in 1847, but Sauternes was known for its sweet wines before that date. The vast majority of the wine produced in the area today is sweet, but this is a risky undertaking in a part of the world where summers are not always hot enough to bring the grapes to dazzling extremes of ripeness and sweetness. Moreover, great Sauternes can be made only from grapes that have been attacked by *botrytis cinerea* ("noble rot"). This is a fungal infection that is provoked by humid conditions, and its effect is to discolour the grapes, shrivel their skins and concentrate their contents of sugar,

Château Suduiraut makes Sauternes of power and opulence.

acidity and glycerol. *Botrytis* effects chemical transformations so numerous that nobody knows exactly how it works, but the result is rich, viscous, honeyed wines that retain a bold dash of acidity that helps the wines to age and improve for decades. As it matures, Sauternes deepens in colour and acquires a drier, almost burnt flavour, sometimes compared to butterscotch.

The cold River Ciron flows through the Sauternes district into the warmer Garonne, and in the autumn this induces mists that blanket the surrounding vineyards. *Botrytis* spores multiply in such mists, and get to work on the grapes. The mist tends to disappear by late morning as the sun burns it off, and growers

hope for prolonged periods of afternoon sunshine to dehydrate the grapes and prevent the transformation of *botrytis* into the ignoble grey rot, which makes the grapes unusable. Only in exceptional years, such as 1990, does noble rot swoop thoroughly across the region, making possible a relatively rapid harvest of properly botrytized grapes. More often than not, *botrytis* infects the vines patchily, and pickers must take care to harvest only those bunches where noble rot has taken hold.

Thus selective harvesting (*triage*) is essential. It also compounds the risk. There are years when *botrytis* either fails to attack to any significant degree, or it occurs very late in the season. If by mid-October the grapes are still healthy and overripe but untainted by noble rot, the temptation to pick can be strong. The result will be a rich sweet wine, but without the distinctive, complex *botrytis* flavour. Perfectionist estates, such as Ch d'Yquem, will if necessary wait until the bitter end, hoping for an eventual onslaught of *botrytis*, sending pickers into the vineyards whenever a significant amount of infection has taken place. In 1985 *botrytis* occurred late, and Yquem was still picking in December, long after most other estates had finished.

A question of timing

The risk in delaying the harvest lies in the worsening weather as the autumn advances. By early November there is a serious possibility that all the grapes still on the vine could be ruined by a week of solid rain. Indeed, this often happens. There are years — 1982, 1991, 1992 — when those who picked early, whether out of luck or lack of nerve, often harvested better-quality grapes than those who left fruit on the vine, only to see it swollen by rain and infected by grey rot. But, as a rule, the highest quality is granted to those prepared to wait for *botrytis* to appear.

In the late 1980s a new piece of cellar equipment, the cryo-extraction chamber, was introduced amid considerable controversy. It is used to dry grapes after they have become sodden by heavy rain. Those who use the chamber stress that it should only be used to "save" botrytized grapes. In hot dry vintages such as 1989 and 1990 the machine stood unused, but in wet years such as 1987 it helped some estates to save part of the crop. Even Yquem has a cryo-extraction chamber, and there is no longer any objection to the machine, provided it is not abused.

Recent improvements

As in the case of dry Graves, there was a great improvement in quality during the 1980s and 1990s. The 1960s and 1970s were mostly lack-lustre years. There were some great vintages, such as 1975 and 1976, but few estates made outstanding wines. Low prices discouraged growers from making badly needed investments in cellar equipment, and the grapes were picked at maximum yields (the regulations allow 25 hl/ha), often before *botrytis* had set in, and they were vinified in neutral tanks. Quality, not surprisingly, was uninspired. All that has changed. New oak barrels for ageing Sauternes, once rare in the region, are now ubiquitous, though certain estates like to age part of their wine in tank to retain freshness. Other estates sometimes overdo the new oak. But on the whole the average quality of Sauternes is now vastly superior to that of the 1970s.

The secret of great Sauternes lies in the harvesting. Once you have picked sweet botrytized grapes, there is little that can go wrong. Top estates such as Yquem, La Tour Blanche and Raymond-Lafon seek to harvest grapes with a potential for 20% to 22% alcohol, resulting in finished wines with about 14% or 14.5% alcohol by volume, and the remainder expressed in residual sugar. In very ripe years, such a high sugar content is almost standard throughout the region; but in less exceptional years selective harvesting is essential if rich musts are to be obtained. The shortcut is to pick overripe grapes with, say, 15% alcohol potential, chaptalize them by an additional 2% to end up with a balance of 13% and 4% residual sugar. The resulting wine is unlikely to be memorable.

The current state of Sauternes

The 1855 Classification (*see* box) had fallen into considerable disrepute by the 1960s, when many classified estates were making wines of miserable quality. Finding great wine, even in fine vintages, had become a lottery. In the early 1980s some producers began to find a way out of this vicious circle — in which poor winemaking justified low prices — and recognized that only a jump in quality could restore the reputation of what is, arguably, the world's greatest sweet wine. The 1983 vintage marked a watershed, and by the end of the decade almost all the great estates were again producing wines that justified their classification and their (inevitably) high prices. Today the consumer, having been offered five superlative vintages unrivalled for a century — 1988, 1989, 1990, 1997, and 2001 — is spoilt for choice. □

THE CLASSIFICATION OF SAUTERNES

(B) indicates properties in Barsac, which may label their wine either Barsac or Sauternes. The order is that established in the 1855 Classification

Premier Cru Supérieur
Ch d'Yquem

Premiers Crus
Ch La Tour Blanche
Ch Lafaurie-Peyraguey
Clos Haut-Peyraguey
Ch de Rayne-Vigneau
Ch de Suduiraut
Ch Coutet (B)
Ch Climens (B)
Ch Guiraud
Ch Rieussec

Ch Rabaud-Promis
Ch Sigalas-Rabaud

Deuxièmes Crus
Ch de Myrat (B)
Ch Doisy-Daëne (B)
Ch Doisy-Dubroca (B)
Ch Doisy-Védrines (B)
Ch d'Arche
Ch Filhot
Ch Broustet (B)
Ch Nairac (B)
Ch Caillou (B)
Ch Suau (B)
Ch de Malle
Ch Romer du Hayot
Ch Lamothe
Ch Lamothe-Guignard

PRODUCERS

It can be difficult to distinguish between the wines from the five Sauternes communes, although Barsac, with its alluvial soils, often stands out: its wines tend to be lighter in colour, and more delicate and elegant in flavour. The richness of some Sauternes, such as Ch Rieussec and Ch Guiraud, can seem overwhelming, and some wine lovers prefer the greater finesse of, say, Barsacs such as Ch Climens or Ch Doisy-Daëne. These are matters of taste, not of quality.

Just north of Barsac there is another *appellation*, Cérons, producing sweet white wines (*see* box, p167). Lightly sweet white wines are also made elsewhere in the Graves and are entitled to the AOC Graves Supérieures; quality is usually indifferent.

The districts of Cadillac, Loupiac and Ste-Croix-du-Mont, on the north bank of the Garonne, also make sweet wines. *See* p168.

Ch d'Arche
2ème Cru Classé Pierre Perromat leased this ancient estate in 1981 and restored its reputation by reducing yields, picking as late as possible, and increasing the percentage of new oak. The result is a rich, sweet, unctuous Sauternes that, being less well known than many others, is reasonably priced.

Ch Bastor-Lamontagne
This large and frankly commercial estate honours the traditions of the region, yet makes no pretence at being as meticulous in its harvesting as the greatest properties. So it is all the more remarkable that for many years the wines have been delicious, spicy, stylish and very well balanced. They are among the bargains of Sauternes.

Ch Broustet
2ème Cru Classé Château Broustet makes a powerful Barsac which often has not enough depth and balance. The wine sold by the Fournier family — the former owners of Château Canon — is still looking for its own style. It is a supple wine and has body. The château has a loyal clientèle.

Ch Caillou
2ème Cru Classé A pretty little château dominates this popular Barsac estate. The overall quality here was not improved by the production of special *cuvées* called Crème de Tête that removed the best lots from the regular blend. The wines are pleasant enough but have little depth and richness, and sometimes noble rot is not apparent.

Ch Climens
1er Cru Classé Ch Climens is one of the few estates in the Sauternes region that can on occasion challenge Ch d'Yquem (*qv*), although the two wines are very different. Climens is a Barsac and has all the subtlety of that commune's wines. In its youth it can seem understated, and is rarely as flamboyant as the wines from Sauternes itself. But after ten years in bottle Climens begins, very slowly, to show the majestic elegance of which it is capable. From the 1983 vintage onwards Climens has not put a foot wrong, and even wines from unremarkable vintages such as the 1972 and the 1973 have proved to be delicious.

Ch Coutet
1er Cru Classé Always one of the best-known estates of Barsac, Coutet had for many years failed to live up to its reputation, and there was also a troubling degree of bottle variation. But in the late 1980s Coutet once again found its form, producing tangy wines that had the Barsac delicacy behind considerable richness of fruit. In the great years a special *cuvée*, Cuvée Madame, is produced.

Ch Doisy-Daëne
2ème Cru Classé Pierre Dubourdieu teasingly claims to dislike Sauternes, and his wine is indeed made in a light and delicate style (except in 1989). Ch Doisy-Daëne appeals with charm rather than power, and in light vintages this lemony style can be disappointing, but in good years Doisy-Daëne can be quintessential Barsac.

Ch Doisy-Dubroca
2ème Cru Classé. Owned by the Lurton family, the proprietors of Ch Climens (*qv*), the wine produced here is made in exactly the same way as its big brother. *Terroir* will out, however, and Dubroca does not have the distinction of Climens.

Ch Doisy-Védrines
2ème Cru Classé This Barsac property, for many years a modest performer, had by 1988 become an outstanding source of fine, complex wine. It is made in a relatively full-bodied style, amply supported by long ageing in new or mostly new *barriques*.

Ch de Fargues
The vines around this crumbling castle are planted on singularly poor soil, yet the wines are rich and luscious. This is because it is made by the same team as Ch d'Yquem (*qv*), since Fargues also belongs to the de Lur-Saluces family. Although marketed at half the price of Yquem, Fargues remains the second most-expensive wine of the *appellation*. It is a triumph of brilliant viticulture and winemaking over modest *terroir*. Fargues often shows better in its youth than Yquem, but with bottle-age Yquem invariably pulls ahead to justify its supremacy. Nonetheless, if you can find a bottle from only 830 cases produced each year, Fargues is a glorious wine.

Ch Filhot
2ème Cru Classé The vineyards of Filhot are grouped around a fine 18th-century château, so it is a shame that the wine is not more exciting. Proprietor Henri de Vaucelles admits to pursuing commercial goals — the large estate is costly to maintain — and in years such as 1976 and 1990 his Sauternes is rich and enjoyable. The Crème de Tête 1990 is a sumptuous wine.

Ch Gilette

This estate is unique in Sauternes. The wines, from low-yielding vines, are produced only in outstanding years, and instead of being aged in *barrique* and then bottled, they are stored in tanks for ten to fifteen years, then bottled and aged for a few more years before being released. In 1999 the vintage on sale was 1979. Consequently the wine evolves much more slowly than other Sauternes, and a "young" Gilette will still taste youthful, and will age for decades more in bottle, long after other Sauternes have begun to tire.

Gilette offers an explosion of honey and apricot aromas and flavours, and the nuttiness of perfectly matured Sauternes. It is extremely expensive, as is any fine Sauternes of comparable age. Annual production is limited to only 480 cases.

Ch Guiraud

1er Cru Classé In 1981 this large but run-down estate was bought by the Canadian Hamilton Narby, who aimed to restore Guiraud's reputation. This has been achieved under Xavier Planty's firm guidance. Guiraud is made in a rich, ample style, a creamy confection of peaches and oak. Guiraud is never chaptalized, because no grapes are harvested unless they contain at least 300 g/l of sugar (18°).

Ch Clos Haut-Peyraguey

1er Cru Classé Jacques Pauly, who owns this small estate in Bommes, stresses that he wants finesse rather than power in his wine. Certainly no one could accuse Haut-Peyraguey of being lush or overblown. But from the 1995 vintage onwards, Jacques Pauly's wines have become more ample and now figure among the five or six "first of the firsts."

Ch Lafaurie-Peyraguey

1er Cru Classé From 1967 to 1977 this wine received hardly any barrel-ageing; it was resolutely unimpressive. With the 1983 vintage this all changed, and since then Ch Lafaurie hasn't looked back. The wine, aged in 50% new oak, is superb: silky in texture, oaky, elegant. It is exemplary Sauternes. In modest years such as 1984 and 1987, Lafaurie produced some of the best wines of the vintage. The credit goes to Domaines Cordier's oenologist, Georges Pauli, in charge in the 1980s.

Ch Lamothe

2ème Cru Classé A new generation has taken over here, so quality will hopefully improve, but Ch Lamothe has been disappointing, and the wines have often been sulphury and lacking in concentration.

Ch Lamothe-Guignard

2ème Cru Classé Since the Guignards bought the property in 1981, they have renovated the cellars and invested in new *barriques*. The improvement in the wine's quality has been spectacular. Since 1986 it has been a delicious wine: rich and sweet, lightly oaky, elegant and complex. With every vintage the quality improves further. Another example of excellent value for money.

Ch Liot

A popular Barsac, Ch Liot is made in a light style, sometimes lacking in *botrytis*, and aged in a mixture of tanks and *barriques*, of which 15% are new. It is relatively inexpensive and makes a sound apéritif Sauternes.

Ch de Malle

2ème Cru Classé This château was known for making fine wines that were too light. But the 1989 and 1990 vintages have revealed the full potential of this estate, which produced rich and unctuous great sweet wines in 1996 and 1998. The château, which is owned by the Comtesse de Bourhazel, is a showpiece.

Ch de Myrat

2ème Cru Classé For 15 years there were no vines at de Myrat, but fortunately there have been new plantings in 1988. The first vintage was released in 1991. After several years of unfavourable climate, the present owner, the Comte de Pontac, has made some fine wines in 1997, 1998, and 2001.

Ch Nairac

2ème Cru Classé Until the late 1960s this wine was sold off in bulk. Then the estate was bought by Tom Heeter and his wife Nicole Tari, and the wine was transformed. From 1972 until his departure in 1987, Heeter made brilliant wines, even in poor vintages such as 1974. A perfectionist, he would make as many as 11 pickings to secure the best

---

CHATEAU D'YQUEM

1er Cru Supérieur. The greatest and also the most expensive of all Sauternes. Its high price has enabled the former owner, Comte Alexandre de Lur-Saluces (who still manages the property), to maintain exemplary standards. His team of 150 pickers harvest for months if necessary, chaptalization is unknown, the wine is aged for three years in all new oak, and the estate will ruthlessly declassify any lots that do not meet its standards. The 103ha (255 acres) of perfectly drained vineyards fall into four parcels that give wines of different character, allowing the blending of the best lots. Yquem, in short, is a hand-crafted wine. This helps to give the wine its profound complexity. Yquem exemplifies the saying that great Sauternes is made in the vineyard rather than the cellar. In a great vintage it comes close to sheer perfection.

fruit. Château Nairac has always been marked by new oak, excessively for some tastes. Since 1988 winemaker Max Amirault has followed admirably in Heeter's footsteps. The 1990 vintage, which spent 30 months in oak, is a classic Barsac. Since 1995, Tom Heeter and Nicole Tari 's son has made some brillant vintages, particularly in 1997.

Ch Rabaud-Promis

1er Cru Classé In the 1960s this château had what were probably the least tidy cellars in Sauternes. That has all changed, and since 1983 the now manager, Philippe Dejean, has been making some of the most delicious wines in the region. It is not conspicuously oaky, has charm rather than power and, in the best years, also a delectable freshness and natural distinction.

Ch Raymond-Lafon

This property belongs to the Meslier family. Pierre Meslier was for decades the manager of Ch d'Yquem (*qv*), and he has applied the same meticulous winemaking standards to his own estate. Yields are very low, and the wine is aged for three years entirely in new *barriques*.

Since 1979, Ch Raymond-Lafon has made a series of sumptuous wines that require long ageing. By harvesting as late as possible, Meslier has made excellent wine even in modest years such as 1985 and 1987. This is the most expensive Sauternes after Yquem and Fargues, but the quality is

superb, and it is well worth the price.

Ch de Rayne-Vigneau

1er Cru Classé A large estate planted on a hillside studded with semi-precious stones, Ch de Rayne-Vigneau used to settle for dull commercial wines. Standards have greatly improved here recently, but progress has not been as rapid as at some other classed-growth estates. Nonetheless Rayne-Vigneau is once again a reliable source of fine Sauternes. Since 1990 — with the exception of 1994 —, the château has produced excellent fine wines.

Ch Rieussec

1er Cru Classé Owned since 1984 by the Rothschilds of Lafite, Ch Rieussec is now back in top form. Under the previous owner, Rieussec made wines that were fat and sumptuous, indeed often delicious, but sometimes overblown and even coarse. And although more recent vintages are still powerful and alcoholic, the richness of fruit seems in better balance. The 1996 and 1997 vintages are among the property's best. Rieussec has undoubtedly recaptured its reputation as one of the great Sauternes estates.

Ch St-Amand

Although the vines are in Preignac, it is easy to mistake this charming, traditionally-made wine for a Barsac. Ch St-Amand's Sauternes is never especially concentrated, but it does have a remarkable elegance. It is also good value for money. The St-Amand wine is sometimes sold under the name Ch de la Chartreuse.

Ch Sigalas-Rabaud

2ème Cru Classé This 14-ha (35-acre) estate is run by the Cordier company, which partly explains the rebirth of

one of the finest Sauternes. The château has twice produced three legendary vintages in a row: in 1988, 1989 and 1990; and in 1995, 1996 and 1997.

Ch de Suduiraut

1er Cru Classé If you are looking for power and opulence in a Sauternes, then Suduiraut is the wine for you. Unfortunately it can also be coarse, and even great vintages such as 1983 and 1986 were disappointing. In 1990 Suduiraut made a magnificent wine. Two years later the estate was sold to the Axa insurance company, which owns many other Médoc estates (*see* p157). So the winemaker, Pierre Pascaud, is no longer accountable to the whims of the five sisters who

previously owned the estate. It is hardly surprising that a vineyard bordering Yquem produces perfect Sauternes.

Ch La Tour Blanche

1er Cru Classé When the 1855 classification was made, this was said to be the best Sauternes château after Ch d'Yquem. Yet the wines of the 1970s and early 1980s were dire. Happily, under the administration of Jean-Pierre Jausserand, standards have risen. Harvesting is much more selective, sub-standard lots are declassified, and 100% new oak has been used since 1990. Since 1988 La Tour Blanche has again been worthy of its *Premier Cru* status.

Ch d'Yquem

See profile.

CERONS

Growers in the three communes of Cérons, Podensac and Illats have the right to the Cérons *appellation* for sweet white wines, but they are also entitled to produce dry white AOC Graves from the same vines. They can harvest a larger (and easier to sell) crop for the dry wine, so there are few Cérons producers these days.

In 1981 Cérons production was 66,500 cases from 790ha (1,950 acres), but by 1989 this was down to 31,000 cases of sweet wine, with 189,000 of dry. At its best Cérons tastes like a light Barsac, but higher yields — 40 hl/ha as opposed to 25hl/ha in Sauternes — make it more difficult to achieve the sugar content of Sauternes. Thus the Cérons wines are lighter and less sweet, and usually show less influence of *botrytis*. This makes them excellent apéritifs rather than lush dessert wines.

Ch de Cérons

Jean Perromat is a long-term defender of the *appellation* and has produced one of the most stylish examples. Yields are below 30hl/ha, and since 1988 part of the crop has been *barrique*-fermented. The 1990 was an exceptional vintage, with a natural sugar content of 23%. Wines are very well balanced and age gracefully.

Grand Enclos du Ch de Cérons

A separate property from the château itself, the Grand Enclos produces about 800 cases of red and white (AOC Graves and Cérons) in a favourable year. In 2002, the estate was bought by Giorgio Cavanna, author of the famous Tuscan Castello di Ama. Worth watching closely!

Other producers

Ch d'Arricaud, Clos Bourgelat (*see* also Graves, p162).

ENTRE-DEUX-MERS

The land between the rivers Dordogne, to the north, and Garonne to the south is a cheerful contrast to the virtually flat, somewhat austere landscapes of the Graves and Médoc. The Entre-deux-Mers ("between two seas" — or tidal rivers) is a rolling plateau, split up by little valleys and dotted with farms and woods.

Long ago, vines were just one more crop amongst the wheatfields, cow pastures and orchards. Today, it is the single largest vineyard area in Bordeau, and the largest AOC in France. The southern edge of the area consists of a line of low but steep hills overlooking the Garonne. These are "the Côtes", the vine-clad slopes where some of the most important medieval vineyards in all Bordeaux were sited.

The area had a name for indifferent, medium-sweet white wines, but the 1980s saw a swing towards diversity. Now it has become a useful source of good-value wines of all styles.

Districts and appellations

The area is a patchwork of wine *appellations*. Much of the red-wine vineyard land is entitled to only the basic Bordeaux or Bordeaux Supérieur AOCs. The latter often offers quite good value. The AOC Entre-deux-Mers covers white wine only.

The hillside vineyards of the Premières Côtes de Bordeaux, which face west across the wide Garonne to the city, produce the best red wines of the area. They are also entitled to use the Premières Côtes AOC for sweet whites; the dry whites are labelled Entre-deux-Mers. These vineyards continue south-east under the name Côtes de Bordeaux St-Macaire.

Within the Premières Côtes are zones devoted to sweet white wines:

Ste-Croix-du-Mont, Loupiac and Cadillac. These three are often considered to be part of the wider grouping of sweet-wine *appellations* centred on Sauternes on the other side of the Garonne, and known in the Bordeaux official statistics as the *"groupe vins blancs doux"*. These same figures show that Cadillac has virtually vanished as an *appellation*, while the other two are showing signs of being in excellent form.

Other zones within the area with their own AOC are: Entre-deux-Mers Haut-Benauge, a white wine sub-zone partly within Entre-deux-Mers and partly outside its borders; Graves de Vayres, on gravel beside the Dordogne; and Ste-Foy-Bordeaux which makes both red and white wines. The Graves de Vayre AOC should not be confused with the Graves AOC on the other side of the river. Its 350ha (865 acres) of vineyard are planted with equal portions of white

PRODUCERS

The area is dominated by cooperatives, which account for 40% of the production. Good châteaux include:

RED WINES
Premières Côtes de Bordeaux:
Brethous, de Chastelet, Dudon, la Gorce, Grimont, du Juge, Lagarosse, Nenine, de Plassan.

SWEET WHITE WINES
Cadillac: Fayau, Manos, Renon, Suau.
Loupiac: du Cros, Loupiac-Gaudiet, Domaine du Noble, Peyrot-Marges, de Ricaud, Rondillon.
Ste-Croix-du-Mont: La Grave, Loubens, La Rame du Mont.

DRY WHITE WINES
Haut-Benauge: le Bos, Haut-Reygnac, Domaine de la Seriziere.
Entre-deux-Mers: Bonnet, Camarsac, Ste-Marie.

and red grape varieties. Château Lesparre produces good red and white wines.

Wine styles

Entre-deux-Mers should be — and usually is — a dry white wine made from Sauvignon Blanc and Sémillon grapes. In the past the AOC rules were frequently ignored, and medium-sweet versions were sold on northern European markets. As this style of wine fell out of fashion, the area declined. A conscious switch back to fresh, dry wines was led by the cooperatives and a few private estates, and sales are increasing. Wines from the Haut-Benauges sub-zone stay dry despite a strong aroma of Sémillon.

The sweet wines of the Premières Côtes and Cadillac are doing everything they can to achieve stardom, but it isn't easy, as *botrytis* (*see* Sauternes p163) is rare in these vineyards and buyers prefer the better-known Sauternes. The local AOCs Loupiac and Ste-Croix-du-Mont are better situated, with sites sloping to the river that can experience *botrytis*. The potential for good sweet wine, up to Sauternes standard and in a similar style, is here. The sweet wines of Loupiac (12,000hl), of Cadillac (6,500hl) and even more so of Ste-Croix-du-Mont (16,000hl) have greatly improved and found their own style.

It is often hard to tell if a red wine comes from this area or from the other parts of the Gironde entitled to the AOC Bordeaux, for there is nothing on the label to say. The Premières Côtes reds can be identified, though: they are often a bargain, and are well-structured, Merlot-based wines of real character. Indeed, it is from these vineyards that are produced the best clarets, light red wines which undergo bleeding during the fermentation process.

BOURG AND BLAYE

Visitors to the Médoc constantly glimpse the wooded slopes of Blaye on the eastern horizon, across the wide brown waters of the Gironde estuary. It is visible, but inaccessible; only to be reached by a sporadic ferry from Lamarque, between St-Julien and Margaux.

The rolling countryside of the Right Bank of the Gironde has many vineyards, even if they are not as dominant as in St-Emilion or the Médoc. There were vines here before the Médoc was planted: Blaye and Bourg were busy medieval wine ports when Pauillac and Margaux were growing corn and raising cows.

Bourg and Blaye produce red and white wines, but the reds are best. The top wines come from châteaux along the riverside row of hills, while the abundant production of inland vineyards is sold to cooperatives. Generally, it can be said that both zones are a good and rich source of good red bordeaux.

Vineyards around the old church at Cars, Blaye.

Grape varieties and wine styles

Merlot and Cabernet Franc are the chief grape varieties, producing red wines that are very much "Right Bank" in style, with echoes of Fronsac and St-Emilion. White wines are made from Sémillon, Sauvignon Blanc and the Colombard variety of nearby Cognac. A proportion of Malbec is used in some of the reds, and Cabernet Sauvignon is also grown.

Historically, Blaye and Bourg red wines had a reputation as robust, dark and long-lived. They were said by a 19th-century writer to need ten years' ageing, and to be superior to ordinary Médocs due to their attractive fruit and structure. This style has remained constant, though Médoc wines have on the whole improved. Today's Bourg and Blaye wines need perhaps three years, and can improve for up to ten in good vintages.

The white wines have no real distinction and are akin to the wines of the Entre-deux-Mers in character.

Areas and appellations

Bourg is the smaller of the two areas, though vine-growing is quite intensive around the port of Bourg. The Côtes de Bourg AOC covers the best land, on the slopes above the river. The *appellations* Bourg and Bourgeais have fallen out of use. Some 3,100ha (7,660 acres) of vines are used mainly for red wine, with a very small amount of white wine.

Blaye is much larger, though the vineyard area is roughly the same as Bourg's. The three *appellations* all cover the same area. AOC Blaye (or Blayais) covers red and white wines, though more reds are made. Côtes de Blaye is for dry white only; Premières Côtes de Blaye restricts the varieties to the Bordeaux classics and demands lower yields. It covers red and white wines. □

PRODUCERS

Cooperatives are important producers, but an increasing number of châteaux bottle their own wine. While the production of white wine is declining, the increasingly popular red wine is making good progress. Among the most reliable red and white wine (indicated by w) producers are:

Barbe, Bertinerie, Les Billauds, Charron, la Croix-St-Jacques, Gardaut Haut-Cluzeau (w), du Grand Barrail, Haut-Bertinerie (w), Haut-Sociando, Les Jonqueyres, Loumède, le Menaudat, Les Petits Arnauds, Pérenne, Peyraud, Segonzac, La Tonnelle, Le Virou.

WINE DISTRICTS OF THE LIBOURNAIS

Wine districts

- St-Emilion
- Lussac, Montagne St-Georges, Puisseguin
- Pomerol
- Lalande-de-Pomerol
- Fronsac
- Canon-Fronsac
- Côtes de Francs
- Côtes de Castillon
- Graves de Vayres

--- *département* boundary
=== major road
=== other road

The Libournais, named after the port of Libourne on the Dordogne, is an alternative name for the Right Bank. The zone covers the vineyards of St-Emilion, Pomerol, Fronsac and their satellites.

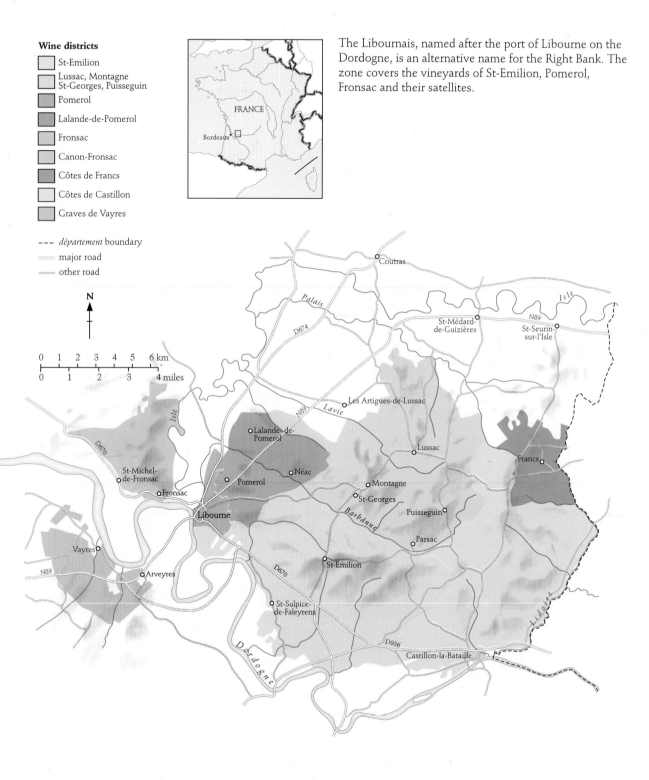

FRANCE

Bordeaux

N

0 1 2 3 4 5 6 km
0 1 2 3 4 miles

Coutras

Palais

D674

St-Médard-de-Guizières

Isle

N89

St-Seurin-sur-l'Isle

Isle

Les Artigues-de-Lussac

N89

Lavie

Lalande-de-Pomerol

D670

Lussac

Francs

St-Michel-de-Fronsac

Néac

Montagne

St-Georges

Puisseguin

Pomerol

Fronsac

Barbanne

Libourne

Parsac

Lidoire

Vayres

St-Emilion

D670

N89

Arveyres

St-Sulpice-de-Faleyrens

Dordogne

D936

Castillon-la-Bataille

ST-EMILION

The golden stones of the medieval town of St-Emilion.

This area produces red wine only and is centred on the village of St-Emilion, some 40km (25 miles) north-east of the city of Bordeaux on the right bank of the River Dordogne. Vines have been cultivated in the area since Roman times. Ausonius, the Roman poet-consul, grew grapes here and Château Ausone is named after him. A large Roman villa has been excavated nearby. The village of St-Emilion itself is called after a hermit who lived on the site in the 8th century.

The visitor to St-Emilion is immediately struck by the sheer beauty of the village, which clings to the limestone hillsides surrounding it rather like an amphitheatre. Its historic remains include the only completely underground church in Europe. Although best avoided in the height of summer, it is a delightful place to stay outside the main tourist season.

The designated vine-growing area covers some 5,200ha (12,850 acres) spread over nine communes. In addition to the nine communes entitled to use the St-Emilion *appellation*, four others are allowed to add this famous name to that of their own commune: Lussac, Montagne, Puisseguin, St-Georges (*see* p176).

Wine zones and châteaux

The area boasts a wide variety of soils, subsoils and micro-climates, so that the types of wine produced vary enormously. There are more than 900 individual producers of St-Emilion, a factor that contributes to the variety. Many of the properties are extremely small, family-run enterprises and Bordeaux's most important cooperative, with more than 200 members, is to be found here.

The top classified properties are concentrated in two distinct zones.

Of the 11 *Premiers Grands Crus Classés*, nine are on the limestone plateau or on the south-facing slopes stretching east to west of St-Emilion for a distance of some 8km (5 miles). Top properties here include châteaux Ausone, Canon and Magdelaine. Two of the three other *Premiers Grands Crus* — châteaux Cheval Blanc and Figeac — are both situated some 4km (2.5 miles) to the west of the village towards the Pomerol border where the soil is gravel and sand.

The Jurade

This body, which today is responsible for the worldwide promotion of the wines of St-Emilion, originated in the 12th century when the Charte de Falaise was signed by Jean-Sans-Terre, son of Eleanor of Aquitaine, permitting the inhabitants of the village to administer their own wine laws. In 1289, under Edward I, these powers were extended to eight further parishes and it is these nine communes that now form the designated area of St-Emilion.

Grape varieties

The late-budding, late-ripening Cabernet Sauvignon, which is widely planted in the Médoc, is generally ill-suited to the north-east of the Bordeaux region because of the cooler clay and limestone soils and lower average air temperatures. The two varieties that perform exceptionally well here are Merlot and Cabernet Franc. In St-Emilion their proportions are generally equal, though châteaux like Magdelaine and Le Tertre Rôteboeuf have an extremely high percentage of Merlot, whereas Cheval Blanc is two-thirds Cabernet Franc. In Pomerol, the cool, iron-rich, clay soil is particularly well suited to Merlot, which accounts for roughly 75%, followed by Cabernet Franc (about 20%) and Cabernet Sauvignon (about 5%). Although Merlot is widely grown throughout the world, it is generally suitable only for light, plummy, early-drinking wines. In Pomerol it appears to have found its natural habitat and the wines attain a depth and richness that can last for 30 or 40 years or more.

The St-Emilion style

The relatively large area, different *terroirs*, great diversity of soils and subsoils, and the large number of producers make it almost impossible to pinpoint a particular St-Emilion style. However, a true-to-type St-Emilion has a youthful appeal with none of the austerity to be found in its Médoc cousins. Its attractiveness is due to the characteristics of the predominant grape varieties: the early-maturing Cabernet Franc and the fleshy, plummy Merlot, which, combined, produce wines that are supple and fruity, have good vinosity and a fair degree of alcohol, backed up by sufficient acidity, tannins and other aromatic components. In some cool vintages, wines from lesser châteaux can be frankly disappointing, appearing quite light and thin, and lacking in fruit: these need drinking within a couple of years of the vintage.

However, the best wines from the finest properties will last easily for 10 to 20 years, if properly cellared. A modest, well-made St-Emilion from a good year will, on the other hand, probably be at its peak from six to eight years after the vintage. ☐

THE ST-EMILION CLASSIFICATION

St-Emilion was omitted from the 1855 Classification. It was first classified in 1955 on the basis of soil analysis, reputation of the property and tasting. In theory if not necessarily in practice, the list is subject to review every ten years, unlike that of the Médoc which, apart from one major change, appears to have been cast in concrete. In St-Emilion the original classification was revised in 1969 and again in 1985 and 1996. Currently, there are 13 *Premiers Grands Crus Classés* and 55 *Grands Crus Classés*. Two of the *Premiers Grands Crus Classés* are listed as "A", the rest are "B".

Premiers Grands Crus Classés

Ch Ausone (A)
Ch Cheval Blanc (A)
Ch Angélus (B)
Ch Beau-Séjour-Bécot (B)
Ch Beauséjour (B)
Ch Belair (B)
Ch Canon (B)
Ch Clos Fourtet (B)
Ch Figeac (B)
Ch La Gaffelière (B)
Ch Magdelaine (B)
Ch Pavie (B)
Ch Trottevieille (B)

Grands Crus Classés

Ch l'Arrosée
Ch Balestard la Tonnelle
Ch Bellevue
Ch Bergat
Ch Berliquet
Ch Cadet-Bon
Ch Cadet-Piola
Ch Canon-la-Gaffelière
Ch Cap de Mourlin
Ch Chauvin
Ch la Clotte
Ch la Clusière
Ch la Couspaude
Ch Corbin
Ch Corbin-Michotte
Ch Couvent des Jacobins
Ch Curé-Bon
Ch Dassault
Ch la Dominique
Ch Faurie-de-Souchard
Ch Fonplégade
Ch Fonroque
Ch Franc-Mayne
Ch Grandes Murailles
Ch Grand-Mayne
Ch Grand-Pontet
Ch Guadet-St-Julien
Ch Haut Corbin
Ch Haut Sarpe

Clos des Jacobins
Ch Lamarzelle
Ch Laniote
Ch Larcis-Ducasse
Ch Larmande
Ch Laroque
Ch Laroze
Ch Matras
Ch Moulin du Cadet
Clos de l'Oratoire
Ch Pavie-Decesse
Ch Pavie-Macquin
Ch Petit-Faurie-de-Soutard
Ch le Prieuré
Ch Ripeau
Ch St-Georges Côte Pavie
Clos St-Martin
Ch la Serre
Ch Soutard
Ch Tertre Daugay
Ch Tour-du-Pin-Figeac (Giraud-Bélivier)
Ch Tour-du-Pin-Figeac (Moueix)
Ch la Tour-Figeac
Ch Troplong-Mondot
Ch Villemaurine
Ch Yon-Figeac

QUALITY FACTORS

Both the geology and soils, and the climate, of St-Emilion and the rest of the Libournais differ from the Left-Bank zones of Médoc and Graves. These factors, allied and linked to the dominant grape varieties of the region, which are Merlot and Cabernet Franc, produce wines of distinct styles. Here the spotlight is on the geology of the St-Emilion vineyards.

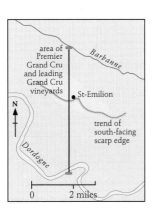

Geology and soils

St-Emilion town is sited on a limestone hill which is in geological terms the edge of a plateau. The scarp slope forming the edge of this limestone faces broadly south. The plateau and the slope (the *côte*) provide the best vineyard sites. Beneath the slope is a zone of sandy gravel, topped in places by river-borne sand. Vines grow here, but the châteaux are not in the first rank. The marshy riverside land has few vineyards. To the north, the plateau slopes gently down to the Barbanne stream. Here the underlying rock is covered with sand and gravel. Some excellent vineyards, and many good ones, are sited here. The wine made on the sand/gravel is typically softer and earlier to mature than that from the limestone plateau and *côte*.

ST-EMILION: PLATEAU AND COTES

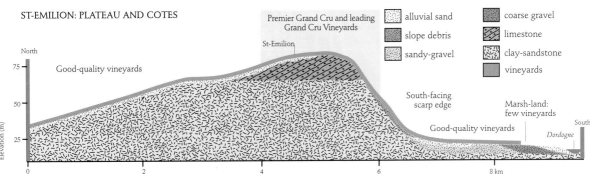

- alluvial sand
- slope debris
- sandy-gravel
- coarse gravel
- limestone
- clay-sandstone
- vineyards

Climate

The climate of the Libournais is broadly that of the Médoc: maritime influences mean fairly mild winters and warm, rather than hot, summers. It is, however, further inland than the Médoc, with slightly cooler winters and warmer summers, but with less rain. The hottest months are July and August, with an average temperature of 20°C (68°F). Most rain falls in winter. However, cool, damp conditions can cause problems at flowering in June, and later in September and early October as the grapes are ripening. The northern part of St-Emilion is relatively far from both sea and river, and is consequently more at risk from spring frosts. Damaging frosts occurred in 1985 and 1991, and the region still remembers 1965, when catastrophic frosts killed large numbers of vines and many vineyards produced little or no crop. Frosts are less damaging on the *côte* as air drainage is more efficient than on the plateau.

Limestone slopes on the *côte* below Château Ausone.

Site and exposure

The land forms are an expression of the underlying geology of the region (*see* Geology and soils). The limestone plateau is the highest point, reaching 90m (300ft) near the town of St-Emilion, while the lowest parts are by the River Dordogne in the south (10m/30ft) and on the northern boundary of the *appellation* (25m/80ft). Altitudes are thus greater than in the Médoc with a slight lessening of average temperatures as a result. The *côte* provides vineyard sites that, while relatively steep, are sheltered from north and west winds and have a desirable southerly exposure. The more open land of the plateau and the northerly slopes are less sheltered. The slopes, as well as the soils ensure good drainage. The limestone of the *côte* is easily quarried, allowing some remarkable, deep *caves* to be dug, many centuries old. These cellars provide ideal, cool conditions for ageing.

PRODUCERS

The St-Emilion châteaux are typically smaller in area than those of the Médoc or Graves, and production is therefore lower. The *appellation* covers seven communes, but most of the best estates are in St-Emilion itself. Elsewhere there are many small properties which either send their grapes to the cooperative (*see* p175) or market their wine directly: this is a fine area for wine tourism.

Ch l'Angélus

1er Grand Cru Classé This is one of the largest of the leading properties in St-Emilion with an average annual production of 12,000 cases. Heavy investment by the owners, the de Boüard de Laforest family, has permitted to make wines that are among the *appellation*'s best. A second wine, Le Carillon d'Angélus, was first introduced in the 1987 vintage.

Ch Ausone

1er Grand Cru Classé Named after the Roman poet-consul Ausonius, this is the leading property of the *appellation*, together with Ch Cheval Blanc. It is beautifully situated at the top of the hillside just outside St-Emilion, and its limestone cellars afford natural temperature control. One of the smallest properties in St-Emilion, it produces just 2,000 cases a year on average and is very difficult to find commercially. This property has undergone a total transfor-

mation since the 1976 vintage, when the new cellar master, Pascal Delbeck, was appointed. Because of family quarrels, Alain Vanthier now runs the estate alone. This great winemaker's 2000 vintage has already become a legend. It costs a fortune, but this hardly matters, as the wine cannot be found anywhere.

Ch Balestard-la-Tonnelle

Grand Cru Classé A fine wine's ancient pedigree is rarely vouched for by a poet — but in this case it is, and by a famous one, no less! Villon refers to it in a poem that is reproduced on the label. The vineyard covers 10ha (25 acres). Balestard-la-Tonnelle is a solid, long-lived wine.

Ch Beauséjour (Duffau-Lagarrosse)

1er Grand Cru Classé Perhaps the least known of the *Premiers Grands Crus*, this château has been undergoing a revival, since the 1990 vintage, and will be well worth keeping an eye on. It used to have a high percentage of Cabernet Franc in the blend, but this is being reduced, and late harvesting has been introduced. This wine has been consistently excellent for the last decade.

Ch Belair

1er Grand Cru Classé Owned by the Dubois-Challon family,

this property produces wine with a lot of Ausone's concentration and some of its tannic backbone, but which matures sooner. Well-regarded for a long time, the estate produced very fine wines indeed in the latter part of the 1980s.

Ch Cadet-Piola

Grand Cru Classé This estate is situated on one of the highest points of the St-Emilion plateau to the north of the village and enjoys a particularly favourable micro-climate. Small in size, it has some 28% Cabernet Sauvignon in the blend so that the wines can be quite tannic when young, although they begin to soften after a few years in bottle.

Ch Canon

1er Grand Cru Classé This is one of St-Emilion's very top properties, which in really fine years can equal Ausone and Cheval Blanc. The quality has improved hugely since 1982, when Eric Fournier, whose family owns it, took over the management. Bought up by the Wertheimer family (of Chanel), Canon is now run by Kolasa (formerly Latour), who had to rebuild the winery from scratch — with the intention of making wines for keeping. The wines often show a cedary, elegant character with bottle-age.

Ch Canon-la-Gaffelière

Grand Cru Classé This property has been totally transformed by its new owners, the Comtes de Neipperg, and is now run by the brilliant young Stephan de Neipperg. His philosophy is to combine the latest technology in vinification with traditional maturation. Some of the vineyards are situated on the hillsides, and some on the flatter sandy soils at the bottom of the slope. Canon-la-Gaffelière produced outstanding wines in 1988, 1996, 1997, 1998, 1999 and 2000.

Ch Cheval Blanc

1er Grand Cru Classé Cheval Blanc vies with Ch Ausone as St-Emilion's leading estate, but has a far more consistent track record. Situated next to the Pomerol border, it is relatively large by St-Emilion standards, producing some 17,500 cases a year. It boasts a wide variety of soils, including gravel, ancient sand and some clay. Part of its uniqueness lies in the combination of grape varieties, with 66% Cabernet Franc — a far higher percentage of this variety than in any other top St-Emilion property. The style of wine is rich, ripe and intense; it can be deceptively approachable when young, but will easily last for 40 years or more.

Ch La Dominique

Grand Cru Classé This estate, situated over towards the Pomerol border, has a long history. It has been a rising star recently, making some very good wines. Since 1969, the owner is Clément Fayat; he is advised by Pomerol's leading winemaker, Michel Rolland. The vineyard has 80% Merlot, and Rolland goes in for late harvesting for maximum maturity.

The wines are extremely concentrated but not overly tannic, very fat and round. The annual production of about 8,350 cases is sold in no time: La Dominique is a great seducer.

Ch Faugères

Grand Cru Formèr film producers Corinne and Péby Guisez have taken to wine making. On 28ha (69 acres) of vines, 70% Merlot and 30% Cabernet make for an ample, balanced and savoury St-Emilion — a must for all wine lovers. Cap de Faugères, a Côte-de-Castillon, benefits from the same meticulous winemaking. The *cuvée* Péby, an homage to the late Péby

Guisez, is amongst the top *Grands Crus Classés*.

Ch Figeac

1er Grand Cru Classé Owned by the Manoncourt family, this is certainly one of St-Emilion's most beautiful estates and is well worth visiting. It is situated towards the Pomerol border, next to Château Cheval Blanc and has a gravel soil with quartz from the Massif Central. Part of the uniqueness of its wines is due to the high percentage of Cabernet Sauvignon — approximately one-third — in the blend. The wines are generally quite concentrated, yet surprisingly supple and appealing when still relatively young. They make very good medium-term drinking.

Clos Fourtet

1er Grand Cru Classé Built next to the collegiate church, on the site of an ancient fort, Clos Fourtet has vast subterranean cellars. Its fine, elegant wines are made in an ultramodern winery.

Clos des Jacobins

Grand Cru Classé This property, which sits in the midst of the St-Emilion *appellation*, produces extremely attractive wines, and the quality is very consistent. The style is generous and velvety, and it makes perfect medium-term drinking. Owned by Domaines Cordier.

Ch Larmande

Grand Cru Classé This old estate lies north of the town of St-Emilion, with a vineyard on sandy soil of 18ha (44 acres) planted in two-thirds Merlot. The Méneret-Capdemourlin family owned the estate for most of this century, until they sold it in 1991. Now part of La Mondiale group, Larmande has been a shining star in the 1990s. Its wine is modestly priced.

Ch Magdelaine

1er Grand Cru Classé With an extremely high percentage of Merlot in the blend, in good years this wine has the opulence and richness normally associated with a fine Pomerol, which is not surprising given that it is owned by the Moueix family, Pomerol's leading producers. The beautifully situated property, overlooking the Dordogne, has vineyards in a horseshoe shape. Its quality places this wine amongst the top *Premiers Grands Crus Classés*.

Ch Pavie

1er Grand Cru Classé Among the biggest producers of all the St-Emilion *Premiers Grands Crus Classés*. Since 1998 the estate has been owned by Gérard Perse, dynamic owner of the excellent Château Monbousquet *(St-Emilion Grand Cru)*.

Ch Pavie-Decesse

Grand Cru Classé Gérard Perse, who bought this property in 1997, has doubled the quality and the price of its wine. The estate produces wines that are quite powerful and have noticeable tannins when young.

Ch Pavie-Macquin

Grand Cru Classé This estate is situated on the Côte de Pavie and enjoys an excellent micro-climate with south-facing vineyards. Its wine is supple and fleshy.

Clos St-Martin

Grand Cru Classé The area's smallest *Grand Cru Classé*.

Although not especially good in the early 1980s, the quality has improved noticeably since 1990.

Ch Soutard

Grand Cru Classé Owned by the de Ligneris family since 1785, this is one of St-Emilion's oldest estates. It is run along traditional lines, and organic viticulture is used. The wines are very dark in colour and quite tannic when young. The finest wines will last in excess of 20 years. The 1990 and 1998 vintages are exceptional.

Ch Le Tertre Rôtebœuf

Grand Cru On this tiny property, where he makes just 2,250 cases a year, François Mitjavile produces a wine that is more like a superb Pomerol. Risk-taking is what he thrives on, harvesting his almost pure Merlot vineyard as late as possible for maximum maturity, employing some whole-berry fermentation and consistently using 100% new oak, even in the lighter years.

Mitjavile came to prominence with the 1982 vintage and has not looked back since, culminating in his extraordinary 1997, 1998, 1999, and 2000 vintages. They are almost impossible to find commercially due to minuscule quantity produced and their international reputation. François Mitjavile has bought a property in the Côtes de Bourg, Ch Roc de Combes, which is also getting the Mitjaville treatment.

Ch Troplong-Mondot

Grand Cru Classé This beautiful property, one of the largest in St-Emilion, has been run by Christine Valette since 1980. Under her management and with the advice of oenologist Michel Rolland (*see* p178), it has produced a superb run of vintages in 1990, 1998 and 2000.

Ch Trottevieille

1er Grand Cru Classé The wines of this property used to be disappointing, but since the mid-1980s there has been a noticeable improvement — probably due to Philippe Castéja's management. Innovations include the use of 100% new oak.

Whereas the wines used to be noticeably lacking in concentration and aged prematurely, Philippe Castéja has been making much more serious wines, designed for medium rather than long-term drinking.

Union des Producteurs de St-Emilion

Of the nearly 1,000 producers in St-Emilion, over 200 are members of the local cooperative, which is the largest in Bordeaux and has an excellent reputation. In addition to the estate wines that it bottles, including several *Grands Crus*, the cooperative also produces a number of specially-blended wines that include the Royal St-Emilion, Côtes Rocheuses, Cuvée Gallus as well as Haut-Quercus.

ST-EMILION'S "GARAGE WINES"

The term *vin de garage*, or "garage wine", is applied to exceptionally good wine that is made in exceptionally small quantities and sold for exceptionally high prices. The rapid success of these wines has inspired many winemakers in St-Emilion and elsewhere.

Ch La Mondotte

Stephan de Neipperg's wine is as rich as it is hard to find.

Ch de Valandraud

Jean-Luc Thunevin's wine is well-structured, impressive and already famous.

Ch Le Tertre-Rôtebœuf

See above.

ST-EMILION SATELLITES

The St-Emilion AOC is but the heart of a much wider vinegrowing zone. Pomerol and Fronsac, to the west, are dealt with separately (*see* pp177 and 180). The villages to the north-east, beyond the Barbanne stream, can add St-Emilion to their names and are listed below. Eastwards are the Côtes AOCs of Castillon and Francs (*see* box).

THE APPELLATIONS

In 1936, when the wine-growing area of St-Emilion was defined, producers in neighbouring areas that fell outside the new *appellation* obtained permission to append the name of St-Emilion to that of their commune. Five communes were accorded this right: Lussac, Montagne, Parsac, Puisseguin and St-Georges. However, in December 1972, in an attempt to rationalize the number of *appellations*, the INAO (Institut National des Appellations d'Origine) decreed that wines from the communes of Parsac and St-Georges could appear under the Montagne label. Today, the Parsac *appellation* is no longer seen (although it still exists) and most of the producers in St-Georges also choose to use the Montagne *appellation* instead.

The wines of the St-Emilion satellites can represent excellent value. The soils and subsoils are fairly similar to those of St-Emilion and neighbouring Pomerol, and the permitted grapes are the same: Cabernet Sauvignon, Cabernet Franc, Merlot, Malbec and Carmenère, making this also a red-wine-only area. In quality, the finest wines are easily the equal of good St-Emilion *Grands Crus* and, because they do not have the prestige of the greater *appellation*, they will usually be more affordable.

Montagne St-Emilion

The largest and probably the best-known of the five satellites, Montagne St-Emilion covers some 1,500ha (3,700 acres) and is situated close to the Pomerol border, to the west of Lussac and Puisseguin. The soil is clay, and clay with limestone and gravel can be found in parts, as can traces of iron in the subsoil. There are two cooperatives. The best properties produce wines that easily come up to good quality St-Emilion *Grand Cru* standard, supple and fruity with some finesse and good ageing potential.

Châteaux of this *appellation* include Calon, Corbin, Maison Blanche, Maison Neuve, Roc de Calon, Roudier and des Tours.

Lussac St-Emilion

Situated 9km (5 miles) to the north-east of the village of St-Emilion, this is the second largest of the satellites, with some 1,400ha (3,400 acres) under vine. The soil varies from clay-limestone hill slopes in the south-east, to a small gravel plateau in the west and pure clay in the north.

Lussac is allied to neighbouring Puisseguin in two ways. A large portion of the production of both areas is vinified at a cooperative they share, and the brotherhood of *Echevins* of Lussac St-Emilion and Puisseguin St-Emilion promotes the wines from both areas, both at home and on the export markets.

Châteaux here include Barbe Blanche, Bel-Air, de Lussac, Lyonnat, Tour de Grenet, Vieux Château Chambeau.

Puisseguin St-Emilion

The most eastern of all the satellites, bordering the Côtes de Castillon, the *appellation* has nearly 700ha (1,730 acres) under vine, and of the 120 growers, roughly one-third are members of the local cooperative. One of the highest points of the Gironde is to be found here, where the undulating countryside reaches 89m (294ft). The soil is predominantly clay and limestone over a stony subsoil.

Châteaux here include: Bel Air, du Branda, Moulin-Listrac and Roc de Boissac.

St-Georges St-Emilion

By far the smallest of the five satellites, with a mere 175ha (432 acres) under vine. Most of the producers declare their wines under the Montagne St-Emilion *appellation* according to the decree laid down by the INAO in December 1972.

Châteaux using the St-Georges St-Emilion *appellation* include Belair St-Georges, Calon, Cap d'Or, St-André Corbin, St-Georges and Tours du Pas St-Georges.

COTES DE CASTILLON AND COTES DE FRANCS

To the east of St-Emilion and its surrounding satellites lie two small and as yet relatively unknown Bordeaux *appellations*.

Côtes de Castillon

The Côtes de Castillon is centred on the ancient market town of Castillon-la-Bataille, which is named after the battle that took place in 1453 and marked the end of the Hundred Years' War. Before 1989 this region was entitled to use the name Côtes de Castillon only when it was preceded by the words *Bordeaux* or *Bordeaux Supérieur*. However, since then it has been allowed its own *appellation*, for red wine only. There are 2,800ha (6,920 acres) under vine, of which 75 (185) grow white grapes for AOC Bordeaux. The wines are not unlike those of the St-Emilion satellites, although perhaps slightly more tannic in youth, requiring a few years in bottle to round out and become more supple. Reliable châteaux include Ch Côte Montpezat and Cap de Faugères d'Aiguilhe.

Bordeaux Côtes de Francs

Ten kilometres (six miles) to the north of Castillon-la-Bataille lies the commune of Francs. Here there are a mere 450ha (1,110 acres) of vines of which just 30 (74 acres) are planted with white varieties. The *appellation* covers both red and white wines, and the latter can be either dry or sweet. Permitted white grapes are Sémillon, Sauvignon and Muscadelle, as for other areas of Bordeaux. The red wines are very well coloured, have an attractive bouquet and are quite fat on the palate.

Châteaux here include Les Charmes Godard, de Francs, Laclaverie and Puygueraud.

POMEROL

Although small in size, this red wine area is one of Bordeaux's greatest assets for the sheer quality and uniqueness of its finest wines.

The mere 730ha (1,800 acres) of Pomerol is situated some 29km (18 miles) east of the city of Bordeaux. It abuts St-Emilion to the east, which is roughly seven times its size and with which it shares two other common borders: the Dordogne River to the south and the stream of La Barbanne to the north, beyond which lies Lalande-de-Pomerol. The noisy N89 highway cuts through the western side of this the most bucolic of Bordeaux's great wine-producing areas, with a few châteaux lying west of the road.

Unlike neighbouring St-Emilion, Pomerol has no real centre unless one counts the ancient river port of Libourne, which was important historically for shipping wines abroad. The major *négociant* house of the area, Etablissements Jean-Pierre Moueix, maintains its offices and warehouses along the quays. The village of Pomerol itself is scattered, noteworthy only for its church which is highly visible across the flat landscape of the region, sitting amidst a sea of vines and little else.

Although grapes have been grown here since Roman times, it is only since World War II that the wines have gained any enduring fame, despite the fact that Château Pétrus, its greatest estate, won a gold medal in the Paris Exhibition of 1878. This historical obscurity is partly due to the small size of the area and to its relative isolation. Most of the leading properties are only a few hectares in size, with an average annual production of a few thousand cases only, compared to the 20,000-plus cases produced at many of the top Médoc properties. Pomerol's isolation continued well into the 19th century, as

The vineyard of Vieux-Château-Certan.

links with Bordeaux were hampered by the lack of bridges across the Dordogne and Garonne Rivers, and the area thus escaped the attention of the powerful Bordeaux wine trade. To this day the leading estates sell their wines direct to their customers, both in France and abroad, without recourse to the leading Bordeaux *négociants*.

No other major wine-producing area in Bordeaux owes its reputation as much to one individual as Pomerol. In the 1930s Jean-Pierre Moueix left his native Corrèze and set up as a *négociant* on the right bank of the Dordogne. Gradually he bought up estates and now owns or part-owns many of Pomerol's leading properties, including Pétrus, La Fleur Pétrus, Latour à Pomerol and Trotanoy. The firm, now run by his son Christian, still acts as a *"metayeur"* and *négociant*, and a significant proportion of sales of all Pomerol and other Right-Bank wines are controlled by the Etablissements Jean-Pierre Moueix.

The appellation

There is only one *appellation*: Pomerol. This region was not included in the 1855 Classification of the wines of the Gironde and, unlike St-Emilion and the Graves, which devised their own lists, Pomerol remains unclassified to this day, to the satisfaction of its major producers. An unofficial ranking does exist, however, based on quality, track record and performance on the market-place.

The style of wines

Only red-wine varieties are grown in this area. The Merlot grape reigns supreme, accounting for some three-quarters of the total area under vine. It is followed by Cabernet Franc which covers roughly one-fifth, and a small amount (approximately 5%) of Cabernet Sauvignon. Other authorized varieties, which are rarely if ever seen, are Cot (Malbec) and Carmenère.

Generally, the wines of Pomerol are ready at a relatively young age, and most are ideal between four and six years after the vintage. Although they do have a tannic backbone, they usually lack the youthful austerity of most Médoc wines, although a vintage such as 1986 would seem to contradict this. After a couple of years in bottle, the lesser wines have a plummy appeal, allied to a fullish, well-rounded palate with no awkward edges. The finest wines have a similar appeal but are far richer and more concentrated, with exotic youthful aromas of spices and herbs. As the finest wines mature, which in the best vintages (such as 1975, 1982, 1989 and 1990) can be for 40 years or more, many of the wines take on a distinctly gamey character, becoming much fuller and fleshier, making them Bordeaux's richest and perhaps most decadent wines.   □

PRODUCERS

The Pomerol estates are usually small, a result of the pattern of sharing inheritances in the area. Most of the best ones are in the north-east of the commune, on the highest part of the gentle plateau.

Ch Le Bon Pasteur

This estate is owned by the family of Michel Rolland, the oenologist who has defined the late-harvest, long-maceration style of many Pomerol châteaux. Tucked away in the north-east corner of the *appellation,* on a site which would appear to have little potential, Le Bon Pasteur makes nevertheless an excellent, good value Pomerol, which in lesser years is ready to drink at three years, but which lasts considerably longer in the finest years.

Ch Bonalgue

This 6.5-ha (16-acre) estate on the edge of Libourne uses 50% new oak, and makes a wine which has to soften before drinking: try it at five to seven years of age. Pierre Bourotte also owns Château les Hautes-Tuileries in Lalande-de-Pomerol (*see* p179).

Ch Beauregard

Bought up by Crédit Foncier, a bank, in 1991, this superb estate has a 16-ha (40-acre) single-vineyard dominated by Merlot, with about one-third

---

CH PETRUS

Long regarded as Pomerol's finest estate, Pétrus is owned by Madame Lacoste-Loubat and the Ets Jean-Pierre Moueix, which also manages it. There are many ingredients in Pétrus: the pure-clay vineyard at the highest point of the Pomerol plateau, ensuring excellent natural drainage and maximum exposure to the sun; the age of the vines, which Madame Loubat refused to pull up after the 1956 frosts, so that many are now 70 years old or more; and finally, the expertise of the brilliant oenologist Jean-Claude Berrouët. The wines are incredibly deeply coloured and dense in youth, developing into unforgettable bottles, the very quintessence of great Pomerol.

Cabernet Franc. Its gravel, sand and clay soil, with a subsoil of iron casse, is typical of the best Pomerol *terroirs.*

Ch Certan de May

This property, located on the highest and best part of the Pomerol plateau, has been owned by the Barreau-Badar family since 1974. It produced consistently brilliant wines in the 1990s, with the sole exception of 1994: enormously rich and concentrated bottles, to be kept for several years.

Ch Clinet

Since 1986, Michel Rolland is the adviser to this property, which has just been acquired by Jean-Louis Laborde. On 9ha (22 acres) of vines, 70% of late-harvested Merlot grapes ensure that this meticulously made wine is amazingly long-lived, but it mustn't be rushed.

Ch La Conseillante

The delightful Dr Francis Nicolas and his family own this beautifully situated property on the eastern flank of the Pomerol plateau, towards St-Emilion. The location may account for the high percentage of Cabernet Franc in the blend. Consistently fine vintages were produced here in the 1980s, culminating in the brilliant 1990, 1995 and 2000 vintages. In the best years these wines will age for 20 years or more.

Ch l'Eglise Clinet

Owned by Denis Durantou, this mainly Merlot estate managed to escape serious damage from the severe frosts of 1956, so the vineyard now has some very old vines. No doubt it is not better known because of the mere 2,000 cases a year produced, yet it makes one of Pomerol's finest wines.

Ch l'Enclos

This property may not rank with Pomerol's finest, but it

can produce extremely good wines that are relatively inexpensive (for the Pomerol *appellation*) and delicious just a few years after the vintage.

Ch L'Evangile

The branch of the Rothschild family that owns Lafite-Rothschild bought a controlling interest in this property in 1990 as a first venture onto this side of the river. The château has always been regarded as one of Pomerol's greatest estates. All wine lovers appreciate the wine's aroma of violets.

Ch La Fleur-de-Gay

Produced from 90% Merlot vines situated in a small parcel of the vineyard of Château La Croix-de-Gay, this wine has only been produced since 1982. Michel Rolland advises on the vinification, and the result is a superb wine with a brilliant track record. One of Pomerol's stars.

Ch La Fleur-Pétrus

Owned by the Moueix family, this is Pomerol's most perfumed, elegant wine. The modest château lies across the road from Pétrus, but the soil is gravel as opposed to the clay of Pétrus, which explains in part some of the differences in character. This wine begins to reach maturity after five to six years, but a really fine vintage will easily last for 20 years or more.

Ch Lafleur

This brilliant château shot to international fame with the 1982 vintage and has remained heavily sought after ever since. Owned by Mademoiselle Marie Robin, the minuscule property produces just 1,000 cases annually. It is made from virtually pure Merlot, and it can equal and even surpass neighbouring Pétrus. Its price and rarity make it virtually impossible to find.

Ch Latour à Pomerol

The vineyard of this property consists of 25 different parcels, some of them around the church of Pomerol, others next to the château itself. It belongs to Madame Lily Lacoste but is managed by the Ets Jean-Pierre Moueix. It ranks in the top dozen Pomerol estates, producing very dense, compact wines, not totally dissimilar in style to Ch Trotanoy.

Ch Nenin

This large estate (27ha/67 acres) has a long history and made one of the leading Pomerols a century ago. For several years, the wine did not live up to its expectations. Now owned by the Delon family (Léoville Las-Cases), the estate is being completely modernized. The 1997 and 1998 vintages have confirmed the owners' ambitions, with prices rising accordingly. The second wine is Fugue de Nenin.

Ch Petit Village

Acquired by an insurance group, AXA, this estate has been put on the market at a very steep price. Gérard Perse (of Pavie, Monbousquet, etc.), showed some interest in 2002, but the transaction wasn't concluded. The estate produces a big, voluptuous style of wine, capable of matching some of the best estates in Pomerol. In the finest years, the wines of Petit Village will last for 20 years or more.

Le Pin

The most minuscule of the great Pomerol vineyards, producing just over 500 cases annually, Le Pin is owned by the Thienpont family, which also owns Vieux-Château-Certan. It only came to prominence in the 1982 vintage, and is therefore one of Bordeaux's most recent stars. Much sought after internationally, and prohibitively priced, the wine is virtually impossible to find.

Ch de Sales

With a production of around 20,000 cases a year, this easily ranks as Pomerol's biggest estate. It is also the only true château in a region where even the greatest estates have only modest country houses, and, in some instances, very simple farmhouses. De Sales does not produce one of Pomerol's greatest wines, but it does make a wine that is precociously drinkable from a few years after the vintage.

Ch Taillefer

This large (for Pomerol) property of 18ha (44 acres) is on sandy gravel soil. Owned by the Bernard Moueix company, Taillefer makes a light, early-maturing style of Pomerol.

Ch Trotanoy

Owned by the Moueix family, Trotanoy, on the western side of the *appellation*, is Jean-Jacques Moueix's home. It ranks as one of Pomerol's top dozen estates, and in its finest years, like 1989, 1990 and 1998, the wine can be almost as dense as Pétrus, with virtually the same potential lifespan, at a fraction of the price.

Vieux-Château-Certan

Owned by the Thienpont family, of Belgian origin, historically this estate was considered to produce Pomerol's finest wine. It was only after World War II that Pétrus entered the ring as a serious challenger to the title. Producing over 5,000 cases annually, this is the largest of Pomerol's top properties. In style, the wine is very different to Pétrus, no doubt partly due to the Cabernet Franc and Cabernet Sauvignon which make up the blend and which can on occasion make it taste quite Médoc-like.

Ch Vray Croix-de-Gay

A small but well-placed vineyard making long-lived and well-regarded wines.

The church at Pomerol is a prominent landmark.

LALANDE-DE-POMEROL

This *appellation* covers land on the northern bank of the Barbanne stream that forms the frontier of Pomerol itself. The wine comes from two communes, La Lande de Pomerol and Néac. The soils are good, with low-lying gravel in La Lande and a higher plateau covered with gravel and sand in Néac. Merlot dominates the blend. The red wines made here have gained from the rocketing price of Pomerol proper, and several châteaux reach quite high standards. The wines mature faster than most Pomerols, and offer a slightly lighter version of the same rich, plummy taste.

As in Pomerol, most estates are small, and sell their wine directly. Thus Lalande-de-Pomerol is not a common name on wine lists.

Leading châteaux include Bel-Air, Belle-Graves, Bertineau St-Vincent, la Fleur St-Georges, Grand Ormeau, les Hauts-Conseillants, Siaurac and Tournefeuille.

FRONSAC AND CANON-FRONSAC

The small red wine area of Fronsac is west of Libourne on the other side of the Isle River. It is only since the early 1980s that Fronsac has started to gain an international reputation, but the area was very well known in the 18th and 19th centuries, when its wines fetched higher prices than those of neighbouring Pomerol, and enjoyed a reputation similar to that of the much sought-after wines of St-Emilion. This recent renaissance is very much due to the interest taken by new investors, such as Ets Moueix (*see* Pomerol p177).

Bounded by the Dordogne and Isle rivers, the Fronsac AOC (800ha/1,980 acres) covers seven communes and has taken its name from a village in the southern part of the region. The Canon-Fronsac AOC (300ha/740 acres) covers St-Michel de-Fronsac and part of the village of Fronsac.

Geologically, the hillsides are a continuation of the St-Emilion côte. The clay-and-limestone soil, with a subsoil of limestone mixed with starfish, is typical of the Bordeaux region. The hilly terrain provides for good drainage, and the nearby rivers protect the vines from frost. The permitted grape varieties are Cabernet Sauvignon, Cabernet Franc, Malbec and Merlot, the dominant variety.

Wine styles

Before the new investment of the 1970s and 1980s, the wines of this area were often criticized for being quite hard and ungiving, perhaps due to too much Cabernet Sauvignon being included in the blend and the wines spending too long in cask. Now, however, this austerity has been replaced by a certain suppleness. The wines from the Fronsac and Canon-Fronsac *appellations* are quite delicate while having a solid tannic build. Slightly spicy, with a flavour of red berries, they are dark-coloured, with a ruby-red robe and can be drunk from about two years after the vintage, but only reveal their full character when kept longer. The best will age for ten years or more. There are no classified estates in the two *appellations*. Wine traditions are upheld by the Confrérie des Gentilshommes du Duché de Fronsac.   □

PRODUCERS

Many estates are small, which makes it hard to find their wines commercially. The leading châteaux are the following:

Ch Barrabaque Canon Fronsac. 9ha (22 acres). Noteworthy *Cuvée de prestige.*
Ch Canon Moueix   Canon-Fronsac. Rich, perfumed wine from old vines.
Ch Dalem   Fronsac. 15ha (37 acres). Restored vineyard and winery. Spicy and balanced wine.
Ch de la Dauphine   Fronsac. Well rounded and harmonious wine made by Moueix from a 33-ha (82-acre) vineyard.
Ch La Fleur Cailleau   Canon-Fronsac. Organic winegrowing on 4ha (10 acres).
Ch Fontenil   Fronsac. Michel Rolland (*see* Pomerol) makes a wine for keeping.
Ch Mazeris-Bellevue   Canon-Fronsac. High Cabernet content: keep five years.
Ch Moulin Haut-Laroque   Fronsac. One of the most attractive Fronsac wines.
Ch Moulin Pey Labrie   Canon-Fronsac. Dense structure: keep ten years.
Ch de la Rivière   Fronsac. A 13th-century estate making rich, fruity wines.
Ch Villars   Fronsac. Quite large, and with rich, concentrated wines.

The river port of Libourne is the gateway to Fronsac. It is from this small port that wine from the Left Bank of the Garonne was once exported.

BURGUNDY

THE RICH AND ANCIENT PROVINCE OF BURGUNDY HAS AT ITS HEART
ONE OF THE GREATEST VINEYARDS IN THE WORLD,
PRODUCING WINES OF OPULENCE AND GRACE.

Château Corton-André, with its towers and unforgettable,
patterned tiled roof, is in Aloxe-Corton, the village at the foot
of the famous Corton hill with its *Grand Cru* vineyards
Corton and Corton-Charlemagne.

With testimonials from the great of every generation from Charlemagne onwards, Burgundy has held the laurels for its fine wines since fine wines began. The red wines of Chambertin, the whites of Montrachet, are unique treasures. But the range of Burgundy's wines, taken as a whole, can be maddeningly inconsistent. This is hardly surprising: in place of the great estates of other areas, there are myriads of tiny vineyards, generally further divided into family-owned plots. An uncertain climate plays across temperamental vines, prone to disappoint when conditions are not quite right. The wines produced by the *négociants* and the many, many small producers in this confusing patchwork of *appellations* ask the wine lover to work harder in order to grasp their subtleties of nomenclature and flavour.

Here the gap between success and failure, between good winemaking and indifferent, between everyday wine and the *Grands Crus* is wider than in any other fine-wine region. But what is great is truly great: arguably the world's finest. Today there is a new generation of winemakers, all open to the best new ideas, and all eager to prove that if Burgundy is laden with laurels, they are not going to rest on them. Burgundy — as the English dubbed Bourgogne — is a large region in east-central France, stretching for 300km (185 miles) north to south, and corresponding to the great medieval province of Burgundy. Though "Grande Bourgogne" covers a large area, only a small part makes wine. Between Chablis in the north and Beaune in the east there is hardly a vine. Here lie the Burgundy uplands: the A6 highway leaves Chablis and climbs steadily until it crests a final hill and emerges in a sea of vines sloping down to the Saône plain. Here is the heartland, the privileged slopes of the Côte d'Or, its famous villages — Meursault, Nuits-St-Georges, Gevrey-Chambertin and the rest — making the greatest red and white wines. Further south, in the Côte Chalonnaise, Mâconnais and Beaujolais zones, wine is the main crop. Burgundian wines are united by their grape varieties: Chardonnay for white wines, Pinot Noir for fine reds. Beaujolais is almost a separate region, with its own red-wine grape variety, Gamay.

Regions of Burgundy

Greater Burgundy — the entire province, in wine terms, including Beaujolais — can be divided into six regions. From north to south they are:

■ **Chablis and the Yonne** Chablis, isolated in the north, makes white wines from Chardonnay in a style echoing that of the Côte d'Or but typically drier and more austere. Chablis makes only white wines, though there are some red-wine vineyards in scattered villages in what is collectively known as the Yonne vineyard. The Yonne borders Champagne, and the upper Loire vineyards are not far away to the west.

■ **Côte d'Or** The well-named centre of fine wine, both red and white. The vineyards lie in a narrow band along the east-facing slope between Dijon and Santenay. Here are made the longest-lived, most complex, and most expensive wines.

■ **Hautes Côtes** The area to the west of the main Côte d'Or slope: vines are found in sheltered parts of this wooded, upland country. The wines are simpler, the country cousins of the Côte d'Or.

■ **Côte Chalonnaise** A string of villages whose vineyards continue the line of the Côte d'Or to the south, but in the *département* of Saône-et-Loire. Reds and whites are made here; not to Côte d'Or standards, but some are serious wines.

■ **Mâconnais** A wide zone further south, west of the town of Mâcon, making middle-rank red and (mostly) white wines. It includes famous white-wine villages such as Pouilly.

■ **Beaujolais** A large zone stretching south almost to Lyons, making soft and approachable red wine from the Gamay grape — the only region not to grow Pinot Noir for red wine.

Site, soil and climate

The underlying rock of much of Burgundy is limestone, or kindred rocks, of the Jurassic era. The geology is however very complex and it is local conditions that matter. Where the limestone reaches the surface, in steep-edged scarp slopes, the rock type becomes important for vine-growing. This formation, and its effect on quality, is displayed clearly by the Côte d'Or (*see* p194). Beaujolais, on the other hand, lies upon mountains formed from granite.

The climate is cool, and in some years the red Pinot Noir grapes fail to ripen fully. A rainy summer is often the culprit. A cold, damp September is not uncommon, and this can ruin the vintage. A good Burgundy year has no spring frost, a warm June for the flowering, steady warmth and modest rain through the summer, and a warm, dry September. Too much summer heat can be damaging to the delicate Pinot Noir.

The careful process of selection of *Premiers* and *Grands Crus* reflects centuries of experience, and these plots are blessed with good micro-climates as well as good exposure and soil.

Grape varieties and wine styles

Any well-made red burgundy, great or minor, will show the character of the Pinot Noir grape. Overlying this will be the qualities stemming from the *cru*, or vineyard, and the vintage. Finally, the winemaker's intentions and abilities have a lot to do with the taste of burgundy.

Pinot Noir wines are never as powerful in colour, tannin, aroma or flavour as, say, those from Cabernet Sauvignon or Syrah. Be it basic or top-level, red burgundy should be subtle and sensuous, not obvious and assertive. Simple red burgundy should offer a smell and taste of fruit — raspberries and cherries are often mentioned — and a kind of gentle sweetness that is wholly natural. The finest wines, as they mature, gain a richness that can almost smell of rot, and older wines develop complex and persistent aromas and tastes. White

BURGUNDY APPELLATIONS

Burgundy has a sophisticated hierarchy of *appellations*. At the base are the regional AOCs, then village AOCs, then *Premiers* and finally *Grands Crus*.

The regional appellations

These cover wine from designated vineyard land anywhere in Burgundy. They can also be applied to wine from specific varieties and/or localities.

Bourgogne Red, white or (rarely) rosé wines from anywhere in the region. Red wines are from Pinot Noir (César and Tressot, two traditional varieties, are also allowed in the Yonne). Whites are from Chardonnay or Pinot Blanc. Chardonnay and Pinot Noir can be used as additional information on labels, as can the names of some villages in the Yonne (Irancy, St-Bris), and some districts (Hautes Côtes de Beaune, Hautes Côtes de Nuits, Chalonnaise).

Bourgogne (Grande) Ordinaire Again from anywhere in the region, but Gamay (for red) and Aligoté (for white) grapes can be used.

Bourgogne Passetoutgrains Red wine made from Gamay and at least one-third Pinot Noir.

Bourgogne Aligoté The Aligoté grape makes a brisk white wine, at its best in Bouzeron in the Chalonnais, where it is labelled Aligoté de Bouzeron.

Village wines, Premiers Crus and Grands Crus

The main villages in the Côte d'Or, and to a lesser extent in other zones, have their own AOCs. Thus wine made within Gevrey-Chambertin can be labelled as such. Within the Côte d'Or villages, and in Chablis, are named vineyards entitled to the rank *Premier Cru*. Wine from here is labelled with both village and vineyard names; for example, Gevrey-Chambertin Les Clos St-Jacques.

Grands Crus are *appellations* in their own right. Vineyards in this top rank, *Grand Cru*, use their name alone — for example, Chambertin.

AOC and commune may not always have the same boundaries: land producing wine below village standard will only receive a regional *appellation*.

Mâcon and Beaujolais

The regional *appellation* system takes in these two zones, but they have their own AOCs (*see* p207 and p209 respectively).

WINE REGIONS OF BURGUNDY

The six regions of Burgundy are shown here, with
Chablis isolated to the north-west (*see* inset) and the
others strung in a line along the eastern edge of the
Burgundy uplands, at the start of the wide Saône valley.
Chablis and the Yonne vineyards are mapped on p187.
The Côte d'Or has its own map on p193, with the
southern regions of the Côte Chalonnaise, Mâconnais
and Beaujolais covered on p204. The Hautes Côtes are
covered by the Côte d'Or map.

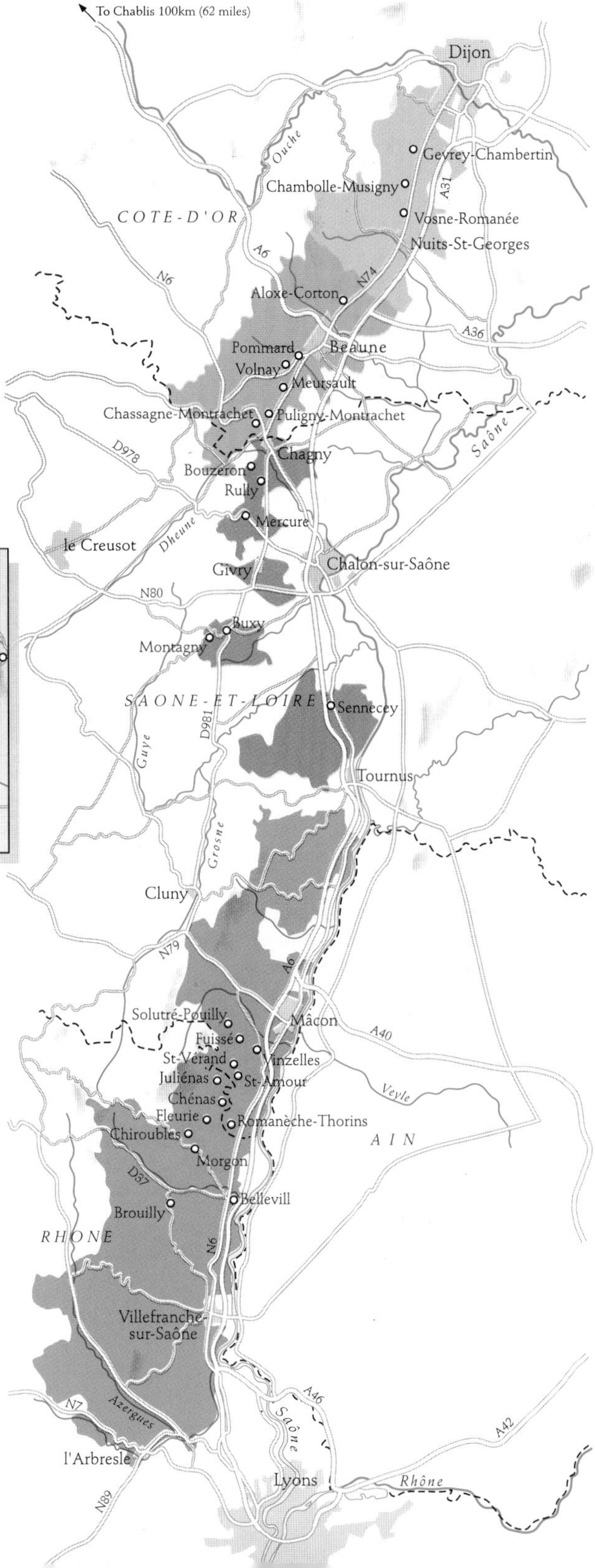

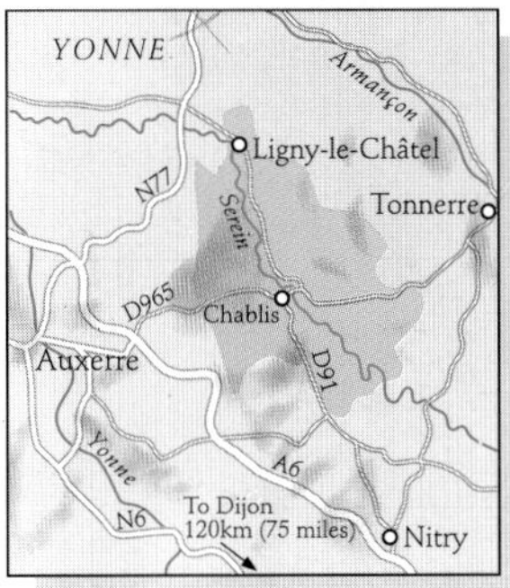

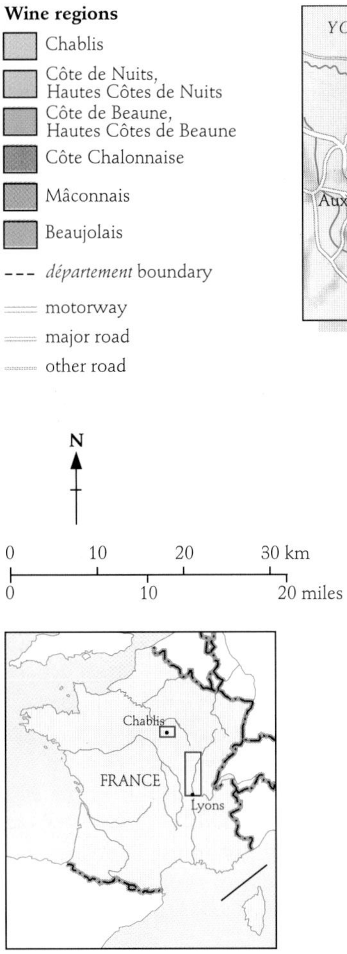

Wine regions

- Chablis
- Côte de Nuits, Hautes Côtes de Nuits
- Côte de Beaune, Hautes Côtes de Beaune
- Côte Chalonnaise
- Mâconnais
- Beaujolais

- - - *département* boundary

motorway

major road

other road

N

| 0 | 10 | 20 | 30 km |

| 0 | 10 | 20 miles |

burgundy nearly always means Chardonnay, a grape that can vary widely in its aromas and flavours, depending on vinification and ageing as much as *terroir*. Tasters learn to spot the toasty, buttery notes in white burgundy that has been fermented in oak, common for Côte d'Or wines. Simple white burgundies — AOC Bourgogne, Mâcon wines, most Chalonnais — never see oak and the flavour should be clean, not over-acidic, and hinting at fruits and honey. The top white wines, like the reds, age into complexity. Great white burgundy inspires terms such as hon-eyed, blossom, nutty. What is most apparent is density and complexity: a very complete mouthful of wine.

Beaujolais is made from Gamay, a distinct variety which is not related to Pinot Noir. Its flavours and quali-ties are described on pp209–212.

Growers and merchants

Burgundy is the land of the small-holder. It has few large estates, and the term "château" rarely has the same connotations of an integrated wine-growing and -making unit as in Bordeaux. Traditionally, the real maker of burgundy wine — as opposed to a grower of grapes — has been the merchant, or *négociant*. They buy new wine from many small-scale growers, blend and mature it and bottle it under their own name. Many *négociants* own some vine-yards; others are purely merchants.

Since the 1960s, however, more producers, even quite small concerns, have been bottling their own wine. Look for the words *"Mis en bouteille à la propriété"* or *"au domaine"*. Talented producers have built worldwide re-putations. Grower-bottled burgundies are, however, often made in small quantities and can be hard to obtain. One advantage of the *négociant* sys-tem is that a merchant can buy and blend enough wine to make a decent quantity from one *appellation*.

Grower-bottled wines are more authentic, for the grower stakes his name on the wine being both what

The village of Volnay is high on the Côte de Beaune slope.

the label says and being true to type. On the other hand the skill of the grower is challenged at every stage, since he is now taking care of every-thing from vineyard to final bottling.

Négociant burgundies are less individual, inevitably — unless they come from a merchant's own vine-yards. Some *négociants* have been criti-cized for making boring, even bad, wines, and for submerging the diver-sity of individual villages and *crus* in their house style. Some of this criti-cism was, and is, justified; but many *négociants* have much improved the quality of their wines in recent years.

Cooperatives are important in Mâcon, the Hautes Côtes, Chablis and Beaujolais. The best co-ops invest in modern equipment and encourage growers to produce better grapes. Their wines can be among the best value in Burgundy.

A new generation of skilled wine-makers began to emerge in the 1980s, greatly improving the wines of grow-ers and merchants alike. At the end of the decade, a price correction made minor burgundies cheaper and once more comparable in value

to New World wines. The top domaines have managed to hold their prices, opening up a larger gap between the great wines and the village and regional AOCs.

Winemaking in Burgundy

While the modern "recipe" for red wine is broadly non-controversial (*see* pp112–113), in Burgundy there is much debate about techniques. Top-ics include vineyard yield, the ways grapes are crushed, the timing and temperature of fermentation, the use and frequency of filtering and other processes, and the extent of ageing needed and the container in which wine should be aged.

Burgundy poses particular chal-lenges due to the grape varieties used, and the climate. Pinot Noir grapes have less colour, tannin and flavour than other varieties such as Cabernet Sauvignon or Syrah, and their juice is more prone to oxidation in the vat. Consequently red burgundy needs to be made gently and carefully.

Burgundy is cool, its climate is very variable from year to year, and it is even less certain than in other quality French wine zones that the grapes will ripen. Successful ripening depends upon both weather and vineyard site. The best vineyards, those graded *Premier Cru* and *Grand Cru*, are those on the most-favoured slopes where all factors — soil, angle of slope, orientation — combine to give optimum ripeness and complexity of taste. Over-ripeness should be avoided with Pinot Noir, however: the best, most subtly-flavoured grapes are only just ripe.

However well-placed the vineyard, two things can mar the quality of its wine, leaving aside straightforward poor viticulture. The first is the clone of Pinot Noir planted, the second is the yield. Pinot Noir is an unstable variety: it has a tendency to mutate, to produce oddities. Modern techniques allow the best plants to be cloned: thus a vineyard owner can plant several hectares of identical vines. The problem is that there are different ideas of "best". Virus-free clones are the top priority of officials; very productive clones appeal to many growers. But these may not make the best wine. Small crops, as elsewhere, spell quality, especially in the Côte d'Or. The limits set by the AOC rules vary from vintage to vintage, and many winemakers restrict yield to less than the figure allowed.

Grapes arrive at the *chais* in whole bunches, and are normally crushed and de-stalked. The Burgundian tradition is to leave the stalks on the grapes, but today most winemakers remove them. Advocates of keeping stalks, however, say that they help to break up the fermenting mass of grape pulp, and also add tannin and an indefinable character to the wine.

The region's cool autumn temperatures affect fermentation, and did so even more in the days before modern methods of heating the must were introduced. A day or two of pre-fermentation maceration — letting the juice and skins mingle — helps draw colour from the grapes. A longer maceration, with whole bunches plus lots of sulphur dioxide

to stave off fermentation, became fashionable in the late 1980s, under the influence of consultant oenologist Guy Accad. His wines are deep, dark and sweet, but no-one knows yet if they will age well.

Red burgundy is fermented at a warmer temperature than most wines, and the *chapeau*, or cap of grape-skins, is regularly mixed back into the fermenting liquid. Then comes ageing: sometimes, at the top domaines, in new oak; but normally in older casks. Too much oak can dominate the subtle flavours in all but the greatest, most concentrated wines of Burgundy. The cold cellars in the region aid slow, gentle maturation, and most good winemakers avoid too much fining, racking or filtering. Some burgundy is not filtered at all: this can produce a deposit in bottle, but connoisseurs accept this in return for the extra complexity and ageing potential.

Making white burgundy

White burgundy is less demanding to produce. The classic wines from the Côte d'Or, and a few from Chablis and the Côte Chalonnaise, are fermented in oak casks — new oak is used for the top wines. Other wines are made in stainless steel, with perhaps a touch of oak for ageing. Wines fermented in cask are left in cask for several months, certainly until after the malolactic fermentation. The wine stays on its lees, and fining and filtration are kept to the minimum. Stirring the lees (*bâtonnage*) adds a creamy complexity to the taste of the wine.

Cask fermentation, when combined with low yield, a well-placed vineyard and long, undisturbed ageing, produces in great white burgundy the unique combination of power, grace and longevity which no New World Chardonnay has yet been able to match. □

READING A BURGUNDY LABEL

Burgundian wine labels have a style of their own: heraldic shields and parchment-coloured paper are reminiscent of medieval Bourgogne, and are found on very ordinary bottles as well as *Grand Cru* wines. They may look similar, but *appellation* rules state precisely what a label has to tell us.

The name of the *appellation* — region, village, Premier Cru or Grand Cru — must be stated in large type and followed by the words "appellation contrôlée" or "appellation d'origine contrôlée" in smaller letters. Thus NUITS-ST-GEORGES will be followed by the words Appellation Nuits-St-Georges Contrôlée.

Premier Cru: wines must have on the label the name of the vineyard preceded by the name of the commune — for instance, Pommard Epenots. This name must be followed by the words Appellation Pommard Premier Cru Contrôlée.
Grand Cru: the name of the *grand cru* — an *appellation* of its own — must appear on the label in large type, followed by

the words Appellation Grand Cru Contrôlée. Thus the red Grand Cru Romanée-Saint-Vivant, produced in the commune of Vosne-Romanée, will be labelled Romanée-Saint-Vivant, Appellation Grand Cru Contrôlée.

This can be confusing for the buyer, as several communes sometimes produce an Appellation Premier Cru wine bearing the same name. The vineyard called Les Perrières can thus be found at Meursault, Beaune, Nuits-St-Georges, etc.

The merchant or grower's name must also appear on a burgundy label, if he has done the bottling. The various terms used to denote domaine bottling, bottling by a merchant, and the distinctions between a grower and a grower/winemaker may or may not be found on the label. Nor need the vintage, the ageing of the wine (in barriques, for instance) or the age of the vines be mentioned on the label. Besides the name and address of the bottler, only the alcohol by volume and the size of the bottle must appear on the label.

CHABLIS

Chablis has become one of the best-known of French white wines — outside of France. Unfortunately some of its notoriety arises because its name has been freely borrowed the world over to describe any dry white wine.

True Chablis, which concerns us here, comes from the most northern wine zone of Burgundy, from vineyards around the small town of Chablis and 19 other villages and hamlets in the Yonne *département*. (For other *appellations* in the Yonne vineyard *see* box, p190.) As with all fine white burgundy, the grape variety is Chardonnay, which is grown here on slopes of Kimmeridgian limestone and clay. These slopes form the southern edge of a geological formation called the Paris Basin, a large bowl-like depression extending from northern France into southern England: the village of Kimmeridge in Dorset, which gave its name to the rock, is on the northern side. Appropriately, the soil is packed with the fossilized shells of a small oyster, *Exogyra virgula*, which contribute to efficient drainage, despite the high proportion of clay.

Climate and the frost problem

The climate of Chablis is northern, essentially continental; there are cold winters and warm summers. Annual fluctuations in sunshine and rainfall result in wide variations in the quality and size of each vintage. The main threat is spring frost, which can cause untold damage to the young vine shoots. April and May are the most critical months.

The 1950s, a decade of particularly inclement springs, saw the first primitive attempts to protect the vines with the introduction of "smudge pots". These oil stoves had to be filled and lit by hand in the early hours of the morning. Since then they

Autumn in the Grenouilles *Grand Cru*.

have become rather more sophisticated: modern *chaufferettes* can be replenished automatically from fuel tanks at the foot of the vineyard slopes. They are efficient but expensive. A second method involves spraying the vines with water when the temperature drops to freezing point, so that a protective coating of ice forms around the young buds. While water freezes at 0°C (32°F), the vine can withstand a temperature of –5°C (23°F) before it suffers. Although frost protection is not infallible, it has made an enormous difference to the viability of Chablis by ensuring a reasonable-sized vintage each year. This has contributed to the expansion in vineyard area.

The appellations

There are four *appellations* in Chablis. In descending order they are *Grand Cru*, *Premier Cru*, Chablis and Petit Chablis. The *Grands* and *Premiers Crus* are specific vineyards: *see* pp188–189. Village or AOC Chablis covers much of the *appellation*, while Petit Chablis is little used at present. Much of the

delimited area remains unplanted, but attempts to scrap Petit Chablis, or rename it, have been resisted.

The Chablis style

The main consideration is the use of oak — or not. There are two distinct schools of thought on the subject — and, consequently, two distinct styles of Chablis. Traditionally Chablis was always vinified and matured in oak casks, for that was the only available storage material. The advent of concrete and stainless steel vats, however, has provided a choice. Some producers have remained with oak; others have given it up completely; while a third school has returned to it. Those who abhor the use of oak believe that it deforms the intrinsic flavour of Chablis; its supporters believe that oak enhances the wine by adding subtlety and complexity.

Curiously, there are examples of mature Chablis, vinified without oak, that with age take on the subtle, nutty flavours normally associated with oak-ageing. Such is the diversity of a wine that, while always dry, today often shows fullness and richness in contrast to its steely, austere reputation. When new it has the immediate appeal of youthful fruitiness, with a firm backbone of acidity. Then it goes through a "dumb" phase before developing the wonderful stony flavours that the French call *pierre à fusil*, or gunflint — the hallmark of fine, mature Chablis. Although Chablis is appealing in its youth, it is much more rewarding with a few years' bottle-age: at least five for a *Premier Cru*, and ten or more for a more substantial *Grand Cru*.

Grand Cru wines offer ageing ability and a great depth of flavour. The various *crus* are hard to distinguish: more often the differences come from the method of vinification rather than the vineyard.

THE CHABLIS AND YONNE WINE AREAS

Chablis is the most important, but not the only, wine in the Yonne *département*. The other vineyard areas are shown in the inset map, right. The large map shows the Chablis zone, with the three main *appellations*: ordinary "village" Chablis, *Premier Cru* and *Grand Cru*. Petit Chablis (with little land actually planted) is not shown.

CHABLIS AND THE YONNE

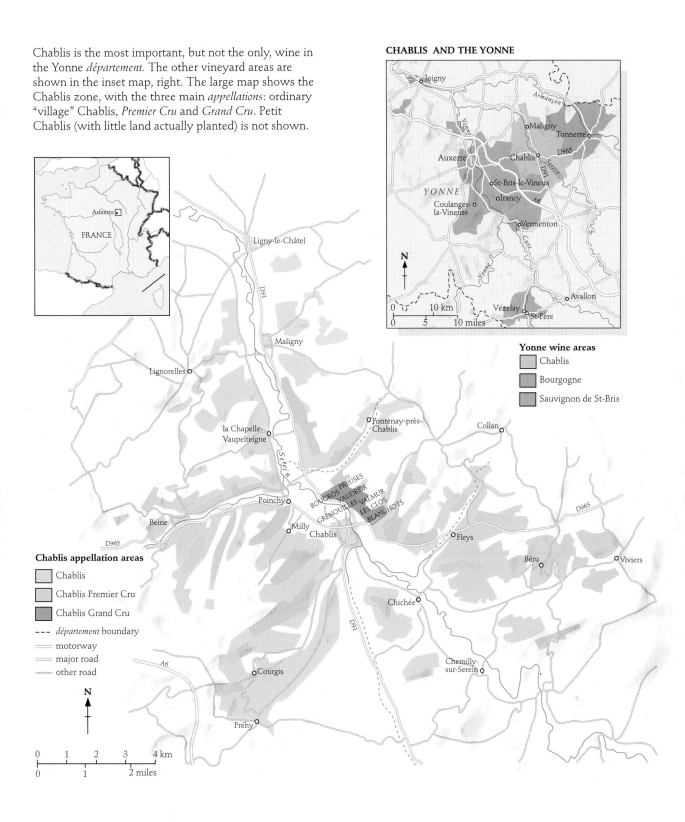

Yonne wine areas

- Chablis
- Bourgogne
- Sauvignon de St-Bris

Chablis appellation areas

- Chablis
- Chablis Premier Cru
- Chablis Grand Cru
- --- *département* boundary
- motorway
- major road
- other road

N

0 1 2 3 4 km

0 1 2 miles

PRODUCERS

Chablis labels indicate the *appellation* — Petit Chablis, Chablis, Chablis Premier Cru and Chablis Grand Cru — and, in the latter two cases, the vineyard. Village names are not used: Chablis is one *appellation*. Land ownership is very fragmented, with several growers owning one *cru*, so quality depends upon the producer. Some growers use one or more domaine or château names in addition to their own. Much wine is still sold by the *négociants* of the Côte d'Or, as well as by those of Chablis itself, and by the local cooperative.

Jean-Marc Brocard

Brocard's Domaine Ste-Claire in the outlying village of Préhy has some 75ha (185 acres) of vineyards, mainly of village Chablis, with a little in Mont-mains and some in St-Bris. He avoids all contact with oak to make pure, flinty Chablis.

La Chablisienne

The local cooperative, La Chablisienne, represents about one-third of the production of Chablis, with some 200 members cultivating about 1,200ha (2,970 acres), and thus plays a significant commercial rôle in the *appellation*. Founded in 1923, it was one of the earliest cooperatives in France. It does not own a press, so its members deliver must, not grapes. Until recently all its wines were made without wood, but now some oak-ageing is used for selected *Premiers* and *Grands Crus*, notably for La Grande Cuvée, a selection from the older vines in the *Premiers Crus*

vineyards. The house style remains firmly representative of good, honest Chablis. As well as selling wine under the label of La Chablisienne, the cooperative causes confusion by using various members' names, as though they were independent producers, and also sells in bulk to *négociants* in both Chablis and Beaune.

Domaine Jean Collet

Jean Collet's son Gilles is now responsible for the day-to-day running of the estate. New cellars have recently been built to cater for the production of 25ha (62 acres), including substantial holdings of Mont-mains and Vaillons as well as small parcels of Valmur, Montée de Tonnerre and Mont de Milieu. Until 1985 the Collets used only *foudres* and *pièces*, large and small barrels, but they now have stainless steel vats as well, mainly for village Chablis. Most of the *Premiers* and *Grands Crus* are fermented in *foudres* and matured in *pièces* for a few months before bottling. The Collets make rich and stylish wines.

René Dauvissat

See profile, p190.

Jean-Paul Droin

One of the new generation in Chablis, Droin is a young man who has taken over his father's estate and stamped his own mark on the wines. His vineyards total almost 20ha (50 acres), with numerous small plots in several *Premiers* and most *Grands Crus*. Vaillons, Montée de Tonnerre, Valmur and Vaudésir are the most important. Since the mid-1980s he has been an enthusiastic exponent of new oak, conducting many experiments in a quest to achieve the ultimate Chablis. Sometimes his wines are enormously successful, and sometimes atypically rich and over-oaked.

Jean Durup

Durup's Domaine de l'Eglantière in the village of Maligny is the largest estate in Chablis, with 130ha (321 acres) in production: 10ha (25 acres) of Petit Chablis, 40ha (99 acres) of Fourchaume and Vaudevey and 80ha (197 acres) of village Chablis. Winemaking methods are simple, with minimal handling of the wine and without a trace of wood. Durup considers oak to be heresy that distorts the true flavour of Chablis. He also uses the names Domaine de Valéry and Domaine de Paulière, as well as Ch de Maligny.

William Fèvre

Domaine de la Maladière, owned by Fèvre, is the largest owner of *Grand Cru* Chablis, with holdings in every one except Blanchots, as well as several *Premiers Crus*, Chablis and Petit Chablis. Fèvre is the leading exponent of new oak, the first to build an underground barrel cellar and the first to build a California-style warehouse in order to produce his Chablis Champs Royaux. The Fèvre estate is now leased

THE CHABLIS GRANDS CRUS

There are seven *Grands Crus*, totalling almost 100ha (247 acres), ranged along one hillside just outside the town of Chablis. They are fully planted, with the annual renewal of some vines. From south to north they are:

Blanchots, with 11.5ha (28.5 acres), is the lightest and most accessible of the *Grands Crus*, for the wines tend to reach maturity earlier than others. The soil is particularly white and chalky, hence its name. **Les Clos** (the name implies a vineyard that was once surrounded by a wall) is the largest *Grand Cru* in Chablis, with 26ha (64 acres), divided among several owners. Les

Clos is generally considered to be the most long-lasting of the *Grands Crus*, the last to reach maturity, with the firmest structure.

Valmur, with 13ha (32 acres), is very similar to Vaudésir, but lacks the intensity and potential longevity of Les Clos. **Grenouilles,** the smallest *Grand Cru*, with just 9.5ha (23.5 acres), lies closest to the River Serein and gets its name from the fact that the vineyard workers could hear frogs croaking on the river bank. The vineyard is shared by Louis Michel (*qv*), Jean-Paul Droin (*qv*) and La Chablisienne (*qv*) cooperative. **Vaudésir** totals 16ha (40 acres), including part of La

Moutonne, a vineyard on the *Grands Crus* slope, but without the status of a *Grand Cru appellation*: a 2.3-ha (5.6-acre) parcel within Vaudésir and Preuses that once belonged to the monks of the nearby Cistercian abbey of Pontigny. Long-Depaquit (*qv*) are the principal producers, making a stylish wine of considerable finesse. **Preuses** is an 11-ha (27-acre) vineyard that shares La Moutonne with Vaudésir. It is generally considered to be more feminine and elegant than Les Clos. **Bougros,** with 16ha (40 acres), bears a close resemblance to Blanchots, with a certain rustic quality.

to Bouchard Père & Fils and has been managed by Joseph Henriot since September 1998. His wines may seem very oaky in youth, but when older they take on wonderfully rich mineral flavours.

Domaine Laroche

One of the leading estates of Chablis, having grown with the *appellation* from 6ha (15 acres) in 1960 to 100ha (247 acres) today, with vines in Les Clos, Blanchots, Bougros, Vaudevey, Beauroy, Montmains, Vaillons and Fourchaume. Laroche's best village Chablis is named Chablis St-Martin, after the patron saint of the town, and the Chablis St-Martin Vieilles Vignes is better still. The most highly priced wine is Réserve de l'Obédiencerie, from a tiny plot of old vines in Blanchots whose grapes are vinified with meticulous care. Michel Laroche also owns a *négociant* business.

Domaine des Marronniers

Légland first rented a few vines in 1976, and since then his Domaine des Marronniers estate has gradually grown to 18ha (44 acres), which include three in Montmains, as well as one hectare of Bourgogne Blanc and one of Petit Chablis. His wines are fine examples of good unoaked Chablis, with all the mineral flinty flavours that result from the soil. Légland also makes a *cuvée bois* as a curiosity and a contrast.

Long-Depaquit

Although owned by the Beaune *négociant* house of Bichot, Long-Depaquit is run independently. Its flagship is the tiny vineyard of La Moutonne. La Moutonne is a clos which has been greatly improved by Albert Long-Depaquit, who has created this estate bearing his name. As well as La Moutonne, it has vines in Les Lys, Vaucoupin, Montmains and Les Clos.

Domaine Laroche in Chablis combines high-tech winemaking with traditional oak-ageing.

THE CHABLIS PREMIERS CRUS

The *Premiers Crus* have expanded in line with the overall growth in the vineyard. In 1982 there were 477ha (1,104 acres) in production, which had risen to 692ha (1,709 acres) by 1991, with the appearance of several unfamiliar names. Many of these date from before the phylloxera crisis, when the Yonne had some 40,000ha (99,000 acres) of vines. It is argued that these revived *Premiers Crus* have the same *terroir* and micro-climate as the older ones. The best-known is Vaudevey, outside the village of Beine. The best *Premiers Crus* are considered

to be Mont de Milieu, Fourchaume and Montée de Tonnerre, which are on the same slope as the *Grands Crus*.

This complete list of *Premiers Crus* includes some that are rarely seen on a label. The producer may prefer to use the better-known "umbrella" name (in heavy type): for example Fourchaume in preference to L'Homme Mort.

Les Beauregards: Côte de Cuissy
Beauroy: Troesme, Côte de Savant
Berdiot
Chaume de Talvat

Côte de Jouan
Côte de Léchet
Côte de Vaubarousse
Fourchaume: Vaupulent, Côte de Fontenay, L'Homme Mort, Vaulorent
Les Fourneaux: Morein, Côte de Prés Girots
Mont de Milieu
Montée de Tonnerre: Chapelot, Pied d'Aloue, Côte de Bréchain
Montmains: Forêt, Butteaux
Vaillons: Châtains, Séchet, Beugnons, Les Lys, Mélinots, Roncières, Les Epinottes
Vaucoupin
Vauligneau
Vaudevey: Vaux Ragons
Vosgros: Vaugiraut

Louis Michel

The great believer in unoaked Chablis. He gave up his barrels 30 years ago and now ferments and ages his wine entirely in stainless steel vats, with minimum handling of the juice and wine. The result is quintessential Chablis, with the classic nerve, steeliness and mineral quality.

He has gradually expanded his estate to 22ha (54 acres), including 14 of *Premiers Crus*, in Montmains, Butteaux, Montée de Tonnerre, Vaillons and Forêt, as well as some *Grand Cru* Grenouilles, Les Clos and Vaudésir. Michel also uses the label Domaine de la Tour Vaubourg.

J J Moreau

The largest *négociant* house in Chablis, now owned by Hiram Walker/Allied Lyons. The Moreau family retain their vineyards, however, with holdings in Vaillons, Les Clos, including Clos des Hospices, small parcels in Valmur, Vaudésir and Blanchots, as well as a large Chablis vineyard, Domaine de Bieville. Moreau's style avoids the use of wood, favouring the fruity flavours of Chablis.

Raveneau

Raveneau is one of the leading names in Chablis, first with François and now his sons, Bernard and Jean-Marie. The estate remains compact 7.5ha (18.5 acres), with the principal holdings in Butteaux, Chapelot and Montée de Tonnerre for *Premiers Crus,* and Valmur, Les Clos and Blanchots in the *Grands Crus*.

Jean-Marie, just like his father, has an empirical approach to winemaking, with no fixed rules about wood-ageing. However, all his wine do spend at least a year in barrels, some new, some up to ten years old. The *Grands Crus* are bottled after 18 months. The result is a combination of weight, nerve and complexity in wines that develop considerable complexity with bottle-age.

A Régnard

Chablis has always excited outside interest, among the *négociants* of Beaune for instance. Patrick de Ladoucette of Ch du Nozet in the Loire Valley (*see* p246), has bought the old-established *négociant* house of A Régnard, which in turn incorporates the old Chablis name of Albert Pic. Considerable investments have been made in new installations, with the house style favouring no wood. This makes for firm wines that are quite austere in their youth.

Other producers

Numerous other growers have come to the fore as the *négociants* lose their market share. Worthy of note are Domaine Barat, Domaine Billaud-Simon, Gilbert Picq & Fils, Jean-Pierre Grossot, Claude Laroche, Domaine des Malandes, Francine and Olivier Savary, Domaine de Vaurou and, among those who vinify in oak, Pinson and Vocoret. Lamblin and Simmonet-Febvre are local *négociants*.

RENE DAUVISSAT

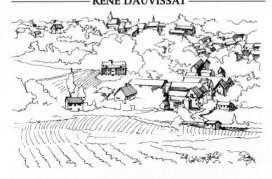

René Dauvissat inherited a tiny holding in 1950 and since then has steadily increased his estate to some 11ha (27 acres), with vineyards in Vaillons, Séchet, Les Clos, Preuses and the *cru* for which he is best known, Forêt. In the mid-1960s he introduced lined steel vats for temperature-controlled fermentation. Even so he still ferments some of his wine in oak, in order to season the new barrels. A gentle maturation in oak was part of his father's style of winemaking and he saw no reason to change — and neither does his son Vincent. Depending upon the evolution of the wine, it spends between six and ten months in wood. The Dauvissats' Chablis are above all wines that demand bottle-ageing and develop wonderfully complex flavours, with the flinty mineral taste of the *terroir*.

APPELLATIONS OF THE YONNE

There are several vineyards other than Chablis scattered about the Yonne *département*. The area is much reduced from 19th-century prosperity, but some isolated areas are reviving.

Bourgogne Rouge and **Blanc** are the principal *appellations*, usually with a village name attached: **Irancy** has had its own *appellation* since 1977, for a red wine made from Pinot Noir, with an occasional drop of César and Tressot. Rosé is also allowed. The best-known vineyard is Côte de Palotte. **Coulanges-la-Vineuse** produces lighter and fruitier red wine than Irancy, from Pinot Noir alone. **Epineuil** also has its own *appellation* for red wine — again only from Pinot Noir. It is the only village that is still making wine in the once-sizeable Tonnerre district.

Chitry covers red and white wine from Chardonnay and Pinot Noir, from the village of Chitry-le-Fort. **Côte d'Auxerre** dates from 1992, and mainly covers vineyards planted with Pinot Noir and Chardonnay in St-Bris-le-Vineux, Auxerre and a few other surrounding villages. **Vézelay** makes red and white burgundy on some well-placed slopes. **Sauvignon de St-Bris,** a white wine made from the only Sauvignon Blanc grown in Burgundy, was granted AOC status in 2002, retroactive to the 2001 vintage. **Crémant de Bourgogne** (*see* p206) is made in the Yonne. The SICAVA cooperative, in the hamlet of Bailly, is well-known for this sparkling wine, and is a useful commercial outlet for the vineyards of villages such as St-Bris and Chitry.

CÔTE D'OR

Burgundy's "golden slope" is an almost continuous but narrow strip of vineyard that traces an east- and southeast-facing slope from Dijon in the north past Beaune and on to the border of the Côte-d'Or *département*. This slope marks the eastern edge of the Burgundian uplands, a complicated and rugged landscape of hills and forests. At its feet, to the east, is the wide plain formed by the River Saône.

The Côte is what geographers call a scarp. Its slope reveals the layers of rock strata that make up the Burgundy hill country, and it is this layer-cake of rocks, and their resultant soils, that are in large part responsible for the Côte d'Or vineyards: *see* p194.

One other location factor has been important for the Côte d'Or: the road at its foot. It was already one of the great routes of Europe when the Romans arrived, and for the centuries since it has linked north and south, Flanders and Provence, Paris and Italy. Today the A6 and A31 motorways join the N6 and N74 roads in keeping up the traffic flow. Not for these vineyards the backwoods obscurity of so many parts of rural France. The names of the great *crus*, walled and tidy above the road, would be familiar to any traveller.

History, as well as geography, has been kind to the Côte d'Or. The area was one of the first centres of monastic life in France, with the great Benedictine abbey of Cluny in the Mâconnais; and then in 1098 Cîteaux, the first house of the Cistercian order, was founded close to Beaune. Within a year, Cîteaux had been given its first vineyard, at Meursault. Under its great abbot, St Bernard, the monks quickly added more vineyard land along the Côte d'Or. The contribution of the monks was vital. They did not find the Côte

Gateway to a *Grand Cru*.

d'Or deserted: the Romans had made wine there, Charlemagne had commended it. But the monks organized it. They built walls around their vineyards — culminating in 1330 in the great wall around the Clos Vougeot, which stands today. They experimented, improved, observed. It was the Cistercians who drew out the quality of the Côte d'Or.

Burgundy was blessed in its temporal as well as spiritual rulers. The Valois Dukes of the late Middle Ages loved grandeur in all things — wine and food especially. And they had the money and the power to demand the best. It was Duke Philip the Bold, around 1375, who turned his attention to red burgundy, bringing forward the "Pineau" grape, ancestor of Pinot Noir, and outlawing the prolific but lower-quality Gamay. His grandson Philip the Good kept up the ban: "The Dukes of Burgundy are known as lords of the best wine in Christendom. We will maintain our reputation."

Revolution displaced the monks and broke the continuity of ownership on the Côte d'Or. After

Napoleon (who gave his personal approval to the future *Grand Cru* Chambertin) few of the monastic *clos* remained in single ownership.

As vineyards fragmented, *négociants*, with the ability to buy and blend from many small plots, became more dominant. The arrival of the railway made them more powerful still: they could export their wine more easily (the Côte d'Or has no handy navigable river), and the unscrupulous among them could bring in southern wine to stretch the great names of burgundy further. This practice went on well into the 20th century, giving the British, for one, the notion that red burgundy was a dark, syrupy brew oddly reminiscent of the wines of Algeria.

Villages and crus
The Côte d'Or is divided in half by Beaune, the city that houses most of its merchants, and dotted with villages that give their names to the vineyards — or in some cases take their names from the vineyards. For example, Chambolle-Musigny is a name concocted from the old title of the village, Chambolle, which has on its patch of hill a famed vineyard, Musigny. Some villages — Volnay, Pommard, Meursault — have enough confidence to stay single.

Each village, or most of them, has its AOC. Within its boundaries are dozens of named vineyards. The most notable are accorded the rank *Grand Cru*, below which come the *Premiers Crus*; the rest are plain AOC. This labelling and classification system is described in detail on p182.

The Côte d'Or is divided into the Côte de Nuits, the northern half, and the Côte de Beaune.

To the west of the main vineyard slope are two AOCs: Hautes Côtes de Nuit and Hautes Côtes de Beaune. These are described on p196.

Wine styles

The Côte de Nuits makes red wine almost exclusively; the Côte de Beaune makes both red and white. Pinot Noir and Chardonnay are the respective grape varieties.

The styles of wine made are legion, as this is the country of the individual in winemaking terms. Each *négociant*, every grower large or small, has his own view as to what constitutes great burgundy and how the personality of each vineyard should be displayed. Care is needed, therefore, when choosing a wine, to establish first its status then the name of the maker.

Generally speaking, wines will increase in complexity, price and age-ability as they rise up the scale from village AOC through *Premier Cru* to *Grand Cru*. However, a boring *Premier Cru* wine, sad and flat when set beside a brilliant bottle from a mere village AOC, disproves this generalization. It is the man who matters, as the local saying has it.

Red burgundy has swung in style from heavy to light, as fashion among both drinkers and winemakers has changed. In the 18th century it was a light, almost rosé, wine. The 19th century, and the first part of the 20th, saw a swing to deep-coloured, tannic wines, and much use was made of sugar to boost the strength. Today there is a return to balanced, perfumed, clean-flavoured wines, lighter in colour and lower in alcohol. However there are several approaches to making red burgundy: *see* pp184–185.

Good winemakers can conjure superb wines from minor *appellations*: buyers seek out the AOC Bourgogne and Côte de Beaune-Villages wines of famous domaines, for these will be made to the same standards as the domaine's *Grands Crus*, and can offer excellent value.

Vintages and ageing

Vintages vary markedly in the Côte d'Or, and conditions differ quite distinctly along the slope. A good vintage in the Côte de Nuits will not necessarily mean a good one further south around Volnay or Meursault. Hail and rot can be very localized in their devastations.

No red burgundy, or white, will keep for as long as a Bordeaux wine of equivalent stature. Think of a decade as the span for the top wines (though they can last for two), and start to enjoy the village reds and most whites at three years old. This is not to deny the existence of great old bottles of burgundy; but they are the exceptions.

Red burgundy is a fragile wine and demands careful transportation and cellaring: many bottles that are exported to faraway countries — especially if they are hot ones — suffer from the trip.

Really good white burgundies can age for longer than their colour suggests: Montrachet from a good vintage, for example, will keep 10 years and longer, and is unlikely to give much pleasure under five. □

Spraying vines at Vougeot. The château is in the middle of the famous Clos, once a monastic vineyard and now a *Grand Cru*.

THE CÔTE D'OR

The Côte de Nuits, named after Nuits-St-Georges, is the northern section of the slope, the Côte de Beaune the southern. To the west, in the hilly country, lie the vineyards of the Hautes Côtes.

Wine communes and areas

- Côte de Nuits commune
- Hautes Côtes de Nuits areas
- Côte de Beaune commune
- Hautes Côtes de Beaune areas

Vineyards

- Grand Cru
- Premier Cru
- Regional and village AOCs

- selected contour: interval 50m (165ft)
- --- selected commune boundary
- motorway
- major road
- other road

N

0   2   4   6 km
0   2   4 miles

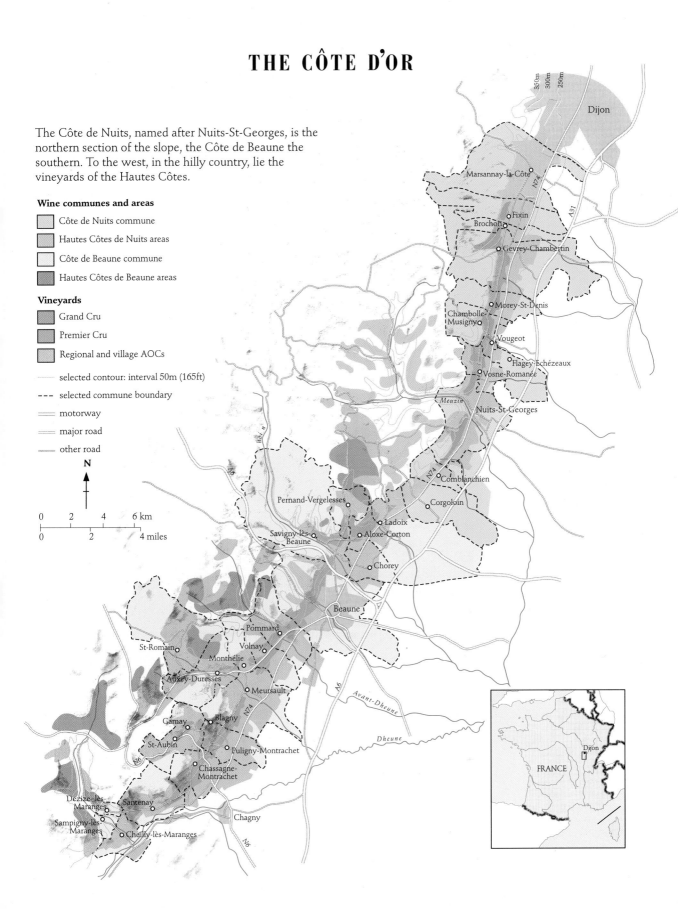

QUALITY FACTORS

The vineyards of the Côte d'Or have been minutely examined to allot them to the various grades of quality, ranging from ordinary regional *appellation,* through communal AOC to *Premier Cru* and *Grand Cru.* The quality formula has three main ingredients: slope, soil and exposure.

Geology and soils

The underlying rock is limestone of two varieties, which, together with associated marl (*see* cross-section), provides the basic structure of the Côte d'Or. The weathering of these rocks has produced soils of various types which gradually slip down the slope under the influence of gravity. Thus the soil at a given point is the product both of the rock strata immediately beneath the ground and that further up, as material is eroded and debris works its way down the slope to mingle with the soil further below. The base of the scarp slope merges into the plain of the River Saône, where the soils are alluvial in origin, and are therefore less suitable for winegrowing.

The *Grands* and *Premiers Crus* occupy a distinct band along the slope where the marl outcrop provides the best soil, particularly for red wines. It is both the best-drained and the easiest to work. White-wine vineyards are concentrated in areas (such as Meursault) where limestone is predominant. Limestone is nearly always found at the top of the slopes: for example, the white *Grand Cru* Corton-Charlemagne is higher up than the red Corton.

Slope

The Côte d'Or is a scarp slope resulting from a geological fault — whereby one section of land has dropped relative to another. The slope formed by this fault is the eroded edge of the tract of higher ground: the Burgundy plateau to the west. To the east, at the base of the slope, is the wide plain formed by the River Saône. The escarpment is not uniform in shape: it is bisected by small valleys that were cut by streams flowing east into the Saône. The vineyards are sited on southeast-facing slopes, between the flat plain to the east and the wooded hills to the west.

THE COTE DE NUITS: SOIL AND SLOPE

West

375
350
325
300
275
250
225

Elevation (m)

Other vineyards

Grand Cru vineyards

Vosne-Romanée

Premier Cru vineyards

Other vineyards

East

0   1   2 km

alluvial sands
limestone-clay conglomerate
marl
limestone
vineyards

Some of the world's most expensive soil at Romanée-Conti.

Site and exposure

The cross-section demonstrates that the typical Côte d'Or commune has its village at the foot of the slope, between the vineyards and the flat land which stretches out to the east. The vine-growing terrain is constrained by height: too far up the slope the micro-climate becomes distinctly cooler; too low down on the flat land and the danger of late frost is greater. Certain places are mysteriously more prone to hail than others; no-one knows quite why.

The slope provides well-drained vineyard sites with suitable soils, and the east and south-east exposure of the slope enhances the warmth gained from the sun and provides protection from rain-bearing west winds.

VILLAGES OF THE CÔTE DE NUITS

This, the northern part of the Côte d'Or, is planted almost entirely with Pinot Noir for red wine: exceptions are mentioned in the text. The slope begins at the southern edge of the city of Dijon, and extends for 22km (14 miles) almost due north–south to Corgoloin, north of Beaune. Each village has its own commune AOC, with *Premier* and *Grand Cru* vineyards within them. The communes are listed from north to south. Growers are named for each village. Some of those who have land in several villages, plus *négociants*, are described on p202. (N) in the lists below indicates a *négociant*'s wine.

Understanding the appellations

The Côte d'Or villages — both Côte de Nuits and Côte de Beaune — glory in an unashamedly complex system of grading their vineyards.

Each village or commune has an AOC. But it is not that simple: some "village" AOCs take in land in neighbouring villages; others do not include all the land within the named commune's boundaries. So AOC Nuit-St-Georges wine may come from Prémeaux, an adjacent village.

Within a commune, there may be vineyards that are not entitled to the village AOC. These will carry the AOC Bourgogne or one of the other generic *appellations*.

Also within a commune are vineyards rated as *Premier* or *Grand Cru*. Their nomenclature is described on p182, but bear in mind that while *in* a village, a *Grand Cru* is not legally *of* it in AOC terms.

Thus we find four grades of wine in a typical commune, of which the middle two (village AOC and *Premier Cru*) will carry the commune's name, while the bottom and top grades, generic AOC and *Grand Cru*, will not.

Côte de Nuits-Villages

This AOC is available for use by vineyards in five marginal villages — Fixin and Brochon to the north, and Prémeaux-Prissey, Comblanchien and Corgoloin at the southern end of the Côte. Because the five villages have obscure names, some growers and *négociants* use the overall *appellation* Côte de Nuits-Villages.

Marsannay

In 1987 Marsannay-la-Côte was given its own commune AOC, for red and white wines produced from the slopes to the west of the N74. Other land in the village, and in adjacent Couchey and Chenôve, is permitted to grow Pinot Noir for Marsannay Rosé, a wine unique in Burgundy. More red than rosé is made.

The red vineyards are expanding, and the wines are improving, as the growers make use of the new AOC. They are solid and well-coloured burgundies, but do not aspire to the levels of the great villages of the Côte. The rosé is one of the best in France: long-lived, dry and intense.

The Marsannay growers include: René & Regis Bouvier, Marc Brocot, Domaine Charlopin-Parizot, Bruno Clair, Domaine Fougeray de Beauclair, Alain Guyard, Louis Jadot (N).

Fixin

Here begins the true "Côte": the slope steepens and the geology beneath Fixin's steeply sloping vineyards is significant: a northern continuation of the limestone band that underlies Gevrey-Chambertin's *Premiers Crus*.

The *appellation* is Fixin, the villages are Fixin and Fixey (and Brochon, which has no AOC but whose best plots can be labelled Fixin). The first five *Premiers Crus* of the Côte de Nuits are here. The superior vineyards are on the middle slopes: Clos du Chapitre, La Perrière, Les Hervelets. These vineyards produce powerful red burgundies that can age well. A small amount of white wine is made.

Fixin growers include: Domaine Bart, Vincent and Denis Berthaut, Régis Bouvier, Bruno Clair, Pierre Gelin, Domaine Huguenot, Philippe Joliet (Domaine de La Perrière), Domaine Marion.

Gevrey-Chambertin

The *Grands Crus* of the Côte de Nuits begin south of the village of Gevrey-Chambertin. Nine vineyards totalling 87ha (221 acres) — more than in any other village — have this status, and a further 28, covering a similar area, have the status of *Premier Cru*.

This is a large *appellation* covering half the commune of Brochon, just south of Fixin, as well as Gevrey itself. The vineyards run up a side valley, giving southerly or south-easterly exposure to a line of *Premiers Crus*. To the south, the *Grands Crus* line the main slope of the Côte, sheltered by a belt of woodland. These are the famous vineyards of Chambertin, Clos de Bèze and half a dozen others that are allowed to add the name Chambertin to their own (for example, Charmes-Chambertin). In addition to the *Grands* and *Premiers Crus*, there is a wide area of straightforward AOC Gevrey-Chambertin land, so the name is frequently found on wine lists.

Chambertin gained fame from the patronage of Napoleon I, who is reputed to have drunk little else — but he diluted his Chambertin with large amounts of water.

The *Grands Crus* can certainly make wine equal to their

COTE DE NUITS GRANDS CRUS

Bonnes Mares	Grands Echezeaux
Chambertin	Griotte-Chambertin
Chambertin Clos de Bèze	Latricières-Chambertin
Chapelle-Chambertin	Mazis-Chambertin
Charmes-Chambertin	Mazoyères-Chambertin
Clos des Lambrays	Musigny
Clos de la Roche	Richebourg
Clos St-Denis	La Romanée
Clos de Tart	Romanée Conti
Clos de Vougeot	Romanée St-Vivant
Echezeaux	Ruchottes-Chambertin
La Grande Rue	La Tâche

status but, as ever in Burgundy, quality varies widely. This is partly due to fragmentation of ownership. There are two dozen owners of land in the 13ha (32 acres) of Chambertin, making an average of 250–300 cases of wine each. Clos de Bèze is less divided, and the standard of wine is higher, than Chambertin. Clos de Bèze may be labelled Chambertin-Clos de Bèze. Both wines demand bottle-ageing. Charmes-Chambertin is another *Grand Cru* with a reputation for consistent, early-maturing wines.

The *Premiers Crus* are superbly sited, the best of their wines (from the best growers) being up to *Grand Cru* standard. Clos St-Jacques is the most famous. Note that Aux Combottes is only ranked as a *Premier Cru*, despite being on the same slope as the band of *Grands Crus* vineyards.

Ordinary "village" Gevrey-Chambertin should be bought according to the grower's reputation: not all the wine is worthy of the village name.

The best Gevrey-Chambertin is powerful, fruity and tannic in character. The top wines have the structure for longevity: they are true *vins de garde* to lay down for perhaps 20 years.

Growers here include: Pierre Amiot, Denis Bachelet, Lucien Boillot & Fils, Bourée Père & Fils, Alain Burguet, Bruno Clair, Pierre Damoy, Maison Delaunay, Joseph Drouhin (N), Drouhin-Larose, Bernard Dugat, Domaine Dujac, Frédéric Esmonin, Michel Esmonin, Louis Jadot (N), Philippe Leclerc, Grillot Marichand, Denis Mortet, Domaine les Perrières, Charles Quillardet, Jean Trapet, Joseph Roty, Armand Rousseau,

Christian Serafin, Domaine Tortochot, Domaine des Varoilles.

Morey-St-Denis
This is a small village that is squeezed between two famous ones, but with all or part of five *Grands Crus* within its boundaries. The vineyards lie on the continuous slope of limestone that runs from Gevrey-Chambertin south through Morey-St-Denis to Vougeot. Two of the Morey-St-Denis *Grands Crus* are old monastic *clos*, which are still

walled — Clos de Tart and Clos St-Denis on the hill above Morey — as is the *Premier Cru* Clos de la Bussière just outside the village. Unusually, some of the *Premiers Crus* lie above the *Grands Crus*, higher up the slope of the Côte than would normally be expected. A tiny amount of white wine is produced.

Clos de Tart is in one ownership (a "monopole"), unusual in Burgundy, and has its own winery and cellars next to the vines. The other *Grands Crus* are Clos de la Roche and Clos des Lambrays (promoted in 1981, and also a *monopole*), and a small part of Bonnes Mares (*see* Chambolle-Musigny below).

Morey-St-Denis produces long-lived red burgundies in the classic, solid Côte de Nuits style: the *Grand Cru* wines can be great, with Clos de la Roche and Clos St-Denis accounted the best. There are some excellent producers here and the overall standard is high. Clos des Lambrays was replanted in 1980 and the vines are still relatively young by *Grand Cru* standards. Clos de Tart has improved markedly in the last few vintages.

Other wines from Morey — both *Premiers Crus* and village wines — offer good value compared with neighbouring *appellations*.

Morey-St-Denis growers include: Pierre Amiot, Guy Castagnier, Domaine du Clos des Lambrays, Domaine Dujac, Faiveley (N), Robert Groffier, Hubert Lignier, Mommessin (Clos de Tart), Domaine Ponsot, Armand Rousseau, Taupenot-Merme.

Chambolle-Musigny
Power matched by elegance and complexity are the hallmarks of the best wines here, which are among Burgundy's greatest reds. They are less tannic and solid than wines

THE HAUTES COTES

To the west of the Côte d'Or is a zone of hilly, wooded country broken by sheltered valleys. The vineyards of the Hautes Côtes, as the area is known, fell into decline after phylloxera ravaged the area. Revival is being led by the regional cooperative, but also involves some rejuvenated private estates.

Chardonnay and Aligoté are the grape varieties grown for white wine, with Pinot Noir for reds. The *appellation* is Bourgogne with the suffix Hautes Côtes de Nuits or Hautes Côtes de Beaune.
■ **Hautes Côtes de Nuits** villages are: Arcenant, Bévy, Chaux, Chevannes, Collonges-lès-Bévy, Curtil-Vergy, L'Etang-Vergy, Magny-lès-Villers, Marey-lès-Fussey, Messanges, Meuilley, Reulle-Vergy, Segrois, Villars-Fontaine, Villers-la-Faye.
■ **Hautes Côtes de Beaune** villages are: Baubigny, Bouze-

lès-Beaune, Cirey-lès-Nolay, Cormot, Echevronne, Fussey, Magny-lès-Villers, Mavilly-Mandelot, Meloisey, Nantoux, Nolay, Rochepot, Vauchignon.
■ These villages in **Saône-et-Loire** are also included in the *appellation*: Change, Créot, Epertully, Paris-Hôpital, and part of Cheilly-lès-Maranges, Dezize-lès-Maranges, Sampigny-lès-Maranges.

Producers
Maison Bouhey-Allex
Marc Bouthenet
Denis Carré
Yves Chaley
Chanson Père & Fils
François Charles & Fils
Claude Cornu
Edouard Delaunay & Ses Fils
Doudet-Naudin
Ch de Dracy
Guy Dufouleur
Guillemard Dupont
Jean Féry
Denis Fouquerand
Marcel-Bernard Fribourg

Maurice & Jean-Michel Giboulot
Jean Gros
Georges Guérin & Fils
Caves des Hautes Côtes
  Groupement de Producteurs
Lucien Jacob
Robert Jayer-Gilles
Jean Joliot & Fils
La Jolivode
Honoré Lavigne
A Ligeret
Ch Mandelot
René Martin
Mazilly Père & Fils
Ch de Mercey
Moillard
Domaine de Montmain
Henri Naudin-Ferrand
Parigot Père & Fils
Domaine du Prieure
Antonin Rodet
Domaine St-Marc
Michel Serveau
Simon Fils
Thévenot-Le Brun & Fils
Alain Verdet
Domaine des Vignes des Demoiselles

from Morey-St-Denis and Gevrey-Chambertin.

The village is tucked into a valley in the Côte which breaks the continuous belt of limestone-based hillside. The commune's two *Grands Crus*, Musigny and Bonnes Mares, are beautifully sited on the east-facing main slope, on the southern and northern frontiers of the *appellation*. The soil here is more pure limestone than further north, leading to lighter wines. Of the *Grands Crus*, Bonnes Mares is reckoned the more powerful and solid, Musigny the more refined and subtle. Among the *Premiers Crus*, Les Amoureuses and Les Charmes are very good. There are some Chardonnay vines in Musigny, and they produce a rare white wine. The standard of the village wines is perhaps less high than in Morey-St-Denis.

Chambolle-Musigny growers include: Amiot-Servelle, Michel Noëllat, Pierre Bertheau, Ch de Chambolle-Musigny, Joseph Drouhin (N), Robert Groffier, Alain Hudelot-Noëllat, Daniel Moine-Hudelot, Georges Roumier, Domaine des Varoilles, Comte Georges de Vogüé.

Vougeot
The Clos, or walled, monastic vineyard, of Vougeot is one of the largest (50ha/124 acres) and most famous *Grands Crus* in Burgundy. Unfortunately for the buyer, it is split between 80 owners. They own small plots dotted about the Clos, and make wines in varying styles. Such a large

vineyard has inevitable variations in soil, and thus some parts make better wine than others. The vineyard slopes from the château, sited beneath the crest of the Côte, down to the N74 road. The best land is at the top, adjoining the Musigny *Grand Cru*; the lowest land is divided by the Clos wall from the adjoining village AOC vineyard and can only be considered superior for historic reasons.

Given the fragmentation, to know the name of the grower is even more essential in choosing wine here than is normal in Burgundy. Standards have improved recently and there is much more reliable Clos de Vougeot on the market. The best wines have a powerful, rich, almost sweet, taste and are long-lived. These are not the most subtle burgundies, but they are full of flavour and with a velvety texture.

Other Vougeot wines include some *Premiers Crus* and village wines that live in the shadow of the *Grand Cru*, and a small amount of white from the Clos Blanc *Premier Cru*.

The medieval château in the Clos is the headquarters of the Confrérie des Chevaliers du Tastevin de Bourgogne, which promotes burgundy through competitive tastings, colourful ceremonies and atmospheric dinners. The Confrérie awards "Tastevin" labels to wines it considers to be good examples of their *appellations*.

Some of the most reliable growers in the Clos include: Domaine Bertagna, Joseph

Drouhin (N), Jean Gros, Alain Hudelot-Noëllat, Domaine Mongeard-Mugneret, Georges Roumier, Château de la Tour, Domaine des Varoilles.

Flagey-Echezeaux
The names get complicated here, even by Côte d'Or standards: Flagey is a village, but the commune name Flagey-Echezeaux does not appear on labels as the non-*Grand Cru* wine (there are no *Premiers Crus*) is allowed to be called Vosne-Romanée. The *Grands Crus* are Echezeaux and Grands Echezeaux, which are both sited on the slope above Vougeot and are closer to Vosne-Romanée than to their named village.

These are powerful, scented wines, the Echezeaux maturing in perhaps a decade, the Grands Echezeaux taking longer. While expensive, they

do not cost as much as the neighbouring *Grands Crus* of Vosne-Romanée.

Among the growers in Flagey-Echezeaux are: Joseph Drouhin (N), René Engel, A F Gros, Méo-Camuzet, Mongeard-Mugneret, Domaine de la Romanée-Conti and Robert Sirugue.

Vosne-Romanée
The home of five *Grands Crus* — La Romanée, Romanée-Conti, Romanée-St-Vivant, Richebourg, La Tâche — and the famous, and fabulously priced, wines of Domaine de la Romanée-Conti (sole owner of the *Grands Crus* Romanée-Conti and La Tâche).

The *Grands Crus* form a block on the hillside above the village, broken only by the strip of La Grand Rue, a *Premier Cru*, bounded by La Tâche and La Romanée-Conti.

DOMAINE DE LA ROMANEE-CONTI

Sole owners of Romanée-Conti and La Tâche, and major owners in Richebourg, Romanée-St-Vivant, Grands Echézaux and Montrachet, the Domaine would be famous for its *Grands Crus* land holdings alone. To these riches it adds its own style of winemaking: late picking for ripe grapes, low yields, a long and warm fermentation, 18 months in new oak casks and minimum filtration. The results can be controversial, but are always rich, heady and incredibly deep in taste. These are wines designed for a very long life. The limited production and consequent high prices make the wines hard to find, but they set a standard for every red burgundy. Other producers may aim for a lighter, more subtle style, but the Romanée-Conti wines are always there as a benchmark.

The Les Argillières vineyard overlooking Prémeaux-Prissey is within the Nuits St-Georges *appellation*.

The *Grands Crus* wines are beyond the wallet of all except millionaires: one recent vintage was priced at the equivalent of £5 a mouthful. Luckily, the village has a clutch of excellent *Premiers Crus* such as Aux Malconsorts (next along the slope from *Grand Cru* La Tâche), Les Suchots, Les Chaumes Aux Brûlées and Les Beaux Monts. Many of these produce outstanding wines to rival those of the *Grands Crus* in their spicy opulence and capacity to age for 10–15 years or more, but they do considerably less damage to one's bank balance.

The commune *appellation* of Vosne-Romanée has had mixed fortunes; some growers once produced clumsy wines while capitalizing on the name, but since the early 1980s the wines have become more reliable and elegant.

Growers include: Robert Arnoux, Sylvain Cathiard, J Confuron-Cotetidot, Forey Père & Fils, Jean Grivot, Jean Gros, Gros Frère & Sœur, Henri Jayer, Leroy, Manière-Noirot, Méo-Camuzet, Mongeard-Mugneret, Denis Mugneret, Pernin-Rossin, Bernard Rion Père & Fils, Domaine de la Romanée-Conti (*see* profile), Robert Sirugue and Jean Tardy.

Nuits-St-Georges
This small town is, after Beaune, Burgundy's second most important wine centre, and home to many *négociants*.

The vineyards are divided into two parts by the valley of a small stream. There are no *Grands Crus*, but around 40 *Premiers Crus* — Les Vaucrains, Les Pruliers, Les St-Georges, Les Argillières, Clos de la Maréchale, to name but a few.

The *appellation*'s vineyards extend for around 7km (4 miles) along the Côte, so it is not surprising that the wines they produce vary greatly in style. Those at the northern end of the AOC zone, such as La Richemone and Les Damodes, adjoin those of Vosne-Romanée, and wines from here share a scented, opulent character.

South of the town, the *Premier Cru* vineyards continue until beyond the village of Premeaux, the most southerly being the Clos de la Maréchale. Here, the vineyards are lower, the soils are heavier, and the wines are full-flavoured, earthy and robust.

The wines of both the *Premiers Crus* and the village *appellation* are usually ready to drink after about five years in bottle, and can remain at their peak for a further three. There is a little white wine.

Nuits-St-Georges has its own Hospice, similar to but smaller than Beaune. The Hospice owns 9.5ha (23 acres) of *Premier Cru* vineyard and its wines reach a high standard.

Growers include: Bertrand Ambroise, Domaine de l'Arlot, Jean-Claude Boisset (N), Jean Chauvenet, Georges et Michel Chevillon, Robert Chevillon, Georges Chicotot, Daniel Chopin-Groffier, Jean-Jacques Confuron, Robert Dubois & Fils, Dufouleur Frères (N), Joseph Faiveley, Henri Gouges, Domaine Machard de Gramont, Hospices de Nuits, Labouré-Roi, François Legros, Lupé-Cholet, Alain Michelot, Moillard, Domaine Moillard-Grivot, Domaine de la Poulette, Henri & Gilles Remoriquet, Daniel Rion, Domaine Thomas and Domaine Fabrice Vigot.

VILLAGES OF THE COTE DE BEAUNE

The southern section of the Côte d'Or begins north of the city of Beaune, where wines are mainly red, from Pinot Noir. The stress on red wines continues south of Beaune to Meursault and Puligny-Montrachet, known the world over for great white wines (from Chardonnay). Further south still, reds begin to eclipse whites once more.

The slope extends for about 25km (15 miles) and includes around 20 villages, each with its own AOC, listed here from north to south. In typical burgundian fashion, however, commune boundaries do not always coincide with *appellation* boundaries. Also, some *Grands* and *Premiers Crus* are shared by two villages.

Growers are named for each village. Some of those who have land in several villages, plus the *négociants*, are described on pp202–203. (N) in the lists below indicates a *négociant*'s wine.

Côte de Beaune-Villages

This red-wine *appellation* may be used by any of the region's villages, with the exception of Aloxe-Corton, Beaune, Pommard and Volnay. It allows growers in lesser-known villages to use a recognizable name, and also means that *négociants* can blend wines from two or more villages to create a balanced wine. A Côte de Beaune AOC exists for wines made near Beaune, but is rarely seen.

Ladoix-Serrigny

This little village on the main road from Nuits-St-Georges to Beaune shelters beneath the enormous vine-clad slope of Corton. This is the dominant feature of the landscape north of Beaune: a big, oval hill capped with woods. *Grand Cru* vineyards clothe three sides of the hill.

Ladoix, the northernmost village of the Côte de Beaune, shares with the village of Serrigny one of Burgundy's for-gotten *appellations*, since the best vineyards of the village are on the hill of Corton, and are entitled to be sold as *Grands Crus* or as *Premier Cru* Aloxe-Corton. Recently, the INAO has recognized *Premier Cru* status to some vineyards. The wines here are mainly red, although some of the higher vineyards, such as Les Gréchons, produce fine whites.

Growers in Ladoix include Capitain-Gagnerot, Michel Mallard and André Nudant.

Pernand-Vergelesses

This village on the western side of the hill of Corton has parts of the *Grand Cru* vineyards of Corton and Corton-Charlemagne (*see* Aloxe-Corton below), and is well-known for its *Premier Cru* Ile des Vergelesses, as well as for its white wines (around 20% of the village's production). The village and *Premier Cru* red wines need at least five years in bottle, and can improve for a further ten years.

Growers include: Bonneau du Martray, Marius Delarche, P Dubreuil-Fontaine and Laleure-Piot.

Aloxe-Corton

The village is dominated by the hill of Corton and the two *Grands Crus*, Corton (the only red *Grand Cru* in the Côte de Beaune, and the largest in Burgundy) and Corton-Charlemagne (for white wine).

Officially, Corton is on the east side of the hill, while Corton-Charlemagne occupies the southern and south-western slopes. The AOC rules have bent the boundaries to co-incide with the soil: the higher vineyards, where the soil is thin, with a high percentage of chalk, are rated as Corton-Charlemagne, whatever the maps may say. They produce some of the finest Chardon-nay wines in the world; their distinguished, nutty, spicy bouquet only begins to open up after five years, and will still be great at 15–20 years.

Further down the slope the soil becomes deeper and red-der, although it varies around the hill, which is divided into a number of vineyards. Wine from these slopes is red, and can be called *Grand Cru* Cor-ton, but the name is usually linked with a specific vineyard — Corton Les Bressandes, Corton Clos du Roi, Corton Les Renardes. These wines are powerfully-flavoured, but earthy and highly tannic when young — they need six or seven years in bottle, after which subtlety, perfume and spicy fruit emerge.

Below on the eastern slope are Aloxe-Corton's red-wine *Premiers Crus*. These wines will be considerably cheaper, but less long-lived, than the *Grand Cru* burgundies.

The lower part of the slope produces red village wines: relatively light, they represent good value.

Among the growers are: Bernard Dubois & Fils, Michel Gay, Antonin Guyon, Louis Jadot (N), Louis Latour (N), Rapet, Daniel Senard, Tollot-Beaut, Michel Voarick.

Chorey-lès-Beaune

Unusually the village, and most of its vineyards, are situated on the eastern side of the N74 "Wine Road". There are no *Grands* or *Premiers Crus* here, but the village wines (nearly all red) are good value for early drinking, of good colour, full of freshness and ripe, soft, red fruit flavours.

Growers here include: Germain Père & Fils, Maillard Père & Fils, Tollot-Beaut.

Savigny-lès-Beaune

The village sits in a valley cut in the side of the Côte, and its vineyards extend up the hills on either side. To the north, they adjoin those of Pernand-Vergelesses; *Premiers Crus* here include Aux Vergelesses, Les Lavières, Aux Serpentières and Aux Guettes. The vineyards around the slope south of Sav-igny, towards Beaune, include

---

COTE DE BEAUNE GRANDS CRUS

Bâtard-Montrachet	Corton
Bienvenues Bâtard-Montrachet	Corton-Charlemagne
Charlemagne	Criots-Bâtard-Montrachet
Chevalier-Montrachet	Montrachet

the *Premiers Crus* of La Dominode, Bas Marconnets and Hauts Marconnets.

Savigny is an important producer of red wines, which are, for Côte d'Or burgundies, very reasonably priced. The *Premiers Crus* are notable for their appealing scent and clean, fruity taste, and they are best drunk at between four and ten years old. Some whites are also made.

Growers include: Pierre Bitouzet, Simon Bize & Fils, Luc Camus, Capron-Manieux, Chandon de Briailles, Daudet-Naudin, Maurice Ecard & Fils, Pierre Guillemot, Antonin Guyon, Laleure-Piot, Jean-Marc Pavelot, Rapet, Seguin, Henri de Villamont.

Beaune

The medieval walled city that lends its name to the entire region is the centre of the wine trade in Burgundy. It attracts tourists throughout the year, but wine lovers are particularly drawn to the three-day wine festival held during the third weekend in November, known as Les Trois Glorieuses. A highlight of the festival is Sunday's auction at the Hospices de Beaune (*see* p201).

The Beaune *appellation* includes by far the largest area (320ha/795 acres) of *Premiers Crus* vineyards on the Côte de Beaune, with about 30 ranged along the hill overlooking the town. These *Premiers Crus* include Les Marconnets, Les Fèves, Les Bressandes, Le Clos des Mouches, Les Grèves, Les Teurons, Les Vignes Franches, and Les Epenottes.

The Côte here slopes more gently, and the band of vines is deeper, than in the Côte de Nuits. Seen from Beaune's medieval walls, the great hill, an unbroken bank of *Premier Cru* vines, is most impressive.

Most Beaune is red, and the large production and high standards make the AOC a benchmark for quality and

good-value red burgundy. The style is softer than the great Côte de Nuits *crus*, but elegance, perfume and a fine, fruity, spicy flavour are all there. Enjoy them at six to ten years old. The white wines are less distinguished and should be drunk younger.

Many of Burgundy's top *négociants* have cellars under the streets of Beaune and holdings in *Premier Cru* vineyards. Drouhin owns a large plot in Clos des Mouches, Louis Jadot's Clos des Ursules is part of Les Vignes Franches and Bouchard Père & Fils has Vigne de l'Enfant Jésus in Les Grèves.

Growers include: Bouchard Aîné & Fils (N), Bouchard Père & Fils (N), Champy Père & Cie, Chanson Père & Fils, Joseph Drouhin (N), Hospices de Beaune, Louis Jadot (N), Jaffelin (N), Lafarge, Louis Latour (N), P de Marcilly Frères, Albert Morot, Patriarche Père & Fils (N), Jacques Prieur, Remoissenet Père & Fils (N).

Pommard

One of the best-known names of the Côte d'Or, Pommard's *"rapport qualité-prix"* is now more in line.

The vineyards continue on south from the Beaune border in a broad belt of quality red-wine land (all Pommard is red). The village, straggling up a small valley, breaks the continuity; then there are more good vineyards that merge into Volnay.

The best *Premiers Crus* (Epenots, Rugiens, Clos de la Commeraine) yield red wines of deep colour, intense aroma, concentrated flavours, full body and complex structure which can improve in bottle for ten years.

Growers include: Comte Armand, Roger Bellan, Jean-Marc Boillot, Domaine de Courcel, Jean Garaudet, Michel Gaunoux, Vincent Girardin, Domaine Mussy, Domaine Parent, Ch de Pommard.

Volnay

The village is high on the slope, with its vineyards on either side and below it. It is known for the high quality of its winemaking, and has a reputation for delicate, silky, violet- and strawberry-scented red wines from *Premiers Crus* such as Caillerets, Champans, Clos des Chênes and Clos des Ducs. They are enjoyable from four or five years old, although they have the ability to age for much longer.

All Volnay wine is red. The *Premier Cru* Les Santenots lies within the next-door Meursault AOC zone, which makes mostly white wine, but produces red wine which is sold under the Volnay name.

Growers here include: Marquis d'Angerville, Jean-Marc Bouley, Joseph Drouhin (N), Hubert de Montille, Domaine de la Pousse d'Or, Joseph Voillot.

Monthélie

This tiny, ancient village, a close neighbour to the south of Volnay and up the hill from Meursault, has some perfect, south-facing sites; but until the mid-1980s its wines (mainly red) were thought of as no more than rather rustic, simple burgundies. Things are now looking up as talented winemakers begin to exploit the potential of their plots, and fragrant, characterful, well-structured red wines from top producers represent excellent value. The best-known of Monthélie's nine *Premiers Crus* are Sur La Velle and Les Champs Fulliot.

Among the growers contributing to the improving reputation of Monthélie are Paul Garaudet, Comte Lafon and Ch de Monthélie.

Auxey-Duresses

The village is tucked into the valley west of Monthélie, two-thirds red wine, one-third white. The *Premiers Crus*, such

as Les Duresses and Clos du Val, are planted with Pinot Noir, and can make fine, raspberry-fruited reds which compare well to Volnays. White Auxey-Duresses, at its best, bears comparison with Meursault — deliciously toasty and nutty — but should be drunk sooner.

Growers here include: Jean-François Diconne, Domaine Leroy, Jean-Pierre et Laurent Prunier, Michel Prunier, Pascal Prunier, Vincent Prunier.

St-Romain

Continuing up the valley for a further 3km (2 miles), one reaches the edge of the Hautes Côtes (*see* p196). From its rocky hillside perch, St-Romain produces roughly equal amounts (17,000 cases each) of fresh, crisp whites (particularly good value) and firm, cherry-flavoured reds.

Growers include: Bernard Fèvre, Maison Germain Père & Fils, Alain Gras, Olivier Leflaive, Louis Latour (N), Leroy, René Thévenin, Charles Viénot (N).

Meursault

Meursault is almost a town, and its vineyards spread wide along the hillsides between Volnay in the north and Puligny-Montrachet to the south. The limestone is predominant, giving excellent conditions for white wine. Despite its size, and the fame of its white wines, there are no *Grands Crus* here, although there are a large number of *Premiers Crus* — Les Charmes, Les Perrières, Les Genevrières, Les Gouttes d'Or.

Red Meursault is made, but the commune's fame comes from white wines of powerful, persistent flavour and good ability to age. The *Premiers Crus* make the finest, most scented wines: the village wines have less character. With its large production, quality is variable, and the most individual wines are usually domaine bottlings.

Growers in Meursault include: Domaine d'Auvenay, Bitouzet-Prieur, Domaine Vincent Bouzereau, Michel Bouzereau, Dominique Caillot, Raoul Clerget, J F Coche-Dury, Domaine Darnat, Domaine J P Dicone, Ch Génot-Boulanger, Domaine Henri Germain, Bernard Glantenay, Albert Grivault, Patrick Javallier, François Jobard, Rémi Jobard, Jean-Luc Joliot, Comte Lafon, Domaine Jean Latour-Labille, Mazilly Père & Fils, Ch de Meursault, Michelot, René Monnier, Pierre Morey, Domaine Prieur-Brunet, Michel Prunier, Ch de Puligny-Montrachet, Ropiteau Frères, Domaine Roulot, Roux Père & Fils, Henri de Villamont.

Blagny

Squeezed between the two famous white-wine *appellations* of Meursault and Puligny-Montrachet, this hamlet sells only red wine — with a positive, slightly earthy style — under its own name. Its white wines take the name of Meursault (from vineyards to the north) or Puligny-Montrachet (if they come from that side of the hamlet).

St-Aubin

St-Aubin is tucked away behind the main Côte, making red and white wines from a well-sited, south-facing slope of vineyards to the west of Puligny-Montrachet. The wines are light, fresh and often delicious, and are usually good value. Growers include: Jean Chartron, Hubert Lamy.

Puligny-Montrachet

The *Grand Cru* of Montrachet, which makes the most expensive and often the best white wine in all of Burgundy, straddles the border between Puligny and Chassagne. Both villages have annexed the great vineyard's name to their own, leading to one of those typically Burgundian confusions whereby large amounts of

white wine can use the magic word "Montrachet" as part of their name.

Puligny concentrates on white wine from its four *Grands Crus* — Le Montrachet, Chevalier-Montrachet, Bienvenues-Bâtard Montrachet and Bâtard-Montrachet — and a clutch of excellent *Premiers Crus*. The great vineyards are superbly sited, with the perfect slope and alignment for making great white wine, facing just south of east and on free-draining limestone-based soil.

The *Grand Cru* wines need plenty of time to reach their potential. Tasters differ, but the consensus is that bottles from the best winemakers in good vintages will last for 20 years or more. In style they are dense, buttery and rich, but with a backbone of acidity which allows them to last in bottle.

The *Premiers Crus* wines of Puligny are more elegant than those of Meursault. Le Cailleret, Les Combettes and Les Pucelles are the heaviest and slowest to mature. Village Puligny-Montrachet is less special and can be expensive. A little red wine is made.

Puligny-Montrachet growers include: Bouchard Père et Fils (N), Louis Carillon, Jean Chartron, Chartron et Trébuchet, Henri Clerc, Domaine Jadot, Marquis de Laguiche, Louis Latour (N), Domaine Leflaive, Olivier Leflaive, Domaine Jean Pillot & Fils, Etienne Sauzet.

Chassagne-Montrachet

Chassagne has three *Grands Crus* — Les Criots-Bâtard-Montrachet, Montrachet and

Bâtard-Montrachet, which it shares with its northern neighbour Puligny; and the assessment above applies equally well to Chassagne's *Grand Cru* wines.

Unlike Puligny, Chassagne makes red wine; indeed almost half the wines are red. These are little known and can be good value.

White Chassagne-Montrachet is very similar to Puligny, with perhaps an extra note of richness due to the southern trend of the slope. Winemaking standards are high. The red wines, often overlooked, are soft, fruity and well-structured. They can age for a decade from good vintages.

Among the growers in Chassagne are: Guy Amiot, Bachelet-Ramonet, Domaine Roger Bellan, Bernard Colin, Marc Colin, Michel Colin-Deléger, Lamy-Pillot, Duc de Magenta, Ch de la Maltroye, Bernard Morey, Marc Morey & Fils, Michel Morey-Coffinet, Domaine Michel Niellon, Domaine Jean Pillot & Fils, André Ramonet and Antonin Rodet.

Santenay and Maranges

This is the southern end of the Côte de Beaune, and here red wine reasserts itself. There are several *Premiers Crus*, and some good wines are made in a rather tough, earthy style. They should not be kept for too long: try them at five to eight years old. The three villages of Dezize-, Sampigny- and Cheilly-lès-Maranges all share the AOC of Maranges with six *Premiers Crus*.

Growers include: Roger-Belland, Ch de la Charrière, René Fleurot-Larose, Mestre Père & Fils, Prieur-Brunet, Louis Lequin.

HOSPICES DE BEAUNE

The Hospices is a charity dating from 1443, when Nicholas Rolin, Chancellor of the Duchy of Burgundy, left his wealth to found a hospital for the poor and sick. The pious have left land, including vineyards, to this day: now the Hospice has 60ha (143 acres) in 39 plots in most of the great villages of the Côte, with the exception of Pouilly-Fuissé donated in 1996. They grow the grapes themselves, and make the wines, but the wines are *élevés* by *négociants*. The wines are sold at a dramatic auction each November: the prices are regarded as a benchmark for the whole vintage. The Hospices wines, both red and white, are traditionally made and extremely reliable — although they tend to be extremely expensive. The Hospices buildings, centred around the dramatic medieval Hôtel Dieu, are one of the treasures of Beaune.

COTE D'OR GROWERS

Major estates, growers and *négociants* (wine merchants) of the Côte d'Or are listed below. These names also occur under the entries for individual villages: *see* Côte de Nuits pp195–198, Côte de Beaune pp199–201.

This list, inevitably incomplete, includes the big *négociants*, the most familiar of which appear on wine-lists worldwide. These firms buy wine or grapes from many places and producers, and then make and market the wine. The list also includes relatively large scale grower-bottlers who make wine from several villages, and finally, those estates whose names are benchmarks for quality burgundy. Producers whose efforts are concentrated in one village are not included: their names appear under the relevant village text.

Inevitably, these categories overlap: some *négociants* also own estates, and some producers sell all or part of their wine to the *négociants*.

This list should be regarded as a starting-point for the exploration of Burgundy's producers: there can be no complete list — in some villages in the Côte d'Or the entire active population makes or sells wine. Many of the smaller producers sell most of their wine directly to visiting consumers, and therefore, despite excellent wine, will never build a reputation outside the Côte d'Or.

Robert Ampeau
Plots in Meursault, Volnay, Puligny-Montrachet and Pommard. This skilled white burgundy specialist based in Meursault also makes good reds.

Pierre André
Aloxe-Corton. Grower (also *négociant*) based at the Château de Corton-André, making sound Corton.

Domaine Marquis d'Angerville
Volnay. One of the pioneers of domaine bottling. Marquis d'Angerville owns land in Volnay, Meursault, Pommard, and elsewhere.

Domaine de l'Arlot
Prémeaux. Land in Nuits-St-Georges. A new estate that is applying clever, modern winemaking techniques to grapes from fine vineyards.

Domaine Roger Belland
Santenay. *Grand Cru* land in Corton and Corton-Charlemagne; other vineyards in Santenay, Puligny and Chambertin. Good, traditional wines, both red and white.

Domaine Bertagna
Vougeot. Top plots include some Chambertin, Clos St-Denis, Clos de Vougeot, etc. German-owned, and making reliable, elegant wines.

Domaine Simon Bize et Fils
Savigny-lès-Beaune. Highly-regarded family estate with land around Savigny.

Ch de Bligny
Puligny, Pommard, Beaune, Aloxe-Corton, Nuits-St-Georges, Vosne-Romanée. This château has been growing wine for about twenty years. The wine, still young, is not without elegance.

Jean-Claude Boisset
This dynamic *négociant* and winemaker is very active in Côte de Nuits, owning numerous wine firms, among them Charles Viénot.

Domaine Bonneau du Martray
Pernand-Vergelesses. Major owner of Corton and Corton-Charlemagne. Superb quality red and white wines.

Bouchard Aîné & Fils
Beaune. A family business going back to the 18 century, taken over by Jean-Claude Boisset in 1994, specialising in winemaking and maturing.

Bouchard Père et Fils
Beaune. *Négociant* on a world-wide scale, with major vineyard holdings also under the name Domaines du Château de Beaune.

Domaine Jean-Marc Bouley
Volnay and Pommard: serious, well-made wines.

Domaine Louis Carillon
Puligny-Montrachet. Serious old family firm with the stress on white burgundies; land in many major Côte de Beaune communes.

Chanson Père & Fils
Beaune. A family business founded in 1750 and taken over by Bollinger in 1999. Owns 38ha (94 acres): *Premiers Crus* and one *Grand Cru*.

Domaine Maurice Chapuis
Aloxe-Corton. Corton estate with very good Corton-Charlemagne.

Chartron & Trébuchet
Puligny-Montrachet. *Négociant* and landowner (Domaine Chartron) stressing white burgundy.

Domaine Robert Chevillon
Nuits-St-Georges. New estate, traditional approach.

Domaine Bruno Clair
Marsannay. A 23-ha (57-acre) vineyard dispersed over 12 AOCs (*Premiers* and *Grands Crus*). Winemaking is respectful of traditional methods..

Domaine Coche-Dury
Meursault. White burgundy specialist: top-rank Meursault, Corton-Charlemagne, Volnay.

Domaine Confuron-Cotetidot
Vosne-Romanée. Good Nuits-St-Georges, Echézeaux, etc.

Domaine de Courcel
Pommard. Long-lived, densely-flavoured classic wines.

Doudet-Naudin
Savigny-lès-Beaune. *Négociant* and landowner. Old-fashioned wines for long maturing.

Joseph Drouhin
Beaune. *Négociant* and important landowner in the Côte d'Or and Chablis. Strikingly well-made and reliable wines.

Domaine Dubreuil-Fontaine
Pernand-Vergelesses. Owners in Corton and surroundings: serious wines.

Dufouleur Frères
Nuits-St-Georges. A *négociant* making wines in the old style.

Domaine Dujac
Morey St-Denis. Owned by Jacques Seysses, a leading winemaker. Land in Côte de Nuits *Grands* and other *crus*.

Joseph Faiveley
Nuits-St-Georges. *Négociant*, major owner of vines; modern methods, good results.

Domaine Michel Gaunoux
Pommard. Very traditional red Côte de Beaune wines.

Domaine Jacques Germain
Chorey-lès-Beaune. Has good

land in Beaune and Chorey, quality wine.

Domaine Machard de Gramont
Nuits-St-Georges. A medium-sized estate using traditional techniques with the stress on keeping the style of each *cru*.

Domaine Jean Grivot
Vosne-Romanée. Côte de Nuits *Grands Crus* at the top level made in the Accad style.

Hospices de Beaune
See profile, p201.

Hospices de Nuits
Nuits-St-Georges. A smaller brother of the Beaune charity: top land in Nuits.

Jaboulet-Vercherre
Beaune. Major *négociant* and owner of Beaune vineyards.

Louis Jadot
Beaune. *Négociant* and important vineyard owner making very good red and white wines.

Jaffelin
Beaune. *Négociant* linked with Drouhin (*qv*).

Domaine Henri Jayer
Vosne-Romanée. A top Côte de Nuits producer using traditional techniques.

Labouré-Roi
Nuits-St-Georges. A *négociant* stressing white wines from the entire region.

Domaine Michel Lafarge
Meursault. Serious wine from Volnay, Meursault, Beaune.

Domaine des Comtes Lafon
Meursault. Top-quality whites (especially Montrachet) and very good red wines (Volnay).

Louis Latour
Beaune. *Négociant*. Red and (especially) white wines from the whole region, which are made to a high standard.

Dominique Laurent
This *négociant* and winemaker is specializing in oak ("200% new oak"). His young firm is very well-known.

Domaine Leflaive
Puligny-Montrachet. Great achievements in white burgundy from Montrachet and its neighbours. Olivier Leflaive is a linked *négociant* business.

Domaine Leroy
Vosne-Romanée. Proprietor and *négociant* owned by the part-owner of Domaine de la Romanée-Conti (*qv*). Recently much enlarged, the domaine has some top sites.

Lupé-Cholet
Nuits-St-Georges. Landowning *négociant* linked to Bichot.

Domaine du Duc de Magenta
Chassagne-Montrachet. Estate whose high-class wines are made by Jadot (*qv*) of Beaune.

Prosper Maufoux
Santenay. *Négociant* which ages all its wines, red and white, in oak.

Domaine Méo-Camuzet
Vosne-Romanée. Corton, Vougeot, other *Grands Crus*: top-class wines.

Domaine Prince Florent de Mérode
Ladoix-Serrigny. Old feudal property with top sites around the Corton hill.

Moillard-Grivot
Nuits-St-Georges. A *négociant* and vineyard owner: good standards.

Domaine Mongeard-Mugneret
Vosne-Romanée. Expanding domaine with well regarded, concentrated red wines.

Domaine Monnier et Fils
Meursault, Pommard, Puligny-

Montrachet. Fine white and red wines, traditionally made.

Patriarche Père & Fils
Beaune. *Négociant* on a very large scale, and owners of the Ch de Meursault.

Ch de Pommard
Pommard. Large walled estate making solid, tasty wine.

Domaine de la Pousse d'Or
Volnay, Pommard, Santenay. Balanced and elegant red burgundies which age well.

Domaine Jacques Prieur
Gevrey-Chambertin, Beaune, Meursault, etc. Fine vineyards and a range of excellent wines.

Domaine Ramonet
Chassagne-Montrachet. Top-class white burgundy from Montrachet and near by.

Reine-Pédauque
Aloxe-Corton. *Négociant* and landowner with fine sites, mostly round Corton.

Remoissenet Père & Fils
Beaune. *Négociant* and vineyard owner. Quality winemaking, with the whites the best.

Domaine Daniel Rion
Nuits-St-Georges. Widespread holdings in the Côte de Nuits yielding wines made in a modern, fruit-dominated style.

Domaine de la Romanée-Conti
See profile, p197.

Ropiteau Frères
Meursault. The vineyard of

this firm has been taken over by Bouchard Père & Fils.

Domaine Armand Rousseau
Gevrey-Chambertin, Morey St-Denis. This pioneer estate-bottler produces very traditional, benchmark wines.

Roux Père & Fils
St-Aubin, Meursault, etc. Landowner in the southern Côte de Beaune and now *négociant*. Modern, clean, typical wines; whites are best.

Domaine Etienne Sauzet
Puligny-Montrachet. Classic white burgundies from *Grands* and *Premiers Crus*.

Domaine Daniel Senard
Aloxe-Corton. Corton reds of the highest repute, now made in the Accad style (*see* p185).

Tollot-Beaut et Fils
Chorey-lès-Beaune. Big estate around Corton and Beaune; robust, long-lived red wines.

Ch de la Tour
Vougeot, Beaune. Accad-influenced winemaking and highly-rated red burgundies.

Domaine des Varoilles
Gevrey-Chambertin. Long ageing is a feature of the red wines from this big Côte de Nuits estate.

Henri de Villamont
Savigny-lès-Beaune. *Négociant* and landowner with vines around Corton, Savigny and Puligny. Good Savigny reds.

Domaine Michel Voarick
Aloxe-Corton. Low yields from fine Corton vineyards mean wines for long cellaring.

Domaine Comte Georges de Vogüé
Chambolle-Musigny. Major owner of *Grands* and *Premiers Crus*.

WINE REGIONS OF CHALONNAIS, MACONNAIS AND BEAUJOLAIS

The Chalonnais, or Région de Mercurey, has five village *appellations* and a host of other vineyards using regional AOCs. Mâcon is the centre of a wide region making white and red wines; Beaujolais is to the south, with its ten *cru* villages at the northern end.

Wine regions

Côte Chalonnaise
- village appellations
- AOC Bourgogne Côte Chalonnaise

Mâconnais
- village appellations
- AOC Mâcon

Beaujolais
- cru
- AOC Beaujolais-Villages
- AOC Beaujolais

- - - *département* boundary

motorway
major road
other road

N

0   10   20 km
0   5   10 miles

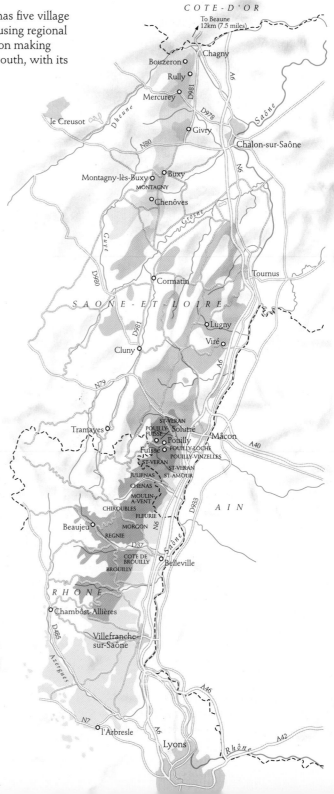

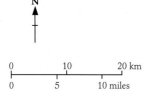

THE CÔTE CHALONNAISE

Wines have been made by the family of the Comtes de Ternay at Château de Rully for six centuries.

The *département* boundary that brings the Côte d'Or to an end at Chagny does not, of course, stop geology dead: the slope of southeast-facing hills continues on into the Saône-et-Loire and the vineyards run on without a pause, but for a small river valley. The political geographers were wise in their choice of boundary, however, for the clean line of the Côte does break down here into a more confused jumble of hills and valleys. The geology is similar to the Côte d'Or, with outcrops of limestone and marl, and some good, steep well-sited vineyards.

This region is known as the Côte Chalonnaise, after the market town of Chalon-sur-Saône. The town is well away from the vineyards, but is a centre for the area. (An alternative name is the Région de Mercurey, after one of the main villages.) The wines are entitled to the general or regional

appellations of Burgundy (*see* p182), and to the qualified regional AOC Bourgogne Côte Chalonnaise; and five villages have the right to use their own names. These are (from north to south) Bouzeron, Rully, Mercurey, Givry and Montagny. A typical Côte Chalonnaise wine will have the village (and AOC) name prominently shown, with the producer next in emphasis. Few vineyards have a reputation, though *Premiers Crus* do exist.

Red and white wines are made (though mainly red), and there is a fair-sized sparkling wine industry. The grapes used are the traditional burgundian varieties: Pinot Noir for red (plus some Gamay, used with the Pinot for Bourgogne Passetout-grains), and Chardonnay for white. Aligoté is also grown for white wines, especially in the village of Bouzeron, which has its own *appellation* for this wine.

The Chalonnaise style

The Chardonnay whites can offer a taste of the real white burgundy style at a realistic price. Less fashionable, they are better value than the wines of Pouilly in the Mâconnais. They never achieve the pungent, concentrated greatness of Montrachet or Meursault, but they do have freshness, personality and charm. Good vintages can age for up to a decade, but most are drunk at two to four years. Aligoté is normally drunk young, but good examples, such as those from Bouzeron, can improve in bottle.

The reds are more variable, but from a good producer in a warm year they are true burgundy, with true Pinot Noir character and the ability to age for four to six years. Wines from the broader region, the AOC Bourgogne Côte Chalonnaise, are often very good buys as the name still does not command a premium price. □

VILLAGES AND PRODUCERS

The villages with their own *appellations* are described from north to south, with some leading producers listed in each. Other vineyards use the AOC Bourgogne. Several *négociants*, with the suffix (N), and estates own land in more than one village.

Bouzeron
Chiefly famed for its Aligoté, for which it gained its own *appellation* in 1979, the small village of Bouzeron also produces some interesting reds. There are no *Premiers Crus*.

Producers include: Bouchard Père et Fils (N), Domaine Chanzy, A et P de Villaine (noted for Aligoté from old vines)

Rully
Rully broods below its castle on its clutch of 19 *Premiers Crus*. Its clear, pleasing reds are on the lighter side, though at their best they are a match for those of Mercurey. Rully's elegant, spice-accented whites are in the majority and tend to take centre-stage; so much so that the wines used for the sparkling Crémant de Bourgogne are these days from farther-off, less well-favoured vineyards. The success of the leading Rully whites has encouraged more growers to use cask-fermentation to add further interest and complexity.

The *Premier Cru* designa-tion covers some, but not all, of the best vineyards, and the best producers make good wine from vineyards of all ranks. They include: Domaine Belleville, Jean-Claude Bre-lière, Chartron & Trébuchet (N), André Delorme, R Dureuil-Jenthial, Domaine de la Folie, Domaine de l'Hermitage, Paul & Henri Jacqueson, Domaine de la Renarde (Jean-François Delorme), Ch de Rully (Antonin Rodet).

Mercurey
Predominantly a red-wine village, though with a little white, Mercurey's vineyard is three times the size of Rully's and has some large and well-run estates and good *terroirs*.

Mercurey from a good producer can be a well-priced and interesting red burgundy, one which can age for four to six years. Several vineyards are classed as *Premiers Crus* and others, though not ranked, have a good name. The best vineyards include Clos-du-Roi, Clos-Voyen or Les Voyens, Clos-Marcilly, Les Champs Martin, Clos-des-Fourneaux, Clos-des-Montai-gus, Clos des Barraults and Clos l'Evêque.

CRÉMANT DE BOURGOGNE

Crémant de Bourgogne is an *appellation* for sparkling burgundy, either red, white or rosé. The term *crémant* originated in Champagne, and referred to wines that were fermented in the bottle at less than half the pressure used in the production of fully sparkling wines. The resulting wines therefore emerged less fizzy.

Controls for quality
The term in Burgundy now applies to high-quality, fully-sparkling wines produced under strict controls that have been agreed with the other wine regions of France that produce *crémants* — Alsace, the Loire, etc.

These controls resemble those applied to the production of champagne and are concerned with the varieties of grape used, the use of second fermentation in bottle (as in champagne) and the time spent in bottle (nine months in burgundy). The main grape varieties used in the production of Crémant de Bourgogne are Chardonnay, Pinot Noir, Sacy, Aligoté and Gamay.

Crémant de Bourgogne is being produced in increasing quantities. The main sources are to be found among the *négociants* of the Nuits-St-Georges area of the Côte d'Or, and the cooperatives and *négociants* of the Côte Chalonnaise and Mâconnais.

The cooperatives at Lugny, Viré and Buxy are in the forefront of Crémant production here. The SICAVA cooperative at Bailly near St-Bris-le-Vineux in the Yonne is a major producer.

Among producers here are: Domaine de Chamerose, Chartron & Trébuchet (N), Michel Juillot, Antonin Rodet (Ch de Chamirey), Hugues de Suremain. The Mercurey cooperative, with 180 members, has a good name.

Givry
The historic centre for wine in the area, with medieval credentials and a preference for red wines. Today the vineyard area is a fraction of that of Mercurey, but some noted red wines maintain Givry's reputation. The wines are powerful, somewhat rustic, but capable of good development in bottle.

There are no *Premiers Crus*, but some vineyard names appear on labels, including the noted Clos Saloman and the Cellier-aux-Moines.

Givry producers include: Domaine du Gardin-Clos Salomon (owners of that entire vineyard), Jean-François Delorme, Domaine Joblot, Louis Latour (N), Domaine Ragot, Domaine Thénard.

Montagny
This *appellation* covers four villages: Montagny-lès-Buxy, St-Vallerin, Buxy and Jully-lès-Buxy. Buxy has an important cooperative, whose members make much of the local wine. The cooperative is involved in production in the wider area of the Mâconnais too. This is a white-wine area, growing Chardonnay exclusively, with no red wines produced at all. All wines that achieve 11.5% alcohol by volume can be labelled *Premier Cru*.

Producers here include: Cave des Vignerons de Buxy (cooperative), Louis Latour (N), Domaine des Moirots, Antonin Rodet (N), Ch de la Saule.

THE MÂCONNAIS

This broad vineyard is where Burgundy begins to feel a breath of the warm South. The town of Mâcon has long had a rôle as a wine-trade centre and river port, and it traditionally drew its supplies from the villages in the pretty, hilly country to the north-west. This zone, the Mâconnais, produces red and white wine under the Mâcon AOC. Within the area are several villages that are allowed to use their own name; some of these, like Pouilly, have built up reputations that set them apart from the wider Mâconnais area.

The countryside of the Mâconnais is idyllic, dotted with lovely villages and rich in livestock and general agriculture. Grapes are one crop among many: not for the Mâconnais the stern monoculture of the Côte d'Or villages. Because the area is further south the climate is less harsh, and summers can be quite hot. Cold winters are still the norm, a reminder that all Burgundy is far inland and open to cold air from the north and east.

The landscape is undulating, with occasional dramatic hills. The vines tend to cluster on the east-facing, most sheltered slopes, tucked amid woods and fields. The underlying geology is complex, with innumerable fault lines; but there are slopes of limestone, suiting Chardonnay, and other areas of granite-type rocks with sandy soil, suiting Gamay. The highest hills, and the best slopes, are clustered in the south of the region. It is here that the most famous villages grow Chardonnay for white wines such as Pouilly-Fuissé and St-Véran. (The similarly named Pouilly Fumé is a Loire wine: see p243.)

Appellations

Red and white wines are made under various AOCs: red wine can be plain AOC Mâcon Rouge, or Mâcon-Supérieur with 1% more alcohol.

White Mâcon Blanc follows the same rule. It is all Chardonnay, while red Mâcon can be Pinot Noir but is normally Gamay. The suffix Villages can be attached if the wine is made in any of 43 named communes, and in the case of white wine the actual name can be attached, as in Mâcon-Azé, or Mâcon-Viré.

Pouilly-Fuissé is white wine from zones within a number of southern Mâconnais villages. Pouilly-Vinzelles and St-Véran are similar. Red wines made from Pinot Noir can be labelled Bourgogne or (with Gamay) Passe-toutgrains (see p182).

Grape varieties and wine styles

White Mâcon, and its sub-AOCs, is made from Chardonnay, a grape which originated here in the village of Chardonnay. Some wines, especially from Pouilly and near by, are recognizably Burgundian, aiming at and sometimes hitting the same marks as a good village wine from the Côte de Beaune, or a Côte Chalonnaise. Much Mâcon Blanc is made in a softer, lighter style, partly due to the warmer climate and partly because a different clone of Chardonnay is grown here.

The area's winemaking is dominated by cooperatives, several of which are large and highly modern. They have found ways of making white wine in a range of styles according to their market: some is aged in new oak for richness and complexity, other cuvées are made in stainless steel for lightness and crispness. This light style is perhaps the most typical, and enjoyable, Mâcon Blanc: pale, almost colourless, light, fresh, clean and appetizing.

Red wines are increasingly from Gamay, and Mâcon Rouge lives somewhat in the shadow of its better-known neighbour Beaujolais. It should be drunk young and fresh.

Pouilly-Fuissé and its neighbours

Well to the south of the Mâconnais, right on the frontiers of the Saône-et-Loire and Rhône départements, is a zone famed for white wines. Here the hills become dramatic sloping-topped cliffs of limestone, and the vines cluster thickly. The name Pouilly-Fuissé gained fame in the USA and other export markets around the middle of this century, which led to increased demand and the consequent over-production and over-pricing of the wine.

The appellation covers land in five villages (see p208), land that is well suited to growing Chardonnay. Some vineyard names are used, though there are no formal Premiers Crus. Most Pouilly-Fuissé is made by the local cooperative, though there are several producers with reputations: see next page. The best Pouilly-Fuissé, made from old vines in good sites, and fermented at least in part in new oak, is a rich, long-lived and serious wine, and deserves its reputation; but much wine is less good than its price would suggest.

The smaller appellations of Pouilly-Loché and Pouilly-Vinzelles cover wine from neighbouring villages. The wines are similar to Pouilly-Fuissé, but usually cheaper. St-Véran is a larger AOC covering land in the very south of the Mâconnais. This overlaps with Beaujolais, and white wine made here can also be called Beaujolais Blanc. The chief St-Véran village is (confusingly) St-Vérand.

All these wines are good alternatives to more expensive white burgundies when they do not attempt to compete with their northern neighbours' high prices. They deserve a year in bottle, and can be relied upon in all but the most atrocious vintages, since the weather here is more consistently kind to Chardonnay than it is further north.   □

APPELLATIONS AND PRODUCERS

The Mâconnais is dominated by cooperatives, with the private estates assuming more importance in the prestigious white-wine villages of the Pouilly *appellations*. The major Beaune *négociants* (*see* pp202–203) usually list these wines; some local *négociants* are named below with the suffix (N).

Mâcon

This wide area makes both red and white wines, with whites in the majority. The grape variety for whites is Chardonnay. The AOC Mâcon is rarely used: most whites achieve the AOC Mâcon-Supérieur (11% rather than 10%Vol), or more often are labelled Mâcon-Villages, which shows the wine comes from one of the 43 supposedly superior villages.

White Mâcon comprises three bottles of white burgundy in four. Nearly all the wine is made by cooperatives, which also make Crémant de Bourgogne (*see* p206). Some good wines come from these co-ops, especially their selected *cuvées*. There are also good growers among the independent producers.

Of the villages entitled to the AOC Mâcon-Villages, some worth looking out for are Chardonnay (home village of the grape variety), Fuissé, Igé, Loché, Lugny, and Prissé, the aptly-named La Roche Vineuse. Mâcon-Viré and Mâcon-Clessé will disappear in 2002 to be replaced by the new *appellation* Viré-Clessé (552ha/1,364 acres), created in 1998.

Producers include: Ch de la Bruyère, Mâcon; Domaine de la Feuillarde, Mâcon; Domaine Jean Manciat, Mâcon; Domaine des Poncetys, Lycée viticole, Mâcon; Domaine d'Azenay, Mâcon-Villages;

Domaine des Bruyères, Mâcon-Villages; Ch London, Mâcon-Villages; Francis Pichet

& Fils, Mâcon-Villages; Domaine Gérald et Philibert Talmard, Uchizy; Domaine Jean Thévenet, Clessé; Trenel Fils (N), Charnay-lès-Mâcon. The *caves coopératives* based at Clessé, Igé, Lugny and Viré all have good reputations.

Pouilly-Fuissé

There are five villages within the AOC: Pouilly, Fuissé, Chaintré, Solutré and Vergisson. Solutré has some excellent vineyards, sited on east- and southeast-facing slopes below the giant limestone rock that is famous as a prehistoric hunting site. The village of Fuissé has a band of well-placed vineyards, again east-facing. Much wine is made by the local Chaintré cooperative and is sold under its brand-names, or that of the major *négociants*, who buy from the co-op and small growers.

Producers selling under their own names include: Auvigue (N), Daniel et Martine Barraud, Domaine Cordier (N), Domaine J A Ferret, Ch de Fuissé, Domaine Guffens-Hynen, Louis Jadot (N), Domaine Roger Lasserat, Pascal Renaud, Domaine Jacques et Nathalie Saumaize, Domaine La Soufrandise, Domaine Thibert, Domaine des Trois Tilleuls, Verget (N) and Ch Vitallis.

Pouilly-Vinzelles and Pouilly-Loché

Few producers use these white-wine AOCs, which cover small areas to the east of Pouilly-Fuissé. The wines are similar, but often cheaper, as the Pouilly-Fuissé name commands a premium. Names that may be seen include: Domaine Cordier; Cave des Crus Blancs, Vinzelles; Domaine Mathias, Chaintré; Domaine St-Philibert, Loché.

St-Véran

This AOC includes land in the villages of St-Vérand (it is a mystery as to why the "d" was dropped from the name of the AOC), Chânes, Chasselas, Davayé, Leynes, Prissé, St-Amour and Solutré, which lie around the "core" *appellation* of Pouilly-Fuissé. Once again this is a Chardonnay white wine, less august than the best Pouilly-Fuissé, but certainly cheaper. The vineyards are on well exposed, limestone slopes, and St-Véran can easily equal its better-known neighbours in terms of quality.

Producers here include: Auvigue (N), Paul Beaudet, Domaine Michel Delorme, Domaine des Deux Roches, Georges Dubœuf (N), Domaine de la Feuillarde, Roger Lasserat, Louis Latour (N), Domaine des Poncetys (Lycée viticole), Domaine des Valanges.

Château Fuissé produces the most expensive Pouilly-Fuissé.

BEAUJOLAIS

One of the best-known wines in the world, Beaujolais suffers a certain identity crisis. Its reputation is for easy-to-drink, unassertive young red wine; its better growers would like it to be taken more seriously. Much of the fame, or notoriety, of Beaujolais stems from Beaujolais Nouveau, the new wine rushed onto the market each November only weeks after the grapes are picked. What was once a local pleasure became fashionable in Lyons, then Paris, then as far afield as Japan.

The knowledgeable decry the *nouveau* wine as a gimmick, but large quantities of the crop — in some years more than half — become Beaujolais Nouveau, and wine merchants outside France sell great amounts of it to people who otherwise rarely buy red wine.

Beaujolais is officially part of Burgundy, but it has little in common with the Côte d'Or except proximity, and the presence of the same firms of *négociants*. Instead of the limestone common in the rest of Burgundy, the Beaujolais soil is based upon the granite and other igneous rocks of a range of mountains which form the watershed between the Loire, over to the west, and the Saône. The grape variety is Gamay, that supposedly inferior vine banned from the Côte d'Or by the medieval Burgundian dukes. The winemaking technique is also different.

The area gained its name from the medieval town of Beaujeu, hidden deep in the foothills. This was the stronghold of the local lords, who ran the area as their own province. The Paris government objected to the extent that Cardinal Richelieu pulled the castle down in 1611. Today Villefranche-sur-Saône and Belleville, both in the main valley followed by the TGV railway and the A6 Autoroute, are the local centres.

Gamay vines in autumnal mist.

Zones and appellations

Beaujolais covers a wide area from just south of Mâcon to the suburbs of Lyons. The Saône Valley forms its eastern edge, and the vineyards rise up over the foothills towards the wooded summits. The highest point in the area is over 1,000m (3,300ft) and the vines rise to around 500m (1,650ft). The hills provide shelter from the westerly winds and the local climate is warm and fairly dry.

There are 60 communes, all of them making wine to some extent. The northern half of the region has the densest vineyards and makes the best wines: the underlying geology here is granitic. Further south, Villefranche-sur-Saône forms the frontier with a different zone, based upon limestone rock.

The whole area can use the AOC Beaujolais, or Beaujolais Supérieur with a little more alcohol. The AOC Beaujolais-Villages is restricted to the hill vineyards in 39 communes of the northern half of the area. Within this restricted zone, in the northernmost portion, are ten villages which use

their own name for their wines: these are the Beaujolais *crus*.

In Beaujolais the term *cru* or *grand cru* (both versions are used indiscriminately) means all the land within these chosen villages, not a specific vineyard as in the rest of Burgundy. There is a considerable difference in quality between an ordinary Beaujolais and a wine from one of the *crus*. In particular, the *cru* wines show a capacity to age in bottle not found in Beaujolais or Beaujolais-Villages. Each *cru* has its own personality, described on the following pages.

This is a rewarding area to visit: the winding roads provide superb views of the vineyards and there are plenty of places to taste and buy wine. Good restaurants abound, though the cuisine is rustic rather than grand.

Winemaking, ageing and wine styles

The normal method of making red wine involves partially crushing the grapes, both to free the grapes from the stalks and to allow the juice to flow and the yeast to get to work. In Beaujolais a local variation of *macération carbonique*, called *macération beaujolaise traditionnelle*, or just "the Beaujolais method", is used. For this, the grapes must be whole as they reach the vat, so picking machines are not used.

The bunches of ripe grapes are tipped, whole and uncrushed, into a vat which is then sealed. The fermentation begins and carbon dioxide is produced, which gathers above the fermenting grapes, slows the process and acts as a disinfectant. The weight of the grapes in the vat crushes the lower ones, allowing the fermentation to begin in the accumulated juice at the bottom of the vat. Some producers pump this juice to the top of the vat to speed up the process.

The heat produced then sparks off fermentation inside the whole grapes, which in turn burst, feeding the process. Once this stage is complete, the grapes are pressed, and further fermentation then takes place. Yeasts are important: particular ones are introduced into the wine destined for *nouveau*.

The point of this technique is to extract maximum colour and aroma: Gamay grapes are particularly suited to it, since their greatest virtue as a variety is their fruity, juicy flavour.

In true *macération carbonique* carbon dioxide is pumped into the vat to prolong the maceration process.

Modern cellars, especially those of the cooperatives and *négociants*, use temperature-control systems to avoid high-temperature fermentation and to maximize aroma and fruit flavours. The traditional technique, still used by some smaller and more quality-conscious Beaujolais estates, allows warmer fermentation, extracting more tannin and colour from the

COTEAUX DU LYONNAIS

The Beaujolais grape varieties — Gamay, and Chardonnay and Aligoté for whites — are used in this 50-commune zone to the south of Beaujolais. Very little white is actually made; while the red wine is a minor cousin of Beaujolais. There are about 400ha (988 acres) under vine, making less wine than one of the Beaujolais *crus*. The zone extends from the southern border of Beaujolais around to the west of the city of Lyons. In the south it touches on the Côte Rôtie of the Northern Rhône. It is a fraction of its former size: in the eighteenth century it extended to 13,500ha (33,300 acres).

The main producer is the cooperative at Sain Bel in the northern part of the appellation, though there are some thriving private estates too.

grapes. In some years, the wine ferments slowly in vats well into the winter, is aged in cask through the spring and summer and is bottled only in the September of the next year. This traditional approach contrasts with the sell-it-quick attitude of the *nouveau*-based wine trade.

Both sorts of Beaujolais are valid wines, to be enjoyed for their own virtues. *Nouveau*, from a ripe year and made well, is an enjoyable purple glassful of wine, welcome in the dank days of November. Mainstream Beaujolais, drunk at perhaps a year old, is fresh, fruity and appetizing, at its best an excellent wine with traditional French country cuisine. The more serious *cru* wines can age over three to seven years into more concentrated, refined bottles that can have an uncanny similarity to Côte d'Or red burgundies — despite the difference in the grape. □

The village and distinctive twin-towered church of Régnié surrounded by its vineyards.

VILLAGES AND PRODUCERS

Most Beaujolais or Beaujolais-Villages is sold under the name of a *négociant* or cooperative (or, in foreign markets, an importer), and carries little clue to its origins. Wines from the ten *crus* offer more local identity, and wines from individual estates, as well as *négociants*, can be found. The main local *négociants* are listed on p212.

Nearly all Beaujolais is red; white is permitted, and is made in small amounts from Chardonnay in the vineyards where the St-Véran AOC (*see* p208) overlaps with Beaujolais. Beaujolais Blanc is merely an alternative name for St-Véran.

THE BEAUJOLAIS CRUS

These are ten villages extending over about 20km (12 miles) from north to south in the north of the Beaujolais region. These villages use their own name, and their wines exhibit their own character. The villages and their vineyards are to be found on easterly spurs or hilly outcrops of the Beaujolais mountains overlooking the valley of the River Saône.

The vines here grow in lime-free granite soils and are cultivated mainly by small farmers, who sell through *négociants* — although there are some large estates. The villages are listed geographically from north to south.

St-Amour

A few kilometres south-west of the city of Mâcon (and, strictly speaking, part of the Mâconnais), St-Amour is the most northerly of the Beaujolais *crus*. It is also one of the smallest. Most of the vines are on east- and southeast-facing slopes at a height of about 250m (825ft). St-Amour produces light, delicately fruity Beaujolais that is made to be enjoyed young but improves after two or three years in bottle. The name, with its romantic connotations, attracts sales; and as only 317ha (783 acres) are under vine there is not enough wine to go round. Accordingly prices can be higher than quality warrants, compared to the other *crus*.

Quite a few of the producers also grow Chardonnay for white wine, which is sold as St-Véran.

Producers are concentrated around the little village of St-Amour-Bellevue. They include Denis et Hélène Barbelet, Domaine Le Cotoyon, Georges Dubœuf (N), Domaine des Ducs, Domaine du Haut-Poncie, François Launay, Domaine du Moulin Berger, Michel Tête.

Juliénas

Juliénas includes some of the oldest wine-producing sites of Beaujolais; indeed, the name is locally claimed to originate from Julius Caesar. Granitic soils on high, steep slopes provide sites with excellent ripening potential.

The wines of this *appellation* are somewhat sturdier than St-Amour and develop plenty of body two to four years after the vintage. There are 600ha (1,483 acres) — twice as much as in St-Amour: the *appellation* extends into the two neighbouring hamlets of Jullié and Emeringes.

Producers in Juliénas include: Cave du Bois de la Salle (cooperative), David Boulet, Domaine du Clos du Fief, Domaine du Granit Doré (Georges Rollet), Franck Juillard, Ch de Juliénas, Domaine Matray, Domaine des Monilles (Laurent Perrachon), Domaine Bernard Santé, Domaine Michel Tête.

Chénas

The *cru* is named after the oak forests that have gradually been replaced by the vine since medieval times. The smallest (285ha/704 acres) and least-known of the Beaujolais *crus*, Chénas borders on, and is almost a part of, Moulin-à-Vent, and the wines of each are very similar. The *appellation* includes part of the commune of Chapelle-de-Guinchy. Chénas' best wines share the character of those of Moulin-à-Vent, and can be quite rich and concentrated, but the wines do not age as well as, for instance, Juliénas.

Chénas producers include: Cave du Château de Chénas (cooperative), Domaine de Chênepierre (Gérard Lapierre), Domaine des Ducs, Hubert Lapierre, Daniel Passot, Domaine des Pierres (Georges Trichard), Raymond Trichard.

Moulin-à-Vent

Taking its name from a windmill sitting astride a hilltop rather than from a village, Moulin-à-Vent is variously described as the grandest, the most serious, and "the King" of Beaujolais or, alternatively, the least typical of the region; it is certainly the most expensive and the most age-worthy. Granite subsoils are overlain with sand that has a manganese content which, some say, contributes to the highly individual character of the wine. At its best it is deep ruby-red in colour and is a powerful and well-structured wine that can still impress after ten years. Some producers age it in oak to make the most of its structure and ageing potential.

Moulin-à-Vent is one of the most productive of the *crus*, with 660ha (1,631 acres) under vine.

Producers here include: Domaine Desperiers Père & Fils, Domaine Les Graves, Ch des Jacques, Ch Moulin à Vent, Domaine de la Rochelle, Domaine des Terres Dorées, Domaine Benoît Trichard, Le Vieux Domaine.

Fleurie

A charmingly named and beautifully sited hilltop village at the heart of the Beaujolais *crus*, Fleurie produces attractive wines that (in part thanks to their easily recognized name) are extremely popular and almost as expensive as those of Moulin-à-Vent. Most of the 860ha (2,125 acres) of vines grow at about 300m (1,000ft) on either rather poor granite sands or clay-rich gravels. Good examples are full of fruit and easy to drink when young, but even better if left for a couple of years.

Leading producers include: Cave Coopérative de Fleurie, Ch des Labourons (Comte B de Lescure), Domaine de la Madone (Jean-Marie Després), Domaine André Metrat, Domaine du Point du Jour.

Chiroubles

High up (between 300 and 480m/1,000 and 1,600ft) in the

hills to the west of Fleurie, Chiroubles (370ha/914 acres) overlooks the whole of Beaujolais and, rather aptly, offers the lightest and, some would say, the most balanced of the region's wines. Light in colour and the most fragrant of the Beaujolais *crus*, it is the first to be ready and should be drunk within two years. Remote but currently fashionable, Chiroubles' wines are not cheap.

Leading producers include: Domaine Emile Cheysson, Henry Fessy (N), Domaine des Gatilles, Domaine de la Grosse Pierre (Alain Passot), La Maison des Vignerons à Chiroubles (cooperative), Domaine Morin, Christoph Savoye, René Savoye.

Morgon

The second-largest *cru*, Morgon (1,100ha/2,718 acres) produces some memorable Beaujolais. The best vineyards are the perfectly exposed sunny sites in a distinctive slate soil called *terre pourrie* on the Mont du Py: the wines from these grapes are particularly rich and full. They are deep in colour, with plenty of body, developing exotic fruit flavours as they age. They are long-lived wines with a highly individual bouquet and the name has given rise to a verb — *morgonner* — describing the similar development of different wines. The *appellation* is wider than this, however, and not all Morgon follows the classic description. Some is unsubtle and heavy — a fault in the poorer wines from each of the *crus*.

Leading producers include: Domaine Aucœur, Jean-Marc Burgaud, Domaine Louis-Claude Desvignes, Domaine de Fontriante, Marcel Lapierre, Dominique Piron, Domaine des Sornay, Domaine des Souchons, Domaine de Thizy.

Régnié

Régnié (700ha/1,730 acres) became Beaujolais' tenth *cru*

only in 1988, yet it vies with Juliénas as the oldest grape-producing district of Beaujolais, dating from Roman times. The wines of Régnié reflect its location between Morgon and Brouilly: to the north they are robust with strong fruit aromas, while from sandier soils in the south of the district they are lighter in colour and more delicate and aromatic in character — more like Brouilly.

Régnié producers include: Ch du Basty, Domaine des Braves, Louis-Noël Chopin, Hospice de Beaujeu, Domaine Dominique Jambon, Domaine de Ponchon, Domaine des Vallières.

Côte de Brouilly

The Mont de Brouilly is a fair-sized hill rising prominently from the vineyards west of Belleville, in the commune of Brouilly. The vineyards which

circle the hill have their own *appellation*, Côte de Brouilly (325ha/803 acres), while the rest of the commune is plain Brouilly. Wines from the Côte de Brouilly are generally reckoned to be superior to those of Brouilly, as they come from the favoured slopes. They are richer, with more character, for grapes ripen well on the Mont de Brouilly and have higher sugar levels (so the wines have a higher minimum alcohol level than the other *crus*). And it is claimed that the distinct blue granite soils (*terre bleue*) on this extinct volcano also contribute a degree of finesse lacking in Brouilly. Côte de Brouilly is best drunk between one and three years after the vintage.

Leading producers include: Dominique Lacondemine, Domaine Large, Ch Thivin and Ch du Grand Vernay (both Claude Geoffray).

Brouilly

The largest, most productive and the most southerly *cru*, Brouilly produces a lot of fairly ordinary wines considered little better than Beaujolais-Villages, but a good Brouilly is grapey with much more substance, and is more long-lived

(two to four years). Because it is produced in larger quantities than elsewhere, Brouilly tends to have a higher commercial profile. The AOC covers several communes (1,300ha/3,212 acres).

Leading producers include: Domaine de Bel-Air, Ch de la Chaize, Domaine Dubost, J Gonard & Fils (N), Bernard Jomain, Jean Lathuilière, Ch Thivin.

BEAUJOLAIS-VILLAGES

The Beaujolais-Villages *appellation* covers the whole of the northern half of the region — the Haut-Beaujolais — and includes 39 communes, as well as the Beaujolais *crus*. In theory, the villages are entitled to use their own name on the wine label, but in practice they do not, so the term Beaujolais-Villages covers, in effect, a range of different wine styles.

The whole of this area has soils that are basically granitic in origin; they are light, warm and sandy, with no limestone content. The wines do not have the keeping power of the *crus* and are intended to be drunk between one and two years after the vintage.

There are hundreds of small estates and producers bottling their own wine, and many wines from cooperatives and *négociants*. It is hard to single out specific producers, as most of the individuals make small amounts of wine, which they usually sell direct.

BEAUJOLAIS

Wines from the southern half of the region, and a few low-lying areas, are entitled to the AOC Beaujolais. Most is sold by *négociants* or cooperatives, but there are some private growers. Most sell direct to their clients, but a few export their wines. At its best at a year old, the simple Beaujolais can be soft, red-fruit-flavoured and highly enjoyable.

BEAUJOLAIS NEGOCIANTS

Beaujolais has its own wine merchants, many centred around Villefranche-sur-Saône. They sell blended wines, and increasingly represent and sell single-estate wines which carry the *négociant*'s name in the small print. Some exist wholly to supply the world with the cheapest Beaujolais they can find. Others stress quality and individual wines. Some leading *négociants* are:

Georges Dubœuf,

Romanèche-Thorins. This is the leading name, seen all

over the world. Dubœuf is both a supplier of wines, using his own name, and a bottler and merchant of individual properties.

Pierre Feraud, Belleville. A small concern with a name for quality wine.

Trenel & Fils, Charnay-lès-Mâcon. A family firm with a good reputation for the *crus*.

Other *négociants* include:

Gabriel Aligne, Beaujeu; Henry Fessy, St-Jean-d'Ardières; Sylvian Fessy, Belleville; Chanut Frères, Romanèche-Thorins.

CHAMPAGNE

CHAMPAGNE'S IMAGE AS A LUXURY DRINK SOMETIMES CONCEALS ITS EXCELLENCE
AS A FINE WINE. OFTEN IMITATED, YET TO BE SURPASSED,
IT IS THE WORLD'S SUPREME SPARKLING WINE.

The cellars of Krug, one of the great Champagne houses, are lined with rows of *pupitres*, special racks which hold the bottles of Grande Cuvée at an angle to allow sediment to slide down into the neck.

The windy landscape of Champagne is an unlikely birthplace for a luxury. The atmosphere here is firmly of the north: dark forests edge the hilltops, the plains are open and featureless, the slopes lie exposed to the harsh east winds of winter. Yet these chalky hillsides gained a reputation as a fine vineyard in early medieval times, and by the time of Napoleon I the sparkling wine of Champagne was a firm favourite with the rich and powerful from Paris to St Petersburg. "In victory you deserve it, in defeat you need it": no-one can be sure who coined the motto, but it has expressed the world's attitude towards champagne, wine of success and consolation, for two centuries.

The wine of Champagne was famous long before it was sparkling. Between 816 and 1825, 37 kings of France were crowned in Reims Cathedral, following the baptism of Clovis of the Franks in 496. St Rémi, his baptizer and the great bishop of Reims, owned vineyards. By the 9th century the wines of Epernay were being mentioned by name. A cluster of monasteries in the region stimulated winegrowing — and wine exports. Great medieval markets held in the region, which is at one of Europe's crossroads, spread the wine's fame. The 16th-century Pope Leo X owned vines here, as did the kings of England, Spain and France. By 1575 champagne was the sole wine at the coronation of Henri III of France. The wine that won royal favour was a pale but intense-tasting red; still, not sparkling. The bubbles in champagne are a natural accident that is carefully fostered. In this cold northern vineyard new wine will often start to gently re-ferment in the spring, as the residual yeasts are woken by warmer weather. One product of fermentation is carbon dioxide gas, which remains in the wine while it is under pressure, but appears as bubbles and froth once the pressure is released. This attractive effervescence needs to be contained in strong bottles, and held down by a firmly-fixed cork. It was the development of bottles and corks that made sparkling champagne possible. Once the bubbles were tamed, champagne became the first world wine, a symbol of celebration in every country. It remains a wine of true excellence, capable of maturing to a subtlety that belies the froth.

The birth of champagne

It is intrinsically unlikely that such an ancient product as champagne could have an inventor. This has not stopped writers from crediting the birth of the wine to Dom Pierre Pérignon, cellarer of the abbey of Hautvillers, near Epernay, in the late 17th century. Dom Pérignon was, according to near-contemporary accounts, a great winemaker. He systemized and refined the making of the already famous local red wine, aiming for a very pale wine, nearly white, but from the best (black) Pinot Noir grapes. Care in harvesting, fast and skilful pressing, then blending the wine from different vineyards are all standard skills in the modern winemakers' repertoire, but Dom Pérignon applied them three centuries ago. He succeeded in making a white wine that could age and improve. But he worked to avoid, not to capture, champagne's naturally-occurring sparkle. For Dom Pérignon and his contemporaries, bubbles were a sign of poor winemaking. It took two more centuries for the words sparkling and champagne to become synonymous.

Ironically, there is good evidence that the English were responsible for the nurturing of the fizz. They were pioneers of strong glass bottles, made using coal, not wood, to fire hotter furnaces. The cork, the second vital ingredient, appeared from Spain at about the same time as the new *verre anglais* (English glass).

Champagne became fashionable in the England of Charles II, after 1660. There are records of buyers ordering bottles and corks at the same time as their casks of champagne. The (red) wine was then bottled in the English aristocracy's cellars. An English author mentioned "sparkling" champagne in 1664. The first French use of the phrase dates from 1712, when the Duke of Orléans' court made the new kind of champagne fashionable. However, sparkling champagne remained a minority of the region's production.

Still white wine (from Sillery, in particular) and red were the mainstays. In the late 18th century only 10% of champagne was fizzy.

Champagne had learnt how to make wine fizz, but not how to control the process. Each year was a gamble: sometimes the wine failed to fizz, in other years the second fermentation was so brisk that most of the bottles burst: cellar workers had to wear masks to protect them from flying glass until glassmaking and winemaking were further refined.

The rise of the merchants

The unpredictable fermentation needed to be mastered, and the violent swings of natural and commercial fortune had to be evened out. The answer for Champagne was the rise of the merchants, who replaced the monastic and aristocratic growers during and after the Napoleonic Wars. The *maisons* had the stability and capital to make, age and distribute (above all, export) sparkling wine.

By the 1840s the sparkling wine business was well established. The merchants were in the forefront of technical advance. They encouraged blending, which evened out the vagaries of the different *crus*. *Dégorgement* (*see* p114) was first practised in 1813. Corking machines and wine muzzles came in in the 1820s and 1830s. But the key discovery was the amount of sugar needed to induce the second fermentation reliably. In 1837 this was more precisely calculated, and the bottle burst-rate dropped to around 5%. Today it is 1%. By the end of the 19th century champagne was established as an industrial and commercial giant, in clear contrast to the bucolic and artisanal wines of other regions. So it remains today.

Making champagne

The winemaking process is described and illustrated on pp114–115. In the vineyard, the key to great champagne is careful selection: pruning is rigorous, and only healthy grapes are used.

Selection continues with the process of blending (*see* p216).

Grape varieties

Three grape varieties are used in Champagne: Pinot Noir, Chardonnay and Pinot Meunier. Pinot Noir gives backbone and longevity to a blend, although it can seem somewhat austere in youth. Chardonnay lends elegance and breeding. Pinot Meunier, a less subtle variety, gives immediate appeal, fills out the body of a champagne and increases its bouquet.

The geography of Champagne

The Champagne region lies some 145km (90 miles) to the north-east of Paris. The underlying rock is chalk, for Champagne is on the rim of the great basin that also forms the English South Downs. The slopes of two areas of chalk upland, the Montagne de Reims and the Côte des Blancs, provide the best vineyards. They include the greatest concentration of villages designated *Grand* and *Premier Cru* (*see* p217).

Three zones (the first three below) form the heartland of the region. Some 100km (60 miles) to the south-east, in the south-eastern corner of the Aube *département*, is another important zone; and there are four outlying zones (*see* map).

■ **Montagne de Reims** The Montagne is a forested plateau south of Reims and the River Vesle, edged by broad, sweeping vine-clad slopes. The vineyards extend eastwards before turning south towards the Vallée de la Marne. This is potentially the coolest zone and some vineyards are north-facing. All three grape varieties are grown, but the cool yet temperate Montagne climate and long growing season particularly suit Pinot Noir.

This zone contains nine *Grand Cru* villages and a number of *Premiers Crus*. The southerly-facing *Grand Cru* village of Bouzy also has a good name for still red wine.

■ **Vallée de la Marne** Stretching from west of Château-Thierry to just east of Epernay, on both banks of the

WINE ZONES OF CHAMPAGNE

The three main vineyard zones of Champagne are the Montagne de Reims, Vallée de la Marne and Côte des Blancs, with subsidiary areas which include the large Aube vineyard (*see* inset map).

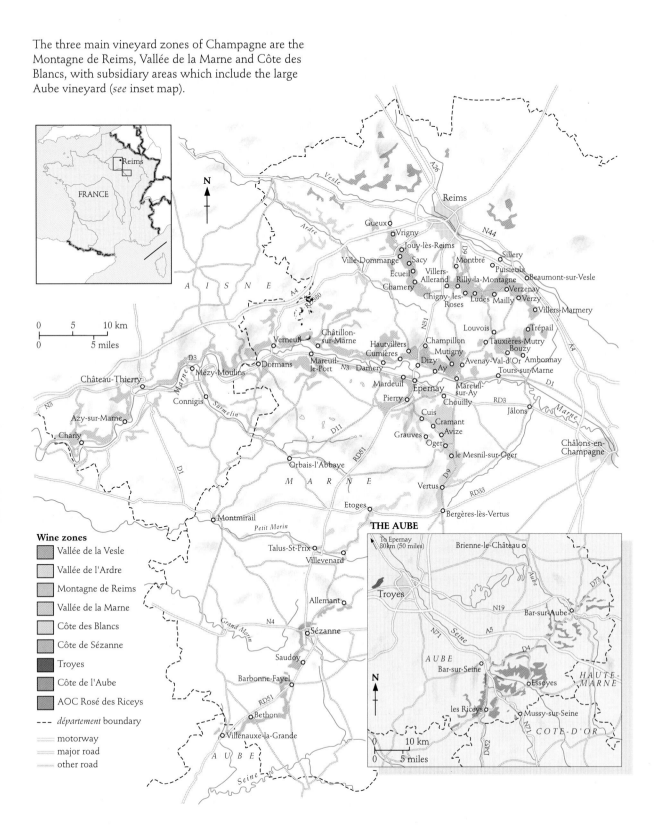

FRANCE

0 5 10 km
0 5 miles

Wine zones

- Vallée de la Vesle
- Vallée de l'Ardre
- Montagne de Reims
- Vallée de la Marne
- Côte des Blancs
- Côte de Sézanne
- Troyes
- Côte de l'Aube
- AOC Rosé des Riceys

- - - *département* boundary
───── motorway
───── major road
········· other road

THE AUBE

To Epernay
80km (50 miles)

Brienne-le-Château

Troyes

Bar-sur-Aube

Bar-sur-Seine

Essoyes

AUBE

HAUTE-MARNE

les Riceys

Mussy-sur-Seine

CÔTE-D'OR

0 10 km
0 5 miles

River Marne, the vineyards of the Vallée de la Marne are generally lower-lying, with less chalk and more clay than in the other two central areas. This area is known for Pinot Noir and Pinot Meunier.

There are two *Grand Cru* villages, Ay and Tours-sur-Marne, although the latter is rated *Grand Cru* only for black grapes. Both are on the north bank with a southerly exposure.

■ **Côte des Blancs** The Côte des Blancs begins just south of Epernay and extends southwards for 21km (13 miles). The ridge, which rises to 250m (825ft), has vineyards on both the western and eastern flanks; the finest are on the east side. The combination of chalk and relative warmth makes this Champagne's finest zone for Chardonnay.

■ **The Aube** Champagne's most southerly zone is more than 100km (60 miles) from Epernay and is much closer to Chablis than to the rest of Champagne. The Aube has a more continental climate, with colder winters and hotter summers, so that the grapes achieve greater ripeness. The soil is richer, with clay and Kimmeridge marl which is also found in Chablis. The vines are 80% Pinot Noir. Much of the Aube's production is bought by the Champagne houses of Reims and Epernay.

■ **Côte de Sézanne** This is Champagne's newest and least-known area, where vineyards were planted only in the 1960s. Its relatively southern position means that the grapes, almost exclusively Chardonnay, ripen very well, lending a rich, slightly exotic feel to the wines.

Qualities and producers

Champagne is unusual among French fine wines in that it is sold according to the name of the producer, not a geographical name. There are a very few single-vineyard, or single-village, wines, but most champagne is a blend. It is also unusual in that most is a blend of vintages. The large champagne companies make most of their living from non-vintage (NV) wines

made according to the house style (*see* Blending, below). Single-vintage wines are made in good years — perhaps three or four a decade. Most houses have prestige *cuvées*, special wines that carry a higher price.

The difference in style between a champagne from a great firm and one

CHAMPAGNE STYLES AND TERMS

WINE STYLES
Blanc de Blancs From Chardonnay grapes only: very fine and delicate wines
Brut nature Non-*dosage* wine
Brut Very dry
Demi-sec Medium-sweet
Doux Sweet
Grand Cru Wine from one or more of the 17 top villages
Grande Marque A house belonging to the Institut des Grandes Marques de Champagne, which dates from 1882. Most, but not all, of the 26 members are the leading houses of today.
NV Non-vintage
Rosé Pink champagne, made usually by adding 10–15% of still red champagne. The perfectionist way is to allow the black grapes to tint the juice in the vat.
Sec In Champagne means medium-dry

LABEL TERMS
Labels must show the small-print codes which tell the origin of a wine:
CM *Coopérative-manipulant*: the wine is from a co-op
MA *Marque auxiliaire*: second label of a producer
ND *Négociant-distributeur*: merchant firm or "house"
NM *Négociant-manipulant*: merchant firm or "house" belonging to the Institut de Grandes Marques de Champagne or to the Institut des Négociants en Vins de Champagne
R *Récoltant*: grower selling his grapes to a co-op and receiving some bottles in return
RC *Récoltant-coopérateur-manipulant*: champagne grown and made by a member of a cooperative
RM *Récoltant-manipulant*: champagne grown and made by a single producer, with or without the help of a co-op
SR *Société des récoltants*: a growers' company

from a small grower or cooperative is considerable. The environmental factors (*see* p217) mean that only a small amount of Champagne's grapes are truly top-class. These come from the best-placed slopes in the top villages. The hard-nosed economics of Champagne supports this: houses will pay most for grapes from these vineyards. A great house will use the best raw material, will age the wine for longer than the minimum 15 months, and will add reserve wines to the blend for its non-vintage. The result will be more complex, more able to age and more expensive than a simpler champagne. A grower with well-placed vineyards can make excellent champagne, but few such wines match the *Grandes Marques* (*see* box) for complexity and longevity.

Blending

Champagne is the world's blended wine *par excellence*. Each year the blender must create a wine that is consistent in style and quality and is in keeping with the image of the house, be it the standard non-vintage or a special *cuvée*. The process begins during the harvest, when a house monitors its resources of grapes from the various zones and varieties. It may buy extra grapes to balance stocks. Early in the new year, when the still wine has completed its fermentation but before the second fermentation takes place, the blender assembles samples of the acidic, raw new wine. combining not just grape varieties, but the same grape variety from many differently-rated vineyards and different zones. He may include a percentage of reserve wine held back from previous vintages. The result may be a blend of up to 70 different wines. The aim is not to make the same wine every year, but to conform to a broad concept of "house style".

Houses differ in the stress they put on white and black grapes, on the use of reserve wines (as low as 15% or more than 30% of the blend), and on the sources of wines, from different zones and villages within zones. □

QUALITY FACTORS

The suitability of the cool, northern Champagne region for quality wine production is not immediately obvious. However, Champagne's particular blend of soil, climate and site lends itself brilliantly to growing reasonably ripe grapes with a high level of acidity.

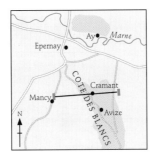

Vineyard classification

Champenois have a rigorous system of vineyard classification called the "Echelle des Crus". More than 200 villages have the right to produce grapes for champagne. Of these, only 17 are rated 100% and have *Grand Cru* status, a further 40 are rated 90–99% and are deemed *Premiers Crus*, and all the remaining villages, rated 80–89%, are *Deuxièmes Crus*. The ranks occasionally appear on labels to show that the wine comes exclusively from, say, *Grand Cru* vineyards. Most champagne, however, is blended from the produce of several villages and/or districts.

- alluvium
- loess and clay
- sandstone and clay with lignite
- belimnita chalk
- micraster chalk
- vineyards

THE COTE DES BLANCS

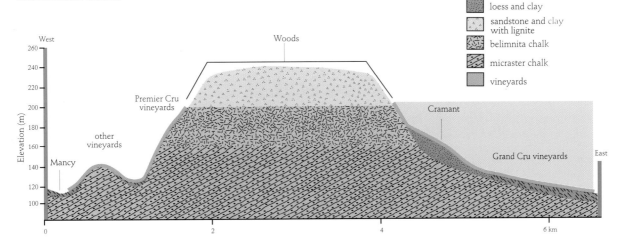

Climate

This is a cool region, although a number of warmer micro-climates do exist. The mean annual temperature is only just above 10°C (50°F), the minimum required to ripen grapes. However, such a climate has two benefits: first, the growing season is long, so the grapes ripen very slowly, accumulating important flavouring components; and second, the grapes keep their acidity, whereas in a warmer climate this would drop sharply as the sugars increased. In a good year, the sugar–acid balance, although not ideal for a still wine, is ideal for the production of a sparkling wine.

Chalk soil in the vineyards of Cramant.

Site

The best vineyards are all on slopes, rising from 80m (260ft) to 210m (690ft). Above this are the woods of the Montagne and the Côte des Blancs. The vines grow best at altitudes of between 90–150m (300–500ft). Below 120m (400ft) there is a greater risk of frost damage as cold air drains down the slopes.

Geology and soil

The better vineyard sites, which are mainly on the slopes of the Montagne de Reims and Côte des Blancs, lie on a deep bed of crustaceous chalk beneath a thin layer of topsoil. This chalk is of two types: *belimnita quadrata*, and Micraster. The former type of chalk is unique to Champagne and is found on the higher slopes. Both not only provide good drainage but also remain relatively humid and can easily supply water and nutrients to the vines' roots when required. The *belimnita* chalk is perhaps marginally better at providing these benefits.

PRODUCERS

Most champagne is made and sold by "houses" — *négociants-manipulants* — which own some (rarely all) of the vineyards they draw on; and make, age and bottle the wine. They use grapes from the whole region, though the prestige firms concentrate on the three main vineyard zones. The biggest and most famous houses are known as *Grandes Marques*. There are currently 26 recognized members of this group. Most growers sell their grapes to one of these houses, though some growers make and sell their own champagne. Others belong to cooperatives.

There are thousands of champagne names, ranging from growers who label wine made for them by cooperatives to the "Buyers' Own Brands" — wines named by the retailer or merchant who sells them. The most commonly seen *négociants-manipulants*, and some high-quality small concerns, are listed below. In the entries NV stands for non-vintage.

Henri Abelé
Based at Reims and owned by the Spanish Freixenet group, this is one of Champagne's oldest houses, founded in 1757. Its traditional style, seen in both the vintage and NV *cuvées*, is quite rich and full-bodied, even perhaps a little blowsy. The recently introduced Les Soirées Parisiennes, however, is much lighter and more elegant.

Agrapart
An Avize-based merchant house, producing only Blanc de Blancs from its 9-ha (22-acre) vineyard on Grand Cru land. The reserve wines are lodged in barrels.

Michel Arnould
This merchant house makes only Grand Cru de Verzenay champagne, one of the most interesting of the Montagne de Reims. The vineyard covers 12ha (30 acres). The champagne has a lot of character.

Ayala
A *Grande Marque*, founded in 1866 and based at Ay. The Grande Cuvée vintage is better than the light, biscuity NV.

Barancourt
A relatively new house at Tours-sur-Marne, founded by three young growers, with a wide range of wines mainly from their 102ha (252 acres) of vineyards in Montagne de Reims and the Côte des Blancs. The best wine is the surprising (still, red) Bouzy Rouge.

Edmond Barnaut
Philippe Sécondé, a grandson of Edmond Barnaut, owns 11.5ha (28 acres) of vines at Bouzy (Grand Cru). His champagne is generous, with just the right *dosage*.

Herbert Beaufort
A family of vinegrowers at Bouzy (Grand Cru), the Beauforts own 17ha (42 acres) of vines. The champagnes are lively, and some of them do not undergo malolactic fermentation.

Beaumont des Crayères
This Epernay cooperative has 210 grower-members with 75ha (185 acres) of vines. Its Cuvée Nostalgie in particular is extremely fine.

Besserat de Bellefon
Marne et Champagne (*qv*) now own this Epernay house. The style is rather light. The Cuvée des Moines — formerly Crémant des Moines — has been consistently successful, particularly in restaurants.

Billecart-Salmon
A small, family-owned *Grande Marque* making wines of exceptional quality that seem to be getting even better. Based at Mareuil-sur-Ay, it has 5ha (12 acres) of vines.

Blin
A dynamic cooperative (85 growers; 110ha/272 acres) at Vincelles, making attractive light, fruity champagnes.

Boizel
Started in 1834, this Epernay house is being run by Mme Roque-Boizel, with Bruno Paillard and associates also owning shares in it. Exports account for a large part of sales, mainly of the NV Brut, a medium-weight champagne with attractive biscuity overtones. Both the Blanc de Blancs and prestige *cuvée* Joyau de France are very good indeed.

Bollinger
Founded in 1829, this prestigious Ay house is owned by descendants of its founder. Unusually for a *Grande Marque*, Bollinger have a large vineyard holding of 143ha (353 acres), producing 70% of their needs. The house uses a high percentage of Pinot Noir which, together with some fermentation in wood and the use of reserve wines, results in an overall style that can be fairly austere in youth, but which after long bottle ageing becomes extremely full-bodied, rich and biscuity.

RD, a wine that has spent a long time on its lees before being "Recently Disgorged" is one of the great champagnes, as is the Vieilles Vignes Françaises, produced in minuscule quantities from pre-phylloxera vines — its rarity being reflected in the price. Their NV Special Cuvée, which went through an uneven patch in the late 1980s, is now back on form, and each bottle bears a back label certifying that the wine has undergone three years' ageing before release.

Bonnaire
This very important Cramant house, with 14ha (35 acres) at Cramant and 8.5ha (21 acres) in the Marne Valley, specializes in Blanc de Blancs. Spécial Club is the best of its always vintaged *cuvées*.

Ch de Boursault
Owned since 1927 by the Fringhian family, this château was built by "Veuve (widow) Clicquot", who lived and died here. Pinot Meunier-based light and fruity wines.

Albert Le Brun
This was one of two houses that used to be based at Châlons-en-Champagne, but the new owner has moved the business. The *cuvée* Vieille France, a Pinot Noir-based blend, is lodged in squat bottles, which imitate an 18th-century flask.

Le Brun de Neuville
A cooperative in the Côte de Sézanne with 145 members and 140ha (346 acres) of vines. Chardonnay-based wines with immediate fruity appeal.

Canard-Duchêne
This champagne was re-launched with new packaging in 1992, and the signs are of a vast improvement in quality.

Vines above the village of Mareuil-sur-Ay in the Vallée de la Marne.

The NV has medium weight, an elegantly fruity style and is very good value. LVMH, the former owner, has sold the business to Alain Thienot in 2003.

De Castellane
Although not well known elsewhere, this house is one of the biggest sellers in France. It produces a 100% Chardonnay *cuvée* in an exotic, almost New World style, but the Cuvées Commodore and Florens de Castellane are outstanding: medium-bodied and elegant with biscuity overtones. Owned by Laurent-Perrier *(qv)*, this house is based at Epernay.

Cattier
Mostly known for its Clos du Moulin (2,2ha/5,4 acres), one of the rare *clos* in Champagne. A fine and complex NV from a blend of three years.

Charles de Cazanove
A large, family-run Epernay house, very popular in France. Its best wine is the prestige *cuvée* Stradivarius, which is a blend of 60% Chardonnay and 40% Pinot Noir.

Charbaut
This Epernay house has been taken over by the highly dynamic Paul Vranken (qv), the Charbaut family having kept their 56ha (138 acres) of vines. The prestige *cuvée* is labelled Certificat; it is an excellent Blanc de Blancs sold in a special clear-glass bottle.

Guy Charlemagne
Based at Mesnil-sur-Oger, this house specializes in Blanc de Blancs. Two outstanding vintage wines.

Cheurlin & Fils
Important house based in the

Aube region, owning a 25-ha (62-acre) vineyard. Supple and fruity wines.

Raoul Collet
Founded in 1921, the oldest cooperative in Champagne produces over 40,000 cases of a solid and masculine champagne a year.

Comte Audoin de Dampierre
Audoin de Dampierre selects excellent wines for his brand. The Blanc de Blancs Prestige cork is held in place by a string-cap of the type used in the 18th century. Outstanding and expensive.

Delamotte
A traditional house, founded in 1760, producing Chardonnay-based wines. Next door to Champagne Salon, it was run by Charles de Nonancourt and

is now owned by Laurent-Perrier (Bernard de Nonancourt), just as its neighbour.

Deutz
This Ay house — founded in 1838 and owned by Louis Roederer since 1993 — produces a fairly forward, fruity style of champagne, especially its Brut NV. The prestige *cuvée* William Deutz is medium-bodied with fine intense flavours — and there is a most elegant Blanc de Blancs.

Devaux
A name used by the Union Auboise, a group of co-ops in the Aube, which has 750 growers and 1,400ha (3,458 acres); 80% Pinot Noir. Fine, fruity and well-made champagnes.

Drappier
A highly regarded family-run

house producing an outstanding range in the Aube region, with 34ha (84 acres) of vines. The wines are rich and biscuity, especially the single-vineyard Grande Sendrée, produced from old vines. The NV Brut is excellent value.

Jacky Dumangin

A Chigny-les-Roses producer with a 5-ha (12-acre) vineyard, making candid champagnes with a delicate fruity flavour.

Duval-Leroy

A large and dynamic Côte des Blancs house that has 140ha (346 acres) of vines but still buys in most of its grapes. The company sells under many labels. Under its own name are an elegantly perfumed rosé and an impressive NV Brut. The vintage Cuvée des Roys is of medium weight with attractive fruit flavours.

Charles Ellner

Though founded in the early 20th century, this label only became a merchant house in 1972. A large vineyard of 54ha (133 acres). The reserve wines are lodged in oak. Chardonnay plays a prominent part in the top range of wines, which aim for elegance.

Esterlin

A brand started in 1985 by the Mancy co-operative, a big producer of champagnes dominated by the Chardonnay wines of the Côte de Sézanne. Easy wines of consistent quality.

Nicolas Feuillate

This Epernay house is owned by 85 cooperatives with 4,000 growers and 1,600ha (3,952 acres) of vines. The best wines here are the prestige *cuvée*, Palmes d'Or, and a vintage Blanc de Blancs.

Henri Germain & Fils,

While heading this house, Germain also ran the Reims football club, when the famous Kopa played there. The label was bought up by Frey, who sold it to Paul Vranken *(qv)*.

Pierre Gimonnet

The Gimonnet family own 26ha (64 acres) of vines in the Côte des Blancs, making very interesting fine champagnes with little or no *dosage*, all of them Blancs de Blancs, of course. They also produce Larmandier Père & Fils — Mme Gimonnet is née Larmandier.

Michel Gonet

The largest grower-producer of the Côte des Blancs has 40h (100 acres), mostly in Grands Crus, and his wines are good value. He also makes and sells Champagne Marquis de Sade.

Gosset

This medium-sized family-owned Ay house joined the ranks of the *Grandes Marques* in 1992, though it is the oldest champagne firm, founded in 1584. It enjoys an excellent reputation for wines that age very well in bottle and which are not released until they are several years old. Both the Grande Réserve and Grand Millésime are fine examples of a rich, weighty, luscious style of champagne.

Alfred Gratien

The new owner of this former family business still makes champagne of a very traditional style, using some wood for the first fermentation. The NV special *cuvée* is dominated by Pinot Meunier, making it quite full-bodied in youth with immediate appeal. Their vintage wines last remarkably well, taking on a rich, nutty character as they age.

Charles Heidsieck

This *Grande Marque* got a boost in the mid-1980s when it was bought by Rémy-Cointreau, which then went on to acquire Piper-Heidsieck *(qv)*. The brilliant winemaker, Daniel Thibault, has completely transformed the NV Brut Réserve. It is now made up of 40% reserve wines, and the two Pinots make up around three-quarters of the blend, with an unusually high proportion of Pinot Meunier. A rich, weighty champagne; one of the best NVs around.

Heidsieck & Cie Monopole

Heidsieck & Cie registered the name Monopole in 1860 and became Heidsieck Monopole in 1923. In 1972, the house was bought by Seagram, who resold it to Paul Vranken *(qv)* in 1996. The wines are called Blue Top and Diamant Bleu (prestige *cuvée*).

Henriot

Founded in 1808, this house owns a superb 125-ha (309-acre) vineyard, most of it in the Côte des Blancs. In 1986, Joseph Henriot became chairman of Veuve Clicquot, bringing with him his vineyard. He left in 1994 to buy up Bouchard Père & Fils *(qv)* and to relaunch his own champagne brand, the Cuvée des Enchanteleurs, a top Souverain Brut wine.

Jacquart

A cooperative based in Reims, whose members own 1,000ha (2,470 acres), Jacquart is well known in France for its light and fruity champagnes.

Jacquesson

This small, 200-year-old firm is known for its enjoyable NV and the bigger, more austere Signature, a special *cuvée* fermented and aged in wood.

Krug

See profile.

Lanson

Lanson's Black Label is one of the world's best-known champagnes. It is fresh, citrussy, clean and perhaps rather lean. The vintage wines have been more impressive. The brand was sold in the early 1990s to Marne et Champagne *(qv)*, but not the vineyard.

Larmandier-Bernier

Mme Larmandier née Bernier and her son own Grand Cru and Premier Cru land in the Côte des Blancs. They produce fruity and lively champagnes and an interesting red Coteau champenois, de Vertus.

Laurent-Perrier

A *Grande Marque* and one of Champagne's largest and finest houses, producing some of the most elegant wines. The Brut NV, which has a high percentage of Chardonnay in the blend, is delicious, with a flowery bouquet and finely balanced palate that improves with bottle-age. There is also a totally dry champagne, Ultra Brut, and a superb prestige *cuvée* called Grand Siècle. Based at Tours-sur-Marne, and with 105ha (260 acres) of vines, Laurent-Perrier is owned by the Nonancourt family. In early 2004, Laurent-Perrier took control of Champagne Trouillard and its 80-ha (198-acre) vineyard, and thus of the houses of Jeanmaire, Oudinot and Beaumet.

Leclerc-Briant

This important house produces an unusual range of wines. Three unblended champagnes — with grapes coming from three selected parcels. The Rosé is the reddest of all rosé champagnes, and the best wine is labeled Cuvée Divine.

Mailly Grand Cru

Only growers with vines in the commune of Mailly can be members of this strange cooperative, founded in 1929. Its single-vineyard champagne is almost always based on Pinot Noir grapes.

Marne et Champagne

One of the region's giants owns no vineyards, and its name is rarely seen on a label: most of the production is sold either as Buyer's Own Brands or under a variety of *sous-marques*. A few of its 300-odd labels include Eugène Clicquot, Gauthier, Gieslier and Alfred Rothschild.

Mercier

LVMH (*see* Moët) owns this house, which is based in Epernay. It makes good, reliable medium-bodied champagne, sold mostly in France.

Moët & Chandon

Producer of the best-selling champagne in the world, and the largest vineyard owner in Champagne, with 558ha (1,378 acres). The quality of the Brut Imperial NV can vary. The vintage version is a consistently fine, fairly weighty champagne, with tropical fruit overtones. Moët also produces one of the great wines of the region, Dom Pérignon, which commands a high price and is particularly sought after in the USA. This wine will easily age for 30 years or more. A tiny quantity of Dom Pérignon rosé is also made.

Moët is owned by Louis Vuitton Moët-Hennessy, the giant luxury-goods firm which also owns several other champagne houses.

Moutard Père & Fils

This *Grande Marque* based in the Aube region offers rounded, full-bodied wines and is the only producer to make a champagne from the still-permitted Arbane grape. (Another grower of old grape varieties is Aubry, based at Jouy-lès-Reims.)

Jean Moutardier

This Breuil house makes a successful wine from pure Pinot Meunier.

Mumm

Mumm may not rate as one of the top *Grandes Marques*, but it certainly is one of the largest, with 70% of its production being exported to 135 countries. Its best-known wine, the NV Cordon Rouge, with its distinctive red band on the label, is a delicately fruity champagne. The prestige *cuvée*, Grand Cordon, an almost equal blend of Pinot Noir and Chardonnay, is very fine indeed, as is Mumm de Cramant, a Blanc de Blancs.

For a number of years, this *Grande Marque* was owned by Seagram before being sold to an American pension fund and, in 2000, to Allied Domecq.

Napoléon

This family-owned house is the least-known of the Champagne *Grandes Marques*, and one of the smallest. Extremely good-quality champagnes — especially the vintage wines.

Bruno Paillard

Founded in 1981 by Bruno Paillard, this Reims house was one of the success stories of the 1980s and looks very well set for the future.

The NV has lots of fruit and finesse and can often be better than a good vintage champagne. Bruno Paillard, a stickler for quality, puts the date of disgorgement on every bottle and has just started doing some fermentation in wood.

Palmer

A highly regarded cooperative (170 growers, with 310ha/766 acres) with a major holding in the *Grand Cru* vineyards of the Montagne de Reims.

Pannier

This Château-Thierry cooperative — the closest one to Paris — uses Pinot Meunier for its wines and produces two prestige *cuvées*.

Joseph Perrier

A *Grande Marque* house in Châlons-en-Champagne with 20ha (50 acres) of vines in the Vallée de la Marne. The NV Cuvée Royale has been inconsistent, and the best champagne is the Cuvée Josephine, an almost equal blend of Pinot Noir and Chardonnay. For a short period, this house was owned by Laurent-Perrier and is now linked to Alain Thienot (*qv*).

Perrier-Jouët

Founded in 1811, this Epernay house was sold by Seagram to Hicks Muse, an American concern, in June 1999, together with Mumm.

In 2000, it was bought up by Allied Domecq. Elegance, finesse and consistency are the bywords for its wines. The stress is on Chardonnay. The finest wine is the Belle Epoque Blanc de Blancs, in its art nouveau bottle decorated with anemones, one of the most elegant and feminine of champagnes. The Grand Brut NV is extremely consistent, with lovely, delicate fruit.

Phillipponat

A small Mareuil-sur-Ay house, unremarkable apart from its fine, weighty single-vineyard champagne, Clos des Goisses. Owned for ten years by the Marie Brizard company, Phillipponat — which is managed by Charles Phillipponat — has been part of Boizel-Chamoine-Champagne (BCC) since 1997.

Piper-Heidsieck

Rémy-Cointreau, owners of Charles Heidsieck (*qv*), also own this house, which is based in Reims. Both have the same winemaker, Daniel

KRUG

Perhaps the greatest name in Champagne, producing big, rich traditional wines that need at least a decade in bottle before they even begin to show off their best. Krug ages its champagnes for many years before sale: the 1988 vintage, for example, was released in the spring of 1999. All Krug wines are fermented in wood. The NV Grande Cuvée is probably the most consistently great wine produced in the region. Brothers Henri and Rémi Krug carry out the blending, which includes a high percentage of reserve wines and of Pinot Meunier, of which they are both firm advocates. Other unique wines include the Collection, older and rarer vintages, and Clos du Mesnil, a single-vineyard, 100% Chardonnay wine. Since January 1999, Krug has been owned by LVMH.

Thibault. Piper is generally lighter, fruitier and slightly leaner in style than its cousin. The Brut NV is dominated by red grapes, although it contains less Pinot Meunier than Charles Heidsieck. The Brut Sauvage is one of the finest non-*dosage* wines produced and the prestige *cuvée*, called Rare, is a grand and elegant champagne.

Pol Roger

A very traditional, family-run firm, with wines of consistently high quality, and longstanding ties to the UK. Elegance and finesse are the hallmarks of the Cuvée Sir Winston Churchill, whose favourite champagne it was, though the special *cuvée* PR is fuller-bodied and richer. Based at Epernay, with 85ha (210 acres) of vines.

Pommery

Some twelve years ago, LVMH took over this *Grande Marque* house and its superb 300-ha (740-acre) vineyard. In 2002, the *Grande Marque* Pommery was sold to P F Vranken, while LMVH has held onto the vineyard, following a strategy already employed during the purchase and sale of Lanson. The NV is well made, but the Louise Pommery Brut and Rosé are outstanding.

Louis Roederer

This family-owned *Grande Marque* house, founded over 200 years ago, makes some of the greatest wines in Champagne. Its 180ha (445 acres) of vines supply most of its needs.

Roederer's NV Brut Premier has a fruity flavour but is nonetheless a rich and weighty wine. The prestige *cuvée*, Cristal de Roederer, was created for Tsar Alexander II, in 1876 and, in great vintages, it is one of the great luxury champagnes.

Ruinart

A *Grande Marque* house founded in 1729 which is relatively unknown, due in part to its small production. Its champagnes are very well made, elegant and flowery in style, and are good value, especially the prestige *cuvée*, Dom Ruinart Blanc de Blancs. Ruinart is based at Reims and owned by LVMH (*see* Moët).

Salon

A *Grande Marque* house, owned by Laurent-Perrier, based at Le Mesnil-sur-Oger in the Côte des Blancs, producing outstanding wine. Its vintage wine, from 100% Chardonnay, is expensive, but much sought after by champagne aficionados.

Jacques Selosse

Anselme Selosse is growing vines at Avize. Being a man of principle, he has decided to produce distinctive champagnes. For fermentation and maturing he uses wood, and his *cuvée* Substance makes use of a technique called *perpétuelle*, where old wines teach young ones how to mature. This Blanc de Blancs specialist — there is one Blanc de Blancs without any added sugar — also makes a lavish Blanc de Noirs.

Taittinger

Dating from 1930, this Reims house is young by *Grandes Marques* standards. Over 50% of its grapes are supplied from its 257ha (635 acres) of vineyards. The overall style aims for delicacy and elegance, although after a decade in

bottle the Blanc de Blancs grows richer and weightier. The NV Brut Réserve is mostly Chardonnay, and their luxury *cuvée*, Comtes de Champagne, is 100% Chardonnay.

Telmont

This house owns 30ha (74 acres) of vines and produces two interesting *cuvées*: Grand Millésime (a blend) and Grand Couronnement (a Blanc de Blancs).

Alain Thienot

Alain Thienot started his brand in 1980 and later took over Marie Stuart, Joseph Perrier and finally Canard-Duchêne. Founded in 1860, the latter house had been taken over by Veuve Clicquot in the early 1980s, before being absorbed, in 1987, along with Veuve Clicquot, by LVMH, who sold it in 2003. Alain Thienot also owns vines in the Bordeaux region, and makes wine at Aniane, in the Languedoc region.

De Venoge

This *Grande Marque*, unfortunately, has had too many owners. Since 1998, it has been part of Boizel-Chamoine-Champagne (BCC). De Venoge's Cuvée des Princes is a great Blanc de Blancs.

Veuve Clicquot Ponsardin

One of the leading *Grandes Marques*, named after Madame Clicquot who, having been widowed young, devoted the rest of her life to building up the house in the early part of the 19th century. Today the wines rank with the finest produced in Champagne.

The NV blend, with its distinctive yellow label, is one of the best of its kind, with a lot of character. La Grande Dame is the flagship wine, a rich blend made up of two-thirds Pinot Noir and one-third Chardonnay. Owned by LVMH (see Moët), and based

at Reims, with 300ha (740 acres) of vines.

Vilmart

A small, top-quality grower with 11ha (27 acres) of vines at Rilly-la-Montagne making all its wines in oak — and the only one to do so in the Champagne region. The wines have a lot of character and need keeping.

Vranken

A new house, founded by Paul Vranken in 1976, it owns 162ha (400 acres) of vines. The emphasis is on Chardonnay, so the wines are light and elegant. Brands include Barancourt, Veuve Monnier, Charles Lafitte, Sacotte, Charbaut-Demoiselle, Heidsieck Monopole, Germain and Pommery.

Other champagne houses and growers

Henri Billot, Gardet, Goulet, Abel Lepitre and de Méric

OTHER WINES

The Champagne AOC is for sparkling wine. Other wines of the region are:

COTEAUX CHAMPENOIS

Appellation for still red and white wines of Champagne. The best reds are from Marne Valley villages: Ay, Bouzy and Cumières.

For climatic reasons, serious reds can only be made three or four times a decade. White wines are more frequently satisfactory.

ROSÉ DES RICEYS

This small *appellation* in the Aube makes one of the rarest rosé wines in France, from Pinot Noir. The slightly warmer Aube climate allows regular production of a serious, dark rosé.

ALSACE

ALSACE DEFIES A NUMBER OF FRENCH WINE CONVENTIONS: MOST WINES ARE WHITE;
AND THEY ARE LABELLED ACCORDING TO GRAPE VARIETY.
BUT IN ONE WAY THEY CONFORM: THEY ACCOMPANY FOOD SUPERBLY WELL.

A 15th-century fortified church overlooks the vineyards of
Hunawihr on the *Route du Vin* in Alsace.
The village's Grand Cru is Rosacker, and the little Clos
Ste-Hune vineyard is also famous.

The Rhine can be glimpsed from the tops of the wooded hills of Alsace, and eastwards beyond it, smoky blue in the summer haze, lies Germany's Black Forest. In many ways, this view provides a key to appreciating Alsace, its wine and its culture. The wide valley of the Rhine and its surrounding hills have more in common with the countries of Central Europe than other regions of France. The wines of the frontier province of Alsace are sometimes compared with their counterparts from neighbouring Germany, but a more helpful parallel is with Austria's full-tasting, dry white wines. Alsace has a repertoire of grape varieties that it shares with Germany: Riesling, Gewürztraminer, Sylvaner. It also uses the Burgundian Pinot Noir (for a small production of red wines), Pinot Blanc — once common in Burgundy but now mostly found in Alsace — and Pinot Gris, also known as Tokay Pinot Gris (in Germany, Ruländer). Baden, facing Alsace from across the Rhine, is Germany's most southerly wine zone. Alsace, in contrast, is (with Champagne) the most northerly French wine region. It is to the north of all the Loire vineyards, and should — by virtue of its latitude alone — be cool. But the Vosges hills, which run north–south parallel to the Rhine, provide both a shelter belt and rain shadow zone. Alsace's vineyards are tucked away in the valleys and warm corners of the Vosges foothills, and benefit from being in one of the driest areas of France. They run in an almost continuous strip for 100km (62 miles) from west of Strasbourg down to the west of Mulhouse. There are a few vines further north of here, in the northern part of the Bas-Rhin *département*, with some right on the German border. Cross this frontier and you are in the south of the Pfalz wine region.

Alsace is a paradise for gastronomes, with many famous restaurants, while its villages reflect the area's long history in their picturesque architecture. It has been wine country for many centuries, despite a sad record of wars and changes of national ownership as a result of its strategic position on the border of France and Germany. Now firmly French, Alsace displays its individuality through its own dialect, a strong regional spirit and its unique wines.

WINE VILLAGES OF ALSACE

The Vosges hills to the west provide shelter for the narrow vineyard strip, which has some of the most picturesque villages and wine country in France. The main villages and towns are named and the locations of some of the most important selected vineyards with the status *Grand Cru* are indicated on the map.

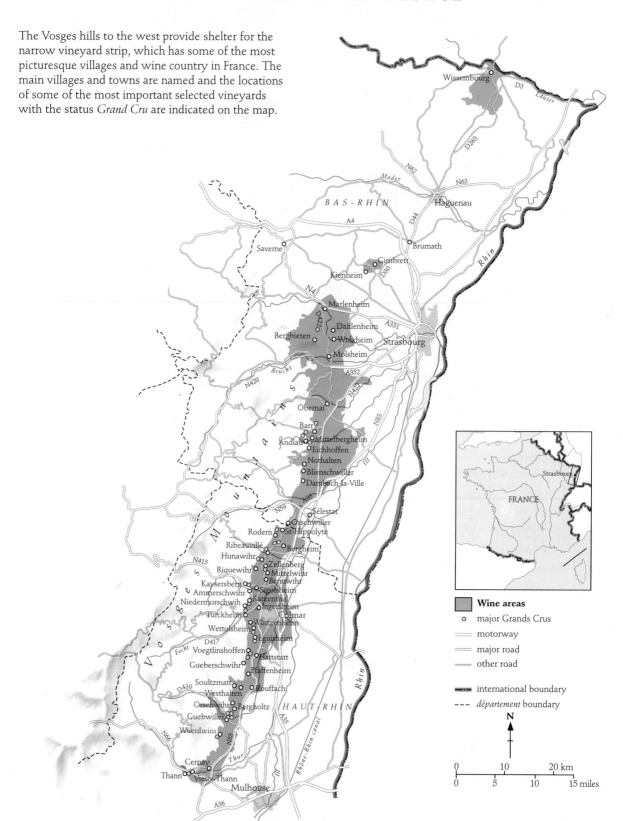

Wissembourg

Lauter

Moder

BAS-RHIN

Haguenau

Saverne

Gimbrett

Kienheim

Rhin

Brumath

Marlenheim

Dahlenheim

Bergbieten

Wolxheim

Molsheim

Strasbourg

Bruche

Obernai

Barr

Andlau

Mittelbergheim

Eichhoffen

Nothalten

Blienschwiller

Dambach-la-Ville

Sélestat

Orschwiller

Rodern

St-Hippolyte

Ribeauvillé

Bergheim

Hunawihr

Zellenberg

Riquewihr

Mittelwihr

Beblenheim

Kaysersberg

Sigolsheim

Ammerschwihr

Katzenthal

Niedermorschwihr

Ingersheim

Turckheim

Colmar

Wettolsheim

Wintzenheim

Eguisheim

Fecht

Voegtlinshoffen

Hattstatt

Gueberschwihr

Pfaffenheim

Soultzmatt

Rouffach

Westhalten

Orschwihr

Bergholtz

HAUT-RHIN

Guebwiller

Rhin

Wuenheim

Cernay

Thur

Thann

Vieux-Thann

Mulhouse

Rhône-Rhin canal

FRANCE

Strasbourg

Wine areas

○ major Grands Crus

motorway

major road

other road

international boundary

département boundary

N

| 0 | 10 | | 20 km |

| 0 | 5 | 10 | 15 miles |

Climate, situation and soils

The sheltered position of the Alsace vineyards produces a favourable climate, with warm springs; dry, sunny summers; and long, mild autumns. Winters are cold, but are rarely severe enough to damage the vines.

The ribbon-shaped wine zone covers a wide variety of rock formations and soils. The geology is complex, with a succession of rock types abutting the ancient granite of the Vosges mountains. Vinegrowers have selected the best sites, on well-drained slopes facing south or southeast, in the many little valleys that punctuate the slope of the Vosges. The result is a strip of vineyard only 1.5–3km (1–2 miles) wide in places.

The Grands Crus

The best-placed vineyards have built up reputations, often for specific kinds of wine. Slowly, since 1975, the AOC authorities have been defining and naming the best vineyards as *Grands Crus*. The list is controversial: some locals say certain sites are not up to standard, and that others have been omitted. Not all Alsace producers make use of the *Grand Cru* names, partly because the laws state that only Riesling, Gewürztraminer, Muscat and Pinot Gris wines can be designated *Grand Cru*. Wine labelled *Grand Cru* must be from vines producing a yield of 65hl/ha or less. This is high for the rest of France (white burgundy at *Grand Cru* level, for example, is restricted to no more than 30hl/ha).

Grape varieties and wine styles

The most important grape varieties planted in Alsace are:

Gewürztraminer Currently 18% of the vineyard — a significant proportion — is planted with this pink-skinned grape. The wine is white; spicy, assertive-tasting and grapey in a fashion akin to Muscat. Good Gewürztraminer from a good vintage is spicy, solid and rich: in disappointing years it can taste oily and flat. It is enjoyable as an occasional treat.

Muscat This aromatic white variety is present in two forms, Muscat d'Alsace and Muscat Ottonel. Alsace Muscat is dry and intensely grapey in taste. It is an unreliable cropper, and is declining in importance.

Pinot Blanc A white variety of growing importance (20% of the vineyard) and interest, Pinot Blanc makes fresh, dry wines of burgundian character. Much of it is used to make sparkling Crémant d'Alsace (*see* below). Regulations allow wine that is made from Auxerrois (a separate variety, and not a true Pinot) to be labelled Pinot Blanc, as can blends of Auxerrois and Pinot Blanc. Klevner is a local synonym for Pinot Blanc.

Pinot Noir This is the only red Alsace grape, and is used to make red and rosé wines. The reds can be good if yields are kept low.

Pinot Gris (or Tokay Pinot Gris) A minority grape, Pinot Gris is nonetheless capable of making full-flavoured, distinguished dry white wines, and great sweet ones. The legendary link with Hungary seems tenuous, and the name Tokay is officially on the way out. In Alsace, Pinot Gris is considered to be the perfect partner to *foie gras*.

Riesling The most distinguished grape grown in Alsace (23% of the vineyard), Riesling makes great, long-lived dry whites and excellent late-harvest sweet wines. Unlike its cousins from lower down the Rhine, Alsace Riesling is almost always wholly dry, and strong in alcohol.

Sylvaner More common in the Bas-Rhin (17% of the total vineyard), Sylvaner makes good, fresh everyday wine, but needs a special site to raise it to the quality of Riesling.

The least special grape variety in Alsace, and the least likely to be named on a wine label, is Chasselas. Wines made from this variety are used for Edelzwicker (*see* below).

Winemaking

Alsace, on the whole, sticks to a fairly traditional, basic white-wine technique. Not here the fashionable maceration of grapes, skin-contact, cold fermentation, nor fermenting or ageing in new oak casks. Wines are stored in large casks (*foudres*) or tanks and bottled 6 to 12 months after the harvest. A few growers ferment and/or age Pinot Gris and Pinot Noir in *barriques*, with good results.

Vintages and ageing

Few Alsace vintages are a disaster: the climate is relatively predictable. A good, or great, Alsace vintage stems from a warm, prolonged autumn, which allows the making of late-harvest wines (*see* below).

Alsace label terms

Alsace makes life easier for the wine drinker by labelling its wines with grape variety names. The other important name on the label is the grower's. Rarely, except in the case of a *Grand Cru*, will an individual village or vineyard be cited.

Other terms that may appear on the labels of Alsace wines are:

Crémant d'Alsace This means the wine is sparkling, made by the *méthode traditionnelle*. Crémants are usually white (from Pinot Blanc, mainly) but sometimes rosé.

Edelzwicker This is a white wine made from a blend of "noble" (*edel*) grape varieties, Chasselas and Sylvaner being most common. The term is less used than it was. Most blends are labelled under a brand name.

Vendange Tardive This describes wine from one of the four main varieties — Gewürztraminer, Pinot Gris, Riesling or Muscat — made using very ripe grapes. Usually, but not invariably, these are picked later than the normal harvest. The German equivalent is *Auslese*. *Vendange tardive* wines can be dry or (more usually) sweet: it is impossible to tell which except by tasting the wine.

Sélection de Grains Nobles This wine is made from individually-selected, nobly-rotten grapes (*see* p163). Made only in very warm years, it is always lusciously sweet and can age for 10 to 20 years. ☐

THE 50 GRANDS CRUS OF ALSACE

In 1975, the INAO first officially recognized Alsatian vineyards as Grand Cru land. (Other decrees followed in 1983 and in 1992.) Most of the *Grands Crus* are located at an altitude of between 200 and 300m (660/980ft). They are listed here from north to south.

Steinklotz
Marlenheim 40.6ha (100.3 acres) on stony limestone, facing south-south-east. Fruity and spicy wines.

Engelberg
Dahlenheim and Scharrachbergheim Facing due south, this 15-ha (37-acre) vineyard on marly limestone makes for well-structured, long-lived wines.

Altenberg de Bergbieten
Bergbieten A *terroir* of 29ha (72 acres) facing south-east. Clayey marl with dolomite shingles. Floral wines with a good length.

Altenberg de Wolxheim
Wolxheim 31ha (77 acres) of clayey marl and limestone produce very long-lived Rieslings with petrolly flavours.

Bruderthal
Molheim This *cru* is sited on a gentle slope. The marly limestone soil is stony toward the upper part. Flowery and persistent Rieslings and Gewürztraminers.

Kirchberg de Barr
Barr Above the village, the Kirchberg rises over a 100m (328ft) to a height of 315m (1,033ft). A composite *terroir* of 40ha (99 acres) dominated by clayey limestone. Long-keeping wines.

Zotzenberg
Mittelbergheim 36ha (89 acres) of marl and Jurassic limestone, facing south and east, produce long-lived wines.

Kastelberg
Andlau This small

(5.82ha/14.38 acres) *Grand Cru* on a steep slope is unique in Alsace for its soil of primary Steige schist and because it is planted exclusively with Riesling grapes. Long-lived fine wine with a mineral taste.

Wiebelsberg
Andlau Sited east of the Kastelberg, this *terroir* on quartzy, ferruginous, flinty soil, facing south and south-east, makes for floral long-lived Riesling wines.

Moenchberg
Andlau and Eichhoffen A 12-ha (30-acre) vineyard on a gentle slope, facing due south and thus favouring the maturation of the Riesling grapes. The wine is as well-structured as it is elegant.

Muenchberg
Nothalten A vineyard stretching over 18ha (44 acres) on gentle slopes, at an altitude of 300m (980ft). The sandy, stony soil is made up of volcanic deposits, producing very elegant, fine Riesling wines.

Winzenberg
Blienschwiller A reputed vineyard of 19ha (47 acres) on a steep slope, facing south and south-east. Its soil, broken-up granite with two micas, suits Riesling and Gewürztraminer, producing lavish wines from very mature grapes.

Frankstein
Dambach-la-Ville This large vineyard of 56ha (138 acres) consists of four parcels facing east and south-east. The granite soil with two micas is filtering. Floral Rieslings and Gewürztraminers.

Praelatenberg
Kintzheim 19 ha (47 acres) on steep slopes, facing east and south-east. The soil, a mixture of gneiss, flint and quartz, brings out the aromatic flavour of native Alsace grapes.

Gloeckelberg
Rodern and Saint-Hippolyte This vineyard covers 23ha (57 acres) on granite soil, sandy and acid, with a brown colour, facing south and south-east.

A traditional sign outside a winery in Turckheim.

Elegant and persistent wines.

Altenberg de Bergheim
Bergheim The vineyard occupies the southern slope of the Grasberg hill, whose red ferruginous, chalky Jurassic marl is planted with 35ha (86 acres) of Riesling and Gewürztraminer grapes. Ample and powerful wines.

Kanzlerberg
Bergheim A vineyard on gentle slopes facing south and south-west. This is the smallest Grand Cru, with 3.23ha (7.98 acres)! A heavy, clayey and chalky soil composed of black and grey Keuper gypsum marls emphasizes the aromatic power of the wine, which needs keeping.

Geisberg
Ribeauvillé A south-facing vineyard of 8ha (20 acres) on a steep slope, which could not have been used without the construction of low walls. The soil is composed of marl, limestone, sandstone and gypsum and seems ideal for exalting the fineness and power of Riesling.

Kirchberg de Ribeauvillé
Ribeauvillé A vineyard as old as the Geisberg, its eastern neighbour, with the same kind of soil, but facing south-south-east. Riesling with plenty of character and a great potential for ageing.

Osterberg
Ribeauvillé A 24.6-ha (60.8-acre) vineyard of similar age and soil as the Geisberg, its neighbour to the east, but facing east and south-east and sited on a gentler slope. It emphasizes the typical Riesling taste but also suits Gewürztraminer and Pinot Gris.

Rosacker
Hunawihr A vineyard of 26ha (64 acres) facing east and south-east. Its heavy soil is composed of limestone and dolomites made lighter by a

scree of sandstone and flint does good justice to the mineral and spicy flavours of Riesling.

Froehn

Zellenberg A *terroir* with a soil of clay, marl and schist, facing south and south-east, which brings out the fruit flavour of Gewürztraminer.

Schoenenbourg

Riquewihr and Zellenberg A vineyard which now covers 53ha (131 acres) on steep slopes, facing south and south-east. The soil is a mixture of marl, dolomite and gypsum, which makes for fine, spicy and long-lived Rieslings. Late-harvesting has shown good results.

Sporen

Riquewihr Facing south-east, on a gentle slope. The marl and clay soil is rich in phosphoric acid and agrees perfectly with the richness of Gewürztraminer and Pinot Gris.

Sonnenglanz

Beblenheim A 33-ha (82-acre) vineyard, facing south-east. The heavy stony and chalky marl soil favours the powerful aroma of Gewürztraminer and Pinot Gris.

Mandelberg

Mittelwihr and Beblenheim A *terroir* of 22ha (54 acres) on a not too steep slope, facing south and south-east. The limestone and marl bring out the finesse and fruit of the wine.

Marckrain

Bennwihr and Sigolsheim Marl and limestone on a gentle slope, facing east and south-east, are good soil for Pinot Gris and Gewürztraminer, whose aromas excel here.

Mambourg

Sigolsheim This superbly sited large vineyard on 62ha (153 acres) of marl and limestone, facing south-east, is excellent for a rich Gewürztraminer which can sometimes be heavy.

Furstentum

Kientzheim and Sigolsheim A fine *terroir* on a very steep slope.

Facing south and south-east, these 30ha (74 acres) of clayey brown and poor soil provide Alsace grapes with strength and finesse.

Schlossberg

Kientzheim The Schlossberg is Alsace's first officially recognized Grand Cru (1975) as well as one of its largest (80ha (197 acres). A steep slope marked by low walls, facing due south. Its sandy limestone is rich in mineral salts, providing the four Alsace noble varieties with richness and finesse.

Wineck-Schlossberg

Katzenthal and Ammerschwihr Facing south and south-east, this hill-side vineyard lies at an altitude of 280-400m (725-1,035ft). A soil of broken granite with two micas gives good expression to the floral freshness of Riesling.

Sommerberg

Niedermorschwihr and Katzenthal The granitic sand of this 28-ha (69-acre) vineyard, facing due south, emphasizes the typical Riesling traits.

Florimont

Ingersheim and Katzenthal The vineyard covers 21ha (52 acres) of chalky marl, facing south-south-east. Sumptuous, elegant and long Gewürztraminer.

Brand

Turckheim 58ha (143 acres) of granitic sand with two micas, facing south and south-east. Riesling in particular makes for rich and long-lived wines.

Hengst

Wintzenheim A vineyard of 76ha (188 acres) on chalky marl, facing south-south-east, producing rich Gewürztraminer and long-keeping Riesling.

Steingrubler

Wettolsheim The upper part (350m/900ft) of this vineyard is sandy clay, ideal for Riesling, while the lower part (280m/725ft) — limestone and marl — suits Gewürztraminer. Well-constituted and long-lived wines from 23ha (57 acres).

Eichberg

Eguisheim Facing south-east, this vineyard covers 58ha (143 acres) of sandy limestone, which exalts the flavours of the great Alsace varieties.

Pfersigberg

Eguisheim and Wettolsheim Facing east-by south-east, the chalky marl and silty clay soil of this large vineyard (76ha/188 acres) at an altitude of 250-330m (650-850ft) gives body and a fruity flavour to Gewürztraminer.

Hatschbourg

Hattstatt and Voegtlinshofen 47ha (116 acres) of silty marl and limestone, facing south and south-east, bring out the aromatic finesse of the four Alsace noble varieties.

Goldert

Gueberschwihr The upper part of the vineyard (330m/850ft) is limestone, the lower part (230m/600ft) clay. These 45ha (111 acres), facing south-east, make the best Gewürztraminers and the finest Muscats.

Steinert

Pfaffenheim and Westhalten This very chalky vineyard coves 39ha (96 acres), facing south-east. The Gewürztraminers, Pinots Gris and Rieslings are all highly aromatic and long-lived.

Vorbourg

Rouffach and Westhalten A large (73ha/180 acres) vineyard on marl and limestone soil, facing south by south-east, excellent terroir for the four noble varieties. Fine, powerful and long-lived wines.

Zinnkoepfle

Soultzmatt and Westhalten At the highest vineyard of Alsace — 420m/1,090ft above sea level —, the vines (68ha/168 acres) are planted right up to the border of the two villages (220m/160ft). The conchiferous limestone mixed with sandstone faces south and south-east. Spicy Gewürztraminers and fine Rieslings.

Pfingstberg

Orschwihr Facing south-east, the vineyard covers 28ha (69 acres) at 250-350m (650-900ft) above sea level. The soil, composed of sandstone mixed with limestone, mica and limestone, is held in place by low walls and exalts the floral aromas of the noble varieties.

Spiegel

Bergholtz and Guebwiller A 18-ha (44-acre) vineyard, facing east, with a soil of marl mixed with sandstone, clay and sand. A fine *terroir* for the four noble varieties, and particularly for Gewürztraminer.

Kessler

Guebwiller Facing south-east, at 300-390m (780-1,010ft) above sea level. The reddish sandy and clayey soil, held in place by low walls, stimulates the floral character of Gewürztraminer.

Kitterlé

Guebwiller A vineyard on a steep slope, at 270-360m (700-930ft) above sea level, whose light, sandy soil is held in place by low walls. The 26ha (64 acres) are planted with Pinot Gris, Gewürztraminer and Riesling, producing dense wines for long keeping.

Saering

Guebwiller 27ha (67 acres) of vines facing east and south-east. The heavy soil of sandy marl is kept in place by low walls. A good *terroir* for the four noble varieties, particularly Riesling.

Ollwiller

Wuenheim The reddish, sandy, clayish soil of this vineyard, facing south-east, makes for fine and elegant Rieslings.

Rangen

Thann and Vieux-Thann Alsace's southernmost vineyard is not only the steepest (68%) but also has a unique soil of volcanic origin: basic lava, sandstone, poor brown soil 19ha (47 acres) facing due south produce the finest Rieslings, as well as powerful and typical Gewürztraminer and Pinot Gris.

PRODUCERS

Alsace wine producers are often both vineyard owners and merchants. They may own land in, and/or buy wine from, several villages. The village named in each case is the company's base. Some cooperatives (*see* p230) also produce high-quality wines.

J B Adam
Ammerschwihr. A family business since the beginning of the 17th century. Mainly a Riesling and Gewürztraminer producer, with occasional *vendange tardive* wines and some Pinot Noir and Pinot Blanc. Winemaking is traditional.

Lucien Albrecht
Orschwihr. Founded in 1772, Albrecht produces wine from all the major varieties, but is noted in particular for its Riesling *Grand Cru* Pfingstberg.

Jean Becker
Riquewihr. Old (1610) family firm making all the major Alsace wines. The best are Muscat, Pinot Noir, Gewürztraminer (from *Grand Cru* Froehn) and Riesling.

Léon Beyer
Eguisheim. Wine merchants since the 16th century, and producers since the mid-19th, Beyer is known for its dry wine style, in particular Riesling, Gewürztraminer (Cuvée des Comtes d'Eguisheim) and Muscat. Labels do not mention the term *Grand Cru*.

Paul Blanck & Fils
Kientzheim. A wide range of wines is produced from all the major varieties, but the Rieslings from *Grands Crus* Furstentum and Schlossberg stand out. The company also uses the Domaine des Comtes de Lupfen label.

Albert Boxler & Fils
Niedermorschwihr. A producer of small amounts of exceptional wine, including the Brand (*Grand Cru*) Pinot Gris (including the *sélections de grains nobles* version), Brand Riesling and Sommerberg (*Grand Cru*) Rieslings.

Domaine Ernest Burn
Gueberschwihr. This handsome 10-ha (25-acre) property produces outstanding Goldert (*Grand Cru*) Riesling and Muscat.

Joseph Cattin & ses Fils
Voegtlinshofen. Cousin of Théo (*see* below), Joseph is a talented winemaker, producing Muscat, Gewürztraminer *Grand Cru* Hatschbourg (including a *vendange tardive* version), and Pinot Noir of particular note.

Théo Cattin & Fils
Voegtlinshofen. Théo is better known than his cousin (*see* above), and produces some good Gewürztraminer — from *Grand Cru* Hatschbourg and from Bollenberg *lieu-dit* — as well as Pinot Gris and a fine Riesling (from *Grand Cru* Hatschbourg), which ages beautifully and for which Cattin is rightfully famous.

Domaine Marcel Deiss
Bergheim. Marcel Deiss is one of the region's three top winemakers. He produces harmonious and unusual wines from every Alsace variety, and his *Grands Crus* are unique.

Dopff & Irion
Riquewihr. This company has the same origins as Dopff Au Moulin (*qv*), and was formed as an offshoot in 1945. It is now owned by the Pfaffenheim co-operative. Its list includes Riesling Les Murailles (from *Grand Cru* Schoenenberg), Gewürztraminer Muscat Les Sorcières, a powerful, long-lived wine, Muscat Les Amandiers, and Pinot Gris Les Maquisards. Having distanced itself from the system for years, the company is now marketing *Grand Cru* wines.

Dopff Au Moulin
Riquewihr. Founded in the 16th century, this company has been, and continues to be, at the forefront of Crémant d'Alsace production, with Cuvée Julien, Cuvée Bartholdi, Blanc de Noirs and Brut Sauvage among the best. It also produces some fine still wines under the Domaines Dopff label.

Rolly Gassmann
Rorschwihr. Gassmann's rich and generous wines have a high content of residual sugar. Gassmann does not own *Grand Cru* land. He makes an excellent Muscat (from Moenchreben *lieu-dit* at Rorschwihr, not the *Grand Cru* at Eichhoffen), a very famous Auxerrois and good *cuvées*, such as Réserve Rolly Gassmann, from every classic variety.

Willy Gisselbrecht & Fils
Dambach-la-Ville. Like many producers in Alsace, Willy

— HUGEL & FILS —

The 13th generation of Hugels (since 1639) is currently running this, the most famous Alsace producer. The company's vast cellars beneath the city of Riquewihr house wines up to a century old. Reliability is the company's keynote. Gewürztraminer is good of the basic generic wines, and the Pinot Blanc de Blancs gets better and better. The Cuvée Tradition and Jubilé Réserve Personnelle ranges represent a progression to real quality. Hugel is the leading producer of *vendange tardive* wines; indeed, this company virtually invented the style. It is similarly experienced in the production of *sélections des grains nobles,* and in this style the Pinot Gris and Riesling stand out. *Grand Cru* wines come from Hugel's Sporen and Schoenenbourg vineyards. Hugel makes large quantities of reliable fine wine.

The painted, half-timbered houses of the wine villages of Alsace date from the 17th and 18th centuries.

Gisselbrecht makes a range of wines of different qualities and *cuvées*, including *Grands Crus* and *vendanges tardives*. His Gewürztraminer is probably his best wine, but the Pinot Gris can be excellent, too.

Domaine André & Rémy Gresser

Andlau. This is a long-established (1667) company, but it has a young, vibrant image. Gresser's reputation was founded on *Grands Crus* Rieslings, Brandhof Pinot Noir and Andlau Gewürztraminer.

J Hauller & Fils

Dambach-la-Ville. This company has a relatively large output of good-value wines from all the Alsace varieties. It stresses Sylvaner, but the best wines include Gewürztraminer *Grand Cru* Frankstein and several Rieslings.

Albert Hertz

Eguisheim. A relative new-comer, Hertz is already considered to be among the best Pinot Noir producers in the region. The wine is elegant and well-balanced. Gewürztraminer and Riesling are also top-quality wines.

Hugel & Fils

See profile.

Zind Humbrecht

Wintzenheim. Leonard Humbrecht campaigns tirelessly for lower yields. His 30ha (74 acres) are extremely well sited and include four *Grand Cru* holdings. Vinification methods are natural and traditional. His Pinot Gris and Gewürztraminer excel.

André Kientzler

Ribeauvillé. A first-class wine-maker who has championed the lesser grape varieties of Alsace — Chasselas and Auxerrois. His top wines include Gewürztraminer (*Grand Cru* Kirchberg de Ribeauvillé), Riesling (in particular *Grand Cru* Geisberg and *Grand Cru* Osterberg) and Pinot Gris.

Kuentz-Bas

Husseren-les-Châteaux. The Kuentz part of the business dates from 1795: it amalgamated with André Bas in 1918. The company produces wines of great quality, in particular the *vendange tardive* versions. The top varietals are Gewürztraminer, Pinot Gris, Muscat and, increasingly, Pinot Noir. The company also makes Crémant d'Alsace.

Domaine Seppy Landmann

Soultzmatt. The Gewürztraminers *Grand Cru* Zinnkoepfle from this talented winemaker are famous.

Gustave Lorentz

Bergheim. A family firm established in 1836, Lorentz produces especially fine Gewürztraminers, particularly *Grand Cru* Altenberg de Bergheim and Cuvée Particulière. Pinot Blanc, Pinot Gris, Riesling and Muscat are good.

Jos Meyer

Wintzenheim. Jean Meyer is very concerned for the future of Alsace varieties other than the four classic grapes that have *Grand Cru* status available to them. Hence his Chasselas "H" (from Hengst *Grand Cru*). His top-quality wines include Jos Meyer Riesling *Grand Cru* Hengst and several Gewürztraminers.

René Muré

Rouffach. Virtually all Muré's own-domaine wines come from Clos St-Landelin (classified as *Grand Cru* Vorbourg) which they have owned since 1935. The company produces Pinot Noir, Riesling and Muscat of note. Riesling Crémant d'Alsace is a speciality.

Domaine Ostertag

Epfig. André Ostertag is certainly not a conventional Alsace winemaker. He is not afraid to experiment, with unexpected failures and stunning successes as a consequence. His best wines are probably Pinot Gris and Riesling from *Grand Cru* Moenchberg, but he has produced a great many wines from all grapes and in all wine styles.

Preiss-Zimmer

Riquewihr. Winemaking has been taken over by the Turckheim Cooperative (although vineyards are still owned by the Zimmers) since the late 1980s, and quality has improved substantially as a result. Gewürztraminer and Riesling are best.

Edgard Schaller & Fils

Mittelwihr. Schaller's style is extremely dry, and his wines need, in some cases, many years in bottle to become more approachable. This is particularly so for the Rieslings (especially *Grand Cru* Mandelberg Vieilles Vignes). He also makes very good Pinot Gris, Gewürztraminer and Crémant d'Alsace.

Domaine Schlumberger

Guebwiller. This family firm has amassed many plots of land over the years and now has the largest holding in Alsace and one of the most important in France. It includes steeply terraced plots that are totally beyond the reach of mechanization, but the *terroirs* are worth the trouble. If one variety established Schlumberger's reputation, it is Gewürztraminer — especially Cuvée Christine, a *vendange tardive*, and Cuvée Anne, a *sélection des grains nobles*. Also of top quality are Schlumberger's Pinot Gris and Ries-

lings from *Grands Crus* Kitterlé and Saering.

Domaine Schoffit

Colmar. This firm is managed by Bernard Schoffit, the lucky owner of a 16-ha (40-acre) vineyard, and more particularly of the Clos St-Théobald in the famous *Grand Cru* of Rangen. To this talented winemaker we also owe rare and highly-priced *vendanges tardives* and *sélection de grains nobles*.

Louis Sipp

Ribeauvillé. The best *cuvées* from Louis Sipp develop their superb flavour over time. Rieslings are best (*Grand Cru* Kirchberg de Ribeauvillé), followed closely by Gewürztraminer (*Grand Cru* Osterberg).

Pierre Sparr

Sigolsheim. Sparr's wines have a rich fruit flavour, sometimes with a hint of sweetness, with Pinot Gris, Riesling and Gewürztraminer the best. The company also produces some

top-quality blended wines, such as Kaefferkopf (Gewürztraminer/ Pinot Gris) and Symphonie (Riesling/Pinot Gris/ Pinot Blanc/Gewürztraminer), as well as sparkling wine.

Trimbach

Ribeauvillé. Along with Hugel, Trimbach has done more than anyone to promote the wines of Alsace the world over. Wines include Gewürztraminer (especially Cuvée des Seigneurs de Ribeaupierre) and Pinot Gris, but the Rieslings are, without doubt, the best of the region.

Cuvée Frédéric-Emile, originating from two *Grands Crus*, is bettered only by Clos Ste-Hune, a vineyard Trimbach has owned for more than 200 years. It is within *Grand Cru* Rosacker, but its wines cannot claim *Grand Cru* status (for legal reasons). A world-class wine, Clos Ste-Hune epitomizes Riesling and is considered by many to be the best wine in Alsace. Alas, not a bottle finds its way into the shops.

Domaine Weinbach

Kayserberg. The Faller family produces impressive wines from its Clos de Capucins vineyard. Three come solely from there: Gewürztraminer Cuvée Théo, Riesling Cuvée Théo and Pinot Gris Ste-Catherine.

Alsace Willm

Barr. Although now owned by the Wolfberger cooperative of Eguisheim, Willm wines retain their distinctive character from the Clos Gaensbroennel vineyard. The Gewürztraminer and Riesling *Grand Cru* Kirchberg de Barr are best.

COOPERATIVES

Leading Alsace co-ops, with a name for quality in wine, include Bennwihr; Union Vinicole Divinal, Obernai; Eguisheim; Caves de Hoen, Beblenheim; Ingersheim et Environs (Colmar); Kientzheim-Kaysersberg; Pfaffenheim-Gueberschwihr; Ribeauvillé et Environs; Sigolsheim et Environs, Kaysersberg; Westhalten et Environs.

COTES DE TOUL & VINS DE MOSELLE

The Côtes de Toul covers about 100ha (250 acres) and has been recognized as an AOC zone since 31 March 1988. Although the region has a long viticultural tradition, it suffers all the climatic constraints of a northern vineyard, so other crops tend to be more important. The main grape is Gamay: there is some Pinot Noir, as well as Auxerrois Blanc and Pinot Blanc for a limited amount of white wine. Gris de Toul, a delicate pink wine made from Gamay, has a crisp acidity, while a sparkling wine (also Gamay), made by the classic method, has some yeasty fruit flavour. Pinot Noir makes a light red wine in warmer years.

Vins de Moselle is a tiny, struggling VDQS produced in the villages in the Moselle Valley near the city of Metz and towards the Luxembourg border. These are the most northerly vineyards of France, and the wines they produce have more in common with those of Luxembourg. The climate here makes growing conditions difficult; spring frost is often a problem and the grapes do not always ripen fully by harvest time. Müller-Thurgau (known here as Rivaner), Auxerrois and Pinot Noir are the main grape varieties in the Moselle.

Vin de Pays des Côtes de Meuse, from vineyards to the west of Metz, is very similar.

THE LOIRE

THE VINEYARDS OF THE LONG AND BEAUTIFUL LOIRE VALLEY OFFER
THE WINE LOVER JUST ABOUT EVERY TASTE AND COLOUR OF WINE
THAT THERE IS TO ENJOY.

The splendid château of Saumur dominates the town and the wide river. Both sparkling and still wines are made in the vineyards around the town, and many sparkling wine firms are based here.

The valley of the Loire is the most widespread of France's vineyard areas, producing dozens of wines with as many different characters. While it is possible to talk of the Loire as making light wines that demonstrate elegance and freshness but rarely power, any single descriptive phrase is sorely inadequate. There are dry, medium-dry and sweet white wines, dry and sweet rosés, reds that can be light and fresh or deep and intense, and a variety of sparkling wines. One of the main factors in the taste of the Loire's wines is the very variable northern climate. A cool year can produce acidic, short-lived wines; a warm summer and autumn can make rich, long-lasting ones. The other great variable is the grape variety. Many are grown, both traditional ones and more recently imported varieties from other regions of France.

France's longest river runs by gentle hills, green fields and vineyards, magnificent châteaux and fine, elegant cities. The rivers define the vineyards: the Loire itself, broad and slow-moving; the Cher, Indre, Allier and Vienne, with their own valleys and wine districts. Smaller tributaries such as the Aubance, Layon, Sèvre and Maine Nantaise create their own vineyard micro-climates and their own landscapes of narrow valleys scarred through the high, flat plateaux. The Loire rises in the southern mountains of the Massif Central. Here are tiny pockets of vineyard, relics of areas once much greater. It is not until it has covered almost half its course to the sea, and is about to take the huge left turn that changes it from flowing north to flowing west, that the first of the three main vineyard areas is reached. The Upper Loire vineyards of Sancerre and Pouilly both make the crisp, herbaceous white wines based on Sauvignon Blanc, whose taste has gone round the world. The second area is the vast tracts of Touraine and Anjou. Here are found a wide range of white wines, still and sparkling, and the Loire's main concentration of red wines. The last division, the Western Loire, is a complete contrast. Here one grape variety, the white Melon de Bourgogne, also called the Muscadet, reigns almost supreme: it produces crisp, sea-tangy white wines. The ocean is never far away, as seen in the higher rainfall of the Pays Nantais.

History of Loire wines

It is believed that even in Gaulish, and certainly in Roman, times there were vines in the Loire region. It is more definitely known that St Martin, who founded his abbey at Tours in AD372, caused the great propagation of the vine to take place — especially in the regions we now know as Anjou and Touraine.

The high point of Loire wines in history was the Renaissance, when the princely châteaux were built, each with its vineyard, and French gastronomy began to blossom amid the wealth and abundance of the Loire Valley. Vinegrowing existed along with market gardening and all kinds of fruits were cultivated. Paris was (and is) a major market for the Loire wines, but export trade also took place through the cities of Nantes and Angers, who were major importers of spices.

Vineyards in decline

Many winemaking areas (Orléans, for example) declined and were not replanted after the phylloxera crisis. There continue to be areas of the Loire where viticulture is in decline. Outlying regions, such as the Coteaux du Loir and Jasnières, each produce only around 15,000 cases a year. Other crops provide the farmers here with an easier income. By contrast, the heart of Loire winemaking seems to be prospering. The red wines of Saumur, Chinon and Bourgueil, the white wines of Vouvray, sparkling Saumur, Muscadet and above all Sancerre and Pouilly, are enjoying varying degrees of success. At the same time, other styles for which the Loire has been well-known — Rosé d'Anjou, for example — are losing their popularity as both the dry whites and reds gain.

Grape varieties and wine styles

Loire wines draw upon a range of local grape varieties and upon those of Bordeaux and Burgundy. Gamay, Pinot Noir and Chardonnay are found in the scattered vineyards at the top

The Le Mont vineyard at Vouvray, with the city of Tours in the distance.

end of the river, pointing to the proximity of Beaujolais and Burgundy. Further north, Sauvignon Blanc becomes dominant. This variety is indigenous to the Loire, as it is to Bordeaux. Burgundy contributes Pinot Noir to the Upper Loire vineyards, a reminder that Sancerre and Pouilly were once in the Duchy. Touraine and Anjou have the dominant Loire white variety, Chenin Blanc — a native vine that is the starting-point for a range of wine styles. Red grapes in the Central Loire include Cabernets Franc and Sauvignon, from Bordeaux.

Using these grapes, winemakers produce a spectrum of styles. The same producer may make red and white, still and sparkling wine. White wine production still enormously overshadows red. On average, red and rosé wines together might total 10 million cases a year; whites around 15 million.

Merchants and estates

The Loire is still a region of small-holdings. There are very few great wine estates, as in Bordeaux, and the tiny parcels of land are reminiscent of Burgundy. But while the Burgundian may have become rich through the renown of his wines, outside a few famous names, such as Sancerre, Muscadet, Pouilly-Fumé and Saumur-Champigny, skill is still meagrely rewarded for many producers in the Loire.

There are few winemaking co-operatives to provide the wine producers with an income. This has meant that the *négociants* are the real power in Loire wines. From bases in the Muscadet region, Saumur and Touraine, the merchants buy grapes (or more usually wine) from up and down the river, and make large quantities of generally innocuous blended wines — and sometimes downright bad ones. As prices are generally kept low by the merchants, producers tend to sell off *cuvées* which are of an inferior quality. This explains why a Sancerre bottled in the Nantes region often turns out to be disappointing. □

WINE REGIONS OF WESTERN AND CENTRAL LOIRE

The Loire is mapped here and on p244 (the Upper Loire). The western vineyards, sometimes called the Pays Nantais, cluster to the south of the city of Nantes. The central vineyards split into two groups: Anjou-Saumur around the old city of Angers and to the east, and Touraine centred on the city of Tours. Various outlying wine zones along tributary valleys survive to a greater or lesser extent.

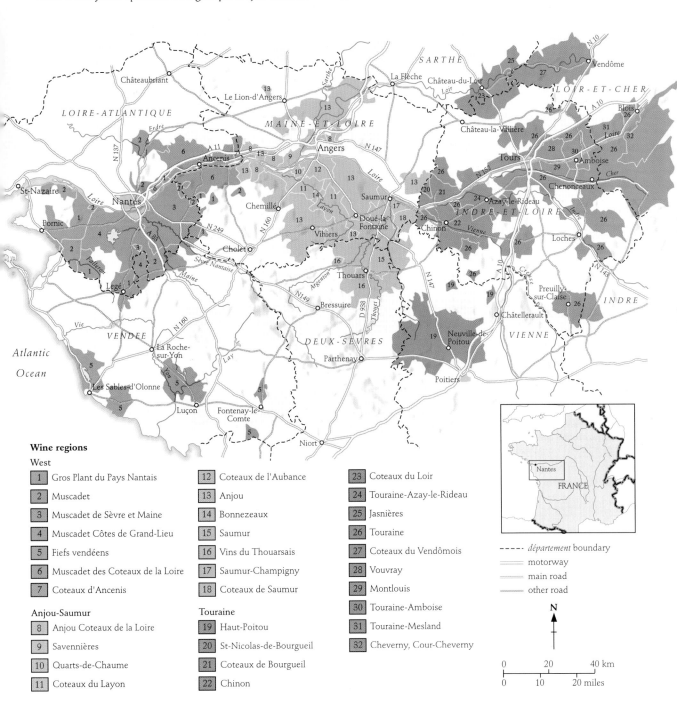

Wine regions

West

1. Gros Plant du Pays Nantais
2. Muscadet
3. Muscadet de Sèvre et Maine
4. Muscadet Côtes de Grand-Lieu
5. Fiefs vendéens
6. Muscadet des Coteaux de la Loire
7. Coteaux d'Ancenis

Anjou-Saumur

8. Anjou Coteaux de la Loire
9. Savennières
10. Quarts-de-Chaume
11. Coteaux du Layon

12. Coteaux de l'Aubance
13. Anjou
14. Bonnezeaux
15. Saumur
16. Vins du Thouarsais
17. Saumur-Champigny
18. Coteaux de Saumur

Touraine

19. Haut-Poitou
20. St-Nicolas-de-Bourgueil
21. Coteaux de Bourgueil
22. Chinon

23. Coteaux du Loir
24. Touraine-Azay-le-Rideau
25. Jasnières
26. Touraine
27. Coteaux du Vendômois
28. Vouvray
29. Montlouis
30. Touraine-Amboise
31. Touraine-Mesland
32. Cheverny, Cour-Cheverny

- - - - - *département* boundary
  ───── motorway
  ───── main road
  ───── other road

N

| 0 | | 20 | | 40 km |
| 0 | 10 | | 20 miles |

QUALITY FACTORS

The Loire vineyards are at the limits of reliable vine cultivation in France. It is because of the favourable micro-climates and drainage patterns created by the rivers that it is possible to practise successful viticulture at all. The shelter conferred by the valleys, the moderating effect of the water in the rivers, even the extra light reflected from their surface, combine to make the difference between marginal and practical vinegrowing. As a result, vintage variation, especially in red wines, is considerable.

	78	200	243	156
	76	193	232	153
	69	173	240	149
	66	175	227	151

N D J F | M A M | J J A S | O
DORMANT PERIOD | SPRING | SUMMER | HARVEST

LOIRE CLIMATE

Nantes
- temperature
- rainfall
- 100 hours of sunshine

Angers
- temperature
- rainfall
- 100 hours of sunshine

Vouvray
- temperature
- rainfall
- 100 hours of sunshine

Pouilly
- temperature
- rainfall
- 100 hours of sunshine

Climate

The chart above shows how the climate varies considerably from one end of the valley to the other, the main variable being the diminishing influence of the Atlantic.

This ocean influence moderates temperature in the west of the region. The Muscadet (Nantes) area also has good amounts of sun. Summer temperatures are highest at Pouilly, far inland, but Angers has the warmest harvest period.

In the spring, there is an ever-present risk of frost until the end of May, and excessive summer rainfall, especially in August and September, can cause rot in the vineyards.

Vintages

Vintages in the Loire can vary in size and quality more than in other parts of France, apart from Champagne.

At the end of the 1980s and the start of the 1990s the Loire, like other areas of France, enjoyed a succession

Cliffs of soft tufa rock at Vouvray, ideal for digging cellars.

of fabulous vintages. The years 1988, 1989 and 1990 all saw the production of richer reds, more luscious sweet whites and fuller, more concentrated dry whites than most *vignerons* had seen in their lifetimes. However, the frost of 1991 brought them back to reality, and the final crop was both small and of only average quality.

Geology and soils

There are four distinct geological regions. The Massif Central vineyards are on granite. Here site matters most: the few vineyards depend on privileged exposure to the south and east for their limited success.

The next, going downstream, is the chalk region of Sancerre and

Pouilly-sur-Loire. This is ideal land, like that of Champagne or Jerez in Spain, for producing white wines. Well-drained hills on both sides of the river offer a range of soils — chalky, clay, flinty — and the various slopes and valleys have their own micro-climates. The third section is by far the largest, comprising the whole of the central Loire Valley and its tributary rivers. Here the rock is a soft limestone called tufa: off-white in colour, volcanic in origin, soft enough for innumerable *caves* to be carved out of it for wine storage. The rivers have sliced through this soft rock, creating cliffs along both banks, and the vineyards are generally planted on the cliff tops, where the drainage is good. Fourth comes the schist soil that forms the plateau beneath the Pays Nantais. The small rivers of the area have cut deep into the plateau, forming well-drained slopes.

WESTERN LOIRE

The wines of the Pays Nantais in the Western Loire have one of the simplest images among French wines. Muscadet and Gros Plant are the wine names, and the tastes are inimitable: crisp, young, fresh white wines that are perfect partners for Atlantic seafood or quaffable thirst-quenchers. These versatile wines have since the 1970s made the fortune of many growers in this region of densely planted vineyards and soft, lightly rolling countryside.

The Muscadet appellations

The wine rules of the region are the least complex of any on the Loire. The largest *appellation* is for Muscadet, which comes in four guises: simple Muscadet (2,200ha/5,400 acres), Muscadet des Coteaux de la Loire (330ha/815 acres), Muscadet Côtes de Grand-Lieu (400ha/990 acres) and Muscadet de Sèvre-et-Maine (11,000ha/27,200 acres). Simple Muscadet is produced mainly in the west of the region, and in comparatively small quantities; on the whole the wine is as simple as the *appellation*. Muscadet des Coteaux de la Loire is from the northern bank of the Loire, between the large port-city of Nantes and Ancenis. Muscadet Côtes de Grand-Lieu comes from the area west of the Nantes-La Roche-sur-Yon road. Muscadet de Sèvre et Maine is from the land around the rivers Sèvre and Maine that lies south and east of Nantes, on the southern bank of the Loire. This is one of the densest vineyard areas in France, with very little in the way of other crops produced. Small villages and towns — the principal wine towns are Vallet, Clisson and La Haie-Fouassière — are dominated by huge churches, which testify to a long tradition of prosperity. There are 23 communes in the *appellation*, producing around 5.5 million cases of wine a year.

Bijou the horse at work near Clisson.

Muscadet was for centuries just a local wine, or was shipped to the Netherlands for distillation. But since the 1970s it has become the epitome of the easy-to-drink dry white wines that have swept the world.

Making Muscadet

The qualities of Muscadet that most captured the imagination of the wine-drinking public were its freshness, crispness and the slight hint of bubbles when it was drunk. These qualities are captured best when the wine is bottled *sur lie* (straight from the cask without first racking it off its lees) in the cellars in which it is made.

A recent trend in Muscadet is to produce prestige *cuvées*, sometimes top blends from the growers, or wines from a single domaine. While they are certainly better than some of the basic Muscadet, the obvious question is whether a wine that is essentially so uncomplicated should be produced in such an expensive way. Part of the answer is that most

vineyards have increased their yields: more than 100hl/ha in the 1980s. On top of this, the area under cultivation has been expanded from 11,000 to 15,000ha (27,000 to 37,000 acres) within a few years. Years with too much sun have produced Muscadets which are less acidic and the quality has suffered from high yields. All these factors explain why some producers wish to stress the characteristics of their own wine.

Other wines

The success of Muscadet has submerged the other wines of the Western Loire. Coteaux d'Ancenis VDQS (300ha/740 acres) comes from both sides of the Loire around Ancenis, an area also covered by the Muscadet des Coteaux de la Loire AOC. Red, rosé and white are allowed, but most wine is red, made from Gamay or Cabernet (Franc or Sauvignon) grapes.

Gros Plant (2,700ha/6,670 acres) is another VDQS, a white made from Folle Blanche, the cognac grape. The wine is very acidic; it is good with local food, if the vintage has been a warm one. The Gros Plant area is broadly the same as that of Muscadet.

The Fiefs Vendéens VDQS (380ha/940 acres), from a separate area south-west of the Loire, produces red wine from Gamay and Pinot Noir (at least 50%) plus one or both Cabernets. There is also some white wine.

Haut Poitou is a VDQS zone to the south, an island of vines where the local cooperative has led the way to export markets with red, white and rosé wine. Grapes are Gamay, Cabernets Franc and Sauvignon, Sauvignon Blanc and Chardonnay. Most of these wines are richly flavoured varietal wines with an emphasis on fruit.   ☐

MUSCADET PRODUCERS

The Muscadet country is one of individual growers rather than cooperatives, and *négociants* are the dominant force. Some of the best of them, and the individual estates, are listed below.

Gautier Audas

The firm of Gautier Audas in Haute-Goulaine sells wine exclusively from selected domaines, of which Hautes-Perrières is the most famous. Their other estates include Domaine de Goulaine, Domaine des Claircomtes in Le Pallet, Domaine de l'Ebaupin and Domaine de l'Ecomandière. There is also a *négociant* side to the business.

Donatien Bahuaud

The historic Château de la Cassemichère is owned by the Bahuaud family. Wine is still produced here, and bottled, *sur lie*, at the château, while this firm of growers and *négociants* also has cellars in the village of La Chapelle-Heulin. Its most famous Muscadet is Le Master de Donatien, a wine from growers selected each year at tastings.

Domaine de Beauregard

Henri Grégoire is reputed for good winemaking and sound management. His straightforward Muscadet de Sèvre et Maine, bottled *sur lie*, is very good value for money. He also makes an unusual red wine from Gamay, sold at an attractive price.

Guy Bossard

Guy Bossard went organic in the 1970s — a brave move in an area that suffers from damp weather and is traditionally devoted to high yields. The quality of his wines and their reputation today suggests his decision was right. He owns 17ha (42 acres) of vineyards in the village of Le Louroux-Bottereau. His estate wine is Domaine de l'Ecu and his top *cuvée* is Hermine d'Or. He also makes Gros Plant and a sparkling Muscadet.

Henri et Laurent Bouchaud

The Bouchauds' 13-ha (32-acre) Domaine du Bois-Joly in Le Pallet produces classic Muscadets, with all the requisite lightness and freshness. Gros Plant and a red Vin de Pays du Jardin de la France made from Cabernet Franc are also produced.

Claude Branger

On his 14.5ha (35 acres), Claude Branger makes soft yet crisp Muscadet Domaine La Haute Févrie, which has won him many awards, and a little Gros Plant. His top *cuvée*, Excellence, is, unusually for Muscadet, worth ageing.

Robert Brousseau

The 9-ha (22-acre) Domaine des Mortiers-Gobin lies near the wooded banks of the Sèvre in La Haie-Fouassière. This is an old estate which has been in the Brousseau family's hands for generations. Methods are still traditional, includ-

The château at Clisson broods over the little River Sèvre.

ing some wood maturation, which produces wines that can age.

Chéreau-Carré

One of the biggest landowners in Muscadet, Chéreau-Carré has 120ha (297 acres) divided among various family members, including the Ch de Chasseloir, which is the largest estate and the heart of the entire operation; Ch du Coing, Moulin de la Gravelle and Ch de l'Oiselinière. All wines are bottled *sur lie* at the individual properties. These estates were pioneers of wood fermentation and ageing for Muscadet, producing a wine that could easily be mistaken for one from Bordeaux.

Bruno Cormerais

An energetic grower who, along with his wife Marie-Françoise, produces a number of wines from his 20-ha (49-acre) estate: Muscadet de Sèvre et Maine, Gros Plant and a Gamay Vin de Pays des Marches de Bretagne are among them. His Muscadet comes in a number of *cuvées*: Domaine Bruno Cormerais, Domaine de la Chambaudière and Cuvée Prestige.

Domaine des Dorices

The curious neo-Norman castle on this estate was built by the Marquis de Rochechouart at the turn of the last century to replace a much older mansion. The whole estate now belongs to the Boullault family, who produce a Muscadet designed for ageing, Domaine des Dorices, from 31ha (76 acres) of vines. They also make a lighter, younger wine, Ch la Touche, as well as Gros Plant and a sparkling white, Leconte.

Domaine Gadais Père & Fils

This 32-ha (79-acre) estate at St-Fiacre produces Muscadets de Sèvre-et-Maine which are excellent value for money. The wines are fine and have a lot of character. A good Gros Plant is sold at a very modest price.

Ch de la Galissonnière

Records of the château go back to the 14th century, but the name actually derives from an 18th-century French admiral. Today the vineyard, now owned by the Lusseaud family, covers 30ha (74 acres). Two *cuvées* are produced: Cuvée Philippe and Cuvée Anne, named after members of the family. A Gros Plant is called Cuvée Valerie. The Lusseauds also own another property, Ch de la Jannière.

Marquis de Goulaine

The estate of the Marquis de Goulaine is among the most famous in Muscadet. Situated in the village of Haute-Goulaine, the Ch de Goulaine was founded over 1,000 years ago. The crop from the 31-ha (76-acre) vineyard is topped up with bought-in wine. Around one-third of the wine is bottled *sur lie*, and there is a prestige Cuvée du Millénaire. Gros Plant is also made.

Domaine Pierre de la Grange

The Luneaus have been growers for seven generations. Pierre Luneau-Papin makes Muscadets at his Landreau estate and outstanding Gros Plants at Domaine de St-Méen.

Domaine "R" de la Grange

Rémy Luneau makes a top range Muscadet de Sèvre et Maine, bottled *sur lie*, which is called Le Grand "R" de la Grange.

Guilbaud Frères-Moulin

Growers and *négociants* owning three estates, Domaine de la Moutonnière, Clos du Pont and Domaine de la Pingossière, for 30ha (74 acres) of vineyards in total. They make a number of prestige *cuvées* including Le Soleil Nantais, a blend from different growers, and Les Hermines, with its specially-embossed bottle.

Domaine de la Louvetrie

At his 26-ha (64-acre) estate, Joseph Landron distinguishes several *terroirs*, each producing a different kind of Muscadet de Sèvre et Maine, which then ages according to its own rythm. Nowadays Bernard Landron works alongside his brother. He has brought in Clos du Château La Carizière, an addition to Amphibolite and Fief du Breuil.

Ch de la Mercredière

This 36-ha (89-acre) vineyard, on the banks of the River Sèvre, surrounds a 14th-century château, a site that was occupied in Roman times. It is now the property of the Futeul family, who also work as *négociants*. Their Muscadets are full and powerful.

Louis Métaireau

In a brilliant move that began the trend towards top-quality Muscadet over 30 years ago, and to stand up against the power of the *négociants*, Louis Métaireau gathered together a group of producers — first three, now nine with 100ha (247 acres) between them — who market their wines under the Métaireau label.

The wines undergo rigorous tastings during vinification and before bottling (carried out *sur lie* at the growers' cellars), and growers have been known to reject their own wines on such occasions.

Métaireau's own estate is Domaine du Grand Mouton.

Ch la Noë

The Comte de Malestroit, whose 17th-century château this is, is a novelist and chronicler of the Pays Nantais. He runs about half the 65ha (160 acres) of vines himself, while the rest is organized on a traditional share-cropping basis, in which growers pay rent in kind. Curiously, considering this is an estate rather than a *négociant* business, the wine is not bottled *sur lie*.

Ch de la Preuille

The Dumortiers at Château de la Preuille — a handsome building — are growing vines on a *terroir* whose soil is composed of porphyric granite with two micas. Their wines, bottled *sur lie*, are dense and age well. There is also a noteworthy Gros Plant (*sur lie*).

Ch de la Ragotière

Gros Plant as well as Muscadet are produced on this 29-ha (72-acre) vineyard surrounding the old château with its 14th-century chapel. The Couillaud family, which owns the estate, makes a young, fresh style of wine.

Gaston Rolandeau

This traditional *négociant*, based just outside the Sèvre et Maine area at Tillières, concentrates on Muscadet. The standard range includes Cave de la Frémonderie, a wine that ages surprisingly well, and a prestige *cuvée* called Signature de la Loire that appears in a Bouteille Nantaise (certifying that it has passed two tasting panels).

Marcel Sautejeau

The firm is based at Domaine de l'Hyvernière, near Le Pallet, and this estate, along with Domaine de la Botinière at Vallet, is the source of its Muscadet. Its turnover of more than 1 million cases a year includes wines from Anjou, Saumur and Vouvray.

Sauvion

One of the most dynamic *négociant* firms in the region, Sauvion has aimed to develop the quality end of the market for Muscadet. Based at the historic Château du Cléray in Vallet, this company markets a number of different brands, including Sauvion du Cléray, Cardinal Richard and Carte d'Or.

Despite buying 80% of its grapes from growers, it has no regular contracts, preferring to base its purchases on tastings, and paying premiums accordingly. Some of these wines are then sold as individual *cuvées*, which are known as Découvertes.

Les Vignerons de la Noëlle

Founded in the mid-1950s, this is one of the biggest cooperatives in the Loire, and the only one for wine in the Pays Nantais (although it also deals in other fruit products). It is based at Ancenis. It makes Coteaux d'Ancenis (red, rosé and white), Muscadet des Coteaux de Loire and *vin de pays* as well as Muscadet.

The cooperative also produces an excellent Gros Plant, which is well balanced and a very good example of the type. Its wines are widely distributed under many labels, including Domaine des Hautes Noëlles for Muscadet.

CENTRAL LOIRE

The ancient provinces of Anjou and Touraine possess some of the most beautiful landscapes of France. It is a land in which nature and man have worked in harmony over the centuries. Royal forests cover the hillsides above the rivers, and the white tufa stone has been used to fashion picture-book villages and fairy-tale châteaux.

The wines from the two provinces are as varied as any found in France. The pattern clears a little if Anjou and Saumur are treated as one unit, and Touraine, to the east, as another. Anjou and Touraine each have a general *appellation* with several others, for specialized wines and/or places, within them.

The wines of Anjou and Saumur
There are almost as many *appellations* and certainly more different wine styles found within a few kilometres of Angers, the capital of Anjou, than in the whole wine region of Bordeaux. It is helpful to identify two distinct enclaves or sub-zones: the white wine district around the River Layon, and the red and sparkling wine district around Saumur (*see* map, p233).

The wines vary from the lusciously sweet whites of Quarts-de-Chaume and Bonnezeaux in the Layon Valley, to the driest possible white wine of Savennières, literally just across the river.

At the other end of the province, on the boundary with Touraine, the wines of the Saumur district have quite a different character. This is most notably an area of crisp, sparkling white wines. These are, however, produced alongside Saumur-Champigny, one of the most fashionable light red wines in France today. This abundance of *appellations* means that for many Anjou producers there is no question of making

Cabernet Franc vines near Chinon make one of the Loire's best red wines.

just one wine. With small parcels of land in neighbouring *appellations*, they can make up to half a dozen different wines, using different names, following different rules, and often with wildly differing results in terms of quality.

The wines of Touraine
Touraine is a little less wholesale in its scattering of *appellations*, which helpfully occur in two pairs, north and south of the river. There are the red wine *appellations* of Chinon and Bourgueil, where the Cabernet Franc grape reaches a quality of expression it seldom finds outside St-Emilion in Bordeaux. On the other, eastern, side of the city of Tours, the Chenin Blanc reaches what many would regard as its apogee in the long-lived white wines of Vouvray and Montlouis.

Surrounding these classic *appellations* is the wider AOC of Touraine, with its associated villages of Mesland, Azay-le-Rideau and Amboise. To the east, as Touraine merges into the Berry region of France, are two developing wine areas: Cheverny et Cour-Cheverny, newly promoted to AOC, and Valençay (*see* map, p244).

Other wines
On the fringes of these major wine *appellations* are a host of lesser names, some in almost terminal decline through lack of local interest, market conditions and notoriously unreliable weather. It would be sad if they disappeared, but the future of the AOCs of the Coteaux de l'Aubance in Anjou, Jasnières in Touraine, and VDQS such as Coteaux du Vendômois, must hang in the balance.   □

APPELLATIONS

The Central Loire region has a wide range of *appellations*, which can be grouped under the headings Anjou and Saumur for the western half of the area, and Touraine for the eastern half.

THE APPELLATIONS OF ANJOU AND SAUMUR
Anjou
This is the general provincial *appellation* for wines that are not covered by one of the more specific AOCs described below. Reds and dry whites are the most commonly produced wines under the general *appellation*. Light reds (Anjou Gamay) and sparkling wines (Anjou *mousseux* and *pétillant*) have separate *appellations*.

Anjou Coteaux de la Loire
A small AOC area near Angers, producing dry and medium-sweet white wines from Chenin Blanc grapes.

Anjou Villages
An *appellation* for the red Cabernet wines of 46 communes south-east of Angers, which are of higher quality than basic Anjou Rouge.

Bonnezeaux
High-class sweet white wines from a village at the southern end of the Coteaux du Layon.

Cabernet d'Anjou and Cabernet de Saumur
Rosé wines made from Cabernet grapes (Franc and Sauvignon). Better than Rosé d'Anjou; can be sweet or dry.

Coteaux de l'Aubance
Medium-sweet to sweet white wines from Chenin Blanc, made by a few producers in the Anjou Villages area.

Coteaux du Layon
Sweet white wines made from Chenin Blanc in the Layon Valley. Certain villages can add their name after the general *appellation* on the label.

Quarts-de-Chaume
A small enclave within the Coteaux du Layon, making particularly luscious sweet white wines.

Rosé d'Anjou
Slightly sweet, pale pink wines made from Groslot grapes. In terms of production, this is still the most important of Anjou's *appellations*, but the wines are losing popularity.

Rosé de Loire
Dry rosé wines, made with at least 30% Cabernet grapes, which can be made throughout the Loire Valley.

Saumur
Red and white still wines from Cabernet and Chenin Blanc grapes, made in 36 communes around the town of Saumur.

Saumur-Champigny
Red Cabernet wines from nine communes near St-Cyr-en-Bourg, east of Saumur.

Saumur Mousseux
Sparkling white wines, fermented in the bottle, made in cellars (often rock caves) around Saumur.

Savennières
Bone-dry white wines from Chenin Blanc, made on the north bank of the Loire. There are two associated high-quality single-vineyard *appellations*: Coulée-de-Serrant and Roche-aux-Moines.

THE APPELLATIONS OF TOURAINE
Bourgueil and St-Nicolas-de-Bourgueil
Red-wine region centred on the town of Bourgueil, on the north bank of the Loire. The grape is Cabernet Franc. The village of St-Nicolas-de-Bourgueil has its own *appellation*, also for red wines.

Cheverny and Cour-Cheverny
This former VDQS zone was promoted to AOC in 1993. Cheverny can be white, red or rosé from Chenin Blanc, Sauvignon, Chardonnay, Gamay, Cabernet Franc, Pinot Noir or Cot. Cour-Cheverny is a characteristic acidic white wine made from the local Romorantin grape.

Chinon
On the south bank of the Loire, opposite Bourgueil, this larger red-wine area is centred on the town of Chinon and the River Vienne. Chinon is at the heart of the area under Cabernet Franc cultivation.

Coteaux du Loir
Red, dry white and rosé wines grown about 40km (25 miles) north of Tours. Today, only 20ha (49 acres) are under vine.

Coteaux du Vendômois
A VDQS zone to either side of the Loir River, making red, white and rosé wines. Production, around 50,000 cases, is almost all consumed locally.

Crémant de Loire
Sparkling white or rosé wine which can be made throughout the Loire Valley, but a high proportion of production is in Touraine. Controls are stricter than for sparkling Saumur.

Jasnières
Small *appellation* for dry white wines (from Chenin Blanc) within the larger Coteaux du Loir *appellation* on the Loir River.

Montlouis
Still wines ranging from medium-dry to sweet, made around the town of Montlouis, east of Tours. Rather in the shadow of Vouvray across the river. Montlouis *pétillant* and *mousseux* are the sparkling versions.

Vins du Thouarsais
A small VDQS zone around the town of Thouars in the Deux-Sèvres *département*, south of Anjou. Red and rosé wines are made from both Cabernets or Gamay, whites from Chenin Blanc.

Touraine
Large *appellation* for white (still or sparkling), red and rosé wines made in a region south of Tours. Some grapes — Sauvignon (for white wines) and Gamay (for reds) — have their own varietal *appellations*.

Touraine Villages
Touraine-Amboise, Touraine-Azay-le-Rideau and Touraine Mesland are the three village *appellations*, all producing better versions of standard Touraine AOC wines.

Valençay
A new AOC zone covering mainly red and rosé wines, with some whites, from around Valençay in the Indre *département*. Whites are made from Menu Pineau (also known as Arbois), Sauvignon Blanc, Chardonnay, Chenin Blanc and Romorantin. Reds and rosés are made from Cabernets Sauvignon and Franc, Gamay and Pineau d'Aunis (a Loire original, also known as Chenin Noir). The wines are not usually found outside the area.

Vouvray
Area centred on the village of Vouvray, east of Tours, on the north bank of the Loire, making high-quality dry to sweet white still wines and (mostly dry) sparkling wines.

PRODUCERS

Producers in both Anjou and Touraine make wines under more than one *appellation*. For example, some in Anjou make Anjou Villages reds, Savennières and Anjou dry whites, and sweet whites from Coteaux du Layon. Where this arises, producers are listed under the *appellation* in which they are based. However, the distinction between Anjou and Saumur on the one hand, and Touraine on the other remains quite clear.

ANJOU
Aubert Frères
One of the largest *négociants* in the Loire Valley, whose interests range from Sancerre in the east to Muscadet in the west. Its Les Hardières estates at St-Lambert-du-Lattay produce Anjou reds and whites, while its Domaine du Mirleau makes Anjou Gamay.

Domaine des Baumard
A family-owned firm, based in the village of Rochefort-sur-Loire, with vineyards in Coteaux du Layon, Quarts-de-Chaume and Savennières. Jean Baumard has handed over to his son Laurent, who has introduced some new ideas. The firm's wines are always beautifully crafted, with a wide appeal. Clos de Ste-Catherine, a medium-dry Coteaux du Layon, and Clos du Papillon in Savennières are good examples of how Chenin Blanc can be attractive young as well as when mature.

Ch du Breuil
From their 36ha (89 acres) in the Layon Valley, Marc and Chantal Morgat make fine sweet Coteaux du Layon-Beaulieu, red and white Anjou, red Anjou Villages, sparkling Crémant de Loire and Vin de Pays du Jardin de la France (red and white). The sweet wines, especially in recent years, have shown astonishing depth and richness, while the dry wines benefit from modern wine-making techniques.

Domaine du Closel
From this vineyard are produced several precise and typical Savennières, particularly Clos du Papillon, the flagship of the range.

Clos de la Coulée de Serrant
Nicolas Joly has achieved some notoriety for his combination of biodynamic farming techniques and a belief in magic and astrology. This might be seen as mere eccentricity were it not for the fact that his Coulée de Serrant, from a single-vineyard *appellation* in Savennières, is a great wine by any standards. The steep vineyard is worked by horse-power. These are wines designed for an immense life.

Ch de Fesles
Formerly owned by Jacques Boivin and later by the famous *pâtissier* Gaston Lenôtre, Château de Fesles has been acquired by the talented Bernard Germain. Its 35-ha (86-acre) vineyard, of which 17ha (42 acres) are planted with red grape varieties, produces the best Bonnezeaux, a rich and fine sweet wine. Bernard Germain's Anjou Villages reds are excellent.

Jacques Lalanne
The largest proprietor in the Quarts-de-Chaume *appellation*, Jacques Lalanne, whose estate is called Ch de Belle Rive, is clearly dedicated to quality without regard to expense. Yields are low, and only botrytized grapes go into the wine, which is fermented in wood during the winter before bottling, which normally takes place in April or May. These wines repay ageing, although they are also attractive in their first year.

Domaine René-Noël Legrand
Curnonsky, a native of the region, patronized this estate, which nowadays has a vineyard of some 15ha (37 acres). René-Noël Legrand makes four different kinds of Saumur-Champigny, all of them delicate and built in a subtle way.

Domaine Ogereau
This 24-ha (59-acre) estate at St-Lambert-du-Lattay is planted with equal portions of red and white grape varieties, allowing Vincent Ogereau to fully develop his gifts as a winemaker. His St-Lambert Coteaux-du-Layon — all botrytized and perfectly aged, often in new oak — are models of their kind.

Hervé Papin
One of the few producers of Coteaux de l'Aubance, from 20ha (50 acres) of vines, Maxime and Hervé Papin's wines suggest that this is an unjustly neglected *appellation*.

Their wines, not only from great years such as 1989 and 1990, but also from 1991, a lesser year, exhibit fine character. They also make red Anjou wines from the Cabernet Franc grape.

René Renou
One of the great advocates of the wines of the Layon Valley, but above all director of the Institut National des Appellations d'Origine (INAO), René Renou makes Bonnezeaux and red wines from 18ha (44 acres) in Thouarcé.

Domaine de Ste-Anne
A 48-ha (118-acre) estate in St-Saturnin from which the Brault family makes red and white Anjou from Chenin, Anjou Villages from Cabernet Franc, and a little sweet Coteaux de l'Aubance.

Domaine Pierre Soulez
At his Ch de Chamboureau estate, Pierre Soulez produces dense, concentrated Savennières and (dry and sweet) Savennières Roches-aux-Moines. His brother Yves has left Chamboureau for St-Aubin-de-Luigné, where he makes interesting Coteaux-du-Layon.

Les Vins Touchais
A large *négociant* and domaine business based at Doué-la-Fontaine. It has amassed large stocks of sweet Layon wines, which, perversely, it sells as Anjou Blanc Moulin Touchais, rather than Coteaux du Layon. These wines can be extraordinary, and show the ageing ability of Chenin Blanc. However, most of the business is in straightforward reds and rosés, which lack the high quality of the sweet wines.

SAUMUR
Ackerman-Laurance
This was the first firm to make sparkling Saumur, in 1811, when Jean Ackerman returned from working in Champagne and realized that the local wines were suitable for the same method. Linked today with the larger firm of Remy-

Pannier, it makes a full range of sparkling Saumur, and a Crémant de Loire (rosé, white).

Bouvet-Ladubay

Without doubt the most enterprising and innovative of the sparkling Saumur houses, Bouvet-Ladubay is headed by Armand Monmousseau, of the well-known Touraine wine-making family, although it is owned by Taittinger Champagne. The range includes two top *cuvées* (both white) — Saphir and Trésor, which includes a high proportion of Chardonnay grapes and is partly fermented in wood.

Ch de Chaintré

This charming 16th-century house with a walled vineyard is in the Saumur-Champigny AOC area. Bernard de Tigny's wine is sometimes (especially in better years) on the heavy side for Saumur-Champigny and needs time to mature. Fermentation is in tank, with some ageing in wood. He also makes a little Saumur Blanc.

Paul Filliatreau

The largest producer of red Saumur-Champigny wines, Filliatreau makes one called Jeunes Vignes from young vines (that is, under 50 years old); a Vieilles Vignes; and a special *cuvée*, Lena Filliatreau, which comes from old vines on silex soil. He also makes Saumur Blanc.

Gratien Meyer Seydoux

One of the largest producers of sparkling Saumur, and the only one to have been founded by a Champagne house, Alfred Gratien, rather than linked more recently through mergers. Its top *cuvée*, Cuvée Flamme (rosé, white), is a blend of old wines, and is usually given some bottle-age before release.

Langlois-Château

Owned by Champagne Boll-

inger, Langlois-Château makes still Saumur and Crémant de Loire (rosé, white), but very little sparkling Saumur. The switch to production of Crémant was made because of the stricter AOC rules behind this wine, and the greater range of grape varieties permitted. The Crémant de Loire brut is made from Chenin Blanc, Grolleau, Cabernet Franc and Chardonnay, while the rosé is made from Cabernet Franc and Cabernet Sauvignon.

Château du Hureau
Philippe Vatan

That Philippe Vatan is making one of the best wines in Saumur-Champigny — as well as a memorable Saumur Blanc — says a lot for his dedication. From huge cellars in the cliffside he produces a standard Saumur-Champigny, a Vieilles Vignes and also a rare sweet white Saumur Moelleux.

Ch de Villeneuve

This estate has 22ha (65 acres) of Cabernet Franc and 6ha (15 acres) of Chenin Blanc. The Saumur-Champigny Vieilles Vignes is a perfect example of white Saumur and Les Corniers gratifies Chenin lovers.

BOURGUEIL AND CHINON
Yannick Amirault

Within a few years Yannick Amirault has become one of the most highly esteemed winemakers in Bourgueil. The intense fruity flavour of his wines is bolstered by supple and abundant tannins.

This fine quality is due to perfectly mature grapes. The St-Nicolas-du-Bourgueil is outstanding, too.

Bernard Baudry

With his experiments with wood and the separation of his wines according to soil type, Bernard Baudry is a serious producer of Chinon. His wines emphasize fruit balanced with wood, and have an ability to age. He has 25ha (62 acres) of vines at Cravant-les-Coteaux, east of Chinon.

Couly-Dutheil

This is the largest producer of Chinon wines actually based in Chinon. It has 65ha (160 acres) of vines, and grapes are bought in from local growers. The top wine is Clos de l'Echo, from a single vineyard that used to belong to Rabelais and is just behind the château.

Pierre-Jacques Druet

The most innovative of Bourgueil producers, who brought his Bordeaux training and attitude to red wines to the Loire. His wines are designed for ageing, but can also be drunk young, as the fruit is so prominent. He makes different *cuvées* from different portions of his vineyard — all of which are on the superior Coteaux zone of Bourgueil. The best is Vaumoreau, and the others — also very good — are Beauvais and Grand-Mont.

Ch de la Grille

This showpiece 60-ha (148-acre) estate above the town of Chinon is owned by Champagne Gosset. A mix of new and old wood is used for maturing, and the result is a red wine that ages well, with a serious balance between fruit, ripe tannins and acidity.

Charles Joguet

Charles Joguet has retired from business, but the estate contin-

ues to bear his name. The vineyards at Sazilly are some of the few on the north-facing slopes south of the River Vienne. From this jewel are made several *cuvées* from different parts of his vineyard: Jeunes Vignes comes from vines less than 10 years old, Clos de la Cure is from vines near the church of Sazilly, then there are Varennes du Grand Clos and Clos de Chêne Vert, and the finest, Clos de la Dioterie, which receives considerable wood-ageing.

Les Caves des Vins de Rabelais

A group of over 100 Chinon producers, some of whose wines go into special *cuvées* such as the garishly-labelled but well-made Cuvée Jeanne d'Arc. The group was founded to help smaller producers survive and struggle against the power of the *négociants*.

Jean-Maurice Raffault

A producer whose wines, when mature, can achieve all the truffle and violet flavours that make Chinon so attractive. He makes a range of *crus* from different parts of his 30-ha (54-acre) vineyard, as well as working with the Caves des Vins de Rabelais *(qv)*.

Joël Taluau

As president of the growers of St-Nicolas, Joël Taluau is an important man in this small *appellation*. His Domaine de Chevrette, 15ha (37 acres) in total, produces a Cuvée de Domaine and a Vieilles Vignes from 40-year old vines.

TOURAINE
Pierre Chainier

This firm was formerly a combination of *négociant* and vineyard-owner, selling wines from the length of the Loire. Since 1991, the business has been reorganized and now produces wines exclusively from its own 200-ha (500-acre) estate and from neighbouring areas in Touraine. Its domaine wines in particular exhibit good *appellation* character.

Ch de Chenonceau

It is appropriate that the Loire Valley's most beautiful château should produce wine, although it is one of the few of the great Touraine châteaux to do so. From a 12-ha (30-acre) vineyard on higher ground away from the river, it makes wines with the AOC of Touraine, including dry and medium-dry whites; reds and a sparkling wine.

Domaine de la Gabillière

The experimental wine school in Amboise makes commercial quantities of wines of high quality from its 16ha (40 acres) of vineyards. Notable are a concentrated Sauvignon Blanc and a sparkling Crémant de Loire (white).

Joël Gigou

One of a handful of growers in the tiny *appellation* of Jasnières within the Coteaux du Loir, Joël Gigou has vines near the hamlet of Lhomme. He makes mostly dry whites from Chenin Blanc grapes and, in rare good years, there is also a little *demi-sec*.

Domaine Henry Marionnet

This estate is also known as Domaine de la Charmoise. With 40ha (99 acres) planted with the Gamay grape and 20ha (49 acres) with Sauvignon Blanc, Henry Marionnet is one of the large producers. His Touraine Primeur is the best in this region. This lucky grower was able to buy up France's oldest vines, which could be found right next to his estate. These vine stocks date back to the period before phylloxera and are 120 to 150 years old. The very rare wine they produce is called Vinifera.

J M Monmousseau

Now owned by the Brédut family, the Monmousseau firm is famous for its sparkling Touraine white, Brut de Mosny, made in large tufa caves at Montrichard. It also makes Vouvray wines from its own estates, and acts as a *négociant*.

La Confrérie des Vignerons de Oisly et Thésée

With 52 members and 275ha (680 acres) of vines, this is a large cooperative for the Loire. It is also extremely good, making a high-quality range of Touraine wines. A high-tech modern winery has been improved and adapted over recent years.

The brand name Baronnie d'Aignan is used for red or white blends, while, for the time being at least, the varietal wines carry the name of the variety. The white Sauvignon de Touraine has been particularly successful in recent years.

Jacky Preys

A large estate of 55ha (136 acres), producing reds from Gamay and Cabernet Franc, including a single-vineyard Gamay wine, Domaine du Bas Gueret, and a wood-aged blend, bearing the name Cuvée Royale. The latter is made of 50% Gamay, 25% Cabernet Franc and 25% Pinot Noir. The estate also produces a small amount of white Valençay.

Philippe Tessier

An important player in the relatively small scene of Cheverny, this domaine has been run by the family for three generations. It makes red and white wines — the whites better than the reds — with a particularly soft spot for the local Romorantin grape, which here produces a crisp, rather than piercingly acidic, white wine.

VOUVRAY AND MONTLOUIS

Berger Frères

A family holding of 20ha (50 acres) located in St-Martin-le-Beau provides all the grapes for the Montlouis wines. Half the production is sparkling wine, the rest still, which in good years can range from a dry to a luscious botrytized *moelleux*.

Domaine Bourillon d'Orléans

Frederic Bourillon, owner of 15ha (37 acres) of vines, is one of the driving forces behind this group of young producers in Vouvray who are doing much to restore the area's reputation. His wines highlight fruit rather than the high acidity that is often dominant in Chenin-based wines. His sweet wines are aged in wood, but he uses both tanks and wood for his dry wines.

Philippe Brisebarre

It is only in exceptional years — such as the classic 1989 and 1990 — that Philippe Brisebarre makes *moelleux* Vouvrays. Normally he makes only one wine, which may be dry or medium-dry, depending on the grape harvest. He also makes a sparkling white wine by the *méthode traditionnelle*, which ages well.

Deletang Père et Fils

A 20-ha (50-acre) vineyard around St-Martin-le-Beau is the source of grapes for this Montlouis business. It specializes in a number of sweeter wines, from different *crus* — including Les Bâtisses and Petits-Boulay — as well as blends to make a domaine wine.

The Deletang cellars are lined with ancient bottles gathering cobwebs, but vinification techniques here are modern. The firm also makes sparkling wines and Touraine AOC reds and whites.

Gaston Huet

The most famous and well-respected name in Vouvray, Gaston Huet wines have maintained high standards, with winemaking now controlled by M Huet's son-in-law, Noël Pinguet. The Le Mont property has been recognized as a top Vouvray since the 1600s. Wines from here, together with those from another property, Le Haut-Lieu, and the third vineyard, Clos du Bourg, are each vinified and sold separately. Huet makes sparkling and sweet wines with only a little still dry wine.

Ch Moncontour

A huge 108-ha (267-acre) vineyard at Rochecorbon, owned since 1989 by the Brédut family. The rise of this estate has boosted the confidence of producers in Vouvray, showing that it is possible to make significant quantities of fine estate wine in a region that has been dominated by *négociants*. The *sec* and *demi-sec* sparkling wines have achieved considerable success. Small quantities of Touraine AOC wines are also made.

Clos Naudin

The Foreau family owns 12ha (30 acres) of vineyard, all on the high ground above the village, and makes the usual range of Vouvray wines — from sparkling through all sweetness levels of still wine.

Prince Poniatowski

Prince Philippe Poniatowski's great-great-uncle was the last king of Poland. The family has owned Le Clos Baudoin since 1910. The house is built half into the tufa cliffs, with the 22-ha (54-acre) vineyard on the plateau above. This is the place for traditional Vouvray, with emphasis on dry and sparkling wines, sold under the name of Aigle d'Or, and with sweet wines made only in exceptional years.

UPPER LOIRE

A s the Loire reaches the halfway mark on its journey to the sea, it makes a huge 90° turn at the city of Orléans, changing direction from south–north to east–west. A short distance upstream of this bend, out-crops of chalk hills, higher on the west bank, low and forming more of a plateau on the east, provide the per-fect situation for vineyards.

To the west, the pretty, fortified town of Sancerre commands a huge arc of vineyards that face south and east, a landscape that is as dominated by vines as anywhere in France, and yet is only a few kilometres in width. Across the river, the village of Pouilly-sur-Loire is surrounded by a small, compact area of vineyards, dropping down on one side to the Loire, on the other climbing gently upwards until the chalk soil runs out.

Wine styles

These two main *appellations* of the Upper Loire have given the world one of its greatest vinous models. White wines made from Sauvignon Blanc grapes have swept from this corner of France to Italy, California, Chile and, above all, New Zealand.

That the fashion started in these two small pockets of viticulture sometimes seems almost forgotten outside Europe. But the two *appella-tions* — the lighter, early-drinking Sancerre and the fuller, longer-lasting Pouilly Fumé — still attract high (some would say too high) prices in restaurants around the world.

When the Californians decided to create a full, wood-aged style of Sauvignon Blanc wine and call it Fumé, they paid an erroneous com-pliment to the wines of a village where wood was simply a container, and where the *vignerons* were in fact trying as hard as possible to move their wines into modern stainless steel. But the term did encapsulate

Flinty soil (*silex*) in Didier Dagueneau's vineyards gives its name to his best wine.

the typically smoky flavour of Sau-vignon Blanc — the herbaceous, grassy bouquet, the taste that is sometimes gooseberries or, when riper, blackcurrants, and the vibrant acidity that offers such refreshment and thirst-quenching flavour. The Sancerrois do not neglect their reds and rosés made from Pinot Noir, but

these are often pale imitations of red burgundy.

Satellite *appellations* (*see* p246) use the same Sauvignon Blanc grape. Though wines from the Quincy, Reuilly and Menetou-Salon *appella-tions* are excellent in their own right, they are not up to a fine Sancerre or a delightful Pouilly Fumé. □

THE WINES FROM THE MOUNTAINS

Two vineyards of the upper, southern end of the Loire have AOC and another two VDQS status.

Côtes Roannaises (AOC)
The *département* of Loire, almost at the source of the river, produces red and rosé wines from Gamay around Roanne. Good Roannaises producers include Paul Lapandéry and Félix Vial.

Côtes du Forez (AOC)
This area has been revitalized by the local cooperative, Les Vignerons Foréziens, with good reds and rosés from Gamay. Beaujolais is just across the mountains to the east.

St-Pourçain (VDQS)
A zone south of Moulins in the Allier *département*, halfway between the Loire

vineyards and Burgundy. The grapes used are Burgundian: Tressallier (known as the Sacy in Chablis), Chardonnay, Aligoté and Sauvignon Blanc for white wines, Pinot Noir and Gamay for red wines and rosés. The local cooperative, Les Vignerons de St-Pourçain, is the main producer.

Côtes d'Auvergne (VDQS)
The wines — from 500ha (1,235 acres) of vineyards around Clermont-Ferrand in the Puy-de-Dôme *département* — are similar to Beaujolais: Gamay for reds and rosés, white for Chardonnay. Some communes can add their name to the wine: Boudes, Chanturgue, Corent, Médargues. The regional cooperative and R Rougeyron are reliable producers.

WINE REGIONS OF THE UPPER LOIRE

The most important vineyards of the Upper Loire are the twin AOCs of Pouilly and Sancerre. The wine areas of the mountain zones to the south are some of the least-known in France.

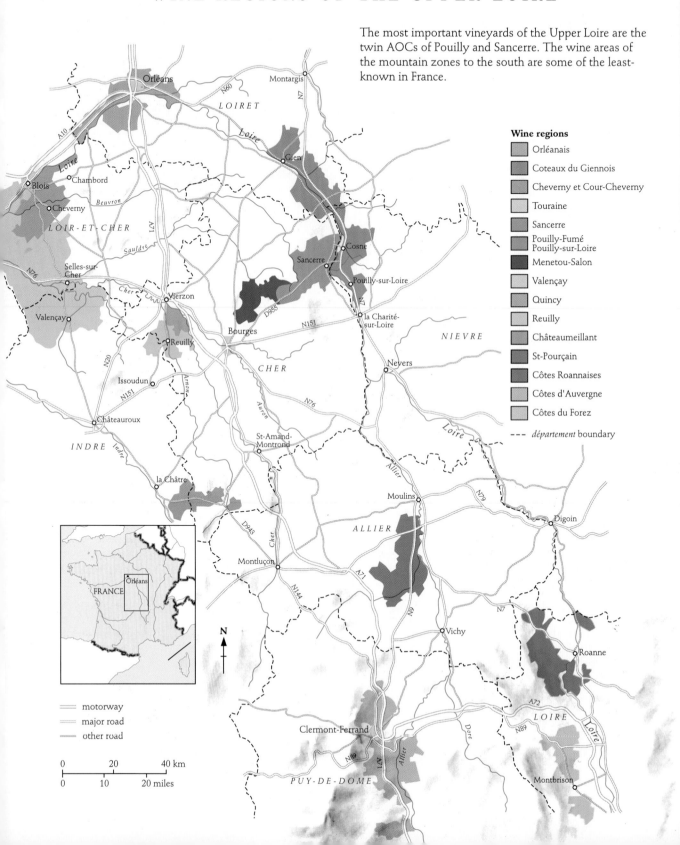

APPELLATIONS AND PRODUCERS

Most producers in the Upper Loire make either Pouilly-Fumé or Sancerre, although some *négociants* market a range of wines. Producers are listed here under their main *appellation*.

SANCERRE
The hillsides of Sancerre have individual vineyards that are among the steepest in France and are generally recognized as producing superior wines. Chavignol is the leading village of the 11 communes protected by the fortified town of Sancerre, with top sites such as Côtes des Monts Damnés and its Grande Côte, situated in the hollow of a natural amphitheatre. Bué is another leading village, with Chêne Marchand and Grand Chemarin. Le Clos du Roi is shared with the village of Crézancy. Verdigny is proud of its Clos de la Reine Blanche.

Bailly-Reverdy
Jean-François is linked through marriage with the Reverdy family, bringing together two important Sancerre names. He has 12ha (30 acres) of vines, two-thirds white, one-third red. The whites are excellent examples of the *appellation*, but Bailly is best known for powerful reds and light rosés.

Domaine Henri Bourgeois
With 60ha (147 acres) of vines, the Bourgeois family are running the biggest firm in the commune of Chavignol. From their old vines, including part of the very steep Côtes des Monts Damnés, they make a prestige *cuvée*, called M.D.
Another superb *cuvée* is La Bourgeoise, a blend of the year's best *cuvées*. The

barrique-aged Pinot Noir is one of the most concentrated and successful of its kind.

Lucien Crochet
A former *négociant*, Lucien Crochet has let his son Gilles take over the business. The 34-ha (83-acre) vineyard, planted with mostly Sauvignon Blanc, includes plots in some of the best *crus* of Sancerre: Chêne Marchand and Grand Chemarin for whites, Clos du Roi for reds.

Vincent Delaporte
This small, but top-quality, family domaine in Chavignol produces mainly white wines and a small amount of red wine. The vineyards, on steep slopes above the village, are worked by hand. Delaporte's wines are found around the world, and in select Paris restaurants.

Fournier Père et Fils
A domaine owner with a *négociant* business. The estate wines go under the name Cave des Chaumières, with a prestige white brand, La Chaudouillonne, while the *négociant* wines from Sancerre, Pouilly-Fumé and Menetou-Salon are sold under a mix of labels: Célestin Blondeau, Patient Cottat, Charles Dupuy, Henry de Chanvre and Léon Vatan.

Gitton Père et Fils
Pascal, René's son, has replaced the old wooden presses with more efficient pneumatic ones. This firm

The Château du Nozet makes excellent Pouilly-Fumé.

likes to emphasize vineyard differences in its bottlings of as many as ten Sancerres and five Pouilly-Fumés. Its cellars are in Sancerre (red, white and rosé). There is considerable barrel fermentation of the whites, which gives them the strong character of olden times.

Domaines Laporte
Now owned by Jean-Marie Bourgeois, this 20-ha (49-acre) estate has modern cellars, making high-quality wines. The top *cuvée* is Domaine du Rochoy, which comes from low-yielding vines and is left on its lees until bottling. Other wines are Clos la Comtesse and Grand Domaine. Laporte also produces a small amount of *négociant* wine.

Alphonse Mellot
One of the most important — and flamboyant — characters in Sancerre, Alphonse Mellot is both vineyard owner, with

50ha (124 acres), and *négociant* of Sancerre and wines from surrounding *appellations*. The family has been making wine here since 1513.

Domaine Natter
On this estate near Menetou-Salon, the Sauvignon Blanc grapes are planted on clay soil, making for powerful wines. There is also a small quantity of Pinot Noir, producing a robust red wine.

Domaine Vincent Pinard
Vincent Pinard's vineyard lies at the heart of the *appellation*, at Bué, and therefore on limestone soil. The wines are left on their lees, either in vats or barrels (which are new for the top range of wines). They are fine, without being insipid, and rich on the palate. There are also Pinot Noir grapes from which Vincent Pinard makes a well-structured red Sancerre.

Clos de la Poussie

A showpiece vineyard in Bué. The 32ha (79 acres) — a large holding for Sancerre — are centred on a spectacular amphitheatre of vines above the village. The wines (of all colours) are sold as Clos de Chailloux in the USA.

Pierre Prieur et Fils

A 12-ha (30-acre) property in Verdigny, including part of Les Monts Damnés. It makes distinguished white and light red and rosé, using modern equipment. The red and rosé come from the Pichon vineyard in Verdigny.

Jean Reverdy et Fils

One of the traditional names of Sancerre, here since the 17th century. Reverdy makes whites from Clos de la Reine Blanche in Verdigny. It also makes red and rosé from a 2-ha (5-acre) plot.

Domaine Jean-Louis Vacheron

This firm specializes in red Sancerre, of which there are fine examples, some matured in new wood. The domaine — a large one of around 37ha (91 acres) — produces Les Cailleries red, Les Romains rosé and Le Paradis white.

Other Sancerre producers

Pierre Archambault; Bernard Balland et Fils; Domaine Joseph Balland-Chapuis; Philippe de Benoist; Fouassier Père et Fils; Pascal Jolivet; Jean-Max Roger; and Domaine Thomas et Fils.

POUILLY-SUR-LOIRE

Villages around the town of Pouilly include St-Andelain, whose vineyards boast especially flinty soil; Les Loges, where the soil is chalky; and Les Berthiers.

Michel Bailly

This small estate of 13ha (32 acres), owned by Michel Bailly, is the result of a division of the former holdings of his father Maurice. Michel's holdings include land in the Champ de Gris, Les Griottes and Les Perriers vineyards.

Caves de Pouilly

This cooperative cellar accounts for about 20% of the *appellation's* production. Under the aegis of its director, Bernard Bouchié, this Pouilly cellar has made itself a name for quality wines. Its special *cuvées* — Les Moulins à Vent and, even more, Vieilles Vignes — have been rewarded with many prizes and distinctions.

Patrick Coulbois

In addition to his main production of Pouilly Fumé and a little Pouilly-sur-Loire, Patrick Coulbois also makes some sparkling wine.

Didier Dagueneau

Known as the wild child of Pouilly, Dagueneau, trained in Burgundy, has questioned many of the local winemaking traditions. He uses new wood for fermentation and makes wines that age well. His top *cuvée*, called Silex, after the flinty soil, is one of the finest being made in Pouilly today.

Jean-Claude Dagueneau

Jean-Claude is Didier's father. His estate is known as Domaine des Berthiers, and consists of 15ha (37 acres) of vines, some in St-Andelain, some in Les Loges. He makes a little Pouilly-sur-Loire, some of which is turned into a sparkling wine. The cellar next door belongs to Jean-Claude's cousin Serge.

Masson-Blondelet

A combination of two long-established Pouilly families, with vineyards scattered around much of the area. The cellars are on the edge of Pouilly, and the firm also has a shop in the same street, from which it sells wine. Its top *cuvée* is Tradition Cullus, and the firm also makes some Sancerre (white).

Ch du Nozet

The most famous as well as the most impressive Pouilly estate is owned by the de Ladoucette family, who also own Comte Lafond in Sancerre. The top wine from the 100-ha (247-acre) estate, Baron de L, is made only in the best years, and attracts high prices and much acclaim.

Michel Redde et Fils

With a large estate of 35ha (86 acres), the Redde family are important producers in Pouilly. They make a straight *cuvée*, and in the best years they also make a deluxe wine, Cuvée Majorum. Their winemaking equipment is modern, and these wines are designed for early consumption.

Guy Saget

The name Saget is now familiar throughout the Loire Valley as a *négociant*, but the family started in Pouilly, where they still work 35ha (86 acres), and in Sancerre, where they have 1ha (2.4 acres). Their wines are attractive, but are made strictly in the commercial mode.

Ch de Tracy

Descended from Scots soldiers who fought for King Charles VII of France against the English, the family of Comte d'Estutt d'Assay has been at the Ch de Tracy, on the Loire not far from Pouilly, since the 16th century. The current vineyard consists of 27ha (67 acres). Recent modernization of the cellars by the latest generation of the family has resulted in some very fine Pouilly-Fumé.

Other Pouilly producers

Bernard Blanchet; Domaine Jean-Pierre Chamoux; Alain Caillebourdin; Didier Pabiot; Jean Pabiot et Fils.

UPPER LOIRE APPELLATIONS

Sancerre and Pouilly Fumé are the leading AOCs: others in the region are:

Châteaumeillant VDQS area in the southern Cher *département*. Small production of reds and rosés from Gamay, Pinot Noir and Pinot Gris grapes.
Coteaux du Giennois An AOC for whites from Sauvignon Blanc and Chenin Blanc, reds and rosés from Gamay and Pinot Noir, produced around Gien, between Sancerre and Orléans.
Menetou-Salon Mainly white, but also red and rosé AOC wines from Sauvignon Blanc and Pinot Noir grapes.
Pouilly-sur-Loire White AOC wines made from Chasselas grapes planted on flinty soil.

Pouilly Fumé White wine from Pouilly-sur-Loire, made from Sauvignon Blanc.
Quincy Elegant AOC white wine made from Sauvignon Blanc grapes, which are planted on sandy and gravelly soil.
Reuilly An old viticultural area with a good name, which has known a revival thanks to its whites, made from Sauvignon Blanc, and its red and rosé AOC wines from Pinot Noir and Pinot Gris grapes.
Sancerre *Appellation* for white wines from Sauvignon Blanc grapes and AOC red and rosé wines from Pinot Noir grapes.
Orléanais VDQS zone, with light reds and rosés from Pinot Noir and Pinot Meunier, whites from Pinot Blanc and Chardonnay.

THE RHÔNE

THE WINES FROM SOME OF FRANCE'S OLDEST VINEYARDS ARE
STRONG IN CHARACTER AND REFLECT THE REGION — SUN-FILLED,
DEEP IN COLOUR AND REDOLENT OF FLOWERS, HERBS AND SPICES.

Granitic soils and an exposed site make the great hill of
Hermitage an ideal vineyard. Syrah vines, on which several of
the Rhône Valley's celebrated red wines are based, thrive
here at the top of the slope around the famous *Chapelle*.

The wines of the Rhône are steadily regaining the high prestige they enjoyed more than a century ago, when Hermitage was numbered among the great reds of France. The Rhône Valley's wines have much in common, but this is by no means a single wine region. Vineyards in a 200-km (125-mile) stretch of the valley from Vienne in the north down to Avignon produce fragrant Syrah-dominated reds from the Côte Rôtie, robust red wines from the region's most celebrated wine zone — Hermitage — and young, fruity, Grenache-based reds from the Mediterranean lands of the Côtes du Rhône. There is a long tradition of vine cultivation in this area: indeed, the vineyards of the Rhône are believed to be among the oldest in France. The superb vintages of the late 1980s and 1990s contributed to the growing international reputation of the wines of this region.

The River Rhône rises in the Swiss Alps and flows for some 800km (500 miles) to the Mediterranean near Marseilles, having crossed the border into France not far from Geneva. The river flows between the young (in geological terms) Alps and the ancient block of the Massif Central, carving gorges in places, more open valleys in others. The vineyards of the Northern Rhône extend from Vienne to Valence; those of the Southern Rhône from Montélimar to Avignon. In the north the climate is continental with warm springs and hot summers. As one travels south it becomes more Mediterranean, although the mistral, a cold northerly wind that can endure for days on end, is a feature of the climate of the Southern Rhône. Red and white grapes are grown throughout the Rhône. Northern reds range from simple, light wines to the dark, full-bodied Syrah-based reds for which the region is renowned. Southern reds are based on several, complementary varieties and tend to be similar across the region — with a pronounced fruit flavour, sometimes spicy or herby, and softer than their northern neighbours. Northern whites contrast sharply between the opulent wines based on Marsanne, and delightful Viognier-based whites. In the parched Southern Rhône white wines have been largely unexciting hitherto, but they are beginning to show more promise.

History of Rhône wines

It has been said that Phocaean Greeks from Asia Minor introduced the vine to the Rhône Valley some 2,400 years ago, and that the Persians brought the Syrah grape from their country. Others believe this variety to be indigenous. Most historians agree that the Romans developed viticulture here and then extended it north into the rest of France.

There is, or has been, a prejudice in certain sections of the wine trade against the wines of the Rhône which goes back to the beginning of the 19th century. For 200 years before that the best *crus* of the Northern Rhône, such as Hermitage, had enjoyed the same status as the *Grands Crus* of the Côte d'Or in Burgundy or the newly-planted estates of the Médoc and Graves in Bordeaux. Grand tours of Europe made by the rich took them past the foot of the great hill of Hermitage as they made their way through France to Italy. Many of them stopped and tasted, and most found the wine good or even great.

Then came the Napoleonic Wars. The British blockade of the French ports robbed Bordeaux merchants of their favourite Spanish wines, which had been used to add strength of colour to claret in all but the very best years. The merchants' eyes fell on the strong, dark wines of Hermitage, which for the next 60 years were condemned to beefing up the weaker wines of Bordeaux and Burgundy.

Oïdium and phylloxera followed. After the destruction of the vineyards by the wine louse, growers were slow to replant the steeper sites. The Depression of the 1930s did not help recovery and many of the best vineyard sites continued to lie fallow. Wines produced in the valley were dismissed as suitable only for local consumption, and it was not until after World War II that the best wines of the Northern Rhône came into their own once again. In many cases prices remained depressed until the late 1970s. In the south, in Châteauneuf-du-Pape, growers had discovered the potential of the high plateau during the interwar years, but again re-planting was slow and it was not until the 1950s that many cherry and apricot trees were uprooted and replaced by vines. Only now can the Rhône Valley vineyard be said to be in full production.

Geology and weather

The rock formations of the Rhône Valley are a product of the geological battle between the Massif Central and the Alps. The River Rhône has, historically, fought its way to the sea between the two. The ancient rocks of the Massif Central in the north provide a volcanic (granite) base for soils which allows vines very good drainage. The fine topsoils of flint, chalk, limestone or mica are often eroded off the steep slopes and have to be redistributed manually. But the same slopes provide good exposure for grapes and are less at risk from damaging frosts and fog.

Further south the valley is broader and steep slopes are few. Subsoils are limestone, sand or clay, and topsoils include boulders and stones left by retreating glaciers. The stones restrict the use of machinery but aid drainage and retain warmth.

As one travels south down the Rhône Valley, the climate becomes more Mediterranean. In the north summers are hot and winters cold, so frost can be a problem. Rainfall sometimes hinders flowering and can spoil the vintage, while summer

Châteaubourg overlooks the Rhône in the south of St-Joseph.

WINE REGIONS OF THE RHONE

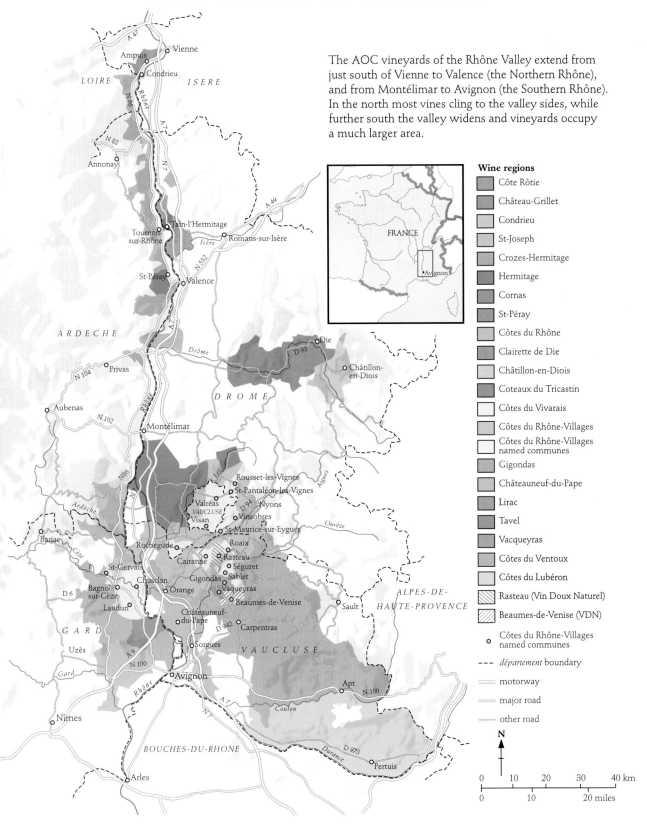

The AOC vineyards of the Rhône Valley extend from just south of Vienne to Valence (the Northern Rhône), and from Montélimar to Avignon (the Southern Rhône). In the north most vines cling to the valley sides, while further south the valley widens and vineyards occupy a much larger area.

Wine regions

- Côte Rôtie
- Château-Grillet
- Condrieu
- St-Joseph
- Crozes-Hermitage
- Hermitage
- Cornas
- St-Péray
- Côtes du Rhône
- Clairette de Die
- Châtillon-en-Diois
- Coteaux du Tricastin
- Côtes du Vivarais
- Côtes du Rhône-Villages
- Côtes du Rhône-Villages named communes
- Gigondas
- Châteauneuf-du-Pape
- Lirac
- Tavel
- Vacqueyras
- Côtes du Ventoux
- Côtes du Lubéron
- Rasteau (Vin Doux Naturel)
- Beaumes-de-Venise (VDN)
- ○ Côtes du Rhône-Villages named communes
- - - - *département* boundary
- motorway
- major road
- other road

N

| 0 | 10 | 20 | 30 | 40 km |
| 0 | | 10 | | 20 miles |

hailstorms can ruin a year's efforts in the vineyard in minutes. Further south climatic conditions are more stable in both summer and winter, although autumnal rainfall may encourage rot or disease, and the mistral blows frequently. This cold, drying north-westerly can blast down the valley for several days at a time and at considerable strength.

Grape varieties and wine styles

In the Southern Rhône people still complain that unscrupulous Burgundian merchants encouraged them to plant Grenache. But this variety still produces most of the great red Southern Rhônes, which are less dense and aggressively tannic than the wines of the north, with raspberry and sometimes herby flavours. Syrah provides the basis of quality wines in the Northern Rhône, producing wines of deeper colour and with more tannin. Their flavour is characteristically of black berry fruits, often with pronounced aromas of violets and spice. Other red grape varieties are Cinsaut and Mourvèdre.

As far as white wines are con-cerned, the Rhône Valley divides in two at the River Drôme, which joins the Rhône south of Valence. In the north Viognier, fabulously scented and often tasting of over-ripe apricots, dominates in Condrieu, while Marsanne and Roussanne take pride of place in Hermitage. Marsanne produces sturdy but sweet-scented wine, while Roussanne is more delicate and aromatic. In the south Grenache Blanc is assuming an ever greater importance, albeit sprinkled with a little Bourboulenc, Piquepoul, Clairette and Picardan. Wines from Grenache Blanc should be drunk young.

On the River Drôme is the town of Die, which lies at the centre of a small wine-producing region. The still white wine made here is Coteaux Diois AOC, but far more interesting are the sparkling wines. Clairette de Die is named after the Clairette grape, although some Muscat à Petits Grains is also used: proportions vary from one wine house to another. Clairette de Die Tradition is made by a locally natural process involving a second fermentation in bottle.

Southern Rhône is the only region outside Languedoc-Roussillon to produce two *vins doux naturels*. The more famous, Muscat de Beaumes-de-Venise, is made from Muscat à Petits Grains. It is a superb dessert wine, luscious and aromatic, with 21% of alcohol by volume. Most of it is produced by the cooperative cellar of Beaumes-de-Venise, but there are also two noteworthy private estates: Domaine de Durban and Domaine des Bernardins.

A Grenache-based *vin doux naturel* is made at Rasteau. Mostly this is a sweet white wine, but the red version is generally better. The cooperative is the main producer, but Domaine de la Soumade makes more interesting wines (including reds).

Growers, merchants and co-ops

During the lean years merchants and cooperative cellars dominated the commercial wine scene. The co-ops protected small growers and gave them a livelihood. Particularly important was the Cave Coopérative de Tain, which still vinifies 65% of Crozes-Hermitage, 25% of Hermitage, 15% of Cornas and 11% of St-Joseph. No other Rhône cooperative aspires to such importance, but in the south village co-ops are still a respectable source of local wine. The co-op in Rasteau, for example, is one of the few places where you can obtain a bottle of the village's *vin doux naturel*.

The backwardness of the Rhône region has benefited the large *négociant* houses. In the Northern Rhône most *négociants* had, and still have, their offices in the twin towns of Tain-Tournon. In the Southern Rhône a number still operate from Châteauneuf-du-Pape. The position of *négociants* in the Côtes du Rhône is further complicated by the presence of merchants from Beaune and other places in Burgundy. Formerly their task was to buy vats of strong wines to fortify their burgundies. This practice is now illegal, but the Burgundians continue to bottle Rhône wines. Generally these wines are among the least impressive on the market. □

READING A RHONE WINE LABEL

Rhône wine labels are simpler to understand than those of Burgundy or Bordeaux. There are no names of *Grands Crus* or *Premiers Crus* to complicate the basic labelling system that tells you where the wine comes from and its status.

Rhône appellations

Some of the Rhône *appellations* are the names of villages or towns, for example Condrieu or Tavel. Others refer to a wider area, such as Côtes du Rhône. Wines produced in the Côtes du Rhône-Villages AOC are allowed to put the name of the village on the label if the wine comes from just that one village. So, for instance, wines from the village of Laudun would have "Côtes du Rhône Laudun, Appellation Côtes du Rhône-Villages Contrôlée". Other *appellations* are named after vineyards — as in the case of Château Grillet — or precisely defined viticultural areas, or *lieux-dits* as they are called (meaning named sites), such as La Geynale in Cornas.

Status

As in the rest of France, the status of the wine is indicated by AOC, VDQS or *vin de pays (see pp136–139)*.

Bottles

In the Southern Rhône only growers within the Châteauneuf-du-Pape AOC are allowed to use a special bottle with a coat of arms (the papal tiara and St Peter's keys crossed beneath it) embossed on the glass. The merchants of Châteauneuf-du-Pape are not permitted to use the same bottle as the growers. On their bottles the crossed keys are above the tiara. You will need to look carefully to see which is which. Merchants from Tain, Burgundy, or anywhere else for that matter, may not use this bottle.

QUALITY FACTORS

Lack of warmth is rarely a problem in the Rhône Valley; rather the reverse. Climate concerns centre around the damaging Mistral, a cold, dry wind that blows fiercely down the valley from the north. The underlying geology provides excellent sites and soils. Quality here depends largely on decisions and actions in the vineyard.

Climate

It does not usually get too hot for vines, at least not in the Northern Rhône. In 1989, however, in Cornas and Hermitage, and in 1990 in Côte Rôtie, the vines did suffer. Grenache vines fare better than Syrah in very hot years, being a Mediterranean variety that is used to the heat. In the Southern Rhône the Mistral wind can dry out the grapes, and wines from desiccated fruit are said to have *le goût du mistral*.

Clones

During the 1970s many vinegrowers in the Rhône Valley replanted their vineyards with high-yielding clones. This unfortunately resulted in wines that were not only thin, but tended to taste the same. The solution to this problem in the 1980s was to make a *sélection massale*. This meant propagating vines from the best plot, which therefore allowed more of the character of the wine to come through. The best of most varieties of vine were those with the smallest berries and the thickest skins. Since the 1980s there has been a far more responsible attitude to cloning among growers in the Rhône.

Geology and soils

The best vineyards in the Northern Rhône are on granite.Topsoils vary and differences show in the wines. In Côte Rôtie, for example, the Côte Blonde has more sand, the Côte Brune more clay. The soils of Hermitage are more complicated. A good wine should combine grapes from different parts of the hill. Of the named plots, Les Bessards is granite shale, Le Méal is sandy and Les Greffieux is rich in clay. Chalky soils are reserved for white wines. In the South the best land is on limestone. Châteauneuf's Plateau de Montredon has its *galets* — smooth pebbles that store heat by day and warm the vines by night.

HERMITAGE AND CROZES-HERMITAGE

| | Hermitage |
| | Crozes-Hermitage |

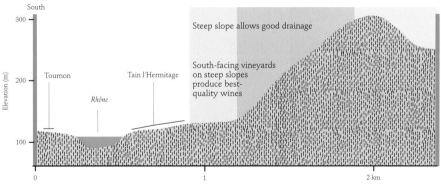

South
North

300
200
100

Elevation (m)

Tournon
Tain l'Hermitage
Rhône

Steep slope allows good drainage

South-facing vineyards on steep slopes produce best-quality wines

0   1   2 km

Vines clinging to the hill of Hermitage above the Rhône.

Yields

For quality wine, yields must be kept low. To some extent this comes from using low-yielding clones, but the growers must also limit their crop. If they crop at more than 80hl/ha, their wines will not be outstanding. Whatever the limits set by the AOC in any given year, Syrah will not produce interesting wines over 50hl/ha, and the best wines are from yields nearer 30hl/ha.

For Grenache, the best growers will tell you that if it yields over 25hl/ha Grenache needs "a pair of crutches" in the form of Syrah and Mourvèdre. Below 25hl/ha Grenache produces superb wines all by itself.

NORTHERN RHÔNE

Great vineyards can be found along much of the Rhône's length, but the most special are in the Northern Rhône Valley. The clue to quality here is the granite bedrock. The first really steep hills appear just to the south of Vienne, an old Roman city 24km (15 miles) south of Lyons. A careful observer can make out the abandoned terraces on which vines grew in the days before phylloxera cut a swathe through the vineyards at the end of the 19th century. Today the Northern Rhône wine region begins in earnest at Ampuis.

Wines of the Northern Rhône

Ampuis is a drab, dusty, overgrown village straddling the route nationale, but on the sheer slopes behind are the vineyards of Côte Rôtie, one of the world's greatest wines. Physically, the slope divides into two — the Côte Brune and the Côte Blonde. There are many intriguing explanations as to how these two names came about, but the most likely is the most banal. The Côte Blonde's topsoils are more sandy, while the thin covering of the Côte Brune has a higher percentage of clay. The subsoil is granite.

Côte Rôtie's wines represent the most elegant expression of the Syrah grape. To some extent this is the result of the addition to the cuvée of a small amount of Viognier — one of the world's most aromatic white varieties — to lessen the tannic quality of the Syrah. Despite increased plantings in the Midi, only in Condrieu AOC, a few kilometres south of Ampuis, and in the tiny, neighbouring AOC of Château Grillet, does the Viognier grape achieve such a level of near perfection.

The best wines of St-Joseph, the next wine district going south, have a light, almost Beaujolais-like elegance; but there are not many of them. After

New oak barrels in the cellars of old-established Ampuis merchant, Marcel Guigal.

the Depression of the 1930s vines were planted chiefly on the alluvial plains, a less suitable site than the hillsides overlooking the Rhône. Efforts are currently being made to redeem St-Joseph: there is great potential for further planting, and the emphasis will be on hillside sites.

On the other side of the river from St-Joseph is Crozes-Hermitage. To some extent the problems of Crozes-Hermitage as an AOC mirror those of St-Joseph: the zone suffered after the authorities extended the limits of the *appellation* in the 1950s to areas not known for their quality. In recent years, however, Crozes has proved the most interesting AOC in the Northern Rhône. Every so often a newly motivated grower decides to bottle his own wines rather than taking his grapes along to the local co-operative. The results have often been impressive.

Crozes lies, quite literally, in the shadow of the great rock of Hermitage, whose famous red and white wines have dominated the Northern Rhône since the 17th century. In style Hermitage wines could be said to be the masculine counterparts of the more feminine wines of Côte Rôtie. At first they can be tough and unyielding, but the best wines reveal a sublimely sensuous fruit once they have passed their eighth year. The whites are unfairly neglected: they are also astonishingly long lived.

The Northern Rhône produces one more great wine, from the vineyards around the village of Cornas on the left bank. If the wines of Hermitage are thought of as masculine, then those of Cornas are supermen — great body-builders with huge, hulking tannins. Classic Cornas is slow to shed this virile image in favour of a more subdued character befitting of the dinner table, but it should never be altogether tame, for the feral nature of this wine is one of its greatest merits.

There are two remaining areas of interest in the Northern Rhône. In and around St-Péray a little white AOC wine is made, predominantly from Marsanne. It can be still or sparkling. To the east of the Rhône, along the River Drôme, is Brézème, which is not a separate AOC, just Côtes du Rhône. It is often overlooked, possibly because, apart from the cooperative cellar, there is only one grower who commits the wine to bottle. Like Cornas, the wines are made from pure Syrah, but, unlike Cornas, they do not soften with age.

Appellations
Throughout the Northern Rhône from Vienne to the River Drôme there are eight AOCs: Côte Rôtie and Cornas which produce only red wines; St-Joseph, Crozes-Hermitage and Hermitage, where wines are red or white; and Condrieu, Château Grillet and St-Péray, where wines are white. There are also pockets of Côtes du Rhône, one of which is Brézème.

As in all the wine regions of France, the AOCs are administered by the INAO (Institut National des Appellations d'Origine), which limits yields, prescribes grape varieties and marks the boundaries of production. In some areas their decisions are controversial: for example, the high plateau at Côte Rôtie is not considered to produce the same standard of fruit as the Côte itself.

Yields vary from 30hl/ha for Condrieu to 50hl/ha for Côtes du Rhône, but are generally about 40hl/ha. Each AOC has a recommended limited yield, but the best growers try to restrict production further.

No rosé is produced in the Northern Rhône. A small amount of sweet white Condrieu is made by stopping fermentation early (by adding sulphur). This wine has limited appeal, and equally limited availability. In Hermitage a few growers continue to

make a *vin de paille* (see p265), but in such minute amounts that fans will go to any lengths to get it. There are moves at Chapoutier (see p256) to make it in commercial quantities.

Grape varieties
The sole black grape permitted is Syrah. In the wines of Côte Rôtie Syrah may be blended with up to 20% Viognier, and in Hermitage Marsanne or Roussanne (up to 15%) are permitted in the blend. In Cornas and Brézème wine must be made from 100% Syrah. The white wines of Condrieu and Château Grillet must be 100% Viognier, although there are some small areas planted to Chasselas. White Hermitage, Crozes-Hermitage and St-Péray wines may be made from Marsanne or Roussanne or both. Marsanne is more popular than the disease-prone Roussanne, though the latter is probably the better grape.

Winemaking techniques
Traditional methods have recently been shaken up by the introduction of new ideas from other wine-producing regions. Cold-temperature fermentation is now being used to produce crisper white wines instead of making them in wooden vats. *Pigeage* and *autopigeage* are gaining ground: this is the practice whereby the "cap" of grape skins that floats to the top of the fermentation tank is mixed back into the liquid, either by human feet or mechanical plungers. There is a great deal more new oak in the Rhône Valley than there was even in the 1980s. Even though well-known producers such as Jaboulet and Guigal (see p256 and p254 respectively) began to use new oak first, it has been the work of Bordeaux-trained oenologist Jean-Luc Colombo that has brought the use of new oak home to the smaller growers of the Northern Rhône.

Producers
It is fair to say that the *négociants* of Tain and Tournon bottle some of the best wines in the Rhône Valley. Some

producers, such as Jaboulet, Chapoutier and Delas, as well as Guigal in Ampuis, own substantial areas of vines in the top AOCs. Even if they do not own vineyards, many *négociants* practise a selective buying policy, which means that their bottlings are generally better than reliable.

Obviously some *négociants* specialize in the wines of this part of the valley, but many of them offer wines from both the Northern and Southern Rhône. Merchants in the north, however, are not permitted to use the special Châteauneuf-du-Pape bottle (see box, p250).

Ageing and vintages
Traditional red wines from the Northern Rhône are legendary for their ageing potential. The Russians, in particular, had a great fondness for old Hermitage in pre-Revolutionary days. Whether modern Rhône reds age so well is a moot point. Certainly most Hermitage does not begin to show its best until it has passed its eighth year; and in some cases not until the decade is out. Cornas is a similar story.

Côte Rôtie generally drinks a little younger. Côte Blonde can be approached at about six years, though the tougher Côte Brune may need a little more time. Crozes-Hermitage and St-Joseph may normally be approached when they are two or three years old. By five or so they begin to lose their charm.

Viognier wines (with the exception of Château Grillet) are at their best between 18 months and four years old. Château Grillet spends longer in cask and takes longer to come round. In general, Condrieu does not keep. White Hermitage is good young and old, but tends to be dull in its middle years. An old white Hermitage wine is truly an experience to savour.

Vintages vary enormously in the Northern Rhône. In the 1980s there were only two mediocre to poor vintages (1984 and 1987): each of the others had a character all its own. □

APPELLATIONS AND PRODUCERS

With the exception of the large cooperative at Tain l'Hermitage, production in the Northern Rhône is largely split between growers who market their own estate or domaine wines, and the *négociants* who buy grapes or wines from the smaller growers and produce their own blends. AOCs are listed alphabetically, with producers under each.

BREZEME
In this small vineyard, only 14ha (35 acres) are planted out of a potential 84 (208). It is the only northern vineyard south of Valence. AOC Côtes du Rhône is made from 100% Syrah. Wines tend to be on the tough side. There are two producers, Jean-Marie Lombard and the *coopérative*, and they both can put Brézème on their wine labels.

CHATEAU GRILLET
With less than 5ha (12.5 acres), Château Grillet is one of France's smallest AOC areas. Since 1830 it has been the monopoly of the Neyret-Gachet family. Château Grillet is a white wine made entirely

MARCEL GUIGAL

This merchant house owns about 10% of the Côte Rôtie vineyard and also buys in grapes to make Côte Rôtie "Brune et Blonde". Marcel Guigal also owns Vidal-Fleury, another established Ampuis merchant house, where he has improved standards dramatically, especially for the top-of-the-range La Châtillonne. Guigal has led the way in promoting individual *terroirs* in Côte Rôtie with his so-called *crus*: La Mouline (Côte Blonde), La Landonne (Côte Brune) and, more recently, La Turque (between the two). From these sites come the rarest, most expensive Côte Rôtie wines, and in some years their prices in New York have exceeded that of Ch Pétrus. Guigal produces wines from throughout the Rhône, including a reliable Hermitage and a Syrah-dominated Côtes du Rhône.

from Viognier, as in neighbouring Condrieu. Unlike most Condrieus, it spends up to 18 months in cask and does not come into its own for five years. Rarity alone seems to justify its high price.

CONDRIEU
The area planted with Viognier occupies about 110ha (272 acres). If all land within the AOC were planted, that might reach 100ha (250 acres). Until recently, vines were old (up to 50 years) and winemaking highly traditional. There has recently been an unfortunate tendency among some growers to put Condrieu in new oak. Yet in the granite and mica soils of this area, Viognier achieves perfection with sensuous apricot-kernel-and-peach notes. New-oak aromas serve only as a distraction. Condrieu is not generally intended for long ageing. In most cases it comes round at about 18 months and should be drunk by its fourth year.

Recommended producers include: Cuilleron; Dezormeaux; Guigal; Delas Frères vines are owned by Michel Delas); Multier at the Ch du Rozay (beware of new oak); Niero et Pinchon; Alain Paret; André Perret; Georges Vernay.

CORNAS
Cornas has 100ha (247 acres) producing red wines from 100% Syrah. Although Cornas' qualities were recognized as early as the beginning of the 19th century, it wasn't until the late 1960s that Auguste Clape (*qv*) began to bottle his wines and sell them to cus-

tomers at home and abroad. By the 1980s Cornas had become one of the most fashionable wines in France, with production frantically trying to keep up with demand. *Négociants* in Tain-Tournon still tend to dismiss Cornas as a rustic wine, and it can be tough in its youth and intriguingly feral in old age.

Auguste Clape
This 5-ha (12-acre) estate brought fame to Cornas. The vines are up to a century old and the Clapes, father and son, combine grapes from their different sites to make a superbly balanced *cuvée*, which takes up to a decade to come round. They also own a small strip of land, classified as Côtes du Rhône, on the other side of the route nationale.

Robert Michel
With 7ha (17 acres), Robert Michel owns about 10% of Cornas. Unlike Auguste Clape, he divides his resources and makes three wines: one from vines planted on the uninspiring flat land on the valley floor; one from a hillside site called La Reynarde; and his top wine, La Geynale, from a small south-facing plot where the vines are 60 to 80 years old. The *lieu-dit* La Geynale seems to produce superb wine even in off-years.

Other producers
Allemande; de Barjac; Bernard; Colombo; Courbis; Juge; Jean Lionnet; Noël Verset; and Voge.

COTE ROTIE
This AOC totals around 210ha (519 acres), most of it on a slope that divides into the Côte Blonde and the Côte Brune. There are a good many *lieux-dits* (*see* box, p250), but no hierarchical *cru* system. The most famous *lieux-dits* are La Landonne, La Côte Boudin, La Turque, La Châtillonne and La Mouline.

Côte Rôtie is made chiefly from Syrah, but there is an allowance for up to 20% Viognier. Traditionally, it was Côte Blonde that received the Viognier, which added its rich perfume to the peony/carnation aromas of the Syrah. In the past most Côte Rôtie was a blend of Blonde and Brune. Increasingly, growers are making wine under more than one label, thereby isolating their best sites.

Domaine Yves Cuilleron

Yves Cuilleron produces two Côte Rôtie (Bassenon and Terres Sombres), three Condrieu and six St-Joseph. His winemaking shows great finesse and precision. He uses grapes from particular plots to create truly remarkable wines.

Marcel Guigal

See profile.

Joseph Jamet

Côte Rôtie wines continue to be made here in a wonderfully traditional way by the two young Jamet brothers, Jean-Paul and Jean-Luc. They have about 6ha (15 acres) on the Côte Brune. Their wines are remarkably supple and aromatic, but they take time to reveal their great character.

René Rostaing

Everyone is talking about René Rostaing in Côte Rôtie. A small landowner in the past, his holdings were increased dramatically when he married the daughter of Albert Dervieux, a traditional winemaker in the area. Since then he has also acquired a large chunk of the plot formerly controlled by Marius Gentaz. Rostaing has continued the winemaking policy of his father-in-law, making separate bottlings of Côte Brune and Côte Blonde wines. He also makes a La Landonne single-vineyard wine. This is a powerful and concentrated

Freshly-picked Syrah grapes from the slopes of the Côte Rôtie.

wine that has considerable ageing potential.

Other producers

Gilles Barge; Pierre Barge; Emile Champet; Chapoutier; Delas Frères; and Jaboulet.

CROZES-HERMITAGE

This AOC covers 1,300ha (3,200 acres) and has in the past had a reputation for producing some of the more lacklustre wines of the Northern Rhône. This was as a result of changes made to the limits of the *appellation* in 1952, when it became possible to make Crozes-Hermitage not just in the hills to the north of Tain l'Hermitage, but also on the less suitable alluvial land to the south of town.

More than 60% of all Crozes-Hermitage is made at the huge cooperative in Tain, which does not isolate the best *terroirs*. In the last few years, however, there has

been a dramatic improvement in quality as new winemaking talents emerge, and Crozes-Hermitage has become one of the most interesting AOCs in the whole of France.

Domaine Combier

This red and white vineyard covers 13ha (32 acres) of fine gravel. Laurent Combier makes excellent wine in both colours. Very great care is taken during (manual) harvesting, winemaking in steel vats and maturing in new — or almost new — casks.

Alain Graillot

Alain Graillot is one of the talented winemakers who have helped revive the flagging reputation of Crozes-Hermitage by raising quality standards. He made his first wines in 1985 and has gone from strength to strength. He now has 20ha (49 acres) in Crozes-Hermitage, as well as 1ha

(2.47 acres) in St-Joseph. He also makes a few barrels of Hermitage. Since 1986 Graillot has made a top-of-the-range wine called La Guirande, which is even more concentrated and packed full of superb Syrah fruit flavour than his generic range of Crozes-Hermitage wines.

Other producers

Belle; Cave des Clairmonts; Combier; Cournu; Desmeure; Jaboulet (Domaine de Thalabert); Roure; and Viale.

HERMITAGE

The wines of Hermitage achieved royal recognition in the second half of the 17th century, when Louis XIV made a present of some bottles to his cousin, King Charles II of England. This royal blessing ensured that for more than a century Hermitage was to be found in all the best cellars and on all the finest English tables.

Winemaking declined in the 19th century, when wines from this area went to bolster the inadequate brews of Bordeaux and Burgundy, but production never ceased. After the devastation wreaked by phylloxera, growers were slow to replant the great hill of Hermitage. Had it not been for the determination of the leading *négociants*, production might well have ceased altogether. It was not until after World War II that the fortunes of wines in the Hermitage region began to improve again, and not until the 1970s did the wines fetch the sort of price they deserve.

Accounts of 19th-century winemaking in Hermitage tell of wines aged in new oak casks for up to six years before bottling. White wines were fermented in new acacia wood. Few, if any, growers these days use 100% new oak for their Hermitages: the wines are tannic enough as it is. There is, however, a great deal more new oak about than there used to be, and of the larger growers, perhaps only Gérard Chave (*qv*) refuses to countenance it flavouring his wine.

From west to east, the main *lieux-dits* of Hermitage are: Les Varognes, Les Bessards, Le Gros des Vignes, Les Greffieux, Le Méal, L'Hermite, La Chapelle, Chante Alouette, Beaumes, Péléat, La Maison Blanche, Les Rocoules, Les Diognières, La Pierreille, Les Murets, La Croix, L'Homme and Les Signeaux. These names rarely appear on labels, since the commonly held view is that Hermitage is a blend of different *terroirs* on the rock. Different topsoils cover the granite and limestone core.

Négociants kept Hermitage going during the lean years, and much of the good land remains in their hands. The cooperative owns a large estate on the hill, and so does Gérard Chave. Smaller growers, however, sometimes have only a fraction of a hectare, and the quality of their wines is often variable.

Chapoutier

With some 30ha (70 acres), Chapoutier has the largest estate on the hill of Hermitage. It also possesses substantial holdings elsewhere: a little under 3ha (6.7 acres) in Côte Rôtie; 2ha (5 acres) in St-Joseph; 5.5ha (13.5 acres) in Crozes-Hermitage; and, last but not least, more than 30ha (79 acres) in Châteauneuf-du-Pape. The company produces more than 83,000 cases of wine a year.

Until the mid- to late-1980s, old wood and old viticultural methods prevented Chapoutier from realizing the potential of its vines. Then Max Chapoutier retired, and the firm was taken over by his two sons, Marc and Michel. They are a powerful team.

Since the 1990 vintage Chapoutier has been on good form, and is possibly the best merchant house now making Hermitage, with its top Le Pavillion and Monier de la Sizeranne labels. Nor has Chapoutier neglected its other wines. The slightly old-fashioned whites are a delight, and at their best when they are old. Also showing well are Chapoutier's Châteauneufs, for Michel is a great believer in the potential of the Grenache grape. In his new Barbe Rac *cuvée* he uses pure Grenache from very old vines (80 years), with excellent results.

Gérard and Jean-Louis Chave
See profile.

Delas Frères
This *négociant* in St-Jean-de-Muzols buys in grapes and wine from throughout the Rhône Valley. Some products still come from the Delas family, which used to own the company. Delas is now in the hands of Champagnes Deutz.

The best wines from this company are Hermitage Marquise de la Tourette and Côte Rôtie Seigneur de Maugiron. Both are reliable wines, although they are no rivals to the front runners in either *appellation*. The Condrieu from Delas Frères is often a good example of wine from that AOC.

Paul Jaboulet Aîné
This *négociant* house in La Roche de Glun, south of Hermitage, produces more than 130,000 cases of wine a year. Grapes and wine are bought in and quality is therefore variable. Jaboulet also owns two quite important estates: 25ha (70 acres) in Hermitage and Domaine de Thalabert, a 35-

ha (84-acre) estate in Crozes-Hermitage. Jaboulet is run by cousins Gérard and Philippe.

The company's top wine is Hermitage La Chapelle, a blend of grapes from Les Bessards, Les Gréffieux, Le Méal, Les Diognières, La Croix and La Maison Blanche. It is among the top three wines of this *appellation*. Jaboulet's wines are more claret-like than those of Gérard Chave. Domaine de Thalabert is also an excellent wine.

Jaboulet's white Hermitage, Chevalier de Sterimberg, is fresher and livelier than some, and is made from a blend of Roussanne and Marsanne. Other wines in the Jaboulet portfolio are more variable, but there are years when the Côte Rôtie Les Jumelles, or Châteauneuf-du-Pape Les Cedres, or Cornas are among the best around.

Other producers
Desmeure; Bernard Faurie; Jean-Louis Grippat; and Marcel Guigal.

ST-JOSEPH
This AOC follows the left bank of the Rhône from Condrieu to Cornas. St-Joseph used to be one of the best wine-producing areas in the Rhône Valley. At the time of the French Revolution, a small *cru* on the border of Tournon and Mauves produced wines that fetched prices as high as the great Hermitage itself. The success of St-Joseph was so great that neighbouring villages borrowed its name.

With the granting of an AOC in 1956, the limits of

GERARD AND JEAN-LOUIS CHAVE

The Chaves, father and son, are probably the best winemakers in the Northern Rhône, but with less than 15ha (36.5 acres) in Hermitage and 1ha (2.5 acres) in St-Joseph, they do not have enough land to satisfy their many fans. The key to Chave's quality is his attention to detail: there are no tricks or gimmicks, just the most careful winemaking imaginable. In his hands Syrah becomes superbly elegant, yet retains the slightly earthy note that sets it apart from other varieties. Chave's *cuvée* is a blend of grapes from several *lieux-dits* — Les Diognières, Beaumes, Péléat, Les Bessards and L'Hermite, in which every component plays an important rôle. Chave's St-Joseph is an extremely rare wine, but it is well worth searching for as it is considered to be one of the best St-Josephs of all.

Vineyards on the splendid hill of Hermitage vary in slope, altitude and soil and produce a range of wine styles.

St-Joseph's wine-producing area were inevitably extended. They were further revised in 1969, allowing less worthy growers to cash in on St-Joseph's good name.

Fortunately, there are some good growers in this large AOC (800ha/1,980 acres). Some of these have started putting the vines back where they ought to be, on the granite *côtes*, rather than down on the alluvial plains. The work began in St-Joseph proper, where growers have planted the steep hillsides with grapes for the first time in decades.

Maurice Courbis

This grower in Châteaubourg is busy replanting hillside sites with the help of his two sons. At present he has about 15ha (35 acres) in St-Joseph and a further 1.5ha (4 acres) further south in Cornas. Courbis' Cornas plot includes some extremely old grapevines planted at the foot of the slope as well as some newer plantings further up the hillside.

Domaine Coursodon

Father and son Coursodon are still the best producers of the St-Joseph *appellation*. Their numerous *cuvées* are all sensational and originate from particular plots. The white wine is less exciting however.

Domaine Pierre Gonon

The two sons who took over from their father have increased the size of the vineyard to more than 7ha (17

acres) planted mostly with Marsanne, Roussanne (white) and Syrah (red). They produce two cuvées of white St-Joseph, one fresh and flowery, the other, labelled Les Oliviers, matured in oak, is rich, fruity, honeyed-like and persistent. The red St-Joseph is vinous, and its tannins are as ripe as its fruit.

Domaine Bernard Gripa

A vineyard with 6ha (15 acres) of Syrah and 4ha (10 acres) of white grapes allows Bernard Gripa to prove each and every year that his wines are reliable and to produce a *cuvée de prestige*, white or red: the excellent and very full Berceau.

ST-PERAY

This *appellation* produces white wines only, either still or sparkling. The sparkling wines are made by the traditional method of secondary

fermentation in bottle. The main grape variety here is Marsanne. Growers are permitted to use the rather better Roussanne, but most are deterred by this grape's tendency to fail at flowering.

At best St-Péray wines are good, minor versions of white Hermitage. The sparkling wines are drunk locally as an apéritif, but they are rarely seen outside the area. Many growers making St-Péray also have estates in St-Joseph or Cornas. Good producers here include Bernard Gripa, Jean Lionnet and Alain Voge.

Domaine du Tunnel

The estate's name alludes to a railway tunnel near the 5ha (12 acres) cultivated by Stéphane Robert. A disciple of Louis Gripat, he uses new oak for his *cuvée* Prestige, a model St-Péray for its finesse, its nervousness and hint of vanilla.

SOUTHERN RHÔNE

The inky Syrah vines of the Northern Rhône peter out south of the River Drôme. Vines reappear south of Montélimar but in quite a different landscape. Stubby vines are trained in the traditional goblet shape, and dry clay and limestone rocks replace the granite peaks north of Valence. Some grape varieties of the Southern Rhône originated in Spain, and were introduced into the region in the 17th century.

Wines of the Southern Rhône

The prime site in the Southern Rhône is Châteauneuf, an *appellation* that bases its pre-eminence on distinctly doubtful papal connections. Many of the district's superior wines are from vines grown in stony and gravelly soils: these include the large white pebbles, or *galets*, of the Plateau de Montredon, which are said to contribute to the characteristic tobacco aroma of the wine.

The wine of Gigondas is often dismissed as *le Châteauneuf des pauvres*. But some great wines are produced here, many of which are superior to the ordinary wines made next door. The landscape is dominated by the famous limestone hills of the Dentelles de Montmirail, and in the main it is the area's chalky soils that make Gigondas a slightly harder wine than Châteauneuf.

Gigondas was the first of the southern Côtes du Rhône to be granted an AOC in its own right. Since then Vacqueyras has been similarly honoured. The top estates here use a lot of Syrah with Grenache to make highly successful, aromatic wines. Lirac and Tavel are both on the left bank of the Rhône. Lirac's wines resemble those of Châteauneuf, but a lot of rosé is also produced, which is not permitted in Châteauneuf. Tavel is an AOC reserved strictly for rosé wines. They are mostly made from

The Dentelles de Montmirail provide a dramatic backdrop in Gigondas.

Grenache, but the better estates combine it with some Mourvèdre.

There are similar Grenache-dominated wines to be found in the Southern Rhône's minor *appellations*, such as the Coteaux du Tricastin, Côtes du Ventoux, Côtes du Vivarais and Côtes du Lubéron, but the best wines are often concealed beneath the enormous blanket *appellations* of the Côtes du Rhône and Côtes du Rhône-Villages. Particularly noteworthy are the villages of St-Gervais, Cairanne, Rasteau, Sablet, Séguret and Valréas (*see* box).

Lastly, there are two regions of the Southern Rhône with the right to produce a *vin doux naturel* — the only examples outside the Midi (*see* p283). Muscat de Beaumes-de-Venise requires no introduction, as in recent years it has become a very popular dessert wine. Made from Muscat à Petits Grains, this is a luscious,

honeyed wine with an alcohol level of 21%. Most of it is made by the *cave coopérative* in Beaumes-de-Venise, but two small estates stand out: Domaine Durban and Domaine des Bernardins.

Less well known is the Grenache-based *vin doux naturel* from Rasteau. Most is vinified as a sweet white, but the red is generally better. The cooperative is the main producer, but better wines (including reds) come from Domaine de la Soumade.

Appellations

There are 11 AOCs in the Southern Rhône and two *vins doux naturels*. Châteauneuf-du-Pape can be red or white; Gigondas is for reds and rosés; and Vacqueyras is limited to reds. Tavel is distinctive in being an *appellation* restricted to rosés. The others — Lirac, Côtes du Vivarais, Coteaux du Tricastin, Côtes du Ventoux,

Côtes du Lubéron, Côtes du Rhône and Côtes du Rhône-Villages (*see* box) — may be red, white or rosé.

Yields are fixed by the INAO (*see* p137), and the same body decides whether a Côtes du Rhône-Villages should be elevated to AOC status. Yields of Grenache are determined up to a point by the grape itself, which has a tendency to fail at flowering, thereby limiting its own production. It is unusual for Grenache by itself to produce 40hl/ha, but permitted yields vary from 50 (Côtes du Rhône) to 28 (Muscat de Beaumes-de-Venise); Tavel is allowed 42, but the limit for other AOCs is 35.

Grape varieties

Grenache is the mainstay of Southern Rhône reds: 13 grape varieties are permitted for the Châteauneuf-du-Pape AOC, but Grenache generally accounts for 80% of the blend. Syrah and Mourvèdre soften or enhance its basic aromas, whereas other varieties, such as Counoise, Vaccarèse, Terret Noir, Cinsaut and Muscardin, are rather used to add spice to the blend.

At the end of the 19th century, Joseph Ducos, an engineer from Auch in the Armagnacais, bought Château La Nerthe, near Châteauneuf, for a song after phylloxera had ravaged the region. He researched the grape varieties that had previously existed on the estate. In addition to Grenache, Syrah and Mourvèdre, he planted Counoise, Muscardin, Vaccarèse, Cinsaut and Picpoul Noir for red wines. For whites he put down Clairette and Bourboulenc. His insistence that these were the correct varieties for the area led to their being enshrined in the AOC legislation in the 1920s, when Terret Noir, Picardan and Roussanne were added.

Ducos' cocktail of cultivars are still to be found on a few estates in Châteauneuf, but for the most part the blend of grapes in this wine area is much the same as in other wine districts of the Southern Rhône region: Grenache Noir packs the

reds; Grenache Blanc, the whites. Other varieties are added in smaller measure, with some of the famous 13 sprinkled on like herbs and spices in a Provençal stew.

There is, however, still an argument for the minor varieties. The Perrins of Château de Beaucastel (*see* p260) set enormous store by the Counoise, a grape that has recently been tried out to good effect in Roussillon. And Domaine du Vieux Télégraphe makes a 100% Cinsaut wine that is extremely good (but hard to find). Elsewhere in the Côte du Rhône, experimental *cuvées* are more likely to be found. There is a growing desire to make wines dominated by Syrah or Mourvèdre, or even *vins de cépage* (varietal wines). Rabasse-Charavin, Domaine de Ste-Anne and Château de Fonsalette are three producers to watch out for.

Clairette was the traditional white variety of the Southern Rhône,

and is still used in the production of the wines of Die (*see* p250), but it is increasingly challenged elsewhere in the region by Grenache Blanc. Interesting wines can be made from Piquepoul, Picardan, Bourboulenc and Roussanne. The latter, in particular, is used by Château de Beaucastel.

Ageing

Southern Rhône wines do not age for as long as their Northern counterparts, nor do they take as long to come round. A good Châteauneuf or Gigondas should last for 20 to 25 years, but it will be drinking well at five or six. The white wines of the Rhône are not considered good cellaring material. Muscat de Beaumes-de-Venise is also drunk young. Some people like to drink Rasteau *vin doux naturel* with bottle-age, when the wine is said to have a *rancio* character, like the more famous Grenache *vins doux naturels* of the Midi. □

COTES DU RHONE-VILLAGES

Today the Côtes du Rhône-Villages AOC covers 16 communes which are allowed to add their name to wine labels. The most interesting villages are profiled below.

Beaumes-de-Venise Now best known for a Muscat dessert wine, which has its own AOC, Beaumes also produces traditional reds.
Cairanne Some believe the red wines of Cairanne share certain characteristics of Châteauneuf-du-Pape, although they do not age as well.
Chusclan Chusclan is known for rosé wines, although more medium-bodied, fruity reds are produced.
Laudun Some of the Rhône's oldest vineyards produce both red wines and whites from Clairette and Roussanne.
Rasteau Best known for its *vins doux naturels* (Grenache-based dessert wines), Rasteau also produces some hearty reds.
Rochegude Production here is mainly of reds based on Grenache and Cinsaut. They are firm, appealing wines.
St-Gervais Some good reds are produced here, mainly from Mourvèdre

and Syrah, as well as a luscious white from 100% Viognier.
Sablet Promoted to Rhône-Villages status in the 1970s, most wines are light and delicate reds or rosés.
Séguret This is another commune known mainly for reds, the best of which exhibit the characteristic tobacco-like aroma of Grenache.
Valréas Much of the wine produced here is early-maturing red. More robust wines are to be had from a few growers as well as the *cave coopérative*.
Vinsobres One of the villages with the best *terroir* for wines of great strength. Unfortunately this potential rarely finds its way into a bottle, as most wines are not sold under the village label, but downgraded to Côtes du Rhône which allows higher yields.
Visan Syrah is being planted at the expense of Grenache here and is producing some good-quality reds.

The other Côtes du Rhône-Villages communes are Roaix, Rousset-les-Vignes, St-Pantaléon-les-Vignes and St-Maurice-sur-Eygues.

APPELLATIONS AND PRODUCERS

Cooperatives play a far greater rôle in the Southern Rhône. Most villages in the wine-producing areas have their own co-op, which provides an alternative to the *négociants* for those growers not wishing or unable to vinify their grapes. AOCs are listed alphabetically, with producers under each. For Rhône Valley *vins de pays, see* box, p262.

CHATEAUNEUF-DU-PAPE

Châteauneuf didn't acquire its papal trappings until long after the popes returned to Rome: even the suffix *du Pape* is a recent addition. In truth, the Popes of Avignon preferred to drink the Muscat of Languedoc. Individual *crus* such as La Nerthe enjoyed a reputation in the 18th century, but the village of Châteauneuf-Calcernier was just one of many producing good wines.

An important figure in the history of winemaking in this district was Joseph Ducos (*see* p259), who was responsible for 10 out of Châteauneuf's famous 13 varieties. His ideas on winemaking would not find many takers in Châteauneuf today: Grenache and Cinsaut should not exceed a fifth; two-fifths should be composed of Syrah, Mourvèdre, Muscardin and Vaccarèse (also known as Camarèse); and three-tenths should come from Counoise and Piquepoul Noir (which has largely disappeared now). White grapes — Bourboulenc and Clairette — should account for the rest. Indeed, Châteauneuf has not

been a fabulous blend of 13 cultivars for quite some time now, but rather a Grenache-based wine spiced up with Syrah, Mourvèdre and others.

Joseph Ducos died before Châteauneuf-du-Pape received its AOC. Nor did he know of the Plateau de Montredon and its famous pebbles. Before World War I this was orchard land covered with olives and cherries. Between the wars the plateau began to be cleared of fruit trees, but the planting of grapevines was not finished until the 1950s.

Soils in the AOC are varied. The heavier soils of Courthézon, for example, are less suitable for Grenache, one reason why so little of it is planted at Ch de Beaucastel.

Ch de Beaucastel

This is a large estate with 100ha (247 acres) in Châteauneuf-du-Pape and a further 30ha (75 acres) in the Côtes du Rhône. It used to be called Cru du Coudoulet, but it is now Coudoulet de Beaucastel. The Perrin family are also *négociants* for Gigondas and Côtes du Rhône wines.

The Perrins are among very few in Châteauneuf who still hold to the 13-variety versions of the wine; not really 13, for they use six reds in their blend and vinify them separately. The wine is currently 30% Grenache, 30% Mourvèdre, 20% Syrah, and 10% Cin-

saut, plus a smattering of others. They set considerable store by Counoise. Beaucastel also differs from other local wines in that the grapes are flash-heated when they come in from the vineyards. This is designed to minimize the need for sulphur dioxide.

Ch Fortia

To a certain extent, this is where the modern history of Châteauneuf began. The 28-ha (69-acre) estate is still owned by a direct descendant of Baron Le Roy de Boiseaumarié. In the 1920s, when AOC legislation was being drawn up, he represented the interests of Châteauneuf growers in protecting the authenticity of the village wines. He used Joseph Ducos' research, and that is how the 13 varieties became enshrined in law.

The present Baron Le Roy makes a highly traditional Châteauneuf from 80% Grenache and is able to make fine wines even in poor vintages.

Domaine de la Janasse

About 50ha (124 acres) of vines — a lot of Grenache — enable the Sabon family to assert their know-how: three "identified" *cuvées* and a Châteauneuf Vieilles Vignes, all of them fruity, spicy and rich.

Ch Mont-Redon

This 150-ha (370-acre) estate dominates the Rhône and the lands of the Vaucluse. All 13 of the *appellation's* varieties are planted here. Their blending accounts for the great depth of

flavour in the traditionally made red and white wines.

Clos des Papes

This 32-ha (79-acre) estate makes red and white wines. It is owned by Paul Avril, who makes his red from a blend of 70% Grenache, 20% Mourvèdre and 10% Syrah. Avril is less pleased with Syrah than Mourvèdre, the variety he refers to as "the Merlot of Châteauneuf". Clos des Papes is a traditional Châteauneuf producer whose wines are among the most elegant and suave in the AOC.

Ch Rayas

Jacques Reynaud has been succeeded by his nephew, Emmanuel, but the legendary and unique Château Rayas is still the same. Its rare wine is made from 100% Grenache from old, low-yielding vines. A second wine, called Pignan, is definitely made from Syrah and probably has Cinsaut in it too. Rayas produces very good, and often the best, wine in Châteauneuf, but beware of inconsistent bottlings. Pignan is also an excellent wine. And in his Côtes du Rhône from Ch de Fonsalette, Reynaud produces some of the best wine to come out of the Châteauneuf *appellation*.

Domaine du Vieux Télégraphe

The Bruniers have about 70ha (173 acres) of Châteauneuf-du-Pape at Vieux Télégraphe. The wine is 70% Grenache topped up with equal quantities of Syrah and Mourvèdre. Vieux Télégraphe is a very consistent wine, always one of the best in the region.

Other producers

Henri Bonnot; Maurice Boiron (Bosquet des Papes); Domaine du Grand Veneur; Gonnet (Domaine Font de Michelle); Ch La Nerthe, Mont Olivet; Chapoutier; La Vieille Julienne.

Beaumes-de-Venise, a Côtes du Rhône Villages commune, also makes a Muscat dessert wine.

COTEAUX DU TRICASTIN

This is a rambling AOC southeast of Montélimar. The wines, which are mostly red, are good enough when consumed locally. One estate to watch here is Domaine de Grangeneuve.

COTES DU LUBERON

This is a fairly new AOC (granted in 1988) to the east of Avignon. The usual medley of grapes is permitted for reds: Ugni Blanc, of Cognac fame, is the mainstay of whites. The large estate, Val Joanis, is a reliable standby.

COTES DU RHONE

This is a huge, best-of-the-rest AOC for wines that do not quite make it into the Côtes du Rhône-Villages AOC. The buyer will find a fair amount of poor wine and a few pleasant surprises. The chief red grape is Grenache again, but for the time being there is

rather more Cinsaut than Syrah or Mourvèdre. Things are changing, however, and the next few years should see a marked improvement in the quality of these wines. White wines are dominated by Clairette, but there is also a little Roussanne and Marsanne.

Négociant wines are often a good bet when it comes to Côtes du Rhône. Jaboulet's (*see* p256) Parallèle 45 has an equal proportion of Grenache and Syrah; likewise Guigal's (*see* p254) Côtes du Rhône often has a strong Syrah character. Chapoutier (*see* p256) are also reliable here.

One or two individual estates deserve mention: Ch du Grand Moulas is good in itself, but its Cuvée de l'Ecu is even better; and Ch de St-Estève is an experimental estate that is constantly turning out new blends. Look out too for Ch de Beaucastel's (*qv*) Coudoulet de Beaucastel,

which has considerable *gravitas* for a Côtes du Rhône (and a price to match), and Jacques Reynaud's (*see* Ch Rayas, p260) rare and expensive Ch de Fonsalette, possibly the best Côtes du Rhône of all.

Côtes du Rhône Villages

This AOC is composed of 16 communes (*see* p259) allowed to add their name on the label. Originally the list of villages included Gigondas and Vacqueyras, each of which has since been awarded its own AOC.

Red wines are based on Grenache, and the best will also have a smattering of Syrah and Mourvèdre in them. Some of the more go-ahead estates have brought out special *cuvées* based on one or other variety. There is rather less white wine produced, although the villages of Chusclan and Laudun count it among their specialities.

Wines to watch out for include those from the top estate of Domaine Ste-Anne in St-Gervais, made from Syrah and Mourvèdre. These wines have inspired a generation of winemakers in the region.

As for Domaine Rabasse-Charavin in Cairanne, it excels at Syrah and produces a wine that could easily be mistaken for a good *cru* from the Northern Rhône.

Domaine de la Soumade in Rasteau is notable not only for its Syrah-dominated reds but also for its *vin doux naturel*, while in Sablet Domaine des Gourberts' wines come from the same stable as a top Gigondas.

Gabriel Meffre's award-winning Ch de Courançonne is largely Grenache-based; and more Syrah is to be found in René Suard's Domaine des Grands Devers in Valréas.

COTES DU VENTOUX

The quality of wine here does not often match up to the beauty of the landscape, with its *garrigues* scented with thyme and lavender. For the time being, the one estate to watch is Malcolm Swann's Domaine des Anges. The Perrins at Ch de Beaucastel in Châteauneuf have a money-spinning, reliable old standby in Vieille Ferme, and Jaboulet bottles some good wine too.

COTES DU VIVARAIS

This is an up-and-coming AOC making decent but light red wines from the usual Southern Rhône varieties, and a certain amount of rosé and white wine. The whites are based on the Clairette, Marsanne and Bourboulenc varieties. Not much Côtes du Vivarais leaves the region, but among the wines that do, look out for those from Domaine de Vigier.

GIGONDAS

Gigondas has always lived a

little in the shadow of its more famous neighbour, Châteauneuf-du-Pape. It produces red and rosé wines made mainly from Grenache, with additions of Syrah, Mourvèdre, Cinsaut and so on, but there are some very good wines indeed to be had from its limestone soils. Grenache is limited to 80% of the *cuvée* and there is a minimum of 15% Syrah and Mourvèdre.

Domaine des Pallières
This is one of the best estates (25ha/62 acres) in Gigondas, making consistently good wines. It was the first to bottle Gigondas at the end of the 19th century and is now owned by the Brunier family of Vieux Télégraphe (*qv* p260). The wines have a touch of hardness that is typical of Gigondas, but they are long lasting.

Domaine St-Gayan
Roger Meffre's 15-ha (35-acre) estate is on the AOC's clay soils and makes big, often aggressively tannic wines. They nonetheless enjoy considerable prestige not only in the region, but also in the rest of France and abroad.

Other producers
Domaine des Goubert and Domaine Raspail-Ay.

LIRAC
The best red and white Lirac wines aspire to the quality of Châteauneuf-du-Pape; the best rosés to those of Tavel (*qv*). One of the best producers is the peripatetic Jean-Claude Assémat, who owns both Domaine des Causses and Domaine des Garrigues. Assémat makes a good Grenache/ Carignan/Mourvèdre/Syrah *cuvée* at Causses, and another wine that is 70% Syrah, which he puts into new oak casks. Other Lirac producers to watch are Domaine Roger Sabon (who also makes fairly good Châteauneuf-du-Pape), Dom-

aine Duseigneur and Domaine Maby (La Fermade).

TAVEL
This *appellation* is restricted to making big, alcoholic rosés. These wines have a wide following in France, where they are consumed in countless Vietnamese and Chinese restaurants. They tend to be exported only when they are past their prime. One of the problems of Tavel is the Grenache Noir, which can oxidize in a rosé just a mite too

quickly: this means that the wines begin to throw a rusty bloom. The answer is to use more Mourvèdre in the blend. Ch d'Aquéria and Domaine de la Mordorée are the top estates.

VACQUEYRAS
This *appellation* emerged from the Côtes du Rhône Villages pack in 1989 with a new AOC for its red wines. The wines have a good depth of colour and flavour, and the elevation of Vacqueyras is considered one of the INAO's wiser decisions.

The best producers are Domaine des Amouriers, Ch de Montmirail and Domaine de la Monardière.

VINS DE PAYS

The *vins de pays* of the Rhône Valley should not be neglected: not only can they yield a pleasant surprise for travellers in the Valley, but they are often on the shopping lists of large supermarkets that are ever on the look-out for the best quality at the lowest prices. Most of the wines are best consumed at their freshest: there is little point in storing them in the cellar.

The *vins de pays* of the Rhône Valley are part of the Rhône-Alpes region, one of several large administrative areas created by the Mitterrand government. Rhône-Alpes produces some 33 million cases of *vins de pays* a year. The wines range from the crisp whites of the mountains around Savoy to the aromatic reds of the Rhône Valley proper.

Vin de Pays des Comtés Rhodaniens
This is a catch-all *vin de pays* for wines from all over the Rhône-Alpes region; but the wines must have satisfied the prior condition of having the right to bear on the label one of the zonal *appellations*: Coteaux de l'Ardèche, Coteaux des Baronnies, Coteaux de Grignan, Collines

Rhodaniennes, Coteaux de Grésivaudan, Balmes Dauphinoises, Allobrogie and Urfé.

Vin de Pays de la Drôme
92% of production is red wine, principally from Grenache, Cinsaut and Syrah. The addition of Gamay, Cabernet Sauvignon or Merlot is permitted. Gamay, in particular, has been quite successful. The wines come from the right bank of the Rhône, between Valence and Montélimar.

Vin de Pays des Collines Rhodaniennes
This *vin de pays* covers what is essentially the hinterland of the Northern Rhône, and where one might assume a reasonable amount of decent Syrah wine was to be had. As much as 60% of the wine is varietal, with the accent not only on Syrah, but also on Gamay and Merlot.

Vin de Pays du Comté de Grignan
This *vin de pays* is on the right bank of the Rhône, around Montélimar. As befits a Southern Rhône *vin de pays*, the wines are dominated by Grenache and the usual Southern Rhône cultivars.

Growers are permitted to make varietal wines from Gamay, Merlot or Cabernet Sauvignon if they wish. Only 1% of production is white.

Vin de Pays des Coteaux de l'Ardèche
A *vin de pays* on the left bank, with its centre at Aubenas. Again the grower may choose between making a commercially appealing Cabernet, Merlot or Gamay wine, or sticking to the more traditional Grenache-based blend. Rosés, including pure Syrah rosés, have been successful from this region. Among the white wines are Chardonnay and Viognier.

Vin de Pays des Coteaux des Baronnies
This *vin de pays* lies in the far east of the region, beyond the olive-oil producing centre of Nyons. Again growers have a choice: they can use traditional grapes of the Southern Rhône or opt for something that might appeal more to a foreign supermarket buyer. Being close to the Diois, they are also allowed to use Pinot Noir. Ugni Blanc, Chardonnay and Viognier are the white varieties permitted, alongside Clairette and Grenache Blanc.

JURA AND SAVOIE

THESE TWO SMALL AND REMOTE VINEGROWING REGIONS OF
EASTERN FRANCE PRODUCE A NUMBER OF DISTINCTIVELY
INDIVIDUAL WINES.

The wines of the Jura and Savoie are little-known outside their regions, but have a guaranteed local market. The Vin de Pays d'Allobrogie made here, in the Val de l'Arve in Haute-Savoie, is popular with skiers.

Mountains make for individuality, cutting off vineyards from outside influences and emphasizing their isolation. So perhaps it comes as no surprise that the wines of the Jura, Savoie and the Bugey bear little resemblance to the others of eastern France — and, indeed, include grape varieties that are not to be found elsewhere in France. The Jura, a land of mountain ridges, forms a remote corner of eastern France on the borders of Switzerland. The scenery is a dramatic combination of craggy cliffs and pastoral scenes of grazing cows; this is also the home of Comté cheese. The town of Lons-le-Saunier stands at the heart of the vineyards, with the broad *appellation* of Côtes du Jura stretching to the north and south. The wines can be red, white or rosé, and even *gris* and *jaune*, as well as sparkling. The *appellation* of Arbois, around that attractive town, provides the best red wine: it is made from Pinot Noir as well as the peculiarly local grape varieties Poulsard and Trousseau. L'Etoile is a tiny *appellation*, mainly for white wine, while the *appellation* of Château-Chalon produces the best *vin jaune*, which is quite the most original wine of the Jura, with its distinctive use of the Savagnin grape. The Savoie vineyards have more in common with those of Switzerland than with the rest of France, for the principal grape variety is the Chasselas. The white Jacquère and the red Mondeuse are also peculiar to Savoie. The main *appellation*, Vin de Savoie, is scattered, with 17 *crus* stretching from south of Chambéry to the shores of Lake Geneva. Roussette, another distinctively Savoyard grape variety, accounts for the *appellation* Roussette de Savoie, with a handful of *crus*, and then there is Crépy, a still white wine, and Seyssel, which may be still or sparkling. The bridge that crosses the Rhône at Seyssel links Savoie to the Bugey, one of those lost regions of France. It lies between the cities of Chambéry and Lyons, on the way to nowhere, with Belley at its centre. Viticulture tends to take second place to other agriculture here. The wines have the status of a VDQS, again with various *crus* of limited importance. Rosé de Cerdon, a rustic sparkling wine, is another curiosity, emphasizing the rural isolation of the mountain vineyards of France.

JURA

The Jura produces some of the most distinctively individual wines of France, from some of the most original grape varieties. There are four *appellations*, encompassing a range of different flavours and colours, and the vineyards are centred on the unassuming town of Lons-le-Saunier, which was the birthplace of Rouget de Lisle, the composer of the Marseillaise.

The climate of the Jura is distinctly continental, with fiercely cold winters, and temperatures that descend well below freezing point with an appropriate amount of snow. Summers are warm and sunny, but rainfall can be heavy, while autumns are long and fine. The soil is a mixture of limestone and clay.

There is one general *appellation*, Côtes du Jura, which covers the broad expanse of vineyards, and three more precise *appellations*: Château-Chalon, L'Etoile and Arbois. The Jura also has a unique style of wine, *vin jaune* (*see* box on facing page).

Côtes du Jura

The Côtes du Jura vineyards stretch both north and south of Lons-le-Saunier over some 72 villages. The majority of the wine is white, from Savagnin and Chardonnay grapes; Pinot Noir, Trousseau and Poulsard are used for red and rosé wine. However, Poulsard is very pale in colour and is sometimes also used for white wine. Chardonnay and Pinot Noir show the close links with Burgundy and the Franche-Comté, while Savagnin, Trousseau and Poulsard are firmly local. Sometimes the wines are pure varietals; sometimes a blend of several varieties.

Château-Chalon

Château-Chalon is the name of a village and of an *appellation*, covering four communes, for *vin jaune*. As the

Vin jaune cellar at Château-Chalon.

village is built on a granite outcrop, it is impossible to build underground cellars there. Consequently all the cellars in the village are only partially subterranean, with the result that there are considerable fluctuations of temperature, which play a big part in the unusual process by which *vin jaune* yeast flourishes.

There are only about a dozen producers of Château-Chalon, who all work closely together, maintaining very high quality standards. In bad years such as 1980 and 1984 they decided not to sell their wine labelled as Château-Chalon but to declassify it all into Côtes du Jura. The rules of the *appellation* impose strict standards: work in the vineyards is checked and yields are restricted to no more than 30hl/ha, although in fact a remarkably low 20hl/ha is more usual.

While the other *appellations* of the Jura include *vin jaune* — with a lower minimum alcohol level of 11.5%Vol — it is at Château-Chalon that this distinctive wine is at its best. The flavour, with the effect of the *flor* and

the searing dry, firm, nutty flavour of oxidation, is most individual. This is one of the most characterful wines in France.

L'Etoile

This note of oxidation found in Château-Chalon wines has spread into the other white wines of the Jura, such as L'Etoile, which means "star" and takes its name from a hillside village outside Lons-le-Saunier, where the soil contains numerous fossilized starfish. L'Etoile became an *appellation* in 1937, for white wine and *vin jaune*. The permitted grape varieties for the white wine are Chardonnay, Savagnin and Poulsard. However, pure Chardonnay is more common, or maybe a blend of Chardonnay and Savagnin; but usually the small production of Savagnin is kept for *vin jaune*.

The ordinary table wine is kept in barrel for two or three years and seems to take on some of the nutty flavours that are original to the Jura. At first taste the wine may seem oxidized, but this is not the case; the underlying fruit is rich and lively.

Arbois

The *appellation* of Arbois is known as the principal red-wine *appellation* of the Jura, although it can also be white, yellow and rosé (sometimes more poetically described as *gris* or even *corail*). Arbois is an attractive old market town, with russet-coloured roofs and an imposing church tower. This is where Louis Pasteur spent much of his childhood: he later used the wines of Arbois as examples in his experiments with bacteria and yeast for his treatise on oenology. Today his former vineyard, just outside the town, is maintained by the firm of Henri Maire.

Arbois prides itself on being one of the very first *appellations d'origine contrôlée* of France, recognized in 1936 along with Cassis and Châteauneuf-du-Pape. The *appellation* covers six villages, of which Pupillin is allowed to add its own name to that of the *appellation* on the label, while Poligny is another important village.

The characteristic grapes for red Arbois, and also red Côtes du Jura, are Trousseau and Poulsard, as well as Pinot Noir. Generally, red Jura wines tend to lack colour, while in contrast some of the rosé wines are often quite dark, as the juice is kept in contact with the skins for considerably longer than is usual elsewhere in France — indeed, for almost as long as for the red wine. Neither Poulsard nor Trousseau have much colour in their skins, although Trousseau grapes tend to have thicker skins, which may make for a fuller flavour in the mouth.

White Arbois is usually made from Chardonnay, maybe with some Savagnin, and occasionally some Poulsard vinified off the skins. Pure Chardonnay will have some varietal character, while a pure Savagnin, or a blend of the two, tends to have the slightly oxidized nose of *vin jaune*, with the typical nutty tang. This demonstrates the main difference between winemaking in the Jura and elsewhere in France. There is not the same attention to the need to keep barrels topped up regularly. Otherwise basic winemaking techniques are not so different. Some cellars are modern and streamlined; others are distinctly more rustic. Accordingly temperature control during fermentation may be a little hit and miss, but is not often necessary, given the cool weather usual at vintage time. Chaptalization (*see*

p109) is allowed in modest quantity and the wine is either kept in concrete vats or large barrels, while small barrels are used for *vin jaune*.

Sparkling wine, vin de paille and Macvin

Three of the Jura *appellations* (with the exception of Château-Chalon) include *mousseux*, or sparkling wine. Chardonnay is the usual grape variety and the method is strictly the classic method developed in Champagne, resulting in some good fruity wines. Several producers make their own base wine and then send it to a company outside Lons-le-Saunier to be turned into sparkling wine. However, Henri Maire's popular sparkling Vin Fou does not use Jura grapes.

There is also a small local custom of *vin de paille*, or "straw wine", which is produced from grapes that were traditionally dried on straw for several weeks from October to January, so that they became quite dehydrated and the resulting juice rich and concentrated. Whereas 100kg (220lb) of grapes normally produce about 70–75 litres of juice, for *vin de paille* this is drastically reduced to 20–25 litres. The fermentation is very slow indeed and may take as long as four years, in small barrels. Although *vin de paille* forms part of three *appellations*, but not Château-Chalon, it is usually made in limited quantity for family and friends. It is deep brown with a rich, sweet, nutty taste.

The final *appellation* of the Jura, created in 1991, is for Macvin, the Jura equivalent of the sweet apéritif Pineau des Charentes. It is a blend of one-third *marc* to two-thirds red or white grape juice.

Vin de pays

A postscript to the wines of the Jura is the Vin de Pays de Franche-Comté, which covers the Haute-Saône and Jura *départements*. A group of growers in the village of Champlitte near Dole make red wine from Pinot Noir and Gamay grapes, and white from Auxerrois and Chardonnay.   □

VIN JAUNE

Unlike virtually all other wines, oxidation forms a vital part of the making of *vin jaune*, the Jura's most original wine. *Vin jaune* could be described as France's answer to fino sherry, for the development of *flor* is essential to the flavour of *vin jaune*, as it is for fino (*qv*). The nutty, salty taste recalls fino too, though *vin jaune* is lighter in alcohol. Its classic partner is the local hard cheese, Comté.

The village of Château-Chalon is considered to produce the finest *vin jaune* of all, although this style of wine also features in the other Jura *appellations*.

The mystery of flor

Vin jaune is made from the low-yielding, temperamental Savagnin grape, which is peculiar to the Jura. Some say it may be related to Gewürztraminer; others that it is from Hungary. In Savoie it has a close cousin, Gringet, which makes sparkling Ayze. For *vin jaune*, the grapes are fermented in the normal way, achieving a minimum alcohol level of 12%Vol, but preferably 13%, then the wine is put into 228-litre barrels for six years. During this time the barrels are neither racked nor topped up, so that a veil of yeast, related to the sherry *flor*, forms on the surface of

the wine. How this happens is the subject of much research.

At Château-Chalon, cellar temperatures vary between 8°C (46°F) and 18°C (64°F) during the year. The *flor* yeast becomes active during the warm summer months and then dies down again in the winter, and thus the distinctive flavour develops. The level of humidity in the cellar and the ratio of the barrel size to the volume of air in the barrel can also affect the yeast activity.

Small yields and high prices

Immense care is taken with the production of *vin jaune*, for there is a very high risk of the wine developing volatile acidity and spoiling. It is tasted and analysed every six months.

A considerable amount of wine is lost through evaporation during the ageing process, which explains the whimsical size of the traditional Jura *clavelin* bottle in which *vin jaune* is sold, for 62cl is what remains from 100cl after six years' maturation in wood. The tiny yields and lengthy production process account for the high price of *vin jaune*. Although it cannot claim to represent good value, it certainly merits a place among the most original vinous flavours of France.

PRODUCERS

There are few large estates in the Jura, although one company, Henri Maire, dominates the region. The other large producer is the cooperative (*fruitière*) in Arbois, which has over 140 members.

Fruitière Vinicole d'Arbois
The cooperative of Arbois is responsible for about a quarter of the vineyards of the *appellation*, and produces only Arbois wines including *vin jaune* and sparkling white wine. Founded in 1906, it has some of the most modern production facilities of the area.

Ch d'Arlay
This château, in the village of Arlay, is one of the oldest estates of the Jura. It dates back to the Middle Ages and now belongs to Count Renaud de Laguiche, whose family are also proprietors in Puligny-Montrachet in Burgundy. The château makes a range of Côtes du Jura wines: white wine from Chardonnay with a small amount of Savagnin, red wine from Pinot Noir, and Corail, a light red wine from all five grape varieties, as well as *vin jaune* and Macvin.

Caveau de Bacchus
Lucien Aviet, in Montigny-lès-Arsures, follows traditional Jura techniques. His rosé wines are usually made from Poulsard and his reds from thicker-skinned Trousseau. He has very little Pinot Noir. He makes white wine from Chardonnay blended with a little Savagnin, as well as *vin jaune*, and some Macvin, following his grandmother's old recipe.

Christian Bourdy
The Bourdy family have been making wine in Arlay since 1781. They have 5ha (12 acres) of their own vines, in both Arlay and Château-Chalon, and also buy grapes as a *négo-ciant*, enabling them to make the complete range of Jura wines, including L'Etoile and *vin de paille*. Their wines are quite traditional; to quote M Bourdy, "oenologically all the wines of the Jura are sick, but we like them like that and we do not want to cure them."

Jean Macle
M Macle is one of the leading producers of Château-Chalon, with cellars that date back to the 17th century in the centre of the village. Although he has vineyards of Chardonnay, his reputation is founded on Château-Chalon, made purely from Savagnin, and he has done much to re-establish the quality of the *appellation*. Meticulous winemaking produces long-lived wines.

Henri Maire
If the wines of Jura have any kind of reputation outside the region, Henri Maire is the man responsible. Although his best-known wine, Vin Fou, a sparkling white wine made by the transfer method (*see* p114), does not contain a single drop of Jura wine, he has in its wake created a greater awareness of the Jura. The family can trace its origins back to 1632 and the firm, a public company since 1986, owns four sizeable estates and also buys in grapes, to account for over half of the total production of the region. The estates, all situated around Arbois, are Domaine de Montfort, de la Croix d'Argis, du Sorbief and de Grange Grillard. The range of wines covers all the different flavours and styles of the Jura, from velvety Arbois to nutty *vin jaune*.

Rolet Père et Fils
This family company based in Arbois has been making wine since the 1940s, with 55ha (136 acres) in both Arbois and the Côtes du Jura. After traditional beginnings, it now has a streamlined warehouse with modern equipment and — unusually for Jura producers — concentrates on single-varietal wines, with a rosé Poulsard, red Trousseau and red Pinot Noir. White wines include some Chardonnay aged in new oak and some Savagnin matured in old oak, as well as sparkling wine, *vin jaune* and Macvin.

Domaine de Montbourgeau
Jean Gros' small estate is known for its dense and elegant white L'Etoile wine.

Harvesting Trousseau grapes for the red wine of Arbois.

SAVOIE

The vineyards of Savoie are scattered over a large part of the two *départements* of Savoie and Haute-Savoie, mixed with fields of cereal and undulating pastures of grazing cows. The city of Chambéry forms the natural centre of the region. The vineyards reach as far as the shores of Lake Geneva in the north, with pockets of vines on the hillside shores of the lake. There is a further concentration of vines around Lake Bourget and the town of Aix-les-Bains, and yet more vineyards to the south of Chambéry in the valley of the Isère, in an area that is sometimes called the Combe de Savoie. Consequently the *appellation* of Vin de Savoie is very fragmented and includes 17 *crus*, of varying importance and differing flavours. Across the Rhône from Seyssel there is also a separate, isolated area, the Bugey, entitled to a VDQS.

Soil and climate

Mountains lead to climatic uncertainty. Winters are cold and hard, usually with ample snowfall. Spring frosts can damage the vines, but any means of protection is totally uneconomic. Hail can be another hazard. Summers are usually warm, but can also be wet.

However, the lakes of Bourget and Geneva create favourable microclimates for the surrounding vineyards, and with such mountainous terrain there is an enormous range of micro-climates, with variations from one hillside to the next, and from one vineyard to another. The soil of both Savoie and the Bugey is a mixture of clay and limestone, mixed with the minerals from the glacial deposits.

Wines and grape varieties

Although this part of France was in fact Italian until 1860, the viticulture of the region has more to do with

The wine-producing town of Seyssel.

Switzerland than with Piedmont. White wines are much more important than red, with grape varieties such as Jacquère, Roussette and Chasselas making delicately ethereal wines that suit the mountain air. The red wines come from Pinot Noir, Gamay and most distinctively Mondeuse — also grown in Italy, where it is known as Refosco and makes a varietal wine in Friuli, at the other end of the Alps.

Grapes for white wine

Jacquère is peculiar to Savoie and the Bugey. In Savoie it is the principal grape variety of the two neighbouring *crus* Abymes and Apremont, where it is also called Plante des Abymes. It is easy to cultivate, for it is not too susceptible to rot or oïdium and only slightly so to mildew. It is less successful in the Bugey, as it needs a warm, sunny aspect, without which it tends to be too green and herbaceous.

There is also Molette, which is used for sparkling wine, since its high acidity means it makes particularly suitable base wine.

Gringet, found in the *cru* of Ayze, is the Savoyard version of Savagnin.

Roussette is another characteristic white grape variety of Savoie. The name originates from the reddish colour of the ripe grapes and locally it is often called Altesse, which translates literally as "highness". It is thought to be related to the Furmint grape used in Hungarian Tokaji. Roussette is also grown in the Bugey, but it is susceptible to both frost and rot, resulting in irregular yields and making it even more difficult to cultivate here than Jacquère.

Chasselas has been grown on the shores of Lake Geneva since the 13th century. It is also to be found in Alsace and in the vineyards of Pouilly-sur-Loire, but in diminishing quantities. It is now generally appreciated as a table grape in France, although across the lake in Switzerland Chasselas really comes into its own as a wine grape, with various regional synonyms, such as Fendant, Dorin and Perlan. In Savoie it is used in the *appellation* of Crépy, as well as three *crus* of Vin de Savoie: Ripaille, Marin and Marignan. Chasselas wine is sometimes criticized for its lack of positive aroma, since it tends to be rather delicate, almost to the point of neutrality.

Chardonnay was introduced into Savoie in the early 1960s. The original objective was to improve the sometimes discreet flavours of the Jacquère, but it has not really lived up to expectations. However as a recognized variety for Vin de Savoie it is sometimes vinified separately and can also be blended with Roussette for Roussette de Savoie. Its local name is Petite Ste-Marie. Generally, however, Chardonnay is more successful in the Bugey district (*see* next page), where it makes some delicately-flavoured wines with good varietal character.

Grapes for red wine

The most characteristic red grape variety of both Savoie and the Bugey is Mondeuse, which in Savoie is grown mainly in the village of Arbin and on the eastern shores of Lake Bourget for the *cru* of Chautagne. Mondeuse was the main variety in the region before phylloxera destroyed so many vineyards; Gamay and Pinot Noir are much more recent arrivals. Mondeuse can be erratic in both quality and quantity, but when it is given a little barrel-ageing its earthy, peppery flavours become more refined. In the Bugey it is successful only on the very warmest sites, since it ripens late and therefore can sometimes be too green.

Growers, merchants and cooperatives

The wines of both Savoie and the Bugey are produced by numerous small growers who usually practise polyculture, so that cereals and dairy farming are as important as vines. They may belong to village cooperatives, such as those in Cruet, Chautagne and Montmélian, or they may sell their grapes or wine to the local *négociants*, who are still an important commercial force in the region.

Very little wine travels outside the region: the influx of tourists, in winter to the ski slopes and in summer to enjoy the tranquillity of the mountains, ensures a ready demand for the local wines.

Techniques and ageing

Methods in the cellars vary in degree of refinement; some are pretty rustic or unsophisticated; others are more streamlined, with stainless steel vats and equipment for controlling fermentation temperatures. The malolactic fermentation may, or may not, be encouraged; chaptalization (the addition of sugar during fermentation to raise the alcohol level) is allowed and is usually necessary. Oak barrels are occasionally used for maturing Mondeuse, but most wines are bottled quite quickly. Generally the wines of Savoie and the Bugey are best drunk when they are relatively young, while they retain their fresh fragrance and fruit. □

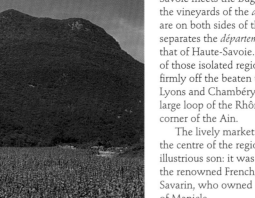

Vineyards near the village of Jongieux, west of Lake Bourget.

BUGEY

Savoie meets the Bugey at Seyssel, for the vineyards of the *appellation* of Seyssel are on both sides of the Rhône, which separates the *département* of the Ain from that of Haute-Savoie. The Bugey is one of those isolated regions of France, lying firmly off the beaten track between Lyons and Chambéry, and contained by a large loop of the Rhône in the south-east corner of the Ain.

The lively market town of Belley is the centre of the region and boasts an illustrious son: it was the birthplace of the renowned French gastronome Brillat-Savarin, who owned a vineyard in the *cru* of Manicle.

Unlike Vin de Savoie, Vin du Bugey (white, red and rosé) and the white Roussette du Bugey have risen no further than VDQS in status; but like Vin de Savoie, they also include several different *crus* of varying importance and individuality (*see* p270). It was the creation of the VDQS in 1957 that saved the wines of the Bugey from complete oblivion, and encouraged the development of the vineyards and the replacement of hybrids with varieties such as Jacquère, Molette, Roussette and Chardonnay for white wine; Mondeuse, Pinot Noir and Gamay for red. There is also a little Aligoté and Poulsard, showing how the region has borrowed from Burgundy and the Jura, as well as from Savoie.

APPELLATIONS AND PRODUCERS

Savoie wine has a complex official structure. The main *appellation*, AOC Vin de Savoie, is used on its own or with the names of one of 17 villages or areas: these are called *crus*. There are also three further AOCs: Roussette de Savoie, Crépy and Seyssel. Also covered here is the neighbouring VDQS, Vin du Bugey.

VIN DE SAVOIE
Vin de Savoie covers a wide spread of vineyards, with 17 individual *crus*. It was created in 1973, from a VDQS that was established in 1957. 70% of the wine is white. The *crus* are described below in order of importance, with notes on their leading producers.

Apremont and Abymes
Apremont lies to the south of Chambéry, around the village of Apremont. Jacquère is the principal grape variety, grown in vineyards where the soil is mainly glacial deposit. The wine has some dry, stony, flinty fruit, with crisp acidity. Some Chardonnay and Mondeuse are also grown. The neighbouring *cru*, Abymes, is so-named after a natural catastrophe: in 1248 part of Mont Granier collapsed, destroying the village of St-André. The vineyards are planted on the rubble from the mountain. Here, too, Jacquère is the main variety and there is a little Chardonnay.

There is a local saying that Apremont ripens in the shade and Abymes in the sun, implying that the wines of Abymes may be a little softer and more supple, Apremont's firmer and more steely.

Pierre Boniface at Domaine des Rocailles is a leading producer of both Abymes and Apremont, as well as some red Vin de Savoie. He owns 15ha (37 acres) of vines and buys grapes from another 25ha (62 acres). His white wines benefit from modern technology, while his red wines, mainly from Mondeuse, are aged in oak *barriques* for extra depth of flavour. Le Vigneron Savoyard, a cooperative, is another good producer at Apremont.

Chignin
Chignin, also to the south of Chambéry, has vineyards on a steep hillside at an altitude of about 360m (1,190ft). Here the predominant white Jacquère grape produces slightly fuller flavours than either Apremont or Abymes. The vineyards face south and south-west, making for a warmer microclimate, while the soil is a mixture of clay and limestone.

Chignin also has a second, quite distinctive white *cru*: Chignin-Bergeron. Bergeron is the local name for the Roussanne grape of the northern Rhône. Nobody quite knows how a pocket of Roussanne vines came to be planted here, but they have been established for over 100 years. Production is tiny, for Roussanne is much more temperamental than Jacquère and much more susceptible to disease, but it also makes wines of greater flavour and depth. There is also a small amount of red wine produced in Chignin, from Mondeuse, Gamay and Pinot Noir. Raymond Quénard is a leading producer.

Arbin and the Isère Valley
Arbin in the valley of the Isère has a reputation for red rather than white wine, for the village never followed the trend towards white wine of the last two decades. Methods tend to be quite traditional, with fermentation in large oak vats and some ageing in smaller barrels, as practised by Louis Magnin.

The other *crus* south of Chambéry in the valley of the Isère are Cruet, St-Jeoire-Prieuré, Montmélian, St-Jean-de-la-Porte and Ste-Marie-d'Alloix. The last two exist solely on paper, as does Charpignat to the north of Chambéry; St-Jean-de-la-Porte prefers to use the overall *appellation* of Vin de Savoie, while there are no vines left in Ste-Marie-d'Alloix. The production of St-Jeoire-Prieuré is also fairly meagre, while Cruet and Montmélian are dominated by the village cooperatives, with Jacquère and some Roussette grapes for white wine and Gamay for red. Nearby Fléterive is an aspiring *cru* and known particularly for its vine nurseries.

Chautagne
The vineyards lie on the eastern shores of Lake Bourget, planted mainly with the red grape varieties Mondeuse, Pinot Noir and Gamay, as well as a little Jacquère, Roussette and Aligoté. Usually they are all vinified as single varieties. The cooperative in the village of Ruffieux is the main producer, providing an outlet for numerous small growers.

Jongieux
A more recent *cru*, created in 1988, with vineyards on south-west-facing slopes west of Lake Bourget. The main villages are Jongieux itself, Lucey, Billième and St-Jean-de-Chivetin. Jacquère is the principal grape variety, with some Chardonnay, which is more successful here than in the Isère Valley as growing conditions are similar to those of the Bugey. Gamay is the most important red variety, making rosé as well as red wine.

Ayze
Ayze has a local reputation for sparkling white wine. The grape is the unusual Gringet, said to be related to the Savagnin of the Jura. Roussette may also be used, and the method is a rustic version of that of Champagne — but usually without any *dosage* so that the taste is crisp, if not eye-wateringly austere.

Ripaille
The *cru* consists of the vineyards of the magnificent 15th-century Ch de Ripaille on the shores of Lake Geneva outside Thonon-les-Bains. Chasselas is the sole variety, making soft, rather light white wine. Methods are traditional; the cellar well-run and functional.

Marignan
Also made from Chasselas; production is very limited.

Marin
The most recently recognized *cru*, a village with vineyards overlooking Lake Geneva,

where Chasselas makes delicate white wine very similar to that of Ripaille.

ROUSSETTE DE SAVOIE

Roussette de Savoie is a white wine AOC. Misleadingly, it can contain Chardonnay as well as Roussette. It is only a pure varietal when one of the four *crus* is named on the label — Frangy (the most important, not far from Geneva); Marestel, near Jongieux; Monthoux, on the south-west shores of Lake Bourget; and Monterminod, east of Chambéry. Otherwise Roussette de Savoie may contain as much as 50% Chardonnay without any mention of the fact on the label. The flavour of Roussette, with or without Chardonnay, is fuller and fatter than a Vin de Savoie made from Jacquère.

CREPY

An AOC in its own right since 1948. The vineyards, on glacial deposits over heavy clay with a chalk subsoil, are on the southern shores of Lake Geneva around Douvaine. Chasselas is the sole grape variety and makes soft, delicate white wines, pleasantly dry and light in alcohol, but without any very positive flavour. Occasionally Crépy may be bottled off the lees to give an impression of *pétillance*. There is also a little experimentation with Chardonnay to enliven the flavour of the rather neutral Chasselas. Fichard and Mercier are the main producers.

SEYSSEL

The oldest Savoie *appellation*, dating from 1942, produces only white wines. The Rhône flows through the town, so that the vineyards are on both sides of its valley. It is best known for its sparkling wine, Seyssel Mousseux, made mainly from Molette grapes, but usually including a little

Roussette for finesse. Molette, with its high acidity and neutral flavour, makes an excellent base for sparkling wine made by the classic method used in Champagne.

The *appellation* Pétillant de Savoie, made from Jacquère, has fewer bubbles and less pressure than a fully-sparkling Seyssel Mousseux, while Roussette de Seyssel is a still wine made solely from that grape variety.

There are two main producers in Seyssel. The house of Varichon & Clerc dates back to 1910, and established the sparkling-wine tradition in Seyssel, the smallest sparkling-wine *appellation* of France. The grandson of the first M Clerc retired in 1986 and the company was bought by a Burgundian, Henri Gabet, who since then has done much to renovate it. Production methods are strictly the classic ones used in Champagne, with the benefit of modern cellar equipment, including *giropalettes* (*see* p110). The firm's best sparkling wine is Royal Seyssel, made mainly from Molette with at least 10% Roussette. It also makes a still Roussette de Savoie, a Pétillant de Savoie, and a sparkling wine with no *appellation*.

Maison Mollex is the largest vineyard owner of the *appellation*, including the renowned Clos de la Péclette. It makes still white wine from Roussette, red Vin de Savoie, and sparkling Seyssel from Molette, with at least 15% Roussette for extra finesse. Methods are simple and traditional, with fine results.

BUGEY

There are two VDQS, Vin du Bugey (white, red and rosé) and the white Roussette du Bugey, both with various *crus* which more often than not exist on paper rather than in the vineyards. The Vin du Bugey *crus* are Virieu-le-Grand, Montagnieu, Manicle, Machuraz and Cerdon; the Roussette du Bugey *crus* are Anglefort, Arbignieu, Chanay, Lagnieu, Montagnieu and Virieu-le-Grand.

Usually the wine is sold simply as Vin du Bugey with the mention of a grape variety such as Jacquère, Chardonnay, Aligoté, Mondeuse, Pinot Noir or Gamay.

Altogether some 63 villages, with a broad diversity of micro-climate, altitude, aspect and soil in the mountainous region around the town of Belley are included in the *appellation*, of which the most important is Vongnes. As in Savoie, Roussette du Bugey may contain a generous amount of Chardonnay.

The family company of Monin, based in the village of Vongnes, is the most important Bugey producer, but its wines are rarely found outside the region. Roussette du Bugey with a high percentage of Chardonnay, some red wine made from Mondeuse, and sparkling wine, a blend of Chardonnay, Jacquère, Aligoté and Molette, account for the greater part of the company's production.

The Caveau Bugiste cooperative also has a good local reputation for its range of wines from the region.

Cerdon

Cerdon is the most individual of the Bugey *crus*, for it stands apart from the rest of the area. The *cru* covers eight villages south-east of Bourg-en-Bresse, of which Cerdon itself, set in an amphitheatre of vines, is the largest.

Sparkling Rosé de Cerdon is made from Gamay, with some Pinot Gris, Pinot Noir and Poulsard. Some still wine is also made, but it is the sparkling that is the most individual. The technique is what is called the ancestral method, which was developed from the inability of the wine to complete the fermentation properly. Nowadays the fermentation is blocked so that some residual sugar remains; the wine is bottled, and fermentation starts again; after about three months the wine is filtered under pressure and rebottled. Sadly there is also a large amount of industrial *vin pétillant gazéifié* — not at all the same thing — as well as some wine made by the classic method in Lons-le-Saunier in the Jura.

Montagnieu and Manicle

Montagnieu is one of the more thriving *crus* of the Bugey, with a production of sparkling wine and some still Roussette.

Manicle is known for its associations with the politician and gourmet Brillat-Savarin; today one lone producer, André Miraillet, continues to make white Chardonnay and red Pinot Noir in the tiny village of Cheignieu-la-Balme. Methods here are pretty rustic, but the flavours are convincing.

VINS DE PAYS

The regional Vin de Pays des Comtés Rhodaniens covers wines made in Savoie, Haute-Savoie and several neighbouring *départements*. There are also two *vins de pays de zone*: Vin de Pays d'Allobrogie (the Allobroges were the Gallic tribe who lived and made wine here at the time of Julius Caesar); and Vin de Pays des Coteaux du Grésivaudan in the *département* of the Isère.

Both wines can be white, red or rosé, although Allobrogie is 95% white.

PROVENCE AND CORSICA

THE VINEYARDS OF PROVENCE ARE THE OLDEST IN FRANCE, AND HAVE A PROUD HISTORY, WHILE CORSICA'S WINES, ONCE OBSCURE, HAVE BEEN WINNING GROWING PRAISE AS THEIR DISTINCTIVE CHARACTER BECOMES KNOWN.

Grapes are ripened in Mediterranean sunshine but the wine is made in cool underground cellars. These are at Domaine Pardiguière near le Luc, in a well-situated valley in the Côtes de Provence zone.

Provence saw the birth of French wine. It was here, some 500 years before the Romans added the province to their empire in 125BC and named it *nostra provincia* — "our territory" — that vines were cultivated by Phocaean and later Greek settlers. Throughout the rich medieval history of Provence, its wines were called for by popes, kings and counts. As with many southern French regions, the crisis of phylloxera jolted Provence into a switch from quality to quantity. Old hill vineyards were abandoned and inferior grapes were replanted on flatter land. However, some pockets of traditional quality wine remained, and gained recognition in the 1930s and 1940s with *appellations* such as Cassis and Bandol. Since about 1975 there has been a revival of interest in red wines — the dominant style was, and is, rosé — as quality-conscious estates have emerged. Most Provence wine is still made by cooperatives and large merchant companies, but the pace-setters are the new, or newly revived, estates. These have invested in modern equipment and led the way in planting non-local grape varieties such as Cabernet Sauvignon, and have revived interest in the region's own quality red grape, the Mourvèdre. Today Provence is a useful source of vigorous red wines of character, but its estates face stiff competition from the similar wines of the reviving Midi and the southern Rhône. Corsica's isolation has led to the growth of an unusual range of wines. For a century until the 1950s, the island's rôle was as a source of strong, cheap reds destined for blending. The 1960s saw further growth in bulk winemaking, as French colonial growers from Algeria tried to re-establish themselves on the island. Recent years have shown a tentative re-emergence of old vineyards, wine styles and grape varieties. The Corsican grape heritage is Italian rather than French, and the styles of wine produced are distinct from those of Provence. The island has its own *appellation*, Vin de Corse, and within this zone are some specific sub-zones and local *appellations*, some thriving, others in decline. Most Corsican wine is drunk on the island by the locals and the large numbers of tourists. For those on the mainland and further afield, it is and must remain a vinous curiosity.

WINE REGIONS OF PROVENCE AND CORSICA

For most of the past century, Provence has had no great
reputation for its wines, with the exception of those
from the four AOC zones of Palette, Cassis, Bandol and
Bellet. A revival of interest in quality means that certain
names now stand out from the broad *appellations* of
Côtes de Provence and Coteaux d'Aix-en-Provence.

Most of Corsica is too mountainous to allow
viniculture — vineyards cling to the hills that rise steeply
from the sea all around the island. The highest
production is from the eastern coastal plain.

--- *département* boundary
— motorway
— major road
— other road

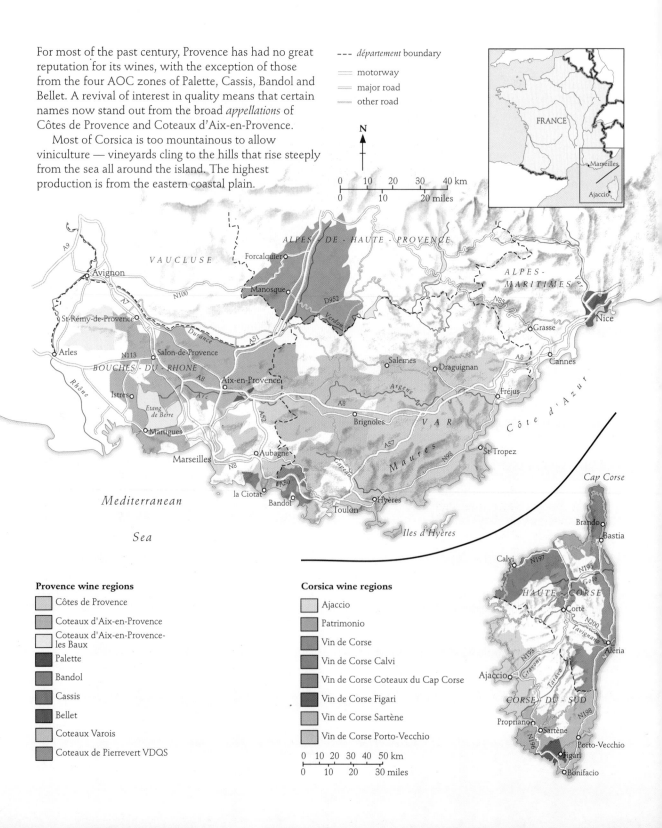

Provence wine regions

- Côtes de Provence
- Coteaux d'Aix-en-Provence
- Coteaux d'Aix-en-Provence-les Baux
- Palette
- Bandol
- Cassis
- Bellet
- Coteaux Varois
- Coteaux de Pierrevert VDQS

Corsica wine regions

- Ajaccio
- Patrimonio
- Vin de Corse
- Vin de Corse Calvi
- Vin de Corse Coteaux du Cap Corse
- Vin de Corse Figari
- Vin de Corse Sartène
- Vin de Corse Porto-Vecchio

PROVENCE

The Provence *appellations* taken together form one of the largest vineyard areas in France, and the vine has always been an important crop in this wide region. Vines appear as a vital part of the famous landscape of olive and forest-clad hills, ancient villages and opulent resorts, and the wines are found on the tables of the region's many fine restaurants.

There are close parallels in climate and soil terms with the wine-producing regions of California and Australia. There is ample sun, adequate winter rain and the topography provides sites protected from the Mistral winds. The terrain offers various soils, all rocky or gravelly, and well-drained hillside sites. Despite all these natural advantages, Provence has been criticized for having a superb winemaking environment but not making great wines. Until recently it concentrated on rosé: the Provence *terroir* producing, unusually, some serious quality wines as well as pleasant holiday drinking; but these by no means exploit fully the potential of the region.

A recent revival of interest in red wines has been in part due to the arrival of estate owners from outside the wine industry (again on the California model). Red wine has reached 35% of Côtes de Provence production (all but 5% of the rest is rosé). Among these reds are some serious and interesting wines, which not only exploit Provençal conditions, but also add "foreign" flavours from non-local grape varieties and benefit from modern winemaking techniques. The best of these wines contribute to an air of excitement and optimism about the prospects for seriously good red wine from Provence though there is still much red that does not as yet match the best from elsewhere in southern France. Rosé and white wines are improving too, as better grape varieties arrive and modern winemaking spreads, but their quality is still patchy.

The wine zones

Provence covers two *départements*, Var and Bouches-du-Rhône, from the Alps in the north and east to the Rhône in the west, with the Mediterranean coast in the south. The vineyards stretch from Nice in the east to the Rhône delta in the west. The *appellations* are potentially confusing: the main one, Côtes de Provence, is mostly in the south, from Toulon eastwards to beyond Fréjus, with isolated patches on the coast close to Marseilles, and inland around Trets. The *appellation* Coteaux d'Aix-en-Provence covers the western part of the region, with the recent (March 1993) AOC Coteaux Varois between it and the Côtes de Provence.

The wide areas covered by these general *appellations* means they are of little help to the wine drinker looking for an idea of a wine's style and quality. In Provence the estate name is both the clue to a local style of wine and some guarantee of quality.

There are, however, some districts that are becoming known for quality wines. The coastal zone has some good sites, but the vineyards are under pressure from development. Inland, the forested hills of the Maures Massif form a barrier between the coast and the wide valley around le Luc, which has some well-placed estates.

There are also four smaller *appellations* — Bandol, Bellet, Cassis and Palette — that identify zones with real local character.

Grape varieties and wine styles

With rosé filling two out of every three Côtes de Provence bottles, there is a stress on innocuous, even boring, grape varieties. Grenache and Carignan are dominant: neither is intrinsically bad, but both need low yields and hill vineyards to make really interesting wine. With the Provence rosé vineyards until now concentrated on flat land and cropped to the limit set by the AOC, flavour and character can be minimal. Cinsaut is potentially more interesting and is used in most red wines to some extent. Syrah has long been at home in Provence, but it is not as dominant as it is in the Rhône Valley. It adds flavour, colour and character to blends. Mourvèdre is traditionally the best Provençal red-wine grape. It is found in neighbouring southern Rhône, where it is used to make Châteauneuf-du-Pape and some of the better Côtes du Rhône wines. In Provence its main presence is in the coastal zone, especially Bandol.

Cabernet Sauvignon, the grape hailed all over the world as the key to making better-quality red wine, has been planted on several of the new-generation Provençal estates. It is most at home inland, in the cooler, hillier vineyards, and in the Aix-en-Provence area, particularly those in the sub-region of Les Baux-de-Provence, which takes its name from the hill village in the startling rocky outcrop of Les Alpilles.

Grapes for the small amount of white wine are Clairette Blanc, Ugni Blanc and the declining Bourboulenc; better varieties are Rolle — use of which is growing — and Sémillon and Sauvignon Blanc, often blended with the local varieties.

Provence rosé shows character only when made by a good estate and when some superior red grape varieties are added to the blend.

Côtes de Provence whites and rosés are generally drunk young, as are many reds, although the more robust and well-made can age well. □

APPELLATIONS AND PRODUCERS

Many of Provence's vineyards are on very small parcels of land, so that nearly half the region's production is from cooperatives. However, certain individual estates actively promote their wines, thanks to the value of the tourist industry.

BANDOL

The largest and most widely known of the smaller Provence *appellations*, AOC Bandol covers an area around the coastal town of Bandol, close to the southern tip of Provence. Most of the wine is red, which must be made from at least 50% Mourvèdre grapes. The balance can include Syrah, Grenache and others. The *appellation* rules also lay down a minimum of 18 months' ageing in cask. The result, from good estates, is an unusual red wine with a strong perfume, a powerful flavour and deep colour. It ages well, sometimes for up to 20 years.

La Bastide Blanche

A 28-ha (69-acre) estate owned by the Bronzo family. They make white and red wines, of which the white *blanc de blancs* is generally seen as the better of the two. In the red, the blend contains a higher proportion of Grenache than is normal in Bandol, resulting in a softer, broader, faster-maturing style of wine.

Domaine le Gallantin

Red wines are the love and speciality of Achille Pascal on this 25-ha (62-acre) estate, one of the smallest in the *appellation*. The wines are fermented at high temperature, which brings out all the colour in the Mourvèdre grapes, and results in wines that are both long lived and among the richest in Bandol. A fresh, lively white and a rosé are also made.

Domaine de l'Hermitage

Gerard Duffort, the owner of this 36-ha (90-acre) property, has completely renovated the vineyard and cellars since buying it in 1974. He now makes some very dense, weighty red wines, which include a small proportion of Syrah in the blend. Wines are vinified in stainless steel before being aged in wood. A white, a blend of Ugni Blanc and Clairette, is made in small quantities, and there is also a particularly good rosé.

Moulin des Costes

The Bunan family owns this estate at La Cadière and also Mas de la Rouvière and Belouve at Le Castellet, making them one of the biggest landowners in Bandol, with 75ha (185 acres) in total. The red wines, blended from the different estates, are 65% Mourvèdre, 14% Grenache and 6% Syrah. Cuvée Spéciale is a red that is made only in the best years, from a higher proportion of Mourvèdre. Techniques here are modern — some say they smooth out too much of the wine's rough edges — but they do result in charming wines in all three colours. There is also a Cabernet Sauvignon red made as Vin de Pays de Mont-Caume, which shows how well Cabernet can perform in this region.

Ch de Pibarnon

The wines from the 48-ha (119-acre) estate of Comte Henri de Saint-Victor are

always winning medals and awards at wine competitions in France. They certainly have an attractive taste, due partly to the presence of new wood and also to the high proportion of Mourvèdre in the blend. The rosé is particularly fruity and fresh, made in stainless steel tanks. The white, which has a percentage of the rare Bourboulenc grape in the blend, is crisp and lightly acidic.

Ch Pradeaux

Sometimes deeply rich and exciting, sometimes overwhelmed by wood, due to ageing of up to four years, the red wines made here can, in short, be either the greatest orthe worst in Bandol. Cyril Portalis continues to run his estate on very traditional lines. He has the benefit of some very old vines, and uses a high proportion (over 90%) of Mourvèdre grapes for his blend, which can make for extraordinary flavours in good years.

Domaine Tempier

Lucien Peyraud has been one of the most influential figures in Bandol. As president of one of the syndicates of wine producers, he set the high percentage of Mourvèdre grapes demanded in the regulations. Nowadays Jean-Marie and François make powerful wines, with huge tannins and fruit, and ability to age for many years. In the 26-ha (64-acre) vineyard and cellars, techniques are not only traditional, but also almost organic, with few artificial fertilizers or chemicals in use.

Two reds are made, a normal *cuvée* and a Cuvée Spéciale, and in exceptional years there are three single-vineyard wines from Tourtine, Cabassou and La Mignona. The Peyrauds also make a rosé, but no white.

BELLET

This tiny zone, restricted by the Alpine foothills and the suburbs of Nice, has only a handful of producers. Red, white and rosé wines are made: the standard is good, with the reds able to age for up to five years, and the whites and rosés combining freshness with interesting and unusual character. The chief grape for red wines is the Braquet (mostly found in Italy), and for whites the Rolle and Chardonnay. As the amount made is so small, little Bellet wine is sold outside Nice.

The largest estate is Ch de Crémat; other significant producers are Ch de Bellet, Clot Dou Baile, Clos St-Vincent and Domaine de Font-Bellet.

CASSIS

The seaside village of Cassis, just east of Marseilles, has long had a name for its white wine, but pressure on land has cut the vineyard area drastically. Grapes grown for white wine include — unusually this far south — Sauvignon Blanc as well as Marsanne and Ugni Blanc. The white wines are savoury and scented with the local herbs. Reds and rosés are in a minority: grapes are the common Provençal varieties, including Mourvèdre.

The leading Cassis estates include Domaine du Bagnol, which makes red and rosé wines as well as a good spicy white; Clos Ste-Magdeleine, which also makes fine white wine; Domaine de la Ferme Blanche, with good reds and whites; Ch de Fontcreuse; and Mas Calendal.

PALETTE

This small area just east of Aix-en-Provence has a long history: the vineyard dates from medieval times and was founded by Carmelite monks. Today only two estates make wine; all three colours are made, the red being the best. Ch Simone is the leading producer, the other being Domaine de la Crémade.

Ch Simone's vineyards have very old vines (Grenache, Mourvèdre and Cinsaut for reds, Clairette, Sémillon and Muscat for whites). Methods are traditional, and the resulting wine has the capacity to age for many years.

COTEAUX D'AIX-EN-PROVENCE

A large *appellation* (3,500ha/ 8,650 acres) in the west of the region, making red and white wines. Much new planting of Cabernet Sauvignon vines has given the AOC a modern profile. Some interesting red wines are now being made here.

Commanderie de la Bargemone

Based on an old Templar commandery, this ancient estate has only recently been restored. The wine produced here relies on a mix of traditional and modern methods; stainless steel and *macération carbonique* combine to achieve maximum fruit. The reds are particularly successful, with 15% Syrah in the blend. The top red wine, Cuvée Tournebride, has 50% Cabernet Sauvignon. Whites are made from Sauvignon Blanc,

Grenache Blanc and Ugni Blanc grapes.

Domaine les Bastides

A 30-ha (74-acre) estate, Bastides uses organic methods of viticulture, producing red and rosé wines. The standard red *cuvée*, Cuvée St-Pierre, is a blend of Grenache, Mourvèdre and Cinsaut; while a top wine, Cuvée Spéciale, includes 40% Cabernet Sauvignon. These wines spend between 16 and 24 months in small barrels. A white wine is also made.

Ch de Beaulieu

This is a large estate — 300ha (740 acres) — producing around 83,500 cases a year. The modern winery is designed to produce easy-drinking wines, which nevertheless have plenty of herby, southern character. The red is made from Grenache, Cabernet Sauvignon, Mourvèdre and Syrah grapes. The rosé blends Cinsaut and Carignan, while the white is Ugni Blanc, Clairette, Sauvignon Blanc and Sémillon. The owners, the Touzet family, have been developing this large property since the 1970s.

Ch Fonscolombe

This is another of the Aix-en-Provence estates that have built a reputation for making good-value, early-drinking wines. It has 160ha (395 acres), producing around 83,000 cases a year. The family of the Marquis de Saporta have been here since the 18th century. Reds make up the bulk of production, with a Cuvée Spéciale at the top of the range, blending Carignan with Cabernet Sauvignon, Grenache and Cinsaut and matured in wood. The estate also produces a Vin de Pays des Bouches-du-Rhône, called Domaine de Boullery.

Ch Vignelaure

After years at the top in Aix-en-Provence — thanks to Georges

Brunet —, this estate was acquired by David O'Brien, who produces top-quality wines with the help of Hugh Ryman. The red wine is as close to bordeaux as is possible in Provence, with its 60% Cabernet Sauvignon, 30% Syrah and 10% Grenache, and long wood-ageing in oak casks. Continuing the bordeaux parallel, a second wine, La Page de Vignelaure, is made, allowing stricter selection to be carried out for the *Grand Vin*.

LES BAUX-DE-PROVENCE

This zone is at the western end of the *appellation*. It produces successful red, white and rosé wines to very strict regulations, from vineyards around the dramatic rock formations of the Les Alpilles range and the fortified village of Les Baux.

Mas de la Dame

The 57-ha (141-acre) vineyard is just east of the Vallée d'Enfer (the Valley of Hell), part of the rocky outcrop of Les Alpilles. It is planted with a high proportion of Grenache, which means that the wines soften comparatively quickly, although they do also have a good backbone of Syrah and Cabernet Sauvignon. There are two red *cuvées*, Cuvée Réserve and Cuvée Gourmande. The Rosé du Mas has a high proportion of Syrah and Cabernet Sauvignon, and is very fruity.

Mas de Gourgonnier

Luc and Frédérique Cartier's Mas de Gourgonnier estate is at the southern end of Les Alpilles. The 35-ha (86-acre) vineyard was carved out of a

much older family estate, and is run on organic lines. Red and rosé are made. The top red *cuvée*, Réserve du Mas, is a blend of 30% Cabernet Sauvignon, 30% Syrah and the balance of Grenache. The regular wine has 10% Mourvèdre and less Cabernet Sauvignon and Syrah. There is also a white wine, which has a high proportion of Sauvignon Blanc.

Domaine des Terres Blanches

Noël Michelin, the owner of this 40-ha (100-acre) property near St-Rémy-de-Provence on the north side of Les Alpilles, is an ardent proponent of organic production, and uses no herbicides or insecticides in the vineyard and few chemicals in the *chai*. He makes a white, a rosé and a red. The red, with 50% Mourvèdre and 30% Syrah, can be a trifle hard when young, but always seems to open out to elegance when given a few years' bottle-age. The rosé is more immediately attractive.

Domaine de Trévallon

Widely acclaimed as the finest estate in Les Baux, and probably among the top estates of Provence, Eloi Dürrbach's Domaine de Trévallon is, however, only allowed to use the Vin de Pays des Bouches du Rhône label. The use of a high proportion of Cabernet Sauvignon grapes in his red wine, and of Marsanne and Roussanne grapes in his white, has cost him his *appellation* status. But this winemaking individualist couldn't care less, and he has history and the market on his side. Indeed, some 150 years ago, Dr Guyot already noted that Cabernet Sauvignon produced fine wines in Provence. Dürrbach's methods, both in the vineyard and the cellar, are organic, and there is no fining or filtering of the wine after the 18 months' barrel-ageing. The wine ages slowly, needing at least five years in bottle before being drinkable, and then developing gradually. It is now the most expensive of Les Baux, principally because it has been taken up by the American market, but it has a wide international following, as well as being found in local restaurants.

COTES DE PROVENCE

The largest AOC in the region, making red, white and rosé wines from a wide variety of sites, soils and micro-climates.

Ch Barbeyrolles

In the hills above St-Tropez, Régine Sumeire's 12-ha (30-acre) estate produces red and rosé wines to a high standard. Her rosé has plenty of fruit, but the red is perhaps more exciting: a blend of Grenache, Syrah and Mourvèdre, it spends up to 18 months in wood and can age well in bottle. A white wine is also being made.

Domaine de la Courtade

This 30-ha (74-acre) estate on the island of Porquerolles has made itself a name for quality wines. The wines are in all three colours. Both the red, made from Mourvèdre, and the white, made from Rolle, have a lot of character.

Domaines Gavoty

Bernard Gavoty, a music critic, used to sign his column in the *Figaro* with the pen name "Clarendon", which also appeared on his best *cuvées*. Roselyn Gavoty, who now manages the two vineyards — Le Petit Campduny and Le Grand Campduny (110ha/ 272 acres, some of it *vin de pays)* —, has kept up this tradition, with a particularly fruity, early-drinking, deep-coloured rosé, a white blended from Ugni Blanc, Rolle and Clairette grapes, and smaller quantities of a wood-aged red, which is a blend of Syrah, Cabernet Sauvignon, Mourvèdre and Grenache grapes.

Les Maîtres Vignerons de la Presqu'île de St-Tropez

This is certainly the most go-ahead cooperative in the Côtes de Provence. It produces a considerable range of wines, of which the Carte Noire red, in the traditional Provençal skittle-shaped bottle, is the best known in export markets. The co-op also has individually named estate wines from some members, including Ch de Pampelonne, which produces a red Grenache and Cinsaut blend and a superior wood-aged red *cuvée* of Grenache, Syrah and Mourvèdre.

Domaines Ott

The Ott family, originally from Alsace, is one of the most influential in the Côtes de Provence and Bandol. They have done more than anyone else to promote Provençal wines, and while their wines now command high prices, they also maintain high standards. Their showpiece Côtes de Provence estates — the 58-ha (143-acre) Ch de Selle (which produces red, white and rosé wines), and Clos Mireille, based on sandy soils right by the coast, which produces only a top-quality white — are at the top of a range that also includes quantities of typical Provençal rosé.

Commanderie de Peyrassol

A document dating from 1256 mentions a production of "400 milleroles" (28,000 litres) of wine. Founded in 1204, this former residence of a commander of the Templars has known only two owners: religious orders and, since 1790, the Rigord family. The husbands having other professions, it is the wives who are managing the estate. In 1977, Françoise Rigord introduced bottling and, in 2001, Philippe Austruy joined in the running of this 55-ha (136-acre) vineyard, which produces two *cuvées* of red (one a *cuvée de*

prestige), a fresh and fruity rosé, and a lively and subtle white wine.

Domaine des Planes

Owned by a Swiss-German family, the Rieders, this is a model 35-ha (86-acre) estate on the slopes of Roquebrune, near St-Raphaël. It produces a good range, including some top red wines made from single varieties: Cuvée Tradition is 100% Cabernet Sauvignon, and there is also a Cuvée Mourvèdre. Blended reds include a Grenache/Syrah blend and a more serious Cuvée Réserve, which mixes Grenache, Cabernet Sauvignon and Mourvèdre. The rare Tibouren grape is grown on the estate, and is used to produce a pleasantly heady, perfumed rosé.

Ch Réal-Martin

This 35-ha (86-acre) inland vineyard produces fine wines in all three colours, which should be drunk after two to five years.

Domaine Richeaume

One of the best red-wine estates in Côtes de Provence is owned by a German, Henning Hoesch. On his 25ha (62 acres) he practises strict organic techniques, and produces three different styles of red wine, as well as a little rosé and white. The top red wine is Cuvée Tradition, which blends local grape varieties; there is also a straight Syrah and a Cabernet Sauvignon. The wines spend up to 18 months in small wooden barrels. An interesting *blanc de blancs* is made entirely from Clairette grapes.

Domaine du Rimauresque

The estate's northwest-facing 36ha (89 acres) produce very fine wines, particularly whites.

Domaine St-André de Figuière

This 15-ha (37-acre) estate near La-Londe-les-Maures has been

owned by Alain Combard since the 1992 vintage. He produces a white, a rosé and three red *cuvées*. Cuvée Marquis has 30% Grenache, and Cuvée Spéciale is dominated by Mourvèdre and Carignan from more than 70-year old vines.

Ch Ste-Roseline

Don't miss a visit to one of the most beautiful cloisters in Provence, a listed historic building, with a tasting of the wines made in a state-of-the-art winery. Bernard Teillaud bought this estate in 1993 and has since restored both the buildings and the 90-ha (222-acre) vineyard. The wines are up to his high standards.

COTEAUX VAROIS

A wide zone between the Côtes de Provence and the Coteaux d'Aix-en-Provence, making red wines for drinking young, and reasonable rosés.

Domaine du Deffends

One of the best. Planted with Syrah and Cabernet Sauvignon.

Ch La Calisse

The vineyard and the buildings were entirely restored in the 1990s. Organic growing. The reds and whites are good value for money.

COTEAUX DE PIERREVERT

This new AOC zone (1998) covers a cooler, upland tract along the Durance River. Red, rosé and white wines are made. The 54-ha (134-acre) vineyard of Domaine de Régusse is the largest in the *appellation*.

CORSICA

Mountains and the sea have shaped Corsica's wines. The sea, isolating yet providing an avenue for trade, brought the ancient Greeks, and their vines, 500 years before Christ. Later, Corsica's position astride the sea-trade routes led to domination by the merchant cities of Pisa and Genoa on the coast of Italy. Vines followed: the island's native varieties have a strong Italian flavour.

The mountains which make up most of Corsica split the island into innumerable small valleys, each of which developed its own wine styles and grape varieties. Some of these have died out as modern communications allowed the introduction of more prolific vines from the mainland, but more than 20 indigenous Corsican vines survive.

Winemaking was a minor, and strictly local, activity on Corsica until the early 1960s. Then several thousand displaced French settlers from North Africa were repatriated to Corsica and set about expanding wine production, in an attempt to capture the bulk wine markets formerly served by Algeria and Tunisia. Large amounts of bad wine were made from the new vineyards, mostly planted on one of the few areas of flat land in the island, the plain south of Bastia. These wines failed to find a market, being submerged instead in the European "wine lake". Government and EC intervention led to the destruction of most of the new vineyards, returning Corsica to the situation as before, with vines on traditional mountain and coastal sites. Indeed, there has been a move to replant some hill vineyards abandoned since the phylloxera crisis.

Wine zones

Corsica has one overall AOC, Vin de Corse, and two local ones, Ajaccio and Patrimonio. In addition, Vin de

Domaine Fiumicicoli, near Propriano, in the sub-zone of Sartène.

Corse may be used with a village name attached to show that the wine comes from certain specific districts (*see* next page). Vin de Corse, used on its own, is most likely to come from the more productive but lower-quality vineyards on the east coast; the name of one of the specific districts on the label leads one to expect more individuality. Ajaccio and Patrimonio are the most serious of the *appellations*, though Ajaccio's small production is all enjoyed locally.

Wine styles and grape varieties

Most Corsican wine is red, with some rosé; only one bottle in ten is white. The most important red grape is Nielluccio, which grows in the north, especially in the Patrimonio *appellation*; and Sciaccarello, the speciality of the Ajaccio area in the west. Both are native to Corsica, but some experts feel the Nielluccio has a link with the Tuscan Sangiovese. The main white grape is Vermentino, which is known on the mainland as Malvoisie or Malvasia, a

very ancient Mediterranean variety.

Reds made from the two main Corsican varieties, or any of the even more obscure native grapes, are the most interesting wines. Nielluccio makes rather pale wine, and is indeed used for rosé. It does however have strength and balance, and can make good, long-lived wines. Sciaccarello, tough-skinned and juicy, has a name for darker, more structured wines with a distinct herby perfume.

Imported varieties include the red-wine grapes Carignan, Grenache and Cinsaut, which are no more interesting here than in the Midi. Syrah is a more welcome immigrant.

Some plantings of "classic" varieties such as Chardonnay, Merlot and Cabernet Sauvignon have been made in the north-east. Their wine is made into Vin de Pays de l'Ile de Beauté. Rosé *vins de pays* from the best producers are excellent.

Small amounts of *vins doux naturels* (dessert wines) are made from Muscat grapes, mostly in the Patrimonio and Coteaux du Cap Corse zones. □

ZONES AND PRODUCERS

Corsica's most characterful wines are those made by small, often family-owned firms. The Corsica *appellations* are listed below, with notes on some of the most reliable producers.

AJACCIO

The *appellation*'s vines lie on the coast and hills around this old city, Napoleon's birthplace, in the west of the island. The AOC demands that the reds be 50% Sciaccarello, and most have a higher percentage. Grenache, Cinsaut and Carignan typically make up the balance. Rosés and whites are also made.

Clos d'Alzeto

Corsica's highest vineyard, with a superb view, produces typical and interesting wines, mainly red.

Clos Capitoro

Jacques Bianchetti makes some of Corsica's most prestigious wines under this name: reds and rosés from Sciaccarello and Grenache, and whites from Vermentino. The red, sold with some maturity, is the best wine.

Domaine Martini

This estate makes traditional red and rosé wines.

Domaine Peraldi

One of the best-known Corsican estates, owned by the Comte de Poix, whose family have had the property for four centuries. Red, rosé and white wines are made. The Clos du Cardinal red wine is aged in oak barrels.

Domaine de Pravatone

At her estate near the prehistoric site of Filitosa — worth a visit —, Isabelle Courrège makes outstanding wines in all three colours.

PATRIMONIO

The vineyards on this particularly steep part of the north coast, around the port of St-Florent, date back to the Middle Ages, but today they are not as extensive as they were earlier this century. The AOC stipulates that 90% of the grapes for red wine must be Nielluccio. White wines come from Vermentino grapes, with some *vins doux naturels* from Muscat.

Domaine Antoine Arena

Antoine Arena has success at his finger tips: fat, lavish whites, extremely powerful reds and fine, rich Muscats.

Domaine Gentile

An estate reviving old local traditions: red, rosé and both dry and Muscat-based sweet white wines are made.

Domaine Leccia

Modern techniques and equipment give this estate's reds a good fruit flavour with some structure. It also produces a good sweet Muscat.

VIN DE CORSE

This *appellation* is at its most interesting when the name of one of the five sub-zones is suffixed to the AOC.

Vin de Corse Calvi

The town of Calvi is on the north-west coast, on the edge of some of the highest and wildest Corsican mountains. The wine zone stretches east and west of the town, an area called the Balagne.

The wines are made from predominantly mainland varieties, and come in all three colours. The white wines are accounted the best.

Producers include Clos Reginu, which makes a good red wine from island varieties spiced with Syrah, Clos Landry (a rosé specialist), and Clos Culombu, which produces wine in all three colours.

Vin de Corse Coteaux du Cap Corse

White wines are best here, with dry ones made from Vermentino grapes and sweet ones from Muscat (AOC Muscat du Cap Corse covers all of Patrimonio). The vineyards are very exposed, balanced on the peninsula at the tip of the island. There are only a few hectares left.

Vin de Corse Figari

This vineyard high up in the island's southern mountains once covered a large area, after displaced French from North Africa settled here during the 1960s. Nowadays their vines have disappeared. The best wine is the *cuvée* Alexandra from Domaine de Tanella.

Vin de Corse Sartène

This AOC insists on 50% traditional Corsican varieties, giving the wines more individuality than some from the other Vin de Corse *appellations*. The area is along a coastal inlet on the west side of the island, south of Ajaccio.

The wines include solid, scented reds which can mature well, and mouthfilling, tasty whites.

Producers include Domaine Fiumicicoli, a modern estate which is nevertheless run by an enthusiast for traditional Corsican grapes; Domaine de San Michele; and the local cooperative, which uses the Santa Barba label.

Vin de Corse Porto-Vecchio

Syrah and Mourvèdre are blended with Corsican red grape varieties here in the south-east of the island. The *appellation*'s leading estate is Domaine de Torraccia, where experimentation and traditional varieties combine to make interesting wines.

VIN DE PAYS DE L'ILE DE BEAUTÉ

Corsica is lucky in the name of its *vin de pays*. Two groups of cooperatives produce a large amount of *vin de pays* from vineyards along the east coast. The Union de Vignerons de l'Ile de Beauté takes a traditional approach, but uses Merlot, Cabernet Sauvignon and Chardonnay to improve wines made from native grapes.

The Union de Vignerons Associés du Levant (UVAL) has a more dynamic attitude, producing wines from mostly "foreign" varieties including some international classics. California is the model for these well-made, fresh wines, which are labelled according to grape variety (Cabernet Sauvignon, Merlot and Syrah reds; Chardonnay and Chenin Blanc whites).

THE MIDI

THE GREAT SWEEP OF MIDI VINEYARDS HAS A REPUTATION FOR BASIC
WINES, BUT INNOVATIVE ESTATES AND COOPERATIVES ARE
CONJURING FRESH FLAVOURS FROM THE ROCKY HILLSIDES.

It is from the hillside vineyards of the Midi, traditionally the best, that the most characterful wines come. The old village of St-Guilhem-le-Désert lies within the extensive vineyards of the Coteaux du Languedoc.

The Midi is currently one of the most exciting wine regions — not just in France, but in the world. Stretching from the foothills of the Pyrenees along the Mediterranean coast to the mouth of the Rhône River, the Midi is a vast vineyard. It encompasses the former provinces of Roussillon and Languedoc, an area which today includes four *départements*: Aude, Pyrénées-Orientales, Gard and Hérault. Not only is the Midi the largest wine-producing area in France, producing 40% of all French wine, it is also the oldest. The Greeks introduced viticulture in the 5th century BC, and the Romans picked up where the Greeks left off. Since then, wine has played a vital part in the region's economy. The period of greatest prosperity came in the late 19th century, when the newly created railway system made it easy to ship southern wine to the thirsty miners and factory workers of the north of France. It was thin, acidic, low-alcohol stuff. At about the same time, Algerian vineyards were beginning to produce the so-called "medical wines" — fuller-bodied, darker and with a higher alcohol content — that were used to "doctor" the wines of the Languedoc and compensate for their lacks. The results of these highly irregular blends were sometimes passed off as burgundies. Then in the mid-1950s, the national consumption of wine in France began to fall for the first time (it has continued to decline ever since). Supply began to exceed demand, creating the European wine glut, for which southern Italy must share the blame. The Midi's wine industry was outdated at every level, from the state of the vines themselves to the means of distribution. Drastic changes had to be made. Until the 1980s, when large quantities of vines were pulled up, Midi vineyards were planted with just one goal in mind: quantity. Quality was of little account. But when serious producers came to realise that the key to success lies in quality, and all that it entails, the Languedoc began its spectacular turn-around. The region now produces AOC wines of an excellent standard, as well as a wide range of *vins de pays*, some of which can rival the very best of French wines.

Midi wine styles

The South produces an immense variety of wine styles. Red wines predominate, under a range of *appellations*, from Collioure in the west to Costières de Nîmes in the east. Amongst the multitude of *vins de pays*, some are of international significance, others of no more than local interest. The sparkling Blanquette de Limoux and Crémant de Limoux come from near the eponymous town in the Aude. The region produces more than 90% of France's dessert wines, or *vins doux naturels*. A few white wines, such as Clairette du Languedoc (see p292), have acquired an *appellation* in their own right, but for the most part, they play a minor role here. The region's rosés are well liked too, especially by summer visitors.

Climate

The Mediterranean climate provides ideal conditions for the vines. The winters are mild, the summers warm and dry, and the rain that falls in winter and early spring suffices for the rest of the year.

The vineyards

The best vineyard sites are in the foothills of the Pyrenees and the Massif Central, and on the rocky slopes of the Corbières. These are areas where little else but olive trees and grapevines will grow. The latter thrive in the arid conditions, and produce intensely flavoured wines whose bouquet is reminiscent of the region's renowned herbs. Soils here are extremely varied, and each spot has its own particularities, so that there can be several different types of soil within a single *appellation*.

New vineyards are being replanted on land where vines were abandoned a century ago, when growers came down from the hills to the more fertile, easier-to-cultivate coastal plains. These vineyards, which can produce only an inferior *vin ordinaire*, are now being pulled up, thanks to government subsidies. So the vines of the plains, responsible for the current wine glut, will eventually disappear altogether.

Grape varieties

Carignan, Cinsaut and Grenache are now predominant throughout the Midi, providing the basis for most of the red wines. Many of the 150 different varieties that grew here during the 19th century have disappeared, destroyed by disease (oïdium and phylloxera) or declining in popularity for lack of productivity. They were replaced by the high-yielding Carignan and Aramon, as well as another notoriously prolific local variety, Alicante Bouschet.

A few *appellations* of the Midi are required by law to contain a certain percentage of what are called *cépages améliorateurs* – varieties that improve the character of the basic product. Grenache was one of the first of them; it has since been joined by Syrah and Mourvèdre.

Today, Cinsaut is being improved by advanced clonal selection, Aramon and Alicante are fated to disappear, and Carignan is holding its own. Cabernet Sauvignon and Merlot are being planted too, as well as Chardonnay and Sauvignon for white. Some growers would even like these varieties to be allowed in their *appellation* wines, but for the time being, their use is more or less restricted to *vins de pays*.

The white varieties that feature in most *appellations* – Ugni Blanc, Vermentino, Bourboulenc and Maccabeo – are used in association with Roussanne and Marsanne. Picpoul, used in Picpoul de Pinet, is having something of a renaissance. Clairette is used for two *appellations*, Clairette du Languedoc and Clairette de Bellegarde. Viognier and other varieties that are foreign to the region are also being planted, but as with the red varieties, for the moment they are allowed for *vins de pays* only.

Winemaking

The main problem arising from a warm climate comes in the winemaking, with the need to control fermentation temperatures and to keep the wine in insulated cellars.

Since the mid-1980s the standard of vinification in the Midi has improved tremendously. The continuous wine-press, which was developed to suit high-quantity production, is gradually being replaced by more gentle pneumatic presses (see p110). The importance of temperature-controlled fermentation for both red and white wines is widely accepted, and cellars are increasingly equipped with this in mind.

The main change in vinification techniques is the widespread use of *macération carbonique*, the purpose of which is to extract the maximum amount of fruit from the grapes, with the minimum amount of tannin. Carignan, which can be rather hard and tannic, and lacking in fruit when it is fermented in the traditional way, is transformed by *macération carbonique*: stressing its fruit and spice, while keeping enough backbone.

The other important development is the increasing use of new oak barrels. The Midi has no tradition of underground cellars, and consequently no tradition of ageing wine. It was stored in large oak vats and sold in the year following the harvest. Nowadays these hard-to-maintain vats have generally been replaced by handier concrete or steel tanks, or, for the most prestigious vintages, by 225-litre barrels or half-hogsheads. Indeed, many barrels from the châteaux of the Médoc enjoy a sunny "retirement home" here in the Midi, where they are giving very satisfying results.

Having discovered all the advantages of oak, vinegrowers are now managing to develop wines with a less woodsy style. The best of them enjoy the barrels for the complexity and depth that they bring to the top vintages, without overdoing an unpleasant "pure wood" taste. The search for a better balance between wine and wood has encouraged the evolution of a uniquely Mediterranean style, rather than copying New World wines.   □

WINE REGIONS OF THE MIDI

The Rhône forms the eastern boundary, and the Pyrenees, the southern, of this vast, ever-evolving wine-growing zone. The Coteaux de Languedoc's hierarchy was recently revamped. The situation is now as follows: Grès de Montpellier (covers nos. 2, 3, 4, 7 and 8 below); La Clape (nos. 13 and 14); Terrasses du Larzac (5 and 6, as well as vineyards near Lodève, Octon and Aniane); Terres de Sommières (west of Nîmes); Pezenas and Cabrières (see no. 9) and Terrasses de Béziers (south of Béziers). A new tiny AOC, Côtes-du-Roussillon-Aspres, was recognized in 2003.

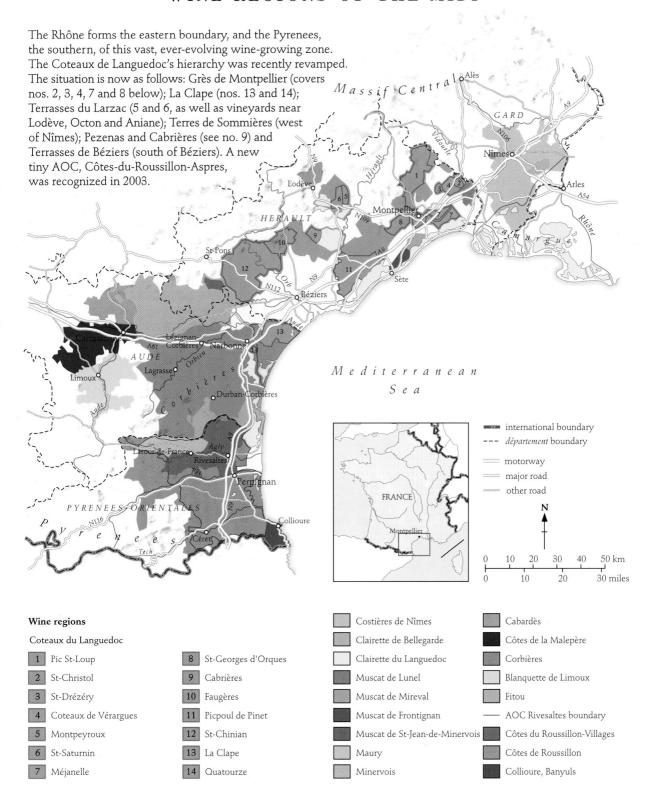

▬▬▬	international boundary
- - -	*département* boundary
═══	motorway
───	major road
───	other road

FRANCE

Montpellier

N

0 10 20 30 40 50 km
0   10   20   30 miles

Wine regions

Coteaux du Languedoc

1 Pic St-Loup
2 St-Christol
3 St-Drézéry
4 Coteaux de Vérargues
5 Montpeyroux
6 St-Saturnin
7 Méjanelle

8 St-Georges d'Orques
9 Cabrières
10 Faugères
11 Picpoul de Pinet
12 St-Chinian
13 La Clape
14 Quatourze

- Costières de Nîmes
- Clairette de Bellegarde
- Clairette du Languedoc
- Muscat de Lunel
- Muscat de Mireval
- Muscat de Frontignan
- Muscat de St-Jean-de-Minervois
- Maury
- Minervois

- Cabardès
- Côtes de la Malepère
- Corbières
- Blanquette de Limoux
- Fitou
- AOC Rivesaltes boundary
- Côtes du Roussillon-Villages
- Côtes de Roussillon
- Collioure, Banyuls

VINS DE PAYS

The *vins de pays,* for which the literal translation is "country wines", were born of the desperate need to grant the hundreds of thousands of anonymous hectolitres produced all over the Midi some form of identity. The idea was to create a certain image. Even now, the Midi still makes around 85% of all French *vins de pays.*

Vins de pays make up a vast category, ranging from simple, enjoyable wines for everyday drinking, to wines on a par with the very best. To a certain extent, they reflect the character of their region of origin, even if *vins de pays* are delimited more by administrative geography than by geology, as is the case for an AOC wine or a VDQS.

Departmental and zonal *vins de pays* are discussed in boxes throughout the chapter, along with their neighbouring *appellations.* Any wine made in the Midi can also use the regional name Vin de Pays d'Oc, which allows for blending between *vins de pays de zone* or *département.*

Grape varieties

The regulations for *vins de pays* allow for an imaginative flexibility as to which grape varieties may or may not be planted. The more adventurous producers have planted unusual varieties, often with exciting results. Cabernet Sauvignon, Merlot and Chardonnay are now quite well established in the Midi, and Sauvignon Blanc, Viognier, Chenin Blanc and many others are also found.

Where a grower makes both an *appellation* and a *vin de pays,* the *vin de pays* may be very much better — or very much worse — than the *appellation.* It may contain anything from the very best varieties — such as pure or blended Syrah or Cabernet Sauvignon — or the very worst, like Aramon or Alicante Bouschet, even though these had seemed to be on the verge of extinction not long ago. □

Mas de Daumas Gassac, producer of a famous Vin de Pays de l'Hérault.

PRODUCERS

Mas de Daumas Gassac
The most exciting *vins de pays* often come from an area where there is no AOC. Mas de Daumas Gassac is the best-known example of a *vin de pays* that has acquired a reputation – and a price to match – that can compete, not only with neighbouring *appellations,* but also with prestigious *Grands Crus* from anywhere in France.

Other Producers
The Gard can boast of Roc d'Anglade, Mas Montel and Petit Chaumont; the Herault: La Grange des Pères, Domaine d'Aupilhac, Mas des Chimères, Domaine de l'Arjolle, Domaine de Clovallon, Domaine de la Colombette, Domaine Perdiguier and Mas d'Aimé; the Saint Chinianais has La Grange des Quatre Sous and Domaine de Limbardié; the Minervois: Domaine Paul Louis Eugène and Clos des Centeilles; Limoux has Jean-Louis Denois; and the Roussillon, Domaine Gauby, Domaine Cazes, Domaine Ferrer et Ribière as well as Le Casot de Mailloles.

To get the best out of their *terroirs,* a growing number of daring vinegrowers had chosen not to submit to the discipline imposed by the AOC label. Sometimes the soil or the climate demand an unauthorized grape variety; other times it may be that the vinification method results in a higher alcohol level than what the rules allow.

And, particularly in the driest regions, a vinegrower may decide to resort to watering his vines – a forbidden practice – in order to improve the quality of the grapes. Elsewhere, a grower who produces a varietal wine, (e.g. one made from 100% Carignan or Syrah grapes) will not be able to obtain the AOC label, and will be forced to sell a perfectly good, perhaps even excellent, wine as a *vin de pays.*

Skalli
The Sète *négociant* Robert Skalli has pioneered reconverting local vineyards to produce varietal wines sold as Vin de Pays d'Oc under the Fortant de France label, which exports very well.

VINS DOUX NATURELS

The term *vin doux naturel*, "naturally sweet wine", is something of a misnomer. The sugar in the wine is indeed the natural product of the grape, but the process of production is perhaps rather artificial as, like any other fortified wine, the fermentation must be stopped by the addition of alcohol, in order to retain the necessary sweetness.

This method of winemaking has a long tradition in the south of France — its discovery is attributed to Arnaud de Villeneuve, a doctor of medicine at the University of Montpellier in the late 13th century. There are several wines made in this way, some red, others white.

The *vins doux naturels* from Roussillon — Banyuls, Rivesaltes and Maury — have long been appreciated in France, not only as dessert wines but also as apéritifs and as partners to foie gras and rich pâtés. The examples made throughout the Midi from Muscat grapes — in Rivesaltes, St-Jean-de-Minervois, Frontignan, Mireval and Lunel — should be served chilled, as an apéritif, or to accompany Roquefort cheese or a fruit cake or pudding.

Banyuls

The best Banyuls has a deep tawny colour, with rich raisin and walnut flavours. Whether they be red, white or rosé, they all tend to become tawny with age. Like Rivesaltes (*see* below), Banyuls can be deliberately oxidised in order to achieve the prized *rancio* flavour, or bottled in a normal manner for a wine similar to port.

Rivesaltes

Around half of all French *vins doux naturels* are from Rivesaltes. Fortified wines were popular enough in the 1930s to make Rivesaltes one of the first *appellations d'origine contrôlée*, in 1936. A lesser *appellation*, Grand Roussillon, was recognized in 1972

for a wine similar to Rivesaltes, but without the same quality; it is hardly ever seen. In theory there are three types of Rivesaltes: *blanc* or *doré*, *rouge* and *rancio*. In practice there are many colours and flavours, not least because the white wines darken and the reds become lighter with age. Red Rivesaltes are made from Grenache, Maccabeo and Malvoisie.

Red Rivesaltes made in the traditional way has the *rancio* flavour due to a gentle oxidation. This is achieved by ageing the wine, either in large oak barrels or in 30-litre glass demijohns, called *bonbonnes*, for at least nine months, so that it is subjected to all the climatic extremes, from the cold of winter to the heat of summer. The wine turns brown with age and the taste is rich, raisiny and nutty, reminiscent of Christmas fruitcake, walnuts and prunes, and is long, with a dry finish. After two years of oxidation, these wines can be sold as Tawny (Tuilé) Rivesaltes, for the reds, or Amber Rivesaltes, for the whites.

Another variation is vintage Rivesaltes. Like vintage port, it is bottled young; the fruitiness develops after several years of ageing.

Muscat de Rivesaltes

This *appellation* was recognized in 1972. Two grape varieties are permitted: Muscat d'Alexandrie and the more aromatic Muscat Blanc à Petits Grains. Sometimes the flavour is quite lemony and honeyed, sometimes fuller and richer, with the taste of pithy Seville oranges. The wine is bottled as soon as possible, in late winter, in order to capture the aroma of the grape. It is best consumed within a year or two of the vintage.

Maury

Maury is a red *vin doux naturel*. The main grape variety in its makeup is

Grenache Noir — *appellation* regulations dictate a minimum of 50% — which gives Maury its distinctive flavour. The grapes are picked when they are overripe, and grape brandy is added after three days' fermentation. The wine must be aged for at least two years, but the best examples are those aged for several more, when they develop a complex, nutty aroma, reminiscent of prunes or fruitcake.

Muscat de St-Jean-de-Minervois

The sole grape variety is Muscat Blanc à Petits Grains, and the grapes are picked when they are almost overripe, with a potential alcohol content of 14%Vol. Producers aim above all to maintain the delicate flavour of the Muscat.

Muscat de Frontignan

Muscat de Frontignan comes from vineyards around the eponymous town, not far from the port of Sète.

The sole grape variety for the *appellation*, which was created in 1936, is Muscat Blanc à Petits Grains; indeed Muscat de Frontignan can also be a synonym for this variety.

The finished wine must have a minimum alcohol level of 15%Vol, with between 5 and 10% by volume of added alcohol. The wines are golden and sweet, with the aroma and flavour of the Muscat grape.

Muscat de Mireval

Mireval is a sleepy town 8km (5 miles) east of Frontignan. It produces a wine very much like that of its neighbour, but which at the moment is of only local interest.

Muscat de Lunel

Much the same could be said for Muscat de Lunel, which is made in the eastern Hérault. Again, the *appellation* demands the use of 100% Muscat Blanc à Petits Grains. □

APPELLATIONS AND PRODUCERS

The *appellations* for *vins doux naturels* are presented below from west to east, i.e. from the Spanish frontier all the way to the mouth of the Rhône. Many of the *appellations* overlap with table-wine areas covered later in the chapter.

BANYULS

Banyuls and Collioure are neighbouring resorts and fishing villages on the Mediterranean coast just before the Spanish frontier, where the Pyrenees meet the sea. The *appellation* Banyuls, which was recognized in 1936, also includes the vineyards of two other coastal villages, Port-Vendres and Cerbère, where the vines grow on steep terraces on the foothills of the Pyrenees, and the soil is infertile schist.

The basic Banyuls *appellation* requires a minimum of 50% Grenache Noir for the reds. Carignan, Cinsaut and Syrah usually make up the rest. The Banyuls Grand Cru *appellation* was added in 1962. In theory this means a higher quality of wine, with at least 75% Grenache Noir and a minimum of two-and-a-half years' ageing.

Producers

Production is dominated by a group of three cooperatives, including the excellent cooperative cellar L'Etoile. Among the best domain wines are those from Domaine du Mas Blanc and from Domaine La Tour Vieille, which uses a system similar to the Spanish *solera* (*see* p423), with three levels, or *sostres*, as they are called in Catalan. In addition, the fine wines of Mas de la Rectorie — known for its *manzanilla*-style white Banyuls — of Domaine Vial-Magnèreset and Clos des Paulilles should not be overlooked.

RIVESALTES

The *appellation* includes 86 villages, mostly in the Pyrénées-Orientales *département*, with a certain amount of overlap with the vineyards of the Côtes du Roussillon. A few of the villages fall within the Aude department, and come within the appellations of Fitou and Corbières. Consequently there are several producers, both cooperatives and private estates, that make both table wine and fortified wine.

Producers

There are several good producers of Rivesaltes, including the Mont Tauch cooperative in the village of Tuchan, Domaine Cazes in Rivesaltes, Domaine Sarda-Malet in Perpignan and Château de Corneilla, in the eponymous village south of Perpignan. The Vieux Rivesaltes from Domaine de Rancy, in Latour de France, and Château Mossé, in St-Colombe-de-la-Commanderie have a fine reputation as well.

MAURY

Maury is a tiny *appellation*, an enclave within the larger *appellations* of Rivesaltes and Côtes du Roussillon Villages. Schist is the dominant soil type in this *terroir*, which covers the vineyards of Maury and three other neighbouring communities.

Producers

The village co-operative is by far the largest producer, but a much more exciting wine comes from Domaine du Mas Amiel, the only private estate of any importance, with 130ha (321 acres), planted essentially with Grenache Noir. At Mas Amiel when the fortifying alcohol is added to the marc, maceration is allowed to go on for three or four weeks, in order to achieve a richer, fuller-bodied wine. The estate also firmly believes in the necessity of ageing its wine in glass *bonbonnes* for a full 12 months, from June to June. It then spends a further number of years in enormous 250-hl vats of Austrian oak, which are topped up at regular intervals to replace the wine lost by natural evaporation.

Mas Amiel sells its Maury in three versions, at 6, 10 and 15 years of age. The latter is the best of all: a delicious concentration of fruit, nuts and prunes, not unlike an old tawny port.

Under the leadership of a new proprietor, Mas Amiel has planted part of its vineyards with Syrah, a quarter of which is now reserved for table wines.

MUSCAT DE ST-JEAN-DE-MINERVOIS

The village of St-Jean-de-Minervois has had its own *appellation* for *vin doux naturel* since 1950. At the beginning of the last century, Muscat was often grown on smallholdings, to be made into wine for home use; the *appellation* arose from this tradition.

Producers

Good wines are made by the village cooperative and by a couple of good independent producers, including Domaine Barroubio, Domaine Clos du Gravillas and the small Domaine de Gimios.

MUSCAT DE FRONTIGNAN

Frontignan's vineyards are of limestone with some alluvium and pebbles. They are on the eastern side of the Bassin de Thau, which, combined with its proximity to the sea, provides a warm micro-climate.

Producers

The local co-operative here accounts for around three-quarters of the total production of the *appellation*, while the leading independent producer is Château de la Peyrade.

MUSCAT DE LUNEL

The town of Lunel lies on the eastern edge of the Coteaux du Languedoc. Growers usually make both Coteaux du Languedoc and Muscat de Lunel.

Producers

Production is dominated by the local cooperative, while the principal independent producers, Château du Grès St-Paul and Domaine de la Croix Saint Roch, make more exciting wines, taking great pains to retain their wines' freshness and proximity to the grape's character.

ROUSSILLON

The ancient provinces of Roussillon and Languedoc, often linked in one all-embracing term to cover the Midi, are in fact quite separate in some respects. Roussillon has historical associations with Spain, and in particular with Catalonia. Indeed, it is viewed by some of its inhabitants as part of Catalonia. The province retains some Catalan influence in both wine and culture; its climate is generally hotter than the rest of France and the wines sturdier and more full-bodied.

The vinegrowing area is bounded by the Mediterranean to the east, the Pyrenees to the south and the mountains of Corbières to the north, so that the hills of Roussillon appear to form an enormous amphitheatre around the fertile plain surrounding the town of Perpignan. River valleys break up the mountainous terrain, the Agly and its tributaries forming tortuous paths through the hills.

The Roussillon region has long been famous for the *vins doux naturels* of Rivesaltes (*see* p283), and it took its first tentative steps away from production of *le gros rouge* that was its unfortunate speciality a bit earlier than the Languedoc did. Various VDQS were created in 1970 and were upgraded in 1977 into the Côtes du Roussillon and Côtes du Roussillon Villages AOC. Four of the villages — Caramany, Latour-de-France, Lesquerde and Tautavel — are even entitled to append their names to the Côtes du Roussillon Villages *appellation* on the label. Roussillon also includes the pocket-sized vineyard of Collioure, granted AOC status in 1971, and the equally small AOC Côte de Roussillon-Aspres, created in 2003.

Styles and grape varieties

Côtes du Roussillon Villages can only be red, while Côtes du Roussillon allows for white and rosé wines as well. The yields for the superior

The picturesque port of Collioure.

appellation are limited to 45hl/ha; the broader one allows 50hl/ha.

The regulations for Côtes du Roussillon Villages implemented better grape varieties much sooner than the Côtes du Roussillon. From 1977, Syrah or Mourvèdre grapes became an essential part of the blend, along

VINS DE PAYS

The area includes six *vins de pays*. Vin de Pays des Pyrénées-Orientales covers the whole *département*, while Vin de Pays Catalan vaguely corresponds to AOC Côtes du Roussillon, covering most of the southern half of the *département*. Vin de Pays des Côtes Catalanes covers the area north of Perpignan, around the town of Rivesaltes and part of the valley of the Agly.

More obscure are Vin de Pays du Val d'Agly and Vin de Pays des Coteaux des Fenouillèdes (both of which lie in the hills to the west of the Vin de Pays de Côtes Catalanes), while Vin de Pays de la Côte Vermeille covers the coastal area around Banyuls and Collioure. Red wines account for 70–85% of production.

with Grenache, Cinsaut and a decreasing amount of Carignan. Syrah, first planted in the area in 1970, is now well established. Mourvèdre is less successful here, as it ripens much later. Carignan also has its fans; they argue that it performs at its best in Roussillon, since it gives low yields of ripe grapes on these arid sun-soaked hills, making warm red wine with soft tannins.

White Côtes du Roussillon has improved greatly in recent years, especially the dry Muscats and the ones made with Grenache (Blanc or Gris). Aside from the best producers' most prestigious vintages, these wines are not meant for long ageing. They were traditionally made to be drunk as soon as possible, although those made from Syrah do particularly benefit from a few years of ageing in the bottle.

Collioure

The Collioure appellation includes reds, rosés, and, since 2003, whites. The varieties that give the best results here are Grenache, Mourvèdre and Syrah. Carignan and Cinsaut are also permitted, while Counoise has theoretically disappeared. Mourvèdre is particularly successful here, enjoying the proximity to the sea that it ripens so well and contributes some rich, sturdy flavours to the wine. Vinification methods are traditional. The grapes are de-stalked and the fermentation very carefully controlled.

Although the regulations do not call for a specific period of maturation, some ageing in wooden casks can enhance the flavour and make Collioure one of the most original and powerful wines in the South of France. It is also a wine that can improve in the bottle for up to ten years, particularly when made by a careful producer.   □

APPELLATIONS AND PRODUCERS

The Côtes du Roussillon vineyards cover a substantial part of the *département* of the Pyrénées-Orientales. The tiny AOC area of Collioure is at the extreme south-east of the *département* on the Mediterranean coast, just north of the Spanish border.

COTES DU ROUSSILLON AND COTES DU ROUSSILLON VILLAGES

The Côtes du Roussillon Villages AOC consists of 32 villages in the northern part of the department, while plain Côtes du Roussillon includes 118 villages further south. The wine-growing area, of 6,500ha (16,050 acres) has a diversity of soils, including schist, limestone-and-clay and pebbly terraces. About 70% of the vinification is performed by the cooperatives, with one in almost every village, but a few good independent producers do manage to express their personalities. Village cooperatives were partly responsible for and Latour-de-France and Caramany being singled out for special mention in the appellation. Caramany was one of the first cooperatives to use *macération carbonique*, as early as 1964, while Latour-de-France was lucky enough to sell its wine to a large national wine merchant, Nicolas, so that the wine, with its catchy name, quickly developed a wide following across France.

Les Vignerons Catalans

Most of the village cooperatives are members of this large producers' union, which is responsible for an enormous proportion of the wines of Roussillon: *vins de pays* and Rivesaltes *vins doux naturels*, as well as the *appellation* wine.

Domaine Cazes

These good-sized *négociants* produce some good Côtes du Roussillon, but also focus on their *vins de pays*, notably the Credo, born of a mixture of Merlot and Cabernet Sauvignon. Among their whites, the dry Muscat is noteworthy.

Domaine Gauby

Gérard Gauby has been nick-named the "uncrowned king of Roussillon". Whether it's AOC or *vin de pays*, he is the region's best-known producer. His Muntada, made essentially from the Syrah variety, is the most sought-out wine in all of Roussillon, but his entire range is of excellent quality.

Other Producers

Among the excellent wine-growers who have attracted attention over the past few years, certain deserve a special mention: Domaine de Casenove, in Trouillas; Domaine des Chênes, Domaine du Clos des Fées and Domaine Gardies in Vingrau; Domaine Ferrer et Ribière, in Terrats (where there is also a good cooperative); Domaines Sarda-Malet, Lafage and Laporte, just outside of Perpignan; Domaines Piquemal and Mas Créamat, in Espira d'Agly; Château de Jau, in Cases de Pène; Domaine des Schistes, in Estagel and Domaine Força Réal, in Millas.

Côtes de Rousillon wines are coming up in the world, as can be seen by the number of investors, from Bordeaux and elsewhere, who have been snatching up the region's vineyards.

COLLIOURE

The villages of Banyuls and Collioure lie next to each other and share the same vineyards on steep terraced hillsides, almost falling into the sea. The soil is poor and stony, and the vines struggle to survive against the wind and drought.

Before Collioure was recognized as an *appellation*, its red wines were sometimes called Banyuls Sec. The amount of Collioure being produced is increasing, and growers, renowned for their VDN (*see* p284) are turning their attention to unfortified red wines.

Producers

The lion's share is done by three cooperatives: Groupement Interproducteurs, the Dominicains, and l'Etoile; while the most exciting Collioure wines come from estates such as et Domaine de la Rectorie, Domaine du Mas Blanc and Domaine de la Tour Vieille.

Cap Oullestreil, between the seaports of Banyuls and Collioure.

CORBIÈRES AND FITOU

The River Aude, which flows northwards from the Pyrenees to the medieval city of Carcassonne, then turning east to enter the Mediterranean north of Narbonne, gives its name to the *département*. It also divides the vineyards of Corbières from those of Minervois (*see* p290). Corbières is the name of both the wine and the rugged hills that dominate the region. The vineyards of Fitou form two enclaves within the larger Corbières *appellation*.

The Corbières *appellation*, which is predominantly red, although it includes a small amount of rosé and white wine, covers a large area south-west of Narbonne. To the north it is limited by the valley of the Aude, and in the south adjoins the vineyards of Roussillon.

Corbières was one of the earliest VDQS of France — created in 1951 — but did not become an AOC until 1985, when an earlier classification of Corbières Supérieures, based on a higher degree of alcohol, was suppressed. At the same time, the delimited vineyard area was drastically reduced, from 44,000 to 19,000ha (108,680 to 46,950 acres), of which only about 15,500ha (38,300 acres) are currently planted.

The nature of the soil ranges from limestone and clay to sandstone to schist, which is quite common. There are many micro-climates (see p288), but overall, the climate is Mediterranean, with mild winters and hot, dry summers.

Grape varieties

There is a general feeling of optimism in the vineyards of Corbières. The area has undergone a gentle transformation with the introduction of improving varieties, particularly Syrah and Mourvèdre, and this has gathered momentum, even if for the moment Carignan remains the

Fitou vineyards in the hills near Tuchan.

backbone of the *appellation*.

White wines represent just 3% of the total production. They are being renovated too, with plantings of the Rhône varieties Roussanne and

VINS DE PAYS

Any *vin de pays* from this prolific vineyard area, producing 150 million bottles annually, may use the departmental name Vin de Pays de l'Aude, and many producers do. But each area does possess its own *vin de pays*, so the Pays de l'Aude is sub-divided into 20 different designations, of which the best known are the Vin de Pays du Val d'Orbieu and the Vin de Pays de la Cité de Carcassonne.

The vast majority of the wine — between 80 and 99% — is red. The exception is the wine from the Upper Aude Valley, near Limoux, a town known for its white and sparkling wine.

In the Corbières, the quality of the *vin de pays* is distinctly lower than that of the *appellation* wines', particularly when these come from the better independent estates.

Marsanne, and the Corsican Vermentino. The quantities of rosé being produced are negligible as well.

Winemaking and wine styles

Macération carbonique is now quite widespread, especially for Carignan, as it enhances the fruitiness. For a classic vinification, the grapes are increasingly likely to be de-stalked, which makes for softer, finer wine.

New oak barrels and insulated or temperature-controlled cellars are now the rule, as are *barriques* for the best vintages. In addition, the harvesting is being done later, and extraction is longer. The wine that is produced in this way will benefit from some bottle-ageing, unlike red Corbières made in the traditional way, which is meant to be drunk within two or three years of bottling.

Fitou

Except for the *vins doux naturels*, Fitou is the oldest *appellation d'origine contrôlée* of the Midi, as it was created in 1948. At that time it was considered far superior to other local wines, but since the 1980s both Corbières and Minervois have taken great strides in the direction of quality.

Fitou is always red, with no white or even rosé wine in the *appellation*, and the grape varieties are those common throughout the Midi, with a substantial proportion of Carignan, as well as Grenache, Cinsaut and an increasing amount of Syrah or Mourvèdre, one or the other of which will soon become mandatory.

Fitou is vat- or barrel-matured for nine months before bottling, and wood-ageing is common for the better wines, in order to obtain fuller-bodied, more complex results. But in Fitou wines, as in those from all over the South, one now notices that the taste of the wood is less marked. □

APPELLATIONS AND PRODUCERS

In the Mediterranean scrubland of the Corbières hills, little will thrive apart from olive trees and vines. A new generation of winemakers has taken up the challenge of producing wines here, and they were rewarded with an AOC in 1985. The two Fitou enclaves have a much longer-established AOC.

CORBIERES

This vast vineyard possesses several cooperatives, the most eminent of which is the Cave d'Embrès et Castelmaure, at the vanguard of the Corbières revolution. Once the tandem Michel Tardieu and Dominique Laurent began advising the cooperative, it invested in equipment and modified its vinification methods. In 1992 it tried using new barrels for its top wine, Cuvée de Pompadour, and today, its "C" and "7" vintages are considered to rank amongst the best wines of the Languedoc.

The diversity of soils and climates within Corbières is such that we can easily understand vinegrowers' desire to sub-divide the *appellation*. The 10 *terroirs* so far delimited give an idea of the style of wine that can be found with this label. They are presented below with their key features and their best producers.

The Corbières region is haunted by the ghosts of a tumultuous past. It was the birthplace and last refuge of the Cathari, the first Languedocians to revolt against both Catholic orthodoxy and the growing influence of the French crown.

Located amongst the ruins of castles that are gradually fading back into the dry and rocky landscape from which they came, the vines enjoy the high altitude that soothes the summer heat and helps pro-tects them from drought. Grapevines are all that grows around here, and they give a wine with powerful mineral aromas, whose red-berry taste gradually melts into roasted notes, and sometimes even hints of chocolate.

On the other hand, on the hills that slope down towards the Aude Valley to the north, and to the seaside to the east, the landscape grows less austere and the climate more moderate, giving birth to rounder, subtler wines. Independent estates are teaming up successfully with the region's influential cooperatives in order to promote both tourism and the local wines at the same time. Holidaymakers are indeed pouring into the region, but so are several star vinegrowers from Bordeaux and Beaujolais, for they too are drawn to the sun and the magnificent landscapes

Boutenac

This territory corresponds to two alluvial valleys surrounding the village of Boutenac. Mourvèdre is at ease here, because it's so close to the Mediterranean. Some of the good producers here are the Châteaux Aiguilloux and la Voulte-Gasparets, and the Domaine du Grand Crès.

Corbières La Méditerranée

This coastal zone is subjected to a strong maritime influence. Mouvèdre grows well on the limestone and clay soil. The best producer is Château de Lastours.

Durban

This large zone in the southeast of Corbières appellation has arid and infertile soil and a climate cut off from any Mediterranean influence by the hills. Among the best producers are Château de Gléon-Montanié and Ch Haut-Gléon.

Fontfroide

This zone owes its name to the Cistercian abbey west of Narbonne. It is separated from the sea only by a small range of hills. One of the driest parts of France, it is well suited to Mourvèdre thanks to the cooling sea breezes.

Haute-Corbières

This is actually the sum of the combination of three former territories: Quéribus, Saint-Victor and Termènes. They are among the highest altitude and the most-untamed zones in the appellation. Among the best producers are Domaines Serres-Marzard and Trillol.

Lagrasse

In the valley of the Orbieu, with vineyards on limestone, this vineyard is planted at an altitude of 150–250m (495–825ft). The Montagne d'Alaric tends to moderate the prevailing winds. Among the better producers, we can name Château des Auzines, Château Prieuré Borde-Rouge and Clos d'Anhel.

Lézignan

On the northern tip of the appellation, this plateau is located at an altitude of only 50m (165ft). It has wide stone terraces. The best producers are Château Etong des Colombes, Château Grand Moulin and Roque-Sestrières.

Montagne d'Alaric

This *terroir* is on the northern flank of the mountain, which is to say at the northern tip of the Corbières *appellation*. It overlooks the plain and enjoys the influences of both the Mediterranean and the Atlantic. The soil is limestone with well-drained gravel. Among the best producers, we can name Domaine des Chandelles, Château Hélène and Château Mansenoble.

Serviès

In the northeastern corner of the *appellation*, limited by the Montagne d'Alaric and the Lacamp plateau. Syrah performs particularly well on the limestone and clay soil here.

FITOU

The Fitou *appellation*, which spreads over some 2,600ha (6,424 acres), is divided into two distinct areas: Fitou-Maritime, which covers vineyards of the coastal plains around the village of Fitou itself, and Haut-Fitou, at a higher altitude. On this higher, drier soil, Syrah is preferred, whereas the later-ripening Mourvèdre performs better in the damper atmosphere of the coast. As a rule, the Fitou-Maritime wines tend to be lighter and ready for drinking sooner than their fuller-bodied Haut-Fitou counterparts.

Producers and merchants

Production is dominated by cooperatives, the most important of which is the Coopérative des Producteurs du Mont Tauch; its main cellar is in the village of Tuchan.

Among private estates, one should note Château de Nouvelles, Domaine Bertrand Bergé, Domaine La Roudène, and Domaine de la Rochelierre, Villa Maria Fita, Clos des Camuzeilles and the Château des Erles.

WESTERN AUDE

Blanquette de Limoux proudly claims to be the oldest sparkling wine of France, with an even longer history than champagne. In 1388 the chronicler Froissart wrote of "delightful drinking sprees of Limouxin white wine", and the discovery of sparkling wine here dates back to as early as 1531.

The town of Limoux lies in the upper Aude valley, southwest of the medieval city of Carcassonne. The vineyards cover quite an extensive area within a radius of 20km (12 miles) around the town.

Grape varieties
Mauzac, the main variety for Blanquette de Limoux, doesn't grow anywhere else but here and in Gaillac. Mauzac has a characteristic apple or pear taste, a certain bitterness on the finish and some firm acidity which makes it particularly well-adapted to sparkling wine. Nevertheless, it must be acknowledged that for more modern tastes in Limoux, Mauzac is somewhat unexciting. This has prompted the planting of Chardonnay and Chenin Blanc.

Making the wine
Traditional Blanquette, which is known locally as the "ancestral" style, is made from Mauzac and nothing else. It is unlike the more modern Blanquette, which is vinified in the traditional method of Champagne (see p114), in which fermentation reoccurs naturally after bottling, which is performed as soon as the vat fermentation is over. The resulting wine has a low alcohol content, and it is usually demi-sec, because of the small amount of residual sugar. Even modern Blanquette has to contain at least 90% Mauzac; Chardonnay and Chenin being authorised up to a combined total of no more than 10%. This is still the most important wine in terms of production in the Limoux, despite a recent phenomenon of younger drinkers preferring ancestral Blanquette.

MALEPÈRE AND CABARDÈS

Two wine-producing areas north of Limoux, in this most westerly part of the Midi, represent the frontier between Languedoc and Aquitaine. The Atlantic influence gives a cooler, damp climate than the rest of the Midi, and richer soils encourage the planting of Bordeaux grape varieties.

There is a VDQS area and a new AOC for red and rosé wines: Côtes de la Malepère, with vineyards southwest of Carcassonne; and Cabardès, north of Carcassonne.

Côtes de la Malepère (VDQS)
For Côtes de la Malepère, the principal grape varieties are Merlot, Cot and Cinsaut, with Cabernets Franc and Sauvignon, Grenache Noir and Syrah as secondary varieties. Some 90% of Côtes de la Malepère is made by cooperatives, including the one in Razès. Nevertheless, a handful of independent vinegrowers, such as Château de Malviès and Château du Routier, bottle at the estate. Their wines are a perfect illustration of the combination of Mediterranean warmth and southwestern structure.

Cabardès (AOC)
The best wines of Cabardès are made from Cabernet Sauvignon, Merlot and Grenache. Cabardès is generally warmer and drier than the Côtes de la Malepère, with vineyards on the better-exposed slopes of the foothills of the Montagne Noire, the last southwestern outcrop of the Massif Central.

In Cabardès, private estates outnumber cooperatives, with Château de Pennautier, Domaine de Cabrol, Domaine de Cointes and Domaine d'Escourrou numbering among the best.

More contemporary in style is the Crémant AOC, a plumper variation on Blanquette. The balance between Chardonnay and Chenin on the one hand and Mauzac on the other has been reversed. The first two can represent up to 90%, Pinot Noir up to 10% and Mauzac is allowed, but it can be entirely absent, too… at least in theory.

The still wines of Limoux, which are simply labelled AOC Limoux, are worthy of note. Each producer can determine for himself the proportions of Chardonnay, Chenin and Mauzac. The grapes are handpicked for this wine, and cask ageing is *de rigueur*.

Last but not least, a red Limoux AOC has been in existence since 2003. Merlot must represent at least 50% of its composition, and in addition, there must be at least two of the following: the two Cabernets, Cot, Syrah, Grenache and Carignan.

Producers
Of the 11 million bottles of sparkling Limoux produced annually, three-quarters come from the modern, well-run Cave Coopérative de Limoux, founded in 1947. It produces a variety of *cuvées*, including Aimery, Cuvée Aldéric and Sieur d'Arques.

Domaine de Martinolles, owned by the Vergnes family, is among the best of the private producers. They have 65ha (160 acres) of vines from which the domain makes stylish Crémant and Blanquette de Limoux and some *vin de pays*.

There are 45 other producers, some of whom vinify their own harvest only, while others buy in grapes or juice. Domaine de Fourn and Domaine de Flassian (Antech) are worth the trouble it can take to hunt them down.

MINERVOIS

The ancient village of Minerve lends its name to a large wine region producing mostly red wine.

The Minervois *appellation* lies across the Aude Valley from Corbières, on the foothills of the Massif Central, partly in the Aude and partly in the Hérault. The *appellation* takes its name from the isolated fortified village of Minerve, founded by the Romans and dedicated to their goddess of wisdom. The village played an important part in the Albigensian Crusade at the end of the 12th century, as one of the last strongholds of the Cathari heresy.

Most of the wine produced here is red, although there are some reasonable rosés and whites, with a little enclave of Muscat *vin doux naturel* in the village of St-Jean-de-Minervois (*see* p284).

Like Corbières, Minervois was granted an AOC in 1985, after becoming a VDQS in 1951. These days, there are very fewer growers left who prize quantity over quality. As a rule, local producers have acknowledged that they need to follow modern viticultural practice, and lower production through more rigorous pruning, green harvesting and carefully selecting the grapes.

Continuous efforts by the co-operative of La Livinière have led to the official recognition of a village *appellation*.

Grape varieties and wine styles

The use of better grapes has improved the taste of Minervois surprisingly well. A good red example is now a solid, full-flavoured wine. There is an increasing amount of Grenache Noir, as well as Syrah and some Mourvèdre.

Syrah is well suited to the warm, dry conditions of the Minervois, and the best wines will contain as much as 75%. Mourvèdre is much more problematic, partly because it is particularly sensitive to fluctuations in the water supply. The proportion of Carignan grapes has been reduced to a maximum of 40% in 1999.

White Minervois, based on Maccabeo and Bourboulenc, is being improved by some Marsanne and Roussanne. Viognier may eventually be allowed for white Minervois, but at present it is restricted to *vins de pays*, along with Chardonnay, Merlot and Cabernet Sauvignon.

Vinification methods are also improving, with considerable investment in new equipment. The process of *macération carbonique* is being refined and oak ageing is becoming more widespread, with the introduction of a few new *barriques*. Greater attention is also being paid to the characteristics of individual vineyards, their soil types and micro-climates leading to the recognition of five separate zones (*see* opposite). □

PRODUCERS

The Minervois appellation spreads across a vast and varied zone of 4,500 hectares (11,120 acres) of vineyards. There are 23 cooperatives, but there are now also 175 private estates, many of which only came into being over the past few years.

Once upon a time, in the Minervois and all over the South of France, they used to produce a mellow white wine. Until the introduction of modern dry whites, it was the only white wine there was. Now they are considering the creation of a new AOC, Minervois Noble, for these very same mellow wines. A few rare examples can already be found, made from late-harvested, or *vendanges tardives*-Grenache Blanc and Maccabeo.

Daniel and Patricia Boyer-Domergue
See profile.

Château Fabas
Roland Augustin is continuing the programme started by his predecessor, Jean-Pierre Ormières, one of the first exponents of barrel maturing.

Château de Gourgazaud
Roger Piquet, the former managing director of the trading company Chantovent, has been at the forefront of experiments with different grape varieties. He first planted Syrah on this estate in the village of La Livinière in 1974.

Domaine Sainte Eulalie
This estate in the village of La Livinière was purchased by Isabelle Cousral. She discovered 100-year-old Carignan vines, and she vinifies the juice in the traditional way, rather than using *macération carbonique*.

Coopérative La Livinière
Cooperatives dominate the appellation; the one in the village of La Livinière is one of the most innovative and energetic. It has encouraged its members to plant the better grape varieties, particularly Syrah, by paying a bonus for them. These efforts have been rewarded by the establishment of La Livinière as a village *cru* of the Minervois, with the implementation of lower yields, higher alcohol and stricter regulations on grape varieties.

Other producers
Names to look for include Domaine Borie de Maurel, Domaine Cathare, Domaine Piccinini, Domaine La Tour Boisée, Château La Grave, Château Massamier la Mignarde, Château Villerambert-Julien, Domaine Aimé, Château de Beaufort, Château de Cesseras, Château d'Oupia, Domaine Saint-Sernin, Château Bassanel, Château Saint Jacques d'Albas and Château la Villatade.

ZONES WITHIN MINERVOIS

Geographically and geologically the Minervois can be divided into five zones. Although these are not yet officially recognized, it is widely agreed that the zones produce wines of quite distinct character.

East: The vinegrowing areas, known as Les Mourels and Les Serres, are on the pebbly plain around Ginestas, where the climate is influenced by maritime winds and rain. They produce light red wines for drinking within a year or two.
North: The Haut-Minervois has vineyards — Le Causse and Les Côtes Noires — at an altitude of 200m (660ft) and a harsher climate influenced by the mountains. The wines are rugged and rustic, and can improve for five or six years.

Central: The vineyards, on the south-facing foothills of the Montagne Noire, are very hot. The vineyard areas, L'Argent Double and Le Petit Causse, produce aromatic, well-structured and long-lived red wines with plenty of warm, spicy fruit.
South-central: West of Olonzac, the south-central zone — Les Balcons d'Aude — includes the villages of La Livinière, Pépieux and Rieux-Minervois; the heart of the *appellation* and the driest, hottest part. Its supple, spicy red wines are best when drunk young.
West: This area, known as La Clamoux, has a more humid climate, with a marginal Atlantic influence. Its vineyards produce red, white and rosé wines.

CLOS CENTEILLES

Daniel and Patricia Boyer create two different wines from their beloved Cinsaut: Campagne de Centeilles, with a hint of Syrah and Grenache, and a light, fresh style that makes it a wine for drinking young, and Capitelle de Centeilles from pure Cinsaut.
A third wine, Carignanissime, is a resounding success, despite the fact that Daniel and Patricia hold Carignan in low regard. And finally, Clos de Centeilles, made from equal amounts of Syrah, Mourvèdre, and Grenache, will age beautifully. All of these wines enjoy a long vatting period, with no ageing in fresh wood.

COTEAUX DU LANGUEDOC

The Coteaux du Languedoc is a large *appellation* that covers a broad sweep of the Mediterranean coast from Narbonne to Nîmes. The AOC label covers 168 villages, in addition to the communes authorized to use the labels Clairette du Languedoc, Faugères and St-Chinian. Depending on the rules of production laid down in the various regulations — which are exceedingly precise for the last three — the wine can be labelled either as Coteaux du Languedoc or as one of the other three *appellations*.

Coteaux du Languedoc was recognised as a VDQS in 1961. The appellation was created in 1985, initially for red and rosé wines only, but it now covers white as well.

The Coteaux du Languedoc region is going through a veritable revolution with the introduction of new grape varieties that display distinctive flavours, and of new winemaking techniques, such as *macération carbonique*.

Grape varieties
The varieties are traditional to the Midi. Since 1990, the law has required that all *appellation* wines contain at least 50% Mourvèdre, Syrah and Grenache. Carignan and Cinsaut together must not exceed 50%.

For the white wines, the principal varieties are Bourboulenc, Grenache Blanc, Roussanne, Marsanne and Rolle. The maximum permitted yield is 50hl/ha for the reds and 60hl/ha for the whites.

Clairette du Languedoc
This is a separate *appellation* for white wine made entirely from the Clairette grape, which can also feature in white Coteaux du Languedoc. The *appellation* zone covers ten villages in the Hérault, between

Château d'Ammelas near Clermont l'Hérault.

Pézenas and Clermont l'Hérault, and it is making a comeback thanks to new vinification techniques. Although Clairette ripens easily, if it is too ripe it can make very heavy, alcoholic wine. Today, the best wine is made at 12%Vol, rather than 13% or 14% as in the past. Clairette also has a tendency to oxidise.

When young, a good Clairette du Languedoc should have an attractive, generous flavour, with hints of almonds, aniseed and fresh fruit.

Among the producers who contributed to establishing the *appellation*'s reputation, both the Jany family at Château la Condamine Bertrand and the cooperative in Adissan can take some credit.

Faugères
This *cru* comprises seven villages in the foothills of the Espinousse mountains, an outpost of the Massif Central. The soil is schist as in St-Chinian. At this point in time, the AOC only covers reds and rosés, but

authorisation for whites is expected shortly. The better wines of Faugères come from estates such as Domaine Jean-Michel Alquier, Domaine Léon Barral, Domaine Saint-Antonin and Château des Estanilles.

Saint-Chinian
This large area covers some 20 villages in the Hérault *département*. Most of the vineyards are on the foothills of the Cévennes, as high as 200m (660ft), so nights are cool and the grapes ripen slowly. The River Vernazobre follows a geological division: to the north the soil is based on schist, which generally gives supple, fruity red wines for drinking young. The south is a mixture of limestone and clay, producing more substantial wines that benefit from some ageing.

Domaine Canet-Valette, Domaine Borie la Vitarèle, Mas Champart, Domaine Rimbert and Château Coujan are quality estates.

CRUS AND PRODUCERS

These are the seven zones of the Coteaux du Languedoc, which have replaced the 14 *crus*. Faugères and St-Chinian received their own *appellations* in 1982. Although they were incorporated into the general *appellation* in 1985, the names Faugères and St-Chinian often stand alone on the label.

Appellation status has led to the creation of an official hierarchy of production zones within the Coteaux de Languedoc. The influence of wind and rainfall, as well as average temperatures and greater or lesser amounts of sun in the coastal, scrub or foothill zones made it possible to distinguish seven climactic zones, the first three of which are named in the *appellation*, which specifies particular production conditions. The other zones are currently working towards official recognition.

La Clape and Quatourze

On the outskirts of Narbonne, the vineyards of La Clape are located on a rugged, rocky outcropping. They enjoy one of the sunniest climates in France, while being cooled off by sea breezes. In addition to the reds and rosés, the white wines are also of good quality here, and vinegrowers here are the only ones in the Languedoc who are allowed to mention the name of the zone on the label. The Bourboulenc grape is particularly successful.

Noteworthy domains include Châteaux Pech Redon, Pech Celeyran, La Mire-Etang, Négly and de Marmorières.

Pic St-Loup

This lively, well-reputed *cru* takes its name from the mountain that dominates the skyline some 20km (12.5 miles) north of Montpellier. The zone covers 13 villages and 12,000ha (29,640 acres). In order to be allowed to use the Pic St-Loup name, the wine must be made from at least 90% Syrah, Mourvèdre and Grenache. These varieties represent about half of the vines in the AOC zone. The other wines, sold under the AOC Coteaux de Languedoc label, can contain Cinsaut and Carignan, which has a strong presence in the zone. Among the better producers we can name Domaines d'Hortus and de Mortiès, Mas Brugière, Clos Marie, Châteaux de Cazeneuve and de l'Euzière, l'Hermitage du Pic Saint Loup, Valflaunès and the cooperative of St-Mathieu de Treviers.

Grès de Montpellier

Large smooth stones and conglomerate soil dominate in the east of this zone, while the west has limestone and clay. This zone encompasses the former *terroirs* surrounding Montpellier: Vérargues (Château de la Dévèze), St Drézéry (Château Puech Haut), St-Christol (*vin de pays* of La Terre Inconnue), La Méjanelle (Château de Flaugergues and Domaine Clavel), St-Georges d'Orques (Château de l'Engarran, Domaines de la Prose, Belles Pierres and Henry). In addition, there is also the scrubland region west of Montpellier (L'Abbaye de Valmagne, Domaine Peyre Rose, Terre Mégère and the *vins de pays* of Mas d'Aimé).

Pézenas and Cabrières

This region includes the vineyards located between Pézenas and Clermont l'Hérault, including some which weren't part of the old *terroirs* and *climats*. The borderline between *vins de pays* and AOC wines is fuzzy here, and several producers are making both. Coteaux du Thongue is expecting to be promoted to *appellation* status shortly. Cabrières is located in the northern part of the zone, near the border with Faugères. Cabrières wines are similar to Faugères, though perhaps in a more rustic style. Among the good producers we can name Le Prieuré de Saint-Jean de Bebian, Les Chemins de Bessac, the Domaines de l'Arjolle, de Clovallon, de la Colombette, La Croix Belle, Deshenry, Perdiguier and Montrose.

Les Terrasses du Larzac

This zone has the advantage of being located at a high altitude, so it is cooler at night, and the vines suffer less from the summer heat than they do elsewhere. The zone covers the former territories of Montpeyroux (Mas Jullien, Domaines Saint Andrieu, l'Aiguilière, d'Apuilhac, Font Caude, Granoupiac, Château de Jonquières and Mas Cal Demoura) and St Saturnin, where the co-operative is in the spotlight. In addition, there are also the villages further north, like Octon and St-Jean de Blaquières, at the foot of the plateau (Mas des Chimères, Mas Haut Buis and Domaine de la Sauvageonne).

Les Terres de Sommières

This zone stretches between the cities of Montpellier and Nîmes, north of the motorway. The *terroir* is easily identified by large, smooth stones, like those found in Châteauneuf-du-Pape. And the wines are often reminiscent of the Rhône style, too. Among the good producers can be named Roc d'Anglade, Domaine Arnal, Mas Granier and Domaine de la Coste.

Les Terrasses de Béziers

The town of Béziers is situated in the Languedocian plains, but nearby there are low-rising terraces that grant vinegrowers the possibility of producing quality wines. These terraces stretch all the way to the coast. The good producers are Château le Thou, Château Font des Prieurs and Domaine du Nouveau Monde, among others.

Picpoul de Pinet

This zone produces everything from Coteaux de Languedoc AOC wines to *vin de pays* in all three shades. But only the whites composed entirely of the Picpoul Blanc variety are allowed to put the zone's name on their label. In this maritime climate, Picpoul brings forth a dry yet fruity white that is the perfect accompaniment to a platter of oysters from the nearby port of Bouzigues.

Mas Saint-Laurent, Domaine Félines-Jourdan, Domaine Gaujal and Domaine Morin-Langaran are some of the best producers.

VINS DE PAYS

Vin de Pays de l'Hérault, covering the whole *département*, is second only to the Aude in terms of production. There are also 28 *vins de pays de zone*, the majority of which are red or rosé. Many of these wines are made from Cabernet Sauvignon, Merlot, Sauvignon or Chardonnay. Wines cut with inferior varieties, like Aramon or Alicante Bouschet, are destined to become anonymous table wines or else find their way to the distillery.

GARD

The *département* of the Gard forms the eastern limit of the Midi, and its main *appellation*, Costières-de-Nîmes, is where the vineyards of the Languedoc meet those of the Rhône Valley. While the area is, like the rest of Languedoc-Roussillon, known mainly for red wine, it is also home to Listel's famous rosé *vin de pays*, and the small white wine *appellation* of Clairette de Bellegarde.

The *appellation* Costières de Nîmes covers a large plateau to the south of the town of Nîmes, and is limited by the Rhône to the east and the Camargue to the south. The motorway, La Languedocienne, is on the northern edge, and to the west are the most easterly vineyards of the Coteaux du Languedoc. The area of the *appellation* has been carefully delimited so that it covers about 25,000ha (61,750 acres) in 24 villages, although only about half of the area is planted with vines, and of those, only about 4,100ha (10,1300 acres) actually produce Costières-de-Nîmes, the rest being *vins de pays*.

The area was recognised as a VDQS in 1951, as Costières du Gard, and was made an *appellation* in 1986. In order to avoid confusion with the departmental Vin de Pays du Gard, the name was changed to Costières-de-Nîmes from the 1989 vintage.

The *appellation* is limited to a particular type of soil, called *grès*, consisting of gravel and large pebbles brought down from the Alps by the Rhône. The large pebbles absorb the daytime heat and radiate it back onto the grapes at night, thus helping the ripening process. The subsoil contains a high proportion of clay, which retains moisture and prevents the vines from suffering from a lack of rain during the summer. The proximity of the sea also has a tempering effect on any potential drought, bringing a degree of humidity.

Grape varieties and wine styles

The list of permitted grape varieties is in a state of flux, as in other parts of the Midi. As recently as 1970 Carignan was predominant. Today, Carignan has decreased dramatically and rarely represents more than 40% of a blend. Since 1990 Grenache has comprised a quarter of all the red wine, and the balance is made up of Cinsaut, with increasing amounts of Syrah plus a bit of Mourvèdre.

Costières de Nîmes is mainly red, although the appellation includes rosé and a smidgen of white, for which the grape varieties are Grenache Blanc, Maccabeo, Ugni Blanc, Rolle and Bourboulenc. A little Marsanne and Roussanne are beginning to add extra interest and aroma to the whites. Chardonnay has also

VINS DE PAYS

The departmental Vin de Pays du Gard is the most common v*in de pays*, while Vin de Pays des Coteaux Flaviens, named after a Roman imperial dynasty, covers the same area and provides some identity for experimental plantings of Merlot and Cabernet Sauvignon, as well as the excess of Carignan.

Vins de Pays des Sables du Golfe du Lion, made famous by Listel, a trade name of the Salins du Midi company, crosses the boundaries of the *départements* of Hérault and Bouches-du-Rhône, with production centred on the sand dunes of the Gard *département*. Around 65% of the wines are rosé (known here as Grains de Gris).

There are ten other *vin de pays* zones, predominantly red, within the *département*, of which perhaps the best-known names are the Vin de Pays du Mont Bouquet and des Coteaux du Pont du Gard.

The regional Vin de Pays d'Oc name is also used, particularly for varietal wines from "new" grapes such as Chardonnay, Chenin Blanc, Cabernet Sauvignon and Merlot.

been planted, but is only permitted for *vin de pays*.

The wines have some of the spicy herbal flavours of the Midi, with some warmth, but not necessarily much body, while the wines from vineyards closer to the Rhône Valley have more weight and richness. These are not wines for long ageing, but for early drinking.

Producers

Unlike most other *appellations* of the Midi, Costières-de-Nîmes is not dominated by village cooperatives; they account for only about a third of the production. The hundred or so independent producers are making considerable efforts to improve the quality of their wine and alter the composition of their vineyards. There have been changes in methods of cultivation — a higher density of vines giving better results — and vinification, with some experimental *macération carbonique*, and oak-ageing in Bordeaux *barriques*.

The recent elevation to *appellation* status has added further incentive, resulting in some good wines, most notably in estate wines from Château de Beck, Château de Rozier, Château de Campuget, Château de la Tuilerie, Château Mourgues de Grès or Domaine du Vieux Relais.

Clairette de Bellegarde

This appellation is reserved for a dry white wine made exclusively from the Clairette grape. Clairette is difficult to vinify well, although when successfully made it has a dry, hazelnut flavour, with some weight and character. Production is a mere 250,000 bottles, coming principally from the Coopérative de Bellegarde and Mas Carlot, where the Blanc family has been making it for several generations, alongside their fine range of Costières-de-Nîmes and v*in de pays*. □

SOUTH-WEST FRANCE

FROM BERGERAC, WHOSE VINEYARDS ADJOIN THOSE OF BORDEAUX,
DOWN TO THE PYRENEES, SOUTH-WEST FRANCE BOASTS A LONG LIST
OF LOCAL GRAPE VARIETIES AND WINE STYLES.

The Château de Crouseilles is owned by the village
cooperative of Crouseilles-Madiran, which did much to
revive the fortunes of this region's wines. The château, in the
foothills of the Pyrenees, produces a fine Madiran.

The wine map of South-West France covers a broad spectrum of different styles, but within this range some patterns do occur. The region corresponds roughly to that of old Gascony, stretching from the boundaries of the Gironde *département* inland and southward, right down to the border with Spain. The vineyards lie along the valleys of the rivers that eventually flow into the estuary of the Gironde: Bergerac on the Dordogne; Cahors on the Lot; Gaillac on the Tarn; and Fronton, Buzet and Marmandais on the Garonne. To the east, around the headwaters of the rivers, viticulture ends in the foothills of the Massif Central, with small, isolated pockets of vines, while the wines of the foothills of the Pyrenees form a sub-group of their own to the south. To the south-east, beyond Toulouse, a wide plain blends with the Aude Valley and the vineyards of the Midi. Inevitably the wines of Bordeaux, red and white, serve as a model and an inspiration for many of the wines of the South-West. The influence of Bordeaux has been felt throughout the development of the region, for historically the city's merchants dominated commerce in the wines of the valleys of the Dordogne, Lot and Garonne, the region that was known in the Middle Ages as the Haut Pays or "high country". Until the area of the Bordeaux vineyard was finally limited to the *département* of the Gironde in 1911, a considerable amount of Haut Pays wine flowed into the Bordeaux trade. The ending of this trade, plus the ravages of phylloxera, struck heavy blows to many of the wines of the South-West. Today, the vineyards are successfully rebuilding their reputations, an effort spearheaded in many places by very active cooperatives and by a new generation of vinegrowers. They are helped by a range of indigenous grape varieties to add to those of Bordeaux. This palette of grapes, several of which are unknown elsewhere, confers individuality on the wines of the South-West. The region offers every style of wine, from the lightest of dry white (still and sparkling) wines in Gaillac to rich, sweet Monbazillac from the Dordogne Valley; from soft country reds to the solid, structured wines of Madiran and Cahors. And the countryside is some of the most beautiful and unspoilt in France.

WINE REGIONS OF SOUTH-WEST FRANCE

Bergerac's vineyards, along with those of the Côtes de
Duras and Côtes du Marmandais, adjoin those of
Bordeaux; here, and in Buzet, the wines produced are
similar in style to those of their famous neighbour.
Cahors has a tradition of robust, tannic red wines which
improve with age. The *appellations* south of Cahors, and
in the hills to the east, offer a palette of unusual wines.
The Pyrenees have their own grapes and wine styles,
from sweet white Jurançon to full-bodied red Madiran.

Wine regions

- Bergerac
- Montravel
- Rosette
- Pécharmant
- Saussignac
- Monbazillac
- Côtes de Duras
- Côtes du Marmandais
- Cahors
- Vins d'Entraygues et du Fel
- Vins d'Estaing
- Marcillac
- Côtes de Millau
- Buzet
- Côtes du Brulhois
- Vins de Lavilledieu
- Côtes du Frontonnais
- Gaillac
- Tursan
- Côtes de St-Mont
- Madiran, Pacherenc du Vic-Bilh
- Béarn
- Jurançon
- Irouléguy

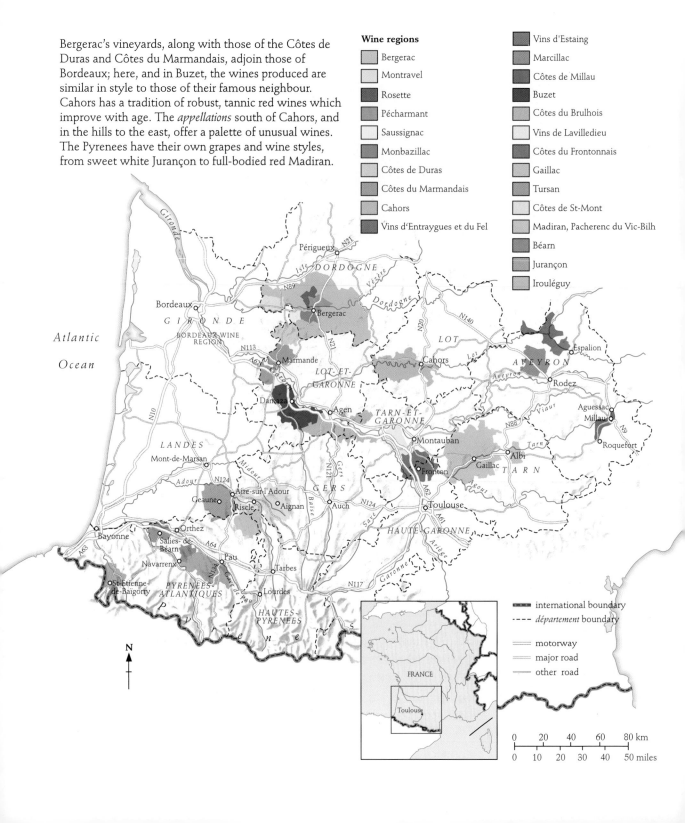

BERGERAC

The pleasant country town of Bergerac lies at the heart of a cluster of *appellations* in the *département* of the Dordogne. The area is rich in agriculture, with strawberries and tobacco, and is also known for walnuts, cep mushrooms and truffles. The undulating hillsides form a natural continuation of those of St-Emilion: it is only the departmental boundary, rather than any physical frontier, that separates Bergerac's vineyards from those of Bordeaux.

Bergerac is the basic *appellation*, covering the whole area: the wines can be red, white or rosé. The *appellation* Côtes de Bergerac, which may also be used throughout the region, denotes an extra degree of alcohol for red wines, 11% by volume as opposed to 10% by volume, while a white Côtes de Bergerac is medium-sweet, or *moelleux*. Other *appellations* can only be produced in limited areas. Pécharmant is a small enclave for red wine, while Monbazillac is the best-known sweet white wine of the Dordogne region.

Among the other white *appellations* are Rosette and Saussignac. These lesser-known names are seldom used: wines entitled to them are often declassified into the more familiar Bergerac or Côtes de Bergerac. Montravel has its own *appellation* for reds and whites, as well as for rosés.

Location, climate and soil
The vineyards cover a broad area, stretching from St-Emilion to beyond the town of Bergerac and including some 93 villages. The climate is similar to that of Bordeaux, with the maritime influence of the Atlantic making for mild winters and moderate rainfall, though perhaps less so than in the Gironde. The average temperature is slightly warmer. Spring frosts can be a hazard, as is hail.

Rouffignac, a Monbazillac commune.

The soil, too, is similar to Bordeaux, and in particular to that of St-Emilion: a mixture of gravel, clay and limestone. Today's Bergerac wines, particularly the sweet whites, are on a par with most bordeaux.

Grape varieties
The grape varieties of the Bergerac region are essentially those of Bordeaux. Others may be allowed in the *appellation* regulations, but in practice are rarely grown.

Traditionally, white Bergerac was made from roughly two parts Sémillon to one part Sauvignon Blanc (and may also have included some Muscadelle and even some Ugni Blanc), but there has been a definite trend towards crispy dry Bergerac, usually labelled Bergerac Sec and made with a large proportion of Sauvignon Blanc. Ugni Blanc has practically disappeared.

Bergerac reds come principally from Cabernet Sauvignon, Cabernet Franc and Merlot grapes, just as in the Bordeaux region. Malbec is sometimes found in the vineyards of Pécharmant.

Techniques and trends
Vinification methods have improved enormously throughout the region. There is a growing interest in the effect of new oak on the maturing wines, more often for reds than for whites, but its use is not always financially viable. Greater care is being taken to control fermentation temperatures of both red and white wine. Experiments with skin contact as well as lees contact have added an extra dimension of flavour to the white wines.

A new generation of energetic growers is making its mark on the *appellation*. These winemakers are highly motivated and prepared to challenge the accepted views of their parents. Some are newcomers to the region, and free of restrictive preconceptions. They are also looking at their vineyards, reducing their yields and working hard to improve the quality of their grapes. As in other vineyards, in France and elsewhere, there is a growing concern and realisation that the quality and health of the grapes are fundamental to the ultimate quality of the wine in the bottle, and have more effect than the calibre of equipment in the cellar.

The red wines of Pécharmant
Pécharmant is considered the most important red wine of Dordogne; it is more structured and has greater staying power and potential for longevity than an average red Bergerac. "Péch" is the local dialect for a hill, so that Pécharmant literally means "the charming hill". It is a small area, east of Bergerac, including four villages with vineyards on gentle south-facing slopes, with about 300ha (740 acres) in production.

The district has superior soils, with some gravel over clay and limestone. It is perfect for Malbec, as well as the Cabernets and Merlot. Not everyone grows Malbec, however, as it is particularly sensitive to crop failure. It can fill a useful role in rounding out the wine and giving it more substance and structure, but only if the yields are kept low.

A good Pécharmant benefits from some ageing, and AOC regulations impose a minimum of one year in the cellar, in vat, cask or bottle, before the wine may be sold, in an attempt to emphasize the ageing potential. The wine can sometimes continue to improve in bottle for ten years or even more.

Although there are some 40 producers in Pécharmant, just 15 of them account for almost three-quarters of the *appellation's* wine. They are working together to improve things. A proportion of new barrels are used, which would once have been considered financially impractical. The *barriques* enhance the ageing potential of the wine, making for finer tannins. Cellars are becoming better equipped with facilities such as cooling equipment. Some estates, like their neighbours in the Gironde, now produce a second wine from young vines, or less successful vats.

The sweet wines of Monbazillac

Monbazillac is the great sweet white wine of the Dordogne and, like Sauternes (*see* p163), true quality depends upon the development of noble rot or *botrytis cinerea*. The vineyards, covering 3,400ha (8,400 acres) in five villages, lie south of the River Dordogne. Perhaps surprisingly, they are mostly on north-facing slopes, but as they face the river, they enjoy the autumn mist that encourages the formation and development of noble rot. Monbazillac wines are from the same grapes as the sweet wines of Bordeaux, usually in the proportions 73% Sémillon, 15% Sauvignon Blanc and 12% Muscadelle.

Monbazillac from a good vintage, such as 1997 or 2001, stands among the great sweet wines of France, full-bodied, and rich, with a concentra-

tion of aromas characteristic of noble rot, as well as an enormous potential for longevity.

Unfortunately, Monbazillac's reputation once suffered from earlier, less-than-honourable habits. More recently however, efforts have been made to improve the quality and reputation of Monbazillac and there are a growing number of producers who are keen to revive it.

The sweet wines of Saussignac

Saussignac, formerly Côtes de Saussignac, is usually a *moelleux* (medium-sweet) white wine. But occasionally, in top vintages like 2001, it can be as rich and sweet as a fine Monbazillac. Before the *appellation* was created, the vineyards were included in the Monbazillac *appellation* as the soil and micro-climate are similar. The AOC is limited to five villages: Gageac, Rouillac, Monestier and Razac de Saussi-

THE MONBAZILLAC REVIVAL

Good Monbazillac must be made with the same attention to detail as the sweet wines of the Gironde.

Hand-picking, with successive *tris*, was made mandatory from the 1992 vintage, and the minimum potential alcohol has been increased from 13%Vol to 14.5%Vol. However, 20%Vol is really desirable in order to avoid the need for chaptalization; in the great years an even higher level of ripeness is attained. Any wine that is deficient in potential alcohol is now declassified into Côtes de Bergerac *moelleux*. Growers who still use mechanical harvesters also have to call it Côtes de Bergerac.

Not only are several *tris* carried out during the vintage, but yields are maintained at a reasonable level. They may be as low as 20hl/ha and certainly no more than 40hl/ha. Most producers ferment in stainless steel vats and rack their wine before ageing it for several months in either large *foudres* or new *barriques*. Others prefer to start the fermentation in vat and, once it is under way, transfer the fermenting juice into small *barriques*, where the finished wine will stay for about 18 months.

gnac, in addition to Saussignac itself. Since 1990, this new *appellation* has made a name for itself and is now recognized and appreciated by an ever-increasing public.

The grape varieties are the same, with a large proportion of Sémillon, as well as a little Sauvignon Blanc and Muscadelle. Vinification techniques vary according to the level of technology in the cellar. Usually the grapes are picked as late as possible, and for traditional Saussignac the ideal balance is 12%Vol of alcohol and 2.5% of residual sugar. This can make for a wine that doesn't have much character, whereas a positively sweet Saussignac is a much more enjoyable drink.

Montravel

In 2002, Montravel became separate from Bergerac, even for the reds and rosés which are nevertheless still made in the Bergerac manner. The white wines that used to be sold either as Bergerac or Côtes de Bergerac, or as Montravel, now almost always bear the name Montravel on the label.

There are three separate *appellations* for white Montravel. Plain Montravel AOC is a dry white wine that can be made in 15 villages. Côtes de Montravel is the *moelleux* version from the same villages, whereas Haut-Montravel is a separate area, covering five villages, of which Fougueyrolles is the centre. The wine is *moelleux*, preferably sweeter than Côtes de Montravel, and made from very ripe, if not nobly rotten, grapes.

Rosette

The tiny Rosette *appellation* is something of an anomaly, yet is has managed to survive. Officially the *appellation* covers a few villages to the north of the town of Bergerac. Like Saussignac and most Montravel, it is essentially a semi-sweet style of white wine, and is most often sold as Côtes de Bergerac. □

PRODUCERS

The Bergerac AOC region covers some 11,900ha (29,393 acres), and many estates make a range of wines under the general *appellations*. Others, particularly in the Monbazillac area, specialize in their local *appellation*.

Domaine de l'Ancienne Cure

This estate's renown is based on its Monbazillac, which is one of the best in this fast-improving appellation. But one shouldn't overlook its well-balanced, aromatic reds, nor its white, a dry Bergerac from 100% Sauvignon Blanc, grown in a vineyard in Colombier.

Château Belingard

Count Laurent de Bosredon, proprietor of this château, is typical of the generation of winemakers in the region: contagiously enthusiastic and ever-willing to challenge accepted ideas. He has looked at macerating with skin and lees, and ageing in oak barrels; and he makes an exciting range of wines: a crisp dry white Bergerac, a substantial red Côtes de Bergerac and a sweet white Monbazillac. His best wines are named after his grandmother, Blanche de Bosredon, who died in the early 1990s, at the age of 102.

Domaine des Costes

Nicole and Jean-Marc Dournel have created an exceptional vineyard in Pécharmant. Between their magnificent acreage at the very gateway to Bergerac, and their *savoir-faire* in the cellar, they have made it to the head of the pack. Dournel wines are the perfect example of what an AOC Pécharmant is supposed to be.

Château Masburel

Olivia Donnan and her husband bought this property in 1997 and have renovated the vineyard entirely. They have acquired a reputation as first-rate vinegrowers, creating Montravels and Bergeracs in all three colours, as well as a sweet Haut-Montravel.

Cave Coopérative de Monbazillac

The co-op owns the showplace Château de Monbazillac, and makes wine from this and four other châteaux: Septy, La Brie, Pion and Marsalet. Vinification takes place at a modern plant, and the co-op produces 2 million bottles a year.

Monbazillac's sloping vineyards above the River Dordogne.

Château de Tiregand

This château is the leading estate of the Pécharmant *appellation*, and the property of the St-Exupéry family, cousins of the famous author of *Le Petit Prince* and also cousins of the owners of Domaine de Pech Céleyran in La Clape (*see* Coteaux du Languedoc, p293).

There are 40ha (99 acres) of vines at Tiregand: Merlot (45%), Cabernet Sauvignon, Cabernet Franc and a little Malbec. The estate makes two red wines, the second from younger vines plus Malbec. The use of a small proportion of new oak enhances the longevity of Pécharmant.

Château Tirecul la Gravière

Monsieur and Madame Bilancini do Monbazillacs only on their 9ha (22.5 acres) in a single stretch... but what Monbazillacs they are! With a generous proportion (up to 50%) of Mus- cadelle and extremely low yield (11hl/per ha) their Cuvée Madame fetches a higher price than many top Sauternes. The wines are barrel-fermented, with half being replenished each year.

Château Tour des Gendres

When an *appellation* is lucky enough to have a pace-setter, the quality of its wines is bound to be exceptional. Alain Brumont has shown this in Madiran. Luc de Conti of Château Tour des Gendres has played a similar role here in Bergerac. Both his red wines and his white wines are outstanding.

These brilliant results have been obtained through meticulous care in the vineyard, perfectly ripe grapes and state-of-the-art winemaking for each type of wine.

Clos Les Verdots

Once known as Berdeaux, Verdots is also the name of the underground river that snakes through the property's cellar, carved out of limestone, in which David Fourtout makes an impressive range of top-notch Bergeracs as well as a good Monbazillac

Other producers

The following estates are known for their Monbazillac: Clos Bellevue, Château La Borderie, Château Le Fagé, Château Poulvère and Château de Theulet; for their Saussignacs: Château Court les Mûts, Château des Eyssards and Château les Miaudoux; for their Montravels: Château Roque-Peyre, Château Puy Sevain, Château de Raz, and Domaine de Gouyat; for their Pécharmants: Domaine des Bertranoux, Domaine Haut-Pécharmant, Château Champarel and Château Terre Vieille; and for their generic Bergeracs: Domaine Constant and Château de la Colline, Château Grinou, Château de la Mallevieille and Château Le Paradis, and Clos d'Yvigne.

DURAS, MARMANDAIS, BUZET

Duras, a small town with a splendid castle, looks west towards the vineyards of Bordeaux, and only the *département* boundary separates its vineyards from Entre-Deux-Mers, while to the north-east its vineyards adjoin Bergerac. This proximity is reflected in the Duras wines. The Marmandais region lies directly to the south, while Buzet is to the south-east along the Garonne Valley. The climate is very similar to that of Bordeaux: perhaps a little warmer and drier, but just as subject to spring frosts and hail. The soil is a mixture of clay (in which the red grape varieties thrive) and limestone, which the whites prefer. The Marmandais has some flint and gravel, which are also good for red wines.

Côtes de Duras

The AOC Côtes de Duras dates from 1937, when most of the wine was white. The rules allow for both dry and *moelleux* (medium-sweet) white wine, as well as red and rosé (although production of rosé wine is insignificant). The production of red wine has increased since the 1970s, and it has now overtaken the white.

The main white grapes are Sauvignon Blanc, Sémillon and Muscadelle. Chenin Blanc, Ugni Blanc and local varieties Mauzac and Ondenc are allowed under AOC regulations, but are rarely found. The red wines are assembled from Cabernet Sauvignon, Merlot, Cabernet Franc and Malbec. Merlot has been known to represent over 50% of the whole.

White Côtes de Duras used to be a rather neutral, slightly sweet wine, made predominantly from Sémillon. Today, with improved vinification methods, the best white wines are pure Sauvignon Blanc, with crisp fruity acidity, following the trend for fresher, drier wines. The ripest grapes, usually Sémillon, go into Côtes de Duras *moelleux*, retaining a couple of degrees of residual sweetness. Red-wine vinification follows Bordeaux practice, with ageing in vat for 12-18 months, sometimes followed by additional ageing in oak. The results are not unlike a young Bordeaux, with an attractive blackcurrant taste.

PRODUCERS

Cooperatives are the most important wine producers in each of these three districts.

Côtes de Duras

The Berticot-Landerrouat cooperative accounts for over half the *appellation's* production. Among the 50 or so private estates, the most notable are Domaine Amblard, Domaine Durand, Domaine de Ferrant, Domaine de Laulan and Domaine du Vieux Bourg.

Côtes du Marmandais

The Côtes du Marmandais is dominated by two cooperatives, Cocumont in the south and Beaupuy in the north. Cocumont is the more modern and dynamic of the two, making good wines that are representative of the *appellation*. But an independent producer, Elian da Ros (Clos Bacquey) is the *appellation's* true star.

Buzet

Les Vignerons Réunis des Côtes de Buzet (now known as Les Vignerons de Buzet) is one of the most impressive and efficient cooperatives in France, producing most of the Buzet wine. It even employs its very own cooper, or barrel-maker.
Château de Gueyze, Château de Padère and Château Mazelières are three private estates whose wine is made by the cooperative.
Among the independent producers, the most notable are Domaine de Pech as well as Château de Savagnères, Château du Frondat and Château des Tournelles.

Côtes du Marmandais

Marmande, in the Garonne Valley, is a centre for market farming. Vines grow among fields of fruit and vegetables: here, and in Duras, very few growers make a living from viticulture alone. The AOC Côtes du Marmandais produces mostly red wines.

After the phylloxera devastation of the late 19th century, hybrid vines were planted until about 1950. The efforts to revive the vineyards were rewarded, in 1955, with VDQS status. In 1983 the grape varieties were further restricted to a maximum of 75% Merlot, Cabernet Franc and Cabernet Sauvignon, and a maximum of 50% Cot, Gamay, Syrah and local varieties Fer Servadou and Abouriou. There is a little rosé, and also some white wine, mostly from Sauvignon Blanc, Sémillon and Muscadelle.

Buzet

Buzet, called Côtes de Buzet until the 1988 vintage, is also mostly red, though the AOC includes white and rosé. The village is on the River Baïse, a Garonne tributary, and the vineyards lie on the south bank of the Garonne, between Agen and Marmande. Grape varieties, and the size and quality of vintages, follow Bordeaux: Cabernet Sauvignon, Cabernet Franc, Merlot and a little Malbec for red wine and Sémillon, Sauvignon Blanc and Muscadelle for the tiny amount of white.

Here, too, the revival in the vineyards came in the 1950s, and the VDQS was created in 1953, followed by the foundation of the cooperative (*see* box) in 1955. Its considerable achievements were rewarded with an AOC for the district in 1973.

CAHORS

Cahors, one of the finer red wines of South-West France, comes from the Lot Valley, mainly from vineyards to the west of the historic town of Cahors. In the 19th century, it was known as a wine that kept well, that could be laid down for many years, then served with game.

Today Cahors varies in body and structure. The best wines are capable of long ageing, with good tannins and fruit, while others are lighter and destined for early drinking. While the Cahors *appellation* is firmly red, this does not preclude some experimental plantings of white grapes such as Viognier, Chardonnay and other varieties, which are not included in the *appellation* but sold simply as white table wine.

Cahors suffered badly during the phylloxera crisis, and many vineyards were abandoned. It was recognized as a VDQS in 1951, but was severely hit by the hard frosts of 1956, so that the vineyard area declined still further. It was not until the 1960s that there was a revival, which was rewarded with the creation of an *appellation d'origine contrôlée* in 1971. Since then the vineyard area has expanded considerably, from 200ha (494 acres) in the early 1960s to 4,300ha (10,620 acres) today. This area represents the feasible maximum, covering all the land under vine before the phylloxera epidemic. The vineyard area now stretches some 40km (25 miles), nearly as far west as Fumel, and includes 45 villages.

Location, climate and soil
The climate is influenced by both the Mediterranean and the Atlantic, for the town is equidistant from each. Being well inland, summers are generally warmer and drier than in Bordeaux. Spring frosts can be a

Spraying the vines.

problem, however, and so can hail. The topography of the vineyards lends itself to a variety of different micro-climates. The River Lot has cut out a long, meandering path, so that it almost turns back on itself, forming dramatically large loops. The vines grow on the terraces of the valley slopes and on the plateau, or *causses,* above.

The great debate in Cahors is over soil and the position of particular vineyards. Broadly speaking, there are two different types of land. The highest vineyards are on the *causses*, the arid plateau above the valley, which is chalky and stony, with only the thinnest layer of topsoil. Below them, there are three terraces on the valley slopes, the lowest, near the river, being on fertile, alluvial soil. The soil is a mixture of clay and chalk, in varying proportions, with some sand, gravel and decomposed rocks. Some argue that the wines of the *causses*, from thin, chalky soil, have better structure, while others find wines from the gravel slopes more subtle and rounded.

A detailed study of the Cahors *terroir*, taking into account not only the soil and subsoil, but also water supply, may eventually result in a classification of *crus*. However, other factors also influence the taste of Cahors, not least the methods of each producer.

Grape varieties
Cahors is unique in South-West France in that the *appellation* does not allow a single drop of Cabernet Sauvignon or Cabernet Franc. The backbone of the wine is Malbec, known locally as Auxerrois. The *appellation* requires at least 70% of it in the wine, but more is often used, even to the extent of a pure Auxerrois. Balance is provided by Merlot and Tannat.

It is Auxerrois that gives Cahors its rugged character, with a firm backbone of tannin. It can be susceptible to *coulure*, which causes considerable annual variations in the size of the harvest. Merlot softens the Auxerrois, filling it out. Tannat adds even more tannin, and is a late-ripening variety. Opinions vary as to its value; some say that it merely exaggerates the defects of the Auxerrois.

Making the wine
Along with the expansion of the vineyards, winemaking techniques in Cahors have been modernized. Stainless-steel tanks have made some headway in replacing cement vats; old oak barrels have been replaced by new Bordeaux *barriques*. Sometimes longer fermentations are used in order to obtain more extract in the wine; sometimes the various grape varieties are fermented separately, followed by a careful *assemblage*. A strict selection of the grapes is made, which may result in a producer making two wines: a standard and a prestige *cuvée*.   □

PRODUCERS

There are some 200 producer-bottlers in Cahors; some are long established and others belong to a a new generation of producers. Some Cahors wine traders also own vineyards. Some 100 growers or so sell their wine to *négociants*.

Domaine de la Bérangeraie
The Béranger family may own just 8 ha (19.75 acres), but their Cahors are known for their authenticity. No chemical weed-killers or fertilizers; traditional vinification, but without filtering; ageing in cement vats and no barrels define the temperament of these long-lasting wines. There are two *cuvées*: Juline, which is more precocious, thanks to the Merlot, and the more virile Maurin.

Château du Cèdre
Charles Verhaeghe's Cahors wines are today the best, and wine lovers are keen to buy his "ordinary" Cahors, as well as his Prestige or Cèdre. All of his "black wine", as the Cahors was once nicknamed, is fleshy and dense, with fine tannins. Winemaking here is state-of-the-art, and maturing uses sophisticated techniques. Excellent work.

Les Côtes d'Olt
The cooperative of Cahors accounts for about one-third of the vineyards and produces a variety of wines, ranging from a traditional sturdy Cahors to lighter, fruitier wines. Its cellars are well equipped with stainless-steel fermentation vats, and some of its better wines are aged in *barriques*. The cooperative is also responsible for about ten individual estates.

Clos la Coutale
This riverside estate near the village of Vire sur Lot is home to the Bernède family, who have been making wine here for over a hundred years.

They move with the times, and have stainless steel vats in which they can control fermentation temperatures. The wine seems to mature fairly quickly, and it often turns out to be well over par in average years like 1999 or 2002.

Clos de Gamot
The Jouffreau family have owned this property since 1610, and have done much to restore the reputation of Cahors. Clos de Gamot is probably the only estate to be planted in Auxerrois alone. It includes some very old vines, which explains why Clos de Gamot has such longevity. The Jouffreaus also own Château du Cayrou, as well as a miniscule vineyard on the *causse*, which produces their best-known *cuvée*, Clos Saint Jean.

Château Lamartine
Alain Gayraud, the owner, has made this 28-ha (69-acre) vineyard a spectacular success. The vines are planted on a terrace above the Lot Valley, in Soturac, at the *appellation's* western outskirts.
The 100% Auxerrois Cuvée Expression, a modern wine with international renown thanks to its elegance and finesse combined with its strength, should not be missed. Nor should the more traditional *cuvées* be overlooked either.

Château la Reyne
The fifth generation of the Vidal family recently took over the reins of this excellent estate. This vineyard's star is rising fast,

Old houses at Puy l'Evêque, west of Cahors.

thanks to Johan Vidal's hard work.
This young vinegrower produces a more modern wine, and his Cuvée Prestige profits from fine-tuned cask maturing.

Château Triguedina
Jean-Luc Baldès is the ninth generation of his family to own this 41-ha (100-acre) estate. His classic wines are made with 25% Merlot, which grants it a pleasantly supple quality. Their Prince Probus Cuvée Prestige is made from 100% Auxerrois.
Jean-Luc also makes a wine in the old style, called New Black Wine, as well as several *vin de pays*, including a remarkable *moelleux* based on Chenin Blanc.

Other producers
Other good estates include Château de Caminade, Domaine d'Eugénie, Château de Goudou, Domaine de la Pineraie and

Domaine des Bateliers, which all have a fine reputation. Among the lesser estates, Domaine de Cause, Domaine de Causse-Maisonneuve and Domaine des Savarines (organic) are worth mentioning.
A few wine merchants have begun buying estates in order to become producers as well. Conversely, a few vinegrowers have taken the opposite route, deciding to market their own production. Among them: Georges Vigouroux (Châteaux Haute-Serre and de Mercuès), the Rigal brothers (Châteaux Saint Didier and de Grézels as well as the Prieuré de Cénac), Alain-Dominique Perrin (Château de Lagrézette) and Marc Delgoulet (Château de Chambert).

GAILLAC AND FRONTON

The region south of Cahors (in the Tarn, Tarn-et-Garonne and Lot-et-Garonne *départements*) can boast of two AOC areas — Gaillac and Fronton — and two VDQS, Vins de Lavilledieu and Côtes du Brulhois. Like Cahors, they are not too far from either the Mediterranean or the Atlantic.

The former accounts for hot summers and dry winds from the south and the south-west, and the latter for rain; the Massif Central mountains to the east are responsible for cold winters and spring frosts. The *département* names — Tarn, Tarn-et-Garonne, Lot-et-Garonne — attest to the importance of the rivers, not least in helping to create a number of microclimates. The wide range of soils allows these regions to grow many of the grape varieties peculiar to the South-West.

GAILLAC

Gaillac is one of the most diverse *appellations* of South-West France, and one of its oldest vineyards: the Romans planted vines here in the 1st century AD. Gaillac gained an AOC for its white wines in 1938; reds and rosés were included in 1970, and red wines now account for around 60% of production.

The vineyards, in the *département* of the Tarn, lie north-east of Toulouse, and encompass some 73 villages around the town of Gaillac. Albi splits the *appellation* into two, with a smaller group of vineyards to the east of the town.

A handful of villages — Broze, Cahuzac-sur-Vère, Castanet, Cestayrols, Fayssac, Lisle-sur-Tarn, Montels and Senouillac — are entitled to use the Gaillac Premières Côtes classification for rich, aromatic, sweet white wines. In theory these vineyards enjoy a better aspect, and their yields are lower, with 40 instead of 45hl/ha.

However, in practice, few producers make use of this distinction.

Soil composition in the Gaillac vineyard is extremely varied: a mix of clay and limestone on the Right Bank of the Tarn, as opposed to alluvial sand and gravel on the left. The terraced vineyards around the picturesque village of Cordes, at the north of the *appellation*, with the most limestone, are ideal for dry white wines.

On the other side, to the west of Albi for instance, the soil, a mix of sand and gravel, fulfills the conditions for producing elegant red wines.

Grape varieties

Gaillac includes an eclectic range of grape varieties, reflected in a corresponding number of different wine styles. The standard Bordeaux white varieties, Muscadelle and Sauvignon Blanc, are mixed with grapes rarely found elsewhere, like Mauzac, for white wine.

Gaillac's oldest variety, Mauzac can compose a wine of varying degrees of dryness, depending on when it is picked. Loin de l'Œil has become increasingly important. For white wine, a vineyard must include at least 15% Sauvignon Blanc, Loin de l'Œil or a mixture of the two.

The most important red variety is Duras, followed by Fer Servadou (known locally as Braucol), Syrah, and for the *primeurs*, Gamay. All together, these varieties must represent at least 60% of the blend. The balance comes from Merlot, Cabernet Franc or Cabernet Sauvignon.

Wine styles

White Gaillac can be *sec* (dry), *doux* (sweet) or *moelleux* (mellow, with an impression of sweetness); *tranquil* (still), *mousseux* (sparkling) or *perlé* (very slightly sparkling).

Gaillac *perlé* is a traditional dry white wine. The authentic method retains a little carbon dioxide from the malolactic fermentation when the wine is bottled: the bubbles in the glass should look like tiny pearls, hence the name.

Sparkling wine is sometimes made by the method used in Champagne and sometimes by the *méthode gaillacoise*, the *méthode rurale* of other parts of France. Originally, the first fermentation was interrupted by immersing the barrels in ice-cold water; today electrical refrigeration is used. After bottling, fermentation recommences the following spring.

Gaillac *moelleux* comes from grapes that are picked late, when they are very ripe. The juice ferments very slowly and the fermentation is stopped to leave some sweetness. Gaillac *doux* must contain 75 grams per litre of residual sugar, while Gaillac *moelleux* depends upon the individual growers' taste.

Two styles of red Gaillac emerge as the most typical, both based on the local Duras grape. In the first, Duras is blended with Fer Servadou for structure and Syrah for colour. The second shows affinities with Bordeaux, blending Duras with Merlot and Cabernet. Red Gaillac benefits from moderate ageing, but is generally ready young.

Red Gaillac Nouveau or *primeur*, made from Gamay grapes using *macération carbonique*, is an agreeable alternative to Beaujolais Nouveau.

FRONTON

Fronton is a small area producing red wine, and a little rosé, but no white, on a plateau between the rivers Tarn and Garonne.

The plateau of Fronton has a distinctive soil: it is this which defines the *appellation* area. The best soil for the vines is red gravel with a high

Château de Lastours is among the leading Gaillac producers.

iron content, locally called *rouget*. Elsewhere the soil is silty *boulbènes* of decomposed clay.

The characteristic fruitiness of Fronton comes from the Négrette grape, which must account for 50-70% of the blend. It produces a supple, fruity wine with a low level of tannin that tends to oxidize easily and age quickly: it needs to be blended with other longer-lasting varieties. Cabernet Sauvignon, Cabernet Franc, Fer Servadou and several others are limited to 25% each. Cabernet Franc seems to be the preferred variety. You can find a pure Négrette, but technically such a wine does not conform to the *appellation*.

LAVILLEDIEU

West of the town of Montauban, and north-west of the Côtes du Frontonnais, lies a small (150-ha/350-acre) *appellation* area of 12 villages centred around La-Ville-Dieu-du-Temple.

The VDQS was granted in 1954 for red and rosé wine made from a blend of Négrette, Gamay, Cabernet Franc, Syrah and Tannat; but many growers concentrate on vins de pays and *vin de table*. The local cooperative vinifies the vast majority of VDQS Lavilledieu.

COTES DU BRULHOIS

Elevated to VDQS from *vin de pays* in 1984, Côtes du Brulhois covers two small areas that are divided by the Garonne, with vineyards in the southeast of the *département* of Lot-et-Garonne and the west of Tarn-et-Garonne. "Brulhois" comes from *brûler* ("to burn") a reference to the local tradition for distillation: this is the edge of Armagnac country.

The VDQS covers red wine and a little rosé, but no white. The principal grapes are Cabernet Sauvignon, Cabernet Franc and Tannat, while Merlot, Malbec and Fer Servadou are permitted, but are less important. Vinification methods are simple, with fermentation and storage in cement vats, making for some rustic red wine, which is produced by two cooperatives and a smattering of independent producers from a 200-ha (494-acre) vineyard.   □

PRODUCERS

In Gaillac, as well as in the smaller zones of Fronton, Vins de Lavilledieu and Côtes du Brulhois, cooperatives were once in complete control of production. Nowadays, some independent estates have come into their own.

Gaillac

A hundred or so independent producers compete with three cooperatives, which are still quite influential. The Cave de Labastide de Lévis and the Cave de Rabastens are the biggest, the Cave de Técou is the smallest, as well as being the best. Most noteworthy among the individual vinegrowers are Vignoble Robert Plageoles et Fils, for their remarkable range of Mauzac-based wines and for their promotion of older varieties like Ondenc and Prunelard; Domaine Causse-Marines, the apostle of Plageoles; Domaine de la Ramaye, another bastion of highly characteristic wine; the more recent Château de Palvié, Domaine de la Chanade, Château d'Arlus, Domaine Labarthe, Mas Pignou, Domaine Rotier, Domaine de Gineste and Domaine de Pialentou, Domaine Barreau and Domaine Salvy. For reds, Domaines de Larroque and Cailloutis are head of the class. For sweet wines, Château de Mayragues, Mas de Bicary, Domaine de Long-Pech and Domaine Borie-Vieille (a lovely *vin de pays* rich in Muscadelle).

Fronton

This *appellation* used to be divided into two zones: Côtes de Frontonnais and Côtes de Villaudric, each with its own cooperative. Today, it is known simply as Fronton, and the only cooperative is in the village of the same name.

Among the 50 or so good producers, Château Bellevue la Forêt is the largest; it really put Frontonnais on the wine map. There is also Château Bouissel, Château Cahuzac, Domaine Caze, Château de la Colombière, Château Coutinel, Domaine de Joliet, Château la Palme, Château Plaisance, Château le Roc, and Domaine de Saint-Guilhem.

Côtes du Brulhois

Aside from the cooperatives of Goulens and Donzac, Château la Bastide and Domaine de Coujétou-Peyret are worth mentioning.

THE PYRENEES

The foothills of the Pyrenees are a land of proudly individualistic wines. The wines of the traditional regions of Gascony, Béarn and the Basque country had been known to pilgrims making their way to Santiago de Compostela in Spain since the 9th century. They won a place in French history in 1553, when Jurançon wine was used to baptize Henri IV, the future king of France. Today the *départements* of Gers, Landes and Pyrénées-Atlantiques have five AOCs — Jurançon, Madiran, Pacherenc du Vic-Bilh, Irouléguy and Béarn — and two VDQS — Côtes de St-Mont and Tursan.

It is difficult to generalize about the climate, which is influenced by both the mountains and the Atlantic Ocean, as there are a host of microclimates. The same applies to soil types, which are quite distinct from area to area, and which account for the individuality of the grape varieties, and therefore the wines.

JURANÇON
The vineyards lie on the lower slopes of the Pyrenees, at an average altitude of 300m (990ft), south of Pau. The *appellation* covers 700ha (1,730 acres) in 25 villages, including Jurançon itself, now little more than a suburb of Pau, and Monein, another well-known village. This is a region of polyculture, with many small parcels of vines scattered among other crops and fields where cattle are grazing.

Grape varieties and wine styles
Jurançon is best known for its fine sweet white wines, although dry whites do exist, and indeed have a separate *appellation*: Jurançon Sec. Both are made from grape varieties quite unrelated to those of Bordeaux: Gros Manseng, Petit Manseng and Petit Courbu.

Gros Manseng, which yields more, gives a dryer juice; while Petit Manseng gives a sweeter juice, as its grapes are richer in sugar. It yields less and is harder to grow. Some growers have no Courbu at all: they feel it detracts from the Mansengs, while others appreciate it for the liveliness it brings to the wine.

Unlike most of the other sweet table wines of France, the concentrated sweetness comes from a process called *passerillage*, whereby the grapes are left on the vines until quite late in the season. Jurançon never acquires *botryris*; Manseng grapes are too thick-skinned for the noble rot to penetrate. In addition, this is a region of long, sunny autumns with warm foehn winds, blowing directly from Spain. The combination of warm days and cool nights shrivels the grapes, which contain a rich, sweet juice, and must be carefully picked several times.

A few producers are experimenting with new oak barrels, although they are aware that over-ageing could affect the delicately pithy character of the Manseng. Jurançon Sec is for relatively early drinking, although it does take on more complex flavours with age. Jurançon *moelleux* ages very well. A bottle from the best vintages need not fear comparison with a good Sauternes, and it develops finesse with age.

MADIRAN AND PACHERENC DU VIC-BILH
These are twin *appellations* for red (Madiran) and white (Pacherenc du Vic-Bilh) wine from 37 villages surrounding the village of Madiran (three in the Gers, six in the Hautes-Pyrénées and 28 in the Pyrénées-Atlantiques). The *appellations* encompass some 1,600 hectares (4,000 acres) situated at about 40 km. (25 miles) from Pau.

Pacherenc du Vic-Bilh almost faded into oblivion at one time, but it is enjoying a revival now, even if production is currently only 1,100,000 bottles, as opposed to 8.5 million of Madiran. Vic-Bilh means *vieux pays* ("old country") in Gascon, and was the old name for the area. Pacherenc is a distortion of *pachet en renc*, or in French "piquets en rangs", implying that the vines were once grown in a row, supported by posts.

The vineyards are on the first foothills of the Pyrenees, with varied soils. The west-facing slopes work well for Pacherenc, while the south-east-facing slopes are better suited to the red varieties. Late spring frosts are one of the worst hazards. Summers are hot enough to cause a drought sometimes. Long, mild autumns can be followed by hard winters.

Grape varieties and wine styles
The most characteristic grape variety of Madiran is a tannic and tough-skinned grape variety called Tannat. A few producers use it alone, while most have got into the habit of blending the 40 to 60% of required Tannat with other, more supple varieties, such as Cabernet Franc (known locally as Bouchy) or, more frequently, Cabernet Sauvignon.

The grape varieties for Pacherenc du Vic-Bilh are Gros Manseng and Petit Manseng, Petit Courbu and a local speciality, Arrufiac, which gives the wine its note of originality.

Most Pacherenc du Vic-Bilh today tends to be sweet, with hints of honey and exotic fruit, true to the grape's roots. Indeed, like its neighbour Jurançon, Pacherenc du Vic-Bilh was traditionally sweet, except in mediocre years when it was dry. Now, Pacherenc follows Jurançon in producing dry or sweet whites depending on the vintage.

In Madiran, the current trend favours an overuse of new barrels. While it is true that seven or eight years of wood can give a certain ample roundness to the wines, the Tannat, as its name implies, has enough tannin all by itself, and hardly needs more from the wood.

IROULÉGUY

This *appellation* takes its name from a tiny village in the Basque country, in the heart of the Pyrenees, not far from the Spanish border. The area suffered badly from phylloxera at the beginning of the last century, and the vineyard had shrunk to just three small villages, which were granted VDQS status in 1952. Ten years later, the area was expanded to the six villages that now comprise the AOC, which was established in 1970.

Red wines make up two-thirds of the production, whites and rosés complete the rest. Tannat makes up the lion's share of the red, but the two Cabernets are important, too.

BEARN

The *appellation* includes three separate areas of the Pyrenees. First, Jurançon, where growers with red grapes will make Rouge de Béarn. Second is Madiran which may make a rosé wine called Rosé de Béarn. The third part of the *appellation* is centred on the village of Bellocq and the picturesque Pyrenean town of Salies de Béarn. Wines from here carry Béarn-Bellocq on the label and may be red, rosé or white.

The vineyards nearly disappeared in the aftermath of the phylloxera crisis, and the tide only turned with the creation of the Cave Coopérative de Salies de Béarn-Bellocq in 1947. Its Rosé de Béarn achieved overnight success in Paris, and Béarn was recognized as a VDQS in 1951. It became an *appellation* in 1975 for red and white wine, as well as rosé.

The dominant grape variety for both reds and rosés is, once again, Tannat, which gives structure and

Tannat grapes form the backbone of Madiran's deep-coloured wines.

body. Cabernet Franc and Cabernet Sauvignon add smoothness and bouquet. White wine from Béarn-Bellocq comes from Raffiat de Moncade, a variety peculiar to that part of Béarn.

Generally Béarn tends to be a rather unsophisticated wine. Some of the best Rouge de Béarn comes from around Jurançon, where most of the producers make some red wine to complement their range. They may give it a few months' barrel-ageing, which helps to round out some of the rugged flavours of Tannat.

COTES DE ST-MONT

The Côtes began as a *vin de pays* and was promoted to a VDQS in 1981. It is now aiming for AOC status.

The vineyards of the Côtes de St-Mont are on the slopes of the hills above the River Adour, to the north of Madiran, around the tiny village of St-Mont. They form a natural continuation of the Madiran and Pacherenc du Vic-Bilh vineyards, and the grape varieties are identical.

TURSAN

Tursan is a VDQS covering 27 villages on the south-east edge of the Landes forest, with the small town of Geaune at its centre. Vieille-Tursan is the biggest village, but the most famous is Eugénie-les-Bains, where Michel Guérard, one of the best chefs in France, has his hotel and restaurant.

Originally it was white wine that made Tursan's reputation. Although red and rosé didn't crop up until the 1960s, their production now outstrips the white's.

The principal grape for white Tursan is the rather uninspiring Barroque. Other varieties are now allowed, in order to provide more flavour and vitality: Sauvignon Blanc, for instance, may now make up 10% of the blend. Usually white Tursan is quite fresh, with some fruity tartness. Red Tursan, from Tannat, Cabernet Sauvignon and Cabernet Franc, tends to be somewhat rustic in flavour. □

PRODUCERS

Cooperatives are still important in winemaking in the Pyrenees, but all of the region's *appellations* have a growing number of reputable individual producers.

JURANÇON
Domaine Cauhapé
Henri Ramonteu has done more than anyone else to enhance the reputation of his *appellation*. Passionate about Jurançon, he makes three dry wines: a standard; a *cuvée* that is fermented in wood; and a *cuvée* Vieilles Vignes from 80-year-old vines. He makes a similar variety of sweet wines: one from Gros Manseng picked in early November; and a Vendange Tardive, from equal parts Gros and Petit Manseng, and matured in wood for 12 months. Noblesse du Petit Manseng spends a total of 18 months in oak, including fermentation. Quintessence du Petit Manseng, for which the grapes are not picked until December, is made only in the very best years. Yields are extremely low, just 8hl/ha, and again the wine is fermented and aged in oak for 18 months. This is Jurançon *moelleux* at its most sublime.

Cave Coopérative de Gan
The co-op in the village of Gan has been instrumental in improving Jurançon's image, particularly with its *vins de propriété*.

Ch Jolys
Robert Latrille bought this estate in 1958. It is the largest estate of the *appellation*, and is planted with 12ha (30 acres) of Petit Manseng and 25ha (62 acres) of Gros Manseng.

Clos Lapeyre
With his organic vinegrowing methods, Jean-Bernard Larrieu is following in the footsteps of Henri Ramonteu.

Clos Uroulat
Charles Hours was president of the producers union for many years. His Cuvée Marie, delicately matured in wood, is among the best of the dry Jurançons.

Other producers
The following growers produce wines that are equal in quality to those mentioned above: Domaine de Bellegarde, whose current proprietor's ancestors emigrated to New Orleans when the vineyards were devastated by phylloxera; Domaine Bordenave, where the young Gisèle Bordenave has taken over her father's vineyard and is producing some of the region's best sweet wines; and Domaine Capdevielle, where the elderly Casimir sticks to traditional methods, like only harvesting in the afternoon, when the sun has had a chance to dry off the grapes.

MADIRAN, PACHERENC DU VIC-BILH
Ch Bouscassé
Alain Brumont, the charismatic proprietor of Châteaux Montus and Bouscassé, created quite a stir in 1982, when he bought one-year-old casks from Château Margaux, thereby introducing maturation in new (or nearly) casks in the Madiran region. Nowadays, most local producers make at least two *cuvées*, including one prestige, with cask-ageing. The same rule applies to Pacherenc, espe-

cially for the *moelleux* wines, although a certain limitation in the use of oak, which can affect the wine's aromas, has been observed recently.

That's the reason why Patrick Ducournau (Domaine Mouréou and Chapelle Lenclos) and his cousins, the Laplaces from Château D'Aydie, have developed a technique known as micro-bubbling, which consists of injecting minuscule quantities of oxygen into the containers, be they vats or casks. This technique speeds up the aeration process by simulating oxidation via the staves, softening the tannins and eliminating the need for the constant pumping over the must that used to be required. Ducournau and Laplace work with Didier Barré (Domaine de Berthoumieu) and Jean-Marc Lafitte (Domaine Lafitte-Teston), sharing ideas and experience for mutual benefit.

Equally admirable are Guy Capmartin and his brother Denis, from Château Barréjat; the wines from Domaine Crampilh, Domaine Laffont and the neighbouring Domaine Labranche-Laffont. The newly established Clos Fardet will also be worth keeping track of.

The cooperatives make quite good wines in these *appellations*. Crouseilles produces Madiran, Pacherenc and *vins de pays* only, while the one at Saint-Mont also accepts growers from the northern part of the Madiran region, over and beyond the *appellation's* borders. The third cooperative, in Castelnau-Rivière Basse, has experienced quite a revival since coming under the leadership of Alain Brumont, whose estate is nearby.

IROULEGUY
In terms of quantity produced, the Cave Coopérative des Vins d'Irouléguy et du Pays Basque dominates this *appellation*, but

there are also a handful of excellent independent producers: Domaine Abotia, Domaine Arretxea, Domaine Brana (with it spectacular cellars carved out of the slopes of the Pic d'Arradoy), Domaine Etchegaraya and Domaine Ilarria. As in the Béarn, they produce a great quantity of rosé, destined to slake the thirst of holidaymakers.

COTES DE ST-MONT
Union Plaimont
The Domaine de Maouries, in the Madiran region, and the Château de Bergalasse, just beyond the border of the Madiran, are both good producers. But they are somewhat overshadowed by the size and renown of the Cooperative des producteurs de Plaimont, which controls virtually all of this VDQS. It is the most impressive cooperative in the South-West. Members must pick by hand, yield is strictly limited, the most up-to-date tracking technology has been put into use, and wood-maturing for certain *cuvées* is in excellent hands. The range of wines is constantly evolving. Their dry whites are very successful, even better than the reds.

TURSAN
Here is another cooperative, the Vignerons de Tursan, that runs its *appellation*. Producing wine in all colours, it also manages a few private estates. The only exceptions to its sovereignty are the formidable enterprise composed of Château Perchade-Perrouchet and the media-hyped vineyard owned by chef Michel Guérard, who, in his elegant Château de Bachen, creates white wines in a New World style, using — as long as the authorities continue to look the other way — a bit of Sémillon to perk up the blandness of the traditional Barroque.

THE AVEYRON AND THE QUERCY

The *département* of the Aveyron has one AOC, Marcillac, and three VDQS zones, Côtes de Millau, Vins d'Entraygues et du Fel and Vins d'Estaing. In the Quercy region, VDQS Coteaux du Quercy covers 420ha (1,038 acres) to the south of Cahors, straddling the *départements* of Lot and Tarn-et-Garonne. Cabernet Franc is the main grape variety.

Marcillac

The Marcillac *appellation* has some very characteristic features. The beautiful countryside has wide sweeps of sloping vineyards, and a few rows just managing to hang on to the exceedingly steep slopes at 300 to 600m (990-1,980ft) above sea level. The soil is mostly red sandstone. As spring frosts can be a problem, there are no vines on the lowest, most frost-prone slopes.

Fer Servadou, known as Mansois locally, accounts for almost 100% of the vines. It makes some wonderfully distinctive red wines, with a certain spiciness and an aroma of black currant. Vinification methods are classic, and the wine usually spends some time in old casks (the cooperative uses vats) before bottling. Although most Marcillac is best drunk young, the best ones show some potential for ageing.

The Valady cooperative produces two-thirds of the wine, but a few independent growers, including Philippe Teulier (Domaine du Cros), Jean-Luc Matha (Le Vieux Porche), Claudine Coste, in Combret, and the Laurens family in Clairvaux, are making some wonderfully expressive wines.

Vins d'Entraygues et du Fel

Before phylloxera, some of the wine from the terraces of Entraygues found its way to Paris. There are now 21ha (52.5 acres) of vines left, grown mainly by two families. Le Fel has built a reputation for its red wine, Entraygues for its white. Today the VDQS covers all three colours; whites are based on Chenin Blanc grapes, reds and rosés on Fer Servadou and Cabernets Sauvignon and Franc. Vinification methods are pretty rustic.

Vins d'Estaing

The 7ha (17 acres) of France's smallest VDQS lie further up the Lot Valley. Methods are traditional, with six growers sharing a communal cellar. The best wine is the white, made from Chenin Blanc softened by some Mauzac. The rosé is quite fruity, and the red made from Gamay, Cabernet Franc and Fer Servadou a little astringent.

Côtes de Millau

This VDQS, which until 1993 was Vin de Pays des Gorges et Côtes de Millau, covers about 50ha (123 acres) of vineyards close to Roquefort and the Tarn Gorges. The cooperative at Aguessac is the main producer, with red, rosé and white wines.

Coteaux du Quercy

VDQS since 1997, this mainly red wine is produced by three cellars: Côtes d'Olt, La Ville-Dieu-du-Temple, and, above all, Vignerons du Quercy at Montpezat-de-Quercy.

Among the 20 or so independent producers, we recommend investigating Domaine d'Ariès, Domaine de la Garde, Domaine Lafage and above all, Domaine du Merchien. □

VINS DE PAYS

Vins de pays are important in South-West France. Many take second place to a geographically identical *appellation* — for example Vin de Pays des Côtes du Tarn, which covers the AOC Gaillac area. Usually both wines are made from the same grapes: the producer selects the best wines for the AOC and sells the rest as *vin de pays*.

Vin de Pays des Côtes de Gascogne

This *vin de pays de zone* has made an impact in its own right. It emerged thanks to the sharp decline in Armagnac sales. The area covers the *département* of the Gers, a slightly smaller area than that of Armagnac.

Around 80% of the wines are white, but some reds were introduced after the *vin de pays* was created in 1982. The white wine is more popular, made from Ugni Blanc, which gives freshness, and Colombard, which provides fruit. More adventurous growers are experimenting with other grapes, especially Gros Manseng.

White Côtes de Gascogne is at its best quite young, for its fresh fruit. The largest producer is the Union Plaimont. The Grassa family has done much to promote the wine; their four estates are the Domaines de Tariquet, de Rieux, de la Jalousie and de Plantérieu. Other good estates include Domaine de San de Guilhem and Domaine de St-Lannes.

Vin de Pays des Terroirs Landais

A *vin de pays de zone* in the Landes *département* with four distinct areas of production: Les Sables de l'Océan, Les Coteaux de Chalosse, Les Côtes de l'Adour and Les Sables Fauves. Half the production is of white wine, a third red, and the rest rosé.

Vin de Pays des Coteaux de Glanes

Gamay and Merlot make tiny quantities of soft, fruity red wine in this zone in the Haut Quercy, in the Lot *département*.

Vin de Pays du Comté Tolosan

This is the regional *vin de pays*, covering 11 *départements* in the Midi-Pyrénées. Red wines predominate, with a small amount of rosés and whites, from a palette of local and classic varieties.

GERMANY
THE BENELUX COUNTRIES
SWITZERLAND AND AUSTRIA

THESE COUNTRIES SHARE A COOL CLIMATE,

A LOVE OF WHITE WINES AND A COMMON HERITAGE OF GRAPES —

THOUGH SWITZERLAND ALSO DRAWS UPON FRENCH

AND ITALIAN VARIETIES.

GERMANY

GREAT GERMAN WINES ARE AMONG THE WORLD'S SUBLIME BOTTLES.
MUCH ORDINARY WINE HAS BEEN DISAPPOINTING, BUT RECENT
SUCCESSES BY YOUNG WINEMAKERS SIGNAL A RENAISSANCE.

The ancient cellars of Kloster Eberbach in the Rheingau
house a museum of winepresses. They were built to hold the
vintages of the great monastic estate, which dates from 1145.
Today Eberbach is the headquarters of the State Domain.

Wherever in the world wine is made, its bouquet, flavour and style are influenced mainly by soil, climate and vine variety. This universal truth is accepted by Germany's many wine producers, but with a different emphasis. A relatively cool climate, probably the most marginal for growing grapes successfully of all the world's major wine-producing regions, has obliged German growers to search out the most suitable sites. If the grapes are sour, characteristics derived from the soil and vine variety count for nothing, so ripeness is all. The result is that many German vineyards lie on south-facing slopes above rivers, benefiting from an equable and warmer riverside climate. Each parcel of land has its own cocktail of viticultural virtues, and, perhaps even more than in France, good and ordinary vineyards adjoin each other. With a background of dangerous living — a few hours of bad weather can ruin a year's work — the archetypal German wine expresses the brinkmanship of the country's vinegrowing. Typically white (though red wines are increasing in importance), it is not strongly alcoholic, and

freshness and elegance are qualities it retains over many years. Its character is perhaps most clearly seen when the Riesling grape is used. Germany's vineyards are mainly in the west and south of the country: only here is the climate suitable for vinegrowing. The vineyards are, as throughout history, grouped along and close to river valleys, notably the Rhein and its tributaries. German wine began with the Romans, who set out the sites of many of the Mosel and Rhein vineyards and who left some fine monuments, including a famous sculpture showing wine casks on a river boat, now in the Landesmuseum at Trier. The monks and princes of the Middle Ages, starting with Charlemagne, were an even greater influence, as were the noble estates — many of which survive. German wine was exported, via the Rhein and other rivers, to most of northern Europe in medieval times.

The rivers of Germany continued to be used for transporting wine until the 1960s. Now their main importance to vinegrowers lies in the sun's warmth, retained and reflected back to the steep vineyards overlooking them, and the wine-drinking

WINE REGIONS OF GERMANY

The 13 *Anbaugebiete*, the official quality-wine regions, are shown here. All German quality wines will carry one of these names on their label. The central Rhein vineyards — the Rheingau, Nahe, Rheinhessen, Pfalz and Hessische Bergstrasse — are mapped on p324. The Mosel-Saar-Ruwer is mapped on p319. The two eastern regions of Saale-Unstrut and Sachsen are in former East Germany and are now emerging into commerce.

Wine regions

- Ahr
- Baden
- Franken
- Hessische Bergstrasse
- Mittelrhein
- Mosel-Saar-Ruwer
- Nahe
- Pfalz
- Rheingau
- Rheinhessen
- Saale-Unstrut
- Sachsen
- Württemberg
- --- international boundary

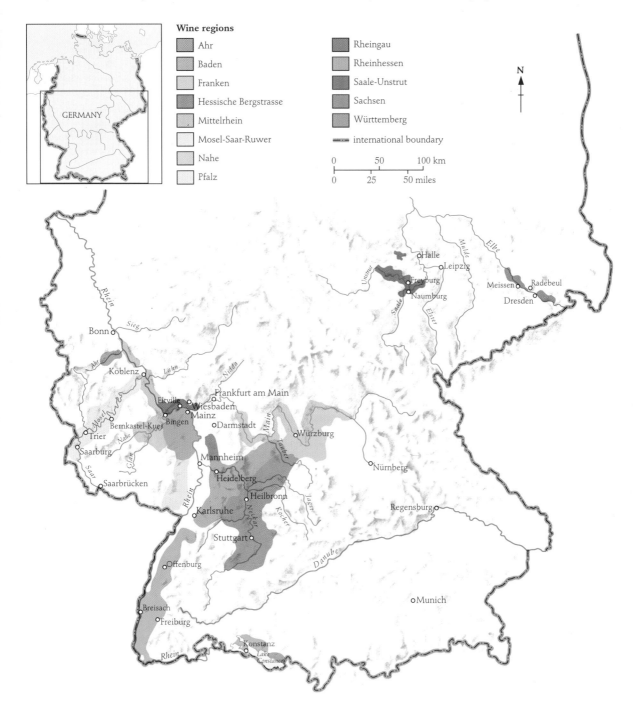

tourists they attract. The largest of these rivers, the Rhein, flows into Germany near Basel, after which it keeps in loose contact with the vineyards of Baden. The Neckar and its tributaries wriggle past many of the steep vineyards of Württemberg, before joining the Rhein at Mannheim. The meanderings of the Main end at Mainz, where it joins the Rhein after unifying some of Franken's far-flung vineyards on the way. The small Hessische Bergstrasse region looks across the Rhein Valley north of Heidelberg. The Pfalz region across the Rhein felt sufficiently independent from the river to drop the name "Rhein" from its title in 1992. Immediately to the north is the Rheinhessen, bounded on the east and north by the river, and facing the Rheingau vineyards on the right, or north, bank. The steep, spectacular vineyards of the Rhein gorge are in the Mittelrhein region. The Nahe, another tributary, has its own wine region.

The Mosel forms one region with the vineyards of the Saar and Ruwer. It is better known outside Germany than any other. The beautiful Ahr region is near the northern edge of vinegrowing in western Germany. In eastern Germany, the rivers Saale and Unstrut form one region, and the vineyards of Sachsen follow the course of the Elbe.

Wine regions and laws
Germany's wine law has codified these geographic — and traditional — divisions into *Anbaugebiete*, or legal wine regions. There are 13 of these: they are shown on the map on p311. These wine regions are further divided into *Bereiche*, or districts.

The names of the many thousands of individual vineyards in Germany were once used by growers to label wine. There are close parallels with the Burgundian system: an *Einzellage*, or single site, is much the same as a *cru*. The law introduced in Germany in 1971 grouped many of these traditional sites into larger,

legally defined, *Einzellagen*. This reduced the number of site names, and thus lessened confusion, but it swept away some important nuances of quality. Further, the 1971 law brought in the *Grosslage*, or collective site. This groups together vineyards which are supposed to have similar characters, although they do not necessarily lie side by side.

Einzellage and *Grosslage* names on a wine label are always preceded by the name of the wine village where they are sited.

It is not possible to learn from a German wine label whether the vineyard site named is a *Grosslage* (and therefore large and unspecific) or an *Einzellage* (usually smaller and more precise). Note too that there is as yet no official ranking of vineyards, as in France, no *Premier Cru* or *Grand Cru*: each vineyard is in theory as capable as any other of producing good wine.

Quality levels
In learning about a German wine, geographic origin is only one piece of the jigsaw. Next comes the official quality level. Germany divides its wine into three broad categories, based upon the sugar level in the grape juice (or "must").

These categories coincide with the EC rule that all wine is either quality wine or table wine. Germany finds it possible to define most of its wine — in some years, virtually all — as quality wine (the equivalent French figure is 64%).

■ **Tafelwein** ("table wine") is the lowest level. An important adjunct is the prefix Deutscher or German, which means the wine is actually grown in Germany. Unqualified, *Tafelwein* can mean wine from elsewhere in the EC bottled by a firm in Germany. Some modern wines of high quality are sold as *Tafelwein* because their producers do not submit them for official testing.

Landwein ("country wine") is a superior sub-category of *Tafelwein*. It has not become as popular as its French counterpart, *vin de pays*.

■ **Qualitätswein eines bestimmten Anbaugebietes (QbA)** is the lower of two bands into which all quality wine is split. The name means "quality wine from a defined region".

■ **Qualitätswein mit Prädikat (QmP)** is the top level of quality wine. The term means "with distinction". The important difference between QbA and QmP wines is that the latter are made from grapes sweet enough to need no added sugar. Each QmP wine is placed into one of six levels of distinction, according to the tested must weight of the grapes. These levels are, in ascending order: **Kabinett:** the most basic QmP level. **Spätlese:** literally, "late-picked". Made from riper grapes, *Spätlese* can be sweeter, but is increasingly the basis for drier wines.
Auslese: made from selected bunches of grapes. In good vintages, the selection will sometimes be of grapes with noble rot (*botrytis cinerea*), producing sweet, luscious wines. Dry *Auslese* is increasingly made.
Beerenauslese: made from individually selected grapes, always overripe, and thus very sweet.
Trockenbeerenauslese (TBA): as above, only the grapes are shrivelled and dry (*trocken*) from the action of noble rot. The concentrated juice produces a wine that is very sweet and very expensive.
Eiswein: literally, "ice-wine". The juice is even more concentrated, since the grapes have been frozen on the vine. An expensive speciality.

Must weight measures natural sugar in the grape juice, but a high must weight does not automatically mean that the wine will taste sweet. Increasingly, winemakers see the virtue of making a drier wine, one in which more of the sugar is allowed to convert to alcohol (*see* Winemaking Today, p99).

The concept of selection
Underlying the official quality levels is the idea that the riper the grapes, the better the wine. This is partly a

reflection of the difficulty of ripening grapes at all in this climate, partly a search for rarity and thus enhanced value. The tradition, enshrined in law, is, where possible, to leave grapes on the vine well into the autumn so that they achieve maximum ripeness. The harvest may take two months, as some vineyards are picked early for *Kabinett* wine, while others linger on in the hope that noble rot will occur and an *Auslese* or above can be made.

Tradition is being questioned in many areas as growers turn away from naturally sweet wines towards the drier ones that consumers demand. This trend is encouraging growers to produce wines from lower yields with more extract, giving the balance that residual sugar would otherwise provide.

Dry and medium-dry wines
A change in the wine laws has allowed wines below certain levels of residual sugar to be labelled as *"Halbtrocken"* (medium-dry) and *"Trocken"* (dry). These styles have prospered with the increased emphasis on drinking German wine with food. A *Trocken* Riesling wine needs good natural sugar and acidity. It is possible to make a *Spätlese Trocken* or an *Auslese Trocken*, with the high must weight translated into alcohol rather than residual sweetness.

Wine styles
Most German wines are white: red grape varieties cover less than 20% of the vineyards, although this percentage is increasing.

The main determinants of wine style in Germany are quality level, as described above, wine district and vineyard, grape variety and the aim of the winemaker. To these must be added vintage: years differ markedly.

Each of the quality levels has a differing minimum must weight in each region. Broadly, in the northern regions wines do not need as much natural sugar to qualify as in more southern ones. Thus a *Kabinett*

Burg Stahleck above Bacharach in the Mittelrhein.

from the Mosel will be lower in alcohol than one from Baden.

The law thus formalizes differences that stem from climate and other environmental factors: the more northern regions are the most sensitive to slight differences in the site, orientation and soil of the vineyard. A German winemaker does not have the homogeneity of the Bordeaux château with its single product from a hundred hectares. One small estate may have a dozen separate plots of vines, and may make three dozen wines from them, defined according to site and ripeness. Discussions about style soon turn, therefore, to specific bottles: it is hard to codify German wine styles.

German wine is, however, when compared with French or Italian, a distinct sort of wine: it stresses the fruit-acid balance rather than alcohol, and the purity of the grape rather

than derived flavours such as those that oak-ageing brings.

Ageing and vintages
Of all the grape varieties used in Germany, it is Riesling, with its marked balance of fruit and acidity, that makes wines which have the greatest capacity to age. In general, the sweeter the wine, the longer it will improve in the bottle, with wines at the top of the sweetness scale, *Beerenauslese* and above, reaching a peak after seven to ten years. Acidity is essential if the wine is to age well: very warm years sometimes make wine which has low acidity but considerable sweetness: these wines last less well than more balanced ones.

Vintages vary considerably in Germany, because the northern climate is marginal and small annual variations can have a big effect on the style of the wine. A warm vintage means high proportions of QmP wine; a cool one may fail to ripen grapes sufficiently to make more than QbA or even *Tafelwein*. For recent vintages *see* p583.

Grape varieties

The white grape variety that forms the style benchmark in Germany is Riesling. It has a great capacity to ripen well in warm autumns, and thus takes full advantage of the QmP levels. Indeed, it could be said that the QmP law was framed around Riesling. As new varieties were developed (*see* below), Riesling lost ground to more prolific and easy to grow vines.

Riesling is one of the world's classic vines and is described in the chapter on grape varieties (*see* p39). In Germany it occupies the best sites: the steeper river-valley vineyards such as those in the middle Mosel and Rheingau. These sites provide the good exposure to the sun, and the autumn warmth, which suit Riesling, which has a long ripening period.

The other classically German white wine variety is Silvaner. It is most associated with the Franken region, but in fact has its biggest plantations in the Rheinhessen. It can make concentrated, lively and long-lasting dry wine, but only when grown in good sites and when a low yield is taken from the vines.

New vineyards and vines

Since the 1960s the German vineyards have expanded by more than 50%. As the best sites had already been planted, often for centuries, most of the new vineyards were inevitably created in rather ordinary sites, providing the cheap wines required by German chain-stores, and their equivalents on the export market. Germany sells abroad some 20% of its wine production, or nearly 17 million cases, each year. Its most important customer is the UK, followed by the Netherlands, Japan and the USA. At the same time it imports over 100 million cases of wine annually, mainly from Italy, France and

Traditional steep terraces above the Mosel at Trittenheim.

Spain. Germany is the largest importer of wine in the EC.

Many of the German vineyards have been reshaped since the 1960s to allow mechanization: this reduces running costs by up to a half. Some of the results of this *Flurbereinigung* (reshaping) are unattractive to look at (notably so in the Kaiserstuhl district of Baden), and in some cases growers have complained about a deterioration in the local climate. But the benefits outweigh the disadvantages.

A parallel trend has been the rise of new vine varieties, competing with and to some extent supplanting the classic Riesling and Silvaner. The new vines are the result of crossing existing varieties: the aim of the plant scientists was to enhance yield, produce higher must weights, reduce vine diseases and provide characterful wine.

The first such crossing was Müller-Thurgau (Riesling x Silvaner),

READING A GERMAN WINE LABEL

German labels are, to non-German-speakers, superficially forbidding. Yet they carry much useful detail.
The name of the producer usually comes first. Terms such as *Weingut* (estate) or *Schloss* (equivalent to château) may precede the actual name.
The vineyard name is always preceded by the name of the village. The village name usually has the letters "-er" added in the German adjectival usage. Thus Bernkastel is the name of the village, Bernkasteler means "from Bernkastel". So Bernkasteler Doctor means that the wine is from the Doctor vineyard in Bernkastel.
The quality category — QbA or QmP — will be stated. On QmP wines the level of distinction will be prominent.

Decoded, the German wine label thus gives us information about who made the wine, the region in which the grapes were grown, and the official quality level awarded to that wine. Other, but not compulsory, data may include the vintage and the grape variety.

A quality wine is vouched for by the AP (*Amtliche Prüfung*: official testing) number, shown on the label. This shows it comes from approved grape varieties, has reached a certain minimum sweetness, and is from the region named.

Erzeugerabfüllung means bottled by the producer, perhaps a cooperative cellar; *Gutsabfüllung* describes an estate-bottled wine. *See also* "Associations and prizes", p315.

which can produce a serious white wine from a small yield when planted in a good site.

Scheurebe (Silvaner x Riesling) is, judged by quality of wine alone, the best of the crossings. Its most successful wines are produced in the Pfalz, where the strong bouquet and high acidity can result in expressive wine for long-term keeping.

Kerner (Trollinger x Riesling) is popular for a robust character, regular and high yields, and must weights that frequently allow the wine to be sold as *Spätlese* or *Auslese*. Although reliable, it lacks the charm or finesse of its Riesling parent.

Red wines and the Pinot family
Red wines are becoming more important in Germany, and their style is changing. They are increasingly made in a consciously French style, with higher alcohol, less residual sugar and wood-ageing. The main red variety is Spätburgunder (Pinot Noir). There is also a growth in the popularity of the white varieties from the Pinot family: Weissburgunder (Pinot Blanc), Ruländer (Pinot Gris) and Chardonnay (allowed since 1991 in the south).

Spät- and Weissburgunder wine of good international class comes from the Kaiserstuhl and Ortenau districts of Baden. Both these Pinot vines are equally at home in the Pfalz, where their wines have a shade more acidity. In fact, high-quality Spätburgunder wine is being produced in many parts of Germany, often by growers with experience in other countries. Other red wine varieties include Blauer Portugieser and Dornfelder, a new crossing.

Growers and cooperatives
With the exception of Baden and Württemberg, almost all the best wines are produced by private estates or by properties owned by a Federal State — such as Rheinland-Pfalz, Hessen, or Bayern — or perhaps by a town. The cooperative cellars receive grapes (but not must or wine) from their members and handle over a third of the German grape harvest. In Baden and Württemberg they cover the whole range of available wine. Elsewhere the quality and style of cooperative wine varies according to the marketing aims of the individual cellar. The growing trend is for cooperative cellars to produce better and therefore more expensive wine, which they sell in bottle as *"Erzeugerabfüllung"*, or "producer-bottled".

New styles of wine
Winemakers are reacting to the market, and producing new styles of wine based on low yields from vines of a reasonable age and from *botrytis*-free grapes. Ecologically-friendly forms of viticulture are in use, including green manuring and a restricted schedule of spraying.

To satisfy the preference of the younger German generation for light, lively, drier, fruity wines, the use of chemicals — other than limited amounts of sulphur dioxide — has been largely replaced by a better cellar procedure. Ageing in new wood, particularly for the Burgunder wines and those of similar structure, is common. Whether this improves the wine or merely changes its style is debatable.

Associations and prizes
Many of the best wine estates are members of the Verband Deutscher Prädikatsweingüter (VDP), an association of QmP-producing estates. The spread-eagle emblem on the capsule of VDP members' bottles is a good indicator of fine-quality wine, although there are still a number of good producers outside the association. In 2002, the VDP introduced a new three-tier system of classification, and provoked some criticism. Wines of the basic lavel *(Guts- und Ortsweine)* bear the name of a region or a village on their label; wines of the intermediate level *(Klassifizierte Lagenweine)* have to be produced from a limited number of sites; and the lop level — *Grosse Gewächse, Erste Gewächse* in Rheingau or *Erste Lage* in Mosel-Saar-Ruwer — aims at rewarding the best wines from the best sites.

The Deutsche Landwirtschaftsgesellschaft (DLG), or German agricultural society, offers gold, silver and bronze awards to wines judged by local panels. These awards are displayed on a small circular label or a strip on the bottle. The DLG also awards *Weinsiegel* (seals): yellow indicates *Trocken*, green for *Halbtrocken* and red for other wines.

LIEBFRAUMILCH AND OTHER POPULAR WINES

Much of Germany's success in wine exports in recent decades has been due to Liebfraumilch and certain other mass-produced medium-sweet white wines. Liebfraumilch is named after a small vineyard near Worms that was once owned by the Church. During the 19th century, the name Liebfraumilch came to be used for wine produced in a much wider area. It was, however, a term used for a high-quality wine.

Under current law, the wine can come from anywhere in the Rheinhessen, Pfalz, Nahe or Rheingau. The principal grapes used in its production are Riesling, Müller-Thurgau, Silvaner and Kerner. It must be a QbA wine with a certain minimum amount of residual sugar. Due to competition in the marketplace, Liebfraumilch is often produced down to a price rather than up to a standard. Despite this fact, it remains an immensely popular — in fact the best-selling — wine in the UK.

The same marketing approach has been applied to wines such as Bereich Bernkastel, Piesporter Michelsberg (a *Grosslage* or wine district) and Niersteiner Gutes Domtal (also a *Grosslage*). Each of these can come from a wide area, allowing scope for the producers to blend. The only guarantee of quality is the producer's name, as the geographical origin is very unspecific. Growers with quality vineyards in, say, Piesport or Nierstein grumble that these ordinary wines devalue the names of their high-quality ones.

AHR-MITTELRHEIN

During the construction of a drainage ditch for the Apollinaris spring in 1853, traces of a row of vines were discovered at a depth of a little over 4m (13ft). Coins dating from AD 260 to 268 were scattered among the vines, confirming that the 25-km (15-mile) wine region of the Ahr has a long history of organized viticulture.

Today, with only 522ha (1,289 acres) of planted vineyard, the region has shrunk to a quarter of its size at the start of the century, but its wines are among the most expensive in the whole of Germany. There is a strong bias towards red wines, as Spätburgunder occupies 268ha (662 acres) and Portugieser 95ha (234 acres). For white wine production, Riesling and Müller-Thurgau cover only 51 and 42ha (125 and 102 acres) respectively.

The River Ahr runs down from the formerly-volcanic Hohe Eifel Hills (maximum height 762m/ 2,500ft), flowing east to the Rhein. The valley, with its strange rock formations and steep slate-covered vineyards, crowned by beautiful woods, relies heavily for its income on the half a million visitors each year. The biggest wine customers are tourists from the Netherlands and the Ruhr district of Germany, whose undemanding tastes the local winemakers aim to satisfy. The tourists, in holiday mood and in such enticing surroundings, are willing to pay a premium for the chance to buy directly from the wine producer. This market is served firstly by cooperative cellars which handle three-quarters of the region's crop.

The type of rosé wine called *Weissherbst* is a speciality of the Ahr. The natural tendency of all north German wines is to have a good proportion of tartaric acid, so that a successful *Weissherbst* from these parts is a lively, refreshing drink, without any of the unripe flavour that comes from too much malic acid. Tartaric acid, which the Germans know as "wine acid", gives to their northern wines the structure a French red wine finds in tannin.

Mittelrhein

Opposite the confluence of the Ahr with the Rhein is the attractive town of Linz in the north of the 700-ha (1,729-acre) Mittelrhein region. The vineyards, which stretch 110km (68 miles) downstream from near Bingen to a little north of Königswinter, have been steadily disappearing for many years, a trend that is not reflected in Germany's other wine regions. Some have given way to housing projects with the increasing urbanization of Koblenz and other towns. Others have been abandoned through a shortage of labour, or because the low selling price of their wine made its production from steep though romantic hillside sites uneconomic. In spite of the rebuilding of many vineyards, over half of the region's 519ha (1,281 acres) of Riesling are more than 25 years old.

However, despite the viticultural gloom that hangs over the lovely Rhein gorge, which has been so much admired by poets and painters of the past, there are signs of improvement in the winemaking industry. The quality of the region's best wines is becoming recognized in the wider world — albeit in a rather limited way.

Vineyards above Mayschoss in the Ahr Valley.

VILLAGES AND PRODUCERS

The Ahr's — mostly red wine — vineyards mingle with a virtually continuous band of small towns, villages and hamlets as the little river runs down from the Eifel Hills to the Rhein. The Mittelrhein vineyards — mostly white — are scattered over a long stretch of the Rhein gorge.

AHR

The entire Ahr Valley is covered by the *Bereich* Walporzheim-Ahrtal.

Bad Neuenahr-Ahrweiler

Where the E31 north-south motorway crosses high over the Ahr valley, the view downstream to the Rhein includes the well-laid out vineyards of Heppingen, part of the Bad Neuenahr-Ahrweiler district. To the west, the inhabitants of Bad Neuenahr-Ahrweiler have created an urban spread, which continues upstream. In most places vines are grown on slopes beyond the reach of the builder, and a short walk into the vineyards takes you an acceptable distance from the bustle below.

The biggest estate besides Weingut Adeneuer of Ahrweiler is Rheinland-Pfalz's own state cellars, the 20-ha (49-acre) Staatliche Weinbaudomäne, Kloster Marienthal. But it is some of the smaller private estates that make what may be the Ahr red wine of the future. It is fully fermented, dry, red and tannic from a traditional fermentation with the grape skins and stalks, and has no appeal to the tourists. The grapes will probably come from extremely steep, warm vineyards, and the wine relies on a malolactic fermentation to help soften it.

Its vinification could be described as French, and it may well have sugar added to the must — thus, incidentally, preventing it from being a QmP. Indeed, for simplicity's sake such wines are sold as "table wine" (*see* p. 312).

Walporzheim and Marienthal

Walporzheim is known for serious red wines, and particularly for the 15-ha (37-acre) Weingut Brogsitters "Zum Domherrenhof", owners of the former Cologne cathedral vineyards, and Weingut Nelles of Heimersheim.

Dernau and Mayschoss

A leader in the modern style of Ahr wine is Weingut Meyer-Näkel of Dernau, whose reputation for interesting, serious, sometimes *barrique*-aged Spätburgunder could not be higher. The production is mainly red wine but also includes Spätburgunder Blanc de Noirs and *Weissherbst*. The cooperative at Mayschoss-Altenahr, the oldest in Germany, is a major wine producer in this area. Top growers also include Weingut Kreusberg and Weingut Deuzerhof.

MITTELRHEIN

In the north of the Mittelrhein a band of volcanic soil running east from the Eifel Hills crosses the region. Elsewhere there is much slate, and even at Koblenz "am Rhein und Mosel", the Mittelrhein white wines have a more earthy flavour than those of the adjacent Lower Mosel. The large volume of water in the Rhein assists a mild climate with an early spring and a late autumn. Although Riesling can tolerate relatively dry conditions, the shallow depth of soil and the speed with which rain flows off the steep vineyards mean that the moderately heavy rainfall from June to August is welcomed. Frost damage in winter and spring is unusual.

Visitors will find attractive riverside villages, spectacularly-sited vineyards and castles, and plenty of chances to try the wine with simple food at the makers' premises.

Bacharach

The riverside village gives its name to a *Bereich* covering vineyards at the south of the region and on the west bank of the Rhein. The vineyards are densest here, facing the start of the Rheingau on the opposite bank.

Six estate bottlers in the Mittelrhein are members of the prestigious VDP (*see* p315), and all are based in the village of Bacharach. These estates include Weingut Toni Jost and Weingut J Ratzenberger.

The deep valleys formed by four streams that flow into the Rhein here have been the source of some of the best branded German sparkling wine for many years. Here Riesling has provided the firm acidity and steely flavour which the Koblenz Sekt makers, Deinhard in particular, have sought. The VDP members have shown that the qualities that make good Mittelrhein Riesling Sekt are the backbone of their still wines.

Boppard

The Hamm vineyard at Boppard has a reputation for fine Riesling from its steep slopes. The name Perll — two estates with the same name — is worth noting.

Koblenz to Königswinter

North of Koblenz, on the east bank, Leutesdorf and Hammerstein are villages with a good local reputation for their white wines. Picturesque Linz is today known more for its buildings than its vineyards. Königswinter has a few vineyards on the Siebengebirge, or seven hills, including the Drachenfels *Einzellage*.

Mühlental and Lahntal

Many of the side valleys of the Mittelrhein are beautiful, and in the wealth of attractive scenery that the region offers, the less dramatically spectacular areas are ignored by the tourists. One such is the Mühlental, a charming rural valley near the fortress of Ehrenbreitstein at Koblenz. It is a picture-book version of steep German vineyards, planted with a wide range of vine varieties.

In the last century Ehrenbreitstein lent its name to a *mousseux*, or sparkling wine, that was sold overseas. Also at that time, the Lahn, which flows through Bad Ems before joining the Rhein, produced Spätburgunder red wine which was well thought of in the district. Today, only seven growers, who concentrate on white wines, remain to carry on an 800-year-old tradition of viticulture in this once important wine valley. Among them are Weingut Haxel and Weingut Arnsteiner Hof — the latter with a history dating back to 1159.

Other producers

Among the leading producers of the region are Weingut Lanius-Knab of Oberwesel and Weingut Weingart of Spay.

MOSEL-SAAR-RUWER

The Mosel-Saar-Ruwer is one of the most consistently spectacular wine regions of Germany. Its 12,980ha (32,073 acres) of planted vineyards follow closely the three rivers whose names the region bears from the Rhein at Koblenz up to the French frontier. Over a quarter of the vineyards are on vertiginous slopes. Since the 1960s a flat area of similar size has been planted with mainly high-yielding vines, on sites once more properly used for fruit trees or even potatoes.

A century ago a good Mosel from those steep slopes cost more than a *Premier Cru* from the Médoc. Partly due to the flood of cheap wines from the new vineyards, the best Mosels are today underpriced.

The Mosel style

At their best, the Mosel vineyards convert Riesling grapes into sublime, subtle white wine. The factors that affect quality are discussed on p320 but the philosophy of the grower is important too. The tradition of late picking and the cool cellars result in some unfermented sugar remaining in the wine. When natural, this is a delightful counterpart to the wine's natural acidity. It is easily overdone, however, especially in the cheaper wines, whose great sales success has harmed the Mosel's reputation.

The best Mosel Riesling is light and refreshing when young, and capable of ageing into a complex and fascinating bottle. In warm vintages the *Auslesen* and above are true reflections of Riesling's wonderful balance of fruit and acidity. No good Mosel wine should be really sweet, however high the *Prädikat*.

Vines and grape varieties

Until the 17th century Elbling was the main vine of the region, and in the early 19th century still covered 60% of the vineyards. It now grows principally in the Upper Mosel, and here and there downstream in the Lower Mosel. Today over half the region is planted in Riesling, and in the best sites, which are essential for this vine, no other is normally grown.

Müller-Thurgau occupies nearly a quarter of the region; Kerner, which can yield around 20% more grape juice than Riesling, covers around 7.5%. Optima, a crossing of European vines that produces musts of high sugar weight but little real quality, was planted by some growers in the 1970s to assist lighter wines, or even itself, to climb into the *Auslese* quality level by the back door.

Now the mood of the times is to return to the quality of wine upon which the reputation of the region was built — and that means Riesling. While Müller-Thurgau has been widely planted in second-class sites and can produce an acceptable wine of Mosel style, the best estates were never seduced by the specious commercial appeal of the more recent new crossings, whose wines were without regional character.

Vines for red wine, mainly Spätburgunder, have recently returned to the region in a small way, in line with the trend in other regions.

The price of the picturesque

The extraordinary steepness of some of the Mosel vineyards has an economic price, and can prompt extraordinary remedies. The saviour of the steep vineyards of Winningen, for instance, has been a system of monorails that carry workers and materials up through the vines to the top of the terracing. Even so, these beautiful vineyards, which everybody likes to look at but in which few wish to work, are immensely expensive to maintain. At the 7ha (17 acres) estate of Richard Richter in the Lower Mosel, 9,000 vines (38% Riesling) are grown to the hectare and each vine requires 30 minutes' work, including the harvest, each year. The reward for this dedication is a yield of one bottle of wine per vine. The costs in the new, flat, vineyards are of course far lower — but the wine is not the same.

The Mosel districts

The map opposite shows the division into *Bereiche* or wine districts. Each has its own character and style of wine. The Lower Mosel, or Bereich Zell, has for long been treated by writers as a poor relative of the Middle Mosel. It does, however, have a high percentage of well-placed vineyards capable of producing good wines. The wines may not reach the heights of the best of the Middle Mosel, but the average standard is high.

The Middle Mosel takes its official *Bereich* name from Bernkastel, which with its twin town Kues across the bridge forms the metropolis of the area. The river twists and turns through enormous bends, providing steep slopes perfectly inclined to the sun — and some not so perfect. Some 25 other villages, some with names that have been famous for centuries — Piesport, Wehlen, Graach — line the river up- and downstream. Here are found the great estates. They make wines up to and including fabulous *Trockenbeerenauslesen*, and in great vintages Middle Mosel wines from the top sites can last in bottle for decades.

The Middle Mosel ends a few kilometres downstream from the city of Trier, and the Upper Mosel starts on the far side of the city. The vineyards of the Saar and Ruwer tributaries are of higher quality than those on this upper part of the main river, producing stylishly delicate wines in favourable vintages. □

MOSEL WINE DISTRICTS

The Mosel is divided into four districts: Lower, Middle and Upper Mosel, and Saar-Ruwer. They correspond to the official German wine *Bereiche* of Zell, Bernkastel, Obermosel and Moseltor, and Saar-Ruwer. The Lower Mosel runs from the junction of the Mosel and Rhein at Koblenz up to and including the village of Zell. The Middle Mosel runs from there to close to Trier, and the Upper Mosel on to the French border. The Saar and Ruwer rivers join the Mosel on either side of Trier.

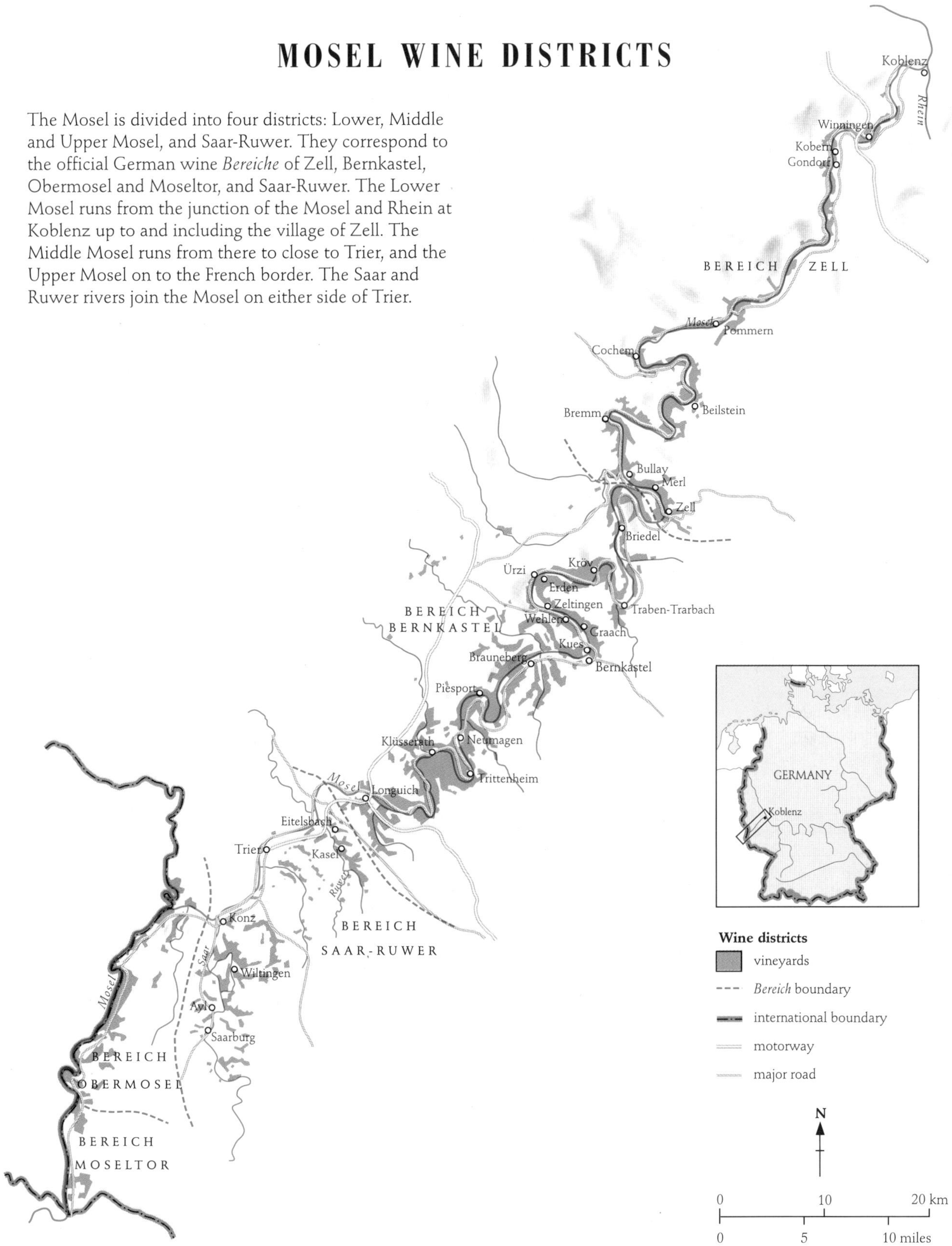

Wine districts

- vineyards
- --- *Bereich* boundary
- international boundary
- motorway
- major road

N

| 0 | 10 | 20 km |
| 0 | 5 | 10 miles |

QUALITY FACTORS

The relatively cool climate of the Mosel-Saar-Ruwer region influences the other factors that decide wine quality — site, vine variety and vintage. To these should be added yield, which to a large extent is determined by the grower.

THE MIDDLE MOSEL: ALTITUDE AND SLOPE

- ☐ best-quality vineyard
- ☐ other vineyards
- ☐ land too high and cold
- ☐ village

—— contour, interval 100 metres

Variety
The classic Mosel vine is the Riesling, which occupies more than half the vineyard. It has the potential to produce the best wine, but it demands the warmest sites because it needs a long ripening period. On the other hand, it can withstand very cold weather.

Site and micro-climate
Riesling grapes will ripen only in sites with a favourable exposure and gradient, resulting in adequate direct sunlight and warmth from April to October; a minimum amount of cold wind and sufficient moisture; reasonably low height above sea level; and a wide horizon. The Mosel lies at a latitude of 50°N — the same as Dieppe, Cornwall and Newfoundland. Sun angles are thus low, even in summer. A steep vineyard, if facing south, will have better exposure to the sun than a gently sloping or flat one. Its position on the slope should not be too high, for the higher up the slope, the lower the temperature. Nor too low, for then spring frost may be a problem.

Here, where every degree of warmth and every hour of sunshine are vital to the growth of the vine, slate — which is also common in the Middle Mosel — is considered to be the best soil, since it stores up and reflects back the sun's heat.

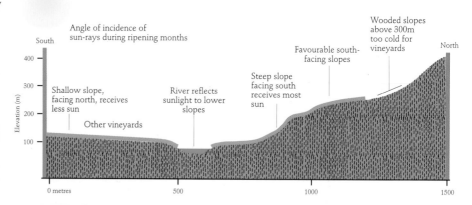

Vintage
Each Mosel vintage presents a special set of challenges. Spring frost or summer rain may cause damage. But it is the amount of sun from August to October that

The steep Sonnenuhr (meaning "sundial") vineyard at Wehlen.

determines the character of the vintage. A cool year will not ripen grapes sufficiently to make more than QbA wines; an average summer will produce QmP wines; while a warm September and October may bring *Auslesen*.

It is in these rare vintages — perhaps one in a decade — that Mosel Riesling shows its truly classic and unique quality.

Yield
German vineyards often give large yields, thanks to technical advances in viticulture — the average for the country in 1982 reached an astonishing 173hl/ha. But progress has its price. Wine from high-yielding vines has less acidity, less concentration, and expresses less vineyard character. This is particularly true of Riesling, which can fall to merely ordinary levels of flavour if over-cropped. The law sets no limits on yield, but some Mosel estates are reducing their yields through pruning and thinning.

New laws, now under discussion, may result in the limiting of the yield per hectare. At present the yield is up to the producer — and the weather.

VILLAGES AND PRODUCERS

The Mosel's best wine villages are concentrated in the Lower Mosel and Middle Mosel: see the map on p319. The region's wine styles are described below, from the north-east, up the river to the south-west.

LOWER MOSEL

The entire Lower Mosel is in the Bereich Zell, divided into six *Grosslagen*. The Mosel Valley, winding and steep, is most attractive here and many wine tourists flock to the riverside villages. The Bereich Zell has good conditions for producing ripe, attractive wines: slate soil and steep slopes. A high proportion of Riesling is grown.

Mosel from this lower end of the river tastes not unlike a Mittelrhein wine. It is well-structured and a little earthy, but usually lacks the finesse and delicacy of the best of the Bereich Bernkastel. The structure of the Bereich Zell wines allows them to be successful as dry (*trocken*) wines, yet these wines are not totally without sweetness; German wine law allows a small amount of residual sugar even in wines classed as "dry".

Winningen and Kobern-Gondorf

Winningen is one of the largest wine villages on the Mosel, and the most important in this part of the river. It shares the top-quality terraced vineyard Winninger Uhlen with its neighbour, Kobern.

In recent years private estates such as Richard Richter, von Schleinitz, von Heddesdorff and Heymann-Löwenstein have become known for their characterful, strongly-flavoured Riesling wines. Heymann-Löwenstein, a particularly free spirit among wine producers, concentrates on high quality and rightly expensive QbA.

Among Germany's most quality-conscious wine-producers' associations is the Deutsches Eck, based at Kobern-Gondorf. All its wines are Rieslings from steep sites, with a maximum yield of 80hl/ha and higher must weights. The president, Franz Dötsch, wants the yield further reduced: he aims for a yield of 50hl/ha or less.

Cochem and Pommern

Cochem is a small town, catering for tourists with its castle and riverside promenade. It is the centre of the *Grosslage* Rosenhang. Weingut Reinhold Fuchs of Pommern, over 90% of whose wines are dry, bottles wines that are almost without any residual sugar.

Zell

The up-river end of the *Bereich* is centred on the town of Zell, with the villages of Merl, Bremm and Bullay also worth noting. The only *Grosslage* in the *Bereich* whose wine is well known outside Germany is the Zeller Schwarze Katz, once 10ha (24 acres) in size but now increased to 410ha (1,012 acres). The *Grosslage* name is widely seen, but not on the better wines. Albert Kallfelz of Merl, a hill away from the district's boundary, emphasizes its own name on its Riesling wines, rather than that of vineyards of varying repute.

MIDDLE MOSEL

The Middle Mosel continues the scenery set by the lower part of the river, but in a slightly less dramatic form. Good vineyards are still very steep but the slopes are cut by large side valleys. The river meanders in great sweeps past a string of well-known wine villages. The nine *Grosslage* names are rarely used for estate wines, the exception being Badstube at Bernkastel, a small vineyard adjoining the famous Doctor. Most great estates have land holdings in several villages. *Einzellage* names are emphasized here in a way not found in less exalted districts. The wine lover learns to look for combinations of great estate names and those of the most noted individual vineyards.

Although wines with a higher alcohol content are now more in vogue in the Pfalz and Baden, the charm of wine from the Middle Mosel remains its finely tuned bouquet and flavour, not a soporific punch. *Filigran* ("complex") is the word the Moselaner likes to use to describe the delicate structure of his Riesling wines.

Briedel to Kröv

The vineyards of Bereich Bernkastel begin at the village of Briedel, and follow several great bends in the Mosel past Traben-Trarbach and Kröv to Erden. None of the estates here has established a great reputation: the wine is fruity, fresh and good without reaching the heights.

Erden to Graach

The important Middle Mosel vineyards begin where the great river bends at Ürzig. The village of Erden faces its vineyards, which lie across the river on the north bank, beautifully open to the sun. The noted vineyards here are Prälat and Treppchen. Ürzig's Würz-garten ("spice garden") is known for the spicy notes in its wine. Good growers here include the Bischöfliche Weingüter, Weingut Dr Loosen, Weingut Mönchhof-Robert Eymael, Weingut Dr Pauly-Bergweiler, Weingut Willi Schaefer, Weingut Erden of Wehlen and Weingut Markus Molitor of Bernkastel-Wehlen.

As the river swings round, it creates a line of superb southwest-facing vineyard sites at Zeltingen, Wehlen and Graach. The top vineyards are Wehlener Sonnenuhr, Graacher Domprobst and Graacher Himmelreich. Growers' names to note include J A Prüm, S A Prüm and Max-Ferdinand Richter.

Bernkastel

The "capital" of the Mosel, the old town of Bernkastel, faces its modern twin, Kues, across one of the rare bridges over the river. Kues is the home of several large wine companies and

THE GROSSER RING

The 27 members of the Grosser Ring, the local section of the VDP, are drawn mainly from estates in the Saar-Ruwer and from the stretch of the Mosel between Erden and Trittenheim. The Ring has held auctions each autumn since it was established in 1908. They are a major regional event and the prices reached are sometimes very high; nevertheless they do not impact upon the market in the manner of those of the Hospices de Beaune in Burgundy (*see* p201). The members of the Grosser Ring, who have holdings in virtually all the best sites, are a source of many of the region's most impressive Riesling wines. Their promotional activities attract a wider interest in all good Mosel-Saar-Ruwer wine.

the Moselland co-op (*see* box). Bernkastel's glory is the incredibly steep Doctor vineyard, which looms above the rooftops. Bernkasteler Doctor is the finest of Mosels in good years: an intense, long-lived, sweet wine comparable in stature (and price: a 1921 *Trockenbeerenauslese* was sold for 3,500 euros) with Ch d'Yquem. The 3.2ha (7.9 acres) Doctor *Einzellage* is owned by the estates Wegeler-Deinhard, Dr Thanisch, Lauerburg and Reichsgraf von Kesselstatt.

Other vineyards capable of producing top-quality wine here are the Graben and Alte Badstube am Doktorberg. The *Grosslage* Kurfürstlay covers a wide area from Bernkastel upstream; it is not used for the best wines.

Bernkastel to Piesport

The river swings on past several average villages and a few top ones: Brauneberg with its Juffer vineyard, Kesten with the Paulinshofberg, Wintrich and Piesport. This village has given its name, and lost much of its reputation, to Piesporter Michelsberg, a *Grosslage* taking in much flat, north-facing land. Piesport itself has top-class vineyards, particularly the large Goldtröpfchen. Top growers here include the great Trier estates: the Bischöfliche Weingüter (a charity); von Kesselstatt; the Vereinigte Hospitien (another charity), as well as the estates Bernkastel, Reinhold Haart of Piesport, Fritz Haag of Brauneberg and Schloss Lieser of Lieser.

Neumagen to Longuich

The upper reaches of the Middle Mosel take in villages such as Neumagen (best vineyard: Rosengärtchen), Trittenheim

FRIEDRICH-WILHELM-GYMNASIUM

This estate, an important owner of vineyards with cellars in Trier, harvests grapes from 21 sites spread throughout Zeltingen, Graach, Bernkastel, Dhron, Neumagen, Trittenheim, Klüsserath and Mehring, and Falkenstein, Oberemmel, Ockfen and Wiltingen on the Saar. The wines are vinified individually, and stored in 400 oak casks. They are further separated according to their official potential quality category, and possibly the amount of sweetness with which they are to be sold, and the vine variety — although 90% is Riesling. The result of this fragmentation is a list of 107 different wines of various vintages and two *Sekte* based on 36ha (88 acres) of planted vineyard. Unquestionably, this is a splendid estate, which has acquired land over many years and has a big following.

(the Apotheke) and Klüsserath (Bruderschaft). An estate name to look for here is Friedrich-Wilhelm-Gymnasium, another charity (*see* profile).

SAAR-RUWER

The run of vineyards is broken by the city of Trier, and two of the Mosel's tributary streams, the Ruwer and the Saar, provide the best vineyards of the upstream part of the region. About half the Mosel-Saar-Ruwer members of the VDP have holdings in the Bereich Saar-Ruwer, the district name for both valleys. Here Riesling covers 70% of the vineyards, with the best sites, as always, being on steep terrain. The district is known outside Germany only for its fine wine. On the home market, cheaper Saar QbA wine is sold under the *Grosslage* name Wiltinger Scharzberg, but much of the cheapest wine with a high level of acidity finds its way to the makers of *Sekt*, Germany's sparkling wine.

The Ruwer

The tiny sub-district of the Ruwer is known for delicate but long-lived Rieslings from two great estates, Karthäuserhof and von Schubert (*see* profile, opposite). The Ruwer makes very little wine, but in good years it can be among Germany's best.

The Saar

The upstream Saar vineyards beyond Saarburg start as they mean to go on, producing firm, steely characterful Riesling wines.

As on the Mosel, the Saar vineyards contain a lot of slate but mainly of a different sort, being softer, more decomposed, and with something of the heavy texture of demerara sugar. In any tasting Saar wines quickly identify themselves through their particularly intense slaty bouquet which Riesling conveys so well.

Estates in the Saar include the great Trier charities (*see* Bernkastel), Schloss Saarstein, Bert Simon, Egon Müller-Scharzhof (the most expensive), Reverchon, von Hövel, Le Gallais of Wiltingen, Forstmeister of Geltz and Weingut Zillingen of Saarburg.

THE UPPER MOSEL

Compared to the Saar-Ruwer vineyards, those of the main stream here are less important. "Gateway to the Obermosel" is how the local guidebooks

THE MOSELLAND

The grapes from 21% of the region's vineyards are processed by Moselland eG, the central regional cooperative at Bernkastel. Of the annual production of three million cases, about a third is sold to large merchants' cellars in bulk. 38% is exported, mainly to the UK, where the cooperative believes there is a good future for its mostly medium-sweet white wine. It believes that the period of great expansion is over and that it must now concentrate on improving the quality of its wines. This thinking has resulted in a range of superior "premium" wines for the supermarkets and cash-and-carry stores of Germany, as well as separate "lines" for the better-quality retail wine merchants. Moselland is also taking part in the modern success of bottle-fermented Riesling Sekt.

Snow-covered vineyards loom above Zeltingen in the Middle Mosel.

describe Wasserliesch, but the notion that the gently rural Bereich Obermosel should have anything so pompous as a gateway, even figuratively speaking, seems out of character. In the rolling, riverside country upstream from Trier, the wine from the 1,100ha (2,718 acres) of planted vineyard cannot be compared with the best from the districts of Bernkastel or the nearby Saar-Ruwer. QmP is a rarity, although a small amount is produced by estate bottlers, even up to the *Trockenbeeren-auslese* level. Most of the grape harvest is handled by the Moselland central cooperative cellars at Bernkastel (*see* box, p322), and the circumstances of the growers are very modest when compared to those of the vineyard owners of Luxembourg, directly across the Mosel.

The slate of the Middle Mosel is replaced in the Upper Mosel by younger soils and *Muschelkalk*, or shell-lime. The deep soil is rich in humus.

Whereas the steep slopes downstream from Trier could never be sown with cereal crops, agriculture has been a rival of vinegrowing in the Upper Mosel for centuries. Today, Weisser Elbling, a long-established vine of unknown origin, covers 87% of the 1,165-ha (2,880-acre) vineyard. Its large yield, which in 1989 reached 221 hl/ha, is often blended with soft wine from Silvaner. From a smaller crop a pleasant, refreshing, *spritzig* (very slightly sparkling) wine is produced by some growers.

Across the Mosel from Remich, the impressively situated Schloss Thorn estate offers a rosé wine from Roter Elbling. Unusually for this part of the river, the estate also lists Riesling wines and a rosé from the Schwarzriesling (Pinot Meunier). Ruländer, Müller-Thurgau, Weissburgunder and Auxerrois — a member of the Pinot family of grapes — are also grown in small amounts in some parts of the Bereich Obermosel. □

VON SCHUBERT

Driving up the Ruwer through Eitelsbach one soon sees a large sweep of hill on the right that runs into a side valley. Here, von Schubert's solely owned Maximin Grünhaus vineyard is divided into three sites which are harvested, vinified and bottled separately. Indeed there is often more than one wine sold under the same name, the difference being marked only by the AP number on the label or by a reference number in the price list. The three sites, Abtsberg, Herrenberg and Bruderberg, consistently produce well-differentiated wines that justify their continued use as selling names. The estate is 98% Riesling, and the majority of the wine is *trocken* or dry. The wines are distinguished and long-lived, and justify their reputation and their high prices.

WINE REGIONS OF THE RHEIN

This map displays the central Rhein vineyard regions —
Rheingau, Rheinhessen, Pfalz, Nahe and Hessische
Bergstrasse — which form the heart of the German
winelands. It reveals the proximity of, say, the Nahe and
Rheinhessen to the Rheingau, and shows how several of
western Germany's biggest cities are close to wine
country.

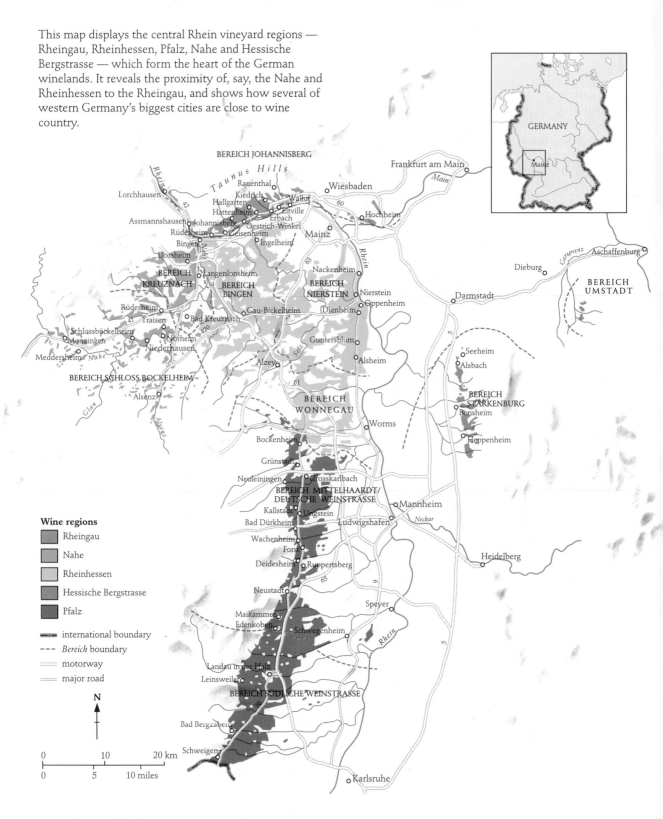

Wine regions

- Rheingau
- Nahe
- Rheinhessen
- Hessische Bergstrasse
- Pfalz

— international boundary
--- *Bereich* boundary
— motorway
— major road

RHEINGAU

In the Rheingau, Germany's most prestigious wine region, life for the estate bottler is a little easier than elsewhere. The Rheingau's reputation commands higher prices, widely thought to be worth paying, for the region makes many of Germany's best white wines. The Riesling grape is superbly suited to these vineyards. Indeed this is the home of the Riesling: the first reference to it dates from 1435. The Rheingau wines are elegant when young, and can age to superbly balanced complexity.

Until the 1980s, the reputation of the region's wines rested almost exclusively on large estates, owned mainly by the aristocracy — Schloss Johannisberg, Schloss Groenesteyn — or the Federal State of Hessen. Since then the bourgeoisie of smaller producers has started to bottle wines of a quality that is admired in Germany by consumers and critics alike. Many grape growers went out of business during the 1980s, but often their vineyards were bought by more determined, younger, and probably better-trained neighbours. Since 1979–1980 the area under vine has risen by some 6% to 3,119ha (7,707 acres), while the number of vineyard owners has dropped by nearly a quarter, from 1,940 to 1,469. Only 304 Rheingau producers own 3ha (7 acres) or more of vineyard, so for the great majority, as throughout the EC, vinegrowing is a part-time activity.

Most of the Rheingau vineyards lie on the lower slopes of the wooded Taunus Hills. To the east, at Hochheim, 356ha (878 acres), completely separated from the main body of the region by the suburbs of Wiesbaden, form a *Grosslage*, parallel to the River Main, known as Hochheimer Daubhaus. To the west, the steep vineyards of Assmannshausen and Lorchhausen have much in common with the Mittelrhein.

A tradition of Riesling

Many of today's large Rheingau estates have been substantial and organized wine producers for hundreds of years. Their vintage records show that over the centuries the grape harvest was frequently small, if not an almost complete failure. In a world where chemicals (with the exception of sulphur dioxide) were rarely used to protect the vine, a balance of nature existed, which some Rheingau producers are now trying to re-create in a more coherent way — as far as air pollution will permit.

St Hildegard's Abbey stands at the top of the wide slope of vines at Rüdesheim.

But the small size of past vintages was also related to the quality of the vines. In the case of Riesling, which now covers 82% of the Rheingau vineyard, clonal selection has resulted in each vine now producing a more regular crop. The average yield in the Rheingau in the 1950s was 51.8hl/ha. In the next decade it climbed to 71.1hl/ha, and in the 1970s and 1980s averaged a little over 81hl/ha.

The mood of the present time would suggest that with more severe pruning and the removal of excessive bunches of grapes during the summer, average yields in the 1990s should drop. The smallest harvests since 1950 have usually been among the worst in quality, while the largest in the 1950s, the 1959 vintage, produced the heaviest must weights since World War II.

About 60% of Rheingau wine is classified as QbA and 10% is converted into *Sekt* (*see* p348) — an industry with which the region has long-established associations. Riesling QbA expresses the regional style well and in the Rheingau it is hoped that its selling price will cover the producer's costs. Profit comes to a traditional Riesling estate through QmP wines, *Spätlese* in particular.

In the Rheingau, when the yield is not excessive, Riesling conveys the flavour from the vineyard well. This helps to justify the use of the *Einzellage* name. In the drier wines, the vineyard flavour will be even more pronounced. Good Rheingau Riesling wine is aristocratic, and often understated in youth. It matures slowly and shares with fine red bordeaux a certain austerity which is never found in wines from warmer climates. Rheingau Riesling, at its best, is one of the world's great wines.

Understanding Rheingau wine names

As in other regions, the perceived importance of the individual vineyard name on the bottle has declined a little in the Rheingau in recent

The Von Simmern estate at Eltville.

years; the coinage has been debased through the overuse on the cheaper wines of *Grosslage* names. Increasingly, Rheingau estates have been promoting their own names. Some

WINE AND FOOD — AND CHARTA

Nearly 50 Rheingau winemakers, including a cooperative cellar, are members of the Charta association, which was founded in 1984.
Its Riesling wines are examined by an official tasting panel, before and after bottling, and are produced to precise minimum standards of must weight and acidity; they cannot be sold until 18 months after their vintage.
To most people they taste dry, although technically and legally they are medium-dry. They are best described as balanced, being neither tart nor noticeably sweetish. Charta wines are sold in a German "flute" bottle, embossed with a double Roman arch and the words "Rheingau Riesling".

This new generation of Charta wine is designed for the German restaurant table and wine merchants. The *mariage des vins et des mets* is a constant topic among many Rheingau winemakers, and has influenced their style of wine since the 1990s.

have developed expensive brand wines, such as Wegeler-Deinhard's estate-bottled Geheimrat "J". In spite of this, and the modest success of the excellent Charta concept (*see* box below), most fine wines still rely partly on their vineyard name on the label to help them find a customer.

The Rheingau's system of wine names is confusing and certainly not "user-friendly". For example, Johannisberger Erntebringer is a *Grosslage* of 320ha (790 acres). Johannisberg is also the name of a village with nine *Einzellagen* or individual vineyards (for example Johannisberger Hölle), while the *Bereich* or district of Johannisberg covers the whole region of the Rheingau.

If matters seem at this point to be somewhat out of control, the Rheingau's most imposing estate, Schloss Johannisberg, manages to rise majestically above it all.

Through the old laws of inheritance, the ownership of vineyards became increasingly fragmented, so in a Rheingau single site there may be as many owners as there are in a Burgundy vineyard. This process has now been stopped and in some places holdings have been swopped or re-allocated. Often this has been achieved in connection with *Flurbereinigung*, an official programme to reconstruct and modernize the vineyards. As half the costs on an estate are wages, it is important to cut travelling by workers from one small parcel of land to another.

Rheingau pageantry

As might be expected of Germany's most profitable wine region, the Rheingau promotes itself through individual and corporate effort in a way of which some other regions can only dream. The thinking behind some of the initiatives is borrowed from France: *die Glorreiche Rheingau Tage*, an annual celebration held at the ancient monastery of Kloster Eberbach in November, owes more than its name to *les Trois Glorieuses de Bourgogne* at the Clos de Vougeot. □

QUALITY FACTORS

The main Rheingau wine region consists of a gentle slope running from north to south. To the north the region is bounded by forest; to the south by the Rhein. This southerly exposure of the slope is an important factor in the quality of the wines produced in the Rheingau vineyards. Late picking of particularly ripe grapes is possible in these favoured sites, and sweet late-harvest wines are a Rheingau speciality.

Riesling is extremely well suited to the variety of *terroirs* and micro-climates in this region, where it is overwhelmingly the dominant variety. Years of clonal selection have produced high-yielding Riesling clones.

Site and soil
None of the Rheingau vineyards is more than 4–5km (2–3 miles) away from the Rhein or Main. Those nearest the woods are cooler because of their distance from the Rhein and their height above sea level. Usually this is a disadvantage, but in years when the grapes ripen before the date at which picking may legally begin, the quality of the fruit in the higher and more slowly ripening vineyards at Rauenthal, Kiedrich or Schloss Vollrads is likely to be better.

At present the start of the harvest is fixed on a regional basis, which ignores the effect of the micro-climate. The argument that some growers are in a better position than others to decide when to gather the grapes in their

Climate
The Rheingau has a sheltered location, shielded from cold north winds by the Taunus hills, and gaining warmth from the moderating effect of the wide waters of the Rhine. These factors moderate the otherwise cool climate, for the region is well to the north of Europe's wine belt — more so than any French region. The rainfall here is fairly low, and the sunshine levels high. However, the northern location means that site and exposure matter considerably: sheltered spots warm up and stay warm, promoting the ripening of the grapes.

 Vineyards

THE RHEINGAU: ALTITUDE AND EXPOSURE

North Taunus Hills — Wood-covered uplands creates sheltered microclimate. Higher vineyards produce slower-ripening grapes. Steep, south-facing slopes receive most sun. Vineyards cover lower slopes. Eltville. South. Rhine.

Vineyards slope up to the woods above Eltville.

different holdings seems worth examining.

At Hochheim in the low-lying east the soil contains clay, sand and gravel; while at Lorch in the steeply sloping west sandstone and slate predominate. Soil is less important than micro-climate in the quality equation.

Selection and sweetness
In the early days of fine winemaking in the Rheingau, it was the Church that provided the discipline and applied intelligence needed to set the date of the harvest and select the grapes. This tradition managed to survive the demise of the monasteries in Napoleonic times.

Grapes attacked by *botrytis cinerea* (noble rot) have been harvested and used for the production of sweet wine since about 1820. Today the trend is to aim for clear and clean-tasting Riesling *Spätlesen* from healthy, *botrytis*-free grapes.

Spätlesen may be gathered seven days after the officially-fixed start of the harvest. An *Auslese* may be gathered at any time, even late into the season.

VILLAGES AND PRODUCERS

The Rheingau is described here from west to east. Most of the wine is white, with red wines coming from Assmannshausen. Large estates are a feature here, and are mentioned according to their headquarters, though most have land in several villages.

Lorchhausen to Assmannshausen

The Rheingau vineyards extend around the corner into the Rhein gorge, down the right bank to Lorch and Lorchhausen, almost opposite Bacharach. At this downstream end of the Rheingau, *Kabinett* wines seem to be a commercially sensible compromise between quantity and quality. Riesling covers over 70% of the vineyards, with some Spätburgunder for red wine. The top Lorch estate is Weingut Graf von Kanitz.

Assmannshausen is known for its red wines from the Spätburgunder. This grape did not arrive in Assmannshausen until 1740 but within 20 years had established its reputation, according to contemporary authors. They noted that two of its advantages were that Spätburgunder was ready for picking 14 days before Riesling, and that even in bad

years it would produce a usable crop. At that time, a late vintage was automatically a bad vintage in which the producer waited desperately for his grapes to ripen. Understanding how to manage a *Spätlese* harvest was to come later. For producers *see* box, below.

The best of the Assmannshausen vineyards lie in parts of the variable 55-ha (135-acre) Höllenberg site. The Assmannshäuser Frankenthal, planted almost equally in Riesling and Spätburgunder, adjoins one of the top vineyards of the Rheingau, the Rüdesheimer Berg.

Top producers include the Assmannshausen estate owned by the state of Hessen, Weingut Robert König, Weingut Krone and Weingut Lorch.

Rüdesheim

Much-visited Rüdesheim has an attractive position below

its famous, steadily rising, vine-covered hill, the Rüdesheimer Berg. Parts, such as the Berg Schlossberg *Einzellage*, are quite steep, and their wines have a flavour from the slaty soil that stands out in a tasting of Rheingau Rieslings.

Among the best-known locally-based estate owners are the State of Hessen (Staatsweingut Rüdesheim), Dr Heinrich Nägler, and Bernard Breuer, a founding member of Charta (*see* p326). Bernard Breuer and Georg Breuer of Rüdesheim are spokesmen of Erstes Gewächs, a more recent association which is now more important than Charta. Other Rheingau estates with land here include August Eser and Wegeler-Deinhard of Oestrich, Balthasar Ress and Schloss Schönborn of Hattenheim, Schloss Groenesteyn of Kiedrich, and the Prinz von Hessen estate of Geisenheim.

Johannisberg and Geisenheim

The village of Johannisberg has nine individual vineyards, and its name has been chosen to label wine from the entire region, but it is best known for the Rheingau's most imposing estate, Schloss Johannisberg (*see* profile, opposite).

Nearer to the Rhein than Johannisberg, Geisenheim is known throughout the wine world for the Hessische

Forschungsanstalt für Wein-, Obst- und Gartenbau — the Hessen Research Institute for Wine, Fruit Growing and Horticulture. It is a training as well as a research institute. Perhaps the most obvious result of its viticultural research is the clonal selection of old-established vines. The institute has its own 20-ha (49-acre) estate with vines in the well-known Geisenheimer Rothenberg and Kläuserweg *Einzellagen*. Geisenheim wines sometimes have an attractive *goût de terroir*. Weingut Freiherr von Zwierlein is one of the top producers here.

Winkel and Oestrich

In contrast to Geisenheim, Winkel produces distinguished Riesling wines without additional flavours. The most famous, characterized by their pronounced fruity-acid style, come from the high-lying vineyards of Schloss Vollrads (now owned by a bank), a leading member of Charta, which has been growing vines for 800 years.

Although neighbouring Oestrich produces very good Riesling wine, it lacks the refinement of the best from the Winkeler Hasensprung vineyard. The best producers of Oestrich are Weingut Peter Jakob Kühn and Weingut Querbach.

Hattenheim

In Kloster Eberbach, tucked into the woods above Hattenheim, the region has an atmospheric centre for its many promotional activities, including wine auctions, tastings, concerts, courses and seminars. Since the 18th century its most famous vineyard, the 31-ha (76-acre) Steinberg, has been walled like its counterpart in Burgundy (also of Cistercian origin), the Clos de Vougeot. Unlike the Clos de Vougeot, however, the Steinberg has one owner, the State

MAKING RHEINGAU RED WINE

Spätburgunder (Pinot Noir) grapes are grown at Assmannshausen to produce a red wine which is very popular in Germany.

Domäne Assmannshausen, owned by the State of Hessen, produces a light-tasting Spätburgunder, often with a little residual sugar, which outsiders find difficult to appreciate. The top wines achieve high prices at German

auctions, and the Domäne is known for its Spätburgunder *Eiswein*.

Some estates have developed a more modern and international style of wine, based on a longer fermentation on the skins. Malolactic fermentation is usual in most Rheingau red wine cellars, but there are different opinions as to how a red wine should be aged.

The enthusiasm of the 1980s for ageing in new *barriques* has declined a little, but has surfaced again recently. Weingut Robert Weiler owns some 100 *barriques*.

The debate continues, with German Hunsrück and Spessart oak being compared with French oak from the Alliers, Nevers and Limousin forests.

of Hessen (Staatsweingut). Its wine has an individual, deep flavour, and firm structure. The 1959 Steinberger Riesling Edelbeerenauslese, tasted 30 years after the vintage, was full of life and style and showed none of the alcoholic heaviness that was characteristic of many wines in that hot and unique vintage. Other producers with land at Hattenheim include Schloss Schönborn, Schloss Reinhartshausen Langworth von Simmern and Weingut Hans Lang.

Erbach

Few would dispute that Erbacher Marcobrunn is one of the finest of the region's many good vineyards. Its 5ha (12 acres) or so, which are divided horizontally and surprisingly by a railway that would hardly be allowed such freedom nowadays, have an underground source of water that serves them well. In average quality, or very dry, vintages, Erbacher Marcobrunn shows its advantages. In great years the competition from all over the region becomes stronger. As commentators search the herb, fruit and vegetable gardens for similes to convey the complexity of Erbacher Marcobrunn, the term "bouquet garni" takes on a new meaning. Whatever the smell and the flavour, the wine is robust in style and needs longer than most to mature in bottle.

The largest owners of Erbacher Marcobrunn include Schloss Schönborn, von Simmern, the State of Hessen (Staatsweingut), Schloss Reinhartshausen, Weingut Jakob Jung and Weingut Freiherr zu Knyphausen — leading winemakers, every one.

On a frost-free island, occupied at various times throughout the year by cormorants, herons, kingfishers, wild duck, natatorial wild boar and manual workers, Schloss

Reinhartshausen has planted an environmentally friendly vineyard. Being concerned with the balance of nature, ecological viticulture takes time to establish itself.

The rot produced by the dampness from the Rhein has so far defeated efforts to grow Spätburgunder in the 16-ha (40-acre) Erbacher Rheinhell vineyard successfully. If the vine is to be retained it must prove its adaptability by 1994. Its relatives, Weissburgunder and Chardonnay, perform satisfactorily here.

Rauenthal and Kiedrich

Near the hills above the Rheingau, the two villages of Rauenthal and Kiedrich produce great wines in good years. Rauenthal's Baiken vineyard is noted for fine wine in warm vintages. Kiedrich is known locally for its church and its choir. Among its estates is that of Robert Weil, now owned 90% by Suntory Ltd of Osaka, Japan, since Weil has bought back 10%.

Eltville and Walluf

Eltville is the headquarters of the wine estates owned by the State of Hessen in the Rheingau and Hessische Bergstrasse. A little further upstream, the J B Becker estate of Walluf produces outstanding, full-bodied red Spätburgunder, as well as concentrated, stylish white Rieslings.

Hochheim

Since the 17th century or even earlier, the name Hochheim has been familiar to Germany's largest export customer, the UK. In the 1680s, according to André Simon, the Countess of Rutland bought "Hockheim" by the *"foudre"* — a cask that varied in size but which could have held the 1,000 litres of the present *Fuder*. The "Old Hock" that was offered in London taverns of the 17th and 18th centuries

probably had little to do with the town of Hochheim. German wine law now defines "Hock" as a table or quality wine (not QmP) from the northern regions of the Rhein.

Hochheim's easterly position, above the Main, rather than the Rhein, has given it a certain independence and, indeed, it has not always been part of the Rheingau. It has a long history of winemaking and claims to have harvested *Spätlesen* at least 160 years before Schloss Johannisberg, and to have grown Riesling as a single variety when elsewhere it was usually intermingled with other vines.

Parts of the best of Hochheim's *Einzellagen* (Domdechaney, Kirchenstück and Hölle) are owned by estates from the central Rheingau, including Schloss Schönborn and Weingut Franz Künstler

(the most famous today). The town also has its own well-known producers in Aschrott (now owned by Künstler), Domdechant Werner, Weingut Königin Victoria Berg, and the State of Hessen (Staatsweingut), and nearly all the 27-ha (66-acre) vineyard holdings of the city of Frankfurt are at Hochheim. Königin Victoria Berg was renamed to mark a visit by Queen Victoria in 1845.

The landscape here is flatter than in the main Rheingau. Most of the sites have sand and gravel in their make-up, and the Hochheimer soil gives its wines an earthy flavour, similar to, but different from, that of Rüdesheim. The structure of the wine here is Rheingau but the taste and bouquet lean in the direction of Franken — with the River Main being the link.

SCHLOSS JOHANNISBERG

On a plateau, surrounded by its 35ha (86 acres) of Riesling vineyards, the Schloss is noticeable from far away. It has an atmospheric cask cellar and a superb wine collection covering all the best vintages since 1842 and some from even earlier. The wines are firm, full-bodied and long-lived, and bear a charming 19th-century-style label. The various categories of QmP are sold with different coloured capsules, continuing a custom that began with wax seals in the middle of the last century. Like many other estates, Schloss Johannisberg has its own *Gutsschänke* or wine bar, a practice that has much increased in the region since the 1970s. The estate puts the stress on dry wines in the modern Rheingau style, but hopes for classic sweet wines when the vintage allows.

NAHE

A thousand years ago the Nahe wine country stretched way beyond the present region, as far north as Simmern in the highlands of the Hunsrück — an area quite unsuited to vines. If wars destroyed vineyards, peace often made sure that only the best sites were re-planted. Most of today's 4,635ha (11,453 acres) under vine lie near the River Nahe itself or its little tributaries, the Guldenbach, the Gräfenbach, the Ellerbach, the Gäulsbach, and the larger Glan and Alsenz Rivers. Water, and the valleys created as it drains from the surrounding hills, explain the siting of the Nahe vineyards.

Soils, wine zones and climate
Upstream, the small town of Idar-Oberstein is known for precious stones, and the soil of the wine region is full of minerals that add flavour to its Rieslings. The soil varies enormously, even within one village, as the growers in Langenlonsheim point out.

The region is divided into two *Bereiche* — Schloss Böckelheim and Kreuznach — (*see* map, p324), but in fact there are three areas with broadly different soils. From the confluence with the Rhein at Bingerbrück to Langenlonsheim, there is quartzite and slate; around Bad Kreuznach there is loess, loam and decomposed red slate; from Bad Kreuznach upstream to Monzingen there is porphyry and coloured sandstone. These three areas equate more or less to the Untere, the Mittlere, and the Obere Nahe (the lower, middle, and upper Nahe), and this is how local people divide their region.

The climate is dry, with 500mm (19 inches) of rain annually. In the few steep vineyards with the necessary equipment, spraying with water is allowed. As in all the northern

Schloss Wallhausen, Bad Kreuznach.

German wine regions the microclimate is more significant than the general overall climate.

Grape varieties and wine styles
The Nahe is essentially a white wine region, but the 10% planted in red vines is increasing; the red-grape crop is used mainly for *Weissherbst*, or rosé. After World War II, the biggest vineyard expansion occurred between 1964 and 1972, the time of the West German "economic miracle". Since then the area has grown by only 4%. Müller-Thurgau and Riesling each cover a quarter of the region, and Silvaner, once an important vine in the Nahe, is starting a slow revival. Estates such as Klören at Laubenheim, which claimed to have planted Bacchus in a moment of mental derangement, now grow the increasingly popular Weissburgunder in heavy soil not suited to Riesling. Weissburgunder is also replacing some of the parcels of Müller-Thurgau on the outstanding Dönnhoff estate at Oberhausen.

The old custom of growing a mixture of vines in one parcel of land is continued, as a curiosity and a link with the past, by a few estates including Crusius of Traisen and Steitz in the Alsenz Valley. Steitz goes a stage further and its "mixed vines" are ungrafted. They are mainly Silvaner and Riesling, but also include Gewürztraminer, Gutedel, Elbling, and the red vines Sankt Laurent and Portugieser. Such a cocktail of vines whose grapes ripen at very different times and yet are gathered in one picking adds interest to the world of Nahe wine.

The Nahe wine style is more forceful than the Mosel's, expressing the drier and warmer climate and varying soils. Local connoisseurs delight in the subtle differences the soils bring to the Nahe wines. Riesling grown here offers delicacy allied with pungent acidity which allows the wine to age well. The Nahe has taken part in the national trend towards dry wine production: some 22% of its quality wine is dry.

Vineyards and estates
There are 1,562 vineyard owners in the Nahe, of which half sell part or all of the crop in bottle. Thirty years ago the names of the best Nahe estates could be mentioned in one breath. They were almost all between Bad Kreuznach and Schlossböckelheim, whereas today good growers are also found around Langenlonsheim, Laubenheim, Dorsheim and up the side valleys of the Nahe. It seems that potentially top vineyard sites are still to be found in this complex and fascinating landscape. On the other hand, the prices for bulk wine are linked to Rheinhessen's — among the lowest in Germany. The cooperative cellars at Bretzenheim near Bad Kreuznach, and Meddersheim in the Obere Nahe, are perhaps the best sources of inexpensive wine. Such wines offer warmth and character. □

VILLAGES AND PRODUCERS

The Nahe region is divided into two *Bereiche*, Schloss Böckelheim and Kreuznach. The villages best known for quality wine are profiled below, with the most frequently seen *Grosslagen* and *Einzellagen* and leading wine estates. Nearly all the wine is white.

SCHLOSS BÖCKELHEIM

This *Bereich* covers the southern half of the Nahe and is named after the chief wine village of the region. As ever, beware confusion between the general and the specific.

Many of the best vineyards of the Nahe lie between Bad Kreuznach and the adjoining villages of Niederhausen and Schlossböckelheim. The *Grosslage* name here is Burgweg.

Schlossböckelheim and Niederhausen

The best vineyards in Schlossböckelheim are Felsenberg and Kupfergrube. The latter is the most famous on the Nahe; owned by the Erich Maurer family since 1998, it is known for concentrated and long-lived Nahe Riesling wine. Estates with land in Schlossböckelheim include Weingut Hans & Peter Crusius and Paul Anheuser.

The smallest *Einzellage* on the Nahe is the 1.1-ha (2-acre) Oberhäuser Brücke near Niederhausen, owned by the Dönnhoff estate of Oberhausen, at present certainly the best Riesling winemaker in Germany. In recent years the site lost the name of Brücke, became part of Hermannsberg, then of Hermannshöhle, after which it was transferred to the *Grosslage* Burgweg, with no single site name. Finally it has become Brücke once more.

Niederhausen is the site of the famous Staatliche Weinbaudomäne or State Wine Cellars, formerly of Prussia (hence the black eagle on the label) now of the State of Rheinland-Pfalz. Training is a function of this model estate, and a number of its previous and present employees run their own wine properties. Nine-tenths of the 40ha (98 acres) of vineyard are on slopes with a gradient of more than 30% and almost all are planted with Riesling. The wines are fresh, fruity and light; those from Niederhausen and Schlossböckelheim can be incredibly elegant while those from the Untere Nahe and Altenbamberg on the Alsenz are earthier and less delicate.

Traisen

At Traisen, the most famous vineyard, planted exclusively in Riesling, is the 2-ha (4-acre) Bastei, directly below the 200m (656ft) Rotenfels rock face. Traiser Bastei wine is full of character and incredibly intense in both flavour and bouquet. The effect of microclimate and soil is obvious. Riesling from the larger Rotenfels is almost as good. Weingut Crusius owns land in both *Einzellagen*; the Staatliche Weinbaudomäne has a holding in Bastei.

KREUZNACH

This *Bereich* takes its name from the spa of Bad Kreuznach. The town is surrounded by vineyards, and the *Grosslage* name is Kronenberg. Some *Einzellagen*, such as Kahlenberg and Steinberg, have high repu-

tations of their own. Among the leading wine estates with headquarters in Bad Kreuznach are August E Anheuser (*see* profile), the Staatsweingut Bad Kreuznach, Weingut Reichsgraf von Plettenberg and Weingut Carl Finkenauer.

North-west of Bad Kreuznach, in the valley of the Gräfenbach, Schloss Wallhausen, Prinz zu Salm-Dalberg'sches Weingut, is a leading estate owned by Prinz zu Salm-Salm. Since 1990 Schloss Wallhausen has used the names of its best vineyard sites only, with the remaining wines being blended to form a *cuvée*. Such rationalization makes the labels of German wines a little more understandable and helps consumer and producer alike.

Rüdesheim

The village of Rüdesheim — not to be confused with the town of the same name in the Rheingau — and the area surrounding it, is the centre of the *Grosslage* Rosengarten. Much pleasant but everyday wine is produced here and labelled "Rüdesheimer Rosengarten".

Bad Kreuznach to Bingen

Further down the valley are the villages of Winzenheim, Bretzenheim and Langenlonsheim, where Riesling's dominance gives way to other varieties. Weingut Erbhof Tesch, based at Langenlonsheim, has a good name for dry wines. Burg Layen, a little way from the river, is the home of Schlossgut Diel, which has its best Riesling vineyards at nearby Dorsheim. The *Grosslage* name Schlosskapelle is often used. Another good producer is Weingut Emrich-Schönleber of Monzingen.

WEINGUT AUGUST E ANHEUSER

Anheuser has long been a well-known name in Bad Kreuznach, where the family has produced Nahe wine since the 17th century. Its Riesling wines are often *spritzig* (with a very slight sparkle) and have the structure to last for many years. As if to emphasize the point, the estate has a rarity list, offering wines in 36 vintages, starting with the 1921 Schlossböckelheimer Kupfergrube Riesling Trockenbeerenauslese. Interesting wines from younger vintages are also available, such as the 1971 Kreuznacher Riesling Auslesen. That such wines can still be offered commercially shows how the region's fine wines are undervalued, and therefore underpriced. The estate is 50ha (124 acres) in size, with vines in some of the best sites in Bad Kreuznach.

RHEINHESSEN

A quarter of Germany's area under vine lies in the region of Rheinhessen. If France still controlled the area of today's Rheinhessen, as it did in the early part of the 19th century, and imposed an *appellation contrôlée*, the small zone of vineyards nearest the Rhein would apply for its own AOC to distinguish itself from the rest of the region, for the Rheinhessen has a reputation as a mass-producer of ordinary wine.

The superior zone, known as the Rheinterrasse ("Rhein terrace") lies in the east of the region (between Mettenheim, north of Worms, via Nierstein to Bodenheim, south of Mainz) and covers about 2,500ha (8,648 acres) — 10% of the Rheinhessen. This is where the famous estates are found. Their wines can be compared in quality to those of the Rheingau, but they are about half the price.

Other areas are now improving too. On the slopes of the hilly countryside that faces across the Rhein to the Rheingau, the two towns of Ingelheim and Bingen prove that top-quality Rheinhessen wine can be made away from the Rheinterrasse. There are some good estate-bottlers in the hinterland of the region, but fewer than in that other one-time desert for fine wine, the southern Pfalz (*see* p335).

The lure of the mass market

The average size of a vineyard holding in the Rheinhessen (3.2ha/8 acres) is a shade less than that in France or Spain, but over twice that in Germany as a whole. With this size of plot, growers had found in the past that it was worth producing a large crop, then making the wine themselves and selling it cheaply in bulk to wine merchants' cellars. Having invested in machinery, they were unwilling to join cooperative cellars which, by their constitution,

Mechanical harvesting in Rothenberg.

can accept grapes only — not must or finished wine.

Judged by volume this business was a great success, but the large quantities of wine could be sold only through chain stores, supermarkets and the export houses selling cheap wine abroad. Having thus become a replaceable commodity, basic Rheinhessen wine could keep its sales only by lowering prices. The results were economically disastrous. The bulk wine producers wrecked the reputation of the region, and so damaged the top estates.

Vines and wine styles

From the 1950s until the early 1980s, it was popularly supposed that increasing sweetness in German wine indicated improving quality. Indeed, this was the basis on which most bottlers in the northern regions worked. *Spätlese* wine was expected to be sweeter than *Kabinett* or QbA, and was much in demand. As traditional vines such as Riesling or Silvaner do not produce *Spätlesen* in the

large amounts the markets needed, "new" vines such as Kerner (*see* p315) and Bacchus were planted. The quality of their over-produced wines may not have been very exciting but their must weights were sufficient to meet the requirements of the German wine law.

The region became known for its cheap, sweet, mostly white wine and the fact that some estates, mainly on the Rheinterrasse, regularly produce wines of stunning quality is still largely overlooked.

Of the 26,372ha (65,164 acres) of planted vineyard, 23% is occupied by Müller-Thurgau, 14% by Silvaner, 8% each by Kerner and Scheurebe, 7% each by Bacchus and Riesling, 6% by Faberrebe (Weissburgunder x Müller-Thurgau), and 5% by Portugieser. Most of the wine is therefore white. Although the area under vine increased by only 8% in the 1980s, Riesling's share rose by 50%. Some say that Riesling has been planted in unsuitable sites; but growing Riesling is usually a sign of seriousness of purpose. The biggest increase, of 78% to 2,173ha (5,369 acres), has been shown by Kerner, which is used in Liebfraumilch (*see* opposite).

It is anticipated that the Rheinhessen vineyard will shrink a little during the 1990s as some grape-growers give up the struggle. The better vineyards will be absorbed by the more profitable estates, the rest will grow other crops.

The virtues of "ordinary" Rheinhessen wine

Although the proportion of drier wine on good estates is much higher, only 13% of Rheinhessen wine as a whole is dry. The customers of many private estates believe that because the cheapest white Rheinhessen wine is sweetish, better-quality wine should be dry. Uninfluenced by other factors, the popular majority taste in the northern half of Germany would probably turn to medium-sweet white wines, and even red wines in the Rheinhessen often contain residual sugar. Producers probe the market with every style of wine of which the Rheinhessen is capable, and the important estates of Anton Balbach, Heyl zu Herrnsheim and others in Nierstein report a swing back to sweeter wines.

About one-third of Rheinhessen wine is exported, principally — though less than before — to the English-speaking and Japanese markets. The quality of its cheap white wine is often derided in a general way by the world's wine writers, but it is usually well received by the same group in blind tastings. It is technically well made, and the large turnover of the stores in which it is sold generally ensures that these wines are drunk at the right moment, when relatively young and fresh.

Nierstein and the Rheinterrasse vineyards seen from the Brudersberg.

The home of Liebfraumilch

In 1992 Germany exported some 28 million cases of wine, of which about 45% was Liebfraumilch (*see* p315). Nearly 60% of this white, medium-sweet, quality wine comes from the Rheinhessen. At least 70% of a Liebfraumilch blend must come from the Riesling, Silvaner, Müller-Thurgau or Kerner grapes. All the grapes must be grown either in the Rheinhessen, Rheinpfalz, Nahe or Rheingau regions.

The wine is hardly sold at all in Germany, and internationally its average shop price is below that of rosé d'Anjou or most red French *vins de pays*. The previous comments about cheap Rheinhessen wine apply equally to Liebfraumilch.

The vineyards around the Liebfrauenkirche (the church of Our Lady) in Worms were once the sole source of Liebfraumilch. Today the merchant house Valckenberg owns 90% of the original Liebfraumilch vineyard, the Wormser Liebfrauen-stift-Kirchenstück. They intend to rebuild its reputation with estate-bottled wines, made mainly from Riesling and Weissburgunder grapes.

The future for Rheinhessen

Gunderloch, the leading Nackenheim estate, likes to think of its best vineyards as "*Grands Crus*" and would dearly love to see a vineyard classification introduced. This is a wish that lies close to the heart of many Rheinterrasse producers. However, having concentrated for over a century and a half on the individuality of German wine based on harvesting dates and methods, vine varieties and a host of vineyard names, the problem of classifying wines by their vineyard of origin in any realistic way is not easy.

The central cooperative cellars are taking part with other producers in a scheme, which started with the 1992 vintage, to sell wines under the heading "Selection Rheinhessen". These are produced from traditional vine varieties, and the grapes must be hand-picked, with a maximum yield of 55hl/ha and a minimum natural alcohol content of 12.2%. The wines are all producer-bottled and bear a capsule common to them all. These dry wines have to pass a tasting examination, ensuring that the high quality standards set are maintained.

Since 1988 the reputation of Silvaner has been slowly re-establishing itself. As a dry QbA it is successful in many cellars. RS (short for "Rheinhessen Silvaner") is dry, and made to enhanced technical and tasting standards by some 50 producers. It was launched in 1986 with a black and orange label, and achieves modest sales of 7,580 cases per year. Many estate bottlers now sell their cheaper wines under the vine variety name only, and these mainly dry wines can be most attractive.

VILLAGES AND PRODUCERS

The northern and eastern boundaries of the Rheinhessen are defined by the inverted "L" shape of the Rhein, while the vineyards in the west feel their way towards the suburbs of Bad Kreuznach in the Nahe. In the south, Worms signals the boundary with the Pfalz. Most Rheinhessen wine is white.

BINGEN AND THE WEST

In the extreme north-west of the region, Bingen faces Rüdesheim in the Rheingau and the vineyards of the Nahe. It gives its name to the *Bereich* covering the entire western half of the Rheinhessen.

From the hill above the town, the 35-ha (86-acre) Scharlachberg *Einzellage* looks south across the rolling scenery of the *Bereich*. It is mainly steep, and one of the few vineyards known outside the district. Weingut Villa Sachsen (22ha, 54 acres) is a leading grower, owned by three families (Prinz Salm, Schriegle and Dietler). Riesling predominates and the well-made, cask-matured wines from Binger Scharlachberg and other sites are crisp and often *spritzig*.

Gau-Bickelheim

To the south, a few kilometres off the E31 motorway which crosses the Rheinhessen diagonally, the village of Gau-Bickelheim is home to the central cooperative cellars of Rheinhessen Winzer. This co-op has no private members, but receives the crop from 16 pressing-stations, which with rationalization will be cut to five. Around 95% of its sales are in Germany. Through its subsidiary the Winzerkeller Ingelheim, the central cooperative intends to build an interesting range of mid-priced superior wines, aimed at retail wine merchants.

One of the leading growers is Weingut Klaus Keller, which competes with German top producers such as Schales of Flörsheim, Michel Pfannebecker of Flomborn, Wittmann of Westhofen and Manz of Weinolsheim.

Ingelheim

Looking across the Rhein from the hills above Ingelheim, Charlemagne is said to have watched the snow melting on the slopes of the Rheingau and planned his future vineyards. The story, according to the historian Bassermann-Jordan, may have some justification, but Ingelheim's main claim to fame for many years has been its red wine from Spätburgunder grapes. A typical and traditional Ingelheim shows very clear Pinot Noir characteristics but seems a little lightweight: elegant but insubstantial. Weingut J Neus is the best-known Ingelheim estate today.

THE RHEINTERRASSE

The influence and vineyards of the ecclesiastics of Mainz once extended to both sides of the Rhein. At Bodenheim, a few kilometres south of Mainz, they were thick on the ground — or more precisely, on the slopes of the Rheinterrasse, the long cliff overlooking the Rhein.

At its northern end, many of the vineyards seem to face the wrong way — east or

north — but that does not stop the Weingut Kühling-Gillot from producing, in good years, a Spätburgunder red wine with over 13% of natural alcohol and a few grams of residual sugar. This and the white wines of similar weight from Grauburgunder grapes are the result of careful grape selection.

Nackenheim

At Nackenheim the Terrasse pushes close to the Rhein. The most famous vineyard here is the Nackenheimer Rothenberg, with its dark terracotta-coloured slate on a 30% gradient. The 80% Riesling estate of Weingut Gunderloch has holdings in the Rothenberg. Like other good estates, Gunderloch has its own minimum levels of must weight for the various official quality categories, below which it will not go. Its Riesling *Spätlese* wines start at a minimum of 12.2% of potential alcohol, and *Auslesen* at 13.8%. (The law requires 11.4 and 12.5% respectively.) There are up to five tours through the Gunderloch vineyards to gather the grapes at the right moment of their development, judged by their level of acidity.

Nierstein

The vineyards of Nierstein are next along the slope to Nackenheimer Rothenberg. Here, and in other villages along the Rheinterrasse, *Flurbereinigung* (*see* p314) has been taking place for some time. In Nierstein, the bill for this is 80,000 DM per hectare, but the costs of working the vineyard there-

after are much reduced. Some growers feel that without modernization, viticulture on the Rheinterrasse would have become terminally uneconomic. The trail of good red soil that storms washed off the vineyards to flow down the Rhein has now ended.

The best vineyards in Nierstein are the Glöck, the Pettenthal, the Ölberg and the Brudersberg. Famous estates among Nierstein's 150 wine producers include Weingut Heyl zu Herrnsheim, Weingut Bürgermeister Anton Balbach Erben, Weingut Sankt Anthony and Weingut Georg Albrecht Schneider. The Grosslage Niersteiner Gutes Domtal spreads over 15 villages — but only 2% of its vineyards fall within the boundaries of the village of Nierstein. The wine behind the label therefore has very little chance of coming from Nierstein. It is possible that this legal misuse of the good name of Nierstein will be stopped before long.

Oppenheim

The unhappy relationship between the town of Oppenheim and the *Grosslage* Oppenheimer Krötenbrunnen mirrors the problem of the growers of Nierstein.

Oppenheim is the biggest town on the Rheinterrasse, the home of a number of good estates, including the State Wine Cellars (Staatsweingut mit Domäne Oppenheim) and Weingut Louis Guntrum, and of the best wine museum in Germany. Sackträger is the top *Einzellage* in Oppenheim.

ALZEY AND THE SOUTH

The town of Alzey, on the south-west of the Bereich Nierstein, is the home of the wine house H. Sichel, a major exporter, and of the Weingut der Stadt Alzey. The southern part of the Rheinhessen is the Bereich Wonnegau, making everyday wines.

PFALZ

The Pfalz wine region is a narrow belt running some 80km (50 miles) from north to south. Most of the 23,045ha (56,944 acres) of vineyard lies on the plain between the Rhein and the high forest country of the Pfälzer Wald, or on the gentle east-facing slopes below the woods, which shelter the district from westerly winds. The climate is dry and mild; the summers and autumns warm.

The Franco-German frontier at Wissembourg forms the southern boundary of the Pfalz, but in reality the region is a continuation of the Alsace vineyard. The topography is the same: the Rhein to the east, the forested hills to the west, the villages in a string along the edge of the slope. This is a welcoming region to visit, with hundreds of wine producers selling direct, and many charming vineyard villages and towns.

Historically, the Pfalz — formerly Rheinpfalz (or in English the Palatinate) — has been a region of ordinary wine with few top-quality estates, concentrated in a handful of villages in the central or Mittelhaardt district. A new generation of estate owners is widening the range of good wines and bringing the Pfalz into the front rank of German wine. In particular, they are raising the reputation of German red wine. The Pfalz is warm enough to ripen red grapes properly, giving enterprising winemakers useful raw material.

While these good young winemakers keep their feet on the ground, success is in the air. The region's image is improving in Germany through the continuing high standards of the traditional quality estates, and the efforts of the newcomers. Most of the latter have been born into small family estates, and trained at viticultural colleges and travelled and worked abroad. They

Traditional carving on a *Fuder* or cask.

are self-critical and have shown that top-quality wine can be produced in villages well away from the traditional top areas. However the broad distinction persists: the southern half of the region, the Südpfalz, is a zone of mass production, the Mittelhaardt is the quality heartland.

Growers, merchants and estates

Nearly half the wine made in the Pfalz is not bottled by the producers, but sold in bulk to wine merchants. Over a third of the quality wine is bottled by merchants on the Mosel, mainly either as Liebfraumilch or under its *Grosslage* name. This tradition of inter-regional trading goes back to a time before 1971, when the German wine law was introduced. Pfalz wine was used to tone down the acidity in cheap Mosel wine. Today, as in the neighbouring Rheinhessen, the number of vine growers in the Pfalz is decreasing, while more of the survivors are becoming "estate bottlers".

Cooperatives are important here. Two very large ones dominate the southern, lesser-quality, half of the region: *see* p337. In the higher-quality zone of the Mittelhaardt, the standing of the cooperative cellars at Bad Dürkheim, Deidesheim, Forst, and Ruppertsberg is confirmed by their continuing success at the national competitions run by the Deutsche Landwirtschaftsgesellschaft (DLG). Many producers use these annual tastings solely to compare their wines with those of their competitors. Some prefer not to publicize their achievements because there can be no guarantee that wines of the same name in successive vintages will be equally good at prize winning. (Inconsistencies of this type are not appreciated by the restaurant trade, in particular.) Reflecting the different markets they supply, the amount of dry wine from cooperative cellars is proportionately less than that of most private estates.

Grape varieties and wine styles

In style terms, this is a region in transition as the old, rather earthy, medium to sweet kind of white wine is being replaced by fresher, drier whites. Red wine is being made on a growing scale. Müller-Thurgau is the most-planted variety with 22%, with Riesling having 20% and Kerner, Portugieser, Silvaner, and Scheurebe also significant. Silvaner is staging something of a revival, with increasing use of cask ageing. Other important vines in terms of quality, and with a significant planted area, are Spätburgunder and Dornfelder for red wine, and Huxelrebe, Bacchus, Ruländer, and Ortega for white wine.

The State Cellars at Neustadt-Mussbach and the small family estate of Knipser at Laumersheim are both experimenting with the Gänsefüsser variety (literally, "goose feet", on account of the shape of its leaf). This vine was once widely grown and its wine was well received, but the crop was uncertain. Another old-time favourite of the Pfalz, Gewürz-traminer, retains its position on a number of leading estates, in spite of its low yield and today's limited interest in scented wines. It can produce dry *Auslese* wines with 15% or more of actual alcohol, for which there is a demand in the south of the region — the Süd Pfalz. It is often at its best with a few grams of residual sugar. In the Süd Pfalz, Weissburgunder makes a wide range of styles extending from base wine for *Sekt* (sparkling wine) to *Auslese* wines with over 16% of alcohol.

A quarter of all Pfalz quality white wine is dry. In the 1982–1992 decade not only did the proportion of "official" dry (*trocken*) wine increase in the Pfalz, but the general bottlings of many producers became drier than they were in the 1970s.

In the Pfalz, *Kabinett* wine can vary considerably in actual alcohol content from the legal minimum for some vine varieties of 9.5%, to 12%. As yet the region has not yet agreed what a *Kabinett* wine should be and thus what it should taste like; often it is a downgraded *Spätlese* and can be a very good wine, but an upper alcohol limit would define the style more clearly. In a fine vintage many *Spätlesen* are (in legal terms) lesser-quality *Auslesen*, as the demand for *Auslesen* is limited. Good estates, in any case, always have self-imposed minimum must weights for the various quality categories, higher than those required by law, usually by a little less than a degree of alcohol.

Thirty years ago the style of Pfalz white wine — nobody spoke of the red — was slightly oxidized, relatively low in acid and, as far as Riesling was concerned, had a pronounced *goût de terroir*. Riesling from the Mittelhaardt today is nearly Rheingau Riesling in structure, being crisp and having a strong backbone of tartaric acid.

Red wines and wood

For red wines, Dornfelder (500ha, 1,235 acres) is said to be replacing Portugieser (2,300ha, 5,700 acres) as a fruity, "café" wine. Although Pfalz Dornfelder is never a great wine, it can gain complexity through ageing in new wood. The Münzberg estate of Godramstein in the south of the region believes it then resembles Merlot. Others prefer Dornfelder to be left to show its natural fruit through being stored in mature oak, without any pick-up of tannin from new casks.

The argument over *barrique*-ageing (*see* p121) is pursued energetically in the Pfalz. Although new wood can change the character of wines of the Pinot family, the Lingenfelder estate of Grosskarlbach treats Dornfelder differently. When fermentation has reached a point at which the sugar level has dropped to the equivalent of about 3% of alcohol, the wine is transferred to stainless steel. After six months in large, well-seasoned, oak casks it is then bottled. There is no fining and only a coarse filtration at bottling. The wine is full of fruit, balanced by its acidity. The recipe works.

In the south of the region, quality (as opposed to everyday) wine is a new arrival, and styles of wine, both white and red, have not yet been fixed for all time. Whether the district's winemakers should develop their own distinctive type of red wine, or try for something more international in character, are questions much discussed. □

Geraniums and vines cover a wine merchant's premises in Ruppertsberg.

VILLAGES AND PRODUCERS

The Pfalz is divided into two *Bereiche* — the Mittelhaardt/Deutsche Weinstrasse which borders the Rheinhessen region to the north, and the Südliche Weinstrasse in the south, down to the French frontier. The most famous wine villages are in the southern part of the Mittelhaardt, between Kallstadt and Neustadt. White and red wines are made.

UNTERHAARDT
The northern part of the Mittelhaardt is known as the Unterhaardt, and once included the valley of the Alsenz and villages that now form part of the Nahe region. The heavy soil of the Unterhaardt was once known as a source of carafe wine, but in the last 20 years its reputation has improved immensely. Today the Pfalz vineyards start just north of Kirchheimbolanden. Bockenheim is the northernmost important wine village, and the end of the Weinstrasse (wine route). Laumerstein and Grosskarlbach are other good villages. In the latter, Weingut K & H Lingenfelder has built a name for red and white wines in an international style.

Weingut Knipser of Laumersheim uses different grape varieties — for instance, Chardonnay and other French varieties — and produces a *barrique*-aged Riesling.

Grünstadt lies on the edge of the woods and marks the boundary of the Mittelhaardt proper.

MITTELHAARDT
A line of vine growing villages on the slopes below the Pfälzer Wald — Kallstadt, Ungstein, Bad Dürkheim, Wachenheim, Forst, Deidesheim, and Ruppertsberg — form the heart of the Pfalz. Here most of the region's members of the VDP associa-

tion have their vineyards.

Kallstadt
The northernmost of the seven top villages: the best vineyard is Steinacker. Good producers include Weingut Koehler-Ruprecht and the village cooperative (Winzergenossenschaft Kallstadt).

Ungstein
Rich, fruity and fiery are among terms used for Ungstein's wine. Red wine is quite important, but the best wines are Riesling whites. Noted estates are Weingut Pfeffingen, J Koch & Sohn and Bärenhof.

Bad Dürkheim
A small spa town with excellent vineyards, and a famous September wine festival, said to be the largest in the world. Good growers include Weingut Fitz-Ritter and Weingut Karl Schaefer.

Wachenheim
A fine-wine village, with famous vineyards such as Gerümpel and Altenberg. Solid, long-lasting white wine is the local tradition, with some estates also making drier wines in a modern style. The dominant producer is Bürklin-Wolf, which has 100ha (247 acres) here and in other Mittelhaardt villages. This, the largest of the three famous Pfalz estates (*see* Deidesheim

below for the other two), uses both wood and stainless steel for storage. The Bürklin-Wolf wines are frequently used as a standard by which others in the region are judged.

Forst
Forst is known for its Riesling: it varies according to the site and the producers but in general its natural, steely, firm character is emphasized by modern vinification.

The largest single vineyard is the Ungeheuer which was greatly increased in size in 1971; the best known is Jesuitengarten, planted 100% Riesling, and perhaps the best is the adjacent Kirchenstück. Basalt rock from the hill to the west of Forst has traditionally been spread over the vineyards: the darker soil is said to hold the warmth better. Weingut Georg Mosbacher produces excellent Riesling.

Deidesheim
Forst's rival as the heart of the Mittelhaardt, with top vineyards like Hohenmorgen, Grainhübel and Herrgottsacker. The village is dominated by two great estates which, with Bürklin-Wolf (*see* Wachenheim above), are among the best-known in Germany. The modernized von Buhl estate, leased to a Japanese group, has 54ha (132 acres), planted 90% with Riesling at Forst, Deidesheim, Ruppertsberg and Friedelsheim. The style of wine is modern, fresh, steely, and made to last.

The 40-ha (98-acre) Bassermann-Jordan estate is all Riesling. Holdings include top sites such as Forster Jesuitengarten and Deidesheimer Hohenmorgen. Unlike von Buhl, Bassermann-Jordan matures its wines in casks of 2,400 litres.

Other good estates include the two Deinhard concerns.

Ruppertsberg
The southern end of the

string, with not quite the reputation of its neighbour Deidesheim, but producing some fine Riesling, Silvaner and Scheurebe wine from the Hoheburg and Linsenbusch vineyards.

Other producers
Leading growers include Weingut Weik of Mussbach-Neustadt, Christmann of Gimmeldingen and Weingut Müller Catoir of Hardt-Neustadt, the Pfalz' most famous producer.

SÜDLICHE WEINSTRASSE
If the style of most Mittelhaardt wine is northern German, that of the Bereich Südliche Weinstrasse, also known as the Südpfalz (southern Pfalz), is nearer that of the Ortenau in Baden, or Alsace in France.

Südpfalz is mainly a producer of basic wine with the second-highest yield in Germany after the Bereich Obermosel. Fine wine production on any wide scale began only in the 1970s.

About 7% of the vineyard is Riesling, and the vines of the Pinot family are very successful in the Südpfalz climate, and for a number of growers the use of new oak *barriques* is a fundamental part of their red winemaking — not an experimental alternative.

The main producers are the district's two large cooperatives: the Rhodt unter Rietburg cooperative and the Deutsches Weintor cooperative. Among private estates, names to look for include Weingut Becker at Schweigen, Weingut Siegrist at Leinsweiler, Weingut Hohenberg at Birkweiler, Weingut Rebholz at Siebeldingen and Weingut Dr Wehrheim at Birkweiler.

HESSISCHE BERGSTRASSE

The small, 400-ha (988-acre) Hessische Bergstrasse region lies on the edge of the Odenwald opposite Worms, which is 20km (12 miles) across the Rhein to the west. It is widely known for spectacular almond, apricot, cherry and peach blossom which seems to arrive overnight in the early days of April. It is an almost frost-free region with a generous annual rainfall of 720mm (28 inches) and a very varied soil in which sand, clay, limestone and loess predominate.

The vineyards are split between two *Bereiche*, reflecting the areas in which they are grouped. Most of the region runs north–south, and is geographically an extension of the Badische Bergstrasse north of Heidelberg (*see* map, p324), and is called Bereich Starkenburg. There is an isolated wine district south of a line drawn from Darmstadt to Aschaffenburg in Franken, set apart to the northeast; this is the Bereich Umstadt.

This is predominantly a white wine region. Riesling occupies over half the area under vine, as it has done continuously since the mid-1960s, during which the wine-producing region has more than doubled in size. Müller-Thurgau accounts for 17%, Silvaner for 8% and Kerner for 4%. Although the vineyards have not been formally reconstructed, the percentage of vines over 20 years old is no greater than it is in the Rheingau, the other wine region in the State of Hessen.

Hessische Bergstrasse Riesling wines compare well with those of the Rheingau, but as production is small they are hard to find, except by visiting the region. These Rieslings have less acidity than the Rheingau ones, and they mature more quickly. Without the breed and elegance of the Rheingau Rieslings, they however have plenty of flavour and charm.

Vineyards above Unterhambach.

About a quarter of the planted area is so steep or so awkwardly placed that it can only be cultivated by hand. Winemaking on a very small scale, using grapes from such expensive sites, is not commercially worthwhile, and as over half the growers each own less than a quarter of a hectare, the main cooperative cellars at Heppenheim receive the harvest from over 70% of the region's vineyards. Growers in the Bereich Umstadt deliver the crop from 29ha (71 acres) to their own Odenwald cooperative.

High costs make viticulture here only marginally profitable. In 1992 it was illustrated in a lecture for wine producers that the net cost to the producer of a Riesling *Spätlese* with a yield of 75hl/ha in a steep site amounted to about 7.10 DM a bottle. With an average selling price of 9 DM for all wines, the Bensheim State Wine Cellars is not overcharging its customers, and neither does the Hessische Bergstrasse as a whole. □

VILLAGES AND PRODUCERS

HEPPENHEIM

At the southern end of the region, the attractive old town of Heppenheim is one of the centres of the Bergstrasse.

Bergsträsser Gebiets-Winzergenossenschaft (BGW)

The region's main cooperative cellar, with a 75-ha (185-acre) vineyard and 570 members of which five are full-time growers. Through a well-judged scale of payments, the co-op's members are encouraged to produce better-quality fruit. The average yield of 84hl/ha is relatively low for a cooperative cellar. Fermentation is spontaneous and left to the natural yeasts on the grape — which, incidentally, presupposes no residues of spray material. Apart from sound QbA the cooperative also offers a full range of QmP, including *Eiswein*. The risk involved in leaving grapes on the vine for *Eiswein* production is covered by the cooperative – not individually by its members.

BENSHEIM

Another scenic old town and the centre of some of the highest-quality vineyards of the region.

Weingut der Stadt Bensheim

About 12ha (30 acres) planted in local sites, which produce the standard range of regional vines plus Rotberger, a Trollinger x Riesling crossing from the Geisenheim research institute in the Rheingau. It produces wine with a high acidity, useful for rosé wine or, as at Bensheim, *Sekt*.

Staatsweingut (State Wine Cellars) Bergstrasse. With 37ha (91 acres), the State Wine Cellars is the most important estate-bottler in the region. It specializes in *Eiswein*, mostly from the 15-ha (36-acre) Heppenheimer Centgericht *Einzellage*. The Staatsweingut list includes six Riesling *Eisweine*. Being a subsidiary of the Hessen State Cellars in Eltville, it follows the Rheingau habit of using foil to protect the grapes left on the vine for the *Eiswein* harvest.

F R A N K E N

Nearly 200 years ago the bailiff of the town of Volkach reported to his superiors that vineyards had been planted where grapes would never fully ripen "even if there were two suns in the sky". Since then the Franken vineyard has grown and shrunk probably more than any other in Germany, according to the political and economic circumstances of the time. In the last quarter of a century it has grown by 169% to 5,918ha (14,623 acres). At its best, Franken wine is characterful, intense and long-lasting, though vintages vary widely. The distinctive *Bocksbeutel*, short and round, rather than tall and slim, is used for many of Franken's wines.

Franken is in the heart of Germany, east of the Rhein, and in an area of harsher climate and broad forests. The vineyards cling to warm corners along the River Main and its tributaries. Vintages can vary quite dramatically in size depending on the weather. With the milder climate of recent years yields have not been much reduced by winter and spring frosts, so while there is never too much good wine, the supply of ordinary wine is probably greater than the demand. In the 1990s good growers are restricting their crop not just by pruning, but also by thinning out the grapes in August.

Vineyards and varieties

The planting of new and reconstructed vineyards has meant that nearly half of Franken's vines are under ten years old. In spite of many centuries of experience, German wine is very open to the whim of fashion — which is not the same as following the wishes of the market. Up to a point, image and stability are offered by leading estates but even these, including the Staatlicher Hofkeller in Würzburg, were attracted by the scented appeal of new vine crossings in the 1970s. Perhaps growers now focus on their future more clearly, for many have replanted with varieties whose worth has been proved over the centuries.

Climate fluctuations make cost forecasting difficult, but high wine prices are supported by the local Bavarian market. The Bavarians' predilection for beer does not diminish their love of their local wine — Franken is politically part of Bavaria,

The steep Innere Leiste vineyard opposite Würzburg is crowned by the Marienberg castle.

or Bayern, a very independent-minded part of Germany.

The emphasis is now on planting Silvaner, the Pinot family and, to a lesser extent, Riesling. But crossings such as Müller-Thurgau (47% of the vineyard area) and Bacchus can produce better wine than they often do.

Scheurebe is not widely planted but its wine often surprises and impresses tasters from outside the region. It needs a good site to ripen its grapes adequately, which means to the level needed for QmP, as does Rieslaner, a locally-bred Silvaner x Riesling crossing.

The Bürgerspital introduced Riesling into the noted Würzburger Stein vineyard and started to bottle it as a single-variety wine at the end of the last century. Good Stein Riesling wine has a convincing air of authority and is undoubtedly very distinguished, with a fine, long flavour. The demand for dry wines, for which grapes with *botrytis cinerea* are not wanted, has meant that the production of sweet *Auslesen* is now smaller than in the past. Riesling, Silvaner, Rieslaner and Spät-, Grau- and Weissburgunder all do well in the Würzburger Stein, and experiments are now being carried out with Chardonnay. In the long run a smaller range of varieties might be better in consolidating the reputation of the vineyard.

Wine styles

Most good white Franken wine has a slight *goût de terroir*, which is strongest in Silvaner wines from restricted yields. Silvaner is Franken's traditional speciality. In the 1970s, Silvaner was sometimes rather fat, lacking acidity, and oxidized; today, produced to modern standards, it is characterful and fresh, and a real pleasure to drink. Over 50% of the production is *Fränkisch trocken*, containing less than four grams per litre of unfermented sugar.

The better half of the region's wine is sold in the dumpy *Bocksbeutel*. This particular shape of green or amber bottle is used in Germany

The baroque beauty of the cellars of Würzburg's Residenz.

exclusively for quality wine from Franken and from a few Baden villages on the River Tauber and near Baden-Baden. Lesser-quality wines are normally sold in litre bottles.

Although the region is known principally for white wine, it has areas of red wine production. The demand from restaurants and producers' private customers for Franken red wine increases, and the small production, mostly from the Steigerwald and the Mainviereck, grows with it. There is a feeling that a further expansion of the present red wine area (5% of the total under vine) could cloud the regional image. However, it is not easy for producers to ignore the success of red wine, and new plantings of Spätburgunder, Portugieser, Schwarzriesling and Domina (Portugieser x Spätburgunder) continue to be made.

Areas, estates and soils

The 31 members of the VDP are distributed widely and unevenly throughout the region, and the holdings of the three large estates based on Würzburg are almost as far flung.

The best sites, that is to say those that produce the ripest grapes, are concentrated on south- or southwest-facing slopes. However, these are more at risk from spring frost damage than lesser sites, as their warmer micro-climate encourages the sap in the vine to rise early in the season. Early spring frost, as in 1985, can ruin an entire harvest. Cooler east-facing slopes are less at risk from frost, but the grapes cannot ripen as well as those in the famous vineyards beside the Main.

While gypsum and keuper are important ingredients of the vineyards on the edge of the Steigerwald, the Würzburg soil is characterized by shell-lime which, disregarding the trials conducted by the state viticultural institute, is said to add finesse to the wine. Since the early 1970s, this institute, which is associated with the Staatlicher Hofkeller, has examined the influence of soil and climate on the flavour, bouquet, and chemical analysis of wine. Its interim conclusion is that "as much as we would like to characterize the wine by the type of soil it is grown in...we now have to begin to take the climate aspect of the site all the more into consideration when talking about the character of a wine".

VILLAGES AND PRODUCERS

The sprawling Franken region is given shape by the River Main, which flows via great bends from east to west. The vineyards are in three *Bereiche:* the Steigerwald to the east, the Maindreieck around Würzburg in the centre, and the Mainviereck downstream to the west. White wines make up 95% of production. The region is reputed for its famous Stein Wein (from one of Franken's best vineyards); the best cuvées, made from Silvaner, are straight white wines which resemble very much French white wines.

STEIGERWALD

The south-eastern boundary of the Franken vineyards is the Steigerwald forest, with the best-known wine villages of the *Bereich* sited south of the E43 motorway.

Castell

The largest estate in the *Bereich* is that of Fürst Castell-Castell, at the charming village at the eastern end of the region that bears the family name. The vineyards are all sloping, if not steep, and, unusually, the estate is sole owner of eight *Einzellagen*.

Iphofen

More often than not the finest wines of the *Bereich* come from the large sweep of modernized, sloping vineyards at Iphofen. Good growers in the Julius-Echter-Berg *Einzellage* will expect their *Kabinett* and *Spätlesen* to have almost a degree of potential alcohol more than the legal minimum.

One of the leading producers here is Weingut Rudolf Fürst, which produces Paul Fürst, one of Franken's most elegant wines. Other good producers are Weingut J Arnold, Weingut Bürgstadt, Weingut E Popp, Weingut Johann Ruck, Weingut Rupp and Weingut Wirsching.

MAINDREIECK

This *Bereich* is centred on the city of Würzburg, the winemaking and cultural heart of Franken.

Volkach

Volkach is a pleasant town where in September 8,000 celebrants sit on benches under chestnut and linden trees, enjoying the annual wine festival. The von Schönborn estate, Schloss Halburg near Volkach, allows its dry Rieslaner wines a malolactic fermentation to reduce acidity; the estate also makes Bacchus wines which show that this can be a serious, good-quality vine if treated correctly.

Immediately south of Volkach, with the aid of a canal, the Main forms a substantial island. The fine sweep of steep vineyards known as the Escherndorfer Lump is among the few *Einzellagen* known outside Franken.

At nearby Nordheim there is one of the good smaller cooperatives, supplied by 265 ha (654 acres) spread out as far as the Steigerwald. In the 17th-century air-conditioned cellar, Müller-Thurgau, Riesling and — more surprisingly because of its balance of acidity — elegant Traminer are stored in wood.

Like the other three important but smaller co-ops at Thüngersheim, Sommerach and Randersacker, Nordheim has a good and improving reputation.

Kitzingen

The harvest from a quarter of Franken's vineyards is processed by the regional cooperative, the Gebiets-Winzergenossenschaft, which is at Kitzingen, down the Main from Volkach. The scale is massive, with 1,500 wines being stored individually each year. Twenty different vine varieties are separated according to the village, the vineyard and their official quality category. The aim is to reduce the list to a total of 600 wines, including a range of small bottlings of superior wine that are destined for wine merchants.

Randersacker

A few kilometres upstream from Würzburg, Randersacker has a good cooperative cellar, a number of rustic wine bars, and some good estates including Weingut Robert Schmitt, which makes a fine QmP range. It is often said that the Randersackerer Pfülben vineyard, with its shell-lime soil and micro-climate suited to Riesling, Silvaner, and Rieslaner, includes some of the best sites in Franken.

Würzburg

The three greatest wine estates of Franken belong to the Bürgerspital, the Juliusspital, and the Staatlicher Hofkeller in Würzburg.

The cellars of the Hof-keller, under the Residenz built by bishops of the von Schönborn family, were severely damaged in 1945 but have been rebuilt and long since refilled with wine from 120ha (296 acres) in 14 vine-growing communities, some on the outer edges of the Franken region. Apart from holdings at Randersacker, the most famous are in the Würzburg sites, and particularly in the Stein vineyard. Of the three great Würzburg estates, many regard the Juliusspital as *primus inter pares* — at the moment. Its 163ha (413 acres) of planted vineyard, accumulated since 1576, include substantial holdings in the region's best-known sites, and 8ha (19 acres) at Bürgstadt west of Würzburg.

MAINVIERECK

This *Bereich* covers the downstream, or western, part of the region.

Bürgstadt

Bürgstadt and neighbouring villages and towns on this part of the Main are known mainly for their red wines. Estates include Rudolf Fürst and the Weingut der Stadt Klingenberg.

Among the more substantial estates in this area of small wine properties is that of Fürst Löwenstein at Kreuzwertheim. Besides the 7,400ha (18,285 acres) of forest and farmland, there are also 26ha (63 acres) under vine, including 9ha (22 acres) in the steep and partly-terraced Homburger Kallmuth vineyard.

EASTERN GERMANY

The reunification of Germany has added two wine regions to the 11 existing under the West German regulations. Other patches of vines are to be found in the east, but the main centres of viticulture are in two designated wine regions: Saale-Unstrut, south-west of Leipzig (over 390ha/963 acres), and Sachsen (320 ha/790 acres), up and down the river on either side of Dresden (*see* map, p311).

Sachsen and Saale-Unstrut both lie further north than the Ahr valley, on the same degree of latitude as the south-east of England. They have a climate somewhat similar to that of Franken, but with even greater — and unexpected — variations. In the winter of 1987 the temperature dropped to –34°C (–29°F), and in late April 1991, with temperatures down to –8°C (18°F), there were 12cm (5 inches) of snow. Vine-growing is possible here only where the micro-climate is favourable. Rainfall is low and the period of vegetation is shorter than in the rest of Germany.

Sachsen has volcanic and loess soil, while the wines of Saale-Unstrut benefit from the chalk in their vineyards: it makes them seem fuller than those of similar strength from the slate soil of the Mosel. It is hard to generalize about yield and production due to the lack of figures. Average yields from run-down vineyards, where dead vines have not been replaced or where clones sensitive to frost are growing, are as low as 34hl/ha, resulting in good levels of extract. When terraces have been rebuilt and vineyards rejuvenated, the region's average yield may be in the order of 50–60hl/ha.

Wine styles and grape varieties

Almost all the wines are white and dry and more closely resemble a Nahe than any other of the western German wines. Their must weights are never as low as the lowest in the Mosel-Saar-Ruwer.

The principal vine of the eastern regions is Müller-Thurgau, followed in alphabetical order by Bacchus, Gutedel, Kerner, Riesling, Ruländer, Silvaner, Traminer and Weissburgunder, plus small amounts of eastern European crossings of *vitis vinifera*. Sachsen also has Germany's only plantation of Goldriesling, a vine, less noble than its name suggests, also grown in small quantities in Alsace.

Producers

In Saale-Unstrut the main producers are the 100-ha (247-acre) Staatsweingut Naumburg established by Cistercians and now owned by the State of Sachsen-Anhalt, Weingut Lützkendorf of Bad Kösen and the Winzervereinigung Freyburg/Unstrut, the cooperative cellar at Freyburg. All the wines of this are sold under the grape name, without the mention of a site or village.

In Sachsen the Winzergenossenschaft Meissen, the cooperative cellars at Meissen, receives the grapes from 160ha (396 acres) owned by part-time growers. At Schloss Wackerbarth, at Radebeul, the State (as opposed to the wine region) of Sachsen has its own wine and *Sekt* cellars, the Staatsweingut Radebeul (100ha/247 acres of leased vineyard).

Since reunification a small number of private estates have been established. The financial difficulties of the producers in both regions can hardly be exaggerated, and in the early 1990s the result of Communist complacency and lack of investment are to be seen everywhere. However, two estates producing quality wines do well: Weingut Schloss Proschwitz of Meissen and Weingut Klaus Zimmerling (organic) of Dresden.   □

Vineyards in the Sachsen wine region near Dresden.

BADEN

Baden is not so much a unified wine region as a conglomeration of districts, some isolated and separated by extensive woods or the Rhein. Most run parallel to the east bank of the river north of Basel, but where the hills meet the frost-endangered Rhein plain, viticulture comes to an immediate halt. Orchards cover the north- and north-west-facing slopes stretching out from the Black Forest, and vines line the slopes that face the sun. Most of the vineyard holdings are too large to abandon, but too small for winemaking to be worthwhile, so there are many cooperatives, including the Badischer Winzerkeller at Breisach, the largest producer cellar in Europe. In total, there are 15,346ha (37,919 acres) under vine.

Grape varieties and wine styles
In the early 19th century nearly 200 vine varieties were growing in Baden; in the 1990s, 92% of the area is planted in seven varieties only, six white and one red. A third of the area is Müller-Thurgau, a quarter the red Spätburgunder, and a third collectively Ruländer, Gutedel, Riesling, Weissburgunder and Silvaner.

In parts of Germany it is now legal to grow Chardonnay commercially. While most of the vines have been imported from France or Italy, 26 Chardonnay clones are on trial in Baden. To be successful in Germany Chardonnay requires a site with the same conditions in which Riesling would flourish, so that there is some resistance to its widespread planting. Surprisingly, the Badischer Winzerkeller is already able to offer a Chardonnay wine, from plants supplied from Alsace in the 1970s as Weissburgunder. A similar error has meant that a cooperative in Markgräflerland can offer Chardonnay *Sekt* from vines that were previously

Durbach is a noted wine town.

thought to be Auxerrois, another member of the Pinot family.

As Baden lies in zone "B" of the EC (the rest of Germany is in zone "A"; *see* p132), the alcohol content of its wine in normal vintages cannot be increased (by adding sugar) by more than 2.5% — a regulation that some districts, such as the Bereich Bodensee, can find difficult to follow. Assuming the yield is not over-large, the southern climate usually makes Baden wine softer and more alcoholic than that of the northern German regions.

Ageing of fuller Pinot wines (of both colours) in new oak *barriques* is common but, in many cellars, still experimental. While a healthy patriotism leads some producers to use locally-grown wood, most turn to Allier, Limousin or Nevers oak from France, and a few have Vosgesian or Slovenian casks on trial.

The quality cooperatives
It is a characteristic of Baden that local cooperative cellars produce good, attractive wines. Indeed, there

is no reason why they should not, as in some cases the cooperative is the only winemaker in a village; it is thus supplied by the best, and not just by the more ordinary, vineyards. Co-operatives such as Sasbachwalden and Kappelrodeck are well-known to wine lovers in Germany. Among their members Spätburgunder is the most widely-planted vine, and because it is not a "speciality" but a standard product, the resulting red wine is very fairly priced.

Technically speaking, average yields of all varieties (including Riesling and Müller-Thurgau) are probably still a shade high, but premium wines are made from grapes with a small crop in the modern way.

Disregarding the complicated matter of balancing quantity and quality financially, the German habit of carefully isolating grapes according to their ripeness seems to have three main disadvantages. It inevitably lowers the standard of the remainder of the crop, leads to an incomprehensible multiplicity of bottlings, and increases production costs. It seems most easily justified in Riesling vineyards in the northern regions, not here in the more prolific south.

Wine and gastronomy
Baden has 3,688ha (9,113 acres) of Spätburgunder (Pinot Noir) vines and no less than 34 Michelin-starred restaurants (as a comparison, the figures for the Côte d'Or are 5,802ha/ 14,336 acres of Pinot Noir and eight starred restaurants). Given the relatively recent German interest in high-quality food, the progress in producing wines (particularly reds) to accompany it has been good — and nowhere more so than in Baden. Without diminishing the efforts of the Rheingau, the structure and variety of Baden wines makes them ideal for a wider range of dishes.   □

VILLAGES AND PRODUCERS

The widely-scattered Baden vineyards are described here from north to south, starting with the area adjoining Franken in the north-east, and ending with those in the far south-east that face Switzerland across Lake Constance. The climate is more continental, more cloudy and wetter than in neighbouring Alsace, and the micro-climate is influenced by the Black Forest. The wine is 75% white. Baden wines are produced from high yields, and the best of them mask their lightness, acidity and thinness with appealing flowery perfumes. While cooperative cellars account for nearly 90% of the production, there exist also a number of estates with old historical ties.

TAUBERFRANKEN

At the north-east corner of Baden, on the last stretch of the River Tauber before it joins the Main, about 700ha (1,730 acres) of vineyards form the Bereich Tauberfranken (formerly known as the Badisches Frankenland). Here the climate is continental, which means there is a serious risk of spring frosts.

Were the district not in the State of Baden-Württemberg it would surely form part of the neighbouring Bavarian wine region of Franken. The quality wines are sold in the Franken *Bocksbeutel*, as if to emphasize the old historical ties. Tauberfranken wines are mostly white, and very similar to those of Franken, but because they are across the state border they are produced according to the wine regulations for the southern zone "B" (*see* preceding page). Two-thirds of the district's vineyards are planted in Müller-Thurgau.

THE NORTHERN RHEIN

The Bereich Badische Bergstrasse/Kraichgau covers nearly 2,000ha (4,942 acres) facing the Rhein Valley north and south of Heidelberg, of which 40% is planted in Müller-Thurgau and 20% in Riesling. Most Bergstrasse/Kraichgau wines are lighter than those from elsewhere in the region.

From Laudenbach at the northern tip of the region, the grapes are delivered to the cooperative cellar at Heppenheim in the Hessische Bergstrasse (*qv*). Further south in the Badische Bergstrasse there are towns with names such as Weingarten and Weinheim, reminding us of a long association with the vine. Three estates are members of the VDP. The Weingut Reichsgraf und Marquis zu Hoensbroech at Angelbachtal-Michelfeld makes almost all its Pinot and Riesling wines dry. Weingut Freiherr von Göler, Burg Ravensburg, at Sulzfeld has 14.5ha (35 acres), of which 60% is Riesling and 20% Lemberger — a mix that recalls the adjacent region of Württemberg.

At Oestringen-Tiefenbach the 25-ha (61-acre) Weingut Albert Heitlinger is planted 45% in Riesling, from which a *Deutscher Tafelwein* of an unusual sort is produced. It is made from *Beerenauslese* grapes, fermented until, with 20 grams per litre of residual sugar, it is almost medium-dry, and then aged in *barrique*. Heitlinger lists some surprising "products" including a spirit made from Jerusalem artichokes. Weingut Seeger of Leimen, is reputed for its Spätburgunder. The large district cooperative, the Winzerkeller Wiesloch, links the Bergstrasse with the Kraichgau, the hilly country between the Schwarzwald and the Odenwald.

ORTENAU

South of the famous spa town of Baden-Baden, the *Bereich* Ortenau district has a good and improving reputation for its wines. Those from the villages of Vernhalt, Steinbach, Umweg and Neuweier, close to the spa are sold in *Bocksbeutel* and tend to be rather expensive. While 30% of the district's 2,244ha (5,545 acres) of vineyard are Riesling, it is the only vine variety in the impressive, steep, 39-ha (96-acre) Neuweierer Mauerberg *Einzellage* near Baden-Baden.

Many of the Ortenau vineyards are steep, with the vines climbing in vertical lines. However, since 1978 some have been terraced so that small tractors can work horizontally across the slopes. As a result, labour costs have dropped; the wind can blow more freely among the vines (thus reducing fungal infections), and the grapes receive more light and sun. The grower contributes towards the cost of conversion to terracing, with the village, the *Land* (provincial government), and the Federal State paying the rest of the bill.

Affental

The Affental, which translates as "monkey valley", comprises a few villages south of Baden-Baden that make a red wine from Spätburgunder grapes well known in Germany, memorable partly for its monkey-embossed bottle.

Durbach

The village of Durbach is a centre of good wine, good restaurants, and spectacular vineyards. There is granite and gneiss in the slopes, which reach a gradient of 86% in parts of the Plauelrain.

Durbacher Riesling wines, for which the village has a good reputation, are similar to those of the Pfalz, although they have less acidity.

Apart from its cooperative cellar, Durbach has very good private estates. Weingut Freiherr von Neveu has 15ha (37 acres) of hill vineyards above the village, making fine Riesling whites and Spätburgunder reds. The Gräflich Wolff-Metternich'sches Weingut is another major estate, dating from 1180. In 1830 the Marquis de Lur-Saluces gave the estate some Sauvignon Blanc vines from his Château d'Yquem, and Sauvignon Blanc is still produced.

The Markgräflich Badisches Weingut Schloss Staufenberg — the estate of the Margrave of Baden — sits high above the village of Durbach in a good defensive position, surrounded on three sides by its precipitous vineyards. Riesling and Traminer were planted here as single vines as early as 1776; today in this part of the Ortenau they are officially known as Klingelberger and Clevner respectively.

Ortenberg

The town of Offenburg has its own estate in the village of Ortenberg south of Durbach. The Weingut der Stadt Offenburg has 30ha (74 acres) under vine, some of which are on amazingly steep slopes. Among a large number of vines, Cabernet Sauvignon is being grown and the wine is matured in new *barriques*.

BREISGAU

The Bereich Breisgau begins south of Offenburg. Vines and fields of maize grow side by side, and there are few estate-bottlers. Much of the wine, similar to that of Kaiserstuhl but lighter and more acid, is produced by the regional cooperative, the Badischer Winzerkeller (*see* profile). The Spätburgunder *Weissherbst* rosé made from grapes grown for the purpose (rather than from rejects from the red wine programme) can be very successful. The vines run up the Glottertal in the Black Forest to a height of 500m (1,640 ft) and there is a vineyard in the important city of Freiburg. Noted estates include Weingut Bernhard Huber of Malterdingen.

KAISERSTUHL

Looking east from Riquewihr in Alsace, the volcanic Kaiserstuhl Hills rise out of the flat expanse of the Rhein plain at a distance of some 15km (nine miles). The Bereich Kaiserstuhl accounts for a third of Baden's vineyards and produces many of the best-known wines of the region. Average temperatures are the highest in Germany, so the structure and style of the general run of wines are not determined by a high level of

acidity, as in the wine regions of the north.

There are a number of first-class estates including four members of the VDP — Weingut Bercher, Weingut Dr Heger, Weingut B Salwey, and Weingut Rudolf Stigler. These names are almost as well-known to wine lovers in Germany as those of the leading properties in the Rheingau. All run their vineyards on environmentally friendly lines and concentrate on the Pinot family and Riesling.

Weingut Rudolf Stigler is a specialist in crisp Riesling wines — some from clones from the Mosel — and, like many in Kaiserstuhl, a producer of serious red Spätburgunder and *Weissherbst* rosé.

The local cooperatives produce 90% of Kaiserstuhl wine, and those in the villages of Achkarren, Bickensohl, Bischoffingen, Oberrotweil, Burkheim and Königschaffhausen are well-regarded. They each crush grapes from a little over 200ha (494 acres) on average, a size at which the cellar master can exercise personal control over all he surveys.

At Achkarren, 40% of the cooperative's 68ha (168 acres) is Grauburgunder. The best wines from this grape (the Alsace Pinot Gris) have a powerful flavour from the vine variety and from the volcanic soil. Grauburgunder is still sold as Ruländer in its older, softer, sometimes *botrytis*-affected form, but it was the cooperative cellar at Bickensohl that in the 1980s launched the successful, crisper style from healthy grapes, gathered before they were fully ripe.

Among the leading producers of the Kaiserstuhl region is Weingut Franz Keller (Schwarzer Adler). Over the last 40 years this grower has made great efforts to improve the quality of German wines.

Ihringen

On the south side of the Kaiserstuhl there is the well-known Ihringer Winklerberg *Einzellage*, which was enlarged in 1971 from 40 to 140ha (98 to 345 acres). As so often happens, the additional 100ha (247 acres) have a different soil formation and micro-climate from the original vineyard, which dates from 1813 (the Romans missed this one). The best wines from the original Winklerberg are produced by the Heger estate and the Ihringen Kaiserstühler cooperative.

Bischoffingen and Burkheim

Other Kaiserstuhl villages with a good name include Bischoffingen, with its large cooperative and the Weingut Karl Heinz Johner, a *barrique*-ageing specialist making red

and white wines. Johner left his home in Baden to run the Lamberhurst vineyard in England before returning to start up this innovative estate. Weingut Bercher at Burkheim also uses cask-maturing to make top-class red Spätburgunder, white Grauburgunder and other wines.

TUNIBERG

To the visitor the high ground of the Bereich Tuniberg resembles a lesser Kaiserstuhl, but it has none of Kaiserstuhl's flavour-imparting volcanic soil. Indeed, much of the soil is deep loess, which is fertile, but not ideal for wine. Nearly half is planted in Spätburgunder, and 43% is Müller-Thurgau. Almost all the crop is processed by the mighty Badischer Winzerkeller to be sold mainly through discount

BADISCHER WINZERKELLER

The mainspring of Baden's wine industry is this remarkable cooperative cellar, the largest in Europe. The enormous premises are at Breisach, close to the French frontier. Size apart — it makes half the wine in Baden — its pioneering work has been important in several ways. First, it developed ways of vinifying hundreds of batches of wine, keeping the individual wines separate. Now it is creating "premium" wines to move into new markets.

The cellar takes grapes from 5,000ha (12,350 acres) making about 800 wines of every class and style, from the basic to *barrique*-aged specialities. The emphasis is increasingly on dry wines. It also owns the Gräflich von Kageneck'sche Sektkellerei at Breisach, a sparkling wine (*Sekt*) producer which uses only Baden wine.

chains and supermarkets in Germany.

MARKGRÄFLERLAND

Between Freiburg and Switzerland, the vineyards of the Bereich Markgräflerland keep a safe distance from the racetrack of the E4 motorway that separates them from the Rhein. They climb gentle hills in pleasant, rural countryside, leading to the 1,300-m (4,265-ft) peaks of the Hochschwarzwald.

The quality of gentleness is shared by the wine from Gutedel, the district's most important and misnamed vine variety. *Gut* (good) it certainly is, but *edel* (noble) it is not. Known in French-speaking countries as Chasselas, Gutedel accounts for 50% of the Markgräflerland vineyard, making some wholesome, digestible, thoroughly pleasant white wine. It does this so well that to find one of the more concentrated versions from the relatively few private estates is a very welcome surprise.

Schlossgut Istein, small (8-ha/20-acre) reputed estate at Lörrach, in the very south close to the Swiss frontier, makes good Spätburgunder among others. There are reliable village cooperative cellars such as those at Auggen, Müllheim, and Wolfenweiler. After Gutedel, they concentrate mainly on Müller-Thurgau (sometimes sold as a light wine under the Rivaner synonym), and Spätburgunder reds (often a little limp and not as good as in Kaiserstuhl).

BODENSEE

The Bodensee area has three *Bereiche*. Two are very small and are attached to the states of Württemberg and Bayern (Bavaria), while the 400ha (988 acres) of the Bereich Bodensee forms part of Baden.

Spätburgunder was growing in the district in the 9th century, but its first recorded plantation as a single variety dates from 1705 at Meersburg. Now it is grown mainly for *Weissherbst*. As in Franken, damage from spring frost causes a great variation in the size of the Bodensee grape harvest. The district has an annual rainfall of 800–1,000mm (23–39 inches) which, with the autumn fog that rises from the lake, creates ideal conditions for rot. Producing red wine with a good colour is therefore not easy, although it is sometimes done.

The large and beautiful Bodensee (Lake Constance) is very much a holiday area, and prices in hotels and restaurants, and of the local wine, are high. Perhaps this explains why the Staatsweingut Meersburg is said to be one of the very few state-owned cellars in Germany to make a profit. This estate is the most important producer in the Bodensee district. Most of the Staatsweingut's vineyards are at Meersburg on the Bodensee. It impressively overlooks its Rieschen vineyard which runs down to the lakeside.

Among its 55ha (135 acres) is the solely-owned Hohentwieler Olgaberg, which at 560m (1,837ft) is the highest vineyard in Germany. Müller-Thurgau, Spätburgunder, Ruländer, Traminer, and Weissburgunder grapes are grown in its volcanic soil.

Vineyards surround the hilltop Schloss Staufenberg estate at Durbach.

BADEN SELECTION

The Baden Wine Growers' Association is aware of the dangers of yet further fragmentation of the market that the flood of new categories of superior quality wine could create. It has, therefore, laid down conditions under which wines may be sold with the title "Baden Selection". They must come from the Burgunder vine varieties (maximum yield 40hl/ha), or from Riesling, Gutedel, or Müller-Thurgau (maximum yield 60hl/ha). At first glance it seems surprising that Müller-Thurgau, and not Silvaner, has been included in the list; however, a Müller-Thurgau wine from a maximum yield of 60hl/ha is very different from one from a yield above 100hl/ha.

"Baden Selection" wines must come from vines that are at least 15 years old, and are labelled with vintage, grape name and district. Interestingly, they cannot carry a village or vineyard name, and have to pass a tasting test. It is hoped that initially the "Baden Selection" wines that have passed the tasting examination will account for up to 3% of the regional harvest. The eventual target is a 10% share — possibly over two million cases. Wines similar to the "Baden Selection" range, of which there are many in the region and in Württemberg, have already won for some cooperative cellars the coveted entrée to good-quality restaurants.

WÜRTTEMBERG

The main part of the wine region of Württemberg lies between Stuttgart in the south and Heilbronn in the north, on both sides of the River Neckar. Much of the 10,314ha (25,486 acres) of planted vineyard is either on the steep, sometimes terraced slopes above the river and its tributaries, or on the south sides of wooded hills. There are six *Bereiche*, but the geographical origin of the wine is less important than the producer in most cases.

Grape varieties and wine styles
Nearly all Württemberg wine is drunk locally, and there is a strong demand in local cafés and stores for a kind of light red wine that in many wine countries would be called rosé.

Over half of the region is planted with red vines and a quarter with Riesling which, with the red varieties Trollinger and Lemberger, occupies most of the best sites. Riesling vineyards are scattered throughout the region but in a number of villages, such as Flein, south of Heilbronn, it has developed a good local reputation. After Riesling, Trollinger covers 22%, Schwarzriesling (Müllerrebe or Pinot Meunier) 15%, and Kerner, Müller-Thurgau, and Lemberger (or Limberger, as it is officially but infrequently spelt), have 9%, 8% and 7% respectively. Samtrot, a mutation of Schwarzriesling, is growing in 90ha (222 acres), and a little Frühburgunder (known here as Clevner) is also found.

Steep vineyards mean steep costs, which can be covered by producing a large amount of ordinary wine or a small amount of more expensive wine. In most cases growers go for a high yield — Trollinger reached an average of 222hl/ha in the exceptional 1989 vintage. The result is a pale red wine — by no means unpleasant as an everyday drink, but of no vinous distinction and short of everything that gives red wine its character. The cooperative cellars, which process 88% of the region's crop, can handle the vast supply of red grapes only by heating them and their juice to 85°C (185°F) for six minutes. The mash is cooled, pressed, centrifuged, further cooled to 18°C (64°F); cultured yeast is added, and fermentation starts. To correct their thinness, grape juice (*Süssreserve*) is blended in just before bottling for sale.

So in spite of its beautiful vineyards set in lovely countryside, its modern hygienic cooperatives where wines are made to a technically high standard, Württemberg is currently the most disappointing of western Germany's wine regions to outsiders. Nonetheless, the older Württembergers love their light red wines, which have no noticeable tannin. They identify closely with them, and the culture of "their" wine is strongly expressed through the region's promotional activities.

However, change is at hand, and the region's potential is being explored. Supermarkets, wholesalers, restaurants and cafés remain the biggest customers, but cooperative cellars would like to sell via wine merchants to those for whom wine is foreground, rather than background, music. So, like their comrades in Baden, at least 14 cooperative cellars are producing superior ranges.

The Württemberg vine that can most easily produce internationally acceptable, slightly tannic and deep-coloured red wine is the Lemberger — the Blaufränkisch of Austria. Like Dornfelder, it can have the weight to withstand being matured in new wood (often Swabian). Although a number of cooperatives now make *barrique*-aged wines, the lead is being given by a few private estates. □

PRODUCERS

The quality of the wine in Württemberg depends more on the aims of the producer than on the site in which the grapes are grown, though there are single sites, or at least parcels of vineyard, that are superior to others. However, judged by the sameness of the selling prices, overproduction usually flattens any peaks of quality or individuality that might appear.

The cooperative cellars process 80% of the grapes. The biggest are the central cellars at Möglingen, north of Stuttgart. All the cooperatives send 15% of their crop to Möglingen, where there is storage capacity for three average vintages.

Apart from the premium wines made by the cooperatives, character and depth of flavour are found in some of the estate-bottled wines, including those of the nine producers who are members of the recently-formed Württemberg branch of the VDP (*see* p315).

Weingut Graf Adelmann at Burg Schaubeck is among the best known; probably more than any other, it shows how good Württemberg wine can be. The average yield from a range of vine varieties is 72hl/ha — compared to the regional figure of 109 hl/ha — and 99% of its wine is dry. Weingut Robert Bauer at Flein produces good, fully fermented wines that are aged in cask. Freiherrlich von Gemmingen-Hornberg'sches Weingut at Burg Hornberg dates from 1612, and uses traditional grape varieties such as Traminer. Schlosskellerei Graf von Neipperg at Schloss Schweigern near Heilbronn, a family estate since 1200, with 32ha (79 acres) of red and white varieties, makes mostly dry wines. Other leading producers include Weingut Ernst Dautel of Bönnigheim, which produces the best wines of the region, as well as Weingut Wöhrwag at Untertürkheim, Weingut Aldinger at Fellbach, Weingut Fürst zu Hohenlohe-Oehringen at Oehringen and Weingut Albrecht Schwegler at Korb.

SEKT

What the EC defines as quality sparkling wine is known in Germany as *Sekt*. In the early part of the century Kaiser Wilhelm II showed his faith in the strength and future of the German *Sekt* industry by imposing a tax upon it to finance the building of his battle fleet. Today, 75–80% of *Deutscher Sekt* is made from foreign base wine, as German wine is too expensive.

The annual consumption of sparkling wine in Germany of about five litres per head is probably the greatest in the world. The term "quality sparkling wine" is an EC deception depending on conditions so broad as to have little impact on the quality of the wine in the bottle. Nearly 98% of German-produced sparkling wine is classified as *Sekt*, and sells at low prices through the supermarkets of Germany. Only 1% of *Sekt* is sold for premium prices.

The major producers

There are nearly 800 *Sekt* manufacturers. The largest bottling plant in the world for sparkling wine, that of Peter Herres in Trier, fills 75,000 bottles every hour, but the majority (86%) of *Sekt* manufacturers produce less than 20,000 bottles each a year. The total annual German *Sekt* output amounts to 41 million cases, of which 60% is produced by just three producers: Henkell-Söhnlein, the Reh group and Seagrams.

The *Sekt* producers are sited in every wine region. The biggest concentration is in the Rheingau, but a study of the industry has identified five producers in the former East German wine regions, and at least one in every other region.

In Germany the preferred style of *Sekt* is what the EC likes to call "dry", which, in the case of sparkling wine, means that it contains between 17 and 35 grams per litre of residual

A *Sekt* merchant in the Pfalz.

sugar. Those who venture into the world of better-quality *Sekt* prefer versions that are *brut* (0–15 grams per litre). These, for the most part, will bear a vintage and be produced from a single vine variety grown in Germany, with Riesling the most popular choice and Weissburgunder gaining ground. They may also be sold under a narrower geographical name than that of the region or district.

Production methods

Until about the mid-1980s, the container in which a *Sekt* developed its sparkle through a second fermentation was not of interest in Germany. Three methods are used: fermentation in tank; in the bottle then disgorged under pressure into vats for bottling; or in the bottle in which it will be sold.

Most opinions about the relative merits of these alternatives are likely to be hopelessly slanted to a commercial interest, but it seems that the type of container is not a quality factor. More important are the suitability of the base wine (high acidity and no strong or "off" flavours), the

choice of yeast and the length of time the wine stays on it — and the wine-making philosophy and dedication of the manufacturer.

Winzersekt

Many producers of still wine offer *Sekt* made from their own base wine either by themselves, or on their behalf by a *Sekt* manufacturer. As production is usually small, fermentation in bottle is ideal and so a virtue is made out of a necessity. The small estate sells its *Sekt* production to its still-wine customers who, unlike the average *Sekt* drinker, are interested in the minutiae of winemaking. For them, a wine produced by the method made famous by champagne has an added value.

Having started in a very small way in the 1980s, about 500,000 cases of this growers' *Sekt*, or *Winzersekt*, are now sold annually at relatively high prices, well above those of the mass-produced *Sekte*.

A producers' association which is based at Sprendlingen, with some 700 members, sells a range of locally-grown *Sekte* — perhaps the only truly successful part of the Rheinhessen wine trade in the 1990s. There is a similar organization on the Saar, and many cooperatives throughout Germany include *Winzersekt* in the programme.

The steady expansion of the *Sekt* industry since the 1950s has been remarkable, and interrupted only temporarily by the effect of increased taxation. However, *Sekt* does not enjoy a good reputation, whether in Germany or elsewhere. Connoisseurs are likely to question the base vine and industrial methods employed for producing most of these sparkling wines. Despite these shortcomings, there are some producers of excellent *Sekt*, such as Menger Krug at Gau Odenheim.   □

THE BENELUX COUNTRIES

DESPITE THEIR NORTHERLY POSITION, BELGIUM, THE NETHERLANDS
AND LUXEMBOURG ALL PRODUCE WINE. LUXEMBOURG PRODUCES
SOME GOOD-QUALITY WHITE AND SPARKLING WINES.

Luxembourg's main vineyard zone is along the valley of the
Moselle, where the vines enjoy good south-eastern aspects
and well-drained sloping sites. This vineyard is close to
Grevenmacher in the north of the zone.

The Benelux coun-
tries do not readily
spring to mind as wine-
producing regions, espe-
cially as they are
situated at what is gen-
erally considered to be
the northern limit of
vine cultivation — at
50–53° North. However,
Luxembourg's Moselle
vineyards are thriving.
Belgian and Dutch
wines, on the other
hand, are something of
an enigma: small pock-
ets of vineyards give the
lie to both nations' more famous beermaking. And
if at present these are just for home consumption,
and often made by enthusiasts rather than strictly
commercially, this was not always so. Although
Belgium lost most of its vineyards – established by
the Romans along the Sambre and Meuse valleys,
and around Leuven (Louvain) – after the French
Revolution, Liège's vineyards were saved by order
of Napoleon Bonaparte. And in 1914 the Germans
destroyed these remaining vineyards, which they
saw as direct competition with the Mittelrhein
region. The destruction of Belgium's vineyards is
historically unfortunate, although the wines did not
aspire to more than everyday quality. The few
authors who have ventured to write about Belgian

wines have not been
kind, suggesting that
they were an acidic and
short-lived beverage that
did not travel (though,
to be fair, few could).
The history of the vine
in Luxembourg, like that
of the country itself, is
relatively untroubled. It
was introduced by the
Romans, when the main
plantings were, as they
are today, on the well-
placed slopes of the
Mosel Valley, the source
of some of Germany's
best-known wines. The vineyards survived the
French Revolution and the Napoleonic Wars that
followed, and made extraordinary progress in the
late 19th century, when local producers were able to
export their wines. The two main grape varieties,
Riesling and Elbling, both white, made the base
wine for German sparkling wines, and certain big
champagne houses also used base wine from Luxembourg. Luxembourg's growers bought more and
more land and became enormously prosperous.
World War I put a brutal end to this wealth, but
after the war the country formed an economic
union with Belgium, which allowed the vinegrowers once again to export a large part of their production, this time to Belgium.

Belgium

Today, around 100 growers make wine in Belgium although the total vineyard area is only about 30ha (74 acres), and the source of good wine is often a well-kept local secret. A few small vineyards have made a name, but only within Belgium.

The main production zones are at Torgny on the banks of the Meuse, at Huy and Saing, at Charleroi and in the Hageland, near Leuven, the only region with vineyards of any size (up to 5ha/12 acres). Hobby vinegrowers are scattered throughout the country. The area name, for example Hagelander or Torgny, is usually prominent on the bottle, although there are no appellation laws in force, or specific labelling requirements other than the basic EC rules.

Most of the vines are either Pinot Noir, for red wine, or Müller-Thurgau, for white, and the wines are best drunk young, at no more than three or four years old.

The Netherlands

There are three commercial vineyards in the Netherlands, two in the extreme south near Maastricht and one further north in Brabant. The main grape varieties are Riesling, Auxerrois, Müller-Thurgau and Optima, a cross between Müller-Thurgau and Silvaner. The white wines are fresh and light in style, akin to those of Luxembourg.

Luxembourg

Luxembourg is one of the smallest of the world's wine-producing countries, yet it has 1,350ha (3,340 acres) planted with vines, a greater area than England. It produces a large amount of wine, thanks to yields of more than 118hl/ha. The Luxembourgeois are great wine drinkers, consuming 60 litres per person annually.

The Moselle Valley, where the majority of the vineyards are situated, has a subsoil of limestone. Its slopes have ideal, south-facing exposures and regular gradients. The river moderates temperatures and the

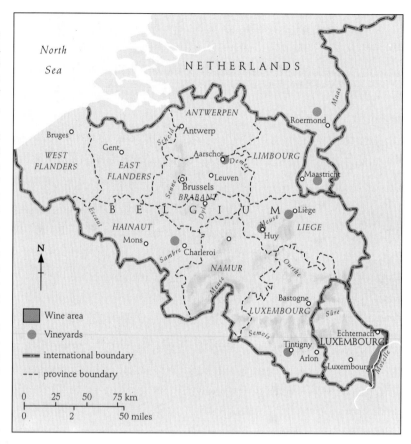

reflection of light off the water helps the grapes to ripen. Luxembourg's vineyards face those of the Upper Mosel in Germany (see p323). They were modernized after the phylloxera outbreak of the 1920s.

Since the 1960s winemaking has made enormous progress, not just in quantity but also in quality. During this period the number of individual winemakers has greatly decreased. Today, 70% of production is from cooperatives, 15% from individual producers; the remaining 15% is from individual growers who sell all their production to *négociants*.

The main grape variety is Rivaner, the local name for Müller-Thurgau, which makes simple, everyday wines and accounts for one-third of plantings. Other varieties are Riesling, Pinot Auxerrois, Pinot Gris, Pinot Blanc and Elbling (12% of plantings). These grapes, all white-wine varieties, make very light wines

that are used as a base for sparkling wines. White wine (still and sparkling) accounts for 99% of Luxembourg's production. The 1% of red wine is made from Pinot Noir.

The *marque nationale*, which corresponds to France's *appellation d'origine contrôlée*, was created in 1935 under the aegis of the Ministry of Agriculture and Viticulture. It was followed in 1985 by the appellation Moselle Luxembourgeoise and in 1991 by the appellation Crémant du Luxembourg (Saint-Rémy cellar at Remich).

An official quality category is established during labelling. Wines tasted by a jury are given marks out of 20. Those awarded 18 to 20 points become *Premiers Grands Crus*, those with 16 to 17.9 *Premiers Crus*, those with 14 to 15.9 points *Vins Classés*; and with 12 to 13.9, *Vins sans mention*. Wines with fewer than 12 points are labelled *Vin de table*. □

SWITZERLAND

SWISS WINES ARE MOSTLY DRUNK LOCALLY BY A PROSPEROUS, WINE-
LOVING NATION. PRICES HAVE ALWAYS BEEN HIGH; STANDARDS ARE
RISING AS OUTSIDE INFLUENCES PENETRATE THE ALPINE VALLEYS.

The village of Aigle, in the Chablais district of the canton of
Vaud, has vineyards on southwest-facing slopes above the
Rhône. Some of Switzerland's best-known wines are
produced here.

Efficiency has long been a necessity in the vineyards of Switzerland, where demand for wine far exceeds the amount that can be produced in often difficult terrain: the Swiss each drink about 20 litres of their own and some 30 litres of imported wine a year. Vineyards clinging to south-facing slopes along the river valleys, and beside lakes (which reflect heat), are difficult to cultivate, and the high production costs make Swiss wine expensive. In the past the drive for efficiency, with excessive use of fertilizers and over-production, often resulted in wines with little acidity. Yields for the better wines are now legally restricted, although some people feel that 112hl/ha is still too much if vines are not to become exhausted too soon.

The average size of vineyard holding — less than half a hectare (1.2 acres) — is one-third of the figure for the EC; most growers leave winemaking to large wineries or cooperative cellars. There is also a growing number of small estate-bottlers, often managed by young people from the viticultural schools of Wädenswil and Changins. For years most wine was simply an everyday drink, but today

training and experience gained elsewhere in Europe and the New World are helping to produce Swiss wines of a quality previously unknown. Vines are grown in most parts, making both red and white wines, but the most important vineyards are found in the French-speaking cantons of Valais and Vaud. Almost all Swiss wines are dry and 56% is white. The main white grape in the French cantons is Chasselas, which generally produces a wine to be drunk within three years, but can surprise by being more than drinkable after 25. To avoid tasting flat it is bottled with some of the natural carbon dioxide retained in the wine. Relatively neutral in taste, good Chasselas can show character and flavour from its soil. In the German-speaking cantons the predominant white variety is Riesling-Sylvaner — the Swiss name for Müller-Thurgau. Pinot Noir, known here as Blauburgunder, is the country's top red grape. It also makes Œil de Perdrix ("partridge eye"), a pale rosé, in the French-speaking cantons. But in the warmer Italian canton of Ticino, Merlot reigns supreme to make some of the country's best reds.

WINE REGIONS OF SWITZERLAND

Away from the steepest of the Alps, vines are grown throughout Switzerland, especially along the many lakes and rivers, which moderate the climate throughout the year. The most extensive vineyards, in the French-speaking cantons, produce white wines from Chasselas grapes, red wines from Pinot Noir and, in Valais, the blend based on Pinot Noir called Dôle. The German-speaking cantons in the north and east tend to make wines for drinking very young; whites from Riesling-Sylvaner (Müller-Thurgau), and reds from Blauburgunder (Pinot Noir). In the south, on the Italian border, the warmer climate ripens Merlot grapes to make fruity red wines.

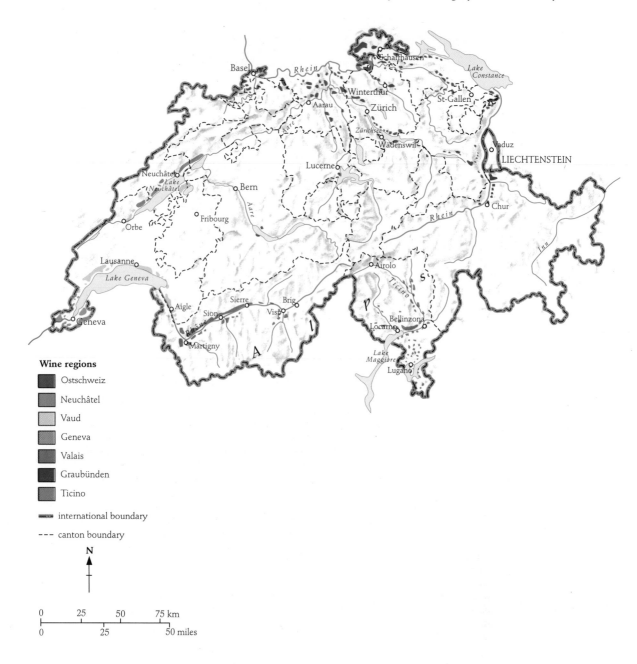

Wine regions

- Ostschweiz
- Neuchâtel
- Vaud
- Geneva
- Valais
- Graubünden
- Ticino

▬▬ international boundary

--- canton boundary

N

| 0 | 25 | 50 | 75 km |
| 0 | | 25 | 50 miles |

REGIONS AND PRODUCERS

Three-quarters of the Confederation's 15,000ha (37,000 acres) of vineyard lie in French Switzerland (Suisse Romande). There are 1,300ha (3,200 acres) in the Italian-speaking canton of Ticino, and the rest is spread over 17 cantons of German-speaking Switzerland. The area of the Swiss vineyard has increased by 20% since the 1960s, with the largest wine-producing canton, Valais, growing by a third.

FRENCH-SPEAKING CANTONS

The west of Switzerland, where its frontier meets that of France, produces the most interesting wine. Valais and Vaud have by far the largest areas under vine, and Geneva and Neuchâtel also produce substantial quantities.

In the French-speaking cantons, there has been a gradual introduction of new grape varieties developed by the research station at Changins: Diolinoir (Diolly x Pinot Noir), Gamaret and Garanoir (Gamay x Reichensteiner) are red-wine varieties, and Charmont and Doral, crossbreeds of Chasselas and Chardonnay, are white-white varieties.

Valais

Valais has 5,250ha (12,970 acres) under vine on the lower slopes of its surrounding mountains. Starting at 1,000m (3,300ft) above sea level, in some of the highest vineyards in Europe, at Visperterminen, the vineyards follow the young River Rhône until its sharp bend at Martigny. Many of the vineyards are intensively planted, sometimes with as many as 15,000 vines per hectare (2.5 acres). Thus the yield per vine may be low, but per hectare it will border on the legal maximum for quality wine.

Valais can be hot and dry; the vineyards around Sierre survive on some 400mm (16 inches) of rain a year, occasionally helped by a little irrigation. Grapes ripen easily and when harvested there is not much difference in sugar content between those grown at 400m (1,320ft) and those at 800m (2,640ft).

The wines found most widely in Valais are the white Fendant (the local name for the Chasselas grape and its wine, which is at its most alcoholic — and expensive — here) and the red Dôle.

Dôle is an attractive Valais speciality — a fruity wine with adequate structure, best drunk within three years of the vintage. It is a blend of Pinot Noir and Gamay harvested at the same time, with Pinot Noir playing the major rôle.

In the absence of fogs, and therefore with less risk of rot, Pinot Noir is a useful vine for Valais — provided it is not grown in the warmest sites. Clones from Burgundy or Switzerland produce wines with adequate acidity and, therefore, structure — unlike many of the wines of the mid-1980s and earlier, which suffered from over-production. Well-trained growers now no longer wait for very high must weights, but harvest when the grapes have 12–13% of potential alcohol and a satisfactory level of acidity. The result is wine that can develop in bottle over a number of years.

Whether it is better to grow Chardonnay and other recently imported vines or to concentrate on traditional varieties is a philosophical and marketing question to which producers find different answers. Those who favour indigenous varieties have some interesting vines to choose from in Valais. Humagne Rouge (there is also a white version) is an exuberant vine; from a crop not larger than 80hl/ha at the most, the wine can be robust, and concentrated enough to withstand ageing in new wooden casks of about 225 litres (*barriques*). Its tannic flavour reminds some tasters of Barolo (*see* p359). In a climate almost as warm as that of the northern section of the Côtes du Rhône, the Syrah grape is also grown.

Grapes from the ancient Valaisan white vine varieties, Amigne and Petite Arvine, and the red Cornalin, ripen late — in October. Carefully produced from small yields, they have much character, the white wines tasting rich and fruity. For sweeter and sometimes highly alcoholic wine, Valais has its Malvoisie (the local name for Pinot Gris) — the most expensive of the canton's traditional wines. Production of these specialities is small.

Good producers in Valais include Charles Bonvin, Simon Maye, Domaine du Mont d'Or and Rouvinez.

Vaud

As the River Rhône leaves Valais and enters Vaud, vineyards continue along its valley, then follow the northern shores of Lake Geneva; it is the considerable presence of the lake that creates the region's temperate climate.

Vaud has 3,850ha (9,510 acres) under vine, divided into five districts: Chablais, Lavaux, La Côte, Côtes de l'Orbe-Bonvillars and Vully, the latter two forming enclaves nearer Lake Neuchâtel. Vaud has traditionally sold its wines under the names of top villages within each district — such as Mont-sur-Rolle, Féchy, Aigle, Epesses, St-Saphorin, Dézaley

---

READING A SWISS WINE LABEL

Wine labelling in Switzerland has in the past been very much at the whim of the producer: wines have been labelled by place name, grape variety or a brand name. Since 1993, wine-producing cantons have introduced *Appellation d'origine contrôlée* regulations which are inspired by the French system. A great deal of legislation is left to individual cantons. There are, therefore, a great number of appellations: 32 in the canton of Geneva and 19 in that of Neuchâtel, which apply to 18 villages. Wine from Chasselas is thus called Dorin in Vaud, Fendant in Valais, and Perlan in Geneva. The red AOC Salvagnin of Vaud is labelled AOC Dôle in Valais (Pinot-Gamay), while the rosé is called Œil de Perdrix in Neuchâtel (and Perdrix Blanche for the Blancs de Noirs). Wines made from rare grape varieties are called Spécialité. Most of them are excellent and rather expensive.

and Yvorne — and these are well-known in Switzerland.

The Chablais covers the right bank of the Rhône, until the river joins Lake Geneva, with vineyards on southwest-facing slopes in villages such as Aigle, Bex, Ollon, Villeneuve and Yvorne. Its white wines, from Chasselas, combine a taste from the soil with the gentle fruitiness of this grape variety.

East of Lausanne, the steep and tidy Chasselas vineyards of the Lavaux are among the most beautiful in Europe. In the warmth reflected by the stone terracing, Pinot Noir is also grown to produce an agreeable but usually not very complex wine. Top villages here include Dézaley, Epesses, Lutry, Rivaz and St-Saphorin.

West of Lausanne, where most of the wines are made by cooperative or merchants' cellars, the district of La Côte is dotted with attractive houses; the vines surrounding them are on rolling or gently-sloping ground, allowing for the use of mechanical harvesters. Again, the grapes are Chasselas for stylish white wines and Pinot Noir for gentle, drinkable reds. Well-known villages include Féchy and Mont-sur-Rolle.

The best producers of this region are the Association Viticole Aubonne, Badoux & Chevalley, Louis Bovard, Henri Cruchon, Hammel, Obrist and J & P Testuz.

Geneva

Vineyards of 1,350ha (3,335 acres) adjoin those of Vaud, north of the lake. About half the production is of white wine from the Chasselas grape (known locally as Perlan), which here takes its light, elegant character from the mineral-rich clay and limestone soil. White wines are also made from the Burgundy varieties, Aligoté and Chardonnay, and light reds from the Gamay of Beaujolais.

Neuchâtel

In cooler parts of the country such as Neuchâtel, where the vineyards (600ha/1480 acres) reach up to 580m (1,900ft), height above sea level helps to determine the ripeness of the crop and the date of the harvest. The climate is tempered by Lake Neuchâtel, and the limestone hills north of the lake can, in good vintages, produce attractive Pinot Noir reds and rosés. The Chasselas grown here makes lively, slightly sparkling white wine.

LIECHTENSTEIN

The principality of Liechtenstein lies between eastern Switzerland and Austria. It was founded in 1719, consisting of the lordships of Schellenberg and Vaduz. In 1921, it adopted a new constitution which considerably reinforced its economic ties with neighbouring Switzerland.

Between the houses of Liechtenstein there are some 15ha (37 acres) of vineyard, owned mainly by the country's prince, Fürst Hans Adam II. His estate cellars, the Hofkellerei des Fürsten von Liechtenstein at Vaduz, are known in central Europe for their Chardonnay wine from low-yielding vines, and for Pinot Noir from old vines. The wines are similar in style and structure to those from the neighbouring cantons of German-speaking Switzerland.

GERMAN-SPEAKING SWITZERLAND

Although much of Switzerland is German-speaking, winemaking is concentrated in the cantons near the border with Germany — a region known as Ostschweiz (east Switzerland). Wines from the Ostschweiz region are generally drunk within a year of the vintage; white wines are mainly from Riesling-Sylvaner (Müller-Thurgau) and reds from Blauburgunder (Pinot Noir, which is also known as Clevner or Beerli).

The *Föhn*, a warm breeze from the Alps, helps to ripen Blauburgunder. The old white varieties, the aromatic Completer and the elegant Räuschling, are grown to a very limited extent. Scattered throughout the region are growers who are trying to make wines with more structure than in the past — using Pinot Noir for red wines and Chardonnay for whites. *Barrique*-ageing is not uncommon.

The largest wine-producing cantons are Zürich and Schaffhausen (although even they buy much white wine from Valais). Most of Zürich's crop is handled by two cooperative cellars in Wädenswil and Winterthur. Some 200 growers also deliver their grapes to the Staatskellereien des Kantons Zürich, the state-owned cellars. Wine is often made on very small estates linked to a restaurant where the wine is sold; apart from the co-ops, one of the best-known producers is Kühn.

ITALIAN-SPEAKING SWITZERLAND

The canton of Ticino (also known as Tessin), in southern Switzerland, is predominantly Italian-speaking. This canton of high unemployment and mountains is known for its red wines made from Merlot grapes, first introduced to the region in 1897. Ticino's hot summers are not well suited to white-wine production, and only 3% of the vineyard area is planted in white-wine varieties (Chasselas, Sémillon, Sauvignon Blanc). Some growers, however, produce white and rosé wine from Merlot and Pinot Noir.

Merlot del Ticino is usually a soft, easy-drinking wine, although some examples are aged in new oak casks for a more complex result, and Cabernet Sauvignon has been introduced to replicate a Bordeaux-style *assemblage* with Merlot. The official "ViTi" badge used to guarantee quality, but some respected producers now disregard the ViTi tasting; according to the wine magazine *Alles über Wein*: "The great days of the ViTi badge are well and truly past. Created in 1949 to protect the quality of Ticino wines, it now stands for controlled mediocrity."

The best wines are those of merchants or small estate-bottlers rather than cooperatives. The best producers are Agriloro, Guido Brivio, Tamborini and Vinattieri Ticinesi.

GRAUBÜNDEN

The canton of Graubünden, or Grisons, where vines were first grown 2000 years ago, has about 300ha (740 acres) of vineyard. Some vineyards are located near the town of Croire, with most of the rest between Croire and Liechtenstein.

Grape varieties are those planted in the French-speaking cantons, as well as several local varieties: the Completer and the Räuschling are two white-wine varieties, and there are even two rather good hybrids, the Seyval Blanc and the Léon Millot (R), which are mainly cultivated in England. The little-known wines of Graubünden are amazingly good.

Good producers include von Tscharner at Schloss Reichenau.

AUSTRIA

SPICY DRY WHITES, OUTSTANDING RICH DESSERT WINES AND
FULL-BODIED REDS — THE QUALITY OF THE WINES NOW ON OFFER
FROM AUSTRIA JUST GETS BETTER AND BETTER.

Old and new: a traditional wooden winepress stands before model rows of carefully-trained vines at an Austrian wine school. A new generation of young winemakers is bringing fresh thinking to Austrian wine.

Grapes have been grown in Austria since before the days of the Romans and this has been confirmed by the discovery of seeds from the *vitis vinifera* dating from the Celtic period. Strengthened by a tradition with its roots firmly in the eastern half of the country, the different vineyards offer a multitude of grape varieties and very distinctive wine styles, which explains the great variety among Austrian wines. Austria is first and foremost a white-wine country. Riesling ripens beautifully in the Wachau and Kamptal-Kremstal regions to give wines that are rich but not sweet. Austria's indigenous white variety, Grüner Veltliner, is widely planted and produces light, peppery wines; and in the Wachau and the neighbouring Kamptal, the grape sometimes gives wines as powerful as the Rieslings. The much cooler Steiermark (Styria) region is the kingdom of aromatic whites; Weissburgunder (Pinot Blanc), Welschriesling, Morillon (Chardonnay), Muskateller, Traminer and brilliant Muskat-Sylvaner (Sauvignon Blanc).

Like everywhere else, great strides have been made to improve the quality of red wines. After a brief infatuation with the ubiquitous Cabernet Sauvignon, winemakers are now refocusing on their indigenous varieties: Blaufränkisch (or Lemberger in Germany and Kékfrankos in Hungary), the St-Laurent and the Zweigelt, a cross between the previous two varieties. The Pinot Noir and Blauer Portugieser are also encountered. The best reds come from the region southeast of Vienna, Carnuntum, and above all from the Burgenland. The Burgenland is also the source of a vast range of exceptional sweet white botrytized wines. The wine scandal that crippled the industry in 1985 was uncovered here (chemicals were added to mimic "noble rot" sweetness). Learning its lesson from past errors, Austria adopted the strictest wine legislation in Europe, at the same time maintaining the specific character of its wines. This is the only country where, for example, you will encounter the bracing rosé called Schilcher or the powerful, spicy white Zierfandler. A young generation of winemakers, more receptive to the outside world and with a better knowledge of winemaking theory, have taken over and are determined to win Austria its place among the best wine-producing countries in the world.

WINE REGIONS OF AUSTRIA

Austria's wine is produced in the east of the country, in
four main zones: Niederösterreich (Lower Austria),
Wien (Vienna), Burgenland and Steiermark (Styria).
Within these zones are 16 delimited wine regions, or
Weinbaugebiet.

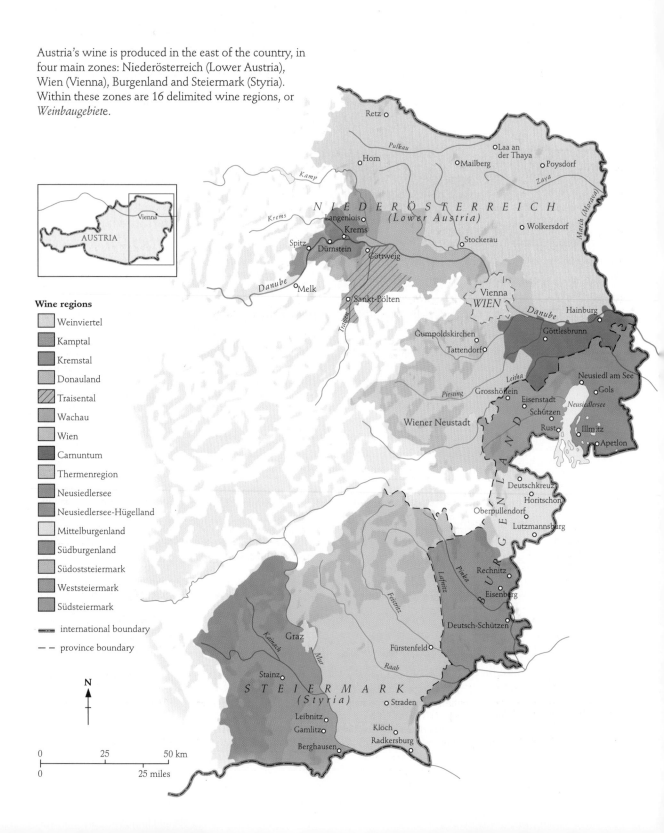

AUSTRIA

Wine regions

- Weinviertel
- Kamptal
- Kremstal
- Donauland
- Traisental
- Wachau
- Wien
- Carnuntum
- Thermenregion
- Neusiedlersee
- Neusiedlersee-Hügelland
- Mittelburgenland
- Südburgenland
- Südoststeiermark
- Weststeiermark
- Südsteiermark

 - - - international boundary
 - - - province boundary

N

0   25   50 km

0   25 miles

REGIONS AND PRODUCERS

The four main zones and the wine regions within them are discussed below in approximate order of importance. Some of the most reliable wine-producing firms are listed in alphabetical order under the regions.

NIEDERÖSTERREICH (LOWER AUSTRIA)

A wide province covering the north-east of the country, bisected by the Danube. Quality wines come from the Wachau hills, the best parts of the Kamptal-Kremstal and the Thermenregion, around the village of Gumpoldskirchen.

Wachau

With 1,448ha (3,580 acres) under vine, the Wachau is one of the smallest wine regions of Austria, but the source of the country's best white wines. The Grüner Veltliner and Riesling grape varieties dominate the area though you may also encounter Neuburger, Sauvignon Blanc and Müller-Thurgau (known locally as Riesling-Sylvaner). South-facing terraced vineyards skirt the Danube gorge for 16km (10 miles). Outstanding volcanic soils and micro-climates give wines that are mineral, powerful and delicately flavoured.

The Wachau has devised its own quality categories, which appear on the label. The lightest wine is *Steinfeder* (10.7% alcohol), followed by *Federspiel* (about 11.5%). The richest wines, equivalent to a German dry *Spätlese*, are designated *Smaragd* and have at least 12%; these are usually made from low-yielding, late-harvested grapes from outstanding sites, and can be world-class wines with considerable ageing potential. Vineyards of singular merit are often specified on the label, prefixed by the word *Ried*.

Top winemakers are Franz Hirtzberger, Emmerich Knoll, F X Pichler and Prager-Bodenstein, followed by Leo Alzinger, Nikolaihof, Josef Jamek, Rudolf Pichler and the Freie Weingärtner Wachau and Dinstlgut Loiben cooperatives.

Kamptal-Kremstal

This area, five times larger than the Wachau, follows the course of the Danube as far as the village of Krems and stretches out to the north towards Langenlois and to the south towards Göttweig Monastery. Riesling and Grüner Veltliner grown on volcanic soil give wines of similar style to the Wachau which, if not as powerful, can be more elegant. Loess terraces produce wines of greater body but less finesse which can also be of outstanding quality. Although white wine dominates, an increasing number of winemakers are turning out promising red *cuvées*.

Best producers include Willi Bründlmayer (excellent Chardonnay; outstanding Riesling and Veltliner), Jurtschitsch, Loimer, Malat, Mantlerhof, Nigl, Salomon and Schloss Gobelsburg.

Donauland-Traisental-Carnuntum

This peculiar region, cut in two by the city of Vienna and following the Danube from east of Krems to the Slovak border, is difficult to define. The soil is often stony, with much clay and chalk. This is promising territory for red wines such as Zweigelt, especially from around the village of Göttlesbrunn.

Good producers here include Glatzer, Leth, Markowitsch, Neumayer, Pitnauer and Zimmermann.

READING AN AUSTRIAN WINE LABEL

All Austrian labels must carry certain information.

The grape variety is usually prominent, indicating that at least 85% of the wine is made from the named variety.

The quality category must be stated. These are similar, but not identical, to German categories (*see* p312), beginning with *Tafelwein* (table wine) and *Landwein* (country wine). All *Qualitätswein* (quality wine) is subject to chemical analysis and tasting and must display a *Prüfnummer* (test number). This confirms that it meets certain standards, such as the sugar content of the must (potential alcohol). In addition to the basic *Qualitätswein* category,

wines can be (in increasing order of sweetness): *Kabinett, Spätlese, Auslese, Eiswein, Beerenauslese, Ausbruch, Trockenbeerenauslese*.

Residual sugars must be mentioned as follows: *trocken* (dry) corresponds to a maximum 9g/l, *halbtrocken* (medium-dry) to 12 g/l, *halbsüss* or *lieblich* (medium-sweet) has 45g/l and *süss* (sweet) has over 45g/l.

The region of origin is indicated on all Qualitätswein. This may be one of the 16 *Weinbaugebiete* (wine-producing regions), a village name or a specific vineyard. Whichever name is used, 100% of the wine must originate there.

Weinviertel

Accounting for 31% of Austria's grape production, the Weinviertel is the largest of the wine regions. It sprawls north and north-west of Vienna, with most wines made in a light, easy-to-drink style.

Some northern producers have decided to concentrate on *Eiswein* production. Much of the Weinviertel enjoys a dry climate that is suited to the gamble involved in this pursuit.

Good producers include Malteser Ritterorden (now part of the Lenz Moser group), Erich Nebenführ, Roman Pfaffl and Helmut Taubenschuss.

Thermenregion

At the heart of this region south of Vienna stands the famous village of Gumpoldskirchen which, although accounting for only 0.5% of all Austrian vineyards, has for many years been a great national favourite. The best wines are the result of a blend of the two local grape varieties, the Zierfandler and the Rotgipfler, which gives a spicy, full-flavoured medium-dry white. A good Gumpoldskirchen is a memorable wine, full of character.

South of Gumpoldskirchen, other vineyards such as Tattendorf are becoming well known for their excellent reds. More and more of the land formerly used to grow the rather ordinary, high-yielding Blauer Portugieser is being given over to the Zweigelt, Cabernet Sauvignon, Blaufränkisch and Saint-Laurent varieties. This latter grape variety, just as tricky to cultivate and vinify as its cousin the Pinot Noir, can produce well-rounded, very elegant wines.

The best producers include Karl Alphart, Manfred Biegler, Franz Kurz, Gottfried Schellmann, Johann Reinisch and Erich Schneider.

BURGENLAND

Accounting for over one third of the country's vinegrowing area, this region — the warmest in Austria — produces red wines (22%), white wines and outstanding dessert wines.

Neusiedlersee-Hügelland

This region stretches from Vienna to the shallow Neusiedlersee. The climate here is excellent and the humidity rising from the lake in Autumn encourages the formation of *botrytis cinerea*, allowing for the production of superb dessert wines. The historic town of Rust is famous for its Ruster Ausbruch, a dessert wine which has been made here for four centuries. Austrian wine law stipulates than an *Ausbruch* should come from grapes with a sugar content somewhere between that of a *Beerenauslese* and a *Trockenbeerenauslese*. For Rust however, this also defines the style of the wine, which is lighter than a *Trockenbeerenauslese* as the fermentation is taken a stage further. Varieties such as the Weissburgunder (Pinot Blanc), the Welschriesling and the Ruländer (Pinot Gris) produce fabulous botrytized wines, as can the Sauvignon, the Neuburger, the Furmint and the Muskateller. The region also produces a range of interesting reds with the Blaufränkisch and Zweigelt standing alongside Cabernet Sauvignons and Merlots.

The best producers include Feiler-Artinger, Kollwentz, Leberl, Prieler, Schandl, Schönberger, Franz Sommer, Rosi Schuster, Ernst Triebaumer and Wenzel.

Neusiedlersee

Between the opposite shores of the lake and Hungary stands the Neusiedlersee region, also known as the Seewinkel. This relatively new vinegrowing region surrounding the villages of Gols, Illmitz and Apetlon covers such a large area that it now accounts for 20% of Austrian wine production.

Here we find the same favourable climatic conditions as in Neusiedlersee-Hügelland, but the sandy soil on the shores of the lake produces wines which are low in acidity. Nearer the village of Gols, however, the soil changes to a composition well-suited to the cultivation of red grape varieties. In warm years, the southern part of the vineyard produces large quantities of botrytized wines. This region now produces a vast range of appellation wines including Chardonnay, barrique-aged Pinot Noir, Schilfweine (made from grapes which have been air-dried on reeds) and some amazing botrytized wines.

There are some remarkably good producers such as Paul Achs, Kracher, Helmut Lang, H & A Nittnaus, Pöckl, Stiegelmayr and Umathum. Also worthy of mention are Gsellmann, Haider, Gernot Heinrich, Velich and the Pannobile production consortium.

Mittelburgenland

South of Neusiedlersee-Hügelland, 95% of this region is planted with red grape varieties, in particular the Blaufränkisch. This variety, which is often blended with Cabernet Sauvignon for added tannin content, can produce unusual, complex reds. This region seems set to become a reliable source of well-structured red wines.

The best producers include Gesellmann, Iby, Igler, Kerschbaum, Kirnbauer, Wellanschitz, Weninger and the cooperative in the village of Horitschon.

Südburgenland

Although geographically large, the Südburgenland accounts for a mere 0.8% of Austria's vineyards. Like the Mittelburgenland it would seem best suited to red wine production.

Good producers include Paul Grosz, Hermann Krutzler and Schutzenhof.

STEIERMARK (STYRIA)

South of the Alps and bordering on Slovenia, Styria is split for wine-producing purposes into three unequal parts: Süd (south), Süd-Ost (south-east) and West Steiermark.

Südsteiermark

The finest wines of Styria come from here. Although the smallest area, more vines are planted here (1,561ha/3,850 acres) than in the other two regions of Styria combined. Its white wines are as prized, and as expensive, as those from the Wachau, though the Südsteiermark wines are made in an entirely different style. The climate is harsher and prone to spring frosts and hail. The wines are both delicate in structure and high in acidity. Only those from low yields attain sufficient maturity to balance the wine, which can have vigour and elegance.

A wide range of varieties is cultivated, including Weissburgunder (Pinot Blanc, known here as Klevner), Riesling, Morillon (Chardonnay), and the popular Welschriesling, as well as Ruländer, Traminer and Muskateller.

Sauvignon Blanc has been planted with immense success here, producing racy, grassy white wines of distinctive varietal character.

Outstanding producers are Polz, Sattler and Manfred Tement, as well as Alois Gross and Lackner-Tinnacher.

Südoststeiermark

Almost as large as the Weinviertel, Südoststeiermark accounts for 1.7% of Austria's vineyards, most close to the Slovenian border. The mix of grape varieties is similar to that of Südsteiermark.

Good producers are Albert Neumeister, Gräflich Stürgkh'sches Weingut and Winkler-Hermaden.

Weststeiermark

Between Graz and the Slovenian border, Weststeiermark has only 280ha (692 acres) of vines, and produces Schilcher, a rosé made from the indigenous Blauer Wildbacher grape. It is characterized by very high acidity and, according to the skill of the winemaker, can be vibrantly refreshing or uncomfortably sharp. It is best drunk young. Its rarity and modishness make Schilcher much sought-after. Some of the best examples of Schilcher come from Erich Kuntner and Günter Müller.

WIEN (VIENNA)

The capital is surrounded by 700ha (1,730 acres) of vines and almost all the wine is consumed locally. In the wine villages on the fringes of Vienna are dozens of *Heurigen*, inns where growers sell their own wines. Most of this light, racy white wine is from the last vintage, and can be of high quality, especially from top sites such as the Nussberg and Bisamberg.

Grüner Veltliner is the most popular grape, but there is some excellent Riesling and Weissburgunder (Pinot Blanc) too. Much of the wine consumed in *Heurigen* is *Gemischter Satz* — a blend of different varieties grown together in the same vineyard.

Good producers include Fuhrgassl-Huber, Johann Kattus (faintly fizzy wines), Franz Mayer, Herbert Schilling and Fritz Wieninger.

ITALY

—

THE ANCIENT GREEKS CALLED ITALY OENOTRIA, THE LAND OF WINE.

GRAPES ARE STILL GROWN THROUGHOUT THE COUNTRY,

AND THE VARIETY OF WINES CONTINUES TO CHALLENGE

AND DELIGHT THE WINE LOVER.

—

The sun-drenched shores of the Mediterranean saw the birth of a number of ancient wine civilizations. Nowadays the vine is still cultivated from one end of Italy to the other and the diversity of its wines is a challenge — and delight — for enthusiasts. Italy and France share the top slot for worldwide and European production. Italy also makes more kinds of wine, with more names, than anywhere else in the world. This profusion stems from the ubiquity of the vine. Virtually every peasant plot and grand estate grows grapes for wine. Every region of this diverse and locally loyal country protects and promotes its own wine names. The result is nearly 300 officially-recognized wine zones, and around one million wine producers. Italy makes every style of wine, including fortified and sparkling, and exploits its myriad micro-climates and sites to add a further layer of variety. The following pages divide Italy into three broad zones: the north, the centre, and the south and islands. The north covers a ring of wine districts from north-west to north-east, mostly in the foothills of the Alps and Apennines. Here are found the quality wines of Piedmont, such as Barolo and Barbaresco, extensive sparkling-wine vineyards, and a range of districts making red and, particularly, white wines. The influence of foreign, especially German and French, wine styles and grape varieties is felt here to a greater extent than elsewhere in Italy. The centre covers the districts in and around Tuscany, whose Chianti vineyards form Italy's most important

Bottles of Chianti dating from 1958 in the cellars of the Selvapiana estate in Pontassieve. Selvapiana, known for its long-lived wines, is in the small Chianti Rufina zone north-east of Florence.

quality wine-producing region. In coastal regions, previously considered unsuitable for quality wine production, and the neighbouring foothills, new terroirs are actively seeking a place in the sun. This quality fever is also making its mark on neighbouring regions, from Umbria to the Marches and Abruzzo. The southern part of peninsular Italy and the islands of Sicily and Sardinia still follow the older wine traditions of the Mediterranean, with sweet, strong wines, powerful reds and specialities such as marsala. These areas have shown spectacular progress over the last few years. Italian wine is changing fast, with international grape varieties, techniques and ideas merging with native ones. Having devoted all its efforts in the 1980s and 90s to the successful production of great Cabernet Sauvignons and Chardonnays, the Italian wine world is now experiencing a swing towards native varieties. This is partly due to a natural affinity to its particularly remarkable heritage but also, and probably more so, due to the realisation that this heritage is a major asset in the current fiercely competitive international market. Wine legislation, which served well for two decades after its introduction in 1963, became outdated in some respects. In 1992 a new law improved the regulations. While these advances are welcome, the conundrum of what an Italian wine is actually like in style and taste, beyond the bare legal requirements, can be solved only by reference to the producer's name.

WINE REGIONS OF ITALY

At present, there are almost 300 *denominazione di origine controllata* (DOC) zones in the 20 administrative regions of Italy.

The colours on the map group the wine regions of the north, centre and south, which are mapped in more detail on pages 364, 380 and 394 respectively.

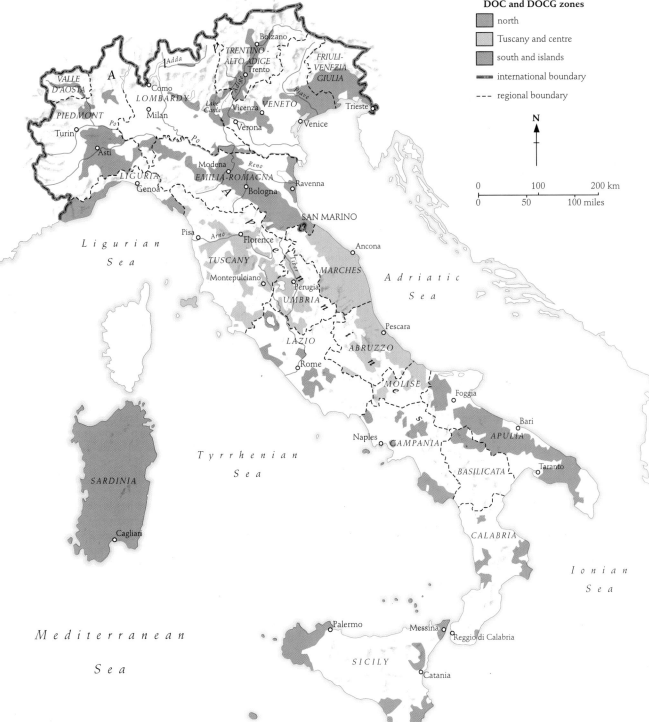

DOC and DOCG zones

- north
- Tuscany and centre
- south and islands
- ▬▬ international boundary
- --- regional boundary

N

0		100		200 km
0	50		100 miles	

VALLE D'AOSTA

Como

Adda

Bolzano

TRENTINO - ALTO ADIGE

Trento

FRIULI - VENEZIA GIULIA

LOMBARDY

Milan

Lake Garda

Vicenza

VENETO

Verona

Trieste

Venice

PIEDMONT

Turin

Po

Asti

Po

LIGURIA

Genoa

Modena

Reno

EMILIA-ROMAGNA

Bologna

Ravenna

SAN MARINO

L i g u r i a n   S e a

Pisa

Arno

Florence

Ancona

TUSCANY

Montepulciano

MARCHES

A d r i a t i c   S e a

Perugia

UMBRIA

Pescara

LAZIO

ABRUZZO

Rome

MOLISE

Foggia

T y r r h e n i a n   S e a

Naples

CAMPANIA

Bari

APULIA

SARDINIA

BASILICATA

Taranto

Cagliari

CALABRIA

I o n i a n   S e a

M e d i t e r r a n e a n   S e a

Palermo

Messina

Reggio di Calabria

S I C I L Y

Catania

The background to Italian wine

Italy's long history of winemaking has left it with a great legacy of superb individual wines, a further huge number of wines with enormous character, and a vast production of very ordinary wine. Until a generation ago this suited a country where wine exports were not a high priority, and where local loyalties meant that people naturally drank the wine of their province — even of their family. No Italian wine, with the possible exception of Chianti, was exposed to the pressures of the world marketplace in the way that the wines of Bordeaux, Burgundy or Champagne were tested.

The 1980s, and even more the 1990s, did however see Italy caught up in the internationalization of wine, with newly critical consumers at home and in export markets very much aware of the quality and value of New World and other European wines. Italian winemakers began to adopt new attitudes and techniques. The limitations of existing Italian wine law, and of indigenous grape varieties, were realized. At the same time the quality of some of Italy's great wines began to be appreciated in London, Paris, New York and elsewhere. Italy is still largely self-contained as a wine country: she grows her own grapes, and has very many varieties; drinks her own wine; and imports comparatively little — there has however been considerable advancement and this is set to continue.

Wine laws

Italian wine law is in a state of change as the limitations of the 1963 DOC law become apparent. This law, which was loosely based on the French AOC system, attempted with some success to codify Italy's thousands of wines. It introduced the idea of the DOC (*denominazione di origine controllata*) zone. This is an area where a certain style of wine is made in a distinctive way. Much weight was placed by the lawmakers on

winemaking tradition. A DOC (like an AOC in France) attempts to codify and regulate traditional practice. This works well in, say, Burgundy, where centuries of trial have isolated the best grape varieties and plots of land. But most of Italy is new to high-quality wine production. Many DOCs fossilized an outdated way of making poor wine. Others slanted the tradition away from quality: the Chianti DOC permitted 30% white grapes in this red wine, and (like many DOCs) allowed 10% of the wine in a blend to come from outside the Chianti zone — sometimes a long way outside. Happily, the 1984 upgrading of Chianti to DOCG (*see* box) tightened the rules.

A new law, passed in 1992, is still being put into effect and any changes this entails are far from finished. The new law is known as the Goria law, after Giovanni Goria, the minister who steered it through. The law clarifies the Italian scene considerably. It establishes, or rather tidies up, a pyramid of quality. At the lowest level is simple *vino da tavola*, basic wine that may be labelled red (*rosso*), white (*bianco*) or pink (*rosato*); but the grape or locality cannot be stated. The next grade is *indicazione geografica tipica* (IGT), similar to the French vin de pays: this is wine from a specific area, which may be vast (covering one or several regions) or very limited (a single commune) and the name of the grape variety may appear on the label. To date, 117 IGT wines have been recognized. Then come the DOC and DOCG names, as before. The Goria law makes it possible for under-used DOCs to be scrapped, and for successful ones to be promoted to DOCG. This is in line with the French system in which AOCs are constantly monitored and adapted when and where necessary.

A new departure is the use of vineyard, estate and commune names within DOCs and DOCGs. Previously, one DOCG covered the whole of Chianti, an area making as much wine as the Médoc and Graves

combined. There was no official provision for showing that a wine came from a given vineyard or commune, just the maker's name. The new law allows the mention (in diminishing order of size) of sub-zones, communes, localities, micro-zones, estates and even specific vineyards. An enormous exercise is going on to define and list all these areas. This restores the importance of location (or *terroir*) to the legal quality system.

Finally, the law allows wines to be assessed at harvest time. If they fail to meet certain standards they will be downgraded — for example from a specified sub-zone to the broad DOC name.

Wine regions

Italy's 20 administrative regions each have their vineyards and their own range of micro-climates and soils. The mountainous nature of much of the country means that conditions can vary widely over a few miles. Generalizations about wine zones are thus less than helpful. To make matters even more confusing, DOC zones sometimes overlap, and producers make wines from several DOC areas. It is possible, however, to spot broad distinctions across the country. The north-east of Italy has much in common with Austria and Switzerland and their light, fresh whites but also produces a number of well-structured, full-bodied wines which are full of flavour. The extreme south, especially Sicily, is part of the Mediterranean wine tradition of rich, strong wines but has also recently attracted great names from the continent — there is much investment and experimentation and the astounding quality revival is set to continue. In between are innumerable zones with excellent conditions for red and white wines, such as Tuscany, Umbria, Marches and Abruzzo.

Grape varieties

Italy has a profusion of native grape varieties. Before the Goria law was put into effect, most DOC regulations excluded the internationally-favoured French classic varieties, though these were increasingly grown and used in *vini da tavola*. One of the reasons for the disenchantment with the DOC system among growers has been the prohibition of non-traditional varieties. Some DOCs do recognize — and have done so for a long time — vines such as Merlot, Pinot Blanc (Bianco) and Pinot Gris (Grigio), which have been established in northern Italy since the 19th century. Cabernet Sauvignon was planted in the Chianti zone of Tuscany two centuries ago, almost as soon as it had been recognized under the current name in Bordeaux.

The native Italian varieties are legion, and the list is made longer still by the profusion of clones and sub-varieties. There is constant debate in central Italy about the vices and virtues of various forms of Sangiovese. This is no esoteric debate: the character of Chianti wines changed considerably in the 1950s and 1960s when there was widespread replanting with an inferior Sangiovese clone. Better producers now recognize the need for careful clonal selection.

The most important Italian grape varieties include:

Barbera Native to Piedmont and now widely planted, making red wines in a variety of styles.
Malvasia This ancient vine, with — usually — pale-skinned grapes, has a pungent flavour and makes dry and sweet, dark and light wines in the southern half of peninsular Italy.
Montepulciano Makes vigorous red wines in central Italy.
Nebbiolo The prime red variety of Piedmont, responsible for Barolo and Barbaresco wines.
Sangiovese The red grape of Chianti and other central wine zones.
Trebbiano The dominant white grape of central and northern Italy.

Among other native grapes is the red Primitivo of the far south, which, it is claimed, is the same as Zinfandel, California's own red variety. ☐

Visitors to Varenna, on the shores of Lake Como, can enjoy local Lombardy wines.

READING AN ITALIAN WINE LABEL

Italian labels are as varied as the wines.

Zones and quality grades
Quality wines come from regulated zones, and these zones are named on labels as *denominazione di origine controllata* (DOC): wines of controlled origin. These zones have names: Soave, Orvieto and so on.

Denominazione di origine controllata e garantita (DOCG) is a higher grade of quality. "Garantita" indicates that the wine adheres to stricter rules. There are now 289 DOCs and 21 DOCGs.

Vino da tavola is table wine. Much of it is ordinary, but some *vini da tavola* are superior wines that are made in DOC areas but not according to DOC rules. The winemaker may use grape varieties, or methods, forbidden under DOC legislation.

Indicazione geografica tipica refers to an intermediate quality level, between DOC and *vino da tavola*, and was created in 1992 for wines of a certain quality, which come from a certain region (*see* p362). Up to date, here are 117 officially recognized IGTs.

Producers and vineyards
Terms for a wine estate include *azienda agricola, fattoria, tenuta* and *podere*: their use on labels implies an estate-bottled wine. Individual vineyards may be identified by the terms *tenuta* (holding), *podere* (plot), *vigna* or *vigneto*. *Cantina sociale* (CS) is a cooperative.

Style and quality
Riserva or *vecchio* describes wine that is DOC or DOCG and has been aged for a longer period than most in cask or bottle or both. *Superiore* usually means the wine has a higher alcohol content (or a little extra ageing) than the standard DOC wine. *Classico* refers to a restricted zone, usually the heart of a wine area. *Novello* is a new wine (as in the French *nouveau*).

Secco means dry, *abboccato* describes gently sweet wine, *amabile* sweeter, and *liquoroso* a true dessert wine which is always fortified.

Frizzante wine is lightly sparkling, *spumante* is a true sparkling wine. If made by the secondary fermentation in bottle method it may be labelled *metodo tradizionale, metodo classico* or *talento*.

WINE ZONES OF NORTH ITALY

Zones with the status *denominazione di origine controllata e garantita* (DOCG) are shown, as are the most significant DOC (*denominazione di origine controllata*) zones. The 1992 Law brought in a number of changes and the number of DOCG zones has for now increased from 5 to 11.

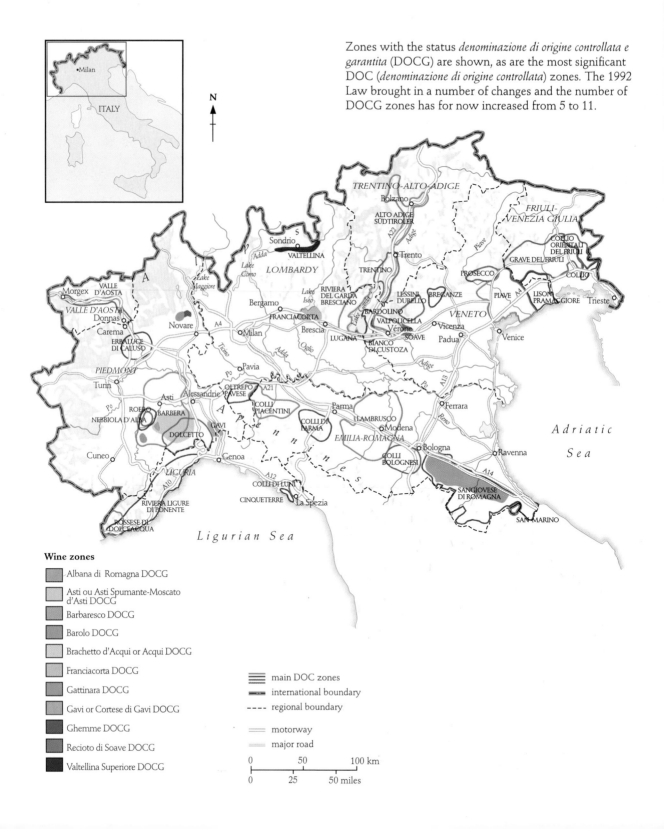

Wine zones

- Albana di Romagna DOCG
- Asti ou Asti Spumante-Moscato d'Asti DOCG
- Barbaresco DOCG
- Barolo DOCG
- Brachetto d'Acqui or Acqui DOCG
- Franciacorta DOCG
- Gattinara DOCG
- Gavi or Cortese di Gavi DOCG
- Ghemme DOCG
- Recioto di Soave DOCG
- Valtellina Superiore DOCG

≡ main DOC zones
▬ international boundary
---- regional boundary
══ motorway
══ major road

0   50   100 km
0   25   50 miles

PIEDMONT

From the crisp, almondy tastes of its dry white wines to the powerful magic of the best red Barolo, Piedmont offers the wine drinker a singular treat. This region of northwest Italy produces unique and exciting wines based for the most part upon indigenous grape varieties.

Piedmont has the sixth-largest vineyard area in Italy; this is despite the fact that around 43% of the region is mountainous terrain, much of which is too harsh to accommodate the vine. The River Po divides Piedmont into two distinct parts. South of the Po and to the south-east of the city of Turin lie the town of Alba and the hills of Monferrato and the Langhe. This area accounts for most of Piedmont's grape production in many overlapping DOC zones. The steep slopes of the Langhe hills produce the grapes for several DOCs, as well as Piedmont's most illustrious red-wine DOCGs — Barolo and Barbaresco. Vineyards north of the Po are planted on craggy Alpine foothills extending from Carema in the west to Novara in the east.

The Barolo style

For centuries Barolo has been a name to conjure with. Tasters sampling the delights of this wine often wax lyrical, detecting hints of tar, violets, chocolate, prunes, tobacco, truffles and autumn smoke. Wines made by top producers and in a good vintage may well exhibit these notes.

Barolo is made from the Nebbiolo grape and the wine is deep garnet in colour with a full, velvety texture, mouthfilling and persistent flavours, and a heady perfume. Firm acidity balances the massive fruit content. The wine is aged for at least three years, two of which are in wood, before being released. It demands further ageing in bottle for anything up to 20 years.

Poppies grow alongside the vines in vineyards near the village of Barolo.

Much of the success of Barolo rests with the winemaker, the vintage and the site. Nebbiolo produces the best wines when grown in calcareous marl soils in a coolish climate. As in Burgundy, producers often name the vineyard on the wine label as an indication of quality (although there is no official hierarchy of *crus*).

Since the late 1970s there has been a trend towards producing wines that are drinkable much earlier. Traditionally, the wine was fermented in contact with the skins for up to two months and was then aged for years in large oak or chestnut barrels (called *botti*). Wines made in this way have a massive concentration of rich fruit and are extremely tannic: they need a decade or more in bottle to become drinkable. There are still producers making this monumental brew, though their methods have changed somewhat and yields have been reduced for greater concentration of flavour. Most contemporary

producers limit skin contact, for an average seventeen days, and age the wine in wood for the minimum time allowed by law, which is two years. Some use small barrels (rather than *botti*) for part or all of the ageing. These Barolos may be ready to drink five or six years after the vintage.

Both styles exhibit great structure and complexity. They are not quaffing wines, and hold no immediate appeal for the neophyte wine drinker, but great pleasure awaits those willing to give them a try.

Barbaresco

East of Barolo in the Langhe hills is the Barbaresco DOCG. Its Nebbiolo vineyards are planted at 200–350m (660–1,150ft) above sea level, and the climate is drier and warmer than in Barolo. The regulations here require only one of the two years of ageing to be in wood. Vineyard site, as always for Nebbiolo, is important. As in Barolo, there is a division of style between traditionalists and those with a more international approach. In general, Barbaresco has an exhilarating perfume that hints of violets. Its lush fruit is balanced by an assertive acidity and tannin. Some wines may need up to ten years in bottle, but most are ready after four or five.

Other vineyards south of the Po

In the south-east corner of Piedmont, the major red grape varieties are Nebbiolo, Barbera and Dolcetto. The area around the town of Alba, between the Barolo and Barbaresco DOCG zones, makes Nebbiolo d'Alba DOC. The soils here are of siliceous clay. Nebbiolo d'Alba varies greatly in style, but is generally less powerful than its well-known neighbours, and it is usually ready to drink within three or four years.

Barbera is Italy's most widely-planted red grape variety, and is regaining prestige in its native Piedmont. It produces a lively, succulent, bone-dry red whose fragrance is reminiscent of blackberries, raspberries and licorice. It is best drunk between two and four years after vintage. Barbera del Monferrato DOC is a light-bodied wine, often *frizzante*. Barbera d'Alba DOC has a fuller style. It is in the province of Asti that Barbera excels itself, however. Barbera d'Asti DOC has a silky texture, with opulent fruit balanced by zesty acidity.

Wine from the Dolcetto grape, prized for easy drinkability, is made in seven DOCs in south-east Piedmont. It is mulberry-hued with bright pink highlights, crisp in taste and well structured, with luscious fruit flavours and a rich perfume. Most of these wines are meant to be drunk young, usually within two or three years of the vintage.

Other indigenous red grape varieties of note are Grignolino, Brachetto and Freisa. Grignolino produces pale, light-bodied reds with floral fragrances and a dry, slightly bitter flavour. Brachetto d'Acqui — upgraded to DOCG in 1996 — is a still or sparkling sweet red whose fragrance is reminiscent of violets and strawberries. Wines made from the Freisa grape are pale cherry-coloured, raspberry-flavoured and thoroughly luscious. There are dry, sweet and sparkling versions of this red quaffing wine.

White and sparkling wines

The most important white grape of southern Piedmont is the aromatic Moscato (the finest member of the Muscat family, this is the Muscat Blanc à Petits Grains); it makes Asti Spumante DOCG, one of the world's best-known sparkling wines. This wine is made by a process traditional to the region, with only one fermentation, in a sealed tank. The must is filtered under pressure before fermentation is complete, leaving a wine that is naturally sparkling, sweet and low in alcohol (7–9.5%). Moscato also makes the elegant, still Moscato d'Asti, which is even lower in alcohol (4.5–6.5%). Both should be drunk as young as possible, before the pure grapey fragrance is lost. The traditional zone of production centres on the town of Canelli, in Asti province, and extends into Cuneo province to the west and Alessandria to the east. The zone became Asti DOCG in 1993.

The dry white wines made from the Cortese grape are crisp and delicately fruity with a hint of lime in the fragrance. The best examples come from the Gavi DOC zone in the eastern part of the Monferrato hills on the border with Liguria; these are wines that tend to be full in style with a silky texture. Sparkling versions are also made. Gavi is best consumed within two years of the vintage, although in good years wines from the top producers can easily last longer.

The Roero DOC zone consists of a sizeable range of hills extending north of the town of Alba, on the left bank of the Tanaro River. The soils are predominantly sandy, rich in fossils and prone to erosion; they are well suited to the production of aromatic and attractively forward whites. The Arneis, an indigenous white variety, produces a lively, dry wine with a soft, fresh flavour. It is best consumed within two years of vintage. The white wine is always labelled Arneis di Roero or Roero Arneis; wine labelled simply Roero is red, based on Nebbiolo.

Northern Piedmont

The principal white grape of the north is Erbaluce, grown around the village of Caluso in the Canavese hills north of Turin. When dry, Caluso DOC wines are crisp and lightly perfumed; they can be either still or sparkling. When Erbaluce grapes are semi-dried before pressing, the resultant wine, called Caluso Passito, is ambrosial. It has a velvet texture and a rich toasted-hazelnut and honey fragrance. Very little of it is made, however. A sweet *liquoroso*, or fortified, Caluso is also available.

The vineyards around the small town of Carema, on the border of Piedmont and Valle d'Aosta, produce some of Italy's finest red wine from the Nebbiolo grape (known locally as Picutener, Pugnet or Spanna). This variety is climatically sensitive and in these glacial terrains produces wines that are lighter in style than southern Nebbiolos. Carema DOC is made wholly from Nebbiolo and is aged for four years — with at least two in small oak or chestnut barrels. It is a deep blackcurrant colour with refreshing acidity, and its appealing fragrance hints at alpine flowers, mint and tar. The wine should be drunk at four to six years old.

In the Vercelli and Novara hills the main red-wine grape variety is again Nebbiolo; here it is usually blended with the local Vespolina and/or Bonarda. At their best the wines are elegant, displaying an enticing aroma that hints at violets. They are usually ready to drink four or five years after the vintage. The best-known wine is that of the Gattinara DOCG zone; wines from the DOC zones of Lessona, Bramaterra, Boca, Sizzano and Fara, and the DOCG zone of Ghemme are very rare. □

QUALITY FACTORS

In Piedmont, as in Burgundy, the concepts of micro-climate and *terroir* are taken seriously. Growers are justly proud of their (frequently tiny and fragmented) plots and often identify the vineyard (designated as a *cru*, or *vigneto* or *vigna* in Italian) and its attributes on the label.

Climate and vintages

In autumn thick fog often lies over the valleys. Winters are damp and cold, and it often snows. In spring, a crucial time for the vine, there can be rain and hail, which may reduce the yield, while summers can be quite hot. As a rule, one can expect between five and eight acceptable-to-great Barolo and Barbaresco years out of every ten. A bad year will usually be the result of a rather dull summer or rain during the harvest. As the harvests for the different varieties can be as much as a month apart, a bad year for one wine might be a good year for another.

 Vineyards

BARBARESCO AND THE ALBA REGION

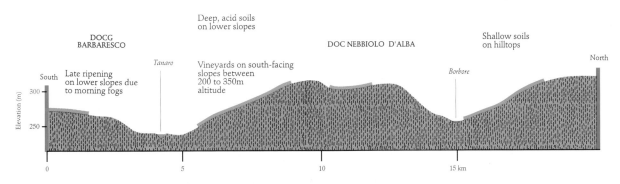

Soil

In the Langhe hills — home of Barolo and Barbaresco — and other south-eastern Piedmont zones, soils are mostly alkaline, being basically calcareous with varying mixtures of sand and clay. The underlying rock of the Langhe hills is calcareous, and the mixture of limestone and associated marl is reminiscent of the Côte d'Or. However, soils vary widely in the tortuous valleys of both Barolo and Barbaresco. Barolo communes are clearly divided by soil type: Monforte d'Alba, Castiglione Falletto and Serralunga d'Alba are on blue-tinged "tortonian" soil, derived from mineral-rich calcareous marls. Wines from these communes show velvety textures and powerful depth of flavour. La Morra by contrast has "helvetian" soil, which is a light-coloured, calcareous marl rich in iron. It produces highly perfumed wines with long ageing potential. The commune of Barolo shares features of both soil zones. Barbaresco soils are similar to those of Barolo, with some more acidic soils on lower slopes.

The Piedmont landscape: slopes and small vineyards.

Site and exposure

This area has gone furthest of any in Italy in identifying vineyard variations in wines. Labels may show terms such as *sorì*, meaning "south-facing", and *bricco* or *bric*, meaning "ridge". Barolo vineyards are usually planted on south-facing hillsides at between 250 and 450m (825 and 1,480ft) above sea level. Barbaresco vineyards are planted at between 200 and 350m (660 and 1,150ft).

Slight differences in exposure, and thus the amount of sunshine or wind, can create marked variations in the development of the Nebbiolo grapes and will therefore influence the resulting wine. Higher and cooler vineyards are often planted with Barbera, which tolerates a wider climatic range than Nebbiolo.

PRODUCERS

The ever-increasing number of Piedmont producers making quality wine are bounding with energy and often produce wines from several appellations, when spared the hail and rain. Only some of the large number of producers are listed below.

SOUTHERN PIEDMONT
Southern Piedmont encompasses the provinces of Cuneo, Asti and Alessandria. Its many famous appellations include the DOCG zones of Barolo, Barbaresco, Asti, and the recent Brachetto d'Acqui and Gavi, as well as Dolcetto, Barbera and Nebbiolo wines from a series of overlapping DOC areas.

Elio Altare
This engaging Langhe character is a testimonial to wines from this area. He has 8.5ha (21 acres) in La Morra and produces magnificent Barolos, a good Dolcetto d'Alba and two fabulous Langhe DOC reds, the Larigi and the Arborina.

Fratelli Bera
This family, which owns 18ha (45 acres) in La Morra, has a very successful range (Barbera d'Alba, Langhe Rosso Sassisto, Moscato Su Reimond and Asti Spumante).

Braida-Bologna
Giacomo Bologna's children are carrying on the good work of this highly skilled winemaker. The Barbera d'Asti DOC still has the place of honour with three crus (Ai Suma, Bricco dell'Uccellone, Bricco della Bigotta) but they also produce a DOCG Brachetto d'Acqui and Moscato d'Asti and a good Monferrato Rosso Il Bacialé.

Fratelli Cavallotto
Good traditional-style Barolo wines (the best being the Bricco Boschis), flavoursome Dolcetto and Barbera d'Alba.

Ceretto
Eight estates with a total of 80ha (200 acres) of vines. The Bricco Asili and Bricco Rocche are top of the range but quality is generally good.

Pio Cesare
This large merchant house in Alba offers a range of compact, full-bodied wines. The most outstanding are the Barolo Ornato and the Barbaresco Il Bricco, not to forget the Piodi Lei Chardonnay and the Barbera d'Alba Fides.

Michele Chiarlo
A reliable reference for the whole Piedmont region. Famous crus include Barolos (Cerequio, Cannubi, Vigna Rionda) and Barbarescos (Asili and Rabajà). Excellent Barbera d'Asti, Gavi, Moscato d'Asti Smentiò and Barilot, a full-flavoured *vino da tavola*.

Quinto Chionetti & Figlio
With 14ha (35 acres) in Dogliani, here we have a pioneer of Dolcetto whose two excellent crus (Briccolero and San Luigi) are snapped up.

Domenico Clerico
One of the best producers in the new-wave Barolo style. From 15ha (37 acres) in Monforte d'Alba (often spared the frosts) he produces first rate Barolos (Pajana, Ciabot Mentin Ginestra) and the equally remarkable Langhe Arte and Langhe Dolcetto Visadì.

Poderi Aldo Conterno
A great name in Barolo wines.

The family owns 25ha (60 acres) and produces wines representative of the best of the 'traditional' school. Top of the range are the Barolo Colonnello, Gran Bussia and Cicala. Very good DOC wines including Barbera d'Alba Conca Tre Pile, Dolcetto d'Alba, Langhe Bussiador and Langhe Favor.

Giacomo Conterno
From 16ha (40 acres) of Cascina Francia vineyards in Monforte d'Alba, this branch of the Conterno family makes really lovely "traditional" long-lived Barolos (Cascina Francia, Monfortino Riserva) plus good Dolcetto and Barbera d'Alba.

Conterno Fantino
Famous for two great Barolos (Sori Ginestra, Vigna del Gris) and the mouthwatering Langhe Rosso Monprà. Flavoursome Barbera, Dolcetto and Freisa.

Luigi Coppo & Figli
This Canelli merchant produces good sparkling wines, an IGT Monteriolo Chardonnay and two Barbera d'Asti wines (Pomorosso, Camp du Rouss).

Matteo Correggia
This 7.5ha (20-acre) estate in Canale, the flagship of the Roero region, is run by an enthusiastic young winemaker. A splendid Barbera d'Alba Marun and Nebbiolo d'Alba Val dei Preti. The very recent Roero DOC Ròche d'Ampsèj is causing quite a stir.

Tenimenti di Barolo & Fontanafredda
Famous for its Barolo crus, this large merchant house also offers good sparkling wines (Contessa Rosa Brut, Gatinera Brut Talento) and a very fruity Diano d'Alba Vigna La Lepre.

Gaja
Angelo Gaja, the figurehead of Italian wine for 20 years — in fact almost a legend — is indefatigable. The future still holds

many challenges for him. After becoming famous world-wide for Barbaresco and Nebbiolo through his Sorì San Lorenzo, Sorì Tildìn and Costa Russi crus, his triumphant success with Cabernet Sauvignon (Darmagi) and Chardonnay (Gaia & Rey) on the steep slopes of the Langhes, the success of Daja Distribuzione, a company importing the best foreign wines, Riedel glasses, etc, and the name of Gaja becoming a synonym for excellence (and steep prices).... we now have a period of expansion: on neighbouring Barolo land (fabulous Sperss and Conteisa Cerequio crus) and in Tuscany, with the acquisition of Pieve S. Restituta in Montalcino and Ca'Marcanda in Bolgheri (65ha, 160 acres of vines currently being planted).

Bruno Giacosa
Owner of 15ha (37 acres) in Nieve and working under contract with numerous winemakers, Bruno Giacosa is another great Piedmont figure: supreme winemaker, never satisfied, modest and enthusiastic. His range of Barbarescos (S. Stefano, Gallina, Asili) and Barolos (Collina Rionda, Falleto) — fine examples of the traditional style — is rounded off by an excellent *spumante* Extra Brut, Dolcetto and Nebbiolo d'Alba.

Fratelli Giacosa
An even better known merchant house in Neive with 15ha (37 acres) of vines. Top of the range wines include the superb Barbera Maria Gioana, the Barbaresco Rio Sordo and the Barolo Vigna Mandorlo.

Elio Grasso
With 15ha (37 acres) of vines and a modernised winery, this Monforte family estate has further strengthened its excellent reputation. Top of the list are the Barbera d'Alba Vigna Martina and the Barolos Gavarini and Ginestra.

Tenuta Cisa Asinari dei Marchesi di Gresy
The di Gresy family own the fabulous Martinenga vineyard and produce the very elegant Martinenga, Gaiun and especially Camp Gross Barbarescos. The excellent Langhe Rosso Virtus is one to remember.

La Scolca
The Soldati family introduced us to Gavi wine in the 1960s and still makes some of the best still and sparkling Gavi wines.

La Spinetta
Having taken their Moscato d'Asti wines to lofty heights, the Rivetti brothers turned to red wines and reaped the benefits with their Pin and subsequently their DOCG Vigneto Gallina and Starderi, two Barbarescos. They also produce an exceptional Barbera d'Alba Vigneto Gallina.

Marchesi di Barolo
A large company, founded in 1861, with 40ha (100 acres) of vines. Its main aim is to offer a large selection of (very) good Barolo wines at a wide range of prices. The excellent winemaker, Roberto Vezza, also produces flavoursome Barbera and Dolcetto wines.

Bartolo Mascarello
Bartolo Mascarello (also known as the Barolo legend) is a fervent, stringent winemaker. He uses traditional methods to blend his various crus to form one single wine, handsome and austere like its creator.

Giuseppe Mascarello
The superb Barolo Monprivato and the Dolcetto d'Alba Bricco are two of the finest wines from this 15ha (37 acre) estate in Castiglione Falletto.

Monfalletto
From 26ha (65 acres) in La Morra, the Cordero di Montezemolo produce beautiful plump, solid wines, matured in small oak barrels. The best include the Barolo Enrico VI, Barbera d'Alba and the rare Curdè Pinot Noir.

Angelo Negro
From its 43-ha (105-acre) estate in Roero, the family produces the flavoursome Roero Sodisfà, Barbera d'Alba Bric Bertu and Arneis *passito* Perdaudin.

CS Produttori del Barbaresco
The Barbaresco cooperative offers a well-produced range of all local appellation wines.

Prunotto
This great name in Alba wines now belongs to Antinori. From its vast range the Barolos Cannubi and Bussia di Monforte, the Barbera d'Alba Pian Romualdo and the Nebbiolo d'Alba Occhetti still stand out but the star of the show has to be the Barbaresco Bric Turot.

Renato Ratti-Antiche Cantine dell'Abbazia dell'Annuziata
The inheritors of this estate, which has played a large part in the redevelopment of the region, produce good Barolos (*cru* Marcenasco), Dolcetto d'Alba, Nebbiolo d'Alba and Monferrato.

Albino Rocca
This Barbaresco estate of almost 10ha (25 acres) produces very good (unfiltered) wines. Top of the range is the Barbaresco Brich Ronchi.

Bruno Rocca
A great protagonist of the Barbaresco, also happy to work with the Barolo. His cru Rabajà has been showered with praise. The rest of the range is noteworthy:Barbera d'Alba, Langhe Chardonnay Cadet, etc.

Rocche dei Manzoni
40ha (100 acres) in Monforte, a modernised winery and the winemaker's passion all come together to produce ten excellent wines. Top position is held by the Barolo crus, the Quatr Nas and fine sparkling wines.

Luciano Sandrone
A clever winemaker and unassuming magician, Sandrone is still dazzling us with his brilliant, sumptuously plump Barolos (Cannubi Boschis, Le Vigne) — true works of art. His other wines (Barberas, Dolcettos, Nebbiolo d'Albas) are of course succulent, elegant and of a rare precision. His fans have only one regret: the estate, including rented vineyards, covers a mere 13.5ha (35 acres).

Paolo Sarraco
The wine produced here is white. Not content with offering two of the best Moscati d'Asti and the great Bianch del Luv Chardonnay, they are also experimenting at this 14-ha (35-acre) estate in Castiglione Tinella: the Langhe Bianco Graffagno is an very promising blend of Riesling, Chardonnay and Sauvignon Blanc.

Paolo Scavino
This outstanding winemaker in Castiglione Falletto produces Barolo *crus* (Cannubi, Bric del Fiasc, Rocche dell'Annunziata), all equally good and of a consistent style. The Barbera d'Alba 'affinata in carati' and Dolcetto round off the range.

Vietti
This family estate in Castiglione Falletto has been producing excellent Langhe wines (Barolo, Barbera d'Alba, Barbaresco, etc.) for a century but its very new Barbera d'Asti are equally as good.

Roberto Voerzio
The yields from this exemplary estate in La Morra are among the lowest in Italy and the wines produced from these passionately tended 10ha (25 acres) battle it out for gold awards. This rings true for the various Barolo crus and the Barbera d'Alba Vigneto Pozzo, the finest example of this long unrecognized grape variety.

Other producers
Marziano & Enrico Abbona, Fratelli Barale, Nicoletta Bocca, Giacomo Brezza & Figli, Brovia, Castello di Neive, La Ca' Nova, Cascina Castlèt, Cigliuti, Giuseppe Contratto, Giovanni Corino, Deltetto, Carlo Giacosa, Icardi, Cascina La Barbatella, Molino, Il Mongetto, Fiorenzo Nada, Nuova Cappelletta, Armando Parusso, E Pira & Figli, F Principiano, Antica Casa Vinicola Scarpa, Scarzello, Scrimaglio, Vajra, Vigna Rionda, Villa Banfi Strevi (*see* p386).

NORTHERN PIEDMONT
The wines of northern Piedmont come from the provinces of Turin (DOC Carema and Caluso) and Vercelli and Novare (DOCG Gattinara and Ghemme). Wines are good but the two DOCG have still not produced the champions they are aiming for.

Antichi Vigneti di Cantalupo
The Arlunno brothers own 25ha (60 acres) in Ghemme from which they produce two robust reds (Collis Breclemae and Collis Carellae). Carolus (white) and Primigenia (red) are two good blended *vini da tavola*.

Antoniolo
This 15-ha (37-acre) family estate produce some of the best Gattinaras (Vigneto Castelle, Vigneto Osso S. Grato).

Travaglini
This winemaker owns 35ha (86 acres) of vines. His sharp, highly tannic Gattinara Riserva has lovely complex aromas.

Other producers
Luigi Dessilani, Luigi Ferrando, Luigi & Italo Nervi, Sella.

VALLE D'AOSTA AND LIGURIA

Mont Blanc, the Matterhorn and Gran Paradiso are among the snow-capped Alpine peaks that separate Aosta from France and Switzerland to the north and Piedmont to the south and east. Most of the wine made here in Italy's smallest province is consumed locally in the restaurants and chalets frequented by skiers.

Aosta's mountainous terrain makes vineyard tending difficult, if not impossible. Most vines are planted on terraces along the steep-sloped valley of the Dora Baltea River. The boundary of Valle d'Aosta DOC follows the river valley which bisects the region. There are seven recognized sub-zones: from north to south these are Morgex et La Salle, Enfer d'Arvier, Torette, Nus, Chambave, Arnad-Montjovet and Donnas.

In the upper valley at Morgex and La Salle are Europe's highest vineyards, planted at between 900 and 1,300m (2,970–4,290ft). The wines, made from local Blanc de Morgex grapes, are zesty, dry whites with delicate aromas.

The red wines of the central valley are based on blends of the native varieties Petit Rouge and Vien de Nus. The wines are dry and deeply coloured with flowery fragrances. The village of Nus also produces Nus Pinot Grigio Passito, a lightly sweet, copper-coloured wine made from semi-dried grapes. Chambave has its Moscato Passito, a richly scented, golden-hued wine. Dry versions of these two wines are also made.

Nebbiolo, known locally as Picutener or Picotendro, is planted around the town of Donnas on sands, clays and gravel soils in the lower valley. The wine, made from a blend of Nebbiolo, Freisa and Neyret, is fresh and crisp with a deep dark ruby colour. Another Nebbiolo-based wine, seldom seen outside the area, is Arnad-Montjovet.

Liguria

Cupped around the Gulf of Genoa in the Mediterranean, crescent-shaped Liguria borders Provence in France to

PRODUCERS

In both regions, many growers struggle to cultivate grapes in tiny plots on steep slopes or narrow terraces. In Valle d'Aosta, six cooperatives provide an outlet for these grapes, making wine for the local population and visiting skiers. Production in Liguria is also small-scale; much of it is sold to sun-seeking tourists, but Liguria's best wines have a reputation within Italy if not beyond.

Valle d'Aosta

Good producers include Les Crêtes d'Aymaville (Chardonnay, Fumin, Petite Arvine, Syrah, Pinot Noir); Charrère (red La Sabla, Les Fourches, Prëmetta); Regional Agricultural Institute (varietals, particularly from Syrah, Pinot Gris, Petit Rouge, and a blended red Vin du Prévôt); co-op La Crota di Vegneron (good Chambave and Nus, excellent Muscatos); Grosjean (red Torette and Fumin, Petite Arvine); Ezio Voyat (Moscato Passito Le Muraglie), Anselmet (Chardonnay). The best co-ops are those of Morgex, Donnas and Arnad (La Kiuva).

Liguria

In the west (Ponente): DOC Pigato and/or Vermentino de Bianchi (Eretico) whites; Bruna, Cascina Feipu, Cascina Terre Rosse (Pigato and red Solitario), Colle dei Bardellini, Tenuta Giuncheo (Vermentino Eclis, Rossese di Dolceacqua DOC), Lupi (Vermentino Vignamare, red Ormeasco), Terre Bianche (Arcana Bianco and Rosso, Rossese di Dolceacqua Bricco Arcagna) and Vio.

In the east (Levante): Colli di Luni DOC (notably Vermentino and sometimes red wines) of Ottaviano Lambruschi, Cantine Lunae Bosoni, Il Monticello, Picedi Benettini and Il Torchio. Cinque Terre DOC by Walter De Battè (excellent) and by the cooperative of Riomaggiore.

the west, then arches round to the south of Piedmont, and curves down to the south-east, bordering Emilia and Tuscany. Mountain ranges shield the region and allow it to enjoy some Mediterranean warmth. The wines, most of which are consumed locally, range from a few long-lived reds to easy-quaffing whites.

The Riviera Ligure di Ponente DOC zone covers much of western Liguria, extending from Genoa to the French border. The four most important grape varieties are Rossese and Ormeasco for red wines, and Vermentino and Pigato for whites. Rossese produces dry, fresh, floral-scented reds. Ormeasco, a local clonal variation of Dolcetto, produces zesty, dry, blackcurrant-coloured wines that can be longer lived than their Piedmontese cousins. Ormeasco Sciacchetrà is a dry, fruity rosé. Vermentino makes delicately scented, firm-bodied whites, while the white wines made from Pigato have floral perfumes with hints of peach.

At Liguria's western tip, by the French border, are the vineyards of Rossese di Dolceaqua, a small DOC zone. The wine is a soft and fruity red with good perfume.

In the eastern part of Liguria, in the Riviera di Levante, are two DOC zones, Colli di Luni and the famous Cinqueterre. Colli di Luni makes good red wines based on the Sangiovese grape variety, and finely-scented whites based on Vermentino.

The steeply-terraced vineyards of Cinqueterre lie along the Ligurian Sea west of La Spezia. This zone's dry white wine is made from a blend of predominantly Bosco grapes, with either Albarolo or Vermentino. At its best the wine is lively with a delicately fruity bouquet. The same varieties that are used for Cinqueterre are semi-dried to make the rich, sweet, tawny-coloured Sciacchetrà.   □

LOMBARDY

Lombardy, east of Piedmont, shares Lake Maggiore with Switzerland and Lake Garda with the Veneto region. The River Po forms much of Lombardy's southern border. Alpine foothills stretching from Lake Maggiore to lakes Como and Iseo and on to Lake Garda provide some of the best vineyard sites in Lombardy. The vast flatlands of the Po Valley are less suited to viticulture. But south of the Po, between Piedmont and Emilia-Romagna, lies a significant wine-producing region — a small, triangular parcel of land called Oltrepò Pavese.

Oltrepò Pavese

Unfortunately, this is the most productive DOC in Lombardy. Its beautiful hilly vineyards could offer the people of Milan much more than a series of everyday wines and, often mediocre, *spumante*, especially considering that some excellent specialists in terroir division were trained at the city's university.

The zone's Rosso, a blend of Barbera and Bonarda grapes, is a lively blackberry-coloured wine with a bitter cherry flavour. The same varieties make red Buttafuoco and Sangue di Giuda wines, often slightly fizzy.

Varietal red wines are made from Barbera (lean and tautly structured) and Bonarda (softer in texture, with brambly fruit). Pinot Nero can be a still red wine, a rosé, or a white (when vinified without skin contact), though it is often blended with Pinot Bianco to good effect in the zone's excellent *metodo classico* wines.

Still, slightly fizzy or fully sparkling dry whites are made from Chardonnay, Cortese, Moscato, Pinot Grigio, Riesling Italico, Rhine Riesling and other varieties. Moscato *liquoroso* is a rare local speciality. This Moscato-based fortified wine is honey-coloured and ranges from lightly sweet to lusciously opulent.

Nebbiolo vines in Valtellina.

Valtellina

Not far from the Swiss border in northern Lombardy are the alpine vineyards of the Valtellina DOC. The zone is a narrow band on the north bank of the Adda River to the east and west of Sondrio, where vines grow on tiny terraces along the precipitous south-facing slopes. The main grape variety here is Nebbiolo, known locally as Chiavennasca. A huge vineyard restoration programme is underway and, if at the same time some of the winemaking techniques are updated, the results should be spectacular — the region has much potential.

Basic Valtellina is best drunk within one to three years of the vintage. Four sub-zones — Sassella, Grumello, Inferno and Valgella — produce Valtellina Superiore (DOCG since 1998), which is aged in wood for at least a year and best consumed at five to ten years old.

Valtellina Sforzato (or Sfursat) is a dry red wine made from semi-dried Nebbiolo grapes; such wines show a concentration of ripe fruit flavours, and have around 14.5% alcohol.

Southern and eastern Lombardy

On the western shores of Lake Garda is Lombardy's largest DOC, Riviera del Garda Bresciano. It produces a dry, refreshing, cherry-coloured red and a zesty rosé, or *chiaretto*, based on the local Groppello grape. This zone overlaps with the Lugana DOC, internationally known for elegant, full-bodied (usually still) white wines from a local sub-variety of Trebbiano. Tocai Friulano (*see* p378) grapes grown in the same zone go into the light dry or *liquoroso* white San Martino della Battaglia DOC. South of Lake Garda, the province of Mantova produces simple reds, whites and rosés in the Garda Colli Mantovani DOC. The flatlands along the River Po have vineyards to make Lambrusco Mantovano DOC, a dry or sweet red *frizzante* wine, similar to Emilia's Lambruscos (*see* p373).

North-east of Bergamo, the Valcalepio DOC produces a medium-bodied red — a blend of Cabernet Sauvignon and Merlot with blackcurrant flavours — a fresh dry white based on Pinot Gris and Pinot Blanc and a Moscato Passito.

Between Brescia and Lake Iseo is the prestigious Franciacorta DOCG, where highly regarded *metodo classico* sparkling wines are made from Pinot Bianco, Chardonnay and Pinot Nero. Franciacorta also makes a still red wine from a Cabernet Franc/Barbera/Nebbiolo/Merlot blend, and a still white from Pinot Bianco, Pinot Nero and Chardonnay.

Three small DOCs in the hills around Brescia make wines that are consumed locally. Cellatica and Botticino are light red blends based on the Schiava grape. Capriano del Colle produces a red wine based on Sangiovese, Marzemino and Barbera, and a Trebbiano-based white wine. ☐

PRODUCERS

Centres of production range from mainly cooperatives in Oltrepò Pavese, to the wine houses of Valtellina and the estates and prestigious boutique wineries of Franciacorta. Producers are listed below by DOC.

OLTREPÒ
Progress is being made in this beautiful region but as yet not all wines are of a good standard (Oltrepò Pavese DOC, referred to below as O.P.).

Fratelli Agnes
This Rovescala estate produces a superb range of reds from the Bonarda (or Croatina) variety, some of them DOC: Campo del Monte, Cresta del Ghiffi, Millenium, Poculum, Loghetto.

Ca' di Frara
A very good 28-ha (70-acre) estate (plus one third trade) in Mornico Losana. Its classics include the O.P. Malvasia and the Pinot Noir Il Raro, Il Frater (a blended red wine) and late harvest wines (O.P. Pinot Grigio, Riesling Apogeo).

Frecciarossa
This 16-ha (40-acre) estate in Casteggio is one of the best in the region: fabulous O.P. Rosso Villa Odero Riserva and Riesling.

Le Fracce
This 'bio-integrated' 42-ha (100-acre) estate in Casteggio is renowned for its O.P. Bonarda and Rosso Cirgà; the whites are not far behind (O.P. Pinot Grigio and Riesling).

Tenuta Mazzolino
The Black and White (one of them O.P. Pinot Nero, the other O.P. Chardonnay) are the star wines of this 14-ha (35-acre) estate in Corvino S. Quirico.

Ruiz de Cardenas
A 5-ha (13-acre) estate in Casteggio focusing on Pinot Noir (O.P. Brumano and Baloss) and Chardonnay, blended in their O.P. Brut Reserve and Extra Brut sparkling wines.

Other Oltrepò producers
Riccardo Albani, Barbacarlo, Il Bosco, Casa Ré, Doria, Fratelli Giorgi, Isimbarda, Castello di Luzzano, Martilde, Montelio, Monterucco, Il Pendio, Bruno Verdi. Cooperatives Casteggio and S. Maria della Versa.

VALTELLINA
This region's growing reputation rests on the efforts of some and the charm of the semi-dried Sfursat.

Nino Negri
This merchant house (Gruppo Italiano Vini) is the flagship of the region. Casimiro Maule produces the splendid Sfursat 5 Stelle and Valtellina Superiore DOCGs (Grumello Sassoros, Inferno Mazer, Sassella Le Tense), which should provide inspiration to many. He works with Enologica Valtellinese.

Aldo Rainoldi
This merchant is making huge progress since the modernisation of his winery. Renowned for his two Sfursat (including the Ca' Rizzieri) and his DOCG range (Sassella Riserva, Crespino, Inferno Riserva).

Conti Sertoli Salis
Claudio Introini makes a Sfursat (Canua) and other lovely wines (Saloncello, Torre della Sirena, Corte della Meridiana) in Tirano for this large merchant house.

Triacca
A fervent supporter of clonal selection, this Tirano merchant produces very good Valtellina wines (Prestigio, Sforzato) and a worthy Sauvignon Del Frate.

Other Valtellina producers
Enologica Valtellinese, Fay, Mamete Prevostini.

FRANCIACORTA
This very dynamic area is best known for the quality of its DOCG *spumante* wines, but the Terre di Franciacorta (T.d.F) still wines (red and white) are equally as good.

Bellavista
This 117-ha (290-acre) estate in Erbusco has a justifiable reputation both for its sparkling wines (Gran Cuvée Brut, Franciacorta Brut, Gran Cuvée Pas Operé, etc) and its still wines: T.d.F. Convento dell'Annunciata and Uccellanda (white) and T.d.F. Solesine, a Cabernet Sauvignon/Merlot red blend.

Guido Berlucchi
One of Italy's main sparkling wine producers. Franco Ziliani, a pioneer of the genre, owns 45ha (110 acres) in Franciacorta. Top of the range wines include the rich Cellarius Brut and two Franciacortas labelled Antica Cantina Fratta.

Ca' del Bosco
Pioneer of sparkling wine and Cabernet, Maurizio Zanella brought Franciacorta out of obscurity by imposing his inimitable style: exuberant but uncompromising in quality. Today, this Erbusco family estate (96ha, 235 acres) is producing prize-winning wines. Stars of the show are the sparkling wines Franciacorta Satèn Millesimato, Brut Millesimato and Cuvée Annamaria Clementi, the IGT reds M. Zanella and Pinero and the T.d.F. Chardonnay.

Cavalleri
This 34-ha (85-acre) estate in Erbusco is well-known for the consistent quality of its many sparkling and still wines. Top of the range wines include the Franciacorta Collezione Brut and Blanc de Blancs, the T.d.F. Bianco Seradina and Rampaneto, the T.d.F. Rosso Vigna Tajardino and the IGT red Corniole (Merlot).

Other Franciacorta producers
Fratelli Berlucchi, Contadi Castaldi, Ferghettina, Enrico Gatti, Guarischi, Lantieri de Paratico, Lo Sparviere, Mosnel, Barone Pizzini, Piomarta, Principe Banfi, Ricci Curbastro, San Cristoforo, Uberti, Vercesi del Castellazzo, Villa.

OTHER WINES
Ca' dei Frati
In Sirmione. Excellent Lugana I Frati and Il Brolettino, white IGT Pratto and *vino de tavola* Tre Filer.

Cascina la Pertica
15ha (37 acres) near Lake Garda. Good Garda DOC Le Sincette and Gropello and a red *vino da tavola* Le Zalte.

La Prendina
30ha (75 acres) south of Lake Garda. Top of the range are the Garda DOC Il Falcone and Vigneto La Prendina. The Piona family also owns La Cavalchina in Venetia (good Bardolino and Bianco di Custoza).

Other producers
Cantrina, Carlozadra, Casella Braga, Costaripa, Marangona, Provenza, Redaelli de Zinis, Stefano Spezia, Spia d'Italia, Cooperatives della Valtenesi e della Lugana, Val San Martino.

EMILIA-ROMAGNA

Although different in many ways — not least in the wines they produce — Emilia and Romagna are linked administratively. Bologna, the capital, lies in the middle, with Emilia to the west and Romagna to the east. The northern border of Emilia-Romagna follows the River Po. The Apennines form the region's western boundary. The mountains keep the region under the climatic influence of the Adriatic: summers are hot and drought conditions are not unknown; winters are damp and fog often lies over the broad plains.

The culinary contributions of Emilia-Romagna outshine its vinous offerings. It is, after all, the land of Parmesan cheese and Parma ham. The only internationally recognized wine from this region is Emilia's sparkling Lambrusco.

Emilia

Many sub-varieties of the native red Lambrusco grape are grown on the broad Emilian plains around the town of Modena, and used in four separate DOC designations. Lambrusco di Sorbara is noted for its dry style, crisp acidity and attractive, grapey bouquet. The adjacent Lambrusco Salamino di Santa Croce produces a similar wine. To the south is the zone of Lambrusco Grasparossa di Castelvetro, whose wines have more tannin and a fuller flavour. Lambrusco Reggiano, to the west, produces — and exports — the most.

In general, Lambrusco is lightly sparkling (*frizzante*), sweet and easily quaffable. It is usually red, although white or pink versions can be made by limiting skin contact during vinification. Sometimes the wine is vinified to dryness, and occasionally it is fully sparkling. Whatever the style, this is a wine for drinking young.

In north-west Emilia is the Colli Piacentini DOC zone, with many sub-categories. Its best-known red wine is a blend of Barbera and Bonarda grapes called Gutturnio, which is usually still and dry, although sweet and *frizzante* (lightly bubbly) versions are also made. Varietal Barbera wine has a deep ruby colour and is generally dry. Bonarda has fresh fruit flavours, a dark blackcurrant colour and may be dry or fairly sweet. Much of the Pinot Nero grown in this area is made into white or rosé sparkling wines.

Varietal whites from Colli Piacentini are Malvasia, Ortrugo, Pinot Grigio and Sauvignon Blanc. These wines are made in a range of styles, from elegantly dry to softly sweet, from still to *frizzante* and *spumante*.

The Colli di Parma DOC, further east, can produce good Malvasia, an aromatic white that comes in dry, semi-sweet and sparkling versions, and a Rosso similar to Gutturnio. *Frizzante* and sparkling wines of the neighbouring Bianco di Scandiano DOC, based on Sauvignon Blanc, are mostly exported.

PRODUCERS

Cooperatives dominate production, accounting for 70%.

Emilia

Good Lambrusco producers include Barbolini, Cavicchioli, Chiarli, Graziano, Ermete Medici & Figli, Moro Rinaldo Rinaldini, co-op Riunite. Monte delle Vigne and Isidoro Lamoretti make good Colli di Parmo wines. Producers from Colli Piacentini include La Tosa, Conte Barattieri, Il Poggiarello, Luretta and, above else, La Stoppa, which also produces excellent *vini da tavola*. Colli Bolognesi DOCs are at the forefront of the region.

Romagna

Good producers include Zerbina, Tre Monti, La Palazza, Castelluccio, Cesari, Leone Conti, Ferrucci, Pandolfa, Fattoria Paradiso, Terre del Cedro and Uccellina.

Currently the most interesting wines and most dynamic producers are to be found in the Colli Bolognesi DOC. This huge appellation has seven sub-regions, including Monte San Pietro, Colline Marconiane and Zola Predosa. Cabernet Sauvignon, Merlot, Chardonnay and Sauvignon Blanc are permitted. Leading producers include Tenuta Bonzara, very well-known for its Bonzarone Cabernet Sauvignon and Merlot Rocca di Bonacciara, and the excellent Vallona and Terre Rosse estates. The Pignoletto is a local white variety which produces pleasant dry or medium-dry still or *frizzante* whites.

Romagna

The main vineyards of this area are concentrated from south-east of Bologna down to the sea. Three grape varieties dominate the region — Albana, Sangiovese and Trebbiano. The indigenous Albana, promoted to DOCG and for many years considered unworthy of this status, is starting to produce really interesting wines, especially passito wines (such as the Scacco Matto from Fattoria Zerbina, the best estate in the region).

The Sangiovese di Romagna DOC still produces light-bodied, quaffable red wines but the best producers are also using it to produce excellent wines. Zerbina's Terre di Ceparano; La Palazza's Pruno; Tre Monditi's Thea; Castelluccio's range of Roncos and Ferrucci's Bottale and Domus Caia, one equally as good as the next.

Following the Adriatic shoreline between the mouth of the Po and Ravenna is the Bosco Eliceo DOC zone. Its wines include Sauvignon Blanc and Bianco — a Trebbiano-based blend — which are both white and usually dry, though they can be still or sparkling. Indigenous Fortana grapes make a still to slightly sparkling tannic red that can be either dry or sweet. □

VENETO

Alpine mountain ranges cover nearly a third of the Veneto and the foothills descend to the flat rice fields of the central plain and, in the west, to the shores of Lake Garda. The Veneto is the most geographically diverse of the Italian wine regions, and offers a broad range of wine styles.

The region's DOC zones fall conveniently into three broad areas: along Lake Garda and around Verona; the hills of central Veneto; and eastern Veneto around Venice and Treviso. In the first of these the wines are usually made from indigenous grape varieties. Wines from further east (with some exceptions) are made from international varieties. Less than half an hour's drive to the east of Verona are the white-wine vineyards of the Soave DOC. North-west of the city lies the Valpolicella DOC, while a little farther to the west are the shores of Lake Garda and the vineyards of the Bardolino DOC. With three of the best-known Italian wine names in the world in such close proximity, it is easy to see why the province of Verona leads the Veneto in premium wine production.

Soave

The best Soaves invariably come from the Classico zone, in the centre of the DOC, which consists of a few hillsides around the communes of Monteforte d'Alpone and Soave. Vineyards are about 250m (825ft) above sea level on gentle slopes of rich, red volcanic soil. Fairly low yields and the micro-climate produce a concentration of ripe fruit flavours in the wine. The main grape variety is the Veneto's white Garganega. Zesty and dry, Soave Classico is bright pale-straw in colour. Its crisp acidity is balanced by delicate fruit flavours that hint of toasted almonds.

Soave's castle, above the Classico zone.

The bouquet is reminiscent of cherry blossom and elderflowers. Basic-level Soaves produced on the plains are of distinctly lesser quality. Some producers make Recioto di Soave DOCG, a sweet wine made from semi-dried grapes that is richer in taste and texture and has a higher alcohol content.

Valpolicella and Bardolino

There are various red wine styles within the Valpolicella DOC: basic Valpolicella, Valpolicella Classico, Valpolicella *ripasso*, Recioto della Valpolicella and Valpolicella Amarone.

Simple Valpolicella is a zesty, light ruby-red wine with an appealing, grapey flavour. It is best consumed young. Wines from the best producers have more concentrated flavours and aromas.

Many Valpolicella producers now choose to make wine by the *ripasso* method, in which the fermented wine is racked onto the lees of the preceding year's *recioto* (*see* next paragraph). *Ripasso* wines are rich and concentrated, with a capacity for ageing. They are dark cherry in colour and have an intense perfume and a tart cherry flavour. The word *ripasso* is not part of the official labelling system, and you will need to be familiar with the methods of an individual producer to identify *ripasso* wines.

The sweet Recioto della Valpolicella and the rich, dry Amarone are made from specially selected grapes that are dried naturally in airy attics from harvest time to about January. With its concentrated flavour, velvety texture and high alcohol level, the deeply-coloured Recioto della Valpolicella is often compared to port and is served in the same way. Amarone is a dry yet stunningly opulent wine.

The Bardolino DOC vineyards extend from the low hills north-east of the town of Bardolino to the shores of Lake Garda. Made from a similar blend of grapes to Valpolicella — the local varieties Corvina, Rondinella, Molinara and others — Bardolino is a bit lighter in style. Bright cherry/ruby in colour, the wine has a crisp acidity and a fresh cherry fragrance. Bardolino Chiaretto is a firmly-structured rosé. In general, these wines are for quaffing while still young.

Other vineyards of Verona

Still whites and sparkling wines are made in Lessini Durello DOC in the Lessini hills north of Soave. High acidity and firm structure make the Durella grape good for high-quality sparkling wine, but the still wines may be a bit too tart for some tastes.

The vineyards of Bianco di Custoza DOC are around the southern tip of Lake Garda. This increasingly popular white wine is usually made to a high standard. Still or sparkling, it makes a good apéritif, whose mellow fruitiness is often compared to greengages and peaches. It is best drunk young.

Central Veneto

The foothills of the Alps extend into central Veneto, where red Bordeaux grape varieties — Cabernet Sauvignon, Cabernet Franc and Merlot — take centre stage; in general they display pleasing varietal character.

The Breganze DOC, on the high plains north of Vicenza, includes red and white varietals. The reds are mainly Cabernet or Pinot Nero, and the dry whites Pinot Grigio and Pinot Bianco. Vespaiolo, a local grape, produces a dry, zesty white wine with a lightly lemony flavour. A Vespaiolo *passito* (a sweet wine made from semi-dried grapes) is also made.

Besides Cabernet and Merlot, the Colli Berici DOC makes reds from Tocai Rosso; its wine is raspberry-coloured with fresh fruit flavours. The major dry whites of the Colli Berici are Garganega, Pinot Bianco, Sauvignon and Tocai Italico. The fruit flavours of these wines are subdued, and they are best drunk young.

The Colli Euganei DOC offers simple Bianco and Rosso plus varietals. Bianco dei Colli Euganei is a soft, dry white blend based on the indigenous varieties Garganega and Serprina. A sweet white Moscato, with an intense floral fragrance, is also made. Rosso dei Colli Euganei is a red blend of Cabernet/Merlot with local varieties.

Among wines made from indigenous varieties, Gambellara DOC is a pleasing, mellow, dry white made from a grape mix similar to that of Soave. Some Recioto di Gambellara is also produced. One of the few Vin Santo wines (*see* p381) outside central Italy is also made here.

Venice and Treviso

In the gentle alpine foothills north of Treviso the Prosecco di Conegliano-Valdobbiadene DOC zone is the home of a sparkling white with a slightly almondy flavour, snappy acidity and a lowish alcohol level. The vineyards of the Cartizze area have been granted their own sub-zone, generally considered superior, although a lot depends on the skill of the producer. The Montello e Colli Asolani DOC zone also makes Prosecco plus dry red varietals from Cabernet and Merlot.

On the plains north of Venice both Piave and Lison-Pramaggiore DOCs produce good everyday varietals that seldom distinguish themselves. A long list of permitted varieties includes Cabernet and Merlot for red wines, Pinot Bianco and Pinot Grigio for whites. Two indigenous grape varieties here are, however, worth a mention. White wines made from Verduzzo have a zesty acidity and a full fruity character, with a hint of almond nuttiness. Verduzzo wines are often bottled slightly sparkling. The Raboso grape produces a deep violet to ruby-coloured wine, with earthy flavours. Rich in tannin, this wine is capable of ageing.   □

PRODUCERS

Small, quality producers — often family firms making single-vineyard wines — are at the forefront in the Veneto.

Allegrini
This famous Fumane estate remains the top reference for the Valpolicella region. Its single-vineyard DOC wines (Valpolicella Classico La Grola, Palazzo della Torre), its Amarone and its Recioto Giovanni Allegrini are all magnificent. The dry *vino da tavola* La Poja (100% Corvina) is one to remember.

Anselmi
Based in Monteforte d'Alpone, Roberto Anselmi, a master of Soave wines, has 70ha (173 acres) in notable Soave Classico vineyards. His crus — Capitel Foscarino and Capitel Croce —, his Recioto di Soave DOCG I Capitelli, a *barrique*-aged white dessert wine of exemplary quality, and his IGT San Vincenzo are highly regarded. His IGT Realda is noteworthy.

Bolla
This Verona wine house produces 1.5 million cases (Veneto, Trentino-Alto Adige, Latium). Top wines are the Amarone and the Recioto della Valpolicella, the Valpolicella Classico Superiore Le Poiane-Jago and the Soave Classico Le Tufaie.

Maculan
Fausto Maculan is a Breganzo producer of international fame (Torcolato and Acininobili, Cabernet Sauvignon Fratta and Ferrata, Merlot Marchesante, etc). Fabulous IGT from Moscato Dindarello.

Masi
The Boscaini family produces 170,000 cases of Valpolicella and Bardolino. Top wines include a series of Amarone della Valpolicella, the Reciotos and the IGTs made from the local Osar, Toar and Brolo di Campofiorin grapes.

Pieropan
Leonildo Pieropan produced the first single-vineyard Soave, the Calvarino. The whole range is wonderful (Soave Classico, Recioto Le Colombare etc.).

Quintarelli
Long fermentation in cask and no filtration make for the rich and complex Valpolicella wines (Classico, Amarone, Recioto) of the almost legendary Quintarelli. Fabulous Amarone and *vino da tavola* Alzero (semi-dried Cabernets).

Venegazzù-Conte Loredan Gasparini
IGT Venegazzù della Casa, the famous bordeaux-style blend, remains one of Veneto's great red wines, only surpassed by its twin, the Capo di Stato.

Other producers
Good Soave and Valpolicella producers include Accordini, Bertani, Brunelli, Bussola, Campagnola, Ca' Rugate, Cantina del Castello, Coffele, Corte Sant'Alda, Dal Forno, Fratelli Degani, Gini, Giuliari, Guerrieri Rizzardi, Inama, La Cappuccina, Le Ragose, Le Salette, Portinari, Prà, Raimondi Villa Monteleone, Tenuta S. Antonio, Fratelli Speri, Fratelli Tedeschi, Zenato, Zeni and Zonin. Noted producers in the other regions include Adami, Bepin de Eto, Case Bianche, Collalto, Col Vetoraz, La Biancara, Le Colture, Le Vigne di S. Pietro, Masottina, Molon Traverso, Ottella, Ruggeri, Serafini & Vidotto, Vignalta, Desiderio Bisol & Figli, Fratelli Bortolin Spumanti.

TRENTINO-ALTO ADIGE

In this mountainous region of north-east Italy only 15% of the land is suitable for cultivation. The wine zones form a Y-shape, following the valleys of the Adige River (called the Etsch in German, the region's second language) and its tributary the Isarco (Eisack) to their confluence south of Bolzano, then continuing south along the Adige.

Trentino and Alto Adige are two distinct regions joined together by a bureaucratic hyphen. The region's northern sector, Alto Adige (also called the Südtirol or South Tyrol), is identical to the province of Bolzano. It borders Lombardy in the west and Austria in the north. Most of its citizens speak German; place names are in both German and Italian; and Germanic grape varieties such as Sylvaner and Müller-Thurgau thrive. The sub-alpine climate means that winters are cold, summer days are hot and nights are chilly all year round. The valley sides are steep and vineyards often have to be terraced.

As the Adige River flows into the province of Trento the valley broadens. The vineyards of Trentino are on average planted at lower altitudes, on gentle, lower valley slopes and on the plains. The climate is warmer and the cultural ambience here becomes noticeably Italian.

Alto Adige
This constantly progressing area enjoys an international reputation for fine dry whites. The white grape varieties — Sylvaner, Müller-Thurgau, Riesling and Welschriesling, Sauvignon Blanc and Pinot Bianco (Weissburgunder) — respond well to the altitude of these sunny valleys, producing crisp, dry wines. Pinot Grigio (Ruländer), a zesty white, takes on a smoky aroma in this area. The distinctive fragrance of lychees produced by Traminer Aromatico

Vines trained on a *pergola trentina*.

(Gewürztraminer) is tamed by early picking and reduced skin contact. The resultant wines are soft and pleasantly floral-scented.

The region's quaffable reds are consumed locally. Four DOC zones are devoted to wines made primarily from the Schiava grape (Vernatsch in German). Schiava, particularly in the Lago di Caldaro (Kalterersee) DOC, usually produces a pale red wine with light cherry flavours and an almondy aftertaste, but it sometimes has a deeper colour and fuller body, as in the wines of DOC Santa Maddalena (St Magdalener).

Other wines of Alto Adige include sparkling wines made from a blend of Chardonnay and Pinot Nero (the Champagne grapes). These varieties are also found in dry, still varietal wines. The indigenous red grape, Lagrein, produces a robust, brambly-flavoured wine known as Scuro (Dunkel), and a fragrant rosé (Kretzer). The golden-hued, sweet Moscato Giallo (Goldenmuskateller) and sweet, pale ruby Moscato Rosa (Rosenmuskateller) are both floral-scented dessert wines.

The vineyards of the Terlano DOC lie on slopes to either side of the Adige River west of Bolzano, and are noted for their fine still varietal whites. Dry sparkling wine is also made here, predominantly from Pinot Bianco.

The high slopes of Italy's most northerly DOC, Valle Isarco, along the Isarco River near Bolzano, produce elegant white varietal wines known for the purity of their aromas.

Trentino
Grown at lower altitudes and therefore in warmer climes, giving slightly higher yields, grapes from Trentino tend to produce mellow wines that have a broader flavour. Most of them are intended to be drunk young.

The Trentino DOC produces many of the same varietal wines as Alto Adige, and crisp *metodo classico* sparkling wines, mainly from Pinot Bianco and Pinot Nero. There are also three notable indigenous grape varieties. Fruit-filled, red Marzemino and white Nosiola produce still dry wines. Nosiola is also the main component of Vin Santo, a sweet, coppery, amber-coloured dessert wine made from semi-dried grapes.

The third indigenous variety is Teroldego, which has its own DOC on the gravel-based soils of the Campo Rotaliano. It produces dry, light, fruity reds and refreshing rosés. Wines from vineyards around Mezzolombardo exhibit greater character and are capable of ageing.

Other zones within Trentino produce simple wines for early consumption: Biancos (based on Nosiola) and Rossos (based on Schiava) from the Sorni DOC, and Schiava-based reds from the Casteller DOC.

The most basic wines come under the Valdadige (Etschtaler) DOC, which covers Alto Adige, Trentino and some of the Veneto. □

PRODUCERS

In Alto Adige and Trentino, cooperatives account for most of the local production. The best Trentino wines are made by private estates, but the Alto Adigo cooperatives sometimes offer splendid wines (Alto Adigo DOC, referred as AA below).

ALTO ADIGE

Viticoltori di Caldaro/Kaltern
This co-op is famous for its great AA Cabernet Sauvignon Campaner and its Moscato Giallo *passito* (Serenade). Outstanding AA Chardonnay, Gewürztraminer, Pinot Nero, Lago di Caldaro etc.

Produttori Colterenzio/Schreckbichl
This co-op at Cornaiano has an excellent reputation: AA Cabernet Sauvignon Lafoa, Chardonnay and Lagrein Cornell; AA Merlot Praedium; AA Rosso Cornelius and IGT Cornelius Bianco Mitterberg.

Tenuta Falkenstein
This Valle Venosta estate produces superb wines from its steep hillside vineyards. Best are the AA DOC wines, a spectacular Riesling, a classic Pinot Bianco and an amazing Gewürztraminer.

Vigneti Hofstätter
From their 45-ha (111-acre) vineyard at Termeno, Paolo and Martin Foradori produce reputed wines, notably the *vino da tavola* Yngram Rosso and the famous Pinot Nero S. Urbano, the first of a high-quality range of AA wines.

Alois Lageder
A well-known wine house of Alto Adige (80,000 cases). The Cor Römigberg, a bordeaux-style red blend, competes with the AA Cabernet Löwengang, only surpassed by the whites (Chardonnay Löwengang, Traminer, Pinot Bianco, Riesling).

Tenuta Manincor
The 35-ha (86-acre) estate of Count Enzenberg is one of the most beautiful of the Caldaro zone. Its highly-regarded wines include the impressive AA Cabernet Sauvignon Cassiano, as well as the Pinot Nero Mason and the Lago di Caldaro Scelta.

San Michele Appiano
This cooperative at Appiano has made good progress: it has probably become the best Italian co-op and competes with the region's top growers. Fantastic range of AA Sanct Valentin white wines at highly competitive prices.

Produttori Santa Maddalena
The Bolzano cooperative is one of the region's big producers. Top wines include the AA Cabernet Mumelterhof, two AA Lagreins and the AA Santa Maddalena Classico, a flavourful red wine.

Castel Sallegg-Graf Kuenburg
This Caldaro estate produces great red and white (Gewürztraminer) wines, but the most sought-after wines are the rare AA Moscato Rosa, a late-harvest sweet wine, and the new *vino da tavola* Conte Kuenburg.

Castello Schwanburg
Wines from this castle at Nalles (27ha, 67acres) are of a consistent high quality, notably the elegant AA Cabernet and the amazing Lagrein reds, followed closely by white wines (Riesling, Sauvignon, AA Pinot Grigio, AA Terlano DOC, etc).

Produttori di Termeno
This rapidly progressing co-op makes first-rate wines, red (AA Lagrein Urbanhof, Pinot Nero et Cabernet Renommée) and white from Gewürztraminer (AA Nussbaumerhof and the *passito* Terminum).

Other Alto Adige producers
Köfererhof, Kössler-Praeclarus, Gojer Glögglhof, Franz Haas, Haderburg, Kränzl-Graf Pfeil, Kuenhof-Peter Plieger, Josef Niedermayr, Ignaz Niedrist, Abbazia di Novacella, Plattner-Waldgries, Popphof-Andreas Menz, Georg Ramoser, Castel Ringberg e Kastelaz Elena Walch, Hans Rottensteiner, Tiefenbrunner Castello Turmhof, Tenuta Unterortl, Vivaldi, Baron Widmann. Cooperatives: Cornaiano/Girlan, Cortaccia, Gries, Merano/Meraner, Prima & Nuova/Erste & Neue.

TRENTINO

Concilio
Based in Volano, Concilio has 500ha (1,235 acres) of vines and produces a·range of good Trentino DOCs (Chardonnay, Pinot Grigio, Merlot Novaline and the bordeaux-style blend Mori Vecio).

Cesconi
The four Cesconi brothers and their small estate at Lavis are held to be one of the rising stars of the region. Top whites include the Pinot Grigio, the Chardonnay, the Nosiola, the Sauvignon, the Traminer Aromatico and the blend Olivar.

Marco Donati
Established since 1863, this estate at the heart of the Teroldego Rotaliani zone is mainly reputed for its splendid Teroldego Sangue di Drago, but the rest of the range is up to it.

Fratelli Dorigati
Dorigati, at Mezzocorona, specializes in Teroldego wines (Riserva Diedri and Rebo). Good Methius *spumante*.

Ferrari
A big Trento producer of *metodo classico* sparkling wines. Top wines include Giulio Ferrari Riserva del Fondatore.

Foradori
This 15-ha (37-acre) family estate is a shrine of the Teroldego zone. Its wines are a testimonial to Elisabetta Foradori's passion and patience. They include, of course, a range of Teroldego wines (Granato, Vigneto Sgarzon, Vigneto Morei and generic wines), the red IGTs Ailampa and Karanar, and the white Myrto.

La Vis
The region's best cooperative holds 800ha (1980 acres) and produces a large and very reliable range of wines, such as the Trentino DOC Ritratti, the Maso range and the late-harvest sweet Mandolaia V.T.

Pojer & Sandri
Based at Faedo, M Pojer and F Sandri still produce Trentino DOC varietals (Traminer, Pinot Nero, Chardonnay, Müller-Thurgau etc). Connoisseurs appreciate the botrytized IGT Essenzia and the white, and even more the red, Faye.

Tenuta San Leonardo
Through the impetus of the marquis Carlo Guerrieri Gonzaga, an amateur of great bordeaux wines, this family estate has acquired worldwide fame. The sophisticated, amazingly fleshy and complex IGT San Leonardo and the Trentino DOC Merlot are delightful.

Other Trentino producers
Maso Cantanghel, Balter, Barone de Cles, Endrizzi, Maso Furli, Istituto Agrario Provinciale, La Cadalora, Letrari, Longariva, Mauro Lunelli, Conti Martini, Castel Noarna, Baroni a Prato, Pravis, Armando Simoncelli, de Tarczal, Zeni. Co-ops: Avio, Cavit, Isera, Nomi, Rotaliana, Vallis Agri.

FRIULI-VENEZIA GIULIA

Friuli-Venezia Giulia, commonly known as Friuli, is in the far north-east corner of Italy. Mountains cover a large part of the region; vineyards are relegated to the foothills (notably the Collio and Colli Orientali zones) and flatlands (the Grave del Friuli zone) of the south.

Careful vine pruning — Friuli has some of the lowest yields in Italy — and technical expertise have gained the region international respect for its clean, crisp dry whites and its fresh, highly-scented reds. These wines are generally made without wood-ageing or malolactic fermentation, allowing the full varietal character of the grapes to be appreciated.

Collio & Colli Orientali del Friuli

The adjacent DOC zones of Collio Goriziano, usually known just as Collio, and Colli Orientali del Friuli lie in the foothills of the Alps bordering Slovenia in former Yugoslavia. Calcium and fossil deposits enrich the soil in many of the terraced vineyards. White wines predominate in both zones: most are varietals and meant to be drunk young.

Tocai Friulano — believed to be native to north-eastern Italy — is the most widely-planted white grape. However, after years of debate the EC has concluded that, in order to avoid confusion with Hungary's Tokaji — made from a blend of Hungarian grapes — Italy's Tocai grape must be renamed; the new name has yet to be decided. It makes wine that is green-tinged pale straw in colour and has an almond-scented fragrance. The indigenous Ribolla Gaialla generally makes lemony dry whites; Verduzzo whites tend to have a nutty flavour. Pinot Grigio makes crisp, dry, relatively full-bodied wine, usually a pale straw colour, but if it receives a bit more skin contact during vinification it

Mateotti Square in Udine, in the centre of Friuli-Venezia Giulia's wine zones.

develops attractive copper tinges. Sauvignon Blanc makes a fine, zesty, highly-scented dry wine, while Malvasia Istriana is dry with a nutty fragrance. Pinot Bianco and Chardonnay also excel here, some made in a fresh young style, others vinified or matured in wood to give richer wines. Picolit and Ramandolo (from Verduzzo grapes) are dessert wines.

Among reds, Cabernet (Franc, Sauvignon or both) is a fresh, deeply-coloured dry wine with herbaceous hints in its blackcurrant perfumes. Some examples improve with age. Merlot has a ruby colour and silky texture, while Refosco is lightly tannic with raspberry and blackberry flavours and an intense bouquet. Refosco, too, benefits from some ageing. Schioppettino, a brambly-scented dry red, improves with a few years' ageing.

One of Collio's most famous wines is not, in fact, a DOC wine — Jermann's Vintage Tunina (see opposite).

Grave del Friuli

This vast, gravelly plain, stretching from east of Venice to the Isonzo River, accounts for about two-thirds of Friuli's total production. Medium- to full-bodied red wines made from Merlot, the Cabernets, Pinot Nero and the indigenous Refosco dominate. Tocai, Pinot Grigio, Pinot Bianco and Chardonnay grapes produce fresh and fruity dry whites for drinking young. A Merlot-based rosé is also made.

Other Friuli wines

In the south-east corner of the region the Isonzo DOC produces excellent, scented reds and delicate whites. The Carso DOC makes sturdy reds from Terrano, a clone of Refosco, and zesty dry whites from Malvasia.

Aquileia and Latisana DOCs, on the lower plains along the Adriatic coast, make small amounts of mainly easy-drinking reds (especially Merlot) and whites for drinking young. ☐

PRODUCERS

Most wine in Friuli is made directly by growers. Plots are very small and fragmented, but even the smallest estate may produce several wines, and estate-bottling is widespread. Lower yields and often meticulous winemaking have improved quality, especially of the whites.

COLLIO AND COLLI ORIENTALI
Borgo del Tiglio
The superb Collios (Malvasia, Ca' delle Vallade, Tocai Ronco della Chiesa, Chardonnay) and the IGTs (Rosso della Centa, Studio di Bianco) are top references for the Cormons zone.

Girolama Dorigo
The Pignolo, a native red grape variety owes its survival to this great Buttrio producer. The Colli Orientali wines (Picolit, Chardonnay, etc) and the red blend Montsclapade are excellent.

Livio Felluga
One of the great historical figures of winemaking in Friuli, Livio Felluga produces delightful Collio Orientali wines at Brazzano di Cormons. His whole range is good, but the white Terre Alte is outstanding. Prestigious white and sweet Picolit, superb Merlot Sosso and Refosco, new IGT Vertigo.

Gravner
Based at Oslavia, in Gorizia province, Josko Gravner is a great winemaker who produces excellent Collio DOCs (such as the Ribolla Gialla) and interesting *vini da tavola*.

Vinnaioli Jermann
Silvio Jermann of Farra d'Isonzo is a winemaker of international fame, who produces only *vini da tavola*, blends or varietals, mostly whites. His best-known wine is the rich Vintage Tunina, a flavourful dry white. Other wines include the recent Capo Martino (Tocai and Pinot), the renowned Chardonnay Where Dreams and the new IGT Pignacoluse made from Pignolo.

Le Vigne di Zamo
The vineyard of the Rosazzo abbey, in Udine, makes Colli Orientali wines, fabulous *vini da tavola* — a white Ronco delle Acacie and a red Ronco dei Roseti —, and the long-lived, very tannic Pignolo.

Miani
Enzo Pontoni is said to live at his vineyard at Buttrio. His wines are in any case proof of the care he takes of them. Fabulous Colli Orientali wines, ranging from the Tocai Friulano to the Refosco Vigna Calvari, as well as a Sauvignon and two *vini da tavola*.

Ronco del Gelso
From his 15-ha (37-acre) vineyard at Cormons, Giorgio Badin produces exceptional Isonzo wines (Tocai Friulano, Sauvignon, Bianco Làtimis, Merlot, etc). A meticulous winemaker (hyperoxygenation) and grower.

Ronco del Gnemiz
This estate in Udine province is famous for its Colli Orientali Chardonnay, but the whole range is equally excellent.

Russiz Superiore
This 60-ha (148-acre) estate at Captriva belongs to Marco Felluga (who also owns a large estate at Gradisca) and to his son. It makes a range of elegant Collio DOC varietals, notably a superb Sauvignon. Interesting IGT Verduzzo.

Mario Schiopetto
The three children of Mario Schiopetto, the brilliant and perfectionist winemaker, are nowadays working with him and have built the winery he always dreamt of. The estate holds 22ha (54 acres) in Collio and 9ha (22 acres) in Colli Orientali. Wines — always among the region's best — include the fabulous Pinot Bianco Amrità, the Tarsia (a Sauvignon aged in French oak), the Tocai Pardes, all DOC wines, and the IGT Blanc des Rosis.

Villa Russiz
This Captriva estate produces a range of remarkable Collio white wines (Tocai, Malvasia, Sauvignon, Istriana, Pinot Bianco, etc), as well as the fabulous Sauvignon and Merlot Graf de la Tour.

Volpe Pasini
Once more, this estate produces high quality wines, which include the Zuc di Volpe range (Pinot Grigio, Chardonnay) and the Bianco Le Roverelle blend.

Other Collio and Colli Orientali producers
Ascevi-Luwa, Conte Attems, Conte d'Attimis, Bastiani, Borgo Conventi, Butussi, Paolo Caccese, Colmello di Grotta, Comelli, Dal Fari, Mauro Drius, Formentini, Giovanni, Edi Keber, Renato Keber, La Castellada, La Rajade, Le Due Terre, Le Viarte, Fratelli Livon, Ronchi di Manzano, Meroi, Perusini, Isidoro Polencic, Primosic, Alessandro Princic, Puiatti, Dario Raccaro, Rocca Bernarda, Scubla, Castello di Spessa, Oscar Sturm, Ronco dei Tassi, Franco Toros, Venica & Venica, Vigna del Lauro, Tenuta Villanova, Andrea Visintini.

GRAVE DEL FRIULI
Pighin
The Pighin family own the largest private estate in Friuli, with 140ha (345 acres) in Grave del Friuli and 30ha (74 acres) in Collio. Their winery at Risano, in Udine province, produces wines from each DOC, as well as two *vini da tavola*, the red Baredo and the white Soreli.

Vignetti le Monde
At Prata di Pordenone, almost in the Veneto, Piergiovanni Pistoni makes good long-lived red wines (Cabernet Sauvignon, Cabernet Franc, Refosco, etc).

Other Grave del Friuli producers
Borgo San Daniele, Cabert, Di Lenardo, Le Fredis, Edi Luisa, Lis Neris-Pecorari, Masut da Rive, Vigneti Pittaro, Plozner, Vistorta, Cooperative La Delizia.

OTHER WINES
Ca' Bolani
This family estate has 180ha (445 acres) of vines (5,000 vines/ha) at Cervignano del Friuli, in Udine province, and is owned by the Zonin family, who run a big wine company. Renowned Friuli Aquileia wines (Pinot Grigio, Refosco, Sauvignon, etc), as well as the Opimio (Chardonnay/Tocai) and the Conte Bolani (Merlot/Cabernet Sauvignon), both excellent blends.

Vie di Romans
This 28-ha (69-acre) estate at Mariano del Friuli produces delightful Isonzo wines, which are among Italy's most elegant white wines. Top wines include the Piere and Vieris Sauvignons, two Chardonnays and the fabulous Pinot Griogio Dessimis.

Other producers
Tenuta Beltrame, Castelvecchio, Stellio Gallo, Edy Kante, Pierpaolo Pecorari.

WINE ZONES OF TUSCANY AND CENTRAL ITALY

With 37 classified DOC and DOCG zones — this is a temporary figure — and countless "super" *vini da tavola*, Tuscany (together with Piedmont) is Italy's most important quality wine-producing region and, without a doubt, the most dynamic. An increasing number of winemakers in the neighbouring region of Umbria are patiently undertaking the task of revamping their *appellations* (11 DOC and 2 DOCG). Across the Apennines, in the Marches, Abruzzo and Molise, the situation is also changing for the better.

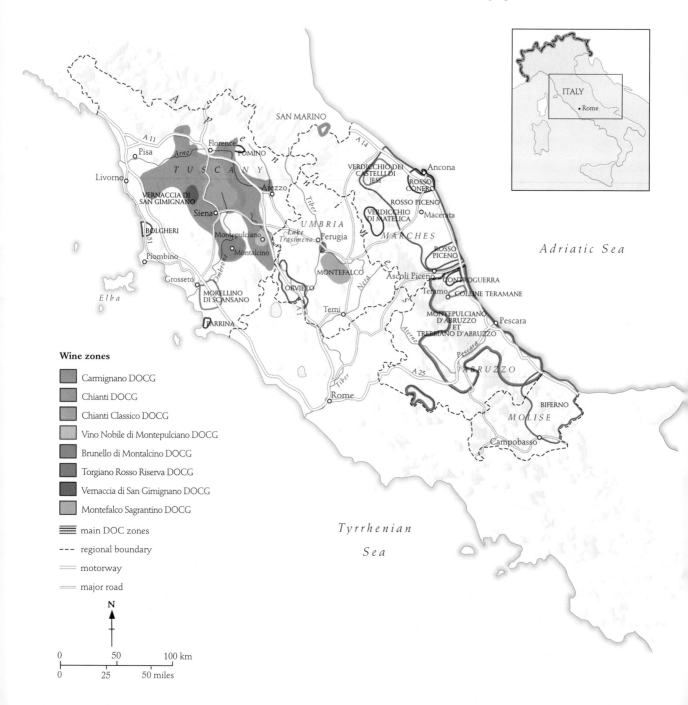

Wine zones

- Carmignano DOCG
- Chianti DOCG
- Chianti Classico DOCG
- Vino Nobile di Montepulciano DOCG
- Brunello di Montalcino DOCG
- Torgiano Rosso Riserva DOCG
- Vernaccia di San Gimignano DOCG
- Montefalco Sagrantino DOCG
- main DOC zones
- regional boundary
- motorway
- major road

0   50   100 km
0   25   50 miles

TUSCANY

Tuscany is a wine region character-ized by constant innovation and renewal, although it almost certainly is home to the oldest continuous wine traditions in Italy, possibly in Europe. When the great renaissance of art, sci-ence and scholarship began in the 14th century, winemaking families such as the Frescobaldi and Antinori were becoming established in Flo-rence. Such families were at the fore-front of the current renaissance of quality wine in Tuscany.

The region is known throughout the world for the red wines of Chi-anti, which in the 1960s acquired a reputation for being thin and dull, and quality plumbed the depths. How-ever, during the 1980s Tuscany has led innovation in Italian winemaking. The impetus has come from the most important Chianti zone, Chianti Clas-sico, and the smaller northern zone of Chianti Rufina, where producers working closely with oenologists such as Giacomo Tachis, Maurizio Castelli and Franco Bernabei have dramati-cally improved techniques.

Further impetus for change came from coastal regions not previously known for wine, such as the area around Bolgheri, where two of Italy's great originals — Sassicaia and Ornellaia — are produced. Sassicaia is a red wine from Cabernet grapes (Sauvignon and Franc) that has been highly acclaimed worldwide (*see* p387). Inspired by its success, imagi-native winemakers in Tuscany and elsewhere now use imported grape varieties to put together unlikely blends. Others, preferring to rely on indigenous grapes, have not neces-sarily used them in the blends or pro-portions laid down by the DOC law.

From this has developed a whole new style of wine, known as the "super" *vino da tavola*. There is no greater contrast than between a basic Italian table wine and these "designer

Hillside vineyards near Greve, in the Chianti Classico zone.

wines". Prices — and packaging — became fantastical, but nowadays the balance is being restored to a certain extent. Sangiovese is equally as prized

VIN SANTO (DOC)

A tradition cherished by many Tuscan winemakers, even the most advanced, is the making of Vin Santo ("holy wine"). This is a *passito* wine, which means that it is made from dried grapes. In Tuscany the grapes (usually white varieties — Malvasia del Chianti, Trebbiano or Grechetto) are hung from rafters to dry, although hot air is used to dry the grapes in modern wineries. The raisins are pressed and the resultant wine is sealed in tiny barrels, *caratelli*, and left for between four and six years. It can be sweet or dry, although its name, suggesting a connection with Mass, implies that it was probably originally sweet. Either version is as the nectar of the gods, especially when drunk with the hard almond biscuits called *cantucci*, which are dipped into it.

as Cabernet. Bolgheri and Bolgheri Sassicaia have obtained DOC status under the Goria Law. The fever has hit the neighbouring Maremmae region from where remarkably good DOC wines are now emerging. In the quest for quality, valuable lessons have been learnt: the use of better clones, and of modern techniques allied to tradi-tional ones.

Gone, too, are the days when Tus-can white wines were old and oxi-dized or heavily sulphured. Good producers discovered that modern technology could make clean, fresh whites *vini da tavola*, while others embraced barrique-ageing for wines made with Chardonnay grapes.

Grape varieties
For red wines, the great Tuscan grape variety is Sangiovese. While it can make indifferent wines when the wrong clone is planted and the yields are pushed high, it can also produce wines to rival anything that is made in

Piedmont from Nebbiolo. Tuscan DOCG wines — the bitter-cherry-tasting Chianti Classico, the rich, powerful Brunello di Montalcino and the more austere Vino Nobile di Montepulciano — are the classics of the grape. In the hills south-east of Grosseto, near the town of Scansano, Sangiovese is known as Morellino, and has its own DOC zone for flavourful red Morellino di Scansano.

Mammolo, a red-wine variety with an aroma of violets, may be used in Vino Nobile di Montepulciano and Chianti. Canaiolo Nero is today a minor Chianti variety.

Trebbiano Toscano is the workhorse white grape variety of the whole of the centre of Italy. Given its essentially neutral character and its high productivity it will never make great wines, but with modern vinification techniques lower yields it can produce eminently drinkable ones. When blended with native grape varieties such as Malvasia del Chianti, or with foreign ones such as Chardonnay, it can form the basis of exciting, previously unheard of wines.

Classification of zones

In 1716 the Grand Duke of Tuscany created some of Europe's earliest wine zones, in Chianti, Carmignano and Pomino. The first zones in Tuscany to be awarded *denominazione di origine controllata* (DOC) status in 1966 were Brunello di Montalcino, Vino Nobile di Montepulciano and Vernaccia di San Gimignano, to be joined very soon afterwards by Chianti and Chianti Classico, then Carmignano and Pomino. All (except Pomino) now have DOCG status. Until the Sassicaia suddenly appeared on the scene, and the ensuing "consecration" of the Bolgheri *terroir*, these six zones could lay claim to the best Tuscan wines. Around 30 others are labelled DOC and the future looks rosy for the "new" Maremma region.

Chianti and Chianti Classico

Currently vineyards in six Tuscan provinces are eligible for the broad DOCG of Chianti, a red wine made from 75-100% Sangiovese, which may or may not be blended with a little Canaiolo and a small proportion of the white varieties Trebbiano and Malvasia del Chianti. Up to 10% Cabernet Sauvignon, Merlot or other red varieties is permitted.

Eight sub-zones are allowed to add their name to the basic denomination, of which the largest, Classico, and the smallest, Rufina, have worked hardest to improve Chianti's image. In other Chianti zones — Colli Senesi, Colli Fiorentini, Montalbano, Colli Aretini, Colline Pisani, Chianti Montespertoli — things have changed less.

The arrival of the DOCG for Chianti Classico in 1984 is now seen as a considerable success. New controls on yields and production brought the quantities down from 380,000hl in 1983 to 280,000hl in 1998 and the presence of white grapes in the blend (a Chianti tradition started in the 19th century by Barone Ricasoli and aimed at softening the harsh tannins in old-style Sangiovese) is now optional.

Much Chianti is still made for relatively early drinking, but Chianti Classico, with its raspberry and black cherry tastes combined with dryness and acidity, is hard to drink young or without food. Chianti Rufina has more of the acidity but possibly better fruit and ageing ability.

Brunello di Montalcino

Slopes near the hill town of Montalcino in Siena province produce this DOCG zone's (1980) powerful red wines. The vineyards, a mix of clay and the stony soil known as *galestro*, enjoy a temperate hill climate. The only grape permitted is Brunello (a Sangiovese clone), and the wines must be aged at least five years — two of which in oak — (*riservas* have an extra year's ageing). They are full in flavour and body, with a pronounced wood taste — some would say excessively tannic and bitter — and will age in bottle almost indefinitely. Rosso di Montalcino DOC covers the same area, for wines that may be sold after one year's ageing.

Vino Nobile di Montepulciano

The beautiful hill town of Montepulciano has been known for its red wine for centuries; it acquired the epithet *"nobile"* in the 18th century. Most of the vineyards, with sand and clay soils, face the Chiana Valley. The main grape is Prugnolo (a local Sangiovese clone), which makes up at least 70% of the blend, softened by Canaiolo Nero and given fragrance by Mammolo. Sometimes the wines are rather lean, but the best have spice and sandalwood notes. Vino Nobile DOCG must be aged in wood for two years; younger wines may be sold as Rosso di Montepulciano DOC.

Carmignano

In this small region west of Florence the red wines must be approved by experts before they can be labelled DOCG. Similar to Chianti, the wines are improved by the inclusion in the Sangiovese-based blend of up to 10% Cabernet grapes (Sauvignon or Franc), which were first planted here in the 18th century.

Bolgheri and Pomino

The majority of grapes used by these two small zones are French varieties. Bolgheri is a recent DOC south of Livorno. This zone, close to the sea, includes wines in the Sassicaia category (*see* p381) which require a minimum 80% Cabernet Sauvignon content. The second of these two regions, Pomino, situated on high hills (up to 700m/2,300ft) to the east of Florence, is dominated by the Frescobaldi family's Tenuta de Pomino. The DOC, created in 1983, allows up to 25% Cabernet and 20% Merlot grapes in its red wine and up to 80% Pinot Bianco and/or Chardonnay in its whites.

Vernaccia di San Gimignano

Vineyards near the medieval towered town of San Gimignano grow Vernaccia grapes to produce a DOC white wine with just a hint of acidity.   □

QUALITY FACTORS

Of all Italy's regions, Tuscany is one of the best suited to the production of quality wine (and olives). The landscape is the key: this is essentially a hilly region, providing ideal sites for vines. Even the less hilly parts, such as the Bolgheri zone to the southwest, have proved to be suitable for fine-wine production.

The Chianti Classico zone
Chianti is made throughout central Tuscany, from the Apennine foothills near Arezzo in the east, to the warmer coastal zone. Most of the best wine comes from the Classico zone between Gaiole and Castellina, where the vineyards are often around 500m (1,650ft) above sea level.

Organization
Organization can be as important as other factors in the sometimes chaotic Italian wine scene. The producers of Chianti Classico have been better organized than others over a longer period, leading to a greater awareness of quality and an acceptance that it is worth paying more for that quality.

TUSCANY: ELEVATION AND WINE ZONES

Wine Zone
Chianti Classico
Chianti

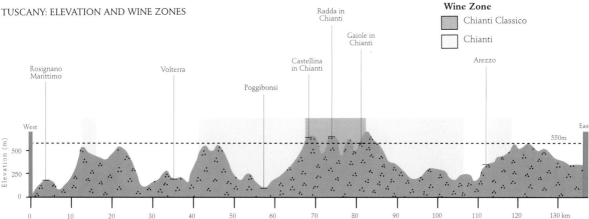

Clonal selection
Sangiovese, the major red grape variety of the centre of Italy, can appear in 14 or 15 clones, the choice of which plays an important part in the quality of the better wines.

Of the two broad categories of Sangiovese — Piccolo and Grosso — the Piccolo is the smaller and thinner-skinned; it is also the easier to grow, with higher yields. It was widely planted after World War II, when the livelihood of peasant farmers depended on selling as many grapes as possible.

Sangiovese Grosso, also known as Sangioveto, makes the better wine. The Brunello grape, a clone of Sangiovese Grosso, has been used in Montalcino since the late 19th

Some of Tuscany's greatest wines are aged in small barrels.

century. Another clone of Sangiovese Grosso, Prugnolo, is used in the Vino Nobile of Montepulciano. Although many old Chianti vineyards are still planted with Piccolo,. the quality of Chianti wines improve considerably as the vineyards are replanted with better clones.

Altitude and soils
Certain zones in Tuscany are distinguished by their altitude. Higher land in this warm region means the grapes keep cool in the summer. The three best Tuscan wine zones are Chianti Classico, Montalcino and Montepulciano, with vineyards on slopes up to 550m (1,800ft) above sea level. Chianti Classico, along with its northern neighbour Rufina, is cooler than the other Chianti zones; it also has better-drained soils, a mixture of lime-based *albarese* and the more stony *galestro*.

The high altitudes also mean that vintages vary more here than in other zones, generally owing to wet weather in the summer.

CHIANTI PRODUCERS

The top names in Chianti are based in the Chianti Classico zone between Florence and Siena, centred on the towns of Greve, Castellina, Radda, Gaiole and Castelnuovo Berardenga, and in the small Chianti Rufina zone north-east of Florence. Many are equally renowned for their innovative *vini da tavola*.

Castello di Ama
This 80-ha (200-acre) estate at Gaiole in Chianti is famous for its Chianti Classico wines from the Bellavista and La Casuccia vineyards, as well as its splendid IGT wines Vigna l'Apparita, Il Chiuso and Vigna al Poggio

Antinori
See profile.

Badia a Coltibuono
This 11th-century monastery, a Mecca of Tuscan sophistication, is owned by the Stucchi family since 1841. The jewel of the 59-ha (146-acre) vineyard is the Sangioveto, a glorious 100% Sangiovese *vino da tavola*, followed closely by the Chianti Classico Selezione RS.

Castello di Cacchiano
This beautiful 33-ha (82-acre) estate at Gaiole has decided to focus production on the Chianti Classico Riserva Millennio: as "grand vin du château" it is made from the superb Sangiovese grapes formerly used only for the no longer existing RF Cacchiano. Flavourful Rosso di Toscana and great Vin Santo.

Castellare di Castellina
The 25-ha (62-acre) estate continues its progress and has a brand new winery. Paolo Panerai's wines are still made by Maurizio Castelli. The Sangiovese/Malvasia Nera-based *vini da tavola* I Sodi di San Niccolo is still the top wine, but the Chianti Classico wines (for instance, Vigna al Pog-giale) and the IGT Canonico (Chardonnay) are excellent.

Castell' in Villa
This 55-ha (136-acre) estate at Castelnuovo Berardenga receives advice from Giacomo Tachis. It produces a Chianti Classico Riserva and a Sangiovese-based *vino da tavola*, the Santacroce, both highly acclaimed.

Cennatoio
From his 13-ha (32-acre) vineyard at Panzano in Chianti, a zone famous for its micro-climate, Leandro Alessi produces very good Chianti Classicos, and the IGTs Etrusco (Sangiovese) and Rosse Fiorentino (Cabernet Sauvignon).

Fattoria di Felsina
This 52-ha (12-acre) estate at Castelnuovo Berardenga has been called the Margaux of Chianti in honour of its rich wines produced under the supervision of Giuseppe Mazzocolin and his consultant, Franco Bernabei. Top wines include the splendid IGT Fontalloro (100% Sangiovese), two Chianti Classicos Riserva, Rancia and Berardenga, as well as the Chardonnay I Sistri and the Cabernet Sauvignon Maestro Raro.

Castello di Fonterutoli
Owned by the Mazzei family since 1435, this 62-ha (153-acre) estate is at the forefront of Chianti quality wines. The Mazzeis produce a range of superb reds: a Chianti Classico and a Riserva, as well as the IGTs Siepi and Concerto, and a flavoursome Morellino di Scansano Belguardo. The Siepi is certainly at present one of the best Tuscan wines.

Tenuta Fontodi
This 61-ha (151-acre) estate at Panzano owned by the Manetti family produces — under the supervision of Franco Bernabei — one of the best Sangiovese-based Tuscan IGT wines, Flacianello della Pieve. The rest of the range is up to it: Chianti Classicos, such as the *riserva* Vigna del Sorbo, good Pinot Noir and Syrah, and the white IGT Meriggio.

Marchesi de' Frescobaldi
The marquis de Frescobaldi have owned vineyards since the 13th century, but started to bottle wines only in the 1960s. Today, most of the production (500,000 cases) comes from 780ha (1930 acres) of vines, which are well-located in the Chianti, Chianti Rufina, Montalcino and Pomino zones. Top of the range are the excellent Chianti Rufina Montesodi and the *riserva* Castello di Nipozzano, as well as the Pomino Bianco Il Benefizio (mainly Chardonnay), made at the splendid Tenuta di Pomino, well up in the Apennines. Noteworthy Brunello di Montalcino Castelgiocondo.

Isole e Olena
From 40ha (99 acres) at Barberino Val d'Elsa, Paolo De Marchi, a California-trained Piedmontese, produces universally acclaimed wines. His trademark is the quality of his Sangiovese vines and his relentless efforts with Cabernet Sauvignon and Syrah grapes — he has been one of the region's pioneers for the latter. The winery is being modernized. The whole range is noteworthy: a great Chianti Classico, the *vini da tavola* (splendid Collezione De Marchi Cabernet and l'Eremo Syrah, the delightful Sangiovese Cepparello) and, last but not least, the Vin Santo.

La Massa
This 22-ha (54-acre) estate at Panzano produces two superb Chianti Classicos made by Carlo Ferrini. The Giorgio Primo is a top reference.

La Sala
This 15-ha (37-acre) estate at S. Casciano owes its growing fame to the passion of two women, Laura Baronti, the owner, and Gabriella Tani, who looks after the vineyard. The wines are amazingly fleshy, dense and clean. Top wines are the Chianti Classico Riserva and the IGT Campo all'Albero.

Antica Fattoria Machiavelli
The 26-ha (64-acre) estate at S. Casciano Val di Pesa is one of Gruppo Italiano Vini's jewels. The writer-politician Machiavel was exiled here, and the Cabernet Sauvignon-based *vino da tavola* Ser Niccolò Solatio del Tani, one of the estate's top wines, is named after him. The two other stars are the superb Chianti Classico Riserva Vigna Fontalle and the IGT Il Principe, one of Italy's great Pinot Noirs.

Melini
The wines of this important Chianti wine house are clearly progressing. Top wines include the Chianti Classico Riserva La Selvanella and the Vernaccia di S. Gimignano Le Grillaie.

Fattoria Monsanto
From 55ha (136 acres) at Barberino Val d'Elsa, Fabrizio Bianchi produces the excellent Chianti Classico Riserva Il Poggio and has given his name to a range of good *vini da tavola*, which include a Sangiovese and a Chardonnay, both reputed.

Castello della Paneretta
The IGT Quattrocentenario and the Terrine of this 16-ha (40-acre) estate at Barberino Val d'Elsa have created a sensation.

Podere Poggio Scalette
Owned by the winemaker Vittorio Fiore, this stony 12-ha (30-acre) high altitude estate at Greve produces the lavish IGT Il Carbonaione, made from Sangiovese di Lamole, a rare and famous clone.

Castello di Querceto
This 55-ha (136-acre) vineyard at Greve produces elegant Chianti Classicos (among them, the *riserva* Il Picchio) and IGT reds (notably the superb Cignale and La Corte).

Agricola Querciabella
Wines from this 29-ha (65-acre) Greve estate include two exceptional *vini da tavola* (Batàr and Camartina), with Giacomo Tachis' characteristic touch. Good Chianti Classicos.

Castelli dei Rampolla
With advice from Giacomo Tachis, the Di Napoli family of Panzano produces two magnificent Cabernet Sauvignon-based *vini da tavola* (Vigna di Alceo and Sammarco), but the Chianti Classicos are up to it.

Barone Ricasoli
Francesco Ricasoli, a descendant of the "Iron Baron" who invented the Chianti style in the 19th century, has recently restructured the production of the Castello di Brolio, a magnificent 227-ha (561-acre) single vineyard. The Castello di Brolio, the top wine of the estate made from a selection of Sangiovese, the Brolio and the *riserva* Rocca Guicciarda are all superb Chianti Classicos. The splendid IGT Casalferro (Sangiovese/Merlot) is another star. The Chardonnay Torricella, the pleasant Formulae red and the Vin Santo, all equally good, complete the range.

Tenuta di Riseccoli
A small 15-ha (37-acre) estate at Greve, where the Romanelli family produce a delicious Chianti Classico Riserva, a classic Vin Santo and a reputed IGT, the Saeculum.

Ruffino
One of Chianti's giants (over 600ha/1480 acres), owned by the Folonari family, who have accomplished spectacular progress. Wines from the large wineries at Pontassieve include three exceptional *vini da tavola*: Cabreo Il Borgo, Cabreo La Pietra and the Romitorio di Santedame, an entrancing typically Tuscan wine. Fine Chianti Classicos. As to the Fattoria di Nozzole at Greve in Chianti, it produces the magnificent IGT Il Pareto and the excellent Chianti Classico Riserva La Forra.

San Felice
This 120-ha (297-acre) estate near Castelnuovo Berardenga produces noteworthy Chianti Classicos, including the excellent Riserva Poggio Rosso, the IGT Vigorello — a classic Sangiovese/Cabernet blend — and two Brunello di Montalcinos.

San Giusto a Rentennano
The 28-ha (69-acre) estate at Gaiole makes two reputed *vini da tavola* (Percarlo and La Ricolma), a masterful Vin Santo and good Chianti Classicos.

Castello San Polo in Rosso
Wines from this 22-ha (54-acre) estate at Gaiole include a great IGT wine made from Sangiovese Cetinaia.

Selvapiana
Owned by the marquis Giuntini, this 45-ha (111-acre) estate in Chianti Rufina is reputed for its long-lived wines, which are sometimes austere when young. Elegant Chianti Classicos, such as the *riserva* Fornace and the Bucerchiale, noteworthy Vin Santo and, since 1993, a good Pomino Rosso.

Fattoria Terrabianca
The 47-ha (116-acre) estate at Radda in Chianti is advised by the winemaker Vittorio Fiore. Top wines of its consistently regular range are two IGT Campaccios and the Chianti Classico Vigna della Croce.

Vecchie Terre di Montefili
A Panzano estate reputed for its excellent range, which includes a Chianti Classico and the IGT wines Anfiteatro and Bruno di Rocca.

Castello di Volpaia
The hamlet of Volpaia, near Radda in Chianti, has one of the highest vineyards in Chianti Classico, at 430-600m (1,410-1968ft). For this reason, wines from this 41-ha (101-acre) estate tend to be long-lived, though austere in certain years. Top wines from the range made by Maurizio Castelli include the IGTs Coltassala and Balifico.

Other Chianti producers
Agricoltori del Chianti Geografico, Casa Emma, Castello d'Albola, Fattoria di Basciano, Borgo Salcetino, Tenuta Bossi, Carobbio, Fattoria Casaloste, Fattorie Chigi Saracini, Colombaio di Cencio, Corti Corsini, Fattoria Corzano e Paterno, Castello di Farnetella, Fossi, La Brancaia, La Madonnina-Triacca, Le Filigare, Meleta, Monte Bernardi, Fattoria Nittardi, Fattoria di Petroio, Fattoria Petrolo, Poggerino, Poggio al Sole, Riecine, Rietine, Rocca delle Macie, Rocca di Castagnoli, San Fabiano Calcinaia, San Vincenti, Fattoria Sonnino, Castello di Verrazzano, Castello di Vicchiomaggio, Fattoria di Vignamaggio, Villa Cafaggio, Villa Pillo, Viticcio.

ANTINORI

From his Florentine palace, the marquis Piero Antinori — together with his daughters Albiera, Allegra and Alessia — runs a wine empire: over 2,000ha (5,000 acres) and 1.25 million cases of wine each year. The company, which has been in the wine business since 1385, has made big investments recently, in Tuscany and Umbria, its traditional bases, as elsewhere: Pouilles, Piedmont, Franciacorta, Hungary, the United States. Top wines include the Tignanello, created in the 1970s by the great winemaker Giacomo Tachis, and the Solaia (80% Cabernets). Other wines include the Brunello di Montalcino Pian delle Vigne and the Bolgheri Guado al Tasso, a great number of Chianti Classicos, the IGTs Santa Cristina and Galestro, the very rare Vinsanto Rosso and the superb range of Castello della Sala at Orvieto (*see* p390).

OTHER ZONES AND PRODUCERS

Most of the DOCG zones of Brunello di Montalcino, Vino Nobile di Montepulciano and Carmignano and the DOC regions of Vernaccia di San Gimignano and Pomino are to be found within the vast Chianti DOCG zone. The producers therefore have a choice: they can either make standard Chianti, a "super *vino da tavola*", or even local DOC or DOCG wines.

BRUNELLO DI MONTALCINO

Altesino

This 28-ha (70-acre) estate, created in 1970, produces several good Brunellos. The generic Brunello and the Montosoli *cru* (from high-altitude, stony soils), as well as the IGT wines Alte d'Altesi and Palazzo Altesi, are all highly acclaimed.

Tenuta di Argiano

A good 20 out of the Marone Cinzano family estate's 37ha (90 acres) of vines are unbroken and this is quite unusual in Montalcino. The Brunello and the Rosso di Montalcino, produced under the supervision of Giacomo Tachis, are well-known but the star of the range is still the Solengo, a *vino da tavola* made from equal parts of Cabernet, Merlot and Syrah.

Banfi

This 3,000-ha (7,500-acre) estate — 800ha/20 acres are under vine —, with its ancient castle at Poggio alle Mura (renamed Castello Banfi), its huge winery, its re-landscaped hillside and artificial lake, is one of Montalcino's main attractions. It was founded in 1978 by the Mariani brothers — owners of Banfi Vintners in the United States and behind Lambrusco's success in that country — who were looking to invest in Tuscany to produce a sweet Moscadello wine. Since then the focus has shifted onto red wines and many very famous wines feature in their current range, including the Brunello Riserva Poggio all'Oro and the flavoursome Rosso di Montalcino, not to forget the whole Sant'Antimo DOC range and the IGT Excelsus.

Fattoria dei Barbi

This estate, founded in 1790, is a fine example of what can be found in the region. It belongs to the Colombini family. Recent investment in the new

Morellino di Scansano DOC has produced good results. Top of the range is the Brunello Riserva Vigna del Fiore. A pleasant Brusco dei Barbi IGT and excellent farm produce can be enjoyed in the restaurant on the estate. Donatella Cinelli Colombini produces two Brunellos (Leone Rosso, Prime Donne) under her own name.

Biondi-Santi

The region's most famous estate is behind the Brunello as we know it today. Around 1880, Ferruccio Biondi-Santi began to produce wine from a particular Sangiovese clone, which he called Brunello. This huge, tannic wine was famous for its long life. There was a time when popularity declined — the wines no longer seemed to be worth the huge price — but the company has now made a comeback. The Brunellos sold by Jacopo Bondi Santi come from the Il Greppo estate, at the heart of the property, and also from

the lovely little Poggio Salvi estate. The stars of the show are the Brunellos, the Sassoalloro IGT and the Moscadello DOC Aurico.

Tenuta Caparzo

This recently reorganised 47-ha (116-acre) estate has once more become a leader in Montalcino. The best wines in the range, still produced by Vittorio Fiore, remain the Brunello Vigna La Casa and Riserva, the IGT Ca' del Pazzo, the lovely Moscadello V.T., enhaced b Sémillon, and the Rosso di Montalcino La Caduta.

Casanova di Neri

This 20-ha (50-acre) estate is producing some of the most interesting wines in the region, including the Brunellos Riserva Cerretalto and Tenuta Nuova.

Tenuta di Castelgiocondo and Luce

Both estates belong to Frescobaldi (*see* p384).

Cerbaiona

A reputed estate. Excellent Brunello and Cerbaiona, a Sangiovese-based *vino da tavola*.

Tenuta Col d'Orcia

One of the two great Montalcino estates belonging to the Marone Cinzano family. It has undergone hugely expensive renovations and other investments are underway (new research into clones grown on the Sangiovese in the Banditella vineyard). Wines from the current vineyards (108ha/266 acres) include the fabulous Brunello Eiserva Poggio al Vento and the Olmaia, an IGT from Cabernet Sauvignon, held to be one of the best in Italy. Excellent Rosso di Montalcino, Rosso degli Spezieri and Moscadello VT Pascena.

Podere Il Galampio

This 12.5-ha (30-acre) estate produces some compact, elegantly-oaked wines.

Grapes are left to dry before being made into Vin Santo.

La Fiorita

The Brunello wines produced on these 5ha (12 acres) — soon to be increased — are known for their ripe fruity flavours but the (well) named Quadratura del Cerchio (Quadrature of the Circle) range in particular offers some astounding *vini da tavola*. Do not miss the "Terzo Viaggio", a fascinating blend of Tuscan Sangiovese and Apulian Primitivo (alias Zinfandel).

La Palazzetta

The 5ha (12 acres) of vines, planted (close together) by Flavio Fanti, are soon to double. Meanwhile, his full-bodied, meaty, complex Brunello and Rosso di Montalcino wines are already collecting awards.

La Poderina

These 20ha (50 acres), owned by an insurance company, produce a lovely Brunello Riserva and an excellent Moscadello.

Lisini

The Lisini family estate covers 11.5ha (28 acres) of fabulous wild countryside in Sant'Angelo del Colle. Its two Brunellos, the classic and Ugolaia, made by Franco Bernabei, have earned a justified reputation as elegant wines of considerable weight.

Mastrojanni

These beautiful, substantial, velvety Brunellos encompass the style of the great consultant-winemaker Maurizio Castelli. The best being the Schiena d'Asino and Riserva. The winery has undergone renovation (temperature control, casks) — always a good sign.

Siro Pacenti

Already famous for his Brunellos, Giancarlo Pacenti is taking a passionate interest in, and contributing to, the research programme set up between Montalcino and the Faculty of Oenology in Bordeaux. There are some promising new wines in the gestation stages.

Pieve Santa Restituta

16ha (40 acres) under the control of Angelo Gaja since 1994 (*see* p368). Fabulous Brunellos (Sugarille, Rennina) and an elegant *vino da tavola,* the Promis.

Salvioni-La Cerbaiola

Wine enthusiasts are snapping up the Brunello wines produced on this tiny estate.

Val di Suga

This 38-ha (95-acre) estate, belonging to a pharmaceutical group, produces fabulous Brunellos, among them Vigna Spuntali and Vigna del Lago.

Other Brunello di Montalcino producers

Castello di Camigliano, Canalicchio di Sopra, Canalicchio di Sotto, Capanna, Andrea Costanti, Due Portine-Gorelli, Fuligni, Il Poggiolino, Il Poggiolo, Il Poggione, La Campana, La Fornace, La Fortuna, La Gerla, Mocali, Agostina Pieri, Poggio Antico, Scopetone.

VINO NOBILE DI MONTEPULCIANO
Avignonesi

The Falvo brothers' 200-ha (494-acre) estate with its 16th-century Palazzo in the heart of Montepulciano produces two of the *appellation*'s best Vino Nobile *riservas*, the Rosso di Montepulciano DOC and a series of IGT wines, ranging from the most "simple" (flavourful Avignonesi Bianco and Rosso) to the most ambitious (Il Marzocco Chardonnay, Grifi Cabernet, etc), as well as a fine Vin Santo and a rare Occhio di Pernice.

Bindella-Tenuta Vallocaia

This estate is owned by a Swiss importer of fine wines, who is a winemaker to the core with a passion for quality. The vineyard will soon reach 30ha (74 acres), of which 12 are newly planted at 7,000 vines/ha. This will go some way to satisfy the great demand for the only two wines: the Vino Nobile DOCG

and the IGT Vallocaia.

Boscarelli

With advice from Maurizio Castelli, Paolo De Ferrari and his two sons produce consistently superb wines from their 12-ha (30-acre) vineyard. Connoisseurs appreciate the two Vino Nobile wines (including the Vigna del Nocio *cru*), which are generously fleshy, elegant and never too woody in taste. Do not miss the "super Toscan" called Boscarelli.

Fattoria del Cerro

This excellent 156-ha (385-acre) estate is owned by the same insurance company as La Poderina. Its rather complete range includes magnificent Vino Nobile wines (notably the Antica Chiusina *cru*) and the IGT Manero (a *barrique*-aged Sangiovese) and Poggio Golo. Noteworthy Chianti dei Colli Senesi and *novello* Brescello.

Fattoria La Braccesca

These 140ha (346 acres), 30 of them inside the DOCG zone, are owned by Antinori (see profile). Major investments and the talent of oenologists Renzo Cotarella and Maurizio Angeletti account for a superb range, the Vino Nobile, the Rosso di Montepulciano Sabazio and a luscious Merlot IGT wine.

Poliziano

This magnificent 90-ha (222-acre) estate is skilfully run by Federico Carletti and oenologist Carlo Ferrini. It is named after Montepulciano's favourite son, the Renaissance poet Poliziano, and has a new winery. The Vino Nobile are model wines, in particular the Vigna del'Asinone *cru*, and the *vini da tavola* Elegia and Le Stanze are worthy of their fame. Excellent Morellino di Scansano Lohsa.

Valdipiatta

This 24.5-ha (60.5-acre) estate is a reliable reference. Its exemplary wines, the Vino Nobile

riserva in particular, are vinified by the talented oenologist Paolo Vagaggini. The new Canaiolo/Merlot-based IGT Trincerone has caused a stir.

Other Vino Nobile di Montepulciano producers

Canneto, Contucci, Dei, Fassati-Fazi Battaglia, Vittorio Innocenti, Lodola Nuova, La Calonica, La Casella, La Ciarliana, Le Casalte, Lombardo, Nottola, Romeo, Tenuta Santavenere-Triacca, Trerose.

OTHER WINES

This category brings together the best of the DOCG Vernaccia di San Gimignano and Carmignano as well as producers of great *vini da tavola*. Incidentally, the whole of Tuscan wine country is currently under renovation. Since the coastal zone of Bolgheri gave birth to the famous Sassicaia, this region has been attracting attention (and considerable investment). The phenomenon now reaches far beyond the Maremma region proper, encouraging vocations and, in time, the creation of new *appellations*. In addition to Bolgheri, several DOC zones, including Montecucco, Montescudaio, Montereggio and Morellino di Scansano, appear to be particularly promising.

Banti

Erik Banti is a demanding and innovative producer. This pioneer of the Scansano zone currently holds 30ha (74 acres) of vines. His Morellino DOC Ciabatta is still one of the best. Noteworthy IGT Anno Primo, which contains a little Merlot.

Capannelle

This small Gaiole estate has won fame through its *vini da tavola*. The new owner has made a fine Chianti Classico, but its most reputed wines are the IGT Capannelle Rosso Barrique and the 50&50, a delicious Sangiovese/Merlot blend.

Tenuta di Capezzana

The Contini Bonacossi family live in a Medici villa on their 90-ha (222-acre) estate. Ugo Contini Bonacossi's wines have established the reputation of the small Carmignano zone, until 1975 part of Chianti Montalbano and upgraded to DOCG in 1990. The use of Cabernet Sauvignon goes back to the 18th century. Fine DOCG reds, such as the *riserva*, but its best known wine is the Ghiaie della Furba. The Carmignano Vin Santo is a classic of its kind.

Tenuta di Ghizzano

From 16ha (40 acres) south of Pisa, count Venerosi Pesciolini produces two first-rate IGTs: the luscious Veneroso, a pioneering Sangiovese/Cabernet-blend, and the fine Nambrot Merlot. Good Chianti and excellent Vin Santo S Germano.

Grattamacco

Piermario Meletti Cavallari continues his research on the Bolgheri *terroir*. The current version of his Grattamacco red, the Bolgheri Superiore, is a blend of 50% Cabernet Sauvignon, 25% Merlot and 25% Sangiovese. Very good.

Guicciardini-Strozzi

The ownership of this estate is the result of a marriage between two old Florentine families. Winemaking here is a thousand-year old tradition; Girolama Strozzi owns a piece of parchment from 944. But, more importantly, one can still feel the fervour and energy which are the prerequisites of success. The estate produces a large range of wines, including several Vernaccia di San Gimignano (excellent *riserva* San Biagio), a flavourful Chianti Colli Senesi Titolato, but the top wines are three superb IGT reds: the Sodole, the Selvascura and the Millani 994, created for the estate's millennium celebrations.

Fattoria La Pierotta

This 10-ha (25-acre) estate at Scarlino is one of the most promising of the new Montereggio zone. Its best representative is the delicious dense, clean and elegant Selvaneta.

Le Macchiole

The Paleo Rosso of this estate is a great Bolgheri Superiore, made from 85% of Cabernet Sauvignon. The IGT Scrio and Messorio are noteworthy.

Fattoria Le Pupille

The owners of this 35-ha (86-acre) estate are among the pioneers of the Morellino di Scansano zone (flavourful classic and *riserva*, magnificent Poggio Valente *cru*), only surpassed by the IGT wines Solalto and Saffredi.

Tenuta di Montecucco

The Montecucco Le Coste of this estate is a great success: a nice wild fruity flavour, mature tannins and a skilfuly managed woody taste.

Morris Farms

This 76-ha (188-acre) estate in Grosseto province is highly reputed for its Morellino di Scansano wines and its splendid IGT Avvoltore.

Tenuta dell'Ornellaia

This magnificent 70-ha (173-acre) estate is the brainchild of Lodovico Antinori (brother of Piero Antinori). Its vineyard has been created from start to finish from the family estate at Bolgheri, next to the Sassicaia estate. The first releases were in 1988. The wines produced here are all internationally famous *vini da tavola*, such as the reds Masseto and Ornellaia and the white Poggio alle Gazze.

Panizzi

This 10-ha (25-acre) estate is currently the best producer of Vernaccia di San Gimignano wines: its owner believes in this grape variety, despite the

very difficult marketing of this often tarnished wine.

Parmoleto

The delicious wine of this small Montecucco winemaker is a testimonial to the great future of this new DOC zone.

Tenuta San Guido

Here started the legend of the Sassicaia, the proud brainchild of the Marquis Incisa della Roccheta. The first release was in 1968 — under the aegis of the Antinori firm. But the famous Cabernet Sauvignon cuttings from the Lafite-Rothschild estate at Bordeaux — a token of the friendship between the two families — had already been planted in 1944. Once the ageing potential of this "family wine" became known, Giacomo Tachis, Antinori's great oenologist, was asked to conceive a wine of international fame. The Sassicaia is a blend of 80% Cabernet Sauvignon and 20% Cabernet Franc and ageing takes places in *barriques* (a third of them new). Year after year, its characteristics are admired: delicate and elegant, with a sophisticated bouquet, mature tannins creating a luscious wild fruity flavour, and a perfect finish.

Fattoria Sonnino

Wines from this 40-ha (99-acre) estate at Montespertoli include the particularly elegant, flavourful IGT Sanleone.

Castello del Terriccio

This superb 1,700-ha (4,200-acre) estate at Castellina Marittima, near Bolgheri, will soon have 40ha (99 acres) of vines. French grape varieties are favoured. A good choice, as is borne out by the Lupicaia Rosso, a Cabernet Sauvignon/Merlot-based *vino da tavola*.

Teruzzi & Puthod

Since 1974, Enrico Teruzzi and his wife, Carmen Puthod, live at the Fattoria Ponte a Ron-

dolino, a 84-ha (208-acre) estate devoted to Vernaccia di San Gimignano wines. Fine wines include two Vernaccias (among them, the Vigna a Rondolino *cru*) and two even more famous IGT whites, the Terre di Tufi and the Carmen.

Val delle Rose

A 33-ha (82-acre) vineyard, which will soon reach twice its surface. Owned by the Cecchi family, this estate is at the forefront of the Morellino di Scansano zone. The *riserva* is a nice "international" wine of great elegance.

Villa Cilnia

This 25-ha (62-acre) estate serves as a model for the Arezzo province. Its wines are vinified by Franco Bernabei. The currently most famous is the IGT Vocato, a Sangiovese/Cabernet Sauvignon blend.

Other producers

Ambrosini (Riflesso Antico, Subertum), Artimino (Villa Medicea), Tenuta di Bagnolo (Pinot Nero), Baroncini (Aia della Macina, Dometaia), Fattoria del Buonamico (Il Fortino, Cercatoja), Cesani (Luenzo), Cima (Vigneto Candia, Montervo, Romalbo), Podere Il Carnasciale (Il Caberlot), La Chiusa, Fattoria La Gigliola (Camporsoli), La Parrina, La Piaggia, Le Calle (Poggio d'Oro), Mantellassi (Le Sentinelle), Meleta (Rosso della Rocca), Merlini (Guadi Piani), Fattoria di Montechiari, Montesalario, Mormoraia (Vernaccia, Neitea, Ostrea), Sorelle Palazzi (Vin Santo), Perazzetta, Fattoria Poggio a Poppiano (Flocco), Poggio Gagliardo (Rovo et Bianco Vigna Lontana), Rascioni & Cecconello (Poggio Ciliegio), Podere San Michele (Allodio), Podere Scurtarola (Vermentino Nero), Serraiola (Vigna Montecristo), Fattoria Sorbaiano (Rosso delle Miniere, Bianco Lucestraia), Fattoria Uccelliera (Castellaccio), Varramistà, Wandanna (Terre dei Cascinieri, Virente).

CENTRAL ITALY

Cypresses, olive trees and vines, medieval hilltop cities and isolated castles; for many people the centre of Italy epitomizes the entire country. The regions of Umbria, the Marches, Abruzzo and Molise are linked by the Apennines, whose sunny foothills provide well-placed vineyard sites. The main grape varieties — Sangiovese (*see* p381) for red wines, Trebbiano Toscano (*see* p382) for whites — provide the unity between the regions, despite the strong personality and rapid expansion of local varieties.

Umbria
Landlocked Umbria, the green heart of Italy, has much in common with its neighbour, Tuscany. Not only are its vineyard sites on cool slopes, it also has a new generation of winemakers who have challenged the DOC rules and created successful "super" *vini da tavola,* before (also) giving themselves over to the region's historic *appellations.* Famous for its Orvieto white wines (*see* box, p390), Umbria is now earning itself a startling reputation as a red wine producing region. It has a total of 11 DOC zones and two DOCG (Torgiano Rosso Riserva and Montefalco Sagrantino).

The River Tiber winds through the region, passing most of the major vineyard areas. The DOC zones of Colli Altotiberini, Colli del Trasimeno, Colli Perugini, Colli Martani and Colli Amerini produce red, rosé and white wines based on Sangiovese and Trebbiano grapes.

Umbria's grape varieties are a fascinating mix of Tuscan, native and foreign varieties; Merlot and Pinot Nero have been particularly successful. The region is very proud of its Sagrantino which can produce great red wines. Sagrantino di Montefalco DOCG wines, of great intensity and colour, may be dry or sweet. The sweet ver-

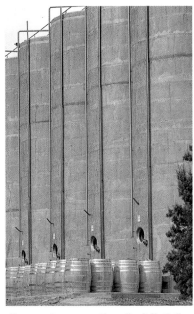

New equipment at Castello della Salla.

sion is made with semi-dried or dried *(passito)* grapes. The Rosso di Montefalco DOC produces a pleasant red wine, based mainly on Sangiovese (60-70%) and Sagrantino (10-15%).

Torgiano DOC has gained an international reputation for high-quality wines thanks to the efforts of the Lungarotti family (*see* p390). The Torgiano red *riserva,* aged for three years, has qualified for prestigious DOCG status since 1990.

Marches
Once destined to be either drunk by tourists or served in amphora-shaped bottles in old-fashioned Italian trattorias around the world, the wines of the Marches are now attracting the attention of wine enthusiasts and the fact that they are good value for money is an added bonus.

The leading white grape variety is Verdicchio, which generally makes light, lemony wines, sometimes sparkling — they are the classic accompaniment to seafood from the Adriatic.

But the efforts of the best producers of the best-known of these wines, Verdicchio dei Castelli di Jesi DOC, have resulted in delicious, elegant, aromatic wines which are full of character. The smaller Verdicchio di Matelica DOC zone also produces good wines, with a slightly higher acidity.

Red wines have the wind in their sails but are still in the minority. The Rosso Cònero DOC, which is making startling progress, is based on Montepulciano d'Abruzzo grapes (sometimes with a little Sangiovese) grown on the slopes of an outcrop of hills near Ancona, the regional capital. This variety (not to be confused with the Tuscan town of the same name, which grows a Sangiovese clone) can, in the right hands, make full, flavoursome, meaty wines. The Rosso Piceno DOC (Sangiovese and Montepulciano) is a much larger *appellation.* The region has seven other, less well-known DOCs including the sparkling red Vernaccia di Serrapetrona.

Abruzzo and Molise
In Abruzzo and Molise the landscape becomes wilder, the cities less sophisticated. For many years known for its very high yields, Abruzzo obviously looks to the south. Molise is still relatively unexplored and uncharted, both for tourists and wine lovers.

The vinegrowers in Abruzzo have begun to realise the potential of their mountainous *terroir* and their star grape variety, the black, highly tannic Montepulciano d'Abruzzo. The wines are becoming more clean cut and elegant. Pioneers of quality (Valentini and Illuminati) have shown that their Montepulciano can achieve the greatness hinted at in the Marches, producing red wines that are generally rich and soft — in the Teramo hills, for instance. Trebbiano d'Abruzzo, the main white grape, makes quaffable, if ordinary, dry white wine. □

UMBRIA PRODUCERS

The supremacy of Orvieto whites has been challenged by many *vini da tavola*, both red and white, which include foreign varieties in the blend. Nowadays focus is again on quality, with Orvieto leading the way, but the ever increasing quality of the red wines is showing a different side of Umbria.

Fratelli Adanti
One of the good Montefalco estates. Firm Sagrantino di Montefalco DOCG, Montefalco Rosso and, foremost, Bianco DOC (Grechetto, Trebbiano and Chardonnay) wines. Pleasant Arquato Rosso IGT.

Antonelli
Complex and strongly flavoured Sagrantino di Montefalco DOCG wines. The Vigna Tonda is a very good *barrique*-aged IGT (100% Grechetto).

Barberani-Vallesanta
This estate is famous for its Orvieto Classico range (superb botrytized Calcaia, off-dry Pulicchio and dry Castagnolo). Noteworthy red IGTs Foresco and Polago, Lago di Corbara DOC (a light wine to be drunk young) and white IGT Pomaio.

Bigi
This big Orvieto wine house (part of Gruppo Italiano Vini) has regained its prestige thanks to its *crus*, such as the dry Orvieto Classico DOC Torricella and the Marrano, a *barrique*-aged Grechetto-based white. Good quality at affordable prices. Annual production is close to 250,000 cases, and more than twice if Bigi's wines from Lazio are included.

Arnoldo Caprai-Val di Maggio
Within a few years, this once obscure Montefalco family estate has been made famous by Marco Caprai, who bought it in 1971. The 60-ha (148-acre) vineyard produces a Sagrantino DOCG star wine, the silky and mature "Selezione 25 Anni" (100% new wood). Others prefer the "simple" version or the elegant Montefalco Rosso Riserva, where 20% Merlot are skilfully combined with Sangiovese and Sagrantino. Pleasant DOC whites Grecante and Vigna Belvedere.

Castello della Sala
This magnificent castle and its 142-ha (351-acre) vineyard are owned by the Antinori house of Florence, a pioneer of quality. Its white wines are still models of their kind, from the dry Orvieto Classico DOC to the prestigious IGTs Cervaro della Sala and Muffato della Sala (botrytized), not to forget the della Sala Chardonnay and the Sauvignon. The Orvieto Classico Campogrande (dry) and Casasole *(abboccato)* offer good quality at affordable prices. A skillful Pinot Noir IGT wine confirms the "red" vocation of the region.

Còlpetrone
Owned by an insurance company, this estate near Montefalco has grown from 5 to 18ha (12 to 44 acres). Its Sagrantino DOCG and its Rosso di Montefalco DOC, both clean, dense and very fruity, are among the best of this *appellation*.

Decugnano dei Barbi
The good and affordable wines from this estate near Lake Corbara are a safe bet for Umbria. The Orvieto Classicos and an excellent red from the IL range

top the list. Two Lago di Corbara DOC and a Chardonnay-based sparkling wine are noteworthy.

La Fiorita-Lamborghini
From expensive cars to wine. The IGT Campoleone 97 has earned 97 from Parker and set tongues wagging. The 32-ha (79-acre) vineyard also produces the Trescone, a fruity and well-groomed Colli di Trasimeno Rosso DOC.

Cantine Lungarotti
The late Giorgio Lungarotti worked relentlessly to prove that Italian wine can be of the highest quality. He has created what is virtually a one-producer DOC (classified in 1968) at Torgiano, near Perugia, and has led the way in using Cabernet Sauvignon and Chardonnay in *vini da tavola,* such as the San Giorgio and the Vessillo (now IGT), and the Chardonnay I Palazzi (now DOC). Italian grapes are much in evidence in the Torgiano DOC, the red Rubesco (Sangiovese) and the white Torre di Giano. The red Torgiano *riserva* is a DOCG wine from Vigna Monticchio, a 12-ha (30-acre) plot of old vines. A good *spumante* Brut and the pleasant red Giubilante complete the range. The Lungarotti daughters are determined to perpetuate the firm's renown, exhibited in a splendid wine museum.

La Palazzola
This 18-ha (44-acre) estate is devoted to international varieties. A luscious Merlot and the Rubino, a fruity and liquorice-flavoured red blend, are the stars. Good Pinot Nero, *spumante* Brut Riesling and Moscato (off-dry and *passito*).

Palazzone
Grape purity, finesse and elegance are Giovanni Dubini's philosophy, applied to 25ha (62 acres) near Orvieto. Exemplary Orvieto Classicos (Campo del Gardiano, Terre Vineate) and IGT wines (Grechetto, Viognier and a botrytized Sauvignon). Noteworthy red IGT Armaleo and Rubbio.

Pieve del Vescovo
Iolanda Tinarelli's and oenologist Riccardo Cotarella's first aim is quality. This 22-ha (54-acre) vineyard in Perugia province produces excellent Colli del Trasimeno reds and whites, notably the Lucciaio.

Sportoletti
Same oenologist, same results at Spello near Assisi. A flavourful and well-groomed range of Assisi DOC and IGT Villa Fidelia wines.

Other Umbrian producers
Colle del Sole, Goretti, La Carraia, Le Poggette, Le Velette, Monrubio, Rocca di Fabbri, Tili. Cooperatives: Cardeto, Colli Amerini, Duca della Corgna, Spoletoducale.

ORVIETO

A handful of producers — notably Antinori, Bigi and an increasing number of private estates — have undertaken to halt the decline of this delicious white wine. The main grape variety is Procanico, the local name for the Trebbiano (40-60%), enhanced by the addition of varying amounts of Grechetto, Verdello, Drupeggio and Malvasia. Focus has been on the production of fresh, dry whites but Orvieto's reputation rests mainly on its sweet wines, no longer the gentle sweet wines of years gone by, but wines affected by noble rot, called *muffa nobile* in Italian. Worth mentioning is a new Sangiovese-based DOC named Rosso Orvietano, which also includes varying quantities of Montepulciano, Merlot, Pinot Nero etc.

MARCHES PRODUCERS

The best-known wine is the white Verdicchio dei Castelli di Jesi DOC but the reds are gaining an increasingly good reputation: the flavoursome Rosso Cònero DOC and Lacrima di Morro d'Alba DOC, made near Ancona, and the Rosso Piceno DOC. Vernaccia di Serrapetrona is a delicate sparkling red, which can be dry or sweet, made from Vernaccia Nera grown in a tiny little area in the province of Macerata.

Boccadigabbia

This small estate, which is famous for its *vini da tavola* (the reds Akronte and Saltapicchio and the Aldonis Chardonnay), has recently bought the Azienda Villamagna (15ha/37 acres), well-known for its excellent Rosso Piceno DOC and its white Monsanulus.

Fratelli Bucci

Ampelio Bucci produces dense and elegant Verdicchio dei Castelli di Jesi Classicos — the best is called Villa Bucci — and the pleasant Rosso Piceno Pongelli.

Fazi-Battaglia

Founded in 1949, this wine house has established the image of the Verdicchio dei Castelli di Jesi, with its amphora-shaped bottle. As other producers have come up, it has been forced to look to its laurels, but with cellar modernization and more rigorous methods, the results are excellent. Fazi-Battaglia owns 365ha (902 acres) in the Jesi zone and, since 1969, 80ha (198 acres) in Tuscany. Very good range of Verdicchios (Castelli di Jesi Classico, the single-vineyard Le Moie and San Sisto, the latter *barrique*-aged). Flavoursome Rosso Cònero and IGT Rutilus.

Gioacchino Garofoli

Founded in 1901, this wine house has always been known for its politics of quality. Noteworthy Rosso Còneros, mainly from its own vineyards (Vigna Piancarda and *riserva* Grosso Agontano); exemplary Verdicchio dei Castelli di Jesi from purchased grapes (Macrina *cru*, *barrique*-aged Serra Fiorese) or from own grapes (Podium).

Fattoria la Monacesca

This family estate (18ha/44 acres at 400m/1,200ft above sea level, renovated winery) is famous for its Verdicchio di Matelica DOC wines, its Ecclesia Chardonnay and the noteworthy Mirum (Verdicchio, Chardonnay and Sauvignon).

Fattoria Le Terrazze

This huge hill estate above Ancona, owned by the Terni family, has made spectacular progress. Brilliant Rosso Cònero Sassi Neri (from selected grapes), astounding Chaos, a brand-new *vino da tavola* IGT (Montepulciano/Syrah/Merlot) with a glorious future, as well as Le Cave, a Chardonnay IGT wine.

Moroder

With 18ha (44 acres) in the heart of the Cònero nature reserve and advice from oenologist Franco Bernabei, the Moroders' fame has been established in no time: their Rosso Cònero Dorico is elegant and pleasantly flavoured.

Alberto Quacquarini

The Vernaccia di Serrapetrona at its best: this producer offers two well-vinified versions, *secco* and *dolce* (Riserva Capsula Nera).

Sartarelli

This 38-ha (94 acre) estate is wholly devoted to quality and to the Verdicchio dei Castelli di Jesi: the entire range — from the basic Classico to the Tralivio, made from old vines, and the splendid late-harvest Balciana *cru* (laureate of London's International Wine Challenge 1999) — is a brilliant testimonial to the elegance of this long-neglected grape variety.

Umani Ronchi

Two separate wineries for the Verdicchio and the Rosso Cònero, almost 200ha (494 acres) of vines (75% of them part of the estate), research into clonal selection together with the University of Ancona, experiments in *barrique*-ageing: the Bianchi Bernetti family are making sure that this firm remains at the forefront of the region. Large range of good quality wines, from classic to *crus* (Verdicchio Casal di Serra, Villa Bianchi and *riserva* Plenio; Rosso Cònero Serrano, San Lorenzo and Cùmaro) and to the star *vini da tavola*: Pelago (splendid Cabernet-Merlot-Montepulciano), Le Busche (Verdicchio-Chardonnay) and Maximo (botrytized Sauvignon).

Villa Pigna

Industrialist and winemaker Costantino Rozzi has left us, but his daughter is carrying on his work: 180ha (445 acres) of vines devoted to quality. Good white wines, noteworthy Rosso Piceno DOC and *vini da tavola* Cabernasco and Rozzano.

Other producers

Bisci, De Angelis, Casalfarneto, Conte Leopardi, Fiorini, Lanari, Mancinelli, Marconi, Oasi degli Angeli, Saladini Pilastri, Santa Barbara, Massimo Serboni, Terre Cortesi, Vallerosa Bonci. Co-operatives Belisario and Valdinevola.

Vineyards of Verdicchio grapes near Montecarotto.

ABRUZZO AND MOLISE PRODUCERS

The classic appellations of Montepulciano d'Abruzzo for the reds and Trebbiano d'Abruzzo for whites have recently been joined by two DOC: Controguerra and Montepulciano d'Abruzzo Colline Teramane. In the Molise region, the Biferno DOC appellation can be used for red, rosé and white wines. The grape varieties used in Abruzzo are also the main varieties here.

Barone Cornacchia
The Montepulciano d'Abruzzo of this reputed estate has been joined by a Trebbiano d'Abruzzo of similarly good quality.

Dino Illuminati
This 70-ha (173-acre) estate is one of the best in Abruzzo. Dense and rich DOC wines, white (Ciafrè, Costalupo) and red (Riparosso). The full-bodied ink-black Zanna and the Lumen, a harmonious blend of Montepulciano and Cabernet Sauvignon, top the list. An unusual red from dried Montepulciano grapes, named Nicò.

Masseria di Majo Norante
The star in the lonely firmament of Molise is the vineyard of Luigi and Alessio di Majo, who are advised by the great oenologist Riccardo Cotarella.

The hot, sandy plain near the sea may be an unusual place to find a quality vineyard, but careful production techniques have led to the creation of some fine wines: the Biferno DOC Ramitello range (a red made from Montepulciano and Aglianico grapes), the Apianae (a sweet Moscato) and the white *vino da tavola* Biblos (Falanghina and Greco).

Gianni Masciarelli
This remarkable producer, near Chieti, has won fame within a short time through his red (Montepulciano d'Abruzzo Villa Gemma and Marina Cvetic) as well as his white wines (Trebbiano d'Abruzzo and Marina Cvetic Chardonnay), all full of character. A new winery and vineyard planted at 3,000 vines/ha clearly show his intentions.

Emidio Pepe
Faultless organic vinegrowing and (arguable) traditional techniques make this estate unique. Emidio Pepe's passion is only surpassed by that of his daughter Stefania, an adept of more modern techniques. Delicious Trebbiano d'Abruzzo, made from old vines; old vintages.

Tenuta Strappelli
7ha (17 acres) near Torana Nuovo and a recent switch to organic methods have led to quick results: a black and dense, long-lived, chocolate-, plum- and coffee-flavoured Montepulciano d'Abruzzo.

Cantina Tollo
One of the best cooperatives in Abruzzo. The Colle Secco range offers safe value for money, particularly the Montepulciano Rubino. Top of the range is the black and velvety Montepulciano Cagiòlo.

Edoardo Valentini
The producer against whom other Abruzzo producers are measured and the first to show the dizzy heights the Trebbiano and Montepulciano d'Abruzzo grapes can reach when properly trained. Valentini owns 65ha (160 acres) of vines, but keeps only 25% of his harvest. With the success of his wines he has been able to command ever higher prices; the wines are difficult to find.

Ciccio Zaccagniani
This small estate in Pescara province is forging ahead with an excellent Montepulciano d'Abruzzo and a red *vino da tavola* made from Cabernet Franc, called Capsico.

Other producers
Fratelli Barba, Bosco, Cataldi Madonna, Di Giovanpietro, Lepore, Marramiero, Montori, Nicodemi, Orlandi Contucci Ponno, Franco Paseti, Sarchese Dora. Cooperatives Casal Bordino and Miglianico.

Hillside vineyards near Chieti, in Abruzzo.

SOUTHERN ITALY

Southern Italy has wine traditions that go back to the ancient Greeks. For them, and for the Romans who followed them, the fertile coastal area was Oenotria, the land of vines.

Until the the late 1970s, little had changed in these regions. Then vast cooperatives appeared on the scene, apparently unable to make the best use of their expensive equipment, other than to use it to obtain the distillation grants they could always rely on. In this depressing climate, the persistence of a few winemakers paid off, resulting in extremely interesting wines, based on native varieties and often excellent value for money. The South is indeed changing rapidly, — finally! — caught up in the quality revival movement which started out in Tuscany and Piedmont. There are still a good many mediocre wines but very good — even great — wines are appearing from winemakers determined to exploit a fabulous wealth of traditional grape varieties, reds in particular. Their success has led to emulation, while the great names of the North have been rushing in with their capital and expertise.

Lazio

The 40,000ha (99,000 acres) of vines in Lazio (or Latium) are still mainly given over to white varieties, the lion's share going to Malvasia, followed by Trebbiano. Red varieties are however on the increase, some of them purely local, such as the Nero Nuono di Cori and the interesting Cesanese, while others are more widespread (Sangiovese, Merlot, Montepulciano). Important work has just begun to improve clonal selection and preserve certain varieties particular to the region. The region has 25 DOC zones which include two of Italy's most well-known appellations, Frascati and Est!Est!!Est!!!. Others are more recent and a DOC region re-

served specifically for French red varieties was even created in 1999 (Atina DOC). Vineyards are found in four main clusters. North of Rome, the Lake Bolsena area produces Est!Est!! Est!!! DOC white wine and the rare, dessert red Aleatico di Gradoli DOC.

Campania

Campania's reputation, well-forgotten since the glory years of Falerne, a favourite wine of ancient Rome, is experiencing a revival. In the space of a few years there has been a real explosion centred around an unparalleled wealth of indigenous grapes: white varieties include Falanghina, Fiano and Greco di Tufo and the reds, Aglianico and Piedirosso. Aglianico, which can produce great wines with ageing potential, forms the basis of the Taurasi, Italy's only Southern DOCG. Behind all this lies exemplary producers such as Mastroberardino and D'Ambra, considerable progress with clonal selection and finally the arrival of great consultant winemakers who have come to work alongside a growing number of enthusiastic winemakers. Great "new" red or white wines are always appearing from zones throughout the whole of Campania: in the historic Falerno zone, north of Naples (Falerno del Massico DOC); in the Irpinian hills, home of Taurasi DOCG and the Greco di Tufo and Fiano di Avellino DOCs; in Ischia, on the Amalfi coast and as far as Cilento, in the area around Salerno.

Basilicata

Basilicata, a small, poor, mountainous region with harsh winters, can lay claim to producing one of Southern Italy's greatest red wines. However only a limited number of estates actually produce Aglianico del Vulture DOC, on the volcanic slopes of Mount Vulture, to such a standard. An increasing number of cooperatives

have however been encouraged by their success, which has also inspired others in the rest of the region. The region also produces some pleasant sweet white Moscato wines.

Calabria

Despite commendable efforts on the part of a handful of producers and its 12 DOC zones, this region still trails far behind. The classic problems of Southern Italy seem to be compounded here by apathy on the part of locals and tourists, who seem happy to drink very ordinary wine. The most well-known wine is the red Cirò DOC (made mainly from Gaglioppo), but unfortunately it very rarely lives up to its reputation.

Apulia

The spirit of revival abounds. Apulia's wine was, until the 1980s, destined for blending and this was in turn abandoned in favour of subsidised distillation. Nowadays, thanks to the example of a handful of invincible companies, the region has been able to redress the balance. More and more pockets of quality have appeared as yields have decreased. The year 2000 marks a new turning point with the arrival of world-class investors: Antinori has bought two estates with a total of 600ha (1,500 acres) of vines and others are about to do likewise. Here too, a wealth of grape varieties is arousing interest: Bombino Bianco and Bombino Nero; Negroamaro, the bitter black grape of Salento (often blended with Malvasia Nera to produce full-bodied reds such as the delicious Salice Salentino DOC); red Uva di Troia and red Primitivo, confirmed as the same grape as California's Zinfandel. Of the 22 current DOCs, Castel del Monte (all three colours), the more southern Locorotondo (the best whites) and above all Salice Salentino, near Lecce, are the most famous. □

WINES OF SOUTHERN ITALY, SICILY AND SARDINIA

The map shows the most important DOCG and DOC zones, but they are still increasing in number. These regions, formerly devoted to overproduction, are moving more and more towards quality.

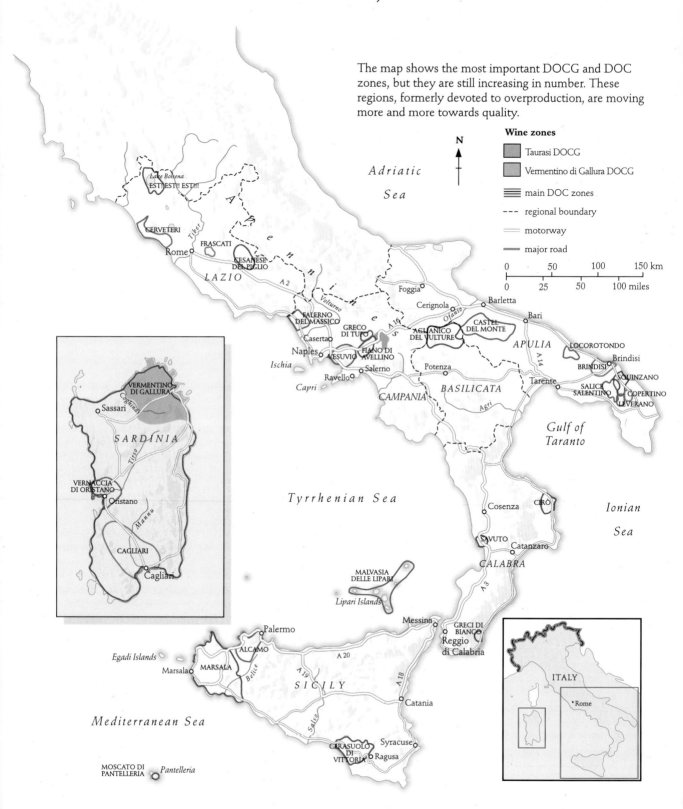

Wine zones

- Taurasi DOCG
- Vermentino di Gallura DOCG
- main DOC zones
- regional boundary
- motorway
- major road

PRODUCERS

As elsewhere in Italy, a great many official wine zones reflect very different realities. The names of the most interesting producers are listed below in alphabetical order for each region.

LAZIO
Casale del Giglio
The 100ha (247 acres) of this bijou estate in the Aprilia plain are devoted to a faultless range of IGT wines and *vini da tavola*. Superb reds (Cabernet Sauvignon, Madreselva and Mater Matuta); fine whites (Satrico).

Castel De Paolis
A high-flying Frascati wine? Here it is!, but also good IGT wines, such as the Selve Vecchie, the Quattro Mori or the amazing Campo Vecchio (Syrah/Merlot/Montepulciano/Cesanese/Sangiovese).

Colacicchi
Stars among the *vini da tavola* of this prestigious 5-ha (12-acre) estate near Anagni are the majestic Torre Ercolana and the flavourful Romagnano Bianco.

Colle Picchioni
An estate at the forefront in Lazio. From 9ha (22 acres) Paola Di Mauro produces the white Marino DOC Selezione Oro and the IGT Vigna del Vassallo (Bordeaux grapes).

Colle di Catone
Winemaker and wine merchant Antonio Pulcini, a producer of good Frascati, is a fan of the Malvasia del Lazio grape, from which he makes several *vini da tavola*: Frascati Superiore DOC Colli di Catone, Villa Catone and Villa Porziana.

Falesco
The Est!Est!!Est!!! Poggio dei Gelsi, the Grechetto, the elegant Montiano Merlot and the Vitiano are all great wines.

Fontana Candida
This firm is part of the same group as Bigi in Orvieto (*see* p390). 625,000 cases a year, mainly of Frascati. Faultless wines, from the classic Superiore to the Terre dei Grifi and the Santa Teresa selection.

Gotto d'Oro
Frascati's best cooperative: 1,800ha (4,448 acres) of vines and nearly 1m of cases each. Excellent value for money.

Mazziotti
The only Est Est Est (without exclamation marks), produced solely from a family vineyard (22ha/54 acres near Bolsena). Delicate classic and a Canuleio from selected grapes. The star is a red IGT, the Volgente.

Sergio Mottura
A 45-ha (111-acre) organic vineyard close to Umbria and brilliant intuitions embodied by IGT wines, the Magone (Pinot Nero/Montepulciano) in particular. The delicate Poggio della Costa, the botrytized Muffo, the Latour à Civitella and the Chardonnay *spumante* are waiting to be discovered.

Giovanni Palombo
A fine example of the new Atina DOC. The stars are the Duca Cantelmi (Cabernet/Syrah) and the Colle della Torre (90% Merlot), both red.

Pietra Pinta-
Colle San Lorenzo
This Cori estate now holds 50ha (124 acres) and aims high. The Colle Amato, a Cabernet/Syrah blend, is excellent.

Villa Simone
Good Frascati Superiore. The stars are the flavourful Vigneto Filonardi and the rare botrytized *cannellino*. Noteworthy *vino da tavola* La Torraccia.

Conte Zandotti
Flavoursome Frascati Superiore, but the stars are the Rumon (Malvasia del Lazio), the Frascati *cannellino* and La Petrosa, an interesting Cabernet/Sangiovese blend.

Other Lazio producers
Alessia, Casale Marchese, Casale Mattia, Dini Limiti, L'Olivella, Pallavicini, Silvestri, Trappolini. Co-op Cerveteri.

CAMPANIA
D'Ambra
This ancient vineyard (full of native varieties) on the island of Ischia has survived thanks to the late Mario D'Ambra, succeeded by his nephew Andrea. Stars are the white Tenuta Frassitelli (Biancolella) and the red Tenuta Montecorvo (Piedirosso), both IGT.

Caggiano
A passionate winemaker with 15ha (37 acres) of vines in the heart of Irpinia. Excellent reds from Aglianico (Taurasi DOCG Vigna Macchia dei Goti, IGT Salae Domini, *vino da tavola* Tauri) and a delicious sweet white called Mel (Fiano/Greco).

De Conciliis
Wines from this family estate near Salerno include the Zero and the Naima, two superb red IGT wines made from Aglianico, and the late-harvest Fiano called Vigna Perella.

Feudi di San Gregorio
A prestigious 45-ha (111-acre) estate in Avellino province. Incredible white wines (Idem bianco, Privilegio and two late-harvest Fianos, the Campanaro and the Pietracalda), luscious Aglianico reds (Idem rosso, Serpico, two Taurasi DOCG).

Galardi
Cousins who are wine enthusiasts, 4ha (10 acres) near Capua and advice from Riccardo Cotarella have led to the Terra di Lavoro, a splendid *barrique*-aged *vino da tavola* made from Aglianico and Piedirosso.

Gran Furor Divina Costiera
6ha (15 acres) of vines in Costa d'Amalfi DOC, devoted to the great local varieties planted at 300-500m (900-1,500ft). Stars of the range are the brilliant Furore Bianco Fior d'Uva and Furore Rosso Riserva.

Maffini
Fascinating and already among Campania's best wines: Cenito and Kléos (red), Kràtos (white).

Mastroberardino
The Taurasi DOCG, the Fiani di Avellino DOC and the Greco di Tufo DOC zones owe their existence to this important firm (250,000 cases) who have always bet on quality. The Vesuvio Rosso DOC is much to the credit of the Lacryma Christi.

Montevetrano
This superb red wine has been a model for many others from Campania, yet its blend of 90% Cabernet Sauvignon and Merlot still causes a stir.

Villa Matilde
The Avallones are devoted to the Southern grape varieties. Years of patience and effort have led to dazzling results: splendid Vigna Camarato, red and white Falerno del Massico DOC and a delicious *passito* from Falanghina (Eleusi).

Other Campania producers
Antica Masseria Venditti, Caputo, Cicala, De Lucia, Di Meo, Episcopio, Grotta del Sole, I Capitani, La Caprense, Marianna, Michele Moio, Mustilli, Ocone, Orazio Rillo, Nicola Romano, Terredora, Vadiaperti. Cooperatives Lavoro e Salute/Telaro, Solopaca, del Taburno.

BASILICATA
D'Angelo
Without Donato D'Angelo, the rediscovery of the splendid Aglianico del Vulture would not have taken place. The stars of his exemplary range are the *barrique*-aged IGT Canneto and the DOC *riserva* Vigna Caselle.

Basilium
This important cooperative produces three delightful, dense and fleshy Aglianico DOC wines and a nice white wine from Greco (I Portali).

Basilisco
This 5-ha (12-acre) estate offers a very fruity Aglianico of impeccable freshness.

Paternoster
This classic producer holds 6.5ha (16 acres) of vines. The stars are three splendid Aglianico DOC wines and the slightly sparkling Moscato IGT Clivus.

Other Basilicata producers
Di Palma, Fratelli Dragone, Armando Martino, Pisani, Progetto di Vino and the cooperative Viticoltori Associati del Vulture.

CALABRIA
Librandi
This important firm (170,000 cases) remains one of the best producers of the Cirò DOC (red Classico and *riserva* Duca San Felice). The stars are three IGT wines: Critone, Gravello and Le Passule *passito*.

Odoardi
The 56-ha (138-acre) vineyard of this beautiful estate has an old reputation. The IGT wines of the Scavigna range, particularly the red Vigna Garrone and the Muscato Valeo now rather outshine the appreciable Savuto DOC (the Vigna Mortila, for instance).

Fattoria San Francesco
The recent progress of this 59-ha (146-acre) family estate has

been spectacular. Exemplary Cirò DOC red wines (Ronco dei Quattro Venti and Donna Madda); the Cirò Rosato is becoming one of Italy's best rosé wines.

Statti
This 500-ha (1,235-acre) family estate has been betting on fine wines (from 35ha/86 acres) and rapidly achieved success with its whites (Lamezia Greco DOC and IGT Ligeia) and reds (two Gaglioppo/Cabernet IGT, the superb Cauro and the fresh Arvina).

Other Calabria producers
Caparra & Siciliani, Lento, Ippolito, Lidia Matera, Serracavallo, Vintripodi, Vivacqua and the cooperative Enotria.

APULIA
Accademia dei Racemi
Under the aegis of Gregorio Perrucci, the Accademia has grouped together several abandoned estates, which have taken up a bet on quality. La Pervini, the leading estate, produces a series of high-quality wines (Primitivo di Manduria DOC Archidamo, I Monili and Primo Amore; IGT Bizantino Rosso). The Accademia also sells wines from the following estates: Casale Bevagna (Salice Salentino DOC Te Deum); Sinfarosa (10ha/25 acres of old goblet-pruned Primitivo wines, which produce a splendid Primitivo di Manduria DOC called... Zinfandel); Masseria Pepe, owned by Alberto Pagano (two delightful Primitivo di Manduria, the Portile and above all the Dunico, made from vines along the seafront); and Felline near Taranto (33ha/82 acres of vines, most of them goblet-pruned). The three Perrucci brothers and their oenologist Roberto Cipresso make three red wines (Vigna del Feudo, Primitivo di Manduria and Alberello) which magnificently illustrate the South's potential.

Francisco Candido
A safe value from the vicinity of Brindisi, this important producer is reputed for his Salice Salentino DOC (three colours), his Aleatico di Puglia DOC (sweet) and still more for his red *vini da tavola*, Duca d'Aragona and Cappello di Prete.

Castel di Salve
Two friends — one born in Salento, the other an Englishman — produce three noteworthy red wines from 37ha (91 acres): the Priante (a *barrique*-aged blend), the Negro Amaro del Salento Armecolo and the Volo di Alessandro.

Leone de Castris
This historical estate with 450ha (1,112 acres) in Salento has remained true to its focus on quality wines. The Donna Lisa Riserva is still one of the best Salice Salentino DOC. The rest of the range (25 wines) is up to it: excellent rosé Five Roses, sweet Aleatico DOC Negrino, several versions based on the Negro Amaro grape and new wines made from Primitivo, the Santera (DOC) and La Rena (IGT).

Pervini
See Accademia dei Racemi.

Rivera
The leading producer (owner of 66ha/163 acres, with links to the Gancia firm) has kept busy. His Castel del Monte DOC are faultless, the stars being the Il Falcone Riserva and the Preludio Chardonnay); its Moscato di Trani DOC Piani di Tufara seduces; and new wines are in the making.

Rosa del Golfo
Damiano Calò has succeeded his father. The Salento Rosato (Negro Amaro with 10% Malvasia Nera) is still one of Italy's best rosés and the Portulano (same blend) one the very good reds of the region.

Taurino
Without Cosimo Taurino's splendid wines, praised to the sky by Parker — in particular the Patriglione and the Notarpanaro — who would have placed a bet on the future of Apulia and of the Negro Amaro grape? This untameable pioneer, who died in 1999, remains a reference for the entire South. The Taurino family faces a difficult task.

Vallone
From 140ha (346 acres) of vines, the Vallone sisters produce famous Brindisi and Salice Salentino DOC wines, as well as a very nice red *passito* called Graticciaia.

Vigneti del Sud
This trademark refers to new estates of the Antinori house (totalling 600ha/1483 acres). The 100-ha (247-acre) Tormaresca estate near Bari, formerly owned by the Gancia firm, already produces two fine IGT wines at highly competitive prices, the Tormaresca Bianco and Rosso, but other, more ambitious wines are soon to be on offer.

Conti Zecca
This huge estate (320ha/791 acres of vines) with a long-standing reputation is being stimulated by the surrounding emulation. Excellent DOC range for Leverano (Malvasia Vigna del Saraceno and Rosso Riserva) and Salice Salentino (Rosso Cantalupi), but the star wine is the *vino da tavola* Nero, a blend of indigenous grapes and of Cabernet.

Other Apulia producers
Michele Calò, Coppi, D'Alfonso Del Sordo, Fatalone, Libra, Masseria Monaci, Pichierri, Santa Lucia, Torrevento and the cooperatives Botromagno, di Copertino, Due Palme, del Locorotondo, Santa Barbara, di Sava and Vecchia Torre.

SICILY AND SARDINIA

Both islands share the problem of high production, dominated by cooperatives, and mediocre wines, but nowadays progress is being made.

Sicily

Sicily's history since the Greeks discovered it in the 5th century BC has left it with a culture that is eclectic, yet curiously narrow. The same is true of its wines. For many years, a handful of producers have battled it out in a climate of general indifference but now their example is being followed by a new generation which has great faith in the island's true potential. Sicily is once again becoming home to some fine wines, especially reds. Here too, large Italian groups have recently bought over hundreds of hectares, famous winemakers are getting involved and emphasis is being laid on the best native grape varieties, Nero d'Avola (red) and Inzolia (white).

White grape varieties prevail, starting with Carraratto (45%), which is followed by the Tuscan Trebbiano. Other interesting varieties include the whites Grillo (in Marsala) and Grecanico and the reds Nerello Mascalese, Perricone and Frappato di Vittoria.

Sicily has 17 DOC regions which only account for a minute portion of production. To the west, Trapani is the largest wine growing area in Italy and produces huge quantities of dry white wines (Alcamo DOC, in particular). It is also the home of Marsala (*see* box). In the east you have historical *appellations* for wines which are virtually unobtainable, such as the red Faro de Messina, Moscato di Noto or di Siracusa. The reds of Cerasuolo di Vittoria DOC and Etna wines are regaining strength. Two little volcanic islands continue to uphold ancient winemaking traditions in their production of dessert wines, Moscato di Pantelleria (between Sicily and Tunisia) and Malvasia delle Lipari (on Salina).

Wine is part of Sicily's ancient culture.

Sardinia

Sardinia has many assets — its climate, the fact it has managed to preserve much of its vinous heritage in the form of local grape varieties and wine styles and talented producers, some of them working for cooperatives. On the other side of the coin you have often little precision in wine making techniques, huge supplies of mediocre white wine, emphasis on native varieties and *terroirs* which are still not showing their full potential.

There is good news, especially on the red wine front, with the production of successful wines from varieties such as Carignano (Carignano del Sulcis DOC), Cannonau (Grenache), Nieddera, sometimes blended with Sangiovese, Cabernet, etc. One of the most interesting white varieties is Vermentino (Vermentino di Gallura is the island's only DOCG). The DOC zones of Vernaccio di Oristano, Malvasia di Bosa and Nasco di Cagliari are capable of producing superb dessert wines. □

MARSALA

Marsala is one of the world's great fortified wines. The categories of Marsala have been revised under new DOC rules, with the intention of steering the wine back on to a course of quality. In its history and potential, it rivals port or madeira (*qv*). Like them, it was created by the British in the 18th century. It is made around the port of Marsala on Sicily's west coast and is based on local white wines made from Catarratto, Grillo, Damaschino and Inzolia grapes and, in recent years, from red wines too.

Most of the grapes are fermented in the usual way, but some are held back to make a sweetening agent. There are two constituents for sweetening, which are blended in varying proportions: the better is *mistella* (also called *sifone*), a blend of fresh or dried grapes and wine alcohol; the other is *cotto*, a reduction of grapes over heat into a burnt syrup. Marsala is required to be fortified with wine spirit.

CATEGORIES
There are five main categories, further qualified by colour (*Oro*, gold; *Ambra*, amber; *Rubino*, ruby) and sweetness (*Secco*, dry; *Semisecco*, medium-dry; *Dolce*, sweet).
Fine: basic Marsala, aged for a minimum of one year, 8 months fo which in wood. The *Cotto* is required for the sub-category *Ambra* (a minimum of 1%) and forbidden for the others.
Superiore and **superiore riserva**: higher in alcohol than *Fine* (18° against 17°), aged in wood for two years (four for the *riserva*).
Vergine and **vergine stravecchio**: always dry, without *mistella* or *cotto*. Aged in wood for five years (ten for *stravecchio*). The term *Soleras* is used as well.

PRODUCERS
Some of the best producers (and their brands) are: De Bartoli (*see* p398); Florio (Terre Arse, Baglio Florio, Targa Riserva 1840); Mirabella (Cudia); Carlo Pellegrino Ruby Fine, Vergine Soleras); Rallo Alvis.

PRODUCERS

Progress is being made in Sicily and Sardinia, the former at a rate of knots and from one end of the island to the other but progress in the latter is more limited. In both cases it is often the red wines which excel.

SICILY

Abbazia di Sant'Anastasia
Wherever Giacomo Tachis, Italy's famous "retired" wine-maker, intervenes, quality is rocketing. Top wines include the Litra, the Bacchante and the Cinquegrani.

Avide
Excellent red wines: two Cerasuolo di Vittoria DOC (Barocco and Etichetta Nera) and the IGT Sigillo.

Benanti
Flavoursome Etna DOC Rosso Rovittello (Nerello Mascalese/Nerello Cappuccio) and delightful IGT Lamorèmio (Nero d'Avola/Nerello Mascalese/Cabernet Sauvignon).

COS
The Cerasuolo di Vittoria DOC zone owes its renewal to a fiery trio of friends who have won their bet. With maturity, their wines have become even better: fine Sciri (100% Nero d'Avola), two delightfully full-bodied Cerasuolo DOC and two white IGT wines, Vigne di Cos and Ramingallo.

De Bartoli
Marco De Bartoli, an obstinate rebel, has saved Marsala from its culinary decline. His Vecchio Samperi Riserva 20 Anni and 30 Anni (not fortified and therefore not DOC), as well as his Bukkuram, which allowed wine enthusiasts to discover the Moscato de Pantelleria, have made him world-wide famous. His fortified Marsala DOC (Vigna La Miccia and Il Marsala Superiore 20 Anni) are still models of their kind.

Donnafugata
The Contessa Entellina DOC zone owes its existence to this important family firm. White DOC Chiarandà del Merlo, reds DOC Milleunanotte and Tancredi. Excellent Ben Ryè, a Moscato passito de Pantelleria.

Duca di Salaparuta-Corvo
The basic Corvo range accounts for most of the production (750,000 cases per year) and offers good value for money. The Duca Enrico (Nero d'Avola) and the Bianca di Valguarnera (Inzolia), both barrique-aged, top the list. In the middle, two flavoursome blends from local grape varieties, the Terre d'Agala and the Portale d'Aspra Rosso.

Firriato
A Sicilian and an Australian are producing 275,000 cases of fine wine from native and French grape varieties (Altavilla, Sant'Agostino etc).

Barone La Lumia
Bottling history is the wish of this reserved original, wildly in love with his vineyard. The Signorio Rosso, the Limpiados and the Nikao — none filtered — are three fascinating examples of the Nero d'Avola grape.

Salvatore Murana
Sun transformed into wine — that's what the Martingana and the Khamma, two Moscato di Pantelleria DOC wines made by this 100% native islander are.

Murgo
This 25-ha (62-acre) vineyard on the hill slopes of the Etna is part of the Etna DOC zone's renewal. Noteworthy Tenuta San Michele.

Palari
Messina's Faro DOC survives thanks to Salvatore Geraci.

Planeta
An excellent range from 250ha (618 acres) of vines. Best are a luscious Chardonnay and an elegant red IGT (Santa Cecilia).

Regaleali
From 300ha (741 acres) of vines the Tasca d'Almerita family produce 250,000 cases of wine, including the excellent Rosso del Conte and Nozze d'Oro, a good spumante Brut and a famous Chardonnay. Three successful new wines: the white Leone d'Oro and the reds Novantasei and Cygnus. Reliable basic range (Regaleali).

Settesoli
This rather huge cooperative (9,000ha/22,250 acres) in Agrigente province has made incredible progress. The Nero d'Avola reds and the white Feudo dei Fiori top the range.

Other Sicilian producers
Caravaglio, D'Ancona, Hauner, Miceli, Milazzo, Pellegrino, Rapitalà, Spadafora, Terre di Ginestra and the cooperatives Nuova Agricoltura, CS di Trapani and Valle dell'Acate.

SARDINIA

Argiolas
The Argiolas family hold 220ha (544 acres) of vines in Cagliari. The island's star is a fleshy, flavoursome red vino da tavola aged in new wood, the Turriga. Magnificent IGT passito Angiolas (Nasco/Malvasia) and good Vermentino di Sardegna DOC and Cannonau di Sardegna DOC.

Tenuta di Capichera
The Ragnedda family own 42ha (104 acres) of vines and produce three exemplary Vermentino di Gallura DOC, notably the splendid Vendemmia tardiva, and a promising vino da tavola (Assajè Rosso).

Gabbas
Giuseppe Gabbas makes two noteworthy red wines: the Lillové, a fruity and dense Cannonau di Sardegna DOC, and the rich Dune.

Cantina Sociale Gallura
This cooperative at Tempio Pausania is one of the best. Wines include the Karana, a Nebbiolo red, and excellent Vermentinos (the DOCG version Canayli and Piras, the vino da tavola Balajana).

Gian Vittorio Naitana
A splendid example of the Sardinian Malvasia. Matchless IGT Planargia Murapiscados, sweet and lively, with apricot and bitter almond flavours.

Sella & Mosca
Stimulated by the ongoing renewal, this Alghero wine firm offers a series of fine wines. The reds Alghero DOC Marchese di Villamarina and Tanca Farrà, the brand-new Raim and the sweet Anghelu Ruju top the list. Whites include the basic Alghero DOC Torbato Terre Bianche, the new Vermentino di Gallura DOCG Monteoro and the Nasco passito Monteluce.

Cantina Sociale Santadi
A very promising cooperative in Cagliari province. The stars are called Terre Brune, Rocca Rubia and Shardana, all reds, and Latinia, a dessert wine made from the Nasco grape.

Other Sardinian producers
Arcadu, Cherchi, Contini, Gostolai, Loi, Mancini, Meloni, Pedra Majore, Picciau, Soletta, Villa di Quartu and the cooperatives Dolianova, Dorgali, Giogantinu, Jerzu, Oliena, Trexenta and del Vermentino.

SPAIN

—

FROM BULK WINE PRODUCER TO QUALITY WINE EXPORTER,

SPAIN'S WINE INDUSTRY HAS BEEN TRANSFORMED,

AND PROMISES EXCITING NEW DEVELOPMENTS

IN THE FUTURE.

—

Although Spain has the largest area under vines in the world, it is however only the third largest wine producing county in the European Union, just behind Italy and France, and fifth world-wide. Reputed for its fortified wines, such as the famous sherry (*see* p424), it also produces a range of red, white, rosé and sparkling wines which include the most basic to the most distinguished. The very unusual geography of Spain is an important influence on its wines. The country consists of a central plateau (the Meseta) at an altitude of about 650m (2,150ft), surrounded on all sides by mountain ranges. The best-quality wines are made from varieties which grow well at high altitudes — for example, up to 500m (1,650ft) in Rioja Alta and Rioja Alavesa, and 700m–800m (2,310–2,640ft) in the Alt-Penedès and in the Ribera del Duero vineyards. Here the sun exposure is good but the ambient temperature, particularly at night, is lower. Most of Spain's top wines come from north of Madrid — from (east to west) Galicia, the Duero Valley, the Ebro Valley and Catalonia. The best sites are in mountain valleys with fairly lightweight topsoils overlying clay subsoils, but there is a good deal of alluvial soil close to the rivers Ebro and Duero. The climate also varies, from cooler, much wetter Atlantic influences in the west, through more continental conditions (hot summers and cold winters) in the north-central valleys, to Mediterranean along the Catalan coast.

Until the second half of the 20th century fortified wine was at the heart of Spanish wine production (together with Rioja, the chief quality wine). This is the *bodega* of the Marqués del Real Tesoro in Jerez de la Frontera.

Spain's rich vinegrowing tradition goes back a long way. The maritime poem written by Rufus Festus Avienus, a Roman historian, tells us that the Phoenicians planted *Vitis vinifera* in Gadir, the present town of Cádiz. More than three thousand years ago at the time when, according to Book II of Strabon's *Geography*, they were building the foundations of the city. A century later, the wines most prized by the Phoenicians came from Xera in southern Spain (now known as Jerez de la Frontera, its wine, now fortified, is known as sherry). According to several reputable studies, the Etruscan amphoras and Greeks arrived in the north east of the Iberian Peninsula around 550 to 525 BC and so we know that wine had arrived in Catalonia by then. The Romans, arriving in Spain towards the end of the 3rd century, brought their own vinification method (treading grapes in a stone trough and allowing them to ferment naturally, now known as the *método rural*), which is still used in some country districts. Vine cultivation continued under Moorish rule, but grapes were eaten rather than made into wine. In 1492 Spain became a united country and, as she prospered, wine became an increasingly important commodity. Rules governing winemaking already existed in regions such as Jerez and Rioja, whose wines flourished in the 19th century, but these were tightened up, and new rules issued for emerging areas like Toro and Rueda in the Castilla-León region.

Then, in the 1860s, phylloxera devastated the French vineyards. *Négociants* flooded across the Pyrenees to buy wine, and found to their delight wines of the right style and quality in northern Spain. Once again exports boomed, but, inevitably, phylloxera arrived in Spanish vineyards. By that time the solution to the problem — grafting European vines on to American roots — had already been discovered. Some regional authorities helped growers replant and encouraged a new approach to vinegrowing and winemaking, and many of today's most respected *bodegas* have their origins in the late 1890s.

In the second half of the 20th century, Spain has made the transition from being mainly a shipper of anonymous, cheap bulk wines 30 years ago, to a leading producer of quality wines today. In the 1970s, Rioja, followed by estates like Vega Sicilia, and later wines from Valdepeñas and Catalonia began to be exported. By the end of the 1980s Spain was producing 322 million cases a year. Now vineyards are being grubbed up, new and better grape varieties are replacing the old heavy-croppers, and what used to be obscure wine-producing areas are coming forward with new ideas to offer the wine-buying world.

Wine regions and styles
Until the constitution of 1978, Spain was a country of 50 provinces. Now there are 17 autonomous regions *(autonomías)*, each encompassing one or more of the original provinces. In terms of wine, Spain can be divided into several large areas which have a common gastronomic, climatic and cultural heritage that determined the kind of wine they made in the past — although they may be producing more, and different, wines today.

Galicia and the Basque country (País Vasco) include some of the most northerly wine-producing areas in the country. The Atlantic Ocean influences the climate, the

economy (based traditionally on the fishing industry) and the wines, which are mainly light, dry whites to partner the fish. Also in the north, Navarra, La Rioja — Spain's best-known wine region — and Aragón make up the wine lands of the Upper Ebro Valley. The three areas share a history of livestock farming and strong cross-border influences from France. Wines tend towards heavier reds that mature with grace, and robust whites to accompany river fish.

Catalonia, at the mouth of the Ebro, has a culture all its own. The fishing industry and Mediterranean climate had traditionally led the region towards white wines. Catalonia was also the birthplace of the Spanish sparkling wine industry.

Castilla-León is a traditional wine-producing region in the Duero Valley. Its climate is continental, although tempered close to the river. The region produces rich red wines, although some "joven" wines have more subtle nuances, and full-bodied dry whites. The region produces rich red wines, and full-bodied dry whites that complement river fish so well. The style is uncompromisingly Castilian, with much less French influence than is evident in the Upper Ebro Valley.

The best Spanish wines come from the above-mentioned regions. But there are large grape-growing areas in central and southern Spain. The vast plains of Castilla-La Mancha and the Vinos de Madrid are found on the Meseta. Historically, this was an isolated area — as important an influence on its wine-making as the strongly continental climate and sheep-farming culture. The area has traditionally produced fairly heavy wines, both red and white. After Madrid became the national capital in 1561, the wines of the region came into their own.

Levante is made up of the *autonomías* of Valencia and Murcia, two provinces with a very strong export mentality: the ancient port of

Valencia is Spain's leading wine-trading centre. A tradition of fishing and a Mediterranean climate bred Valencia's traditional whites, but the region discovered very early a talent for making wine any way the customer wanted it.

Andalucia in the south of Spain is a single, very large *autonomía*. The legendary sherries are now being drunk differently and seen in a different light. The wines are certainly still fortified but are being produced over a lengthy period under flor. When it comes to characterising the wines, the soil type is a more important factor than the alcoholic content. Andalucia may be heralded as the one wine region in the world which is producing wines of a generally high quality and is offering wines with an ageing potential which, when the elaborate production process is taken into account, are among the cheapest.

Finally, Spain's islands produce small amounts of wine. The Balearic Islands' geology is similar to that of Catalonia, and the wine industry developed as part of that region's maritime culture. Light and fruity reds and crisp, dry whites in the *joven* (young) style are made mainly for the holiday market. The Canary Islands are totally different: the bedrock is volcanic and the soils completely black in places. Wines are mainly red, again in a light, fresh *joven* style, for the tourist resorts.

Grape varieties
The low-quality Airén is the most abundant (white) grape, and the principal variety in central Spain. Garnacha Blanca is also widespread, especially in Catalonia, making full-bodied white wines with a high alcohol content. Other important white varieties are the high-quality Albariño of Galicia, and Verdejo, considered to be one of the best whites in Castilla-León. Macabeo (or Viura), Parellada (a very productive, high-quality variety) and Xarel.lo make Cava sparkling wines

and are important throughout Catalonia and the Upper Ebro Valley.

The finesse and highly aromatic qualities of Tempranillo make it the star of Spanish red grape varieties. Also known as Ull de Llebre, Cencibel, Tinto Fino, Tinto del País and Tinta de Toro, it is a principal variety in Castilla-La Mancha, Castilla-León, the Ebro Valley and parts of the Duero Valley and Levante. It may have a common ancestor with the Pinot Noir grape of France. Garnacha Tinta is the most widely-grown red grape, particularly in central Spain, the Ebro Valley and Catalonia. Cariñena, which produces robust, well-balanced wines, blends well with Garnacha. It is widely grown in Catalonia and Rioja (where it is known as Mazuelo), but is hardly used in the DO wine of its native region of Cariñena. Graciano produces low yields but highly-valued wines under the *crianza* ageing process — hence its use in Rioja. It is not widespread and is often mixed with other grapes. Classic international varieties are also grown in several areas (see under specific regions).

Structure of the wine industry
A mainstay of the Spanish wine industry for the last 100 years has been the cooperative, which freed small farmers unable to afford wine-making equipment from being forced to sell their grapes to the local *señor* at whatever price he wished to pay. In the days when growers were simply paid by the kilogram for their grapes, the co-ops worked splendidly. However, as demand for bulk wine fell and quality became paramount, badly run cooperatives, with low yielding and badly sited vineyards, became insolvent.

A new generation of entrepreneurs has grown up since the beginning of the 1980s, either buying up old cooperatives or contracting them to produce quality grapes. At the same time, the price of new-technology winemaking equipment

has fallen to the point where quite small companies can afford to buy it.

Spanish wine companies are usually known as *bodegas*. A *bodega*, literally, is an above-ground wine store, in contrast with a *cava* or below-ground cellar. Cava wines are so-called because, needing long storage at low temperatures, sparkling wines are stored in the *cava*, while still wines in cask, which benefit from atmospheric changes through winter and summer, are stored in the *bodega*.

Recent developments
Since 1985, the quality of Spanish wines has increased on an unprecedented scale and the presence of more and more great Spanish names on foreign markets bears testimony to this. These include some of the country's best wines which, with the exception of Vega Sicilia, had until then not found an opening on the international market.

The wine industry has therefore changed in a country comprising seventeen autonomous regions (*autonomías*), each one not only a decentralised, almost Federal, state but also producing very distinctive wines depending on wine growing techniques, legislation and finance. In the same way as there has never been a single national dish — the famous paella is historically linked only to the Mediterranean coast — the wines are nowadays highlighting the differences that bulk wine and the predominance of Rioja had tried to erase.

Also, we cannot forget the intricacies of the Spanish appellation system which is based on the French system. These laws restrict wine production to average grape varieties which are not always those favoured by the winemakers. The same applies to the length of time the *crianzas* and *reservas* must spend in the cask and the bottle. For example, regulations stipulate that *gran reservas* must spend 24 months in the cask and 36 months in the bottle. In more recent times Rioja

wines, often sold directly on the New York market to get round these restrictive laws, have been darker in colour and are being released earlier.

The art of the matter
New winemaking techniques have also been emulated in Spain. The emphasis laid on raw materials, fruitiness and concentration is being felt on both sides of the Pyrenees.

Catalonia, producer of Cava, the best-selling sparkling wine in the world for over a century, has now rediscovered the Garnacha grape, of which Spain has the largest quantity in the world.

A few years ago in the DO Priorato, Alvaro Palacios, a young winemaker originally from Rioja, had the audacity to make what was to become one of the most expensive Spanish wines from grapes which, until then, had been given very little credit: the 93 Ermita is made from 80% Garnacha, 10% Carignan and 10% Cabernet Sauvignon and has been cask-aged for 19 months and then aged in the bottle for the remainder of the time. René Barbier, pioneer of the revival of this DO, brought out a wine made from 25% Syrah and equal quantities of Garnacha and Cabernet Sauvignon. Also in this region, word is spreading about a Poboleda which very few Spaniards have tasted as it is more easily found in New York.

Having invaded the DO Priorato and colonised Ribera del Duero, wine industry investors now have their claws in the DO Toro ... and the markets are following.

Another leading light in new-age Spanish winemaking is Peter Sisseck, the Danish owner of the Dominio Pingus estate, who worked for many years in Bordeaux and Ribera del Duero where he acted as advisor to companies such as Hacienda Monasterio. In Libourne, Peter Sisseck became friends with Jean-Luc Thunevin, the man behind the great St-Emilion Château de Valandraud, a wine which did not exist in 1990 but which is on its way to becoming the most expensive Bordeaux wine. Inspired by Thunevin, Sisseck himself started to follow closely every detail of the manufacturing process: hand picking of each individual grape, two periods in new wood, not to increase aromas but to find the ideal barrels and oxidation levels, very little SO_2... The result is the Dominio Pingus, a little treasure which came on the scene only a few years ago and is now Spain's most expensive wine: a bottle of Dominio Pingus 1995 can fetch over £350!

This price may surprise a Frenchman but not an American: in New York they buy Dominio Pingus by mail order — if they can get their hands on it, that is — and place it of course in their cellar alongside their Viña Costeira Clos Erasmus, made exclusively from Treixadura, a Galician grape variety. DO Montilla-Moriles, formerly Sherry's poor relation, has also woken up and is now producing wines sought after by connoisseurs, such as Don P.X. (100% Pedro Ximénez) and in particular Fino Eléctrico, of which some bottles go back to vintages prior to 1959. Finally, in Jerez itself, producers are unearthing some fine old bottles which are also pushing the prices up — the only point in common of Spain's 17 autonomous regions. Bottles such as Carchelo, Abadía Retuerta 96 cuvée El Campanario (a wine produced by Pascal Delbeck which, according to Parker, is worth 94+), Organistrum, Borsao, Vega Sinda Chardonnay and Clos Erasmus — are getting connoisseurs excited and those who have only just unravelled the mysteries of the Tempranillo grape will find that varieties such as Garnacha, Monastrell, Mencía (wines from El Bierzo, in León, and neighbouring Galicia) are becoming more prominent in most of the new wines, as is the delicate Graciano, which in the past gave the best Riojas their tannins, colour and aroma.   □

SPANISH WINE LAWS

Since 1986, Spanish wines have complied with standard EC regulations laid down for wine-producing countries, and are categorized as Vinos de Mesa (table wines) and VCPRD — Vinos de Calidad Producidos en Regiones Determinadas (quality wines produced in specific regions).

Quality levels
Vino de mesa is the basic grade of table wine, and may come from anywhere in Spain. It may not show area of origin or a vintage date. *Vino de mesa* followed by a regional name is an intermediate grade between simple *vino de mesa* and *vino de la tierra*. There are 28 regions (*comarcas*) that have the right to use their local name to describe the wine, for example, Vino de Mesa de Betanzos. This category is known colloquially as *vino comarcal* (local wine). This naming format is also used for wines that fall outside the DO system (see below), for example, Yllera in Castilla-León, which may append the name of their province or *autonomía*, as in Vino de Mesa de Castilla-León. This allows a vintage date on the label.
Vino de la tierra is "country wine" (like the French *vin de pays*) from one of 28 differently specified areas that over the years have shown their own character, and aspire to full DO status in the future.
Denominación de origen (DO) is the first "quality wine" category, comparable to the French *appellation d'origine contrôlée* or the Italian *denominazione di origine controllata*. In June 2000, Spain had 51 DOs. It is applied to wines that meet international standards for grape varieties, method of production and geographical origin. A Spanish equivalent to the French Institut National des Appellations d'Origine (INAO), the INDO, was created in 1970.
Denominación de origen calificada (DOC) is a "super-category" for wines that can meet very special criteria of quality and consistency. So far the only example is Rioja, which was promoted to the new level as from the 1991 vintage.
Denominación de origen calificada (DOC) is a "super-category" for wines that can meet very special criteria of quality and consistency. So far the only example is Rioja, which was promoted to the new level as from the 1991 vintage.

The status of Spanish wines
Spanish wine laws have been harmonized to ensure the consistent use of terms on the label that tell the wine drinker the ageing status of the wine.
Vino joven ("young wine") is wine intended for immediate drinking and bottled straight after fining. It is also known as *vino del año*. The Instituto Nacional de Denominaciones de Origen (INDO) is trying to encourage the use of the term *joven* instead of *sin crianza*, meaning wines that have spent no time in oak.
Vino de crianza must have two full calendar years' storage, with a minimum of six months in *barricas* (oak casks). Some regions, like Rioja, insist on more than six months. A *crianza* may be released in its third year. White and *rosado* (pink) *crianzas* must spend one year in the *bodega*, of which six months must be in *barricas*. They may be released in their second year.
Reserva red wines must spend three calendar years in the *bodega*, of which at least one must be in *barricas*. They may be released in their fourth year. White and *rosado reservas* must spend two years in the *bodega*, of which six months must be in *barricas*. They may be released in their third year.
Gran reserva reds are permitted only in particularly good vintages (before the introduction of vintage control in 1979, vintages were on occasion invented) and must have spent at least two calendar years in barricas and three years in bottle. They may be released in their sixth year. White and *rosado gran reservas*, now very rare, must have been aged for four years, with at least six months in *barricas*, and may be released in their fifth year.

Reading a label
The important information is on the back label (*contraetiqueta*), or sometimes on a paper seal across the cork. The *contraetiqueta* carries the official logo of the Consejo Regulador (the DO's regulatory body) for that wine, a serial number by which the wine can be traced, and often a map. The main information is the status of the wine: *crianza, reserva* or *gran reserva*. If none of these words appear, then it is a *vino joven*. The front label shows the wine's quality level.

WINE REGIONS OF SPAIN

Spain's vineyards are widely scattered across the dramatic physical landscape — a large, central plateau ringed by mountains cut by important rivers. The most striking feature of Spanish vineyards is their diversity: some are as high as 1,000 m (3,280 ft), there are some where temperatures drop 20°C in the evenings and go from −10°C in winter to 40°C in summer, not forgetting the wide range of local grape varieties to which foreign varieties have been added. The vineyards of the Canary Islands, on the same latitude as the Sahara Desert, and those in Jerez, just off the African coastline, are further examples of this. Broadly, the north produces table wines; the centre bulk wines; the south sherry-type apéritif and dessert wines. The map shows 39 of the 51 DOs.

LA RIOJA

Rioja Alavesa has large areas of Tempranillo grapes planted in clay soils.

When the Romans came to Rioja in the Upper Ebro Valley 2,000 years ago, they found that the local tribespeople, whom they called the Celtiberi, were already cultivating the vine and making wine. Ever willing to spread the benefits of new technology, as well as fulfilling their own needs, the legions tutored the locals in advanced winemaking.

By the beginning of the second millennium, production of Rioja wine was big business, and its making and quality control were the subject of city ordinances in Logroño and throughout the region.

The story of modern Rioja began in the 1860s, when Camilo Hurtado de Amézaga, the Marqués de Riscal de Alegre, returned from a period in Bordeaux armed with new ideas, new vines and, most important of all, new oak casks. His kinsman in nobility, the Marqués de Murrieta, had similar notions, and they set about planting Cabernet Sauvignon

and Merlot vines and preparing to vinify and age the wine in what was then the Bordeaux style. The Marqués de Riscal was the impetus behind Alava Council's appointment of Jean Pineau, a winemaker from Bordeaux, who was given the task of improving the wines from various local producers. The wines made by the two marqués soon began to fetch prices undreamed of in the Rioja region. Some local winemakers, who did not have the same means to get hold of imported grape varieties, were introduced to the process by the Marqués winemakers. To their great surprise, these winemakers discovered that the local grapes with which they'd been working for years — particularly Tempranillo — responded extremely well to the new methods, with or without Cabernet Sauvignon.

Meanwhile, north of the Pyrenees, first oïdium and then phylloxera ravaged the French vineyards,

and *négociants* from Aquitaine and further afield came looking for wine to buy. They were particularly pleased to find a newly developed wine industry, using French methods, so close to home. Rioja wines boomed, and local growers and winemakers rushed to switch to the new ways.

During the 20th century Rioja has established its reputation as Spain's finest red-wine region. In 1991 the wine was promoted to the new super-category of DOC (*denominación de origen calificada*) and new, stricter regulations governing grape sources, vinification and ageing now apply.

Districts, climate and soils

Rioja wine is made in the *autonomía* of La Rioja, and in the neighbouring *autonomías* of País Vasco and Navarra, and there are some vineyards, although no *bodegas*, in the province of Burgos. However, the Rioja DOC is run from Logroño, the capital city of La Rioja, and the most important sub-divisions of the region are the traditional ones of Rioja Alavesa, Rioja Alta and Rioja Baja.

Rioja Alavesa is the area of vineyards north of the Ebro in the province of Alava (País Vasco).

Rioja Alta, which includes the Burgos enclave, is south of Alava.

Both districts are in the Riojan highlands, 400–500m (1,320–1,650ft) above sea level, with slightly cooler temperatures that give wines of the highest quality. The climate is moderated by Atlantic influences, whilst being sheltered by the Cordillera Cantábrica from the severest effects of northerly winds. Early spring sunshine leads into long, hot summers and mild autumns with cool breezes at night. Winters can be very cold with frost and snow in places.

Rioja Baja, which includes the Navarra areas, occupies the southeast of the region, sloping down to about 300m (990ft) above sea level. The climate is more Mediterranean than in the rest of the region: it is hotter and drier — semi-arid in some places — with longer hours of sunshine, thus producing ripe grapes earlier. Wines from this area are softer and more early-maturing, with a higher alcohol content, than their northern counterparts.

The clay soil of Rioja is "striped" with limestone and iron in the northwest, while sandy, alluvial soils are found in the Rioja Baja.

Grape varieties

The principal grape variety for red wine is Tempranillo. In most of northern Spain, and especially in Rioja Alta and Rioja Alavesa, it is the main quality red grape. It is thick-skinned and glossy black, and gets its name (*temprano* means early) because it ripens in mid- to late-September, about two weeks earlier than Garnacha. By itself Tempranillo would not age for the length of time and in the graceful manner

for which Rioja is renowned, so it is nearly always mixed with other grapes.

Garnacha Tinta (or Garnacha Riojana) is the main red variety of Rioja Baja, and is used in nearly all Rioja wines. However, it needs long, hot autumns to come to full ripeness, as in the Rhône Valley where it is known as Grenache. Graciano also produces high-quality wines. There has been renewed interest in this grape since Rioja was awarded the DOC, as Graciano adds a dash of real finesse as the wine ages.

Other red varieties include Mazuelo (grown elsewhere in Spain under the name Cariñena), which provides Rioja with tannin and acidity; and Cabernet Sauvignon, which is still grown by the Marqués de Riscal, but elsewhere is classified as an "experimental" variety. A traditional red Rioja "mix" might be 70% Tempranillo, 15% Garnacha, 10% Mazuelo and 5% Graciano.

White Rioja has changed a good deal since the shift of emphasis away from oak-aged wines towards crisp, cold-fermented *joven* styles, which favour the Viura grape. Traditionally Viura used to be added in small quantities to red Riojas to add fire and brilliance to the colour, and it is still added to some Alavesa wines (10% maximum) to help the acid balance. Modern *joven* white Rioja is likely to be 100% Viura. Malvasía Riojana is Viura's partner in white Rioja. It is a vital ingredient in the oak-aged whites, adding an extra dimension to the rather neutral Viura, combining perfectly with the oak. Garnacha Blanca produces good quantities of reasonable-quality wine, if a little lacking in acidity.

Winemaking and ageing

Traditionally, Rioja was made in stone troughs, the grapes trodden by foot and the fermentation process left to the mysteries of nature. Methods since 1856 have been more scientific. Most *bodegas* now ferment in stainless steel or epoxy-lined vats.

Once the wine is made it rests for a while in vats before being put into 225-litre oak casks (*barricas*). There are very strict rules on minimum ageing but *bodegas* are free to adopt the periods — over and above the minimum — best suited to their house style. A good deal of experimentation is under way with different kinds of oak: with some 600,000 *barricas* in use in Rioja, every combination has been and is being explored.

White wines are now almost universally fermented in stainless steel, although those houses that still produce traditional styles (that is, for oak-ageing) may ferment the grapes at a slightly higher temperature.

It is the ageing process that makes Rioja unique. Spanish wine law lays down strict criteria as to what may be called *crianza, reserva* and so on, but in Rioja the rules are stricter still. Rioja *joven* (formerly *sin crianza*) describes wines that have spent no time in oak or those that have spent less time than the minimum laid down for *crianza*. Some *bodegas* are experimenting with just a hint of oak — say, two or three months — but the wine so aged is still, legally, only *joven*. These wines can be released early in the year after the vintage.

Rioja *de crianza* is the name applied to a wine released in its third year, having spent at least 12 months in *barricas*. In practice, *crianza* wines are usually released with about a year's bottle-age as well. Red Rioja *de reserva* may not be released until its fourth year, having spent at least 12 months in *barricas* and 12 months in bottle. White and *rosado* wines must spend six months in oak and may be released in their third year.

Rioja *de gran reserva* is reserved for red wines made in particularly good years, and which may not be released before their sixth year, having spent at least 12 months in oak and at least 12 months in bottle. White and *rosado gran reservas* — now very rare — must spend six months in oak and may be released in their fifth year.   □

RIOJA PRODUCERS

Virtually all Rioja is made by *bodegas*, which range from modest to very large. They mostly own vines, but also buy in grapes and wine from farmers, many of whom work very small plots. Growers without winemaking facilities often sell their grapes through cooperatives who supply must or wine to the merchant *bodegas*. *Bodegas* age the wine, so their barrel stock is an important statistic. Given the range of wines, colours are shown as (w) white, (p) pink, (r) red.

Bodegas AGE

Formed by the union of three old firms, AGE (50 ha/123 acres) now belongs to Bodegas y Bebidas and buys in most of its grapes. Major brands include Romeral and Siglo (w, p, r), Marqués del Romeral (r), Siglo Saco (r) and Azpilicueta (*crianza* and *reserva*).

Bodegas Berberana

Established in 1877, this is now a large producer with a substantial vineyard holding (5,600ha/13,830 acres) and an annual production of 1.4 million cases. Main brands: Carta de Oro, Carta de Plata and Preferido (w, p, r), Lagunilla *crianza* and Berberana (r).

MARQUES DE MURRIETA

One of the two historic pioneers in the production of Rioja, this *bodega* was established in 1852 and is proudly old-fashioned in its approach. All the grapes come from the *bodega*'s own vineyards at Ygay near Logroño, which were recently extended to 300ha (740 acres). The wines are produced by totally traditional methods and nurtured in cellars that have also been enlarged. One of those traditions is to age all the wines in wood (for a minimum of two years and usually much longer than at any other *bodega*), and there are 14,000 casks for that purpose, some of which are very old. The *bodega* produces a small range of wines that includes Marqués de Murrieta (w, r), the glorious Castillo Ygay (w, r), a very rare and expensive *reserva*, and, more recently, 41,329 bottles of Dalmau (r).

Bodegas Bilbaínas

An old-established (1901) *bodega*, with 255ha (630 acres) and an average annual production of some 83,000 cases. Main brands: Cepa de Oro, Viña Paceta (w); Ederra, Gran Zaco, Imperator, Viña Pomal (r); Viña Zaco and Vicalanda.

Bretón y Cia

This 106-ha (260-acre) *bodega*, founded in 1985, produces fine examples of modern-style Rioja, of which Alba de Bretón (100% Tempranillo from old vines, unfiltered) and Dominio de Conte (90% Tempranillo, 10% Graciano) are the best.

Bodegas Martínez Bujanda

Highly respected *bodega* that now makes wines exclusively from its own vineyards of 383ha (946 acres) with meticulous precision. This is among Rioja's finest producers. Main brands: Valdemar (w, p, r) and Conde de Valdemar (r).

Bodegas Marqués de Cáceres

Founded in 1970 by Enrique Forner, a pioneer of new technology for white and *rosado* wine-production in Rioja. With grapes supplied by a linked growers' grouping, the Unión Vitivinícola, annual production averages 555,000 cases of high-quality modern wine (r, p, w).

Bodegas Campo Viejo

Part of the giant Bodegas y Bebidas group, and the biggest firm in Rioja, Campo Viejo was founded in 1963. Many of its grapes come from the company's own vineyard holdings (510ha/1,260 acres). A very wide range is produced: main brands are Albor (r, w); Campo Viejo, San Asensio, Selección José Bezares (w, p, r); Marqués de Villamagna, Viña Alcorta (r).

CVNE (Compañía Vinícola del Norte de España)

Founded in 1878, this *bodega* has gained a reputation for serious quality. About half its

grapes come from its own vineyards (500ha/1,235 acres). In 1990 the company installed an ultra-modern vinification plant in Rioja. Main brands in a reliable range are Corona *semi-seco* (w), Cune (w, r, p), Monopole (w), Imperial (r), Viña Real (r).

Cosecheros Alaveses SA

The Artadi Pagos Viejos, Viñas de Gain Crianza and Viña El Pisón produced by this company, established in 1985 (70ha/170 acres of vineyards and 800 oak barrels) rank it among the best producers of modern-style Riojas.

Bodegas Domecq

Riojan offshoot of the famous sherry firm (*see* p426), founded in 1973. One of the biggest landowners in Rioja Alavesa, with some 500ha (1,235 acres) of vines, producing 500,000 cases of soft, agreeable wines. Main brands: Viña Eguia (r) and Marqués de Arienzo (w, p, r).

Bodegas Franco-Españolas

Established in 1890, this *bodega* has an annual production of 388,000 cases from bought-in grapes. It belongs to the same group as Federico Paternina. Main brands: Diamante *semi-seco* (w), Viña Soledad (w), Rioja Bordón (r).

Finca Allende

This 22-ha (55-acre) *bodega*, founded in 1995, sells 150,000 litres per annum, 70% of which is exported. Tasters have been particularly enthusiastic about its Aurus (85% Tempranillo and 15% Graciano) and its Allende (100% Tempranillo).

Granja Nuestra Señora de Remelluri

The Spanish love the Remelluri Crianza and Reserva from this 1967 *bodega* (100 ha/250 acres, 360,000 litres per annum); 70% is sold on the home market.

Bodegas Martínez Lacuesta

Old-established (1895) and

proudly old-fashioned *bodega* still making wine in oak vats. Main brands: Campeador (r) and Martínez Lacuesta (r).

Bodegas Lan
Lan was founded in 1974, using the initials of Logroño, Alava and Navarra, the three provinces that were then producing Rioja. The *bodega* owns 80ha (198 acres) of vineyards but buys in nearly 90% of its grapes to make 155,000 cases annually to a good standard. The company owns 25,000 oak casks, and its main brands are Lan (w, p, r) and Viña Lanciano.

Bodegas Barón de Ley
A new *bodega* (1985) based in a restored ducal hunting lodge, called the Coto de Imaz. Surrounded by almost 100ha (247 acres) of vineyards, it has a cellar of 4,000 oak casks, which are mostly French. Barón de Ley is a white wine made from 100% Viura and Barón de Ley *gran reserva* is a red made exclusively from Tempranillo.

Bodegas Faustino Martínez
Established before 1860, when Rioja was still made by the *método rural*, this *bodega* now farms 500ha (1,236 acres) of its own vineyards and has a stock of some 25,000 oak barrels. Main brands: Faustino V (w, p, r) and Faustino I (r).

Bodegas Montecillo
Established in 1874, this *bodega* makes approximately 250,000 cases of wine a year. Ageing is done in 25,000 oak casks, mostly French. Main brands: Viña Cumbrero (w, r), Montecillo (p, r), Viña Monty (r).

Bodegas Muga
A family-controlled *bodega*, established in 1932, which still ferments traditionally in wooden vats and fines with egg-whites. Muga has 60ha (148 acres) of vineyards and makes 50,000 cases of wine a year. Main brands: Muga (w, r),

Wooden fermenting vats in the Muga cellars at Itaro.

Torre Muga and Prado Enea (r).

Bodegas Marqués de Murrieta
See profile.

Bodegas Palacio
Established in 1894, this *bodega* uses grapes from its own vineyards (10ha/25 acres) but mainly buys in to support a production of 220,000 cases of wine a year. Main brands: Glorioso (w, p, r) and Cosme Palacio y Hermanos (w, r).

Bodegas Federico Paternina
This is part of the same group as Bodegas Franco-Españolas, and one of Rioja's largest producers (20m litres, 40,000 oak casks). Main brands: Banda Dorada, Federico Paternina (w); Banda Rosa (p); Banda Azul, Conde de los Andes, Viña Vial (r).

Bodegas La Rioja Alta
Established in 1890, this *bodega* produces 155,000 cases of impressive wines annually.

Grapes come from its own vineyards (300ha/740 acres) as well as local growers. Some fermentation in oak vats and an old-fashioned approach to ageing (30,000 oak casks, some of them 20 years old) make this one of Rioja's greatest *bodegas*. Main brands: Viña Ardanza (w, r); Reserva 904, Reserva 890, Viña Alberdi, Viña Arana (r).

Bodegas Riojanas
Established in 1890, this family-owned *bodega* farms 200ha (495 acres) of vines and buys in grapes and wine (about two-thirds of its needs) to support an output of 277,000 cases a year. The cellars have about 20,000 oak casks. Main brands: Canchales, Monte Real, Puerta Vieja (w, p, r); Viña Albina (w, r), Viña Albina Centenario (r).

Roda SA
This company (60 ha/150 acres and 1,200 oak casks), established in 1986, exports 70% of the 5,000 cases of

Roda I Reserva (100% Tempranillo) it produces.

Señorío de San Vicente
Set up in 1974, this *bodega* (18ha/45 acres; 400 oak casks) exports half of the 4,200 cases of San Vicente (100% Tempranillo peludo) it produces.

Bodegas R López de Heredia Viña Tondonia
Founded in 1892, this *bodega* maintains a very traditional approach: half the grapes come from its own vineyards of 170ha (420 acres), all wines are fermented in oak vats and transferred by hand into 14,000 oak casks, and fining is still done with egg-whites. Main brands are Viña Gravonia (w, r), Viña Tondonia (w, p, r), Viña Bosconia (r), Viña Cubillo (r).

Viñedos del Contino
This *bodega* (60ha/150 acres; 2,000 oak casks), founded in 1974, produces Contino, one of the stars of the modern Rioja style, and a curious little wine called Contino Graciano.

Vinos de los Herederos del Marqués de Riscal
Founded in 1860, this firm started the new-wave wine-production in Rioja at the end of the 19th century and is still owned and run by the descendants of the founders. The first company to introduce French grape varieties in 1868, although in only 9 out of its 39ha (22 out of 96 acres) of vineyards, Riscal invented the famous wire net to prevent counterfeit. 40% of the grapes come from the company's own vineyards (200ha/495 acres), where the original Cabernet Sauvignon is still grown, although it is now mostly used in the 85% Cabernet Barón de Chirel rather than in mainstream Rioja reds. 21,000 oak casks are being replaced in rotation. Main brands: Marqués de Riscal and Barón de Chirel Cabernet Sauvignon (r).

NAVARRA AND ARAGÓN

Wine has been made in Navarra since before Roman times, and has been one of its main products (and export earners) since the end of the 18th century. The French connection with these naturally prosperous, mixed-farming regions in the Upper Ebro Valley paid dividends in the mid-19th century, when French merchants sought wines from Navarra and Aragón to make up a shortfall following French vineyard disasters.

The DO Navarra wineland sits east of Rioja and north-west of the wine-producing areas of Aragón. It is divided into five sub-zones, with vineyards up to 560m (1,850ft) in the wetter, cooler north (Tierra Estella, Valdizarbe and Baja Montaña) and down to 250m (825ft) in the hotter, drier south (Ribera Baja). Between the two lies Ribera Alta, the largest sub-zone which is transitional in climate and altitude. Soils in the first four sub-zones are remarkably similar: deep, fertile topsoil over gravel, with a chalky bedrock. Only in Ribera Baja does the soil become light, sandy, and less suitable for vines.

The principal grape is Garnacha (73% of the vineyard) but the Consejo Regulador has encouraged the planting of Tempranillo, aiming for a split of 34% Garnacha, 31% Tempranillo and 11% Macabeo (Viura) for white wines.

The government of the *autonomía* of Navarra operates a research establishment called EVENA (Estación Viticultura y Enología de Navarra), which grows every variety of grape on every variety of rootstock in all soil types throughout the region to determine the best vinous practices. The results are impressive, and a testament to the region's capabilities.

Navarra's fame within Spain is for big, powerful and delicious *rosados* that are among the best pink wines

Puente la Reina in Navarra.

in the world and which, tasted blindfold, might pass for light reds on the palate. A quest for quality has proven successful: in 1998, the market share held by *crianza* wines increased by 58.8% in Spain and 27.11% abroad and the exported red *reserva* wines even came within a hair's breadth of 219%.

Aragón

Since the 1980s the wines of Aragón, formerly just supplying a burgeoning local market, have started to make an impact abroad. There are four DOs in this region: Cariñena, Calatayud, Campo de Borja and Somontano.

Cariñena is the most established of Aragón's DOs. It gave its name to the grape, but only 1.5% of the vineyard is given over to Cariñena. Most is Garnacha (60%) and Viura (21%). Vineyards are situated from 400 to 800m (1,320 to 2,640ft) on mixed soils, and the climate is continental. Cariñena's best-known wines are young or *crianza* reds, though it also produces young, fresh whites and

rosados. The region is also classified for production of Cava (*see* p418).

Calatayud is the most recent of Aragón's DOs (1990) and the second-largest. The vineyards are high (500–900m/1,650–2,970ft) and the climate continental with low rainfall, resulting in low yields. The main red grape is Garnacha, with some Tempranillo, Juan Ibañéz and Monastrell. *Rosado* wines are made from Garnacha, and white wines are made mainly from Viura with some Garnacha Blanca. All wines produced are in the *joven* style.

The vineyards of Campo de Borja are at slightly lower altitudes. Again, the main red grape is Garnacha (more than 80% of the vineyard), and red and *rosado* are the main styles, as well as a sweet (non-DO) *mistela*, made from Moscatel, which is a mixture of grape juice and spirit.

Halfway up the Pyrenees, Somontano has little in common with other DOs in Aragón or, indeed, the rest of Spain, but promises to be one of the most exciting of Spain's new DOs. Before 1900, all of its export wine went to France, and it is only since the DO was awarded in 1985 that winemakers have appreciated what the region has to offer. Wine styles here are fairly unique, and include highly individual reds, light fruity whites and *rosados*. The vineyards range from 350 to 700m (1,155 to 2,310ft) in altitude, are on rich soils and often terraced into valley sides.

The main red grape is Moristel (unique to Somontano and not the same as Monastrell), which occupies about 25% of the vineyard, followed by the Tempranillo. The main white is Viura, closely followed by Alcañón, another local speciality. New *bodegas* are experimenting with non-Spanish varieties side by side with traditional grapes. □

PRODUCERS

The cooperative tradition is strong in both regions. Contract growers are encouraged to experiment with new grape varieties, and are modernizing equipment. Wine colours are shown as (w) white, (p) pink, (r) red.

NAVARRA

Ninety per cent of grapes in DO Navarra are supplied to producers by cooperatives.

Bodegas Julián Chivite

Established in 1647, this *bodega* is a widely respected family business, making wines from its own 350ha (865 acres) of vines as well as bought-in grapes and wine, maturing them in 15,000 oak casks. Chivite is the largest exporter from Navarra, and its 125th anniversary red has passed into legend. The main brands include Gran Feudo (w, p, r), 125 Anniversario (r), Gran Feudo de Moscatel (sweet) and Viña Marcos (r).

Guelbenzu SL

The Guelbenzu Evo et Lautus from this traditional *bodega* (1851) with 38ha (95 acres) of vineyards, have been coming out on top at wine tastings in recent years.

Luis Gurpegui Muga

The *rosado* and red Monte Ory from this company, founded in 1921, are both held in high esteem.

Bodegas Irache

Founded in 1891, this family business expanded as it approached its 100th birthday, and now has some of the most modern oenological facilities in Navarra. Grapes come from the *bodega's* own vineyards (50ha/124 acres) as well as being bought in, and average yearly production reaches 1.3 million cases. The *crianza* cellar can house 4,445 oak casks. Main brands include Castillo Irache (p, r), Gran Irache (r) and Real Irache (r).

Vinícola Navarra

One of Navarra's oldest *bodegas* (founded in 1864), this winery nevertheless has much in the way of modern plant, and belongs to the giant Bodegas y Bebidas group. Grapes come partly from its own vineyards (12ha/30 acres), but mainly from contract growers. The cellar includes some old 2,000-litre oak casks for show purposes, but *crianza* is produced in 2,000 *barricas* of more modern design. Main brands include Bandeo (w, p, r), Las Campanas (w, p, r), Viña Alaiz (w, p, r), Castillo de Javier (p) and Castillo de Tiebas (r).

Bodegas Ochoa

This is a small (88,000 cases annually) *bodega* run by Javier Ochoa, who also works with EVENA. Grapes come from its own vineyards of 17ha (42 acres) as well as being bought in. Maturation takes place in some 300 oak casks. The best wine is labelled Ochoa Moscatel.

Nuestra Señora Del Romero

This cooperative, set up in 1951, produces 330,000 cases each year from its 1,100ha (2,720 acres) of vineyards and 2,200 oak casks. In Spain, its Malon de Echaide is deemed to be one of the best *rosados*.

Señorío de Sarriá

A traditional *señorío* — a large private estate — of 1,500ha (3,700 acres). 200ha (495 acres) of vines include Chardonnay and Cabernet Sauvignon, and the cellars have the latest technology, with some 10,000 oak casks. The main brands are Señorío de Sarriá (w), Viña del Portillo (p), Viña Ecoyen (r), Gran Vino del Señorío de Sarriá (r) and Viña del Perdón (r).

ARAGON

Aragón producers — most (90%) of them cooperatives — are listed alphabetically within each *denominación*.

CARINENA
Bodega Cooperativa San Valero

This is the largest cooperative in the region, the biggest exporter in Aragón, and one of the most innovative *bodegas*, promoting the planting of high-quality grapes as well as testing experimental varieties. Its wines, which range from everyday bottlings to *gran reservas*, regularly win prizes. It produces 1.7 million cases of wine a year from its members' 5,500ha (13,590 acres) of vineyards. Main brands are Don Mendo (w, p, r) and Monte Ducay (w, p, r).

Grandes Vinos y Viñedos SA

Founded in 1997, this 5,500-ha (135,000-acre) *bodega* has made a name for itself with its Monasterio de la Viñas, a Cabernet Sauvignon, and Corona de Aragón, made exclusively from Tempranillo grapes.

CALATAYUD
Castillo de Maluenda

This *bodega*, set up in 1945, has a vast area under vines (3,500ha/8,650 acres) and produces a well-balanced red exclusively from the Garnacha grape, its Castillo de Maluenda Garnacha Selección.

CAMPO DE BORJA
Bodegas Bordeje

A very small — 250ha (618 acres) — old-established (1770) *bodega*, with cellars built into the hillside outside the village. Grapes come from the *bodega's* own 80ha (198 acres) of vineyards, and the style is very old-fashioned, with much of the wine aged in giant wooden vats. Main brands: Rosado de Garnacha (p), Abuelo Nicolas (r), Don Pablo (r).

Sociedad Cooperativa Agrícola de Borja

This 1,450-ha (3,580 acre) cooperative is considered to be one of the best. The main wines it produces are its Borsao (r) and Gran Campellas (r).

SOMONTANO
Pirineos SA

This *bodega*, founded in 1993, supports the indigenous varieties with its 100% Parraleta or Moristel reds and a fabulous Moristel and Tempranillo, Montesierra Crianza.

Viñedos y Crianzas del Alta Aragón SA

This 1991 *bodega*, with its 300ha (740 acres) of vines and 2,500 oak casks, is number two in the DO, thanks in particular to its Enate wines (Chardonnay, Cabernet Sauvignon, Gewürztraminer, and a 70% Tempranillo).

CASTILLA-LEÓN

This is the original Spanish heart-land: the capital cities of the eight provinces that make up the *autonomía* of Castilla y León all have historic connections with the reconquest of Spain. Castile and León were independent kingdoms until the middle of the 11th century, when they united under Alfonso VI. In 1469 the queen of Castilla-León, Isabella, married Ferdinand, who was heir to the throne of Aragón, and the seeds of a united Spain were sown.

The River Duero passes through seven of the eight provinces, and influences the micro-climatic and geological conditions in four of the region's five DOs (Ribero del Duero, Rueda, Cigales and Toro). Before the

very recent explosive success of Ribero del Duero wines, followed by Toro wines, which are now exported, these wines were produced to serve three local communities: Castilian noblemen, church dignitaries in the cathedral cities, and academics at the University of Salamanca. These were people with money and a taste for quality. The red and rosado wines are robust, powerful, alcoholic and just the sort of thing the local Marqués would enjoy with his roast wild boar.

The fifth (and newest) DO of Castilla-León — Bierzo — is separate from the other four, and owes more in style to neighbouring Galicia. Different grapes are grown here and the wines are in a lighter, fresher, style.

Ribera del Duero

This is the most important DO in the Duero Valley and in Castilla-León. In the mid-19th century, while the Marqués de Riscal and the Marqués de Murrieta were importing Bordeaux grapes and winemaking practices to Rioja (*qv*), something similar was happening near the village of Valbuena in the province of Valladolid. A new company, called Bodega de Lecanda, was established in 1864 with Bordeaux technology: when it passed to another owner in 1890 the name was changed to Vega Sicilia, although the first bottles of Vega Sicilia go back to 1915 or 1917. For the first 118 years of its existence Vega Sicilia — then, as now, one of the world's rarest and

Sixteenth-century houses surround the bullring at Peñafiel, the wine capital of Ribero del Duero.

most expensive wines — was classified simply as *vino de mesa*. In 1982, however, after vigorous lobbying by other winemakers, the DO was awarded. The most exciting aspect of this, which had already been proved by Vega Sicilia, was that the local red grape, Tinto Fino, or Tinto del País (actually Tempranillo), could, with the right husbandry, produce world-class wines. Vega Sicilia now uses mostly Tinto Fino in drier years, and Cabernet Sauvignon in wetter years.

The Ribera del Duero vineyards follow the course of the Duero River from Soria to Valladolid, mostly at an altitude of 700–800m (2,310–2,640ft). The soil is deep, light and sandy over clay and limestone, with occasional outcrops of chalk. The vineyards are at the climatic limit of vine cultivation in these parts, which explains why yields average only 24hl/ha. The climate is fully continental.

The grapes have good acidity, and the finished wine is of high quality and expensive. Tinto Fino occupies 60% of the vineyard. Whereas in Rioja it needs the help of other grapes to make the perfect "mix", the high altitude and cool climate in Ribera del Duero enable it to produce a wine of balanced acidity and complexity by itself. Only red and *rosado* wines are produced here, and there is some Garnacha on an experimental basis. Valbuena (home of Vega Sicilia) and a few other villages are allowed to replant Bordeaux varieties. There is some *joven* red, but most wine goes into *crianzas*, and the region's *reservas* and *gran reservas*, at their best, are matched only by the greatest Riojas.

Rueda

The history of Rueda wine is long and respectable, and in the days when Valladolid was the national capital, Rueda's wines were in great demand among its noble families. However, after phylloxera struck in the 19th century, much of the vineyard was replanted with high-yielding Palomino, simply because growers were paid by the litre for the wine

they produced, regardless of quality. There was another local grape, the Verdejo, but it produced only small quantities of juice, which was rather unstable. Some winemakers tried to make the best of the Palomino, and Rueda started to gain a reputation for lightly fortified sherry-type wines in the early 20th century. However, these were of little interest to the export market.

Rueda's leap back into the limelight came in the 1970s, at the hand of one of Spain's innovators, the Marqués de Riscal (*see* p406). The Riscal *bodega* had been looking for somewhere to make a white wine to carry the Riscal name, having made a decision many years ago not to make white wines in Rioja. What attracted Riscal's winemakers to Rueda was something the locals had hardly bothered with for years: the Verdejo grape. They discovered that the grape had tremendous potential for quality white wines as long as the juice was not allowed to oxidize on its way to the press. Riscal had the technology to pick and protect the grapes, transport them to the winery at speed, and press and handle them under an inert gas blanket to preserve the freshness of the must: a genuine case of a grape realizing its full potential thanks to new technology. Riscal went on to plant many other experimental varieties, and to make a Rueda based on Sauvignon Blanc.

Other *bodegas* followed the Verdejo trail, and the epithet Rueda Superior is now reserved for wines that are at least 85% Verdejo. There have also been successful experiments with a modest amount of oak-ageing: the original regulations in Rueda demanded a minimum of six months, but this was set aside when it became obvious that the region's future lay in crisp, dry, fresh wines. Then Riscal produced a *reserva* Limousin with six months in French oak, which reopened the debate.

However, many *bodegas* continued to make the old, sherry-type wines (now known as Rueda Pálido for drier

styles aged under *flor*, and Rueda Dorado for oloroso types) in the hope that the market would turn in their favour. There is little sign yet that this is going to happen.

Rueda's vineyards are found on rolling countryside at an altitude of 600–780m (1,980–2,575ft), and the best of them tend to be closer to the Duero, on iron-rich soils with a limestone bedrock. This is Spain's central Meseta, so the climate is solidly continental, with occasional years (usually of exceptional quality) when rainfall is evenly spread.

The main grape is now Verdejo (47% of the vineyard) which must be present to at least 85% for the DO Rueda Superior and also for the new sparkling wine category DO Rueda Espumoso. (Having lost the right to produce Cava in 1989, Rueda has taken matters into its own hands.) Palomino is the second most widely planted grape (25%) and is in decline, as are the Rueda Pálido wines that it makes. Viura (21%) blends well with Verdejo for still and sparkling wines, and newcomer Sauvignon Blanc (7%) has recently been granted "authorized" (as opposed to "permitted") status after having been introduced by the Riscal *bodegas*.

"Experimental" varieties include Tempranillo, Chardonnay and even a little Cabernet Sauvignon, in spite of the fact that no red (or *rosado*) wines are as yet permitted under the DO. However, there are plans to extend DO Rueda to include reds and *rosados*.

Cigales

Cigales won its DO status in 1991, but has been making wine for centuries, concentrating on excellent *rosados*. The region sits north and west of Ribera del Duero (famed for its reds) and Rueda (some of Spain's best whites), so this is literally a good middle ground. In addition, Cigales makes some excellent reds and these promise well for the future.

Geographically, the vineyards lie north of the city of Valladolid at an altitude of 800m (2,640ft). The land is flat and the soil is stony with limestone bedrock. The climate is mainly continental with good rainfall, and is generally sympathetic to the cultivation of the vine.

The main red grape is Tempranillo (Tinta del País: 50%), followed by Garnacha Tinta (30%) and Granacha Gris. White varieties are Verdejo, Viura, Palomino and Albillo, which together account for over 20% of the vineyard, although the area under the latter two is decreasing. Cigales wines are very interesting, with some pioneering work on *crianza rosado*, including six to eight months in oak, and some experimental work with Cabernet Sauvignon, though not in DO wines. Reds from Tempranillo promise extremely well, but current production is 80% *rosado*, mostly *joven*-style wine pressed from a mixture of red and white grapes.

Toro

This is the wine — heady and uncompromisingly Castilian — that since 1215 has been served at the high tables of the University of Salamanca. The local grape is Tinta de Toro (Tempranillo again), which can achieve 14° alcohol and even higher strengths quite naturally, one of its most prized qualities for 800 years.

However, winemaking was fairly primitive in this area until relatively recently. More modern wineries have been taking advantage of the upsurge in interest in Toro since the awarding of the DO in 1987, and new *bodegas* with stainless-steel tanks and high-technology fermentation control are making their mark. Mariano García, winemaker at Vega Sicilia for twenty years, the Lurton brothers, Antonio Sanz and even Vega Sicilia, Pesquera and San Vicente have become extremely fond of this DO.

The town of Toro sits on the River Duero with vineyards all around it, although the best of them are in the north-east of the zone. From time immemorial this has been known as the Tierra del Vino (wine country) to distinguish it from the vast cereal-

Medina del Campo, at the centre of Rueda, has been a market town for centuries.

farming uplands of Castile, known as the Tierra del Pan (bread country). The wineland is at an altitude of 600–750m (1,980–2,750ft), and soils are limestone-based in the north of the zone, but more alluvial near the confluence of the Duero and the Guareña. The climate is solidly continental, but, like Rueda, Toro can often receive unexpected rainfall borne on westerly winds.

The only "preferred" grape in Toro is Tinta de Toro (Tempranillo), which occupies 58% of the vineyard. A red wine must be a minimum of 75% Tinta de Toro: and somewhere between a quarter and a third of all red wines go for *crianza* under DO regulations. Minority grapes include Garnacha, Malvasía and Verdejo, and these produce the region's small quantity of *rosado* and white wines.

Bierzo

The region is known as El Bierzo, but the DO wine, classified at the end of 1989, is simply Bierzo, and centres on the mining town of Ponferrada in the province of León.

Bierzo is in a sheltered mountain valley contiguous with the DO Valdeorras (across the River Sil, in Galicia). The vineyards are mainly at an alti-

tude of 500–650m (1,650–2,145ft), and soils vary from alluvial at the lower (river-valley) levels to slate in the highlands, under reasonably fertile, deep topsoil. The climate is temperate with plenty of sunshine.

The main red grape is Mencía, found only in Bierzo and Valdeorras, and believed to share a common ancestor with Cabernet Franc. Current research suggests that it has considerable potential, and it occupies 62% of the vineyard. The other red grape is Garnacha Tintorera. The quality white grapes of the region are Godello and Doña Blanca, but these are still overshadowed by Palomino.

Winemaking generally is in a state of change in the Bierzo region, with concrete vats being replaced by stainless steel ones, and pneumatic presses replacing the old continuous-screw equipment. The red wines of Bierzo are made in all styles from *joven* to *gran reserva*, but wines are good and promise well. White wines from Godello and Doña Blanca are fresh and pleasant, though many *bodegas* still mix in some Palomino, simply because there is so much of it about. However, progress is still being made towards replanting with other grape varieties. □

PRODUCERS

Here, too, old ways are being updated. Many growers, though still owning small plots, have organized themselves into cooperatives, and huge investment is being made. Producers are listed alphabetically within each DO.

RIBERA DEL DUERO

Bodegas y Viñedos Alión SA
Set up in 1990 by Vega Sicilia, this *bodega* is already one of the region's leading producers.

Alejandro Fernández-Tinto Pesquera SL
The Pesquera (100% Tempranillo) of this *bodega* — founded only in 1972, but well-established — has won universal acclaim. Alejandro Fernández is one of the DO's leading producers.

Felix Callejo SA
This firm and its Gran Callejo Gran Riserva have earned a good reputation.

Condado de Haza SL
This new firm (1993) has added to its Condado de Haza an explosive Alenza Crianza.

Bodegas Peñalba López
Founded in 1903, this *bodega* (200ha/494 acres) using ultra-modern equipment ferments its grapes in 4,500 oak casks.

──────── VEGA SICILIA ────────

Established in 1864, this *bodega* laid the foundations of winemaking in the Duero Valley. The French grape varieties (Cabernets, Merlot and Malbec) brought from Bordeaux survive today, but there are increasing amounts of Tinto Fino. All the grapes come from the *bodega*'s own vineyards, which cover 250ha (618 acres). Yields are low and production averages only 27,000 cases a year. Demand far exceeds supply. Methods are traditional and the wines are matured in 6,000 oak casks. Vega Sicilia's highly individual wines, which are immensely powerful with a high alcohol content and excellent fruit quality, are sold as Valbuena (r), matured in *barricas* for three to five years, and the *reserva* Vega Sicilia Unico (r), matured for up to ten. The Valbuena, held to be a second wine, is however a different wine, which is sometimes extraordinary.

Matarromera SA
This firm, founded in 1988, has caused quite a stir with two superb wines made exclusively from Tinta Fina grapes: Matarromera Gran Reserva and Magnum Matarromera Reserva.

Mauro SA
With competent advice from Mariano García (formerly Vega Sicilia), this firm, founded in 1980, has brought up to world-class level its Terreus, San Román and other Mauro *crianzas*, which however do not have the DO label.

Monasterio SL
This firm was set up well-equipped in 1991: 68ha (168 acres) and 1,500 oak casks, which produce the outstanding Hacienda Monasterio Riserva.

Montebaco
The Montebaco Crianza of this firm, founded in 1989 (50ha/124 acres and 400 casks) has been highly acclaimed.

Hermanos Pérez Pascuas SL
The Viña Pedrosa (*crianza* and *reserva*) is made from 100ha (247 acres) of vines, almost all of them Tinta del País grapes.

Dominio Pingus SL
This estate produces a "vin de garage": Pingus, made exclusively from the Tinto Fino grape. Prices are rocketing…

Bodegas Ribera-Duero
A cooperative cellar since 1927. Its main brands are Peñafiel and Protos.

Bodega Vega Sicilia
See profile.

Abadía Retuerta SA
Since 1990, the Bordeaux oenologist Pascal Delbeck has newly planted this 204-ha (504-acre) vineyard. With four vintages, this firm has become one of Spain's leading producers: El Palomar, El Campanario, Valdebellón and Negralada.

RUEDA

Alvarez y Diez SA
The Mantel Blanco Rueda Superior and a Sauvignon varietal of this firm, established in 1941, are models of their kind.

Belondrade y Lurton
Founded in 1994 by Brigitte Lurton, of the Lurton dynasty, this firm produces an average 2,100 cases of wine per year.

Angel Lorenzo Cachazo
Since 1988, this firm produces its excellent Martivili Rueda Superior, a testimonial to the virtues of the Verdejo grape.

Grandes Vinos SL
The Mirador Rueda Superior is the DO's "vin de garage".

Vinos Blancos de Castilla
Founded in 1972, this *bodega* is an embassy of the Marqués de Riscal, with an average annual production of 225,000 cases of good quality wine.

CIGALES

Cooperativa de Cigales
This co-op (1957) produces over 125,000 cases of wine.

TORO

Cooperativa Vino de Toro
The region's main producer.

Fariña SL
Founded in 1940, this *bodega* is a reference. The Colegiata and the Gran Colegiata are showcases for wines made from the Tinta de Toro grape.

Mauro-Toro SA
The San Román, a brainchild of Mariano Rodríguez, is a wine likely to win contests.

BIERZO
The DO is dominated by large, modern cooperatives.

Prada a Tope
Founded in 1984, this *bodega* makes wines from 15ha (37 acres) of vines and bought-in grapes.

GALICIA & BASQUE COUNTRY

The north-west of Spain differs most markedly from the rest of the country in terms of climatic influences, which come from the Atlantic Ocean and the Bay of Biscay; but it is also rather cut off from the rest of the country by the Cordillera Cantábrica. Its historical links are with Celtic culture (via the Roman Empire), while today it has much in common with neighbouring Portugal. This region is often referred to as "Green Spain" because of the richness of its vegetation, the result of the temperate climate, plentiful rainfall and rich soils. There are three DO wines (Rías Baixas, Ribeiro and Valdeorras) in the *autonomía* of Galicia, and one (Txakoli) in the north of País Vasco, which is Basque country.

Rías Baixas

This is the newest and, some would say, the best of Galicia's DO wines: the other two DOs remained virtually undiscovered until this one burst upon the international scene in 1988. The principal grape is the Albariño, a variety of such excellence that almost the whole wine industry in the province of Pontevedra has been built upon it. There is much activity throughout the DO: old *bodegas* are being updated with new technology, new ones are being built, and a lot of attention is being paid to quality control during wine production. The result is one of the most exciting of Spain's "new" wines.

There are three sub-zones of Rías Baixas: Valle del Salnés (Val do Salnes in the local language, Galego) on the west coast around Cambados; El Rosal (O Rosal) on the Portuguese border; and Condado del Tea (Condado do Tea). Soils are generally granite-based and the climate is Atlantic-maritime: winters are cold and rainfall plentiful. The wines are possibly the best whites in Spain:

Wine stored *sur lattes* at Lapatena.

Miguel Torres, founder of the modern Catalan wine industry, believes the Albariño is the Riesling of Germany, allegedly brought by German monks making pilgrimages to Santiago de Compostella.

Ribeiro

Ribeiro wines enjoyed considerable popularity three or four hundred years ago in northern Europe, but their recent history has been rather obscure. Although the DO was established in 1957, it is only with the publicity given to Rías Baixas that interest in Ribeiro has revived. The wines have great potential, and new investment is evident everywhere.

Ribeiro vineyards (in Orense province) are mainly in three river valleys on unexceptional alluvial soils with a granite base. The climate is temperate, with a greater temperature range and less rainfall than on the coast. The main grapes are Treixadura (white) and Caiño (red).

Ribeiro produces light and fresh whites and reds in the *joven* style. There is also *enverado*, a wine made

from grapes picked while still underripe (giving an alcohol level of 8–9%) to retain freshness and acidity. There is a small amount of *crianza*, but most wine is intended for instant drinking.

Valdeorras

Easternmost of the Galician DOs, Valdeorras is contiguous with Bierzo in Castilla-León and makes wine in a similar, light, fresh *joven* style. This area is still influenced climatically by the Atlantic Ocean, although it is more continental, with a greater temperature range for example, than elsewhere in the region.

Most vineyards are in the Sil River valley on fertile soils with some limestone. The main red grape is the Garnacha (35%), although the Mencía (8%) is "recommended", and the main white is the Palomino (25%), with the Godello (16%) "recommended". The areas under Doña Blanca and a newcomer called the Lado are increasing as the wines from these grapes start to show well. The future seems to lie in wines from the excellent Godello grape.

Txakoli

Spain's northernmost wine is made in the *autonomía* of País Vasco. The region consists of three provinces: Vizcaya and Guipúzcoa in the north, and Alava in the south. Alava is part of DOC Rioja, but the northern provinces have their own traditional wine in DO Txakoli (or Chacolí), the smallest DO in Spain. Bordering on the Bay of Biscay, the climate is maritime, and the vineyards are situated in the foothills on alluvial soils. A light, fresh, dry white (90% of production) and light red wine are made from the local Hondarribi Zuri (white) and Hondarribi Beltza (red) grapes, and both are in the *joven* style. The white wine is drunk as an apéritif or with shellfish.   □

PRODUCERS

Producers in north-west Spain are small-scale: many growers farm less than 1ha (2.5 acres) of land that has been carved up over the generations by inheritance laws. Cooperatives can have several hundred members, or even more. There has been much modernization, and replanting with high-quality grape varieties is encouraged and is now extensive. Producers are listed alphabetically within each DO. Wine colours are shown as (w) white, (p) pink, (r) red.

RIAS BAIXAS
Granxa Fillaboa
A family-owned winery that has 30ha (74 acres) of Albariño in a delightful plantation. The brand name is Fillaboa, one of the best wines of the DO.

Bodegas Morgadío-Agromiño
A modern *bodega* — established in 1988 to produce quality wines — with some 30ha (74 acres) of Albariño in new vineyards.

Bodegas Salnesur
Founded in 1988, this *bodega* owns 140ha (346 acres) of vines. Its wines are labeled Condes de Albarei.

Bodegas de Vilariño-Cambados
Established in 1986, this *bodega* is a co-op serving 140 members who farm 100ha (247 acres) of Albariño. The brand name is Martín Codax.

Bodegas Marqués de Vizhoja
This winery owns 18ha (44 acres) of vines. Main brands are Torre la Moreira (w) and Marqués de Vizhoja (w).

Santiago Ruiz
This 40-ha (100-acre) *bodega*, founded in 1892, bears the same name as the much missed patriarch of the DO and the street in which it stands. The label is just as original as the wine, which is made from 70% Albariño, 20% Loureiro and 10% Treixadura.

Terras Gauda SA
Since 1990, Terras Gauda — Albariño, Loureiro, Caiño Blanco — has ranked amongst the best wines in the region.

RIBEIRO
Cooperativa Vitivinícola del Ribeiro
This cooperative (670ha/ 1,650 acres) was formed in 1967 and has managed to produce quality white wines: Amadeus and Pazos de Ulloa.

Portela SAT
This *bodega* with 8ha (20 acres) of vineyards, founded in 1987, produces Sol da Portela, a white wine made exclusively from Palomino grapes, and Señorío de Beade, a red blend of 40% Caiño, 30% Ferrón and 30% Souson, both of which are made in the modern Ribeiro style.

Emilio Rojo
The label of the white wine which is the figurehead of this producer — made from five varieties (Lado, Treixadura, Loureiro, Torrontés and Albariño) — bears the name of one of the personalities of the DO.

VALDEORRAS
Bodegas A Tapada
This 10-ha (25-acre) *bodega*, founded in 1993, produces two whites exclusively from Godello grapes. One is *barrique*-aged, the other isn't — the choice is yours!

GETARIAKO TXAKOLINA
Eizaguirre
Established in 1930, this small *bodega* belongs to the Eizaguirre family and farms its own small vineyard as well as buying grapes in from other growers. Main brands are Berezia (w), Eizaguirre (w), Hilbera (w), Monte Garate (w).

Txomin Etxaniz
The owner of this 21-ha (50-acre) vineyard in Cantabria is well-known both on the agricultural scene and in Basque politics. Excellent white (85% Hondarribi Zuri and 15% Hondarribi Beltza, a red variety used for making white wines).

Vineyards in autumn near Carballino in Galicia.

CATALONIA

Like other northern Spanish *auto-nomías*, Cataluña (the Castilian spelling) or Catalunya (the Catalan) had a long history as an independent country before the union of Spain in 1492, when Barcelona, its capital, was the seat of government. Barcelona's importance as a port gave it a key role in the wine-exporting business from the 13th century onwards, although Catalonia's wines were unexceptional.

Until the middle of the 19th century, the region made oxidized white wines from a variety of unsuitable grapes and matured them into *rancios* — dark, almost sherry-like wines with a nutty-brown colour, matured in carboys half-buried in sand for many years. The breakthrough came in 1872 when the first bottle of Cava — sparkling wine made by the traditional method (*see* box) — was produced by the Raventós family. Josep Raventós had seen the rise of champagne's popularity on his travels through France and northern Europe, and decided that Catalonia could compete. Suddenly the region, and Barcelona in particular, had an unquenchable thirst for sparkling wine. Better-quality white grapes were planted, and many growers found that surplus grapes could be turned into a pleasant, fresh, dry white wine, especially in the higher vineyards. There was also experimentation with reds, and it became clear in the 1950s and 1960s that Catalonia had real potential. There was also experimentation with reds, and it became clear in the 1950s and 1960s that Catalonia had real potential. The region now has ten DOs: Catalunya and Plá de Bages have recently been added to Penedès, Conca de Barberà, Costers del Segre, Alella, Ampurdán-Costa Brava, Priorato, Tarragona and Terra Alta. The *autonomía* is also responsible for the production of more than 90% of the wines of DO Cava.

Catalunya

The DO Catalunya covers some 60,000ha (150,000 acres) and adjoins several other DOs. Between January and June 2000, the brand new DO

Many Catalan vineyards are in lush river valleys, as in Priorato at the historic heart of the region's winemaking.

Catalunya label was affixed to some 10 million bottles. According to Carles Andreu, the first secretary of the DO's Consejo Regulador (Regulating body), this deluge was the result of a consensus between winemakers and producers to allow the smaller DOs of the region, such as DO Conca de Barberà, to use this label in order to find an outlet on the market. Furthermore, DO Catalunya may, in time, absorb wines made from grapes grown in one DO and bottled in another.

Plá de Bages

This, the most recent of the Catalan DOs, has brought together small parcels of land which hitherto had been satellites in the Cava universe. Valentí Roqueta, Secretary General of the DO, confirms that, according to a Medieval manuscript *(Miracula Sancti Benedict)*, the name Bages comes from Bacchus, god of wine. Predominant grape varieties include Macabeo, Chardonnay and Picapoll for the whites and the red varieties Ull de Llebre, Cabernet Sauvignon and Merlot. A small amount of Sauvignon Blanc, Garnacha, Pinot Noir and Malbec are also grown and there are experiments underway with Syrah, Gamay and Gewürztraminer.

Penedès

Since January 2000, new regulations demarcate the best land and an 'educational' back label is now compulsory in a DO which has done more than most to bring the Catalan wine industry up to date. Forty years ago there were no more than three or four winemakers making a concerted effort to produce and sell fine wines for export, but most were still turning out old-fashioned, heavy, semi-fortified wines. In 1960 the mayor of Barcelona suggested that Penedès would be a good source of everyday red wine for the city, and offered incentives to winemakers.

The more forward-looking *bodegas* — like Torres and Jean León — immediately started to experiment, and Spain saw its first stainless steel fermentation tanks, temperature control, and new-technology winemaking. The pioneers experimented with "foreign" grapes like Cabernet Sauvignon and Chardonnay; sooner or later other bodegas followed suit.

Penedès is immediately south of Barcelona city, in the provinces of Barcelona and Tarragona, and the regional centre for still wines is Vilafranca del Penedès. The vineyards are planted at three levels: the Bajo-Penedès is the coastal strip up to 250m (825ft) altitude, with a hot climate and fairly ordinary wines. The Medio-Penedès has vineyards up to 500m (1,650ft), and the cooler climate produces much better grapes (most of the Cava vineyards are at this level). The Alt-Penedès rises up to 800m (2,640ft) in the foothills of the mountain ranges surrounding Spain's central Meseta. The region's best grapes, particularly red varieties, are grown at this level.

The regulations of the DO allow for 121 varieties of grapes in Penedès, but most growers stick to a much smaller selection. Reds in order of popularity are Ull de Llebre (Tempranillo), Garnacha, Monastrell, Cariñena, Cabernet Sauvignon and Samsó, with Cabernet Franc, Merlot and Pinot Noir permitted. Principal white grapes are Parellada, Xarel.lo, Macabeo and Subirat-Parent (Malvasía Riojana), with permitted varieties including Chardonnay and Sauvignon Blanc.

Conca de Barberà

This is a small DO zone between Tarragona in the south and Costers del Segre in the centre of the region. It was delimited after a long wait in 1989. Historically, its fortunes have been linked with Cava, and most grapes grown have traditionally been sold to the Cava houses. There are

CAVA SPARKLING WINES

Unlike sparkling-wine producers in many other parts of the world, Josep Raventós (*see* opposite) concentrated on native Catalan grapes and finally settled on Macabeo (known elsewhere as Viura), Parellada and Xarel.lo. These may be used in any combination, and some modern houses also use Chardonnay. Cava from outside Catalonia may be made exclusively from Viura.

Cava vineyards are found in the Medio-Penedès, on land high enough for the good acidity necessary for excellent wine, but low enough to provide economic yields. Some of the best vineyards draw a proportion of their grapes from the Alt-Penedès, but the wines tend to be expensive.

Cava is also made in the Catalan provinces of Girona, Tarragona and Lleida (Lérida), and the DO covers demarcated vineyards in Aragón (Zaragoza), Navarra, La Rioja, País Vasco (Alava) and some transitional zones in Valencia, Castilla-León and Extremadura.

Modern Cava winemaking takes place in some of the world's most up-to-date wineries, and follows the traditional method of secondary fermentation in bottle (*see* p110). Cava must spend a minimum of nine months in bottle, and most bottles spend between one and three years in the cellars.

PRODUCERS

The two largest producers are in San Sadurní de Noya in Barcelona province.

Codorníu

This was the first Cava producer (in 1872) and is still the largest. The company was founded by the Raventós family in 1551. Elegant landscaped gardens conceal a modern winery which can take in 1,000 tonnes of grapes from as many growers at vintage time. Main brands: Anna de Codorníu, Extra Codorníu, GranCodorníu, Non Plus Ultra, Jaume de Codorníu.

Freixenet

The second-oldest Cava producer, this is also family-owned. While it is the second-largest producer of Cava, Freixenet is the world's largest producer of sparkling wine generally, with interests worldwide. Main brands: Freixenet Brut Nature, Brut Barroco, Carta Nevada, Cordon Negro, Reserva Real, Cuvée DS, Segura Viudas, Aria, Castellblanch, Conde de Caralt.

moves in DO Penedès to get Conca de Barberà annexed to Penedès, but Conca does have a vinous identity of its own and, since the award of a provisional DO in 1972, there has been increased interest in the area's own, still wines which are fresh and fruity.

The basin (*conca* in Catalan, *cuenca* in Spanish) of the rivers Francolí and Ganguera is protected by mountain ranges, and, at an average 500m (1,650ft) altitude, offers the sort of cool climate in which high-quality grapes can be grown. The soil is chalk- and limestone-based.

The main grapes are Macabeo and Parellada for white wines (about 70% of the vineyard) and Trepat, Garnacha and Ull de Llebre (Tempranillo) for reds, with a little experimental Cabernet Sauvignon. Wine production is 80% *joven* whites.

Costers del Segre

This DO is named after the River Segre, which flows down from the Pyrenees to join the River Ebro south of Llebre (Lérida). The region is fragmented into four sub-zones: to the east are the sub-zones Valls de Riu Corb and Les Garrigues; to the north is Artesa, and to the west is Raimat.

Raimat is a large estate which has made its name using Californian techniques with Cabernet Sauvignon and Chardonnay grapes, as well as Tempranillo and others. Elsewhere in the DO, a good deal of grapes are sold to Cava producers or in bulk.

The land lies between 200m (660ft) in the north of the region and 400m (1,320ft) in the south, but the soil is surprisingly uniform throughout — sandy topsoil over limestone. The main grapes are Macabeo, Parellada, Xarel.lo, Chardonnay and Garnacha Blanca for white wines; and Garnacha, Ull de Llebre (Tempranillo), Cabernet Sauvignon, Merlot, Monastrell, Trepat and Mazuelo (Cariñena) for reds.

Alella

Barcelona once threatened to swallow up Alella and surrounding vineyards in its advancing commuter development. However, new upland areas accredited for planting since 1989 (in four new districts known collectively as Vallés) have preserved Alella as the centre of a wine area with an advancing reputation.

The vineyards run inland from the coast towards the foothills of the Cordillera Catalana from altitudes of up to 90m (295ft) near the coast, to 90–160m (295–530ft) in the central area, and 160–260m (530–860ft) in the Vallés. The bedrock is granite in the higher vineyards, and the topsoils become increasingly sandy towards the coast. The climate here is Mediterranean, but cooler in the higher western vineyards, and the principal grapes are Pansá Blanca (Xarel.lo) and Garnacha Blanca for white wines, Ull de Llebre (Tempranillo) and Garnacha for reds and *rosados*.

Ampurdán-Costa Brava

This is Catalonia's northernmost DO, in the province of Girona on the French border and contiguous with the French wine areas of Banyuls and Côtes du Roussillon. Greater Catalonia, of course, once encompassed lands on both sides of the Pyrenees. The vineyards are in the Pyrenean foothills, at an altitude of 200m (660ft) at their highest point, sloping down to sea level on good soils with a reasonable limestone content. The climate is Mediterranean, cooled by the Tramontana which blows from the north, but still hot and humid.

The main grapes are Garnacha and Cariñena for red and *rosado* wines, and Macabeo and Garnacha Blanca for whites. However, old-style *rancio* dessert wines are still made from Garnacha by the *vin de paille* method (by which grapes are dried on straw mats before pressing) under the name Garnatxa.

Priorato

This is the heartland of traditional Catalan winemaking ... and nowadays of new winemaking practices and trade. Vineyards range in altitude from 100–700m (330–2,310ft), often on terraced mountainsides, and the *llicorella* soil is unique in Spain. The main grapes are Garnacha, red and white, and the wines range from modern light, fresh *joven* whites to the reds which are now more subtle-flavoured.

Tarragona

Historically, Tarragona made a fortified, sweet red wine, often called "poor man's port". It is still produced (under the DO Tarragona Clásico), but has long since been superseded in production terms by light wines (red, *rosado* and white) mainly in the *joven* style, but with some reds reflecting the heavyweight style of Priorato. The main grape for red wines is Cariñena, and for whites Macabeo, but there is still some traditional Moscatel, and reds made with Tempranillo are starting to make an appearance.

The region divides into three sub-zones around the town of Falset: Tarragona Campo (up to 200m/660ft altitude around Tarragona city, and representing 70% of the DO area), Falset-Comarca (at 360m/1,200ft in a mountain valley), and Falset-Ribera del Ebro on the Ebro delta (at 100m/330ft altitude). Soils tend towards the alluvial, and the climate is hot and Mediterranean.

Terra Alta

The highest and most southerly DO in Catalonia, Terra Alta, borders on the *autonomía* of Aragón. The vineyards average 400m (1,320ft) in altitude and are planted in inaccessible mountain valleys. However, the bedrock is limestone and drainage is good, encouraging vines to flourish. The climate is continental and the high altitude gives the grapes good exposure to the sun without their becoming overheated.

The main grape is Garnacha Blanca (77% of the vineyard) and the traditional style is the sweet or oak-aged *rancio*. However, modern technology is producing some lighter, fresher wines. □

PRODUCERS

Many changes are underway in the Catalan vineyards: new owners, a revival of indigenous varieties and experimentation with foreign varieties, more widespread bottling, the appearance of the concept of *masía* (equivalent to the French Château) and new DO regions. Wine colours are shown as (w) white, (p) pink, (r) red.

PENEDES
Albet i Noya
This company, founded in 1978 and pioneer of bio-dynamic vinegrowing, produces a good red wine made exclusively from Syrah grapes, Col.lectió.

René Barbier
The 300ha (740 acres) of vineyards belonging to this *bodega* (part of the Freixenet group) meet only part of its requirements. Two whites, its Mediterraneam made from three local grape varieties, and René Barbier Selección, are excellent.

Can Rafols dels Caus SL
Since 1980, this 50-ha (125-acre) *bodega* with 150 oak casks has made a name for itself with several wines in the Gran Caus range and a Caus Lubis, made exclusively from Merlot grapes.

Cellers Puig Roca SA
With 30 years of winemaking experience behind him, Josep Puig uses his 10-ha (25-acre) *bodega* and 130 oak casks to produce his award-winning Augustus wines and Forum *barrique*-aged vinegars.

Chandon SA
Since 1987, this branch of Moët & Chandon, in a *masía* designed by the architect Oscar Tusquets, has been producing a good Cava and a well-balanced Eclipse Chardonnay.

Juvé & Camps SA
This Cava company (430ha/ 1,060 acres), founded in 1921, has found a niche in the market with its Ermita d'Espiells

(Macabeo, Xarel.lo and Parellada) and its Casa Vella red (Cabernet Sauvignon).

Josep Maria Raventós i Blanc
This company, predominantly a Cava producer, has managed to make a name for itself in still white wines with its 100% Xarel.lo and its El Preludi.

Miguel Torres
Since 1870 this *bodega* has collected together 800ha (1,975 acres) of vineyards but it still needs to buy in grapes and, more importantly, thanks to the much-missed Miguel Torres, it transformed the Spanish wine industry with its constant quest for improved quality. The winemaker Miguel A. Torres, who now runs a company with a presence in around 100 countries, has skilfully found the right balance between quality and quantity and has recently even bought over Jean León, another pioneer in the DO.

COSTERS DEL SEGRE
Cellers Castell de Remei
This family-owned *bodega* has 100ha (247 acres) of vineyards. It has recently benefited from extensive investment. Main brands include Castell del Remei (r) and Gotim Bru (r).

Raimat
Established in 1918, the most forward-looking *bodega* in the region makes wines in an ultra-modern winery from virus-free clones of mainly French grape varieties. 1,250ha (3,000 acres) produce approximately 770,000 cases annually.

Owned by the Raventós family, it also makes Cava in this area (Raimat label). Still wines include Chardonnay (w), Cabernet Sauvignon (r), Tempranillo (r) and several blends.

ALELLA
Alta Alella
This company incorporates Parxet, which makes Cava: the two were merged in 1987. The *bodega* is privately owned and farms 40ha (100 acres) of vines, making it the largest proprietor in Alella. Main brand: Marqués de Alella (w).

AMPURDAN-COSTA BRAVA
Cavas del Castillo de Perelada
For some years now, this castle has been the venue for one of the most prestigious summer festivals but it also houses a casino and two restaurants. In addition to this, there are some fairly decent whites and the excellent Castillo Perelada Gran Claustro (r), produced in a 1923 *bodega* covering 100ha (250 acres) with 1,200 oak casks.

PRIORATO
Alvaro Palacios SL
Alvaro Palacios, an ex-pat from his native Rioja and trained in Bordeaux, settled here in 1989 on the advice of his friend, René Barbier. His Ermita (80% Garnatxa), at the time the most expensive wine in Spain, raised the stakes and other wines have followed since then — as have doubts about the ageing qualities of Garnachas. Despite this, the other winemakers hold their colleague in high esteem – even if he is a spoilsport.

Cellers Fuentes Hernández
Using 80% Garnatxa from old vines, winemaker Josep M. Fuentes has created a remarkable Gran Clos 1995 which is almost black in colour.

Clos Mogador
René Barbier, with his 20ha (50 acres) of vineyards, has caused

a real stir in this DO. His Clos Mogador and Clos Erasmus, entirely different from his Penedès wines, are absolutely wonderful.

Costers del Siurana
Thanks to the Catalan Arnaud de Villeneuve, the Dolç de l'Obac has rediscovered its former sweetness, while the Clos de l'Obac has quite a kick.

Mas Martinet Viticultors
The Clos Martinet from this *bodega* ranks it among the great names of the DO.

Vall-Llach Mas Martinet
In this *bodega* we have the Catalan folk singer Lluís Llach trying his hand at winemaking with his Cims de Porrera Classic (Cariñena, Garnatxa and Cabernet Sauvignon).

TARRAGONA
Josep Anguera Beyme
The Joan d'Anguera (Syrah, Garnatxa, Cabernet Sauvignon) produced by this *bodega*, founded in 1830, is very good value for money.

Celler de Capçanes
This *bodega* was established in 1933 on 240ha (590 acres) of vineyards. It has adapted to modern tastes with its Val del Calás Crianza and even produces really good white and red kosher wines.

Cellers Scala-Dei
The original winery dates back to the 16th century. The present company produces about 5,000 cases annually from 110ha (272 acres) of its own vineyards. The best wine is Cartoixa, a magnificent, heavy red wine.

TERRA ALTA
De Muller
This *bodega* (1851), also working in the Tarragona and Priorato DOs, produces a traditional communion wine, De Muller vino de Misa.

CENTRAL AND SOUTHERN SPAIN

South of the city of Madrid and north of sherry-producing country is the land of everyday wine, although, here too, the production of quality wines is the ultimate dream. In this country, where the climate is hot and the vines hardy, the technology is leading-edge and the customer is king.

This large area can be divided up into Levante in the east; Castilla-La Mancha around and to the south of Madrid; Andalucia in the south; and, finally, Spain's islands.

Levante

This region extends along the east coast of Spain and includes the *autonomías* of Murcia and Valencia, Spain's second largest wine growing area in terms of surface area.

Valencia is the name of a DO as well as the *autonomía* that includes two other DOs — Alicante and Utiel-Requeña. Wine producers in Valencia hope to have a generic DO for the whole *autonomía* with sub-divisions. To an extent that is what they already have; it is currently possible to blend wines from any of the three DOs and call them "Valencia".

The vineyards range from almost sea level in Valencia itself to 300–400m (990–1,320ft) in Alicante, and above 800m (2,640ft) in Utiel-Requena, so both the grapes and wines are varied. The climate ranges from Mediterranean on the coast to continental in the high lands, and soils range similarly from alluvial to limestone. The main red grapes are Monastrell, Garnacha, Bobal and Tempranillo; the main whites are Merseguera and Macabeo. Most of the widely available wines from this region take their source grapes from any or all of the three DO regions.

Bodegas in Valencia have long catered for export markets, from the cheapest everyday blends under the client's own label to some reasonably

Stone jars, or *tinajas*, are traditional in the south for fermenting and storing wine.

impressive *crianza* and *reserva* reds, as well as sweet wines.

A new DO, Bullas, has been added to Jumilla and Yecla, Murcia's two DOs situated in semi-arid country inland from Alicante, which have more or less always evolved at the same pace as Valencia. Phylloxera finally arrived in Jumilla in the 1980s, forcing growers to replant but allowing them to make an informed choice of vines.

Vineyards are planted up to 700m (2,300ft) on good soils overlying limestone bedrock. Altitude this far south does little to mitigate the power of the sun, and good husbandry is essential to ensure that the grapes retain some acidity by harvest time. Monastrell and Cencibel (Tempranillo) are favoured for red wines and Merseguera and Airén for whites. There is a trend towards *joven* styles, with some work on *crianzas* using American oak casks.

Castilla-La Mancha

The *autonomía* of Castilla-La Mancha is a vast area covering the southern half of the Meseta. Although it produces half of Spain's wine — from vineyards covering almost 8m ha (nearly 20m acres) — it has only five DOs: Almansa, La Mancha, Méntrida, Mondéjar and Valdepeñas.

Almansa is the easternmost zone and owes more to Levante than the other La Mancha DOs. The vineyards are planted on the flatter "lowlands", on reasonably good soils, and the climate is continental, bordering on the semi-arid. Almansa is red-wine country (at least one *bodega* makes wine up to *reserva* level), and the main grapes are Monastrell, Cencibel (Tempranillo) and Garnacha. Some Merseguera (white) is blended with red grapes to make *rosado*.

DO La Mancha, granted in 1966, is the largest in Spain. It had a name for low-quality bulk wine, but new investment is changing this. The region is naturally best for red-grape production, but growers have perversely planted mostly white-grape vines. The new investors were determined to make use of the ubiquitous Airén grape, and by the mid-1980s, with careful, new-style vinification, Airén was producing large quantities of cheap and cheerful wines.

The vineyards are high (500–650m/1,650–2,150ft) and dry, and the climate is baking hot in summer and freezing cold in winter. However, the soil is reasonably good, and the altitude and extremes of temperature mean that the vines have no mould or insects. The wines are nearly all *jovenes* in all three colours, and represent some of the best-value everyday wines in Spain.

Méntrida is another mass-production zone, east of Madrid. However, the last few years have seen changes in DO regulations with regard to alcoholic strength, and there may yet be some surprises from here. The grapes — mainly Garnacha and Cencibel — have great potential.

Just outside DO Méntrida, in the province of Toledo, is a good example of what could be achieved in this area. Carlos Falcó (the Marqués de Griñón) is himself a graduate in winemaking of the University of California (Davis), but he also imported Bordelais know-how to his vineyard at Malpica de Tajo. He planted Cabernet Sauvignon and Merlot, and irrigates on the Californian drip-feed system (strictly forbidden in Spain except for "experimental" vineyards). Ten years on, his wine, although classified simply as Vino de Mesa de Toledo (like a Tuscan *vino da tavola)*, is one of the best in Spain.

The five *bodegas* in the new DO Mondéjar produce 7,000hl of red wine, which is sold young, from some 750ha (1,850 acres) of vineyards spread over 20 villages.

Valdepeñas is the one area of Castilla-La Mancha that has traditionally, and consistently, produced

good-quality wines. Geographically, it is almost an enclave within La Mancha: on south-facing slopes vineyards are well placed, at an altitude of 700m (2,300ft), and are protected from the prevailing winds by mountain ranges. The soils are limestone-based and the climate verges on the semi-arid, but there is a deep, chalky

THE ISLANDS

Balearic Islands Spain's first offshore DO — Binissalem in Majorca — was granted in 1991. It lies north-east of Palma in the centre of the largest of the Balearic Islands at an altitude of 250–300m (825–990ft). The principal grape is the local Manto Negro (red). The DO permits white, *rosado* and red wines, but the whites (mainly the local Moll with some Parellada) and *rosados* are made only as *jóvenes*, and in much smaller quantities. The Plá i Levant, a *vino de la tierra* (country wine), made from 1,000ha (2,470 acres) of vineyards in the valleys of central and eastern parts of the island, is shortly to receive DO status.

Canary Islands Seven DOs in the space of a few years and two "winegrowing regions", despite the fact the first DO, Tacoronte-Acentejo in Tenerife, was not awarded until 1992. The other DOs are Abona, El Hierro, La Palma, Lanzarote, Valle de Güímar, Valle de la Orotava and Ycoden-Daute-Isora. 185,000hl of wine were produced in 1997 from vineyards covering almost 800,000ha (1,980,000 acres) with a subtropical climate. There are two local grape varieties, Listán Negro and Negramoll, not forgetting Malvasía.

PRODUCERS
Franja Roja, Binissalem (Majorca)
The *bodega* of José Ferrer, the island's most important producer. Established in 1931, it is the most forward-looking of all Mallorquín wineries, farming 78ha (190 acres). Main brand: José L Ferrer (w, p, r).
Carballo SL (DO La Palma) produces the very unusual Carballo Malvasía Blanco 1997 and the red Negramoll 1988 as well as the Mozaga Malvasía Dulce 1998, which is made in DO Lanzarote.
Bodegas Monje (DO Tacoronte-Acentejo) Producer of an excellent red wine called Monje de Autor.

subsoil that retains water. These favourable factors have kept the region at the forefront of production.

The grapes are the same as in La Mancha but with more of an emphasis on Cencibel and red wines. White wines are in the *joven* style, but better reds (from 100% Cencibel) are made up to *gran reserva* level.

The vineyards of the DO Vinos de Madrid have traditionally produced good, everyday wines for the capital. Most wines today are in the *joven* style, but some producers believe Madrid's future lies with *crianza* reds made from Tempranillo.

Andalucia
Southern Spain comprises one huge *autonomía* — Andalucia. This is where the Spanish wine industry began, in Jerez, and wine production throughout the region has been traditionally in the sherry mould. DOs Jerez and Málaga are discussed elsewhere (*see* p424 and p430), but Andalucia has two other DOs: Condado de Huelva, near the Portuguese border; and Montilla-Moriles in the province of Córdoba.

When the sherry market started to contract, Condado de Huelva began to diversify, producing new-style, light *joven afrutado* (cool-fermented) wines from the Zalema grape. The regions has however continued to produce its old-style fortified wines, known as Condado Pálido and Condado Viejo, which are on par with Olorosos.

Montilla-Moriles has managed to make a name for itself in its own right, as well as going down the *joven afrutado* route. Today Montilla makes *jóvenes*, *vinos crianzas* (unfortified) and *vinos generosos* (fortified and aged in a *solera*, like sherry). The main grape is the white Pedro Ximénez. The Montilla vineyards are at altitudes of 700m (2,310ft) down to 300m (990ft), where the Meseta descends to the south coast: the climate is semi-arid/continental. The best soils are chalky *albarizas*, as in Jerez, and these better vineyards are known collectively as the Superior region. □

PRODUCERS

In these areas, traditionally the producers of bulk wines with occasional little treasures such as Fondillón wines, both cooperatives and privately owned bodegas are investing in technology that will enable them to diversify production. Wine colours are shown as (w) white, (p) pink, (r) red.

LEVANTE
ALICANTE
Bodegas
Gutiérrez de la Vega
Founded in 1973, this *bodega* (10ha/25 acres; 5,000 cases per annum) revolutionized the market for new Moscatels with its Casta Diva, Cosecha Dorada and Cosecha Miel.

Salvador Poveda
Since 1918 a leading company in the region. Amazing Fondillón (a 100% Monastrell sweet wine), a Moscatel and even a red wine, again 100% Monastrell, called Viña Vermeta.

Primitivo Quiles, NCR
The Fondillón produced here is one of the most famous Mediterranean dessert wines: the austere King Philip II gave a gift of a bottle to the Emperor of Japan and Dumas' musketeers held it in great esteem. The Fondillón Rancio Primitivo Quiles is one of the best.

UTIEL-REQUEÑA ET VALENCIA
Vicente Gandía Plá
This Valencia *bodega* (1885) sells its wines to 60 countries. Wines include the popular Castillo de Liria (r, p) and a good red wine, Hoya de Cadenas (Tempranillo-Garnacha).

JUMILLA
Agapito Rico
This 100-ha (250-acre) *bodega*, founded in 1989, produced the Carchelo 1997 (an un-oaked wine from 80% Monastrell and 20% Merlot), a Spanish wine everyone is talking about.

BSI San Isidro
Created in 1935 with 20,000ha (49,500 acres) of vineyards, BSI is still on track today — thanks to its Sabatacha (w), made exclusively from Airén grapes, its Gémina 1998 (r) and its dessert wine, Lacrima Viña Cristina.

Encarnación Olivares Guardiola
Although not producing wines under the DO label, sales are high and the company is held in high regard. Olivares Dulce (a sweet wine made exclusively from Monastrell) has an unusual kick with nuances of charcoal and candied fruit.

YECLA
Castaño
This company (1950) exports 60% of the wines it produces. Its white Macabeo Castaño and its Castaño (90% Monastrell), Hércula and Dominio Espinal (r) are fine examples of the DO's production.

CASTILLA-LA MANCHA
ALMANSA
Bodegas Piqueras
This *bodega*, an institution since 1915, produces its very modestly-priced Castillo de Almansa in all three colours (Airén; Monastrell-Cencibel).

LA MANCHA
Ayuso SL
This company was set up in 1947 but a recent change of ownership may call for a little prudence. It made a name for itself with its Estola (100% Cencibel) which is sometimes too oaky.

Centro Españolas SA
This company has been producing an Allozo Crianza and a Reserva 100% Tempranillo, both entirely convincing wines, since its creation in 1991.

Cooperativa Jesús del Perdón
The Yuntero brand from this 3,500-ha (8,850-acre) cooperative (1954) is well established; the *crianza* version is a successful blend of Cencibel (75%) and Cabernet Sauvignon.

Vinícola de Castilla SA
This huge operation produces the subtly different Balada Cencibel Ecológico, a biodynamic red.

VALDEPEÑAS
Miguel Calatayud SA
The Vegaval Plata Cencibel, produced by this 50-ha (125-acre) *bodega* (1960) competes against a Cabernet Sauvignon.

Cosecheros Abastecedores
This *bodega* (1875) produces classic wines; outstanding 100% Cencibel Pata Negra and Señorío de los Llanos.

Casa de la Viña
This 200-ha (500-acre) estate is part of Bodegas y Bebidas. The Cencibel grape finds expression in their value for money Casa de la Viña crianza.

Félix Solís
This estate, established in 1952, is the largest producer of 75cl bottles on the Spanish market. In the everyday wine, Los Molinos, and the more elaborate Viña Albalí, the Cencibel grape is at its best.

Videva SA
This company was set up by six winemakers in 1967. Their new wine, Pago Lucones, aged for 18 months in oak casks, is made from Cencibel — vines more than 30 years old from a *pago* (the Spanish equivalent of a Burgundy *clos* — and 10% Cabernet Sauvignon.

Viñedos y Bodegas Visan SL
A bottle of the excellent Castillo de Mudela Reserva 1987 (100% Cencibel) still cost less than £10 in February 2000.

ANDALUCIA
CONDADO DE HUELVA
Vinícola del Condado Soc. Cooperativa
Set up in 1956, this cooperative (2,500ha/6,200 acres; 2,200 oak casks) produces its Privilegio del Condado using the DO's main grape variety, Zalema (w), and the splendid Mioro Pálido, a blend of Palomino, Listán and Garrido Fino.

MONTILLA-MORILES
Alvear
The oldest estate in the DO (1729) is still being run by a member of the Alvear family. Excellent Fino C.B. and Pedro Ximénez 1927, absolutely amazing Pedro Ximénez 1830.

Gracia Hermanos SA
The María del Valle (100% Pedro Ximénez) sets the tone of this 1962 *bodega*.

Navisa
(Ind. Vinícola Española SA)
Since 1950 this 200-ha (500-acre) estate has been producing Finos (Cobos, Pompeyo) and the delicious sweet Tres Pasas.

Pérez Barquero
In existence for 100 years, 125ha (310 acres) and a brand, Gran Barquero, which ranks among the best in its class.

Bodegas Toro Albalá SA
If you are looking for character, there is no need to look any further: since 1922 this *bodega*, built on a former electricity power station, has being making a name for itself with its Eléctrico Fino del Lagar and the unusual Don PX (short for Pedro Ximénez), a natural sweet wine "unfiltered and free from additives". Don't miss its Marqués de Poley, made from Pedro Ximénez from the 1945 vintage.

SHERRY

Sandeman's vineyards, planted on *albariza*, or chalk, the ideal soil for sherry.

The sherry vineyards are to be found in the centre of a triangle formed by three towns to the north of Cádiz: Jerez de la Frontera at the apex inland, and Sanlúcar de Barrameda and Puerto de Santa María on the estuary of the Guadalquivir River and Cádiz Bay respectively.

The climate is generally warm, and can be hot and very dry in the summer, the heat tempered by the proximity of the ocean. Two prevailing winds — the dry Levante from the east, the wet Ponente from the Atlantic — blow alternately. The soil of the main vineyards, called *albariza*, is of chalk, and it is the combination of this soil — ideal for making white wines — and the hot, somewhat humid climate that produces the conditions ideal for growing the grapes.

The sherry region is fast becoming one of a single grape variety. The white Palomino grape — Palomino Fino as it is technically called — occupies 90% of the vineyard area, leaving little (and decreasing) room for the other permitted varieties, also white: Pedro Ximénez (which makes a sweet wine, still used occasionally for turning dry sherry sweet) and Moscatel Fino (rarely found today).

Making the wine

Harvesting in the sherry region is generally in the first half of September. The grapes are taken in small, plastic crates to pressing stations. Traditionally, they were trodden by workers wearing hob-nailed boots; today continuous horizontal or modern hydraulic presses are used. The juice is then fermented fully into dry white wine, with an alcohol level of at least 13.5% Vol. It is at this point that sherry changes from an ordinary white table wine into something unique and almost magical. Although sherry comes in different styles (*see* box, p427), the two quintessential styles are fino and amontillado.

Once fermented, the wine will be put into wooden casks, called locally butts, which hold 500 litres but are not filled to capacity. As the wine ages in the large, cool storage buildings of the *bodega* (winery), a yeast covering called *flor*, carried on the moist Ponente wind, grows naturally on the wine. This preserves it from oxidation from the air space in the cask, as well as lending a yeasty character to the mature, dry wine. Two things are curious about *flor*: first, that it occurs naturally in only one other wine area in the world (in the Jura in France) and secondly that it affects no two butts, even neighbouring ones, equally. One butt may have a splendid frothy layer of *flor*, the next one hardly any at all.

It is for this reason that sherry is classified into styles at an early stage of its development. Those butts with *flor* are classified as *palmas* and are put aside for ageing as fino (with the

THE SOLERA SYSTEM

The essence of sherry is blending, across years as well as between casks.

The *solera* system, used for all styles of sherry, operates by a series of blendings: a proportion of the youngest wine in the *bodega* is blended into a butt of wine from the preceding year, where the younger wine begins to take on the character of the older.

To make room for this process, a third of the butt of second-year wine is transferred to the third-year wine, while a third of the third-year butt is moved into the fourth-year wine. Each of these stages is called a *criadera* (the Spanish word for nursery).

After an average of five such movements a third of the butt of oldest wine (called the *solera*, because traditionally this was at the base of a tier of butts resting on the floor, or *suelo*) is drawn off for bottling. Wine can be drawn off at an earlier stage for different qualities of sherry, but it must by law go through at least three stages.

Sherry is therefore a blended wine in many senses. The final bottle will contain wines from a number of different *soleras* which are blended in a further series of butts before bottling.

possibility of further ageing into amontillado after the *flor* has done its work): they are lightly fortified with brandy up to 15.5% Vol. Those without *flor* are classified as *rayas* and are destined for oloroso: these are then immediately fortified up to 18% Vol alcohol (*flor* only survives up to 17.5% Vol) and are put aside for separate ageing.

History of sherry

Vines are thought to have been grown in the Jerez region for 3,000 years. It is claimed that Jerez is of Phoenician origin, founded as Xera in 1100BC. However, the creation of sherry as it is known today needed the arrival of the Arabs in the 7th century and their invention of distillation. By the late Middle Ages the trick of adding brandy to the wine to protect it on sea-voyages to England had been discovered. The English were early buyers of Jerez wines — and "sherris sack", the wine approved by the Shakespearian character Falstaff, became the vogue in Elizabethan taverns. In the following centuries, despite the outbreaks of war with Spain, sherry remained a staple in England, and many British shippers set up in the Jerez region to work alongside the Spanish and French .

The 19th century was a heyday for sherry in Britain. Demand outstripped supply, however; corners were cut, and the quality of sherry suffered. The shippers then grouped together to control quality, and after World War I sherry enjoyed another boom spurred by the popularity in the UK of the "sherry party" (a promotional idea credited to Williams & Humbert). After World War II, sales continued to grow, with the development of the important Dutch market, until the 1980s, when a series of mergers creating the huge Rumasa group led to a serious crisis of oversupply in sherry, and a reputation for poor quality. The response to this and to Rumasa's collapse was the setting up of a major plan for improving the image of a product that seemed at

odds with the world's desire to drink light white wines as apéritifs.

This has meant that today sherry — the official *denominación de origen* of Jerez-Xérès-Sherry y Manzanilla-Sanlúcar de Barrameda — is the most tightly controlled wine in Spain. Plantings, yields and the price of grapes and the sale price of the matured wine are all controlled by the Consejo Regulador, the industry's governing body. Wine has to mature for a minimum of three years, while a *bodega* can sell only 29% of its stock each year, to encourage longer maturing. In addition, the Consejo Regulador controls those firms which are allowed to export: other sherry producers (called *almacenistas*) must sell to an exporter.

In 2000, there were 2,440 vinegrowers cultivating 10,350ha (25,575 acres) of vineyards and working with 57 *bodegas* to produce over 100,000 tons. With sherry exports reaching

67 million litres, there is no doubt that the DO has managed to put right once and for all the errors committed in the 1990s. In Spain, however, sherry is still not given the recognition it deserves, as scarcely 15% of production is sold on the home market.

The best news of the 20th Century had however come four years earlier: on 1st January 1996, after a 10-year struggle, Sherry earned exclusive rights to its name, but not without a price — 6,900ha (17,000 acres) of vineyards had to be ripped up to contain production. British and Irish imitations no longer had the right to use the name. According to those who know the damage that can be caused by the misuse of words, we need to go a step further: if we use Champagne and Cognac when talking about the wine and brandy produced in these regions, why not insist on Jerez, the name of the birthplace, instead of sherry?   □

Barbadillo's *bodega* in Sanlúcar de Barrameda.

PRODUCERS

Sherry companies are based in the towns of Jerez de la Frontera — the boundary between Christians and Muslims —, Sanlúcar de Barrameda and Puerto de Santa María. All own vast wineries and bottling plants as well as large above-ground maturing cellars (bodegas) where thousands of casks are piled up to five high to be used for the blending process, la solera. Since 1999, the Sacristías or Reliquias, wines which, reserved for the families, had been left dozing in casks marked 'no', have been arriving on the market and pushing prices up.

Manuel de Argüeso

Founded in 1822 by Don Leon de Argüeso, this Sanlúcar bodega is famous for its almacenistas, the best cuvées of the best vintages, which are never blended.

Its most famous sherry — beside Pedro Ximénez El Candado — is Manzanilla Señorita, which is aged in Sanlúcar, while the Fine Amontillado and Cream of Cream sherries are both from Jerez wines. Its fino, Colombo, and dry amontillado, Coliseo, are both well-known in the Jerez region, as are its two brandies, Tres Unios and Genesis.

Herederos de Argüeso SA

This company's manzanilla, Las Medallas de Argüeso, and especially its San León, are every bit as good at the Oloroso Argüeso.

Antonio Barbadillo

This bodega, founded in 1821, is still run by the Barbadillo family. It owns 500ha (1,235 acres) of vineyards, cellars to house 65,000 bottles and half the manzanilla oak casks in the Jerez DO.

The old bodega in the town centre has modern premises on the outskirts. Its vines, jointly owned with Harveys (see p428), are in Jerez Superior. Eva, Solear, Muy Fina, La Pastora and Mil Pesetas are good manzanillas and its Amantillado Príncipe is on an equal par. Barbadillo was one of the first companies to produce a non-fortified dry white wine, Castillo San Diego, made exclusively from the Palomino grape.

In 2000, Barbadillo brought out its Reliquias, a palo cortado produced in four versions, each of scarcely 600 bottles. Each bottle was sold for 150 euros.

Hijos de Rainera Pérez Marín

This bodega, with 300ha (740 acres) of vines and 16,000 botas (the characteristic oak casks), was founded in 1865. It has become very popular thanks to its Manzanilla La Guita, especially since young people in Spain, and in Madrid in particular, discovered a taste for this wine.

Sánchez Romate

Set up by Juan Sánchez de la Torre in Jerez in 1781, this family bodega has 80ha (200 acres) of vines and 5,600 casks. Around two thirds of the annual production of over 3 million litres is exported. In the 30,000 m² of town centre cellars, its wines – Fino Marismeño and Macharnudo, Amontillado N.P.U. and La Sacristía de Romate, Dulce Cardenal Cisneros and La Sacristía de Romate PX... — are ageing alongside the top-of-the-range brandies Cardenal Mendoza and Cardenal Cisneros.

Hijos de Agustín Blázquez

One of the oldest sherry firms, founded in 1795. This is now part of the Domecq group (qv), but sherries and brandies are still produced under the name. Bodegas in Jerez and Puerto de Santa María produce a range of which the most familiar are the Carta Blanca fino and Carta Oro old amontillado.

Bobadilla

Abroad, this bodega is probably better known for its brandy — Bobadilla 103 is one of Spain's most ubiquitous brandies — than for its sherry. However, in Spain, both the brandy and the sherries are familiar sights in many bars. The style of all the Bobadilla sherries is comparatively dry (no doubt to suit the Spanish palate), and its best wine is undoubtedly the Victoria fino.

Luis Caballero

A rapidly-expanding Puerto de Santa María bodega, under the control of Luis Caballero Florido. Apart from its own brands, and those of John William Burdon, Caballero now controls Emilio Lustau (qv), whose name it uses as its main export label. The Caballero bodegas are housed in expansive and picturesque premises in the centre of Puerto de Santa María; Luis Caballero also owns the castle there, an old Moorish fortress

Croft

On the ring road of Jerez, the imposing installation of Rancho Croft belies its modernity with classic bodega architecture. Behind the façade all is high-tech, as befits one of the more recent arrivals in Jerez. Not that Croft sherry is new (the firm was started in 1678), but Croft's presence as a producer rather than purchaser of sherry only dates from 1970.

In the 1960s Croft revolutionized the sherry market by its creation of Croft Original Pale Cream, a pale-hued sherry that looked dry, but tasted sweet through the addition of dulce apagado (sweet wine). The firm controls about 18% of the sherry trade, mainly through sales to the UK of Croft Original.

Delgado Zuleta

A medium-sized, family-owned Sanlúcar bodega with a long history, going back to the year 1744. It started life with a different name — that of the founder, Don Francisco Gil de Ledesma — adopting its present name when José Delgado Zuleta made the change at the end of the last century. The top brand, Manzanilla La Goya, is named after a famous flamenco dancer, and with its old-fashioned black, white and gold label is a familiar sight in Spain. The amontillado is made from old wines — very good Quo Vadis? —, and the cream, Puerto Lucero, is often served as a dessert wine in Sanlúcar restaurants.

Pedro Domecq

Certainly one of the best-known names in sherry,

famous equally for its flagship La Ina fino sherry and for Fundador and Carlos I brandies. The firm dominates the sherry trade. Curiously, it was started by an Irishman, Patrick Murphy, in 1730, and only in the 19th century did the name change with the arrival of Pedro de Domecq, a Frenchman, to take charge of the firm. Today, it owns spectacular *bodegas* in Jerez, a large modern plant for bottling and a spectacular palace in the centre of Jerez, which is used for entertaining. The firm is now part of the Allied Lyons group.

While Domecq has made a name for itself with La Ina fino sherry, its Rio Viejo and Sibarita dry olorosos, its Cortado Capuchino palo and its dulce deserve to be known as well.

Duff Gordon

Now part of the Osborne group (*qv*), this is certainly a famous name in sherry, founded in 1768 by Sir James Duff, British consul in Cádiz, and run by Duffs and Gordons until being sold to Thomas Osborne in 1872.

Garvey

The fino San Patricio is the most famous wine from this fine *bodega* in the centre of Jerez, and its naming after Ireland's patron saint indicates the strong Irish connection in this firm, founded by William Garvey in 1780. Garvey is a large landowner in Jerez Superior, with 600ha (1,482 acres). San Patricio is the best-known brand from this firm, which also produces the Cortado Jauna palo and the Gran Orden Pedro Ximénez.

Miguel M Gomez

A Puerto de Santa María *bodega* which was founded in Cádiz in 1816 and only reached Puerto in 1969. The *bodegas,* although therefore

THE STYLES OF SHERRY

Sherry is a fortified white wine, naturally dry, which is produced commercially in a variety of styles ranging from very dry to very sweet. In its dry version it is more of a white table wine than a fortified one. It is a wine to drink as an apéritif, or with food; at the beginning of a meal, or the end: sherry is the most versatile of the fortified wines.
Sherry divides into two broad categories, fino and oloroso, which form the starting-points for the various styles. Fino-category sherries are affected by *flor*, olorosos are not.

FINO CATEGORY
Manzanilla

Manzanilla is a style of very dry fino from *bodegas* in the seaside town of Sanlúcar de Barrameda. The driest and lightest of all sherries, it is supposed to gain a salty tang from the sea. Before shipping it is fortified up to 15.5% Vol.

In Spain, manzanilla is highly popular, particularly among young people.

Manzanilla pasada

Manzanilla pasada is an old manzanilla fino that has lost its *flor* and begun to age. In Jerez this is called fino amontillado; in Sanlúcar, pasada.

Fino

Fino belongs into the driest category of sherry, made in Jerez and Puerto de Santa María. Jerez fino is fuller, Puerto fino is softer and lighter. Fino is matured under a layer of *flor* yeast, which preserves its freshness and avoids oxidation. The wines are 100% Palomino, and before

shipping will be fortified up to between 15.5% Vol and 17% Vol. In Jerez itself, fino is drunk unfortified.

Fino amontillado

Fino amontillado is a fino that has lost its *flor* yeast, but that has not yet arrived at the amontillado stage.

Amontillado

Amontillado is a wine that has gone beyond the fino amontillado stage and has developed an amber, almost golden colour, and a depth and nutty flavour. Since this cannot happen until the wine has been in the *solera* system for at least eight years, cheaper amontillados are produced by killing the yeast *flor* in order to speed up development. Amontillado should be a dry wine.

Medium

Medium is a sweetened amontillado, designed for the northern European market. The sweetening was traditionally done with Pedro Ximénez, but extra-sweet Palomino wine is now normally used.

Palo cortado

Palo Cortado is a wine that started life as a fino, was left to develop into an amontillado, but on the way became sidetracked onto an oloroso route. It will be classified as *dos, tres* or *cuatro cortados* according to age. A dry wine that is rare and therefore expensive.

OLOROSO CATEGORY
Oloroso

Oloroso is the style of sherry that never developed *flor*, and was fortified up to 18% Vol

at an early stage in its ageing. With maturation, the alcohol will increase: up to 24% Vol. Like true amontillado, true oloroso is always dry, rich and very concentrated.

Cream

Cream is a dark, sweetened oloroso, designed for the same export markets as medium sherry. Colour comes from sweetening wines, the sweetness comes from the use of grape must.

Pale cream

Although based on fino, palo cream is blended with light oloroso and sweetened with *dulce apagado* (sweet wine made by arresting fermentation with brandy) to give an oloroso taste but a fino appearance.

Brown sherry

Dark and rich, brown sherry is made from a blend of olorosos and *rayas* (lesser-quality olorosos).

OTHER TERMS
East India (or Amoroso)

A term used to describe sherry whose maturing had been speeded up during travel from Spain to India. The style is still made, but not via a sea voyage.

Almacenista

Sherries matured by small wholesalers who cannot sell direct to the public or export. Many are blended, but some are bottled and sold as separate lots.

new, are modelled on the old style with cathedral roofs. The best wines are almost certainly the fino Alameda and the Mentidero, an oloroso. The firm is family-owned.

Gonzalez Byass

While the return of this company to completely Spanish ownership, with the purchase of the Byass family shares by the Gonzalez family, has ended a long link with Britain, this has enabled the firm to concentrate on improving its already formidable quality. From spectacular *bodegas* near the castle in Jerez, complete with the La Concha *bodega* designed in the shape of a shell by Eiffel, this company continues to produce its top-of-the-range fino, Tio Pepe, and La Concha amontillado, from *soleras* which date back to the last century. Its very old wines, Amontillado del Duque, the dry oloroso Apostoles, and Matusalem sweet oloroso, as well as the Noé (dulce) are justly regarded as some of the finest sherries made.

John Harvey

It may seem strange that the biggest sherry producer did not have any production facilities of its own in Jerez until 1970, when it purchased the small Mackenzie *bodega*. Until then it had been buying sherry from other firms. It has since bought a number of other *bodegas*, including Palomino y Vergara (*qv*) and de Terry (*qv*) as well as the now defunct firm of Marqués de Misa. This gives it *bodegas* in Puerto de Santa María as well as Jerez.

Harvey's major brand is a dulce, Bristol Cream, which is the world's biggest seller.

Emilio Hidalgo

A small, family-owned Jerez *bodega* which acts as *négociant,* buying wines from growers. Fino Pañesa, Oloroso Gobernador and Privilegio brandy are among its best-known products.

Vinicola Hidalgo

Manzanilla La Gitana is the most famous wine from this family-owned *bodega,* housed in old offices in the centre of Sanlúcar. All the wines, even the amontillados and olorosos, have a light, Sanlúcar character. The new Pagollano is a dry white wine.

Bodegas de los Infantes Orleans-Borbón

This regal-sounding firm was founded by descendants of the Duc de Montpensier, who was related to the Spanish royal family. The family's vineyard in Sanlúcar had been used to make wine for their own consumption, and the remainder had been sold to sherry companies.

In 1943, when sherry was first produced under the family label, it was made by Barbadillo (*qv*), who now own 50% of the company. Since this is a Sanlúcar firm, it is not surprising that the manzanilla Torre Breva is its best sherry. Most wine is exported to Austria and the Netherlands.

Emilio Lustau

This is the innovative firm that launched the idea of *almacenista* sherries onto the world market — registering them as a brand name —, and has followed this up by Landed Age sherries, which are bottled in the country of export and aged in bottle before being sold. Experts are praising the Pedro Ximénez, the San Emilio, the Moscatel Emilín, the oloroso Emperatriz Eugenia, the Lustau Almacenista 1/50 Vides and many others of Lustau's brands.

Osborne

See profile.

Herederos del Marqués del Real Tesoro

The Marquis of the Royal Treasure was a title created by King Charles III in 1760 for Joaquin Manuel de Villeña of the Spanish navy, who had used his own silver in place of cannon balls when ammunition ran out during a sea battle against pirates.

The *bodega* was founded by the marquis's grandson in 1879, and today it is run by his heirs. They make two ranges: a top range of Ideal Fino, Almirante Oloroso and old amontillados, and a more commercial range of sherries under the Real Tesoro label sold mainly in the Netherlands. A short while ago the company acquired a true status symbol, Fino Tio Mateo, one of the classics of the DO, and established its Manzanilla La Bailaora on the market.

Pedro Romero

Sanlúcar *bodega,* whose main brand name is Viña el Alamo, but which is best known for its Manzanilla Aurora. Their range of brandies includes the splendidly titled Indiscutible.

Sandeman-Coprimar SA

The familiar black silhouette figure of the Don, with his sombrero and *copita*, was created in the 1920s. Today, although the firm is part of the

OSBORNE

In the very heart of Puerto de Santa María stands the huge 30-ha (74-acre) Osborne complex: a warren of shaded courtyards, gardens, and 40 *bodegas* situated around the old house of the Duff Gordon family, acquired along with that brand name by Osborne in 1872. Today Osborne is still family-owned, but it is at the forefront of experimentation in the Jerez region. Size and modernity doesn't seem to have done any harm to the family's sherries. For many, these are the quintessential Puerto sherries, soft, elegant and light, without the tang of Sanlúcar's manzanillas or the weight of Jerez fino. Fino Quinta is the best-known brand on export markets, but the dry amontillado Coquinero, and Bailen, a dry oloroso, are of equal quality. The 10RF is a slightly sweetened, full oloroso.

giant Canadian Seagram group (and also one of the biggest producers of port), the Sandeman family still has a management interest.

The firm was started in 1790 in London by George Sandeman with initial capital of £300. Large investment in recent years has meant a considerable increase in quality of brands such as Don Fino, and the old amontillados and olorosos like Royal Ambrosante amontillado and Imperial Corregidor oloroso, which are based on long-established *soleras*.

José de Soto
Still family-owned, de Soto was founded at the end of the 18th century. It is probably best known in Spain for its Ponche Soto, a blend of herbs, brandy and sherry.

But the fino Don José María, the amontillado José de Soto and the dry oloroso Soto also have a following. A member of the family in the 19th century devised grafting systems in Jerez after phylloxera.

Bodegas Fernando A de Terry
The huge arcaded courtyard of the old de Terry *bodega* on the edge of Puerto de Santa María was once used as a show-ground for the Carthusian (Cartujanos) horses which drew the firm's collection of carriages. This was when the firm was still family-owned. But expansionist tendencies led to the building of a huge *bodega* on the main road to Jerez which bankrupted the company and forced its sale, first to Rumasa, then to the Harvey group (*qv*), and finally to the Allied Lyons group.

Although today the name de Terry is best known for brandies, its sherry production is still important, often appearing in bottles with retailers' own-brand labels.

Pouring manzanilla pasada from Barbadillo's 100-year-old *solera* in Sanlúcar.

Valdespino
Valdespino is neither the best-known nor the biggest sherry firm, but it is certainly the oldest — the family has been established in the Jerez region since 1264. For many sherry aficionados, the small, high-quality Valdespino range of sherries is the very best.

The firm, headed by Don Miguel Valdespino, is sherry tradition preserved. Much fermentation is still carried out in barrels (although a little stainless steel has been permitted in recent years). Wines are classified in the time-consuming way, barrel by barrel. Increased production to meet demand is eschewed since there might be a risk to quality.

The finest sherry the firm produces, the full but elegant fino Inocente, comes, uniquely for Jerez, from one ancestral vineyard just outside the city. Valdespino is also known for the dry, nutty amontillado Tio Diego, the sweet Oloroso — and for fine sherry vinegar.

Williams & Humbert
For long an independent firm, Williams & Humbert was quoted on the London Stock Exchange until a controlling shareholding was purchased by the Rumasa group in the 1970s. The firm is now owned by the Medina group). The buildings of the *bodega,* situated in beautiful gardens in the centre of Jerez, are some of the most expansive in the city. Along with its horses, which run on the local racecourse, and the former office of the British Consul (now run as a museum), this is a major tourist attraction.

The firm's top brand, Dry Sack, the bottle in the sack (an imitation of the way barrels of sherry were covered with sacking during transport) was certainly better known in the 1970s than it is now, but it is a very good commercial blend of amontillado, oloroso and Pedro Ximénez. The Dulce Pedro Ximénez Don Zoilo is a beautifully intense sherry.

Wisdom & Warter
Founded in 1854, Wisdom & Warter was a household name in the 19th century. Punch coined the phrase "Warter makes the wine and Wisdom sells it". It remained an independent company until it was acquired by Gonzalez Byass, from whose high standards of production it now benefits. The manzanilla La Guapa, the fino Los Búhos and the amontillado Very Rare Solera are all sound, if unexciting, wines.

MÁLAGA

Nowadays there are less than 10,000ha (25,000 acres) of vineyards left in the Málaga DO. A few years ago even, local viticulture seemed destined to disappear under the threat of property developments for the leisure industry and a high market demand for raisins. Furthermore, the very sweet wines were no longer popular with consumers and they did not regain their popularity until the mid-1990s. Under these circumstance, no producers seemed prepared to carry on the work of Scholtz — a legend at the time when Port, Madeira, Tokay and Malaga were considered perfect dessert wines.

Málaga's decline began towards the end of the 19th century with the arrival of phylloxera — the vineyard of Axarquía, in the hinterland, was the first to be devastated by the epidemic. Some winemakers, including the López brothers, set themselves up as merchants in Málaga. Demand recovered but Málaga's main market, central Europe, disappeared with the arrival of the Great War and then the requisitions during the Spanish Civil War (1936-1939) emptied the cellars. In 1937, one of the bosses of the López firm, Rafael de Burgos Carrillo, in order to help the emigrants, socialists like himself, managed to set up a network of representatives in America and create a large market for málaga and brandies. Nowadays this *bodega* is responsible for 90% of the wines sold under the Málaga label, which it still produces by traditional methods.

Grape varieties and soils
The main grape variety is the Pedro Ximénez (over 50%), known locally as Pedro Ximén, followed by Airén (Lairén), Moscatel and Doradilla. The soils range from a red chalky composition beside the sea to the crumbly slate of the steep slopes in the Axarquía region. The climate on the coast is Mediterranean (400mm rainfall per year) but inland it is continental, with severe frosts (over 550mm of rain).

Making the wine
Málaga is fortified with grape spirit, which is added after fermentation. The character of the wine comes from the addition of *arrope* (a reduction of boiled grape juice) — technology going back to Roman times — which gives it its dark colour, sweetness and depth. There are four other wine additives used in the region to fortify málaga: *Mistela* (fortified grape juice which has not been allowed to ferment), *Vino de color* (a highly concentrated *arrope*), *Vino maestro* (grape juice which has been fortified up to 7% Vol and then fermented up to 16% Vol) and *Vino tierno*, a very sweet wine made from grapes which have been dried in the sun before being fermented and fortified. These different additives are blended with the wine in accordance with the degree of sweetness and type of wine required. The future málaga is then matured in chestnut casks *(conos)* and undergoes a *solera* system similar to the one used for sherry. The final quality of the wine depends on the period of maturation and the best can be kept in the bottle for decades, even centuries.

A distinction can be drawn between málaga, made from the first must, and Pedro Ximénez and Moscatel, which are made using single grape varieties. Since 1995, the production of dry white wines (Málaga Blanco Seco) and natural sweet whites, i.e. where the alcoholic strength is not increased artificially, has been permitted in the region.

STYLES AND PRODUCERS

Until 1997, the styles were classified according to the maturation period, the level of sweetness and the grape variety: *dulce* (sweet), *lágrima* (originally the juice oozing from the grapes as they hung to dry, then the free-run juice from the grapes before the first pressing); *Málaga dulce color* (containing a significant amount of *vino de color*); *Málaga Moscatel* (made exclusively from Moscatel grapes), *Málaga Pedro Ximén* (100% Pedro Ximén); *pajarete* (medium dry), *seco* (dry); and *soleras* (wines showing the date the first solera began. These are considered to be the best málaga).

New regulations classify the wines according to age:
Málaga Un-aged or less than 6 months;
Málaga Criadera 6 months to 2 years;
Málaga Noble 2 to 3 years;
Málaga Añejo 3 to 5 years;
Málaga Trasañejo 5 years or more.

PRODUCERS
Gomara SL The 200 casks in the Gomara bodega produce a Fino, a Málaga Cream, a Moscatel and, for the connoisseurs, a Málaga Trasañejo.
Larios SA Although better known for its gin, Larios has 2,000 casks and produces an average of 500,000 litres of wine per annum. The company now belongs to the Pernod-Ricard group but the exquisite Oloroso Seco Benefique and Málaga Larios Dulce still have their ardent followers.
López Hermanos This exemplary company, founded in 1885, for a century took on the role of protector for the rest of the DO. Now a mere 250 ha (620 acres) are all that is left from its winegrowing past. In 1997, the world-famous label of its flagship wine, Málaga Vírgen, was changed to read 'sweet' in place of Pedro Ximén. Don Juan Pedro Ximénez, Don Salvador Moscatel and Seco Trasañejo Pedro Ximénez are all great names.
Tierras de Mollina From the 775 ha (1,900 acres) of vineyards belonging to this company (1977), we have Montespejo, a dry white, and Carpe Diem málagas – an Añejo and a Dulce Natural – made for export.

PORTUGAL
AND THE MEDITERRANEAN

—

FROM PORTUGAL THROUGH GREECE, CYPRUS AND TURKEY

TO THE LEBANON AND ISRAEL, AND ON ROUND

THE NORTH AFRICAN SHORE, THE WINE AND THE OLIVE

DOMINATE THE HILLY LANDSCAPES.

—

PORTUGAL

STRONG TRADITIONS, A WIDE RANGE OF GRAPE VARIETIES AND A
VARIED CLIMATE ALLOW PORTUGAL TO MAKE SOME STYLISH WINES,
AS WELL AS FORTIFIED PORT AND MADEIRA FOR WHICH IT IS FAMOUS.

Cellars at Azeitão on the Setúbal Peninsula. The wines of
southern Portugal are improving rapidly as winemakers from
outside the region bring not only their skills, but also the
money to keep cellar equipment up to date.

Portugal is a land of contrasts. This narrow country occupies a mere seventh of the Iberian Peninsula, and on the map it looks overwhelmed by the bulk of neighbouring Spain. But few countries of Portugal's size can lay claim to as many different styles of wine. Place a glass of dark, spicy port alongside a glass of light, slightly sparkling Vinho Verde. No two wines are less alike, yet they are produced in adjacent regions. Topography plays a vital part. Wines from the coast are shaped by the Atlantic, the moderating effect of which diminishes beyond the mountains. Annual rainfall, as high as 1,500mm (60 inches) on the coast, is less than 500mm (20 inches) inland. Vines cover Portugal from north to south. Only the highest mountains are too cold to support some form of viticulture. Between the River Minho, which marks the northern frontier with Spain, and the Algarve coast 560km (350 miles) to the south, there are nearly 400,000ha (988,000 acres) of vineyard producing an average of 94 million cases of wine. Two great rivers divide the land into three distinct winemaking areas. In the north the Douro bisects granite mountains that soar to nearly 2,000m (6,600ft), and from its valley come not only port, but also a range of table wines. Central Portugal, from the Douro to the Tagus (Tejo), has a hospitable climate and the large wine-producing region of the Ribatejo, as well as the well-known zones of Dão and Bairrada. South of the Tagus lie the vast hot plains of the Alentejo region, and the more touristically orientated Algarve. Many of the contrasts inherent in the landscape extend to Portugal's wine industry. Ultra-modern wineries are found alongside tiny cellars making wines for local consumption in the same way as they have for centuries. Since joining the EC in 1986, Portugal has had the incentive to change. With money to invest, the Portuguese are making a determined effort to improve their wines and capture new markets. However, certain traditions are unlikely to be swept away. In the past only a handful of vines have crossed Portugal's borders, and growers are reluctant to uproot their treasure-trove of indigenous vines and replace them with imported interlopers. Even the most forward-thinking winemakers tend to resist planting foreign varieties.

WINE ZONES OF PORTUGAL

Portugal's vineyards stretch the length of the country. The 40 DOC *(Denominação de Origem Controlada)* zones — shown in colour — are the superior zones. The most famous of these are Porto (1761), Douro (1982), Dão (1908), Madeira (1908), Moscatel de Setúbal (1907), Vinho Verde (1908-1929) and Bairrada (1979). *Indicação de Proveniencia Regulamentada* is the second *appellation* tier, followed by *Vinho Regional* which is equivalent to the French *vin de pays*.

Atlantic

Ocean

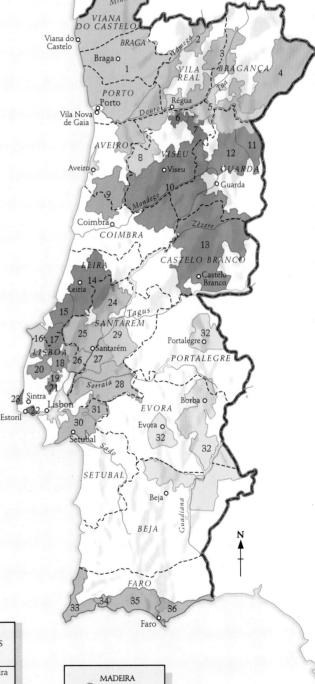

DOC zones

1	Vinho Verde	21	Bucelas
2	Chaves	22	Carcavelos
3	Valpaços	23	Colares
4	Planalto-Mirandês	24	Tomar
5	Porto e Douro	25	Santarém
6	Varosa	26	Cartaxo
7	Encostas da Nave	27	Almeirim
8	Lafões	28	Coruche
9	Bairrada	29	Chamusca
10	Dão	30	Setúbal
11	Castelo Rodrigo	31	Palmela
12	Pinhel	32	Alentejo
13	Cova da Beira	33	Lagos
14	Encostas de Aire	34	Portimão
15	Alcobaça	35	Lagoa
16	Lourinhã	36	Tavira
17	Òbidos	37	Madeira
18	Alenquer	38	Biscoitos
19	Arruda	39	Pico
20	Torres Vedras	40	Graciosa

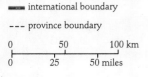

▬▬ international boundary

--- province boundary

0	50	100 km
0	25	50 miles

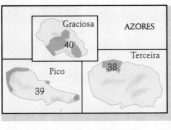

NORTHERN PORTUGAL

Wine has been exported from the Atlantic shores of Iberia since the 12th century when Portugal first became a nation. By the 1650s, foreign merchants were settling around the port of Viana do Castelo, but wines from this damp region proved disappointing, and early traders moved inland in search of more robust reds. They found them in the steeply-terraced vineyards of the Douro Valley upstream from Oporto, starting a huge trade in sweet, later fortified wine eventually christened "port" (*see* p440).

Vinho Verde

The largest demarcated wine region in Portugal covers the whole northwest. Rain-bearing winds support intensive cultivation, and the countryside between the Rivers Minho and Douro is some of the most densely populated in rural Iberia.

Around 80,000 grape-growers farm 25,000ha (61,750 acres). The vines grow over special pergolas, leaving room for other crops to grow underneath. Raising the vineyard canopy also reduces the risk of disease in hot weather.

Vinho Verde (meaning "green wine") is frequently misinterpreted. The name has no connection with the colour of the wine, which may be either red or white. Nor is it made from "green" grapes harvested before they are fully ripe (although wines are low in alcohol and high in natural acidity). It is so named because it is made to be drunk young and fresh, retaining a slight *pétillance* or sparkle.

Douro

The dry red wine from the mountains of the Douro valley was discovered towards the end of the 17th century by the English, who gradually turned it into the famous fortified wine known as port. However, even today, around half of the wine produced in Douro, which has been a DOC region since 1982, is sold as table wine.

For a long time the Douro table wine was treated as the poor relation to port and reserved for local consumption. Over the last ten years, however, an increasing number of fine wines have been produced in wineries throughout the whole region. Several large companies with ultra-modern equipment also buy grapes from the small producers.

The main grape varieties used to produce Douro red table wines are the same ones used to make port. The main varieties used to make white wines are Malvasia Fina, Viosinho and Gouveio. □

The valley of the Douro near the Spanish frontier, lined with terraced vineyards.

PRODUCERS

The northern vineyards divide between the DOC areas of Vinho Verde and the Douro. The best Vinhos Verdes are made and bottled by individual *quintas*. Port producers (*see also* pp442–445) use new techniques to make soft red Douro table wines from port grapes, and balanced, dry white wines from white grapes grown in the higher, cooler margins of the Douro.

Adega Cooperativa de Ponte da Lima

The cooperative wineries in the north of Portugal have not always had a good reputation for quality but the Ponte da Lima co-op produces very good red Vinho Verdes and an excellent white from the Loureiro grape.

Aveleda

This family concern in Penafiel, about 30km (19 miles) from Porto in the heart of Minho, has a rich history going back over more than three centuries. It has always concentrated on the production of quality wines and has long had a reputation in Portugal and abroad for its Vinho Verdes and Adega Velha brandy, considered by many to be the best spirit produced in Portugal. More recently Avelada has also gone over to the production of Douro wines and its Charamba brand has been a great success. Aveleda is the largest Vinho Verde producer, producing 2 million cases annually, of which 60% are exported to 39 countries.

Borges

Over the years, the premises belonging to this Vila Nova de Gaia company, founded in 1884 by the brothers António and Francisco Borges, have become the focal point of a large concern which has made a name for itself by producing a vast range of wines from various Portuguese DOCs (port, Douro, Vinho Verde, Bairrada, Dão, Rosé de Trás-os-Montes) as well as sparkling wines. Borges exports its wines to almost 50 countries spread over all five continents.

Solar das Bouças

This 25-ha (62-acre) property on the banks of the River Cavado belongs to the van Zeller family. The Loureiro grape produces a light, perfumed dry white Vinho Verde wine.

Palácio de Brejoeira

This remarkable estate is regarded as a "first growth" among Vinho Verde *quintas*. Maria Herminia Pães planted 17ha (42 acres) of vines around her rambling 18th-century palace near Monção, 4km (2.5 miles) south of the Spanish border. The wine is made entirely from (white) Alvarinho grapes, and is typically round with more body than most Vinho Verdes.

Quinta do Côtto

This *quinta*, owned by Miguel Champalimaud, produces a highly concentrated, spicy red wine under the Grande Escolha label. This very special *cuvée* is only produced in the best years. Both the wine and the owner have rapidly gained a solid reputation in the region.

Quinta de Covela

The Quinta de Covela has been established since the 16th century in the Douro valley, on the right bank of the river, on the border between the Vinho Verde and Douro DOCs. It is set in an area of exceptional beauty, overlooking the river and surrounded by 14ha (35 acres) of vineyards, orchards and bushland (16ha/40 acres). This company's respect for the environment is evident from the precision with which its buildings have been rebuilt.

Ferreira

Barca Velha, named after the old barges which ferried wine down-river, was launched in 1952 and is Portugal's greatest red wine. It is made from high-quality port grapes in a remote corner of the Douro close to the Spanish border. It is the brainchild of Ferreira's chief winemaker, Fernando Nicolau de Almeida, who was inspired by a visit to Bordeaux. Like vintage port, it is declared only in exceptional years, the remainder being declassified as Reserva Especial.

Luís Pato

Here we have a man who is passionate about Bairrada. His 60ha (150 acres) of vineyards produces red, white and sparkling wines which are full of character. Since the 1995 vintage, Luís Pato has been producing a red wine from the Baga grape using ungrafted vine stocks planted on the sandy soil of the Quinta do Ribeirinho. Yields exceed 9hl per ha. In the same year he also started to produce wine from the same species of vine on a chalky-clay soil. As a result, the name of the vines the wines originate from can be shown on their labels: Vinha Pan and Vinho Barrosa.

Real Companhia Vinícola do Norte do Portugal

The table wine arm of the port house Royal Oporto and one of the largest wine-producers in Portugal. Its red and white wines are sold under the Evel label.

Sogrape

This, Portugal's largest wine company, goes back to 1942. The Mateus brand, originally the mainstay of the company's business, is currently sold in 130 countries. Thanks to an innovative marketing policy and high tech production facilities and vinification methods, Sogrape now markets an extensive range of well-balanced, often award-winning, wines from Portugal's main DOC regions. In 1987, Sogrape took over the company A.A. Ferreira & Offley.

Conde de Santar

One of the few single estate Dão wines. Its red and white wines have improved since the 1970s.

Domingos Alves Sousa Quinta da Gaivosa

Over the last ten years, Domingos Alves de Sousa has been one of the great discoveries in Douro wines, not only from a quality point of view but due to the varied range he offers. With five *quintas* in Douro, including Quinta da Gaivosa, Quinta do Vale da Raposa and Quinta da Estação, he owns almost 100ha (250 acres) of vineyards. Over and above the port supplied to exporters, the company produces 12,500 cases of Douro DOC wines. The brands bear the name of the *quinta* from which they originate and the Quinta das Caldas was added to the list in 1996.

Over the last few years, Domingos Alves de Sousa wines have been amongst the highest acclaimed by Portuguese and foreign specialist press alike.

CENTRAL PORTUGAL

The land between the rivers Douro and Tagus is some of the most productive in Portugal. A wide variety of crops flourish in the warm, maritime climate: maize and beans in the deep soils on the coast, tomatoes and citrus fruit along the fertile river valleys inland. Vines grow in profusion, producing all manner of wines.

The DOC regions of Dão and Bairrada (*see* below) are well-known for their firm-flavoured red wines. Further south, the Oeste (meaning west) coastal area produces more wine than anywhere else in Portugal but, except for one or two *quintas*, most is fairly ordinary wine destined to be sold in bulk or distilled. The country's second-largest wine-producing area, the Ribatejo, straddling the River Tagus, is the source of some of Portugal's best *garrafeiras*: mature red wines bottled without any denomination of origin but selected from the cream of the crop.

Lisbon has all but swallowed three historic DOC regions near the Tagus estuary. Carcavelos is left with one vineyard (Quinta dos Pesos) producing fortified sweet amber wine. Colares, once renowned for deep red wines from its phylloxera-free Ramisco vines growing in coastal sand, is close to extinction. Only Bucelas, making dry white wines from the acidic Arinto and Esgana Cão ("dog strangler") grapes, is showing sure signs of a revival in fortune.

Dão

One of Portugal's best-known wines is named after the small River Dão which cuts through mountains south of the Douro. The granite-based soil is ideal for the production of good wine, yet since the 1950s much opportunity has been squandered. In common with much of north and central Portugal, the land is split into smallholdings, most of which grow

The walled town of Obidos, north of Lisbon, capital of the Obidos wine zone.

grapes for one of ten local cooperatives. Merchant bottlers often have difficulty in selecting Dão wines and have to make do with some fairly rudimentary winemaking, but a handful of independent companies are now trying to undo the cooperative stranglehold.

Over two-thirds of Dão wines are red, made from anything up to nine officially authorized grapes. A similar number of local varieties is permitted for the whites. Dão reds should be firm, but frequently taste hard and austere from prolonged maceration on the stalks and skins. Another problem is that few wines are bottled sufficiently early and the ripe, fruity flavours of a young red or white Dão often fade with protracted age. However, the first results from the modern wineries look promising.

Bairrada

Overlooked as a wine region until it was awarded demarcated status in 1979, Bairrada now rivals Dão as one of Portugal's best-known wines. The region covers an area of fertile clay soils between the mountains and the Atlantic south of Oporto. Over 80% of Bairrada's wines are big, ripe, fruity reds made from the tannic Baga grape. Traditional red Bairradas need time in bottle to soften, but some of the larger producers are blending more Castelão Francês to make wines for drinking young.

Most white grapes are used to produce sparkling wines for the domestic market, though there are a few still white wines made from a blend of Maria Gomes grapes and Bical, another local variety. The best are deliciously crisp and aromatic. □

PRODUCERS

Large cooperatives and big private estates have long dominated production of the varied wines of Portugal's central zone. However, since the deregulation of the wine trade has led to the disappearance of the exporters' monopoly, a great number of small estates are ambitiously attempting to produce quality wines. These changes have also affected vine plantings. International grapes are appearing in these vineyards alongside traditional Portuguese varieties.

Adega Cooperativa de Cantanhede

The largest cooperative winery in the historic region of Bairrada can be found in the town of Cantanhede. Founded by 100 partners in 1954, this winery is one of the good examples of the national cooperative system and one of the best units in the country.

Although located in an area which is steeped in tradition, it has managed to bring itself up-to-date and to keep up with industry developments.

Fiuza & Bright, LDA

The Australian winemaker Peter Bright, manager and founder of this company, worked with J P Vinhos until

───── PALACE HOTEL, BUCACO ─────

The small hill town of Buçaco, between Bairrada and Dão, is within neither demarcated region, so the wines made here are not subject to official legislation. The Palace Hotel owns 9ha (22 acres) of vineyard, and hotel manager Jose Rodrigues dos Santos doubles up as a winemaker. The firm supplements production by blending wines from some of the best growers in nearby Dão and Bairrada. Reds tend to be big, dark and impressive; whites are dry but rich, honeyed and concentrated. The wines, labelled simply Buçaco, are sold only in the hotel and its sister establishments in Curia, Coimbra and Lisbon. Built in the early 1900s as a royal hunting lodge, the Palace's cellars are the resting place for some remarkable wines. Vintages go back to 1927 and most years since 1945 are still available in the dining room.

1992. Bright Brothers Vinhos (Portugal), founded in 1993, produces wines in the various regions: Douro, Bairrada/Beiras, Estremadura, Ribatejo, Cartaxo and Palmela/Terras do Sado.

Fiuza & Bright is a joint venture set up in 1994 between Joaquim Fiuza and Peter Bright. The 60ha (150 acres) of vineyards are planted with French grape varieties.

Caves Acácio-Caves Moura Basto

This company was founded in 1954 by Acácio Moreira da Rocha, in Arcozelo — Vila Nova de Gaia. As a result of increased sales and successive investment, the premises now cover an area of 30,000 sq m and have a storage capacity of 5 million litres. In 1987 the company took over the Caves Moura Basto in Amarante, a company which had been producing and selling Vinho Verde since 1940. Caves Acácio sell everyday wines, DOC wines (Vinho Verde, Dão, Douro and Bairrada) and brandies.

Caves Aliança

This, one of Portugal's main wine companies, located in the heart of the Bairrada region, was founded in 1927 to produce sparkling wines and brandies. Since then, whilst continuing to produce these drinks, it has broadened its range over the years to include wines from other regions. For the past ten years the company has placed its bets on wine it itself has produced and owns several hundred hectares of vines and wineries in some of the best winemaking regions in Portugal.

In addition to its Bairrada wines, Caves Aliança produces and sells Douro and Dão wines, Vinho Verdes, Palmela, Alentejo and Regional Beiras wines.

Messias

This company, founded in 1926 by Messias Baptista, is located in Mealhada, in the Bairrada region, where, in addition to its huge wineries, it owns 160ha (400 acres) of vineyards divided among various *quintas*. The most significant of these is the 70-ha (170 acre) Quinta do Valdoeiro. In the Douro valley, right in the heart of the Cachão da Valeira, through which the famous river Douro flows, the company owns two *quintas*, Quinta do Cachão and Quinta do Rei. They cover a total of 200ha (500 acres), of which 110ha (270 acres) are planted with vines for Port production and, in the Quinta do Cachão, Douro wine production.

Caves São João

Small Bairrada firm owned by two fastidious brothers who make some of the best, long-lasting red wines in the region. Frei João Reservas develop for 20 years or more. They also bottle good, solid, traditional red Dão under the Porta dos Cavaleiros label.

Quinta da Pancas

A 16th-century property near the peaceful town of Alenquer in Oeste. Proprietor Joaquim Guimaraes has supplemented traditional grape varieties with Chardonnay and Cabernet Sauvignon, making wines with international flavour.

Quinta da Lagoalva de Cima

This estate, one of the largest in Ribatejo, stands around 2km (one mile) from the little town of Alpiarça and extends over 5,500ha (13,600 acres). Vines are grown over 60ha (150 acres) and, as part of a recent reorganisation, have been transferred from alluvial soils to poorer quality sandy soils, which actually improves the quality of the raw material.

SOUTHERN PORTUGAL

The River Tagus is the rough dividing line between the poor agricultural smallholdings of the north and central areas and the vast estates, or *latifúndios*, that cover the south. The hills give way to a broad expanse of flat, low-lying plain.

With the exception of the Setúbal Peninsula (*see* below) this is hardly natural grape-growing country. South and east of Lisbon the landscape is progressively more arid as the climate becomes more severe. Green after the winter rains, the countryside turns an ever deeper shade of brown as the thermometer hits 40°C (104°F). With few rivers to provide irrigation, drought is a common problem for farmers. Deep-rooted cork oaks are one of the few crops to survive the summer months.

The south used to be something of a joke among people from Lisbon and the north. In the 19th century they christened it *terra de mau pão e mau vinho* — land of bad bread and bad wine. The region was further set back in the wake of the 1974 revolution as many of the large landlords were dispossessed by radical farm workers. The Algarve, despite its four wine zones, is preoccupied by tourism, and is unlikely to make much headway with wine. But with the help of modern winemaking technology and a degree of know-how, the southerners of Setúbal and the Alentejo may be about to have the last laugh.

Setúbal Peninsula
The port of Setúbal lends its name to the land between the rivers Tagus and Sado. Setúbal is also a demarcated region for a sweet, fortified wine made predominantly from Muscat grapes growing on the limestone slopes of the Serra da Arrábida hills. Two styles of Setúbal are sold commercially: an aromatic, spicy 5-year-old and a dark, intensely sweet 20-year-old. In spite of the suburban invasion by Lisbon to the north, since the 1970s the peninsula has become one of the most exciting wine regions in Portugal. This is largely due to three enterprising companies which have tried different grape varieties (including some foreign imports) and pioneered new styles of red and white wine.

Alentejo
The plains of the Alentejo extend from the Atlantic coast in the west to the Spanish frontier in the east, occupying about a third of Portugal. The region is relatively new to commercial winemaking, but seven vineyard zones have recently been awarded DO status. Of these Borba, Redondo and Reguengos are the most important, with local cooperatives making good use of foreign expertise. Private estates, again with overseas links, are also emerging. Full-flavoured red wines made from a blend of ripe Aragonez (the Tinta Roriz of the Douro) and Trincadeira and other native grapes are currently showing more promise than the rather fat, blowzy whites. □

The grape harvest at Ferreira, in the Alentejo.

PRODUCERS

Although there are currently four DOC regions in the Algarve, the wines are for a large part made by cooperatives and drunk by tourists. More exciting wines are being made by enthusiastic winemakers in modern wineries in the Alentejo and on the Setúbal Peninsula.

Adega Cooperativa de Borba
One of Portugal's most modern cooperatives, which uses state-of-the-art technology combined with careful attention to detail to produce balanced red wines in the hot climate of the Alentejo.

Quinta do Carmo
Traditional private estate still treading grapes in *lagares*: open tanks built with local marble. With 70ha (173 acres) of vineyard near Borba in the Alentejo, Carmo is producing one of the best reds in southern Portugal. The Rothschilds have recently taken a stake in the property.

Fundação Eugénio de Andrade
This charitable foundation has set itself up in a former 16th-century monastery outside the town of Evora, in Alentejo. With 7,000ha (17,300 acres) of vines and modern wine-making equipment it produces wines which are better known under the name Herdade de Cartuxa. The white wines are full of exotic aromas and the reds are well-structured with hints of mint.

Herdade do Esporão-Finagra
Finagra came about as the result of an ambitious project in the 1970s which turned into a sure bet. This company, 2km (1 mile) from Reguengos de Monsaraz, in the heart of the sub-region of Alentejo of the same name, has 600ha (1,500 acres) of vineyards planted with traditional Alentejo varieties and a small percentage of international grape varieties. The wines are cellared, stored and aged in impressive premises. Each year the Alentejo wines of the most consistent quality are produced here and many of them have already received awards in Portugal and abroad. Finagra recently opened an excellent tourist complex centred around wine which forms part of the Alentejo Wine Route.

José Maria da Fonseca
This company has been producing fine examples of Azeitão wines for over a century and a half and is now the second largest producer of Portuguese wine, with sales exceeding £500,000 in 1998, 75% of which was exported. Latterly, through the purchase of land in the most productive areas, JMF has come to own over 650ha (1,600 acres) of vines, mainly in Setúbal and Alentejo, where the company has its own wineries.

J P Vinhos
This company was established in 1922 under the name of João Pires & Filhos, Lda. In the past it bought in grapes from producers in the region to make wine which was then sold in bulk. At the end of the 1970s, António Avillez, who had become the biggest shareholder in the company, took charge of the company's destiny. With incredible dynamism, he had 200ha (500 acres) planted under vines, refurbished and modernised the cellars and created new brands of bottled wine. These are high quality, innovative examples of what is being produced in the Portuguese wine industry as a whole. Production capacity is around 12 million litres.

José da Sousa Rosado Fernandes
This time-warp winery at Reguengos de Monsaraz in the Alentejo is little changed since it was founded in 1878. Bought by the Setúbal firm of José Maria da Fonseca in 1986, the wines continue to be vinified in enormous *talhas* or clay pots in a cool underground cellar. The wines, all red, are robust and spicy.

Southern Portugal is best known as a producer of cork, from the bark of the cork oak tree.

PORT

More myths seem to have grown up around port than any other of the world's great wines. Maybe this comes from the nature of the land in which it is grown — the harsh, rugged countryside of the Douro Valley of northern Portugal, still one of the most remote areas of western Europe. Maybe it comes from the tradition-loving British in particular, who consumed vast quantities of the wine in the 18th and 19th centuries, "passing the port" around the table to the left, clockwise, once the ladies had left the table; standing to drink the loyal toast in vintage port, guessing the vintage of the wine that was being drunk, and never, ever, leaving the table until the decanter was empty.

The province of Tras-os-Montes (across the mountains), home of port, is the last frontier of Portugal. Until very recently the only way to reach the high Douro Valley, where the river pours through gorges and past tiny, isolated villages, was by labouring mule or by the little railway which hugs the river bank. Today, new roads have been built and the river dammed, but the land is still inhospitable, fit only for vines; staggeringly beautiful in spring, brown and parched in summer.

The demarcated area of the port vineyards covers some 2,600 sq km (1,000 sq miles) on both sides of the River Douro and its tributaries, stretching from just west of the town of Peso da Régua eastwards as far as the Spanish frontier. About 10–12% of this area is planted with vines. Port vines are planted on schist soil, while other vines in the area, planted on granite soil, can only be used for Douro table wines and DO wines.

The climate in the Douro is one of extremes. Winters can be cold; colder in the east of the region, wet-

These *barcos rabelos* used to be the only way to bring port down the Douro.

ter in the west. Summers, by contrast, can be fearsomely hot — temperatures in the mid-40s°C (*circa* 110°F) are not uncommon — and generally dry. Vines were traditionally planted on stone-walled terraces, but these are becoming rarer as new plantings are on earth-buttressed terraces called *patamares*, or in vertical rows, depending on the gradient.

In times past, up to 48 different grape varieties have been permitted for port production. They were planted randomly in the vineyard, so that port was made from a blend of grape varieties. In the more recent past — since the 1974 revolution —, those 48 have been rationalized into a list of five red varieties. They are: Touriga Nacional, Tinto Cão, Tinta Roriz, Tinta Barroca and Touriga Francesa.

The vineyard land is heavily divided. There are 25,000 growers permitted to produce grapes for port. They will sell either grapes or wine to shippers (the firms that mature, bottle and sell the wine) or to cooperatives (who since 1986 have also been allowed to bottle and export wine).

Making the wine
The vast proportion of port is red, though white is also made. Both styles are made by the addition of brandy during fermentation, which stops the fermentation before its completion, leaving a more or less sweet wine. Harvesting in the Douro starts in mid-September and runs for up to a month. At a critical stage in the winemaking (one normally determined under strict supervision by the purchaser of the wine), a clear, colourless grape spirit called

aguardente will be added to stop fermentation, at the rate of 100 litres of brandy to 450 litres of wine.

At this point, it becomes port. Although there are now growers who mature the port on their own property, most port will be taken downriver in the spring following the harvest to the town of Vila Nova de Gaia at the mouth of the Douro (opposite the city of Oporto), where each shipper has a "lodge" — the headquarters where the wine is matured and bottled. This tradition of transportation, unique in the wine world, came about because the moister air of Vila Nova was considered better for maturing port in wooden casks; and in any case, the wine was shipped from there.

The port is matured in wooden casks for varying periods, depending on the style that is being made (*see* box). These casks, called *pipas* (in English, pipes), contain 630 litres. While the least expensive rubies and tawnies can still be exported in bulk, all other port is now bottled in Portugal (this is indicated by a paper seal which is fixed over the cork or around the bottle capsule).

History of port

Port began its rise to fame as a wine which was exported to the British, and which was developed by them: British factors (traders) set up merchant houses in Portugal from the 17th century onwards. At first, what was exported was red table wine — Red Portugal, as it was called. It was never fortified until the 18th century, when it was found that the addition of brandy stabilized the wine on its sea journey. Even in the early 19th century, there was fierce discussion as to whether red Douro wine should be sweetened and fortified — an argument fortunately won by the proponents of fortification.

As port began a decline in Britain in the 1920s, so the French market for tawny and light ruby port as an apéritif opened up: today, despite the reputation port has in the UK,

France is by far the largest export market (with a small, but growing, interest in the top vintage wines), followed by the Benelux countries and Germany, and the United States.

Port regulations

Port was the first wine in the world to be regulated as the first measures date back to 1756 when the Marquis of Pombal, then Prime Minister of Portugal, demarcated the vineyards of the Douro valley, thus creating the first DOC area. He also established a government wine monopoly, the Companhia Geral da Agricultura dos Vinhos do Alto Douro. (It now exists in a privatized and non-regulatory form as one of the shippers, the Royal Oporto Wine Company.) The idea was to protect the grape-growers from the low prices offered to them by the British shippers, and to control the quality of the wine and the yields of the vines.

From this action stem most of the controls that, today, make port the most regulated wine in the world. The controls start with the vineyard. All vineyards in the port region are classified from "A" down to "E", according to location, aspect, soil, climate, vine varieties planted, age of vines, vine density, yields and the quality of vineyard maintenance. The higher the rating, the higher the price paid for grapes and the higher the percentage of production that can be turned into port (the rest will become table wine). Shipments of port are also controlled. A shipper or grower may only sell one-third of his total stock in any year. This means that port has to be aged for at least three years before sale.

Finally, each sample of port is labelled by professional tasters from the Instituto do Vinho do Porto, a quasi-government body, which also carries out research.   □

STYLES OF PORT

Port wine refers mainly to a specific geographic area. The Douro valley does not produce one but several types of wine and the production and ageing regulations are set by the law. The Instituto do Vinho do Porto, an institute dependent on the State, is each year responsible for setting the maximum quantity of must which can be made into port and for quality control: approval, analysis, tastings...

White port   made from white grapes only and aged in wood, it can be dry, medium dry or sweet.

Ruby port   made from various blends and aged in wood, its clear bright red colour reminds you of the jewel of the same name.

Tawny port   meaning 'russet-coloured'. As it ages in the cask, the wine is oxidised through the wood and the red colour of this port takes on orange hues. As the wine ages it becomes smoother and more elegant. This is the best-known port in

France where it is sold after 3 to 5 years ageing.

Aged tawnies   made from a blend of wines from several vintages. The average age ('10 years', '20 years', '30 years', 'over 40 years') is given on the label.

'Colheita' (or 'Reserva') tawnies from one vintage and cask-aged until it is bottled. The date of bottling and the vintage must appear on the label.

Late Bottled Vintage or LBV   Wines from a single year, that have been kept in wood for between four years and six years before bottling. The time spent in the cask makes it lighter than a true Vintage port.

Vintage   port from a single exceptionally good year. A vintage will be declared two years after a harvest when the port is improving well and showing all the qualities required for a very lengthy ageing period. It will continue to age in the bottle. It should not be drunk until it is 8 to 10 years old, or even 15 to 20 years for certain great vintages.

PRODUCERS

The port trade is dominated by the shippers, who are traditionally known as "British" or "Portuguese", though many other nations are involved. The shippers age, bottle and export the wines from their lodges in Vila Nova de Gaia; nearly all own port-producing *quintas* (estates) in the Douro, and also buy wine from other growers.

Andresen
A small Portuguese-owned group which includes under its marques Mackenzie, Pinto Pereira, and Vinhos do Alto Corgo. Mackenzie is probably the best-known of its brands: founded in the 19th century by a sherry shipper, Kenneth Mackenzie, its name has been revived recently by the declaration of vintage ports.

Barros Almeida
Barros & Almeida was founded in 1913 by Manuel de Almeida, who later joined forces with his brother-in-law, Manoel de Barros. The latter injected a great dynamism into the company and led it through the difficult eras of the first and second Republic, the new Fascist regime and the two world wars. Nowadays the Barros group comprises several companies which have been bought over or created over the years. These include Kopke, Hutcheson, Feuerheerd & Associados and H.& C. J. Feist — Vinhos S.A. The group currently has a 5% share of the port market. Barros & Almeida is one of the most reputable port companies, known mainly for its aged tawnies and Vintage ports.

It also produces all the other types of port and Douro wine and sells wines from Bairrada and Dão and natural sparkling wines. The company has a presence in practically all the markets which import port.

Sociedade dos Vinhos Borges
See p435.

Broadbent Selections, Inc
Broadbent Port was launched with the 1994 Vintage by Bartholomew Broadbent, son of the esteemed wine author, Michael Broadbent. Its 1994 is a custom blend made from 70-year-old Tinta Amarella and Roriz grapes, 20% of which were foot-trodden in traditional stone *lagares*, while the remainder was fermented in modern auto-vinificators. Their second Vintage was 1997 which was made by Dirk Niepoort and had the Touriga Nacional added to the blend.

J W Burmester
Founded in the 18th century by a family of German origin, this shipping house has an excellent reputation for its aged tawnies and its *colheitas*. It is still owned by the family and buys from good growers in the Alto Douro. During the 1980s, its vintages were superb.

A A Cálem
One of the largest family-owned shippers, Cálem has recently established a formidable reputation outside its traditional market of Portugal for its vintage, late bottled vintage and *colheita* wines. A considerable landowner at Pinhão, Cálem's flagship *quinta* is Quinta da Foz, where

wine is made in open *lagares* (stone treading troughs), and is also released as a single-*quinta* wine. Cálem has recently purchased Quinta de Ferradoza from Borges & Irmão. Its winery near Vila Real produces tawnies, sold under the Tres Velhotes label.

Churchill Graham
A small house, it was set up in 1981 by John Graham of the Graham port family, which had sold its own port house to the Symington family in 1970. The range includes two single-*quinta* wines, Quinta da Agua Alta and Quinta de Fojo, both of which are owned by John Borges from whom Churchills buy the bulk of their fruit. The wines, labelled Churchills, include aged tawnies and an LBV.

Cintra
See Taylor *(qv)*.

Cockburn Smithes
More familiarly known as Cockburn's, this is one of the most famous names in port. Founded in 1815 by Robert Cockburn, it became Cockburn Smithes in 1848 when Cockburn was joined by Henry and John Smithes. In 1961, Cockburn's purchased Martinez Gassiot *(qv)*, while in 1962 it was taken over by Harveys of Bristol, now part of Allied Lyons. It has big vineyard interests in the Douro, at Tua and Pinhão (Quinta do Tua and Quinta da Eira Velha are sometimes released as single-*quinta* vintages) and in the Vilariça Valley high up the Douro which is a brand-new

and extensive development.

In the UK, it sells the leading brand of port, Cockburn's Special Reserve, along with the almost equally popular Fine Ruby: both are well made, commercial wines, and as such are typical of Cockburn's ports in general. Aged tawnies, a new departure for Cockburn's, are among the best around. Cockburn's declares vintages less often than other houses: but its releases in 1983 and 1985 showed that the style is softer and more velvety than the wines from some houses — although they last as long.

Croft
One of the oldest of port shippers, founded in 1678 — although the first Croft, John, did not arrive until 1736. It remained in family hands until 1911 when it was sold to W & A Gilbey, who themselves were bought by International Distillers and Vintners (part of Grand Metropolitan). It is managed jointly with the Croft sherry company in Jerez. Two other firms owned by Croft are Delaforce and Morgan Brothers *(qqv)*. It makes a full range of ports, many of which, like Distinction Finest Reserve are of sound, rather than exciting quality. However its aged tawnies and vintage wines (which include a single-*quinta* Quinta da Roeda) are up with the best.

Delaforce
Delaforce, founded by a Huguenot family in 1868, has been part of International Distillers and Vintners since 1968. But there are still Delaforces involved in the business, and the wines are still made in a separate lodge, and are based on separate vineyards. Paramount ruby is important in the Netherlands and Germany, while France receives shipments of basic ruby and tawny. In English-speaking markets,

His Eminence's Choice, an old tawny, is well regarded. The vintage wines are based on the Quinta da Corte in the Torto Valley, giving elegant wines, with some delicacy and less longevity than some of the blockbusters of the trade.

Dow
See Symington profile, p444.

H & C J Feist
Owned by the Barros family (*see* entry), this brand is best known for rubies and tawnies on the French market. It was founded by two German cousins in London in 1836 and bought by Barros in the 1950s.

Ferreira
See profile.

Feuerheerd

Now owned by the Barros family, this firm was founded by a German, Dietrich Feuerheerd, in 1815. It has long had a place on the French market for wines such as Commendador, Royal Banquet and Marques de Soveral. Feuerheerd's former *quinta,* Quinta de la Rosa, remained in family hands when the rest of the firm was sold to Barros.

Fonseca Guimaraens
Some of the finest vintage ports come from this firm, which has been owned by Taylor's (*qv*) since 1948. Their style — rich and plummy and generally quite sweet — is consistent and completely different from the Taylor style. That difference comes from

the Pinhão vineyards, Quinta do Cruzeiro and Quinta do Santo Antonio, which provide 80% of the vintage Fonseca wines. In lesser years, a Fonseca Guimaraens vintage is declared while from the other *quinta* owned by the firm, Quinta do Panascal, there is a single-*quinta* vintage. The most famous wine in the Fonseca Guimaraens range is Bin 27, a vintage character wine, but its aged tawnies are improving all the time. The firm was founded in 1822 by Manuel Pedro Guimaraens who came from Braga in northern Portugal: his descendant, Bruce Guimaraens, makes the wines for both Fonseca and Taylor.

Forrester
This is one of the most famous names in port history. Baron Joseph James Forrester, who was drowned in the Douro in 1861, was the first to map the upper Douro and to devise a cure for the oïdium fungus that had devastated the vineyards in the 1850s. His uncle had joined with the Offley family in 1803 and for many years the firm was called Offley Forrester: now the wines are called Offley but the firm, under the ownership of Martini & Rossi, is called Forrester. The principal vineyard, Quinta da Boa Vista, also lends its name to a vintage port as well as, confusingly, to an LBV. There is also a single-*quinta* vintage, from Quinta do Cachucha, aged tawnies which are often underrated, and the Duke of Oporto ruby.

Gould Campbell
See Symington profile, p444.

W & J Graham
See Symington profile, p444.

Gran Cruz
Gran Cruz, the world's largest port exporter, followed on from the company Assunção

& Fos in 1887. It has its own ageing cellars in Portugal and two *quintas* with 200ha (500 acres) of vines in the heart of the Douro valley: Quinta da Granja and Quinta do Castelo.

Porto Cruz, created in 1955 by Jean Cayard, founder of the company La Martiniquaise, is the largest brand in France. The company is well-known for its wide range of ports: Tawny, White, Special Reserve, Aged tawnies (10, 20 and 30 years), Colheita, LBV and Vintage.

Quinta do Infantado
This estate derives its name from the word 'Infante' (meaning "heir to the throne"), as it originally belonged to Prince Dom Pedro, son of the King of Portugal, Dom João VI, before being bought over by João Lopes Roseira. Until 1978, the

estate sold its *vinhos finos* — the name given to port before the Vila Nova de Gaia enterprise was set up — to exporters in the town, holding back varying quantities to be aged on the *quinta*. In 1979, Quinta do Infantado sold the first estate-bottled ports, reviving a tradition which had been lost around fifty years previously. Since the 1986 changes in the law, these wines, once sold exclusively in Portugal, are also exported. All Quinta do Infantado ports are estate-bottled and each bottle is dated and numbered.

C N Kopke
This is one of the firms owned by the Barros family (*see* entry). It is also the oldest port shipper, having been started in 1638 by Cristiano Kopke, son of the consul for the Hanseatic cities in Lisbon. Today it is the

FERREIRA

Ferreira was one of the most important firms in the development of the Douro as a vineyard area, when Dona Antonia Ferreira, the *grande dame* of 19th-century port, opened up the Douro Superior vineyards almost to the Spanish border. Although it was bought in 1989 by the owners of the Sogrape (Mateus Rosé) group, it continues to produce great ports. It is perhaps best known for its aged tawnies, of which the 20-year-old Duque de Bragança is often regarded as the finest of its type. The Quinta do Porto 10-year-old tawny is also respected for its rich, fruity style. The vintage wines, until 1991, were not released until they were ready for drinking; they are on the sweet side, very much in the Portuguese tradition. Ferreira also owns the Hunt Roope and Constantino brands.

star of the Barros portfolio, producing some excellent *colheita* wines and pleasant aged tawnies. Vintage wines, based on the Quinta de São Luiz, are soft and fast-maturing, although getting better.

Martinez Gassiot
Although wholly owned by Cockburn's, this shipper is treated separately, with its own lodge at Régua where many of the wines are matured. This gives them the "Douro bake": richer, nuttier than wines matured in Vila Nova de Gaia, with a slightly burnt taste. This characteristic is of particular benefit to the aged tawnies, which manage to keep an impressive amount of fruit even at the 20-year-old level. However, the vintage-style LBVs and vintage character tend to lose colour.

Martinez wines also come from different *quintas* to Cockburn's: Quinta do Bartol high up the Douro, Quinta da Adega at Tua and Quinta da Marcela at Pinhão. Vintage ports have plenty of fruit.

Messias
A popular brand in Portugal and the former Portuguese colonies in Africa and South America, Messias is a family-owned firm started in 1926, and perhaps even better known for its table wines from Dão, Douro and Bairrada. *Quintas* include Quinta do Cachão and Quinta do Rei, upstream of Tua at Ferradosa.

Morgan Brothers
Owned today by Croft, Morgan Brothers is one of the oldest names in port: it was founded in 1715. Literary afi-

cionados will remember that Morgan's Double Diamond is mentioned in Charles Dickens' *Nicholas Nickleby*. Today much of the business is in own-label wine for retailers, but some vintage port is made from *quintas* in the Rio Torto and Ronção Valley.

Niepoort
A small shipper, owned by the Niepoort family, with a fine reputation for *colheita* ports and aged tawnies. The vintage ports, too, are very fine and often underrated. The firm was founded in 1842 and Rolf and Dirk van der Niepoort, currently in charge, are the fourth and fifth generations. Grapes are bought in from *quintas* in the Pinhão Valley, but Niepoort owns no vineyards of its own.

Offley Forrester
See Forrester *(qv)*.

Osborne
Owned by the sherry firm of Osborne *(qv)*, this is a relatively new house. Only set up in 1967, it initially used the production facilities of Quinta do Noval, but now has its own lodge. A full range of wines is made, most of which are exported to western European countries. The firm owns no vineyards at present.

Manoel D Poças Junior
This family-owned firm, founded in 1918, is known mainly in France, Belgium and Portugal. The firm owns three *quintas*: Quartas, Santa Bárbara and Vale de Cavalos. It sells

good vintages, *colheitas* and excellent aged tawnies.

Quarles Harris
See Symington profile.

Quinta de São Pedro das Aguias
"Saint Peter of the Eagles" is the name of Douro's oldest *quinta*, created in the 11th century by monks. They probably appreciated an environment propitious to prayer and meditation, built their monastery and planted vines. The Cistercian monks left their abbaye only in 1834, after the civil war. In 1986, the Quinta de São Pedro was bought over by Paul Vranken, a wine merchant from Champagne. Since then the property, which had been abandoned, has been given a new life. The abbey has been restored, new vines have been planted and the first release was in 1988. The quinta produces a range of tawnies (sold under the São Pedro and San Marta labels) and a white port.

Quinta do Noval
The steeply-terraced vineyards of the Quinta do Noval in the Pinhão Valley are among the most photographed and most impressive in the whole port region. It would be a mistake, however, to think that all Quinta do Noval ports come from the *quinta* itself. Only the two vintage ports are truly estate wines: the regular vintage, itself a classic Portuguese style, sweet and fruity; and the Nacional, produced in tiny quantities from a small plot of ungrafted vines on the estate — a wine which can command high prices.

The rest of the Noval range is of good quality: from the Late Bottled Noval (it recently dropped the vintage designation on this wine) to the aged tawnies. The firm, until recently called A J da Silva and

---

SYMINGTON GROUP

Graham's, Dow's, Warre's, Quarles Harris, Gould Campbell, Smith Woodhouse... all familiar names to lovers of fine port, but few know that they are owned by the same family firm. However, a Symington started work at Graham's over a century ago, became a partner in Warre in 1892, and the family bought Dow in 1912. In 1970 they acquired Graham's. Warre, the oldest of the British-owned shippers, was founded in 1670 (Dow in 1798, Graham's 1822). Dow, based at Quinta do Bomfim, is known for its dry style; Graham's, whose *quinta* is Malvedos, rich and sweet; Warre (whose *quintas* are a half of Bom-Retiro and da Cavadinha), wines of immense power. Symingtons now own the showpiece Quinta do Vesuvio and sell its single-*quinta* vintage under the Symington name.

owned by the van Zeller family, is now owned by AXA Millésime, the Bordeaux château group.

Adriano Ramos-Pinto

One of the most innovative firms in the port trade, with considerable research in viticulture and winemaking. Until recently it was owned by 42 members of the Ramos-Pinto family, but now control is in the hands of the Roederer Champagne house.

The firm owns five *quintas*: Santo Domingos, Bom-Retiro, Urtiga, Bons-Ares and Ervamoira. Two of its aged tawnies are released as single-*quinta* wines: Bom-Retiro (a 20-year-old) and Ervamoira (a 10-year-old); the firm also produces vintage wines that are known for their considerable elegance.

Robertson Brothers

Although now owned by Sandeman (*qv*), Robertson Brothers still have an independent existence through their Rebello Valente brand, a name acquired in 1881. Most famous is the vintage port which has a long and distinguished existence, even though produced in tiny quantities. The LBV is a crusted wine which needs decanting, and has considerable flavour; the aged tawnies include the 20-year-old Imperial.

Royal Oporto Wine Company

By far the largest producer of port, Royal Oporto also has one of the most interesting histories. It was set up in 1756 by the Portuguese government as the controlling body for the whole port trade when port was suffering from scandals to do with sharp dealing and adulteration. Its job was to control the making of the wine and then to sell it on to the shippers.

This monopoly was abol-

ished in 1858 and now it is a privately-owned firm, which at present owns the largest vineyard in the Douro region.

Rozes

A major name on the French market, and owned by the Louis Vuitton-Moët Hennessy group, it is appropriate that this firm should actually have started life, in Bordeaux in 1855, as a shipper of ports to France. Today the bulk of its business is with inexpensive rubies and tawnies, and Rozes port is well-known in France. Some vintage wines are made, from vineyards in the Pinhão area, but have never achieved a great reputation.

Sandeman

Founded in 1790 by Scotsman George Sandeman, the House of Sandeman, owned by Seagram, but still family-run and linked with the sherry firm of the same name (*qv*), is one of the largest producers of port. Much of that is strictly basic stuff, which is sold in quantity to France and other western European markets. But there is a core of fine wine, from the aged tawnies (the 10-year-old Royal tawny is attractively fruity), to the soft, relatively fast-maturing vintage wines. Founder's Reserve is the standard blended ruby which is found in English-speaking markets. Until 1974, Sandeman did not own vineyards, but bought from growers in the areas around Régua and Tua. However it now owns Quinta de Confradeiro and de Celeiros in Pinhão and Quinta das Laranjeiras near Poçinho.

C da Silva

This small, Spanish-owned firm produces port under a number of names: Presidential and Dalva, as well as da Silva. Most wines are light, soft and commercial, sold mainly in European export markets, but there are also quantities of

very fine old *colheita* wines, which are bottled to order.

Smith Woodhouse
See Symington profile p444.

Taylor, Fladgate & Yeatman

For many the epitome of vintage port. Taylor (known as Taylor, Fladgate in the United States to avoid confusion with the Taylor Wine Co) is still a family-controlled partnership, which also incorporates Fonseca Guimaraens (*qv*). It was founded in 1692, but did not achieve its present name until the 19th century.

Pioneering has been very much in the Taylor tradition: the first British shipper to own property in the Douro from the original purchase of Casa dos Alembiques in Régua — now a vinification centre — to the showpiece Quinta de Vargellas high up the Douro, bought in 1893; the first to commercialize a Late Bottled Vintage (now the best-selling LBV on the British market); and more recently the first to introduce a new style of undated port, First Estate.

Along with innovation rests tradition in the continued use of treading grapes in open *lagares* to produce vintage ports at Quinta de Vargellas; these lie next door to computerized stainless steel fermentation tanks for lesser wines. The range goes from the classic vintages, regarded as some of the finest made, through the single-*quinta* Quinta de Vargellas and some excellent aged tawnies (of which the 20-year-old is almost certainly the best) to basic rubies and tawnies and vintage character wines which are never less than well made. In France, they also use the Cintra brand.

Vieira de Sousa

Owned by the Barros family (*qv*), this brand was created in 1925 by Alcino Vieira de

Sousa. Today its main concern is with cheap ruby and tawny ports which are sold chiefly in Belgium and Germany.

Warre
See Symington profile.

Wiese & Krohn

A firm that was founded by two Norwegians in 1865, and which was taken over by the Carneiro family in 1922. While they have been principally involved in *colheitas* and other fine tawnies, they also produce a small amount of vintage ports which are achieving a good reputation. The style of wines is sweet and rich.

Wiese & Krohn buy most of their grapes from growers in the Rio Torto Valley, but also own a small property, Quinta do Retiro Novo.

OTHER COOPERATIVES

Under the 1986 regulations it is now possible to ship port direct from the Douro. This enables farmers and cooperatives to bottle and sell their own port, rather like a port château operation. The list includes: Adega Cooperativa de Alijó; Adega Cooperativa de Mesão Frio; Adega Cooperativa de Santa Marta de Penguião; Aida Coimbra, Aires de Matos e Filhos; Albertino da Costa Barros; Cooperativa Vitivinicola do Peso de Régua; Henriqué José de Carvalho; Jaime Acacio Q Cardoso; Jaime Machado Aires Lopes; Manuel Carlos Agrellos; María Fernanda Taveira; Montez Champalimaud Quinta do Cotto; Quinta do Infantado Vinhos; Serafim dos Santos Parente; Sociedade Agricular Quinta do Crasto; Sociedade Agricola Romaneira; Quinta de Val de Figueira.

MADEIRA

The island of Madeira, 600km (375 miles) west of Casablanca in the Atlantic Ocean, gives its name to the only wine in the world that is baked in an oven. The archipelago, which also includes the smaller island of Porto Santo, was discovered in 1418–1419 by a Portuguese sea captain, Zarco the Cross-Eyed, and has been part of Portugal ever since.

The name Madeira comes from the Portuguese word for wood: when it was discovered, the lush mountainous island — which rises to 1,750m (5,740ft) on sheer cliffs which fall, beachless, into the sea — was covered with dense forest. This was burnt by the Portuguese, and the resulting rich volcanic soil, full of potash, has proved fertile and very suitable for vinegrowing. Vines were imported from Crete in 1453.

Madeira was a good watering-point on the sea trade routes: very soon British settlers established trading posts and, later, moved into the wine trade. The wine from the island quickly became a standard part of a ship's cargo, and as the wine travelled around the world in small wooden ships, the tropical heat was found to improve its quality immeasurably. The wine producers on the island only discovered this when, one day, a shipment returned unsold. From that time onwards, madeira has been heated either in special ovens or by running hot pipes through the wine. The system is called *estufagem*, from the Portuguese for oven, *estufa*. The heating gives madeira its unique burnt character with high acids, and also allows it to last seemingly for ever once bottled (and for a long time even when the bottle is opened).

The 200ha (494 acres) of vineyard are scattered, and greatly outnumbered by banana plantations. The main vineyards are at Câmara de Lôbos, just west of Funchal, the

Vines climb volcanic cliffs.

island's capital, and at Santa Anna on the north coast.

A major problem ever since the phylloxera epidemic of the 1870s has been a great shortage of the four noble grape varieties (*see* box). Most cooking madeira (which still forms 80% of exports) is made from a different, and inferior, grape, the red Tinta Negra Mole.

New regulations, introduced since Portugal joined the European Community, now mean that if a wine is labelled with one of the noble grape varieties, it must contain at least 85% of that noble grape. Many younger madeiras, including 3- and 5-year-olds, cannot now achieve this thanks to the lack of grapes, and are labelled with no mention of the variety. Plantings of noble vines are expanding, but they are low-yielding and farmers are loath to uproot their productive Tinta Negra Mole.

Making madeira

Madeira, like other fortified wines, is a wine that is a blend of years. After fermentation, which generally, like port, is stopped by the addition of the fortifying grape spirit (although some firms ferment dry and add sweetened grape juice and grape spirit later), madeira is aged in casks, sealed with a banana leaf and a cork. It is then blended before bottling. □

GRAPES, STYLES AND QUALITIES

There are four principal varieties of noble grape on the island, and each produces one of the four classic styles of madeira, which are named after them:

Sercial Makes the driest style of madeira. It can be astringent when young, but ages extremely well, producing wine with a nutty character.
Verdelho Medium-dry golden wines come from this grape.
Bual A medium-sweet wine, which is full and rich but never cloying.
Malmsey From the Malvoisie or Malvasia grape; rich, luscious wines, which become slightly drier with age.

QUALITIES
While old vintage madeiras are sometimes for sale, most that is sold falls into a series of age categories, which are all available in the four styles corresponding to the four classic grapes — the age referring to the youngest wine in the blend:

3-year-old Basic madeira, much of which goes for cooking. The Tinta Negra Mole will be the grape variety, and the label will simply indicate that the wine is dry, medium dry, or sweet.
5-year-old reserve The first level at which noble varieties can be used.
10-year-old reserva velha or special reserve.
15-year-old extra reserve or exceptional reserve.
Fresqueira 20-year-old vintage A wine from one year, made 100% from the noble grape varieties, which spends 20 years in cask.

PRODUCERS

Apart from a few family concerns, a large number of well-known Madeira brands are grouped together under the Madeira Wine Company (MWC), formerly an association of English merchants now taken over by the Blandy and Symington families (*see* p444). This company ships 25% of total Madeira production and 52% of Madeira exported in bottle. The Madeira Wine Institute controls and approves the quality of the wines produced on the island.

Barbeito

The youngest of the madeira producers, founded in 1946 and now run by the daughter of the founder. From cramped premises perched on a cliff, they make a range of wines that are characterized by a softness and lightness. Island Rich and Island Dry are their two 3-year-old wines, while the 5-year-old range appears under the Crown brand. They also have stocks of venerable wines which were purchased when the company was created. Barbeito owns no vineyards, buying grapes to make their wine.

Blandy Brothers

The most familiar name for madeira in the British market. The firm was founded by John Blandy, who arrived in 1807 to garrison the island against the threat of Napoleonic invasion. The family is still a principal shareholder in the Madeira Wine Company — and of Reid's Hotel, the most prestigious on the island. The range includes the set of four 5-year-old wines named after British dukes: Duke of Sussex sercial, Duke of Cambridge verdelho, Duke of Cumberland bual, Duke of Clarence malmsey. Blandy's 10-year-old special reserve wines are among the best. The historic Blandy lodges at São Francisco in the centre of Funchal are a must for any visitor to the island.

H M Borges

Family-owned firm which makes a range of 5-year-old wines that tend to be dry and with good acidity.

Broadbent Selections, Inc.

Broadbent Madeira ranges back to the 1933 Malmsey Vintage. The brand belongs to Bartholomew Broadbent of Broadbent Selections, Inc. and the blends were selected by his father, Michael Broadbent of Christie's fame. The Rainwater, the 5-year-old Reserve, the 10-year-old Malmsey and 45-year-old Terrantez are notable wines but they also produced a 1964 Bual, a 1934 Verdelho, 1940 Sercial and 1954 Verdelho.

Cossart Gordon

Another major brand name, now part of the Madeira Wine Company. The firm is one of the oldest on the island: it was founded in 1745 by Francis Newton and William Gordon, with William Cossart arriving in 1808. As a curiosity, during the 19th century, the firm sold madeira with a shot of quinine to the British in India to ward off disease. The Cossart Gordon style is comparatively light and on the elegant side. Good Company is the basic range, Finest Old is the name for the 5-year-old reserve wines, while Duo Centenary is the name for the 15-year-old exceptional reserve range.

Henriques & Henriques

This is the largest firm outside the Madeira Wine Company. It was set up by a vineyard owner in Câmara de Lôbos in 1850, and still is a considerable (for the island, that is) owner of land in the area. Harveys of Bristol's own-label madeiras are made by this firm, which also produces a range of madeiras under its own name and those of other wine merchants. It also owns other brands: Belem and Casa dos Vinhos de Madeira.

Justino's Madeira

The wines produced by this company (1870) have been enjoyed in Europe for nearly a century and have been adopted by the United States and Canada over the last ten years; more recently, its superior quality wines have found their way to Japan. In 1993, a winery equipped with the most up-to-date technology was built, strictly in keeping with the traditional methods of manufacture of this very special wine. Thanks to an increase in quality, demand for its wines has significantly increased and Vinhos Justino Henriques has decided to join forces with one of France's largest distribution groups, thus becoming one of the leading companies on the export market.

Leacock

Leacock is another member of the Madeira Wine Company, and was founded in 1741 at much the same time as Cossart Gordon. One of the Leacock family, Thomas Slapp Leacock, who lived in the 19th century, is credited with restoring the madeira vineyards after the phylloxera epidemic. The firm produces two main ranges: Saint John is the basic range, while Special Reserve is the 10-year-old range. The house style is on the dry side, which makes the sercials in particular good apéritif wines.

Lomelino

The full name of the firm is T Tarquinio da Câmara Lomelino. Although founded as a Portuguese-owned house, it is now part of the Madeira Wine Company. Reserve 5-year-old and Imperial Reserve 10-year-old ranges are produced, with a pronounced burnt taste to the drier wines and good rich flavours in the sweeter ones. Lomelino madeiras are found in many countries of western Europe.

Madeira Wine Company

The companies which originally came together to form the Madeira Wine Company, some of whose names are preserved today, were: Aguiar Freitas, A Nobrega, Barros Almeida, Bianchi, Blandy, C V Vasconcelos, Cossart Gordon, F F Ferraz, F Martins Caldeira, Funchal Wine Company, J B Spinola, Krohn Brothers, Leacock & Co, Luiz Gomes, Madeira Victoria, Miles Madeiras, Power Drury, Royal Madeira, Rutherford & Miles, Socieda Agricola da Madeira, Lomelino, Vinhos Adudarham, Madeira Meneres, Vinhos Donaldson, Shortridge Lawton, Welsh Brothers.

Pereira d'Oliveira Vinhos

A small family-owned firm, founded in 1820, with a lodge in Funchal and a winery and vineyards in San Martinho and Câmara de Lôbos. They produce a range of wines which is light and dry and generally fresh. Like many producers, they also have stocks of older vintage wines which they sell as single bottles to visitors to their premises in Funchal.

Veiga França

Veiga França is a firm that specializes in wines which appear frequently in French kitchens. Their bual and malmsey wines are particularly sweet.

THE MEDITERRANEAN

THE VINEYARDS OF THE EASTERN MEDITERRANEAN AND OF NORTH
AFRICA HAVE A GLORIOUS PAST. TODAY, ONLY A FEW POCKETS OF
QUALITY WINEMAKING SUBSIST.

The north-eastern corner of the Mediterranean, the Aegean
Sea, is seen here below the vineyards of the innovative
Domaine Carras, in the Côtes de Meliton appellation area
of Sithonia, northern Greece.

The shores of the Mediterranean Sea were the cradle of wine. Greece has a wine tradition which dates back 3,000 years, and those of Turkey, Lebanon and Syria are even older. The Romans planted vines on every shore of the inland sea, including North Africa and Spain. Today the vineyards are beset by problems ranging from religious disapproval in the Muslim lands to changing consumer tastes in the more westernized countries. However, the wine traditions live on, and some surviving wine styles show a clear line of descent from classical times. Other wines, as yet a few, are the product of recent investment in vineyards and cellars and are firmly aimed at northern European buyers. A third group, sadly the majority, comprises poorly-made, heavy wines with a purely local, and probably declining, market.

The common threads in the Mediterranean wine tradition are sweet, dark wines and wines whose tastes are augmented by additives. Retsina, the pine-scented Greek white wine, is the sole survivor of the latter group; in Roman times wines were flavoured with anything from honey to seawater.

The dark, rich wines are made from grapes dried in various ways to concentrate their flavours. These wines survive in Cyprus and Greece, as well as in Italy and Spain. Grapes are left to dry on the vine, on mats in the sun, or in dark attics. Further ageing and oxidation in small casks adds to the unfamiliar, antique flavour. The best examples of the Greek Mavrodaphne (*mavro* means black) and of Cyprus Commandaria are comparable with the Italian Vin Santo and the Spanish málaga and Priorato, which are other branches of the same tradition.

Makers of light wines struggle to cope with a dry, hot climate that without skilled winemaking can easily ruin the fruitiness and acidity, especially of white wines. There is nothing in the Mediterranean climate beyond the power of modern wine technology, as California, Spain and southern France have shown, but the level of investment is still relatively low. Pockets of quality winemaking in Greece, the Lebanon, Israel and North Africa prove that these lands of sun and stony hillsides, and of fascinating grape varieties, could make great wines again, as they did in the time of the Caesars.

WINE REGIONS OF THE MEDITERRANEAN

The eastern and southern shores of the Mediterranean have a wine tradition that goes back to Antiquity, but of which little is left today.

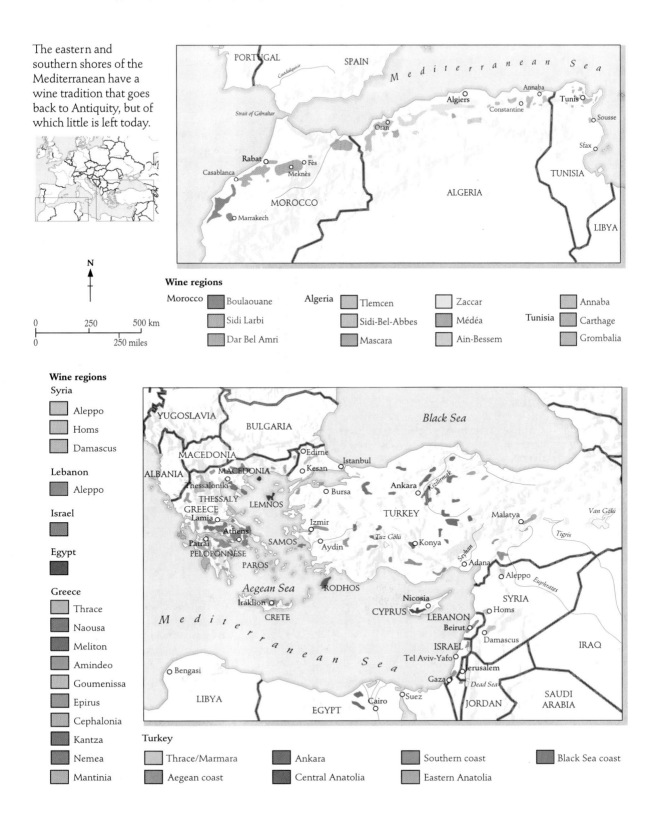

N

0 250 500 km

0 250 miles

Wine regions

Morocco		Algeria					Tunisia	
Boulaouane		Tlemcen		Zaccar			Annaba	
Sidi Larbi		Sidi-Bel-Abbes		Médéa			Carthage	
Dar Bel Amri		Mascara		Ain-Bessem			Grombalia	

Wine regions

Syria
Aleppo
Homs
Damascus

Lebanon
Aleppo

Israel

Egypt

Greece
Thrace
Naousa
Meliton
Amindeo
Goumenissa
Epirus
Cephalonia
Kantza
Nemea
Mantinia

Turkey
Thrace/Marmara
Aegean coast
Ankara
Central Anatolia
Southern coast
Eastern Anatolia
Black Sea coast

GREECE

In the ancient world, wine from Greece was considered very fine and was widely exported. During the many centuries of Ottoman domination winemaking dwindled into a localized agricultural product. The long-drawn-out battle for freedom from the Turk left a modern emerging nation exhausted and with major economic problems, only to be faced by two world wars and a bitter civil war. It is small wonder that today's Greek wine industry should be thought of as a new enterprise which began in the 1960s.

In fact, a number of the large companies were founded in the 19th century, but their main concerns were brandy and ouzo, with wine very much an afterthought. Such wine would be sold directly from the barrel, and only during the 1960s did the idea of bottling before sale slowly spread. Moreover, the taste of these wines was dictated by the Greek palate of the day, which on the whole was for wines high in alcohol, low in acidity and frequently oxidized.

During the 1960s to 1980s the picture was altering. The Wine Institute in Athens had been created in 1937 to help and advise winemakers, and from 1952 it began to formulate a quality wine system which became law in 1969. The most spectacular advances came during the 1980s, with the arrival of temperature-controlled technology combined with a new wave of young, enthusiastic oenologists, many of whom had trained in France, Italy or Germany. At the same time the national palate was also changing, with a growing demand for fresher, clean and fruitier styles.

Today the Greek wine trade has a new element. The major firms, who may own vineyards, buy most of their grapes from small farmers and often produce wine in a number of different areas throughout Greece.

The Meteora rocks, Thessaly.

Local cooperatives produce wine from their members' grapes. They may sell under their own label, or sell on to other producers, or both. Now there is a third type of company: the small, often family-run enterprises that grow their own grapes, and occasionally buy those of growers with whom they work very closely.

RETSINA

A Greek speciality, retsina in strict terms is an aromatized wine, with links back to classical times when wine was transported in pottery amphorae that needed to be sealed. The seal, made with a mixture of plaster and resin, excluded air and enabled the wine to keep better. This seal lent a slight flavour to the wine and it came to be believed that this was the reason the wine lasted. This led to the practice of adding resin to "keep" wine.

Today retsina is made like any other dry white wine, but small pieces of resin from the Alep pine are added to the must, and are then left until the first racking of the young wine.

Production here is relatively small and is mostly sold on the home market, where there is a big demand, but some is available for export.

By and large the export market is dominated by some 20 firms: the best-known are Boutari, Kourtaki, Tsantali and Achaia-Clauss. Other names that can be found include estates such as Hadjimichali, Lazaridi, Gerovassiliou, Carras, Kokotos, Strofilia, Tselepos and Gaia, and the Muscat wines from the co-ops of Samos, Lemnos and Patras.

Climate and soil
Lying between 33° and 40° north, Greek vineyards are in the hotter zones, but this is often alleviated by the influence of the sea and sometimes by planting at considerable height, 650m (2,145ft) or more. Climatic conditions tend to be stable, but there are still vintage variations.

Generally the soil is poor, with no predominant type. It is usually rocky, with chalk, schist, loam, clay, sand and, particularly on some of the islands, notably Santorini, with volcanic subsoil and pumice.

Grape varieties
There are about 300 native grapes in Greece, many of them highly local and with distinctive flavours. Just over half the 150,000ha (370,500 acres) planted are for winemaking; the rest are for eating or for the dried fruit industry.

Important white-wine varieties include Assyrtiko, which holds its acid well, has a lot of flavour when it is fermented with temperature-controlled technology, is found on Santorini and is spreading to other areas; Rhoditis, a pink-skinned variety from the Peloponnese, also now being planted in Macedonia and the area around the city of Thebes; and Savatiano from the Mesogea area in

Attica, the basic grape for the best retsina but now found, on the right sites, to produce good dry white wine. Other white-wine grapes include the pink-skinned, delicate, aromatic Moscophilero from Mantinia, the Robola from Cephalonia and the Vilana of Crete.

Important red varieties include Agiorgitiko, or St George, which produces the wines of Nemea; Limnio, an ancient variety originally from Lemnos, but now growing successfully in Halkidiki in northern Greece, where it makes full-bodied wines with ageing capacity; and Xynomavro, native to northern Greece. Mandelaria is widely planted on the islands, giving tannic wine of enormous colour, while Mavrodaphne, found mainly around Patras, makes a fortified red wine of considerable character.

During the last decade, there have been plantings of international varieties everywhere in Greece, but only in small quantities (less than 5%). These varieties include Cabernet Sauvignon, Merlot, Syrah (with excellent results), Grenache, Chardonnay, Sauvignon Blanc, Gewürztraminer, Ugni Blanc and a tiny amount of Viognier in southern Greece.

Wine styles

Greece makes a large range of wines: dry white and red wines, sweet Muscats, fortified red Mavrodaphne, and sparkling wines. Between 65 and 70% of the annual average production of around 3.5 million hectolitres is in white wine, but this includes retsina. Most of the wines, particularly the whites, are made for early drinking; but areas such as Naoussa and Nemea can produce wines that will age. And a number of the new small estates make wines, mainly from Cabernet Sauvignon, that will take long ageing.

Wine laws

Greek wine law provides for two categories of wine: quality wine from a delimited area and table wine, each subdivided into two classes. The term Controlled Appellation of Origin is applied to sweet wines from the Muscat and Mavrodaphne only, and each bottle bears a blue seal under the capsule. Dry wines take the term Appellation of Origin of Superior Quality, and their seal is printed red on pink. There are about 50 wines from 27 delimited areas. Labels may also show the words Reserve or Grande Reserve, indicating wines of extra quality with longer ageing.

Cava is a term used to describe high-quality table wine that is produced in small quantities, and aged for a long time.

Table wines also embrace *vins de pays*. Greece has a number of these areas, producing some interesting wines. Permitted grapes for *vins de pays* often include non-Greek varieties, and many of the wines blend Greek and non-Greek grapes. Important *vins de pays* include Crete, Attica, the Peloponnese and Macedonia.   □

MAIN GREEK WINE REGIONS AND APPELLATIONS

The North
Northern Greece, consisting of Macedonia and Thrace, specializes in red wines. The Xynomavro grape dominates the areas of Naoussa, Amindeo and Goumenissa. Amindeo also produces a sparkling rosé wine.

The other appellation area is Côtes de Meliton in Sithonia, where a mixture of grapes is grown, producing white wines from Rhoditis, Assyrtiko, Athiri and the rare, flavoursome Malagouzia, sometimes blended with Sauvignon Blanc; and red wines from Limnio and Cabernet Sauvignon.

Central Greece
Central Greece (Epirus and Thessaly) has three appellation areas. North-west of Ioanina, Zitsa produces a dry, or medium-dry, lightly sparkling white wine. Rapsani, on the foothills of Mount Olympus, is home to red wine (always dominated by the Xinomavro grape), while Ankialos is a dry white from Rhoditis and Savatiano grapes.

The Peloponnese
The southern peninsula has a large number of appellations. On a high plateau near Tripolis, the Moscofilero grape makes the aromatic white wine of Mantinia, while Nemea, near Corinth, makes a fruity red wine from the St George. This native variety of enormous colour is held to have a great potential for fruity quality wines, with fine and silky tannins, which can greatly improve when aged in new oak.

The appellation Patras is given to the dry white wine from the Rhoditis grape grown on the hillsides around the town of the same name. Muscat of Patras (or Rion de Patras) is a dessert wine, a *vin de liqueur*, while Mavrodaphne of Patras is a fortified red wine of about 15%Vol, made from the grape of the same name, and well matured in oak.

The Islands
Among the Ionian islands Cephalonia alone has appellation wines; the most important is the Robola, a big, dry white.

The Aegean islands of Lemnos and Samos produce fine sweet wines from Muscat grapes. Muscat of Lemnos is a *vin de liqueur* made by adding wine distillate to unfermented must; a dry version is also made but it is seldom seen off the island. Wines from Samos can be *vin de liqueur* (Samos Doux), *vin doux naturel*, made by stopping fermentation, or Samos Nectar from sun-dried grapes.

Paros and Santorini are the major appellations in the Cyclades, the former giving a dry red wine from a blend of deep-coloured Mandelaria with white Monemvassia, while Santorini makes a powerful dry white wine from Assyrtiko, and a sweet wine called Vissanto.

Rhodes is home to a dry white wine from the Athiri and a dry red from the Mandelaria, but also makes sparkling table wines by different methods.

Crete has three appellations for dry (and also sweet) red wines — Archanes, Daphnes and Siteia — while both white and red wines are made at Peza. Cretan wines tend to be rich and powerful, made from local varieties such as Kotsifali and Liatiko (red) and Vilana (white).

TURKEY

Turkey has a history of winemaking longer, probably, than any in the world, but since most of its population is Muslim it might not seem best placed to take advantage of it. Kemal Atatürk did his best to revive the wine industry in the 1920s, but even now, although Turkey is the world's fifth biggest producer of grapes, with some 600,000ha (nearly 1.5 million acres) under vine, only about 1.5% of the grapes are turned into wine (about 250,000 hectolitres).

This is not because of a great aversion to alcohol. The population may drink only an average of one litre of wine per head, but they get through 1.5 litres of raki (aniseed-flavoured and 40%Vol of alcohol) and four litres of beer. Raki is the drink around which culinary culture is based; wine is for social drinking. This is aided by Turkish law, which states that wine must be between 11% and 13%Vol of alcohol, but hindered by high taxes which raises its price by about 35%; and there is no imported wine.

All this sounds like the recipe for an embattled wine industry, using old techniques to produce wine for a local minority taste, with no awareness of the outside world. But things are not that bad. The vineyard area has been shrinking but yields have risen, particularly in the Aegean and Thrace, so overall production has not fallen by the same amount. And while the government may not actively promote the wine industry, in fact the state-owned producer, Tekel, is the biggest in the country.

State production accounts for nearly 90% of the total, though neither state nor private sectors are working at full capacity. The grapes are grown by peasant farmers, who sell them to the 22 state-controlled and 124 privately-owned companies; it is quite common for grapes to be trucked long distances from vineyard to winery. At least one private producer, Diren, picks and moves grapes only at night to avoid the risk of spoilage. Most vines are bush-trained and the official number of grape varieties is 1,250, though only 50 or 60 are grown commercially. European varieties tend, not surprisingly, to be concentrated in the west. Production is split almost equally between red and white wines, with only a very little rosé made. Vinification and maturation is often in cement or in old wooden barrels, with the larger companies now being equipped to make wine to suit Western tastes.

These wines make a fascinating comparison with those of other Black Sea countries (see p470), most of which are emerging from collectivized Communist systems. There is the same solidity of fruit, the same old-fashioned and highly characterful reds (old-fashioned need not be a derogatory term). Some whites are not bad, but the high alcohol levels and lack of temperature-controlled fermentation tells against them.   □

REGIONS AND PRODUCERS

The seven main wine-producing regions, and producers, are described below.

Tekel
The state producer. Hosbağ, a Gamay from Thrace (Trakya) is one of theirs, as is Buzbağ, a powerful red made from Boğazkere grapes in Anatolia.

AEGEAN
This region, based on the districts of Izmir, Manisa and Denizli, accounts for some 20% of Turkish wine production. Grape varieties, red: Çalkarasi, Grenache, Carignan; white: Sémillon.

BLACK SEA
A coastal region based on Çorum and the Tokat Valley. Grape varieties, red: Dimrit, Sergikarasi, Boğazkere, Öküzgözü; white: Narince, Kabarcik.
Diren A family company based in the Tokat Valley, with an annual production of about 500,000 cases of wine. The best bine is Karmen Reserve, made from Boğazkere and Öküzgözü grapes.

EASTERN ANATOLIA
Wine production is centred on Elaziğ. Grape varieties, red: Öküzgözü, Boğazkere; white: Narince.

MEDITERRANEAN REGION
Centred on Burdur. Grape variety: the red Dimrit.

MID-ANATOLIA
Winemaking is centred on the cities and regions of Ankara, Kirikkale, Neuşehir, Kirşehir and Niğde. Anatolia has very severe winters and hot summers. Grape varieties, red: Kalecik Karasi, Papazkarasi, Dimrit, Irikara, Çalkarasi; white: Emir, Hasandede.
Kavaklidere An old-established private winery near Ankara, producing one of the country's best red wines from the local Ozel Beyaz grape.

SOUTH-EASTERN ANATOLIA
Centred on the districts of Gaziantep, Mardin, Urfa and Diyarbakir. Grape varieties, red: Horozkarasi; white: Dökülgen, Kabarcik.

THRACE AND MARMARA
The heart of Turkish wine production, accounting for 40% of the whole. Centred on Tekirdağ, Canakkale, Edirne, Kirklareli and Bilecik. Grape varieties, red: Papazkarasi, Adakarasi, Karaseker, Gamay, Pinot Noir; white: Yapincak, Beylerce, Sémillon, Clairette, Riesling.
Doluca A private company founded in 1926, near Istanbul and the Marmara Sea, with an annual production of 625,000 cases of wine. Villa Doluca (Gamay, Cabernet Sauvignon and Papazkarasi) is Turkey's most popular red. There is also a semi-sweet, slightly sparkling Moskado.

THE LEVANT

The Eastern Mediterranean, if Turkey (*see* opposite) is included, is a region which every wine lover ought regularly to toast. Every time a bottle of vintage port is decanted, or champagne lifted from the ice bucket, thanks should be given to the Levant: because here, in this parched landscape of fig and olive, is where it all began.

For thousands of years before Christ, wine was being made here: it was a staple of life, produced as routinely as bread or fruit. It continues to be so, but the world's vinous attention has moved elsewhere: it was the cradle of the vine, but wine has long since grown up and left home.

There have been attempts over the years to modernize the various national wine industries in this part of the world, and some of them have succeeded and are succeeding. The climate is hot and dry, the vines are usually hardy but not necessarily of high quality and the winemaking, on the whole, is equal only to the requirements of the local market. Parts of California and Australia turn out perfectly creditable wines in conditions equally unpromising. There is nothing wrong with the wine industries in any of these countries that could not be cured by research and investment, but it would take years of one and millions of pounds of the other.

Château Kefraya and Château Ksara in the Lebanon prove that quality can be achieved; they make the finest red wine not just of the Lebanon but of the whole region. Some way behind in quality come the Golan Heights wines of Israel. Being kosher, they point to another major influence on the development of wine in this area: religion.

Three of the world's major religions, Christianity, Judaism and Islam, are widely practised here.

Pruning vines in Cyprus.

Judaism demands kosher wines, and this has shaped the Israeli wine industry. Islam's prohibition of alcohol appears sometimes to be more honoured in the breach than the observance, but where a large part of the population is Muslim, the wine industry is unlikely to be either high-quality or flourishing.

ISRAEL

Modern Israel's wine industry was founded by Baron Edmond de Rothschild, who established vineyards in the 1880s, using French varieties. In 1906 the company became a growers' cooperative, Carmel, which exports its kosher wines to a worldwide Jewish market. There are currently 3,035ha (7,500 acres) of vines in Israel, producing grapes for Carmel and 13 other companies.

Kosher wines for religious purposes are customarily sweet and red. They are produced to high standards of purity but either the juice or the

wine is usually pasteurized, which reduces quality. Israeli tastes have, in recent years, swung to drier wines, but even so the most important point for a practising Jew is usually that a wine is kosher: taste tends to come second. But when the new Golan Heights Winery began to attract attention in the early 1980s with kosher red and white wines that were grown in cooler climates, from grapes such as Sauvignon Blanc, Chardonnay and Cabernet Sauvignon, its effect was to galvanize the whole Israeli wine world. The Golan vineyards, like Château Musar's in the Lebanon, are planted at high altitude (up to 1,100m/ 3,630ft) and coincidentally are also in a disputed zone. The Carmel cooperative, which had been suffering from under-investment, has since put $8,000,000 into new equipment. The complacency of the captive market has gone.

LEBANON

Lebanon's two main producers are Château Kefraya and Château Ksara, each with an annual production of 1,600 to 2,000 tons of grapes and 12,000 to 15,000hl of wine; grapes of low quality are used for distillation of arak, an aniseed-flavoured local drink. Both estates have some 300ha (740 acres) of vines under cultivation. New plantings of international grape varieties during the 1990s have shown excellent results, producing several wines of worldwide fame.

Château Musar, founded in the 1930s by the father of the present owner, Serge Hochar, is probably the best-known Lebanese estate. Its cellar houses millions of bottles with vintages from 1953 onwards. The property buys its grapes from growers in the Bekaa Valley and has a winery in Junieh on the coast.

CYPRUS

Improvement has seemed imminent in Cyprus for some years, but has yet to happen. The fortified wine has the potential for high quality, but seldom achieves it. The table wines are made from grapes grown at an altitude of up to 900m (2,970ft) in the Troodos Mountains but have generally spent too long sitting in the sun between picking and processing for the results to be fresh and fruity. There is, however, a government vine-pull scheme to reduce the poorest, coastal vineyards, and the alcoholic, tannic, unexciting red Mavron grape may no longer be planted. Even so, it accounts for 70% of the vineyards with the runner-up, the white Xynisteri, taking only 13%. Other vines grown are Cabernet Sauvignon, Grenache, Lefkas, Malaga, Shiraz, Palomino, Chardonnay and Riesling.

The famous Cyprus dessert wine, Commandaria, was popular with the crusading order of the Knights Templar in the 12th century. White Xynisteri and black Mavro Kypriako grapes are dried on mats in the sun to concentrate the sweetness for about ten days before fermentation. There are 14 villages included in the classified zone, the best being Yerasa, Zoopiyi and Kalo Chorio, but most Commandaria these days is simple commercial wine.

Cyprus sherry, generally low-quality fortified wine, may no longer call itself sherry after 1995.

OTHER COUNTRIES

Egypt, a secular state, has one wine producer, Gianaclis; most of the vineyards are given over to table grapes, raisins or grape juice. Syria, Jordan and Iraq all have vineyards, but only a little wine is made, and it is rarely seen on export markets. □

REGIONS AND PRODUCERS

The biggest commercial wine producers in the area are in Israel and Cyprus. Lebanon and Egypt each have one sizeable concern.

ISRAEL
Israel's wine regions are divided into several sub-regions:
Shomron, with sub-region Sharon, in Samaria.
Negev
Shimshon in Samson, with sub-regions Dan, Adulam and Latroun.
Galil in Galilee, with sub-regions Canaan, Nazareth, Tabor and Cana.
Harei Yehuda in the Judean Hills, with sub-regions Jerusalem and Beth-el.

Golan Heights Winery Known locally as the Hatzor winery, and collectively owned by eight local settlements, it has currently about 500ha (1,235 acres) in production. The vineyards produce good-quality red and white wines from French varieties in a cooler climate — they rise from the foot of snow-capped Mount Hermon. The Gamla range is the most basic, with Golan in the middle and Yarden at the top. All are kosher, though since the winery is outside the Biblical area of Israel it does not need to leave the vineyards fallow every seventh year. The soil is volcanic and techniques Californian.
Carmel The biggest Israeli wine company, with 70% of the market, producing only kosher wines. The company is a growers' cooperative and was for years unwilling to update its equipment; as a result the wines, while still meeting kosher standards of purity, have been poor by other criteria. That has now changed, and the new-style wines are just beginning to appear. The top of the range is the Rothschild series.

LEBANON
Château Kefraya With a sub-soil of 55% of clay and proper rootstocks, no irrigation is needed for this vineyard. Its Grande Cuvée 1996 — 60% Cabernet Sauvignon, 20% Syrah and 20% Mourvèdre — has received 91 from Parker.
Château Ksara A radical change has taken place with the arrival of Charles Ghostin, who has brought to this estate Europe's best grape varieties. Delightful

Chardonnay, aged in new oak and stirred on the lees, as well as good reds.
Château Musar Until recently Levant's top wine estate. There have been several superb vintages, particularly in 1977.
Other producers Ch Nakad, Ch Massaya, Nathalie Touma, Abou Nader and El Adem.

CYPRUS
Cyprus wineries generally make a range of wines: sweet Commandarias as well as dry red and white table wines. There are 24,000ha (59,300 acres) of vineyards, concentrated in one large area stretching south and west from the Troodos Mountains. The big four Cyprus producers between them control 75% of the market. Sometimes Commandaria from small producers can be found: it is worth seeking out.
Etko Cooperative with a brand called Nefeli which is a relatively fresh white wine made from the Xynisteri grape. Other brands are Olympus, Cornaro Grenache and Carignan, Rose Lady, Semili, White Lady and Grand Commandaria.
Keo One of the big four producers whose best-known brands are Othello, Aphrodite, Bellapais, Thisbe and Commandaria St John.
Laona "Arsos" Model Winery Government-run producer, concentrating on experiments with superior grape varieties. It makes only table wines.
Loel One of the big four producers whose brands include Palomino, Amathus, Orpheo Negro and Commandaria Alasia.
Sodap Producer whose brands include Afames, Arsinoe, Danae, Kolossi, Kokkinelli, Santa Marina and Commandaria St Barnabas.

EGYPT
Gianaclis
Egypt's only wine-producer, making 66,000 cases a year from Cabernet Sauvignon, Colombard, Grenache, Muscat, Palomino and Ruby Cabernet. It is based in Abu Hummus, north-west of the Nile delta. It makes such brands as Omar Khayyam (which should not be confused with the Indian sparkling wine of the same name) and Reine Cléopâtre.

NORTH AFRICA

France colonized North Africa in stages, and she left it in stages. Her first stop was Algeria, where French colonists settled as early as 1830; Tunisia followed, but only in 1881, and Morocco was not colonized until 1912. In each country they developed large-scale wine industries. Fifty years later the French were preparing to leave: Tunisia in 1955, Morocco in 1956 and Algeria in 1962. They took with them most of the best winemakers, who settled in Corsica and the Midi and started again; and they left behind them a legacy of French grapes, French tastes and French wine law.

These days that legacy is wearing pretty thin. Islamic fundamentalism is a threat to wine, especially in Algeria, but there have been other blows, too. France had originally envisaged Algeria as a market for French wine, but in the late 19th century Algeria turned supplier instead. Indeed all three colonies exported bulk wine to France, which was widely used for blending with less concentrated, less alcoholic and less well-coloured wine — most famously Burgundy.

When France left, that trade stopped. With little domestic market, each country pulled up vines and sold what it could to the thirsty USSR; but by the late 1980s that outlet, too, was disappearing. General economic decline at home and the rising prices of raw material have been more insidious enemies. In each country the area of wine grapes has shrunk to less than half what it was pre-independence, and yields have fallen as the vineyards have been neglected.

Vineyard areas

North African vineyards are all near the coast, with the better-quality wines coming from the hills a little way inland. Morocco is the only country with an Atlantic coast, and

Horse-drawn plough at work in a vineyard at Enfidaville, Tunisia.

the cooling effect of this benefits its wines; as in the other countries, however, huge areas of the coastal vineyards have been uprooted. In the hills the vines may grow up to 1,200m (3,960ft); the cooler climates found at high altitudes are crucial to the quality of the wines.

Grape varieties and wine styles

There is still an ethnic market in France for North African wines, but it is hard to see why anyone else should want them. They most resemble the unimproved wines of the Midi, but these days there is so much fruit and freshness flowing from the south of France that consumers are increasingly unwilling to tolerate anything else. Indeed it is all too easy to forget that Carignan, left to itself in a hot climate, can make spectacularly fruitless and harsh wine, as can Cinsaut, Aramon and Alicante Bouschet, all of which red varieties are North African staples. There are also non-French varieties such as Farhana, Hasseroum,

Rafsai, Zerkhoun; and there are some very good French grapes such as Cabernet Sauvignon, Syrah and Mourvèdre. Grenache tends to get over-alcoholic and flabby, and Pinot Noir thrives best in much cooler climates than North Africa's, although both varieties are planted. But it is Carignan that dominates. White wines are made from Clairette and Ugni Blanc, with the best whites being Muscats from Tunisia. These have their own appellations and can be sweet or dry.

The best North African red wines come from Morocco. Moroccan winemaking is probably the most up-to-date in North Africa. The majority (85%) of production is red, and most of the rest is rosé, a very pale, almost white, wine sometimes called *vin gris*. The reds can be rich and chewy, but the whites are not successful.

Algeria has had a well-developed quality wine system since colonial days, when there were 12 VDQS areas. The best wines are the reds from the mountain vineyards. □

WINE REGIONS

Algeria, Morocco and Tunisia all base their wine law on the French system of *appellations d'origine contrôlée*. Many of the vineyard names reflect this heritage. Wine names vary: much wine is exported in bulk, not bottle, and label names depend on the bottler.

ALGERIA

The quality wine zones are concentrated in the provinces of Oran and Alger on the Mediterranean coast. Seven zones are officially recognized for producing *appellation d'origine garantie* (AOG) wine.

ORAN

Oran has always been the largest winemaking province, with the best-quality wines.

Coteaux de Mascara

An AOG zone, traditionally making Algeria's best wines, big rustic reds. Noted vineyards include Clos Faranah and Sidi-Brahim. Whites are also made.

Coteaux de Tlemcen

Another high-quality AOG area, on sandstone hills near the border with Morocco, making red, white and rosé wines of fair quality: powerful yet quite soft.

Other zones in Oran

Ain-Temouchent, Ain-el-Turk, Sidi-Bel-Abbès, Messarghin, La Sanca, Arzen. Monts du Tessala is AOG.

ALGER

The country's second-largest winemaking province has some superior vineyards in the cool mountainous areas.

Miliana

One of the esteemed "mountain" vineyards, celebrated for their quality in colonial days, which continues to make strong red wines.

Médéa

An AOG zone of high-altitude vineyards, making red wines of some finesse.

Dahra

More mountain vineyards, close to the sea, on the borders of Alger and Oran provinces. Haut Dahra makes red and white AOG wines.

Mostaganem-Dahra

This region splits into four sections: Picard-Dahra for low-yielding hillside vines; Dahra-Mostaganem for red, white and rosé wines of some power; Mostaganem for the same; Rivoli-Mazagran for low-yielding strong reds, stronger rosés and whites.

Other zones in Alger

Ain-Bessem and Coteaux du Zaccar are AOG areas; the former generally produces better wines. Oueds Issers and Sebdou make mostly wine for everyday drinking.

MOROCCO

Morocco has 15,000ha (37,000 acres) devoted to wine grapes, with 12 *appellation d'origine garantie* (AOG) regions.

Berkane and Angad

A small area in the east, making earthy red wines.

Meknès and Fèz

The biggest region, producing good reds from high-altitude vineyards beneath the Atlas Mountains. Appellations here include Guerrouane, Beni m'tir, Sais, Beni Sadden and Zerhoune. The wines can be rich and chewy.

Gharb

This includes the appellations of Gharb and Zemmour. From here and to the south comes Gris de Boulaouane, a popular, light rosé.

Rabat

Here on the Atlantic coast are the appellations of Chellah and Zaer, making light red wines.

Casablanca

Coastal vineyards that include the appellation of Zenata.

TUNISIA

Under a wine law of 1957, Tunisia has a four-level classification system: *vins de consommation courante, vins supérieurs, vins de qualité supérieure*, and *appellation d'origine contrôlée*.

The vineyards are in the north-east of the country, east and west of the capital, Tunis. Red wines were the best under French rule, though Tunisian rosé was fashionable for a time after World War II.

Today, it is the Muscats that provide the country's best wines. The vineyards around Bizerte in the north specialize in Muscat, as do those near Hammam-Lif outside Tunis, and around Grombalia and Bou-Arkoub in the east of the country.

The royal stables at the wine town of Meknès, Morocco.

THE DANUBE
AND THE BLACK SEA

—

AMONG THE COUNTRIES IN THIS WIDE AREA

SOME ARE WELL-KNOWN FOR WINE, SUCH

AS HUNGARY; WHILE OTHERS, SUCH AS MOLDOVA,

ARE EMERGING FROM DECADES OF OBSCURITY.

—

THE DANUBE AND THE BLACK SEA

Hungary is on the same latitude as Burgundy; Romania as Bordeaux. The Danube basin has vineyards as large as France, with a further belt following the Black Sea coast from Moldova round to Georgia.

Wine regions

‑‑‑ international boundary

N

| 0 | 100 | 200 | 300 km |
| 0 | | 100 | 200 miles |

BOHEMIA
Prague
CZECH REPUBLIC
Brno
Valtice
MORAVIA
SLOVAKIA
Pezinok
Nitra
Bratislava
Tokaj
BUKKALJA
MATRAALJA
Eger
Sopron
Budapest
Satu Mare
COTNARI
Iaşi
Oradea
HUNGARY
Kecskemet
Maribor
Ljutomer
SLOVENIA
PODRAVSKI
NORTH
TRANSDANUBIA
Lake
Balaton
GREAT PLAIN
POSAVSKI
Ljubljana
PRIMORSKI
SOUTH TRANSDANUBIA
Pécs
Szeged
Zagreb
VOJVODINA
BANAT
Arad
Timişoara
Tirgu Mureş
TIRNAVE
NICORESTI
ODOBESTI
Galaţi
CROATIA
Novi Sad
ROMANIA
STEFANESTI
DEALUL MARE
Ploieşti
Belgrade
DRAGASANI
MURFATLAR
Craiova
Bucharest
Constanţa
SEGARCEA
Split
SERBIA
Vidin
Danub
Silistra
Russe
NORTHERN
Svishtov
Dobrich
Shumen
EASTERN
Varna
Adriatic
Sea
Pleven
Turgovishte
Preslav
Niš
Iskür
Suhindol
BULGARIA
Sofia
Karlovo
SUB BALKAN
Sliven
Burgas
Black
Sea
Dubrovnik
KOSOVO
Kyustendil
Plovdiv
Stara Zagora
SOUTHERN
SOUTH
WEST
Assenovgrad
Haskovo
Skopje
Melnik
MACEDONIA

Elbe
Vltava
Vah
Morava
Danube
Tisza
Drava
Sava
Mureş
Morava
Olt
Jiu
Prahova
Siret
Prut
Iantra
Maritş

KAZAKHSTAN
UKRAINE
MOLDOVA
RUSSIA
ROMANIA
Caspian
Sea
BULGARIA
Black Sea
GEORGIA
AZERBAIJAN
ARMENIA

| 0 | 500 km |
| 0 | 250 miles |

THE DANUBE

FROM AUSTRIA'S FRONTIER EAST TO THE BLACK SEA, VINEYARDS DOT
THE HILLS AND PLAINS OF SOUTH-EAST EUROPE, RICH WITH
INTERESTING WINES BOTH OLD AND NEW.

The countries of south-eastern Europe, although clearly individual, share a sense of tradition which has readily absorbed outside influences. The Tîrnave region in Romania uses both indigenous and imported grape varieties in its wines.

The countries with vineyards in the Danube basin have a very real wine tradition in common, sharing grapes and wine styles. Many influences play upon the wines of this area, however: in particular the great importance of Germany as an export market, and the arrival of French classic grape varieties such as Cabernet Sauvignon and Chardonnay. The frontier of the Roman and, later, the Byzantine empires ran along or north of the Danube. The legions brought vines and wine-presses, and their rôle was taken up later in history by the monks, along with the German colonists of the Middle Ages who roamed far south and east, carrying the vine along the Danube. The long occupation by the Turks (at its height in the 16th century) halted winemaking in many areas: the Turks reached the gates of Vienna twice, and only in the late 19th century did the countries we know today take shape. After World War II, four decades of Communism switched the emphasis from peasant proprietors to large cooperatives and collective farms. Now land is being returned to its pre-Communist owners. So today we find the old wine traditions — the local grapes, styles and techniques — overlaid by the new, in the form of international grapes and wine styles, and recent if not totally up-to-date technology. Wine drinkers look to the Danube countries for good-value everyday wines, and for the occasional arcane classic like Hungary's Tokaji. For everyday wines, advice and technology from Western countries is being rapidly imported as newly vibrant wine industries seek out export markets for their products. To the wine drinker, this means more and more Danube wines with familiar names on their labels: classic grapes such as Merlot and Cabernet Sauvignon. Each of these countries has a personality, if a fast-changing one. The western half of the region — the Czech Republic, Slovakia, Slovenia and, to some extent, Hungary — takes its lead from Austria and Germany, with white wines in the majority. Romania, Bulgaria and Serbia use their own grapes and French classics and make both white and red wines. But every valley in this complex area hides a wine tradition that may be dormant now, but might well emerge in these changing times.

HUNGARY

There is something irrepressibly individual about Hungary. This comes from a national identity — Magyars isolated among Germanic and Slav races — and the lavish legacy of the Austro-Hungarian Empire. Proud of this sense of identity, which survived the attempts of communism to wipe it out, the Hungarians do things their own way. Their language is one of the most complex in Europe, as is the range of grape varieties planted in their vineyards; varieties which cannot be found elsewhere. For example, these are the people who brought us the Tokaji wine, the likes of which cannot be found anywhere else in the world. Hungary was already producing wines under Roman rule and has maintained a good winemaking tradition ever since, with a few interruptions while under Turkish occupation. Tokaji wines were being sold in Europe as far back as the 17th century and their reputation grew under Austrian rule.

The last few years have seen the establishment of many family businesses, some of which are producing wines of a remarkable quality. Particularly successful are the estates in the Villány region, in the south of the country. In the Tokaji region in particular, there are also many medium-sized businesses (50 to 150ha — 123 to 370 acres), often relating to historical estates, which have benefited from foreign investment. Finally you have large scale operations which generally buy grapes from the small producers: co-operatives, State farms (very few), former State farms, now privatised, and newly established companies with Hungarian or foreign capital.

Grapes and wine styles

Hungary is predominantly a white wine producer. Only 30% is red, and this comes mostly from the south of the country, especially around Villány

Training vines in Hajós.

and the Great Plain. Most reds are quite light in style, and even Bulls Blood is not quite as powerful as its

QUALITY LEVELS

Existing wine laws set out four levels of quality.

Asztali bor (Table Wines): generally sold in 1 litre bottles with a minimum alcohol content of 8% and a minimum of 9% sugar in the must.
Tájbor (Country Wines): originating from a specific region, they must have a minimum of 9% sugar in the must.
Minőségi bor (Quality Wines produced in a specific region): sold in 75cl bottles. They must have a minimum alcohol content of 10%. The place of origin, the grape variety and the vintage must be stated on the label. Maximum permitted yield is 100 hl/ha.
Különleges minőségü bor (Wines of Superior Quality): same criteria as the Minőségi bor but they must have a minimum 12% sugar in the must and the maximum yield is limited to 75 hl/ha. All dessert wines (late harvests, Szamorondi and Aszˉ) are included in this category.

name might suggest. The whites, when made to the local taste, are spicy and often sweetish. There is a sprinkling of noble grape varieties, both white and red — among the latter, Pinot Noir and Merlot have potential — but it would be a great shame if Hungary were to concentrate on these to the detriment of her native grapes. Investigating the qualities of these may take longer, but of the reds Kadarka — hard work to grow, and susceptible to winter frosts, but promising in quality — could be interesting. There is Kékfrankos, too, but this seldom makes exciting wine, and some Zweigelt, also found in Austria, where growers like it because it yields heavily.

The most widely planted white grape, indeed the most widely planted of all, is the Olaszrizling, alias Laski Rizling or Welschriesling. There is a lot of the rather neutral Leányka, plus Furmint, Hárslevelü, Tramini (or Traminer), Muscat Ottonel, Juhfark, Rhein Riesling (Rajnai Rizling), Müller-Thurgau (Rizlingszilváni) and Pinot Gris (Szürkebarát).

The centre and south

Hungary has around 128,000ha (316,160 acres) under vine, scattered all over the country except the far south-east. More than half the total are on the Great Plain, the name of which could not be more appropriate, both for size and flatness. The Great Plain lies south of Budapest and east of the River Danube. The climate here is one of extremes: the summers bake, the winters freeze, and the wind races across the grasslands. It races so much, indeed, that the sandy soil is apt to blow and erode, and one means of holding it down is to plant vines. The sand and the summer heat combine to produce wines that are ripe and low in acidity, quite light and without much positive regional character; most of it is white, and mostly from Olaszrizling, a grape with equally little character of its own. The Great Plain wine region is divided into three districts:

Kiskunság Mostly white wine from Olaszrizling, Ezerjó, Chardonnay and others.

Hajós-Vaskuti Mostly red wine from Kadarka, Cabernet and others.

Csongrád Mostly red wine from Kadarka, Merlot and Cabernet.

The south-west

To the west of the Great Plain, on the other side of the Danube which splits Hungary in two, lie the vineyards of the Southern Transdanubian region.

Villány-Siklós Villány-Siklós is the southernmost winemaking district of Hungary. Villány makes plummy, earthy Merlot and Cabernet Sauvignon reds that are exported, but the local specialities are the red Kékfrankos and Kékoportó grapes; the latter, with its round flavour and low acidity, is perhaps more to domestic Hungarian taste. Siklós is known for whites. The best producers are Tiffán, Gere Attila, Gere Tamás, Bock, Malatinszky, Kúria and Vylyan.

Mecsek A little further north, around Pécs, is the Mecsek district, making mainly white wines. The vineyards are on the slopes of the Mecsek hills, and grapes include Olaszrizling, Furmint, Chardonnay and Cirfandli (the Zierfandler of Austria). The soils are volcanic sand or slate, and the wines tend to sweetness.

Szekszárd Another step northwards brings red wines back into dominance. Kadarka rules in this hilly area, but there is also Cabernet, Merlot, Kékfrankos and Kékoportó, with some whites from Chardonnay, Tramini and Rizlingszilváni. The best producers are Dúzsi Tamás, Vesztergombi, Vida Péter and Möcsényi Kastélybor.

Dél-Balaton The Dél-Balaton, or South Balaton, district makes still and sparkling whites from Olaszrizling, Sauvignon Blanc and Chardonnay, plus reds from Cabernet Sauvignon. All, even the Cabernet, are on the

Vineyards run down towards the shores of Lake Balaton.

sweet side. The huge Balatonboglár wine farm and research station is on the southern shore of Lake Balaton. The vineyards are newer than those on the north shore, and include more non-native grape varieties. Noteworthy producers include Légli Ottó, Szt Donatus Pincészet and Öregbaglas.

Lake Balaton

The main Balaton vineyards are included with several other districts in the Northern Transdanubian region. The importance of the enormous Lake Balaton to viticulture in the region can hardly be overstated. It is the biggest lake in Europe, and brings with it all the tempering effects on the climate that large expanses of water can offer. The soils are sandy and volcanic.

The main grape variety of these vineyards north of the lake is Olaszrizling, but the best varieties are the native Furmint, Kéknyelü and Szürkebarát. Improved winemaking here could yield aromatic wines of great individuality.

Districts of the Balaton region are:

Badacsony Area centred on an extinct volcano towards the western end of the lake which makes white wines from Kéknyelü, Szürkebarát, Olaszrizling, Sauvignon Blanc, Rajnai Rizling, Zöldszilváni, Muskotály, Rizlingszilváni and Tramini. Szt Orbán Pincészet (Szeremley) is a good producer.

Balatonfüred-Csopak Further east, again on the lake shore, making whites mostly from Olaszrizling. Good wines are produced by Figula.

Balatonmellék Produces mostly white wines from near Lake Balaton. Kál-Vin and Dörgicse Bor are two good producers.

Somló Hungary's smallest wine district, with 500ha (1,235 acres), situated on another extinct volcano, away from the lake to the northwest. Somló produces white wines from Furmint, Juhfark, Muscat Ottonel, Olaszrizling and Tramini. Noteworthy producers include Györgykovács, Inhauser and Fekete.

Mór and Sopron Further away from the lake, but still in the Northern Transdanubian region, Mór and

Sopron yield wines with higher acidity, white in Mór and red in Sopron.

Sopron is more temperate in climate than the rest of Hungary, situated in the first foothills of the Alps in the west of the country. Sopron borders another lake, the Fertö Tó or Neusiedlersee of Austria (*see* p358). Winters are milder here, and summers cooler and wetter. Sopron makes red wines from Kékfrankos, Pinot Noir and Cabernet, and whites from Zöldveltelini, Tramini and Leányka. Most of Sopron's red is from Kékfrankos, though the Cabernet can be more exciting.

Mór is a district midway between Budapest in the east and Sopron in the west, quite close to the Slovakian frontier. It specializes in the white Ezerjó, fairly neutral but with good acidity on this loess and sandy soil. Hilltop Neszély and Weninger are two good producers.

The northern region

It is the north of the country that produces most of the wines that have built Hungary's greatest fame abroad. Bulls Blood comes from here, and on a rather higher level, so does Tokaji. Here, too, is the Australian-inspired Gyöngyös estate.

Eger The old city of Eger is the capital of a district whose most famous product has been the red wine known as Bulls Blood, or Egri Bikavér. Bulls Blood is made mostly from Kékfrankos grapes, with some Cabernet Sauvignon, Cabernet Franc, Merlot and Kékoportó. Once made principally by the Egervin winery, under present wine laws both Egri and Szekszárdi Bikaver are recognized. The original legend maintains that the 17th-century siege of Eger by the Turks was overcome by the Magyars because of their copious consumption of the wine, leading the Turks to think their opponents drank the blood of bulls. Today's Bulls Blood, a commercial blend, rarely lives up to the legend. Good producers include Gál Tibor, Thummerer, Pók Tamás, Tóth István and Vincze Béla.

Checking for clarity in the cellars of the Tokaji Wine Trust at Tolcsva.

Bükkalja A sizeable district in the foothills of the Bükk Mountains, near Egri, specializing in white wines.

Mátraalja A large and diverse district on the southern slopes of the Mátra Mountains, west of Eger, producing mostly white wines of all styles from Olaszrizling, Rizlingszilváni, Tramini, Szürkebarát, Zöldveltelini, Leányka and Muscat Ottonel. At the Gyöngyös estate Australian-trained winemaker Hugh Ryman produces clean, crisp Sauvignon Blanc and Chardonnay. He was one of the first Western winemakers to invest in Hungary and has revolutionized winemaking at the estate. The wines are soundly made, immensely attractive varietals that compete in both price and quality with middle-ranking Australian wines. Other good producers are Szölöskert (Mátra Hill) and Szöke Mátyás. Nagyréde, a village in the Mátraalja district, has gained a reputation for fresh, fruity wines, including good rosé. The northern region of Tokaji is described below.

The future of wine in Hungary

Prior to the ending of Communism in Hungary, winemaking standards had fallen behind what the rest of the world expected, yet the wineries are well-equipped, with up-to-date presses and vinification equipment, and the vineyards are in good heart with the right clones, and yields that are not too high. Yet however modern the winery, and however good the grapes, if they are mishandled the wines will not be up to standard — and that, all too often, has been the case. Like those of most of eastern Europe, Hungary's wine industry was wedded to quantity, while its greatest hope for the coming years lies in quality, to coax much-needed hard currency from abroad. A new wine law to bring the wine industry in line with EC patterns is in the making, but it is outside investment that will really change the face of Hungarian wine. This has started with the internationally popular grape varieties; applied to Hungary's best native grapes it could produce something very special.

TOKAJI

Louis XIV of France hailed the Tokaji as the king of wines. At the time it was the most prized wine in Europe, valued as much for its medicinal qualities as for its rich flavour and refreshing character. Today it is just as remarkable, if only because of the original way in which it is made. Its ageing potential is astounding: the best vintages can be aged for two centuries. The 7,000ha (17,297 acres) of vineyards in the Tokaji region are planted on volcanic soil in Hungary and eastern Slovakia, not far from the Russian border. They overlook the Bodrog valley where autumn mists cause the noble rot, or *Botrytis cinerea* (see Sauternes, p163), in the two main grape varieties, Furmint and Hárslevelü. The third variety, Yellow Muscat, is sometimes sold separately.

How Tokaji is made

Described for the first time by the Monk Szepsi Laczkó Máté in 1631, the method used to produce Tokaji wine is completely unique. The botrytized, concentrated grapes (*aszú* berries) are picked individually during successive harvests beginning at the end of October. The *aszú* berries, initially stored separately, are then incorporated in dough form (or whole) to wine or must (base wine or base must), soaked for a period of one to three days, and then pressed. Fermentation often lasts for many months. The number of hods (*puttonyos*, sing. *putton*) of *aszú* berries added to each 136 litre cask (Gönci cask) determines the richness and quality of the wine: 3,4,5,6 *puttonyos*. The richest of all is the Aszú Eszencia. The *aszú* wines are aged for several years in oak casks stored in age-old cellars, sometimes several kilometres long, where temperature and humidity levels remain constant. The walls of these cellars are covered in a unique fungus, the Cladosporium caellare, which contributes to the good climatic conditions of the cellar.

Nowadays, however, controlled oxidation (in full *barriques*) is preferred. The *barrique* ageing period has been reduced by law to a minimum of two years for the *aszú* wines, although current practice is between two and four years depending on characteristics. The bottle ageing of *aszú* wines is of great importance.

Wine produced in Tokaji is not always *aszú*. In years when the noble rot has not affected all the bunches of grapes and the botrytization process has been hampered by unfavourable climatic conditions, the healthy grapes and those affected by noble rot are vinified together in the usual way. The wine produced in these lesser years is called Szamorodni, which may be dry or sweet. At the other end of the quality spectrum is Eszencia, from the name of the juice which runs freely from the *aszú* grapes. It is so rich in sugars that it may only reach an alcohol content of 3% after several years fermentation. This nectar, too rich and syrupy to be drunk on its own, is generally kept for blending but anyone who has tasted this (incredibly expensive) wine will not forget it in a hurry.

Recent developments in Tokaji

Unfortunately the centralised State Farm has been bending the rules and, for some time now, the age-old traditional Tokaji winemaking process has been replaced with industrial practices and you will not find a single putton in the cellars. Only a few small farms have been actually blend-ing the botrytized berries with the wine in the manner described above. The State Farm officials adhered to the correct proportions of the blend, thus gaining some sort of authenticity for the last forty vintages of Tokaji wines.

Since 1991, several historic estates have been re-established, among them the former imperial estate of Hetszölö. Due to the extremely lengthy ageing process, it will be ten years before the newly independent estates will achieve their target: a return to the *aszú* wines specific to each vineyard which made the region famous. The State Farm did however manage to produce remarkably good wines, given the scale of production, and so the division of this great vineyard into smaller units should lead to a significant increase in quality.

Main investment in the Tokaji region has been in the Disznókö Estate (AXA-Millésimes, France), Hetszölö (GMF, France-Japan), Oremus (Vega Sicilia, Spain), Degenfeld (Lindner, Germany), Château Pajzos et Megyer (Laborde, France) and the Royal Tokaj Wine Company (a British group of which Hugh Johnson is a member). Initial results are very promising and these estates are producing complex, fruity *aszú* wines which are elegant, yet powerful. The best recent vintages are 1993, 1997 (very limited quantities) and 1999.

The best producers are Disznókö, Szepsy, Hetszölö, Oremus, Gergely Vince, Pajzos, the Royal Tokaj Wine Co. and Degenfeld.   □

STYLES OF TOKAJI

WINE	Sugar contente	Extract	Years in cask
Dry Szamorodni	0–10	25+	2
Sweet Szamorodni	10–50	25+	2
Aszú 3 *puttonyos*	60–90	30+	5
Aszú 4 *puttonyos*	90–120	35+	6
Aszú 5 *puttonyos*	120–150	40+	7
Aszú 6 *puttonyos*	150–180	45+	8
Aszú Eszencia	180–240	50+	10–20

(Sugar content and extract expressed in grams per litre)

BULGARIA

Of all the countries of eastern Europe, it is Bulgaria that has made the greatest impact on the wine drinkers of the West. Since the mid-1970s ripe, well-made Bulgarian Cabernet Sauvignon has been a regular feature of many a table in Britain, Scandinavia and Germany, a rival to the minor clarets; but since the end of Communism in Bulgaria it has no longer been enough to think of the wine generically, as simple Bulgarian Cabernet Sauvignon. The picture has become more diverse, with more wineries, more grapes and more varied styles of wine appearing on export markets; and the white wines, traditionally less exciting and less well-made than the reds, are improving rapidly.

Bulgaria, situated between the Black Sea in the east and the republics of the former Yugoslavia in the west, is in the part of the world that might have been intended by Nature for vinegrowing. It has a broadly continental climate of hot summers and cold winters, with the temperature ranging from 40°C (104°F) to –25°C (–13°F). The Black Sea tempers these extremes in the east of the country, but the west is more firmly continental.

History and structure

Whether Nature or man provided the initial impetus, wine was grown in Thrace, what is now Bulgaria, 3,000 years ago: Thracian wine is mentioned in the Iliad of Homer. But while this is a long history it is not an uninterrupted one: domination by the (Muslim) Ottoman empire meant that from 1396 to 1878 vinegrowing went on only on a local scale. Only after 1918 did winemaking really begin to thrive. The advent of Communism after World War II meant the collectivization of the vineyards along with the rest of agriculture, and

it was only in the mid-1970s that the wines began to take their familiar modern shape.

The need to export wines shaped the present wine industry. Demand came first from the former USSR, which had a seemingly insatiable thirst for sparkling wine and sweetish table wine. Western involvement came with the US firm Pepsico, which wanted to sell its fizzy soft drink in Bulgaria but did not want either Bulgarian currency (had such a thing been possible) or, say, tractor parts in return. In order to get wine that would be saleable in the West, it put the Bulgarians in touch with such leading figures of the Californian wine industry as Professor Maynard Amerine of the University of California, Davis. Certain wineries, fired with Californian enthusiasm, began to forge ahead.

Great swathes of Cabernet Sauvignon and other classic varieties were planted on the wide, rolling countryside north and south of the Balkan Mountains, which divide the country horizontally. Before collectivization there had been vineyards not just here but also on the steeper slopes of the foothills; these however were neglected in the rush for higher and higher yields and have yet to be replanted. When they are, these old hill vineyards might yield Bulgaria's finest wines yet.

The structure of the Bulgarian wine industry is thus geared to producing large volumes of well-made wine tailored to foreign (but not always Western) tastes. Progress was by no means uniform. The *Controliran* regulations, which define the geographical origins of the better wines, were supposed to reflect regional character, and were a step forward. Some wineries seized the export opportunities offered, while others lagged behind in quality. The princi-

pal wine zones were divided more according to administrative convenience than by soil or climate. There was a limit, too, on the degree of individuality encouraged in wineries. A standard training system of just over 1m (3.3ft) high was established for all vines, even though some, like the native Mavrud, might benefit from a different approach: possibly bush training. And as in other Communist countries, marketing was carried out by a central organization, Vinimpex; another central body, Vinprom, controlled production.

Bulgarian wine today

From the mid-1970s until the mid-1980s the Bulgarian wine industry flourished. The first intimation of change came in 1984, when President Gorbachev of the USSR took the first of his measures to restrict the alcohol intake of the Soviet citizens; aimed primarily at vodka, this nevertheless affected all Comecon wine-exporting countries. Bulgaria's exports of wine to the USSR fell from 25 million cases to 14 million cases in a single year, and then to 8.3 million cases the next year. The result was a massive vine uprooting programme, combined with restrictive measures like a freeze on the price of grapes: nearly half of Bulgaria's vineyards were destroyed, and some of the rest were neglected. There has been some replanting since, particularly of Chardonnay, but in 1990 production of wine was 20 million cases, down from 50 million in 1985.

In 1989 the Communist government fell and in 1990 the wine industry was liberalized — at 36 hours' notice. In 1991 the Law of Restitution was passed, which sought to restore land to those who could prove family ownership prior to 1947. Most of the vineyards were then quickly transferred to private hands. No change in the use of the land is permitted for five years, but the law cannot enforce proper care of vineyards, and the new owners may live in the cities and be unable to look after their new acquisitions, or they may just not be interested in viticulture. Privatization for the wineries was more gradual.

Vines and vineyards

Whatever the uncertainty of the early years after Communism, the basics are unlikely to change. Roughly half of Bulgaria's wine is red and half white, and it is made in over 130 "agro-industrial complexes" that grow a large number of other crops besides grapes.

Vines cover about 110,000ha (270,000 acres), or 4% of the country. Three-quarters of the vineyards are planted with non-native varieties; and of red grapes, a massive 75% are either Cabernet Sauvignon or Merlot. The Cabernet Sauvignon in fact is king, followed by Merlot and Pamid, and then Gamza, Mavrud, Melnik, Pinot Noir and Gamay, among the red grapes; of the whites, the most planted variety is the Rkatsiteli.

Each winery uses a wide variety of grapes, and while there are regional leanings — to red wines in the south, and whites in the east — nowhere is there the sort of specialization found in western European countries, with grape varieties selected to match local conditions. Greater specialization would be to the advantage of quality. It would have to be instigated by the wineries themselves, which are the driving force of the industry in the aftermath of Communism.

It would be a shame, however, if market forces were to dictate that every winery should concentrate on Cabernet Sauvignon and Chardonnay to the exclusion of native varieties. Mavrud, for example, has great quality potential. It is grown in the central southern region, with 100ha (247 acres) around Assenovgrad, where most of it is found. It has small berries and low yields and

The Melnik grape, growing beneath sandstone cliffs near the Pirin Mountains.

is difficult to cultivate, but when it ripens properly (which is late in the year) it gives dense, tannic and long-lasting wine that can be compared to that from the Mourvèdre of southern France.

Melnik is another indigenous red variety. It comes from around the town of the same name in the southwestern region, near the border with Greece. The local wineries don't do as much with it as they could, and both vineyard care and vinification could be better.

Gamza is widely grown — possibly because it has large berries and will suck up water to give large yields, if it is allowed to. In these instances it makes pallid, thin wine that oxidizes quickly; it needs lower yields to produce its best wines with depth and the ability to age.

Of the native white varieties, neither Dimiat nor Misket (a crossing of Dimiat and Riesling) offer great quality, though they can be attractive when properly made. Rkatsiteli is not strictly speaking a native grape, since

it is found in other countries bordering the Black Sea, and may have been imported from Georgia. It is rather neutral in flavour, though could have potential if it is well made.

Not all Bulgarian wineries are equipped to get the best out of any grape, native or imported. The top ones have rank upon rank of stainless steel fermentation tanks, perhaps with *barriques* for ageing some of the reds and the best Chardonnay; others may lack the basic equipment to control fermentation temperatures and the malolactic fermentation. Where the latter is the case, red wines are more likely to survive in drinkable shape than whites. It is therefore increasingly important for wine drinkers to differentiate between one winery and another, just as one would in any other serious wine region.

Labels will need to be studied with more care: it is no longer enough to ask for just "Bulgarian Cabernet". Some of the best wineries are listed over the page.

WINE REGIONS

Bulgaria is divided into five wine regions, which between them account for the entire country except for the area around the capital, Sofia. The Balkan Mountains (in Bulgarian, *Stara Planina*) divide the country climatically as well as physically, separating the hotter south, with its rich, full wines, from the cooler north, where the wines are more refined and imported, classic grape varieties dominate. Native Bulgarian grapes are concentrated more in the south.

Wines are clearly labelled, with winery name (often that of the district) and grape variety, plus quality category (*see* box).

The town of Melnik in the South-western Region.

South-western Region

The South-western Region, close to the Greek border, is by far the hottest. Its speciality is the red Melnik, grown around the town of that name. The wineries at Petrich and Harsovo, while improving, are not among Bulgaria's best and do not really do justice to Melnik's potential. The Cabernet Sauvignon is soft and ripe.

Southern Region

The hot Southern Region is predominantly a red-wine producer, at least in terms of quality. Mavrud and Pamid are important here (the former especially in Assenovgrad) and there is some Cabernet Sauvignon, Pinot Noir and Merlot — the last being particularly good from the Haskovo, Stambolovo and Sakar areas.

Mavrud from Assenovgrad is a *Controliran* wine; dark and spicy, it can age well. The district is sited where the ground rises to the Rhodope Mountains that form the border with Greece.

Eastern Region

The Eastern Region, which takes in the whole of Bulgaria's coast, benefits from the cooling effects of the Black Sea and produces Bulgaria's best whites, including those from the Preslav and Shumen dis-

tricts. Despite great improvements, quality can still be unreliable. The best producers are Trimontium and the Boyar estate at Shumen and Yambol, which produces ordinary wines but also *barrique*-aged quality wines.

The Preslav winery is one of Bulgaria's white wine stars. It was selected in the mid-1970s to export whites to the West, and still makes the best in the country. It controls the wineries of Khan Krum and Novi Pazar, and used to include Shumen, which is now independent. Khan Krum could surpass Preslav in quality in the future. Both make good Chardonnay, of which the Reserve wines are aged in new oak.

The winery at the spa town of Burgas on the Black Sea coast has a typically Eastern Region bias towards white wines (about 65% of the vineyard). The Country wines can be attractive, particularly those made from the Aligoté grape.

Sub-Balkan Region

The Sub-Balkan Region, as well as making attar of roses, grows a lot of white grapes, plus Cabernet Sauvignon and Red Misket from the district of Sungulare.

Northern Region

The best red wines come from the hilly Northern Region. It is here that the Suhindol winery is located. Suhindol built the international fame of Bulgarian Cabernet Sauvignon, and incidentally made a name for itself in the process, but today it is not necessarily the best producer.

Suhindol was the first exporting winery in Bulgaria to be handed over to private owners. It also controls the Vinenka winery, which is one of the country's oldest, producing very good Cabernet Sauvignon and good Merlot.

The Russe winery is one of the best in Bulgaria. The most important single grape variety here is Cabernet Sauvignon, and the wine is made to high standards in a well-equipped and up-to-date establishment.

QUALITY LEVELS

Under the wine law of 1978 there are four quality categories:

Country Wines are young, intended for early drinking, and are usually blends of two grape varieties.

Varietal Wines are wines of denominated geographical origin. The reds generally have some age, the whites do not. Some, particularly the Mavrud, are sold as Premium Wines.

Special Reserve Wines are from selected vineyard sites, from grapes that have been carefully selected. They are made in small volumes.

Controliran Wines are made from named grape varieties in specific vineyard sites. To gain *Controliran* status, three consecutive vintages must be submitted to the state authority. In subsequent years the wine may be declassified if it is not up to standard. There are about 27 *Controliran* wines. Names include those of many of the leading wineries. The word *"Controliran"* is prominent on labels.

Reserve Wines may be from any quality category, provided that they have two years' ageing (for whites) or three for reds. Most Reserve Wines are, in practice, the better Varietal Wines.

ROMANIA

Romania has a long winemaking history: the Greeks brought vines to the Black Sea 3,000 years ago, and later the medieval Saxon colonists introduced Germanic grape varieties to the region of Transylvania. However, phylloxera struck in the 1880s, destroying many grape varieties. Replacement vines, such as Pinot Noir, Cabernet Sauvignon, Merlot and Sauvignon Blanc, were introduced from France, while some indigenous varieties have remained, including Tămaiîoasă Romanească, Fetească Albă and Fetească Regală (white), and Fetească Neagră (red).

With about 260,000ha (640,000 acres) Romania is high in the table of the world's wine-producing countries — well ahead of its Balkan neighbours — and grapes are an important part of the rural economy. Most of the wine is consumed locally, with the result that only a tiny amount travels outside the country.

The vineyards are split into eight regions, which in turn are divided into 50 appellations. The system of appellations is modelled on France, while the classification scheme looks to Germany, with wines graded according to their potential alcohol and time of harvesting. The lowest classification is table wine of no specific origin (8.5% to 10.5% of alcohol); then there are country wines, still without a specified origin (10.5% to 11.5% of alcohol); and finally appellation wines (with a minimum of 11.6% of alcohol). Chaptalization is virtually unknown: any application for permission is hampered by bureaucracy, but more significant is the fact that sugar is simply too expensive. For the same reason most Romanian vineyards are virtually organic, as they cannot afford chemicals to control rot and treat disease.

As the most northern wine-producing country of the Balkans,

Romania has the coolest climate and consequently white wines predominate. In all but the most southerly of the wine areas, red grapes ripen with difficulty except in particularly warm vintages.

Wine regions and styles

The best wines of Romania, and those most likely to be seen outside the country, come from four main regions: Tîrnave; Cotnari; Dealul Mare; and Murfatlar. The region of Tîrnave in Transylvania, north of the Carpathian Mountains, has vineyards in poor soil on a plateau between two rivers, the Tîrnave Mare and Tîrnave Mică, and benefits from a mild microclimate. The vines — Fetească Albă

COTNARI

In the last century the pale, honeyed sweet wines of Cotnari acquired a certain reputation alongside Hungarian Tokaji. In the Cotnari region in the north-east of Romania, near the city of Iaşi, autumns are usually dry and sunny, which enables the grapes to be left on the vines until late in the season so they become dehydrated and shrivelled and their juice rich and concentrated. Noble rot is rare, occurring only in exceptional years.

Cotnari is made from Grasă, Fetească Albă, Tămaiîoasă Romanească and Francusa (all of which may also be found as single-varietal wines). Grasă provides richness and can be susceptible to noble rot; Fetească Albă contributes finesse; Tămaiîoasă, said to smell of frankincense, gives aroma; and Francusa adds acidity to a wine that could otherwise be cloyingly sweet.

Each variety is vinified separately and then blended, usually 30% each of Grasă and Fetească Albă and 20% each of Tămaiîoasă and Francusa. Large oak barrels are used, both for fermentation and maturing the wine for a couple of years before bottling. Cotnari can age well, especially from the best vintages.

and Fetească Regală, Riesling Italico, Muscat Ottonel, Sauvignon Blanc and Pinot Gris — make white wines with good aroma and firm acidity.

On the southern foothills of the Carpathians are the vineyards of Dealul Mare, near the industrial town of Ploieşti, north of Bucharest. Here the climate is warmer and some red grape varieties are grown, most successfully Pinot Noir, as well as some Cabernet Sauvignon, Merlot and Fetească Neagră. Tămaiîoasă is also good here. There is a research station, with modern facilities.

The warmest region, and also the driest, is Murfatlar, near the port of Constanţa. Here Cabernet Sauvignon is at its best, benefiting from the warming influence of the Black Sea to produce some ripe flavours.

There are other appellations producing wines of less interest on the Banat plain in the west; Segarcea, Stefanesti and Drăgăşani in the south; Odobeşti and Nicoreşti in the east.

The future for wine in Romania

Like everything else in Romania, the wine industry is in a state of transition. Land is being returned to its former owners as the enormous state farms are dismantled and the cooperative system abandoned. However, farm and cooperative wineries remain, for at present they alone have the capacity to vinify the grapes and bottle the wine. Cellar facilities vary considerably, but some have benefited from investment in new equipment and technology. Danish and British investors are taking an interest in wineries and the GTZ, a German technical co-operative body, is advising Romanian producers. The Carl Rey winery has planted 200ha (494 acres) of vineyards. The problems are all too apparent but the potential to make good wine is undoubtedly there. □

SLOVENIA

S lovenia is a very recent country, resulting from its split with the former Yugoslavia in 1991. With a population of two million, it now has 21,400 ha (52,879 acres) of vineyards.

At the time when Slovenia was still part of Yugoslavia, it only accounted for 6% of Yugoslavia's annual wine production. Along with Serbia and Kosovo, Slovenia was a large wine exporter. Nowadays Slovenian wineries are fairly well-equipped with stainless steel vats standing alongside old oak casks and concrete vats. Although most of the vineyards have been rapidly privatised, each region has its own central winery and these alone account for 97.5% of the country's annual wine production (700,000 cases in equal quantities of red and white). The rest is produced by a growing number of private producers, around 150 of which already bottle their own wines. They are proud of their cellars, whatever their size (one or two vats or a line of black oak casks).

Under the communist regime, each person was allowed to own 10ha (25 acres) of land. In actual fact, most people own less than that and, as it is traditionally used to cultivate various crops, many growers own less than a hectare of vines. Most choose to grow a mixture of grape varieties and these vary from region to region.

The best producers are the Movia Estate, which has for years played an avant-garde role, the Bjana Estate in the south-west, the Kupljen Estate, Vipava Cellars (1,700 ha/4,200 acres) in existence in the Primorska region since 1894 and the Valdhuber Estate. Of the other eight republics in the former Yugoslavia, Croatia was the largest wine producer (46%, two thirds of which white), followed by Serbia (17%, 70% of which was red). In the aftermath of a painful period of peace, it is Serbia which

Harvest time in the Podravski region.

should be best equipped to produce quality wines. Croatia, with 54,000ha (13,345 acres) of vineyards producing a good red for everyday drinking, has got off on the right footing. The Amselfelder, one of the best-selling brands of red wine in Europe, came from Kosovo. It is a Pinot Noir wine originally aimed at the German market. As a result of the war, the brand's owners were forced to move production to Italy where its rather sweet commercial style can be reproduced with ease.

Quality categories

Until the republics of the former Yugoslavia pass their own separate wine laws, the Yugoslavian wine law of 1974 is still in force in Slovenia. This allows for High Quality Wines, Quality Wines, Table Wines with Geographic Origin and Table Wines. The wines are allocated a category by a tasting panel and so, in theory, they can vary in their category from year to year. The tasting is backed up by a chemical analysis. No chaptalization (*see* p109) is permitted for the High Quality Wines. □

WINE REGIONS

Slovenia has three major wine regions: the Primorski or Littoral region, on the Adriatic coast near Italy; the Podravski or Drava Valley region, in the north-east, near Austria; and the Posavski or Sava Valley region, in the south-east. Major investments have been made in the following regions:

Primorski
Part of this region is a continuation of Italy's Collio area, in the Friuli-Venezia Giulia region, and the wines from here are distinctly Italianate in style. Among red wines there is good Merlot, sometimes *barrique*-aged; and Cabernet Sauvignon. Often excellent whites include ripe, dry and spicy Pinots Gris and Blanc, light, well-structured Chardonnay and often subtle, apricoty Malvasia. The local speciality is the red Refošk: dark, acidic and an acquired taste.

Podravski
The country's best wines, and certainly the best whites, come from the Podravski region in the north-east, which includes the Ljutomer sub-region. Here there are grape varieties, and white wine flavours, reminiscent of Germany and Austria at their best: Rulandec (or Pinot Gris), Rhein Riesling, Traminéc (or Traminer), very good, pungent Sauvignon Blanc and *botrytis*-affected dessert wines. Even the Laski Rizling, when drunk locally rather than exported, can be fresh and attractive.

The Ljutomer-Ormoz sub-region has the country's best-quality vineyards and two huge cellars, Ljutomer and Ormoz. Ormoz is the larger and has a distinct edge in quality terms; the wines exported under the Lutomer label come from both wineries and, it should be said, are a poor advertisement for both. The potential of the *terroir* has yet to be reached. There are a number of good villages in the region: one, Jeruzalem, is supposed to have been founded by Crusaders on their way to fight the Saracens, but who liked the wines too much to leave.

Posavski
Wines from south-east Slovenia are generally sound but less than exciting.

CZECH REPUBLIC AND SLOVAKIA

The wines of the former Czecho-slovakia were, until the demise of Communism, among the least known in Europe. Most countries of the Eastern bloc exported wines to their Comecon neighbours, but not Czechoslovakia; with the exception of a trickle of wine to Poland, Czechoslovakia kept the produce of its vineyards entirely to itself, and imported beer as well.

When this inward-looking wine industry did seek guidance, however, it sought it from the USSR, with the result that the wineries were run by one ministry and the vineyards by another, grape prices were heavily subsidized by the state and the wine, after facing numerous hazards during the winemaking process, was finally bottled in re-used bottles which might contain traces of detergent or other undesirable substances. That so many wines retained enough potential to attract Western invest-ment proves the underlying promise.

Regions and grape varieties

Quality, and potential quality, is fairly equal across the two Czech regions of Bohemia and Moravia (16,000ha/ 49,500 acres), and the state of Slova-kia. Bohemia, being the coldest region, has the fewest vineyards, just about 400ha (988 acres) north of Prague. Moravia, to the east, comes second and Slovakia has 26,000ha (64,245 acres), some two-thirds of the former Czechoslovakia's vineyards.

Grape varieties are unsurprising in a country that borders Germany, Austria and Hungary: principally Frankovka (Germany's Limberger) and St-Laurent, plus a little Pinot Noir, for reds; and Pinot Blanc, Traminer, Roter and Grüner Veltliner (both, despite their names, are white grapes), Müller-Thurgau, Silvaner, Rhein Riesling, Laski Riesling, the native, aromatic Irsay Oliver, a little

Sauvignon Blanc, and Pinot Gris for the whites. About 60–85% of the wines are white.

Vines are grown on collective farms, which might extend over thousands of hectares, with grapes being only one crop among many; however, the vines usually seem to get the most suitable spots.

Privatization — or restitution — surged ahead early in Czechoslova-kia, although changes in the use of land over the decades of Commu-nism complicated the issue. Privat-izing the wineries was a simpler matter, with each central winery (those with a bottling line) and its satellite wineries (those with just vinification and storage facilities) becoming a separate company.

Wine styles

The wines of the Czech Republic and Slovakia can be compared in style to those of Austria and Hun-gary: when well made they are dry, ripe and crisp, often quite light, with very good varietal fruit. The red wines from Pinot Noir, when they are good, are very good. The climate is continental; warm and dry in sum-mer with cold winters. Since the har-vest is in October or November, problems with overheating fermen-tations are minimal, even without cooling systems.

If most of the wines are northerly in style, the exceptions are those that come from Tokaji. These vineyards, generally thought of as producing a uniquely Hungarian wine, in fact extend a little way over the Slovakian border. (Some of the cellars are reputed to pass beneath the frontier.) Under the Communist regime the Czechoslovakian government leased these vineyards to Hungary in exchange for beer, but in the early 1990s the 700ha (1,730 acres) were returned to Slovakian control, along with the right to the name. Develop-ments are awaited with interest. □

PRODUCERS

Wineries are emerging from state control and establishing individual identities, and small producers and cooperatives are also active.

Nitra

One of the major wineries in Slovakia, taking its grapes from southwest-facing hills in the west. More by accident than design, wines from the spicier, more aromatic grapes, such as Irsay Oliver, tend to be made here, with Western advice.

Pezinok

A Slovakian winery in the Little Carpathians region in the west of the country, making a variety of wines under Western supervision.

Saldorf

A relatively small Moravian (Czech) winery producing, among other varieties,

Ruländer, Rhein Riesling, Sauvignon Blanc, Müller-Thurgau and Grüner Veltliner, exported to the West under the Archioni label. Some of them (not the Grüner Veltliner) age well.

Valtice

A medieval castle once owned by the Liechtenstein family, now having access to 1,100ha (2,718 acres) of vineyards in Moravia (Czech Republic). With Western advice it makes white wines from Rhein Riesling, Grüner Veltliner, Welschriesling and the rare Grüner Sylvaner; reds from Frankovka and St-Laurent.

Znovin-Satov

A large Moravian (Czech) winery producing sturdy wines imported to the UK and elsewhere under the Moravenka label, more old-fashioned in style than Nitra's Western-influenced wines.

THE BLACK SEA

THE COUNTRIES AROUND THE BLACK SEA WHICH HAVE EMERGED
FROM THE FORMER USSR HAVE THE POTENTIAL TO ADD INTERESTING
STYLES AND FLAVOURS TO THE WORLD'S WINE LIST.

Bottles nearly a century old slumber in the Tsars' cellars at
Massandra in the Crimea. The calibre of these old vintages
alerted the outside world to the potential for the making of
quality wines around the Black Sea.

The USSR used to be the great puzzle of the vinous world. It grew grapes for wine all along the Black Sea coast; it was variously reported as being the third or fourth largest producer in the world, and visitors came back with travellers' tales of sweet "champanski" — and of bottles which were labelled identically but which clearly contained different wines, probably from different regions and different grapes. The few examples that found their way to Western markets were generally damned as being well-nigh undrinkable.

Then in April 1990 Sotheby's in London auctioned 124 different wines, including vintages from 1830 to 1945, from the Russian Imperial Cellar at Massandra in the Crimea: over 13,000 bottles in all. Lots of them were good; some were very good. Suddenly there was evidence that Russia had once known how to make wine. Around the same time proof of more recent skills began to appear. Splendid, sturdy reds from Moldova (formerly Moldavia) from vintages in the 1960s, 1970s and the 1980s attracted attention. As the old USSR disintegrated, it began to be possible to assess each of the winegrowing republics. These are, from west to east, Moldova, the Ukraine (including the Crimea), Russia, Georgia, Armenia and Azerbaijan. In the past their wines could be sent in bulk to be bottled anywhere in the USSR; this goes some way to explain the odd lack of correlation between label and wine. It also explained the often appalling quality: everything was geared to hot bottling, a technique which effectively cooks the wine and stops any danger of refermentation or bacterial infection. Such wine is stable — and dead. Even before its journey to the bottling plant, the wine would have been well-travelled. The structure of the old USSR wine industry is still in place in the republics. It is based on a system of "first-stage" wineries, which ferment the must and send the wine on to "second-stage" wineries, whose task it is to age and sometimes bottle it. The vineyards are generally separately run. The future of these vineyards is uncertain, as political and technical change accelerates. Already Moldova shows signs of becoming a supplier of good-value red wines. The other Black Sea states are not far behind.

Modernization

The Black Sea countries face problems of modernization as great as any in eastern Europe, and greater than most. The biggest limiting factor in each country is the lack of that most basic (if least interesting) item, the up-to-date bottling line. Because so much bottling was done outside the wine regions in the past, many wineries have no bottling line of any sort, and those that do have one generally have the wrong type, not suitable for producing quality wines.

Other shortages are equally fundamental: 75cl bottles, essential for exporting to the EC, are hard to come by, and labels, corks and capsules can all be rarities. One British importer solves the capsule problem by taking bottles sealed over the cork with sealing wax, in the way that vintage port sometimes is.

In the past wineries used to share resources, so any shortages could be eased by cooperation. But the break with Moscow has resulted in greater autonomy, and wineries that previously worked together are now, to some extent, in direct competition.

Privatization has been slower than in eastern Europe. Wine is a crucially important industry in these countries — particularly in Moldova, where it is the most important of all — and no government is rushing to relinquish control. However, as individual wineries take over their own marketing, more and more wines will be seen abroad.

With a steady trickle of Western winemakers arriving to investigate the prospects of making wines specifically to suit Western tastes, the wines are likely to become fresher, fruitier and more commercial.

MOLDOVA

The further east one goes, the less familiar the wines are likely to be to Western palates. Moldova is the most European: there are more European varieties in its 160,000–200,000ha (395,000–495,000 acres) of vineyards than in any other republic, and the huge wine farms may have 18,000ha (44,460 acres) at a time of Chardonnay, Cabernet Sauvignon, Sauvignon Blanc, Aligoté and the Pinot family. The native red Saperavi is an excellent grape, rich, spicy and tannic; the native white Rkatsiteli seems mostly dull and neutral, but some observers believe it has a future, if well made. It's a small country, not more than 350km (217 miles) from north to south, and vines are grown everywhere except the far north; the best, however, come from the middle and round the Dniester River, and while there are undoubtedly some top-class sites, they are still awaiting identification. Yields are remarkably low — 20–40hl/ha.

Moldovan equipment and techniques, while ahead of those of its neighbouring republics, are still behind those of, say, Hungary — but the potential, particularly for red wines, is enormous. Much of the ageing is slow and careful, in old oak barrels, and vintages from the 1960s can taste astonishingly fresh.

Moldova produces 44–50 million cases of wine a year, which puts it on a par with Bordeaux. Its wines are categorized by a system of "vintages", a "vintage" being a year that produces ripe grapes with a natural sugar level of ten Baumé or over. In the more northerly vineyards only one year in three qualifies as a "vintage"; in the south, where the best reds come from, every year is a "vintage".

UKRAINE

Moldova's neighbour along the Black Sea coast is the Ukraine, a country with vineyards that are flatter than those of Moldova and, like the latter, on the same latitude as Bordeaux. The similarity cannot be taken much further, however. Ukraine's speciality is white wine and, particularly in the Crimea, sparkling wines. It produces Sauvignon Blanc, among other grapes, but the style of the still white wines is not close to Bordeaux.

The range of grapes is not as great here as in Moldova. The Ukraine's principal grapes are Rkatsiteli and Aligoté, and while there is some Rhein Riesling its style owes little to the Rhein.

As well as sparkling wine, the Crimea region of the Ukraine makes a speciality of fortified and dessert

GRAPE VARIETIES

The Black Sea countries between them can muster a great many grape varieties — there are said to be over 1,000 in Georgia alone. The former USSR did a huge amount of research on the subject. Access to this research (which is in Russian, and in Moscow) would, no doubt, help to establish how many of these are actually synonyms for the same variety. Major grape varieties grown in these countries include:

WHITE
Aligoté: widely grown
Chardonnay: Moldova, Ukraine
Fetjeaska: Moldova, Ukraine
Furmint: Moldova
Italian Riesling: Moldova
Krakhuna: Georgia
Mtsvane: found in Georgia; often blended with Rkatsiteli

Muscat: widely grown, high quality
Pinot Blanc, **Pinot Gris**: Moldova, Ukraine
Rhein Riesling: widely grown
Semillion: synonym for Sémillon
Tsitska: Georgia
Tsolikouri: Georgia

RED
Aleatico: Crimea
Bastardo: Crimea
Cabernet Sauvignon: widely grown
Malbec: Moldova, Ukraine
Matrassa: Ukraine, Azerbaijan
Merlot: Moldova
Muscat: widely grown, high quality
Plechistik: Russia
Saperavi: widely grown, high quality

wines, from grapes grown along a narrow coastal strip of land. The vineyards are sloping but mostly low-lying, and even with irrigation, yields are low. The climate here is warm, with mild winters and summers that are not excessively hot. The sparkling wines come from further north and may be made by the traditional method of secondary fermentation in bottle, the *cuve close* method, or by the Russian "continuous" system, an invention that pumps base wine and yeast through a series of tanks with finished wine constantly emerging at the other end.

Winter vineyards near Kishinev, in central Moldova.

RUSSIAN REPUBLIC

Sparkling wine is made in most of the ex-USSR countries, but in the Russian Republic the greatest potential might be found in still red wines, made from grapes which include Cabernet Sauvignon. Reds are made in the south and east of the country, with whites and sparkling wines being produced in the north and west. The grape varieties include Muscatel (for dessert wines), Silvaner, Riesling, Cabernet Sauvignon, Aligoté, Pinot Gris, Pinot Noir, Plechistik, Pukhjakovsky, Tsimlyansky and the ubiquitous Rkatsiteli.

GEORGIA

Georgia is a giant step away from the familiar in both vines and winemaking. There are few European grape varieties apart from Muscat.

There are three basic methods of making wine in Georgia. The "European" method involves fermenting the must without the skins. The Imeretian method means vinifying the must partly with the skins in large underground jars that in some respects resemble the *pithos* of Ancient Greece and the traditional *tinajas* of Spain.

The third method, the local Kakhetian system, means the skins are left in contact with the wine for three to five months. White wines (or

rather dark yellow, tannic wines) made this way are not at all to Western tastes, but the Georgians themselves love them.

In addition, the old USSR wine law stated that all wines, red, white or fortified, in all the republics, had to be aged for three years in wood before bottling. Not surprisingly, local palates are not attuned to fruit or freshness in their white wines.

Georgian taste also runs to high sugar levels, in reds as well as whites. On the home market wines are still identified by the very Soviet system of giving them a name and a number, the name being that of either the grape variety or the place where they were made — or, it seems, just about anything else: Saamo No. 30 is sweet Rkatsiteli from the village of Kardanakhi in Kakhetia, and "Saamo" means "pleasant".

ARMENIA, AZERBAIJAN, KAZAKHSTAN

Armenia and Azerbaijan both concentrate on dessert wines, with some highly alcoholic red table wines in the former and some dry whites and reds in the latter. The only other wine region to be found in the former USSR is in Kazakhstan, where white and sweet dessert wines are made from grapes grown on the shores of the Caspian Sea.　□

PRODUCERS

Wineries with long traditions are reawakening; newer ones are emerging as they modernize. Three which show the latent potential of these vast lands are:

MOLDOVA
Krikova
A Moldovan winery that has equipped itself with a brand new Italian bottling line. It makes good red Kodru, Krasny and Cabernet Sauvignon, rich and ripe.

Purkar
A Moldovan winery established in 1827, on the banks of the River Dniester. The limestone cellars are cut out of the rock and so provide ideal conditions and constant temperature. Negru de Purkar is a rich and long-lived red blend of Cabernet Sauvignon and Saperavi.

UKRAINE
Massandra
The Massandra winery in the Crimea (Ukraine) no longer makes wine, but ages it both in bottle and in barrel. It is the central winery for the coastal vineyards of the Crimea, taking wine from other wineries, but was originally built to supply wine to the Tsar's summer palace at Livadia. The wines, principally dessert and fortified, were modelled on those of western Europe: there were "ports", "málagas", "madeiras", "tokays", "marsalas", "cahors" and of course "champagnes". Many were of extremely high quality, and the dessert wines can live 100 years or more.

NORTH AMERICA

—

CALIFORNIA'S WINE MADE A MAJOR IMPACT ON THE WINE WORLD IN
THE 1970s, NOT LEAST FOR ITS EMPHASIS ON WINES NAMED BY GRAPE
VARIETY. IT HAS BEEN JOINED BY MANY OTHER STATES OF THE USA
AND FOUR CANADIAN PROVINCES.

—

Tales of the history of wine on this continent generally begin with the story of the Viking explorer Leif Ericson, who landed on Newfoundland about AD 1000. On seeing an abundance of wild vines growing there, he called this unknown land Vineland. Right from the early years of colonisation, pioneers attempted to vinify the indigenous grape but did not succeed in obtaining a quality wine and it was not until the second half of the 19th century that wine production took on some importance. The introduction of Prohibition in 1920, applying to all the United States, practically wiped out wine production and it only recovered slowly after its abolition in 1933. It is only in the last 25 years that the rest of the world has come to realise that there actually is a North American wine industry: the quality of Californian wines was met with widespread astonishment and New World wines became a force to be reckoned with. Since then, Californian wines have continued to win over connoisseurs but not all North American wines come from California. Wine is now produced in almost all the other states and in Canada, although producers, as well as consumers, are very unevenly distributed across this vast continent.

From this continent, with as diverse a range of landscapes, soils and climates as it is possible to find, comes a staggering variety of wines — from the unfamiliar Léon Millot and Seyval Blanc in the winelands east of the Rocky Mountains, to the Cabernet Sauvignon and Chardonnay that have brought California worldwide fame. The concept of varietal wines — those based on a single grape variety — is as much a part of the North American wine scene as it is in Australia and New Zealand. North America has its native varieties, which, while largely replaced by many different kinds of hybrid (usually describing a cross between French *vitis vinifera* and American *vitis labrusca*) and classic European varieties for the production of fine wines, have made an unforgettable contribution to the history of world winemaking in the form of their resistance to phylloxera. Innumerable vines around the world are now grafted onto *labrusca* rootstock. This creative solution was a product of innovative thinking, adaptability and boundless enthusiasm — the hallmarks of New World winemakers. Their enthusiasm and determination were evident in the 1970s and 1980s when efforts at grass-roots level successfully removed onerous state regulations and tax structures imposed after Prohibition to restrict the wine industry.

The modern history of North American winemaking began with the establishment of small, family-owned wineries by people who had previously worked in other (often unrelated) professions — another characteristic America shares with Antipodean wine producers. Free from the constraints of tradition, American winemakers have not been reticent in using technology: irrigation makes vine cultivation possible in the desert, and fermentation, barrel-ageing and bottling are often monitored by computer in the most sterile and antiseptic of environments. Winemaking has even been turned into something of a tourist attraction: Napa Valley in California, for example, ranks second only to Disneyland in the number of tourists that visit each year; and Canadian wineries located along the Niagara Peninsula encourage visitors to come and sample their wines.

Until the mid-1980s wines produced in the USA, even by major companies, were not made with export markets in mind, but this state of affairs is changing fast. In 1984 the total of wine exported was just over three million cases; today that figure has reached 20 million. Other than Canada, the two top markets for US wines are the UK and Japan, but new ones are opening up all the time. Compared to those of Europe, the wine industries of North America are still in their infancy. Many wine-producing regions are in an embryonic stage of development — 95% of all US wine, for example, originates in only four states (California, New York, Washington and Oregon). In the years ahead the USA especially may indeed compete with traditional, long-established wine producers in the world marketplace. When that occurs, it may deserve to be described as a vast vineland.

WINE REGIONS OF NORTH AMERICA

Vines grow from coast to coast across the USA and in four provinces of Canada. In many areas other than the major wine-producing regions — California, the Pacific North-west and New York — winemaking is relatively small-scale. It is, however, developing fast in a vast range of *terroirs* and micro-climates, the variety of which is hard to match elsewhere in the wine world. Winemaking regions are therefore likely to become more extensive.

Wine regions

- other wine areas
- international boundary
- state boundary

N

| 0 | 500 | 1000 km |
| 0 | 500 miles | |

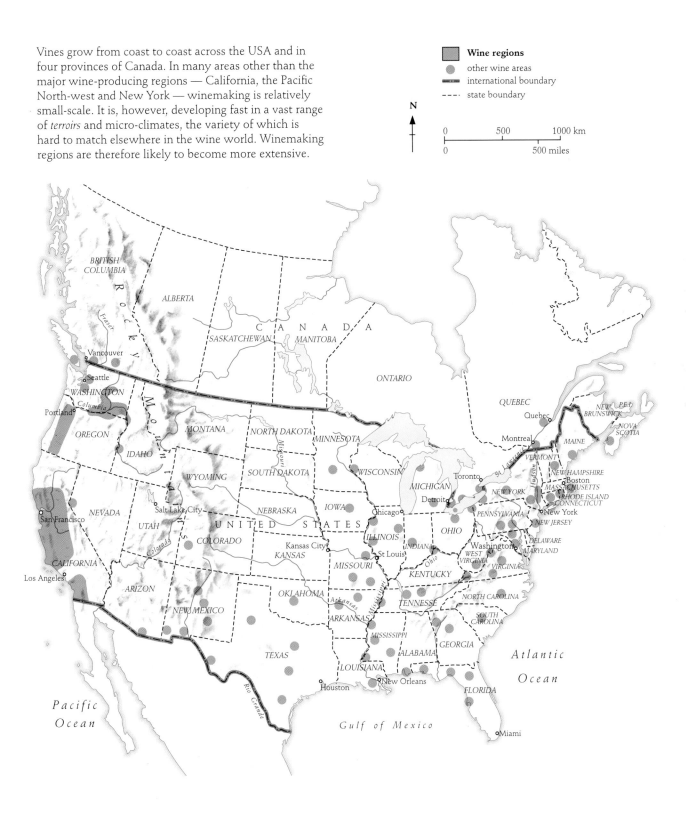

History of wine in North America

There is little doubt that by the 17th century, if not before, vines grew wild along the eastern seaboard of North America from Georgia to Canada. The first cultivated wines produced were for sacramental use. By the middle of the 17th century Jesuits were making wines at their missions in Quebec as did Franciscan missionaries in New Mexico along the Rio Grande River. (Vines may, in fact, have arrived in New Mexico from the south by 1580.)

Those vines found growing wild along the north-east and mid-Atlantic coasts were *vitis labrusca*. The best-known variety is Concord, a red grape which was developed and propagated in 1850 by Ephraim Bull,

a resident of Concord, Massachusetts. This hardy, high-yielding and disease-resistant vine was eventually planted throughout New England, the Mid-west and the mid-Atlantic coast. In the deep South another native vine, *vitis rotundifolia*, grew wild and was later domesticated. The most popular white-wine grape variety of that species, the Scuppernong, was planted from the Carolinas to Florida and then westwards to Mississippi and neighbouring states.

The earliest references to commercial winemaking are from Pennsylvania, the New England states, Kentucky and the Carolinas, using native vines. Many producers tried to find grapes suited to making European-style wines as native varieties, especially

vitis labrusca, produced wines with an unpleasant "foxy" flavour. Attempts were therefore made to import European vine cuttings of *vitifera*. The new varieties were however not resistant to diseases and parasites.

West of the Rocky Mountains, where no native grapes grow, the first wines made were from the red Mission (Criolla) grape that had been brought from Mexico. In the 1850s hundreds of vine cuttings of *vinifera* varieties from Europe were introduced into California where they adapted extremely well to the Mediterranean-like climate and growing conditions.

It was only during the second half of the the 19th century that wine production became important, at first in California (over 1 million hectolitres at the end of the century), then in Ohio, Missouri and along the East Coast, including New York State.

Prohibition

Prohibition in the USA greatly disrupted winemaking. Before this, in both the USA and Canada, winemaking enjoyed some success thanks to the energy and expertise of European immigrants. In the 19th century thriving wine industries in Ohio, Indiana and Virginia coincided with those in Missouri, New Mexico and California. But their success was short-lived, as phylloxera found its way into California by the 1880s and other vine diseases hit the Mid-west.

The vineyards that survived Prohibition were mainly those producing native varieties for grape juice, jams and jellies. In addition to Concord, popular varieties were Catawba, Norton and Isabella (all red), and Delaware, Niagara and Dutchess (whites). They were at the time good enough to produce sweet wines and the popular fortified wines — in the styles of port and sherry.

At the time Prohibition was introduced, the United States produced some 2 million hectolitres of wine, and Californian wines were reputed even in Europe. Five years later, production had dropped by about 95%

READING AN AMERICAN WINE LABEL

American wines are simply named: the name of the producer or winery is followed by the name of the grape variety, which may be qualified by "Special Reserve" status or the like.

Proprietary names once denoted cheap, everyday wines. However, innovative winemakers are increasingly producing top-quality blends and giving them original names.

Wine type   The most common wine type is the varietal, named after the dominant grape variety used, which according to US federal law must comprise at least 75% of the wine in the bottle. Oregon's varietal wines must be 90% from the named variety (with the exception of Cabernet Sauvignon, to allow for some bordeaux-style blending).

Generic wine names (such as burgundy, chablis, chianti, port, sherry, dry white, blush) are widely used by large producers, the idea being that they give a clue to the style of a wine — although the use of a European name does not mean that the wine is made from European grape varieties: any grapes or blend may be used. Oregon is, again, the exception: European place names may not be used on the label.
Region of origin   The most general regional name is "American", used for a blend from two or more states. The

regional name can also be that of a state; wines labelled California must be made wholly from grapes grown in the state. Next comes the county name: at least 75% of the grapes must come from the named county — except in Oregon, which requires 100%.

However, counties are political boundaries, not wine zones; and since 1980 US law has recognized Viticultural Areas (VAs), modelled partly on Europe's appellations, which may cross county boundaries. The VAs follow natural climatic boundaries, topographical regions or zones of specific soil. If wines bear the name of an approved VA, at least 85% of the grapes must originate in the area cited (again, Oregon's strict state law demands 100%).

The smallest regional division is the individual vineyard; if a vineyard is named, 95% of the grapes must have been grown there.
Vintage   A vintage date is optional but, if used, the wine must be at least 95% from the vintage designated.
Other information   Alcohol content and health warnings appear on all wine for sale in the USA. (Health warnings are not used on wine for export to Europe.)

In Canada, although wine laws and officially defined wine zones are different (*see* p517), wine labels present very similar information.

and in 1933, when Prohibition was abolished, Europe had all but forgotten about American wines. Many states did not resume winemaking for decades after the repeal of Prohibition, and until the early 1960s all wine-producing regions, including California, focused on fortified wines and sweet, standard table wines.

The wine scene today

Most North American wine producers did not exist prior to 1966. At least 70% of California's wineries have been founded since then; and in New York State at least 80% of the active wineries have been created since 1976. In Ontario, Canada, the first new winery licence since 1929 was issued in 1975.

In 1991 the USA became the fourth-largest wine producer in the world, after Italy, France and Spain and ahead of Argentina. During the 1980s production averaged more than 200 million cases. But when one looks at per-capita consumption compared with European countries, US figures are paltry: 8 litres per capita compared to 67 litres in France and 62 litres in Italy. The attitude to wine is different in the USA: it is generally considered to be a special-occasion drink, if it is drunk at all. Six states — California, New York, Florida, Texas, Illinois and New Jersey — consume half of the wine sold.

American grape varieties

Native *labrusca* varieties produce wines with a characteristic "foxy" flavour. Wholly American hybrids retain the *labrusca* character, whereas European/American hybrids produce wines of much more acceptable flavour. The best quality wines are those produced from *vinifera* strains.

A wide range of *vinifera* varieties are now grown across America. Any one variety can produce a range of wine styles depending on where it is grown. A Chardonnay or a Sauvignon Blanc from California, for example, can taste very different from that produced in Washington.

Wine regions

North America has six significant wine-producing regions or states.

California totally dominates US wine production. This domination is bound to continue, given the state's hospitable climate, well-established *vinifera* varieties and the international reputation of its producers.

North-western USA, which in wine terms is largely Washington and Oregon, is a fast-developing wine area that is rapidly gaining a reputation for high-quality wines.

North-eastern USA includes New York State, which is the second-largest US producer, though it represents only 3% of the total. New York typifies developments in other eastern states, where there is a shift to *vinifera* varieties in an attempt to produce more traditional wines. Other North-eastern states producing wine include the states of New England, and New Jersey, Pennsylvania and Maryland, where some of the earliest wine production on the continent took place.

The **South and Mid-west USA** may not produce significant quantities, but there are some good wines tucked away in not necessarily the most obvious places.

Canada is perhaps a surprising wine producer, given its reputation for harsh weather, but grapes were harvested here long before they were in the USA, and a quality wine industry is emerging today. □

NATIVE GRAPE VARIETIES AND HYBRIDS

Native American grapes are still widely grown, though hybrids are more widespread and *vinifera* varieties (*see under each region*) are on the increase.

Aurora Franco-American hybrid used for still and sparkling white wines that are generally unexciting.

Baco Noir French hybrid that produces quite acceptable, dark-coloured red wines.

Catawba Native American red hybrid for sparkling and blush wines.

Cayuga White Franco-American hybrid that produces a firm, dry white wine of reasonable quality.

Chambourcin Successful French hybrid making full-bodied, flavourful red wines and also used in blends.

Chancellor French hybrid producing fruity, if unexciting, red wines.

Chelois French hybrid used in blended reds and blush wines.

Concord Native American red grape producing dark, rather dull wines with characteristic native "foxy" flavour.

Cynthiana *See* Norton.

De Chaunac Franco-American hybrid producing fruity, basic red jug wines.

Delaware Native American, used for still and sparkling wines, one of the least "foxy" unless very dry.

Dutchess Native American variety, (which like Delaware does not have much of a future) with no foxy character, producing basic-quality dry white wines.

Elvira Old, native American white variety. Little grown today.

Isabella Old, native American red variety, foxy in character and dying out.

Léon Millot French hybrid producing decent, full-bodied red wines capable of ageing.

Maréchal Foch Widely-grown Franco-American hybrid producing palatable reds.

Melody Recent hybrid derived from Pinot Blanc, producing fruity, slightly sweet white wines.

Niagara American hybrid related to the Concord and the most pungently foxy grape grown. It is often used for sweet white wines.

Norton Old, native American red variety producing full, foxy wines.

Ravat Ravat Blanc, also known as Vignoles, is a Franco-American hybrid derived from Chardonnay and almost always made in a sweet (white) style.

Seyval Blanc Franco-American hybrid derived from Chardonnay and producing fruity white wines.

Vidal Blanc Hybrid derived from Ugni Blanc, used in a range of reasonable white wines including ice wines.

Vignoles *See* Ravat.

Villard Franco-American hybrids producing dull red and white wines.

CALIFORNIA, WASHINGTON AND OREGON

California's cool coastal zones yield the finest wines; the fertile, hot Central Valley 85% of everyday wine. Cooler, damper Oregon has much in common with northern European zones such as Burgundy. Washington State's hot summers, cold winters and, more importantly, cold nights mean good levels of acidity in the grapes.

California: North Coast and Northern Central Coast

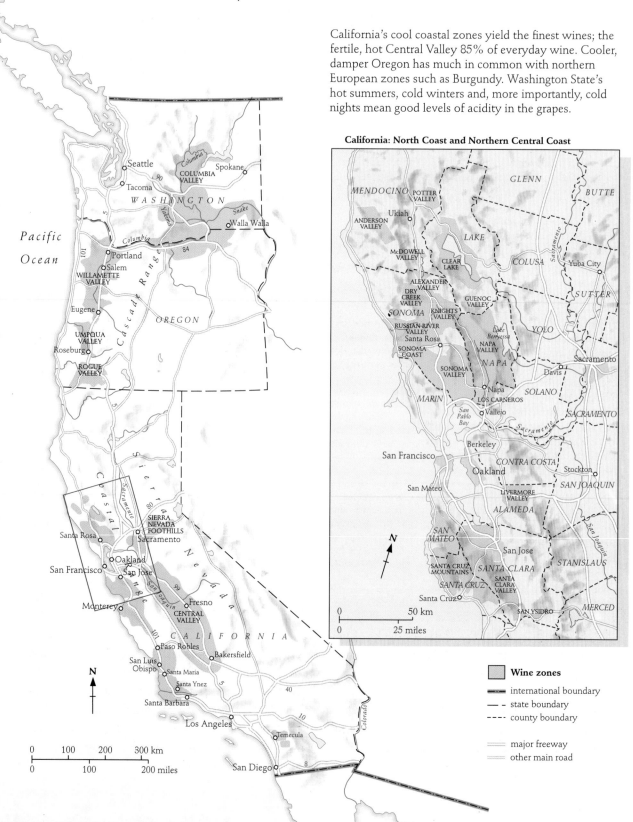

Wine zones
international boundary
state boundary
county boundary
major freeway
other main road

CALIFORNIA

A VAST RANGE OF VINEYARD SITES AND GRAPE VARIETIES, AND A HOST OF DEDICATED WINEMAKERS WITH A SCIENTIFIC APPROACH HAVE COMBINED TO MAKE THIS ONE OF THE MOST DYNAMIC AND POWERFUL WINE REGIONS IN THE WORLD.

The Napa Valley is California's foremost wine-producing region. Vichon Winery, near Oakville in the heart of the Napa Valley, is owned by Robert Mondavi, one of America's leading winemakers.

With its gamut of hospitable climates, California had been making wine for nearly 200 years; but it was only in the 1960s that sophisticated consumers in San Francisco, Los Angeles and other Californian cities began to demand an accessible source of fine wine, and winemakers with the money and determination to make such wine soon met the challenge.

The grape came to California from Spain, by way of Mexico and the Franciscan padres, who erected a chain of missions along El Camino Real (the "King's Highway", now US 101). They brought Christianity to native Americans, along with the wine necessary to celebrate the Sacrament. The Gold Rush of 1849 spread winegrowing throughout the state. Hordes of young men who had picked at the earth for flecks of yellow metal settled into more stable modes of earning a living. One of the consequences of the lively mix of settlers from varied European backgrounds was a love of wine, and the Golden State's diverse regions provided a range of vinous micro-climates under its year-round sunshine, from the chill oceanic zones along the Pacific Coast, home of fine wines, the searing heat but fertile land of the San Joaquin Valley, to the little vineyards that make distinguished wine in the snow-capped foothills of the Sierra Nevada. Having lived through recurring depressions (the big one in the 1930s), the plague of the phylloxera mite (once in the 1880s, again in the 1990s), and the deprivations of Prohibition in 1920–1933, California once again has a strong and thriving wine trade. The state produces some 170 million cases of wine each year — that is, around 90% of all the wine made in the United States.

California today is as diverse as any place the world of wine has ever known. If most of its wineries produce dry whites (from Chardonnay grapes, in the main) and dry reds (mostly from Cabernet Sauvignon and California's own Zinfandel grape), there are also enough pale pink or "blush" wines, red (and some white) Rhône-style blends and Italian varietals, enough sweet whites made from botrytized Riesling and Gewürztraminer grapes, fortified and sparkling wines, and an unending list of "miscellaneous others" to keep the most devoted oenophile happy for aeons.

California's vineyard

Of the state's 350,000ha (865,000 acres) of vines, slightly more than half are geared to wine. (Most of the remainder produces raisins, and 10% are picked as sugar-rich table grapes.) By way of crude comparison, California has about 50% more land devoted to wine than Bordeaux, yet produces three times as much wine, due in large part to grape yields of 95–190hl/ha in the interior valley. Napa and Sonoma average around 50hl/ha, similar to Bordeaux.

Wine regions

The diversity of California's wines mirrors the almost unlimited array of growing sites: grapes are grown in 47 of the state's 58 counties. To paint the picture in the broadest strokes, California can be divided into three main climatic zones. These are, from west to east:

■ the areas of coastal influence (which are found from Mendocino County in the north almost to San Diego, at the far south of the state)
■ the huge, hot Central Valley
■ the cool foothills of the Sierra Nevada Mountains.

The coastal zones are by far the most important in terms of quality wine production. The regions close to the Pacific — such as Napa Valley, Sonoma County, Lake County, Anderson Valley in Mendocino County, Livermore Valley and the Santa Cruz Mountains around San Francisco Bay, Monterey County, San Luis Obispo County, Santa Maria Valley in Santa Barbara County — are blessed with ocean, bay and river fogs that keep daytime temperatures down. This means that natural acidity in grapes is retained, so that quality table wines — crisp and lively — can be produced. Napa and Sonoma have by far the greatest proportion of land under vine and the highest concentration of wineries.

The Central Valley provides standard table wines ("jug wines") that form the economic foundation upon which quality wines are crafted. Up to 85% of California wines originate in this fertile farmland that stretches from Bakersfield to north of Sacramento. The great valley is also the source of superb dessert wines.

Increasingly, individual wineries are taking advantage of the breadth and diversity of California's vinous locations. Kendall-Jackson, from its base in Lake County, has made a name for itself with Chardonnay drawn from throughout the state. Beringer, Franciscan, Mondavi and a number of others own wineries in several major growing regions.

California is home to the world's most productive winery — Gallo in the Central Valley — but there are countless modest producers, often to be found in edge-of-town "business park" locations, who make their wine more or less as a hobby. Most wineries, large or small, buy grapes from, or own plots in, a variety of vineyards: the winemaker's skill is in blending. Grapes from

GRAPE VARIETIES ON THE LABEL

The custom of labelling wine by grape variety — rather than place of origin — is now common to all New World wine producers. It gained momentum in California, where the most important grapes — and thus wine names — are:

RED WINES

Zinfandel   One of the world's most versatile grapes is rarely found outside California. Not only does it make red wines in a wide range of styles, it is also used to make paler wines, ranging from absolutely colourless, to pale copper, to light rose, to deep pink; they are labelled White Zinfandel and/or "blush", usually have a strawberry fragrance and are slightly sweet to medium-sweet.

Cabernet Sauvignon   The great red bordeaux grape has long been successful in California's coastal regions.

Grenache   Widely grown in southern France and Spain, a large proportion of the planting is used for "jug wines" in the Central Valley. Some growers are now using it for superior Rhône-style blends.

Pinot Noir   The red burgundy grape grows well in cooler zones such as Carneros, Sonoma's Russian River Valley, and other northern coastal regions. It is used in the blend for sparkling wines, and is increasingly seen as a varietal.

Merlot and **Cabernet Franc**   Once planted mainly to blend with Cabernet Sauvignon; now increasingly used for varietal wines.

Petite Sirah   No relation to the Rhône's Syrah, it is used in generic blends and as a dark, tannic varietal.

Carignane   An everyday variety from southern France and Spain, Carignan (spelt with an additional "e" in

California) is widely grown for use in bulk wines, but seldom seen as a varietal.

Barbera   This Italian variety keeps its acidity well in hot climates. Used in generic red blends; varietals are rare.

Gamay   Grapes known as Gamay are not necessarily the same variety as that grown in Beaujolais, but are used to make Beaujolais-style wines in Napa and Sonoma.

Syrah   Small plantings; used mainly in Rhône-style blends.

Nebbiolo and **Sangiovese**   One or two producers use these Italian grapes for varietal wines.

WHITE WINES

Chardonnay   Burgundy's great white grape makes dry white wines in a wide range of styles.

Colombard   Originally from southwest France, this variety has high acidity and performs well in California.

Chenin Blanc   Used for everyday, easy-drinking wines and occasionally in Loire-style dry and sweet wines.

Sauvignon Blanc   Grown in the coastal counties; made as a dry white varietal (sometimes known as Fumé Blanc) and used in bordeaux-style blends.

Muscat Blanc   Sometimes known as Muscat Canelli; generally used to make sweet wines.

Riesling   The great German grape (often known as Johannisberg Riesling or White Riesling) makes aromatic dry, off-dry or sweet wines.

Gewürztraminer   Grown in the cooler zones and used for off-dry (occasionally dry) wines.

Sémillon   Used in bordeaux-style blends, and occasionally as a varietal.

cooler locations provide acidity, those which come from warmer sites have a fuller flavour. Thus the two most important keys to a wine's style — the producer's name and the main grape variety — are usually the most prominently displayed on the label.

Wine names

The majority of California wines, especially quality wines, are varietal wines: in other words they are named after the grape variety from which they are made (*see* box). They need not be 100% from the variety named on the label, but that grape alone must form at least 75% of the contents.

California winemakers have long realized that (as in bordeaux, for example) a pure varietal does not necessarily mean the best wine (a careful blend often improves the wine). The advent of what are dubbed "Meritage" wines allows more room for blending in the bordeaux style, if the winemaker uses the bordeaux varieties (Cabernet Sauvignon, Merlot, Cabernet Franc, Petit Verdot and Malbec for red wines; Sauvignon Blanc, Sémillon and Muscadelle for Meritage whites). Such wines may not use varietal labelling, but are superior to everyday table wines. Some producers use the name Meritage, while others have created their own brand names.

The names of highly regarded wine regions such as Napa and Sonoma will help sell a wine, but they may be used only if a high proportion of the grapes has been grown in the named region (*see* box, p476).

Sparkling wine made by the traditional method developed in Champagne is increasingly being known and labelled as classic-method (rather than champagne), but California still makes use of European names — chablis, burgundy, port and sherry — to describe generic wines which often bear no more than a passing resemblance to their namesakes.

California wineries increasingly use oak for fermenting or maturing wine.

Vintages and ageing

California's benign climate results in far less variation between vintages than is found in Europe's fine-wine-producing regions. While unseasonal rain, cold or heat may occur in specific micro-climates, a poor overall vintage is very rare in California.

Because of the way the wines are made, most California wines can usually be drunk young: a year or two after the vintage for white wines, three to five for standard red wines. The better white wines — Chardonnays and Sauvignon Blancs from Napa and Sonoma — can improve with seven or eight years' bottle-age. Well-made reds, especially Cabernet Sauvignons and Zinfandels from the best coastal zones,

may improve over longer periods — 20 years or more — but are enjoyable younger than the classed-growth bordeaux and *Grand Cru* burgundies that they emulate.

California is home to many idiosyncratic and innovative winemakers, and two of the world's most advanced wine schools — the University of California at Davis and California State at Fresno. Fermenting and maturing wine in oak is just one of the subjects under constant experimentation. Many producers offer both red and white wines in fresh, fruity, early-maturing styles and richer, oak-aged versions made from the same grape variety.   □

QUALITY FACTORS

California is the direct inverse of north-west Europe when it comes to seeking the ideal in viticultural *terroir*. European winemakers are looking for the warmer nooks in what is, for the grape, a rather chill and forbidding climate; California growers have an overly hospitable, tending-toward-hot climate, and thus seek the cooler edges where the grape must struggle to reach full flavour maturity (good) rather than heat ripeness (bad) — ideally at the end of each variety's growing season. They also have different priorities for soil, site and exposure. The myriad potential and actual vineyard sites are only just beginning to be explored.

Climate

Where Europeans go north for the cooler climes needed for Pinot Noir, Riesling and the highly acidic grapes used for sparkling wines, California's winemakers look west, towards the coast.

In Santa Barbara County's Santa Ynez Valley, for example, the day's temperature climbs 1°F for every mile one moves east (about 0.5°C per 1.6km), inland up the Santa Ynez River. Close to the Pacific, Pinot Noir is favoured.

A bit inland, Chardonnay does better; up towards Lake Cachuma it is warm enough to ripen Sauvignon Blanc, and even Cabernet Sauvignon in warmer years. And Santa Ynez is well south of the Napa Valley, where Cabernet is more at home.

Local climate, rather than soil type, is the deciding factor for selecting the grape

Site and exposure

Hill slopes are prized for rich Cabernet Sauvignons and Zinfandels. A southern exposure is not welcome in most regions here — growers find it too hot. A site facing east, or even north — a bit cooler, more capable of maturing fruit — is more likely to be appreciated.

Techniques

California, with its many competing wineries, is where every technique in winemaking will be tried, and where some have made a dramatic contribution. Temperature-controlled stainless steel fermenting tanks and French oak barrels are among key tools here.

NAPA VALLEY VA AND SUB-AREAS

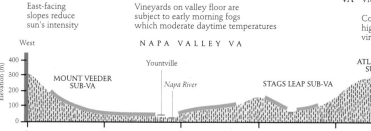

Vineyards

VA Viticultural Area

Colder, higher altitude vineyards

Fog sweeping in from the sea cools vineyards in Sonoma.

variety that will perform best.

In the coastal regions inland and north of San Francisco Bay, particularly Napa and Sonoma, a further factor comes into play. Breaks in the chains of mountains that run parallel to the coast allow sea breezes and cool,

damp fog to moderate the heat of the valleys. This explains the apparent paradox of Carneros, in the south of Napa and Sonoma Counties, being cooler than areas further north: the sea air from San Francisco Bay moderates the conditions in Carneros.

Soils

Since the 1970s, California winegrowers have learned that each plot of ground has its own identity, its own expression of flavour. Cabernet Sauvignon grown on well-drained gravelly ground can produce a classic bordeaux-style red, while the same vines grown nearby in heavy clay will barely ripen grapes, and the wines will be herbaceous, grassy, and even asparagus-like.

Save for those growers who consider limestone essential for Pinot Noir (Calera in San Benito, Chalone in Monterey), the importance of soils is limited to considerations of texture, slope and exposure.

Well-drained soils are essential. Hill soils are less fertile than those in the rich valley floors: this poverty leads to more intensely flavoured fruit.

WINE ZONES OF NAPA AND SONOMA

The heart of the California quality-wine industry is found north of San Francisco Bay, in the counties of Napa and Sonoma. The Napa Valley has several sub-zones that are more closely defined by soil type and micro-climate (*see* box, p485). The warmest zones are in the north; the coolest, Carneros, overlaps into Sonoma County. In Sonoma the wine zones (*see* box, p491) are more scattered, and thus more diverse, than in Napa.

Wine zones

Sonoma County
- Alexander Valley VA
- Dry Creek Valley VA
- Knights Valley VA
- Russian River Valley VA
- Chalk Hill sub-VA
- Green Valley sub-VA
- Sonoma Coast VA
- Sonoma Valley VA
- Sonoma Mountain sub-VA

Napa County
- Napa Valley VA
- Howell Mountain sub-VA
- Diamond Mountain sub-VA
- Spring Mountain sub-VA
- Rutherford sub-VA
- Oakville sub-VA
- Atlas Peak sub-VA
- Mount Veeder sub-VA
- Stags Leap District sub-VA
- Los Carneros VA

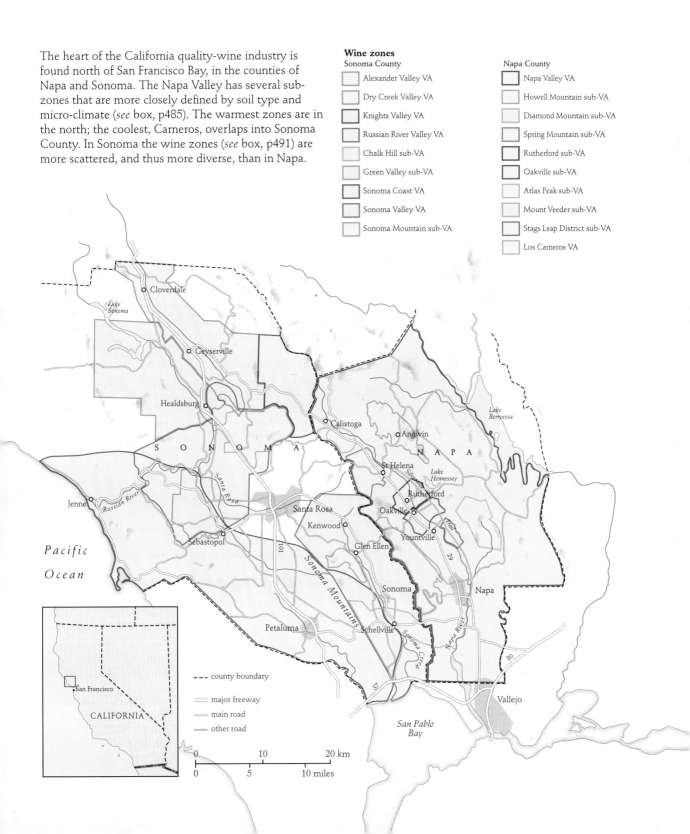

--- county boundary
major freeway
main road
other road

0   10   20 km
0   5   10 miles

NAPA

The crescent-moon-shaped Napa Valley is the best-known wine region in America because it is utterly and completely focused on one thing, and one thing only: wine. Napa Valley devotes 30,000ha (74,000 acres) to vinegrowing (in excess of all the Médoc, plus St-Emilion, in Bordeaux). Napa County is less than half the size of Sonoma County, yet has twice the number of wineries. Napa's grape acreage represents just one-tenth of California's wine-grape total, yet its 250 or so wineries account for almost a third of the state's total.

Highway 29 is "the Wine Road" for good and glorious reason. Running parallel to the Napa River, it sees a mix of vineland, cellar and tasting room almost continuously from Trefethen's winery at Oak Knoll Avenue, just north of Napa, to Storybook Mountain's hillside Zinfandel plantings at the Sonoma County border 48km (30 miles) to the north.

Napa's history
That Napa is well-suited to the grape is documented not only by its climatic zones (*see* box), but also by 150 years of enduring empirical evidence. Stone cellars remain gracefully ageing monuments to a vinous history that created a rugged foundation for the growth that was to come.

The great Greystone, on the north edge of St Helena (now the western home of the Culinary Institute of America); the exquisitely rebuilt Far Niente at Oakville; the sturdy block façade at Calistoga's Château Montelena; the ivy-covered length of Inglenook; the small stone structure that now forms the core of Beaulieu — without the underpinnings of history, Napa's extraordinarily rapid growth in the middle years of the 1970s might have been cataclysmic instead of merely chaotic.

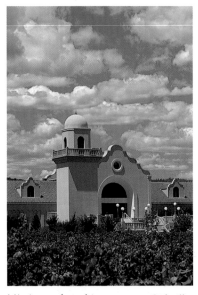
Mission-style architecture near Oakville.

The valley's first wine was made around 1840 by Missouri Indian fighter George Yount, who settled at what is now Yountville in 1836, planting vine and orchard in 1838. By 1860 he was making 5,000 gallons of wine each harvest.

But Napa Valley winemaking before the Civil War (1861–1865) was mostly an adjunct to farming: an orchard here, a vegetable garden there, a few rows of grapes where the sun shone best. Napa's true vinous pioneer was the Prussian Charles Krug, who began making wine in the early 1860s. He used the first mechanical winepress and built the first commercial winery of any size in Napa Valley, at St Helena. He also trained many of California's great early winemakers — Clarence Wetmore (who founded Cresta Blanca), Jacob Beringer, Carl Wente.

By the 1870s, wine was evolving to industry, with people like Jacob Schram and Hamilton Walker Crabb elevating hobby to business. The Scottish writer Robert Louis Stevenson, after visiting Jacob Schram at his Calistoga estate, described the wine as "bottled poetry".

Crabb, meanwhile, was planting To Kalon Vineyard (he said it meant "the boss vineyard" in Greek) on the west side of Oakville, testing more than 400 grape varieties. What was To Kalon remains a testing ground to this day: part of Crabb's vineyard is now the University of California at Davis Experimental Station; part is Mondavi's Block P, for its Reserve Cabernet Sauvignon.

The Napa Valley of 1889 had at least 142 wine cellars, although phylloxera did great damage in the 1880s and 1890s.

Prohibition was a blight to wineries, but the growing of grapes actually increased through its 13 years. Spurred by home winemakers, the consumption of wine more than doubled from the onset of Prohibition until its repeal. Large cooperatives ruled the roost in the turbulent post-repeal days and through the war years.

The 1940s saw tiny mountaintop winemakers — Stony Hill, Souverain (now Burgess), Mayacamas — begin the swing from dessert wines and generic table wines to varietally labelled Cabernet Sauvignon and Chardonnay.

In 1943 Robert Mondavi's father rescued Charles Krug's winery from disrepair. When Robert founded his own winery at Oakville in 1966, it was the first new winery of any size built in the Napa Valley since the end of Prohibition. More than 95% of the wineries in Napa Valley today were built after Mondavi's Spanish mission-style cellars.

The real boom in the Napa Valley, and elsewhere in the Golden State, came in the mid-1970s and on into the 1980s, when Americans began reading about wine, visiting wineries, and tasting everything from

Chenin Blanc to Chardonnay, Pinot Blanc to Pinot Noir. Eleven new wineries opened in the Napa Valley in 1972, including Stag's Leap Wine Cellars and Clos Du Val. Another eight signed on in 1973, and from that point on, the race was as hot as a forest fire.

Today the Napa Valley is well equipped to receive the 250,000 visitors a year who drive along Highway 29 and its eastern parallel, the Silverado Trail. There are restaurants and tasting rooms alongside the wineries, and early on fog-free mornings the sky will be dotted with colourful hot-air balloons offering a bird's-eye view of the vine-carpeted valley.

Grape varieties and wine styles

Most of California's main grape varieties (*see* p480) are represented in the Napa Valley, and the majority of wines are named after the variety upon which they are based.

Napa is dominated by Cabernet Sauvignon for red wines and Chardonnay for whites, which each combine to make up more than half of Napa's plantings. Other primary grape varieties are Pinot Noir and Merlot for red wines; the versatile Zinfandel, which is used not only for spicy, raspberry-fruited reds, but also for dry and slightly sweet blush (rosé) wines; Sauvignon Blanc for dry whites; and Chenin Blanc, which makes Loire-style dry and sweet white wines as well as wines shamelessly labelled Vouvray.

Recently, there has been a strong trend toward those varieties most used in the bordeaux-style or Meritage blends (*see* p481): Cabernet Franc, Malbec and Petit Verdot for red, Sémillon and Muscadelle for white. These wines point away from the early bluster of high alcohol, heavily extracted, over-oaked varietal wines and toward more complex, more subtle elixirs. As consumer sophistication rises, so do grape varieties as well as wine prices. □

WINE ZONES OF NAPA

Napa has one main viticultural area (VA), covering the whole county, and several sub-zones. Thirteen zones have been officially recognized. Napa Valley grapes command high prices, so the name is usually prominent on the label. Most wineries own vineyards in several of the sub-VAs, and some are beginning to focus their identities on a single area. However, the VA may be used on the label only if at least 85% of the wine originates there.

Napa Valley, the main VA, encompasses every single vine planted in Napa County.

Mount Veeder VA runs along the Mayacamas Range from immediately north and west of the town of Napa to Bald Mountain; its hill slope vineyards are planted at altitudes ranging from 120–800m (400–2,600ft) above sea level. Well-drained volcanic soils make for low yields — never more than 40hl/ha — and intense, well-defined Cabernet Sauvignons and Chardonnays.

Spring Mountain VA spreads up the hills west of St Helena. Old vineyards provide densely-flavoured fruit for wine. Leading wineries are Cain Cellars (Cain Five, a Meritage red), Smith-Madrone (a flinty white Johannisberg Riesling) and Robert Keenan (Merlot).

Diamond Mountain, south of Calistoga, is one of the steepest vineyard sites this side of the Rhein or Mosel. Some of the terraces at Sterling's Diamond Mountain vineyard are head-high, and low yields make for lean Chardonnays and hard, sharply-focused Cabernet Sauvignons.

Howell Mountain VA — flanking Deer Park Road as it twists its way over the hill from St Helena, through Angwin, on the Vaca side of the valley — was approved in January 1984. All of its 80ha (200 acres) or so of vines are above 425m (1,400ft) in elevation, nearly always above the morning fog belt. Zinfandel is Howell Mountain's historic variety, but new plantings provide Dunn's Cabernet Sauvignon, a wine compact and hard when young, but opening up with patience and bottle-age.

Atlas Peak VA, with 4,500ha (10,000 acres), north of Napa, is the private domain of Atlas Peak Vineyard, now part of Allied-Hiram Walker. The vineyard has received technical assistance from Champagne Bollinger and Piero Antinori, the famous Chianti producer. This VA accounts for over one-fourth of all California's Sangiovese plantings.

Stags Leap District VA, east of Yountville, is known for the "iron-fist-in-velvet-glove" Cabernet Sauvignons of Clos Du Val, Stag's Leap Wine Cellars, Stags' Leap Vineyard, Shafer, Pine Ridge and Silverado. It competes with Rutherford for producing the best bordeaux-style red wines.

Rutherford and **Oakville**, in the middle of the valley, each have their own VA, sometimes linked as the Rutherford-Oakville Bench. The bench is a wide, flat, low terrace along the side of the valley, formed by the Napa River: thus the soils are rich alluvial and well-drained gravel. Rutherford in particular is famous for distinctive Cabernet Sauvignons: red wines with firm, tannic structure and somewhat herbaceous flavours. Oakville, further south, has more varied soils, and other grapes are grown alongside the Cabernet Sauvignon.

Los Carneros is the county's southernmost VA, a thin-soiled, bay-cooled region that extends round into the Sonoma Valley. Chardonnay plantings dominate, while the Pinot Noir which yields such juicy, strawberry-fruited wines represents a third of the plantings. Merlot is now being planted in increasing amounts.

Chiles Valley, in the north-eastern part of the county, enjoys a particular climate, running from northwest to southeast.

St Helena VA (1999) spreads to the northeast of Rutherford VA.

Yountville, a recent VA (1999), extends between Mount Veeder and Stags Leap District.

Wild Horse Valley, the most recent VA (2001), counts a single vineyard.

PRODUCERS

In spite of the increasing interest in viticultural areas (VAs) in Napa, as in the rest of the USA, the most reliable guide to quality remains each producer's reputation. The winemaker's skill lies in blending wines with different characteristics. The following wineries are based in the Napa Valley, although they may draw in grapes from further afield. Most wines are named after their grape variety: *see* p480.

Beaulieu

The reputation of this venerable Rutherford house rests on Georges de Latour Private Reserve Cabernet Sauvignon, named after the Frenchman who settled at Rutherford in 1899, and perfected over nearly four decades by Russian winemaker André Tchelistcheff. This is one of California's world-class reds, made solely from Cabernet Sauvignon, matured only in American oak; and it can age gracefully for decades.

Beringer

Brothers Frederick and Jacob Beringer founded the winery just north of St Helena in 1876, reconstructing their family's original, exquisite Mainz "Rhine House" (now a tasting room) beside caves dug by Chinese labourers. Star wines are the massive-but-balanced blackcurrant Private Reserve Cabernet Sauvignon and the toasty-oaked, clove-filled Chardonnay. The Napa Ridge label is for softer table wines.

Caymus

The Wagner family began farming Napa Valley in 1906, growing grapes in 1941, and making wine here in Rutherford in 1972. Early on they proved that fancy buildings weren't needed to make great wines — like the stunning Special Selection Cabernet Sauvignon — but they now work out of a handsome, stone-faced winery. Conundrum is a barrel-fermented dry white blend of Muscat, Sauvignon Blanc, Chardonnay and Sémillon.

Clos Du Val

French-born Bernard Portet, whose father was *régisseur* at Ch Lafite-Rothschild in Bordeaux, brings a decidedly French flavour to this Stags Leap District winery, most interestingly in a blackberry-studded Zinfandel and an unusual white wine: a silky, oily dry Sémillon. Clos Du Val (on the Silverado Trail just north of the town of Napa) also owns the nearby St Andrew's, where a tropical-fruited Chardonnay is the focus, and Taltarni Vineyard in Australia (run by Bernard's brother Dominique).

Clos Pegase

Founded in 1984 in a flurry of architectural controversy, the unusual lines and rose-red hue of Clos Pegase have since become part of the landscape south of Calistoga. The wines are a lean, lemon-pear Chardonnay, a broad, blackcurrant Merlot, a herbaceous Cabernet Sauvignon, and a juicy Meritage red blend of Cabernets Sauvignon and Franc, with Merlot.

Cuvaison

Founded in 1970, Swiss-owned since 1979, the winery is in Calistoga but most grapes come from its estate in Carneros. Winemaker John Thacher transformed rather dense wines into soft, elegant, more flavourful creations. The Chardonnay is creamy, with hints of apple; Merlot is packed with chocolate and currant; Cabernet Sauvignon stresses tobacco and redcurrant; a Carneros Pinot Noir has concentrated strawberry, clove and mushroom aromas.

Diamond Creek

Four tiny vineyard plots amounting to merely 8.5ha (21 acres) on Diamond Mountain each have their individual soil and exposure, providing four distinctive Cabernet Sauvignons. Volcanic Hill has balanced, ash-grey earth that

Beringer's German-style tasting room at St Helena.

yields austere wines; Red Rock Terrace is iron-red, its wines plummy, with blackcurrant flavours; Gravelly Meadow is cool, giving hints of iodine and black cherry fruit; Lake is tiny, the wines intense and expensive, released only in excellent years.

Domaine Carneros

Eilene Crane once worked at Domaine Chandon (*qv*), then designed and made sparkling white wines for Gloria Ferrer (Sonoma). She now does the same at Domaine Carneros, south-west of Napa. The winery looks like a French château and is a collaboration between the French Champagne house Taittinger and distributor Kobrand.

Domaine Chandon

Moët-Hennessy invaded the Napa Valley in 1973, buying vineyards in Carneros, Yountville and atop Mount Veeder. The sparkling white wines are shown off in the Yountville winery's elegant salon and exquisite French restaurant, whose wine list features still and sparkling wines from throughout the Napa Valley. Etoile is a fine, tangy, *tête de cuvée* sparkling white wine. Another creation, Panache, is a fortified grape juice apéritif rather like Pineau des Charentes.

Far Niente

Built by Captain John Benson in Oakville in 1885, this stone cellar was restored a century later by Oklahoma nursery-man Gil Nickel. The grounds are manicured and the wines

match. Chardonnays are rich and ageable; Cabernet Sauvignons lush with blackberry and violets; Dolce is a sweet white botrytized Sémillon/Sauvignon Blanc blend in the style of Sauternes.

Franciscan

After ups and downs and multiple ownership changes, Franciscan, near Rutherford, is now settled, owned by the German Eckes family. Cabernet Sauvignons are made from Oakville fruit, Merlot from Alexander Valley (Sonoma) and Chardonnays from Monterey County south of San Francisco Bay. The company also owns Mount Veeder Winery and property in Chile.

Freemark Abbey

The stone cellar north of St Helena dates from 1886, but was never an abbey. The first winery to make a sweet white botrytized Riesling in Napa Valley (called Edelwein, in 1973), Freemark focuses on Chardonnay and Cabernet Sauvignon. The former makes floral and fresh white wines, bursting with fruit; the latter produces red wines that tend toward cedar, tobacco, cherry and tar. In good years the Cabernet Sauvignons age remarkably well.

Grgich Hills

Croatian-born winemaker Miljenko "Mike" Grgich is known for his generous, well-proportioned and slow-maturing Chardonnays. After an apprenticeship at Robert Mondavi, Grgich moved to Château Montelena where he made the internationally-acclaimed 1973 Chardonnay. In 1977 he founded this Rutherford winery with partner Austin Hills. Some Cabernet Sauvignon and Zinfandel (for red varietals), and Sauvignon Blanc and Johannisberg Riesling (for whites) are also vinified here.

Heitz Cellars

Joe Heitz's winery south-east of St Helena is famous for its Martha's Vineyard Cabernet Sauvignon, one of California's most revered red wines, known for its identifying eucalyptus scent and classic structure. Joe's son David now handles winemaking.

Inglenook

The ivy-covered stone structure west of Rutherford was one of many built by Hamden W McIntyre over a century

ago. The winery is known for Cabernet Sauvignons that show their Rutherford origins with cedar, eucalyptus and tobacco flavours. Inglenook's Gravion is a dry white bordeaux-style blend of Sauvignon Blanc and Sémillon.

Charles Krug

The cellar dates to 1861, when Charles Krug planted grapes north of St Helena and began his career as winegrower guru to most of the early vinous pioneers of Napa Valley. Owned by Peter Mondavi and his sons, Krug is known for its bell-pepperish Vintage Selection Cabernet Sauvignons and the silky, sweet grass and hay-scented Chenin Blanc whites.

Louis M Martini

Louis M Martini's grandson Michael and granddaughter Carolyn now run this St

ROBERT MONDAVI

Robert Mondavi is the most vital force in the American wine industry. He founded his Oakville winery in 1966 when he left Charles Krug, and created Fumé Blanc, a complex, barrel-aged Sauvignon Blanc that took the varietal to exciting heights. He also makes structured Cabernet Sauvignon (with cherry, bell pepper and violet aromas); richly-fruited Chardonnays (lots of clove and vanilla); supple Pinot Noirs (black cherry, mushroom). Affordable table wines — all varietals — are made at Woodbridge winery in Central Valley; his Opus One (a partnership with Mouton-Rothschild) is a bordeaux classed-growth-quality Cabernet Sauvignon; and he also owns Vichon (known for Chevrignon, a silky Sauvignon Blanc-Sémillon blend) and Byron (fine Pinot Noirs from Santa Barbara County).

Helena winery known for its Cabernet Sauvignons of finesse and ageability. Martini Cabernets from the 1940s to 1960s command high auction prices. A special treat is Martini's Muscato Amabile, a low-alcohol, spritzy, fresh, floral, grape-tasting sweet white wine like Piedmont's Asti *spumante*.

Robert Mondavi
See profile, p487.

Château Montelena
The old stone château, north of Calistoga, still houses excellence in winemaking: apple-fruited, richly textured Chardonnays, firm blackberry and blackcurrant Cabernet Sauvignons, zingy raspberry and peppercorn Zinfandels, and velvety, apricot-laden, off-dry Johannisberg Rieslings. An authentic Chinese junk graces the lake in Château Montelena's garden.

Mumm Napa Valley
This joint venture (France's Champagne Mumm, Canada's spirits giant Seagram) based west of Rutherford is known for moderately priced classic-method sparkling white wines. The Blanc de Noirs is delicate, with soft cherry fruit; the Winery Lake is stony and flinty when young, oily and graceful when aged.

Joseph Phelps
Century-old railroad timbers form the gateway to Phelps, the St Helena winery built in 1973. German-born winemaker Walter Schug made the winery famous for sweet and dry Rieslings and massive, dense Cabernet Sauvignons (Insignia) from the Eisele vineyard before leaving to found his own winery. Now winemaker Craig Williams puts his stamp on Phelps with strong attention to Rhône-style wines, from a red, rose-petal-scented Syrah and a delicately spiced

Grenache red to a tangy white based on Viognier grapes.

Rutherford Hill
Merlot, the grape of the legendary (and expensive) Pomerol reds of Bordeaux, is getting increasing attention from consumers and critics alike. Owned by many of the same partners as Freemark Abbey (*qv*), Rutherford Hill, which lies north-east of Rutherford, uses more Merlot to blend with its Cabernet Sauvignon than Freemark, and employs Limousin oak to age its Chardonnay.

St Clement
The lovely Victorian house north of St Helena was built in 1878, and the basement winery was begun in the 1960s under the name Spring Mountain. Renamed St Clement in 1975, it was sold to the Japanese brewer Sapporo in 1987. Sauvignon Blanc is made in a lean, limey Graves style; Chardonnays are rich without being flabby or overoaked.

St Supéry
A delight for visitors to Rutherford, with a demonstration vineyard and the Atkinson House living museum of Napa Valley wine history, where taste stations offer a noses-on explanation of why one grape tastes different, as wine, from another. Owned by the French Skalli family (owners of the Fortant de France brand in the Midi, *see* p282), St Supéry is run by Michaela Rodeno. There is a fine, complex Sauvignon Blanc, crisp with freshly mown grass.

Saintsbury
Deep in the heart of the Carneros district south-west of Napa, Dick Ward and David Graves focus wholly on Pinot Noir and Chardonnay. Garnet is a lighter, fresher Pinot Noir that bursts with cherry fruit.

Schramsberg
Former management consultant Jack Davies, and his wife Jamie, kick-started classic-method sparkling wine in California. They founded Schramsberg in 1965, based on an old Calistoga wine estate dating to 1862. Both Blanc de Blancs and Blanc de Noirs age beautifully, the former with lemon and bread-dough aromas, the latter with flinty, berry flavours.

Silver Oak
The winery, in Oakville, is founded entirely on reds made from Cabernet Sauvignon. There is a Napa Valley Cabernet, an Alexander Valley (Sonoma) Cabernet, and a Bonny's Vineyard Cabernet (from a small vineyard owned by Justin Meyer's wife Bonny). All are powerful, violet-scented statements of pure Cabernet Sauvignon.

Silverado
This elegant, stone-faced winery notched into a knoll below the Silverado Trail produces graceful wines. Sauvignon Blanc is tight with flinty grassiness; Chardonnay is viscous and rich with licorice and lemon; Merlot has blackcurrant and blackberry fruit; Cabernet Sauvignon has subtle hints of cedar and tobacco, with iodine as spice.

Stag's Leap Wine Cellars
At his winery on the Silverado Trail east of Yountville, former University of Chicago lecturer on political science Warren Winiarski makes Chardonnays that are neither over-oaked nor flabby with ultra-ripe fruit, and Cabernet Sauvignons with a firm tannin backbone underlying a silky, olive-pepper cloak. The Cask 23 special *cuvée* red uses Cabernet Sauvignon and other Bordeaux varieties. The Winiarski wines attract worldwide praise.

Sterling
Sterling, once owned by Coca Cola, is now part of Seagram. The white-walled fortress looks rather like a Greek monastery, perched atop its Calistoga hilltop. Merlot is consistently exquisite, Diamond Mountain Ranch Cabernet Sauvignons and Chardonnays are dense and focused; the Winery Lake Pinot Noir is lush and supple.

Sutter Home
The oldest wooden wine building in Napa Valley (1874) still serves as tasting room at Sutter Home, just south of St Helena. It has grown in the last decade from a 50,000-case Zinfandel-only winery to nearly five million cases, which include the country's most popular White Zinfandel (pale cherry colour, slightly sweet), a light, fruity red called Soleo (a blend of Zinfandel, Barbera, Gamay and Pinot Noir), and new alcohol-free wines. It also owns Amador County's Monteviña Winery in the Sierra Foothills.

Trefethen
The pumpkin-coloured Eshcol Winery just north of Napa is the second-oldest wooden winery in the valley, restored by Gene Trefethen and his family. Prune and walnut trees were replaced by a 243-ha (600-acre) vineyard, which now produces Chardonnay (lean and steely), White Riesling (tangy apricot), Cabernet Sauvignon (chocolate ripe). The blended Eshcol Red and Eshcol White are both well-priced and popular.

SONOMA

Size and geography determine Sonoma as a county of vinous diversity. Sonoma County is two-and-a-half times the size of Napa County, yet has virtually the same vineyard acreage. Where Napa is a monoculture of wine-grapes, Sonoma dazzles with horticultural variety. Where Napa retains the patrician Bordelais mould, Sonoma is Burgundian, a county of gardeners, with fields of flowers, orchards of apples and plums, and grazing for dairy cows and goats.

Sonoma's history

The county's history is one of exploration. Spanish priests extended their chain of missions from Mexico into California, the first appearing in San Diego in 1769, the last built in the town of Sonoma in 1823. With the padres came grapes, for crude sacramental wines and the "firewater" (*aguardiente*, brandy) that helped them to sleep. The Russians settled Fort Ross and named Mount St Helena for their princess. Later, the sons of Italy extended the culture of the vine, the settling family names being Rossi, Sbarboro, Pastori, Nervo, Mazzoni and Seghesio.

Today the names have a far more international ring. French, English, Japanese, Spanish and German firms all have major winery holdings in Sonoma, and large tracts of vines are owned by wineries on the Napa side of the Mayacamas Range.

Sonoma was also home to the likeable Hungarian confidence trickster "Count" (sometimes "Colonel") Agoston Haraszthy. He and the town's Mexican governor, General Mariano Vallejo, swapped tales of growing grapes. Two of Haraszthy's sons married Vallejo's twin daughters and in 1857 Haraszthy founded Buena Vista Winery, imported over 100,000 cuttings of European vines, allegedly including Zinfandel (1861), but was forced out for financial irregularities in 1866.

Sonoma's history of selling its wines in bulk to wineries in other regions died out with the wine boom of the 1970s. As new wineries popped up all over the county, local pride prospered and Sonoma wines began to be recognized for both their diversity and their distinctiveness.

Sonoma's wine industry

Today Sonoma County is vinously stable, with 160 wineries and 15,000ha (37,000 acres) of vinelands. Twenty years earlier the numbers were 30 wineries and barely 4,450ha (11,000 acres) bearing. To say that the

Ferrari-Carano's impressive underground cellar north of Healdsburg.

world's interest in Sonoma wines has grown would be an understatement.

If, in the past, Sonoma wine-growers have resisted self-promotion and limelight, today several entities exist to let the world know of their fine wines and, better, agreeable prices. It is a beneficial sign of the times that grape-growers and wine-makers — once the bitterest of antag-onists — often work hand in glove on such projects.

The best of these organizations is the Carneros Quality Alliance, which not only put growers and winemakers on the same side of the quality fence, but also financed a seri-ous, scientific examination of Pinot Noir's identity in the region. And though a Sonoma Valley group has seriously proposed a seal of approval, it remains prudent to trust the repu-tation of individual producers for quality assurance.

Visitors thrill to visit wineries where the owner is as likely as not to pour their sample and answer their questions. Even more than other wine regions on America's west coast, Sonoma County is uncompro-misingly hospitable, with plenty to occupy tourists with an interest in food and wine.

Climate and soil

The interest in Sonoma wines is quality-driven, and the quality clue comes from the crops — apples, hops and prunes — that once held primacy here. All, but especially the apples, require climatic conditions a bit cooler than California's norm. What that means to the vine is a longer, slower growing season, one tem-pered by the intrusion of fog up the Russian River from Jenner, its outlet to the Pacific, or inland across the Carneros region and up into Sonoma Valley from San Francisco Bay. For the grape it means flavours that are vine-ripened instead of sun-shriv-elled. In the wine that means flavour that carries through into the bottle, from precocious youth to the elegant veneration of old age.

Zinfandel, California's own "classic" vine, is rarely found outside the state.

Sonoma's individuality is a reflec-tion of the wide variety of soil tex-ture, sun exposure, rainfall and ocean influence (see box). Where the upper Alexander Valley is inland and warm, with vines planted in gravel soils that retain and reflect the day's heat at night, Cabernet Sauvignon and Sauvignon Blanc thrive. Only miles away, around a few bends of the Russian River, in Green Valley, colder soils and the close proximity of Pacific Ocean morning fogs create perfect conditions for Pinot Noir and Chardonnay — sometimes for table wine, often for sparkling.

Though Sonoma County is per-haps best understood through its zones (the viticultural areas or VAs: see opposite), it is important to remember that the name of a good producer is a far more reliable key to quality than any regional name that appears on the label. That is partly due to the fact that no viticultural area is any better than the worst winemaker entitled to the name. While a wine bearing the name of a small VA or individual vineyard may be one producer's best wine, other winemakers will put just as much care into blending a wine that is not entitled to use a VA name on the label because less than 85% of the wine comes from the region. Also, VAs often have overlapping boundaries.

Grape varieties and wine styles

Where most of the world's wine regions have a sharp vinous focus, Sonoma offers a colourful array, its diverse viticultural areas allowing wines to be made in many styles, from the full palette of California's grape varieties (see box, p480). Dry white wines made from Chardonnay grapes and red wines from Cabernet Sauvignon head the list, but there are good-sized crops of Zinfandel (for reds and rosés), Pinot Noir and Mer-lot (for reds), Sauvignon Blanc, Chenin Blanc, Colombard and Gewürztraminer (for whites) and Cabernet Franc (for lighter reds).

The majority of wines are named after their predominant grape variety. This varietal name, in conjunction with the name of the producer or winery, is the key to the style and quality of the wine.   □

WINE ZONES OF SONOMA

Sonoma County has ten major viticultural areas (VAs), discussed here roughly from south to north. While any wine produced here may be sold under the county name (or under that of Northern Sonoma, for the northern part of the county), some of the VAs — Sonoma Valley, Russian River Valley, Alexander Valley — are much larger than VAs in Napa and have become well-known in their own right. They increasingly appear alone on a label — if 85% of the grapes are from the area.

Los Carneros, Sonoma County's southernmost VA, extends into Napa Valley to the east; its western aspect is the southern part of Sonoma Valley VA. The Spanish word for ram — named after the sheep that once dotted these low, thin, hard clay-alluvium soils — Carneros is an area cooled by the San Pablo Bay (the northern reach of San Francisco Bay) and steady afternoon winds that funnel through the Petaluma Gap from the Pacific. Thus, most of its vineyards are planted with Pinot Noir and Chardonnay.

Sonoma Valley VA is shaped like a crescent moon, sliding north-west from the bay to the Santa Rosa Plain, paralleling Napa Valley's larger crescent to the east. Sonoma Valley radiates out on all sides from Sonoma town's historic plaza. Its vineyards are devoted to Cabernet Sauvignon, Merlot and Sauvignon Blanc, which thrive on the valley floor and benches (wide natural terraces). Upper slopes are home to radiant, raspberry-fruited Zinfandel.

Sonoma Mountain VA, at the north-western end of the valley, is a small sub-zone of Sonoma Valley VA. Some of its vineyards, ranging up to nearly 440m (1,000ft) above sea level, are higher than most morning fogs. Thus the warm-blooded varieties — Cabernet Sauvignon, Zinfandel and Sauvignon Blanc — are favoured for their ripe chocolate, rich raspberry and mellow melon (respectively) flavours. Chardonnay is also grown here, but one must wonder why.

Russian River Valley VA (3,400ha/8,400 acres) is a cooler southern extension of the Alexander Valley, demarcated by the river's westward bend toward the ocean. Russian River once emptied into San Francisco Bay, but an eruption of Mount St Helena aeons ago re-routed it sharply toward the sea. Pinot Noir, Chardonnay, flinty White Riesling, and nutmeg-spiced Gewürztraminer ripen slowly along the bends of gravelled riverbeds. Much of the crop is devoted to crisp, delicately-fruited sparkling wines.

Green Valley is one of the two sub-zones within Russian River; it is on the cooler, ocean side of the VA, a mere 16km (10 miles) from the Pacific. Most of the vineyards are devoted to Chardonnay and Pinot Noir.

Chalk Hill lies within the warmest, easternmost boundaries of Russian River Valley, at the southern edge of Alexander Valley. Its dun-coloured, volcanic ash soils — in the very shadow of the mountain that created them — are planted mostly in white-wine grapes Sauvignon Blanc and Chardonnay.

Sonoma Coast VA is, at its best, a region where fog immersion makes for intense, vine-matured fruit flavour profiles. However, it was something of a political creation, and the areas within it are linked only by their contact with the seashore.

Knights Valley VA, though politically part of Sonoma County, is really a geographical extension of Napa Valley, going north (or Alexander Valley going south). Initially farmed by William Knight, who arrived in 1845, and isolated from ocean and bay, its warmth and low pH soils point to Cabernet Sauvignon, Merlot and Sauvignon Blanc. Beringer (based in Napa) owns most of the vines.

Alexander Valley VA, settled in 1833 by Cyrus Alexander, a typical trader-trapper-miner-hunter pioneer, stretches from the banks of Russian River to the foothills of the Macayama range, and overlaps the northern part of the Russian River Valley. Deep, rich, river soils yield grapes for luscious late-harvest (botrytis-infected) White Rieslings and Gewürztraminers and fleshy Chardonnays, while thin soils on the benchland above the river produce soft, accessible (no Merlot required) Cabernet Sauvignons and steely-backboned Sauvignon Blancs.

Dry Creek Valley VA is a smaller parallel to Alexander Valley, to the south and west, a bit closer to the Pacific. The climate is hotter and more humid than in its neighbouring regions. Its volcanic benches and gravelled lowlands provide a home to all the Bordeaux varieties, red and white, plus a recent expansion of Italian and Rhône grape cultivars, which also like a bit of sunshine. Notable are several sites of stubby, century-old Zinfandel vines that yield piercingly concentrated, raspberry-toned reds.

Carneros' cool climate is ideal for Pinot Noir.

PRODUCERS

The diversity of Sonoma wines comes not only from a broad palette of grape varieties (*see* p480), after which the wines are generally named, but also from the county's distinctive viticultural areas (*see* p491), each with its own combination of micro-climates and soil types. Most producers make a range of wines: red and white, still and sparkling.

Arrowood

Richard Arrowood's fame came from creating diverse Chardonnays and luscious botrytized Rieslings as founding winemaker at Château St Jean (*qv*) in the mid-1970s. He now maturely crafts graceful Chardonnay, Cabernet Sauvignon and Merlot from a palette of vineyards, as well as a Viognier and a Pinot Blanc, working in a white and blue-grey winery at Glen Ellen.

Buena Vista

Agoston Haraszthy founded the winery in 1857; United Press International boss Frank Bartholomew brought vines and reputation back to life in the 1940s. Now German-owned, Buena Vista focuses on its vineyard in Carneros, altruistically promoting the region almost as much as itself. Winemaker Jill Davis does well with the usual varieties (Chardonnay and Pinot Noir), but also stretches the region with soft, silky Merlots and rich, blackcurranty Cabernet Sauvignons.

Clos du Bois

See profile.

Dry Creek

Since 1972 owner David Stare has made a ferny, figgy, grassy Fumé Blanc (Sauvignon Blanc) his calling card. That even his first Fumés continue to drink well — with a lovely, oily texture — is a tribute to both the variety and the way it is handled at Dry Creek. The winery is in the centre of the Dry Creek Valley VA, north of Healdsburg. True to the region is a piercing, raspberryish Zinfandel and a cedary, raspberry-loaded Meritage Red.

Gary Farrell

Working out of the Davis Bynum Winery, on Westside Road, Healdsburg, winemaker Gary Farrell draws as much berried succulence and juiciness out of Russian River Pinot Noir as is imaginable. Farrell is one of several talented winemakers producing wines for his own label under the benevolent lease of someone else's facility. He also makes Davis Bynum's wines.

Ferrari-Carano

Don and Rhonda Carano own this Healdsburg winery, with a 1,500-barrel (19,500-case) underground *chai*. A figgy, melon Fumé Blanc (Sauvignon Blanc) and tropical-fruited Chardonnays are the main wines here, and the Italian red-wine grape variety Sangiovese is being grown and studied also.

Gloria Ferrer

Jose and Gloria Ferrer own Spain's giant sparkling wine house, Freixenet, outside of Barcelona. In 1982 Jose satisfied a long-held dream of expanding his work to California, where his creamy, elegant classic-method Brut sparkling wine is nearly nine-tenths Pinot Noir. The toasty, fuller-bodied Carneros Cuvée, three years on the yeast, is closer to an equal blend of Pinot Noir and Chardonnay. Some table wines are also made at the winery south of Sonoma.

Foppiano

Louis Foppiano Jr carries a lot of history in the winery — a strong stone's throw from where the Russian River flows under Highway 101 on the south side of Healdsburg — founded in 1896 by his great-grandfather. At the top end of the market, Cabernet Sauvignon and Chardonnay are sold under the Fox Mountain label; the lowest-priced varietals are labelled Riverside Farm. In between, dubbed just plain Foppiano Vineyards, are reasonably priced, easy-to-drink reds from Petite Sirah, Zinfandel and Cabernet Sauvignon, and whites from Chardonnay and Sauvignon Blanc.

Gallo-Sonoma

In 1993 E & J Gallo released their first Sonoma Estate Chardonnay — creamy, elegant and restrained. Next came a high-priced Cabernet Sauvignon from their estate of more than 800ha (2,000 acres) north of Healdsburg.

Geyser Peak

Once held by Schlitz Brewery and later partly Australian-owned (Penfolds), Geyser Peak, near Geyserville, has returned to the Trione family,

---

CLOS DU BOIS

Imagine making 170,000 cases a year of barrel-fermented Chardonnay. Then imagine doing it well — it's creamy, with fresh lemon fruit — and selling it for little more than the price of an everyday wine. Clos du Bois totals more than 330,000 cases of wine a year. Merlot is an equally popular speciality, rife with blackberry and ripe blackcurrant fruit that is soft, silky and lingering. Winemaker Margaret Davenport also produces single-vineyard Chardonnays (lean, austere Flintwood, rounder, more fleshy Calcaire) and Cabernet Sauvignons (redcurrant Briarcrest and blackcurrant-filled Marlstone). Clos du Bois is part of Allied-Hiram Walker, which also manages Callaway in southern California, and Atlas Peak and William Hill Winery (both in Napa Valley).

with an Australian winemaker. Hence the spirited and thoroughly delightful dry white Sémillon/Chardonnay blend from Daryl Groom, who once fashioned the praised Grange Hermitage for Penfolds. Reserve Alexandre is a complex Meritage red.

Glen Ellen

Though the winery — in Glen Ellen — made a big splash with affordable Proprietor's Reserve Chardonnay and Cabernet Sauvignon, it is quite adept on the highest side of the quality spectrum, especially with an oily, ageable Sauvignon Blanc. Glen Ellen's "Imagery Series" artfully examines inventive new ways of treating unusual red-wine varietals, such as Aleatico, Trousseau, Syrah and Cabernet Franc. Glen Ellen has been sold to Heublein.

Gundlach Bundschu

Jim Bundschu is the fourth generation of his family to farm Rhinefarm Vineyard at Sonoma, which was planted in 1858 by Charles Bundschu and Jacob Gundlach. Today there are 120ha (300 acres), which include the Kleinberger vineyard, which makes a dry white Riesling-style wine, and Merlot that ferments out full of blackcurrant-flavoured intensity.

Hanzell

This 3,200-case, 13-ha (32-acre) jewel of an estate just north of Sonoma features a winery which was designed after the north-facing façade (inner courtyard) of Burgundy's famous Clos Vougeot. Founder J D Zellerbach was enamoured of Burgundian wines, planting Chardonnay in 1953, then Pinot Noir. He was a pioneer in bringing French oak and employing stainless steel. Grown on a warm, south-west slope, a focused Chardonnay does quite well here.

Iron Horse

The chilly climes of Green Valley are ideal for Pinot Noir and Chardonnay, crafted both for sparkling wine (the Brut Rosé and the berry-fruited Wedding Cuvée are notable; Laurent Perrier is working with Iron Horse) and for table wine. Cabernet Sauvignon comes from winemaker Forrest Tancer's vines, more than 48km (30 miles) distant from this Sebastopol winery, in Alexander Valley.

Jordan

Tom Jordan built his winery in Healdsburg in the style of a Bordeaux château; but his white wines are made from the burgundy grape, Chardonnay. The Cabernet Sauvignon is soft, with blackcurrant fruit that endures; the Chardonnay is oily with licorice and anise. Jordan also makes a small amount of botrytized, sweet white Sémillon/Sauvignon Blanc and a toasty, apple-fruited classic-method sparkling wine called "J".

Kenwood

Kenwood quietly and consistently produces over 200,000 cases of good and interesting wines each year. These include pepper-spiced Zinfandel, refined Artist Series Cabernet Sauvignon, herballemon Sauvignon Blanc, supple Pinot Noir, crisp melonfruited Chenin Blanc, creamy Chardonnay. The Lee family bought the rustic old Pagani Brothers winery near the small town of Kenwood in 1970.

Kistler

Steve Kistler worked three vintages at Ridge (San Francisco Bay) to learn what he calls "non-interventionist" winemaking. His successes with Chardonnay — lean and tight up front, yet creamy and viscous in the finish — have translated into a tidy new 25,000-case winery at Glen

Ellen, with seven individually cooled and humidified barrel rooms. Some Cabernet Sauvignon and Pinot Noir are also produced here.

Korbel

Set along meandering, gravelled Russian River banks a short hop from the Pacific, Korbal, at Guerneville, is a visitor's delight, from the antique rose garden to the old vine-covered brick buildings. Founded over a century ago by Czech brothers Francis, Joseph and Anton Korbel and owned by the Heck family since 1954, Korbel produces over a million cases a year of affordable sparkling wines and a third that of brandy.

Laurel Glen

Patrick Campbell transforms grapes grown on the fog-free slopes of Sonoma Mountain west of Glen Ellen into one of the finest Cabernet Sauvignons in the country. Plushly lined with violet, blackberry and black cherry fruit, Campbell's Cabernet Sauvignons are firmly structured for age with a framework of tannin and a backbone of acid.

Matanzas Creek

Any winery whose motto is "Extremism in the pursuit of quality is no vice" has got to be a force to be reckoned with. Proprietors Sandra and Bill MacIver employ dual winemakers to experiment and investigate every possible quality profile. The focus is on Chardonnay, the results are rich with ripe butterscotch and vanilla, accented by clove,

apple and licorice notes. A lean Merlot lasts, in glass and in bottle; Sauvignon Blanc is its white equivalent.

Pedroncelli

This Geyserville winery was founded in 1927; the grapes were Carignane, Burger and Petite Sirah. Now the children and grandchildren of John Pedroncelli run things, and the grapes are Chardonnay, Sauvignon Blanc, Chenin Blanc, Cabernet Sauvignon and Zinfandel (made as pale blush, rosé and red). The prices remain reasonable and the following strong.

Piper-Sonoma/Rodney Strong

Once under the same corporate roof, Piper and Strong still stand side-by-side near Healdsburg. The former, owned by Piper Heidsieck, though producing superb sparkling wines, has scaled down due to falling consumption. Strong now takes the name of its founding winemaker Rod Strong, whose Alexander's Crown Cabernet Sauvignon is noteworthy.

Preston

Sauvignon Blanc and Zinfandel define this Dry Creek Valley house north of Healdsburg, but increasing attention is paid to Rhône varieties such as white Marsanne and Viognier, and red Carignane, Syrah, Mourvèdre, Grenache and Cinsaut; there is also a particularly tasty red Barbera. Lou Preston's "old vine" Zinfandels ripple with blackberry and peppercorn fruit that dances on your tongue.

Ravenswood

Joel Peterson focuses on intense, berry-laden Zinfandels that account for more than half the Sonoma winery's production. A Merlot and a Meursault-like Chardonnay — both equally intense — are also made. The Ravenswood label features three interlocked ravens.

St Francis

The 40-ha (100-acre) parcel of land once grew walnuts and prunes. Now Merlot is king at Joe Martin's Kenwood winery. Martin's winemaker, Tom Mackey, who made wine in New York's Finger Lakes district, also makes a little aromatic, off-dry white Muscat Canelli, as well as Cabernet Sauvignon, Cabernet Franc and Zinfandel.

Château St Jean

From its 1973 founding to the present, Chardonnay defines St Jean, near Kenwood, accounting for 70% of its 225,000-case output. The Chardonnay from the Robert Young Vineyard is massively creamy and toasty, that from

Belle Terre Vineyard is both toasty and pear-like, and there is a Sonoma County Chardonnay. Reds are making a comeback (an earthy, meaty Pinot Noir is intriguing), the honeyed, botrytized Riesling and Gewürztraminer still scintillate, and a separate facility makes sparkling wine.

Sebastiani

Founded in 1904 by Tuscan immigrant Samuele Sebastiani, this downtown Sonoma giant has evolved through several incarnations. Once strictly

bulk, August Sebastiani introduced everyday varietals; his son Sam downsized the winery dramatically for high quality, most notably a flinty, floral, dry white called Green Hungarian; now second son Don has volume back-up under a profusion of labels.

Simi

Giuseppe Simi and his brother Pietro bought their Healdsburg winery for $2,200 in 1881. A stone cellar, the core of the present winery, was built in 1890. Surviving Prohibition, the winery was refurbished first by Russ Green, eventually by Moët-Hennessy. Former winemaker, now president, Zelma Long oversees intense vinicultural research. Chardonnays feature ripe clove, apple and anise, the Cabernet Sauvignons are round and soft with violet

scents, and there is a new blend of Sémillon and Sauvignon Blanc (Sendal) which is fleshy with ripe fig and honeydew melon fruit.

Sonoma-Cutrer

At this elegant winery, just off one runway end of Sonoma County Airport at Windsor, Chardonnay is the be all and end all. A high-tech cooling tunnel prevents grape overheating; workers sort the fruit by hand before fermentation. The vineyard-designated wines are Les Pierres (40ha/100 acres), Cutrer (40ha/100 acres) and Russian River Ranches (85ha/210 acres).

Château Souverain

Now part of Nestlé (along with Beringer), Souverain is a prime example of fine Sonoma wines that are undervalued and hence underrated. A handsome restaurant shows winemaker Tom Peterson's wines in their best light: spicy Zinfandel; supple Pinot Noir; silky Chardonnay.

Viansa

When Sam Sebastiani left the winery his grandfather founded, he started his own small operation next to the Schellville Airport south of Sonoma, in Carneros. California-Italian is the theme, with olive trees (for oil), Italian grapes such as Sangiovese, and a marketplace-like tasting room. The best wine, however, is the well-balanced, dusty, blackcurrant-fruited Cabernet Sauvignon.

Williams Selyem

Burt Williams and Ed Selyem simply make the best Pinot Noir in town — Healdsburg — fermenting Russian River fruit in old stainless steel milk tanks. The Pinot Noirs are spicy, succulent and lengthy. Ask about their killer Zinfandel, vibrant with blackberries and coffee notes.

Château St Jean, near Kenwood, in the Sonoma Valley.

OTHER COASTAL REGIONS

Beyond Napa and Sonoma are a number of places that fully display the wild and interesting diversity of California. While a few wineries take the European lead of linking their vinous identity to a single place, a single wine, the norm is a panoply of wines drawn from near and far over a broad spectrum of style and substance. Any of California's main grape varieties (see box, p480) may be used — and a number of others also appear. It is common for a single winery to produce red, white and rosé (blush), a sparkling wine, and perhaps even a dessert wine or three.

Lake and Mendocino
North of what is jokingly called "Sonapanoma" are Lake and Mendocino counties. Although less well known internationally than Napa and Sonoma, with far fewer wineries, they too form part of what Californians call the North Coast; they are north of San Francisco and share many of their neighbours' cool-climate advantages — particularly in Mendocino's highly regarded Anderson Valley.

Surrounding Clear Lake, Lake County is inland from the Pacific Ocean, having a warm climate that is suitable for Sauvignon Blanc (for white wines) and Cabernet Sauvignon (for reds); together these two varieties comprise more than half of the county's plantings. Soils are largely volcanic in nature, the residue of ancient blasts from Mount St Helena and Mount Konocti. Growers consider themselves outpost pioneers, far removed from normal channels of commerce. To this day not a single railway line enters Lake County to serve its half-dozen wineries. Many of the vineyards are owned by Napa-based wine companies, such as Sutter Home, Louis Martini and

Fog on the California coast.

Beringer (now part of Nestlé).

Mendocino County splits into two primary zones: the warm interior Ukiah Valley and the chilly Anderson Valley running west to the Pacific Ocean. Three dozen wineries draw from about 5,000ha (12,000 acres) of vineyards. Chardonnay (for white wines) accounts for a quarter of the plantings, followed by three red-wine varieties: peppercorn and raspberry-laden Zinfandel (grown mostly on high, redwood-forested ridges), Cabernet Sauvignon and workhorse red Carignane. Pinot Noir is on the upswing, but is largely used to make sparkling white wines (Roederer, Scharffenberger). One viticultural area (VA), Cole Ranch, encompasses but a single vineyard, and is the source of some excellent Cabernet Sauvignon.

Bay Area
The area surrounding San Francisco Bay embraces a wide variety of vine-growing sites, from the gravelled

lowlands of Livermore Valley viticultural area to the rainforest slopes of the Santa Cruz Mountains VA, and wineries in historic stone cellars to industrial park tin sheds housing stainless steel fermentation tanks and French oak barrels. In this region there are downtown wineries, such as Audubon and Rosenblum, drawing fruit from many viticultural areas, as well as small estates focusing tightly on a particular patch of ground (Ahlgren, Cronin, Fogarty, Hallcrest, Roudon-Smith, Santa Cruz Mountain Vineyard, Woodside).

Livermore Valley's likeness to Graves in Bordeaux is mirrored by plantings of mostly Cabernet Sauvignon for red wines, Sauvignon Blanc and Sémillon for whites. The cool mountains above Santa Cruz and Santa Clara counties see predominantly Chardonnay and Riesling for white wines, Zinfandel and Pinot Noir for reds.

Monterey and San Benito
Travelling south, the counties of Monterey (on the coast) and San Benito (inland) offer a still greater range of viticultural sites.

Monterey, with its long, sunny growing season, is a land made by irrigation. This was pioneered in the early 1960s by Paul Masson, Mirassou and Wente, who brought sprinklers and drip emitters to Salinas Valley. Natural rainfall is often less than 250mm (10 inches) a year — not enough for a crop that requires upwards of twice that. With irrigation, and loose sandy soils that discourage phylloxera, Monterey reached a high of nearly 16,200ha (40,000 acres) by the mid-1970s, mostly planted in Cabernet Sauvignon which, with all that water, turned vegetal as wine.

In the Salinas Valley today (which comprises the viticultural areas of

Santa Lucia Highlands, Arroyo Seco, San Lucas and Chalone), acreage is down to under 12,100ha (30,000 acres), nearly a third of which is Chardonnay (for white wines). Cabernet Sauvignon (for reds), now better understood (irrigation is cut off after June), is second most planted, followed by Chenin Blanc and Riesling for whites, Zinfandel and Pinot Noir (which does very well near Monterey Bay) for reds, and Sauvignon Blanc and Pinot Blanc (the latter mostly for sparkling wines). Delicato, a Central Valley-based winery, owns the San Bernabe Vineyard near King City, at 3,450ha (8,500 acres) one of the largest contiguous vineyard plantings known.

The red-wine variety Merlot does well up in the Santa Lucia Highlands (Smith & Hook is excellent), fleshy red Pinot Noirs come out of cool spots (Pinnacles, Morgan), Chardonnays possess a distinctive tropical fruitiness (Estancia, Lockwood), and J Lohr makes a red Gamay with pepper-cherry fruit that dances on the palate. Carmel Valley VA, a warm pocket west of the Salinas River, is known for its chocolate-ripe Cabernet Sauvignons.

Once a part of Monterey County, San Benito used to be known for the large Cienega Valley planting by Almaden and its winery, earthquake-bisected by the San Andreas Fault. Calera's Pinot Noirs are the county's claim to fame today.

San Luis Obispo
Paso Robles is the largest viticultural area (VA) in San Luis Obispo County — where 40 wineries farm nearly 4,000ha (10,000 acres) of vine — but Edna Valley VA (south of the city of San Luis Obispo) and Arroyo Grande VA are increasingly important.

Paso Robles, particularly in the warmer region west of Highway 101, is known for its fruity, soft, accessible red Cabernet Sauvignons (Castoro, Eberle, Meridian).

In 1913 the Polish pianist Ignace Paderewski bought 800ha (2,000

acres) west of the town of Paso Robles to plant almonds and Zinfandel grapes. Today the town of Templeton, just south of Paso, is revered by connoisseurs for its peppercorn-fruited red Zinfandels (Ridge, Mastantuono). Paso Robles hosts a major wine festival each May. The York Mountain VA, just 12ha (30 acres) on high ground west of Templeton, is the exclusive domain of York Mountain Winery, founded in 1882.

The Edna Valley is best known for its creamy Chardonnays (Edna Valley Vineyard, Corbett Canyon), while Arroyo Grande has become home to crisp sparkling wines (Maison Deutz). The southernmost edge of the county takes in a small part of the Santa Maria Valley VA, most of which extends over into Santa Barbara County.

Santa Barbara
Santa Barbara sits on what is a geophysical curiosity for California: though virtually all of California's coast faces west, this channel shoreline — from Point Conception to Carpinteria — offers 80km (50 miles) of southern exposure, strikingly similar to the Spanish-French Mediterranean coastline.

The grape first came to Santa Barbara County with the northern expansion of the missions: Santa Barbara (1786), La Purisima Concepcion (Lompoc, 1787) and Santa Ines (Solvang, 1804). As in many areas of California, a thriving wine industry grew through the last half of the 19th century, only to be cut short by Prohibition in the early 20th. Albert Packard's La Bodega was a three-storey adobe structure erected in 1865, with walls 1m (3ft) thick. The wagon road through his vineyard is, to this day, the street De La Vina.

Santa Barbara's revival began in 1962, when Canadian Pierre Lafond founded Santa Barbara Winery. Based then on fruit wines, the winery is now known for cherry-filled red Pinot Noir, juicy white Johannisberg

Riesling and zingy red Zinfandel. The county's big push, though, came from former tyre salesman Brooks Firestone, whose name and altruistic promotion of the region helped put Santa Barbara on the vinous map.

Nearly 4,000ha (10,000 acres) of vine now compete with celebrities and horse ranches. More than half of Santa Barbara's vines are Chardonnay, producing creamy, lush, tropical-fruited white wines, but Pinot Noir gets a disproportionate amount of attention because of the red wines from star-quality vineyards Bien Nacido, Sierra Madre and Sanford & Benedict. The prime VAs are Santa Maria Valley, the flatlands in the north-west corner of the county, and the Santa Ynez Valley, which follows the wildly meandering course of the Santa Ynez River from Lake Cachuma to the Pacific. More than two dozen wineries busily transform grapes to wine.

Southern California
There is a considerable amount of winegrowing south of Santa Barbara County. Los Angeles was the site of California's first commercial winery, founded in 1824 by Joseph Chapman. He was followed by Jean Louis Vignes, a native of Cadillac in France, whose El Aliso Ranch was the basis of a thriving wine business. After the mid-19th century Gold Rush — as the vine moved to Napa, Sonoma and the Sierra Foothills — wine in Los Angeles declined by disease (Pierce's) and development.

Today, aside from around a dozen "business-park" winemakers in the Los Angeles area, there are more than 8,000ha (20,000 acres) planted in Riverside County, most picked as table grapes. But the sandy soils of the Temecula VA, in the south-west corner of the county (north of San Diego, south-east of Los Angeles) are noted for Chardonnay, both as still white (Callaway) and sparkling wine (Culbertson, renamed Thornton). The smaller VA of San Pasqual Valley has barely 40ha (100 acres) to vine. □

PRODUCERS

California winemakers often own vineyards in several viticultural areas, or even over several counties, and may also buy grapes from other growers. The winemakers of California's coast are discussed here according to the region in which the winery is based. As in the rest of California, most quality wines are labelled according to grape variety (see p480).

LAKE AND MENDOCINO

Fetzer
Founded by Barney Fetzer in Hopland, Mendocino, in 1969, Fetzer has grown into a sizeable, yet still premium, wine producer, now owned by the big distiller/distributor Brown-Forman (the producer of Jack Daniels whiskey). A large commercial organic garden shows how Fetzer grapes are grown, and a cookery school teaches wine and food pairings. Barrel Select Cabernet Sauvignon and Barrel Select Chardonnay are much admired. The Sundial Chardonnay, fresh with pear and apple fruit, is particularly good value for money. There is a second label, Bel Arbors.

Guenoc
The vineyard near Middletown, once the ranch of British actress Lillie Langtry, overlaps the border between Lake and Napa counties. Guenoc's Langtry Red is a Meritage blend of blackcurrant suppleness; the Langtry White is oily with olive and licorice. Guenoc's Reserve Chardonnay is also distinctive, with rich yet restrained creamy lemon fruit.

Kendall-Jackson
Built as tiny Château du Lac at Lakeport in 1983, attorney Jess Jackson's vinous empire has grown to nearly a million cases a year through the acquisition of wineries J Stonestreet (Sonoma), Cambria (Santa Maria Chardonnay) and Edmeades (Anderson Valley). Kendall-Jackson made Chardonnay a generic term for white wine with its popular, pineapple-fleshed, slightly sweet version. The Cardinale, an expensive red Meritage blend, is big and bold, with cassis, iodine and tobacco fruit.

Navarro
Ted Bennett and his wife Deborah Cahn own 20ha (50 acres) near Philo, in the cool quiet of Mendocino's remote Anderson Valley. Crisp dry Chardonnays and supple Pinot Noirs compete with sinfully sweet white botrytized Riesling and Gewürztraminer. The latter is also made as a grape juice for children visiting the winery.

Parducci
John Parducci's father founded the winery in 1932 and, like other old Italians, Parducci quietly goes about his business, making sound, affordable wines such as his Petite Sirah, with its plum and berry spiciness, from his 140ha (450 acres) vineyard. But the word got out, so thousands of visitors make the trek to Ukiah to visit winery, gift shop, art gallery, restaurant and tasting room.

Roederer
Jean-Claude Rouzaud brought Champagne Louis Roederer to California in 1985. This experiment by the French house in making classic sparkling wine the far side of the Atlantic extended to blending in the Anderson Valley just as it does in Champagne. It therefore bought land differing in its altitude and proximity to the ocean. Roederer's plot closest to the sea is 18km (12 miles) from its most inland. The goal is 100,000 cases from almost 162ha (400 acres) of vines. The Estate Brut, which is oak-aged, is elegant, with lemon and bread-dough aromas.

Scharffenberger
Champagnes Pommery and Lanson (part of Louis Vuitton Moët-Hennessy) are partners with John Scharffenberger in Philo, Mendocino. John's sparkling white wines tend toward the lean and austere, though his Brut Rosé has rich, toasty aromas, plum and strawberry fruitiness.

BAY AREA

Bonny Doon
Randall Grahm courts publicity, and makes wholly distinctive wines, a few from his Santa Cruz Mountain home base. His tasty Rhône-style red, Le Cigare Volant, full of cranberry and cherry aromas and flavours, is labelled with a spoof of French UFO (*cigare volant*) sightings. He also makes a pear *eau-de-vie*, an intensely sweet Muscat Canelli in the style of a German *Eiswein*, and other eclectic take-offs.

Concannon
The Concannon saga dates to its 1883 founding by the Irish bookseller James Concannon. Prohibition saw the cellars productive, thanks to ties with San Francisco's Catholic hierarchy (and the legitimate need for sacramental wines). Concannon (now part of Wente) is one of the last producers of Petite Sirah, a bold, somewhat rustic red wine full of plummy flavour that grows well in the gravelled ground of the Livermore Valley.

Mirassou
The fifth and sixth generations of Mirassous date their Santa Clara Valley vinelands to 1854, and the winery itself is in San Jose. However, since the 1960s Mirassou's vineyard emphasis has shifted south to 300ha (750 acres) of Monterey County vineland, where it produces velvety Pinot Noir and bold bell-peppered Harvest Cabernet Sauvignon reds, and several sparkling white wines — the Au Natural is crisp and biting — that show off Monterey's cool climate.

Ridge
Founded by a group of scientists who made wine on weekends, Ridge, which is based at Cupertino, is now Japanese-owned. But veteran winemaker Paul Draper continues to produce the most distinctive Zinfandels extant from vineyards as disparate and distant as Lytton Springs (Sonoma) and Dusi (Paso Robles). The dense, almost black York Creek (Napa) Petite Sirah has long been a favourite with collectors.

Wente
Like their Livermore neighbours, the Concannons, the Wentes set up winegrowing in 1883. Since that date the Wente estate has remained family-owned: they have recently remodelled the former Cresta Blanca winery into a restaurant and sparkling wine centre, and buying

Concannon Vineyard as well. Wente raises beef cattle next to its Livermore vines, and has extensive vine holdings in Monterey County. Wente's Sémillon has lovely melon-fig fruitiness.

MONTEREY AND SAN BENITO

Calera

Josh Jensen's passionate love of burgundy led to a search for a limestone-laced patch of earth where he felt that Pinot Noir would feel at home. He found what he was looking for in an old lime kiln (for which *calera* is the Spanish word) in the hills above Hollister in San Benito County. The winery cascades down the slope in seven levels. Each estate vineyard — Jensen, Reed, Selleck and Mills — makes a distinctive Pinot Noir, but each has a rich and recognizable cinnamon/cherry spiciness. Some Viognier grapes are grown, making wine in an austere, white Rhône style.

Chalone

To the east of the town of Soledad, on the Monterey side of the basalt Pinnacles rock formation from Calera, is Chalone. This winery, too, focuses on the old Burgundian methods of extracting maximum character out of Pinot Noir and Chardonnay grapes. Chalone's expansion, coupled with partner Ch Lafite-Rothschild of Bordeaux, links it with Edna Valley (San Luis Obispo), Acacia (Napa), Carmenet (Sonoma) and Woodward Canyon (Washington State) in an exciting corporate venture.

Jekel

Jekel, based at Greenfield, is a famous exception to the rule "Riesling doesn't work in California." Monterey Bay fog means that the Jekel grapes retain enough acidity, so even dry Riesling keeps its tart apricot-like fruit depth, while a sweet botrytis-affected dessert wine is lush with fruit. Chardonnay is also successful; and the Cabernet Sauvignon tends towards a chocolate ripeness.

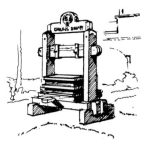

The Monterey Vineyard

Founded in 1974, near the small town of Gonzales, The Monterey Vineyard is now owned by Seagram Classics. Its forte is the Classic line of affordable, easy-drinking wines, particularly Classic Pinot Noir and the blended Classic Red.

SAN LUIS OBISPO

Eberle

Former footballer Gary Eberle first planted grapes east of Paso Robles in 1972 for Estrella River Winery (now Meridian), and then began his own label in 1980. A low-yield clone of Cabernet Sauvignon, planted on its own roots, accounts for soft and well-balanced berry-like wines. Eberle produces also Chardonnay and tiny amounts of red varietal wines from Barbera, Syrah and Zinfandel, white Viognier and a flower-scented Muscat Canelli.

Martin Brothers

Winemaker Nick Martin and salesman Tom Martin bring an undying love of Italian culture to their Paso Robles wine venture. They have made the prime Piedmontese grape Nebbiolo popular as a varietal wine, with its tar, violet and pomegranate fruit (the labels on the bottles feature reproductions of Italian Renaissance art). A supple, dry white Chenin Blanc is distinctive. A Vin Santo (*see* p383), rare outside Italy, is made from Malvasia grapes, and a *grappa* (grape spirit) is distilled from Nebbiolo.

Meridian

The original Estrella River Winery in Paso Robles was quickly bought by Beringer (itself owned by Nestle/Wine World) when family squabbles forced its sale. Master winemaker Chuck Ortman oversees an annual production of 300,000 cases — two-thirds of which are a creamy, melon and vanilla Santa Barbara Chardonnay. Cabernet Sauvignon, Syrah and Zinfandel are made from the Home Vineyard.

Wild Horse

The Templeton winery sits on a plateau east of the Salinas River, just 23km (14 miles) east of the Pacific. Chardonnay is supple with apple fruit; Pinot Noir is stunning, with floral rose petal, "forest floor" mushroom and cherry; Merlot is tangy with camphor, eucalyptus and tobacco. Owner/winemaker Ken Volk believes in making his wines accessible, but they are good, too.

SANTA BARBARA AND SOUTHERN CALIFORNIA

Byron

In 1984 Byron Kent "Ken" Brown founded Byron, which overlooks Santa Maria Valley's vinelands to the west. The early success of Brown's creamy, appley Chardonnay, his supple, mushroom- and strawberry-laden Pinot Noir and lemony, grassy, bell-pepper Sauvignon Blanc prompted Robert Mondavi to purchase the winery in 1990. There is even a Cabernet Sauvignon, with sweet tobacco and soft redcurrant fruit, and an excellent Pinot Blanc.

Callaway

Ely Callaway, a retired textile magnate, founded his winery in the wilds of Temecula (97km/60 miles north of San Diego, in Riverside County) in 1969. Callaway sold to Hiram Walker in 1981. The winery specializes in a buttery, non-oak-aged Chardonnay called Calla-Lees. Also popular are a complex Fumé Blanc (barrel-aged Sauvignon Blanc), and a fruity Sauvignon Blanc (made in stainless steel).

Firestone

Brooks Firestone found the Santa Ynez Valley (Santa Barbara County) suitable for grape vines. At his Los Olivos winery he focuses on apricot-fruited Johannisberg Rieslings (some dry, some sweet), a rose-perfumed Pinot Noir, and a silky Merlot that lingers in the mouth. His wife Kate runs nearby Carey Cellars.

Sanford

Rich Sanford began planting vines on the south bank of the Santa Ynez River just west of Buellton in 1971. His experience in the area shows in butter-and-grapefruit Chardonnay, Pinot Noirs that are rich with black cherry, herbaceously ageable Sauvignon Blancs, and a tangy, orange-peel and rose-petal Pinot Noir Vin Gris (a dry *blanc de noirs*). Star quality.

Santa Barbara

This is the oldest winery in the county of Santa Barbara, since it was found in the 1960s. It produces excellent burgundy style wines, Pinot Noir and Chardonnay, as well as Sauvignon Blanc and Zinfandel.

INTERIOR REGIONS

The two inland wine-producing regions, which do not benefit from the influence of the Pacific Ocean, nonetheless offer some interesting wines in every conceivable style. Besides the usual California varieties (*see* p480), Portuguese grapes are grown to make port-style wine in the Central Valley.

Central Valley

California's Central Valley stretches out over 640km (400 miles) from the the foothills of Mount Shasta in the north to Bakersfield in the south, about 100km (63 miles) from Los Angeles. It has six recognized viticultural areas (VAs) running from north to south: (1) North Yuba (1985), northeast of Sacramento, on the right banks of the Yuba, enjoys the most temperate climate; (2) Dunnigan Hills (the most recent, 1993), in the county of Yolo, north-west of Sacramento, already has over 500ha (1,230 acres) of vines; (3) Clarksburg (1984), south of Sacramento, benefiting from the sea mist which rises up from San Francisco Bay, is especially famous for its very lively Chenin Blancs; (4) Lodi (1983), stretching out over the south of Sacramento and the north of San Joaquin, produces its famous raspberry-scented Zinfandels from vineyards planted on the plains and terraces; (5) Merritt Island, in San Joaquin, also benefits from a temperate climate thanks to the sea mists; (6) Madera, stretching over the counties of Madera and Fresno, has 15,000ha (37,000 acres) given over to grapes for wine production and produces a large quantity of eating grapes and raisins.

In the San Joaquin Valley, occupying the southern half of the Central Valley, vines grow alongside fields of wheat and cotton. While warm daytime temperatures deplete acidity and prevent the production of high-priced premiums, there is balance enough

El Dorado County, Sierra Foothills.

for charming, affordable table wines. Thompson Seedless grapes are used for white wine, brandy base and table grapes, as well as for raisins.

French Colombard, Chenin Blanc, Zinfandel, Grenache, Petite Sirah and Barbera contribute to the vast quantities of "jug wine" which overshadows the fine white Chardonnay, red Cabernet Sauvignon and chic sparkling wines that are also made here.

The variety does not stop there. In the 1930s and 1940s most of California's wines were sweet and fortified. Today those wines are almost an afterthought, but not far from the world's largest winery — Gallo's output is more than a million cases for each week of the year — are tiny producers (Quady and Ficklin) of excellent dessert wines. In the neighbourhood are anonymous giants (Sierra, Vie-Del, Noble) who quietly ferment wines for others, offshoots of more prestigious operations (Heublein, Mondavi, Sebastiani), and producers of brandy and clean

standard wines (Delicato, Franzia, Bronco, Giumarra, Guild).

Two of the world's top wine schools are here in the Central Valley: the University of California at Davis and California State at Fresno.

Sierra Foothills

Along the eastern edge of the great Central Valley are the foothills of the Sierra Nevada range, a transition from hot dry plains to mountain ski resorts. The majesty of the Sierras may offer different scenic vistas from valley wine regions, but densely fruited wines — reds from Zinfandel and Cabernet Sauvignon, whites from Chardonnay and Sauvignon Blanc — are equally appealing.

California's foothill counties are, in order of plantings: Amador (800ha/2,000 acres), El Dorado (200ha/500 acres), Calaveras (80ha/ 200 acres), Tehama (60ha/150 acres) and Nevada (50ha/125 acres).

Long before anyone had associated Napa or Sonoma with the grape, gold-seeking pioneers had grown wine where lowland oaks give way to upland pines. In the mid to late 19th century more than 100 wineries existed among the mountain streams and crannies of played-out mines. Then phylloxera and Prohibition, along with the absence of cheap transport, put the foothills out of the wine business for half a century.

Vinicultural rebirth came in the 1970s, when Amador County Zinfandels, made by Sutter Home and Ridge, hit the market. Soon, names such as Boeger, Karly, Stevenot, Madrona and Monteviña spread the region's renown. The reasons were simple enough. Hillside vines, at 460–910m (1,500–3,000ft) above sea level, give lower yields and focused flavours. The absence of fog reduces mould problems. Lower land costs reduce production costs and wine prices. □

PRODUCERS

The Central Valley produces nearly 90% of all California's wine, but most of this is "jug wine" — blended wine for easy drinking. The same region has a tradition of fortified and dessert wines.
High altitudes in the foothills of the Sierra Nevada Mountains give intense flavours to the wines produced here, although they are made from many of the usual California grape varieties (*see* p480).

CENTRAL VALLEY
J F J Bronco
Bronco is the sixth-largest US winery, with a storage capacity of some 20 million cases. Most of its production is standard table wine and sparkling wine, sold under J F J Cellars and CC Vineyard labels, but Bronco began the 1990s by purchasing premium labels Grand Cru, Hacienda, Laurier, Black Mountain and J W Morris Ports.

Ficklin
The Ficklin family began planting grapes at Madera in 1912, although they did not begin making wine until 1948. Traditional port-style wines are what the Ficklins make, from Portuguese grape varieties Tinta Madeira, Tinta Cão, Touriga and Souzão. The old cellar is of adobe, covered with ivy; the wines it shelters are fairly priced and wonderful, with fluid black cherry and sweet currant fruit, and just a hint of black walnut.

Gallo
Modesto's winery got to be the largest in the world — 65 million cases a year — by Ernest Gallo's making good his boast that he could sell more wine than his late brother, grower/winemaker Julio Gallo, could make. Most of the wines — table, sweet and sparkling — are inexpensive, but soundly made. Hearty Red Burgundy, a slightly sweet red wine, brought Gallo initial attention, but the Sauvignon Blanc varietal white has star quality. The range is now very wide, with something for every taste from "pop" wines to oak-aged Chardonnay.

R H Phillips
Out in the Dunnigan Hills, east of famed Napa Valley, is the Giguiere family's 250,000-case R H Phillips winery. Its fresh and fruity blends and varietals are priced nowhere near their quality level, mainly because land is cheap in Yolo County (near the University of California Davis wine school). Night harvesting makes crisp, clean wines — particularly the Sauvignon Blanc.

Quady
Bringing a new respectability to dessert wines, Andrew Quady has become known as the "Muscat King of California" with his floral Orange Muscat called Essensia, the silky, black-cherry-flavoured Black Muscat (Elysium) and a 4% alcohol, spritzy Orange Muscat (Electra). The Madera winery also makes fortified port-style wines, some of them labelled Starboard (the opposite of port on a ship).

SIERRA FOOTHILLS
Boeger
In 1972 Greg and Susan Boeger founded their vineyard and cellar just east of Placerville in El Dorado County, where vines are rooted in ground up to 900m (3,000ft) above sea level, which means cool temperatures in the absence of fog. Boeger's raspberry-filled Merlot and silky, peppercorn Zinfandel are equally alluring.

Ironstone
John Kautz founded his winery in the county of Calaveras only in 1994. Although his vines are still young, he already produces excellent wines from Cabernet Franc and Syrah.

Monteviña
Monteviña became known in the 1970s for its powerful red Zinfandel wines made from grapes planted in 1972 in the red, decomposed granite of Amador County. The winery was bought by Sutter Home (Napa) in 1988, and began to focus on Italian red-wine varieties on a site that has, from the first, produced California's most reliable varietal Barbera wine. New plantings of Nebbiolo share space with trial plantings of varieties such as Sangiovese, Refosco and Aleatico.

Renaissance
The stunningly terraced vineyards of the winery above the town of Renaissance in the county of Yuba produce lush, late-harvest (botrytized) white dessert wines made from Riesling and Sauvignon Blanc.

One of the large, modern wineries typical of the Central Valley.

NORTH-WESTERN USA

WITH ONLY A BRIEF HISTORY OF VINEGROWING, AMERICA'S NORTH-
WESTERN STATES, PARTICULARLY WASHINGTON AND OREGON, HAVE
EMERGED WITH A PALETTE OF EXCITING FINE WINES.

Oregon is known above all for its red wines made from the
Pinot Noir grape. This winery, Elk Cove, produces Pinot Noir
wines from three individually named vineyards in the north
Willamette Valley, the heart of Oregon's wine industry.

The states of Washington and Oregon are not known for year-round warmth and sunshine like California. But, like their southern neighbour, their climate is influenced by the ranges of mountains and hills that provide a host of micro-climates to challenge and to inspire winemakers who have been attracted to the region.

In Washington State, most of the vineyards are located inland and are cut off from the influence of the Pacific Ocean by the Cascade Range. The latter forms a barrier against rain and creates a desert. Vines can therefore only prosper in the valleys of the Columbia River and its tributaries. Irrigation and a scientific approach to vinegrowing allow for a wide range of wines. Most popular are dry and off-dry whites from Chardonnay, Riesling, Sauvignon Blanc and Sémillon grapes, and reds from Cabernet Sauvignon and Merlot. The best of them tend to be varietals.

Oregon's main vine zone is the Willamette Valley, which is sheltered by the coastal range and the Cascades, to the east. Its climate being cooler and wetter than California's, it enjoys conditions similar to those in Burgundy: Pinot Noir, the great burgundian red-wine grape, is the most widely-grown variety while Chardonnay and Pinot Gris make elegant dry white wines. Oregon is one of the few New World regions in a position to challenge Burgundy; French investment in vineyard land has but compounded the excitement.

Winemaking is a relatively new industry in these states. From the ending of Prohibition (1933) until the mid-1960s there were just half a dozen wineries in Washington State — and these made wines from fruit (rhubarb, raspberries, pears). In 1962 a group of amateur winemakers planted a small plot with classic European grape varieties. By 1967 the success of their wines had inspired a wealthy local rival firm to turn its attentions from native grapes to *vitis vinifera* varieties, and since then Washington viniculture has grown apace, in size and in quality.

Oregon's wine history is equally short and the industry has remained small, but the quality of the wines, particularly those made from Pinot Noir, is possibly second only to Burgundy's.

WASHINGTON

Washington State is steadily catching up with New York State, the second-largest US producer of quality wine. Washington is on an upward cycle and produced 3 million cases in 1997. New York, with 11 million cases in 1988, was recently down to half that figure. Neither will ever threaten California. Washington State's output comes from about 15,000ha (37,000 acres) — a tenth of California's wine-grape plantings. However, only 6,000ha (15,000 acres) are *vinifera* plantings, and California's wine production is more than 30 times that of the Evergreen State. Two-thirds of Washington's plantings are of Concord grapes, used for juice, not wine.

Climate
East of the Cascade Range, central Washington has a continental climate, with hot summers, cold winters and low rainfall. In the rain shadow of the Cascades (Mount Rainier is 4,367m/14,410ft above sea level), the Columbia Valley is an arid, high desert region, with an annual rainfall of just 200mm (8in). It took irrigation to bring *vitis vinifera* grapes east of the Cascades; huge, gangly, centre-pivot systems that reach long arms out to embrace a circle of nearly 65ha (160 acres) at a time.

Of equal viticultural importance is hardening off vines to prepare them for the frozen winters common to the high plains. Cutting off water and nutrients (usually mid-August) well before autumn's first frost ensures that the pre-dormant vines will survive the winter. In 1979, before the need for hardening off was fully appreciated, over 400ha (1,000 acres) of vineyard were killed statewide.

As in northern Europe, Washington growers look for south-facing slopes, both to take full advantage of

Sampling the fermenting wine.

WINE ZONES

Washington has four viticultural areas (VAs): Columbia Valley, located inland, is one and a half time the size of Belgium and extends into Oregon; it encompasses two minor VAs, Yakima Valley and Walla Walla Valley. The fourth VA is Puget Sound, near Seattle.

Columbia Valley is the primary VA, with over 4,000ha (9,000 acres). It takes the form of an upside-down "T". The upright column of the "T" is the Columbia River, flowing south until it forms the border with Oregon State.
Walla Walla Valley, the eastern arm of the "T", accounts for only 0.5% of the state's plantings, but produces wines of very high quality.
Yakima Valley, the western arm of the "T", accounts for 40% of Washington's plantings. Its prosperity is due to irrigation.
Puget Sound on the Pacific coast provides good conditions for the German grapes Müller-Thurgau and Siegerrebe.There are also Pinot Noir plantings.

summer sunlight and to mitigate the winter chill. The close proximity to a major river — the Columbia or Yakima — also tends to moderate temperature extremes. Cool nights mean good acidity in the grapes. Washington's harvest is later than California's, starting mid-September and often running into November.

Grape varieties and wine styles
The white-wine grapes Chardonnay and Riesling (often referred to as White Riesling) are the most planted varieties in Washington, followed by the red-wine varieties Merlot and Cabernet Sauvignon. Sauvignon Blanc (for white wine) is gaining ground. Although not so widely planted, Sémillon has its supporters; in Washington it is sometimes made as a varietal white wine, as well as being blended with Sauvignon Blanc. Cabernet Franc and Syrah are expanding while Riesling is down from previous totals.

Washington has made its vinous name with whites from Chardonnay, whose fruit is crisp and fresh, Rieslings with bright, steely apricot definition and depth, reds from Merlot, crackling with currant fruitiness, and low-tannin Cabernet Sauvignons whose fruit fairly leaps from the glass. The fruit comes through strongly because the grapes are matured slowly and evenly by the warm, but not hot, sun of Washington's northerly latitude. Vine maturity (fruit flavour) as opposed to sun ripeness (dehydration) shows in the wines.

The industry is young, so styles vary greatly — some winemakers give a few months' oak-ageing to their Chardonnay and Sémillon whites, as well as their reds.

Sparkling wines are receiving increased attention, particularly at Château Ste Michelle, the state's largest producer.

PRODUCERS

The history of quality winemaking in Washington really began with the Columbia winery, followed by Château Ste Michelle. An ever-increasing number of wineries began to open in the 1970s and 1980s. Washington's 85 wineries, with about 6,000ha (15,000 acres) of vineyards, produce mainly varietal wines.

Arbor Crest
Arbor Crest first gained attention through its creamy, richly fruited Chardonnays. Its tasting room, the Cliff House, perches on a basalt outcrop above the Spokane River, a few miles east of Spokane. The Mielke brothers' vineyard is on the Wahluke Slope, a south-facing site in the Columbia Valley, producing an outstanding Sauvignon Blanc and a generously fruity Merlot full of currant and berry aromas.

Columbia
Founded as Associated Vintners in 1962 by a group of dedicated hobbyists with 2ha (5.5 acres) in the Yakima Valley, Columbia achieved prominence through winemaker David Lake's superb, lean Cabernet Sauvignons grown at some of Yakima's top individual vineyards: Otis, Red Willow and Sagemoor Farm. Columbia now produces over 80,000 cases a year, with red varietal wines from Cabernet Sauvignon, Merlot, Syrah and Cabernet Franc, and white wines from Chardonnay, Riesling, Gewürztraminer and Sémillon.

Covey Run
Originally named Quail Run, this Zillah (Yakima Valley) venture was founded by a group of fruit growers who turned to growing winegrapes. The fragrant, stainless-steel-fermented Lemberger, a most unusual red, is a speciality, along with White Riesling

and Chardonnay. La Caille de Fumé is a dry white Sauvignon Blanc/Sémillon blend.

The Hogue Cellars
The Hogues run a diversified 570-ha (1,400-acre) farm and 240,000-case winery near Prosser in the Yakima Valley; grapes compete with asparagus, hops and apples. But a silky white Sémillon and some minty red Merlots moved the family into serious winemaking. Their list now includes reds from Cabernet Sauvignon and Cabernet Franc.

Latah Creek
At this Spokane winery, owner Mike Conway puts a personal stamp on crisp Chardonnays (his Feather Chardonnay is delicately appley) and an oak-aged red Lemberger.

Leonetti
Gary Figgins began making distinctive Merlot and Cabernet Sauvignon out of a basement cellar at Walla Walla, but raging success soon allowed a handsome stone cellar to be erected. Red wines remain a speciality: 5ha (12 acres) of Merlot grapes surround the house (with a little Syrah and Sangiovese). A bordeaux-style blend carries the title Walla Walla Valley Select.

Preston
The 20-ha (50-acre) vineyard that was planted on the sandy, high desert flatlands just north of Pasco in 1972 has expanded to 73ha (181 acres) and production has grown to 35,000

cases. Dry Chardonnay and sweet, late-harvest Riesling have long been Preston's specialities, and the Gamay Beaujolais Rosé is fresh and fruity.

Quilceda Creek
Though only 1,000 cases of Cabernet Sauvignon are made each year since 1979 at Quilceda Creek — at Snohomish, north of Seattle, from bought-in Columbia Valley grapes — they are eagerly scooped up by those who know Washington wines. Paul Golitzin makes the wine, the legendary André Tchelistcheff (nearly 40 years at Napa Valley's Beaulieu) consults.

Château Ste Michelle
See profile.

Paul Thomas
Working the unusual dry side of fruit wines, Paul Thomas

made Crimson Rhubarb — a *blanc de noirs* made from rhubarb — a household word in western Washington. A barrel-fermented Chardonnay is complemented by a red Cabernet Sauvignon-Merlot blend. In 1993 the winery was purchased by Associated Vintners (Columbia — *qv*).

Woodward Canyon
Red wines from Cabernet Sauvignon (blackcurrant and dill) and Merlot (coffee and tobacco) are winemaker Rick Small's specialities, but he also makes a white burgundian-style — barrel-fermented, malolactic fermentation, extended lees contact — Chardonnay (clove and butter). His Meritage (bordeaux-style) red is called Chabonneau. He owns vineyards near his winery in Walla Walla Valley, and buys in from Columbia Valley.

——— CHATEAU STE MICHELLE ———

A company based in suburban Seattle, making wine from native grapes and other fruit, became the most influential winery in Washington in 1967, when major investment brought in André Tchelistcheff (from Napa Valley, California) as a consultant, and attention shifted to varietal wines made from *vinifera* grapes. Château Ste Michelle now makes 500,000 cases a year, with a range of varietal wines (flinty Rieslings, Cold Creek Cabernet Sauvignon from Yakima Valley) and Domaine Michelle sparkling wines. The parent company, Stimson Lane, also owns another large winery — Columbia Crest at Paterson, known for its easy-drinking white wines — and the smaller Snoqualmie, with a Late-Harvest (sweet) White Riesling and an off-dry Muscat Canelli.

OREGON

Oregon's reputation for wine growing has nothing to do with the quantity of wine it produces. It all happened on a famous day in 1979 when, during a blind tasting organised by Robert Drouhin, David Lett's 1975 Eyrie Vineyard Pinot Noir beat Drouhin's phenomenal Clos de Bèze 1961 to second place, after the Chambolle-Musigny 1959 from the same producer. At that time, Oregon had only just over 100ha (250 acres) of Pinot Noir.

Nowadays Oregon has around 3,000ha (7,400 acres) of vineyards (half of which are planted with Pinot Noir), less than 2% of the total area California dedicates to grape growing for wine production.

Climate and soil

Most of Oregon's winegrowing takes place west of the snow-clad Cascade Range, which runs north-south parallel to the Pacific Ocean, about 160km (100 miles) inland. It is a cool, wet region, with a lot more in common with Burgundy and other northern European vineyards than either California or Washington.

Just inland from Tillamook is the heart of Oregon winegrowing, Yamhill County, which accounts for a quarter of the state's land under vine. The northernmost section of Willamette Valley (*see* box), Yamhill County's core is McMinnville, population 10,000. There, each July, the International Pinot Noir Celebration (IPNC) is held at Linfield College.

Willamette Valley, once an inland sea, has soils that are also volcanic in origin (from an ancient Idaho eruption), and are particularly rich in rust-red iron oxide in the Red Hills of Dundee area, though some of Yamhill's western slopes have yellowish sedimentary layers. Yields are generally a mere 30–40hl/ha in the Willamette Valley, which provides

Vines in the Red Hills of Dundee.

up to three-quarters of Oregon's wine-grapes.

In this cool region, harvest usually runs from early October into mid-November. The Rogue Valley, a bit warmer, generally comes in earlier, except where the perennially late Cabernet Sauvignon is grown.

Oregon's first wine-grapes were planted in 1961, when Richard Sommer saw hope for ageable Riesling west of Roseburg. Sommer's Hill-Crest Vineyard winery was licensed

WINE ZONES

Besides part of Columbia Valley, Oregon currently has three viticultural areas (VAs), the largest and best-known being the Willamette Valley:

Willamette Valley extends south and west from Portland to Eugene.
Umpqua Valley is further south, extending down to Roseburg.
Rogue Valley — which includes Applegate and Illinois Valleys — is just north of the California border, ringing the tourist city of Grants Pass.

in 1966. The first *vitis vinifera* plantings in Yamhill County came in 1966 at The Eyrie Vineyard, where David and Diana Lett proved that Pinot Noir doesn't have to be dark to be good and age well. "Cabernet Sauvignon has a distinct flavour profile, no matter where it is grown," David Lett says. "But Pinot Noir is so site- and winemaker-specific, it varies so widely, that people can't get an easy handle on it. Which is what makes it so intriguing."

Grape varieties and wine styles

The red-wine variety Pinot Noir is planted in nearly half of Oregon's land under vine. White-wine varieties account for most of the rest: Chardonnay holds second position, followed by Riesling and Pinot Gris.

Though Pinot Noir attracts most attention, the 1980s spawned two new developments. One was the explosion of attention given to Pinot Gris, once an Italian afterthought (Pinot Grigio), now made into a steely-flinty dry white.

Quiet evolution marked Chardonnay's transition from the overblown California style to Oregon's subtle, more elegant stamp (apple fruit, sweeter spices like clove, ginger, allspice, vanilla). Oregon's white wines, especially Chardonnays, can age for three or four years in bottle. The Pinot Noir reds vary widely — between winemakers and vintages — but most are ready to drink at between four and six years old, although the best continue to improve for much longer.

The 1980s brought respected winemakers to the region from California (William Hill, Carl Doumani, Steve Girard), France (Domaine Drouhin and Laurent Perrier) and Australia (Brian Croser) with money and talents to stretch Oregon's winegrowing experience. □

PRODUCERS

Oregon's wineries, like Washington's, mostly date from the 1970s and 1980s. Unlike Washington's, however, the majority are family-run businesses that concentrate on wines made from their own, locally-grown grapes. Most of the following are in the northern Willamette Valley, between Portland and Salem. As is usual in the USA, most wines are labelled by grape variety.

Adelsheim
David and Ginny Adelsheim began planting their 19-ha (48-acre) vineyard on the slopes of Chehalem Mountain in 1971, with equal amounts of Pinot Noir and Pinot Gris, then Chardonnay, Pinot Blanc and White Riesling. Ripe black cherry, mushroom and truffle define the Pinot Noir; the Pinot Gris is a flinty dry white.

Amity
Half of Myron Redford's 6-ha (15-acre) vineyard, planted in 1970, is Pinot Noir, some of which is annually made in the *nouveau* style: light, very fruity, ready to drink just months after harvest. Cinnamon-spiced white Gewürztraminer is noteworthy, as is the rarely produced, peppery red Gamay Noir.

Bethel Heights
Twins Ted and Terry Casteel began planting their 21ha (51 acres) in the Eola Hills, 19km (12 miles) north-west of Salem, in 1977, and have made estate-only wine since 1984. Nearly half the vines are Pinot Noir, producing a supple red wine, with hints of truffle, tar and black cherry. Chenin Blanc gives a "lemon-and-pineapple" dry white wine.

Domaine Drouhin
After the success of the Californian David Lett's (The Eyrie) Pinot Noir during a blind tasting, Joseph Drouhin founded a winery at Dundee. His first vintage Pinot Noir, in 1988, has astounded the other producers.

Erath
Lumberman Cal Knudsen and winemaker Dick Erath founded Oregon's largest estate winery (now 40,000 cases) west of Dundee in 1972. Half the production is a mint-spiced, black-cherry-filled Pinot Noir. A honeysuckle Riesling is made both dry and in a Mosel style (2% residual sugar). French-oak-fermented, lees-aged Pinot Gris is new, and some Pinot Noir is made as a fruity, dry Vin Gris (rosé).

The Eyrie
See profile.

Henry Estate
The Henry family began planting grapes along the Umpqua River, 20km (13 miles) north-west of Roseburg, in 1972; the winery was completed in 1978. Though it is warmer than the Willamette Valley here, Pinot Noir is still the leading wine, with fragrant rose-petal aromas and meaty richness. White wines are Chardonnay, aged in American oak, Gewürztraminer and Müller-Thurgau.

Oak Knoll
Ron and Marge Vuylsteke own no vineyard, but buy grapes. An oak-aged Chardonnay leads the list, followed by silky Pinot Noir, apricot-laced Riesling and dry Pinot Gris.

Ponzi
Just 24km (15 miles) south-west of Portland is the 28-ha (70-acre) vineyard of Dick and Nancy Ponzi. Racy Rieslings and taut, richly-built Pinot Noirs (black cherry, mushroom, clove) excite. Chardonnay is barrel-fermented in Allier oak, a wood that accents the wine's sweet lime fruit.

Rex Hill
Owners Paul Hart and Jan Jacobsen founded Rex Hill in 1982. Winemaker Lynn Penner-Ash focuses on flavourful Pinot Noirs — from seven different vineyards — which account for 60% of the winery's 30,000-case production. The Chardonnay is flinty dry, richly scented with clove.

Sokol Blosser
Susan Sokol Blosser and her husband Bill first planted vines in the Red Hills of Dundee in 1971; the first vintage was 1977. Honeysuckle identifies the Müller-Thurgau (white); the Chardonnay is rife with floral pine and lemon; black cherry Pinot Noirs are juicy and fresh.

Tualatin
California winemaker Bill Fuller and businessman Bill Malkmus established the 34-ha (85-acre) estate in the tiny town of Forest Grove in 1973. The flinty, apricot Riesling, smoky-clove Pinot Noir, and Chardonnay rich with oak toastiness and clear clove are much favoured. White wines are also made from Sauvignon Blanc, Gewürztraminer, Flora (a Sémillon x Gewürztraminer crossing) and Müller-Thurgau.

THE EYRIE

The winery, in a spare bit of industrial space on the outskirts of McMinnville, Yamhill County, is the birthplace of quality wine in Oregon. The vineyards, planted in the Red Hills of Dundee in 1966 by David and Diana Lett, are the oldest *vinifera* plantings in the Willamette Valley. The wines they produce are simply legendary. The Pinot Noirs have a cherry, black pepper and peppermint thread running through them. Intense in youth, they can age just as well as some of the red burgundies on which they are modelled — the best vintages of the 1970s lived for 20 years, while the wines of lesser years drink at between five and ten years. Pinot Gris and Chardonnay are good too. The Eyrie's more unusual offerings are a subtle dry white Muscat Ottonel and a little rare red Pinot Meunier.

NORTH-EASTERN USA

HAVING PRODUCED WINES SINCE COLONIAL TIMES, THE NORTH-EASTERN USA IS NOW LOOKING FORWARD TO A FUTURE BASED ON MORE INTERNATIONALLY-STYLED WINES.

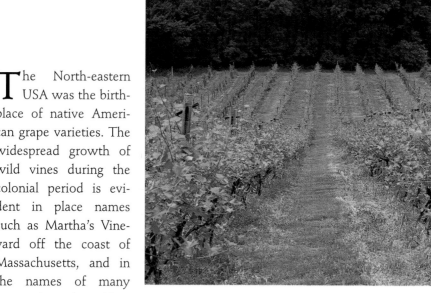

The vineyards of Tewksbury Wine Cellars, in the hills of Hunterdon County, New Jersey, are part of a winemaking revival in the state. The mainly *vinifera* varieties are highly susceptible to spring frosts in these northern climes.

The North-eastern USA was the birthplace of native American grape varieties. The widespread growth of wild vines during the colonial period is evident in place names such as Martha's Vineyard off the coast of Massachusetts, and in the names of many towns throughout New England and nearby states. These hardy, enduring wild vines were the forebears of the Concord grape variety, the mainstay of the *vitis labrusca* family. There was an early assumption that if vines grew wild, then European varieties would also thrive. For this reason, many settlers rejected the native vine. In 1683 William Penn of Philadelphia imported vine cuttings from France and Spain in the first of many failed attempts to establish European varieties in the New World. However, the Concord vine was domesticated in the 1850s and widely cultivated in the North-east thereafter.

The primary purpose of grape cultivation in the early days was not winemaking. Concord was widely planted because of its versatility; it has long been used for making grape juice, jams and jellies. Other *labrusca* varieties (Delaware, Dutchess, Elvira and Catawba) were cultivated for sparkling, table and fortified wines at some time prior to Prohibition. Whether before or after Prohibition, eastern wines developed a poor reputation within the USA. Their image was based on sweet wines made from American grape varieties and on kosher wines, which, because they were made from Concord grapes, were automatically associated with eastern winemaking. Outside New York State, French hybrids and *vinifera* grapes were not planted much before the end of the 1960s, when changes in state regulations encouraged the emergence of cottage or "farm" wineries by, for one thing, reducing previously prohibitive licensing costs. As a result, the number of wineries in the North-east (New York, New England, New Jersey, Pennsylvania and Maryland) has grown to more than 200, with about half of those in New York State. With this increase in small wineries there has been a corresponding increase in the attention given to planting hybrids, *vinifera*, or both, with the result that some good still wines and some fairly good-quality sparkling wines are now being produced.

History of North-eastern wines

The oldest wine region in the North-east is New York State's Hudson River Valley, where the Brotherhood Winery, founded in 1839, is thought to be the oldest operating winery in the USA. By 1860 wine was also being made in the Finger Lakes district further west. This became the centre of North-eastern wine production and retained its importance both before and after Prohibition.

New York State dominated grape-growing and winemaking in the North-east. Growers in Pennsylvania, New Jersey and even in Canada often sent their fruit to a major wine-maker or juice company in New York for processing. The region became known for Welch's grape juice, *labrusca* flavoured wines, kosher wines and cheap fortified wines.

Introduction of non-native vines

It was widely believed that the North-east's cold climate, short growing season and summertime humidity conspired to prevent the cultivation of any vine except native American varieties. During the 1960s a few growers in New York and neighbouring states began working with French hybrids that were tolerant of the cold and resistant to many vine diseases. Philip Wagner, of Boordy Vineyard in Maryland, had already dedicated many years to researching hybrids grown under continental conditions. He carefully matched hybrids to the most suitable micro-climates and developed frost-free strains. Wagner established a vine nursery and supplied a range of French hybrid varieties to grape-growers throughout the North-east and Mid-west.

Charles Fournier and Konstantin Frank were also pioneers in the search for hardy rootstock for growing *vitis vinifera* in cold climates, and in 1957 their experimental vines survived the otherwise disastrous winter freeze in Finger Lakes. *Vinifera* thus became a choice for growers in the North-east.

Barrels and demijohns at the pioneering Montbray Wine Cellars in Maryland.

Grapes and wine styles

It is not uncommon for producers to make wines from all three types of grapes — native American, hybrids and *vinifera*. Which types are grown depends on what is available to the winemaker and the demands of the market. Some producers sell only to local residents; others reach more affluent tourists or the sophisticated retail and restaurant market both within and beyond their area.

Even winemakers trying to compete in the world market will more than likely offer inexpensive, sweet, user-friendly wines to tourists at the winery door. Many wines made from hybrids are given a proprietary name that usually is more appealing to the novice (and easier to pronounce) than the hybrid variety's name.

Over the years the North-east has performed a great service to the wine world by its unofficial testing of so many cold-climate hybrid grape varieties in different sites and soils. The Franco-American hybrid Aurora became very popular when native hybrids failed to deliver good-quality wines, but is itself now being phased out in favour of Cayuga White. Other proven white hybrids that have emerged from the pack as leaders and become popular among winemakers in North-eastern USA are Seyval Blanc and Vidal Blanc. Ravat (which is also known as Vignoles) is proving to be one of the more versatile white grapes, being made into dry, sweet wines as well as sparkling wines.

The best performers among the red hybrid varieties are Baco Noir (the first to prove itself anywhere), Chambourcin, Chelois, de Chaunac, Maréchal Foch and Villard Noir. But no one red hybrid has proved itself a cut above the rest as yet.   □

NEW YORK STATE

For as long as records have been kept, New York State has been acknowledged as the second-largest wine-producing state in the USA. It has long been dismissed by serious wine lovers for turning out mass-produced sweet wines. For years most wines were produced from Concord, Catawba and other *labrusca* grape varieties, and the wines were indeed on the sweet side to mask the harsh, unpleasant flavours associated with those native grapes.

Native American varieties dominated planting in the Empire State up to the 1980s, and a few large wineries dominated production. The situation began to change with the Farm Winery Act of 1976, which lowered licensing fees and allowed small wineries (those producing less than 20,000 cases) to sell directly to consumers. Of 88 wine producers recorded in 1993, 73 had been founded since 1976. Most of them were small family-owned enterprises.

Concord, though declining, still accounts for 75% of total plantings. Although the total grape acreage is declining as unproductive vines and unwanted varieties are removed, the area under hybrids and *vinifera* varieties has been increasing. The leading white hybrids are Aurora, Seyval Blanc, Cayuga White and Vidal Blanc, while the main reds are Baco Noir and de Chaunac. The most widely planted *vinifera* variety, and seventh overall in grape acreage, is Chardonnay. Riesling and Gewürztraminer are on the increase.

There are five primary grape districts within New York. To the southwest of Buffalo, 95% of the Lake Erie district is planted with Concord, most of which is destined to become grape juice. The four other districts are very much alive for quality wines. The Finger Lakes is enjoying a fresh start with new, quality-minded

Winery on Lake Erie, New York State.

producers working with hybrids and *vinifera* grapes. The Hudson River Valley, which has a fine record for flavourful, well-made hybrids, is now working with *vinifera* varieties. The two other regions, on the eastern tip of Long Island, have staked their future entirely on *vinifera* wines. In recent years New York's wine industry has not grown, however: annual production averages 15 million cases.

The Finger Lakes

This district has close to 40 wineries producing more than 85% of the state's wine. All three grape types — *labrusca*, hybrids and *vinifera* — can be found. Although the vineyard area has decreased, many new vineyards have been established along the slightly more protected shores of Cayuga Lake and Seneca Lake, and there is a shift away from both *labrusca* and hybrids to *vinifera* varieties. Most of the older companies — Taylor, Great Western, Gold Seal — were established near Keuka Lake and Canandaigua Lake, where the Canandaigua Wine Company, one of

the largest US wineries, is sited. Leading small wineries make excellent Chardonnay, Riesling and Gewürztraminer, and in most vintages Seyval Blanc and Cayuga White remain reliable hybrids.

The Hudson River Valley

The state's oldest wine region, the Hudson River Valley, is 110km (70 miles) north of New York City. There are more than 20 wineries, all relatively small. Most of them, in deference to the humidity, began by using French hybrids — mainly Seyval Blanc. However, the length of the growing season, ranging between 180 and 195 days, has prompted a recent interest in *vinifera*, especially Chardonnay and Cabernet.

Long Island

The eastern side of Long Island divides into two wine districts — North Fork, which is rural, and The Hamptons, a smart residential area. Almost all wineries are located on North Fork, where the sandy clay soils and the tempering ocean sound create a surprisingly favourable site for the aristocratic *vinifera* varieties. Sixteen producers make wines of varying quality, and they can rely on New York City as a ready market.

Since 1973 Hargrave Vineyards have convinced even the most cynical to believe in this vineyard region. Hargrave's success with Cabernet Sauvignon and Merlot inspired others to plant *vinifera* vines. Over its first 20 vintages, Long Island has yielded many rich, near-classic Merlots and good Cabernet Sauvignons. Recent efforts focusing on bordeaux blends — Cabernet Sauvignon, Merlot and Cabernet Franc — could prove successful. Chardonnay and Sauvignon Blanc are the two most widely planted whites. □

PRODUCERS

Large wineries making essentially low-quality wines from native grape varieties are at last being challenged by a growing band of individuals dedicated to making wines from the best hybrids and *vinifera* varieties. There remains a battle against the cold climate and the preference of many New York City drinkers for Old World wines.

FINGER LAKES

Canandaigua Wine Co
Producing more than 8 million cases a year, this wine company in Orange County is one of America's largest, and includes its oldest wine label — Virginia Dare. Canandaigua makes many *labrusca* wines but also some premium varietals, including Muscat.

Glenora Wine Cellars
Founded in 1977 in Yates County, Glenora has always emphasized vintaged varietal wines made from hybrids and, more recently, from Chardonnay and Riesling. It supplements its own vineyard on Seneca Lake with grapes from local growers. Glenora produces fine balanced Riesling and rich, barrel-fermented Reserve Chardonnay. The traditional method sparkling wines (blends of Chardonnay and Pinot Noir) can be outstanding.

Knapp Vineyards
Making a wide array of *vinifera* and hybrid varietals, Knapp has won numerous awards in recent years. Established in 1982 in Seneca Falls near Cayuga Lake, Knapp has its own 26-ha (65-acre) vineyard, with another 53ha (130 acres) leased long term. Knapp's record for white wines, including both dry and late-harvest Rieslings, Seyval Blanc and Vignoles, is impressive.

Wagner Vineyards
Since its first harvest in 1978, Wagner has become the premier producer of Chardonnay in the Finger Lakes region (Seneca County). It produces only estate-grown wines, and about half the 20,000-case annual production is of *vinifera* wines, including Chardonnay, Riesling, Pinot Noir and Gewürztraminer. Other wines of note are the barrel-fermented Seyval Blanc and a pleasing Reserve White. In 1988 Wagner made two extraordinary ice wines (from frozen grapes) from Ravat Blanc and Riesling.

HUDSON RIVER VALLEY

Benmarl Wine Co
Mark Miller started making wines in Marlboro in 1971, long before it was *de rigueur*. He planted 30ha (72 acres) primarily to hybrids, and then added Chardonnay and Cabernet Sauvignon. In order to finance this pioneering project Miller sold vine rights to 400 shareholders who help during the year. The leading wines are Seyval Blanc, Baco Noir, Chelois and Vignoles.

Clinton Vineyards
Clinton has carved out a niche for itself as a Seyval Blanc specialist, and includes a sparkling version. Chardonnay and Riesling are also made. The winery in Dutchess County produces 10,000 cases a year.

Millbrook Vineyards
Owner John Dyson patented a unique trellising system that enables him to grow 100% *vinifera* varieties at Millbrook east of the Hudson. Chardonnay, including a barrel-fermented Reserve, accounts for more than half of Millbrook's production. As it nears its 12,000-cases-a-year target, Millbrook is featuring Cabernet Franc, Pinot Noir and Tocai, and experimenting with Rhône and Italian varieties.

Rivendell Winery
Rivendell made a cautious start at New Paltz west of the Hudson in 1983, but became one of the most sought-after brands within its first decade. This unblemished reputation was built upon Chardonnay, barrel-fermented Seyval Blanc, Vidal Blanc, Cabernet Sauvignon and proprietary blends.

LONG ISLAND

Bedell Cellars
This is a small (5,000-case) winery on the north coast run by Kip and Susan Bedell since the early 1980s in a restored potato storage barn. The first few vintages of Merlot and Cabernet Sauvignon were so rich and seemingly long-lived that they immediately placed Bedell among the best producers outside the West Coast.

Bridgehampton Winery
One of only a few producers on South Fork, this compact, state-of-the-art winery has made a name for itself with Chardonnay, Merlot and an occasional dessert-style, late-harvest Riesling.

Hargrave Vineyards
Founded in 1973, this north-coast winery was the first in the modern era of North-eastern winemaking. Hargrave enjoys greater success with red wines, notably Cabernet Sauvignon, Merlot and Cabernet Franc. Its best white, Chardonnay, is slightly inconsistent, however. The company also makes Sauvignon Blanc, Riesling, Gewürztraminer and Pinot Noir, and is running at full capacity of 12,000 cases a year.

Palmer Vineyards
Founded in 1983 by New York City advertising executive Robert Palmer, this 10,000-case producer is located on the area's oldest country estate on North Fork. Palmer has made great strides with Gewürztraminer and Merlot, and also makes Cabernet Sauvignon and Chardonnay.

Pindar Vineyards
With 85ha (210 acres) planted in North Fork, Pindar is Long Island's largest winery, producing 45,000 cases a year. Offering a wide range of wines, and with a sophisticated distribution system, Pindar has gained international attention with its Merlot and Mythology, a red bordeaux-style blend. Chardonnay has also been impressive.

OTHER NORTH-EASTERN STATES

In winemaking terms the rest of North-eastern USA consists of certain states in New England, together with New Jersey, Pennsylvania and Maryland. The story of winemaking here is similar to that of New York.

The states of New England

Massachusetts claims a long history of winegrowing. The island of Martha's Vineyard was discovered by Europeans in 1602 and so named because of the *labrusca* grapes found growing there. Today it has an impressive range of *vinifera* varieties.

All six New England states have played a rôle in the modern winemaking renaissance. In 1973, White Mountain Vineyards of New Hampshire became the first new winery to open its door since Prohibition. Unfortunately, this pioneer of *vinifera*, which grew successfully until the particularly harsh winter of 1983, did not survive.

New England's best wine-growing regions are found near the coast or in the mountains inland. There are currently between 30 and 40 active wineries throughout the region. Depending upon the vineyard's proximity to the ocean or upon its elevation, the growing season can be as short as 145 days or as long as 210. All told, vineyards presently extend to 400ha (1,000 acres), with about half that area planted to *vinifera* varieties and half to French hybrids.

The leading states today are Connecticut and Massachusetts, each with ten wineries, many of which are to be found in a narrow band along the coast. Many producers make other items, usually fruit and berry wines or cider. South-eastern New England has emerged as a popular VA, used by producers in Connecticut, Rhode Island and Massachusetts. Those who have vineyards in western Connecticut prefer to use the

A well-known Pennsylvania winery.

Western Connecticut Highlands VA. The former has much the warmer climate of the two and is therefore more suitable for growing *vinifera*.

New Jersey (Warren Hills VA)

With the passage of the Farm Winery Act in 1981, New Jersey experienced a modest winemaking revival. Known as the Garden State, it has approximately 260ha (650 acres) under vine, 75% of which are planted to French hybrids. Many producers with vineyards in Hunterdon County use the Central Delaware Valley VA. There are 19 producers in all, and most of them have enjoyed success with hybrids, especially Seyval Blanc and Chambourcin.

Pennsylvania

Pennsylvania has seen its vineyard area decline in recent years; it now has 3,650ha (9,000 acres) under vine, with 80% planted to *labrusca* varieties. The first wine producer in the state's modern era, Conestoga Vineyard, opened in 1963. In 1968, after the state voted to allow wineries to

sell their own wines, several were established and their number has grown to more than 40. Prime land for hybrids and *vinifera* exists in the south-eastern corner, where growing conditions are similar to those in neighbouring Maryland.

Maryland

Maryland was a wine-producing state before the others as a result of pioneering work conducted by Philip Wagner, who founded Boordy Vineyards in 1945. By the late 1960s Montbray Cellars near Baltimore was devoting all its efforts to growing *vinifera* grapes. Those who followed in the 1970s planted hybrids or began experimenting with Chardonnay, Riesling and Cabernet Sauvignon.

All recent plantings have been to *vinifera*. Maryland now has 130ha (320 acres) planted roughly equally with hybrids and *vinifera* varieties. Most vineyards are in the eastern corner of the state near the border with Virginia. Cabernet Sauvignon and Chardonnay are the leading *vinifera*, Seyval Blanc the main hybrid. Commercial wineries find themselves in an odd situation in Maryland in that there are so many home winemakers that there is great competition for grapes. Home winemakers usually offer higher prices, and the only winners in this situation are independent growers.

Though most producers have been labelling their produce "Maryland" wines, the state has been awarded three VAs. Cumberland Valley extends into Pennsylvania and encompasses many outstanding vineyards. This appellation may be used much more in the future. Catoctin, in the mountains west of Baltimore, is an area that has shown great potential for the cultivation of *vinifera* varieties. The third VA, Linganore, has yet to reveal what it can do. □

PRODUCERS

Producers throughout the North-east have always faced financial uncertainty as a result of, until recently, unhelpful state legislation, unfavourable climatic conditions and the vagaries of a market prejudiced against non-*vinifera* varieties.

NEW ENGLAND

The leading wine-producing states of New England are Connecticut and Massachusetts. Rhode Island has half a dozen very small wineries.

CONNECTICUT
Chamard Vineyards

The second most successful Connecticut winery, Chamard is a modern winery, run by the Chaney family at Clinton. It concentrates on *vinifera* varieties — Chardonnay, Pinot Noir and Cabernet Sauvignon, and also Merlot and Cabernet Franc for blending purposes. Production is expected to increase substantially.

Haight Vineyards

As the state's first new winery, Haight planted experimental vineyards in 1978 and began commercial winemaking six years later. Located in Litchfield County in the north-western corner of the state, Haight's hillside vineyard extends to 12ha (30 acres) and produces 8,000 cases a year. The list includes Riesling, Chardonnay, a blend of red and white predominantly hybrid varieties and bottled under the Recolte label, and limited quantities of sparkling Blanc de Blancs made by the *méthode traditionnelle*. The winery favours the Western Connecticut Highlands VA.

MASSACHUSETTS
Chicama Vineyards

One of the first North-eastern wineries to commit to growing *vinifera* grape varieties, Chicama was founded in 1971 by the Mathiesen family. Located on the island of Martha's Vineyard off the coast of Massachusetts, Chicama grows an impressive assortment of *vinifera* varieties, including Chenin Blanc, Chardonnay, Sauvignon Blanc, Gewürztraminer, Cabernet Sauvignon, Merlot and Pinot Noir. (The name Martha's Vineyard is actually used by a producer in Napa Valley, California.) Chicama's winemaker Tim Mathiesen rates the company's red wines in particular, but the sparkling Chardonnay, Sea Mist, is showing a lot of promise. Most wines are only available at present to tourists or locally within Massachusetts. The former farm switched to vine-growing in 1986 and started to produce wine in 1989. It is now New England's largest vineyard.

RHODE ISLAND
Sakonnet Vineyards

This Newport County producer struggled until it was acquired by the Samson family in 1987. They have expanded the vineyard to 17.5ha (44 acres), as well as buying in fruit from neighbouring states, and make 25,000 cases a year. The vineyard provides Vidal Blanc, Chardonnay, Gewürztraminer, Pinot Noir, and Cabernet Franc. The winery's best-selling wines are two blends, America's Cup White and Spinnaker White, both made in part from Vidal Blanc and Cayuga White.

OTHER NORTH-EASTERN STATES

South of New York State are New Jersey, Pennsylvania and Maryland. None is a top wine-producing state, but there are pockets of interesting viticultural development.

NEW JERSEY
Renault Winery

Located in Egg Harbor City, this is the oldest (founded in 1864) and still one of the most successful wineries in the state. Founded by French champagne producer, Louis Renault, who came to the USA in the mid-19th century, the company produces 25,000 cases of assorted wines. Not surprisingly, however, sparkling wines, such as Spumante, head the list.

Tewksbury Wine Cellars

One of the first new wineries to open in decades (in 1979), Tewksbury is in Hunterdon County in north-eastern New Jersey, where most of the better vineyards are located. Owner and veterinarian Dan Vernon has developed 8ha (20 acres) of hillside near his farm, and has enjoyed success with Chambourcin, Riesling and Gewürztraminer.

PENNSYLVANIA
Chaddsford Winery

Eric Miller, whose family owns Benmarl in New York State, started his own winery in Chester County in south-eastern Pennsylvania in 1982. He produces several hybrids and blends that are sold to tourists and locally. Buying grapes from the Philip Roth

and Stargazer vineyards in the Piedmont region, Miller has won accolades for his excellent barrel-fermented Chardonnays. Cabernet Sauvignon is also produced.

MARYLAND
Boordy Vineyards

Boordy produces more than 8,000 cases a year, making it Maryland's largest winery. With grapes from its own small estate vineyard and supplied by local growers, it produces a range of hybrids. Now owned by the Deford family, who bought this historic vineyard (which dates from 1945) from founder Philip Wagner, Boordy's winery has been moved out from the suburbs of Baltimore city to the Deford family's farm in rural Hydes.

Catoctin Vineyards

Jerry Milne only ever intended to be a vineyard owner, but circumstances forced him to turn his hand to winemaking, and his wines have turned out to be top notch. Located in Montgomery County, his winery produces 4,000 cases of wine a year as well as supplying grapes to several other wine producers. The leading wines made at Catoctin are the Cabernet Sauvignon and the Chardonnay.

Montbray Wine Cellars

G Hamilton Mowbray, who owns this winery at Westminster in Carroll County, has quite a reputation in the state, having been making wines since the mid-1960s. He produces a range of *vinifera* wines, as well as Seyval Blanc, which is a good example of its type.

SOUTH & MID-WEST USA

MANY STATES HAVE ONLY HAD WINE INDUSTRIES SINCE THE 1970s
AND 1980s, BUT, WITH THE AID OF TECHNOLOGY AND NEW VINE
STRAINS, THEY FACE AN EXCITING FUTURE.

The Naked Mountain Vineyard, near Markham in the
wooded hills of Fauquier County, Virginia, is one of many
estates to concentrate increasingly on *vinifera* varieties as the
state re-establishes its once-pioneering wine industry.

The native grapevine encountered by Sir Walter Raleigh and other early explorers in the South-eastern USA belonged to the *rotundifolia* species, also known as the Muscadine family. For years the most widely planted variety in the South was the Scuppernong Muscadine, which still grows well in the warm, humid climates of the Carolinas, Georgia and Mississippi. Wine historian Leon Adams maintains that the first wine ever made in North America was Scuppernong from Florida, which he traces back to 1565. Virginia Dare, the most popular and best-known North American wine before Prohibition, was made from Scuppernong, a grape that bears no resemblance to *vinifera* varieties. It is often described, perhaps with tongue in cheek, as "God's gift to the sunny South".

Working under conditions very different from those in the east, growers throughout the Mid-west initially favoured *labrusca* vines. Before Prohibition Ohio and Missouri, relying on domesticated native grape varieties such as Catawba and Delaware, dominated US wine production. Around 1900 each state was making more wine than California, but the industry was almost completely wiped out by Prohibition. Signs of a reawakening did not occur until the late 1960s. By the 1970s most of the Mid-west (Ohio, Indiana, Michigan, Missouri) had eased back into winemaking to some degree, using *labrusca* and hybrid varieties. Today each state in the Mid-west makes wine in some commercial quantity, including Wisconsin and Minnesota. Two states, Ohio and Missouri, are leading the way in the Mid-west. The former has made progress with French-American hybrids and is turning its attention to *vinifera* plantings. Missouri, while showing little inclination toward *vinifera*, is turning out an array of quality wines from hybrids and even a few select native vines.

The new and as yet unchallenged leader in the South is Virginia, which has gained international recognition for its classic-style *vinifera* wines. As the US population continues to shift south (and south-west), those regions with as yet untapped wine potential — especially Tennessee, Georgia and North Carolina — may ultimately make the South second only to the West Coast for quality wines.

The South

In the South, Virginia is rich in viticultural history, thanks to Thomas Jefferson's vineyards at Monticello, where Jefferson — unsuccessfully — tried to grow *vinifera* vines, but the state has been a late developer in the modern era. Traditionally the state produced *labrusca* and fortified wines. Today the vineyard area has expanded to 600ha (1,500 acres), two-thirds of which are planted with Chardonnay, Cabernet Sauvignon and other *vinifera* vines, both red and white. Today more than 200 grape-growers supply fruit to 50 wineries ranging in scale of production from a few hundred cases up to more than 100,000. Though wineries are scattered throughout seven VAs, most are in central Virginia along the Blue Ridge Mountains.

Tennessee, North Carolina, Georgia, Florida, Arkansas and Mississippi each have several producing wineries. Tennessee in particular has joined the ranks of wine-producing states and now has 240ha (300 acres) under vine, 15 producers and land available for expansion. Georgia has increased its wineries to six, but only 5% of the state's 500ha (1,200 acres) of vineyards are *vinifera*. North Carolina's six wineries devote about 20% of the state's 160ha (400 acres) to *vinifera*. Florida has six producers and 240ha (600 acres) under vine.

Producers in all these regions face climatic problems with *vinifera*, whether it be winters that are too warm in Florida or too frosty in North Carolina. A range of native varieties — including extensive plantings of Scuppernong Muscadine, particularly in North Carolina and Mississippi — hybrids and local blends produce a large variety of wine styles in addition to those from *vinifera* varieties.

South-western states

Texas had one winery and 8ha (20 acres) of vines in 1975: within a decade those figures were 26 and almost 2,000 (5,000), and several pioneering wineries seemed poised for success. However, it became clear that certain grape varieties, such as Carignan and Ruby Cabernet (a Cabernet Sauvignon/Grenache cross) were poor choices for the conditions. Some producers, especially those with ties to the oil business, experienced financial difficulties during the 1980s, and several others failed to live up to expectations.

Texas ranks fourth in the USA, with an annual production approaching one million cases. By the early 1990s, a sufficient number of fine wines had been made from Cabernet Sauvignon, Sauvignon Blanc, Chenin Blanc and Chardonnay to raise hopes for the future of winemaking in Texas.

With five VAs, Texas claims one of the USA's biggest in Hill Country, covering 40,000 square kilometres (15,000 square miles). Most grapes are grown in three regions of the state: on the flat High Plains (at 999m/3,000ft) near Lubbock; to the west of Austin in Hill Country; and in West Texas, whose vineyard belongs to the University of Texas. Climatic and soil variations over such large areas create very many wine styles.

New Mexico's winemaking history goes back to 1580, when missionaries planted vineyards along the Rio Grande. A small wine industry survived for over 300 years, by which time the state had more than 1,200ha (3,000 acres) under vine. After Prohibition ended that run, a renaissance did not begin until the 1980s, when 160ha (400 acres) of *vinifera* vines began to supply the first few new commercial wineries. Vineyards lie along the mesas (plateaux) following the Rio Grande, and there are three VAs: Mesilla Valley, Middle Rio Grande Valley and Mimbres Valley. Almost all the 2,000ha (5,000 acres) are *vinifera*. Several producers make good Cabernet Sauvignon and Sauvignon Blanc, and the record so far for sparkling wine is impressive.

With 100ha (250 acres) of *vinifera* grapes planted primarily in the Sonita VA, Arizona is still in its infancy as a wine region. Sonita's vineyards are at 1,500m (5,000ft): the warm, dry climate combined with lots of available land is likely to encourage others to join the six pioneering wineries.

The Mid-west

Michigan grows 4,500ha (11,000 acres) of grapes, but only 800ha (2,000 acres) of that are wine varieties, primarily hybrids with a little *vinifera*. The Concord production goes to New York State for making into grape juice. Now ranked 14th in the USA, Michigan has 18 wineries. Most vineyards are along the shores of Lake Michigan, with smaller plantings near Lake Erie. The state has four VAs: Fennville, Lake Michigan Shore, Leelanau Peninsula, and Old Mission Peninsula.

With strong support from its legislature, Missouri has been on a steady course to regain its former position within the US wine industry. Total plantings stand at 520ha (1,300 acres). Catawba, used for red table and sparkling wines, is the most widely planted. Vidal and Seyval Blanc are two of Missouri's best white hybrids. Norton (Cynthiana), which produces a full-flavoured red wine, shares top honours with Chancellor and Chambourcin among the reds. *Vinifera* plantings are negligible. Missouri's 30 wineries produce a range of varietal and blended wines from hybrids. There are four VAs: Augusta, Hermann, Ozark Highlands and Ozark Mountain.

There are modest developments in both Ohio and Indiana after years in which hybrids paved the way for hit-and-miss performances from *vinifera* wines. Ohio has 1,000ha (2,500 acres) of vineyards, half of which are devoted to wine varieties, both French hybrids and *vinifera*. Future plantings will be of *vinifera*. The most promising varieties planted in Ohio have been Riesling, Gewürztraminer and Chardonnay. Cabernet Sauvignon has enjoyed some success, and several growers are experimenting with Pinot Gris. There are four VAs: Grand River Valley, Isle St George, Lake Erie and Ohio River.

PRODUCERS

Many producers in fledgling state industries are still experimenting to find which grapes best suit their conditions. Some buy in supplementary grapes from, say, the West Coast. Wherever possible, especially with irrigation in warmer states, *vinifera* varieties are encouraged, but cooler climates necessitate hybrids.

VIRGINIA
Meredyth Vineyards
The state's oldest winery, in Middleburg, skilfully produces wines from hybrids and *vinifera*. Its 22-ha (56-acre) vineyard is situated in the scenic Bull Run Mountains. Decent Merlot recently joined the consistently fine Seyval Blanc.

Montdomaine Cellars
Located in Charlottesville, this wine estate relies on its 20-ha (50-acre) vineyard in the Monticello appellation. The winery concentrates on Chardonnay and bordeaux-style red blends, and earned great respect in its early vintages for Cabernet Sauvignon and Merlot.

Piedmont Vineyards
In the Middleburg region, not far from Washington DC, the Piedmont winery grows first-rate Chardonnay and Sémillon, and since its foundation in 1973 has consistently produced an attractive Seyval Blanc from its 25-ha (60-acre) vineyard. A red bordeaux-style blend is new to the list.

Prince Michel Vineyards
With 45ha (110 acres) in the Montpelier region, Prince Michel has a reputation for barrel-fermented Chardonnay and a pricey bordeaux-style red called LeDucq Meritage.

NORTH CAROLINA
Chateau Biltmore
Located in Ashville, this winery is just a part of an historic 3,250-ha (8,000-acre) estate

and mansion built in 1880 by the Vanderbilt family, and now a popular local attraction. The estate-grown Cabernet Sauvignon and Chardonnay are from a 45-ha (107-acre) vineyard that was planted in the early 1980s. A sparkling Blanc de Blancs is also produced.

TENNESSEE
Tennessee Valley Winery
Originally a partnership of home winemakers, this Loudon County winery is now operated solely by the Reed family. It produces wines from native American varieties, hybrids and *vinifera* vines. The best wines are Aurora, de Chaunac, and Maréchal Foch. Chardonnay and Cabernet Sauvignon have been erratic in quality.

GEORGIA
Chateau Elan
About 48km (30 miles) north of the city of Atlanta, Chateau Elan is not just a winery, but a restaurant and museum complex that attracts more than 250,000 visitors a year. The 80-ha (200-acre) vineyard is planted mainly to Chardonnay, Sauvignon Blanc, Riesling, Cabernet Sauvignon and

two popular hybrid varieties, Chambourcin and Seyval Blanc. Two flavoured Muscadine wines are also produced. Selling half of its total production locally, Elan is aiming to produce 60,000 cases a year.

ARKANSAS
Wiederkehr Vineyards
Founded in Altus in 1880 by the Swiss Wiederkehr family, these historic cellars have been expanded several times, and Wiederkehr is now one of the largest producers east of the Rockies. With two-thirds of the 263-ha (650-acre) vineyard containing *vinifera* varieties, the company produces a large range of wines. Riesling and several Muscat-based wines top the list.

TEXAS
Cap Rock Winery
Built in Lubbock in 1988, this high-tech winery changed hands before its first harvest. Relying on its 48-ha (120-acre) vineyard, Cap Rock concentrates on Chardonnay, Cabernet Sauvignon and Sauvignon Blanc, producing each one at three price levels. Chenin Blanc and blush and sparkling wines are also made.

Fall Creek Vineyards
With 32ha (80 acres) on the shores of Lake Buchanan in Llano County, the Aulers have built a replica of a French château and are making Chardonnay, Cabernet Sauvignon and Sauvignon Blanc. A limited amount of Reserve Chardonnay is made and has been impressive.

Llano Estacado
A leader in the renaissance of the Texan wine industry, this Lubbock winery is now the second-largest in the state, averaging 75,000 cases a year, and producing relatively good Chardonnay, Chenin Blanc and Sauvignon Blanc. Cabernet Sauvignon is its next challenge.

Pheasant Ridge
Another pioneering winery, also in Lubbock, Pheasant Ridge does exhibit inconsistency, but also flashes of greatness. Owner Bobby Cox produces Chardonnay, Sauvignon Blanc, Chenin Blanc and Cabernet Sauvignon — the latter being the most promising of all his wines.

NEW MEXICO
Anderson Valley Vineyards
In the northern Rio Grande Valley, Anderson, founded in 1973, was the first quality producer in New Mexico. With 47ha (115 acres) of vineyards around Albuquerque, it has made a name for itself with Cabernet Sauvignon, Sauvignon Blanc as well as other *vinifera* wines.

Gruet Winery
Established in the Anderson Valley in 1984 by the Gruet family — originally from Champagne in France — this producer specializes in traditional method sparkling wines — Brut, Blanc de Noirs and a vintage Blanc de Blancs.

MICHIGAN
Chateau Grand Traverse
Founded in 1974, this winery is owned by the O'Keefe family, who grow only *vinifera* vines in the Leelanau Peninsula VA at the northern end of Lake Michigan. More than half the Chateau's 35,000-case production consists of Riesling, made in a range of sweetness levels, including an occasional dessert version.

St Julian Wine Co
Founded in 1921, St Julian is one of the few wineries in the once-bustling Paw Paw region that is still going strong. The company has enjoyed success with a broad range of table wines made from hybrid varieties, and sparkling wines, but the company's success increased dramatically when

it added non-alcoholic, carbonated grape juice to its list. There are now 14 different flavours of grape juice as well as their wines, and the tasting rooms today attract many visitors. Annual wine sales have exceeded 200,000 cases, and by conservative estimates St Julian makes 50% of all Michigan's wines.

OHIO
Chalet Debonne
One of Ohio's hard-working wine pioneers, in Madison, Lake County, Debonne started with hybrids in 1971. It has since added *vinifera* to its 25-ha (60-acre) vineyard. Hybrids include the reliable Cham-

bourcin, and, when the vintage is merciful, surprisingly good Chardonnay and Riesling are produced.

Firelands Winery
Firelands is owned by Paramount Distillers of Cleveland, whose president, Bob Gottesman, has single-handedly kept the Ohio wine industry alive. Paramount, which owns Lonz

Winery, Mon Ami Wine Company and Meier's Wine Cellars (all of them in Ohio), invested heavily in Firelands. Situated on the Isle St George (VA) in Lake Erie, the winery is reached by ferry and is enormously popular with tourists. With 16ha (40 acres) of *vinifera*, Firelands focuses on Chardonnay, Cabernet Sauvignon and Gewürztraminer.

MISSOURI
Hermannhof Winery
A long defunct brewery in Hermann was revived in the early 1980s by local banker James Dierberg. He renovated from the cellars up. Popular with tourists, the winery produces a

range of French hybrids. The wine most in demand is Hermannhof's Cynthiana and a range of sparkling wines.

Mount Pleasant Vineyard
This historic winery was founded in 1881, and revived in 1968 by Lucian Dressel, its owner and winemaker. He built it back up to a 20,000-case winery making a range of varietals and sparkling wine from his 28-ha (70-acre) estate vineyard. The Vidal Blanc is often top-notch, along with Seyval Blanc, a delicate Missouri Riesling and port-style fortified wine. Dressel helped define Augusta as a Viticultural Area, the first in the USA to be federally approved.

Stone Hill Wine Co
One of the original giants (founded in Hermann in 1847), Stone Hill was the country's second-largest winery by 1910. Re-opened in 1965, it makes a wide range of wines, in part from its 25-ha (60-acre) vineyard. Its massive ageing cellars draw thousands of tourists who enjoy the *labrusca* and hybrid wines. Catawba and Norton remain popular, while hybrids earning considerable respect include Seyval Blanc, Vidal and Vignoles among white wines, and Villard Noir among reds.

MINNESOTA
Alexis Bailly Winery
A lawyer by profession, David Bailly became interested in wine as a hobby. He had to be very courageous as the climate is so harsh that vine stocks have to be buried during winter time. During the 1970s, he planted a few acres to hybrids on his farm south-east of Minneapolis, and then constructed a small winery. Maréchal Foch and Léon Millot are the red hybrids planted. Produced as varietals, they are dark in colour and in most vintages balanced and flavourful.

Fall Creek Vineyards in Texas illustrates ranch-style grape-growing in the southern states.

CANADA

DESPITE OFTEN ADVERSE CONDITIONS, CANADA IS BEGINNING TO
MAKE A NAME FOR ITS WINES — SOME SPECIALIZED, OTHERS WITH
WIDER INTERNATIONAL APPEAL.

Waddington Bay, in British Columbia, typifies much of
Canada's mountainous scenery — rarely hospitable to the
vine. Yet the country's winemakers are taking advantage of
specific micro-climates to produce wines in a range of styles.

Perhaps surprisingly in a country that is known worldwide for its long, cold winters, over 70 wineries make wine in four Canadian provinces — Ontario and British Columbia, and, to a lesser extent, Nova Scotia and Quebec — from a total of more than 8,000ha (20,000 acres) of vines. Canadians, too, consume more wine per capita than their neighbours south of the border. More than half of the wine sold in Canada is white, but the trend is nowadays towards red wines — thanks to the health implications of the "French Paradox": in 1992 a doctor in a much-publicized television interview suggested that the French sustain a low incidence of heart disease, despite a high cholesterol intake, because of their regular consumption of red wine.

One of the best-kept secrets in the wine world is that Canada is the largest producer of the rare, sweet white *Eiswein* (ice wine). Year in, year out, between November and Christmas, temperatures in Ontario and British Columbia drop so low that the late-harvest grapes freeze solid on the vine; they are pressed when the berries are as hard as marbles.

The preferred grapes for ice-wine production are Riesling and the thick-skinned white hybrid, Vidal. While this expensive nectar has garnered gold medals in competitions from Bordeaux to Verona and London to New York State, the dry table wines made from European *vitis vinifera* varieties are also beginning to make an impact both on the domestic and international fronts. The emergence of quality wines from Canada has much to do with the institution of the Vintners Quality Alliance, an *appellation* system established in 1988 by the country's largest wine region, Ontario, and adopted by British Columbia two years later.

Although the wine industry in Canada dates back to the beginning of the 19th century it was not until the 1960s that such hybrids as Seyval Blanc, Vidal, Baco Noir and Maréchal Foch and classic European grapes began to take the place of the native North American *vitis labrusca* varieties. The unkillable Concord grape was the backbone of Ontario wines for decades, producing mainly sweet, strong products labelled "port" and "sherry". These labels will probably disappear soon.

Today the emphasis is on varietally-named table wines made from European *vinifera* varieties: Chardonnay, Riesling, Pinot Gris and Pinot Blanc for white wines; Pinot Noir, Cabernets Sauvignon and Franc, Merlot and Gamay for reds. As well as ice wines, sweet white late-harvest Riesling and Vidal from Ontario and British Columbia are particularly worth searching out. Some sparkling wine is made by the traditional method and called "Canadian Champagne"; the old-style "ports" and "sherries", and low-alcohol (7%) wines are still in evidence.

History of Canadian wine

According to Norwegian sagas, the Viking explorer Leif Ericson discovered grapes when he landed on the American continent in around AD 1000. He named the place Vinland.

However, the history of Canadian winemaking is not that old. Johann Schiller, a German corporal who fought in three American wars, is acknowledged as the father of the Canadian wine industry. In 1811 he was retired with a land grant just west of Toronto, Ontario. He planted a small vineyard from cuttings of wild vines he found growing along the Credit River. He made wine from these domesticated grapes and sold it to his neighbours. Thirty-five years later the "estate" was bought by an aristocratic Frenchman, Justin de Courtenay, who had unsuccessfully tried to replicate the taste of red burgundy in Quebec. He had better luck in Toronto, and his Gamay won a prize at the 1867 Paris Exposition.

The first real commercial Canadian winemaking operation began in 1866 when three gentlemen farmers from Kentucky acquired land on Pelee Island in Lake Erie, Canada's most southerly point, and planted 12ha (30 acres) of native American Catawba grapes. A few months later they were joined on the island by two English brothers, Edward and John Wardoper, who planted their own vineyard, half the size.

Gradually, vineyards were planted on the mainland, moving east to the Niagara Peninsula where the major concentration of vineyards is situated today. By 1890 there were 41 commercial wineries in Canada, 35 of them in Ontario. In the Okanagan Valley of British Columbia and along Quebec's St Lawrence shoreline it was the Church rather than the regions' farmers who encouraged the planting of vineyards and fostered the art of winemaking.

During Canada's 15 years of prohibition (1919–1933) the making and selling of wine was not illegal (thanks to an aggressive grape-growers' lobby, which managed to have wine exempted from the Act) and Canadians could buy sweet, *labrusca*-based products with an alcohol content of 20%. Following the end of prohibition, the liquor board system was set up across the country. Each provincial government had jurisdiction over the sale and distribution of beverage alcohol. Government liquor stores were established and the products they sold were heavily taxed to control consumption and to raise revenue. This system persists in Canada to this day, although Alberta and Manitoba have decided to turn retailing operations over to the private sector, while maintaining control of the wholesaling pricing.

The Canadian wine industry today is divided into three classes of winery: large commercial enterprises that like to style themselves "major" (as opposed to commercial) wineries, estate wineries and small-scale, farm-gate operations.

Climate

As a cool-climate grape-growing country, quality from vintage to vintage can vary as significantly as it does in the vineyards of northern Europe.

For many years it was believed that *vitis vinifera* vines would not survive the rigours of Canadian winters and the freeze-thaw-freeze cycle of the early spring. As a result, the major plantings were in the winter-hardy native North American *labrusca* varieties (mainly Concord for red wine, Niagara for white) and the early-ripening and heavy-bearing hybrids. Happily, *labrusca* grapes, with their "foxy" bouquet and flavour, have been banned for table-wine use since 1988 in Ontario (they are still used for "ports", "sherries" and 7%-alcohol wines), and the hybrids are giving way more and more to classic European varieties.

Wine laws

The production and sale of beverage alcohol is a provincial jurisdiction, which means that wine regulations vary from province to province. As a bilingual country, all wine labels are partly printed in both French and English; the basic information is that found in the USA (*see* p476).

Vintners Quality Alliance (VQA) is Canada's equivalent to the *appellation contrôlée* system. At present it applies only in Ontario and British Columbia. In order to conform with VQA standards, wines from Ontario and British Columbia must be 100% grown and bottled in those provinces, from a list of approved varieties.

VQA has two categories: provincial and geographic.

The provincial designation allows hybrid or *vinifera* grapes, with 75% minimum of the named grape variety. The label will say Product of Ontario or Product of British Columbia.

Geographic designations refer to specific viticultural areas, which will be named on the label. Only *vinifera* grapes can be used, with 85% minimum of the named variety. A blended wine, such as Chardonnay/ Riesling or Cabernet Sauvignon/ Merlot, must contain at least 10% of the second named variety. Vintage-dated wines must contain a minimum of 95% of wine from the vintage.

VQA wines are tasted by a professional panel for typicity and quality. Wines approved are given a black VQA seal. Wines that receive 15 out of 20 points are granted the higher quality designation of a gold seal.   □

REGIONS AND PRODUCERS

Canada has two major wine-producing provinces — Ontario in the east and British Columbia in the west. Nova Scotia and Quebec, also in the east, have much smaller areas under vine.

Ontario

The vineyard areas of Ontario, where at least 85% of Canadian vines are grown, are on roughly the same latitude as France's Midi and Italy's Chianti Classico zone. But the climate in terms of heat units and rainfall is more akin to that of Burgundy. In hot, dry years, bordeaux-style red wines made from Cabernet Sauvignon or Cabernet/Merlot blends can be achieved, as well as flavourful burgundian-style Pinot Noir and Gamay. In most years Chardonnay and Riesling provide very drinkable to fine quality white wines thanks to the warming micro-climates provided by lakes Ontario and Erie and the wind effect produced by the Niagara Escarpment. This former shore of a prehistoric lake acts as a buffer to the breezes from Lake Ontario, lowering the risk of frost.

There are three designated viticultural areas in the province of Ontario: Niagara Peninsula, Lake Erie North Shore and Pelee Island. Under the province's Wine Content Act, Ontario wineries can produce VQA wines from 100% locally-grown grapes (labelled Product of Ontario) or they can blend as much as 75% wine produced elsewhere with locally-made wine to make non-VQA products that will carry the term Product of Canada on the label.

At the time of writing there are 30 wineries in Ontario, ranging from Brights (which recently bought Cartier-Inniskillin to make it the tenth-largest winery in North America) to tiny farm wineries making less than 5,000 cases.

Recommended producers include: Cave Spring Cellars, Château des Charmes, Henry of Pelham, Hillebrand Estates, Inniskillin, Konzelmann Winery, Marynissen, Pelee Island Winery, Reif Estate, Southbrook Farms, Stoney Ridge, Vineland Estates.

British Columbia

The Okanagan Valley, where most of British Columbia's wineries are located, is technically a desert. The southern part of the valley, which borders Washington State in the USA, can have daytime temperatures that reach 35°C (95°F), with very cool nights. It is on the same latitude as Champagne and the Rheingau but, unlike these northerly European regions, the intense heat of summer, the lack of rainfall and the cool evenings require that the vines be irrigated. Many lesser-known German white-wine varieties have been planted (Optima, Ehrenfelser, Siegfried Rebe), as well as Riesling, Gewürztraminer, Bacchus (Silvaner x Riesling x Müller-Thurgau) and Auxerrois Blanc. The reds, mainly Pinot Noir, Merlot and hybrids, are not yet up to the standard of the whites, with a few notable exceptions.

British Columbia has 30 wineries operating in its four designated viticultural areas: Okanagan Valley, Similkameen Valley, Fraser Valley and Vancouver Island. The growth of vineyards since 1988 has been impressive, with 40–60ha (100–150 acres) being planted each year. New plantings are all *vitis vinifera*. The major growth has been in farm-gate and estate wineries.

Under British Columbian regulations only the major wineries can bottle "imported" wine, which may be blended with local wine. Estate wineries and farm-gate wineries must bottle wines made only from locally-grown grapes. These are entitled to the VQA designation if they pass the taste test.

Recommended producers include: Blue Mountain Vineyard, Brights, Cedar Creek, Domaine de Chaberton, Gehringer Brothers, Gray Monk, Hainle Vineyards, Lang Vineyards, Le Comte Estate, Mission Hill, Sumac Ridge, Summerhill.

Nova Scotia

Nova Scotia, which is midway between the equator and the North Pole, boasts three farm wineries and a total of 60ha (150 acres) of vineyards, which concentrate mainly on hybrids as well as unfamiliar Russian red grape varieties such as Michurinetz and Severnyi. The short growing season restricts the number of varieties that can be planted in the Annapolis Valley and Northumberland Strait. Much effort is being put into finding early-ripening clones.

Nova Scotia has not yet accepted the VQA standards, which could ultimately give Canada a national appellation system. The three wineries in this province (most notably Ste Famille Wines) are serviced by 38 growers.

Quebec

Quebec is the least likely of all Canadian wine regions. The centre of the province's small but enthusiastic vinegrowing region is the old town of Dunham, where 15 wineries have been licensed since 1985. The wineries, strung out along the American border, battle the elements to produce wine for the tourist trade. During the winter months the vines have to be covered with earth by the method of back-ploughing in order to protect them from the cold; they are uncovered by hand in the spring. Average sunshine hours during the growing season in Dunham are 1,150 (in Bordeaux they are 2,069), but topographical features create highly localized warm spots that allow the hardiest of vines to survive, if not flourish.

Quebec's cottage wineries produce mainly (90%) white wine, mostly very fresh Seyval Blanc. These wines are available only from the wineries, but the scenery along the way makes the trip (80km/49 miles south of Montreal) well worth the effort.

Recommended producers include: Vignoble de l'Orpailleur, Vignoble Dietrich-Joos, Vignobles le Cep d'Argent.

Unfortunately, neither Nova Scotia nor Quebec have yet applied the VQA standards to its winemaking.

SOUTH AMERICA
AND CENTRAL AMERICA

—

THE VINEYARDS OF MEXICO ARE THE OLDEST IN THE NEW WORLD;
THOSE OF CHILE AND ARGENTINA ARE RESPECTED AS SOURCES OF
BULK WINE AS WELL AS QUALITY WINES OF INCREASING INTEREST
AND SOPHISTICATION.

—

Spanish conquistadors introduced the vine to the Americas. Viticulture was spread by missionaries, who needed wine for sacramental purposes. Hernán Cortés, who was responsible for the colonization of New Spain (now Mexico) in the 16th century, instructed every settler to establish 1,000 vines annually, and viticulture spread from Mexico to the north and south of the New World. It reached Peru in the late 16th century, and then Chile and Argentina. By the next century it had reached California, also by way of Mexico. The vines adapted to their new sites and were prolific enough to be used for making both wine and brandy. With modest demands made upon them, a few vines with vague Spanish ancestry, such as País in Chile and Criolla in Argentina, soon proliferated in the warm, dry climates. Both countries are blessed with climatic conditions envied by grape-growers around the world. Between latitudes 32° and 26° South various *vinifera* grapes — planted in Argentina and Chile at about the same time, the mid-19th century — receive more than adequate warmth to bring them to maturity without need of chaptalization. Most vineyard sites in Chile would be too warm for sensitive grapes were it not for cooling breezes blowing off the nearby Pacific Ocean. Only an occasional pre-harvest cold spell or frost has been known to unsettle Chilean growers. The natural resources of South America, even more than the climate, are the envy of winemakers elsewhere. Santiago and Mendoza, the respective wine capitals of Chile and Argentina, are only 240km (150 miles) apart, but separated by the towering Andes, which provide plentiful water to cultivate vines.

The reputation of the Central and South American wine industries was for decades damaged by local political and economic difficulties. Throughout the 1980s greater stability in many countries attracted foreign investors, and wine producers were able to turn their attention to export markets and the quality, rather than the quantity, of their wines. New wine styles, capable of competing with those of Europe, California and Australia, have emphasized fresh fruit flavours in the white wines, and full-bodied, deeply coloured and intensely flavoured reds.

In the mid-19th century an influx of European immigrants to South America heightened an interest in wine and encouraged experimentation with a range of wine varieties. In the 1850s the first significant plantings of *vitis vinifera* from France took place in both Argentina and Chile. The French impact on Chilean winemaking was longer-lasting, but limited the choice of grape varieties until recently. Italian grapes and wine types are more noticeable in Argentina and Brazil. Over time the influence of the French, Italians and Germans manifested itself in the acceptance of wine as a natural part of the daily diet. But in Mexico and most of Central America fledgling wine industries went without the benefit of an invigorating influx of wine-knowledgeable immigrants. Later in the 19th century, as phylloxera, the dreaded root louse, was taking its toll in European vineyards, a number of winemakers and others with rudimentary cellar skills made their way to South America, where the *vitis vinifera* vines familiar to them were flourishing.

Once the plentiful water resources of the Andes were controllable through irrigation schemes, vineyards were easy to establish. In Chile most vineyards are located near main rivers flowing west to the Pacific Ocean. These rivers and their tributaries, generously fed by mountain streams, flow non-stop all year round. Using canals and ditches, growers have devised an irrigation system based on open furrows, which enables rows of vines to be irrigated whenever it is necessary.

Growers on the other side of the Andes in Argentina have developed a more elaborate and sophisticated irrigation system of dams, reservoirs, canals and ditches to first trap the snow and then tap into the meltwater. Since adequate, naturally-flowing water supplies are not available year-round, this system enables sufficient quantities to be collected and then used to irrigate vineyards at the foot of the Andes in the growing season later in the year.

WINE REGIONS OF CENTRAL AND SOUTH AMERICA

The principal wine regions of South America lie to either side of the Andes Mountains — in Chile and Argentina. Between latitudes 32° and 26° S the climate is particularly favourable to the production of good-quality wines based on *vinifera* grape varieties. Wine is produced in several other countries, including parts of Brazil, Mexico, Uruguay and, to a much lesser extent, in Peru, Colombia, Paraguay, Bolivia and Ecuador.

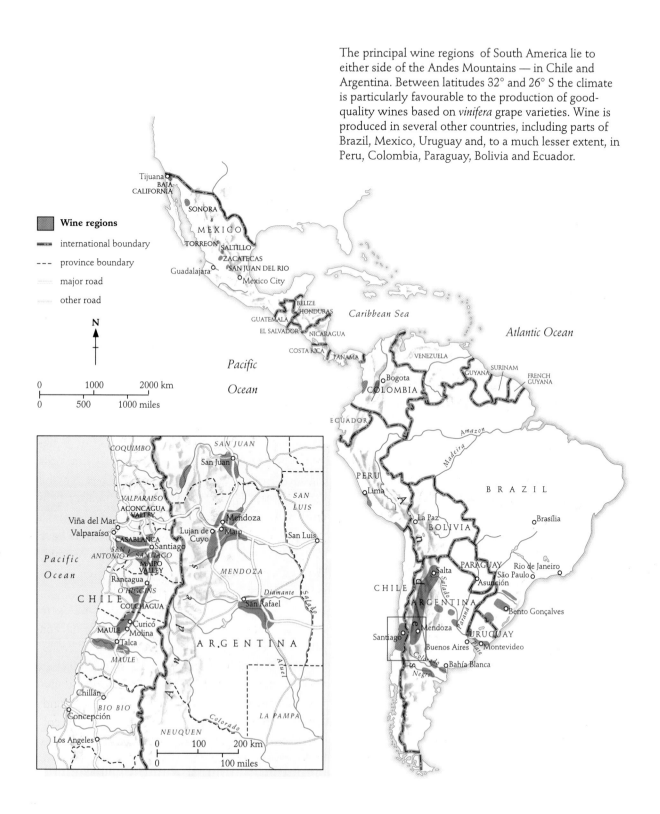

Political and economic instability

Mexican viticulture was dealt two serious blows at the beginning of the 20th century; one in the form of phylloxera, and the other the Mexican Revolution of 1910. In Chile, although isolated to a certain extent by the Andes and thus protected from phylloxera, winemakers had to contend with exorbitant taxes on wines in 1902, and then an outright ban on planting new vines from 1938 to 1945. During the early 1970s in Chile many wine estates were dismantled during a land reform. Throughout the 1970s various South American countries experienced periods of runaway inflation and rocketing interest rates, which not only harmed domestic markets but also discouraged foreign investment.

A wine revolution

As political and economic conditions stabilized during the 1980s, foreign investors looked closely at potential vineyard land in South America. Established international companies began to invest. The timing could not have been better: in both Chile and Argentina the domestic markets, which once consumed most of the wine produced, were slowing down.

Wine producers are now focusing on exports for their long-term survival. As a consequence, they have been compelled to rethink their methods. Most major exporters have modernized their facilities and evolved new wine styles and winemaking techniques, including the use of small oak barrels for ageing premium wines such as Chardonnay and Cabernet Sauvignon. Wine cellars built over a century ago stand in sharp contrast to rows of shiny stainless steel tanks, centrifuges, state-of-the-art presses and bottling lines. Some traditionalists are opposed to these developments, but most producers see it as the only option.

By the early 1990s, Chile had won acceptance in many wine markets and was clearly showing the way. Argentina was preparing to follow along the export path. One of the biggest obstacles faced by wine producers remains the natural inclination of growers in South America to allow the vines to carry far too big a crop. As the 21st century approaches, South America has access to whatever winemaking technology it wants and can afford. A revolution is likely in the vineyard as the conflict between high yields and wine quality is played out, and as the wines of Central and especially South America become more readily available and therefore play an increasingly significant rôle in the world marketplace.

Wine regions

Mexico may be the oldest American wine producer but its quality wine industry is relatively new. Peasant wine and brandy production still dominate, and Mexico remains overshadowed by its neighbours to the north and south.

Chile has emerged as the king of wine exports. It is now the third major wine importer to the USA, sailing past Australia and Germany and trailing only Italy and France. It achieved this by offering wines under familiar varietal names and at attractively low prices.

Argentina is South America's awakening giant and has such vast amounts of land available for planting that it could become the main player. It is the largest wine-producing region on the continent, and has the most potential. Its best-known winemaking facilities are relatively modern, but technology traditionally has been aimed at mass production.

Brazil is South America's third-largest wine producer, and is enjoying an improved economy. With 60,000ha (150,000 acres) under vine, Brazil is starting to export: domestic consumption is relatively small by South American standards. ☐

The century-old brick-arched cellars of Santa Rita, in the Maipo Valley, Chile.

MEXICO

With its rich history and pivotal rôle in American winemaking history, Mexico presents itself as a real anomaly. Here is a country that introduced grapes and winemaking to countries both north and south of its borders, yet is often considered too hot and inhospitable to wine grapes. Though half of Mexico is in the torrid zone south of the Tropic of Cancer, wine is grown on the mile-high Central Plateau and in Baja California.

History of winemaking in Mexico
At the end of the 19th century, California's pioneering winemaking family, the Concannons of Livermore Valley, persuaded the Mexican government to take advantage of the country's grape-growing potential, and introduced dozens of French *vinifera* grape varieties to many parts of Mexico. James Concannon left Mexico in 1904, but six years later Antonio Perelli-Minetti, who was another winemaker from California, introduced another battery of varieties as he planted hundreds of acres near Torreón.

However, by 1900 a large proportion of Mexico's vineyards were being blighted by phylloxera, and political problems dogged the country for many years after the Revolution. All thoughts about a wine revival had to be suspended until the early 1940s when farmers gradually began replacing their cotton crop with grapes.

The modern wine industry
The top priority then and today is growing grapes for brandy. Several international brandy firms have invested in Mexican viticulture, and set up their own facilities there in order to avoid heavy import duties into Europe, especially on brandies. The Domecq wine family of Spain was the first to make a significant investment, in 1953. With Mexico City as its headquarters, the company now has brandy and winemaking facilities at 11 locations. Other well-known firms with a big stake in Mexico are Gonzalez Byass and Freixenet from Spain, Hennessy and Martell from France, Martini & Rossi and Cinzano from Italy, Suntory of Japan and Seagram from North America. Devoting considerable time and money to wine production as well, Domecq has emerged as the leading quality wine producer, and some of its lines are now exported to the USA.

Today Mexico's vineyards exceed 40,000ha (100,000 acres). Close to 80% of the wine-grape harvest goes directly into brandy or vermouth production. Traditional wine production has been on the increase since 1980. As more vineyards are devoted to noble grape varieties and suitable land on coastal or high-elevation sites is developed, the modest momentum achieved by the 1990s should be sustained. ☐

REGIONS AND PRODUCERS

Production is mainly in the hands of large international companies. In fact, small producers are discouraged by bureaucracy and the fact that most Mexicans prefer Mescal, Tequila and beer to wine.

Baja California
The northern part of this region has a relatively fresh climate by Mexican standards and most vineyard expansion is here — more than 10,000ha (25,000 acres) are currently under vine. Most of the vineyards can be found in the Guadalupe and Santo Tomás valleys and around Ensenada. The most well-known producer, and one of the longest established, Santo Tomás, produces very promising Cabernet Sauvignons and Chardonnays. L.-A. Cetto produces wines from the Cabernet Sauvignon, Nebbiolo, Petit Syrah and the Californian Zinfandel Variety. Cabernet Sauvignons produced by Cava Valmur and Pedro Domecq are also well-known.

Parras, Saltillo
The Parras Valley, in the north of Mexico, is said to be the cradle of American wine. The best vineyards can be found at 1,500m (5,000ft) where the climate is suitable for the production of quality wines. Venedos San Marcos, a modern operation, is best known for its Cabernet Sauvignon and sparkling wines. Bodegas de San Lorenzo (which belongs to Casa Madero), established back in 1626, produces a range of *vinifera* wines and brandy. There are several distilleries in the area.

Laguna, district of Torreón
In this district, where cotton production dominates, the climate is too hot for growing noble grape varieties. Vergel, a company established in 1943 and the best-known in the district, has modernised its winery and uses temperature-controlled stainless steel vats.

San Juan del Rio
This wine growing region, 160km (100 miles) north of Mexico, is a fairly recent development. Most of the vineyards are at an altitude of 1,800m (6,000ft). Cava de San Juan sets the example with noble *vinifera* wines such as Cabernet Sauvignon and Pinot Noir (under the Hidalgo label) and a sparkling wine (Carte Blanche). Martell produces quality still wines here.

Sonora
Almost 20,000ha (49,420 acres) of vineyards, mainly given over to the cultivation of Thompson Seedless and other eating varieties as well as a wine grape used for distillation.

Zacatecas
At 2,000m (7,000ft), this is the highest and coolest wine region. Wine growing began here in the 1970s and the first producer was Bodegas de Altiplano.

CHILE

Chile is one of the few important wine producing countries not affected by phylloxera. The deadly aphid, which ravaged all the vineyards in Europe and North Africa, did not make it past the Andes cordillera nor the great expanse of desert in the north and was unable to reach the coastal vineyards. As Chilean vines do not require grafting, wine enthusiasts are passionately watching the progress of Chile's methods of cultivation and vinification which should result in this country bringing us wines which rank among the best in the world. Foreign producers are also aware of the opportunities this privileged position offers. Thus, Catalan Torres was enticed by the Chilean adventure as far back as 1979, soon to be followed by producers from Bordeaux (in particular Cos D'Estournel, Margaux and Lafite), Chablis, Alsace and then California. A Chilean Cabernet Sauvignon from Bodega Los Vascos in the Rapel Valley, run by the Lafite Rothschilds, caused a sensation at the Vinexpo by standing its ground among the best of the Bordeaux châteaux.

Furthermore, to increase the quality of their wines, some purely Chilean operations have enlisted the assistance of French winemakers (in particular Michel Rolland, Jacques Lurton and Jacques Bassenot), flying winemakers from Australia and New Zealand, among them Brian Bicknell, and Californian advisers such as Edward Flaherty. Chile has 144,000ha (355,000 acres) of land under vines (a little more than half for wine grapes) and production (including wine for distillation) is around 5.5 million hectolitres. Three quarters of Chilean fine wines are exported.

Wine Regions
Under the *appellation contrôlée* system introduced in 1995, there are five

Vines at Molina, near Lontué, Chile.

regions, subdivided into several different valleys:

Atacama (Copiapó and Huasco valleys). A northern region stretching from the coastline at the foothills of the Andes, where mainly eating grapes are grown and no quality wine is produced.

Coquimbo (Elqui, Limari and Choapa valleys). Vineyards dispersed in a mountainous region, mainly producing eating grapes and mediocre wine used for distillation of *pisco*, the national brandy.

Aconcagua (Aconcagua and Casablanca valleys). A region close to the port of Valparaíso, about 100km (62 miles) north-west of Santiago.

■ In the Mediterranean-style climate of the Aconcagua Valley, mainly red Bordeaux grape varieties and, for a few years now, the noble Syrah, are grown on the alluvial or gravely soils.

■ The fairly recently-developed Casablanca Valley (there was not a single vineyard to be found here in 1980) benefits from the fresh breezes from the Pacific. The sandy-chalky

soil is ideal for cultivation of the Chardonnay grape, which produces a delicately flavoured wine. The Merlot and Sauvignon Blanc varieties are also grown successfully here.

The **Central Valley**, sitting halfway between the Pacific and the Andes (with, in increasing order of importance, the Maipo, Rapel, Curicó and Maule Valleys — almost 45,000ha (110,000 acres) of vines.

■ The Maipo Valley, near Santiago, is Chile's oldest wine producing area and still has the highest concentration of vineyards in the country. Soil conditions here are very varied and the wines are of a high quality.

■ In Summer the largest part of the Rapel Valley, prone to a little more rainfall that the Maipo Valley, is tempered by the southerly winds. The 1990s saw spectacular development in this area where red wine varieties are particularly at home.

■ Almost 200 km (125 miles) south of Santiago, the Curicó Valley is famous for its Chardonnay wines but it also produces good reds from the Cabernet Sauvignon, Merlot and Pinot Noir varieties.

■ The Maule Valley is the most southerly, and so the coldest, in the Central Valley. A large amount of País is still produced here but this mediocre variety is gradually being replaced by noble varieties such as Chardonnay, Sauvignon Blanc and Merlot.

Southern Region (Iata and Bió-Bió Valleys)

■ The legacy of the colonial period is still very evident in the Iata Valley, which is largely given over to País, although noble varieties are being introduced in response to an increasing demand for quality wines.

■ The Bió-Bió Valley, the most southern wine-growing area in Chile, has relatively few vineyards. Chardonnay, Pinot Noir and Riesling grow well at this latitude. □

PRODUCERS

Most producers call their export wines by the name of the grape variety: Cabernet Sauvignon, Merlot, Chardonnay and Sauvignon Blanc are the most common. It is however becoming common for producers to bottle one or several grape varieties at various price levels and/or under several names.

Almaviva
A Franco-Chilean operation established in 1997, in which the Mouton Rothschilds and Concha y Toro, Chile's largest producer, hold equal shares. The main contribution from the Chilean partner was a small vineyard of about 40ha (100 acres) located in the southern outskirts of Santiago, which had been under cultivation for about a decade. Almaviva offers a single wine from the two Cabernet varieties. Current production of this Bordeaux-style wine, which likes to rank itself among the classed growths, scarcely exceeds 34,000 cases.

Aquitania
This estate close to Santiago, established several years ago in Quebrada de Macul, in the Maipo Valley, belongs to Bruno Prats (who ran the Château Cos d'Estournel in Saint-Estèphe), Paul Pontallier (Château Margaux) and Felipe de Solminihac (one of the best oenologists in Chile). It currently produces just over one million bottles of Cabernet Sauvignon sold under the Domaine Paul Bruno label.

Caliterra
This ultra modern operation, set up in Curicó in 1989, now belongs to the Chadwick family, the owners of Errázuriz, and Robert Mondavi, whose ambition is to produce here the Chilean equivalent of his Opus One. It cultivates some 230ha (570 acres) of vines in Casablanca, Maipo, Rapel and Curicó and produces around 600,000 cases of Cabernet Sauvignon, Merlot, Chardonnay and Sauvignon Blanc.

Canepa
This company in the Maipo Valley, going back to the 1930s, cultivates several large vineyards in the Maipo, Rapel, Curicó and Maule valleys. Following recent modernisation, it produces 125,000 cases of wines from the red and white Bordeaux grape varieties as well as less common varieties such as Zinfandel and Gewürztraminer. Wines are labelled according to their destination: Petroa, Montevenuto, Rowan Brooks, or carry the buyer's brand name.

Carmen
Viña Carmen in the Maipo Valley, established in 1850, is one of Chile's oldest wine making operations. It has belonged to Santa Rita since the 1980s and was completely modernised in 1992. It produces over 30 000hl under the direction of Alvaro Espinoza, one of the best oenologists in the country. In addition to the usual Bordeaux varieties, the range of wines on offer includes Pinot Noir, Petite Sirah and Grande Vidure.

Casa Lapostolle
The French Marnier-Lapostolle Group — producer of Grand Marnier, the famous orange- and cognac-based liqueur, owner of Château de Sancerre — wishing to diversify into New World wines, enlisted the assistance of the oenologist Michel Rolland, acquired a 51% shareholding in a *bodega* in the Rapel region in 1994, renamed the estate Casa Lapostolle and fitted it out with the most up-to-date equipment. In addition it bought 300ha (740 acres) of vines: the Casablanca vineyard in the valley of the same name (mainly Chardonnay and Pinot Noir), the Requinoa vineyard (Cabernet Sauvignon and Sauvignon Blanc) and the Apalta vineyard (old vines of red Bordeaux varieties). 60% of the grapes come from these vineyards, the balance coming from wine growers working under contract. They currently produce 150,000 cases of ranges coming under the names of the Casa Lapostolle (Sauvignon, Chardonnay, Merlot and Cabernet Sauvignon); Cuvée Alexandre (Chardonnay, Merlot, Cabernet Sauvignon) and Clos Apalta (an up-market blend of Merlot, Carmenère and Cabernet Sauvignon).

Concha y Toro
Founded in 1883 in the Maipo Valley, this *bodega*, which was modernised in the 1980s, is Chile's largest producer with around 11 million cases of wine, half of which is exported. It produces wines from traditional Bordeaux grape varieties as well as from Pinot Noir and Syrah. Its wine labels are, in order of increasing quality, Concha y Toro, Trio or Explorer, Casillero del Diablo, Marqués de Casa Concha, Amelia (a barrel-fermented and barrel-aged Chardonnay) and Don Melchior (Cabernet Sauvignon).

Cono Sur
A company set up in 1993 by Concha y Toro in Chibarongo, in the Colchagua (Rapel) Valley, originally calling on the assistance of the Californian Edward Flaherty to produce wines exclusively for export. Cono Sur operates vineyards in Casablanca, Rapel and Bió-Bío and produces some 500,000 cases of a wide range of wines (whites include Chardonnay, Gewürztraminer and Viognier and the reds Cabernet Sauvignon, Merlot, Pinot Noir and Zinfandel), distributed under the Cono Sur, Tarconal (supermarkets) and Isla Negra (top of the range) labels.

Curicó Cooperative
For many years this cooperative, founded in 1939, produced wines for the local market only. With the market for better quality wines increasing, it modernised its plant in the 1980s and enlisted the assistance of the flying winemaker Peter Bright. Its Cabernet Sauvignons, Merlots and Sauvignon Verts, exported under the Los Robles label, account for around half of the 50,000hl produced.

Errázuriz
The Errázuriz operation was established in 1870 in Panquehue, in the Aconcagua Valley north of Santiago, at a time when the Maule Valley, south of the capital, was the preferred location. Since 1983 it has belonged to the Chadwick family, who called on the assistance of the flying winemaker from New Zealand, Brian Bicknell, and then the Californian Edward Flaherty, to produce wines with plenty of character. The company operates several vineyards totalling over 350ha (865 acres) in the Aconcagua, Casablanca, Maipo and Curicó valleys, cultivating mainly Cabernet Sauvignon, Merlot, Chardonnay and Sauvignon Blanc varieties, depending on the soil.

Cousiño Macul
When the Cousiño family's estate was established in 1865

in Macul, near Santiago, it was right in the heart of the countryside. Nowadays its vineyards covering some 250ha (620 acres) are increasingly threatened by urban development and are, like the neighbouring vineyards, likely to disappear shortly. The Cousiños have therefore bought land further south which they intend to turn into a vineyard and winery. Today the Macul estate is known for its Cabernet Sauvignon, Merlot and Chardonnay. These wines are generally produced from old vines and are of a style which is more European than American.

Montes

In 1988, four partners with a great deal of experience in the world of wine selling, formed the Discovery Wine Company — which has since taken on the name of their oenologist, Aurelio Montes — to produce wines

--- LOS VASCOS ---

A famous estate founded in 1750 in the Limari Valley, in the Colchagua region, by the Basque Miguel Echenique. The founder's descendants, whose land was expropriated during the agricultural reform in the 1960s, re-established the vineyard bit by bit in the 1970s. This exercise incurred financial difficulties and so the owners were forced to look for a partner and the Château Lafite Rothschilds took a 50% stake in the company in 1988 (the Eyzaguirre-Echeniques were to sell their shareholding to Santa Rita in 1996). The French partner immediately began to modernise the plant, had hundreds of small oak barrels sent over from Lafite and began to implement the methods used in Pauillac. It is not surprising therefore that the style of the Los Vascos Cabernet Sauvignon is closer to that of a Medoc than a Californian wine.

for export. The operation, located in the Curicó Valley, has 220ha (550 acres) of vineyards and produces over 250,000 cases of the usual varieties: Cabernet Sauvignon, Sauvignon Blanc and Chardonnay under various brand names. They also produce an exceptionally good Merlot.

San Pedro

San Pedro is an example of the recent revolution in the Chilean wine industry. Established in 1865, the company remained in the hands of the same family for 75 years before being sold to the country's largest brewer. Production continued on a small scale, using dilapidated equipment, until the beginning of the 1990s. In less than 10 years it has become one of the largest and most modern wine-making companies in Latin America. It has over 2,000ha (4,950 acres) of vineyards under its control, stores its wine in an impressive array of huge stainless steel vats, produces the best wines in thousands of small French and American oak barrels and sells some 400,000 cases per annum. Assisted by the Bordeaux oenologist, Jacques Lurton, San Pedro is mainly known for its wines sold under the Gato Negro and Gato Blanco labels, which together account for almost 50% of exports. It also distributes wines under other labels, such as the prestige *cuvées* Santa Helena and Castillo de Molina. The famous San Pedro name is reserved mainly for Chardonnay and Merlot wines for export.

Santa Carolina

Established in Santiago in 1875, Santa Carolina was one of the first operations to be modernised. The original vineyard has fallen victim to urban development but the company owns over 600ha (1,480 acres) of vines in the Casablanca, Maipo and Rapel valleys and buys a large quantity of grapes from independent growers. Under the guidance of the talented cellar master, Maria del Pilar Gonzalez, it produces over 250,000 cases of the usual ranges: Cabernet Sauvignon, Cabernet Sauvignon/Merlot, Merlot, Sauvignon Blanc and Chardonnay — supplemented by a small quantity of Malbec, Syrah and even Gewürztraminer.

Santa Ema

The Pavone family, of Piedmontese origin, which had been cultivating vines on Maipo island since 1931, set up the Viña Santa Ema in 1955 to produce its own wine rather than selling its grapes to other producers. The acquisition of land in the Rapel Valley increased its wine-growing area to some 300 ha (740 acres). As most of the wines — mainly Cabernet Sauvignon, Merlot, Chardonnay and Sauvignon Blanc aged in French and American oak — are aimed at the United States market, it is

produced in a typical North American extrovert style.

Santa Emiliana

This ambitious company was founded in Maipo in 1986 by several of the main shareholders of Concha y Toro, in association with Banfi Vintners. It has several vineyards in the Casablanca, Rapel and Maipo valleys and produces almost 1.8 million cases of Cabernet Sauvignon, Merlot and Chardonnay as well as sparkling wines made by the Charmat method. Its wines, sold under the Walnut Crest label, are very popular in the United States, its main export market.

Santa Mónica

In 1976, the Bordeaux-trained Chilean oenologist, Emilio de Solminihac, and his wife Monica purchased a winery in Rancagua, in the Rapel Valley — at a time when the future of Chilean wine was for the very least uncertain. At the same time as producing bulk wine for other companies, they modernised the winery, developed the estate vineyards, which today cover 93ha (230 acres) and began to bottle some of their own wine. All the wines exported nowadays by Santa Mónica originate from this vineyard, which is unusual by Chilean standards.

Solminihac likes to be creative and so he also produces Rieslings, in addition to the usual Cabernet Sauvignon, Merlot and Chardonnay varieties — the best of which are barrel-fermented. For the time being, the company output is less than 85,000 cases, the remainder still being sold in bulk. The best export wines are sold under the Tierra del Sol label.

Santa Rita

Founded in 1880 in Buin, in the Maipo Valley, modernisation of the Santa Rita winery began in 1980 and the area under vines was increased to 2,000ha (4,950 acres) in the Casablanca, Maipo and Maule valleys. Contracts were entered into with other wine growers for deliveries of additional grapes of a high quality and emphasis was laid on export (25,000 cases in 1985, 415,000 in 1994 and, in 1998, 1 million out of almost 1.4 million cases produced). Small French oak barrels are used widely for vinification and/or ageing of the best wines. The three main export labels are, in order of increasing quality, "120", Riserva and Medalla Real. In addition to the usual range, you will also find Carmenère, Semillon/Viognier, Petite Syrah/Merlot and Pinot Noir wines.

Tarapacá ex-Zavala

This vineyard, founded under the Rojas name in the Maipo Valley in 1874, was bought over by Antonio Zavala, who then gave it his name. A divorce in the Zavala family then caused a problem which remained unresolved until the President of Chile, nicknamed "the Lion of Tarapacá", decreed that the estate should be renamed "Ex-Zavala". Finally it took the name of Tarapacá ex-Zavala. The operation remained small scale until it was bought over in 1992 by the Holding Fosforos which has invested no less than 50 million dollars in constructing and fitting out new buildings, buying land and planting vines. The first 440ha (1,100 acres) of new vines went into production in 1995. Tarapacá now produces over 1 million cases of Cabernet Sauvignon, Merlot, Chardonnay and Sauvignon Blanc, the best wines being aged in American or French oak, depending on their destination. The 1988 Cabernet Sauvignon and the 1999 Sauvignon Blanc were Gold medal winners at the 1999 Vinando in Mendoza, Argentina.

Miguel Torres

This highly innovate company was set up in 1979 when Miguel Torres, from the famous Spanish family of wine producers,

The vineyard of Los Vascos, near Peralillo, in the Limari Valley.

bought an old vineyard in the Curicó Valley. Ultra-modern equipment was installed, allowing for the production of 100,000 cases per annum, which was then increased to 167,000. Torres introduced temperature-controlled stainless steel vats, modern winepresses and small French oak barrels into Chile. In the vineyards, improved vine management and controlled irrigation improved quality and these methods have largely inspired other producers. In its three main vineyards in Curicó and Maule (over 300ha/740 acres), Torres concentrates on the Sauvignon Blanc, Chardon-

nay and Cabernet Sauvignon varieties while experimenting constantly with the Carignan, Syrah and Gewürztraminer. The company also produces a very dry sparkling wine by the traditional method, using Chardonnay and Pinot Noir grapes. Almost three quarters of wines produced are for export.

Undurraga

Established in 1885, Undurraga was one of the first companies to export to the United States at the beginning of the 20th century. Equipped with up-to-the minute technology, it now exports over 800,000 cases

throughout the world with 8 million bottles being consumed on the home market. The grapes produced in its Maipo and Maule vineyards (almost 1,000ha/2,750 acres) are supplemented by supplies are bought in from independent growers. An assortment of the Bordeaux varieties and Pinot Noir are used to produce the wines, the best of which are fermented and/or aged in wood.

Valdivieso

This company, which dates back to 1879, was best known for its sparkling wine until it was taken over by the Mitjans family around 1950. It was modernised in 1990 and continues to produce 90% of the sparkling wine sold in Chile (over 400,000 cases, about half of which are produced by the Charmat process) but also produces some still wines, especially reds using Pinot Noir, Cabernet Sauvignon and Malbec, almost all of which are for export.

Los Vascos

See the profile

Villard

In 1989, the Frenchman Thierry Villard bought a piece of land in the Casablanca Valley, planted a small vineyard, set up a company in which Santa Emiliana took a minority shareholding, installed some modern equipment and imported some small French oak barrels. The grapes come from this small vineyard and the Maipo Valley. Since 1997 Villard has been producing a still very limited quantity of Chardonnay, Sauvignon Blanc, Cabernet Sauvignon, Merlot and Pinot Noir wines.

ARGENTINA

The first vineyards were established at the foot of the Andes in the middle of the 16th century by missionaries and conquistadors from Peru and Chile. This region, now known as Mendoza, is still Argentina's main wine growing area. In the 19th century, following independence and then the building of the Buenos Aires-Mendoza railway line, the Andean vineyards became very important and successive waves of Italian, French and Spanish immigrants planted varieties from their country of origin. In the 20th century, more and more land was planted with vines until it reached a peak of 320,000ha (790,720 acres) in 1980. The area under vines has since decreased (210,000ha/518,910 acres in 1998). Nevertheless, producing 12,673,000hl, Argentina still ranks as the fifth wine producing country in the world behind Italy, France, Spain and the United States. Consumption per head of population has fallen from 90L in 1980 to 50L in 1997 (sixth highest in the world). Exports, on the other hand, have increased dramatically: 1,205,000hl in 1997 compared to 220,000hl in the 1980s. The vineyards extend for over 1,770km (1,100 miles) in the west of the country, where they benefit from irrigation, so essential under the inland climatic conditions. Melted snow is brought to reservoirs in the wine growing country along a network of canals and this system is supplemented by deep high pressure bore holes. The province of Mendoza, the focal point of the country's wine-making industry, lies some 960km (600 miles) from Buenos Aires — on the same latitude as Santiago and Chile's best wine growing regions — and produces around 70% of Argentina's wines. Most of the vineyards are to be found in the valleys and the plateaux of the lower Andes. The noble varieties, in particular Cabernet Sauvignon and Malbec, are grown to the south of the town of Mendoza, in two regions set at a higher altitude with

Most vineyards of the Mendoza region are in the valleys or on the plateaux of the Andean foothills.

a cooler climate, Maipu and Lujan de Cuyo. To the east, at the foot of Tupungato peak, Chardonnay and Merlot varieties can be grown successfully. San Juan, the country's second largest wine growing region, north of Mendoza, is much hotter. It produces very little quality wine. Most wine produced here is for brandy, Vermouth and a large quantity of grape concentrate. The other regions produce smaller quantities. Salta, still further to the north, is near the Tropic of Capricorn. Its vines are cultivated at 1,700m (5,600ft) where the cool climate is suited to white grape varieties. Although accounting for only around 5% of the country's production, the most southerly region, Rio Negro in Patagonia, is even cooler than the northern wine-growing regions so is ideally suited for growing good quality white varieties and producing base wines for sparkling wines.

Grape varieties and wines

Although first to go when it came to reducing the area under vines, the variety inherited from early colonisation, the Criolla, still produces huge quantities of basic red wine. Malbec is

at its best in Argentina, producing well-structured wines with a deep colour and rich ripe blackcurrant and spicy flavours. Bonarda is equally good at producing large quantities of quality red wines. Cabernet Sauvignon is becoming more popular — in response to demand from the international market — often blended with Merlot and/or Malbec to soften the edges. In addition to the Bonarda, Italian immigrants introduced other red varieties such as Barbera Dolcetto and Sangiovese. Finally, the Spanish Tempranillo is not altogether insignificant. Initial results from Syrah are promising but once again the Pinot Noir is proving to be a difficult variety to master.

The most interesting white variety is the Torrontes, which produces lively, fragrant wines with a pleasant spicy flavour. Muscat of Alexandria and Pedro Giménez are plentiful, the Ugni Blanc and Chenin Blanc varieties produce fairly mediocre wines and international-style Chardonnays are produced mainly for the Anglo-Saxon markets. Sémillon and Viognier are also grown.   □

PRODUCERS

Argentina exports a fairly high quantity of its wines in bulk. The purchaser then bottles it and often gives it a name of its choice. As a result, the same wine may be sold under different labels depending on the importing country or even the distributor. On the Argentine market, most sparkling wines are called *champaña*, whether they are locally produced or imported or made by the Charmat process or the traditional method.

La Agricola
With the aim of making its mark on the international market, La Agricola has modernised its operations and enlisted the assistance of two flying winemakers, the Californian Edward Flaherty and the Australian David Morrison. The Bonarda/Sangiovese is excellent value for money and without a doubt the most interesting in the Santa Julia range (sold under the name of Picajuan Peak by a large British supermarket chain). La Agricola also produces a lively, aromatic Torrontes.

Bodegas Balbi
Belonging to the Domecq group, this company produces various wines for export, including, with help from the oenologist Thierry Boudinaud, a complex red wine from a blend of four varieties — Cabernet Sauvignon, Malbec, Merlot and Syrah — distributed under the Barbaro label.

Bianchi
Part of the Seagram group. This company's best wines are a Chardonnay and a Malbec but it also produces a *champaña*.

Luigi Bosca
Bosca produces varietal wines — Cabernet Sauvignon, Malbec and Chardonnay — for the export market.

Humberto Canale
Southern wines from the Rio Negro region in Patagonia. The Sémillon and Malbec are particularly noteworthy.

Catena
Large quantity of value-for-money wines sold on the local market under the Trumpeter label and, mainly for export, Malbec, Cabernet Sauvignon and Chardonnay wines with an international style, sold under the Alamos, Catena, Viña Esmeralda, Rutini and San Felician names. Its prestige *cuvées* are marketed under the Catena Alta label.

Domaine Chandon
Founded in 1960 by the champagne company, Moët & Chandon, this company, the largest *champaña* producer, has diversified into still wines for the local market and export, including a Chardonnay and a blended red wine under the name of Castel Chandon.

Etchart
Etchart (Pernod-Ricard group) produces a wide range of good wines including delicious Torrontes (the 1999 was awarded a gold medal at the Vinalies 2000 in Paris) and Chardonnays, both from the Salta region, and Malbecs and Cabernet Sauvignons in the Mendoza region.

Finca Flichman
This long-standing company, recently modernised, has enlisted the assistance of the flying winemaker Hugh Ryman. Its range of wines produced from the classic greats — Malbec, Cabernet Sauvignon and Merlot — is supplemented by the Italian Barbera and Sangiovese varieties, the Spanish Tempranillo and Syrah from the Rhône valley. It offers a wide range of varietal and blended wines. The Cabernet Sauvignon, distributed under the Caballero de la Cepa label, is well aged and richly flavoured. The Fond de Cap label is reserved for its top of the range wines.

Bodegas Lurton
A recent company set up by Jacques Lurton, from Bordeaux, and Nicola Catena, from Argentina, exporting a Tempranillo/Malbec blend and a very good Cabernet Sauvignon under the Gran Lurton label.

Navarro Correas
A brand name used by three producers for export of a range of wines, in particular to the Anglo-Saxon markets, which include a Malbec and a Syrah as well as a Merlot/Malbec blend labelled Colección Privada.

Peñaflor
Peñaflor, Argentina's largest wine making group, has enlisted the assistance of the famous flying winemakers Peter Bright and John Worontschak. On the domestic market the group sells mainly red wines for everyday consumption. Most of its wines for export are produced by its subsidiary Trapiche (see below).

Henri Piper
This is the name used on the Argentine market for the *champaña* produced locally by the Champagne company, Piper Heidsieck.

Finca El Retiro
Established in the Mendoza region in 1912, this family concern enlists the skills of an Italian oenologist, Alberto Antonioni. It produces concentrated red wines, especially those made from the Spanish Tempranillo grape.

San Telmo
This large-scale producer shows great skill in producing wines of an international style: Malbec, Cabernet Sauvignon and a Malbec/Cabernet Sauvignon blend (labelled Cuseta del Madero).

Trapiche
The winery belonging to the giant Peñaflor group which relies from the omnipresent oenologist, Michel Rolland. The most well known reds include a Cabernet Sauvignon, Malbec, Syrah and a Bordeaux-style blend called Medella; white wines include Chenin, Chardonnay and Torrontes wines. It also produces a top of the range Cabernet Sauvignon under the name of Andean Vineyard.

Vistalba
This French company in the Mendoza region produces a range of Cabernet Sauvignon, Malbec, Syrah and Barbera wines, most of which are destined for the international market.

Bodegas Weinert
This company, which dates back to the end of the 19th Century, is called after the Brazilian Bernardo Weinert, who modernised it in 1975. Since then, the company has climbed among the ranks of the best Argentinean producers with its Chardonnay, Merlot and Cabernet Sauvignon. The Cavas Weinert is an exceptional Merlot/Malbec blend. Weinert's red wines, often aged in oak casks, are the finest expression of traditional Argentinean style.

BRAZIL AND OTHER COUNTRIES

Brazil ranks as the third largest wine producer of the sub-continent with a production of almost 2,800,00hl. The first vineyards were set up in the Rio Grande do Sul by the Jesuits in the 17th Century, using the Criolla grape from Argentina, but were abandoned when the missions were destroyed. In the 17th century the Portuguese tried to plant varieties from their own country but met with little success as the tropical climate caused the vinifera to rot before the grape ripened. From the 1830s, the hybrid Isabella, a red variety better suited to the climate, was imported from the United States. This variety is still found today, alongside other American and European hybrids such as Couderc Noir and the white varieties Delaware, Niagara, Dutchess and Seyval Blanc. It was later immigrants, principally Italians, who introduced *vinifera* grapes into the province of Rio Grande do Sul. Nowadays the most common *vinifera* varieties — although still only accounting for around 20% of plantings — are the reds Barbera, Bonarda, Cabernet Franc, Cabernet Sauvignon and Merlot and the whites Malvasia, Muscat, Trebbiano (Ugni Blanc) and Semillon.

Wine regions

Most producers, numbering almost 600, are to be found in the provinces of São Paulo, Santa Catarina and in particular Rio Grande do Sul where there are a number of new, very promising hillside vineyards enclosed in a triangular area set between three cities: Bento Gonçalves, Garibaldi and Caxias do Sul. Along the border with Uruguay, the Frontera region is fast developing around Bagé and Livramento.

Many international companies have been attracted to Brazil. National Distillers set up a subsidiary of Almaden Vineyards in the 1970s, followed by Cinzano, Martini & Rossi, Rémy Martin and Moët & Chandon.

Other South American countries

Uruguay, with 1,132,00hl, is South America's fourth largest wine producer. More than half of the area under vines is dedicated to *vinifera* varieties (mainly Cabernet Sauvignon, Merlot, Semillon and Pinot Noir).

Peru produces 120,000hl of wine, a large quantity of which is used to distil *pisco*. Among the very few wines which find their way onto the international market are those from the Tacama vineyard (150ha /370 acres) in the Ica Valley, at 400m (1,300ft) altitude. Traditional Bordeaux varieties and several others, including the Chenin and Ugni Blanc, are grown here.

Colombia has only 1,500ha (3,700 acres) under vine, growing mainly the Isabella variety. The country produces mainly fortified wines.

Paraguay, Bolivia and **Ecuador** produce very small quantities of poor quality wine.

BRAZILIAN PRODUCERS

Vinicola Aurora
Brazil's largest producer and main exporter is this huge cooperative, producing some 20 million hectolitres of wine, which was founded in 1931 in Bento Gonçalves in the province of Rio Grande do Sul. It has over 1,000 members cultivating more than 20,000ha (49,500 acres) of vines. Some of the 1.1 million cases produced are sold under the American Marcus James brand (see below). The company enlisted the skills of the flying winemaker John Worontschack to help improve its wines. The best are sold under the Conde de Foucauld (Cabernet Sauvignon) and Clos des Nobles (Cabernet Franc) labels.

Casa Moët & Chandon
The large Champagne company has set up a venture equipped with temperature-controlled stainless steel fermentation tanks in Garibaldi, in the Serra Gaucha (Rio Grande do Sul). Here they produce a sparkling wine, of course, sold as Champaña and also some table wines.

Dreher
Founded by Heublein, this company has established *vinifera* vineyards in the mountains near Bagé in the newly established Frontera region which borders with Uruguay. It exports Cabernet Sauvignon, Barbera and Castel Marjolet, a Cabernet Sauvignon/Merlot blend.

De Lantier
This company, set up by Martini & Rossi in the Serra Gaucha region (Rio Grande do Sul) uses its modern equipment to produce mainly still wines from noble vinifera varieties which it sells under the Baron de Lantier label and its De Gréville sparkling wines which are produced by the traditional method.

Riograndense
Brazil's *vinifera* pioneer from as far back as the 1930s, this company near Caxias do Sul (Rio Grande do Sul) has some 60ha (150 acres) of vines planted under Merlot, Cabernet Sauvignon and Trebbiano (Ugni Blanc). Most of its wines are distributed under the Granja União label.

Marcus James
This brand name belongs to the American Canandaigua Wine Company but its wines are produced at Vinicola Aurora. It offers a wide range of varietal wines which include Chardonnay, Cabernet Sauvignon, Merlot and Zinfandel. Annual production is near to 1 million cases.

Palomas
This company in the Frontera region, which came under the control of Seagram in 1989, has over 1,000ha (2,500 acres) under *vinifera* varieties. Its winery has undergone modernisation which has resulted in a significant increase in quality.

AUSTRALIA
AND NEW ZEALAND

—

WINES FROM AUSTRALIA AND NEW ZEALAND

ONLY "ARRIVED" INTERNATIONALLY DURING THE 1980s,

BUT ALREADY THEY HAVE ESTABLISHED A REPUTATION FOR

DISTINCTIVE FLAVOURS AND EXCELLENT VALUE.

—

AUSTRALIA

AUSTRALIA MAKES DELICIOUS GOOD-VALUE WINES, FULL OF FRUIT
AND FLAVOUR, PLUS A GROWING RANGE OF FINE WINES. THE
AUSTRALIAN STYLE IS ACCEPTED, AND COPIED, THE WORLD OVER.

The Southern Vales wine region of South Australia
is centred on McLaren Vale, whose rolling hills
are densely covered with vineyards that bask
in an almost Mediterranean climate.

The distinctive Australian wine style emphasizes brightness, freshness and retention of primary fruit flavour. The wines reflect the sunny climate: they are soft, fruity and densely-flavoured; they are "user-friendly" in that they provide just the style of wine that the market demands; and they display their charms from the moment they are bottled. This description is, however, a generalization that will be proved as much by the exception as by the rule. The very best wines are complex, tightly structured and long-lived: Sémillon and Riesling whites can be magnificent when 20 years old, Cabernet Sauvignon reds at 30 years, and Penfolds' Grange Hermitage (made from Syrah) at 40 years or more. While large companies make highly polished, predictable wines, the remaining over 800 producers make wines of every grade of quality and style. In 1999, production reached 7,930,000hl, of which slightly over 27% were exported. An additional 580,000hl were used for distillation.

The vine first arrived in Australia from the Cape of Good Hope in 1788 and was planted in Governor Phillip's garden in what is now the centre of Sydney.

Its cultivation spread rapidly — away from the high humidity and summer rainfall of the coastal areas, first to Sydney's western suburbs and the Hunter Valley, and eventually to Tasmania, Western Australia, South Australia and Victoria. Wine production on a commercial scale was seriously under way in all these locations by the end of the 1830s, and expanded continuously through to the end of the century. Australia's wines remained largely ignored by the wine world, however, until a century and a half later. By then, somewhat less isolated globally, encouraged by an extremely enthusiastic domestic market, and with the massive aid of technology — irrigation transformed vast areas that were hitherto far too hot and arid — Australian producers were making the sort of wine that was in demand internationally. They suddenly found that their wines were being appreciated and acclaimed throughout the world for quality and value. The reputation of winemakers from this part of the southern hemisphere is still growing, and their wines will continue to surprise and excite as their potential is fully realized.

Wine regions

Although vines are grown in some part of each of Australia's states and territories (you will even find a small vineyard in the extremely hot Northern Territory), the main wine growing areas are located in the south-east — along the coastline and in the basins of the River Murray and its tributary, the Murrumbidgee — and the far south-west, mainly in the following four states:

■ **New South Wales,** the oldest and hottest of the wine-growing states, where you will find the famous Hunter Valley, north of Sydney, and the great irrigated region of Murrumbidgee in the west. The second-argest wine producing state in Australia, accounting for 34% of production, New South Wales produced 26% more wine in 1999 than in 1997.

■ **South Australia.** The vineyards are concentrated in the south-eastern part of this state which, accounting for 46% of production, ranks as Australia's top wine-producing state, with a mere 9% increase between 1997 and 1999. Some of Australia's best wines are produced here (in the Barossa Valley, for instance) and inland, in the Riverland north-east of Adelaide, a huge quantity of everyday drinking wines is produced and sold in wine-boxes.

■ **Victoria**. The smallest and most southerly state, yet this state has more wine growing regions than any other. Ranking third, with 17% of Australia's wine production, it offers a very varied range of wines, the general quality of which is ever increasing, some of them figuring among Australia's finest wines. Production increased by 18% between 1997 and 1999.

■ **Western Australia.** The last state to go over to wine production and which — despite a 59% increase in production between 1997 and 1999 — only accounts for 3% of Australia's wines. The vineyards are concentrated in the south-west, near the state capital, Perth. Here the climate is varied, but lack of water is the growers' major concern.

Vintages and weather

The diversity of Australian wines is accentuated by vintage variation. Growing-season conditions, contrary to common belief, have a marked impact on style (first and foremost) and quality in all the premium regions. It is true that poor vintages in the European sense — low natural sugar and high levels of mildew and *botrytis* — are rarely, if ever, encountered. But vintages do vary: each has its particular character, easily identified by an experienced taster.

Everyday wine and fine wine

The view of Australia as a hot, sunny continent is true for 90% of its land mass. It is not, however, true for many of its finest wine regions, which are situated in the far cooler — albeit sunny — remaining 10%. To begin to understand the relationship between the Australian climate, *terroir*, wine style, wine quality and choice of grape variety, you have to make the distinction between fine wine and beverage wine, between *Cru Classé* and *vin ordinaire*.

Just as France has its basic wine lands in Provence and Languedoc, and

California has the Central Valley, Australia has the Riverlands of the Murray and Murrumbidgee river systems, where New South Wales, Victoria and South Australia meet. Here the climate most definitely *is* hot and sunny, but irrigation has transformed near-desert into high-yielding, verdant vineyards producing low-cost grapes of utterly predictable quality. These make the wine that fills the wineboxes and flagons that account for two-thirds of Australian domestic sales, and also the bulk wine for export. In all, the area makes 60% of the wine, and will continue to play a leading rôle well into the 21st century.

Wine names

Most Australian wines, especially quality wines, are named after the grape variety from which they are made (*see* box). Australians began to use variety names when these words were still obscure technical terms to Europeans. They also used European names to identify wine styles, so shelves displayed Coonawarra Claret and South Australian Chablis. Another naming convention, the use of "Bin" numbers to indicate a consis-

MAIN GRAPE VARIETIES

The face of the Australian wine industry has been greatly altered by the planting of new vineyards. As a result, production has doubled in less than 10 years, and some of the more mundane grape varieties have been replaced by noble varieties. Thus Chardonnay, more or less non-existent in 1970, occupied the prime position in 1999, which is now held by Syrah. The five main noble grape varieties, together accounting for over half of production, are listed below in order of quantity (the figure in brackets refers to production in tons in 2001):

Syrah (311,045). This noble variety of the Rhône valley — known as Shiraz in these parts — can produce some of Australia's finest wines, as in the Barossa Valley and Hunter Valley, for instance, and some of its poorest, as in the vast quantity of everyday

red wines produced in the irrigated regions.
Cabernet Sauvignon (249,288). The famous variety used in the great Bordeaux wines is at home in Australia, either alone or when blended with Shiraz and Merlot.
Chardonnay (210,770). This variety, famously used in white Burgundies and Champagne, has become an international star. In Australia it produces rich, fruity wines, full of character, which often benefit from oak ageing.
Sémillon (88,427). This Bordeaux variety produces excellent white wines. Those produced in the Hunter Valley rank among some of the finest in the world.
Merlot (80,142). Used mainly to soften the edges of the Cabernet Sauvignon.
Colombard has been abandoned in France, but the Australians appreciate its capacity to produce very lively white wines in hot climates.

tent style, survives. New laws and labelling agreements have clarified the situation (*see* box, p536).

Increasingly the name of the region, and sometimes of the company, is becoming more familiar. There are as many wine styles as producers, but the growing emphasis is on identifying the source of the grapes — down to named vineyards ("paddocks") — which means that the interplay between variety and *terroir* is coming to the fore.

Oak and ageing

Those white grape varieties that suit oak treatment, such as Chardonnay, Sémillon or Sauvignon Blanc, are increasingly being barrel-fermented. Maturation in French oak *barriques* is, typically, six to nine months for premium wines. Aromatic varieties, such as Riesling and Gewürztraminer, are usually tank-fermented and bottled soon after.

Quality red-wine producers age wines increasingly in small oak casks: Cabernet Sauvignon and Shiraz can benefit from between six months and two years in wood.

Australian white wines tend to reach maturity fairly quickly, at between two and six years old, the exception being certain Hunter Valley Sémillons, which can improve for 20 years. The red wines, too, are designed to be drinkable more quickly than their European counterparts. Only a few fine wines (such as Penfolds' Grange) are intended for long bottle-ageing: most reach their peak at five to ten years old. Australian climate conditions are inimical to private cellars, and some producers release fine wines for sale only when they are mature. The rapid pace of change in the industry means maturity track-records for styles or properties are often lacking or incomplete.

The history of Australian wine

If one were to compare viticultural maps of Australia in 1890 and 1990 they would look much the same, but the fortunes of wine producers fluc-

tuated wildly between those dates. Phylloxera had arrived in Geelong, Victoria, in 1875 and caused wholesale destruction throughout that state (though, mercifully, not in others). The great bank crash and depression of 1893 affected the whole of the wine industry, as did the abolition of interstate taxes following the federation of states in 1901. It was now much easier for producers to sell their wines in other states, greatly aiding South Australia's expanding wine industry — based on the Riverlands area and the Barossa Valley — which was also stimulated by a growing demand for fortified wines, particularly from Victorian Britain.

Fortified wines dominated the market at the expense of other wine styles until the 1960s, when table

wines became more popular, though quality was poor. From then on, a number of factors helped shape the industry into what it is today, not least of which were the development of a high degree of technical expertise and the increased planting of Cabernet Sauvignon (from 1960) and Chardonnay (from 1970) in response to a greater demand for quality wines. Literally hundreds of small wineries were established, led by Dr Max Lake at Lake's Folly, New South Wales, in 1963. He was followed by a veritable flood of doctors, lawyers and businessmen and women who started weekend or retirement wineries, covering a range of *terroirs* and climatic zones as diverse as that found from Champagne to Languedoc.

Chardonnay grapes waiting by a traditionally-designed basket press at Padthaway.

WINE ZONES OF AUSTRALIA

Australia's vineyards are concentrated in the south-eastern and south-western corners of this vast continent, either relatively close to the coast or along the courses of two great rivers — the Murray and the Murrumbidgee. The names on the maps are those of newly delimited zones and regions which are part of a legal framework that defines Australia's wine-producing areas and winemaking parameters.

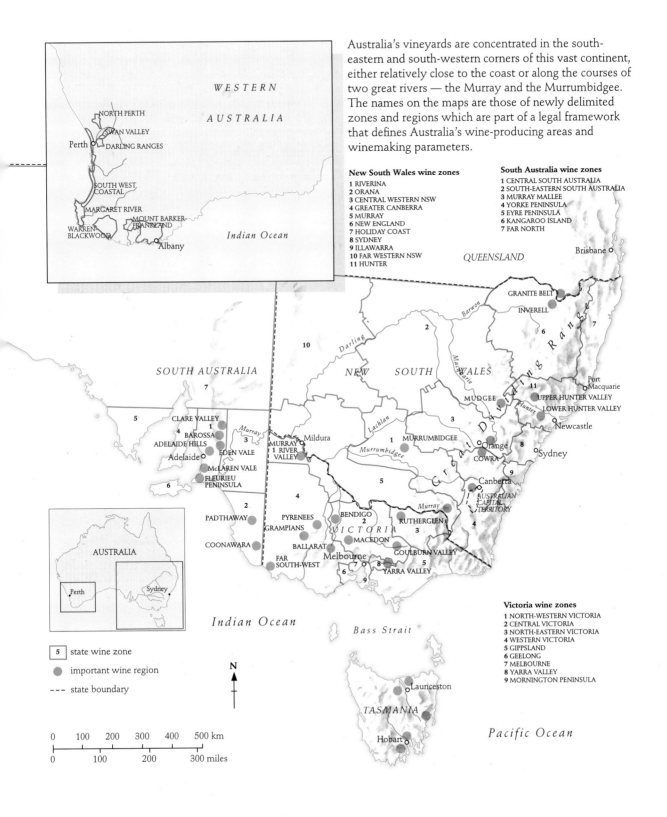

New South Wales wine zones

1 RIVERINA
2 ORANA
3 CENTRAL WESTERN NSW
4 GREATER CANBERRA
5 MURRAY
6 NEW ENGLAND
7 HOLIDAY COAST
8 SYDNEY
9 ILLAWARRA
10 FAR WESTERN NSW
11 HUNTER

South Australia wine zones

1 CENTRAL SOUTH AUSTRALIA
2 SOUTH-EASTERN SOUTH AUSTRALIA
3 MURRAY MALLEE
4 YORKE PENINSULA
5 EYRE PENINSULA
6 KANGAROO ISLAND
7 FAR NORTH

Victoria wine zones

1 NORTH-WESTERN VICTORIA
2 CENTRAL VICTORIA
3 NORTH-EASTERN VICTORIA
4 WESTERN VICTORIA
5 GIPPSLAND
6 GEELONG
7 MELBOURNE
8 YARRA VALLEY
9 MORNINGTON PENINSULA

WESTERN AUSTRALIA

NORTH PERTH
SWAN VALLEY
Perth
DARLING RANGES

SOUTH WEST COASTAL

MARGARET RIVER

MOUNT BARKER-FRANKLAND

WARREN BLACKWOOD

Albany

Indian Ocean

QUEENSLAND

Brisbane

GRANITE BELT
INVERELL

Barwon

SOUTH AUSTRALIA

Darling

NEW SOUTH WALES

Macquarie

Port Macquarie

MUDGEE
UPPER HUNTER VALLEY
LOWER HUNTER VALLEY

CLARE VALLEY
BAROSSA
ADELAIDE HILLS
Adelaide
EDEN VALE
McLAREN VALE
FLEURIEU PENINSULA

Murray

Mildura

MURRAY RIVER VALLEY

Lachlan

MURRUMBIDGEE

Murrumbidgee

Orange

COWRA

Newcastle

Sydney

Canberra

AUSTRALIAN CAPITAL TERRITORY

PADTHAWAY

PYRENEES
GRAMPIANS

BENDIGO

VICTORIA

RUTHERGLEN

Murray

COONAWARA

BALLARAT

MACEDON

GOULBURN VALLEY

FAR SOUTH-WEST

Melbourne

YARRA VALLEY

AUSTRALIA

Perth

Sydney

Indian Ocean

Bass Strait

Pacific Ocean

TASMANIA

Launceston

Hobart

5 | state wine zone

● important wine region

--- state boundary

N

0 100 200 300 400 500 km

0 100 200 300 miles

Fine wines on the increase

The winds of change are blowing hard through the vineyards of Australia: in 1985 one-third of Australia's production was of premium grape varieties; by 1999 it was almost two-thirds. In 1970 Riesling and Sémillon were the only premium white varieties grown in commercial quantities. Less than 50 tonnes of Chardonnay grapes were crushed in that year, but the 1999 harvest provided over 210,000 tonnes — more than any other variety. Riesling, locally called Rhine Riesling to distinguish it from many so-called Rieslings, ranks second. It is used for producing brilliant and subtle dry and off-dry white wines of a style that is rather French than German. Premium white-grape varieties, such as Colombard, are thus inexorably replacing the old low-quality, local varieties as the principal grapes in Riverlands vineyards. A similar trend can be observed for red grape varieties but Pinot Noir is mainly used for producing sparkling wines and, in the coolest regions, some varietal wines of good quality.

Technology in the wine industry

Australian wine is the product of an industry possessing a level of technological expertise unsurpassed elsewhere. This is largely attributable to the Australian Wine Research Institute, as well as to the University of Adelaide and the Charles Sturt University in New South Wales.

The technological revolution in the Australian wine industry began, in effect, in the mid-1950s, with the introduction of stainless steel vats for Riesling and Sémillon. Within 20 years the importance of technical expertise had been recognized, especially as producers realized that if they were to make high-quality wines they had to combat the hot and arid conditions prevailing in many vineyards.

Irrigation — a practice frowned upon in many traditional wine-growing areas of the world — is essential almost everywhere in Australia to enhance the quality of the fruit and maintain high yields. Today all sorts of canopy management techniques are employed while the vines are growing, and there is continuous experimentation with new, cooler hillside sites and clonal selection. Mechanical harvesting at night makes sure the grapes are cool when picked, refrigeration provides cool storage during transport, and temperature-controlled procedures throughout the winemaking processes can today ensure a top-quality end-product.

The impact of technology has been coupled with a remarkable willingness on the part of winemakers to share their knowledge with their peers. Every two years a national technical conference is held which attracts expert contributors from around the world. Local conferences are also held in most wine regions.

The wine shows

The highly developed wine-show system attracts a lot of attention (and not a little criticism) because those who market Australian wines make such enthusiastic use of the trophies and medals awarded to their clients. Each of the seven state-capital wine shows brings together 20 or so leading winemakers for four days to judge 2,000 wines under highly controlled conditions. During this time there is also much discussion on technique, style and future trends   □

WINE LAWS AND LABELS

The Australian Wine and Brandy Corporation — the industry's statutory body — have recently introduced a "Label Integrity Programme" which completes a legislative system that both prescribes and enforces (through wide-ranging audits) the essential elements of appellation control: any claim of vintage, variety or region must be correct and be able to be proved correct.

New names

A wine agreement concluded with the EC will see the gradual phasing out of all names such as "chablis", "champagne", "burgundy" and "claret" on domestic wine labels (they have long since disappeared from export labels).

In their place the major wine producers will continue to develop brand names such as Orlando's Jacobs Creek, Mildara's Jamiesons Run, Penfolds' Grange Hermitage and Koonunga Hill, and Lindemans' Bin 65 Chardonnay. For these brands, region and variety are of little or no importance (except, of course, such talismans as Chardonnay). The reason is one of pragmatism: the four largest companies — Southcorp (including, among others, Penfolds, Lindemans and Seppelt), BRL Hardy, Orlando and Mildara Blass — make 80% of Australia's wine, and to achieve such volumes they have long relied upon blending varieties (Cabernet Sauvignon and Shiraz, for example) and wines from regions as disparate as the Hunter Valley in New South Wales and Coonawarra and the Clare Valley in South Australia.

Small wineries focus on grape variety and region, and of course their name. While all leading small companies have estate vineyards, many supplement their own grapes, usually from the region in which the winery is located.

Wine labels

None of this helps when it comes to understanding Australian wine labels elsewhere in the world. If one ignores the propaganda and the mandatory disclosures on the back label, the front label is disarmingly simple. But it requires knowledge of legal regulations, a good grasp of geography and a certain amount of instinct to determine whether the location of the maker and the origin of the wine have anything in common. In short, while winemakers are obliged to disclose their address or place of business, they do not have to reveal the origin of the grapes (and hence the wine). If they elect to do so, 85% of the grapes must be from the nominated district. Similarly with varietal wines; if a grape name is given, 85% of the wine must have been made from the named variety. If multiple districts or varieties are specified, they must be listed in descending order of importance.

NEW SOUTH WALES

New South Wales was the first Australian state to cultivate grapevines. Today, in the Hunter Valley close to the coast, some of Australia's finest wines are made. With two additional areas inland — Mudgee and Murrumbidgee — the state accounts for more than a third of Australia's total wine production.

Three figures stand tall in the development of this state's wine industry. Captain John Macarthur, best known as the father of the Australian wool industry, travelled through France and Switzerland in 1815 and 1816 collecting vines and studying their cultivation, and planted a commercial vineyard on the western outskirts of Sydney in 1820. Gregory Blaxland, better known as a pastoralist and explorer, exported the first Australian wine to England in 1822. And James Busby, a Scottish gardener, brought back more than 600 vine cuttings from Europe in 1831. They included virtually every known variety of *vitis vinifera*.

In 1825 Busby bought a property in the Hunter Valley and installed his brother-in-law, William Kelman, as manager. Vineyard development began in earnest following Busby's return from Europe in 1831, the same year as George Wyndham, founder of what was to become the Hunter Valley's largest producer, successfully planted vines at Dalwood near Branxton. A year later there were ten vineyards in New South Wales, varying in size from a half to a little more than one hectare (2.5 acres).

The Hunter Valley
Aided by the development of the Upper Hunter Valley (briefly in the 1860s and 1870s but more significantly from the 1960s), the continued domination of the Hunter Valley Zone is assured. Yet in viticultural terms it is something of an anomaly

Arrowfield Estate in the Upper Hunter.

that can only be partly explained by its closeness to Australia's largest population centre, Sydney. For the Lower Hunter in particular appears to be a wretched place in which to grow vines: most of the rain falls at the wrong time (frequently just as the vintage gets under way); much of the soil is poorly drained, heavy clay; and summer temperatures are very high. In its favour are afternoon cloud cover, sea breezes, and high humidity, all of which help to ameliorate the vine stress that would otherwise result from the high temperatures. In addition, yields are low so grape quality is good, and there is an inexplicable affinity between the *terroir* and Sémillon and Shiraz grapes.

The Hunter Valley produces the world's greatest dry Sémillon, once exemplified by the majestic 20- to 30-year-old wines from Lindemans. The particular vineyards that produced those unique white wines went out of production in the early 1970s, but McWilliams, Tyrrells and Rothbury (and Lindemans on a diminished

scale) still make superb and distinctive wines. The magic of Hunter Sémillon — made without the use of oak — is the way it evolves from an anaemic, faintly grassy, thin wine in its youth to honeyed and grilled-nut opulence in its full maturity.

Shiraz, too, undergoes a remarkable metamorphosis over a similar time span. But with this red variety the development is in the opposite direction: from tightly knit and moderately tannic to a velvety *mélange* of earth, leather, chocolate, coffee, straw and berry aromas and flavours.

Chardonnay has overtaken Sémillon as the most widely planted white variety, while among the reds Cabernet Sauvignon is fast closing the gap on Shiraz. These four varieties now account for 75% of the vineyard.

The Upper Hunter is predominantly a white-wine region, with the ubiquitous Chardonnay producing a soft, peachy and early-maturing wine aimed at the commercial market. Cabernet Sauvignon is grown for red wines, but does better in the Lower Hunter, even if regional characteristics dominate with age.

Mudgee
The Mudgee Region is in the southeast corner of the vast Orana Zone, at a similar latitude to the Hunter Valley, but to the west of the Great Dividing Range. The first vines were planted here in 1858 by Adam Roth, a German "vine dresser". Vineyard and winery (Craigmoor) remained in the family until 1969.

Notwithstanding that Mudgee was best known for its intensely coloured, richly flavoured and concentrated Shiraz (and more latterly Cabernet Sauvignon) reds, Roth's grandson obtained some white-grape vine cuttings from Laraghy's Kaluna Vineyard in 1930. Towards the end of the 1960s these were identified by the French ampelographer Dr Denis Bourbals as a particularly high-quality clone of virus-free Chardonnay, and became a significant source of that variety in its subsequent march around Australia.

With its somewhat drier climate and better soils, Mudgee became an often unacknowledged but very reliable supplier of grapes and wine to the Hunter Valley and elsewhere, and it came as no surprise when the Hunter Valley's Wyndham Estate acquired the Montrose (by far the largest producer), Craigmoor and Amberton wineries and vineyards at the end of the 1980s. Rothbury Estate in the Hunter Valley has now leased Mudgee's large Augustine Vineyards, while Rosemount Estate and Tyrrells are other Hunter wineries that have long-term purchase arrangements with growers in the Mudgee Region.

Murrumbidgee
Both Mudgee and the Hunter Valley (which, each, account for an annual production of several thousand tonnes) pale into insignificance compared with the 123,000 tonnes of the Murrumbidgee Region (formerly the Murrumbidgee Irrigation Area) in Riverina Zone. Seventy per cent of production is of white wine, and more than half of that is Sémillon and Trebbiano; Shiraz accounts for half the red wine. With one notable exception — botrytized Sémillon — the wines are of everyday quality. Quantity and economy of production are the driving forces here: there is little spring and summer rainfall, and a total reliance on irrigation results in prolific yields.

The rest of New South Wales
The high-altitude western slopes of the Great Dividing Range are at last being systematically explored for possible vineyard sites. Tyrrells has established a sizeable vineyard at Inverell in the New England Zone, and Rosemount's chief winemaker Philip Shaw has formed a partnership with Rosemount to grow grapes at

Orange in the Central Western Zone. The first Rosemount Orange Region wines were released in 1993, joining Bloodwood Estate (also contract-made by Rosemount) as the first commercial producers, but there are others waiting in the wings.

The Central Western Zone also incorporates Cowra Region, which is further south but at a much lower altitude, and is an important producer of fleshy, buttery Chardonnay for Cowra Estate and Rothbury Estate. A little further south again, but at a higher altitude, is Young Region (in the Greater Canberra Zone); here McWilliams now owns Barwang Estate, producing limited but increasing quantities of excitingly good Sémillon and Shiraz. A number of other growers here either make small quantities of wine themselves or sell their grapes to producers in Greater Canberra, which is home to a thriving group of wineries dotted

around the perimeter of the Australian Capital Territory. The zone has 16 wine regions in all.

In the south of New South Wales, in the uncompromisingly cool climate of the Snowy Mountains, is the Tumbarumba Region, which is part of the Murray Zone. Southcorp, the giant South Australian company, is the major customer. They use Chardonnay and Pinot Noir in their premium sparkling wines, and, with the 1992 vintage, they released a scintillating Sauvignon Blanc employing a blend of grapes from Tumbarumba and Padthaway in South Australia.

Finally there are the coastal wineries from Cassegrain at Port Macquarie in the Hastings Valley in the north to the Grevillea Estate at Bega in the south. With the exception of Cassegrain, production at most of these small coastal wineries is directed at the tourist trade, and quality is mediocre at best.   □

QUEENSLAND

Queensland, the north-eastern state of Australia, has a very small area under vine. If one ignores outposts such as Roma (in remote and blazing hot central-west Queensland), the Atherton Tablelands and Ipswich, all Queensland's wineries are situated in the Granite Belt, a fruit-growing region at the southern end of the Darling Downs, a few kilometres away from the New South Wales border, hence the state's inclusion in this chapter.

Winemaking, the Catholic Church and the Italian community have been interlinked in this region for a century. However, it was not until 1970 that the primitive wineries began to move away from table grapes as their raw material when Angelo Puglisi of the Ballandean Estate planted 6ha (15 acres) of Shiraz and Cabernet Sauvignon.

The vineyards are all 750–900m (2,500–3,000ft) above sea level. Budburst is late here and spring frosts are a real hazard. And after a hot summer, temperatures rapidly fall again. Rainfall is plentiful during the growing season and can spread into the vintage. The two most suitable grape varieties are tangy

Sémillon and peppery-spicy Shiraz, but Chardonnay and Cabernet Sauvignon are also prominent at Ballandean.

Overall production is small, and much of the wine is sold direct to tourists.

PRODUCERS
Bald Mountain
Denis Parsons is a meticulous grape-grower. His smooth Sauvignon Blanc and Chardonnay whites, and spicy Shiraz red are made elsewhere under contract.

Ballandean Estate
This is the senior winery of the region, producing diverse wines, including oddities such as Auslese Sylvaner (white) and some smooth reds.

Rumbalara
Rumbalara is a Sémillon specialist that produces some fine wines, though quality is variable. There is also an occasional silky Cabernet Sauvignon.

Stone Ridge
This company initially made its mark with vibrantly peppery Shiraz, but has now added a nicely crafted Chardonnay.

REGIONS AND PRODUCERS

With Riverina the notable exception, the wine regions of New South Wales have a tradition of small, family-run concerns and were at the forefront of the spread of the "weekend winemakers" revolution. The most important regions are listed alphabetically, followed by significant rest-of-state producers. For a full list of zones, regions and sub-regions, *see* pp591-592.

LOWER HUNTER VALLEY

With the Barossa Valley, this is Australia's most historic and famous wine region, though its output is relatively small. Variable soils, warm to hot summers and modest rainfall (usually when it is least needed), pose problems. Yet great wines — slow-maturing Sémillon, quick-developing, buttery Chardonnay, long-lived velvety Shiraz and regionally accented Cabernet Sauvignon — are made here.

Allandale

The emphasis is on Sémillon, Chardonnay, Shiraz and Cabernet Sauvignon , all made in the usual regional style.

Allanmere

Owner Newton Potter and winemaker Geoff Broadfield produce superb Chardonnays and Sémillons, and above-average reds. Durham is the Reserve label.

Broke Estate

A high-flying newcomer, drawing upon expert consultancy, that has made its debut with an outstanding Cabernet blend and solid Chardonnay.

Brokenwood

One of the most highly regarded small Hunter wineries, providing a high-quality range of wines from estate-grown Graveyard Hermitage (red) to Sauvignon Blanc/ Sémillon and Cabernet/Merlot (Cricket Pitch label). Hunter Valley Chardonnay and Cabernet Sauvignon are also strong performers.

Drayton's

A family-owned winery, dating from 1853, making modestly priced but reliable wines. Verdelho (white) and Hermitage (red) are specialities.

Evans Family

The family estate of wine "guru" Len Evans, growing Gamay (red), Pinot Noir and Chardonnay, only the last of which is notable.

Lake's Folly

Dr Max Lake founded the first of the weekend wineries that are now so much a part of the Australian wine scene. Son Stephen is now winemaker, and the Cabernet Sauvignon and Chardonnay are better than ever.

Lindemans

An old-established winery, founded in 1870, with a proud history of winemaking that includes Sémillon-based wines and Shiraz, which is the best bet today, along with some sophisticated Chardonnays.

McGuigan Brothers

With marketing genius Brian McGuigan in charge of production, this largely export-oriented company, producing some unashamedly commercial wines, is likely to continue the spectacular growth it has experienced since 1992.

McWilliam's Mount Pleasant

This is the prestige arm of the Riverina-based McWilliam clan, a prolific family firm (since the 1880s) that was once more dominant than it is today. The quality of the wine cannot be faulted: Elizabeth Sémillon, released when it is six years old, is a jewel.

Murray Robson Wines

Robson has had his ups and downs, but, with a wealthy patron, is now flourishing, with many labels and styles, including Chardonnay, Shiraz, Sémillon and Cabernet Sauvignon.

Richmond Grove

Part of the Wyndham group (now owned by Orlando of South Australia), this winery gets most grapes from an ultra-modern Cowra vineyard, and makes pedestrian wines at modest prices.

Rothbury Estate

The creation of Len Evans (*see* above) is now a public company. It produces 250,000 cases a year, including buttery Cowra Chardonnay, Hunter Chardonnay and a typically dense Shiraz, but do not overlook the Sémillon.

Tulloch

This winery's reputation has suffered since the Tulloch family sold out in 1969, having run the company since 1895. Despite now being part of the Southcorp group, Tulloch shines only very occasionally, chiefly with Chardonnay.

Tyrrells

See profile, p540.

Wyndham Estate

The largest producer by far in the Hunter Valley, Wyndhams (Orlando group) has a very long history (it was established in 1831). The winery today is a product of the heady days of the 1970s under Brian McGuigan. Its products — a wide range of varietals — say more about marketing than winemaking.

UPPER HUNTER VALLEY

Widespread deep soils produce higher yields than in the Lower Hunter: Chardonnay and Sémillon whites are the wines for which this region is best known. There are two large vineyards, Denman Estate (owned by Rothbury) and Segenhoe Estate (owned by Tyrrells).

Arrowfield

Now Japanese-owned, this winery's best wines have come from elsewhere, even from New Zealand. Heavy oak dominates the whites.

Reynolds Yarraman

Former Houghton (Western Australia) winemaker Jon Reynolds produces flavoursome, solid wines. Most notable are Chardonnay and a Cabernet/Merlot blend.

Rosemount Estate

Founded in 1969 and a success since day one, Rosemount produces remarkably consistent wines. Voluptuous Roxburgh Chardonnay and Show Reserve wines are flagships.

MUDGEE

Rainfall in the growing season is lower, nights are cooler, but summer days are hotter than in the Hunter Valley. Pleasant Sémillon (overshadowed by that of the Hunter), honeyed, peachy Chardonnay, intense berry-and-earth Shiraz, and chocolate-and-cigar box Cabernet Sauvignon are best.

Botobolar
Gil Wahlquist was an early convert to organic grape-growing. He produces eclectic whites and textured Shiraz and Cabernet Sauvignon.

Craigmoor
The second-oldest winery in Australia (founded in 1858) and beautifully sited, Craigmoor is a tourist attraction. It is now part of Wyndhams. Its smooth, peachy Chardonnay is recommended.

Huntington Estate
Self-taught Bob Roberts produces lovely Cabernet Sauvignon, Cabernet/Shiraz and Shiraz reds, which hold their sweet and earthy, berry-fruit flavour for several decades.

Miramar
Contrary to the Mudgee norm, Ian MacRae produces more white wines than reds, including Riesling, Sémillon, Sauvignon Blanc, Traminer and Chardonnay.

Montrose
This winery (Orlando group) produces substantial quantities of smooth, supple whites and reds at their commercial best under the Poets Corner label. Montrose produces occasional jewels such as the peach-and-melon 1991 Chardonnay.

Steins
Bob Stein produces dark cherry, berry and spice-filled Shiraz to rival the best.

TYRRELLS

Murray Tyrrell has taken the small winery established in the Hunter Valley in 1864 by Edward Tyrrell from relative obscurity to international prominence. Since 1888 the winery has known only two masters — "Uncle Dan" Tyrrell, who made 70 consecutive vintages up to 1958, and Murray Tyrrell, (with son Bruce as general manager). Murray has cleverly balanced tradition with commercial demands. He was the first winemaker to realize the potential of Chardonnay: his quaintly named Vat 47 Chardonnay, launched in 1971, was for a decade unchallenged as the best in Australia, and retains a great reputation. It heads a list including "Vat" identified wines and the Old Winery range. Tyrrells also produces excellent Sémillon for which the region is justly renowned.

Thistle Hill
Dave Robertson is capable of producing extremely good smoky/tropical Chardonnay, and gently earthy Cabernet Sauvignon.

MURRUMBIDGEE
Formerly the Murrumbidgee Irrigation Area (MIA), this region came into being when near-desert was transformed by a vast irrigation scheme engineered from 1906 to 1912. Grapes are mainly white, with Sémillon the most important; the only red of significance is Shiraz. The area's speciality is botrytized (sweet) Sémillon.

De Bortoli
One of the fastest-growing wineries in Australia. De Bortoli was founded in 1928 and produces three million cases a year. Its luscious, botrytized Sémillon, Noble One, is a great wine and a flagship.

Lillypilly
A family-owned boutique winery, unusual in Riverina Zone, Lillypilly is run by Robert Fiumara. The sweet whites are best: spicy botrytized Muscat of Alexandria and botrytized Riesling are best.

McWilliams Mount Pleasant
Founded in 1877, McWilliams produces nearly 1.5 million cases of wines. The company is ambitious, but still depends on sherry and port, with as yet utilitarian table wines.

Miranda
A high-flying company that has transformed quality with the purchase of a Barossa winery (Rovalley) and grapes from South Australia. Tangy Chardonnay and limey Riesling (Wyangan Estate label) are particularly successful.

CANBERRA
There is no freehold title in the Capital Territory, so wineries huddle around the boundary,

heavily dependent on cellar-door sales. The climate is continental, and most vineyards are at 500m (1,650ft) or higher. Cabernet Sauvignon, Riesling and Chardonnay are the best.

Brindabella Hill
Roger Harris is doing very well with limey Riesling, lively herbal blend of Sémillon and Sauvignon Blanc and bright and fresh Cabernets.

Doonkuna Estate
The late Sir Brian Murray was Australia's only vice-regal winemaker; his widow carries on, with full-flavoured Riesling, subtle Sauvignon Blanc and elegant Chardonnay at the top of the list.

Helm's Wines
Ken Helm is a tireless ambassador for the district. The quality can be variable, but Riesling and Cabernet/Merlot are good.

Lark Hill
This is considered by many to be the best winery in the region. Riesling, Spätlese Riesling/Chardonnay (sweet) and Cabernet/Merlot are best.

OTHER PRODUCERS
Camden Estate
Camden Estate is not far from Sydney, and very close to one of Australia's first vineyards. The Chardonnay is a full-bodied and complex wine.

Cassegrain
Cassegrain, in the Hastings Valley, is best known for rich, textured Chardonnay, and a lively *nouveau*-style Merlot.

Trentham Estate
Tony Murphy's family has long grown grapes on the New South Wales side of Mildura on the Murray River. The winery at Trentham has quickly made a name for itself with an impressive range of modestly priced wines.

VICTORIA

Victoria has more wine regions than any other Australian state, and produces many styles of wine, but the wine industry here has had a chequered history. Today many of the quality-minded wineries are making exciting wines and there are high hopes for the future.

The first vines arrived in Victoria from Tasmania in 1834, but their fate is unknown. Three years later William Ryrie came over the Snowy Mountains from New South Wales and established a farm in what is now the Yarra Valley, planting vine cuttings he had brought with him.

By the end of the 1840s three regions boasted significant wine production: Melbourne Metropolitan (around the state capital), Geelong and the Yarra Valley. While all these were to remain important areas until the 1880s, the discovery of gold at Ballarat in Central Victoria in 1851 changed the course of history — briefly making Australia the wealthiest country (on a *per capita* income basis) in the world. This led to the rapid expansion of vineyards northwards through Ballarat, Bendigo, Great Western and Rutherglen.

Vines had been fortuitously planted at Rutherglen the year gold was discovered by pastoralist Lindsay Brown, who said: "To get gold you need sink (mine) only about 18 inches and plant vines". By the last quarter of the century, Victoria had become by far the most important wine-producing state: by 1890 it produced well over half Australia's wine.

The fall and rise of Victoria

But, in 1875, phylloxera appeared in Geelong, then moved progressively northwards through Bendigo, laying waste to Rutherglen and Milawa by the turn of the century. Some areas — notably the Yarra Valley and Great Western — were mysteriously

High-altitude vineyards (750m/2,500ft) in the foothills of the Great Dividing Range.

spared. Victoria remains the only state to have been significantly affected by phylloxera.

The decline in wine production continued. The federation of the Australian states was followed by the removal of state trade barriers and duties. At the same time there were changes in the pattern of wine consumption as the demand for low-cost fortified wines and full-bodied dry reds increased. Both these developments aided the wine industry of South Australia which became dominant at neighbouring Victoria's expense. All the wine regions in southern Victoria went out of production, leaving scattered outposts such as Chateau Tahbilk.

The renaissance of the wine industry began in the latter part of the 1960s, when there were less than a dozen wineries outside the North-Eastern Zone. Twenty-five years later there were over 200, with new ones being established almost daily.

The scheme delimiting Australia's wine regions, proposed by the wine industry, divides the state into nine zones: North-Western Victoria (the Murray River Valley), Central Victoria, North-Eastern Victoria, Western Victoria, Gippsland, Yarra Valley, Geelong, Melbourne and Mornington Peninsula. The zones are in turn divided into 17 regions and 82 sub-regions. In some instances the sub-regions are so esoteric as to be meaningless even to the most avid student of Australian wines, while in other cases the boundaries represent clear demarcations between areas that have markedly differing *terroir* and climate. Not all zones and regions are commercially significant.

Wine regions and climate zones
While generalizations are inevitably hazardous, there are three basic climate regimes within the state.
■ **Very warm** Murray River Valley Region, Central Northern Victoria (a Region of Central Victoria Zone) and North-Eastern Victoria Zone (excluding the high-altitude sub-regions of King Valley Region) are very warm, with high daytime temperatures and cold nights. They produce fortified wines of the highest quality and, particularly in the Murray River Valley, considerable quantities of white table wines, the latter helping fill the wine-cask pipeline.
■ **Temperate** The Western and Central Victoria zones include the newly-named Grampians (formerly Great Western), Pyrenees, Bendigo and Goulburn Valley regions. The climate is temperate, ideally suited to full-bodied, rich and textured Shiraz and Cabernet Sauvignon. Full ripeness is always achieved, but the climate is not so warm as to diminish varietal character.
■ **Cool** Regions technically falling within these two zones, but which climatically belong with the southern part of the state, are the Far South-West (notably Drumborg), Macedon and Ballarat regions. These are grouped with Yarra Valley, Geelong, Mornington Peninsula and Gippsland as cool areas.

Pinot Noir flourishes in cooler climes, as does Chardonnay, and is used both for table and sparkling wines. At their best, the Pinot Noirs and Chardonnays assume a distinctly burgundian cast, which accentuates rather than diminishes as the wines approach full maturity (typically three to five years for Pinot Noir and up to ten years for Chardonnay).

Harvesting grapes at Coldstream Hills.

It falls to the particular attributes of the micro-climate and/or of the particular vintage to determine whether or not later ripening varieties such as Cabernet Sauvignon and Shiraz achieve optimum ripeness and hence flavour. Sauvignon Blanc and Merlot are two grapes that ripen a little earlier, and plantings are certain to increase.

Murray River Valley
This famous region produces more than 80% of Victoria's grapes, and it is therefore not surprising that Australia's largest single winery — Lindemans' Karadoc, with a storage capacity of 64 million litres — is situated at the western end of the valley, not far from the city of Mildura. There are other major wineries in this region. Mildara's principal establishment — located on the eastern outskirts of the same city — looks somewhat antiquated compared to that of Lindemans. A short distance to the south at Irymple is the Alambie Wine Company, for long an anonymous supplier in bulk to other wineries, but now successfully promoting its own brands of Salisbury Estate and Somerset Crossing.

Finally, on the other side of the Murray and hence technically in New South Wales, is the Buronga Hill winery, part of the BRL Hardy group.

The rest of Victoria
When one looks more closely at statistics, the importance and nature of the rest-of-state production comes into focus. Almost half the Murray River Valley's output is of Muscat Gordo Blanco and Sultana — non-premium grape varieties that are continually declining in importance. On the other hand, 65% of the four premium red grapes (Cabernet Sauvignon, Shiraz, Pinot Noir and Merlot), and almost 40% of the premium white varieties (Chardonnay, Riesling and Sauvignon Blanc) are grown south of the Murray.

During the coming years, the contribution of the rest of the state to premium wine production will steadily increase. It would require either blind optimism or extreme parochialism to suggest that Victoria will resume the leading role it had in the late 19th century, but there is no denying that since 1970 more has happened in the wine industry in this state than in any other part of Australia, and the pace of development shows no sign of slackening.

Had the north–south boundary between South Australia and Victoria been drawn 20km (12 miles) further west, Coonawarra — the most prestigious red-wine district in the country — would have belonged to Victoria; had the boundary been 30 km (19 miles) further west, then the premium white wines of Padthaway might have been Victoria's. It is arguable that the climate and wine style of these two famous wine-producing regions have more in common with those of Victoria than those of the rest of South Australia. For the influences of altitude, latitude and the confluence of the Indian Ocean and Tasman Sea provide an extraordinarily rich viticultural tapestry spread across the length and breadth of the state. □

REGIONS AND PRODUCERS

Although bulk-wine producers dominate, small quality-conscious wineries established in the last decade are increasingly important. In the Murray River Region, Victoria shares many of New South Wales' large-scale producers. The most commercially important zones, or regions within zones, are listed alphabetically below. For a full list of zones, regions and sub-regions, *see* pp592-593.

BENDIGO

Bendigo is red-wine country. Scattered vineyards are surrounded by eucalyptus forests, believed to contribute to the character of the wines — deeply coloured, full-bodied Shiraz, Cabernet Sauvignon and Shiraz/Cabernet blends.

Jasper Hill

Ron and Elva Laughton produce two reds: Georgia's Paddock Shiraz and Emily's Paddock, a blend of Shiraz and Cabernet Franc. Both are powerful, long-lived wines that are in much demand.

Mount Ida

Owned by Mildara Blass, Mount Ida makes an excellent, cherry-flavoured Shiraz.

Passing Clouds

Graeme Leith makes delicious red-berry- and mint-accented Shiraz, as well as sundry Cabernet blends.

Yellowglen

Using grapes from all over south-eastern Australia, Yellowglen has improved the quality of its top *cuvées*, producing good profits for owner Mildara Blass.

GEELONG

The cool, often windswept and largely treeless plains and the gentle slopes of Geelong are well suited to fragrant, authentic Pinot Noir and Chardonnay. Spicy Shiraz, Cabernet Sauvignon, Sauvignon Blanc and Riesling are also produced here.

Bannockburn

Low-yielding, fully mature estate vineyards and strongly French-influenced winemaking methods produce superb, complex Sauvignon Blanc and Chardonnay, and even more complex Pinot Noir (the speciality) and Shiraz.

Clyde Park

Gary Farr is winemaker at Bannockburn (*qv*) but has his own vineyard at Clyde Park. His wines are complex and highly individual in character, with Chardonnay the best.

Idyll Vineyard

The Seftons have been making wines here since the 1960s, producing idiosyncratic and flavoursome Traminer plus wood-aged Shiraz and Cabernet Sauvignon.

Prince Albert

One of two Australian wineries to produce Pinot Noir alone, and on a site planted in the last century. The wines are pretty but rather light.

Scotchmans Hill

This company has produced some winners since 1990, including soft, generously flavoured, well-priced Chardonnay, Pinot Noir (especially) and Cabernets.

GIPPSLAND

Large distances separate small vineyards that dot the flat, often parched landscape. Typically very low yields produce highly concentrated and textured Chardonnay and a few magnificent Pinot Noirs; Cabernets are also produced.

Bass Phillip

This is the other solely Pinot Noir winery. Phillip Jones makes some very stylish, burgundian-accented wines that have fanatical followers.

Briagolong Estate

Dr Gordon McIntosh makes highly individual but flavoursome Chardonnay and Pinot Noir as a weekend hobby.

McAlister Vineyards

The single product here is the McAlister, a blend of Cabernet Sauvignon, Cabernet Franc and Merlot, which is powerful, brooding and sinewy.

Nicholson River

Teacher Ken Eckersley makes remarkable Chardonnay that is voluptuously weighty and redolent of honey, butterscotch and toasty oak.

GOULBURN VALLEY

Wine production has always been centred around the town of Tabilk and Chateau Tahbilk, with Mitchelton a newer neighbour. Shiraz, long-lived Cabernet Sauvignon and powerful, limey Riesling are best.

Chateau Tahbilk

A family-owned, historic winery that has made wine since the 1860s: some Shiraz vines planted in 1862 still produce. Elegant Marsanne (white) and long-lived, sometimes tannic but always concentrated Shiraz and Cabernet Sauvignon are specialities.

Mitchelton

A clever producer of a wide range of wines, enjoying a strong export base. Oaky Marsanne (white), good fleshy Riesling and a richly fruited, top-of-the-range blend of Shiraz and Cabernet Sauvignon stand out.

GRAMPIANS

Gold and wine have been inextricably linked to this region, formerly Great Western, for 140 years, with Shiraz — ranging from dark cherry to liquorice-and-spice — a continuous, high-quality theme. Smooth, fleshy Cabernet Sauvignon and peachy Chardonnay are important.

Best's

This historic vineyard includes some of the original vines that were planted during the 1860s and grape varieties unknown anywhere else in the world. The silky-smooth Shiraz and Cabernet Sauvignon, and tangy melon-and-peach Chardonnay are excellent wines.

Montara

Chardonnay, Riesling, Ondenc (white), Chasselas (white), Pinot Noir, Shiraz and Cabernet Sauvignon all come from estate plantings. Pinot Noir occasionally excels here — against all odds as the climate, in theory, is too warm.

Mount Langi Ghiran

Trevor Mast makes some of Australia's greatest Shiraz. His wines are wonderfully textured and richly endowed with spice, liquorice and dark berry-fruit flavours.

Seppelt Great Western

Founded in 1866 by Joseph Best and purchased in 1918 by Seppelt, this is the production centre for all Penfolds' sparkling wines under the Seppelt, Seaview, Minchinbury and Killawarra labels. Quality has improved since the mid-1980s as Chardonnay and Pinot Noir replace lesser varieties.

MACEDON

Macedon's districts are vastly different: Sunbury is on the flat plains, while Kyneton and the Macedon Ranges are in hill country. They share relatively tough, granite soils, howling winds, and very cool growing conditions. Highly distinguished Cabernet Sauvignon and Shiraz are made in warmer vintages; in cooler years they may fail altogether, leaving sappy Pinot Noir and fine-boned Chardonnay.

Cleveland

This winery does best with Pinot Noir and Chardonnay. It also produces sparkling wine and a Cabernet Sauvignon.

Cobaw Ridge

Self-taught winemaker Alan Cooper produces Chardonnay and Shiraz.

Cope-Williams

Expatriate English architect Gordon Cope-Williams produces an excellent sparkling white called Macedon Brut.

Craiglee

Craiglee is the reincarnation (in 1976) of an historic Macedon winery at Sunbury. It produces quite wonderful Shiraz and seductive Chardonnay.

Goonawarra

Originally founded in 1863, this is another winery to have been revived (in 1983) in a superb bluestone building. Estate-grown Sémillon, Chardonnay and Cabernet Franc grapes make three high-quality wines.

Hanging Rock

John and Ann Ellis produce a wide range of wines from expensive estate-grown sparkling brut to inexpensive Picnic White and Picnic Red.

Rochford

Light- to medium-bodied Pinot Noir with a sappy burgundian edge is the one to watch from this winery.

Virgin Hills

A single, superlative red wine (the best barrels bottled under a Reserve label) is made without the use of sulphur dioxide from estate Cabernet Sauvignon, Shiraz and Merlot which are grown organically.

Wildwood

After an uncertain start in 1983, Wayne Stott is doing well with fragrant Pinot Noir and minty Cabernets.

MORNINGTON PENINSULA

Formerly the summer playground of wealthy Melbourne residents, this region has 35 wineries, most of them catering for tourist and cellar-door trade and producing wines of a consistently high standard. The cool, maritime climate produces delicate, elegant wines, with Chardonnay, Pinot Noir, Shiraz, Merlot and Cabernet Sauvignon the most important grape varieties.

Dromana Estate

Immaculate vineyards produce Garry Crittenden's much admired, fragrant Chardonnay and Cabernet Merlot (Dromana Estate label). Grapes from other sources are used for an eclectic range under the Schinus label.

Elgee Park

Bailleu Myer pioneered the 20th-century renaissance of the Mornington Peninsula, adding interest with Australia's first Viognier (the Rhône white variety). Chardonnay and Riesling are best.

King's Creek

Consultant winemaker Kathleen Quealy fashions small quantities of extremely stylish Chardonnay and Pinot Noir.

Main Ridge

Nat White picked one of the coolest sites on the Peninsula for this vineyard, and he has sometimes battled to ripen the grapes fully. His Chardonnay, Pinot Noir and Cabernet Sauvignon are light, crisp and lively wines.

Massoni

Melbourne restaurateur Leon Massoni and former Yellowglen owner Ian Home plan to increase production of full-flavoured, complex Chardonnay, Pinot Noir and a sparkling white wine.

Merricks Estate

This winery is the weekend occupation of Melbourne solicitor George Kefford and his wife Jacquie. Their vibrantly juicy and spicy Shiraz, made elsewhere under contract, has won numerous awards.

Moorooduc Estate

Since 1983 Dr Richard McIntyre has made strikingly textured, toasty Chardonnay and elegant Pinot Noir and Cabernet Sauvignon.

Port Phillip Estate

Leading Melbourne lawyer Jeffrey Shera released his first Pinot Noir, Shiraz, Cabernet/Merlot, and estate-grown Chardonnay in 1991.

Stoniers Merricks

A fast-growing winery that makes a lot of wine for others.

BROWN BROTHERS

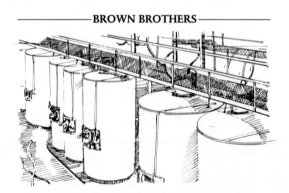

Brown Brothers epitomizes much of what is good about the Australian wine industry. Established in Milawa (North-Eastern Victoria) in 1889, the company has always managed to stay one leap ahead of the field. Much of the credit goes to John Charles Brown — the third generation to make wine — who produced his first vintage in 1934. His four sons continue the tradition. Brown Brothers' great contribution has been the systematic evaluation of countless previously untried grape varieties, and the development of high-altitude, cool-climate vineyards in the foothills of the Australian Alps. They specialize in single varietal wines, and produce many. Whites include Dry Muscat Blanc and Family Reserve Chardonnay, while the best red is the delicious Koombahla Cabernet Sauvignon.

The quality is exemplary, with high-toned plummy/strawberry Pinot Noir leading the list and throwing down the gauntlet to the top Yarra Valley producers.

T'Gallant

This quixotically named business is run by husband-and-wife consultant winemaking team Kevin McCarthy and Kathleen Quealy, and produces unoaked Chardonnay, Holystone (a still white Pinot Noir/Chardonnay blend) and Pinot Gris (white).

Tuck's Ridge

Established in 1993, this still modest winery promises to become the largest in the region once its newly planted vines will start to produce. It makes Riesling, Chardonnay, Pinot Noir and Cabernet Sauvignon.

MURRAY RIVER VALLEY

The mighty Murray forms most of the border between New South Wales and Victoria, rising in the Great Dividing Range and reaching the Southern Ocean 1,000km (620 miles) to the west near Adelaide. Viticulture along the river's course is wholly dependent on irrigation, and high yields of everyday white wine are the region's life blood.

Lindemans Karadoc

This is the vast production centre of the Lindemans arm of the Southcorp group, with over 400,000 cases of Bin 65 Chardonnay annually going to the four corners of the globe.

Mildara

The name goes back to 1888, but the winery is now a somewhat outdated facility owned by Mildara Blass, one of Australia's four big wine companies. It offers a large range of products from Riverlands-sourced table wines to sherries and brandy. Most of its premium wines are made elsewhere.

Salisbury Estate

Labelled wine is but a fraction of the 1.7 million cases of wine sold to other wineries.

Tisdall

Tisdall has been part of Mildara Blass since 1993. It is likely that the wide product range will be trimmed. A consistently good Cabernet/Merlot has been the best wine.

FAR SOUTH-WEST

Seppelt Drumborg vineyard (Southcorp) is the most significant enterprise, although grapes are processed at Great Western. The at times cold and uncertain weather makes growing difficult, but superb sparkling-wine base material, a few scintillating botrytized Rieslings and occasional intense Cabernet Sauvignons are the compensation.

Crawford River

Part-time winemaker John Thomson defies all odds in making technically perfect and excitingly flavoured Riesling, botrytized Riesling, Sémillon/Sauvignon Blanc and Cabernet Sauvignon.

YARRA VALLEY

This beautiful valley, rimmed by substantial mountains, has a climate that is cooler but drier than Bordeaux (though warmer than Burgundy) and ancient but well-drained soils that are suited to producing elegant Chardonnay, spicy Shiraz, sumptuous Merlot and high-quality Cabernet Sauvignon. But it is with Pinot Noir that the region has had exceptional success, producing wines of world-class quality and re-establishing its pre-eminent reputation.

Coldstream Hills

Founded and still run by James Halliday (the best-known writer on Australian wines), this winery has won more awards than any other in the Yarra Valley, having particular success with Pinot Noir and Chardonnay. It has been sold to Southcorp.

de Bortoli

The largest (170,000 cases) of the Yarra Valley wineries and expanding rapidly, de Bortoli produces generously flavoured wines under the de Bortoli name, and keenly priced ones labelled Windy Peak.

Diamond Valley

While David Lance makes Riesling, Chardonnay and a Cabernet blend with skill, he surpasses himself with classically velvety, rich plummy Pinot Noir.

Domaine Chandon

This is Yarra Valley's showpiece, owned by Moët et Chandon, and making various *cuvées* of sparkling wines of outstanding quality and style (labelled Green Point in some export markets).

Long Gully Estate

A substantial winery producing a wide range of table wines with a strong export base. Quality has been uneven.

Mount Mary

Regarded by many as the region's foremost producer, John Middleton makes small amounts of long-lived and perfectly balanced Cabernets, fine, racy Pinot Noir, and austerely elegant white wines.

Oakridge Estate

With vines planted in red, volcanic soils, this is a Cabernet Sauvignon specialist making beautifully articulated wine of the highest class.

Seville Estate

Peter McMahon produces great wine, with a Rhône-like Shiraz and small quantities of heavily botrytized Riesling adding variety.

St Huberts

The first of the revivalists, and now owned by Rothbury Estate (Hunter Valley), St Huberts makes excellent Chardonnay and Cabernet Sauvignon.

Tarrawarra

Clothing magnate Marc Besen produces Chardonnay and Pinot Noir of awesome power, concentration and longevity.

Yarra Edge

Founded in 1982, this winery has started to sell its wines (notably a good Cabernet Sauvignon) under its own label only in 1990.

Yarra Ridge

This winery has grown at a furious pace since its first commercial vintage in 1989, and is likely to continue to do so, having formed a partnership with Mildara Blass. Grapes from all over Victoria make hugely successful Cabernet Sauvignon, amongst other wines.

Yarra Yering

Bailey Carrodus produces very fleshy, complex red wines — Dry Red No 1 (Cabernet-based) and Dry Red No 2 (Shiraz-based).

Yeringberg

Swiss Baron Guillaume de Pary makes voluptuous wines in a tiny corner of the three-storey winery built by his grandfather in the 1860s: Marsanne (white) and Roussanne (white) are specialities.

SOUTH AUSTRALIA

S outh Australia contributes slightly less than half of the country's total wine production. It includes indifferent cask wines from the high-yielding Riverlands area, but also red, white and sparkling wines that are among Australia's best.

Precisely who made the first wine for sale in South Australia remains a matter for debate. One of the contenders, Walter Driffield, sent a case of 1844 vintage white to Queen Victoria in England, and was promptly prosecuted for making wine without a licence. What the Queen thought of the wine was not recorded. Winemaking began in the garden suburbs of Adelaide, but soon spread south to Reynella and north to the Barossa and Clare valleys. Much of the Barossa Valley was developed by German Lutherans from Silesia.

The first grape-growers found the climate of South Australia much more conducive to vine cultivation than that of their native Europe. The varied but generally well-structured soils held the winter and spring rainfall in sufficient amounts to see the vines through the dry summers. Good yields of disease-free grapes were virtually guaranteed and high grape-sugar levels a matter of course.

Climate and wine zones
Adelaide, the capital of South Australia, is at latitude 35°S, and compares climatically with California's Central Coast. Much of South Australia is strongly maritime-influenced, with cool seas ameliorating conditions that might otherwise be far too warm for high-quality wine.

South Australia produced 75% of all Australia's wine in the 1940s and 1950s. While this figure has slipped to 46%, the state's continued importance is self-evident. It has three important zones: Central, South-Eastern and Murray Mallee. (Four

The famous *terra rossa* soils of Coonawarra produce superb Cabernet Sauvignon.

others — Yorke Peninsula, Eyre Peninsula, Kangaroo Island and Far North — are of academic interest.)

The Central Zone can fairly be described as the engine room of the Australian wine industry. The only major wine company not to have its headquarters here is Lindemans, although that is now part of the Penfolds group. This zone includes the state's traditional — and most well-known — winemaking regions.

Barossa
Barossa is by far the most important — and internationally best-known — region. Yet, during the 1970s in particular, it went through a difficult period as the cool-climate wine regions of Australia came to the fore, and as Chardonnay usurped Riesling and Cabernet Sauvignon likewise replaced Shiraz as the most desirable grapes and wines. The vineyard area declined, and, as the cult of the small winemaker took hold, the factory image of the large Barossa wineries counted against it. Much of Aus-

tralia's cask wine is blended and packaged by large companies in the Barossa Valley.

The decline in the importance of Barossa Region stemmed from the removal of low-yielding vines that had been used principally in the production of fortified wines. However, red grapes from the remaining plantings of old, untrellised, unirrigated bush vines of Shiraz, Mourvèdre and Grenache are now much in demand.

The nature of this renaissance reveals the attributes of the Barossa Valley: it is ideally suited to producing rich, full-bodied and generous dry red wines, exemplified by Penfolds' Grange Hermitage. As a matter of expediency, it continues to provide large amounts of white such as fleshy Riesling and the ubiquitous Chardonnay, but red-grape production far exceeds that of white.

Clare and Eden valleys
It is in the Clare Valley, north of Barossa, and the Eden Valley, between Barossa and the Adelaide

Hills, that Riesling, usually called Rhine Riesling, comes into its own. It is made in a peculiarly Australian style: crystal-bright juice is cold fermented in stainless steel to dryness or with precisely controlled trace amounts of residual sugar. This distinctive, crisp style of white wine is utterly unlike the Riesling style found in Alsace or Germany, and it matures beautifully in bottle for between 10 and 20 years.

The Clare Valley has a distinct climate, continental rather than maritime, and which, curiously, is equally well suited to the red varieties Cabernet Sauvignon, Shiraz and Malbec. The wines produced from these grapes are deeply coloured, concentrated and powerful, yet not in any way jammy or overripe.

McLaren Vale

The McLaren Vale, at the centre of the area known as the Southern Vales, about 40km (25 miles) south of Adelaide, built its reputation on a century's or more production of massively extracted, ferruginous dry reds. While it continues to produce utterly distinctive Shiraz and Cabernet Sauvignon, many of its vineyards are ideally suited to white grapes such as Sauvignon Blanc, Sémillon and Chardonnay. Usually these vineyards have a maritime climate, and perform best in cooler vintages.

Adelaide Hills

Parts of the baking plains around the city of Adelaide were the birthplace of South Australia's wine industry. Urban development has driven, and a cooler climate has lured, many grapegrowers into the Adelaide Hills. In the Clarendon sub-region to the north of the Adelaide Hills, potent Riesling and particularly fine, cassis-accented Cabernet Sauvignon are grown. With greater altitude north towards the Piccadilly Valley sub-region, the climate becomes distinctly cooler, and Chardonnay and Pinot Noir dominate, mainly for sparkling wines. Further north-east,

the Lenswood sub-region produces all the classic grape varieties of both Bordeaux and Burgundy.

South-Eastern Zone

Several hundred kilometres south-east of Adelaide is the South-Eastern Zone, which includes two very important Regions — Coonawarra and Padthaway. Coonawarra's climate has proved ideal for Cabernet Sauvignon: while strongly maritime, it is warm enough to ensure that no excessive vegetal flavours intrude, yet cool enough for the varietal character to develop.

Shiraz, too, has always flourished in Coonawarra; in cooler years peppery spicy notes are evident, in warmer vintages dark cherry and redcurrant flavours predominate. Cabernet Sauvignon and Shiraz share the same supple, silky texture: the tannins are fine and soft.

Advanced — and controversial — vineyard techniques are used by some of the large wine companies.

These ensure high yields and reduce production costs to low levels but they do not maximize the potential quality of the wines.

Nearby Padthaway, further north and a little warmer, favours white grapes, although all major varieties are grown in both regions. Padthaway Chardonnay, in particular, has a very distinctive regional character, with a strong grapefruit-like edge to its aroma and flavour. Here again, generous yields are the norm.

Murray Mallee

The hot, arid plains through which the Murray River flows westwards from the border with Victoria constitute South Australia's famous Riverlands area — in the Murray Mallee Zone. Viticulture is made possible by large-scale irrigation, and vast quantities of very ordinary, but very popular, mainly white table wines are produced for cask or bag-in-box sales or bulk exports. Mechanized production and high yields are standard.   □

TASMANIA

Tasmania is an island state off the coast of south-east Australia. Its production of grapes and wine is minuscule, yet it has been of endless fascination since Bartholomew Broughton offered his first wine for sale in 1827, and Diego Bernacchi allegedly tied artificial bunches of grapes to his vines on Maria Island to attract investors in 1889. The opinion of the Tasmanian Department of Agriculture at that time was that the climate of Tasmania was much more suited to apple orchards than vineyards. Grapes are now grown in six distinct parts of the island, but progress has been frustratingly slow. In 1999 only 3,000 tonnes were harvested, almost 75% of it Chardonnay and Pinot Noir.

The three principal areas have been Pipers Brook (north-east of Launceston), the Tamar Valley (north-west of Launceston) and the Derwent Valley (north of Hobart). Three burgeoning areas are the Coal River (north-east of Hobart), the East Coast (roughly halfway up) and the Huon Valley (south-west of Hobart).

PRODUCERS

Several dozen wineries produced together over one million cases in 1999 (against only 200,000 in 1997).

Heemskerk

This company produces Jansz sparkling wine in a joint venture with Roederer of Champagne, as well as stylish Pinot Noir, scented Riesling and austere Chardonnay.

Morilla Estate

Beautifully situated on the Derwent River, Morilla is trying hard with Pinot Noir but does best with Riesling, Chardonnay and Gewürztraminer.

Pipers Brook

This rapidly expanding operation is run by Andrew Pirie. A highly regarded Chardonnay and Pinot Noir lead the way.

Smaller producers worthy of note are Freycinet and Spring Vale (East Coast), Holm Oak and Marions Vineyard (Tamar) and Domain A (Coal River).

REGIONS AND PRODUCERS

Until fairly recently the large winemaking concerns of the Riverlands have dominated the South Australian wine industry at the expense of the small boutique-winery producers. Many smaller producers are now organizing themselves into groups in order to wield more power and influence. The most commercially important regions are listed alphabetically. For a full list of zones, regions and sub-regions, *see* pp592-593.

ADELAIDE

The northern suburbs of Adelaide include many once-famous wine districts such as Magill, Woodbury, Tea Tree Gully and Hope Valley. Urban encroachment means grape-growing these days is largely restricted to Angle Vale and Gawler River on the hot plains north of the city.

Penfolds Magill Estate

Five precious hectares (12 acres) of Shiraz vines remain around the house built by Christopher Rawson Penfold when he arrived from England in 1844. They produce silky smooth Magill Estate Dry Red.

Primo Estate

Roseworthy (University of Adelaide) gold medallist Joe Grilli uses a range of innovative techniques to produce zesty Colombard, concentrated Joseph Cabernet Sauvignon and botrytized Riesling.

ADELAIDE HILLS

Vineyards are at an altitude of 400–600m (1,300–2,000ft) so the climate is far cooler than that of Adelaide, half an hour away. The region consistently produces wines of great elegance and finesse.

Ashton Hills

Stephen George, also consultant winemaker at Wendouree in the Clare Valley, makes elegant Riesling, Chardonnay, Pinot Noir and a blend of Cabernet Sauvignon and Merlot.

Grand Cru Estate

Former Seppelt director Karl Seppelt has a substantial vineyard from which he produces full, smooth Chardonnay and Shiraz, as well as Cabernet Sauvignon made under contract elsewhere.

Petaluma

Top-quality wines are made by Brian Croser with grapes from the Piccadilly and Clare valleys and Coonawarra. The sparkling wine is called Croser; the second label (for still wines) is Bridgewater Mill.

Stafford Ridge

Former Hardy chief-winemaker Geoff Weaver has expanded his own operation at Stafford Ridge. The tangy and intense Riesling, Sauvignon Blanc and Chardonnay are outstanding.

BAROSSA

The moderately warm climate with winter/spring rainfall and a generally dry summer, coupled with varied but generally well drained soils, mean the region has always been suited to the production of full-bodied dry reds. Penfolds and others make great red wines from low-yielding vineyards up to 100 years old.

Basedow

A stalwart producer, dating from 1896, of very dependable wines, such as the oak-matured Sémillon known as White Burgundy in Australia.

Charles Melton

Graeme (Charlie) Melton is at the forefront of the Barossa Valley's rebirth, especially with his velvety, liquorice-and-prune Nine Popes red, blended from Shiraz, Grenache and Mourvèdre.

Elderton

The Ashmead family were formerly grape-growers, but now make wine as well (via contracts). Smooth, red-berry Shiraz and Cabernet Sauvignon are best.

Grant Burge

Former Krondorf founder Grant Burge accumulated large vineyard holdings for this venture, founded in 1988, and produces red and white wines.

Kaiser Stuhl

Founded in 1931, this former cooperative is now part of Southcorp and produces 1.7 million cases of wine a year. Only the Red Ribbon Shiraz has any pretensions to quality.

Krondorf

Now part of Mildara Blass, Krondorf is a commercial success story. Grapes come from all over South Australia.

Orlando

Now owned by Pernod-Ricard of France but originally established in 1847, and with Wyndham and a host of others in the group, Orlando makes the world-famous Jacobs Creek, both white and red. Other labels include St Hugo, St Helga, Gramps and RF, all with varietal subtitles.

Penfolds

See profile.

Peter Lehmann

Flavour-filled Riesling, Sémillon, Chardonnay, Shiraz, Cabernet Sauvignon and a blend of Cabernet Sauvignon and Malbec, all from Barossa fruit, are mainstays.

Richmond Grove

Founded in 1931, Leo Buring's winery has long been regarded as the maker of Australia's greatest Rieslings — white wines that evolve magnificently for 20 years or more. Today the company is owned by the Orlando group who have given it its new name, while the Leo Burling label has been acquired by Southcorp.

Rockford

Rocky O'Callaghan is an old-style winemaker using old vines to produce wines of voluminous character, including Riesling and Shiraz.

St Hallett

See profile, p550.

Tollana

Dating from 1888, Tollana is part of Penfolds, but has forged its own identity with deep, lime-juice Eden Valley Riesling, tangy, spicily oaked, barrel-fermented Sémillons, Sauvignon Blancs and Chardonnays, and elegant, slightly sappy reds.

Tolley

Owned and run by the same family since 1892, Tolley produces a conventional range of well made and reasonably priced varietal wines with one speciality — a fragrant, flowery Gewürztraminer.

Wolf Blass Wines

Since the 1960s Wolf Blass has developed one of Australia's most successful brands with multi-regional, multi-varietal blends, all influenced by vanillin American oak. Blass has merged with Mildara (*qv*).

Yalumba

Dating from 1863 and producing 850,000 cases of wine a year, Yalumba is one of the great Australian family firms, and enjoys great success with its budget-priced Angas Brut sparkling wine and Oxford Landing varietals, plus up-market brands.

CLARE VALLEY

Clare contrasts sharply with Barossa. Wineries are smaller, the majority of them are family-owned and -run, and most use local fruit. Wines include superb, long-lived Riesling, powerful Shiraz and a regional speciality — a complex Cabernet/Malbec blend. Both Sémillon and Chardonnay do well.

Eaglehawk Estate

Formerly Quelltaler, founded in 1856, before being bought by Wolf Blass, this company now makes a limited range of pleasant wines.

Grosset

Jeffrey Grosset makes fine Riesling and Chardonnay, as well as a superb Cabernet Sauvignon/Merlot-based red called Gaia.

Jim Barry

The prolific Barry family owns some outstanding vineyards, making undervalued Riesling and, at the other end of the spectrum, a classy pretender to Penfolds' Grange throne, The Armagh.

Leasingham

A 20-year ownership by H J Heinz failed to capitalize on the reputation Leasingham once enjoyed (the company dates from 1893). Now owned by BRL Hardy, it produces solid Riesling, Chardonnay, Shiraz and Cabernet/Malbec.

Mitchell Cellars

Andrew and Jane Mitchell have since 1975 made classic Riesling and firm, dusty Cabernet Sauvignon, now adding Chardonnay and a minty Shiraz to their list.

Pikes

Brothers Neil and Andrew (viticulturist with Penfolds), produce a crisp Sauvignon Blanc and concentrated, powerful Cabernet Sauvignon.

Sevenhill

Established (in 1851) and still run by the Jesuit Manresa Society, Sevenhill makes good secular wine from usual and unusual varieties including Crouchen (white), Grenache (red) and Touriga (red).

Skillogalee

Hilly vineyards produce richly concentrated Riesling, Shiraz and a Cabernet Sauvignon/Cabernet Franc/Malbec red.

Taylors

Lofty aspirations (all grapes are estate-grown and hand-harvested) and marketing pragmatism (modest quality and pricing) work amazingly well for Taylors' Chardonnay and Cabernet Sauvignon.

Tim Knappstein

This company was bought by Petaluma in 1993, but is still run by talented Tim Knappstein, who produces stylish Riesling, Chardonnay, Fumé Blanc and Cabernet/Merlot, an exceptional botrytized Riesling, and Sémillon and Pinot Noir from Lenswood.

Wendouree Cellars

Established in 1895, these vineyards have a unique micro-climate, and produce small amounts of dry reds of great depth and concentration including Shiraz, Mourvèdre, Malbec and Cabernet Sauvignon.

Wilson Vineyard

John Wilson makes eclectic wines, including Zinfandel and sparkling burgundy, both red.

COONAWARRA

This has all the attributes of a true *appellation*: a particular limestone-based soil (coloured red by iron impurities) called *terra rossa*, and a single, cool macro-climate. The region produces Australia's greatest Cabernet Sauvignon and high-quality Shiraz in abundance; Riesling, Sauvignon Blanc and Chardonnay also flourish.

Balnaves

Grower Doug Balnaves has some of his grapes made under contract into exceptionally smooth and richly fruited Chardonnay, Cabernet Sauvignon and Cabernet/Merlot.

Bowen Estate

Doug Bowen is a highly-regarded small producer, excelling with chunky, berry-and-spice Shiraz and concentrated Cabernet Sauvignon.

Brands Laira

Technical input from recent half-owners McWilliams has improved the range of Riesling, Chardonnay, Shiraz, Cabernet Sauvignon and Cabernet/Merlot. Watch out for Original Vineyard Shiraz.

Hollick

Ian Hollick produces finely-crafted reds, while his partner Patrick Tocaciu (formerly winemaker at Tolana) makes very good Riesling and subtle melon-and-fig Chardonnay.

PENFOLDS

Penfolds, formerly the most important winery in Australia and the largest group of wineries under common ownership, has become part of Southcorp in 1994. Traditionally, Penfolds' strength lies with its red wines, from Grange Hermitage (the country's finest) to Koonunga Hill; with Magill Estate, Bin 707 Cabernet Sauvignon, St Henri, Clare Estate, Bin 389 Cabernet Shiraz, Bin 128 Coonawarra Shiraz and Bin 28 Kalimna Shiraz in between. Ageing is mostly in small American oak barrels: in some cases French oak is also used. A philosophy of picking only fully ripe grapes, deliberately blending regions to achieve balance, and strictly controlled fermentation and barrel-ageing techniques give the wines tremendous depth and complexity. Since 1990 Penfolds has successfully moved into white wines.

Katnook Estate

This is part of Coonawarra Machinery Company, the largest independent group of grape-growers in the district. Pristinely crisp Sauvignon Blanc, stylish Chardonnay and slightly leafy Cabernet Sauvignon head the Katnook range. John Riddoch is the name of the volume second label.

Leconfield

Ralph Fowler makes high-quality, classic Riesling and Cabernet Sauvignon.

Lindemans

Very well known in the Hunter Valley of New South Wales, Lindemans (Southcorp) established itself in Coonawarra in the 1960s. The emphasis is on red wines, with St George Cabernet Sauvignon and Limestone Ridge Shiraz/Cabernet at the top of the list.

Mildara

Mildara, now merged with Wolf Blass (qv), was founded in 1888 at Mildura (Victoria) and the group's headquarters are still there. Mildara purchased land in Coonawarra in 1955 and premium wines are made there. With Wynns, it has been a key player in the region's renaissance. The succulent Jamiesons Run blend brought commercial success.

Parker Estate

This is a partnership of three families that makes two Cabernet Sauvignons, the best of them under the Terra Rossa First Growth label. It is extremely concentrated, using lots of new oak and the best grapes available.

Penley Estate

Complex citrus-and-melon Chardonnay and dark chocolate, vanilla and red-berry Cabernet Sauvignon are best, and will soon be estate-grown.

Redman

A famous name that has disappointed for many years, but has recently returned to form with its Claret (Shiraz) and Cabernet Sauvignon.

Rouge Homme

A separate brand of Lindemans aimed at the mid-market. The Shiraz/Cabernet blend and Chardonnay are both excellent value.

Rymill

Peter Rymill moved from grape-growing to winemaking in 1987. His Cabernet Sauvignon is intense, his Shiraz rich and his Chardonnay excellent.

Wynns Coonawarra Estate

Founded at the end of the 19th century, Wynns is possibly the most famous, but certainly the most successful producer in the region. John Riddoch Cabernet Sauvignon and Michael Hermitage (red) are the opulent, low-volume flagships. Wynns (now part of Southcorp) also makes Rieslings and Chardonnays.

Zema Estate

The Zema family still hand-prune and hand-pick, a rare practice in the Coonawarra region. They make deeply coloured and flavoured Shiraz and Cabernet Sauvignon.

EDEN VALLEY

The windswept northern end of the Adelaide Hills has always seen itself as an extension of the Barossa Valley. Riesling does very well here, rivalling that of the Clare Valley in terms of quality, but with its own slightly fruitier, lime-juice-flavoured style. The relatively cool climate is also suitable for elegant Chardonnay, Shiraz and Cabernet Sauvignon.

Heggies

This is the second foray into high-altitude (570m/1,900ft) grape-growing by Yalumba (qv). Steely, citrussy Riesling, intense, limey botrytized Riesling, and flavoursome Chardonnay are best.

Henschke

This is one of Australia's greatest small wineries, dating from 1868 and run with dedication and skill by Stephen and Pru

Henschke. They make a wide range of usually superlative wines headed by the velvety Hill of Grace Shiraz, made from 120-year-old vines.

Hill-Smith Estate

Hill-Smith draws upon two vineyards — at 380m (1,250ft) and 550m (1,800ft). They provide a third brand for Yalumba (qv); and Sauvignon Blanc, Chardonnay and Cabernet/Shiraz have all done well.

Mountadam

David Wynn and son Adam make concentrated, complex Chardonnay, Pinot Noir and Cabernet Sauvignon from low-yielding estate vineyards.

Pewsey Vale

This vineyard, owned by Yalumba (qv), marked the first move away from the Barossa Valley floor for almost a century. Firm, steely, toasty Riesling has been the reward.

FLEURIEU PENINSULA

The Peninsula is a maritime-influenced area, and is much cooler than one would expect. The Langhorne Creek sub-

——— ST HALLETT ———

If the reputation of the Barossa Valley suffered from 1965 until 1985, small wineries such as St Hallett have done a great deal to restore the situation. The driving force is Bob McLean (ex-Orlando), who formed a partnership with winemaker Stuart Blackwell and long-term Barossa *vigneron* Carl Lindner. They transformed St Hallett with Old Block Shiraz, made from a series of vineyards containing vines not less than 60 years old. While the flavours of dark cherry, redcurrant, plum and peppermint are intense, the wine is neither tannic nor harsh. The supple, silky texture has been augmented by the use of high-quality new American oak. They also produce a tangy, unoaked Poachers White, a Sémillon/Chardonnay/Sauvignon Blanc blend, and a Barossa Shiraz at a lower price.

region, uniquely relying on total winter flooding, has long supplied grapes to the large Barossa Valley producers, the slightly herbaceous-flavoured fruit blending well with that of warmer regions.

Bleasdale Vineyards

An historic gem — founded in 1850 and still run by the Potts family — making Verdelho (white) in an aged, madeira-like style and as a lightly-oaked table wine.

Currency Creek

This cool, maritime-influenced vineyard makes stylish Sauvignon Blanc, Chardonnay and sparkling wines.

MCLAREN VALE

Since the turn of the 19th century, McLaren Vale has been the home of the small professional winery. The region has a special charm and produces great wines, particularly in cooler vintages. Sauvignon Blanc, Chardonnay and Cabernet Sauvignon are the most successful wines.

Andrew Garrett

A high-flyer in the 1980s, but quieter under Japanese (Suntory) ownership, and now as part of Mildara Blass, this winery makes attractive Riesling, Chardonnay, Shiraz and Cabernet/Merlot.

BRL Hardy

The marriage of convenience between the historic family firm Thomas Hardy, founded in 1853, and Renmano (*qv*) produced one of Australia's four large wine groups. The Hardy side of it produces over 800,000 cases of wine a year. Brands are many and various, providing more honesty than excitement. Top-of-the-range wines can be outstanding.

Chapel Hill

A success story of the 1990s thanks to consultant wine-maker Pam Dunsford and capital from new owners. Her spectacularly opulent Chardonnay, Shiraz and Cabernet Sauvignon have all had wine show success.

Chateau Reynella

Founded in 1838, Chateau Reynella is now the headquarters of the BRL Hardy Group, producing limited quantities of fine table wines under the Stony Hill label and a great vintage port.

Coriole

The Lloyd family produce superb dark chocolate-and-cherry Shiraz, a Sangiovese (red), a couple of dry whites and fine virgin olive oil.

D'Arenberg

D'Arry Osborn and son Chester fashion red wines of rare individuality and quality from old vine plantings of Shiraz and Grenache.

Geoff Merrill

Merrill is one of the industry's great characters, making surprisingly elegant wines under this label, and more exotic wines under the Mount Hurtle and Cockatoo Ridge labels.

Ingoldby

A much respected name in the region, Ingoldby is now owned by Bill Clappis, who consistently produces well structured, and generously flavoured Cabernet Sauvignon amongst many other wines.

Kay Bros

Colin Kay continues a century of family tradition. Briary, bitter-chocolate Block 6 Shiraz is the best wine.

Normans

A family firm dating from 1851, Normans consistently produces very fine and often under-appreciated wines, the best being Shiraz and Cabernet Sauvignon (under the Chais Clarendon label).

Pirramimma

Another family firm established at the end of the 19th century, Pirramimma has slipped in recent years, but it has some fine estate vineyards upon which to draw. Recovery efforts are being made with Riesling, Chardonnay and Shiraz.

Richard Hamilton

Richard Hamilton also owns Leconfield (*qv*) and employs the same skilled winemaking and marketing team for both. Succulent Chardonnay and spicy old-vine Shiraz are best.

Shaw & Smith

Former "Flying Winemaker" Martin Shaw and Australia's first Master of Wine Michael Hill-Smith produce high-quality melon-and-gooseberry Sauvignon Blanc and tangy barrel-fermented Chardonnay.

Wirra Wirra

An energetic and successful operation long known for crisply herbaceous Sauvignon Blanc and fine, complex Chardonnay, and now adding the excellent The Cousins sparkling white wine and the silky smooth The Angelus Cabernet Sauvignon.

Woodstock

Scott Collett enjoys life to the full and makes wines accordingly, the best being dark-chocolate and red-berry Cabernet Sauvignon, and a searingly intense, botrytized sweet white.

MURRAY MALLEE

This is desert and salt-bush country brought to life solely through irrigation. A warm, dry summer, free-draining sandy soil and unlimited water produce large yields of very useful white grapes — chiefly Chardonnay, Riesling,

Chenin Blanc and Colombard — as well as less exalted varieties used principally for bulk table wines, fortified wines and brandy.

Angove's

An impressive array of modest varietal white and red table wines, fortified wines and very fine brandy are all produced from estate-grown grapes. The vineyard has vine rows totalling 1,500km (930 miles), and produces 800,000 cases a year.

Berri Estates

A former cooperative that is now part of BRL Hardy (Southcorp), Berri Estates produces principally cask wine and bulk wine for export (4.5 million cases), much of it going to Scandinavia and the EC.

Renmano

This represents the BRL half of the Hardy group (Southcorp), which produces the Chairman's Selection, Riesling, Cabernet Sauvignons, as well as a Chardonnay and a tawny "port".

PADTHAWAY

Padthaway is virtually the exclusive domain of some of Australia's largest wine companies: Southcorp (Lindemans, Seppelt, Wynns, BRL Hardy) and Orlando between them own more than 90% of the plantings, and there is only one small resident producer — Padthaway Estate. With a climate slightly warmer than that of Coonawarra and very well drained and structured soils, the region produces good yields of high-quality grapes, especially Chardonnay, Riesling and Sauvignon Blanc. A large proportion of the grapes produced are anonymously blended, particularly those used in sparkling wines.

WESTERN AUSTRALIA

Western Australia is the newest wine state. Between 1997 and 1999, the region's plantings have increased by 48%. A region of great climatic contrast, its wines are similarly varied. The Swan Valley is the traditional wine-producing region, but the cooler, up-and-coming areas to the south of Perth now offer the most interest.

The settlement of Western Australia began with the arrival of the sailing ship Parmelia in 1829. Among its passengers was a botanist, Thomas Waters, and in his baggage were grapevines. He was granted a 20-ha (50-acre) property at Guildford on the Swan River. He planted vines there and dug the cellar of Olive Farm, the oldest winery in Australia.

Swan Valley
In 1840 John Septimus Roe planted the Sandalford Vineyard in the Swan Valley, establishing a viticultural dynasty that was to last 130 years. At about the same time Houghton, now Western Australia's largest winery, was founded near by.

Viticulture remained concentrated in the Swan Valley until the mid-1960s, Yugoslavian settlers being the mainstay (like the Lutherans in the Barossa Valley). At one time there were more wineries in the Swan Valley than in either New South Wales or Victoria, mainly supplying the local community, and with the emphasis on fortified wines and heavy table wines.

Changing lifestyles and demand, inroads made by cask wines from South Australia via the supermarkets, and the emergence of the cooler growing regions to the south began to alter the picture. As recently as 1979 the Swan Valley contributed 58% of Western Australia's grape production; by 1992 that proportion has been reduced to 25%, though

Picking Chardonnay in the Perth Hills.

production has stabilized.

The climate is the hottest of all the Australian wine regions, with the least summer rainfall and the most sunshine. Vintage commences at the end of January and is largely over by the end of February. Two-thirds of production is of white varieties. Apart from a little Cabernet Sauvignon, much of which is used to make Houghton Rosé, the only red grape of significance is Grenache, destined mainly for fortified wine. Chenin Blanc is the most important white variety, followed by Verdelho and Chardonnay, then Muscadelle and Sémillon. Most of the region's white grapes are used to make Houghton White Burgundy (known overseas as Houghton Supreme), for years Australia's best-selling dry white. Today, the region is in decline.

The southern regions
The Margaret River Region, 250km (155 miles) south of Perth, has gained an international reputation for the quality of its wines: it is also a place of unique character and beauty.

All the major grape varieties have been tried in the temperate climate: in descending order of success are Cabernet Sauvignon, Sémillon, Merlot, Sauvignon Blanc, Chenin Blanc, Chardonnay and Shiraz. Two varieties that have not succeeded are Riesling and Pinot Noir; on the other hand, the small planting of the Californian speciality Zinfandel has been an unqualified success.

The cooler Mount Barker-Frankland Region is in the extreme south, running north from the old whaling town of Albany to Mount Barker. The first vines were planted near Mount Barker in 1966, a year earlier than at Vasse Felix in the Margaret River. Right from the outset tightly knit, steely, long-lived Riesling whites and classically austere Cabernet Sauvignon reds established a position of dominance. Sauvignon Blanc, Chardonnay, Pinot Noir (especially at Albany) and Shiraz have done well since without challenging the primacy of Riesling and Cabernet Sauvignon.

Halfway between Margaret River and Mount Barker-Frankland is the Warren-Blackwood Region, much better known by either of two of its sub-regions, Manjimup and Pemberton. High hopes are held for this still nascent region, and in particular for Pinot Noir and Chardonnay.

The South-West Coastal Region is an eel-like strip running from the Margaret River to north of Perth, the unifying feature being the fine Tuart sands in which the vines grow. The climate is significantly hotter at the northern end than the southern.

The Darling Range, east of Perth, has a few, mainly small wineries. The climate here is only slightly cooler than in the Swan Valley. Finally, there is the Northern Perth Region, which is very hot and produces mostly white grapes.

REGIONS AND PRODUCERS

Many producers in the newer, cooler Western Australian areas are small, and concentrate on more complex wine styles. Isolated from the main domestic markets in eastern Australia, some have yet to realize their potential. For a full list of zones, regions and sub-regions, *see* pp592-593.

MARGARET RIVER

The relatively warm waters of the Indian Ocean and the absence of nearby mountains conspire to give the Margaret River one of the most temperate climates in the wine world. It produces wonderfully tangy Sémillon, Sauvignon Blanc and Chardonnay whites, and powerful Cabernet Sauvignon reds that mature gracefully.

Amberley Estate

South African-born Albert Haak has produced commercial winners by concentrating on an easy-drinking, affordable Chenin Blanc.

Ashbrook Estate

The Devitt brothers make consistently impressive and finely crafted varietal wines sold mainly at the cellar door and by mail order.

Brookland Valley

This beautifully sited winery, complete with restaurant, produces crisp but light Chardonnay and Sauvignon Blanc.

Cape Mentelle

This is one of the region's great producers, majority-owned by Veuve Clicquot of Champagne. The company makes a pungent, gooseberry-and-passionfruit Sémillon and Sauvignon Blanc blend, and a tangy barrel-fermented Chardonnay, as well as voluptuous Zinfandel (red), Shiraz and Cabernet Sauvignon.

Chateau Xanadu

Xanadu's bottles have striking labels, though the quality of the wine is rather uneven. Crispy, herbaceous Sémillon has been the most consistent.

Cullen Wines

Kevin Cullen, wife Diana and daughter Vanya, the winemaker, have produced many great wines, with berry-plum and dark chocolate Cabernet/Merlot always to the fore.

Devil's Lair

Production is set to increase here — from a striking new winery — with flowery, tangy Chardonnay and powerful berry and vanillin oak Cabernet Sauvignon.

Happ's

Erland Happ is looking to specialize with Merlot but he is currently succeeding best with a complex Chardonnay.

Hayshed Hill

This company opened its doors to the public in 1993, with brightly fruity Cabernet Sauvignon and a generously-oaked, rich Sémillon.

Leeuwin Estate

Massive promotional expenditure — which included, for example, bringing the Berlin Philharmonic Orchestra to the vineyard — has helped to establish the reputation of both Leeuwin's and the Margaret River region. Glorious,

long-lived Chardonnay and classic Cabernet Sauvignon lead the way.

Moss Wood

Keith Mugford makes lovingly crafted Sémillon (both unwooded and oaked), voluptuous Chardonnay and the region's most sensual Cabernet Sauvignon, as well as an excellent Pinot Noir, all wines of great style.

Pierro

Michael Peterkin makes some of Australia's most spectacularly complex and highly textured Chardonnay. Also good is the Sémillon/Sauvignon Blanc blend.

Vasse Felix

The most senior of the region's wineries is now owned by the Holmes à Court family. It produces crisp Classic Dry White, outstanding botrytized Noble Riesling and velvety Shiraz.

Willespie

A consistent producer of attractive, full-flavoured Sauvignon Blanc, Verdelho (white) and Sémillon. An impressive Merlot is being developed.

MOUNT BARKER-FRANKLAND

The climate of this scenically striking region ranges from maritime but cool in Albany, where Chardonnay, Sauvignon Blanc and Pinot Noir flourish, to the equally cool but much more continental climate further north where Riesling, Shiraz, Cabernet Sauvignon and Malbec grape varieties are dominant.

Alkoomi

This is a notable producer of tightly structured, long-lived Riesling and Chardonnay; earthy, cassis-tinged Cabernet Sauvignon; and the occasional lush Malbec.

Castle Rock

The view from estate vineyards on the slopes of the Porongurups is second to none, although the crisply delicate Riesling and Chardonnay, plus similarly weighted Cabernet Sauvignon, give the Diletti family a more tangible return on its investment.

Chatsfield

Ken Lynch and daughter Siobhan produce delectable melon-and-grapefruit Chardonnay, limey Riesling, and cherry, spice and leaf Shiraz (made under contract at Goundrey).

Frankland Estate

Winemaking is a diversification at Barrie Smith and Judy Cullam's sheep station. They make fruit-scented Riesling and crisp Sauvignon Blanc.

Galafrey

Ian and Linda Tyrer have had great success with herbaceous lime-juice Riesling, dense Shiraz and Chardonnay.

Goundrey

The largest winery in the region, at Mount Baker, belongs to flying winemaker Goundrey. It makes wine for itself and for smaller vineyards with their own labels. The premium Windy Hill and lower-priced Langton labels can be good value, particularly Chardonnay and the Sauvignon Blanc/Sémillon blend.

Howard Park

Plantagenet winemaker John Wade produces immaculately crafted Riesling and spicy, oaky, cherry-flavoured Cabernet Sauvignon/Merlot of the highest class at his own winery, established here in 1986. Madfish Bay is a newly introduced second label.

Plantagenet

Plantagenet, the first to grow grapes at Mount Baker, is a respected producer of stylish, intense Chardonnay, spicy Shiraz, and silky Cabernet Sauvignon. A contract winemaker of note.

Wignalls

This vineyard is exceptionally well suited to the production of fragrant, sappy, burgundy-style Pinot Noir. The Chardonnay and Sauvignon Blanc are also good. All three are made at Plantagenet.

SOUTH-WEST COASTAL

This is surely one of the most unusual wine regions in the world, consisting of a narrow coastal strip 250km (155 miles) long by 20km (12 miles) wide. The *raison d'être* of the wine industry is the unusual soil — a fine Tuart sand. Wine styles are diverse.

Baldivis Estate

This company produces pleasant, light-bodied whites from Sémillon, Chardonnay and Sauvignon Blanc, as well as a Cabernet/Merlot red.

Capel Vale

Peter Pratten employs the skills of Rob Bowen as winemaker to produce at times scintillating Riesling, fig-and-melon Chardonnay that ages well and Baudin, a Cabernet Sauvignon/Merlot-based red.

Killerby Vineyards

Killerby was established by the late Barry Killerby and is now run by daughter Anna and her winemaker husband Matt Aldridge (formerly at Rosemount). They make finely crafted white wines and excellent Cabernet Sauvignon.

Paul Conti

Paul Conti is a gifted winemaker who produces an unostentatious range. The pristine, spicy-grapey *vendange tardive* (late harvest) Frontignac (white) and fine red-cherry Manjimup Hermitage (red) are consistently good.

SWAN VALLEY

While the climate is fearsomely hot and dry in summer, the deep alluvial soils have very good water-holding capacity. But trends in the industry have contributed to the decline of many wineries and to the concentration of production at Houghton.

Evans & Tate

The winery and one vineyard (Gnangara) are here, but the best wines come from vineyards in Margaret River, including fresh and fragrant Sémillon, lively and tangy Chardonnay, silky, red-berry Merlot, and structured, toasty oaked Cabernet Sauvignon.

Houghton

See profile.

Lamont

The late Jack Mann's daughter, Corin, uses his methods to produce White Burgundy, Light Red Cabernet, Hermitage (red) and Chardonnay.

Moondah Brook Estate

This is a brand of Houghton, drawing its excellent Chenin Blanc and Verdelho from the Moondah Brook vineyard, and its Cabernet Sauvignon from Margaret River and Frankland.

Olive Farm

The oldest winery in Australia, Olive Farm was built in 1829. Today it maintains a low profile, while competently making a wide range of table and fortified wines sold in Perth and at the cellar door.

Sandalford

Sandalford was founded in 1840. It has a large Margaret River vineyard, but was consistently disappointing until Bill Crappsley arrived as winemaker (from Evans & Tate) prior to the 1993 vintage. Cabernet Sauvignon is the biggest seller, but Verdelho whites show most promise.

Westfield

John Kosovich, whose father founded the vineyard in 1922, has long worked magic with Swan Valley Verdelho, Chardonnay and Cabernet Sauvignon, and will soon harvest the first grapes from his small vineyard at Pemberton.

WARREN-BLACKWOOD

This is one of the newest wine regions in Australia. Altitude varies, but has a significant cooling effect, and increases rainfall in winter and spring. Most major grape varieties are being tried, but most attention is given to Chardonnay and Pinot Noir.

Producers include:

Donnelly River, Gloucester Ridge, Mounford, Piano Gully, Smithbrook, Warren Vineyard.

DARLING RANGE

The Darling Range (or Perth Hills) is 15km (9 miles) from Perth. Most vineyards are at 150–400m (500–1,300ft), and irrigation is not necessary. The chief varieties are white — Chardonnay, Sémillon and Sauvignon — but total little more than 50ha (125 acres).

Producers include:

Avalon, Carosa Vineyard, Chittering Estate, Coorinja Vineyard, Cosham, Darlington Estate, Hainault, Piesse Brook, Scarp Valley.

─────HOUGHTON─────

Houghton was established in 1836, and John Fergusson made the first wine in 1859, beginning a century of family ownership. The appointment in 1930 of the late Jack Mann, a highly skilled winemaker, was the most important event in Houghton history. His Chenin Blanc/Muscadelle blend became the best-selling white wine in Australia, and single-handedly put Swan Valley on the map. No less remarkable is the wine's capacity to develop in bottle over ten to fifteen years, gaining a honeyed, nutty richness like a Hunter Sémillon of similar age. (Neither has ever relied on oak.) Jack Mann's successors have refined the style a little by including Chardonnay and reducing the Muscadelle. Houghton is now part of BRL Hardy (Southcorp).

NEW ZEALAND

THOUGH PRODUCING TEN TIMES LESS THAN ITS NEIGHBOUR,
AUSTRALIA, NEW ZEALAND RANKS HIGH ON THE INTERNATIONAL
MARKET, NOTABLY THANKS TO ITS WHITE WINES.

Te Mata Peak overlooks vineyards near Hastings in Hawke's Bay, one of the chief grape-growing regions, on the east coast of New Zealand's North Island. The widely-spaced vines allow full mechanization in these modern vineyards.

The modern wine industry of New Zealand is still considered to be in its infancy, yet it has achieved a worldwide renown out of all proportion to both its size and its maturity. With the slogan "The Home of Cool-Climate Wines", New Zealand's wines have established a style and a character that are immediately both memorable and popular. They are crisp and fruity, balancing acidity and concentrated flavours, and eschewing the fullness of Australian wines in favour of elegance and poise. Not surprisingly, New Zealand has export customers throughout Europe, the Americas and the Far East.

The style is epitomized by two white wine styles that have captured the imagination of wine lovers around the world. The first is based on Sauvignon Blanc, the white grape renowned in the Sancerre and Pouilly-Fumé wines of France, which in New Zealand has achieved new heights of intensity and a superb fruit flavour. The second is made from Chardonnay, another grape variety that in New Zealand has a delicious natural acidity that is balanced by a honeyed malolactic fermentation, the use of new wood and, again, excellent fruit quality.

To these two can soon be added another distinctive style that is coming up fast, based on blends of red grape varieties — Cabernet Sauvignon with a little Merlot — and producing wines with the sort of elegance that is more often associated with Bordeaux. Latitudinally, one would expect New Zealand to have a hot climate — rather like that of the Spanish vineyards. In reality, the country's isolated position in the southern Pacific Ocean gives it changeable weather patterns, with strong, often cold southerly winds blowing from the Antarctic. The Northland region at the northern tip of North Island is, in fact, semi-tropical, while the far south of South Island, around Dunedin and Invercargill, can experience bitterly cold winters and only cool summers. Vineyard areas are found on both islands between these two climatic extremes. Those of Auckland are now in decline, but new plantings continue at a pace from Northland to Otago on South Island, though they tend to be concentrated in the more temperate belt from Gisborne and Hawke's Bay in central North Island to Marlborough in the north of South Island.

History of New Zealand wines

While the modern wine industry — the making of fine varietal wines (predominantly from one variety) from mainly French grapes — has developed fast since the 1970s, New Zealand's viticulture is, like Australia's, as old as the country's European settlement. The first vines were introduced in 1819 by an English missionary, the Reverend Samuel Marsden, who planted cuttings brought from Australia at Kerikeri in the Northland region. The first recorded wines were made by James Busby, who was a major influence on the development of Australian viticulture. He arrived in New Zealand in 1832, and within four years of planting vine cuttings was making wine at Waitangi, also in Northland.

Apart from the early British enthusiasts, there were French, German and Dalmatian settlers who arrived as gum diggers (who dug for the fossilized resin of the Kauri tree), but who were later to make a great contribution to the growth of the wine industry in the 20th century.

In addition to the problems from which all 19th-century vineyards suffered — in particular pests and diseases such as phylloxera, which reached New Zealand in 1895 — the country's winemakers were hampered by a widespread temperance movement. The effects of this legacy of abstinence continued to be felt until 1990, when supermarkets were for the first time allowed to sell wine.

Recent trends

Until the 1970s much of the wine made was fortified and sold as "sherry" or "port", according to style and sweetness. In the 1960s and 1970s farmers — and not just winegrowers — were encouraged by the New Zealand government to plant spare land with vines and to treat them like any other commercial crop. (This explains the supply of many grapes for the industry today by contract growers.) At that time, more than two-thirds of vines were hybrids — produced by crossing American and European vines — although with governmental encouragement to plant, many poor-quality hybrids were dug up, and today hardly any remain.

Since the 1970s an increasing emphasis has been placed on table wines in New Zealand. And the wine industry continues to evolve. Only since the 1980s have vineyard areas been definitively established as suitable for particular grape varieties, and experimentation continues.

When the planting of European varieties took precedence over hybrids, it was decided to use German vines, particularly the white grape Müller-Thurgau. Growers realized slowly that the New Zealand climate resembles that of central France rather than Germany, and Sauvignon Blanc was introduced in the early 1970s, and Chardonnay in the mid-1980s. German grape varieties, which formed the basis of the production of inexpensive "cask", or "bag-in-box", wines (everyday wine in a plastic bag inside a box), are giving way to French ones which are considered the best varieties for New Zealand's distinctive wine styles. Among red grape varieties, Cabernet Sauvignon alone has a long history, having first been planted by wine pioneer James Busby.

After the campaign launched in 1986 to rip up almost a quarter of the vines, as a result of over-production, the area given over to vine growing, especially that of noble grape varieties, has begun to increase again, going from 5,000ha (12,000 acres) in 1988-1990 to 9,000ha (22,000 acres) in 1998. Nowadays the increase in production depends mainly on the world market. Exports have increased spectacularly: 23,000hl on average per annum between 1986 and 1990, 131,000hl in 1997 (out of 550,000hl produced). New Zealand's future is as a quality, rather than volume, wine producer. Although it can easily compete with Australia in terms of quality, it will experience more problems when it comes to price.

Structure of the wine industry

To supply domestic and export markets, the wine industry has both polarized and diversified. In 1992 there were only three really big producers, who between them had 85% of sales, 78% of production and 65%

WINE LAWS

In general, New Zealanders are less concerned about legalistic labelling than Europeans, believing that a wine sells on taste rather than provenance.

Like other New World countries, New Zealand's wine producers for years used French and German wine names to authenticate the style of their wines. Since 1983 wine laws have been tightened, with grape varietal labelling now being the most common practice. A varietal wine must contain 75% of the variety named: if it is a blended wine, the predominant grape is named first. Other information is standard: vintage, producer, contents and alcohol level. The words "estate-bottled" may be seen, but this is less significant in New Zealand where it is common for grapes to be moved hundreds of kilometres from vineyard to winery.

Regional names appear on wine labels if the grapes are predominantly from that area: Marlborough and Hawke's Bay are the most common regional names seen. The Wairarapa/Martinborough region has a voluntary labelling system whereby a wine can be certified as 100% from that area by carrying a sticker that says "100% Martinborough Terrace Appellation Committee".

It is hoped that by 1995 a system of "Certified Origin" will be in force for New Zealand wines. This will guarantee the geographical origin of the grapes when a regional name is claimed on the wine's label. It will also guarantee the grape varieties and the vintage of wines whose labels claim a geographical origin. This system will include all New Zealand wines that carry a geographical locator on their label.

WINE REGIONS OF NEW ZEALAND

Vines are grown from Northland in the north of North Island to Otago in the southern half of South Island, extending through a range of climates and soil types. Auckland, Gisborne and Hawke's Bay were the first of New Zealand's major wine regions to become established: Wairarapa, Marlborough and the other areas of South Island are the "new" wine-producing regions that have only come to prominence since the beginning of the 1980s and are still being developed.

Wine areas
- major wine-producing areas
- other wine-producing areas
- -- regional boundary

of exports, but there were also 163 smaller wineries. While big companies dominate the industry, smaller ones proliferate.

In this, as in so many ways, the New Zealand wine industry mirrors that of Australia. In both countries there are monoliths that dominate, but that, luckily, also offer a quality range. There are boutique wineries (small wineries where most sales are at the cellar door) that provide some of the best wines and often high-profile public relations. Between the two is a group of wineries that offers some top-quality wines in relatively large quantities. There is cross-Tasman investment; one of the most famous Marlborough wineries, Cloudy Bay, is run jointly with Cape Mentelle of Margaret River Region in Western Australia.

Evolution of the wine regions

New Zealand's wine industry developed from the Auckland region southwards. Viticulture was begun in many areas more for social than climatic reasons, so vineyards have not necessarily been where one would expect. Many wineries that used to grow their grapes in Auckland now buy in from contract growers in more suitable growing areas. While some still process the grapes on the spot, others truck grapes from vineyard to winery in refrigerated lorries.

Many regions, even the more recently cultivated, receive high or fairly high rainfall, so the main problem in vineyards in many regions is the rampant growth of the vines. Severe pruning during the growing season and the training of vines so that the grapes receive maximum exposure have been developed. Such canopy-management techniques (see pp102–103) are copied elsewhere.

North Island

Two-thirds (in 1992) of grapes are grown on North Island still, despite its climatic unsuitability, but the trend is for producers to look south for their grapes, either by acquiring or planting vineyards, or buying in.

■ **Auckland** is New Zealand's oldest wine region, but the humid climate, with high autumnal rainfall that encourages mildew, is inhospitable to the vine. Soils tend to be heavy clays, so good drainage is essential.

Although the total acreage under vine has diminished — the area now produces less than 4% of New Zealand's grapes — there are still significant growing areas in Henderson, Kumeu, Huapai and on Waiheke Island in Auckland Harbour. Auckland is largely a red-wine region, with Cabernet Sauvignon the main variety. While many wineries are based here, they rely more and more on grapes from other areas.

■ **Waikato** and **the Bay of Plenty**, south of Auckland, are two distinct areas, but are relatively close to each other. This part of the country was settled later than others because of land wars in the 19th century between the Maori and the Europeans, but has long been associated with vinegrowing. At the end of the 19th century, an Italian viticulturalist, Romeo Bragato, was invited over from Australia by the New Zealand government to assess existing vineyards as well as the potential for new ones. He established an experimental vineyard here. The New Zealand government's wine research station used to be at Te Kauwhata.

Climatically, the risk is still from autumnal rainfall and the consequential loss of fruit through disease. Soils are mixed. The Waikato vineyards are near Hamilton and around the Firth of Thames, while the Bay of Plenty is further east. The most widely-grown varieties throughout

GRAPE VARIETIES AND WINE STYLES

Chardonnay   The most widely planted white grape variety in New Zealand, and found in every vinegrowing area, with Marlborough and Hawke's Bay producing the most familiar styles. Wines produced from Chardonnay are usually oak-aged, normally with the secondary malolactic fermentation, and they balance lovely acidity with ripe tastes.

Sauvignon Blanc   The second most-planted premium grape variety, making white wines with a characteristic, intensely herbaceous flavour. Marlborough is the most familiar source for these wines, with Hawke's Bay producing a more smoky, sometimes woody, fuller style.

Riesling   Only a little is planted in New Zealand, principally in South Island, but also in Hawke's Bay. It produces classically floral, dry white wines and intensely sweet, botrytized styles.

Müller-Thurgau   Though not a premium variety, this is second only to Chardonnay in terms of area planted. It produces medium-dry or sweet white wines, used in cheap blends or boxes. This grape is grown chiefly in Gisborne.

Other white varieties   Grapes grown in smaller quantities include Sémillon, Gewürztraminer, Chenin Blanc and Palomino (used for sherry-style wines).

Cabernet Sauvignon   The principal red variety in New Zealand. Chief growing areas are Auckland, especially Waiheke Island, now famous for its Bordeaux-blend wines; Hawke's Bay, which produces full-flavoured wines; and Marlborough, which is just beginning to establish a reputation for good Cabernet wines. This grape is increasingly blended with Merlot to produce better-balanced wines. Cabernet Sauvignon on its own produces a slightly herbaceous flavour.

Pinot Noir   While the Wairarapa/Martinborough area has produced most of New Zealand's well-known Pinot Noirs, other areas, notably Canterbury and Central Otago, have produced the occasional exceptional wine, which suggests there is great potential for this grape variety. At present, a lot of Pinot Noir is blended with Chardonnay to make bottle-fermented sparkling white wines, especially in Marlborough.

Merlot   Occasional straight Merlots from Hawke's Bay and Marlborough indicate that New Zealand is capable of producing world-class wines of this type. But, at present, the greater ripeness this grape normally achieves is used to bolster the sometimes-green Cabernet Sauvignon wines, thus producing classic Bordeaux-style blends.

are Sauvignon Blanc and Chenin, which have replaced Müller-Thurgau.

■ **Gisborne**, south-east of the Bay of Plenty, used to be the bulk wine-producing area of New Zealand. Much of the wine went into casks for bag-in-box products made by major producers located in other areas. As a result, there are only a few local wineries, among them New Zealand's only winery applying organic methods. Today most bulk wine is imported from Australia. Gisborne has rich, alluvial loam soils that give high yields. Rainfall does occur in autumn, but not usually enough to damage the crop. This is mainly a white-wine region, with Müller-Thurgau still the chief variety, followed by Chardonnay, Dr Hogg Muscat, Reichensteiner and Sauvignon Blanc.

■ **Hawke's Bay** — on the east coast of North Island between Napier and Hastings — has long been a pioneering area. The region is well suited to vine cultivation: it receives plenty of sunshine and low autumnal rainfall, so ripening is good. Spring frosts are a possibility, however. The best soils are well-drained gravel and shingle.

Chardonnay is the most widely planted grape, followed by Müller Thurgau, Cabernet Sauvignon and Sauvignon Blanc. The region produces some of New Zealand's finest red wines. Other areas buy grapes from Hawke's Bay, North Island's second-largest, premium-quality grape-growing area after Marlborough.

■ **Wairarapa**, at the southern tip of North Island, is still relatively small, but is internationally renowned for red wines made from Pinot Noir. A latecomer to the wine scene, the first modern vineyards being planted in 1978, this is New Zealand's most fashionable "new" wine region. Some white varieties, including Chardonnay, Sauvignon Blanc and Riesling, are also grown.

The heart of Wairarapa is the town of Martinborough, which lies in the centre of a small plateau called

Gibbston Valley Vineyard in Central Otago in the cool south of South Island.

the Martinborough Terraces. This area is in the rain shadow of the Tararua Mountains, so annual rainfall is low. The only problem is wind, which necessitates the planting of windbreaks. The best soils are the well-drained, gravelly silt loams around Martinborough.

South Island
Although originally planted at the same time as North Island, most vineyards fell into disuse, and only during the 1970s did winemakers appreciate the potential here.

■ **Nelson**, on the north coast, is a small grape-growing region, though vine cultivation dates from the 1860s. It is the warmest part of the island, with long hours of sunshine, although there is a risk of autumnal rains and spring frosts. Chardonnay and Riesling are the main grapes.

■ **Marlborough**, south-east of Nelson, on the flat, wide Wairau Plains, is now the largest grape-growing area of New Zealand, with 2,070ha (5,110 acres) achieved since 1973 when Montana, the largest wine group in the country, planted the first vines. This is one of the driest and sunniest parts of the whole country, although

spring frosts are possible. The slow ripening conditions suit white varieties — Müller-Thurgau, Sauvignon Blanc, Chardonnay and Riesling. Cabernet Sauvignon is the main red variety, but its wines are strongly herbaceous as a result of lack of sun. Several Auckland wineries buy grapes from Marlborough, or have wine made here. Most vineyards are on well-drained, alluvial soils.

■ **Canterbury-Christchurch** French settlers planted vines in this area in 1840, but current interest in the region dates from the early 1970s. There is still much confusion about which style of wine producers should concentrate on in an area that is certainly on the cool side. Low rainfall and long autumns with warm days and cool nights are highly suitable for viticulture, despite regular spring frosts. Soils are silt loams overlying river gravel.

■ **Central Otago**, further south, is the country's smallest grape-growing area. Pinot Noir, Gewürztraminer and other white grape varieties do particularly well in this climate. The growing season is short, but autumns are very sunny and dry. □

PRODUCERS

Four-fifths of grapes used in the New Zealand wine industry are supplied by contract growers and not grown by winemakers, hence the relative importance of where the grapes are grown in the list below. Even the smallest wineries are equipped with the latest wine technology and are characterized by self-sufficiency and the enthusiasm of a relatively young industry.

NORTH ISLAND

The majority of the longest-established wineries are based in North Island.

Ata Rangi

A small but top-quality vineyard in Wairarapa, producing full-flavoured Pinot Noir typical of the Martinborough style, and a red blend of Cabernet Sauvignon/Merlot/Syrah called Célèbre.

Babich Wines

One of the many wineries founded by Dalmatians, and still owned by the Babich family. They have 50ha (124 acres) of vines in Henderson, north of Auckland, and they buy in grapes as well. Irongate, from Hawke's Bay, is the top range: it includes a Chardonnay and a Cabernet/Merlot blend. A Sauvignon Blanc comes from Marlborough, and a Sémillon/Chardonnay blend from Gisborne.

Brookfield

Peter Robinson owns a 3,5ha (8,5 acre) vineyard in Hawke's Bay and buys the remaining grapes in the region. His two main wines are a Chardonnay and a Cabernet/Merlot blend.

Collard Brothers

Collards is one of the few producers to make successful Chenin Blanc whites. It also makes Chardonnays from all four of New Zealand's major viticultural areas: Auckland, Gisborne, Hawke's Bay and Marlborough. Collards has 40ha (100 acres) of vines at its base in Henderson.

Coopers Creek Wines

This attractive winery in Huapai, north of Auckland, produces a wide range of varietal wines. The most famous is probably Swamp Reserve Chardonnay, made from local fruit. A Chardonnay from Parker's Vineyard in Gisborne was added in 1992. Coopers Red is based on Pinot Noir, and there are plans for a sparkling wine from the same grape.

Corbans Wines

The second-largest wine company in New Zealand, Corbans makes a range of wines from three-litre boxes to fine estate wines. The group has wineries in Te Kauwhata, Hawke's Bay, Gisborne and Marlborough. The finest wines are the Stoneleigh Vineyard wines from Marlborough — Chardonnay, Sauvignon Blanc and, more recently, reds such as Malbec. Rhine Rieslings have long been a speciality (Corbans label). The Cooks label is reserved for wines from Hawke's Bay.

Delegat's Wine Estate

Delegat's, a family-owned winery in Henderson, has rationalized a diffuse product range. From Hawke's Bay comes an inexpensive varietal range as well as the superior Proprietor's Reserve wines. Chardonnay and Sauvignon Blanc are made from Marlborough fruit and released under the Oyster Bay label.

De Redcliffe Estates

This small boutique winery is part of a resort complex in the Waikato region. From 14ha (35 acres) supplying half the estate's needs, and grapes bought in from the Marlborough region, De Redcliffe produces a varied range, from a full-flavoured Marlborough Rhine Riesling and typically herbaceous Marlborough Sauvignon Blanc to seriously wooded Sémillon whites. From Hawke's Bay come a toasty, oatmealy Chardonnay, and a creditable Pinot Noir.

Dry River Wines

Neil McCallum has diverted this small vineyard away from mainstream Wairarapa styles. Although he makes Pinot Noir, he devotes more time to aromatic white varieties such as Riesling, Gewürztraminer and Pinot Gris. He is particularly successful with Gewürztraminer in a dry style, and Pinot Gris, from which he extracts all the dry peppery flavours a white wine like this would exhibit in Alsace.

Esk Valley Estate

The turnaround at this Hawke's Bay winery since it was purchased in 1987 by Villa Maria (qv) has been remarkable. It now specializes in fine wines, following in the Villa Maria tradition of good Cabernet/Merlot blends. Sauvignon Blanc and Chardonnay are also good.

Goldwater Estate

Waiheke Island made its name with Goldwater's Bordeaux-style wine. This Cabernet Sauvignon/Cabernet Franc/Merlot blend needs some maturation, but is always full of dusty, sweet fruit. A Dalimore Vineyard Chardonnay and a barrel-matured Sauvignon Blanc Fumé are also produced here.

Kumeu River Wines

Styles here have evolved from fortified wines to what is now unashamedly French, with honeyed Chardonnays, barrel-fermented Sauvignon Blanc, and a classic Bordeaux-blend red of 40% Cabernet Sauvignon, 40% Cabernet Franc and 20% Merlot. The winery, owned by the Brajkovich family, still uses Auckland grapes.

Lincoln Vineyards

Another Dalmatian-founded winery that has moved from fortified to table wines. The Fredatovich family's wines include a Chardonnay from the Parklands Vineyard in Brighams Creek, Chenin Blanc, and Cabernet Sauvignon/Merlot reds from Auckland and Hawke's Bay.

Martinborough Vineyard

Pinot Noir and the Martinborough Vineyard are inextricably linked in wine culture. It is less than ten years since the first vintage of this wine — considered by many people to be the best Pinot Noir outside France. Chardonnay, Sauvignon Blanc and Gewürztraminer are the other main wines produced.

Matawhero

This winery in Gisborne produces, among others, a Chardonnay, a Gewürztraminer, a Cabernet/Merlot blend, a Pinot Noir and a Shiraz. The owner, Denis Irwin, uses only natural yeast.

Matua Valley Wines

One of the most innovative wineries, Matua Valley produces a large range of varietals at its Waimauku winery, north of Auckland, including M (one of New Zealand's finest sparkling wines) made from 70% Pinot Noir, 30% Chardonnay. Wines sourced from Marlborough and released under the Shingle Peak label include an award-winning Sauvignon Blanc, Riesling and Chardonnay. Top-of-the-range Ararimu wines include Cabernet Sauvignon and Chardonnay.

The Millton Vineyard

This reputed winery is in Gisborne, where the Millton family produce a highly regarded, barrel-fermented Chardonnay and a botrytized Riesling, plus a Loire-like Chenin Blanc. The biodynamic system of cultivation uses plants, not chemicals, to repel pests and disease.

Mission Vineyards

Now almost 150 years old, Mission in Hawke's Bay is owned by a religious order and produces a huge range of good, inexpensive varietals. An indication of new quality standards comes from the St Peter Chanel Vineyard Reserve Chardonnay, which has an excellent intensity and flavour.

Montana Wines

The country's largest wine group and one of the most innovative, Montana was the first to plant Sauvignon Blanc in Marlborough. A top-quality, bottle-fermented sparkling white wine, Deutz Marlborough Cuvée (a joint venture with Champagne Deutz of France), is made from Marlborough fruit. Another joint venture with Penfolds aims at improving the red wines. Montana also has recently acquired vineyards in Hawke's Bay (Church Road labelled wines). It produces a large range of affordable vines, some of which are highly popular: Wohnsiedler, Blenheimer, Chablisse and Chardon. It has wineries in Gisborne, Hawke's Bay, Marlborough and Auckland.

Morton Estate Winery

This Bay of Plenty winery has earned a serious reputation, especially for its Chardonnay. Winemaker John Hancock uses Riverview Vineyard fruit (from Hawke's Bay) for the top-quality, award-winning Black Label Chardonnay. The Cabernet/Merlot blend is a solid, rich red, and there are two Pinot Noirs and three bottle-fermented sparkling wines in the range. The company has expanded into the Marlborough region.

Ngatarawa Wines

Alwyn Corban runs this 15-ha (37-acre) Hawke's Bay vineyard, using organic methods. The Ngatarawa range offers Glazebrook Cabernet/Merlot, Alwyn Chardonnay and a botrytized Riesling.

Nobilo Vintners

This is one of the larger wineries, owned by the Nobilo family. Grapes come from Gisborne, Hawke's Bay and Marlborough, as well as the winery's vineyards. While its largest production is of Chardonnay, Nobilo makes a full range, including one of the few wines from Pinotage (a South African red variety) to be produced in New Zealand.

Palliser Estate

Palliser is one of the newest arrivals in Wairarapa (first vintage in 1989), and one of the largest, with 30ha (74 acres) under vine and more planned. The best wine is a Pinot Noir.

C J Pask Winery

Chris Pask has 35ha (86 acres) of vines in Hawke's Bay and, with award-winning wine-maker Kate Radburnd, produces Chardonnay, Sauvignon Blanc and a Cabernet/Merlot blend as well as the less expensive Roy's Hill range.

Selaks Wines

With grapes from 45ha (111 acres) by the winery in Kumeu (Auckland), their own vineyards in Marlborough, and from Gisborne and Hawke's Bay, Selaks' top-of-the-range Founder's label includes an oak-aged Sauvignon Blanc, a Chardonnay, Cabernet Sauvignon and Mate I, a sparkling white wine.

Stonyridge Vineyard

The best wine from this red-only estate is Larose, a Bordeaux-style blend of Cabernet Sauvignon, Merlot, Cabernet Franc and Malbec, regarded by many as New Zealand's finest wine in this style.

Te Kairanga Vineyard

An ambitious project of 32ha (79 acres) in Wairarapa, Te Kairanga produces fruity Pinot Noir, Cabernet Sauvignon, a fresh, unoaked Chardonnay as well as a barrel-fermented Reserve Chardonnay, a barrel-fermented Sauvignon Blanc and a light red called Nouveau Rouge, a blend of Pinot Noir, Cabernet Sauvignon and Durif (California's Petite Sirah).

Te Mata

See profile.

Vidal Wine Producers

Founded in 1905, this Hawke's Bay winery is now part of the Villa Maria group (*qv*). The Reserve Cabernet Sauvignon/Merlot is a big, bold, but always elegant wine. The Reserve Cabernet Sauvignon is also good: both benefit from careful wood

———— TE MATA ESTATE ————

Te Mata is the most famous winery in Hawke's Bay, and the oldest in the country, producing New Zealand's most prestigious wines. There were vines here in 1892, but after the depression of the 1930s the vineyard declined: only in 1974, when the winery was purchased by John Buck and Michael Morris, did its fortunes revive. The recently restored white-plastered winery and homestead are striking examples of modern architecture. Top wines from this estate are the lavishly fruit-filled Coleraine Cabernet Sauvignon/Merlot and the rich Elston Chardonnay, two single-vineyard wines. There is also Awatea, a Cabernet Sauvignon/Merlot blend, a less expensive Te Mata Cabernet/Merlot, Castle Hill Sauvignon Blanc and good-value rosé and dry white blends.

maturation. Reserve Chardonnay has also been judged highly. The Private Bin label is less expensive.

Villa Maria Estate

This is New Zealand's third-largest producer. George Fistonich is behind the success of the group's red wines. There are Reserve and Private Bin ranges, plus the Cellar Selection, produced with grapes from Hawke's Bay and Marlborough, including Cabernet Sauvignon, Cabernet/Merlot blends and Shiraz. Whites wines include Chardonnay, botrytized Riesling, Sauvignon Blanc and Gewürztraminer.

Waimarama Estate

John Loughlin produces top-quality, Bordeaux-style reds at this Hawke's Bay winery. His first releases in 1991 were a Cabernet Sauvignon/Merlot blend and a straight Cabernet Sauvignon.

SOUTH ISLAND

Winemakers have only truly appreciated the potential of South Island's growing conditions since the 1970s.

Cellier Le Brun

Daniel Le Brun comes from a long line of French champagne producers. Although his Marlborough winery has been sold, he continues to produce a series of great wines, the best of which are the vintage-dated *cuvée*, a non-vintage Blanc de Blancs and a rosé.

Chard Farm

This 12-ha (30-acre) vineyard on a hill slope in Central Otago specializes in Chardonnay and Pinot Noir: Riesling is also planted.

CLOUDY BAY

Cloudy Bay's Sauvignon Blanc made New Zealand's great reputation for this wine. With its full, rich but always herbaceous style, the wine has captured the essence of cool-climate winemaking that is New Zealand's hallmark, and that caught the imagination of the wine world in the late 1980s. Under the direction of winemaker Kevin Judd, it is one of the very best of its kind. Also excellent is the Chardonnay, a wine that ages well and again shows the right balance of wood, fruit and acidity that is Marlborough's style. Newer wines from this winery, with its 32-ha/79-acre vineyard (now owned by Veuve Clicquot Champagne and part of Cape Mentelle in Western Australia) are reds — a Cabernet Sauvignon/Merlot and a Pinot Noir — and a sparkling wine, Pelorus.

Cloudy Bay Vineyards

See profile.

Gibbston Valley Vineyards

These vineyards by the Kawarau River were first planted in 1981. They produce a range of wines — while still deciding what works best in the short growing season and continental climate of Central Otago — including Riesling, Müller-Thurgau, Gewürztraminer, Pinot Gris, Sauvignon Blanc, Chardonnay and Pinot Noir.

Giesen Wine Estate

Canterbury's largest wine estate (20ha/49 acres) was founded by the Giesen brothers in 1984. They make exciting, botrytized, late-harvest Rieslings, and good Chardonnay and Sauvignon Blanc.

Grove Mill Wine Company

Grove Mill has rapidly made its mark in Marlborough, particularly with the buttery Landsdowne Chardonnay. Other wines include Gewürztraminer, Sauvignon Blanc and a fruity Cabernet Sauvignon.

Hunter's Wines

Sauvignon Blanc is the star here: the version not matured in oak respects the traditional, piercing, fruit-flavoured Marlborough style. The 18ha (45 acres) vineyard also produces a barrel-fermented Chardonnay in a soft, exotic style; a soft, slightly sweet Gewürztraminer; and a peppery Cabernet Sauvignon.

Jackson Estate

This is a brand new winery in Marlborough, although the vineyard has been supplying local wineries since 1987. The Stitchbury family released their first vintage in 1991, and the Sauvignon Blanc made an immediate sensation, rivalling that of Cloudy Bay (*qv*).

Neudorf Vineyards

The Finns farm this small estate of 5ha (12 acres) in Nelson, producing a rich Chardonnay, Sauvignon Blanc, Riesling and Pinot Noir.

Omihi Hills

This winery aims at producing high quality wines from Pinot Noir and Chardonnay from its 6,5ha (16 acres) vineyard north of Canterbury. Its first important release goes back to 1992.

Rippon Vineyard

Rippon released its first wines in 1989, and has rapidly established a reputation, particularly for Pinot Noir, Sauvignon Blanc and Chardonnay.

St Helena Wine Estate

From a high point in 1982, with a Pinot Noir that established Canterbury as a serious wine region, St Helena has had many ups and downs. Now on a more even keel, it also produces Chardonnay, Pinot Blanc and Pinot Gris.

Seifried Estate/Redwood Valley Estate

This is the largest estate in Nelson, with 40ha (100 acres) of vines owned by Hermann Seifried. A botrytized Riesling and a dry Riesling are among the best wines.

Vavasour Wines

In developing vineyards away from the centre of the Marlborough region (in the Awatere Valley), Peter Vavasour took a risk, but it has paid off. His Cabernet Sauvignon is considered to be one of the best South Island reds, and a rival to Hawke's Bay. Good Chardonnay and Sauvignon Blanc are also produced.

Waipara Springs Wine Co

Award-winning Chardonnay, Pinot Noir and Sauvignon Blanc are produced in this newly established winery in North Canterbury.

SOUTH AFRICA

—

SINCE THE POLITICAL OPENING UP OF THE COUNTRY,

SOUTH AFRICA'S WINE INDUSTRY HAS BEEN UNDERGOING

RADICAL CHANGES AND IS ON ITS WAY

TO BECOME A LEADING EXPORTER OF QUALITY WINES.

—

Soon after Jan van Riebeeck established the Dutch East India Company's fuelling station at the Cape of Good Hope in 1652, he sent to Europe for vine cuttings in the belief that sailors would suffer less from scurvy if they drank wine. On 2 February 1659 he wrote in his diary: "Today, praise be to God, wine was pressed from Cape grapes for the first time". Simon van der Stel, van Riebeeck's successor as governor and a wine enthusiast, planted vineyards at Constantia with the help of French Huguenot refugees skilled in viticulture and winemaking. The industry then went from strength to strength.

After wine duties between Britain and France were drastically cut in 1861, the next half-century's triple disasters of phylloxera (1886), the consequent replanting and overproduction despite the lack of a market, and the Anglo-Boer War (1899-1902), saw the industry hit by chaos and hardship.

This tendency to overproduce at the beginning of the 20th century was accentuated by the fact that, as luck would have it, the vineyards did in fact recover fairly quickly from the terrible disease and attracted producers who had been affected by the collapse of the ostrich feather market. These farmers, many in number, sold their grapes to co-operatives and powerful merchants had a hold on prices. This resulted in the creation in 1918, on the farmers' initiative, of the Ko-operatieve Wijn-bouwers Vereniging (KWV), a government-backed cooperative set up to administer and control legislation, reduce production (by means of a quota system), create marketable products and to stimulate demand. For many years the KWV maintained the full powers bestowed upon it by the state in all wine matters, from production to marketing, including the oenological sector, planting rights and wine industry statistics.

Inevitably, isolation led to inertia and failure to keep up with world trends, in particular in grape varieties. Strict quarantine laws kept Chardonnay out for decades. The role of the KWV is now altering. It still acts as administrator for the industry, but independently of government, but it no longer controls production with quotas, thus allowing growers to plant vineyards and varieties at will and to compete in a free market. KWV also functions as a wine company, operating vineyards, making wine and selling it on domestic and international markets. In 1996, the huge cooperative began restructuring to enable it to stand its ground in a highly competitive international market. It was turned into a group of private companies in 1997, the members themselves becoming the shareholders.

Today South Africa's winemakers and growers are embracing the trends and techniques of the international wine world. Winemaking has changed dramatically over the past few decades, beginning in the 1960s when Cape winemakers introduced cold-fermentation techniques in order to make fresh, aromatic wines in the hot climate. Quality-conscious producers are experimenting with French oak barrels for maturing wines. The standard of harvest care, cellar treatment and general hygiene has also improved.

As for the vineyards, the wine industry put in place a virus detection and equipment certification programme back in the 1960s, following serious problems with infection in the first half of the 20th century. In 1986, a Vine Improvement Board, with representation from independent producers, the KWV, merchants and nurserymen, was set up in order to put the best certified plants on the market. However the problems of virus and disease to which the South African vineyards had so often fallen victim, in particular leaf roll, persisted.

Many winemakers are travelling extensively to gain experience, particularly in handling the classic European grape varieties now being widely planted, or working a vintage in Europe or California. Some are taking oenology degrees in France, Germany, Australia or New Zealand. All are aware of commercial necessity — that they must make wine styles the consumer demands.

WINE REGIONS OF SOUTH AFRICA

The Wine of Origin Scheme dates back to 1973. Four major regions are sub-divided into districts, which are in turn sub-divided into wards: Coastal Region with the districts of Paarl, Stellenbosch, Swartland and Tulbagh; Breede River Valley with the districts of Robertson, Worcester and Swellendam; Klein Karoo with the single district and ward of Calitzdorp; and Olifants River. Outside these regions, there are another three districts: Overberg, Piketberg and Douglas.

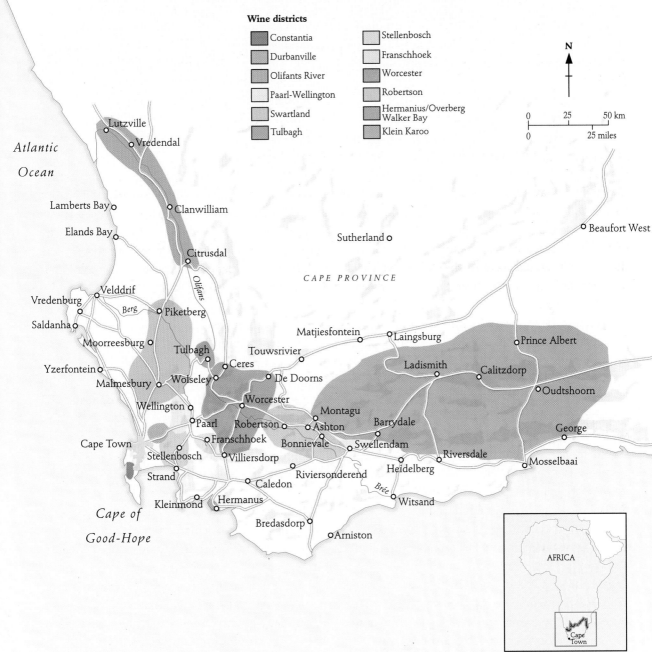

Wine districts

- Constantia
- Durbanville
- Olifants River
- Paarl-Wellington
- Swartland
- Tulbagh
- Stellenbosch
- Franschhoek
- Worcester
- Robertson
- Hermanius/Overberg Walker Bay
- Klein Karoo

Vineyards near Stellenbosch are harvested in March and April: six months earlier than in the northern hemisphere.

Opening up to the world

After the abolition of Apartheid in 1991, then the election of Nelson Mandela in 1994, South Africa's wine industry was finally able to open itself out to the world and to establish business relationships with nations which had until then been boycotting the country. The wine industry, which had been operating a policy of economic self-sufficiency, had to review the way it worked, especially since it was lagging well behind, being isolated at the very moment when, in the 1980s, technical progress and wine-making techniques in the rest of the world had taken a huge leap forward. One of the main changes involved moving away from brandy production, which had dominated until then, and back to growing grapes for wine production. The farmers, previously concentrating on yields, had to change their philosophy and turn their minds to quality. This involved converting part of the vineyards from varieties used for bulk production and brandy over to the so-called noble varieties, such as Chardonnay, Sauvignon, Cabernet Sauvignon, Merlot, Syrah and Pinotage, which were much more likely to appeal to international tastes. In 1997 these varieties only accounted for 19% of all vines planted, a huge majority of vines were still Chenin Blanc, an all-purpose variety which could produce dry white wines, sweet white wines and brandy.

In 1997 the noble varieties gradually took over from the Chenin Blanc (32% in 1987, 28.5% in 1997). White grape varieties being predominant, there is still very little land under red varieties and the lack of quality red wines is keenly felt. Great wines are produced, but in very small quantities and often from the same areas: Constantia, Simonsberg and Helderberg. The South African wine industry is in some ways following international trends: it is undergoing complete change and is at the stage of looking for interesting terroirs for growing quality grapes. Between 1995 and 1996 exports grew by 35% from 8.2 million to 11.1 million 12 bottle cases, generating a revenue of 550 million Rand. In 1990 they were 855,000 cases, representing a leap of 1,300% in the space of seven years. In 1999 they totalled 129,193,314 litres compared to 118,407,948 in 1998: the growth trend continues.

Since the market opened up and quotas are no longer on the agenda, export, formerly the exclusive domain of the KWV, has become the producers' sweetheart. The South African Wine and Spirit Exporters' Association has gone from five members in 1990 to 160 in 1997 and 350 in 2000. Most South African wines are sold in the United Kingdom and the Benelux countries but the South Africans are counting more and more on markets such as Scandinavia, Japan, Canada and the United States. Between 1998 and 1999, white wine sales increased by 29% in the United Kingdom (South Africa's largest market accounting for 40% of export sales), 42% in the Netherlands and 41% in the United

States. In 1999, consumption of South African wines in Scandinavia was, at around 7.5 million litres, just as high as in Germany.

Wines for export are carefully monitored by the Nietvoorbij Wine and Spirit Board, where they are analysed and tasted. Each bottle is awarded an official seal which guarantees its origin, vintage and grape variety.

Some cooperatives, to shed their "coop" image, are keen to become privately-owned companies. Numerous producers have launched an attack on the huge international market. These include winemakers who were once employees but, encouraged by the export boom, decided to set up their own operation and sell their own wine. They do not even own their own vines or winery. They buy in the grapes and rent out a building — the raw materials and casks being the only investments required — and sell their wines in the higher price ranges. This is the origin of the so-called garage wines (*cuvées* of a very high quality produced in extremely limited quantities): Etienne Le Riche, Nico Vermeulen, Signal Hill, Kleinvallei or even David Trafford. The new political situation, although still very shaky, has attracted Swiss, German, Belgian, Italian, American and also French investors.

Another sign of the changes: black empowerment is beginning to creep into the vineyards. The involvement of black or half-caste workers is giving rise to joint ventures between them and estate owners and more and more money is being allocated to their education. We are also starting to see the first non-white winemakers but, as we enter this new century, this is still in the early stages...

Much National Enthusiasm

Strongly influenced by the Anglo-Saxons, the South African consumer in the Cape region very quickly got involved in the game. He is proud of his wines and, like the English, keen to know all there is to know about wines and winemaking. He will do everything in his power to ensure you cannot catch him out. Tasting clubs of all types, formal and informal, are on the increase, including commercial clubs, student clubs and clubs where budding winemakers get together to exchange their questions and knowledge in wine matters. Finally there are clubs of enthusiasts who meet at each other's houses in turn where they hold a blind tasting of a range of wines and attempt to guess the grape variety, the year, the estate and the winemaker behind each sample tasted. In actual fact, the winemaker plays such an important part in the eyes of the South African consumer that, each year, an inter-club blending competition is held. The idea is to put together the best blend from given varieties, as the winemaker himself would do.

The Cape Wine Academy is another sign of how seriously wine is taken here. Set up in 1979 by players in the winemaking industry to encourage sensible consumption, more than five thousand pupils throughout the country attend this academy each year. Full courses are on offer, endorsed by exams. The highest grade is the Cape Wine Master which is modelled on the British Master of Wine qualification.

A sign that the country is opening up, each region has a very well established, well documented wine route and visitors are given a warm welcome and guided tour around most of the wineries. At lunchtime they can relax in the magnificent grounds with a picnic basket and a glass of wine made on the premises.

South African producers hold regular wine fairs and competitions as part of their efforts to establish themselves in an increasingly demanding international wine market. They also keep a close watch on what is happening in the New World countries such as Australia, New Zealand and Chile, where marketing and brand names are strong.

Grape varieties and wine styles

Cape wines were well-known in Europe in the 19th century, most notably the sweet Constantia wine (made from Muscat grapes) requested by the exiled Napoleon and enjoyed by Russia's tsars. Fortified wines and liqueurs are also part of South Africa's heritage.

South Africa is traditionally a white-wine producing country, the main varieties being Steen, the local name for Chenin Blanc, with 23.8% of all plantings; Hanepoot (Muscat of Alexandria), 4.3%; Colombard, 11.2%; Sauvignon Blanc, 5%; and Cape Riesling (originally Crouchen Blanc from south-west France), 2.7%. Plantings of Chardonnay (5.7%) are currently rising fast.

Chenin Blanc is used for many wine styles, from fresh, dry, cold-fermented whites to medium-dry, sweet and botrytized wines.

The main red grape varieties are: Cinsaut, with 3.6% of plantings; Cabernet Sauvignon, 6.7%; and Pinotage (a grape created in 1926 by crossing Cinsaut with Pinot Noir), 5.5%. Shiraz (Syrah), Merlot, Cabernet Franc and Pinot Noir are also becoming ever more popular. It was Dr I A Perold of the KWV who originally had the idea to cross the Pinot Noir with the Cinsaut and this was then developed by Professor C J Theron. The first bottle was not actually sold until 36 years later, in 1961, by the Stellenbosch Farmers' Winery. There are five other crossed varieties, all white, called Chenel, Weldra, Colomino, Grachen and Follet but only the Pinotage has found a place alongside international grape varieties and in actual fact this variety alone portrays the image of South African wine.

As in America and Australia, wines are generally sold under the name of a grape variety (known here as a cultivar), with the producer's name prominent on the label.

Climate and soil

Although the life-cycle of a vineyard here is very much comparable to one in Europe, being on the Southern hemisphere, the year is completely inverted: when grapes are being harvested in France, the vines in South Africa are only just starting to come to life after lying dormant for the whole winter. January marks the start of summer when early varieties begin to ripen and harvest is in full swing between February and April.

The south-western Cape has a cooler climate than its position 35° south of the equator would suggest. The Atlantic and Indian oceans and the cold Benguela current flow north up the coast from Antarctica, acting as a moderating influence, so the climate is generally Mediterranean. Annual rainfall, which varies from 100mm (4 inches) inland to 1,000mm (39 inches) around the coast, falls mainly between May and August. Summers are generally warm, though they can be quite hot in central areas, while winters are mild with little frost. Grapes in some of the Cape's hotter areas are likely to suffer from heat stress or ripen too quickly, but if the correct amount of water is available at the correct time, any potential problem can be averted. Irrigation is vital and legitimate.

Years of research and experimentation have established the suitability of different vineyard micro-climates for specific grape varieties from South Africa's rich viticultural heritage (Steen, Hanepoot, Shiraz). Work is still being done on more recently imported varieties.

Similarly, experimentation is taking place, as in several New World countries, to discover the best soils, sites and aspects. There are great variations between soils, not just within the south-western Cape but also between different vineyards in the same region. Generally, soils on the coastal plains range from Table Mountain sandstone in the west to granite compounds in the east. Shales predominate in the Karoo while in the valleys, where most of the vineyards are situated, the hillsides have stony soils and the floors have sand and gravel.

Furthermore, South Africa is making every effort to take environmental issues into account in their winemaking developments. This trend is supported by laws, research at the Nietvoorbij Vine and Wine Centre and by the implementation of a 2000 programme by the Wine and Spirit Board. The whole wine industry, from cooperatives to private producers, is to be involved.

Wine regions

Worcester and Paarl have the largest area under vines (16.5%), followed by Stellenbosch (15.3%), Orange River (14.7%), Robertson (11.7%), Olifants River (8.7%) and Klein Karoo (3.1%). As regards production, Worcester is also in the lead (22.7%), then Robertson (15.6%), Paarl (14.5%), Olifants River (14.1%), Stellenbosch (12.4%), Orange River (8.5%) and Klein Karoo (3.9%).

In 1973, with the introduction of the Wine of Origin system (WO), South Africa's wine lands were divided into a series of official regions, districts, wards and estates, in decreasing order of size. The area of most concentrated wine production, within a 50-80km (30-50 mile) radius of Cape Town, has two main regions: Coastal and Breede River Valley. The Boberg Region appellation is used for fortified wines from parts of the Coastal Region (see p569). There are eight districts that lie outside the main regions. A wine may carry the more specific appellation of a ward (a sub-district) if it is made from grapes grown entirely within that ward.

The WO system emphasizes grape variety — 75% minimum if a single variety is named on the label, or 85% if the wine is to be exported — rather than controlling basic quality factors, such as yield.

If the vintage appears on the bottle, at least 75% of the bottle contents are from that year (85% if the wine is for export to the European Union). Furthermore, the vintage may only appear on the label if the wine has been certified by the Wine & Spirit Board.

Each bottle sold has a lot number to ensure traceability — the manufacturing process can be traced right back to the grape pressing stage.

The wine industry

There are 4,515 growers cultivating 104,179ha (257,500 acres) of vines throughout the south-western Cape. Three main types of producer exist: cooperatives, private producers and estate wineries. Many of the 69 cooperatives can now offer good quality and value for money. Private producers, numbering 337, include prestigious companies such as Bellingham, Distillers Corporation and Stellenbosch Farmers' Winery (who merged in December 2001 to form a company called Distell). These companies make wine from grapes grown in their own vineyards, as well as buying in grapes and wine and blending wine under brand names. There are 92 estate wineries, which use only grapes grown on their own or nearby land.

South Africa ranks as the world's seventh-largest producer, with just over 3% of total world production. In 1999, 5,959,075 hectolitres were produced. Annual consumption is 9.5 litres per head. Historically, most wines were sold through domestic wholesalers but with the lifting of sanctions and more receptive foreign markets, an increasing amount is now exported. □

REGIONS AND PRODUCERS

South Africa's main wine-producing areas are to the south-west of Cape Town. Further north are several isolated wine lands along the Orange River. The main producers are listed by Wine of Origin (WO) zone.

COASTAL REGION WO
This is the largest appellation, comprising six of the Cape's best-known areas: Constantia, Durbanville, Stellenbosch, Paarl, Swartland and Tulbagh.

Constantia District WO
Constantia has a wealth of history as this is where Simon van der Stel planted his own vines in the 17th century. The vineyards, situated south-east of the Cape Peninsula, enjoy a Mediterranean-style climate — irrigation is unnecessary — and benefit from the mountain's shade in the afternoon and from cool sea breezes. Constantia has mainly Chardonnay, Sauvignon Blanc and Riesling for white wines, Cabernet Sauvignon and Shiraz for reds. The Sauvignon Blanc is rich and powerful.

Main producers include Buitenverwachting (with an elegant Chardonnay), Groot Constantia and Klein Constantia (notable for Vin de Constance, a sweet Muscat reviving the tradition of Constantia wine, as well as Chardonnay and Sauvignon Blanc).

Durbanville District WO
Situated on the granite-based slopes of the Dorstberg Mountains among Cape Town's northern suburbs, four wine estates remain, concentrating on reds, particularly Pinotage and Shiraz.

Paarl District WO
Paarl (Afrikaans for "pearl"), 50km (30 miles) north-east of Cape Town, is a major wine district, with 19.5% of South Africa's vineyards, some of its best producers and innovative cooperatives. It is also the centre of KWV's international activities and the venue for the annual Nederburg wine auction.

The region lies on exactly the same latitude in the Southern Hemisphere as the Jerez vineyards in Spain in the Northern Hemisphere. The climate is typically Mediterranean with hot, dry summers and wet winters. Irrigation is necessary only in very dry years. Soils vary from sandstone in the fertile Berg Valley, granite around Paarl itself and weathered slate in Malmesbury in the north-east. Although mainly a white-wine district, with good Chenin Blanc, Sauvignon Blanc and Chardonnay, higher-altitude vineyards are well suited to the production of fine red wines: among the most successful are Cabernet Sauvignon and Pinotage. A new wine festival is held each year on Paarl mountain or at one of the estates.

Paarl embraces the ward of Franschhoek WO ("French Corner" — settled by Huguenots). The area has retained its French character, reflected in the oaked wines and the country's best Cap Classique (traditional-method) sparkling wine made at Clos Cabrière.

There are many good producers, including Fairview, Glen Carlou, Simonsvlei, Villiera and, in the Franschhoek ward, Bellingham, Boschendal, Cabrière, Chamonix, Dieu Donné, La Motte, La Provence and Mont Rochelle.

Stellenbosch District WO
The attractive town of Stellenbosch, whose university has a department of viticulture and oenology, has the greatest concentration of fine wine estates in South Africa, and 15.6% of the country's vineyards. It has three types of soil: Table Mountain sandstone in the west (favoured for white wines), alluvial soils around the Eerste River, and granite in the east (best for reds), where the ward of Simonsberg-Stellenbosch WO is situated in the mountain foothills.

Plantings include Cabernet Sauvignon, Cabernet Franc, Merlot and Shiraz. The Stellenbosch district is also the home of some of the best Pinotage wines (which mature earlier than the Cabernet). Many of the top wines are blended reds, often aged in oak barrels.

Top producers include Beyerskloof, Delheim, De Trafford, Kanonkop, Louisvale, Meerlust, Morgenhof, Mulderbosch, Neethlingshof (for Weisser Riesling Noble late-harvest), Overgaauw, Rustenberg, Rust-en-Vrede, Simonsig, Stellenzicht, Thelema, Vriesenhof, Warwick (Trilogy, a bordeaux-style blend).

Swartland District WO
Swartland has 12.9% of South Africa's vineyards, around the towns of Darling, Malmesbury and Riebeek. Irrigation is generally necessary. This area has traditionally been the source of high-quality fortified wines from varieties such as Hanepoot; robust, full-bodied reds from Cinsaut, Tinta Barocca, Pinotage and Shiraz and good, inexpensive whites from Riesling, Colombard, Bukettraube and Fernão Pires.

Good producers include Allesverloren (for port-style wines), Spicefoute and Swartland co-op.

Tulbagh District WO
Surrounded on three sides by the Winterhoek Mountains — which create a number of micro-climates — Tulbagh's vineyards are situated on the eastern border of Swartland. The climate is hot and relatively dry, making irrigation necessary for vineyards sited on the sandy valley floors, though less so for those planted on wetter hillsides.

The most famous producer is Twee Jongegezellen.

Boberg Region WO
This appellation is used only for fortified wines made in the districts of Paarl and Tulbagh.

BREEDE RIVER VALLEY REGION WO
This region covers the three districts of Worcester, Robertson and Swellendam, through which the Breede River runs, and Wolseley, currently not important for viticulture.

Worcester District WO
This district has around 20 highly efficient cooperatives making 22% of the country's wine, including some good whites from Riesling (Weisser Riesling), Sauvignon Blanc and Colombard, and dessert wines from white and red Muscadel. It is also South Africa's most important brandy-producing area. Worcester covers many of the Breede River's tributaries, each of which has a markedly different micro-climate. The Nuy co-op is a good producer.

Robertson District WO
This district's lime-rich soils are particularly suited to growing

grapes, and 12.3% of South Africa's vineyard is here. With mountains on its northern and southern borders and a hot, arid climate, viticulture became possible only when a large dam was constructed at the beginning of the 20th century. Today Robertson's estates and co-ops are the source of some of the Cape's most esteemed Chardonnay and Shiraz wines, as well as sparkling wines and traditional fortified dessert wines.

Top producers include Graham Beck Winery (sparkling wines), Bon Courage, De Wetshof, Rietvallei, Rooiberg cooperative and Weltevrede.

Swellendam District WO

An area where wine is produced in bulk by cooperatives.

OTHER DISTRICTS
Klein Karoo District WO

The region stretches from Montagu in the west to Oudtshoorn in the east. Its vineyards require irrigation and tend to be planted in or near river valleys. Chenin Blanc, the Cape's versatile grape variety with naturally high acidity, thrives here, making a range of styles from dry whites, to sweet and rosé wines. The fertile red shale-based Karoo soils and the deep, rich alluvium closer to the various rivers are better suited to Muscadel and other dessert wines, for which the area is well known. Most grapes are processed by co-ops. Boplaas produces excellent port-style wines.

Olifants River/ Olifantsrivier District WO

The region stretches in a broad belt north to south along the valley. Vines grow on sandstone or lime-rich loams. Summers can be hot and rainfall relatively low, but with careful canopy management to ensure that grapes are shaded by the vine's leaves, and with modern winemaking techniques, Olifants River is emerging as an important source of good, value-for-

money wine, especially from the Vredendal co-op.

Overberg District WO

Overberg, south of Paarl and Stellenbosch, is potentially one of the most exciting viticultural districts in South Africa. Pockets of vineyards nestle between large tracts of wheat, especially in the Walker Bay WO ward. These vineyards, which benefit from Atlantic breezes, have soils of weathered shales, ideal for cool-climate grapes: Chardonnay and Pinot Noir thrive here.

Top producers include Bouchard-Finlayson, Hamilton Russell and Vergelegen.

Piketberg District WO

This large flat district, between Swartland and Tulbagh to the south and Olifants River to the north, has very high summer temperatures and low rainfall: irrigation is common. Most of the wines are port-style reds made by co-ops. Investment in improved vineyard techniques has led to the emergence of easy-drinking, dry wines.

Other districts

Douglas and Andalusia are both WO areas around Kimberley in the centre of the country. Each has a single co-op. Benede-Oranje (Lower Orange) is a WO near Augrabies in the Orange River Valley, also in the centre. These districts produce mostly bulk, and some dessert wines.

ZIMBABWE

The only other southern African country to make wines of any note is the Republic of Zimbabwe.

Viticulture began in Zimbabwe when table grapes were planted in the 1940s. Twenty-five years later, wine grapes were planted, and commercial production reached its zenith in the early 1980s. There are now some 300ha (750 acres) under cultivation and wine production is shared between two large companies, African Distillers (140 ha/350 acres) and Cairns Winery (120 ha/ 300 acres); other producers sell on their grapes.

The climate is not really suited to viticulture. Very mild winters and hot summers do not help the vine produce good-quality fruit. Irrigation is essential, as is a programme to control the numerous pests. The soils are of poor quality and some of the plants, which were imported from South Africa, were virus-infected or from low-quality vines. With hard work, optimism and ingenuity, and the aid of modern technology, even these problems have been overcome. Zimbabwe produces over 6.6 million bottles of still and sparkling wine annually.

The main grape varieties are Cabernet Sauvignon, Cinsaut and Pinotage for red wines, Colombar(d), Steen (Chenin Blanc), Clairette Blanche and Hanepoot (Muscat of Alexandria) for white.

Over the last ten years Zimbabwe has planted noble grape varieties (Merlot, Pinot Noir, Sauvignon Blanc, Syrah and Chardonnay) in order to produce better quality wines and to export.

The political and economic

problems the country experienced in Spring 2000 did not spare the wine industry, which requires imported products, and have in particular put a stop to investment projects.

Producers
African Distillers (Afdis)

African Distillers Limited is Zimbabwe's largest wine and spirits company, founded in the 1940s. Alongside its own brands, African Distillers' portfolio includes brand names from shareholding companies (International Distillers & Vintners Ltd, Stellenbosch Farmers' Winery Ltd, etc). Its wine division, Stapleford Wines, owns three estates: Green Valley Vineyards, Bertrams Vineyards and Worringham Vineyards. It also buys in wines produced under the supervision of a company winemaker. A planting project is underway: in 1998 and 1999, 45,000 plants were imported from South Africa and planted in an area of almost 40 ha (100 acres) near Harare.

Cairns Winery

Cairns Winery, belonging to Zimbabwean investors, owns 120 ha (300 acres) of vines and produces 2 million litres: 75% white wines, of which 95% are dry and medium whites and 5% sparkling wines, and 25% reds. It also produces a Tawny port. In 1979 Cairns bought over the Mateppe Winery, founded in 1965, and created the Mukuyu Winery, which uses modern equipment and techniques. The vineyards are situated in the Ruzawi River Valley, south of Marondera. Over the last fifteen years, Cairns' Makuyu label has won many medals in Britain, South Africa and Canada.

REST OF THE WORLD

—

IN ENGLAND GROWERS STRUGGLE AGAINST COLD AND RAIN TO

MAKE MAINLY CRISP WHITE WINES;

IN INDIA, CHINA AND JAPAN, A STILL MODEST WINE INDUSTRY HAS

STARTED TO PRODUCE SOME FINE WINES.

—

ENGLAND AND WALES

As a wine importer, England has a long and illustrious history. As a producer of wine, its history is just as long, yet little known.

As in so many European countries, winemaking began with the Romans. However, the vines they brought from Italy were not ideally suited to the cold, and more wine was imported than produced in Britain. There is evidence of vineyards in Saxon times, from Cambridgeshire in the east to Gloucestershire in the west, and after the Norman Conquest in 1066 winemaking flourished on a modest scale for almost 500 years, in both aristocratic and monastic estates. The tradition lingered until this century, when World War I sounded the death knell for Britain's commercial vineyards.

The current revival of English winemaking began in a small way in the 1950s, when a handful of winemakers began to experiment to find vines suited to the cool, damp climate. While the cold is moderated by the proximity of the sea, waterlogged roots make poor wine: a well-drained site is vital. Spring frosts are a hazard that can seriously reduce yields, and the vines also need wind protection. The harvest takes place throughout October, timing being a problem: the grapes need to ripen for as long as possible, but must be picked before rain or frosts can rot the bunches.

This early research paved the way for serious commercial viticulture, which began in the early 1970s; ten years later there were 450ha (1,100 acres) of vines, and by 1994, over 1,000ha (2,500 acres). Today, nearly 500 well-established vineyards produce around 200,000 cases a year.

Grape varieties and wine styles
The majority of English wine is white, light, with a flowery aroma and good acidity; some wineries are

Winter in Denbies' vineyard, Surrey.

beginning to make sparkling and red wines. Most are drunk young, although some can age successfully for up to ten years in bottle.

REGIONS AND PRODUCERS

Grapes are grown for wine as far north as Yorkshire, but the climate confines most vineyards to the southern half of the country, where almost every county, from Cornwall in the west to Suffolk in the east, plus Wales and the Channel Islands, boasts a wine industry on some scale. The main concentration is in the south-east, in Kent, East Sussex and West Sussex. The average holding is 2–3ha (5–7.5 acres), but vineyards range from less than 0.5ha (1.2 acres) to about 25ha (62 acres).

England's largest wine estate by far is Denbies in Surrey, with more than 100ha (250 acres). Other producers on a serious scale include Adgestone (Isle of Wight), Barkham Manor (East Sussex), Biddenden (Kent), Breaky Bottom (East Sussex), Carr Taylor (East Sussex), Lamberhurst (Kent), Nutbourne Manor (West Sussex), Pilton Manor (Somerset), Tenterden (Kent), Thames Valley (Berkshire), Three Choirs (Gloucestershire), Wootton (Somerset).

German crossings such as Müller-Thurgau, Bacchus, Reichensteiner and Schönburger account for nearly half the vineyard area. The frost-resistant hybrid Seyval Blanc accounts for around 13% of plantings, but the industry is still young and rife with experimentation; more than 30 other varieties are recorded.

Plantings of red-wine varieties such as Pinot Noir, Triomphe d'Alsace, Dornfelder and Dunkelfelder remain small, although both red and rosé wine are made.

Wine laws
The most important distinction is between English wine and British wine. English (or Welsh) wine is made from grapes grown and freshly picked in UK vineyards. British wine is an industrial product made from concentrated, imported grape juice.

Most English wine is labelled "Table Wine" because of an EC rule that wine from hybrid grapes may not be described as quality wine — even though some of England's most successful bottles come from the white hybrid Seyval Blanc. However, the English Vineyards Association, the trade body that represents most commercial vineyards, has a gold Seal of Quality label, awarded to wines that pass a stringent analysis and tasting by a panel of Masters of Wine.

The official EC designation "English Vineyards Quality Wine" should soon appear on qualifying bottles, since the EC is defining the UK quality wine regions and revising its rules.

The name of the vineyard or the local winery that bottled the wine is usually prominent. The label may also bear a description, such as "dry white", or a named grape if it accounts for at least 85% of the contents. If two grapes are named, they may be used in any proportion, but with no other varieties in the blend. □

INDIA, CHINA, JAPAN

The making and drinking of wine has never really formed part of the culture of India and the countries of the Far East, although grapes have been grown, and wine produced, in zones where the climate permits. A few grapes of the *vitis vinifera* family are native to India and Japan, and many other species are found throughout this vast area — one of which, *vitis amurensis*, has been crossed with *vinifera* to produce China's hybrid Beichun grape.

INDIA

Wine has been known and made in India for 2,000 years, but it took the 16th-century Portuguese colonists to establish a wine industry with any continuity. Goa's Portuguese varieties are still producing wine, but there is a new wave of technically-competent winemaking producing conscious imitations of modern European wines with some success. European grape varieties such as Chardonnay, Ugni Blanc, Muscat, Pinot Noir, Merlot and Cabernet Sauvignon are now being planted with increasing seriousness.

India has around 43,000ha (106,000 acres) of vineyards, but less than 1% is used for wine (167,000 cases a year). Production is centred east and north-east of Bombay in the Deccan area, a highland zone with a tolerable, if not ideal, grape-growing climate. Government restrictions used to force entrepreneurs to export all their wine, but in 1988 regulations relaxed to allow 25% of production to be sold at home. A number of Indian wine companies are now linking up with Western investors who can help with export sales, in return gaining entry into India's massive market of 800 million people.

Traditionally, Indian wines are thick, sweet — and sold in screw-cap bottles. But 1985 saw the launch

Work in Suntory's vineyard, Japan.

of Omar Khayyam, a "traditional method" sparkling white wine. This award-winner has captured the imagination of the international wine world. More recently, Grover Vineyards, a French-Indian joint venture, has achieved fame with wines made from French grape varieties.

CHINA

Growing wine-grapes is not alien to the Chinese culture, but historically it has been of little importance. Vineyards were established early in the 20th century by European missionaries and merchants in the Shantung (Shandong) Peninsula of north-east China. Most of today's 30,000ha (74,000 acres) of wine grapes are still found here, and the area produces about a million cases of wine a year. However, exact production statistics for the country are elusive.

Most of China's vineyards are in cool-climate zones, with winter temperatures of 3°C (37°F) and summer ones of 26°C (79°F). Rainfall is however high, particularly during the growing season in July and August,

and summer typhoons can do damage. The best vineyards tend to be those on south-facing slopes on alluvial, well-drained soil. The more southerly vineyards are humid and can have botrytis problems.

The missionaries' imports of white-wine varieties such as Rkatsiteli, Welschriesling and Gewürztraminer, and the black grape Muscat de Hambourg remain important. Beichun, a versatile red hybrid relatively resistant to fungal diseases and cold, and the table-grape varieties Dragon's Eye, Cow's Nipple and Cock's Heart are all widely used to make traditional, semi-sweet, predominantly white Chinese wines: the most famous, Kui hua chen chiew, is exported throughout the Far East.

China has around 90 wineries, a third of which are serious about making wine of reasonable quality. In the 1980s a new mood of openness encouraged foreign investment, and several multinational companies now provide funding for equipment and expertise. Local grapes are bought from small family-owned vineyards on contract while new vineyards, planted with classic European varieties, mature.

The aim is for consumer-friendly, predominantly white, medium-dry blends that can be marketed at home and abroad. Besides Rémy Martin, Hiram Walker and Pernod-Ricard (*see* box, p574), Impexital, the Italian international finance group, and Seagram are also involved with joint ventures in China.

Significantly, the more progressive state-run wineries are beginning to make Western-style wines, putting pressure on scarce grape resources such as Riesling and Chardonnay, which are consequently rising in cost. As are the wines, which command higher prices than traditional-style wines.

JAPAN

The Japanese, although not a wine-drinking nation, have a long history of wine production. In 1186 Japan's only native *vinifera* variety, Koshu — which can make fruity white wines — was cultivated in vineyards around Mount Fuji, south of the Kofu Valley and west of Tokyo. This is still the most important wine district, the best vineyards lying on gravelly, volcanic soils on south-facing slopes. The majority of Japan's wine-producing districts are in the southern half of the main island. Hokkaido island in the north has two districts, Kyushu in the far south has one.

The most widely-planted vines are American hybrids, a legacy of Japanese researches abroad in the late 19th century. The dull, red Campbell's Early; Delaware (a delicate though acidic white particularly suited to sparkling wines); Muscat Bailey A (a hybrid of Koshu and *vitis labrusca*, making acceptable rosés), plus Koshu, account for approximately 85% of Japan's vineyards. The rest has varieties such as Sémillon, Riesling, Chardonnay, Cabernet Sauvignon and Merlot. In 1997 the total vineyard area, 21,400ha (52,900 acres), produced 250,900 tons of grapes, but only 27,700 were used for wine.

The hybrids are better suited to this inhospitable archipelago than European or Asian varieties. Freezing winters, typhoons, monsoons and salt winds contrast starkly with Mediterranean climates of the same latitude. The foxy flavours associated with hybrid wines are partially masked by the legal allowance of up to 260 grams of sugar per litre — sweetness is favoured by the ordinary consumer.

Japan's first winemaking company, Dainihon Yamanashi Budooshu Gaisha (now Mercian), was founded in 1877. Two years earlier, two young men, Takano Masanari and Tsuchiya Ryuken, had left for France to study wine-growing and winemaking techniques which they applied upon their return to Japan.

The 1970s saw far-reaching developments: first was the introduction of French and German grapes and foreign (mainly French and Australian) wine expertise. Second, three multinational Japanese companies, Mercian, Mann and Suntory, set up gleaming, high-tech wineries for the home market.

In 1997, Japan officially had 335 winemakers, but the three main brands (Mercian, Suntory and Sapporo) account for 65% of the wine market. Japan's average consumption per head is just above 3 litres, with most wines being imported.

Most Japanese wines are blended with imported bulk wine and are labelled "Produce of Japan". If the imported bulk wine is more than 50%, this must be stated on the label. Such wines are disappearing as imported wines are more widely and competitively distributed. □

REGIONS AND PRODUCERS

INDIA
C I Ltd
Multi-millionaire Sham Chougule owns a high-tech winery 150km (90 miles) inland from Bombay at Narayangaon, in the Sahyadri Mountains. The vineyard is on east-facing, lime-rich soil at 750m (2,475ft). This partly mitigates India's hot, dry climate. What startled Western palates about the winery's dry sparkling wine, Omar Khayyam, was that it had an extraordinary European character and appeal. With his joint-venture partner Pernod-Ricard, Chougule has launched several wines on the Indian market, including Marquise de Pompadour, a *demi-sec* version of Omar Khayyam, and Riviera, a white made from Thompson Seedless and Chardonnay grapes.

Grover Vineyards Ltd
In the mid-1980s, Kanwal Grover, a rich industrialist and wine enthusiast, persuaded Georges Vesselle, a former technical director of champagne producer Mumm, to launch a joint venture in the Bangalore region. The vineyard on the Karnataka plateau is on clay soil and the climate is dry and cool. There is no winter and little rain during the monsoon, allowing for two harvests every year. Rigorous selection of grape varieties, imported from France, have shown very promising results. A light, supple Cabernet Sauvignon, a Blanc de Blancs de Clairette and a fresh, fruité rosé are considered to be among the country's best wines.

Since then, Veuve Clicquot (LVMH) has acquired an interest in the company and Michel Rolland is working as a consultant oenologist. Annual production will soon reach 82,500 cases of wine.

CHINA
Beijing Friendship Winery
Pernod-Ricard's joint venture makes 40,000 cases of white Dragon Seal, using blended French and Chinese grapes.

Hua Dong Winery
The company, partly owned by Hiram Walker, is associated with Shandong Peninsula's Qingdao state winery. Australian consultants have helped set up the venture, including an experimental Chardonnay vineyard. Best-known export is white Tsingtao brand wines.

Rémy Martin
The first modern-style Chinese white wine was Great Wall, made in 1978 in conjunction with the Tianjin Farm Bureau. This venture now produces 120,000 cases of Dynasty (red and white), for home and export markets.

Imperial Court, a traditional-method sparkling white wine using Chardonnay, Pinot Noir, Petit Meunier and Ugni Blanc, is produced at a winery near Shanghai.

JAPAN
Japan's reputation for genuine, though expensive, quality wines rests largely with Château Lumière (owned by the old family firm of Toshihiko Tsukamoto) and Château Mercian (owned by Sanraku) whose Chardonnays, Cabernet Sauvignons and Merlots have great concentration and depth.

The most exclusive wine is Suntory's Sauternes-style Château Lion, made from botrytized Sémillon grapes at a price comparable to Château d'Yquem.

A 1992 spicy white Miyozakae from the Kitazima Sake Company has been acclaimed in international tastings.

REFERENCE SECTION

WHAT THE QUALITY WINE LABEL SHOWS

The label on a bottle of quality wine (as opposed to table wine — *see* p580) must carry certain information, following regulations in the country of origin. The regulations set out what must be included, what may be included and — sometimes — what may not appear on the label. The chart below summarizes the situation in the world's most important quality wine-exporting countries.

Key
Mandatory = M
Permissible = P
Neither = X

	FRANCE	ITALY	GERMANY	SPAIN	PORTUGAL	ENGLAND	HUNGARY	GREECE	AUSTRIA	CYPRUS	ISRAEL	BULGARIA	ROMANIA	USA	AUSTRALIA	NEW ZEALAND	CHILE	ARGENTINA	SOUTH AFRICA
1 The word "wine"	0/X	X	X	X	X	X	X	X	M	M	M	M	M	M	M	M	M	M	M
2 Country of origin	M	M	M	M	M	M	M	M	M	M	M	M	M	M	M	M	M	M	M
3 Denomination of origin	M	M	M	M	M	M	M	M	M	P	M	P	M	P	M	P	M	M	M
4 Quantity in the bottle	M	M	M	M	M	M	M	M	P	M	M	M	M	M	M	M	M	M	M
5 Alcohol content	M	M	M	M	M	M	M	M	M	P	M	M	M	M	M	M	M	M	M
6 Name and address of the "responsible" bottler/brand owner or lot number	M	M	M	M	M	M	M	M	M	M	M	P	P	M	M	M	M	P	M
7 Quality status	M	M	M	M	M	M	M	M	P	P	P	M	P	M	P	P	P	P	X
8 Sulphite/additives declaration	X	P	X	X	P	X	P	X	P	X	P	P	X	M	M	P	X	X	X
9 Grape variety(ies)	P	P	P	P	P	P	M	P	P	X	M	P	P	P	P	M	P	M	P
10 The term "estate" (meaning grapes grown only on the estate)	P	P	P	P	P	P	P	P	P	X	P	P	P	M	P	P	P	P	M
11 Vintage	P	P	P	P	M	P	M	P	P	X	P	P	P	P	P	M	P	M	P
12 Sweet/dry description	P	P	P	P	P	P	M	P	M	P	M	M	P	P	P	P	P	P	P
13 Test (tasting/laboratory analysis) of quality	X	P	M	M	P	X	P	X	M	X	P	M	X	X	P	P	X	M	P
14 Official seal (placed under capsule/over cork)	M	P	P	P	M	X	P	M	M	M	X	P	X	X	X	X	P	X	M
15 Single-vineyard specification	P	P	P	P	P	P	P	P	P	P	X	X	P	P	P	P	P	X	P

The notes below refer to the points numbered on the chart opposite. For further information on reading a wine label, *see* pp44-46.

1. The word "wine" need not appear on quality wine labels from EC countries as it is rendered superfluous by the individual countries' controlled appellation systems (*see* pp578–580). The exception is French VDQS wines. Any wine entering the EC from outside, or produced in a non-EC country, must also state the word "wine" clearly on the label.

2. The country of origin need not appear on the label if the wine is destined solely for the home market. Otherwise, it is mandatory for any wine, anywhere in the world.

3. The denomination of origin is usually based on a geographical region (eg Rioja in Spain) or on a vine variety (eg Barbera d'Alba in Italy).

4. The quantity in the bottle is normally expressed in centilitres (75cl).

5. The alcohol content (mainly ethyl alcohol), is often expressed as a percentage (12%) of the total volume but can also be expressed in degrees (12°). This must be exact to 0.5% and is now mandatory in virtually every country, not least as evidence of a responsible attitude to alcohol.

6. The name and address of the bottler or brand owner has become mandatory information on all EC, and most non-EC, wine labels. If a product is bottled by one company under contract to another, the liability lies with the company for whom the bottling is carried out. If it is an "own label" product, liability rests with the company whose name and address appear on the label. Similar to this is "lot marking", a reference code allowing the consumer to initiate a complaints system which traces the contents of an individual bottle back to the exact batch of grapes.

7. The quality status for EC wines is inherent in the controlled appellation system (*see* pp578–580); likewise for non-EC countries with a similar system. In reality, this is often only a partial guarantee of quality; the name of a good producer/winemaker is more reliable.

8. A sulphite/additives declaration is now mandatory on all wine labels in the USA, and any wines imported into the USA. Sulphite in wine is sulphur dioxide (SO_2), used as a preservative in wine, as in many other products, and found naturally in the human body. The EC's permitted levels are 160 mg per litre for white wine, 210 mg per litre for red and 260 mg per litre for sweet wine, excluding *Beerenauslese* and *Trockenbeerenauslese*. The trend throughout the world is to use as little as possible. In December 1993 Austria introduced a maximum of 110 mg per litre, but any wine which contains more than 50 mg per litre must put the word "*geschwefelt*" (contains sulphur/sulphites) on the label. The use of additives — natural products such as ascorbic acid (Vitamin C) and sorbic acid — is strictly regulated in the winemaking process. Pesticides used in the vineyard may in future have to be declared on US labels.

9. Labelling wine by its grape variety(ies) is now the most popular system of nomenclature worldwide. The percentage of the variety(ies) in the bottle is strictly regulated. Wine from an EC country which mentions one variety must contain a minimum of 85% of that variety; if two varieties are named on the label they must constitute 100% of the grape blend, the larger proportion being stated before the smaller. No EC wine label may list more than two varieties. In countries outside the EC, a wine must contain between 75 and 100% of the named variety. A number of non-EC countries may name two varieties, among them Australia, Austria, Bulgaria and Chile.

10. The term "estate" (meaning wine made from grapes grown only on the estate) is generally permitted on labels but is often a misnomer. In South Africa for example, "estate" can be used if the grapes have been grown on an adjacent estate or one nearby with the same soil and micro-climate.

11. If the vintage is stated on the label, at least 85% of the wine (or 95% in the USA) must come from that vintage.

12. A sweet/dry description is generally allowed on the label, either in the form of words or, for white wine, symbols, which are now widely used throughout the world. For sparkling wines in the EC a sweet/dry description (eg Brut, Demi-Sec) is mandatory.

13. A test (tasting/laboratory analysis of quality) is becoming a more important part of many countries' labelling requirements. All German quality wine labels carry an AP number (*Amtliche Prüfungsnummer*) on the label and Austrian wines a *Staatliche Prüfnummer*. The Italian DOCG regulations now specify a tasting both before bottling and after ageing. The Show System (tasting competitions) in Australia and New Zealand is tantamount to a tasting test, though more overtly commercial.

14. Official Seal (placed under capsule/over cork). This is a method by which the regional controlling authority authenticates the wine's origin and quality. In South Africa and Austria this is a "banderol" conferred by the government. No official authority exists in Australia for issuing such seals but voluntary schemes exist, such as the New South Wales government's quality wine logo.

15. The name of a single vineyard is almost universally permitted as a sign of extra quality and is an integral part of the quality system in France, for example, with its Burgundian *crus* and Bordeaux classed growths.

REGULATIONS FOR QUALITY WINE

Most of the world's wine-producing countries have strict regulations to control every stage of quality-wine production. Unless a wine conforms to these regulations, it will not be eligible for quality-wine status, and will fall into a lower category (*see* p580). *See* the notes on the facing page for more information.

Key
Yes = ✔
No = ✗
Permissible = P

	FRANCE	ITALY	GERMANY	SPAIN	PORTUGAL	ENGLAND	HUNGARY	GREECE	AUSTRIA	CYPRUS	ISRAEL	BULGARIA	ROMANIA	USA	AUSTRALIA	NEW ZEALAND	CHILE	ARGENTINA	SOUTH AFRICA
1 Controlled indication of origin	✔	✔	✔	✔	✔	✔	✔	✔	✔	✔	✔	✔	✔	✔	✔	P	P	✔	✔
2 Controlled appellation system	✔	✔	✔	✔	✔	✔	P	✔	P	✔	✗	✔	✔	✔	✗	✗	✔	✔	✔
3 Grape varieties: type	✔	✔	✔	✔	✔	✔	✔	P	✔	✔	✔	✔	✔	✔	P	M	✔	✔	✗
percentages	✔	✔	✔	✗	✔	✔	✔	✗	P	✗	✔	✗	✗	✔	P	M	P	✗	✔
4 Viticultural practices other than planting density	✔	✔	✔	✔	✔	✗	✔	✔	✔	✔	✔	P	✔	✔	✗	✗	✔	✔	✗
5 Planting density	✔	P	✔	✔	✗	✗	✗	✗	✗	✔	✔	P	✔	✗	✗	✗	P	✔	✔
6 Irrigation allowed	✗	P	✗	✔	✗	✗	P	✗	P	✗	✔	✗	✔	✔	✔	✔	✔	✔	✗
7 Production methods: sparkling	✔	✔	✔	✔	✗	✔	✔	✔	✔	✗	✔	✗	✔	✗	✔	✗	P	✔	✔
fortified	✔	✔	✗	✔	✗	✗	✔	✔	✗	✔	✔	✗	✔	✗	✔	✗	✗	✔	✗
8 Maturation/ageing process	P	✔	✔	✔	✔	✗	✔	✔	✔	✔	✔	✔	✔	✗	P	✗	P	✔	✗
9 Sulphur dioxide/additives level	✔	✔	✔	✔	✔	✔	✔	✔	✔	✔	✔	✗	✔	✔	✔	✗	✔	✔	✗
10 Bottling at source	P	P	✔	P	✗	✗	P	✗	P	P	✔	✔	✗	✗	✗	✗	P	✔	P
11 Levels of ripeness/alcohol	P	✔	✔	P	✔	✔	✔	✔	✗	✔	✔	✔	✗	✔	✗	✗	✗	✔	✗

The notes below refer to the points numbered on the chart opposite.

1. Controlled indication of origin is inherent in appellation systems based, like the French, Italian and Spanish, on geography or grape varieties. Most of the world's wine-producing countries now have legislation to insist that, if a region or district is named on the label, a large percentage of the grapes in the wine must originate there. However, in New World vineyards the origin of the grapes has, until very recently, been relatively unimportant; only now are the best vineyard sites beginning to be defined.

2. The wine world today is in a state of flux regarding appellation systems. Several countries which have long-established appellation systems are seeking fewer restrictions to allow experimentation; other countries are seriously looking into developing such systems. The controlled appellations of France, Germany, Spain, the USA and Australia are listed in detail on pp581–593. The most interesting appellations in other countries are discussed in their individual chapters.

3. Grape varieties: all EC quality wines must be made from vines belonging to the *vitis vinifera* family and "recommended" or "authorized" for that particular wine, and region, by the wine authorities of the individual country. England is fighting for permission to use Seyval Blanc in English/Welsh quality wine. As a French-American hybrid it is currently not permitted, however good the wine. In other countries, such as the USA and Canada, hybrids are allowed, and there is more experimentation. However, when grape varieties are named on the label they must constitute a certain percentage of the wine (*see* p577, Note 9).

4. Viticultural practices, apart from planting density, are usually strictly regulated in EC countries, particularly pruning and training, which have a direct bearing on yield. German regulations have long been based on the number of buds allowed on the vine (and on must sugar levels), which encourages volume rather than quality. Non-EC countries, many of whose wine industries are in their infancy, have a more flexible approach to viticulture aimed at encouraging experimentation.

5. Planting density is a particularly topical subject among viticulturalists but it is not often regulated. Regions such as Burgundy, traditionally a high-density area, are experimenting with lower density planting, while in Australia, where low density planting was the norm, newer vineyards are being established with a far higher number of vines per hectare.

6. In EC countries, wines in experimental status areas such as Raimat in Spain, and vineyards which are in the process of being established even in England's damp climate, allow irrigation. Generally, however, appellation-controlled vines in EC countries are not allowed to be irrigated. In warmer, non-EC countries, the better the quality of the wine, the less irrigation the vine receives. In countries such as Australia and Chile, and in specific regions of other countries such as the Wachau in Austria and Robertson District in South Africa, viticulture can be practised only if irrigation is carried out — to a greater or lesser extent — at various periods of the vine's cycle.

7. Generally, if a country makes sparkling or fortified wines, these are regulated by specific legislation.

8. Specific regulations apply to the maturation/ageing process of specific wines in specific appellations. For example, Austrian *Spätlese* wines must be aged until 1 March of the year following the harvest, and higher *Prädikat* wines until 1 May. Such regulations are fairly widespread. In Hungary, legislation exists only for Tokaji. Australia has specific maturation requirements for bottle-fermented sparkling wine.

9. Sulphur dioxide/additives level. *See* p577, Note 8.

10. Bottling at source is preferred by appellation authorities to enhance the prestige of the area and of the product but it is against EC regulations to insist upon it. In Alsace (France), bottling at source is mandatory for historical reasons, and similarly in marsala (Italy), to prevent the bulk transportation of inferior quality wine. Technical reasons necessitate certain styles being bottled at source, such as sparkling wines, where the secondary fermentation takes place in the bottle in which the wine will be sold.

In other countries, such as South Africa, information may be misleading. Estate status may be conferred upon a wine even if a tanker transports the just fermented juice to a bottler or wholesaler outside the district, who then fines, filters and ages it.

11. Levels of ripeness and alcohol content. Certain countries' appellation systems, and within that those of certain regions, specify either a level of ripeness, such as the German and Austrian systems (*Spätlese*, *Auslese* etc) which are based entirely on this criteria, or a minimum level of alcohol.

In France, Muscadet, exceptionally, is based on a maximum level of alcohol. In Spain, certain DOs specify a level of ripeness. In Argentina, the must, or unfermented grape juice, must reach a Baumé level of between 10 and 14° (this indicates the potential alcohol content of the wine).

QUALITY LEVELS

The appellation of origin system was first introduced in France to protect quality wines from certain traditional regions. Since the 1960s other European countries have established similar systems which are widely regarded as indicators of quality (the chapters on individual countries give more details). The EC normally recognizes four levels of quality: the chart shows how parallels can be drawn between these four levels in various countries.

COUNTRIES	TABLE WINES		QUALITY WINES	
	Table wine	Table wine from a designated region	Quality wine from a designated region	Top quality wine from a designated region
France	Vin de table	Vin de pays	Appellation d'origine vin délimité de qualité supérieure (VDQS)	Appellation d'origine contrôlée (AOC)
Italy	Vino da tavola (VDT)	Indicazione geografica tipica (IGT)	Denominazione di origine controllata (DOC)	Denominazione di origine controllata e garantita (DOCG)
Germany	Deutscher Tafelwein	Landwein	Qualitätswein eines bestimmten Anbaugebietes (QbA)	Qualitätswein mit Prädikat[1] (QmP)
Spain	Vino de mesa	Vino de la tierra	Denominación de origen (DO)	Denominación de origen calificada (DOC)
Portugal	Vinho de mesa	Vinho regional	Indicação de proveniência regulamentada (IPR)	Denominação de origem controlada (DOC)
England	Table wine	Regional wine	English/Welsh Vineyards Quality Wine	Nil
Hungary[2]	Asztali bor	Tájbor	Minöségi bor	Különleges Minöségü bor
Greece	Table wine. Cava	Vin de pays	Controlled Appellation of Origin (sweet wines) Appellation of Origin of Superior Quality (dry wines)	Reserve ou Grande Reserve
Austria	Tafelwein	Landwein	Qualitätswein Kabinett Prädikatswein[3]	Vinea Wachau[4]

1 The Prädikat, or distinction, refers to six levels of ripeness and quality: Kabinett, Spätlese, Auslese, Beerenauslese, Trockenbeerenauslese, Eiswein.

2 Hungary has applied for membership of the EC.

3 The Prädikat, or distinction, refers to eight levels of ripeness and quality: Spätlese, Auslese, Beerenauslese, Trockenbeerenauslese, Eiswein, Ausbruch, Strohwein, Bergwein.

4 The best wines of the Vinea Wachau region refer to their own levels of ripeness and quality: Steinfeder, Federspiel, Smaragd.

VINTAGE CHARTS

Any assessment of a vintage is a generalisation — wines from different properties will vary — and a guess: no-one can be sure how wines will develop in bottle. The "When" column gives broad advice on when to drink:

D means drink now; (D) probably past its best; K means drink now, but can be kept; L means lay down for the future: the figure (L 10+) gives an estimate of likely time to maturity from the vintage. Ratings are out of 10.

BORDEAUX
Red: Médoc and Graves
Ratings are for classed growths; other wines will mature sooner. Recent vintages are proving attractive earlier than is traditionally the case, but good years will still have a good life. *See also* pp148, 158.

	Rating	When	Comment
2003	7	L	Despite heat wave, no damage to the Cabernet Sauvignons
2002	8	L	Vintage salvaged by good weather in late autumn
2001	6	G	A tough year for the Cabernets
2000	9	L	Ripe grapes, plenty of tannins
1999	6	K	Patchy; better in southern Médoc and Graves
1998	7	K	Sometimes watery; few long-lived wines for keeping
1997	6	L7+	Relatively ripe grapes; some wines for keeping
1996	8	L10+	Good classic vintage; very promising; superb Cabernet-Sauvignons
1995	9	L10+	Excellent vintage; some brilliant wines
1994	7	L	Promising, despite September rains
1993	6	D	Spoilt prospects due to September rains, but still fair to good
1992	6	D	Large crop; light but well-balanced wines
1990	9	L	Excellent and well-built wines, with rich tannins of great finesse
1989	9	K	Large, ripe, opulent but patchy
1988	8	K	Classic vintage; fruity wines
1986	8	K	Very ripe grapes; a high concentration of tannins
1985	8	K	Ripe, round wines
1983	9	K	Tough Cabernet-based wines that have become supple.
1982	10	K	High quality, elegant wines

Red: St-Emilion and Pomerol
The pattern for these "Right Bank" wines differs from that of the Médoc and Graves. Most wines mature more quickly, and vintages do not always follow those of the Left Bank. *See also* pp171, 177.

	Rating	When	Comment
2003	6	L	Merlots suffered during heat wave
2002	7	L	Patchy; interesting exceptions
2001	8	L	Great Merlots
2000	9	L	Perfectly ripe grapes
1999	9	L	Full-bodied, mellow, round wines
1998	8	K	Ripe, powerful, deep-coloured wines
1997	7	D	Full-bodied Merlots, elegant wines
1996	7	L	Less regular than in Médoc because of a rainy harvest, but some fine wines
1995	9	L10+	Superbly ripe Merlot; excellent wines
1994	8	K	Ripe grapes after a hot summer; superb Merlots
1993	6	K	Great Merlots, excellent Pomerols
1992	5	D	Wet year, light wines
1990	10	K	A great vintage with concentrated wines
1989	9	K	Ripe, rather tannic wines
1988	9	K	Excellent vintage, fine fruity structure
1987	6	D	Merlot wines are better than in Médoc; average vintage
1986	8	K	Fine wines, the best are for keeping
1985	8	K	Ripe, delicious, early-maturing wines
1983	8	K	Good vintage, irregular wines
1982	10	K	Hot year, luscious wines

White: dry
Comments are for Graves classed growths. Most minor whites will be at their best under three years old, though the vintage quality will follow the comments and ratings below. Improved winemaking now means few truly poor vintages. *See also* p158.

	Rating	When	Comment
2003	6	D	Not enough acidity
2002	7	L	Some great wines
2001	6	K	Just enough ripeness
2000	8	K	Early harvest, ripe grapes
1999	7	D	Large crop, yields too high
1998	7	D	Supple wines, not for keeping
1997	6	D	Small crop, light-bodied wines
1996	8	L8+	Powerful, well-balanced and well-structured wines
1995	8	L8+	Fine, powerful wines, as in 1988

1994	7	K	Good, well-balanced wines
1993	6	K	Fine wines with a lot of fruit
1990	9	K	Excellent vintage for elegant white wines
1989	9	D	Ripe crop, opulent wines
1988	8	D	Full-bodied wines

BORDEAUX
Sweet wines

Sauternes and Barsac have had a decade of good luck since 1980. Vintages differ in the amount and quality of botrytis, which gives extra concentration and character. The vagaries of nature make for excellent or more or less moderate sweet wines. *See also* p163.

	Rating	When	Comment
2003	8	L	After-season favoured *botrytis*
2002	8	L10+	Well-balanced wines; good *botrytis*
2001	9	L10+	Excellent vintage; well-balanced wines
2000	7	D	Mixed weather during autumn
1999	8	D	Rich, well-structured wines
1998	7	D	A *botrytis* vintage, some easy wines
1997	8	D	Full-bodied and supple wines
1996	9	L8+	Very fine vintage, October weather favoured *botrytis*
1995	9	L	Fast-developing *botrytis* during first half of October
1994	8	L	Another small vintage, but good where rigorous selection was practiced
1993	6	K	Small crop, good wines
1992	6	K	Moderate
1990	10	K	Superb vintage; highly concentrated wines of rare elegance
1989	10	K	Excellent vintage, elegant classical wines
1988	9	K	A *botrytis* vintage, excellent wines
1986	8	K	Good wines, the top ones for ageing
1985	7	D	Patchy: some good wines
1983	10	D	Superb, luscious vintage

BURGUNDY
Red

The most capricious of wines: the myriad growers and *négociants* make markedly different wines, and weather can cause big local variations. Comments are based on Côte d'Or *Premiers Crus. See also* p181.

	Rating	When	Comment
2003	8	L	Patience rewarded with excellent wines
2002	7	K	Just enough ripeness

2001	6	D	No overall ripeness
2000	6	D	Crop too large, as in 1999
1999	7	D	Fine wines despite the rain
1998	7	D	Moderately ripe, harsh tannins
1997	7	D	Irregular, supple and pleasant wines
1996	9	L8+	Patchy, but top wines outstanding
1995	8	L	Good wines : delicate fruit and colour
1994	6	D	Uneven due to bad weather, some good wines
1993	7	K	Good vintage
1992	7	D	Moderate
1991	8	D	Good vintage, but small crop (frost)
1990	9	K	Third great year in a row
1989	9	K	Excellent wines, very dense
1988	9	K	Outstanding vintage; distinctive wines for keeping

White

Côte de Beaune wines, at *Premier Cru* level, form the basis of these ratings. Chablis: see notes at foot of chart. *See also* p181.

	Rating	When	Comment
2003	7	L	Very fleshy, full-flavoured wines
2002	7	K	Grapes of high quality
2001	7	D	Healthy crop, sufficient ripeness
2000	7	D	Ripe, healthy grapes
1999	7	D	Light, but well-balanced wines
1998	7	D	Rainy harvest. A better 1997?
1997	7	D	Easy and pleasant wines, not for long keeping
1996	9	L	Outstanding vintage, very sweet , light acidity
1995	9	L	Small crop, superbly balanced wines of exceptional concentration, as in 1990, but with higher alcohol content
1994	7	K	Better than 1993, better than the reds
1993	6	D	Good vintage, fruity wines
1992	8	K	Good, typical wines
1991	7	D	Balanced wines
1990	8	K	Third great year in a row: ample, elegant wines
1989	9	D	Oustanding year, full-bodied wines
1988	8	(D)	Great year, light and fruity wines

Chablis: 1997, 1996 and 1995 were exceptional years, particularly 1996, with wines for keeping. 1993 and 1994 were good years. 1992: large crop of full, fat wines. 1991: hard hit by frost, small crop due to frost, top wines can be good. 1990: very good year for top wines, to be kept for ageing. Older vintages of *Premier* and *Grand Crus*: 1989, 1988, 1986, 1985 and 1983 were all good.

Key   D: drink now; (D): probably past its best; K: drink now but can be kept; L: lay down; L 10+: likely time to maturity from vintage.

CHAMPAGNE

For most champagne the vintage is irrelevant: makers blend wines of different vintages to produce a consistent blend. Vintage-labelled wines are produced by the top champagne houses only in very good years.

Outstanding vintage champagne from a *grande marque* house deserves to spend about a decade in bottle to reach its best.

Since the classic 1996 vintage with its balanced, long-lived wines, the Champagne region has produced large crops, including in 2000. But nothing that is up to the 1996 par. 1988, 1989, 1990 and 1995 have been vintage years. But there are still abundant stocks of older vintages. 1985 is a very good fruity and elegant vintage. 1983 is less vivid, but has better cuvées from red grapes with white juice. 1982 remains luscious, particularly in the pure Chardonnay cuvées. *See also* p213.

ALSACE

Most everyday Alsace wines can be drunk at 1–4 years old; *Vendange Tardive* and *Sélection de Grains Nobles* wines can have a longer life. *See also* p223.

	Rating	When	Comment
2003	7	L	Excellent ripeness, moderate acidity
2002	6	D	Rain and just enough ripeness
2001	6	D	Very patchy
2000	6	D	A difficult climate for some exellent wines
1999	4	D	Wines even more watery than in 1998
1998	5	D	Wines as watery as in 1997
1997	5	D	Supple, watery wines
1996	8	L	Fine, well-structured typical dry wines, but moderate *botrytis*
1995	7	K	Good vintage, strong wines
1994	6	D	Vintage spoilt by rain
1993	6	D	Smaller and better crop than 1992
1992	5	D	Large crop
1990	8	K	Good vintage with typical wines
1989	10	K	Outstanding vintage
1988	9	K	Powerful wines for a long life
1985	8	D	Rich, elegant and fruity wines
1983	10	K	Outstanding vintage of very powerful wines

LOIRE

The dry wines of Pouilly and Sancerre, from Sauvignon Blanc, are at their best under 5 years of age, with rare exceptions. Sweet whites of Anjou and Touraine from Chenin Blanc can, in the rare great years, last for decades. *See also* p231.

	Rating	When	Comment
2003	8	K	Excellent red and white wines
2002	8	K	Superb reds, whits in full bloom
2001	6	D	Nice after-season; some fine wines
2000	6	D	Fruity whites, light and delicious reds
1999	5	D	Rainy harvest, no great wines
1998	6	D	Red and white wines light in style
1997	8	D	Ripe grapes for red wines; great sweet wines
1996	9	L	Second great year
1995	9	L	Excellent vintage; outstanding sweet white wines
1994	7	D	Some good red wines and some very fine sweet ones, *moelleux* and *liquoreux*
1993	7	(D)	Average vintage
1990	9	K	A great year for fine sweet wines, *moelleux* and *liquoreux*
1989	10	D	Best vintage of the century; top are sweet wines made from the Chenin Blanc grape

Good older Anjou and Vouvray wines: 1988, 1985, 1978, 1976, 1975, 1964 et 1959.

RHÔNE
Reds

North and South Rhône conditions can vary: the comments make that clear. The ratings and when-to-drink notes are for the longer-lived, Syrah-based wines of the north, and wines such as Châteauneuf and Gigondas in the south. *See also* p247.

	Rating	When	Comment
2003	7	K	Tiny crop, wines of overall good quality
2002	6	K	Harsh climate; stunted wines
2001	6	K	Grapes ripe enough, but patchy results
2000	7	K	Perfectly ripe grapes
1999	7	K	Better in north than south, better reds than whites
1998	8	K	Better reds (north and south) than whites
1997	5	D	Reds and whites very (too ?) supple
1996	7	L	Moderate; large crop, but not ripe enough; excellent white wines
1995	9	L	Excellent vintage, powerful and well-structured wines
1994	7	D	Patchy, rain during harvest
1993	6	D	Better in south than north, better whites than reds
1990	9	K	Superb: ripe, balanced for lkeeping
1989	9	K	A great year for tannic concentration
1988	10	K	Best vintage of the century

Key   D: drink now; (D): probably past its best; K: drink now but can be kept; L: lay down; L 10+: likely time to maturity from vintage.

GERMANY
Mosel

Vintages here differ not just in quality but in style: traditionally, the best years are warm ones, those yielding lots of sweet (*Auslese* and above) wine. Cooler years, with good *Kabinett* wines, are not to be despised. Keeping suggestions are for *Spätlese* and above. Great vintages can be kept for decades, and even *Kabinett* wines can, in the right years, improve for 8–10 years. *See also* p318.

	Rating	When	Comment
2003	7	L	Concentration and good acidity
2002	6	D	A lot of rain; wines sometimes watery
2001	7	D	Good overall
2000	6	K	Rainy harvest, good sweet wines
1999	8	K	Elegant, mature wines, rainy harvest
1998	5	K	A lot of acidity; fine *Eisweine*
1997	9	L	Powerful wines for keeping
1996	7	L	Small crop of inconsistent quality; best Rieslings from harvests in late October or November
1995	8	L	Initially much acidity, but grapes ripe at harvest time, few *Eisweine*
1994	9	L	Good to excellent; fine, well-balanced Rieslings
1993	8	D	Good despite challenging conditions

Older vintages which made wines for keeping: 1990, 1988, 1985, 1983, 1976, 1975, 1971, 1964, 1959.

RHEIN REGIONS

Subtle but important differences between Mosel and Rhein: the Rhein wines, especially the Rheingaus, usually age for longer — say 12 years plus for great vintages; but do not keep Rheinhessen wines beyond eight years without giving them a trial. For keeping suggestions refer to Mosel. *See also* p325.

	Rating	When	Comment
2003	8	L	Ample Rieslings
2002	6	D	Unstable climate, average wines
2001	8	L	Excellent crop
2000	7	K	Moderate to good
1999	7	K	Large crop
1998	6	D	Patchy
1997	8	L	Balance and ripeness
1996	8	L	Good *Auslese* and *Beerenauslese* in the Rheingau, moderate in the Pfalz
1995	7	K	Variable, early harvest due to rot

Older vintages which made wines for keeping: 1990, 1989, 1983, 1976, 1975, 1971, 1964, 1959.

TUSCANY
Reds

Chianti Classico and Rufino, and Brunello di Montalcino, plus the growing legion of "super" *vini da tavola*, are wines worth keeping. These notes apply to them. Simpler Chianti does not need more than 3–4 years' ageing. *See also* p381.

	Rating	When	Comment
2003	6	L	Irregular crop
2002	6	L	Difficult climate; bleak wines
2001	8	L	Some very fine wines
2000	7	L	Irregular wines
1999	8	L	Balanced
1998	8	L	Good structure
1997	8	K	Good ripeness
1996	7	L	Patchy. Full-bodied, deep-coloured Chiantis
1995	8	L	Superb vintage
1994	9	L	Good to excellent for DOCG wines and *vini da tavola*
1993	8	K	Good vintage
1990	9	K	A great year

Older vintages for red wines: 1988, 1986, 1985, 1983, 1978, 1971, 1968, 1967.
White wines: 1994 and 1993 were good vintages for Umbria and Tuscany.

PIEDMONT
Reds

Piedmont's Barolo and Barbaresco reds demand bottle-age, though the more modern style of winemaking favoured by some producers means faster-maturing wines. Old-fashioned Barolo from good vintages may take 10 years to become approachable, and will last for 20 years. Barbaresco starts to become accessible in 4–5 years. *See also* p365.

	Rating	When	Comment
2003	6	L	Very irregular
2002	7	L	A difficult year, but some great wines
2001	9	L	Fine full-bodied wines
2000	9	L7+	Excellent
1999	9	L9+	Full-bodied wines
1998	7	L	More concentration than fruit
1997	8	L	Good vintage
1996	8	L	High-quality vintage
1995	7	L	Late-harvest Nebbiolo produced top-quality wines
1994	7	D	Patchy, better Barolos
1993	7	K	Irregular vintage
1992	6	D	Fairly light and early-maturing

Key   D: drink now; (D): probably past its best; K: drink now but can be kept; L: lay down; L 10+: likely time to maturity from vintage.

1990	9	K	Superb conditions, many stylish wines for keeping
1989	7	D	Hail reduced the crop, but some good wines nevertheless
1988	8	K	Excellent vintage. The best are classics.

Older classic Barolo vintages: 1986, 1985, 1983, 1978, 1971, 1964.

VINTAGE PORT

Only a small part of any port crop becomes "vintage", and in some years there is none — a vintage is not "declared". Vintage port is designed for long bottle-ageing: wines a century old can be superb. The following years have been declared by some or all of the major shippers.

Ratings cannot be usefully given until the wine has been bottled (at two years old) and acquired a few years' ageing, as character can alter. A query below indicates years where it is too soon to assess quality. Owing to the longevity of port, "When" information is in a different form: the likely period of optimum pleasure.

Some houses declare single-quinta wines in non-vintage years. These may be expected to mature in 8–12 years. *See also* p440.

	Rating	When	Comment
2003	?	L?	Great hopes for the vintages
2002	?	L?	Uneven climate; some excellent wines
2001	?	L?	A lot of humidity at first, but a good after-season has salvaged this vintage.
2000	9	L12+	A small crop of high quality
1999	8	L10+	Perfectly ripe grapes
1998	8	L7+	Perfectly ripe grapes
1997	9	L10+	Superb vintages
1996	7	L12+	Large crop of moderate to good quality. Universal declaration unlikely
1995	8	L12+	Almost no vintage declared
1994	9	L20+	Small crop, excellent wines. Vintage
1992	8	L	Probably an outstanding vintage
1991	7	L	Vintage of great extraction
1985	7	K	Good, but not top-class
1983	7	K	Good
1982	7	K	Some but not all shippers declared
1980	8	K	Vintage improving with ageing
1978	7	K	Vintage starting to reveal its fruit, but still very much closed and a bit light

Older fine vintages, still in good condition: 1977, 1970, 1967, 1966, 1963, 1960, 1955, 1945.

CALIFORNIA

The enormous size of the California vineyards, and their great variation in conditions, make useful vintage judgements hard to come by. The focus of these comments is Napa and Sonoma; the "When" suggestions concentrate on Cabernet Sauvignon reds from the top producers. Most California wines are enjoyable young, though a limited number of top reds, and Chardonnay whites, are designed for bottle-ageing. Prestige Chardonnays can gain from 5 years or more in bottle. *See also* p479.

	Rating	When	Comment
2003	6	L	Extremely patchy
2002	6	L	Grapes just ripe enough; unbalanced wines
2001	7	L	Great Cabernet Sauvignons
2000	?	K	A lot of rain, average wines
1999	7	K	Patchy; fine Zinfandels
1998	5	D	Unstable weather; light wines
1997	9	K	Rich and full-bodied wines
1996	7	L	Small crop of excellent quality
1995	8	L	Good quality, though less for whites
1994	8	D	Good red wines from a small crop
1993	7	D	Variable quality
1991	9	D	Fine reds

Older classic Cabernet Sauvignon vintages: 1985, 1980, 1978, 1974, 1970.

AUSTRALIA

The great variety of Australia's regions and wines make generalisations impossible. Contrary to myth, conditions can and do vary: drought, floods, bush fires and heat waves add to the confusion. Ratings and "when to drink" data are thus omitted.

In general, Australian red wines such as Cabernet Sauvignon, Pinot Noir and Shiraz are ready sooner than their northern hemisphere equivalents. White wines for ageing include Rieslings and Sémillons which can last 20 years; Chardonnays are mostly made to drink young.

However wines from the same grape, and area, will differ in their ageing potential according to the maker's methods and intentions. Mass-produced wines are far less subject to vintage variation than more expensive ones, and are made to be drunk as soon as they are released for sale. Some vintage wines are aged by their makers and only released when ready.

Harvest in Australia is in February-April, so all wines are six months older than northern hemisphere wines of the same vintage date. *See also* p532.

Key   D: drink now; (D): probably past its best; K: drink now but can be kept; L: lay down; L 10+: likely time to maturity from vintage.

WINE ZONES AND STATISTICS

The following pages list wine areas and wine production statistics for the major wine countries of the world where figures are available. Figures show wine production (in hectolitres, or hl) and area under vine, in thousands of hectares (ha) and acres. Area figures can be imprecise as non-bearing vineyards are often included.

EUROPE . . . . area under vine . . . . . . production
Albania 5 (12) 105
Austria . . . . 49 (121) 2 703
Belgium . . . . n.a. 1
Bosnia-Herzegovina** 4 (10) 54
Bulgaria . . . . 109 (269) 3 308
Croatia* ** . . . . 59 (146) 2 277
Czech Republic ** 13 (32) 450
France . . . . 914 (2,285) 52 671
Germany . . . . 106 (262) 10 834
Greece . . . . 129 (319) 3 826
Hungary . . . . 131 (324) 4 180
Italy . . . . 899 (2,221) 54 188
Luxembourg 1 (2.5) 160
Macedonia (former Republic of)* ** . . . 31 (77) 1 803
Malta 1 (2.5) 32
Portugal . . . . 260 (642) 3 621
Romania . . . . 253 (625) 5 002
Spain . . . . 1,180 (2,916) 30 320
Slovakia 20 (49) 490
Slovenia** 20 (49) 894
Switzerland . . . . 15 (37) 1 172
United Kingdom 1 (2.5) 12
Yugoslavia (Serbia and Montenegro) . 82 (203) 4 025
Sub-total EUROPE . . . . . . 4 282 (10,581) 182 128

USSR (former)
Armenia* 22 (54) 80
Azerbaijan* ** 66 (163) 650
Belorussia* ** 4 (10) 232
Estonia** . . . . n.a. 7
Georgia* ** . . . . 73 (180) *650*
Kazakhstan* ** 12 (30) 191
Kirghizstan* ** 8 (20) 20
Latvia** . . . . n.a. 114
Lithuania* ** 5 (12) 197
Moldova** . . . . 159 (393) *2 194*
Russia* ** . . . . 85 (210) 2 100
Tajikistan* ** . . . . 38 (94) *195*
Turkmenistan* ** 28 (69) 168
Ukraine** 125 (309) 728
Uzbekistan* ** . . . . 132 (326) 1 470
Sub-total USSR (former) . . . . . 757 (1,870) 8 996

AFRICA . . . . area under vine . . . . . . production
Algeria 56 (138) 360
Egypt* 56 (138) 26
Libya . . . . 7 (17) . . . . –
Madagascar 2 (5) 90
Morocco 50 (123) 298
South Africa . . . . 111 (274) 8 156

Tanzania . . . . 3 (7) . . . . –
Tunisia 27 (67) 352
Other African countries 1 (2.5) 26
Sub-total AFRICA . . . . 313 (773) 9 308

AMERICA . . . . area uder vine . . . . . . production
Argentina . . . . 210 (519) 12 673
Bolivia 4 (10) 20
Brazil . . . . 60 (148) 2 782
Canada 7 (17) 343
Chile* . . . . 144 (356) 5 475
Mexico . . . . 41 (103) 1 112
Paraguay . . . . n.a. 92
Peru 11 (27) 120
Uruguay* . . . . 11 (27) 1 132
USA . . . . 364 (899) 20 450
Venezuela . . . . 1 (2.5) 12 673
Other American countries 5 (12) 5
Sub-total AMERICA . . . . 858 (2,120) 56 877

ASIA . . . . area under vine . . . . . . production
China* . . . . 194 (479) 3 550
India* . . . . 43 (106) . . . . –
Japan . . . . 22 (54) 1 301
Korea* . . . . 30 (74) . . . . –
Pakistan . . . . 9 (22) . . . . –
Taiwan . . . . 3 (7) . . . . –
Thailand . . . . 3 (7) . . . . –
Other Asian countries 19 (47) 4
Sub-total ASIA . . . . 323 (798) 4 855

MIDDLE EAST . . . . area under vine . . . . . . production
Afghanistan* . . . . 52 (128) . . . . –
Cyprus 20 (49) 710
Irak* . . . . 53 (131) . . . . –
Iran . . . . 270 (667) . . . . –
Israel 8 (20) 90
Jordan . . . . 15 (37) . . . . –
Lebanon* . . . . 26 (64) . . . . –
Syria* . . . . 86 (212) . . . . –
Turkey* 602 (1,487) 278
Yemen* . . . . 24 (59) . . . . –
Sub-total MIDDLE EAST . . 1 156 (2,856) 1 078

OCEANIA . . . . area under vine . . . . . . production
Australia . . . . 98 (242) 7 415
New Zealand 9 (22) 606
Sub-total OCEANIA . . . . 107 (264) 8 021

(*) Area under vine for wine production x 1,075.   (**) mean value 1992/1995.
Source : Office International de la Vigne et du Vin (January 2001) for 1998.

FRANCE: APPELLATION CONTROLEE ZONES

These zones are listed in alphabetical order, with their region and the colour of wine(s) produced. (*See* also pp132–4.) Regions are: Alsace (A), Bordeaux (Bord), Burgundy (Burg), Champagne (Ch), Loire, Jura and Savoie (J & S), Midi, Provence and Corsica (P-C), Rhône, South West (SW), VDN *vins doux naturel*. R, p, w, sp, vj, vp means red, pink, white, sparkling, *vin jaune* and *vin de paille*. Asterisk (*) indicates a VDQS.

Ajaccio ....P-C........r, p, w
Aloxe-Corton ....Burg .....r, w
Aloxe-Corton
 Premier Cru ....Burg .....r, w
Alsace ou vin d'Alsace ..A ....w (r, p)
Alsace Grand Cru..........A ....w
Anjou ....Loire.....p, w (r)
Anjou Coteaux-
 de-la-Loire ....Loire.....w
Anjou Gamai ....Loire.....r
Anjou Mousseux...........Loire.....sp
Anjou Villages ....Loire.....r
Anjou Villages Brissac ...Loire.....r
Arbois ....J & S ...r, p, w,
....vp, vj
Arbois Mousseux ....J & S ....sp
Arbois Pupillin..............J & S ...r, w,
....vp, vj
Auxey-Duresses ....Burg .....r, w
Auxey-Duresses
 Premier Cru ....Burg .....r, w
Bandol...........................P-C.......r, (w)
Banyuls ....VDN ....r, p, w,
....*rancio*
Banyuls Grand Cru ....VDN ....r, *rancio*
Barsac...........................Bord .....w
Bâtard-Montrachet.......Burg .....w
Béarn ....SW ....r, p, w
Béarn-Bellocq ....SW ....r, w, p
Beaujolais......................Burg .....r (p, w)
Beaujolais Supérieur......Burg .....r (w)
Beaujolais-Villages ....Burg .....r (p, w)
Beaune ....Burg .....r (w)
Beaun Premier Cru........Burg .....r (w)
Bellet............................P-C.......r, p, w
Bergerac........................SW ....r, p
Bergerac Sec ....SW ....w
Bienvenues-Bâtard-
 Montrachet.................Burg .....w
Blagny...........................Burg .....r, w
Blagny Premier Cru.......Burg .....r, w
Blanquette de Limoux...Midi .....sp
Blanquette
 méthode ancestrale ...Midi .....sp
Blaye ....Bord .....r, w
Bonnes-Mares ....Burg .....r

Bonnezeaux...................Loire.....w
Bordeaux ....Bord .....r, w
Bordeaux Clairet ....Bord .....r
Bordeaux
 Côtes-de-Francs ....Bord .....r, w
Bordeaux
 Haut-Benauge...........Bord .....r, w
Bordeaux Mousseux .....Bord .....sp
Bordeaux Rosé ....Bord .....p
Bordeaux Sec................Bord .....w
Bourg ....Bord .....r, w
Bourgogne ....Burg .....r, w (p)
Bourgogne Aligoté ....Burg .....w
Bourgogne Chitry ....Burg .....r, w
Bourgogne
 Côté chalonnaise.......Burg .....r, w
Bourgogne
 Côte Saint-Jacques ....Burg .....r, w
Bourgogne
 Côtes d'Auxerre ....Burg .....r, w
Bourgçgne
 Côte du Couchois .....Burg .....r, w
Bourgogne
 Coulanges-la-Vineus .Burg .....r, w
Bourgogne Épineuil.......Burg .....r, w
Bourgogne Grand
 Ordinaire ....Burg .....r, w
Bourgogne Grand Ordinaire
 Rosé ....Burg .....p
Bourgogne Hautes Côtes
 de Beaune ....Burg .....r, w
Bourgogne Hautes Côtes
 de Nuits ....Burg .....r, w
Bourgogne La Chapelle
 Notre-Dame ....Burg .....r, w
Bourgogne
 Le Chapitre...............Burg .....r, w
Bourgogne Montrecul ...Burg .....r, w
Bourgogne Mousseux ...Burg .....sp
Bourgogne Ordinaire ....Burg .....r, w (p)
Bourgogne Ordinaire
 Rosé ....Burg .....p
Bourgogne
 Passetoutgrain ....Burg .....r (p)
Bourgogne Rosé ....Burg .....p
Bourgogne Vézelay ....Burg .....w
Bourgueil ....Loire.....r, p
Bouzeron ....Burg .....w
Brouilly ....Burg .....r
Bugey* ....J & S.....w
Bugey mousseux*..........J. et S....sp
Bugey pétillant*.............J & S.....sp
Buzet.............................SW. ......r, p, w
Cabardès........................Midi .....r, p
Cabernet d'Anjou ....Loire.....r, p
Cabernet de Saumur .....Loire.....p
Cadillac.........................Bord .....w
Cahors ....SW ....r
Canon Fronsac ....Bord .....r
Cassis............................P-C.......r, w, p

Cérons ....Bord .....w
Chablis ....Burg .....w
Chablis Grand Cru........Burg .....w
Chablis Premier Cru .....Burg .....w
Chambertin ....Burg .....r
Chambertin Clos
 de Bèze......................Burg .....r
Chambolle-Musigny.....Burg .....r (w)
Chambolle-Musigny
 Premier Cru ....Burg .....r (w)
Champagne ....Ch ....sp
Chapelle-Chambertin ...Burg .....r
Charlemagne ....Burg .....w
Charmes-Chambertin...Burg .....r
Chassagne-
 Montrachet................Burg .....r, w
Chassagne-Montrachet
 Premier Cru ....Burg .....r, w
Château-Chalon............J & S .....w
Château-Grillet ....Rhône ..w
Châteaumeillant* ....Loire.....r, p
Châteauneuf-du-Pape ..Rhône ..r, w
Châtillon-en-Diois ....Rhône ..r, p, w
Chaume ....Loire.....w
Chénas ....Burg .....r
Chevalier-Montrachet ..Burg .....w
Cheverny ....Loire.....r, p, w
Chinon ....Loire.....r (p, w)
Chiroubles ....Burg .....r
Chorey-lès-Beaune........Burg .....r (w)
Clairette de Bellegarde..Midi .....w
Clairette de Die ....Rhône ..sp
Clairette du Languedoc..Midi .....w
Clos de la Roche ....Burg .....r
Clos de Tart..................Burg .....r
Clos de Vougeot...........Burg .....r
Clos des Lambrays ....Burg .....r
Clos Saint-Denis ....Burg .....r
Collioure.......................Midi .....r, p, w
Condrieu ....Rhône ..B
Corbières ....Midi .....r (p, w)
Cornas ....Rhône ..r
Corse ....P.-C; ....r, p, w
Corse Calvi...................P-eC .....r, p, w
Corse Coteau du Cap
 Corse ....P-C ....r, p, w
Corse Figari ....P-C.......r, p, w
Corse Porto-Vecchio .....P-C.......r, p, w
Corse Sartène ....P-C.......r, p, w
Corton ....Burg .....r (w)
Corton-Charlemagne....Burg .....w
Costières de Nîmes.......Midi .....r (p, w)
Côte de Beaune ....Burg .....r, w
Côte de Beaune-
 Villages ....Burg .....r, w
Côte de Brouilly............Burg .....r
Côte de Nuits-Villages ..Burg .....r (w)
Côte Roannaise ....Burg .....r, p
Côte Rôtie ....Rhône ..r
Coteaux Champenois ...Ch ....r, p, w

Coteaux d'Aix-en-Provence.....P-C ......r, p, w
Coteaux d'Ancenis* ......Loire.....r, p, w
Coteaux de l'Aubance ..Loire.....w
Coteaux de Die ....Rhône ..w
Coteaux de Pierrevert ...Rhône ..r, p, w
Coteaux de Saumur ......Loire.....w
Coteaux du Giennois....Loire.....r, p, w
Coteaux du Languedoc.Midi ....r, p, w
Coteaux du Layon ....Loire.....w
Coteaux du Loir ....Loire.....r, p, w
Coteaux du Lyonnais....Burg .....r, p (w)
Coteaux du Quercy*.....SW ....r, p, w
Coteaux du Tricastin ....Rhône ..r, p, w
Coteaux du Vendômois ....Loire.....r, p, w
Coteaux Varois.............P-C ....r, p, w
Côtes d'Auvergne*.......Loire.....r, p, w
Côtes de Bergerac ....SW .....r, w
Côtes de Blaye ....Bord .....w
Côtes de Bordeaux Saint-Macaire ....Bord .....w
Côtes de Castillon.......Bord ....r
Côtes de Duras.............SW ....r, p, w
Côtes de la Malepère*...Midi ....r, p
Côtes de Millau* ...Midi ....r, w, p
Côtes de Montravel ......SW ....B
Côtes de Provence ....P-C ....r, p, w
Côtes de Saint-Mont* ...SW ....r, p, w
Côtes de Toul ....A ....r, p, w
Côtes du Brulhois*........SW ....r, p
Côtes du Forez ....Burg .....r, p
Côtes du Jura...............J & S....r, p, w, vp, vj
Côtes du Lubéron ....Rhône ..r, p, w
Côtes du Marmandais ..S.O.....r, p, w
Côtes-du-Rhône...........Rhône ..r, p, w
Côtes-du-Rhône-Villages ....Rhône ..r, p, w
Côtes du Roussillon......Midi ....r, p, w
Côtes du Roussillon Villages ...Midi .....r
Côtes-du-Roussillon Villages Caramany....Midi ....r
Côtes-du-Roussillon Villages Latour de France....Midi ....r
Côtes-du-Roussillon Villages Lesquerde....Midi ....r
Côtes-du-Roussillon Villages Tautavel....Midi ....r
Côtes du Ventoux ....Rhône ..r, p, w
Côtes du Vivarais* ......Rhône ..r, p, w
Cour-Cheverny............Loire.....w
Crémant d'Alsace.........A ....sp
Crémant de Bordeaux ..Bord ....sp
Crémant de Bourgogne.Burg ....sp
Crémant de Die ....Rhône ..sp
Crémant de Limoux......Midi ....sp
Crémant de Loire ....Loire.....sp
Crémant du Jura...........J & S.....sp

Crépy............................J & S.....w
Criots-Bâtard-Montrachet.............Burg .....w
Crozes-Hermitage........Rhône ..r, w
Échezeaux ....Burg .....r
Entre-deux-Mers ....Bord .....w
Faugères....................Midi ....r, p
Fiefs Vendéens*..........Loire.....r, w
Fitou..........................Midi .....r
Fixin ....Burg .....r (w)
Fleurie ....Burg .....r
Fronsac.......................Bord .....r
Fronton ....SW ....r (p)
Frontignan ....VDN ....w
Gaillac........................SW ....r, p, w
Gaillac Mousseux..........SW ....sp
Gaillac Premières Côtes ....SW .....w
Gevrey-Chambertin.......Burg .....r
Gevrey-Chambertin Premier Cru..............Burg .....r
Gigondas ....Rhône ..r, p
Givry..........................Burg .....r, w
Givry Premier Cru ....Burg .....r, w
Grand Roussillon ....VDN ....r, p, w, *rancio*
Grands Échezeaux ....Burg .....r
Graves........................Bord ....r, w
Graves Supérieures ....Bord .....r, w
Graves de Vayres ....Bord ....r, w
Griotte-Chambertin......Burg .....r
Gros-Plant ou Gros-Plant du Pays nantais*........Loire.....w
Haut-Médoc ....Bord ....r
Haut-Montravel ....SW .....w
Haut Poitou*...............Loire.....r, p, w
Hermitage ou Ermitage ....Rhône ..r, w, vp
Irancy.........................Burg .....r
Irouléguy ....SW ....r, p, w
Jasnières.....................Loire.....w
Juliénas ....Burg .....r
Jurançon.....................SW ....w
Jurançon Sec ....SW ....w
L'Étoile ....J & S....w, vp, vj
L'Étoile Mousseux ....J & S.....sp
La Grande Rue ....Burg .....r
La Romanée..................Burg .....r
La Tâche ....Burg .....r
Ladoix ....Burg .....r, w
Ladoix Premier Cru.......Burg .....r, w
Lalande de Pomerol ......Bord .....r
Latricières-Chambertin.Burg .....r
Les Baux-de-Provence...P-C ....r, p
Limoux ....Midi .....sp
Lirac..........................Rhône ..r, p, w
Listrac-Médoc ....Bord .....r
Loupiac ....Bord .....w
Lussac Saint-Émilion.....Bord ....r
Mâcon........................Burg .....r, w (p)

Mâcon (Rouge et Rosé).Burg .....r, p
Mâcon Supérieur..........Burg .....r, w, B
Mâcon-Villages.............Burg .....w
Madiran ....SW .....r
Maranges ....Burg .....r, w
Maranges Premier Cru..Burg ....r, w
Marcillac ....SW ....r, w
Margaux ....Bord ....r
Marsannay...................Burg .....p, w (r)
Marsannay Rosé...........Burg .....p
Maury ....VDN ....r, p, w, *rancio*
Mazis-Chambertin........Burg ....r
Mazoyères-Chambertin ....Burg .....r
Médoc ....Bord ....r
Menetou-Salon............Loire.....r, p, w
Mercurey ....Burg .....r, w
Mercurey Premier Cru..Burg ....r, w
Meursault ....Burg .....w (r)
Meursault Premier Cru .Burg .....w (r)
Minervois ....Midi .....r (p, w)
Minervois-La-Livinière .Midi .....r
Monbazillac.................SW .....w
Montagne Saint-Émilion.............Bord .....r
Montagny....................Burg .....w (r)
Montagny Premier Cru.Burg .....w (r)
Monthélie ....Burg .....r (w)
Monthélie Premier Cru.Burg .....r (w)
Montlouis-sur-Loire ......Loire.....w
Montlouis-sur-Loire Mousseux ....Loire.....sp
Montlouis-sur-Loire Pétillant......................Loire.....sp
Montrachet..................Burg .....w
Montravel ....SW ....w, r
Morey-Saint-Denis ....Burg ....r (w)
Morey-Saint-Denis Premier Cru..............Burg ....r (w)
Morgon ....Burg .....r
Moselle*......................A ....r, w
Moulin-à-Vent ....Burg .....r
Moulis, Moulis-en-Médoc ....Bord ....r
Muscadet....................Loire.....w
Muscadet Coteaux de la Loire.................Loire.....w
Muscadet Côtes de Grandlieu.............Loire.....w
Muscadet Sèvre-et-Maine ....Loire.....w
Muscat de Beaumes-de-Venise ....VDN ....w
Muscat de Frontignan ..VDN ....w
Muscat de Lunel ....VDN ....w
Muscat de Mireval ....VDN ....w
Muscat de Rivesaltes ....VDN ....w
Muscat de Saint-Jean-de-Minervois ....VDN ....w

Muscat du Cap Corse ...VDN ....w
Musigny ....Burg .....r (w)
Néac.............................Bord ....r
Nuits ou Nuits-Saint-
    Georges ....Burg .....r (w)
Nuits ou Nuits-Saint-Georges
    Premier Cru ....Burg .....r (w)
Orléans*.....................Loire.....r, p, w
Orléans-Cléry* ....Loire.....r, p, w
Pacherenc du Vic-Bilh ...SW ....w
Pacherenc du Vic-Bilh
    Sec..........................SW ....w
Palette ....P-C.......r, p, w
Patrimonio..................P-C.......r, p, w
Pauillac.........................Bord .....r
Pécharmant..................SW ....r
Pernand-Vergelesses .....Burg .....r (w)
Pernand-Vergelesse
    Premier Cru ....Burg .....r (w)
Pessac-Léognan ....Bord .....r, w
Petit Chablis ....Burg .....w
Pomerol ....Bord .....r
Pommard ....Burg .....r
Pommard Premier Cru..Broug. ..r
Pouilly-Fuissé ....Burg .....w
Pouilly Fumé ....Loire.....w
Pouilly-Loché ....Burg .....w
Pouilly-sur-Loire...........Loire.....w
Pouilly-Vinzelles ....Burg .....w
Premières Côtes-
    de-Blaye...................Bord .....r, w
Premières Côtes de
    Bordeaux ....Bord .....r, w
Puisseguin
    Saint-Émilion............Bord .....r
Puligny-Montrachet......Burg .....w
Puligny-Montrachet
    Premier Cru ....Burg .....w, r
Quarts-de-Chaume ......Loire.....w
Quincy........................Loire.....w
Rasteau ....VDN ....r, p, w
                                        rancio
Régnié ....Burg .....r
Reuilly ....Loire.....r, p, w
Richebourg ....Burg .....r
Rivesaltes....................VDN ....r, p, w

Romanée Conti ....Burg .....r
Romanée-Saint-Vivant..Burg .....r
Rosé d'Anjou................Loire.....p
Rosé de Loire................Loire.....p
Rosé des Riceys.............Ch ....p
Rosette.........................SW ....w
Roussette de Savoie ......J & S ....w
Roussette du Bugey*.....J & S ....w
Ruchottes-Chambertin ..Burg ....r
Rully ....Burg .....r, w
Rully Premier Cru ....Burg .....r, w
Saint-Amour..................Burg .....r
Saint-Aubin ....Burg .....w (r)
Saint-Aubin
    Premier Cru ....Burg .....w (r)
Saint-Bris ....Burg .....w
Saint-Chinian ....Midi ....r, p
Saint-Émilion................Bord ....r
Saint-Émilion
    Grand Cru ....Bord ....r
Saint-Estèphe................Bord ....r
Saint-Georges
    St-Émilion................Bord ....r
Saint-Joseph.................Rhône ..r, w
Saint-Julien ....Bord ....r
Saint-Nicolas-de-
    Bourgueil ....Loire.....r, p
Saint-Péray ....Rhône ..w
Saint-Péray Mousseux ..Rhône ..sp
Saint-Pourçain*..............Loire.....r, p, w
Saint-Romain................Burg .....r, w
Saint-Véran..................Burg .....w
Sainte-Croix-du-Mont ..Bord .....w
Sainte-Foy Bordeaux.....Bord .....r, w
Sancerre ....Loire.....w (r, p)
Santenay......................Burg .....r (w)
Santenay
    Premier Cru ....Burg .....r (w)
Saumur.........................Loire.....r, w
Saumur Mousseux ....Loire.....sp
Saumur-Champigny......Loire.....r
Saussignac ....SW ....w
Sauternes.....................Bord ....w
Savennières...................Loire.....w
Savennières
    Coulée-de-Serrant .....Loire.....w

Savennières
    Roche-aux-Moines ....Loire.....w
Savigny ou Savigny-
    lès-Beaune ....Burg .....r (w)
Savigny-lès-Beaune
    Premier Cru ....Burg .....r (w)
Seyssel ....J & S.....w
Seyssel Mousseux ....J & S.....sp
Tavel ....Rhône ..p
Touraine ....Loire.....r, p, w
Touraine-Amboise ....Loire.....r, p, w
Touraine-Azay-
    le-Rideau..................Loire..... p, w
Touraine-Mesland........Loire.....r, p (w)
Touraine Mousseux ......Loire.....sp
Touraine Noble-Joué.....Loire.....p
Touraine Pétillant........Loire, sp
Tursan* ....SW ....r, p, w
Vacqueyras ....Rhône ..r (p, w)
Valençay ....Loire.....r, p (w)
Vin de Savoie...............J. etS.....r, p, w
Vin de Savoie Ayze
    Mousseux ....J & S ....sp
Vin de Savoie Ayze
    Pétillant...................J & S ....sp
Vin de Savoie
    Mousseux ....J & S....sp
Vin de Savoie
    Pétillant...................J & S.....sp
Vins d'Entraygues
    et du Fel*..................SW ....r, p, w
Vins d'Estaing* ....SW ....r, p, w
Vins de Lavilledieu* ......S.-O......r, sp
Vins du Thouarsais*......Loire.....r, sp
Viré-Clessé ....Burg......w
Volnay ....Burg.....r
Volnay Premier Cru ......Burg.....r
Vosne-Romanée...........Burg.....r
Vougeot ....Burg.....r
Vougeot Premier Cru ....Burg.....r
Vouvray ....Loire.....w
Vouvray Mousseux.......Loire.....sp
Vouvray Pétillant..........Loire.....sp

(Source: www.inao.fr, 10 March 2004)

Main grape varieties

(Source: www.onivins.fr, 4 April 2004)

WHITE WINE VARIETIES (262,261HA/648,047 ACRES): Ugni Blanc (90,341ha/223,233 acres), Chardonnay (36,302ha/89,702 acres), Chenin Blanc (9,836ha/24,305 acres), Muscat à Petits Grains (6,933ha/17,131 acres), Colombard (6,896ha/17,040 acres), Grenache Blanc (6,461ha/15,965 acres), Maccabeo (5,223ha/12,906 acres), Riesling (3,407ha/8,419 acres), Mauzac (3,251ha/8,033 acres), Chasselas (3,124ha/7,719 acres), Muscat d'Alexandrie (3,063ha/7,569 acres), Clairette (2,971ha/7,341 acres).

RED WINE VARIETIES (606,518HA/1,498,706 ACRES): Carignan (95,744ha/236,583 acres), Grenache Noir (95,717ha/236,517 acres), Cabernet Sauvignon (53,412ha/131,981 acres), Syrah (50,676ha/125,220 acres), Cabernet Franc (36,094ha/89,188 acres), Gamay (34,535ha/85,336 acres), Cinsaut (31,592ha/78,064 acres), Pinot Noir (26,337ha/65,079 acres), Meunier (10,599ha/26,190 acres), Aramon (9,084ha/22,447 acres), Alicante-Bouschet (8,763ha/212,653 acres).

GERMAN WINE PRODUCTION

The regions are divided into *Bereiche*, listed after the region.

Ahr. *Bereich:* Walporzheim/Ahrtal
Mittelrhein. *Bereiche:* Siebengebirge, Loreley.
Hessische Bergstrasse. *Bereiche:* Umstadt, Starkenburg.
Franken. *Bereiche:* Maindreieck, Mainviereck, Steigerwald, Bayerischer Bodensee.
Württemberg. *Bereiche:* Remstal-Stuttgart, Kocher-Jagst-Tauber, Württembergisches Unterland, Oberer Neckar, Württembergischer Bodensee.
Baden. *Bereiche::* Tauberfranken, Badische Bergstrasse/Kraichgau,Ortenau, Breisgau, Kaiserstuhl Tuniberg, Markgräflerland, Bodensee.
Mosel-Sarre-Ruwer. *Bereiche:* Zell/Mosel, Bernkastel, Saar-Ruwer, Obermosel, Moseltor.
Nahe. *Bereiche:* Kreuznach, Schlossböckelheim.
Pfalz. *Bereiche:* Mittelhaardt/Deutsche Weinstrasse, Südliche Weinstrasse.
Rheingau. *Bereich:* Johannisberg.

Rheinhessen. *Bereiche:* Bingen, Nierstein, Wonnegau.
Saale-Unstrut. *Bereiche:* Schloss Neuenburg, Thüringen.
Sachsen. *Bereiche:* Dresden, Elslertal, Meissen.

Main grape varieties

WHITE WINE VARIETIES (84,036HA/207,650 ACRES): Riesling (23,009ha//56,854 acres), Müller-Thurgau (22,757ha//56,232 acres), Sylvaner (7,421ha/18,337 acres), Kerner (7,412ha/18,315 acres), Scheurebe (3,521ha/8,700 acres), Bacchus (3,435ha/8,488 acres), Pinot Gris (2,523ha/6,234 acres), Pinot Blanc (1,936ha/4,784 acres), Faberrebe (1,806ha/4,463 acres), Morio-Muskat (1,460ha/3,608 acres), Huxelrebe (1,417ha/3,501 acres), Chasselas Blanc (1,279ha/3,160 acres), Ortega (1,212ha/2,995 acres), Elbling (1,111ha/2,745 acres),

RED WINE VARIETIES (20,958HA/51,787 ACRES): Pinot Noir (7,556ha/18,671 acres), Blauer Portugieser (4,552ha/11,248 acres), Frankenthal (2,543ha6,284 acres), Pinot Meunier (2,152ha/5,318 acres), Dornfelder (2,125ha/5,251 acres),

ITALIAN WINE PRODUCTION

There are currently 21 DOCG and 289 DOC zones in Italy's 20 provinces.

Main grape varieties

WHITE WINE VARIETIES (417,964HA/1,032,775 ACRES): Catarratto Bianco Commune (64,982ha/160,568 acres), Trebbiano Toscano (58,477ha/144,495 acres), Trebbiano Romagnolo (21,257ha/52,525 acres), Malvasia Bianca di Candia (15,523ha/38,357 acres), Moscato Bianco (13,533ha/33,440 acres), Garganega (13,048ha/32,241 acres), Ansonica (12,711ha/31,408 acres), Trebbiano d'Abruzzo (11,951ha/29,531 acres), Catarratto Bianco Lucido (9,792ha24,196 acres), Malvaisa del Chianti (9,341ha/23,081 acres), Nuragus (8,667ha/21,416 acres),

Malvasia Bianca (7,629ha18,851 acres), Prosecco (7,073ha/17,477 acres), Pinot Blanc (6,852ha/16,931 acres), Tocai Friulano (6,852ha/16,931 acres), Chardonnay (6,180ha/15,271 acres).

RED WINE VARIETIES (460,261HA/1,137,289 ACRES): Sangiovese (86,196ha/212,987 acres), Barbera (47,121ha/116,434 acres), Merlot (31,872ha/78,755 acres), Negro Amaro (31,387ha/77,556 acres), Montepulciano (31,008ha/76,620 acres), Primitivo (17,250ha/42,624 acres), Calabrese Nera (14,188ha/35,058 acres), Aglianico (13,042ha/32,226 acres), Nerello Mascalese (12,269ha/30,316 acres), Grenache (11,459ha/28,315 acres), Dolcetto (10,416ha/25,738 acres), Gaglioppo (7,017ha/17,339 acres), Nerello Cappuccio (6,550ha/16,185 acres), Monica (6,229ha/15,392 acres), Cabernet Franc and Carmenère (5,782ha/14,287 acres), Nebbiolo (5,246ha/12,963 acres).

SPANISH WINE PRODUCTION

There are currently 51 appellation zones in Spain.

Rioja. Rioja DOC.
Navarra. Navarra DO.
Aragón. Calatayud DO, Campo de Borja DO, Cariñena DO, Somontano DO.
Castilla-León. Bierzo DO, Ribera del Duero DO, Rueda DO, Rueda Superior DO, Rueda Espumosa DO, Toro DO, Cigales DO.
Galicia and Basque Country. Rías Baixas DO, Ribeiro DO, Valdeorras DO, Chacolí de Guetaria, Chacolí de Vizcaya DO.
Catalonia. Alella DO, Catalunya DO, Conca de Barberà DO, Costers del Segre DO, Empordán-Costa Brava DO, Penedès DO, Plá de Bages DO, Priorato DO, Tarragone DO, Terra Alta DO.
Levante. Alicante DO, Bullas DO, Jumilla DO, Valencia DO, Utiel-Requena DO, Yecla DO.
Castilla-La Mancha/Madrid. Almansa DO, La Mancha DO, Méntrida DO, Mondéjar DO, Valdepeñas DO, Vinos de Madrid DO.

Andalucia. Condado de Huelva DO, Málaga DO, Montilla-Moriles DO, Jerez DO.
Islands. Binissalem DO, Tacoronte-Acentejo DO, Abona DO, El Hierro DO, La Palma DO, Lanzarote DO, Valle de Güímar DO, Valle de la Orotava DO, Ycoden-Daute-Isora DO.

Main grape varieties

WHITE WINE VARIETIES (639,633HA/1,580,511 ACRES): Airén (389,819ha/963,230 acres), Pardilla (41,090ha/101,532 acres), Macabeo (40,457ha/99,968 acres), Palomino Fino (25,551ha/63,136 acres), Pedro Ximénes (20,435ha/50,494 acres), Parellado (10,390ha/25,673 acres), Xarel.lo (9,879ha/24,411 acres), Zamela (8,506ha/21,018 acres), Merseguera (7,978ha/19,713 acres).

RED WINE VARIETIES (390,890HA/965,876 ACRES): Grenache Noir (104,404ha/257,979 acres), Bobal (91,305ha/225,612 acres), Monastrell (73,873ha/182,538 acres), Tempranillo (45,511ha/112,456 acres), Grenache Tintorera (15,826ha/39,106 acres).

UNITED STATES VITICULTURAL AREAS

Viticultural Area	State
Alexander Valley	California
Altus	Arkansas
Anderson Valley	California
Arkansas Mountain	Arkansas
Arroyo Grande Valley	California
Arroyo Seco	California
Atlas Peak	California
Augusta	Missouri
Bell Mountain	Texas
Ben Lomond Mountain	California
Benmore Valley	California
California Shenandoah Valley	California
Carmel Valley	California
Catoctin	Maryland
Cayuga Lake	New York
Central Coast	California
Central Delaware Valley	New Jersey/Pennsylvania
Chalk Hill	California
Chalone	California
Chiles Valley	California
Cienega Valley	California
Clarksburg	California
Clear Lake	California
Cole Ranch	California
Columbia Valley	Washington
Cumberland Valley	Maryland
Diablo Grande	California
Dry Creek Valley	California
Dunnigan Hills	California
Edna Valley	California
El Dorado	California
Escondido Valley	Texas
Fennville	Michigan
Fiddletown	California
Finger Lakes	New York
Fredericksburg in the Texas Hill Country	Texas
Grand River Valley	Ohio
Grand Valley	Colorado
Guenoc Valley	California
The Hamptons, Long Island	New York
Hermann	Missouri
Howell Mountain	California
Hudson River Region	New York
Isle St George	Ohio
Kanawha River Valley	West Virginia
Knights Valley	California
Lake Erie	New York/Pennsylvania/Ohio
Lake Michigan Shore	Michigan
Lake Wisconsin	Wisconsin
Lancaster Valley	Pennsylvania
Leelanau Peninsula	Michigan
Lime Kiln Valley	California
Linganore	Maryland
Livermore Valley	California
Lodi	California
Loramie Creek	Ohio
Los Carneros	California
Madera	California
Martha's Vineyard	Massachussetts
McDowell Valley	California
Mendocino	California
Merritt Island	California
Mesilla Valley	New Mexico
Middle Rio Grande Valley	New Mexico
Mimbres Valley	New Mexico
Mississippi Delta	Mississippi/Louisiana/Tennessee
Monterey	California
Monticello	Virginia
Mount Harlan	California
Mount Veeder	California
Napa Valley	California
North Coast	California
North Fork of Long Island	New York
North Fork of Roanoke	Virginia
North Yuba	California
Northern Neck George Washington Birthplace	Virginia
Northern Sonoma	California
Oakville	California
Ohio River Valley	Ohio
Old Mission Peninsula	Michigan
Ozark Highlands	Missouri
Ozark Mountain	Missouri
Pacheco Pass	California
Paicines	California
Paso Robles	California
Potter Valley	California
Rocky Knob	Virginia
Rogue Valley	Oregon
Russian River Valley	California
Rutherford	California
San Benito	California
San Francisco Bay	California
San Lucas	California
San Pasqual Valley	California
San Ysidro District	California
Santa Clara Valley	California
Santa Cruz Mountains	California
Santa Maria Valley	California
Santa Ynez Valley	California
Shenandoah Valley	Virginia/W Virginia
Sierra Foothills	California
Solano County Green Valley	California
Sonoita	Arizona
Sonoma Coast	California
Sonoma County Green Valley	California
Sonoma Mountain	California
Sonoma Valley	California
South Coast	California
South-eastern New England	Connecticut/Rhode Island/Massachusetts
Spring Mountain	California
Stags Leap District	California
Suisun Valley	California
Temecula	California
Texas Davis Mountains	Texas
Texas High Plains	Texas
Texas Hill Country	Texas
Umpqua Valley	Oregon
Virginia's Eastern Shore	Virginia
Walla Walla Valley	Washington
Warren Hills	New Jersey
Western Connecticut Highlands	Connecticut
Wild Horse Valley	California
Willamette Valley	Oregon
Willow Creek	California
Yakima Valley	Washington
York Mountain	California
Yorkville Highlands	California
Yountville	California

Source: Federal Bureau of Alcohol Tobacco and Firearms (as of April 2000)

Main grape varieties

WHITE WINE VARIETIES: Chardonnay (34,782ha/85,945 acres), Colombard (18,633ha/46,042 acres), Chenin (8,639ha/21,347 acres), Sauvignon Blanc (4,513ha/11,151 acres), Muscat of Alexandrie (2,084ha/5,149 acres), Riesling (1,650ha/4,077 acres).

RED WINE VARIETIES (85,900HA/212,256 ACRES): Zinfandel (19,972ha/49,350 acres), Cabernet Sauvignon (17,996ha/44,468 acres), Merlot (15,093ha/37,294 acres), Grenache (4,656ha/11,505 acres), Barbera (4,455ha/11,008 acres), Pinot Noir (4,427ha/10,939 acres).

ARGENTINIAN WINE PRODUCTION

Main grape varieties

WHITE WINE VARIETIES (60,398HA/149,241 ACRES): Pedro Ximénez (20,647ha/51,018 acres), Muscat of Alexandrie (10,184ha/25,164 acres), Torrontes Riojano (8,692ha/21,478 acres), Torrontes Sanjuanino (4,914ha/12,142 acres), Chenin (4,013ha/9,916 acres).

RED WINE VARIETIES (42,580HA/105,214 ACRES): Bonarda (12,186ha/30,111 acres), Cot (10,457ha/25,839 acres), Tempranillo (5,659ha/13,983 acres), Sangiovese (3,014ha/7,447 acres), Cabernet Sauvignon (2,347ha/5,799 acres), Béquignol (1,273ha/3,146 acres).

CHILEAN WINE PRODUCTION

Main grape varieties

WHITE WINE VARIETIES (23,284HA/57,534 ACRES): Sauvignon Blanc and Sauvignonasse (6,723ha16,612 acres), Muscat of Alexandrie (5,955ha/14,715 acres), Chardonnay (6,589ha/16,281 acres), Sémillon (2,422ha/5,985 acres).

RED WINE VARIETIES (46,820HA/115,691 ACRES): País (15,436ha/38,142 acres), Cabernet Sauvignon (20,812ha/51,426 acres), Merlot and Carmenère (8,317ha/20,551 acres), Carignan (512ha/1,265 acres).

AUSTRALIAN WINE PRODUCTION

Main grape varieties

WHITE WINE VARIETIES (35,516HA/87,759 ACRES): Chardonnay (13,713ha/33,136 acres), Sémillon (4,803ha/11,868 acres), Riesling (3,423ha/8,458 acres), Muscat of Alexandrie (3,410ha/8,426 acres), Doradilla (2,200ha/5,436 acres), Sauvignon Blanc (1,725ha/4,262 acres), Colombard (1,231ha/3,042 acres).

RED WINE VARIETIES (35,763HA/88,369 ACRES): Syrah (13,410ha/33,136 acres), Cabernet Sauvignon (11,219ha/27,722 acres), Limberger (2,677ha/6,615 acres), Merlot (2,461ha/6,081 acres), Grenache (2,014ha/4,977 acres), Pinot Noir (1,986ha/4,907 acres).

Wine Regions
Proposed wine zones and regions (subject to final approval):

New South Wales
Riverina Zone   Regions: Griffith, Leeton, Murrumbidgee, Hay, Carrathool, Narrandera ,Coolamon ,Lockhart, Temora, Junee, Wagga Wagga, Cootamundra, Gundagai, Tumut.
Orana Zone   Regions: Mudgee, Cobar, Bogan, Bourke, Brewarrina, Walgett, Coonamble, Warren, Narromine, Gilgandra, Coonabarabran, Coolah, Wellington, Dubbo.
Central Western Zone   Regions: Cowra, Forbes, Orange, Blayney, Lachlan, Bland, Parkes, Weddin, Cabonne, Evans, Oberon, Rylstone, Greater Lithgow, Bathurst.
Greater Canberra Zone   Regions: Young, Yass, Canberra, Boorowa, Harden, Crookwell, Gunning, Mulwaree, Queanbeyan, Goulburn, Tallagande, Eurobodalla, Cooma-Monaro, Snowy River, Bega Valley, Bombala.
Murray Zone   Regions: Wentworth, Balranald, Wakool, Windouran, Murray, Conargo, Jerilderie, Urana, Berrigan, Corowa, Hume, Culcairn, Holbrook, Tumbarumba, Deniliquin.
New England Zone   Regions: Moree Plains, Yallaroi, Inverell, Severn, Tenterfield, Bingara, Narrabri, Barraba, Manilla, Uralla, Gunnedah, Quirindi, Nundle, Walcha, Dumareso, Guyra, Parry.
Holiday Coast Zone   Regions: Tweed, Kyogle, Lismore, Richmond River, Copmanhurst, Maclean, Nymboida, Ulmarra, Bellingen, Coffs Harbour, Kempsey, Hastings Valley, Grafton, Byron, Ballina, Nambucca, Casino.

Sydney Zone   Regions: Hawkesbury, Wyong, Gosford, Wollondilly, Blue Mountains.
Illawarra Zone   Regions: Woolongong, Wingecarribee, Shoalhaven.
Far Western Zone: Region: Central Darling.
Hunter/HunterValley/Hunter River Valley Zone
Sub-zone: Upper Hunter. Region: Upper Hunter/Upper Hunter Valley/Upper Hunter River Valley. **Sub-regions**: Scone, Denman, Muswellbrook, Jerrys Plains, Merriwa.
Region: Lower Hunter/Lower Hunter Valley/Lower Hunter River Valley. **Sub-regions**: Allandale, Dalwood, Belford, Ovingham, Pokolbin, Rothbury, Broke/Fordwich, Milfield, Cessnock, Greater Taree, Greater Lakes, Gloucester, Dungog, Port Stephens, Newcastle, Lake Macquarie, Singleton, Maitland.

Victoria
North-western Victoria Zone
Sub-zone: Murray River Valley. **Sub-regions**: Nangiloo, Red Cliffs, Mildura, Robinvale, Merbein, Irymple, Karadoc, Wood Wood, Swan Hill, Lake Boga, Beverford, Mystic Park.
North-eastern Victoria Zone   Region: King Valley. **Sub-regions**: Milawa, Oxley, Markwood, Meadow Creek, Edi, Myrrhee, Whitlands, Cheshunt, Whitfield, Hurdle Creek.
Region: Owens Valley. **Sub-regions**: Buffalo River Valley, Buckland River Valley, Porpunkah, Beechworth.
Region: Rutherglen. **Sub-regions**: Wahgunyah, Barnawartha, Indigo Valley.
Region: Kiewa River Valley. **Sub-region**: Yakandandah.
Region: Glenrowan.
Central Victoria Zone
Sub-zone: Daylesford.
Sub-zone: Maryborough.
Region: Central Northern Victoria. **Sub-regions**: Picola, Katunga.
Region: Goulburn Valley. **Sub-regions**: Avenel, Dookie, Murchison, Shepparton, Nagambie, Tabilk, Mitchellstown, Mount Helen, Seymour, Graytown, Strathbogie Ranges, Yarck, Mansfield.
Region: Bendigo. **Sub-regions**: Bridgewater, Heathcote, Harcourt, Graytown, Rodosdale.
Region: Macedon. **Sub-regions**: Sunbury, Macedon Ranges, Kyneton.
Western Victoria Zone   Region: Grampians. **Sub-regions**: Great Western, Halls Gap, Stawell, Ararat.

Sub-zone: Ballarat.
Region: Pyrenees. Sub-regions: Avoca, Redbanl, Moonambel, Percydale.
Region: Far South West. Sub-regions: Gorae, Condah, Drumborg.
Region: Ballarat. Sub-region: Smythesdale.
Yarra Valley Zone   Sub-region: Diamond Valley.
Geelong Zone   Sub-regions: Anakie, Moorabool, Bellarine Peninsula, Waurn Ponds.
Mornington Peninsula Zone
Gippsland Zone   Region: West Gippsland. Sub-regions: Moe, Traralgon, Warragul.
Region: South Gippsland. Sub-regions: Foster, Korumburra, Leongatha, Westernport.
Region: East Gippsland. Sub-regions: Bairnsdale, Dargo, Lakes Entrance, Maffra, Orbost.
Melbourne Zone

South Australia
Central South Australia Zone   Region: Adelaide. Sub-regions: Magill, Marion, Modbury, Tea Tree Gully, Hope Valley, Angle Vale, Gawler River, Evanston.
Region: Adelaide Hills. Sub-regions: Piccadilly Valley, Mount Pleasant, Clarendon, Lenswood.
Region: Barossa. Sub-regions: Barossa Valley, Lyndoch, Rowland Flat, Gomersal, Tanunda, Nuriootpa, Greenock, Angaston, Marananga, Seppeltsfield, Dorrien, Lights Pass.
Region: Clare Valley. Sub-regions: Clare, Watervale, Auburn, Sevenhill, Leasingham, Polish Hill River.
Region: Eden Valley. Sub-regions: Eden Valley, Springton, Flaxmans Valley, Keyneton, High Eden, Pewsey Vale, Partalunga.

Region: Fleurieu Peninsula. Sub-regions: Langhorne Creek, Currency Creek.
Region: McLaren Vale. Sub-regions: Happy Valley, McLaren Vale, McLaren Flat, Seaview, Willunga, Morphett Vale, Reynella, Cromandel Valley.
South-East Zone   Regions: Coonawarra, Padthaway, Buckingham-Mundulla, Penola.
Murray Mallee Zone   Region: Murray Valley. Sub-regions: Riverland, Nildottie, Renmark, Berri, Barmera, Loxton, Waikerie, Morgan, Lyrup, Moorock, Kingston, Murtho, Monash, Qualco, Ramco.
Yorke Peninsula Zone
Eyre Peninsula Zone

Western Australia
Region: Northern Perth. Sub-regions: Gingin, Bindoon, Muchea, Moondah Brook.
Region: Darling Ranges. Sub-regions: Chittering Valley, Toodyay, Perth Hills (Bickley, Darlington, Glen Forrest), Orange Grove, Wandering.
Region: Swan Valley. Sub-regions: Upper Swan, Middle Swan, West Swan, Guildford, Henley Brook.
Region: Mount Barker-Frankland. Sub-regions: Mount Barker, Porongurup, Albany, Denmark, Denbarker, Frankland.
Region: Margaret River. Sub-regions: Yallingup, Willyabrup, Cowaramup, Margaret River, Augusta.
Region: Warren Blackwood. Sub-regions: Donnybrook, Bridgetown, Blackwood, Manjimup, Pemberton.
Region: South-west Coastal. Sub-regions: Wanneroo, Mandurah, Bunbury, Capel, Baldivis. Region: Esperance.

GLOSSARY

This glossary defines some of the terms most frequently encountered in the world of winemaking, labelling and tasting. Further tasting terms are discussed on p80. The following abbreviations are used for foreign words and phrases: Fr = French; Ger = German; It = Italian; Port = Portuguese; Sp = Spanish. Asterisks (*) refer to other entries in the glossary.

Abboccato (It)   A gently sweet wine.

AC (Fr)   *See* Appellation d'Origine Contrôlée.

Acidity   Various acids are present in wine: some from the grapes, others produced during fermentation. Acidity is one of the main elements of wine; without it, wine tastes dull and lifeless, although excess acidity makes wine taste sharp. Volatile acidity, from acetic acid, is a winemaking fault that makes wine taste vinegary.

Adega   (Port) Winery.

Alcohol   An important element in wine, but not the only one. Produced during fermentation when enzymes created by the yeasts change the sugar content of the grape juice into alcohol, carbon dioxide and heat. The alcohol content of wine, expressed in degrees or as a percentage of total volume, varies from around 7%Vol to around 15%Vol.

Amabile (It)   A sweeter wine than *abboccato**.

Amber   As it ages, white wine takes on deep golden, amber-like tints. This colour change results from oxidation* of the colouring matter.

Amontillado (Sp)   Sherry that has matured beyond the fino* stage and has developed an amber colour, and a depth and nutty flavour.

Ampelography   The science of defining grape varieties.

Anthocyanin   A pigment in grapes that gives red wine its colour. The purpley-red of young wine is caused by fairly unstable anthocyanin molecules that, in the course of ageing, join up with tannins*; the wine then takes on a ruby-red colour.

AOC (Fr)   *See* Appellation d'Origine Contrôlée.

Appellation d'Origine Contrôlée (AOC) (Fr)   The top grade of French quality wine. The term created by French authorities (the INAO*) to guarantee the origin of wine (and other products such as cheese). AOC rules establish specific areas of production, grape varieties, minimum levels of sugar in the must* and of alcohol in the wine, maximum yield per hectare, pruning practices, and cultivation and vinification methods.

Aroma   The scent that a wine gives off. Aroma refers specifically to smells that come from the grape. Three levels of aromas are distinguished by specialists in tasting: primary, varietal aromas; secondary aromas resulting from the fermentation; and tertiary aromas that develop as the wine ages and together form its bouquet*.

Assemblage (Fr)   The blending of wine from different grape varieties, fermentation vats, and/or vineyard plots. This "assembling" of several wines (or spirits) results in a balanced final product.

Ausbruch (Ger)   Austrian wine that is sweeter than *Beerenauslese**, less sweet than *Trockenbeerenauslese**.

Auslese (Ger)   German or Austrian wine made from selected bunches of particularly ripe grapes, usually resulting in a naturally sweet wine, although dry *Auslese* is increasingly made. In good vintages, the selection may be of grapes with noble rot (*botrytis cinerea**).

Azienda agricola (It   Wine estate.

Barrica (Sp)   Cask in which wines are matured, usually with a capacity of 225 litres.

Barrique (Fr)   A barrel mainly associated with Bordeaux, holding 225 litres (24 cases of 12 bottles), and today used for ageing wine, although formerly also for transporting it. The capacity of a *barrique* may vary from one region to another: in the Muscadet area, it contains 228 litres; in Anjou andTouraine it holds 232 litres. A traditional English equivalent is the hogshead: in France other names are used depending on region and capacity. *See also* Foudre.

Baumé   Scale for measuring degree of potential alcohol by "weighing" the must*. It is in fact by chance that the measurement given corresponds approximately to the wine's degree of alcohol after fermentation.

Beerenauslese (Ger)   German or Austrian wine made from individually selected grapes that are always overripe (probably affected by noble rot*), and thus very sweet.

Bereich (Ger)   District.

Blanc de blancs (Fr)   White wine made from only white grapes. Most commonly used to describe champagne made from only Chardonnay grapes.

Blanc de noirs (Fr)   White wine made from black grapes.

Blending   *See* Assemblage.

Blush   Term originating in the USA to describe rosé wine.

Bodega (Sp)   Wine cellar, not necessarily underground. Can describe the building where wine is made and matured, or the firm that makes it.

Body   Describes the combined effect of alcohol content and extract* in a wine.

Bordeaux mixture   *See* Bouillie bordelaise.

Botrytis cinerea The fungus known as noble rot* which, when it attacks healthy grapes in favourable conditions is highly prized in the vineyard. Botrytized grapes make some of the world's greatest sweet wines, such as Sauternes, Hungarian Tokaji and *Trockenbeerenauslese**.

Botrytized Describes sweet wines made from from grapes affected by *botrytis cinerea**.

Bouillie bordelaise "Bordeaux mixture": a fungicidal spray used against vine diseases such as mildew*, made from copper sulphate and slaked lime.

Bouquet Complex emanation of smells from a wine, resulting from a combination of aromas*. Bouquet refers to the smells that develop as a result of wine being matured in wooden casks, and from subsequent ageing in bottle.

Boutique winery Term used in the USA and Australia to describe a small winery making quality wines.

Branco (Port) White.

Brown sherry Dark sweet sherry.

Brown wine White wine of a much deeper colour than is the norm.

Brut (Fr) Usually the driest style of champagne and, by extension, other sparkling wines.

Brut nature (Fr) Very dry sparkling wine style — with no *dosage**.

Budburst The stage in the vine's annual cycle when the buds get bigger and open up.

Canopy management Science of grapevine growing and training.

Cantina sociale (It) Cooperative winery.

Cap (Fr *chapeau*) The solid matter (pips, skins, stalks) that rises to the surface of the must* during fermentation*.

Carbonic maceration Wine-making technique in which red-wine grapes are put into sealed vats without being crushed. Carbon dioxide is pumped into the vats. Fermentation takes place naturally inside the grapes, which split under their own weight. This extracts aroma and colour from the grapes.

After a week or so the grapes are pressed; fermentation* of the free-run* and pressed wine is then completed in the normal way. *See* Beaujolais method, p209.

Cava (Sp) Cellar. Also a definition of Spanish *méthode traditionnelle** sparkling wine, and a Greek term for high-quality table wine.

Cave (Fr) Cellar.

Cave coopérative (Fr) Co-operative winery.

Cépage (Fr) Grape variety.

Chai (Fr) Buildings for winemaking, ageing or storage. Much used in the Médoc, where these overground cellars are the norm.

Chaptalization The technique of adding sugar (cane or beet or rectified, concentrated must) to the must* before fermentation* to give the wine a higher alcoholic content.

Charmat Method of making sparkling wine, also known as *cuve close*. Wine, sugar and yeast are placed in a large vat for secondary fermentation to take place. The wine is chilled, filtered, transferred under pressure to a second tank, sweetened with *liqueur d'expédition* and bottled. *See* Dosage.

Charta (Ger) Association of Rheingau producers committed to making medium-dry and dry Riesling wines.

Château (Fr) Literally castle or country house; in wine terms a unit of land, with or without a dwelling, which is run as a wine estate. The INAO* may devise a more precise definition.

Chef de culture (Fr) Vineyard manager or foreman.

Clairet (Fr) Red wine, light in body* and colour. The word claret is derived from it. Usually used today for pale red wine from Bordeaux.

Classed growth Translation of *Cru Classé**.

Classico (It) A restricted zone, usually the heart of a wine area.

Climat (Fr) Term used in Burgundy for a legally defined geographical area.

Clonal selection Selection of

vines reproduced by cloning* in order to plant vines that are particularly disease-resistant, early-cropping or high-yielding.

Cloning Horticultural technique of propagation from a single source: the resulting plants, or clones, will all be identical.

Clos (Fr) Generally refers to a vineyard surrounded by a wall, in Burgundy particularly.

Collage (Fr) *See* Fining.

Cooperative Union of grape-growers who jointly own winemaking facilities and sometimes bottle and market wines.

Corked Describes wine that has a strong smell of rotten cork. This rather rare occurrence is caused by the development of certain moulds.

Coulure (Fr) Shedding of vine flowers and consequent failure to set grapes: usually caused by rain or cold during the flowering season.

Courtier (Fr) Wine broker: a middleman arranging sales by châteaux* to *négociants**.

Cream Sweetened oloroso* sherry, usually dark.

Crémant (Fr) Describes gently sparkling wine in Champagne; elsewhere in France a wine made by the *méthode traditionnelle**.

Crianza (Sp) *See* Vino de crianza.

Cru (Fr) Literally meaning growth: an area that reflects a particular soil and climate. In Bordeaux, a wine from a specific estate or château*, and from this, the various ranks of wine estates; see below:

Cru bourgeois (Fr) The category below classed growths in the Médoc.

Cru Classé Classed growth: in the Médoc, a château placed in one of five ranks by the 1855 Classification (*Premier Cru, Deuxième Cru,* etc).

Crushing The act of splitting open the grapes before fermentation so that they release their juice.

Cultivar South African term for a grape variety.

Cuvaison (or *cuvage*, both Fr) The stage in winemaking from when the must* is put into the fermentation vats up to the draining off or *décuvage*.

Cuve (Fr) Vat or cask to hold the fermenting must*, or to store wine.

Cuvée (Fr) Literally, a vatful: the word signifies a selection of wine that may or may not have been blended. Also describes a batch of wine with the same characteristics.

Cuverie, cuvier (Fr) *See* Vat-room.

Decanting The process of moving the wine to another container, usually in order to separate the sediment from the clear wine.

Demi-sec (Fr) Medium-dry; in champagne, medium-sweet.

Denominação de Origem Controlada (DOC) (Port) The top tier of Portugal's appellation system.

Denominación de Origen (DO) (Sp) The most common grade of Spanish quality wine.

Denominación de Origen Calificada (DOC) (Sp) A "super-category" for Spanish quality wines meeting special criteria of quality and consistency.

Denominazione di Origine Controllata (DOC) (It) Italian quality wine.

Denominazione di Origine Controllata e Garantita (DOCG) (It) A higher grade of Italian quality wine than DOC.

Deposit The sediment of solid particles found in wine. In the case of white wines, these are often fragments of colourless crystals of tartrate; in red wines, they are usually a combination of tannins and pigments. *See* Decanting.

Disgorging (Fr *dégorgement*) Stage in the *méthode traditionnelle** in which accumulated yeast deposits are eliminated after the second fermentation in the bottle.

DO (Sp) *See* Denominación de Origen.

DOC (Port) *See* Denominação de Origem Controlada.

DOC (Sp) *See* Denominación de Origen Calificada.

DOC (It) *See* Denominazione di Origine Controllata.

Doce (Port) Sweet.

DOCG (It) *See* Denominazione di Origine Controllata e Garantita.

Domaine (Fr) Equivalent to château*; a wine estate. The inference is that the wine is made, and bottled, by the landowner.

Dosage (Fr) The process whereby sugar is added to champagne after disgorging*. Sugar is added in the form of *liqueur d'expédition*, a mixture of brandy and sugar, the sweetness of which varies depending upon whether the champagne is brut (maximum 15 grams per litre or gr/l), extra dry (from 12 to 20gr/l), sec (from 17 to 35gr/l), demi-sec (from 33 to 50gr/l).

Doux (Fr) Sweet; applies to wines with a sugar content of over 45 grams per litre.

Dry In Champagne, sec, or "dry" in fact means sweet, the driest champagne being brut.

Dulce (It and Sp) Sweet.

Eiswein (Ger) Literally, "ice-wine". Made from grapes frozen at the time of picking. When pressed, the water in the grapes remains as ice and the concentrated juice flows out.

Elevage (Fr) Literally "raising". The treatment given to wine between fermentation and bottling.

En primeur (Fr) Wine sold before it has been bottled. Common in Bordeaux when classed growths are sold in the year after they are made.

Encépagement (Fr) The balance of different grape varieties used in a vineyard or a blend.

Extra dry Style of sparkling or still wine. *See* Dosage.

Extract Soluble solids in wine; high extract denotes a full-bodied wine.

Fattoria (It) Wine estate.

Fermentation, alcoholic Transformation of the sugar contained in the must* into alcohol and carbon dioxide, prompted by yeasts.

Fermentation, malolactic Follows the alcoholic fermentation in some wines. Malic acid in the young wine is affected by specific bacteria and converted into lactic acid and carbon dioxide. The wine

becomes softer and less acidic.

Filtering Process of separation of unwanted elements such as lees* or dead yeast from the wine.

Fining (Fr *collage*) Clearing or clarifying wines before they are bottled. A substance such as beaten egg white, fish glue or bentonite (a type of clay) is added to the wine to absorb suspended particles and to fall with gravity to the bottom of the container. The wine is then drawn off (racked) and sometimes filtered before bottling.

Fino (Sp) A pale, dry sherry aged under flor*.

Flor (Sp) A particular type of yeast that develops on the surface of fino* sherry, protecting it from oxidation and giving it its distinctive flavour.

Fortified wines Wines to which brandy or another spirit are added, usually before fermentation is complete. This preserves grape sugar, thus sweetness in the wine, and adds to the alcohol level.

Foudre (Fr) Large cask with a capacity of 200–300hl.

Foxy Describes wines with gamey smells, particularly those made in the USA from native (and some hybrid) vines.

Free-run wine (Fr *vin de goutte*) Wine derived from the grape juice obtained before pressing, through the natural bursting of the skins.

Frizzante (It) Slightly sparkling.

Garrafeira (Port) A red wine from an exceptional vintage that has been matured for at least two years before bottling, with a further year in bottle prior to sale.

Goblet (Fr *gobelet*) Way of pruning a vine in which it takes the shape of a goblet, with several branches coming out of the main stem.

Grafting Horticultural technique; particularly used of uniting European (*vitis vinifera*) vines with phylloxera*-resistant (*vitis labrusca, vitis riparia, vitis rupestris*) roots.

Grand Cru (Fr) Top-quality French wine: the term is used differently in Bordeaux, Burgundy, Champagne and Alsace.

Grande marque (Fr)   A champagne-producing firm belonging to the Institut de Grandes Marques de Champagne. Most, but not all, of the 28 members are the leading champagne houses of today.

Grand vin (Fr)   The best, or first, wine of a château*.

Gran reserva (Sp)   Red wines that are made only in particularly good vintages, and must have spent at least two calendar years in *barricas** and three years in bottle.

Grey rot   *See* Rot, grey.

Halbtrocken (Ger)   Medium-dry.

Hectolitre (hl)   100 litres.

Hybrid   Crossing of two species of vine.

INAO (Fr)   The Institut National des Appellations d'Origine is a French public body which controls the *Appellation d'Origine Contrôlée* wines.

Indicação de Proveniencia Regulamentada (IPR) (Port)   The second tier of Portugal's appellation system.

Joven (Sp)   Young.

Kabinett (Ger)   The basic QmP* level of German and Austrian wines.

Landwein (Ger)   Literally country wine, this is a superior sub-category of *Tafelwein**.

Lees   Made up of dead yeasts, tartaric acid and other residual matter from fermentation, the lees form a dark yellow deposit at the bottom of the cask. They are removed by racking*.

Liqueur d'expédition (Fr)   *See* Dosage.

Liquoroso (It)   Fortified dessert wine.

Macération carbonique (Fr)   *See* Carbonic maceration.

Maderized   When a white wine oxidizes badly and browns in colour usually because of poor storage and/or excessive age), it is said to have maderized. The phenomenon takes its name from the taste of Madeira.

Magnum   Large bottle with a capacity of 1.5 litres (the equivalent of two ordinary bottles). Great

wines age more slowly in magnums than in 75cl bottles.

Malolactic fermentation   *See* Fermentation, malolactic.

Manzanilla (Sp)   The driest and lightest style of sherry.

Medium   Describes a sweetened amontillado* sherry.

Méthode traditionnelle (Fr)   The method of making sparkling wine that was developed in Champagne in France and has been copied the world over. A secondary fermentation in the bottle results in bubbles of carbon dioxide becoming trapped in the wine. *See* p114. The winemakers of Champagne have fought to maintain the exclusivity of their name and, following an EC directive, the term may no longer appear on any wine from outside the region. The use of the former term, *méthode champenoise*, is now forbidden everywhere.

Méthode rurale (Fr)   Sparkling wine method: the wine is bottled before fermentation is over, producing a sparkle.

Metodo classico, metodo tradizionale (It)   Term for the *méthode traditionnelle** production of sparkling wines.

Mildew   Various parasitic moulds which attack the green parts of the vine in warm, humid conditions.

Millésime (Fr)   Year; vintage.

Mistela (Sp), **Mistelle** (Fr)   Grape juice that, through fortification (the addition of grape spirit), has not been allowed to ferment. The result is sometimes sold as a drink which is stronger and sweeter than wine.

Moelleux (Fr)   Describes sweet white wines.

Mosto (It)   Grape concentrate used as a sweetener.

Must   Unfermented grape juice obtained by crushing or pressing.

Mutage (Fr)   Fortification.

Négociant (Fr)   Merchant who buys grapes or wine from growers to mature it and/or sell it to wholesalers or foreign importers.

Noble rot   *See* Rot, noble.

Nouveau (Fr)   Refers to wine of

the most recent vintage, which means that, after 31 August of the year following the vintage, wines can no longer claim this *appellation*.

Novello (It)   New.

NV   Means non-vintage; often applied to champagne.

Oenology   The study of wine.

Oïdium   Disease of the vine caused by a microscopic mould that attacks the flowers, leaves and fruit.

Oloroso (Sp)   Style of sherry that never developed flor*. True oloroso is dry and rich.

Oxidation   When oxygen in the air comes into direct contact with the wine it causes changes in colour and taste. Such changes are usually detrimental, but oxidation is an essential part of the winemaking process in some wines.

Paddock   In Australia, a named vineyard.

Pajarete (Sp)   Medium-sweet.

Palo cortado (Sp)   A sherry that started life as a fino*, but has the flavour of an oloroso*.

Pale cream   A style of sherry based on fino*, and sweetened.

Pasada (Sp)   A manzanilla* sherry that has been aged.

Passito (It)   Describes sweet wine made from dried grapes.

Pasteurization   To "stabilize" low-quality wines and get rid of any micro-organisms, wine can sometimes be pasteurized, ie heat-sterilized like milk.

Pétillant (Fr)   Slightly sparkling.

Petit château (Fr)   Bordeaux term for an unclassified wine château.

Phylloxera   Vine disorder caused by the *phylloxera vastatrix* aphid, which attacks the roots of the vine. Caused devastation of European vineyards in the second half of the 19th century after its accidental introduction from America. The only cure is to graft vines onto phylloxera-resistant American rootstocks.

Podere (It)   Wine estate; plot.

Predicato (It)   Term for Tuscan quality wines meeting certain local criteria.

Premier Cru (Fr)   Officially-defined vineyard or estate in a ranking system. Definitions vary; the term is used in Bordeaux, Burgundy and elsewhere.

Press wine (Fr *vin de presse*)   Wine obtained by pressing the solid matter left over in the vat after the draining off of the free-run wine*. Part or all of the press wine is sometimes blended with the free-run wine at a later stage.

Pressing   The operation whereby the grape juice or wine is produced.

Primeur (Fr)   Wines made to be drunk very young; they are marketed from 21 November till 31 January of the following year. (Not to be confused with *en primeur*.)

Qualitätswein eines bestimmten Anbaugebeites (QbA) (Ger)   The lower of two bands into which all German quality wine is divided. The term means "quality wine from a defined region".

Qualitätswein mit Prädikat (QmP) (Ger)   Literally "quality wine with distinction". The higher of two bands into which all German quality wine is divided. The important difference between QbA* and QmP wines is that the latter are made from grapes sweet enough to need no added sugar. Each QmP wine is placed into one of six levels of distinction, according to the tested must* weight of the grapes. These levels are: *Kabinett; Spätlese; Auslese; Beerenauslese; Trockenbeerenauslese; Eiswein.*

QbA (Ger)   *See* Qualitätswein eines bestimmten Anbaugebeites.

QmP (Ger)   *See* Qualitätswein mit Prädikat.

Quinta (Port)   Farm, estate or vineyard.

Racking (Fr *soutirage*)   Operation involving separating wine from its lees* by transferring from one container to another.

Rancio   A pungent taste found in old, maderized*, fortified wine.

Recioto (It)   Sweet Italian red wine prepared with grapes that have been left for a time to dry on racks, or

hanging, to concentrate their juice.

Récolte (Fr)   Crop.

Rendement (Fr)   Yield or crop.

Reserva (Sp)   Red wines that must spend three calendar years in the *bodega**, of which at least one must be in *barricas**. White and rosé *reservas* must spend two years in the bodega, of which six months must be in *barricas*.

Reserve (Fr)   Term used for special *cuvées** put aside for ageing and future use.

Residual sugar   Natural grape sugar left in wine after fermentation. Fermentation is sometimes halted by the winemaker to leave some residual sugar (or RS).

Rich   For champagne, very sweet.

Rosado (Sp), **Rosato** (It)   Rosé.

Riserva (It)   DOC or DOCG wines with additional ageing in cask or bottle or both.

Rot, grey   Rot which affects grapes damaged by hail or pests, caused by the same mould family as the noble rot*, *botrytis cinerea**. Grey rot affects the quantity of the harvest, and can lead to a wine disorder called oxydasic casse.

Rot, noble   When conditions are favourable, with a dry, sunny end of autumn, grapes develop a beneficial form of decay thanks to the development of *botrytis cinerea**, the celebrated mould that shrivels the skins of the grapes, producing a concentrated juice.

Rôti (Fr)   Literally "roasted". Characteristic of sweet wines with aromas of dried grapes resulting from noble rot*.

Ruby (Port)   A basic red port that undergoes three years' maturation.

Sec (Fr), **Seco** (Sp and Port), **Secco** (It) Dry. In champagne, sec means medium-dry.

Second vin   The second wine of a château, as opposed to its *grand vin**.

Selection by mass   Selection of vines not from a single clone, but from a group of plants whose genetic structure varies.

Selection, clonal   *See* clonal selection.

Sélection de grains nobles (Fr)   This expression, used particularly in Alsace, is also seen in other regions such as Sauternes, Monbazillac and Coteaux du Layon. It applies to wines made from late-picked grapes affected by noble rot* or from grapes which have begun to dry on the vine with a natural concentration of sugars.

Sin crianza (Sp)   Wines that have spent no time in oak, or less than the legal minimum for crianza* wines.

Solar (Port)   Mansion, similar to a French château*.

Solera (Sp)   A system of blending all styles of sherry, across years as well as between casks. *See* p424.

Sparkling   Wines bottled with dissolved carbon dioxide, which forms bubbles when the wine is opened. There are several ways of making a sparkling wine, the most important being the *méthode traditionnelle**, and the Charmat* or *cuve close* method; effervescence may also be produced by adding carbon dioxide.

Spätlese (Ger)   Literally, "late-picked"; late-harvest QmP* wine. Made from riper grapes than *Kabinett**, *Spätlese* can be sweeter, but is increasingly the basis for drier wines.

Spumante (It)   Sparkling.

Stabilize   To help wines keep well in bottle, different treatments, such as refrigeration, pasteurization*, racking* and filtering* are available to winemakers; these operations, generally referred to as "stabilizing", aim to stop any undesirable development.

Sulphur dioxide   Used as a disinfectant in winemaking. It checks premature fermentation in the harvested grapes, destroys undesirable yeasts, eliminates microbes and bacteria, protects against oxidation, and is used to prevent sweet white wines from refermenting in the bottle. Sulphur dioxide is now used either in gaseous form, or diluted in water. Too much sulphur dioxide produces a smell of rotten eggs and induces headaches.

Superiore (It)   Describes wine that has a higher alcohol content (or a little extra ageing) than the standard DOC* wine.

Sur lie (Fr)   On the lees* (unracked). Used of wines (especially Muscadet) bottled without being racked.

Tafelwein (Ger)   Literally table wine, this is the lowest grade of German wine. An important adjunct is the prefix Deutscher or German, which means the wine is actually grown in Germany. Some modern wines of high quality are sold as *Tafelwein* because their producers do not submit them for official testing.

Tannin   There are many different types of tannin, found in nuts, wood, bark, berries and of course grapes. The stalks, skins and pips contain tannins which are released during pressing and fermentation, giving the wine its character and contributing to its capacity for ageing. Storing the wine in new wood allows the addition of tannin from the wood.

Tawny   Port wine that has been aged in wood for five years until some of its colour has faded, and then bottled.

Tenuta (It)   Wine estate; holding.

Terroir (Fr)   A winegrowing environment, covering soil, site and local climate.

Tinto (Sp and Port)   Red.

Tries (Fr)   Selective harvesting is called *vendange par tries*: the practice of picking only those grapes deemed ripe enough, or affected by *botrytis**.

Trocken (Ger)   Dry wine. Do not confuse with the next entry.

Trockenbeerenauslese (Ger)   The top QmP* grade. As with *Beerenauslese**, it is made from individually selected grapes, which are always overripe and thus very sweet; in this case the grapes are shrivelled and dry from the action of noble rot*. The concentrated juice produces a wine that is very sweet and very expensive.

Varietal (Fr *vin de cepage*)   Wine

made from a single grape variety. In France the wine must contain 100% of the same variety; in some other countries small proportions of other varieties are allowed.

Vat-room (Fr *cuvier*)   Where the vats or *cuves* are kept.

VDN (Fr)   *See* Vin doux naturel.

VDQS (Fr)   *See* Vin Délimité de Qualité Supérieure.

Vecchio (It)   Wine that has been aged for a longer period than most in cask or bottle or both.

Vendange (Fr)   Grape harvest; vintage time.

Vendange verte (Fr)   Literally "green vintage". Early summer cull of unripe grapes to prevent over-abundant crop. Any work *en vert* refers to procedures carried out during the growing period.

Vendange tardive (Fr)   Means late-harvest, referring mainly to sweet Alsace wine.

Veraison (Fr)   Stage in the ripening of the grape when the fruit changes colour.

Vigna (It)   Vineyard.

Vigneron (Fr)   A wine-grower or vineyard worker.

Vigneto (It)   Vineyard.

Vignoble (Fr)   Vineyard, which can be just one plot or an entire region, as in "the Bordeaux *vignoble*".

Vin de l'année (Fr)   Wine of the most recent vintage.

Vin de garde (Fr)   A wine made to be aged.

Vin de goutte (Fr)   *See* Free-run wine.

Vin Délimité de Qualité Supérieure (VDQS) (Fr)   The grade of French quality wine below AOC*.

Vin de liqueur (Fr)   *See* Mistelle.

Vin de paille (Fr)   Literally, straw wine. Sweet wine made from grapes dried on straw mats.

Vin de pays (Fr)   Country wine: A superior grade of *vin de table** produced according to regulations concerning grape varieties, yields and localities.

Vin de presse (Fr)   *See* Press wine.

Vin de table (Fr)   The lowest grade of wine defined in French law. It

cannot claim a specific origin and is usually sold under a brand name.

Vin doux naturel (VDN) (Fr)   Literally, naturally sweet wine. Wines that are rich in natural sugar are fortified* to preserve residual sugar*.

Vin gris (Fr)   A kind of rosé made from red grapes. Most grapes, whether red or white, have white flesh. Vin gris is made by leaving the flesh for a short time with the (red-coloured) skins, before pressing and fermentation.

Vin jaune (Fr)   Wine made in the Jura which is affected by flor*.

Vin ordinaire (Fr)   Everyday wine that is included in the classification *vin de table**.

Vin santo (It)   A *passito** wine, made from dried grapes.

Vino da tavola (It)   Table wine. Much of it is ordinary, but some *vini da tavola* are superior wines that are made in DOC* areas but not according to DOC rules.

Vino de crianza (Sp)   Literally, wine of breeding. Quality wine that must have two full calendar years' storage (one for white and rosé *crianzas*), with a minimum of six months in *barricas**.

Vino joven (Sp)   Literally, "young wine". This wine is intended for immediate drinking and is bottled straight after fining. It is also known as *vino del año*.

Vino de mesa (VdM) (Sp)   The basic grade of Spanish table wine, which does not have to show area of origin or a vintage date.

Vino de la tierra (VdT) (Sp)   Country wine (like the French *vin de pays**) from one of 28 areas that have shown their own character.

Vintage   Originally means the grape harvest; as there is only one per year, the term has come to refer to the wine made from the harvest of a particular year.

Vitis labrusca   Vine species of North America.

Vitis vinifera   The European, or "wine" vine.

Volatile acidity   *See* acidity.

INDEX

INDEX OF GRAPE VARIETIES

ACKNOWLEDGMENTS

With thanks to:
Birchgrove Products
Caves Saint-Vincent
Champagne Veuve Clicquot
Christopher Sykes Antiques of Woburn
Dampoux
Dartington Crystal Ltd (décanteur)

L'Esprit & Le Vin
John Lewis
The Hugh Johnson Shop
Puiforcat
Riedel
Riedel Screwpull®

CONTRIBUTORS TO THE FIRST EDITION

General Editor
Christopher Foulkes

Introductory Essay
Michael Broadbent

Other contributors
The following list includes those who have written one or more chapters, and those who have contributed
their expertise in the form of statistics, technical information and expert comment.

Jim Ainsworth	Anne-Frizet-Manette	Richard Paul Hinkle	Richard Mayson	Michael Schuster
Maureen Ashley	Catherine Frugère	Dr Miloslav Hroboň	Andrew Montague	Alain Senderens
Tony Aspler	Patricia Gastaud-	Ian Jamieson	Françoise Peretti	Gabrielle Shaw
Vicky Bishop	Gallagher	Dave Johnson	John Radford	Peter Schleimer
Eric Boschman	Rosemary George	Kate Kumarich	Maggie Ramsey	Tamara Thorgevsky
Stephen Brook	Philip Gregan	Maxwell Laurie	Margaret Rand	Roger Voss
Kenneth Christie	Patricia Guy	André Lurton	Norm Roby	
Bertrand Denoune	James Halliday	Giles MacDonogh	Michel Rolland	
Hildegard Elz	Helena Harwood	Maggie McNie	Jacques Sallé	
Magdaléna Fazekašová	Cameron Hills	Catherine Manac'h	Pierre Salles	

In addition to those named here, the General Editor and the publishers wish to thank those many people in the wine
trade all over the world who responded to requests for information from the editors and contributors.

PICTURE CREDITS

Ian Booth 28; 30; 32; 33; 53; 60; 61; 65; 70; 71; 72; 73.
The Bridgeman Art Library 81.
Cephas/Jerry Alexander 127; 484.
Cephas/R. A. Beatty 397; 446.
Cephas/ Nigel Blythe 169; 301; 320; 323; 332; 333;
    335; 340; 573.
Cephas/Andy Christodolo 263; 279; 330; 349; 519; 524.
Cephas/Rick England 522; 559.
Cephas/M. J. Kielty 226.
Cephas/Lars Nilson 468.
Cephas/Alan Proust 563; 566.
Cephas/Mick Rock 2-3; 7; 19; 47; 54; 99; 100; 104;
    108; 111 (except bottom, second from the left); 113
    (top left, top right, centre left, centre right); 115; 117;
    118; 119; 121; 122; 123; 125; 131; 133; 137; 138; 139;
    141; 145; 163; 173; 179; 186; 189; 198; 208; 209; 210;
    213; 217; 223; 231; 232; 235; 236; 238; 243; 245; 247;
    248; 251; 252; 255; 257; 258; 261; 264; 266; 267; 271;
    277; 295; 297; 299; 306; 313; 336; 338; 343; 346; 348;
    351; 359; 360; 365; 367; 371; 374; 376; 383; 386; 389;
    391; 392; 415; 416; 424; 429; 432; 436; 438; 448; 449;
    457; 459; 462; 465; 466; 473; 482; 486; 490; 494; 500;
    502; 504; 506; 507; 508; 510; 512; 531; 532; 534; 537;
    541; 542; 546; 552; 555; 572.
Cephas/Peter Stowell 355.
Cephas/Ted Stefan 479.
Cephas/Helen Stylianou 453.
Cephas/Mike Taylor 455.
Christie's 79.
Colorific/Alon Reininger 460.
Corbis-Sygma/Ric Ergenbright 571.

C. M. Dixon 22.
Patrick Eagar 171; 219; 310; 326; 381.
E. T. archive 21; 25.
Fall Creek Vineyards 515.
Robert Harding Picture Library 316.
Larousse/Diaf Studiaphot/Hervé Gyssels 27; 59; 62;
    63; 64; 66; 67; 75; 77.
Network/Wolfgang Kunz 342.
Photothèque-TV-France/Desseigne 111 (bottom, second
    from left).
Russia & Republics Photo Library 470.
Scope/Charles Bauman 528.
Scope/J. Guillard 8, 107, 431.
Scope/Jean-Luc Barde 399.
Scope/Jean-Daniel Sudres 14; 456.
Scope-Kactus/Hugues 527.
Tony Stone Worldwide 516.
Trip Photographic Library/V. Kolpakov 472.
Alan Williams 50; 55; 113 (bottom left, bottom right);
    116; 148; 150; 158; 177; 180; 181; 184; 191; 192; 194;
    205; 229; 268; 282; 285; 286; 287; 290; 292; 302; 304;
    309; 325; 327; 339; 400; 405; 408; 409; 411; 413; 417;
    421; 425; 434; 439; 440; 481; 489; 491; 499; 501.
Zefa 314; 363; 378; 461; 495.

Studio photography (Paris): Photography Hervé Gyssels,
    DIAF Studiophot, stylist Isabelle Dreyfus,
    Sommelier Jean-Christophe Renaut.
Studio photography (London): Photographer Ian Booth,
    styling and props Diana Durant.